History of Indigenous Education in the Panjab

History of Indigenous Education in the Panjab

Since Annexation and in 1882,

By

G. W. Leitner, LL.D.,

GYAN

Published by

Gyan Publishing House
5, Ansari Road
Daryaganj, New Delhi-110002
Phone: 011-47034999, 9811692060
E-mail: books@gyanbooks.com

Distribution Network
gyanbooks.com
India, USA, Canada, UK, Australia, France

ISBN : 978-81-212-6490-7 (PB)
First Published, 1882

2nd Impression 2022

Printed at: Gyan Press, Delhi.

HISTORY OF INDIGENOUS EDUCATION IN THE PANJAB
Author: G. W. Leitner

HISTORY

OF

INDIGENOUS EDUCATION

IN

THE PANJAB

SINCE ANNEXATION AND IN 1882,

BY

G. W. LEITNER, LL.D.,

DOCTOR OF ORIENTAL LEARNING OF THE UNIVERSITY OF THE PANJAB; OF THE MIDDLE TEMPLE, BARRISTER-AT-LAW; LATE ON SPECIAL DUTY WITH THE EDUCATION COMMISSION APPOINTED BY THE GOVERNMENT OF INDIA; FORMERLY PROFESSOR OF ARABIC WITH MUHAMMADAN LAW AT KING'S COLLEGE, LONDON.

1882.

Publisher's Note

It may look unprogressive to bring out another reprint of a book which was first published as far back as the later years of the nineteenth century. It is possible that lot of further research might have taken place in this subject during the succeeding years, yet these works maintain their own reference value. The idea behind the present venture is to make available these rare works to most libraries and readers

The British and other Western scholars rendered great service to this land and their works still have great bearing on the Language, Culture and History of the Punjab. The Languages Department has planned to bring out reprints of the most valuable works, including the present one, for the benefit of most readers, scholars and research workers.

LAL SINGH
Director
Languages Department,
Punjab.

Patiala
April, 1971

LIST OF CONTENTS.

PAGES

Introduction to a History of Indigenous Education in the Panjáb since annexation, including a Parliamentary Report on the Panjáb University movement . . . . i to viii

HISTORY OF INDIGENOUS EDUCATION IN THE PANJAB.

PREFACE AND SUMMARY . . . . 1 to 16

Including a

CLASSIFICATION OF INDIGENOUS SCHOOLS, PAGES 10 TO 13

and

NOTES ON THE CENSUS RETURNS OF 1881, PAGES 13 TO 16.

PART I.

A.—THE RELIGIOUS AND NATIONAL FOUNDATIONS OF INDIGENOUS EDUCATION . . . . 17 to 27

Including an account of the

Influence of indigenous education on schools in England (pages 20 and 21), and quotations from Hindu, Sikh, and Muhammadan sacred writings on education (pages 23 to 26).

B.—VERNACULAR INDIGENOUS EDUCATION IN THE PANJÁB . . . . . 28 to 45

Including

I.—SIKH VERNACULAR INDIGENOUS EDUCATION (PAGES 28 TO 37)

With an account of Sikh authors, of Sikh initiation, and of the Gurmukhi School (pages 29 to 37).

II.—CHATSALAS; MAHAJANI AND LANDÉ SCHOOLS (FOR THE TRADING COMMUNITY) (PAGES 37 TO 45).

C.—QUASI-VERNACULAR INDIGENOUS EDUCATION IN THE PANJÁB . . 46 to 51

Including an account of

III.—QUASI-VERNACULAR SCHOOLS (URDU AND HINDI) (PAGES 46 TO 51).

D.—SEMI-CLASSICAL INDIGENOUS EDUCATION IN THE PANJÁB . . . 52 to 65

Including an account of

IV.—PERSIAN SCHOOLS

(Their text-books, schemes of study, &c.).

E.—CLASSICAL INDIGENOUS EDUCATION IN THE PANJÁB . . . . . . 66 to 96

V.—KORAN SCHOOLS (PAGES 66 TO 72).

(Including the child's contract with the Deity; a letter from a Koran school teacher complaining of official persecution, &c.)

VI.—ARABIC SCHOOLS (PAGES 72 TO 79).

(Including an account of the scheme of studies at the Deoband School; the list of Arabic books used in Indigenous Schools; the curriculum vitæ of a Panjabi Maulvi, &c.).

VII.—SANSCRIT TEACHING (PAGES 79 TO 96).

(Including an account of Sanscrit learning in the Panjáb, of the educational limits of castes, a list of Sanscrit books used in Indigenous Schools, and extracts from Mr. Adam's Report on Sanscrit learning in Bengal in 1835, a sketch of a model Indigenous Sanscrit School, and of the educational career of a Panjábi Pandit).

F.—FEMALE INDIGENOUS EDUCATION . . . . 97 to 112

Including an account of Panditani Ramabai and her brother, of the existence of female education in the Panjáb prior to annexation, of the widow re-marriage question in the Panjáb, the cause of its advocacy in certain castes, female life in the Province, and the solution of the problem of female education by employing the priests of the

PAGES

various denominations in schools for boys and their wives as teachers in female schools in households. Opinions of various witnesses before the Education Commission on the subject of female education).

G.—OPINIONS OF WITNESSES BEFORE THE EDUCATION COMMISSION ON THE SUBJECT OF INDIGENOUS SCHOOLS IN THE PANJAB, AND NOTES THEREON . . . . . 113 to 144

H.—THE PANJAB BEFORE AND ON ANNEXATION . . . . . 145 to 202

(Including an account of the Indigenous Schools and their endowments before annexation compared with their present condition, the resumption of rent-free tenures in part or whole or after the death of incumbents at the time of annexation by the State or by Jaghirdars, the value of the services of Missionaries, the manner in which redress can be afforded and indigenous education be revived, improved, and rendered permanent, at no cost to the State, and, indeed, to its pecuniary advantage, &c.; also an account of—

(a) Gurmukhi Schools before annexation on page 150.
(b) Arabic and Persian schools before annexation on page 151.
(c) Learned teachers of the present time on page 152.
(d) Hakims on page 152.
(e), (f), (g) Baids, Patshalas, Artists, on page 153.
Remarks on learning generally in the Panjáb before annexation on pages 153 to 155.

PANJÁB ADMINISTRATION REPORT FOR 1849-51, ON POPULAR EDUCATION . . . . 155 to 157
AMBALA SETTLEMENT REPORT FOR 1852 . . . . . 157 to 159
LUDHIANA DITTO 159
HUSHIARPUR DITTO 159
SIALKOT DITTO 160
EXTRACT FROM ADMINISTRATION REPORT FOR 1851-52 . . . . . 161 to 165
DITTO DITTO DITTO 1854-55 AND 1855-56 . . . . . 165 to 169
DITTO DITTO DITTO 1856-57 AND 1857-58 . . . . . 169 & 170
THE RESUMPTION OF RENT-FREE LANDS INCLUDING THOSE BELONGING TO SCHOOLS OR CONNECTED WITH TEACHING . . . . . 170 to 174
THE NON-REGULATION LAW OF THE PANJÁB AND ITS EXECUTION AS REGARDS RENT-FREE TENURES . . . . . 174 to 180

INSTANCES OF RESUMED "MUAFIS" BELONGING TO MAULVIS, PANDITS AND BHAIS . . . . . 180 to 183
PRINCIPLES WHICH WERE ACTED ON IN RESUMING RENT-FREE TENURES . . . . 183 to 187

(Including an account of "Jaghirs and Pensions" from the first Administration Report (1849-51), and showing the prospect of the annexed territory yielding a "net profit," within fifteen years, of fifty lakhs per annum by the lapses of Jaghirs and Pensions; also extract from Administration Report for 1851-52 and 1852-53).

EXTRACT FROM HUSHIARPUR SETTLEMENT REPORT FOR 1852 . . . . 187 & 188
" AMBALA DITTO DITTO . . . . . 188 to 190
" JALANDHAR DITTO DITTO . . . . . 190 to 193
" PANJAB ADMINISTRATION REPORT FOR 1856—58 194
" AMRITSAR SETTLEMENT REPORT FOR 1860 . . . . 195 to 199
" LAHORE DITTO DITTO . . . . . 199 & 200
" FEROZEPUR DITTO DITTO 1859 200
" GUJRANWALA DITTO DITTO 1860 . . . . . 201 & 202

PART II.

CONTAINING THE DETAILS REGARDING EVERY ASCERTAINED SCHOOL IN THE VARIOUS DISTRICTS OF THE PANJAB, THE NAMES OF LOCAL *SAVANS*, &c

I.—THE DELHI DIVISION . . . . . 1 to 16

(a) Delhi District (pages 1 to 10).
(b) Gurgaon District (pages 11 to 13).
(c) Karnal " (" 14 to 16).

II.—THE HISSAR DIVISION . . . . . 17 to 26

(a) Hissar District (pages 17 to 19).
(b) Rohtak " (" 20 to 23).
(c) Sirsa " (" 24 to 26).

PAGES

III. THE AMBALA DIVISION . . . . 27 to 38

(a) Ambala District (pages 27 to 31).
(b) Ludhiana „ („ 32 to 37).
(c) Simla „ (page 38).

IV.—THE JALANDHAR DIVISION . . . . 39 to 51

(a) Jalandhar District (pages 39 to 44).
(b) Hushiarpur „ („ 45 to 49).
(c) Kangra „ („ 50 & 51).

V.—THE AMRITSAR DIVISION . . . . 52 to 74

(a) Amritsar District (pages 52 to 59).
(b) Sialkot „ („ 60 to 70).
(c) Gurdaspur „ („ 71 to 74).

VI. THE MULTAN DIVISION . . . . 75 to 92

(a) Multan District (pages 75 to 78).
(b) Jhang „ („ 79 to 84).
(c) Muzaffargarh „ („ 85 to 88).
(d) Montgomery „ („ 89 to 92).

VII.—THE LAHORE DIVISION . . . . 93 to 132

(a) Lahore District (pages 93 to 119).
(b) Gujranwala „ („ 120 to 127).
(c) Ferozepur „ („ 128 to 132).

VIII.—THE RAWALPINDI DIVISION . . . . 133 to 164

(a) Rawalpindi District (pages 133 to 143).
(b) Shahpur „ („ 144 to 150).
(c) Jhelum „ („ 151 to 157).
(d) Gujrat „ („ 158 to 164).

IX.—THE PESHAWAR DIVISION . . . . 165 to 170

(a) Peshawar District (no returns).
(b) Kohat District (pages 165 & 166).
(c) Hazara „ („ 167 to 170).

X.—THE DERAJAT DIVISION . . . . 171 to 181

(a) Dera Ghazi Khan District (pages 171 to 175).
(b) Bannu „ („ 176 to 179).
(c) Dera Ismail Khan „ („ 180 & 181).

PART III.

A.—GENERAL STATEMENT SHOWING THE NUMBER OF PUPILS IN INDIGENOUS SCHOOLS IN THE PANJAB, AS ALSO THE NUMBER OF PERSONS "UNDER INSTRUCTION" ACCORDING TO THE CENSUS OF 1881 AND THE NUMBER OF PUPILS IN GOVERNMENT AND AIDED SCHOOLS (SEE PAGES 14 TO 16 OF THE PREFACE TO THIS REPORT.) . . . 1

B.—STATEMENT SHOWING THE NUMBER OF (a) MAKTABS AND MADRASAS, (b) PATSHÁLAS, (c) GURMUKHI SCHOOLS, (d) MAHAJANI SCHOOLS, AND OF THEIR RESPECTIVE PUPILS ON 30TH OCTOBER 1882 THROUGHOUT THE PANJAB . . . . *ib.*

C.—A GENERAL ABSTRACT OF THE INDIGENOUS SCHOOLS IN THE PANJAB ACCORDING TO DIVISIONS AND DISTRICTS . . . . 2 to 13

PART IV.

CONTAINING NOTES ON PART I—(nineteen pages).

1. THE SIKHS AND THEIR EDUCATION . . . . 1 to 4

(a) The Páhul . . . . . . (page 1).
(b) Obligation of every Sikh to read . (page 1).
(c) Gurmukhi text-books . . . (page 2).
(d) Discipline in Gurmukhi schools . (page 2).
(e) Remuneration of the teacher . (page 2).
(f) Account of Gurmukhi education by Bhai Gurmukh Singh (pages 2 to 4).

	PAGES
2. AN ACCOUNT OF MAHAJANI TEXT-BOOKS . . . . (Including extracts from Mr. A. P. Howell's "State of Education in India during 1866-67").	4 to 9
3. APPENDIX TO THE MEMOIRS OF STATISTICS ON INDIGENOUS EDUCATION IN THE NORTH-WESTERN PROVINCES, PRINTED 1850.	9 to 11
4. ROUGH NOTES AND PROPOSALS REGARDING INDIGENOUS SCHOOLS, PARTLY BASED ON A PERUSAL OF THE REPORTS FROM THE NORTH-WESTERN PROVINCES.	11 to 17
5. CONDITION OF INDIGENOUS EDUCATION IN DISTRICTS OF THE NORTH-WESTERN PROVINCES BEFORE THEIR INCORPORATION IN THE PANJAB.	17 & 18
6. TERMS USED IN INDIGENOUS SCHOOLS	18 & 19

PART V.

LIST OF MAULVIS, PANDITS, BHAIS, PANDHAS, HAKIMS, BAIDS, AUTHORS, AND POETS IN THE PANJÁB, ARRANGED ACCORDING TO DIVISIONS AND DISTRICTS	1 to 32
PRÉCIS OF, AND CONCLUSIONS FROM, THE RECORDS OF THE PANJÁB GOVERNMENT, AND OF THE PANJAB EDUCATIONAL DEPARTMENT BEARING ON THE SUBJECTS OF THE VILLAGE SCHOOL CESS AND OF INDIGENOUS SCHOOLS	1 to 52

CHAPTER A.

Précis of, and notes on, the contents of the "Extracts from the Reports of the Panjáb Educational Department, and from the Reviews thereon by the Government of the Panjáb between the years 1856-57 and 1880-81." (See Chapters C, D, and E)	1

CHAPTER B.

Conclusions from above, and statements regarding the income and expenditure from the Village School Cess since 1856-57, the statistics of indigenous Schools, the misapplications from the Village School Cess from 1856 to 1881, and the principal items of expenditure in 1881-82	10

CHAPTER C.

Introduction to the "Extracts" as above, consisting of a summary of the Breaches of the Educational Despatches of 1854 and 1859 of the Secretary of State, and of an extract from the Proceedings of the Supreme Government forwarding the Despatch of 1859, by the Panjáb Educational Department	22

CHAPTER D.

Official documents connected with the raising of the Village School Cess	25

CHAPTER E.

"Extracts" (above alluded to) from the Panjáb Educational Reports and from the "Reviews" thereon by the Panjáb Government between 1856-57 and 1880-81	33 to 52

APPENDICES.

APPENDIX	I.—Appointment of an Educational Syndicate for British Burma	1 & 2
APPENDIX	II.—Special reports on (a) Hindu Indigenous Schools	1 to 7
	(b) Sikh " "	8 to 10
	(c & d) Muhammadan Indigenous Schools . . .	11 to 18
APPENDIX	III.—Papers connected with the origin of the Itimad-ud-dowla Fund . . .	1 to 9
APPENDIX	IV.—List of 389 books in the Gurmukhi characters in the possession of Sirdar Atar Singh of Bhadaur (For further lists see Dr. Leitner's paper submitted to the Imperial Simla Text-book Committee in 1877) . . .	1 to 6
APPENDIX	V.—LIST OF VERNACULAR SCIENTIFIC BOOKS PUBLISHED BY THE PANJAB UNIVERSITY COLLEGE, OR USED BY CANDIDATES FOR THE DEGREE STANDARDS IN ARTS	1 to 6
APPENDIX	VI.—EXTRACTS FROM PANJAB ADMINISTRATION AND EDUCATIONAL DEPARTMENT REPORTS BEARING ON INDIGENOUS AND GOVERNMENT VILLAGE SCHOOLS .	1 to 25
APPENDIX	VII.—Survey of Mahajani, Landé, Sarafi and other commercial characters in various parts of the Panjáb, the North-West Provinces and Sind (ninety-three pages).	

(a) Introductory 23 pages.
(b) Part A 34 "
(c) Part B 36 "
} See special "List of Contents" prefixed to Appendix VII.

INTRODUCTION

TO

A HISTORY OF INDIGENOUS EDUCATION IN THE PANJAB SINCE ANNEXATION.

I AM about to relate—I hope without extenuation or malice—the history of the contact of a form of European with one of Asiatic civilisation; how, in spite of the best intentions, the most public-spirited officers, and a generous Government that had the benefit of the traditions of other provinces, the true education of the Panjáb was crippled, checked, and is nearly destroyed; how opportunities for its healthy revival and development were either neglected or perverted; and how, far beyond the blame attaching to individuals, our system stands convicted of worse than official failure. Whether it is possible to rouse to renewed exertion, on behalf of its own education, the most loyal population that has ever been disappointed, is a question which the following pages will only partially attempt to answer. Much will, of course, depend on the wise adaptation of the noble principle just propounded—of "local self-government"—to a department of the Administration,—that of education,—in which, above all others, it can be introduced with perfect safety and the greatest political advantage.

Respect for learning has always been the redeeming feature of "the East." To this the Panjáb has formed no exception. Torn by invasion and civil war, it ever preserved and added to educational endowments. The most unscrupulous chief, the avaricious money-lender, and even the freebooter, vied with the small landowner in making peace with his conscience by founding schools and rewarding the learned. There was not a mosque, a temple, a dharmsála that had not a school attached to it, to which the youth flocked chiefly for religious education. There were few wealthy men who did not entertain a Maulvi, Pándit, or Guru to teach their sons, and along with them the sons of friends and dependents. There were also thousands of secular schools, frequented alike by Muhammadans, Hindus and Sikhs, in which Persian or Lundé was taught. There were hundreds of learned men who gratuitously taught their co-religionists, and sometimes all-comers, for the sake of God—"lillah." There was not a single villager who did not take a pride in devoting a portion of his produce to a respected teacher. In respectable Muhammadan families husbands taught their wives, and these their children; nor did the Sikhs prove in that respect to be unworthy of their appellation of "learners and disciples." In short, the lowest computation gives us 330,000 pupils (against little more than 190,000 at present) in the schools of the various denominations who were acquainted with reading, writing, and some method of computation; whilst thousands of them belonged to Arabic and Sanskrit colleges, in which Oriental literature and systems of Oriental Law, Logic, Philosophy, and Medicine were taught to the highest standards. Tens of thousands also acquired a proficiency in Persian, which is now rarely reached in Government and aided schools or colleges. Through all schools there breathed a spirit of devotion to education for its own sake and for its influence on the character and on religious culture; whilst even the sons of Banyas who merely learnt what they absolutely required in order to gain a livelihood looked with respect, amounting to adoration, on their humble Pándhas, who had taught them the elements of *two* "r's."

We have changed all this. The annexation disturbed the minds of believers in Providence, and all that was respectable kept, as much as possible, aloof from the invader,—just as the best Englishman would not be the first to seek the favour of a foreign conqueror. At the same time, the single-mindedness of the first English officials in the Panjáb, and the religious earnestness which they showed, reconciled the people to foreign rule; and the mutiny of 1857 found the Province still possessed of sufficient national life to aid us effectually in the struggle for self-preservation. Unconsciously no doubt, as we felt safer, we began to think less of the prejudices of the people, and the energies of our best officers were devoted to the introduction on a virgin field of reforms of doubtful success in Europe, which wasted their time but gave them a reputation, rather than to the natural development of what elements of progress already existed in indigenous civilisation. These officers were surrounded by ambitious and needy adventurers, many from the North-Western Provinces, whose knowledge of Perso-Urdu, which they shared with us, was the key to the mysteries of government and to the exploitation of the Province, just as a smattering of English is a coveted possession of the class, eager for place and political power, which we have created out of the rejected members of chiefly the middle and lower castes. Urdu, therefore, became synonymous with education; and on its supply failing, and intellectual darkness in the meanwhile creeping over the Province, in consequence greatly of the resumption of rent-free grants, we began to cast about for means to provide ourselves with cheap subordinate agents in the various branches of the administration. No doubt, higher motives also led to the establishment of an Educational Department; but its principal characteristics will not be fully understood unless the above circumstances are borne in mind.

Now, although Persian had been taught for ages in the Panjáb to a large number of pupils, and was exerting a natural and beneficial influence on their various vernaculars along with Arabic and Sanskrit, Urdu was a subject of study rather for Europeans than Natives, to whom it was said to come incidentally through Persian. The substitution, therefore, of Urdu for Persian was looked upon as a limitation of education, and led to its disuse as the spoken and written language of gentlemen. However, Urdu and, subsequently, English were welcomed as an avenue and claim to employment under Government by the more needy in the community and by those who wished to ingratiate themselves with the authorities. Thus, education was first degraded by us from an object of mental and moral culture to a means for purely worldly ambition. The religious basis of education was similarly undermined; for, looking upon Maulvis, Pandits, and Gurus as possible leaders of dissaffection, we treated them and their learning with suspicion.

Instead of identifying them with our interests, everything in their literature which appeared ridiculous to our hasty examination was held up to tacit scorn,—a course which was calculated to destroy the sense of reverence among their co-religionists. The cultivation of the sacred classical languages, without which the vernaculars cannot be developed, became more and more restricted to the practising priestly classes, whose influence for good was not utilised by a wise Government. They accordingly withdrew into the background, in consequence of which many of the classical colleges or private schools, conducted "for the sake of God," died out, just as the practical deprecation of Persian for the sake of Urdu led to the cessation of numerous institutions in which "the language of gentlemen" was taught. Similarly, our primary schools injured the Mahajani schools, with which they are now being incorporated, although many of the latter still survive, and, along with the Lundé character, teach a system of mental arithmetic which is as invigorating to the mind of a tradesman's boy as it is practically useful to him. Gurus still continue to teach the sacred Granth to thousands of Sikh boys in the character which commits to writing the words which came from the mouth of the founder of their religion, in "Gurmukhi"; but then, as now, the alphabet and the language—Panjábi—which it renders were considered to be barbarous, and were not used by us for purposes of elementary secular instruction.

Still, the influence of old associations and of the striking inventions of modern times, combined with the prestige of the ruling race, rendered the people susceptible to any form of education that Government might wish to foster; and when the Educational Cess was first levied for the avowed purpose of establishing schools in the contributing localities as far as possible, great expectations were raised. These were not fulfilled, to the astonishment and scarcely disguised indignation of the rural population. Nor should the name of "Educational Cess" mislead us. It was originally the "*Village School* Cess," as admittedly imported from the North-Western Provinces. Whatever their own tyrants had done, they had not come with the words of progress and enlightenment to take the money out of their pocket for their education, and then appropriate it to something else. In 1857 there was a balance of R1,14,562 from the Educational Cess, whilst only R23,472 had been expended on village schools. In a village on the frontier a school was demanded in return for the cess, and on its refusal an outbreak took place, which had to be suppressed by the despatch of troops. My own appeal to start schools by subscription in backward districts was everywhere met with the rejoinder that the Government had raised a fund for a school and had not given them one. The resumption of grants of rent-free lands was an act of which Muhammadan bigotry might have been guilty as regards Hindu endowments; but the faith of the agricultural population in the general honesty of the alien Government was strong when it received its first blow on the money raised for education being devoted to they knew not what. This faith will not be restored unless some equivalent for that money is devoted to the objects for which it was raised.

As regards the trading classes, the more ambitious of them gladly availed themselves of the Government system of education, which promised them elevation in social rank, or rather gave them the opportunity, in the event of being employed in the public service, of exercising power over those higher castes that had hitherto despised them. The moral and educational obligations are not so great on the "lower" as they are on the "higher" castes of Hindus; but the temptation to become practically a higher caste through official preferment, by means of falling in with the Government system of education, was too strong to be resisted. The opportunity also of dispossessing the Muhammadans from the teacher's seat, which they held throughout the province, was too good to be neglected. Thus, the less respectable or less conservative of these classes hailed the advent of Urdu along with all the official loaves and fishes which it brought, in the hope that even this weakened agency of Muhammadan influence would also eventually disappear. When English became one of the main avenues to higher employment, the most ambitious members of these classes still more readily availed themselves of it as the easiest means for acquiring political power and for taking the place of the Brahmans as the intellectual leaders of the people. Thus, after the subversion of the religious principle, by the elimination of the priestly classes from our educational councils, was introduced a social *bouleversement*, in which neither birth nor traditional rank, nor the reputation of piety, liberality, or courage, seemed to weigh with Government—the Native's Providence on earth—against the apparently more practical usefulness of the supple *parvenus* who began to monopolise official favour.

The rank and file, however, of the trading classes went on, much as before, satisfied with such education as their Pándhas could give to their sons, but also largely attending Government and Missionary schools. These Pándhas chiefly taught mental arithmetic, the multiplication table, and a kind of short-hand of Nágri, called "Lundé" or "Landé," which means "tailless," because that character is deprived of unnecessary flourishes and is generally written without vowels. It is alleged that the Lundé of each district, if not of each city or larger cluster of villages, differs from that of another. Perhaps a more careful investigation will show that, substantially, all the various forms of commercial writing, whether called "Lundé," "Landé," "Sarafi," "Mahájani," &c., are the same; that they are all modifications of Nágri, which they endeavour to render more tachygraphic in emulation of the quick Persian writing; and that they offered a means of primary education by the adoption of the salient features common to all these handwritings, which we have neglected. Certainly, when it is remembered that these Pándhas were also called Gurus, we must admit that the Síkhs made a wiser use of the vulgar characters by developing them into "Gurmukhi," the characters in which the sacred Granth has now collected the words which fell from the "*mouth of the Guru*" = Gurmukhi—a conjecture which may account for the spread of that character in the Panjáb. Guru Nanak did not write himself; his disciples (Síkhs) preserved his sayings orally, but Bhai Balá communicated them to the second Guru Angat, who wrote them down in the Landé character, in which he also recorded his own precepts. It was he who then invented the *Gurmukhi* character; but he committed nothing to writing in it, except the history of Guru Nanak, a large volume. The third Guru, Amar Das, also recorded his sayings in Landé, an example which was followed by the fourth Guru. The books of both are at Goindwál near Amritsár. It was only the fifth Guru, Arjan, in whose time all the sayings and records of the previous four Gurus and his own were collected into the "Adi Granth" and written in Gurmukhi (which had by that time become widely used) above the signature of Bhai Gurdas—a Granth which still exists at Kartarpur in the house of Guru Sadhu Singh.

It was with the oppressed and despised trading community that we sought and obtained some popularity. To them we came indeed as social saviours. They were lightly taxed, though of their taxation next to nothing was even attempted to be devoted to their traditional education. The Kamiana tax, a portion of which was to be given to schools for the manufacturing classes, was no sooner imposed than it was abandoned for taxes like the license tax, no portion of which has ever been given to education. But the trading and manufacturing classes largely availed themselves of the schools provided out of *general* taxation or the cesses of the agricultural community, to which a stone was given when they demanded bread; and, finally, a state of things has been reached when nine-tenths of those who benefit by middle and higher education belong to those *nouvelles souches sociales* from which, with the disappearance of the influence of the aristocracy and of the priesthood, those grave disorders may be expected in India as in Europe.

Turning now to the landed gentry, the petty Chiefs, and the Raises generally, their greater wealth and family pride enabled them either to dispense with education for their sons, or else to provide private tutors for them. They had been disappointed by the new order of things; but their confidence in Government was still unshaken, and they were not disinclined to have their children taught in Government schools, provided their rank received due deference. With this view, for instance, they asked Lord Canning for a college at Lahore, intending it to be reserved for their sons. A higher department was accordingly created in connection with the Lahore District School, in which, as in the older Universities of England, the distinction between patricians and others was kept up. Some of them passed the Entrance Examination of the Calcutta University; and the Government College, Lahore, was at last established (1864); but the distinction between noblemen and commoners was abolished, the Raises fully recognising the truth of the official suggestion that learning should know no difference of birth, but at the same time withdrawing, to a great extent, their children from contact with plebeians. Thus, the opportunity was also lost with the aristocracy of identifying its younger generation with the new civilisation, and of providing the people in future with enlightened leaders, whose interest and smallness of number made them completely amenable to guidance by the State.

The above was the condition of things which I found on my arrival at Lahore in November 1864. With the exception of the trading and manufacturing classes, the educated members from which were no source of strength to the Government, nor had yet betrayed symptoms of becoming one of mischief, I found all that was respectable in the country either alienated or disappointed. A Parliamentary Report, quoted further on, describes a state of affairs which was partly remedied afterwards, but which has now given way to, I fear, the hopeless disillusion of all whose support is necessary to true progress and the stability of an enlightened administration. Sometimes with the best intentions, at other times from motives of self-preservation, the Educational Department, from which the despatch of 1854 expects an alacrity, not common to human nature, for self-effacement, misinterpreted, ridiculed, opposed, delayed, and crushed almost every effort at national government in matters of education, and almost every aspiration of the people that was not compatible with its ascendancy and prestige. Nor has that department, like other departments, been a handmaid to the State; but it has acted as if education were something apart from the general administration, and not merely one of many agencies for strengthening the hold of an enlightened and progressive Government upon the people, and for identifying their interests in one common devotion to the welfare of the State. On the contrary, it has sown dragon's teeth, which are springing up in a harvest of disaffection, destructive alike of the ancient civilisation of the country, of the possibility of any genuine, because gradual, development from within and of the natural adaptation of all that may be suited to India in a foreign civilisation.

I cannot more fitly conclude this "introduction" than by quoting some extracts from the Parliamentary Report (1874, C. 1072—II, Part III) to which I have already referred, at the risk of being accused of vanity and of introducing matter the relevancy of which may not be at once perceived by the ordinary reader. The importance, however, of the provincial interests at stake, and the necessity of describing the revival of the educational spirit of enterprise in the Panjáb, now threatened by collapse, unless its official obstacle is removed, should place one above all personal considerations, among which the desire of praise or the fear of blame for redundancy are, indeed, of small moment—

"In 1864 the Panjáb Government offered the Principalship of the Lahore Government College (just founded) for public competition. Dr. Leitner applied for and obtained the appointment. He reached Lahore in November 1864, and there found a state of things which he at once set himself to remedy. He describes the Government educational system as having little real hold on the people, who in sullen silence felt themselves to be disregarded, and their ancient civilisation despised. There was, indeed, we are told, a system of so-called English education, consisting chiefly of instruction in mathematics and random or fragmentary selections of more or less known authors. One of the courses contained portions of Dr. Dixon's 'Life of Bacon,' Prescott's 'Essay on Chateaubriand's Essay on Milton,' Campbell's 'Rhetoric,' and Roger's 'Italy,' as a curriculum of English literature for advanced students; whilst in mental philosophy, Abercrombie; in history, a few notices of the history of the Jews, and of Rome, or Greece, were deemed sufficient. As regards the elementary schools, we learn from Dr. Leitner that some of the maps in use actually made the Sahara run through Spain, an error the peculiar character of which would seem to indicate that these maps may have been inaccurate reproductions of information originally derived from a Moorish or Saracenic source.

"The educational despatch issued by the India Office in 1854 furnished the basis for Dr. Leitner's operations. Its main principle was 'to pave the way for the abolition of the Government schools by means of voluntary organisation,' but its provisions, such as, for instance, the grant-in-aid rules, were imperfectly known or understood by the natives, and decisive steps to carry it out were still to be taken.

"Dr. Leitner began by endeavouring to arouse a spirit of self-reliance among the natives, especially among their natural leaders—the chiefs, the priests, and the wealthier merchants. He founded an association, the 'Anjuman-i-Panjáb,' for the diffusion of useful knowledge, the discussion of subjects possessing literary and scientific interest, and for the free expression of native opinion on questions of social and political reform. The association flourished and spread through the province. It opened a 'Free Public Library' and free 'Reading-Room,' and popular lectures and recitations of native poets were ere long added to its other attractions. It has taken a leading part in the discussion of matters of social, provincial, and imperial importance.

"Two movements inaugurated by the society call, however, for more especial notice. One of its native members, an eminent Sanskrit scholar, Pandit Radha Kishn, the President of the Sanskrit section of the society in its literary department, addressed a letter to Government, suggesting that steps should be taken for the preservation and cataloguing of Sanskrit manuscripts—a movement which is now being carried out all over India. He received a letter of acknowledgment from His Royal Highness the Prince of Wales, then President of the London Sanskrit Text Society, and Patron of the 'Anjuman'—a gracious act, which not only stimulated the labours of the society, but gave a considerable impetus to the second movement referred to, *viz.*, the 'Oriental movement,' whose importance in affecting the whole course of the Indian system of education must necessarily be great. Its distinguishing features are described as follows :—

"1. *The foundation of a National University in the Panjáb,*—implying the development of self-government among the natives in all matters connected with their own education. The first step towards this end was to associate with the officers of Government in the control of popular education the donors by whose contributions the proposed University was to be founded, together with the learned men among the natives of the province.

"2. *The revival of the study of the Classical Languages of India, viz.,*— Arabic for the Muhammadans, and Sanskrit for the Hindus; thus showing the respect felt by enlightened Europeans for what natives of India consider their highest and most sacred literature, without a knowledge of which it was felt that no real hold upon their mind can ever be obtained by a reformer.

"3. *The bringing European science and education generally within the reach of the masses.*—This was to be done by developing the vernaculars of India through their natural sources—the Arabic, Sanskrit, and Persian,—and by translating works of interest or scientific value into those vernaculars.

"4. *The elevation of the standard of English education to the level of the reforms which are ever being carried out in Europe, and by studying languages, history, philosophy, and law on the 'comparative method,' as adapted to the mental disposition of Muhammadans and Hindus respectively.*—The University was to be not only an examining body, but also a teaching body, differing in this respect from the other three Indian Universities, those of Calcutta, Bombay, and Madras, which merely examine. It was also to be a centre of discussion on all subjects affecting education, and, finally, a matter of peculiar interest to us in Europe, it was to be an academy for the cultivation of archæological and philological investigations, and for giving a helping hand to European Orientalists, whose enquiries it would advance by researches on the spot, whilst it would itself benefit by popularising European Oriental learning, and bring its critical method to bear on the literary labours of native savánts (*vide* Panjáb University College Papers and Statutes).

"The scheme thus conceived enlisted warm native support, and most liberal contributions poured in. Sir Donald Macleod, the Governor of the Province, gave his approval to the movement, and under his auspices a committee of European supporters issued in its favour a manifesto. It was opposed, however, by the Educational Department and by the Calcutta University, although one of its Vice-Chancellors, Mr. Seton-Karr, generously declared that, in his opinion, the time for the formation of a fourth University for Upper India had arrived. A long controversy ensued. Its progress may be traced in the files of the Indian newspapers, and a reference to them will show the active part which Dr. Leitner took therein. A portion of the general Panjáb scheme, *viz.*, the movement in support of vernacular literature, was at length adopted in the North-Western Provinces, and eventually the Calcutta University was induced to make substantial concessions to the popular requirements and in favour of Oriental learning.

"Early in 1870 a 'University College' was established at Lahore, and the Government Colleges of Lahore and Delhi, the Medical Schools (English and vernacular), an Oriental College, law classes and apparently a school in arts and industry, were affiliated to it (*vide* Prospectus).

"On the recommendation of the Panjáb Government the Government of India, in its order No. 9, dated 10th June 1869, sanctioned the foundation of the University College, it being stated at the time that the name of 'College' had been added to that of 'University,' in order to mark that this arrangement was temporary, and that as soon as the University College created a larger number of students and candidates for examinations than had existed before, the full rights of a University would be conceded to it.

"Meanwhile it is interesting to observe that the Lahore Government College, which began in 1864 with four students, counted in 1872 over 60 undergraduates in attendance, a proof that the impetus given to Oriental education has not diminished the demand for English. The men who have left the Lahore College are said to be among the most successful of native officials, employés, or private practitioners, and seem, as Lord Northbrook is reported to have said when on a visit to that institution, fully to realise their duties to their fellow-countrymen.

"Two Universities, as may have been gathered from what has been already said, influence education in the Panjáb.

"Under these Universities are, first, District, *i. e.*, 'Zillah Schools,' which prepare for the Entrance Examination of the Calcutta University in English, and in English and the vernacular for the Panjáb University College. There are also mission schools, normal schools, adult schools, and private students preparing for the 'Entrance Examination.' Below the 'zillah' schools, which are subdivided into higher, middle, and lower, and are chiefly Anglo-Vernacular, are a number of town and village schools, where Persian, geography, the vernaculars, and the 3 r's. are taught. There are also special schools, such as the Medical College of Lahore, the normal schools for teachers, &c., at Rawalpindi, Lahore, and Amritsar; and, finally, *there is a vast number of indigenous religious schools for Muhammadans and Hindus.* These indigenous schools are almost entirely conducted by priests, some of whom are believed to be profound Oriental scholars; but the studies in these schools are chiefly confined to the grammar and religious literature of the two classical languages of India, *viz.*, Arabic and Sanskrit. In some of them also Persian, caligraphy, and a peculiar commercial cyphering are taught. The arrangements for discipline, regular attendance, &c., are very defective, but *these schools being numerous and popular cannot be ignored in any popular system of public instruction* (*vide* Dr. Leitner's report as Inspector of the Ráwalpindi Circle, and the amusing photograph of the rod in vogue in such schools, exhibited by the Indian Government). According to the grant-in-aid rules of the Indian Government, *they appear to be entitled to a grant from Government*, not exceeding half their annual expenditure, so long as they teach secular subjects in a satisfactory manner. Practically, the Christian missionary schools have hitherto been the only semi-religious schools that have received grants-in-aid from Government, and there seems to be no doubt that India is indebted to the missionaries for much of her education, and for the formation of a higher standard of practical morality.

"In order to familiarise the native priests, who, to a great extent, constitute the learned classes, with the results of European criticism, Dr. Leitner assisted in founding a critical Arabic journal for the Maulvis, and a Sanskrit journal (both weekly) for the Pandits. He also wrote the *Sinin-ul-Islam*, a book of which Part I has appeared, containing 'the History of Muhammadanism and its Literature, and their Place in Universal History.' It was written for the use of the Maulvis, and its object is to familiarise them with the idea that their learning did not, as they have fondly supposed, stand alone in the world, but that it borrowed from Western sources, just as, on the other hand, the European schools of the middle ages availed themselves of the labours of the Arabs.

"In all the schools, whether indigenous or 'aided,' the teachers naturally vary in status and attainments. Generally it may be said that in the private 'aided,' as well as in the Government schools of the middle and higher classes where English is taught, the teachers are well or fairly qualified; a few graduates of European Universities being found among them. Above the head-masters of the upper district schools are the four Inspectors of the Umballa, Lahore, Ráwalpindi, and Multan Circles, and the Professors and Principals of the Government Colleges of Lahore and Delhi. These officers are 'graded,' *i. e.*, they have a vested interest in promotion to higher pay and position according to seniority and services; they are all graduates of European Universities. The Director of Public Instruction under whom they are placed has hitherto been a military man or a member of the Indian Civil Service (*vide* Panjáb Educational Reports).

"Much as our Indian system of education has, in spite of its imperfections, undoubtedly done, it cannot be said to have given culture, one of the highest marks of 'education.'

"Native elegance and refinement, wherever they still linger, are evidently of Persian origin; thorough mental discipline and scholarly habits exist with Pándits and Maulvis, whilst a smattering of various branches of 'instruction,' to be more or less offensively paraded, is what we have given to the natives with our so-called English education. That this is not an overcharged statement will appear upon reference to the official 'Remarks' published by order of the Lieutenant-Governor of the Panjáb (Proceedings, No. 606, dated 18th February 1873)—

"'Neither the English language nor literature is taught upon any scientific or intelligent system, and the success of English education, as a consequence, has not hitherto been marked in the Panjáb. Nor has the system which produces few scholars been more successful in producing gentlemen. The Lieutenat-Governor desires that the department take especial care that the good manners natural to Oriental youth are not lost at school. This matter has hitherto been neglected. If the result of sending boys of good family to school is, as is now often the case, that they return pert, conceited, and studiously rude and familiar, it is no wonder that parents desire to educate their children at home. English education is not a desirable thing if it only signifies sufficient acquaintance with the English language to write and speak ungrammatically, sufficient acquaintance with English literature to be shallow, and with English history to be insolent. English education is to be penetrated with the spirit of the great English authors; to imbibe some portion of their strength and beauty, and nobility and gentleness, and wisdom, to mould the life and character upon the models they have furnished. This is the standard of education to which the department must endeavour to rise.'

"True learning and taste among the natives of India are still Oriental, not English. The elaborate manuscripts, whether written in tracing, on paper, on leather, bark of the birch tree, canvas, or wood, by the hand or the toe, show an attention to detail and finish which cannot be too highly rated. The illuminated pages of manuscripts, written 1,000 years ago, are fresher than any combination of colours in English show-books; the pictures, in spite of a want of knowledge of perspective, very often seize the salient characteristics of a person, action, or scene, more vividly and minutely than the dark reflection of the photograph, or the conventional drawing-room painting. A happy combination of Western with Eastern ideas, as shown in the Panjáb movement, and for which Dr. Leitner has so earnestly contended, may be accepted as a wholesome reaction against an unreasoning condemnation of everything Oriental. Each, surely, may learn from the other. The subtle Eastern wit may quicken, while in turn it is steadied by the matter-of-fact touch of the European; and something of its minute thoroughness be turned to profitable account as a corrective of superficiality and of hurried generalisation. The one will no longer consider that he has everything to teach and nothing to learn, nor will the other hold aloof, in sullen and apprehensive silence, as he sees one landmark after another of his ancient civilisation inconsiderately swept away. Each will take an enlarged view of things. The character of each will be raised and strengthened.

"The care which natives take of their manuscripts, the ceremonious way with which they treat their sacred writings, and the costly layers of wrappers in which they are embosomed, are remnants of a reverence with which the spread of printing is everywhere calculated to interfere. Yet in Tibetan printing from wood blocks, probably far more ancient than the era of its appearance in Europe, the leaves are preserved with a religious care which might well be commended to the attention of European students. And whatever the value of Central Asian geographies in the Turki language, or of the Tibetan astronomical tables, or of other historical, ethical, and poetical works may be as educational models, they can scarcely fail to arrest the attention and enlist the sympathy of every intelligent and unprejudiced educator."

HISTORY

OF

INDIGENOUS EDUCATION IN THE PANJAB SINCE ANNEXATION.

PREFACE AND SUMMARY.

I FEAR that my account of the decline of indigenous education in the Panjab may offend some prejudices and oppose some interests. I have to appeal to rulers to put themselves in the position of the ruled, if they wish to under stand them, and to criticise a Department to which I am attached by a long career and several friendships. The task that has been imposed on me involves the sacrifice of considerations which few can ignore, even in the greatest of causes. Yet if it is to be discharged, however imperfectly, both the writer of these pages and their reader must endeavour to divest themselves of every preconception. Indeed, the man has so often described the struggle with the lion, that it would be well to sketch a picture which the lion might have drawn had he been a painter, in other words, to consider the effect of our system of education on indigenous civilization from combined European and Native standpoints.

The Panjab is classic ground. Not merely the celebrated country between the Sutlej and the Jumna, but also the whole province teems with noble recollections. The history of its culture will tell us of a simple worship which long withstood the superstitions of the priests and warriors whom it had itself sent to conquer the South; of an ardent republicanism allied to the most chivalrous devotion to chiefs; of a capacity for self-government not equalled elsewhere; and, above all, of the universal respect for learning and of the general spread of education. The priest was a professor and poet, and in several tribes, castes and classes, as will be shown further on, education was a religious, social or professional duty.

As the wanderer through villages or unfrequented suburbs of towns, remote from the visits of Europeans, passes unperceived along the deserted streets or lanes, after the oil-lamp has been lit in the Native household, he will hear snatches of songs or fragments of poems telling of departed grandeur, of duty to the Deity, of the fear of God which overcomes the fear of man. Love, which has ever inspired poetry in all ages and countries, will be celebrated in chaste and tender strains, except where the influence of Urdu has colored the description of that passion. Here a minstrel will praise Ranjit Singh or recount the glories of the "Dharm Raj" when God's law alone was King. There a boy will chant a chapter from the Koran or a "sweet-voiced" reader recite portions of the "Ramayana." Elsewhere, the sound of some saying of a Sikh sage or of the verses of a favorite Panjabi poet, unknown to print, but living in the mouths of the people, will strike the attentive ear. Indeed, the taste for poetry, chiefly Panjabi, Persian, and now Urdu, is still the native resource for a prosaic life. Few are the shops, houses or even huts in which there are not periodical gatherings, though their recurrence is rarer than before annexation, to hear readings or recitations from religious books; many there still are who have committed portions of the "Mahabharata" to memory in polyglot versions; in the humblest household will often be heard those charmingly compiled stories of prophets and saints which have been written for the use of girls; the driest grammatical or philosophical disquisition will collect and keep an audience in the Village Hall or shop whose owner wishes to become a public benefactor, and even the frivolities of the Holi are sobered at numerous places, as, for instance at Amritsar, by the concourse of Pandits to discuss some subtle point in the Vedanta and of "Mastersingers" in Panjabi. These "Battles of the Bards," whether of priests or poets, "Mubáhisas" or "Mushá'ras," attract numerous listeners from all creeds, whilst every night at the "Durbar Sahib" of the sacred City of the Sikhs may still be heard, though in less enthusiastic tones, discussions on religion and science. Even at Simla, within the shadow of the stronghold of the Education Commission, and undeterred by the presence of several "Lát" and numerous "Bara" Sahibs and "Councilis," there are, in the small row of shops near the Elysium Hotel, repeated nightly gatherings for prayer or praise, or to hear religious or philosophical recitations, which are generally hushed into temporary silence at the sound of approaching Jampanis or of a cavalcade taking European riders to their belated rest.

It is only where the influence of a Government school has extended that these signs of a national intellectual life are disappearing. The boy who brings home his Urdu lesson does not often read it out, even to his Muhammadan parent, for the language is not the Perso-Panjabi of the Province, but the Delhi dialect, into which strange and rustic idioms are introduced by the Educational Department under the impression that it is promoting purism. Besides, the source of the boy's lesson is profane and it is studied not in order to develop the mind or character, but as a step towards an appointment. Few parents, who feel the pettiness of such an ambition, can spontaneously make the lesson in question a basis for the inculcation of moral maxims, nor does the boy listen with deference to a father whom he is, more or less consciously, learning daily to despise. The language and sentiments which the boy brings back from school, being imperfectly understood both by himself and by his parents, can, therefore, awaken no response, and are not attached to any associations of family or faith. In every case in which we have taught a boy through the medium of a foreign vernacular, we have lost the teaching power of his parents, especially as regards instruction in morality and in the practical duties of life. The lessons of the schoolmaster are, therefore, not continued in the pupil's home, and they are not extended to his brothers and sisters, as would be the case if they were given in his real vernacular, and if they were based on what is best in his own associations. Incidentally also, the present system retards female education, and stops the former supply of female teachers trained in their own families. There are, however, still numerous households in which the child, back from an indigenous school, tells the lesson fresh from the Pandit, Maulvi, Bhai or even Pádha to his admiring parent, who will comment on it, and who, living his own childhood over again, will take the opportunity of instilling into the mind of his offspring the wise saws which he may have heard, and the practical applications of what has the sanction of learning and of religion.

It may now be asked, "what is this indigenous education which is so held up to admiration? Where are these indigenous schools, and how are they supported?"

These questions, which Mr. Arnold, the first Director of Public Instruction in the Panjab, put to himself in his first Report, have not yet been answered. More than 26 years have elapsed since the foundation of the provincial Education Department, and, in spite of constant pressure by the Panjab Government, its attempts to elicit information have invariably failed. Numerous explanations have been given of this want of success, of which the only plausible one is the law of self-preservation as applied to the Education Department. Before its formation Sirs Henry and John Lawrence had no insuperable difficulty in ascertaining the particulars regarding indigenous education, so far as their enquiries extended. In backward districts, like that of Hushiarpur, the Settlement Report of 1852 shows a school to every 19·65 male inhabitants (adults and non-adults), which may be contrasted with the present proportion of 1 Government or aided school to every 9,028 inhabitants, or 1 school to every 2818·7 inhabitants, including the present number of ascertained indigenous schools throughout the province, a significant contrast to the proportion of

1 school to every 1,783 inhabitants in the most backward division of the Panjab in 1849 when brought under British rule after a period of confusion following on war and annexation!

The explanations, however, given by successive Directors of Public Instruction in the Panjab of the failure to ascertain the correct number, if not the nature, of indigenous schools, and their consequent inability to aid or improve them, in accordance with the policy of the Educational Despatches of 1854 and 1859, and with the repeated instructions of the Local Government, well deserve consideration. They are given at length in the "Extracts from Educational Reports and Government Reviews" thereon, which I have thought it my duty to add to this report. They may, however, be summarized as follows: (1) that it was difficult (if not, in the words of one Director, "impossible") to ascertain the number of these schools; (2) that the education given in them was worthless; (3) that there were few indigenous schools; (4) that all those worthy of the name of school had already been absorbed into the Department; (5) that they could not be absorbed into our educational system (6) that only the District Officers could properly attend to them; (7) that the grant-in-aid rules did not apply to them, or that only these rules applied to them; (8) that the Village School Cess was available for them, or that it was not available for them; (9) that they *refused* aid even on the most lenient conditions; (10) that the statistics collected regarding them by District Officers were untrustworthy; (11) that the statistics collected by Chief Muharrirs were, for certain good reasons, equally unreliable; (12) that no European Inspector had the time to inspect them; (13) that several European Inspectors did inspect many of them regularly; (14) that a special agency for their inspection and more funds were required; (15) that (on more funds being appropriated to education generally) they could not be dealt with by the Department, and their statistics were accordingly, on more than one occasion, omitted from the Educational Returns.

Possibly, and with some show of fairness, educational officers may reply to the above enumeration of inconsistent excuses for not fully and faithfully discharging their obvious duty to the State, that the alleged explanations were not offered either simultaneously or in the bluntness of my wording or that some of them were not offered at all. I can only point out that the statements in the Reports which I have quoted and in other documents with the Local Government tell their own tale, and that they can give no other meaning to an unprejudiced reader, acquainted with official phraseology, even in the rare instances in which the words are not the *ipsissima verba* of my summary. The fact at all events remains, as will be proved further on, that nothing was done for indigenous schools except to injure or destroy them; that indigenous education has greatly declined without a corresponding increase in Government and Aided Schools; and that, although the attention of the Director was called to the practice of other provinces, the Panjab, which spent nearly 16 lakhs (exclusive of Rs. 69,880 by the Panjab University) during the last year on 110,649 pupils among a population of 18¾ millions, or 1 pupil to every 169, there were 81,000 pupils under instruction in the Central Provinces among a population of 8,215,167, or 1 pupil to every 101 (according to Mr. Alexander Mackenzie's statement published this year), and 1,106,619 pupils in Lower Bengal among a population of about 68 millions, or 1 pupil to every 61 (the number given by Mr. Mackenzie, late of the Madras Legislative Council, is 62,724,840). It must be borne in mind that, in the Bengal enumeration, the Koran Schools, which form the larger proportion of Panjab indigenous schools, are not counted, whilst I doubt whether all the indigenous schools are included in the returns of the Central Provinces. In 1860-61, there were 37,280 pupils in the Panjab, costing Rs. 4,18,510, or Rs. 11-3-7 per head. In 1865-66, there were 102,418 pupils, costing Rs. 8,66,766, or Rs. 8-7-5 per head. In 1881-82 the cost per pupil, exclusive of the expenditure of the Panjab University (the latter chiefly on higher education), rises to Rs. 14-6-3, and, inclusive of that amount, to Rs. 15-4-8, whereas there can be no doubt that it was quite possible to add the extra 8,000 pupils of last year to the number in 1865-66 without any extra expenditure whatever, instead of nearly doubling the same. (The above expenditure is on Government and Aided Schools and, occasionally, on a few *nominal* Indigenous schools, as shown in the annexed "conclusions from the Educational Reports and Government Reviews thereon.") In 1860-61 there were 8,449 schools, and 119,547 pupils, including 6,559 indigenous schools with 82,267 pupils (so far as was then ascertained, the numbers being admittedly *under*-stated). In 1875-76 there were 6,471 schools and 163,981 pupils, including 4,406 indigenous schools with 48,697 pupils. In 1880-81 there were 6,750 schools, and 157,950 pupils, including 4,662 indigenous schools with 53,027 pupils. It seems to me to be clear from above that there has been a falling off in indigenous schools, even during the operation of the Educational Department as well as after annexation, without an increase in Government and Aided Schools corresponding in any degree to the increase of expenditure, the increase of the population and the increase of pupils in other Provinces. For this state of things, I profoundly regret to be compelled to say, great and persistent mismanagement coupled with passive resistance to the policy of the Government and an intentional neglect of opportunities, are alone to blame, as it will be my painful duty to establish further on.

The incomplete Census of 1854-55, which greatly understates the population, and is exclusive of Delhi and Hissar, gives a population of 12,717,821 souls in the then British territory in the Panjab, which may serve as some basis for our educational calculations. To quote paragraph 188 of the Administration Report for 1854-55, "there were then 26,210 villages in the Panjab with an average of about 450 persons in each; 2,124 small towns containing from 1,000 to 5,000 inhabitants; 76 containing from 5,000 to 10,000; 31 cities containing from 10,000 to 50,000; and four first-class cities, containing more than 50,000 inhabitants, *i.e.*, Amritsar with 122,184 souls, Lahore with 94,153, Peshawur with 53,294, Mooltan (including suburbs) with 55,999 souls." (At all events, we have here a definition of what is meant by "a village," a very significant circumstance when taken in connection with the Village School Cess which was then being raised for aiding Indigenous Schools in villages and for providing Government village schools to serve as models to Indigenous Schools.) By the last Census we have 29,848 villages and towns against 28,879 in 1854-55, and 15,631,386 inhabitants by the last census against 12,717,821 *for the same districts*, surely no very startling increase in 28 years of general peace and prosperity under British administration when the accuracy of the last census is compared with the incompleteness of the census of 1854-55. It is to be regretted that the opportunity was not taken at the last census, as suggested on previous occasions, to obtain a return of indigenous schools, which could have been done easily, because incidentally, without creating suspicion, or, at all events, of the number of mosques and other sacred edifices, which would have equally served to give, at any rate, the approximate number of indigenous schools before annexation, for there was no such edifice without a school, whilst there were innumerable schools, in addition, held in private houses, in the village halls, in shops and in the open air. As there was no village or town without, at any rate, one sacred edifice, we get, at least, 28,879 schools, which, if attended by only ten pupils each, would contain nearly 300,000 pupils; but there are reasons, which will be mentioned in the body of the report, for estimating a larger number.* After 26 years of the operations of the Educational Department, we have, *including* the number of indigenous schools as returned in 1878-79, 157,950 pupils in schools of every description in 1880-81, or about half of the numbers before annexation. The cost also of the Government and aided schools per pupil, according to the report of 1881-82, is, apparently, 15 times higher than that of an indigenous school, where one rupee per head is implied to be the general average. We shall, of course, not have done our duty to the people, unless, at the *same* expenditure on education as at present, we succeed in, at least, quadrupling our present numbers, which can be done, with an earnest effort on the part of the district authorities, and a complete change in the *personnel*, administration

* A very large number of villages had more than one school, whilst towns like Delhi had 279 schools (see Mr. A. Roberts' Report for 1849). Some villages, even now, have more than one school, *e.g.*, Atawa and Firozpur in the Gujranwala District; Hariana, Baribasi, and Gurh Shankar in that of Hushiarpur, &c. (see Appendix II). Hundreds of villages, however, where dharmsalas and other sacred edifices still exist, are now deprived of the schools which were formerly connected with them. The City of Amritsar has still 143 schools; Sialkot 38; Batala 10, &c.

and system of instruction of the Educational Department, in the course of a few years, or, better still, by the abolition of the Educational Department at a considerable saving to the State, to be devoted to the foundation of *more* schools, high and low, English and Oriental, as also to the award of more scholarships for proved merit, and for the special encouragement of any subject or any section of the community that may be in need of such stimulus.

The following table compares, so far as I have been able to ascertain, the number of indigenous schools and their pupils with that of the corresponding Government primary vernacular schools, although it may be said, *en passant*, that many of the indigenous schools, as will be shown from their scheme of studies, published in the body of this report, should more fitly be called high schools and, in some instances, colleges, than schools :—

Year.	Schools.			Pupils.			Expenditure by Government on Government and Aided schools.
	Indigenous.	Government.	Total.	Indigenous.	Government.	Total.	
							Rs.
1856-57	5,024	456	5,480	30,196	6,064	36,260	1,28,864
1857-58	3,461	1,336	4,797	26,317	12,024	38,341	2,27,131
1858-59	6,173	2,029	8,202	32,023	26,377	58,400	2,57,482
1859-60	6,309	1,704	8,013	63,090	37,000	1,00,090	2,85,789
1860-61	6,559*	1,886	8,445	82,267*	32,165	1,14,432	3,77,953
1866-67	5,434	1,660	7,094	33,063	53,757	86,820	9,49,065
1867-68	4,888	1,555	6,443	46,947	51,326	98,273	9,49,176
1868-69	5,222	1,462	6,684	55,454	51,100	1,06,554	9,84,685
1869-70	3,995	1,128	5,123	52,479	43,486	95,965	9,98,816
1870-71	4,133	1,087	5,220	50,551	43,080	93,631	10,18,640
1871-72	4,292	1,057	5,349	54,612	44,429	99,041	10,60,525
1872-73	4,154	1,042	5,196	48,771	45,178	93,949	12,56,919
1873-74	4,463	1,148	5,611	54,445	52,511	1,06,956	11,41,606
1875-76	4,406	1,218	5,624	48,697	61,131	1,09,828	14.51,161
1876-77	4,803	1,264	6,067	56,642	57,972	1,14,416	14,57,552
1877-78	5,581	1,295	6,876	61,818	57,829	1,19,647	14,44,512
1878-79	4,662	1,210	5.872	53,027	54,065	1,07,092	13,69,146

* This is taken from paragraph 11 of No. 147, dated Lahore, the 13th March 1860, from Secretary, Panjab, to Government of India, acknowledging the receipt of the Educational Despatch of 1859.

The following Statement shows the number of Colleges and Schools, scholars, and total expenditure on Government and Aided Schools from all sources at intervals of five years from 1860 to 1881, as also the ascertained number of indigenous schools and of their pupils :—

	1860-61.	1865-66.	1870-71.	1875-76.	1880-81.
I.					
Colleges and Schools.					
Arts Colleges	...	3	2	2	1
Secondary Schools	146	165	151	205	225
Primary Schools	1,696	1,701	1,283	1,495	1,524
Schools for Girls	40	1,032	465	352	323
Special Schools	8	7	10	11	15
Total of Government and Aided Institutions ...	1,800	2,968	1,911	2,065	2,088
Total of ascertained indigenous schools ...	6,559	...	4,133	4,406	4,662
GRAND TOTAL ...	8,449	...	6,044	6,471	6,750
II.					
Number of students in					
Arts Colleges	...	51	102	113	94
Schools for boys	35,957	82,022	72,546	1,03,978	94,396
Schools for girls	872	19,561	11,819	10,556	9,695
Special schools	451	294	415	637	738
Total of students	37,280	1,02,418	84,782	1,15,284	1,04,923
Total of ascertained indigenous schools ...	82,267	...	50,551	48,697	53,027
GRAND TOTAL ...	1,19,547	...	1,35,333	1,63,981	1,57,950
III.					
Total expenditure from all sources on Government and Aided schools.	Rs. 4,18,510	Rs. 8,66,766	Rs. 10,18,640	Rs. 14,51,161	Rs. 13,92,584
IV. Cost per pupil in Government and Aided schools.	Rs. A. P. 11 3 7	Rs. A. P. 8 7 5	Rs. A. P. 12 0 3	Rs. A. P. 12 9 5	Rs. A. P. 13 4 4

NOTES.—Between 1866 and 1870 a grant of Rs. 10,000 per annum from Imperial Funds for female education was withdrawn. It had been wrongfully taken from the Village School Cess, which was itself, as on other occasions, constituted a source for *giving* grants to Government and Aided Schools. Village Schools were reduced on account of the exhaustion of educational cess balances, which, although derived from the Village School Cess, had been largely misapplied to purposes other than those for which it had been raised, and by a new rule by which the minimum pay of a teacher was raised from Rs. 5 to Rs. 10 per mensem, thus making him a Government servant and rendering him independent of the good opinion or support of the village or town in which he taught, with disastrous effect to the numbers and efficiency of the schools and the morality of both teacher and pupils. Had these Rs. 5 per mensem been continued to the teacher and had he been allowed to take fees, he would have had a stimulus for exertion and his school might, indeed, have become a model to indigenous schools. The Rs. 5 given to raise the Village School teacher's salary from Rs. 5 to 10, might more fitly have been given to the development of existing indigenous schools or to the creation of new Schools, instead of choosing a time, when the misapplied balances had been exhausted, to *double* the pay of teachers, *reduce* the number of schools and *increase* the salaries of their Inspectors.

In 1873, about two lakhs of additional income accrued from Local Rates, which were not duly spent in increasing the number of village schools in villages. In 1870, superior officers were graded and received a considerable increase of pay. In 1880-81, about 100 Primary Schools, which were formerly included with Secondary Schools, are shown separately. In the first Educational Reports the names of the towns and villages in which Schools are situated are given. This is not done in the later Reports, so that it is impossible now to ascertain how many Government Vernacular Schools are in Villages or where they are, what is spent on them from the Village Cess, &c., whilst, in spite of making up a number of Zila schools into three Divisions (High, Middle and Primary), and thus showing three schools, where there is really only one school, often taught by the same masters, there were only 1,284 Government Vernacular primary schools in 1881-82, when the expenditure on education is nearly 16 lakhs against 2,029 real Village Schools in 1858-59, when the expenditure was only Rs. 2,57,482, *or about a sixth part of the present expenditure.*

In order to give an account worthy of the Education Commission and of the Government regarding indigenous education, a whole year, at least, should be devoted to the collection of the necessary information by a person well acquainted with the subject and in thorough sympathy with it. It is not likely that what the Educational Department has failed to accomplish during 26 years with its thousands of teachers throughout the province under military orders, many of whom are able to furnish, at any rate, the bare statistics so far as their own localities are concerned, whilst all the resources of district officers have equally been available for places in which there are no Government schools, will now be accomplished in a few weeks by a man broken down in health and with none of these agencies at his command. When it is also taken into consideration that in numerous places the indigenous school has literally been frightened out of its home by the Tahsildar, if in the most remote possible competition with a Government school, and that the bulk of the teachers, however generally well disposed to aid in such an enquiry, fear to incur departmental displeasure for assisting in any of the supposed aims of the Panjab University College, the difficulty of the task is greatly increased. It was not thus, as it were, at a minute's notice that the hedge schools of Ireland were dragged into light, received a local habitation, and formed the basis of the present "national" system of education in that country. The innumerable hedge schools of the Panjab will, therefore, not be dealt with in this Report. Even as regards the apparently "fixed" 4,662 indigenous schools mentioned in the Educational Report for 1878-79 (after which no reference to these institutions again appears), it is needless to point out that the mere statement of the above number gives no indication of the localities in which these schools are to be found, nor is it likely that a Department which has not yet been able to furnish the list of *Government* Vernacular Primary Schools situated in villages, properly so-called, and that can give no information as to the precise amount spent on such schools from the Village School Cess which it has itself misapplied to purposes other than that for which it was raised, will be able to furnish any information regarding the exact whereabouts of these institutions, while it does not possess a single officer capable of inspecting what it has all along looked upon as a rival that should be crushed. The consequence of this relation of the Educational Department to the Indigenous Schools of the country has been that many Maulvis, Pandits and Bhais would be afraid to give information regarding these schools or the subjects taught in them to any officer of Government, lest their doing so might lead to the absorption or destruction of these schools or to the imposition of a tax on a generally precarious income. The tendency, therefore, of indigenous teachers is to *under*-state their income and the number of their pupils, in order to obtain safety by their assumed unimportance, and this view it is also to the interest of the Government schoolmaster to promote, though for different reasons. But even when the required statistical information has been elicited, there still remains the difficulty of ascertaining the precise value of the subjects taught. When one officer deposes that he *knew* Sanscrit and the vernacular, and that he had yet found, against the fact, that the Indigenous Schools were *deficient* in grammar and when another officer, who is equally acquainted with English and Urdu, is of opinion that books beyond the F. A. standard cannot be translated into the latter language, it is easy to perceive what the result of any enquiry would be, if conducted by persons out of sympathy with it or, worse still, whose personal interests, and certainly present leisure, would be affected by its success.

Under these circumstances, it seemed to me that the only possible way for arriving at the desired information in the short time at my disposal was to proceed extra-officially, and with this view I addressed the subjoined circular to the Maulvis, Pandits, Bhais and Munshis of the Lahore Oriental College. Teachers and students, however, were engaged in the Examinations preceding the Long Vacation, though some of them furnished me with valuable information which has been printed in Appendix II to this Report. The circular was also sent out with the Journals of the Anjuman-i-Panjab in English, Urdu, Gurmukhi, and Hindi to members and subscribers, as also to the priests of the various denominations. It was also circulated, as a matter of courtesy and professional etiquette, among teachers of Government schools, 21 of whom have kindly replied. To them my best thanks are due, for they have shown themselves to be above professional jealousy, whilst some have also contributed information of value. Most, however, appear to have been afraid to give any information regarding institutions which are deemed to be under the ban of "the Department."

In one district, at least, the rumour was spread that, as I had already given my evidence on the 8th July last, it was no longer necessary to supply me with the required information. Elsewhere, it was suggested to me to leave its collection exclusively to the teachers of Government schools, as they were *impartial* (? !) and not to ask the masters of the indigenous schools themselves, the only people who were really able, if only willing, to communicate the necessary details regarding their schools. In one district, abounding in indigenous schools, I was told that there were *none*, and in a town proverbial for its twenty Koran schools the return showed *one*. Sometimes the list of *Government* schools was sent to me, and, at other times, the indigenous schools were dismissed with the observation that there was none "of any celebrity." Of course, had I not been hurried, I should have gradually ascertained the existence of many more indigenous schools than are now "returned," by continuing my enquiries through friendly and trustworthy priests of various denominations; but, as it was, I had to take the readiest means at my disposal, and this was to obtain the information through officials and others, but in an *unofficial* manner. I accordingly also addressed Dr. W. H. Bellew, C.S.I., the eminent Sanitary Commissioner of the Panjab, in the hope that he would allow the chowkidars who bring in the weekly returns of births and deaths to ascertain also the whereabouts of indigenous schools and the names of local indigenous medical practitioners (Hakims and Baids), if not of celebrated Maulvis, Pandits and Bhais generally, so as to enable me, once I knew the precise locality of a school, to address its Manager as well as local celebrities direct on the subject. Dr. Bellew suggested my applying to Colonel Bamfield, the Inspector General of Police, who with a kindness and public-spirit, which deserve the recognition of the Education Commission, at once placed his Police clerks, 500 in number and posted in a corresponding number of "Circles" all over the province, at my disposal. I cannot sufficiently express my gratitude to that officer for his readiness in assisting my enquiries and for the trouble which he took whenever I had occasion to complain of the insufficiency or inaccuracy of any return, but a mistake occurred which nearly frustrated his efforts. The police, nowhere a popular body, also in the Panjab do not receive the recognition which they deserve, and educational enquiries *officially* conducted by them are calculated to create suspicion. It had been arranged that the information was to be elicited incidentally and privately, and to be paid for, and that the police clerks, being Hindus, Muhammadans or Sikhs, were themselves to be interested in a measure likely to benefit their respective communities. Unfortunately, by far the bulk of the information collected by the police clerks was elicited officially, and the consequence is that their returns, although correct so far as they go, are *far below* the actual numbers.

I then addressed a letter, which will be found further on, to some of my acquaintances and friends to the cause among civil officers, and, as ever, found among them the most intelligent and warm-hearted appreciation of measures intended for the public good. I am convinced that had the returns obtained from Deputy Commissioners regarding indigenous schools by the Educational Department been published *in extenso* in the educational returns, and had they been amplified or checked by further information received from the teachers of these schools themselves, and from the masters of Government schools, there would have been no necessity now, after 26 years of supposed attempts and failures, to take the very first step towards the utilization of the indigenous schools as an agency for creating good citizens and for advancing civilization, *viz.*, to ascertain precisely where they are and what they teach.

No office clerks, translators or money were placed at my disposal in a task which involves correspondence with several thousand teachers and others whose names have now been elicited, and who should be addressed, by their own friendly *colleagues*, for further information. On no account should any further enquiry be conducted by a member of the Educational Department, as my long experience of its action regarding all independent or semi-dependent educational enterprise, as well as the future requirements of indigenous and mass-education which I propose to sketch, render it absolutely indispensable that no share should be given to that Department in any matter, directly or indirectly, affecting indigenous education. It is not desired to take the masses *out* of the masses by converting them into aspirants for Government service, and this must be the inevitable effect of allowing that Department to have anything whatever to do with indigenous education, not to speak of the abolition of the "Indigenous Schools," *as such*, which must follow on departmental interference. The indigenous education of the country, instead of being preserved and developed, for its own sake, will then give way to a pretentious and shallow system of preparation for office-hunters; the trades and traditional professions of the pupils will be abandoned; what there is left of the religious feeling will be destroyed; and the country will be overrun by a hundred thousand semi-educated and needy men, for whom it will be impossible to provide, and who will have been rendered unfit for their own occupations. I should indeed regret if my persistently drawing the attention of Government and of the public since 1865 to the neglect of indigenous and of religious education should only result in inflicting a death-blow on the only conservative element of this country, and on its last hope of a genuine, *because* indigenous, civilization

What has been done in the face of apparently unsurmountable difficulties is :—

(1) The localities of over 6,000 schools, with, *at least*, 88,320 pupils, have been named and fixed, and numerous details regarding them have been ascertained. From a comparison also of the Census returns with my own, as explained further on, there are 96,585 persons "under instruction" not given in Government and aided schools.

(2) The names of over 2,000 leading Maulvis, Pandits, Munshis, Bhais, Authors, Hakims and Baids have been ascertained, and it now only remains for the authorities of the Panjab University College to put themselves into sympathetic relations with them for the advancement of the various specialities which their labours represent and for the general promotion of educational measures.

(3) The names of over 4,000 teachers have been elicited, with whom it will be necessary to enter into further correspondence.

My thanks are especially due to :—

(1) Colonel A. H. Bamfield, Inspector General of Police, and to his officers and subordinates generally.

(2) Mr. J. A. E. Miller, Officiating Deputy Commissioner of Rawalpindi.

(3) Sirdar Thakur Singh, Sindhanwalia.

(4) Mr. W. Coldstream, C.S., Deputy Commissioner of Simla.

(5) Mr. Carr Stephen, Judicial Assistant of Ludhiana.

(6) Mr. S. S. Thornburn, F.R.G.S., Officiating Deputy Commissioner of Dera Ismail Khan.

(7) Pundits Guru Parshad, Rikhi Kesh and Kaka Ram,

(8) Moulvis Muhammad-ud-din, Ghulam Mustafa, Abu Sayid Muhammad Husain, Altaf Husain, Zafruddin, and other Moulvis,

(9) Bhais Drit Ram, Jawahir Singh, and Gurmukh Singh,

} of the Oriental College—Contributors of Appendix II

(10) The Editors of the English and Urdu Journals of the Anjuman-i-Panjab for distributing the circulars.

(11) Pirzada Muhammad Husain, McLeod Arabic Fellow, and Lala Chuni Lal, H. A. Pleader, for their assistance in translation.

(12) Pandits Ishar Parshad and Achint Ram.

(13) Babu Navina Chandra Rai, Assistant Registrar of the Panjab University College.

I cannot profess to have accomplished a task which requires the most ample time, in addition to a very special and profound knowledge of native institutions, to my own satisfaction, and I therefore cannot expect to have deserved the approbation of the Education Commission and of the Government, except for the courage or temerity in attempting to undertake a work of such magnitude within a few months, undeterred by the depressing failures of similar attempts during the last 26 years, and for having, I hope, become the "pioneer" of a more successful and exhaustive future inquiry. If so, the discovery of the "people's own Department of Public Instruction" in the Panjab will be due to the initiative of the President of the Education Commission and of Sir Charles Aitchison, who deferred my furlough for nearly three months in order to enable me to collect statistics regarding an educational material which, from his knowledge of the universality and importance of indigenous education in Burmah, he rightly inferred might also be extensive and valuable in the Province of his warmest affection and early official career. To use the motto prefixed to the first treatise on Political Economy in Turkish, written by my pupil at King's College, London, 20 years ago, Dr. Charles Wells, in spite of the vague assertion that the oriental vernaculars were incapable of rendering European thought or science,

On le peut; je l'essaie; qu'un meilleur le fasse.

Montaigne.

CLASSIFICATION OF INDIGENOUS SCHOOLS.

A few words are necessary in explanation of the appended circular. I had to consider that its recipients were generally men unacquainted with our forms of "returns," and certainly unable to fill them in within the short time at their disposal. Dividing the schools, therefore, according to *subjects* would have unduly increased the number of forms, and would have led to confusion. Dividing them according to *religions* would have perpetuated the mistake of calling all Hindu schools patshalas, including the purely secular and Mahajani Schools. Dividing them according to *languages* would have led to the growing abuse of the term, "Hindi" being also applied to Landé and Saráfi as well as Nagri, if not Gurmukhi Schools. I, therefore, chose a middle, if somewhat rough, course, by dividing them into "Maktabs or Madrasas," "Patshalas," "Gurmukhi Schools," and "Mahajani Schools." I made no enquiry about female indigenous schools, as such a course would have thrown suspicion on the whole circular, and would also have endangered the success of future action regarding indigenous schools generally. The information, therefore, which the following report contains regarding Native female teachers, has been elicited spontaneously and incidentally.

By "Maktab" or "*place of writing*" is meant a Persian school, whether confined to Muhammadans or open to all sects.

By "Madrasa" or "place of lesson" is meant an Arabic school from its humble beginning, the "Koran schools" (properly spelt "Qurán") up to institutions imparting the highest knowledge in the language, literature, law and the sciences contained in Arabic. Whether "Madrasas" also taught Persian and subjects of general knowledge was not a reason for separate classification, as this would be elicited in the returns themselves.

By "Patshála" is meant a school in which Sanscrit, in however elementary a manner, is taught, and *one* of the aims of which, at any rate, is *religious*. The term, therefore, includes schools in which the "Nagri" *character*, miscalled the "Hindi" *language*, is taught as leading up to Sanscrit, whether the eventual teaching includes high or elementary, secular, or only religious teaching.

By "Gurmukhi schools" are meant schools, chiefly for the Sikh population, in which Gurmukhi is taught.

"*Mahajani* Schools" are schools for the commercial or trading community, in which the various tachygraphic forms of Landé and Saráfi are taught in addition to the multiplication table. These schools also sometimes teach the "Nagri" character, for which, as also for "Landé," the term Hindi is misused. These schools are conducted by "Pádhas," among whom in the Punjab are numerous Muhammadans.

I have also added specimens of the commercial cypher in use in Upper India, if not in other parts of this country, in order to show that they *do* afford a basis for a general character for purposes of elementary education, or that, at any rate, they do not so perceptibly vary from place to place, or that the careful writer cannot read his own writing half an hour after he has written it, as is alleged. This inability has been known to happen with English scrawls, but has not been used as a ground for the abolition of the Roman character. The first Banya I picked up in the row of shops near the hotel in which I am living, could read a *number* of commercial characters current all over India. He happened to be a native of Kangra, and read what he called his own Mahajani with great fluency, which, however, turned out to be "Thakari" or "Thankri," a character used in Kangra and, with Nagri additions, in Mandi, Kulu and other adjoining districts.

The schools started by natives on the model of Government schools, which are almost all Anglo-Vernacular, could scarcely be called "indigenous," although this term is given to them in the reports of the Educational Department. At all events, I should have run the risk of the recipients of the circular confounding them with Government schools. As their number is small, and can be partially ascertained in the reports above referred to, I do not think that the objects of this report are affected by their omission. At the same time, it was desirable to show that "unaided schools" also exist on the English pattern, which have been ignored by the Educational Department, although they may have been conducted with considerable efficiency during many years. I have accordingly given an account of some of the *unaided* schools.

The indigenous Schools in the Panjab may also be classified as follows :—

I.—Sikh indigenous Education.

1. Gurmukhi Schools.

II.—Muhammadan indigenous Education.

2. Maktabs.
3. Madrasas, religious and secular.
4. Koran Schools.

III.—Hindu indigenous Education.

5. Chatsalas (for the trading community).
6. Patshalas (religious).
7. Patshalas (semi-religious).
8. Secular Schools of various kinds and grades.

IV.—Mixed indigenous Education.

9. Persian Schools.
10. Vernacular Schools.
11. Anglo-Vernacular Schools.

V.—Female indigenous Education.

12. (*a*) Female Schools for Sikh girls.
    (*b*) Do. Muhammadan girls.
    (*c*) Instruction at Hindu homes.

With a more minute subdivision the indigenous schools might have to be classified as follows :—

I.—Maktabs or Madrasas.

1. Arabic Schools and Colleges (of various grades and specialities).
2. Perso-Arabic Schools and Colleges (do. do.).
3. Koran Schools (where merely or chiefly the Koran is read).
4. Perso-Koran Schools.
5. Koran-Arabic Schools.
6. Perso-Koran-Arabic Schools.
7. Persian Schools.
8. Persian-Urdu Schools.
9. Persian-Urdu-Arabic Schools.
10. Arabic Medical Schools.
11. Perso-Arabic Medical Schools.

II.—Gurmukhi Schools.

12. Gurmukhi Schools.
13. Gurmukhi and Landé Schools.

III.—Mahajani Schools.

14. Landé Schools of different kinds (Chatsalas).
15. Nagari-Landé Schools (Chatsalas).
16. Perso-Landé Schools.

IV.—Patshalas.

17. Nagari-Sanscrit Schools.
18. Sanskrit religious Schools.
19. Sanscrit secular literary Schools (cultivating various branches).
20. Sanskrit semi-secular Schools (do. do. do.).
21. Sanskrit Medical Schools (chiefly).
22. Hindi-Sanscrit Schools.
23. Sanskrit astrological or astronomical Schools (chiefly).

V.—Female indigenous Schools (classified as above).

The transliteration of names of places adopted in this Report, sometimes varies according to the idiosyncracies of the *contributors* of returns, and there has been no time to adopt a uniform system of spelling throughout in correcting the proofs. I prefer "tsh" for "ch" in "charm" in order not to confound it with "ch" in "character" or the strong aspirate "ch" as in German.

Form of a Circular in English (and translated into Urdu, Hindi and Gurmukhi) distributed to Police Clerks, to Teachers of Government and Indigenous schools, to Members of the Anjuman-i-Panjab and its branches, to the Staff of the Lahore Oriental College, to District Officers, and to Maulvis, Pandits and Bhais throughout the Panjab.

SIR,

Kindly inform me, at your earliest convenience, whether any, and "if so" what, schools exist in the towns or villages in your circle (*Halqa*) which are unconnected with Government. I principally refer to schools for the religious and other instruction of Muhammadans, Hindus and Sikhs, which are often found attached to mosques, temples and dharmsalas, respectively, and in which Arabic and Persian, Sanscrit and Hindi or Gurmukhi respectively are taught. I should also like to know whether there are any schools in your circle conducted by Pádhas to teach Mahajani, Landé and Saráfi; and I should like to have a specimen of the Mahajani character and multiplication table used in those schools. Any information regarding the approximate number of boys attending either the religious or the Mahajani schools, the subjects taught in them, whether the teacher is a learned man, and whether his pupils pay him in money or kind, and an approximate estimate of his monthly income, as well as any other information which you may have to give, will much oblige, &c., &c.

Questions—	*Answers—*
Mention the name of the most eminent Hakim, Baid, Maulvi, Pandit and Bhai in your circle.	
A.—Maktabs or Madrasas.	
I.—(*a*) Where is the largest *Maktab* or *Madrasa* in your circle?	
(*b*) Is it attached to a mosque? Or is it held in a private house?	
(*c*) What is the name of the teacher or teachers?	
(*d*) What are his or their qualifications?	
(*e*) About how many pupils attend that school?	
(*f*) What are the subjects taught in it?	
(*g*) How is the head teacher paid (in money or kind), and about how much per mensem?	
B.—Patshálas.	
II.—(*a*) Where is the largest *Patshála* in your circle?	
(*b*) Is it attached to a temple?	
(*c*) What is the name of the head teacher?	
(*d*) What are his qualifications?	
(*e*) About how many pupils attend his schools?	
(*f*) What are the subjects taught in it?	
(*g*) How is he paid, and about how much is his monthly income, whether in money or kind?	
C.—Gurmukhi Schools.	
III.—(*a*) Where is the largest school for teaching Gurmukhi in your circle?	

(b) Is it attached to a Dharmsala or as a bunga to a Gurudwara or Sikh temple?

(c) What is the name of the head teacher?

(d) About how many pupils attend his school?

(e) What are the subjects taught in it?

(f) What is the teacher's monthly income, by fees, &c.?

D.—Mahajani Schools.

IV.—(a) Is there a school for teaching Mahajani, Lundé and Saráfi?

(b) What is the name of the head teacher?

(c) What are his qualifications?

(d) About how many pupils attend his school?

(e) What are the subjects taught in it?

(f) What is the teacher's monthly income by fees, &c., &c.?

N.B.—Further information or general remarks may be added here regarding the Maktabs, Madrasas, Patshalas, Gurmukhi and Mahajani Schools in your Circle.

(At the end of the above Circular two pages were added, which it is scarcely necessary to reprint, of a "General Statement of Indigenous Schools in the —— Circle" to be filled in for the minor schools of various kinds in the towns and villages in the particular Circle.)

The same Circular, accompanied by the following letter, was addressed to acquaintances and friends of the cause among Civil Officers.

"May I venture to draw your attention to the forwarded letter regarding indigenous schools, which I am circulating by the permission of His Honour the Lieutenant-Governor, who is himself interested in the success of the enquiry.

The circular is intended for head masters of indigenous schools, and for those who, in your opinion, are best able to answer the questions regarding these indigenous institutions, which, I fear, we have too much neglected, and which it is now proposed to foster and improve.

It would be well if the Pandits, Maulvis, and Bhais, to whom the circular may be sent, were clearly given to understand that the enquiry is for their benefit and for that of their respective learning.

The collection of statistics on the subject of indigenous schools has hitherto been greatly impaired by a natural reluctance on the part of their teachers to give information, for they saw that the effect of our present system hitherto was to destroy or to absorb their schools.

I need hardly add that anything which you may be pleased to do to further the present enquiry will be esteemed a great personal favour."

The following "General Statement" is based on the Census returns and on the statistics furnished in the Report of the Director of Public Instruction for 1880-81 and in his Report No. 4 S., dated 22nd September 1881. It compares the number of pupils in Government and Aided schools (Primary, Middle and High) with the number of persons stated to be "under instruction" in the Census returns in each district of the Punjab. The balance remaining after deducting the pupils in Government and Aided schools from the number of persons "under instruction" ought to give, as approximately as possible, the number of pupils in indigenous *schools*, though they would probably not give the large number of pupils reading privately with Maulvis and Pandits, or of females reading in their own homes. It has, however, been considered right to deduct from the number "under instruction." also the total of girls reading in Government and Aided female schools. Although such a course is calculated unduly to decrease the number of pupils in indigenous schools, there would still remain 60,168, which corresponds with the numbers separately ascertained by me in the Police and other Returns, which are very much below the full number. The statement also gives the approximate revenue of each district, and the number of village schools that could be supported from the Educational one per cent. cess, in all 3,145 *village* schools (against 1,284 Primary schools now existing *both* in towns and the larger villages) at a cost of Rs. 60 per annum for each school, besides fees and income from other sources to be detailed hereafter.

It is deserving of notice that whilst the returns of the Punjab Educational Department (see paragraph XVI of Director's No. 48., dated 22nd September 1881) give 9,177 girls, nearly all of a tender age, as attending the Government and Aided female schools, the Census Returns only give 6,101 females as "under instruction," which, presumably, includes females of a more advanced age reading in their homes, as also girls reading in indigenous schools, regarding which my Report gives, incidentally, some account. The only explanation that can be offered is either that the Returns of the Educational Department *over*-state the number of girls in its schools, or that many respectable females, who are able to read and write, decline to admit this accomplishment, for reasons which I attempt to give elsewhere. Even if the 6,101 females supposed to be "under instruction" in the Census Returns were deducted from the "balance" left under that head, which is necessarily allotted to indigenous schools, the total number of pupils in those schools would amount to 63,244, but I have preferred to take the larger number of girls stated in the Educational Returns, and to reduce the number of pupils in indigenous schools to 60,168. As an instance of the difficulty of ascertaining the *full* number of pupils in indigenous schools, not to speak of the large number reading in private houses, which is scarcely returned at all, I would refer to the returns, say, of *Rawalpindi*. Of this district the police returns gave 171 schools with 3,700 pupils; the first returns of the district officers for 1878-79 gave 802 schools with 5,454 pupils, but when Mr. Miller took the matter in hand, the existence of 681 schools with 7,145 pupils was ascertained.* Similarly, in the *Gujrat* District there were 574 schools with 7,880 pupils in 1871-72. (See my Report as Inspector of Schools of the Rawalpindi Circle, paragraph 13, and Statistics, page XXXII, annexed to the Departmental Report for that year.)

I *then* considered that those numbers were about *half* of those actually attending the indigenous schools in that district. *This* year the police returns give only 135 schools with 2,577 pupils, whilst the District Inspector of Gujrat reports 264 schools with 3,518 pupils, or *less than half* the number in 1871-72. The private returns, however, which I have received, give 366 schools with 5,418 pupils. As regards the *Jhelum* District, which had 675 schools with 6,904 pupils in 1871-72, the present year only gives 249 schools with 4,080 pupils in the combined police and private returns.

From this it is clear that, although indigenous education has decreased in all those schools which had been *ascertained* to exist by the Educational Department, in the Rawalpindi District itself, the schools that had *not* been reported still continue to flourish. This state of things, I believe, applies to the whole province, so that, although there has been an enormous decrease in indigenous schools, there can scarcely be less than 120,000 pupils in the Panjab *even now* attending these institutions or reading in private houses, which shows that, in spite of persecution, indigenous education is still endowed with some vitality, and that it, practically, represents the protest of the people against our system of education.

* As this is going to Press, the *second* set of *revised* police returns has come in and gives, together with *other* schools mentioned only in the district and private returns, a total of 816 schools with 12,076 pupils! I had made Rawalpindi the "*test*" district, and I have no doubt that, if enquiries were carried on with similar minuteness in other districts, far larger numbers of schools and pupils than are now "*returned*" would be elicited throughout the Punjab.

Statement comparing the number of pupils in Government and Aided Schools with those in indigenous schools, and with the population in each District of the Panjab, and showing the number of schools that might be maintained in the villages in each district from the one per cent. Villages School Cess, at an expenditure of Rs. 60 per annum (besides fees and other income to be detailed hereafter) on each village school.

District.	Population of the District.	Number of Scholars in Primary, Government, and Aided Schools.	Number of Scholars in Government and Aided, Middle and High Schools: English.	Number of Scholars in Government and Aided, Middle and High Schools: Vern.	Total.	Number of Persons under instruction in Government, Aided, and Indigenous Schools: Males.	Females.	Total.	Balance, i.e., the number of scholars in the indigenous schools.	Revenue of the District.	Number of schools which can be maintained by 1 per cent.
Delhi ...	643,515	3,916	249	152	4,317	6,443	293	6,736	× 2,419	850,170	146
Gurgaon ...	641,848	2,929	89	130	3,148	3,341	47	3,388	× 240	1,062,969	177
Karnal ...	622,621	1,800	63	59	1,922	2,715	63	2,778	× 856	629,687	105
Hissar ...	504,183	1,400	36	6	1,442	1,711	26	1,737	× 295	424,109	71
Rohtak ...	553,609	2,260	52	66	2,378	2,864	33	2,897	× 519	882,696	147
Sirsa ...	253,275	606	16	...	622	1,655	34	1,689	1,067	175,692	29
Umballa ...	1,067,263	4,857	136	236	5,229	6,201	164	6,365	1,136	774,088	129
Ludiana ...	618,835	3,122	183	269	3,574	4,962	291	5,253	1,679	784,581	131
Simla ...	42,945	418	61	...	479	797	416	1,213	734	13,592	2
Jullundur ...	789,555	5,517	207	396	6,120	7,329	433	7,762	1,642	1,205,701	201
Hoshiarpur ...	901,381	4,276	135	309	4,720	8,112	65	8,177	× 3,457	1,240,433	207
Kangra ...	730,845	2,311	46	43	2,400	5,038	94	5,132	2,732	611,871	102
Amritsar ...	893,266	5,427	284	81	5,792	8,656	450	9,106	3,314	782,431	130
Gurdaspur ...	823,695	5,003	176	80	5,259	7,438	177	7,615	2,356	1,044,330	176
Sialkot ...	1,012,148	4,203	110	170	4,483	9,525	455	9,980	× 5,497	1,098,989	183
Lahore ...	924,106	4,772	317	190	5,279	9,815	657	10,472	× 5,193	524,337	87
Gujranwala ...	616,892	4,093	172	70	4,335	7,277	295	7,572	3,237	457,748	76
Ferozepore ...	650,519	2,295	61	119	2,475	3,342	181	3,523	1,048	505,229	84
Rawalpindi ...	820,512	4,169	58	75	4,302	8,899	516	9,415	× 5,113	685,916	114
Jhelum ...	589,373	3,374	61	58	3,493	4,561	99	4,660	× 1,167	581,785	97
Gujrat ...	689,115	3,530	135	72	3,737	5,831	163	5,994	× 2,257	565,961	96
Shahpur ...	421,508	2,024	54	27	2,105	3,562	97	3,659	1,554	379,979	63
Mooltan ...	551,964	3,352	170	24	3,546	7,025	216	7,241	3,695	518,578	86
Jhang ...	395,296	1,729	185	44	1,958	3,651	127	3,778	1,820	283,072	47
Montgomery ...	426,529	1,377	12	53	1,442	3,393	63	3,456	2,014	295,800	49
Muzaffargarh ...	338,605	1,565	22	25	1,612	3,279	122	3,401	1,789	488,908	81
Dera Ismail Khan	441,649	1,862	48	48	1,958	3,039	41	3,080	1,122	302,519	50
Dera Ghazi Khan	363,346	1,774	65	56	1,895	3,349	85	3,434	1,539	347,368	58
Bannu ...	332,577	1,146	21	15	1,182	2,080	36	2,116	934	388,389	65
Peshawar ...	592,674	1,755	44	15	1,814	8,183	321	8,504	× 6,690	661,608	110
Hazara ...	407,075	960	12	14	986	2,274	20	2,294	1,308	190,615	32
Kohat ...	181,540	356	19	...	375	1,276	21	1,297	922	86,015	14
TOTAL ...	18,842,264	88,178	3,299	2,902	94,379	157,623	× 8101	165,724	69,345	20,901,137	3,145
NOTE.—Add Total of girls in Government and Aided Schools.					9,177	Deduct Total of girls ...			9,177		
Grand Total of boys and girls in Government Schools.					103,556	Total number of pupils in indigenous schools.			60,168		

The balance, however, of 60,168 "under instruction" according to the census is greatly under the mark. It is clear that when more pupils are returned as attending indigenous schools than are given by the census as being "under instruction" (apart from pupils in Government and aided 'schools), that not only must the real number under public instruction be larger than is reported, but also that a further increase must be allowed for those under private instruction. In the cases, however, in which, in consequence of the incompleteness or non-arrival of the police, district and other returns, the number of pupils attending indigenous schools is below that shown by the census as being "under instruction," it seems to me that to adopt the figures of the census would still be below the mark, especially in such a district as Peshawar, where so many are under private instruction. As regards a place, however, like Simla, I cannot take the much higher figure of the census, because it evidently includes a number of Europeans and Eurasians who may be "under instruction," though not at school, but who cannot obviously enter into the calculation for the purpose of the present enquiry. Taking all these circumstances together, I venture to consider that adopting the higher figure, whether of the census or of my returns, would still be below the mark, for, in any case, the very large numbers under purely private instruction would still be generally excluded. One thing is certain that whether one accepts the figures of the census or those of my returns, the number of pupils "under instruction," which is *not* given in Government or aided schools, amounts to, at least, 96,585 in the Punjab, and this I take to be the lowest number of the recipients of "indigenous education" in the Province. The following instances may illustrate my meaning: The Delhi District, to which the police returns only gave 120 indigenous schools with 1,764 pupils, has now been ascertained to possess 216 of these schools with 3,314 pupils, whereas the census only gives 2,419 as "under instruction," so that there must be, at least, 905 persons more than are returned "under instruction," not counting those who receive private instruction. Similarly, the census gives 240 for Gurgaon, in which district there are 55 indigenous schools with 650 pupils. Karnal has 856 in the census against 1,042 pupils in 77 schools, according to my returns. Hisar is allowed 295 "under instruction," whilst I have 766 pupils in indigenous schools. Rohtak gets 519 against my 763 in 63 schools. Simla, however, gets 734, whereas I prefer the lower figure of 176 in 11 indigenous schools for reasons which have already been explained. For Rawalpindi the census gives 5,113 as "under instruction," whilst Mr. Miller's returns show nearly two thousand more for that district, or 7,145 pupils in its indigenous schools. For Gujrat the census gives 2,257, but the District Inspector of Schools 3,518 indigenous pupils only, or 1,461 more. For Jhelum the census has only 1,167 "under instruction," as already explained; there it appears that the work of devastation of indigenous schools, caused by the attitude of the Educational Department, has been most successful, but my returns give 4,080 pupils, or 2,913 more than the census,—no doubt a great falling off since 1871-72, when 6,904 pupils were reported as attending indigenous schools, but still better than the number of the census. On the other hand, up to the moment of writing, only 224 schools with 2,414 pupils have been reported by the Police Clerks for the Hoshiarpur District, but it is obvious that there must be a larger number, as the census mentions 3,457 as "under instruction." I am now awaiting the district and private returns which are sure to add to that number. Sialkot has 5,497 "under instruction," whilst the district returns give only 383 schools with 4,379 pupils, and the police and private returns have not yet been examined. Lahore is given 5,193 by the census and 6,097 by the police and private returns; whilst the district returns have not yet reached me. For more detailed information, I must refer to the tabular statements at the end of this report.

To sum up. Although 60,168 pupils, the lowest number, according to the census, probably attending indigenous schools in the province, or even 96,585 under instruction not given by Government or aided schools (not to speak of my conjecture that presumably 120,000 persons receive indigenous education in the Punjab), may be considered to be a great falling off from the 300,000 pupils who, according to my lowest estimate, attended school before the annexation of the Punjab, it is obvious that there still exists a considerable educational material that may yet be saved from destruction and that may even be largely increased and improved, provided the steps are taken that I will venture to indicate hereafter.

INDIGENOUS EDUCATION IN THE PANJAB.

PART I.

A.—THE RELIGIOUS AND NATIONAL FOUNDATIONS OF INDIGENOUS EDUCATION.

The various forms of indigenous education in the Panjab are synchronous with the establishment in the Province of Hinduism, Muhammadanism and Sikhism respectively. As regards Hindus, their education began when the Kshatria King confined himself to rule and war and relinquished legislation to the Brahmin. To strengthen the reason for his existence the latter made the four stages, of studentship, teaching the Vedas, asceticism and meditation, into which his life was divided, obligatory on himself, together with a moral and ceremonial code far more stringent and minute than on the remaining castes, and which, indeed, would have been intolerable to any class not aiming at spiritual and intellectual domination. Teaching was, therefore, the link which connected the Brahmin with other castes and, at the same time, secured his preservation and ascendancy. It was, accordingly, his aim to make education neither "too cheap" nor too inaccessible, and, punished as the Sudra was, if he presumed to *dictate* in law or religion, to the extent of exclusion from the instruction in these subjects, he was willingly admitted to all other *secular* teaching, provided he bore himself with humility. Indeed, the necessities and relations of life often compelled the Brahmin to enlarge his circle of disciples, whilst an ascetic from any caste or even outcaste could raise himself to the level of the gods by education and the practice of virtue. These considerations are very important in dealing with the subject of education among Hindus. To begin with, the moral obligations are in a somewhat descending scale as the caste is lower, so that, in dealing with a Hindu educational question, it is essential to ascertain the nature, traditions and aims of the caste that either raises it or which it affects. Then it should never be forgotten that the caste-system is intended to create a pride in the discharge and perfection of the hereditary profession, so that, whilst humility is taught to the caste above one's own, the limits and duties of one's own caste have a divine sanction, and are watched with jealousy against transgression from all outsiders, whether higher or lower in Hindu society. Thus even the "Sweeper", the Mehter or Prince, has his prototype in the house of God. Finally, it should always be remembered that every Hindu movement, notably that of Buddha, Nanak, and in modern times that of the educated Natives, has one great aim—the throwing-off the intellectual yoke of the Brahmin. With the two reformers it had the further objects of, first, making all classes equal by a high standard of practical morality and, secondly, of *popularizing* the education which the Brahmin doled out through the medium of Sanscrit, by rendering its treasures into the vulgar tongue. Thus, the Sikhs transplanted into a dialect, partly Panjabi and partly Hindi, in the widest sense of the latter term, many of the books and ideas till then clothed in a Sanscrit garb. Among the so-called educated Natives, the acquisition of, for instance, the Entrance, First Arts and B. A. Certificates is, often, a marketable commodity, which *inter alia* raises the dowry that they can ask from the parents of their bride, whilst in the highest caste teaching is an obligation which cannot be paid for, and which, if imparted for payment, can only be excused on the ground of *angusta res domi*. The efforts, therefore, of Khatris, Kayaths, Súds and others to acquire the language of their rulers, whether Persian or English, is, first, a tradition of their caste, and, secondly, an attempt to secure a monopoly of appointments which may give them both political power and social prestige over those higher than themselves in the Indian scale. The bulk, however, of the Hindu population is well content with the wise and elastic domination of the Brahmin, and is ever ready to respond to appeals on behalf of Sanscrit learning. We thus find endowments throughout India made to Sanscrit teaching by members of all castes and classes. These endowments were chiefly in land, and were either held separately or in connexion with temples. So much so is this still the case that, in some parts of India, in order to avoid a division of ancestral property among all the members of a family, it is often consecrated to a temple, of which the eldest son of the donor is constituted the hereditary custodian. The Hindu village community also dealt with the soil as the caste did with the person, including that of the teacher; in other words, just as the highest instruction in law or religion was, generally, confined to the Brahmin caste, whilst secular learning was, practically, thrown open to all, so the allotment of the soil belonging to the village community proceeded on the assumption that both the priest and the secular teacher had a right to a share. Nothing can more mark the decline of the Panjab—the Koh-i-nûr among the diamonds of the English Crown—than the inability of nearly all the witnesses recently summoned by the Education Commission to answer the question "How far are indigenous schools a relic of an ancient village system"? Of course, intelligent Panjab villagers (and there are still many wise and honest men among them) could, even now, answer the question, but, as no villager was summoned for obvious reasons, I will endeavour to do so in the words both of authors of repute and of official despatches, corroborating or correcting their statements by what may have come within my own humble knowledge and experience. From passages in "Ludlow's British India" the following extracts may be quoted: "Where the village system has been swept away by us, as in Bengal, there the village school has equally disappeared." "The third great characteristic of Hinduism—(are) its municipal institutions, as embodied in the village system . . which deals with the soil in an essentially personal way. . . The occupants of a given space of land are no mere aggregation of human units, but an organised body, to which certain functionaries are necessary, which enjoys, as a body, certain rights over the soil, . . . even though within that community (certain persons) should be entitled to rights of what we should call absolute ownership. Everywhere the community has certain officers representing all those functions which appear to be most essential to village life. First, is the headman, representing the whole community as towards the Government; next, is the accountant, keeping a description of all the village lands, with the names of holders and terms of holding, and the accounts of individuals and of the village, drawing up deeds, writing letters. Then the police-officer, not a mere paid watchman, but a member of the village, hereditary, as I have said, in his functions; enjoying as the price of them a certain definite amount of land. The priest, often a Brahmin, is another of these officers, hereditary in like manner; in like manner holding the priest's land. The schoolmaster, often also the astrologer (though in other cases they are distinct functionaries), is another. And do not suppose that this is an office which has fallen into desuetude . . . . *In every Hindu village which has retained anything of its form . . . the rudiments of knowledge are sought to be imparted; there is not a child, except those of the outcastes (who form no part of the community), who is not able to read, to write, to cipher; in the last branch of learning they are confessedly most proficient* . . . . . The astrologer . . . has to keep account of lucky or unlucky days for all manner of operations; . . . . . *and part of his duty is to prepare an almanack every year.* The money-changer and silversmith assists the headman, assaying all money paid. The smith is another village functionary, together with the carpenter, the barber, the potter, the leather worker, and such other tradesmen as the necessities of the village may require; including, it may be, the tailor, washerman, cowkeeper, physician, musician, minstrel (*who is also generally the village genealogist*) . . in other parts even a "superintendent of tanks and water-courses becomes a component part of the village system."

"It is only the hereditary character of these functions, and their connexion with the tenure of land, which can explain the wonderful permanency of the village system. It varies, of course, infinitely in its details. The functionary who is here paid by the ownership or from the produce of a given field, receives elsewhere a certain share of the general produce,—every twentieth handful of grain, or the like—or even a money fee. The village corporation again, as Elphinstone shows, is often distinct from the . . . village landholders, who have under them permanent and temporary tenants and labourers, besides shop-keepers . . . The joint ownership of the village land, by the village community, must have been originally the rule throughout the whole of India. Of course not only the joint ownership, but the idea of the village community itself has been wholly swept away in many instances, partly in more. But even in these it lingers yet in the speech and minds of men; it clings, as it were, to the soil. Even where the functionary has disappeared, his land retains the memory of his functions. THE 'SCHOOLMASTER'S FIELDS,' the 'watchman's field' never disappear from the village books; and *the restoration of them to their original purpose is always hailed as an act of justice.*"

As for the places of instruction, whether in towns or villages, the great object of the Hindu legislator of bringing teacher and pupils into personal relations of respect on the one side and of affection on the other was everywhere carried out to minute details, which seemed to anticipate every possible circumstance. The larger proportion of schools were, therefore, held in the houses of the most liberal patron, or were invested with a religious or popular sanction by being attached to, or held in, temples, the enclosures to the huts of Fakirs and in the Chaupals or Village Halls. Above all, was the effort of both wealthy individuals and of communities directed towards the emancipation of all teachers, especially those of religion, from worldly cares, on the tacit or express assumption of their imparting instruction gratuitously, for nothing so degrades education in the native mind, except in what may be called the worldly castes of Khatris, Kayats, Sûds, Kalâls and others who are now benefiting by English education, as they formerly flocked to the Muhammadan Perso-Kuranic schools, as the imposition of a regular fee. We, accordingly, find that most of the education given by Brahmins, certainly to members of their own caste, was gratuitous, as it, indeed, still is, whilst in innumerable instances, now unfortunately reduced to an ascertainable number, the teacher both fed and instructed his pupil. Even now, wherever the indigenous teacher of the higher order has any other means of livelihood, as, for instance, when he is a family priest or physician (a profession which, low in its origin, has been raised by learning), he will gladly impart gratuitous instruction, not only to the sons and relatives of his client, but to all others who may wish to avail themselves of it. Indeed, I am not acquainted with any Native, Hindu, Muhammadan or Sikh, who, if at all proficient in any branch of indigenous learning or science, does not consider it to be a proud duty to teach others. Even among those "educated natives" who have not thrown aside social or religious restraints, I have known men devoting half of their slender incomes to maintaining schools or pupils at them. It is only those who have benefited exclusively by our system of education that have not contributed to educational endowments of any kind—one of the first thoughts of a Native as soon as he is somewhat freed from household anxieties.

As for the mode of instruction, it also bore in every one of its features the emphatically practical as well as ideal aim of the Hindu legislator. It is all very well to laugh at regulations regarding dress, times of reading, manner of addressing the teacher, friends and fellow-pupils, when we either ignore the circumstances which gave them point, or when these circumstances have been swept away. Suffice it to say, that from the humblest beginnings in education up to the highest courses in Hindu metaphysics and science, great wisdom was displayed. Traces of the "Kindergarten" system are still found. The simplest means for arresting and keeping attention are still often resorted to. The moral and mental capacities of children, according to their spheres of life, were, everywhere, carefully studied and cultivated. A respect for learning was inculcated, which was the solace of the humblest in his daily avocation, who only awaited opportunities for acquiring it. A taste for poetry, and for philosophical and religious enquiry, spread even to the lowest castes, if not to outcastes. Among the many names that are still remembered, we need only refer to the inspired weaver, the Juláha *Kabir*, the Chumar *Ram Das*, the Dhobi *Nam Deo*, and the immortal *Valmiqi*, the author of the Ramayana, whom popular report holds to have been a highway robber of the despised Chúra outcaste.

True, there was no class-instruction, as in our schools, reducing all intellects to the same level and retarding the industrious for the sake of the dullard; but disputations in Sanscrit among the students and the repetition of the day's lesson in chorus on the dispersion of the school encouraged such emulation as may be necessary, whilst the separate instruction of the pupil and his devotion to his work during the time that he was not reading with his tutor, stimulated those habits of reflection and of private study, in which the student in our Government schools is sadly deficient. Then again, when he grew older, he travelled to learn philosophy under one tutor and law under another, much in the same way as students of German Universities visit various seats of learning in order to hear, say, International Law at Heidelberg, the Pandects at Berlin, &c. Indeed, the term Indo-Germanic may be applied to other affinities of the Indians at one end and the Germans at another besides those of language. The practice of every German Doctor being allowed to teach in the "*faculty*" at the University where he has graduated, which, indeed, is the meaning of "*Doctor*," has its counterpart in both the function and the signification of "Acharya," the Muhammadan "Hakím" and the humbler Guru. Every student, who has finished his course, teaches what he has been taught or takes up a sub-division of the same subject, much to the advantage of his speciality, a practice which has greatly contributed to the intellectual activity of German Universities, where professors and graduates are not merely "teachers," *Lehrer*, but "increasers," *Mehrer*, of their science, by the admirable method of co-operation in the delivery of lectures and by the stimulus which is thus afforded for original investigation. Thus, in the parallel between the relics of the "Kindergarten" system, the omnipresence of moral and religious instruction, the learned "disputations" of students, the peregrinations from one eminent professor to another, the "*faculty*" of teaching conferred on "absolved" graduates, we have a parallel between India and Germany, which should induce the ordinary English critic to pause before he condemns indigenous education. Above all, was it in the manner of teaching grammar that Panini became a model to European philologists, whilst in philosophical reasoning there is not a single European system in which it has not been preceded by an Indian school or thinker. Even in enquiries connected with natural history and with man, the numerous Sanscrit monographs still extant on the influence of sound on the passions, on the diseases of animals, &c., afford a mine of research, which we would do well to explore, before it finally closes with the immediately impending extinction of their traditional expounders or possessors, owing to our unwarrantable neglect of the indigenous civilisation of this country.

I need scarcely explain that my account of the ancient methods and means of instruction in indigenous schools must be contrasted with the reports of their remnants throughout the various districts of the Panjab, before a faithful picture can be drawn of the present state of things. The enumeration, for instance, of the books which are taught in Sanscrit schools does not mean that they are all taught in *all* the schools; but that these books ought to be taught wherever they are available, which, with the exception of the Rigveda and one or two other books only taught, as far as I know, at the Lahore Oriental College, is generally the case. We must remember that the country is in a state of educational despondency; that, in very many places, official influence has been brought to bear to drive away or to suppress the indigenous school; that the religious feeling has received a great shock, first, owing to the annexation of the province by non-believers, and secondly, by the influence of a foreign rule and of a secular education. When, however, we still find that over 80,000 pupils receive their education in indigenous schools in spite of all discouragements during the 26 years of the repressive action of the Educational Department, and that in all the ancient traditions of teaching are not yet dead and can be easily revived and utilised, provided the province does not continue to be sacrificed to the personal interests of a few European officers, we are put into the possession of a material for education which it will be our fault if it is not developed into useful, loyal and religious citizens. Just as the introduction of specimens of the art-industry of India has tended largely to develop the present artistic taste among English workmen, so did the *methods of instruction pursued in indigenous schools influence the schools in England*. Lest this statement be considered an unsupported assertion by those Englishmen who are not aware of the debt of gratitude which they owe to indigenous schools, I will quote a paragraph from the first Educational Despatch of the Court of Directors which was issued on the 3rd June 1814. After speaking in terms of praise of the mode of instruction at Hindu homes*, and offering encouragement to its further prosecution by a gradation of honorary marks of distinction, khillats and titles in conformity with the immemorial usage of Eastern Governments as regards learning, the Court of Directors proceed to point out that the indigenous village schools are a part of the village system, and that they have formed a model to schools in England. Mr. A. P. Howell, in his "Education in British India prior to 1854 and in 1870-71," introduces the passage in question in the following words :—

"The following paragraphs from the same despatch are remarkable for their reference to the indigenous schools, and to THEIR METHOD OF INSTRUCTION WHICH WAS ACTUALLY BORROWED FOR ADOPTION IN ENGLAND, as also to the principle, afterwards developed throughout the several provinces in India, of local cesses levied for the establishment and maintenance of elementary rural schools :—

"We refer with particular satisfaction upon this occasion to *that distinguished feature of internal polity* which prevails in some parts of India, and by which *the instruction of the people is provided for by a certain charge upon the produce of the soil, and by other endowments in favour of the village teachers, who are thereby rendered public servants of the community.*

"*The mode of instruction that from time immemorial has been practised under these masters has received the highest tribute of praise by its adoption in this country, under the direction of the Reverend Dr. Bell, formerly Chaplain at Madras; and it is now become the mode by which education is conducted in our national establishments, from a conviction of the facility it affords in the acquisition of language by simplifying the process of instruction.*

"*This venerable and benevolent institution of the Hindus is represented to have withstood the shock of revolutions, and to its operation is ascribed the general intelligence of the natives as scribes and accountants. We are so strongly persuaded of its great utility, that we are desirous you should take early measures to inform yourselves of its present state, and that you will report to us the result of your inquiries, affording in the meantime the protection of Government to the village teachers in all their just rights and immunities, and marking, by some favourable distinction, any individual amongst them who may be recommended by superior merit or acquirements; for, humble as their situation may appear, if judged by a comparison with any corresponding character in this country, we understand those village teachers are held in great veneration throughout India.*" Mr. Howell comments on this as follows :—

"There is no doubt that from time immemorial indigenous schools have existed, as here alleged. In Bengal alone, in 1835, Mr. Adam estimated their number to be 100,000; in Madras, upon an enquiry instituted by Sir Thomas Munro in 1822, the number of schools was reported to be 12,498, containing 188,650 scholars; and in Bombay, about the same period, schools of a similar order were found to be scattered all over the presidency. It is much to be regretted that, as each province fell under our rule, the Government did not take advantage of the time when the prestige of conquest or gratitude for delivery from war and oppression were strong in the popular mind, to make the village school an important feature in the *village system that was almost everywhere transmitted to us. Had this been done, and had the numerous village*

* "We are inclined to think that the mode by which the *learned* Hindus might be disposed to concur with us in prosecuting those objects would be by our leaving them to the practice of an usage, long established amongst them, of giving instruction at their own homes, and by our encouraging them in the exercise and cultivation of their talents, by the stimulus of honorary marks of distinction, and in some instances by grants of pecuniary assistance.

"The influence of such communications could not fail to be strengthened by your causing it to be made known that it is in the contemplation of the British Government to introduce and establish amongst the natives a gradation of honorary distinction, as the reward of merit, either by the public presentation of ornaments of dress, in conformity with the usage of the East, or by conferring titles, or by both, as may be deemed most grateful to the natives, who should be invited to communicate their ideas to you upon points so much connected with their feelings."

allowances been diverted to this object, and had the Government devoted itself to the improvement of school-books and school masters, instead of establishing a few new schools of its own, and thereby *encouraging the belief that it was for the State, and not for the community, to look after education*, the work of general improvement would have been substituted for the work of partial construction, and we should now have had in every province a really adequate system of national primary education. Sir Thomas Munro aimed at this in Madras, as did Mountstuart Elphinstone in Bombay and Lord William Bentinck in Bengal; but their views were overridden by men who, if less far-seeing, were more persistent."

"The Despatch concluded by a request that the Governor General would take "the earliest opportunity" of submitting for consideration any plan calculated to promote the object in view.

But the Government was then engaged in the war with Nepal, and subsequently in tranquilising Central India, and the expense and financial embarrassments entailed by these measures prevented immediate attention being paid to the views of the Court of Directors in regard to education. It was not until these wars were concluded and the finances restored, that Lord Moira took up the subject in a manner which led to the more decisive action of his successor in 1823, when the Parliamentary grant was for the first time appropriated. This seems the best explanation of "THE GREAT OMISSION" which was commented on in the Parliamentary enquiry of 1853."

It was, however, natural that a commercial Government, like that of the Directors, should eventually sympathise with the Indian shop-keeping class, which desired that their children should be raised above their sphere, and which paid for English education, whereas Oriental education, although it stimulated native liberality in the form of endowments, had to be paid for. Accordingly, under the pressure of the Babus and Anglicists, Lord Bentinck ordered, in his Resolution of the 7th March 1835, that "all the funds appropriated for the purpose of education would be best employed on English education alone"; "that no stipend should be given to any student that may hereafter enter at any of these (Oriental) institutions"; and "that no portion of the funds shall hereafter be employed on printing Oriental works." Although the "General Committee of Public Instruction" (to which honorary body India is more indebted than to any paid Educational Department) reconciled this Resolution with the ultimate aim of both Anglicists and Orientalists,—namely, the diffusion of knowledge through the media of the vernacular languages,—the Asiatic Society, in language which may be deemed too strong, but which was prophetic when the present state of the decline of indigenous education is considered, not incorrectly described this Resolution as "destructive, unjust, unpopular, not far outdone by the destruction of the Alexandrian Library itself," as is, indeed, the case in the loss of Sanscrit manuscripts alone since the date of that Resolution. Mr. Howell's remarks on the subject of the consequent neglect of indigenous education deserve to be quoted: "It will be a matter of regret to those who have marked the important part played by the clergy in all countries in the work of State education, that measures were not taken at this stage to secure the cordial co-operation of the Maulvis and Pandits—the clergy of India—in the new policy."

A few quotations from the Hitopodesá, Niti Mala, Manu and the Mahabharata, sent to me by Babu Navina Chandra Rai, may be interesting as incidentally showing the importance of education in raising the lower classes, the great value attached by Hindus to wealth as a means for the practice of virtue, and the teaching power (which our system has nearly destroyed) that natural affections and religious duty vest in the father *and mother* (thus implying the existence of female education). The gradation of studies in indigenous Hindu schools of, first, reading the text, then committing it to memory, a practice, to which we largely owe the preservation of the Vedas and of many other

treasures of Sanscrit learning, then understanding its purport, and, finally, carrying out its precepts, still follows the instructions of Manu, XII, 103 :—

On the merits of learning and teaching from the Hindu Sháśtras.

SELECTIONS FROM THE HITOPODESA.

Knowledge* is the best among all things, for it can neither be lost, nor sold, nor destroyed.

* Or learning.

It is knowledge only which, when attained, even by a low man, brings him to an intercourse with the haughty King and thence to fortune, just as a river leads one to the ocean.

Knowledge gives humility; from humility one obtains ability, from ability wealth, from wealth virtue, and from virtue happiness.

There are two kinds of knowledge which glorify a man—the knowledge of *Shastra*, arms, and the knowledge of *Shástra*, literature and science. The former becomes ridiculous to an old man, but the latter is ever esteemed.

Learning removes numerous doubts; it shows things invisible; it is like eyes to all; whoever does not possess it, is indeed blind.

One learned son is better than hundred illiterate ones; one moon removes the darkness, which all the stars together cannot do.

A father who contracts debts is an enemy; a mother who is unchaste is an enemy; a wife who is beautiful is an enemy; and *a son who is not learned is an enemy.*

A boy becomes learned by the training he receives from his *mother* and father. No one can become a learned man as soon as he is born.

A mother is an enemy and a father is an enemy who has not taught (her or his) child, (for such a child) is not suited to the society (of learned men), just as a heron is not suited to the society of swans.

Those who are gifted with beauty and youth, and descended from a high family, do not look well if they are illiterate, as the flowers of the *palks* tree (though beautiful) do not look well for want of good smell.

The time of the wise passes in literary pursuits (literally, in practical and literary amusements), but the fools spend their time in evil pleasures, sleep or quarrel.

The illiterate have thousands of occasions every day for sorrow and hundreds of occasions for fear. Not so the learned.

There are two delicious fruits of this world the poisonous tree, *viz.*, the nectarine taste of *poetry* and literature, and the society of good people.

On the merits of acquiring knowledge.

Knowledge is a man's superior beauty and hidden treasure. Knowledge is the cause of enjoyment, fame, and happiness. Knowledge is the teacher of teachers. *Knowledge is one's friend in a foreign country.* Knowledge is highly divine; knowledge, *and not wealth,* is respected by Kings. One who is wanting in knowledge is a brute.—(Niti Málá, p. 99.)

Who can vie with those whose internal wealth consists of knowledge, which is invisible to a stealer, which nourisheth always, *which increases by being given away* to the solicitous, and which is not destroyed even at the destruction of the Universe. The King hears those who possess knowledge.—(Niti Málá, p. 100.)

Trifle not with those learned men who have attained the highest object of life. The vulgar *Lakshmi* (wealth), which is like a straw, cannot overcome them, just as the soft fibre of a lotus tree cannot bind the elephant, whose black cheeks have got the fresh lines of lusty youth.—(Niti Málá, p. 101.)

The jewel of knowledge is the greatest of all riches, for it cannot be carried away by relatives as a share of inheritance, or by thieves, nor is it reduced by being given in charity.—(Niti Málá, p. 102.)

Among all things, knowledge is invaluable, as it can never be lost, sold, or reduced.—(Niti Málá, p. 104.)

As jewels are without dress, food without *ghee*, a woman without breasts, so is life without knowledge.—(Niti Málá, p. 105.)

It is not equal to be a learned man and to be a King, for the King is only honoured in his own country, whereas a learned man is honoured everywhere.—(Niti Málá, p. 108.)

A learned man possesses all the good qualities, while an illiterate man has only vices. Therefore one learned man is superior to thousands of illiterate men.—(Niti Málá, p. 109.)

What is the use of high family if a man has no talents? *A learned man, even if he cannot boast of good family, is honoured by the gods.*—(Niti Málá, p. 111.)

The moon is the ornament of the stars, the husband is the ornament of the wives, the King is the ornament of the earth, but knowledge is the ornament of all.—(Niti Málá, p. 112.)

Elixir should be extracted out of poisons, gold should be extracted out of excrescence, *good knowledge should be obtained even from a low man.* A good wife should be taken even from a low family.—(Niti Málá, p. 113 and Manu.)

A wise man, when striving after knowledge or wealth, should think of himself as one who is never to die or to become old; but when performing a religious action he should consider himself as being dragged by the hair, by death.—(Niti Málá, p. 114 and Hitopodesá.)

One who seeks after pleasures should give up (his hope of obtaining) knowledge. One *who seeks after knowledge should renounce pleasures, for one who hankers after pleasures cannot attain knowledge, nor vice versá.*—(Niti Málá, p. 116.)

He is not an old man who has grey hairs; if a young man is learned, he is considered by gods to be elderly.—(Mahabharát.)

Those who have *read* books are superior to the illiterate; those who have *committed to memory* (the subject, they have read) are superior to the mere readers of books; those who *understand* the purport are superior to those who commit books to memory; and those who *follow the precepts* are superior to those who merely know them.—(Manu, XII, 103.)

A few quotations from the Adigranth, Sar-uktawálí, and Chánaka, although more properly belonging to my account of Sikh indigenous education, furnished to me by Bhais Dhrit Singh and Jewahir Singh, may also be referred to in this place:—

Translation of some of Sloks from Sikh religious books, original or adopted from Sanscrit.

(1) After completing his *education*, he feels his interest to be in doing good to others.* (*Nanak's Rág Asa, Shabad 25.*) (2) The more he *studies* under a tutor's directions, the greater the popularity and respect he gains. (*Rág Prabhat Shabad 7.*) (3) As he *studies* deeply, so shall he find precisely, what truth is; and shall thereafter meditate and pray to the true God. (*Rág Rámkali Pause 53.*) (4) To speak truth day and night, and to live in the company of *educated* men, is pleasant; for these men distinguish virtues from sins, and cause falsehoods to be discarded. "The *learned*," says (learned) Nanak, "argue that true happiness abide with God alone.—(*Rág Magh-ki-Var Sloke 18, after Pause 17.*)

5. An *illiterate* man, like a flower without smell, is regarded to be of no value (respect), though he may be handsome, have wealth, puberty, a noble family and many relatives.—(*Sár Uktávali*, Chap. 3, verse 19.)

6. A *learned* man is an ornament even in the assembly of saints, though he may have no ornaments, or clothes, and though he be ugly in appearance.—(*Sár.* c. 3, *v.* 20.)

7. *Knowledge* is *a* power, causing man to be successful in every business. It is the giver of honor and wealth; therefore the liberal-minded ought to cultivate it.—(*Sár.* c. 3, *v.* 24.)

8. *Read* again and again, and thy *knowledge* shall increase a thousand fold. · As the water standeth on the lower part of the earth, so should the *knowledge* acquired be kept in the foremost point of the tongue.†—(*Sár.* c. 3, *v.* 25.)

9. There are five treasures of happiness, which are undecaying, and have no fear of being looted:—(1) *learning*, (2) activity,‡ (3) a knowledge of a handicraft, (4) sound judgment, and (5) good manners.—(*Sár.* c. 3, *v.* 10.)

10. A hidden, vast and immeasurable treasure is *knowledge*,—nay, believe it to be the substance of man. *Knowledge* provides reputation, happiness and enjoyment, and makes the *leader* of men.—*Sár.* c. 3. *v.* 21.)

11. *Knowledge* is a friend in a foreign country, and is higher than a god (Dev). It is respected by Kings, and is the killer of sins; without *knowledge*, man is nothing more than an animal. (*Sár.* c. 3, *v.* 12.)

12. Sleeping, eating, cohabiting, and fear are equally seen in both man and animal. It is *knowledge* which distinguishes man from animals, otherwise the former is no better than the latter. (*Sár.* c. 3, *v.* 13.)

13. Men without righteousness, suavity, virtue, liberality, devotion, and *knowledge*, are but burdens on this perishable earth. They, though in a human body, live like deer. (*The same, v.* 14.)

14. A deer furnishes five things,—hide, flesh, and horns, &c.,—to mendicants (Munis), hunters, and trumpeters, &c., respectively. Thus a deer, by virtue of five things, is more useful and generous than a man devoid of the six principles (mentioned in last-preceding quotation).

15. Can a man judge right from wrong without *knowledge*? The blind can make no distinction among the shades of different colors. (*The same, v.*, 16.)

---

* Dr. Trumpp translates the passage as follows:—

"(When one) is meditating on science, then he is rendering services to others."

† I take this to mean that "as it is the natural tendency of water to flow downwards, so it is the duty of learned man to keep his knowledge always ready for immediate communication at the tip of his tongue."

‡ "Uddam" is rather being ever-ready for work and is opposed to procrastination.

16. An illiterate man is served in his own home, a land-owner is respected in his village, a King is obeyed in his kingdom, but *the learned* is worshipped everywhere. (The same *v.* 17.)

17. One who does not obey the commands of his teacher—be he a teacher only of one letter—will, after transmigrating into different bodies of a hundred dogs successively, be born in the house of a sweeper. (*The same, v.* 18.)

18. *Knowledge* protects like a mother, cherishes like a father, and loves like a wife. It is a remedy of grievances, and a source of comfort. (*The same, v.* 23.)

19. The mother and father, who do not look after their children's *education*, are their enemies; because uneducated men are never respected in society, as a heron in an assembly of swans. (Adapted from the Hitopadesa.)

20. It is thorough learning which enables man to reason in politics; without politicians the country cannot rise.

21. Wearing a crown, armlets, bracelets, ear-rings, and pearl-necklaces, having a face as the moon, eyes attractive as the lotus-flower, a body as that of Kám (god of love); and marrying a wife as beautiful as Rati (wife of Kám) who, after bathing, polishes her body with rubbed sandal-wood and saffron, and weaves every hair with delicious perfumery, are, no doubt, things which beautify any man, but are worthless, even disastrous, in the end.

22. The only ornament which surpasses in rank all others (quoted in last preceding passage) is *Vedic education*, which, in a short period, beautifies and adorns man, and causes him to taste all the fruits that spring up from this essence of light. Brahma has created fourteen worlds, but nothing is more precious in his creation than learning. Therefore, says Hardyal,* a man ought always to cultivate learning, if he wishes to gain the four *Padaraths* (*i. e.*, righteousness, riches, enjoyment, and salvation).

As regards Muhammadans, they emphatically value education "for its own sake" and, *therefore*, singular as this may sound to us, they avoid, as a rule, the Government schools, in which neither their religion is taught nor are the mind and character cultivated, but *only* worldly advantages are secured. I have myself been partially educated in a Muhammadan school, where I learnt Arabic and committed large portions of the Kuran to memory. The system followed and the instruction imparted in the precepts of morality and prudence have, with some defects, a number of excellences which would be sought for in vain in Government schools. I might quote numerous passages from Arabic, Persian and Turkish authors to show that the advantages of popular education and the importance of self-government and of the impartial treatment before the law of all sects are religious duties incumbent on all Muhammadans, which Turkish over-zeal and the subsequent predominance of the Sûras given at Madina over those delivered at Mecca may have occasionally obscured when Islam was fighting for its existence with other creeds. What Muhammadanism is capable of as an agency of civilization in the highest, even modern, sense of the word, may be gathered from General Khairuddin's book "on the ways of governing," a rather free translation of "Al-masálik fil memálik," now translated into Urdu. I wish, however, to confine myself in my quotations to what is most generally known in India, and there, above all, I find a significant saying current, which shows the duty of the State towards religion: "*Al-mulk wad-dín tawámáni*"="*Government and religion are twins*," for no Government can expect to be permanent that neglects the religion of its subjects. Nor is the "Dín" referred to in this place the Muhammadan religion exclusively, for the saying is quoted by the wise Minister Abulfazl of the wise Akbar in justification of his supporting all denominations alike as a Government official. Besides, the meaning which underlies "Dín" is that of an *obligation*, as in incurring a debt, and is equivalent to the same sense in *religion*, as still further brought out in the French "religieux," a man who is under a vow or obligation to be a monk, an idea which is similarly paralleled in the root meaning as well as application of the Mur*ábit* monks of Kabylia from "rabata" = he bound. "Al-*'ilm* farizatun a'la kulli Muslimin wa Muslimatun = learning is obligatory on every Muhammadan man or woman" may be interpreted to refer only to religious learning, were the *Hadís* or tradition of the sayings of the prophet not explaining that "Al-*ilm ilmáni*, ilm ul abdan, wa ilm-ul-adyan = science or learning consists of two parts, the science of bodies (of the natural) and the science of religions." The plural here seems almost to indicate not only religious matters generally, but the study of more than one religion. Again, "Utlub al-

* Hardyal's Suktavali, from which the saying "Patience is an armour" has become proverbial. His compilation of Sar-uktavali and his Sabhajit or "victory in Courts" contain numerous sayings like the above.

ilm wa in kana fis-Sini = seek for knowledge even if it is (to be found only) in China," which clearly shows that whatever reputation for the cultivation of sciences distant China may have had in Arabia, these sciences were certainly not orthodox from a Muhammadan standpoint. What European science and literature owe to the Arabs and to the Spanish, Sicilian, French and even English "schools" which they taught can never be sufficiently recognized. In comparative chronology Al-Birúni is still a master, whilst in saving portions of Plato and Aristotle from oblivion and in laying the foundation of clinical medicine, the Muhammadans have laid Europe under an obligation which it has not yet discharged to the adherents of that creed in India. When I come to describe the indigenous system of Muhammadan education, I may have occasion to refer to the important mathematical, astronomical and philosophical works still studied in their schools. I quote, however, some passages from the Koran and Hadís, sent to me by Munshi Karam Ilahi, as current in the Panjab, for, let it be remembered, that even where the boy learns the Kuran only by rote, he obtains a knowledge of its general meaning, from the practice of his religious duties, as also from the explanations of his father, which the latter derives, however illiterate he himself may be, from the experiences of his longer life, so that words derived from Arabic and used in Urdu translations are often more familiar to the vulgar than newly-coined terms in its own vernacular.

Extracts from the Kuran, and the Hadis on the Merit of Knowledge from a compilation by Munshi Karam Ilahi and passages from the "Hadis" by Maulvi Abdul Hakim.

1. Whoever has been given wisdom has indeed been given what is best.

KURAN.
(*Section, Tilkarrusul, Ruku' 3.*)

2. The learned and the illiterate are never equal in rank.

KURAN.
(*Section 23, Ruku' 1.*)

3. Those who have eyes and those who have not are never equal in rank.

KURAN.
(*Section 24, Ruku 6, Sura Momin.*)

4. Of God's creation those alone fear God who are learned.

KURAN.
(*Section 22, Ruku' 4.*)

5. Those who have believed and have received knowledge, God exalts in rank.

KURAN.
(*Section 27, Ruku' 1.*)

6. God gives him knowledge of the true faith whom He wishes to make good.

KURAN.

7. One hour's teaching and learning is more righteous than a whole night's prayer.

HADIS.

8. When a man dies, his acts die with him, except three, namely, a perennial charity (a permanent charitable endowment), or his *learning* whereby (posterity) is benefited, or a virtuous son.

HADIS.

9. Two men are enviable; he who spends his wealth in alms and he who benefits others by his learning.

HADIS.

10. The dwellers of Earth and Heaven and the fishes of the waters crave forgiveness for the learned. *A learned man is as superior to a (mere) devotee as the light of the full moon is superior to that of the stars.* The learned men are the heirs of the prophets. Indeed, the prophets have not left behind them silver and gold coins but have left knowledge. Hence whoever has attained knowledge has received their full inheritance.

HADIS.

11. *A learned man is as superior to a (mere) devotee as I (Muhammad) am superior to the least amongst you.*

HADIS.

12. The world is damned and so is everything that is in it—except the remembrance of God and those who remember Him, as well as the learners and the teachers of knowledge.

HADIS.

Intimately connected with the subject of indigenous education is the question of the absence of religious teaching from Indian Government schools, in defiance of the educational experience of both Europe and Asia, on which Mr. Howell comments as follows: "In India, not only is there no religious teaching of any kind in Government schools, but even the aided schools under native managers are generally adopting the same principle. I believe this result was never anticipated, and I am sure it requires attention. Looking to the rapid growth of our educational system, and to the enormous influence for good or evil that a single able and well-educated man may exercise in this country, and looking to the dense but inflammable ignorance of the millions around us, it seems a tremendous experiment for the State to undertake, and in some provinces almost monopolise, the direct training of whole generations above their own creed, and above that sense of relation to another world upon which they base all their moral obligations; and the possible evil is obviously growing with the system. It is true that things go smoothly and quietly, but this is attained by ignoring not only the inevitable results of early training on the character and the great needs of human nature, especially in the East, but by also ignoring the responsibility which devolves on the Government that assumes the entire control of direct education at all. If, therefore, while fanaticism is raging around, there is a calm in our schools and colleges, it is an ominous and unnatural calm, of impossible continuance, the calm of the centre of the cyclone.

"The subject is one of extreme difficulty that grows with the consideration devoted to it. Of course, it is out of the question to recede in any degree from the pledges of the past. And it is probable that the evil is less serious in primary schools where the instruction given does not necessarily destroy religious belief, whereas our higher instruction does. Therefore, although the State may establish and maintain primary schools where no local effort is forthcoming, it would still seem very desirable that it should retire as rapidly and as completely as practicable from the entire control of all direct instruction, and especially higher instruction, and leave it to local management to be encouraged by the State, and aided in conformity with the English principle which, without any interference in the religious instruction imparted, practically ensures by the constitution of the Local Boards that some religious instruction is regularly given."

B.—VERNACULAR INDIGENOUS EDUCATION IN THE PANJAB.

Having given an account of the religious, and, to some extent, of the national, foundations of indigenous education in the Panjab, I now proceed to its vernacular development, either as a protest against the educational monopoly of the priestly classes, or as a supply for the demand of the trading community. The former, which is by far the more important, is represented by the rise of Sikhism and with it of Gurmukhi schools; the latter, which is of considerable practical value, is represented by the Mahajani schools in which the Landé writing and mental arithmetic are taught in the vernacular of the locality. There is also a third class of schools which have been brought into existence by the requirements of our rule, but I doubt whether they can be called indigenous. I refer to the schools in which Bengali or other employés in our offices get their children taught Bengali, Hindi, Urdu or English (as the case may be), or in which Brahmo, Arya, and other Somajes of recent origin instil their tenets along with such instruction as their promoters consider to be useful or desirable. I also believe that the schools conducted by "aided" or "unaided" managers, preparing for any of the public examinations, of which English may form an essential part, can scarcely, as yet, be called indigenous. I am also doubtful whether I can speak of "female indigenous schools," although, above all others, the instruction given to Muhammadan girls in the Kurán and, sometimes, in Persian and in the "lives of saints," to Hindu girls in Hindi or Panjabi in the Nagari character, and to Sikh girls in Gurmukhi, is, emphatically, indigenous, although generally confined to the family circle and to immediate neighbours and friends. About "Gurmukhi" and Landé schools, however, there can be no doubt, and as, I believe, they greatly affected one another, there is the less hesitation for bringing them under the heading of this chapter.

I.—Sikh Vernacular Indigenous Education.

The Sikh is the Protestant of Hindu politics, society and religion. He is above all the worshipper of "the book," of his Bible, and should be an "ahl-Kitáb". His great aim is to destroy the monopoly of learning, and of the social or religious ascendancy of one class, and to make education the property of the masses of his community. In their search for a general vernacular in which to render the best ideas contained in Sanscrit, Persian and Arabic, the authors of the Granths made use of all the vernaculars of India with which they came in contact. This explains the heterogeneous character of their diction, and much of the confusion of the controversy as regards the meaning of the terms "Gurmukhi," "Panjabi", "Hindi" and "Bhásha", which opponents, following really different aims, but professing one object, hurl at one another in varying senses. It would be well, therefore, constantly to bear in mind, on the one hand, the origin, character, and aims of Sikhism, as opposed to the monopoly of caste, class, or of the learned languages, especially Sanscrit, although eagerly studying all learning; and, on the other, the never-relaxing efforts of Hindus of all classes to restore the wandering children to the fold. Sikhism wishes to create a race of warriors and students; Hinduism aims at class monopoly, however conciliatory or latitudinarian its forms, whether exercised by the Brahmin, whose intellect has been developed to the highest excellence by the hereditary cultivation of ages, or by the class now aiming at power, through a smattering of English.

All Sikhs are equal; Hindus are unequal. Sikhs are conservative democrats in religion and politics, loyally subordinate to elected rule or office, and admitting the hereditary principle, even for the descendants of Gurus Nanak and Govind Singh, only by courtesy, whilst they consider their chiefs, including Ranjit Singh, merely as *primi inter pares* and as representative servants of the commonwealth. There are four "platforms," *Takhts*, or councils, of Sikhs, in which all matters concerning their faith and, in former times, concerning their community generally, may be discussed—of Akalbunga, Anandpur, Patna and Abchalnagar, Nader, in Hyderabad. To them all good "Sikhs," a term to be explained hereafter, are admitted; but, wherever Sikhs assemble in the Guru's name, that is, for the benefit of their faith and for the suppression of idolatry, there is a fifth "platform;" but the "takht" is merely the seat, surrounded by the *Diwán* or General Parliament of Sikhs, in which all members of that community, men or women, can, and do, take part. The Sikhs, in proportion as their characteristics are preserved, are the backbone of our rule in the Panjab. Brave, liberal, truthful and loyal, the Protestants of India have every claim on the Protestant and liberal Government of Great Britain.

Above all, are the Sikhs, by name and history, a community of "learners" and "disciples." Their organization indicates a republicanism of letters, with liberty in all studies, the equality of all "Sikhs" or students, and the fraternity of "Bhạis," an excellence to which all can aspire. The crucial test of a good Sikh is good conduct, and the mass-education of that community is aimed at by its free access to every kind of learning within its reach, and by making the power of interpretation and explanation of the mysteries of Sanscrit and other philosophies or sciences the most important qualification of a "Gyani."

I begin this chapter with an account of Sikh indigenous education, reversing the order of antiquity, which would give the first place to Hindus, the second to Muhammadans, and the third to Sikhs; because I wish to show that even the most elementary instruction in this province, in what is officially stated to be a barbarous dialect, is full of lessons for our Educational Department, and because the humblest beginnings at reading and writing of the child at a Gurmukhi School are similar to those in all other indigenous schools in which other subjects are added.

Before, however, entering into these details, I wish to draw attention to the extensive Literature which exists in Gurmukhi. Appendix IV shows books, in the library of Sirdar Atar Singh only, which are in the Gurmukhi character, and, to a great extent, composed in a language largely mixed with Hindi, but, otherwise, essentially Panjabi, archaic, mediæval and modern. For, it should be remembered, that the Sikh sacred writings were intended for the general apprehension of Hindus throughout India, and that they, in consequence, drew largely not only on the then existing Hindi dialects but also on Sanscrit, from which numerous translations were made, whilst Panjabi, which has its own history of phonetic development or decay different from that of Hindi proper, had largely drawn on the Persian court-language of the former rulers of the province. We, accordingly, find, both before annexation and now, that Hindi was nowhere spoken or written in the Panjab (see last Census, in which not even one person is returned as speaking Hindi in the province), but that what is called Hindi is really the Bhásha or vernacular of the Panjab, namely Panjabi, which the Hindus wrote in the Nagari or Landé characters, the Muhammadans in the Persian characters and the Sikhs in the Gurmukhi characters, the language being affected by dialectic and scholastic influences, in some parts closely resembling one of the Hindi *patois* of adjacent territory in the North-Western Provinces. The "Adi Granth" is an invaluable treasury of various mediæval vernaculars of India, and, accompanied by traditional explanations, which Dr. Trumpp has, perhaps too summarily, rejected in his admirable translation, is a mine of information to the student of Indian languages, religions, and customs.

"Gurmukhi," however, is not a name for a mere *character*, as is supposed both by Natives, including now even the Sikhs themselves, and by Europeans. Etymologically and historically, it is the name of the *language* which flowed from the "mouth of the Guru" Nanak, and, although his sayings were committed subsequently to *writing* by Arjan, the characters, though not the *name*, existed *before* Nanak. For instance, at *Athúr*, in the Ludhiana District, there is a mausoleum, so Sirdar Atar Singh, the Chief of Bhadaur, tells me, on which there is an inscription dated 50 years before the advent of Guru Nanak, written in characters which are evidently the same as the present Gurmukhi, though the difference between them and the earlier Sikh writings and between these writings and present Gurmukhi is somewhat greater.

The number of Gurmukhi manuscripts on various subjects connected with science and religion scattered all over the province, in the possession of Bhais and shrines, is very considerable, though every day increases the chances of their being lost or destroyed owing to our neglect of the real vernacular literature of the province. They are both translations of Sanscrit works and original productions, chiefly in Panjabi verse. That their value is not small may be inferred from the following enumeration of authors before annexation, whose writings are still read:—

BABA AMIR DAS, who died about 15 years ago, has left us 200 books, chiefly of Panjabi poetry of a religious character, of which the "RATAN HAJARA" is the most famous. He was also an eminent author on the Baidak system of medicine.

BHAI BUD SINGH was one of the most successful translators of Sanscrit works into Gurmukhi.

BHAI SANT SINGH, GYANI, and BHAI BISHAN SINGH, GYANI, both of Amritsar, were illustrious as teachers and poets, whilst the descendants of the latter still endeavour to maintain the literary traditions of their family.

As a poet, the name of BHAI NIPAL SINGH is still deservedly popular, whilst his rival in reputation, BHAI SANTOKH SINGH of Kantal in the Karnál District, has rendered his name immortal among his co-religionists by an encyclopædia of sciences written in verse. His renderings of Sanscrit works into Gurmukhi poetry are said to be master-productions. Certainly, his great work, "the SURAJ PARKÁS," a history of the Sikhs, the translation of which into, I believe, Urdu is being undertaken by His Highness the Raja of Jhind, will yet receive the admiration of European scholars. As a traveller also, Santokh Singh was justly renowned, and he made it his object to visit all places where Sikhs had ever flourished or Gurus had lived. This tendency among the Sikhs to go the round of places where their co-religionists had been has had no mean effect, as we shall see further on, if not to stimulate indigenous education in other parts of India, at all events to affect its terminology.

Who also could omit from a record of Gurmukhi savans the name of the great Grammarian and Vedantist, BABA GANGA RAM, who translated and adapted Sanscrit grammar and philosophy into Gurmukhi, and who so completely conquered the prejudices of the Brahmins at Benares, where he long resided, against his "protestant" body of reformers, that, from his time, date the establishment of Dharmsalas in the sacred city of the Hindus?

What greater proof, again, can be afforded of the importance of Gurmukhi literature and poetry, than the reference to the fact that the Court of GURU GOVIND SINGH, the warrior-poet and reformer of the Sikhs, was composed of the "52 immortals," the great Gurmukhi poets of all denominations, including even the hated Mussulman, who wrote on theology, moral philosophy, history and State economy (*siasat mudan*), in verse which was only surpassed by the "unsurpassable" Guru Govind himself, who corrected their manuscripts with his own hand? One of these manuscripts, *extending to 4,000 pages*, still exists at Anandpur, in the Hushiarpur District, and is corrected throughout in the very handwriting of the second founder of the Sikh faith. Nor was the effect of Sikhism lost on other denominations. The famous Mathematician and Arabic Scholar HASHIM SHAH wrote numerous *novelettes* in Panjabi, which are still much read; he got a Jaghir near Jagdeo in recognition of his literary eminence, and his Arabic scholarship secured his pardon from the ever-forgiving *Ranjit Singh*, when he had once joined in a revolution against the Sikh "Sirkar," the "servus servorum" of the Panjab. Hashim Shah's "Shirin Ferhad" in Panjabi, his story of "Sassi Pannu," and of "Soni Mehiwal," still form the delight of thousands.

Nor were the Sikh Sirdars, as is generally alleged, illiterate. RANJIT SINGH himself had *forgotten* his letters, for there is evidence that he left school for the turmoil of life at the age of 9. SIRDAR LEHNA SINGH MAJITHIA was no mean Mathematician and Engineer. He is said to have translated Euclid from Arabic into Panjabi. Several European contemporaries testify to his skill in devising machinery, of which a leather gun, useful for artillery purposes, seems almost mythical were its existence not attested. KAUR NAO NIHAL SINGH, AJIT SINGH and LEHNA SINGH MAJITHIA studied the higher branches of Mathematics and Astronomy under the famous AKHWAND ALI AHMAD, who was specially called from the *frontier* to Lahore. Lehna Singh, moreover, combined a knowledge of Arabic with that of Sanscrit, so did AJIT SINGH SINDHANWALIA, as also ATAR SINGH of the same illustrious house, and KAUR NAO NEHAL SINGH, in addition, of course, to considerable proficiency in Persian. *Now* I only know two natives in the Punjab who know *both* the classical languages of the East, Arabic and Sanscrit, and both of them are Sikhs. One is the young Sikh Sirdar, Gurdial Singh of the Civil Service, who was trained in the respective indigenous schools before he carried everything before him in the Amritsar Government School and the Lahore Government College. The other is the oldest representative of the great Sindhanwalia family, Sirdar Thakur Singh, Extra Assistant Commissioner, who has written a treatise on "Diabetes," is a distinguished Persian and Gurmukhi scholar, and who is now writing what promises to be a monumental history of the Panjab. (Natives, of course, who know Sanscrit and Persian are not rare, whilst men who know both Arabic and Persian may still be found in considerable numbers.) At the present moment, we have still Gurmukhi scholars and authors, but their number is yearly decreasing. Among them may be named BHAI GYAN SINGH, the illustrious son of an illustrious father, to whom I have already referred; BHAI BISHN SINGH of Amritsar, a prolific author in Grammar, Philosophy, including Logic, and History, who refused repeated offers of Jaghirs from Ranjit Singh, and has, therefore, left his descendant to the gratitude of posterity.

BABA UDA SINGH BEDI of Gunachaur in the Jalandhar District, is also an author of merit. He is very poor, for we have confiscated his Jaghir which, it is alleged, the Sikh Government gave to his family "in perpetuity" "al-ed-dewám."

SARDAL SINGH, son of GYAN SINGH, also an author, similarly carries on a struggle for existence as a petty Inspector, "Girdáwar," of Female Schools at Amritsar on Rs. 20 per mensem.

The Udási Fakir of Amritsar, a poet and author, also deserves to be noticed, as also BAWA SOMER SINGH of Wassowal in the Amritsar District, a famous author, who, *inter alia*, has written a well-known "History of Govind Singh."

My object in referring to past and present Sikh authors is merely to show that the Gurmukhi language and literature is not the contemptible and barbarous idiom which Educational Reports and the interested statements of Hindu and Muhammadan underlings make it out to be, but that it is still living with a glorious tradition, and with the possibility of development to a still more glorious future, if it be cultivated and encouraged as the national language of the Panjab, as the Rev. Dr. Trumpp once suggested with so much earnestness in his Report on the Lahore Oriental College, then in its infancy, and without a single class for the teaching of Panjabi.

I have before me a Gurmukhi treatise, the title of which recalls both classical and Scandinavian mythology. It is the "AMRIT CHAKÁON-DI VIDI," or "instructions for giving the AMRIT," the sacred drink, mixed with sugar, honey and spice, to the candidate for initiation into the mysteries of studentship or Sikhism, which we will find to be an indication of the course of studies pursued in Gurmukhi schools. When the gods succeeded against the Rakshasas in churning the ocean, the quintessence of which gives them the delightful beverage AMRIT to be quaffed in their heaven, they obtained both the nectar and AMBROSIA, the food of Olympus, and it is, no doubt, AMRIT which the heroes drink in Walhalla. It is in connection with Sikhism that the appellation of the sacred city of the Sikhs, AMRITSAR, will alone be understood. It is not merely "Amrita Saras," or "pool of immortality," as generally rendered, but it is the inexhaustible fountain from which he who drinks deep derives immortal knowledge, and with it immortality.

On these instructions are the seals of both the Akalbunga and Anandpur Parliaments or *Takhts*.

After the Amrit is prepared, the following instructions are given to the candidate as essential to studentship :—

"This is essential :

"The reading of the *Japji*, of the *Jápji*, of the *Reh-rás* (an evening prayer), of the *Sohilá* (a prayer before going to sleep), of the *Anandji* (with the evening prayer), of the *Chandipát*, the *Gurmantr* (a motto from the well-known book of prayer of the Sikhs, the first-named "Japji.")

Saddh Sangat (the communion with good men).

Dinwár purub kerna (rejoicing on the festivals of the Guru).

Káta Kirtán (worship).

Sikhon da adr kerna (be respectful to Sikhs).

Nitnám Siri Guruji pat kerna (hear or read the Granth daily, a frequent employment of Bhais by pious Sikhs).

Darshan kerna (to see the Granth, which implies visits to the temple or sacred repository where it is kept). (In other words, "see, hear or read the Bible or sacred book of the Sikhs.")

Shastr Vidya sikhna = the study of *military affairs.*

Gorde charn sikhna = learn to *ride.*

Satsh bolna = speak the truth.

GURMUKHI VIDYA SIKHNA = STUDY GURMUKHI SCIENCE.

DHARM KI KIRT KERNA = DO YOUR BUSINESS RIGHTEOUSLY.

Khairát kerna = give alms.

Mata pitada adr kerna = Honor father and mother.

From this it is clear that the education of a Sikh, not unlike that of the ancient Persian, consists in speaking the truth, learning to ride and being a warrior, in addition to his main duties, that of worship, reading the sacred books and *studying Gurmukhi literature.*

I need not add that the "Amrit" or "Pohol" is given alike to women and men.* In the "principles" of the Amritsar Guru Singh Sabha, "the right of women to express an opinion at the meetings or to send it in writing" is expressly guarded. Indeed, in former times, no one, man or woman, could be a proper Sikh without knowing to read and write, and it is a significant fact that the Sikh carpenters are still highly proficient in Gurmukhi, and that many of them become Bhais. Three sales were considered to be unpardonable: the sale of girls, by taking a dowry for them (which is now commonly done), the sale of cows, and the sale of land. If a man gave a dowry to his wife, it was to herself in jewels, but, on no account, would he or any of his relatives even take food or water in the same village from which his wife came, for a Sikh wife, like that of Cæsar, should be above the suspicion of having become the object of a pecuniary consideration. If the Bédis, descendants of Guru Nanak, killed their daughters, it was because they were too proud to ally them with other Sikhs; but they were rightly anathematized in consequence. Guru Govind strictly forbids the association with killers of daughters (*kurí már*) and others whom it is not necessary to mention here; but the deference paid to the fair sex may be inferred from the saying, which speaks of the security enjoyed in the best Sikh times that "virgins could walk alone by day and night," being fully guarded by the general respect.

If a "disciple" (whose Gurmukhi course, in which it may be noticed that writing has to precede reading) wished to advance from studentship to fellowship, and become a "*Bhai*" or "brother" secular or spiritual, he had to study the two Granths, the Gurmukhi Grammar, *Pingal* (Prosody in Gurmukhi), *Itihás* (a Sikh application of the term to History), and Arithmetic (in Gûrs or rules of which each letter contains a meaning), and the elements of Sanscrit. The above were the compulsory subjects, but, if he wished to reach a higher grade, he would study the Niaya system of Logic, the Vedanta and the Patigánt, which are all to be found in a translated or adopted form, in Gurmukhi. Highest of all, however, ranked the "*Gyani,*" the "I'rfán," who could explain the mysteries of philosophy and religion in popular language, and would communicate them, as a preacher, to the people, thus showing that the essence of Sikhism is the popularization of knowledge. The Panjab University has adopted the title of "*Gyani*" for the highest proficiency in Gurmukhi literature, in which an examination is held. Prelim-

* For a description of the origin of the "Pohol" see Part IV, Note 1.

inary to it is the "*Widwan*" or "knowledge" test, which, in its turn, is preceded by an entrance or ability, "*Buddhiman,*" examination, in which this year a Sikh lady has passed with credit. It is to be hoped that these examinations will do something towards the revival of a literature, and the cultivation of a language, which superciliousness alone can term "barbarous."

To the nightly scientific discussions at the Durbar Sahib in Amritsar, and to the periodical gatherings of Panjabi poets and of pandits, I have already referred. Whilst, however, it was one of the great aims of the Sikh reformers to bring knowledge of every kind within the reach of all classes, it was equally their object to show that knowledge, dissociated from strength of body and purity of life, was profitless. This is why, in the various memorials from Sikhs to the Education Commission, the physical, mental and moral degeneracy of that community, in consequence of the neglect of Gurmukhi, is referred to, and why, from the development of their sacred language, not only educational, but also social and physical, benefits are expected to flow. In fact, nothing is so strongly impressed on the Sikh mind as "*mens sana in corpore sano.*" The Granth's description of "who is a real Pandit" is a protest against the exclusiveness of the learned caste.

Sô Pandit jo man per bôde = He is a Pandit who teaches his mind (knows himself).
Rám Nám atam meyn sôde = Who with his soul remembers God (Rám).
Rám Nám sar rás pîwe = To whom God's name is the sweetest drink (reference to Amrit).
Us Pandit ke up dês jag jîwe = From the teaching of such a Pandit the world would live.
Har ke charu hir de basáwe = He who impresses God's (Hari) footsteps on his heart.
So Pandit phir jôn ne áwe = That Pandit will not again return to life on this earth (by transmigration).
Bêd, Purán, Smrit, budhe mûl = He will (indeed) understand the Vedas, Puranas and Smritis.
Sukháiu meyn janne astûl = In a moment he will have the comprehension of universal things.
Chau Varna ko dè up dês = *He* will (indeed) be able to give instruction to the four castes (obviously the supposed privilege of the Brahmin alone).
Nanak us Pandit ko sadá adês = Nanak (himself) will ever salute such a Pandit.

THE GURMUKHI SCHOOL.

The child should enter it at 5 years of age and not after 7; the practice however is that he is sent to school at 6 (unless, in consequence of the contempt into which learning has fallen, he is not sent to school at all, which is now generally the case). Both boys and girls attend the same primary school. As fingers have been created before pens were invented, he first writes on the ground, which is prepared by a layer of *Pandhu* or *Ganjni* (*Pindôl* in Hindustani). Several Europeans have undergone this practice, including General Pollard, R.E., much to their advantage, in acquiring dexterity in Oriental penmanship. The economy, simplicity, greater compass, and ease in effacing wrongly-formed letters, of writing on the ground, seem to have much to recommend the practice, which is also alleged to have the effect of teaching the child to be more careful of the slab or paper in not smudging it, as is now so often the case, in the attempt to improve the form of the letters. Be that as it may, the child, who has now learnt the forms of the letters of the alphabet, accompanied sometimes, even at this stage, by the oral recitation of alphabetically-arranged moral maxims, which he will write down hereafter, is promoted to the dignity of a wooden slab or *pati,* which is first blackened over with soot, then dried in the sun or near a fire, and which may then be written on with Pandhu, which can be easily washed off, the "pati" being also glazed over with ground glass, called "gota." The pen used is easily obtainable from every thatch or hedge of Sarkerá (white or yellow reed, the well-known Munshi's *Kalam* being cut from the finer and rarer Nâza reed of black reddish colour, those of Wâsit between Bassora and Baghdad being the most famous).

The children then learn the forms of the numerals and simple enumeration; also the signs for weights and measures. It is not considered necessary for the ordinary Sikh child to learn the Pahara or multiplication table. If he wishes to do so (and this is generally only the case with the sons of Lamberdars and Patwaris, who may have afterwards to deal with village accounts), he can attend the Padha's school, about which more hereafter.

The children now write down the names of God, of the people of the house in which they are, of surrounding objects, of eatables, and indeed of everything that can be pointed out to them or that can create an interest.

Guru Angat, like Professor Huxley, did not consider it to be beneath his dignity to write primers for children, and he accordingly wrote a number of mottos and moral maxims which accompany the letters of the alphabet, *e. g.* :—

"D." *Gurmukhi* "dada"=" Dôs na dîje kahu; dôs karmá apnea" (do not attribute your failure to others; attribute it to destiny). Most mottos are, however, much more simple, as is shown in an appended specimen, *e. g.*—

"J." *Jaja*= . . . "Juth mat bolna," tell no lies; or, "jo jo jappé, so iski gát howe" (whoever prays, has salvation).

"S." *Sasa*= . . . "Saddh sang páwe, jàu kóe" (whoever associates with good men, &c., &c.).

The child then reads the *Japji*, which chiefly deals with the eternity of God and other books or chapters from the Granths in the following order:—

The Rai rás (a corruption, probably, in Perso-Panjabi of Rah-rást=the straight or true road,) in which the learner's attention is drawn to examples of God's providence in nature, *e. g.*, "Udud áwe sai kosán, tis pátshe batshre tsherea, tin kaun khiláwe, tin káun piláwe"=" The (migratory) bird comes from (the distance of) hundreds of kôs, leaving behind its young, who (but God) feeds them; who (but God) gives them to drink?" Therefore, the inference is, fear not, lest He allow thee to hunger.

The Arti Soila is an allegory intended to prevent idolatrous practices, by showing that nature is God's temple, the sun and moon the temple's lights, &c., (so as to prevent worship of the Brahmin's salver, with its oil-lamps, his bells, &c.)

The Sidh Gosht is a conversation with holy men, showing that there is no necessity for miracles, when the human body itself is the greatest miracle. (Guru Govind anathematized Ram Rai and the latter's disciple called Ram Ráyya, for having performed the miracle of restoring a dead cow to life, as he considered that the exercise of miraculous gifts created spiritual pride, whereas a "Sikh" or learner should be humble.)

The Unkár shows the skill of the creation and its objects, and enjoins the worship of the Creator.

The Báibár, or 22 stories illustrative of God's work and calculated to deprecate intolerance.

The child may then read the whole of the Adi Granth, followed by the "5 Chapters" of Guru Govind Singh, which are models of poetry; he may then read the latter's entire Granth (it may be incidentally mentioned that in Guru Govind's time Panjabi gradually increased over the Hindi element in Gurmukhi compositions).

I need scarcely point out that with such a system of primary education the parent can easily co-operate with the schoolmaster. The child repeats his lesson at home. Father and mother, who ought to be able to read and write Gurmukhi, can assist him in his work by advice, and by confirming the instruction of the school from the experience of their lives. Education thus becomes an agency connected with the best daily associations of the pupil, instead of, as now, estranged from them. By instructing the son of the agriculturist through the medium of Urdu, we have deprived him of the teaching power of his parents in Panjabi; we have disconnected him from the past, and yet have given him no education which will enable him to cope with the difficulties of the present, or to make him a loyal and useful member of the community.

To resume my account of the course of studies pursued at a Gurmukhi school:

The child then reads the *Hanuman Natak*, an adaptation of this famous drama by Hindu Ram, which is composed in mixed Hindi and Panjabi, and written in the Gurmukhi character.

Tulsi's *Ramayana* then follows, written in classical Hindi, but in the Gurmukhi character.

A chapter of the *Bhagwat* in Gurmukhi and other books are now read.

The well-known "*Janam Sakhi*" being in prose is read at home by the pupil (Bhai Man Singh's is considered to be the most trustworthy account).

The *Gurbilās* (History of the first six Gurus and of the tenth Guru) is now read.

The pupil who wishes to devote himself to medical practice now reads the *Nigant* (drugs), *Saringdhar* (prescriptions and pathology), and the *Nidan* (causes of diseases and diagnosis) in Gurmukhi.

The study of astrology is not respected among Sikhs as it is among Hindus, whose priests often derive from its practice a livelihood, which enables them to cultivate some scientific or literary speciality, and to give gratuitous instruction to pupils. The Sikhs, however, have a little book of divination called Parekshas or Examination.

Rhetoric or *Sahitkab* was much studied in Gurmukhi, which combined both Panjabi and Hindi. The text-book by Fakir Amir Das of Amritsar, to whom allusion has already been made, is the most famous. It consists of 8 or 9 volumes, which, *inter alia*, include "a guide to polite conversation, manners and etiquette"; "when to praise; explanation of allusions, &c.," as well as "Prosody"-"Chand", all subjects in which a native, brought up under the present system, is deficient, and is, therefore, unable to claim a liberal education, either from the mediæval stand-point of Europe or that of gentlemen of any country.

The Vedant, as I have already stated, is read in Gurmukhi, but it is not a part of the ordinary school course, of which I have given the traditional *model* course.

The name of the teacher or Guru has received the widest application, not only in the province but throughout India. Where the traditional guide or Brahmin is not also the spiritual or secular teacher, a Guru from another caste often takes his place. Among Sikhs there are three kinds of Gurus, educational, religious, and spiritual (the Guru who initiates the "Sikhs" on taking the Pohol).

The discipline of the Gurmukhi school is like that of the Landé school, which will be described further on. The income of the teacher is derived from land, from the contributions of his fraternity, the endowment of his dharmsala, or from the presents of his pupils or of their parents. The subject of the landed endowments for Gurmukhi schools will be treated elsewhere. Suffice it to say that Ranjit Singh was particularly liberal to them, and that he recommended all who came near him to read Gurmukhi.

The protesting child of Hinduism, the Sikh community, is constantly exposed to temptations to return to the fold. Surrounded by the influences of Brahminical literature in their own education and daily associations, it is not to be wondered at that the Sikhs only offer a feeble front to the attacks on the systems of Nanak and Govind, which are now so vigorously made by Hindus. Some of the Sikh leaders themselves find in a compromise with Hindu notions that spiritual domination over their co-religionists which is so dear to the nature of man, but against which the genius of Sikhism protests. Already has the tendency to relapse into idolatry been commented on by the recent *Takht* at the Akalbunga, but it will become irresistible if we continue our present denationalizing system of education, which deprives the Sikhs of their mental, moral and physical training, and which plays into the hands of Hindu proselytism. For, let it be remembered, that in spite of caste exclusiveness, the Brahmins are ever on the look-out for neophytes to Hinduism from among Sikhs, Buddhists and the aboriginal races, though not to any particular caste. This ardent proselytism, which will cross mountains and deserts in order to make a convert, I pointed out as early as 1866, and it has since succeeded in establishing the Brahmin as a latitudinarian priest in many districts where formerly the Lama reigned supreme. All ideas and deities are welcomed by Brahminism, and their connexion with the Hindu Pantheon is established in some way or other. The new worshippers are also promoted to the dignity and exclusiveness of a caste for themselves, added to some existing classification. A similar danger from another quarter is also threatening the Sikhs. The educated Hindus, whose one great aim is the consolidation of all non-Muhammadans of India into *one nation*, are endeavouring to substitute Nagri for Gurmukhi, and some dialect of Hindi for the Bhásha or vernacular of the country. As long as their efforts are confined to the promotion of the Nagri character among their Panjabi co-religionists, their efforts deserve every encouragement, but the tendency to supplant Gurmukhi by Nagri should be steadily resisted. Unfortunately, there are a great many traitors in the Sikh camp, whilst the gentleness, pliability and versatility of the ever-persistent Hindu will be more than a match for the ingenuous Sikh, unless we restore to him that education which will again make him strong to become a mainstay of good government in the Panjab.

From the annexed lists of Dharmsalas and Gurmukhi Schools throughout the province, it will be clear that, whilst both buildings and teachers are still available for Gurmukhi teaching, there is a great decline in the number of pupils, as the parents prefer that they should learn nothing at all than the system in vogue in Government Schools which unfits them for their livelihood. At the same time, it will be seen that almost in every village where there are Sikhs a strong desire is expressed for Gurmukhi teaching, not only by that community generally, but also by lamberdars and patwaris, whose interest would rather prompt them to support the extension of the Government system, including Urdu, than to advocate the all-levelling Gurmukhi. It will also be seen that there is scarcely a village in the Panjab which, if inhabited by Sikhs, does not still contain persons who can read Gurmukhi, as well as one or more Dharmsalas, so that there are educational appliances at hand throughout the Panjab which it would be criminal to neglect. In some places, like Babe-di-Ber in the Sealkot district, out of a population of 250 persons, 70 still know Gurmukhi and 7 Urdu, whilst only 26 of the young generation read Gurmukhi and the rest apparently nothing. Here is a typical Sikh village, in which every one, before annexation, could read and write, but which an alien system has tended to deprive of the kind of education which it had, because no longer equally useful, and, at the same time, has given no other education instead, thus replunging the country into barbarism. Take, for instance, the case of the village Churian Kalan in the Sealkot district. Out of a population of 1,500, of whom more than half are Hindus and the rest Mussulmans, only 10 persons know Gurmukhi and one Urdu. Only six boys attend the neighbouring Government school and 20 read privately, of whom 10 read Urdu and 10 Gurmukhi. (For an account of the decline of Gurmukhi education and for a summary of the memorials on its behalf, see Part IV, Note 2.)

The present chief seats of Sikh learning are AMRITSAR, the DAMDAMA Dharmsala in the village of Raipur in the Ludianah district and Ferozepur. In AMRITSAR alone, besides the golden temple and the bungahs attached to it, as also the Mushá'aras and Mubáhisas to which I have alluded, there are over 300 Dharmsalas in which Gurmukhi is taught (See Bhai

Dhrit Singh's Report on page 8 of Appendix II). **Raipur** has a special notice in my account of the indigenous schools of the Ludianah district, which will, incidentally, show whether land or wells granted rent-free to teachers by the Sikh Government have been resumed or assessed by us in the very refuge of Guru Govind Singh (Damdama), one of the most sacred of Sikh Dehras, in which was once the rural University of the Sikhs, the village Raipur. It will also be seen from that and other accounts that fees in cash or kind are preferentially given to the Dharmsala or Dehra rather than to the Bhais in person, though some of their income is, no doubt, derived direct from those pious zamindars who send for them to their houses in order to read the Granth to them. Saddhu Bhup Singh teaches crowds of fakir-pupils from every part of the Panjab. Whilst there is much imposture among fakirs, though not more than in any class of any community in any country, there is often real piety and sometimes considerable learning. Indeed, the fakirs have been the chief means for the popularisation of religion, irrespective of caste. The Right Reverend T. V. French, D. D., Bishop of Lahore, whose opinion on the subject of fakirs is not likely to lean on the side of undue partiality in their favor, deposed in his evidence before the Education Commission that "*some of the best teachers in the world, I should think, are some of the Hindu Fakirs, Sanyasis, Jogis and the like, doing* Guru's work, but they teach nothing at present except their own philosophies and religious systems." I have seen these fakirs, whose learning and insight into philosophical and religious controversies have often created my profound admiration, treated worse than dogs by Europeans, simply, forsooth, because they looked "uncanny." Yet they exercise a most healthful influence on the village. The mind of the peasant and of his boy is "lifted up," as was expressed to me, when they pass the fakir's hut, who is often a standing example of self-abnegation and a monitor of morality to his surroundings. No wonder, then, that any attempt to resume their rent-free well is considered to be unlucky by the peasantry, for their removal from a place is often followed by an increased disregard in the community that is left behind of moral obligations. No wonder also that some of the so-called "educated natives" who have cast off the trammels of their faith, do not look upon them with favor. The fact remains that, in some respects, educational, moral and religious, they are a valuable aid in the preservation of much that is good in Indian Society.

I trust that I have shown that Gurmukhi has a history and literature, and that it cannot be called "barbarous," unless, indeed, we assume that Πᾶς μὴ Ἄγγλος βάρβαρος, which would be as unjust as the counter-statement of the native would be who sees one landmark after the other of his ancient civilisation swept away by the conqueror, to use the words of a Parliamentary report, that Πᾶς Ἄγγλος βάρβαρος. Even, however, if Gurmukhi were barbarous, it has a right to be respected and cultivated as the language of those who so nobly stood by us in the days of the mutiny of 1857, or as English had a right to be raised from a "barbarous" vernacular, when it superseded Latin and French for literary purposes, to its present proud position of being the most widely diffused of modern civilised languages.

II.—Chatsálas: Mahajaní and Landé Schools.

The influence of these schools has extended to the trading classes all over India. Our earliest reports of the North-West Provinces show Panjabí schools established at Delhi. Ancient and familiar as the term of "Guru" is, it became popularised through the Sikhs as a vernacular guide of faith, if not as a vernacular secular teacher. Even the term "Lundé," "Landé" or "Mundé" for boy, as well as in its real sense of "tail-less," has spread far beyond this province to designate various commercial handwritings in India. A table which I have affixed to this Report, as well as the specimens of the Mahajaní, Landé and Sarafi characters which I have collected, will show that, just as it was unjust to call a language like Gurmukhí "barbarous" which contained so many literary treasures, so also is it scarcely true that "no one can read Landé an hour after he has written it," or that "each form of Mahajaní is confined to the district in which it is used." It is simply an abbreviation of the Nagrí character for tachygraphic purposes, though I admit that it is not so readable (which, indeed, no Hindi quick-hand or short-hand can be) as the ordinary "Shikasta" against which so much abuse is raised. At the same time, it can be easily read by the members of the particular trade whom it concerns, and this is, after all, what is wanted. Even English spelling is ideological rather than phonetic, and is unintelligible to those who merely speak the language, but have not learnt to read it. Again, "Landé" is not a mere trade-cyphering, though, even as such, it formed a basis of elementary instruction throughout Upper India, at all events to the commercial community, which we have ignored. The evidence, collected from the Panjab and, I believe, also from the North-West Provinces, is unanimous in regarding "Landé," or "Mundia" merely as a form of transliteration for trade purposes, confined to single trades, and does not know of its use for higher literature. In my "Introduction" to this Report, I have endeavoured to show how Gurmukhí was developed from Landé, and that the original writings of some of the Gurus were in that despised character, manuscripts which are still religiously preserved in one or two places which I have indicated. That the Sikh reformers should endeavour to adopt the most universally-spread form of writing, in order to disseminate their creed, was merely a part of their general aim to popularise knowledge. The effort was not, however, continued with persistence, owing to the absence of sufficient intercourse and comparison with different parts of India, and the Gurmukhí character was adopted as being the one which could be most easily acquired by all classes, whilst also laying claim to greater beauty than any of the forms of "Landé."*

The teachers of these schools are generally called PANDAHS or PÁDAHS though, in many places, the term "Guru" is applied to them; whilst, if they are Muhammadans, which many of them are in the Panjab, they are often designated "Mians," a term more suited to the elementary teacher of Persian. These Pádahs are generally Brahmins, if Hindus, or Rawals, if Muhammadans, though it is said that the Muhammadan Pádahs are descendants of Brahmins who were forcibly converted to Islam. The profession of Pádahs is hereditary in that class, whether Hindu or Muhammadan. Every class of the community, except the lowest, however, contributes its quota to the fraternity of Pádahs, especially the Khatris in the Panjab, and the Kayets in the North-Western Provinces. Banya Pádahs and others also travel from town to town, offering to teach the children of Banyas, at various localities, the multiplication-table and ciphering, if not book-keeping and drafting bills, &c., within a certain time, and for a certain remuneration. This circumstance has given rise to the erroneous supposition that indigenous schools were here to-day and there to-morrow, and that, in consequence, their statistics could not be collected. In several parts of this and other provinces and countries, there are indigenous village schools, which are open when agricultural work is slack, and which are closed when the assistance of the boys is required by their parents in the fields. Again, private tutors are, as a rule, no more fixtures in the Panjab than they are in England; but all this would not justify the conclusion arrived at in the Panjáb Educational Reports, that accurate statistics regarding schools that *are* settled in various localities, cannot be collected either here or in England, if a conscientious effort were made to collect them, and if it were really wished to obtain and to utilise the information so often in vain sought for by the Government.

The remuneration of the Pádahs, about which more hereafter, is often very considerable, for it depends on their reputation as trainers of good businessmen and on the practical utility of their instruction generally, for which natives will always be ready to pay handsomely, just as they are ever liberal to their religious teachers. It is only to attend *our* schools that they either pay little or require to be paid by stipends or scholarships, for these schools give neither a practical nor a religious education, but are merely intended, like the Persian schools of old, which they have supplanted to a certain extent, for aspirants to employment in Government offices, and are accordingly mainly frequented by that class.

The initial steps of writing, first on the ground (in villages) and then on "patis," wooden boards, prepared for the purpose, have already been sufficiently explained in my account of Gurmukhi Schools. What gives the Landé School its special character is its arithmetic, both mental and oral. By the latter I mean the repetition of the multiplication-table, whether ordinary (1 to 10) ×

(1 to 10) ; superior or " bara gyára " (11 to 30) × (11 to 30) ; fractional (1 to 50) × ($1\frac{1}{4}$, $1\frac{1}{2}$, $2\frac{1}{2}$, $3\frac{1}{2}$, $4\frac{1}{2}$, $5\frac{1}{2}$, &c.) ; some fractions into fractions—*e. g.*, $1\frac{1}{4} \times 1\frac{1}{2}$; $1\frac{1}{2} \times 2\frac{1}{2}$; $2\frac{1}{2} \times 3\frac{1}{2}$, &c. ; whilst by mental arithmetic I chiefly refer to the rules or *gurs* by which, chiefly business, calculations of the most intricate kind, especially as regards fluctuations in the grain market, can be carried on with ease, mentally, much to the astonishment, and often confusion, of our mathematical M. A.s, helped by every convenience of writing material, scientific methods, and double the amount of time. The Educational Department, however, instead of collecting these *gurs*, which are often the heirloom of the Pádahs, excuses its neglect by offering the Mahajani Schools to contempt, and more or less fully, in the annual reports, repeats the substance of the following remarks of the first Director of Public Instruction, Panjab (paragraph 23 of Report dated 6th July 1857): "The LANDÉ Schools are those in which the children of shop-keepers are taught the mysteries of book-keeping, and in which that *vicious system of accounts which is daily deprecated in our Civil Courts* is perpetuated." I regret to find this sneer by an officer, for whose name I have respect, against an excellent system of book-keeping and of accounts, unaccompanied by a proposal to introduce a *scientific* system, acceptable to the trading community, such as one naturally expects would be made by the educational chief of a province.

"I have seen several of these schools, and, considering the tales we have all heard of the marvellous arithmetical quickness of Hindu boys, have been rather disappointed." I do not know whether Mr. Arnold expected to see the performance of arithmetical miracles, but it is clear from his subsequent statement that he could not have seen the best of these schools, and that what he did see was well worthy of adoption by a thoughtful educator.

"One or two boys in each school can, indeed, perform *wonderful feats* in the multiplication-table up to limits *far beyond* the orthodox twelve times twelve, and can work rule-of-three problems quickly in their heads; often, at the same time, quite unable to work them on paper." As the boys did these "wonderful feats" and solved these problems mentally, both with quickness and, I presume, accuracy, there is no reason why they should have also solved them on paper, especially as they had not been taught to do so; but I suppose that in arithmetic, as in everything else, "orthodoxy is my doxy and hetorodoxy is your doxy." "But the majority do not seem to me to acquire any *great quickness* at figures." In what school in England do the majority of boys acquire any "*great quickness*" at figures? On the contrary, they have nothing like the arithmetical talent of Banya boys, "*and certainly if they do not gain this, they gain nothing.*" This I venture to doubt. A man may be a slow, or only a moderately fast, reckoner, and yet find the accomplishment useful in his vocation, "for the power of *writing a character which neither they themselves nor anybody else can decipher an hour after it has been written, cannot be called an accomplishment.*" It is really extraordinary how a responsible officer reporting to Government can so mislead his employers. If Mr. Arnold and those who have followed him in his strictures had only examined for themselves and *had wished to find the truth, even if detrimental to the departmental system*, they would, at any rate, not have confounded during 26 years these CHATSALAS or Pádah schools with the PATSHALAS, about which more hereafter, and which are, generally, as different from one another, as a French elementary school is from a German University.

Perhaps, also, it has not occurred to educational officers that native teachers, not unlike better-paid Europeans, do not object to deriving both personal profit and reputation from the sale of what, in the absence of a better term, we may call "primers." If, therefore, a Bhai sells his alphabet or a Pádah his multiplication-table at, say, one anna each, to the pupil when he enters the school, it is not surprising that he should not welcome with an exaggerated enthusiasm the introduction of a printed treatise which only puts money into the pockets of Mr. Smith or of the Government Book Depôt. Again, just as an European writer of school-books considers that he is entitled to remuneration, if not recognition by Government, if he compiles, with scarcely a line of difference, the fiftieth *réchauffé* of a reader, or of a treatise on mensuration, when indeed he does not merely put his name to the work of others, so also may a Pádah be excused, if he wishes to be paid for the communication of the mysteries of his profession, its *gurs*, or other marketable commodities.

As regards the Landé character, it also serves to perpetuate the secret trade-dialects, which I discovered some years ago, and which are not merely used for the purpose of the concealment of the "tricks of trade," but which have also carried along with artificial words and phrases, several idioms and many ordinary words, as well as the inflections of ancient dialects, of which they are, accordingly, partial survivals, and should therefore be of the very highest interest to the philologist, ethnographer, guild-historian, and sometimes, indeed, to the Police Officer. At all events, the writers may not wish outsiders to "decipher what they have written," although, if they desire to conceal their meaning, the *words*, and not the Landé *writing*, would be unintelligible.

As for the system of account-keeping taught by these Pádahs, so far from being "deprecated by our Courts," they have often been admitted as the best unsupported evidence there can exist of the correctness of an entry, as nothing can exceed the regularity and accuracy with which, *e. g.*, Bahi-Khatas (Ledger and Index) are kept, and the difficulty which the system offers against fraudulent entries or falsification of accounts. As regards the discipline of the Landé schools, I consider that it compares favourably in substance, though not in appearance, with that of Government schools. Both kinds of institutions, so far as the attendance of the younger children are concerned, are nurseries rather than schools,—in other words, are intended to keep the children out of mischief and to relieve the parents of attending to them in homes which are often crowded, if not noisy. Even here, however, the comparison is to the advantage of the Landé school; for, in the first place, the Pádah, as a rule, goes round every morning to the pupils' houses to collect them, or else sends a senior boy to enquire about an absentee, whilst he also in the course of the day calls out the names of boys at irregular intervals, when they have to answer to the call and to be found engaged in their work, or else he will know the reason "why." In the second place, the Pádah is authorised, in the generality of cases, by the parents to inflict corporal punishment on naughty boys, not only for misconduct whilst at school, but also for misconduct at his own home. The indigenous schoolmaster and the parents therefore co-operate, which has a salutary effect on the boy's mind; whereas the Government schoolmaster does not trouble himself about the conduct of his pupils out of school-hours, and is not trusted by the parents to inflict both just and yet merciful chastisement, in spite of the native equivalent to our "spare the rod and spoil the child," *viz.*, "the child's bones belong to the parents, the child's skin belongs to the teacher"—in other words, native tradition justifies the teacher to inflict any punishment short of a permanent corporal injury. The parent knows that the religious restraints of the Brahmin Pádah or the fellow-feeling of a caste-teacher, together with the personal interest which he has not to offend a customer whose presents of cash and sweetmeats last almost throughout the life of his son, are sufficient checks on any propensity for merciless beating of a negligent or disobedient boy. The stories told of the severe punishment inflicted in indigenous schools, I have ascertained to be mostly false, as, indeed, it is only natural that they should be. Those who spread them have generally derived their information from ex-pupils of Government schools, where the teacher is mostly a stranger to the parents of his pupils, is sometimes of low caste, and always independent of their favour, whilst he will sometimes even presume on the fact of being a Government official, who has merely to please his own superior and, *mirabile dictu, his pupils*, with whom, accordingly, as reports will mention in terms of praise, he is "popular," much to the destruction of his influence for good on them. Indeed, the boys look upon themselves as being far more necessary to the teacher than he is to them, for do they not help him to credit or promotion by passing examinations? In short, whereas in indigenous elementary schools the teacher co-operates with the parent, much to the advantage of his pupil, in Government schools, the teacher seeks the favour of his charges, greatly to the increase of their conceit and subsequent want of pliability or judgment in the practical exigencies of life. If in Government schools many pupils still revere their teachers, it is simply because old traditions and home influences have not yet entirely lost their weight, though this must soon be the inevitable result of persistence in our present system.

Then, again, the official inspection of registers of attendance is a great incentive to false entries, which come to the knowledge of absentee boys, who purchase, by their silence on this point, immunity for other offences. Finally, the Inspector's visits, especially when he calls in schools from varying distances to his camp, are occasions on which teachers have been known to connive with pupils and well-read outsiders to cheat the Inspector. Indeed, it has been asserted on good authority that, on the Inspector's tours, especially in one district, a set of clever boys personate the higher classes of different schools by changing their turbans, &c., a very easy attempt, as the inexplicable superciliousness of most Europeans in their dealings with natives prevents their gaining a distinct impression of native faces that they may have only occasionally seen. That these statements are not overdrawn may be inferred from quotations from the Educational Reports themselves. First, as regards attendance—" The great discrepancy", says an Inspector, " between the numbers on the registers and the numbers taught, seems to be due to a system of official pressure which produces only superficial results " (Panjab Report, 1865-66, page 47). " The registers are not always trustworthy " (Panjab Report, 1866-67, page 14). " Mr. P.", remarks the Director of Public Instruction, Panjab, " was asked for suggestions how to make attendance more regular, and how to secure more trustworthy returns. His reply was, that *attendance must be irregular* among an agricultural population, and that it was no use punishing for incorrect returns " (Panjab Report, 1865-66, page 60). When a Bengal Inspector was deputed to visit the schools of the Panjab in 1868, he found that in 16 village schools, the numbers on the rolls of which were returned as 776, there were only 480 present, although his visit naturally attracted all within possible reach.

Then, as regards the effect of Inspectors' visits to schools not in their site, but from 16 to 60 miles away from them, as the Bengali Inspector states to be the practice in the Panjab and the North-Western Provinces, an accusation which my own experience as Inspector does not enable me to contradict, certainly as regards the shorter distance : " I have known *very fairly prepared classes to be improvised* at a *moment's notice if it was the teacher's interest to make me believe that he had been working steadily* * * * a distribution of sweetmeats is sufficient to attract *all the educated youths in the neighbourhood* " (Panjab Report for 1866-67, page 51).

Now as to the course of study in the CHATSÁLA, one of the humblest of indigenous educational institutions. To learn how to calculate mentally, to keep business correspondence and bahi-khatas is no mean accomplishment, whilst the connexion of writing or reciting the alphabet, &c., with short sentences, sometimes in verse, containing lessons of morality and prudence, impresses both on the youthful intellect. It is in *our* schools that the boys read by rote. To quote the Bengal Inspector's report on Panjab schools—" There was one thing, however, which struck me most markedly at all the examinations, whether of joint or of separate schools. The pupils answered more from memory than from any intelligent appreciation of their text-books. They were more ready with rote work and felt more confident when only repeating than when required to think. If, for instance, I asked from their history, " Who was *Ruzia Begum* ?" the answer invariably began with " *Ruzia Begum burri hushiar thi, hurroz Quran purthi thi* ", and so on, and on, would they proceed repeating until stopped. If I asked them to name the principal places on the river Ganges, the answer always commenced with naming Hurdwar, and proceeded smoothly enough to Calcutta. But if directed to begin from some intermediate station, such as Allahabad, Benares, or Patna, there would be terrible faltering, and in most cases a perfect standstill. In mental arithmetic there appeared to be a marked deficiency. The native system of solving rule-of-three problems by aliquot parts seemed to have been generally neglected, although the text-book used has a chapter especially on that subject. The reading was fluent from the text-books, and, generally speaking, the answers were correct to those questions in grammar, synonyms, and etymology of words, which the Deputy Inspectors asked at my request; but after a few examinations these questions seemed to me to have become stereotyped on the memories of the Deputy Inspectors themselves, and they could not vary them with much ease or readiness on being desired to do so. In one respect, and in one only, I can offer my praise without any hesitation. The handwriting of the village school pupils, whether of the Panjab or the North-West, is, so far as I have seen, quite excellent. On the whole, my impression is that the pupils who attend the village schools of those parts are made to take great pains to learn, and that they excel in everything in which intelligent guidance is not particularly needed. The vernacular education of the North-West has evidently not escaped the evils of "cram."

In another place the Inspector touches the root of the present evil, which is the decadence of indigenous schools:

"The indigenous education of India was founded on the sanction of the *Shastras*, which elevated into religious duties and conferred dignity on the commonest transactions of every-day life. The existence of village communities, which left not only their municipal, but also in part their revenue and judicial administrations, in the hands of the people themselves, greatly helped to spread education among all the different members of the community. He will see the fruits of the indigenous system in the numberless pathshalas, chatsals, and tols which still overspread the country, and which, however wretched their present condition, prove by their continued existence, in spite of neglect, contempt, and other adverse circumstances of a thousand years, the strong stamina they acquired at their birth. At the present day, the religious sanction is growing weak, the village communities are nearly gone, manufacturing industry has come to the verge of ruin, the heaviest incidence of taxation is falling upon land, and a foreign language has become the language of court and commerce. The natural incentives to popular education being thus weak, its progress will depend on the efforts of an enlightened Government inclined to compensate to the people for their losses under foreign rule. Until a healthy political, economical and social condition has been regained under the security of British administration, artificial stimulants must supply its place as well as they are able.'

The fact is that whilst indigenous education is based on religious sanction, fortified by considerations of the practical requirements of life and, above all, by the ever-present *personal* influence of the teacher, the personal influence of the teacher is wanting under our system, and its place is supplied by the more artificial stimulus of the chance of employment under Government. We have at great expense sown dragons' teeth, with the inevitable result. We have not made the new generation more intelligent, but more restless and, unless we restore the traditional teacher, the Maulvi, Pandit or Bhai, to his *cathedra*, and arm him with disciplinary power, the whole future generation of India will become a source of mischief to itself and to us.

And talking about discipline, one Pádah, with a slight switch or rod, is able to maintain it in a school composed of 100 boys. As he lifts the emblem of authority, a pin may be heard to drop. In the East, all that represents authority is revered, and is a stimulant to the noblest exertions, whether for religion, for the Government, or for one's fellow-countrymen. In a relaxing climate, a stimulant is necessary, and without it, the respect for parents, the elders, the authorities and the teacher, and the fear of God, would die out, as it is dying out in India. The moment that our secular education will convince the Indian youth that there is no personal God, and he will see himself surrounded by many of the same mode of thinking (for now he is still slapped on the mouth with his mother's slipper if he repeats his atheism in his own home), the fear of Government will vanish with the fear of God. "The teacher's rod, whether under the form of tutorial, parental, Government or religious 'hukm,' is the moral regenerator of the East."

As for the punishments inflicted, they consist ordinarily in calling a boy who comes late to school *Piddi* or *Pisiddi*, or laggard, whilst the boy who comes first is called *Miri* or chief. This distinction is often found sufficient to ensure punctual attendance. In worse cases, caning on the hand, standing with his face to the corner of a room, or pulling the ear are the usual punishments.

Fines are not inflicted, because no scholarships or stipends are given from which they can be deducted, and because the parents would resent it. Sometimes, I believe, the boy has his heels drawn up, and gets a few blows on the soles of his feet. Often, a senior boy is ordered to cuff a young recalcitrant.

The lessons are given separately to each boy, as has already been stated; but at the end of the day, all boys j M chorus in the multiplication-table, and disperse with a moral song sung together. Sometimes, the Nagri character is also taught in these schools. The morning is usually devoted to arithmetic (or reading in other indigenous schools); there is a break of two hours about noon for meals, and the afternoon is usually devoted to writing.

The income of the best Pádahs sometimes amounts to nearly Rs. 100 per mensem. It is often Rs. 50, and windfalls frequently happen to the tutor from a pupil who has been successful in his business, for, as a rule, the indigenous teacher is gratefully remembered, which is not often the case with youths whom we have taken out of their spheres, and trained at our expense at Government schools and colleges. Before, though not immediately preceding, annexation, when, in spite of what sycophants may say, the people were wealthier than they are now, 2 pice per week used to be paid, usually on *Sundays*, to the Pádah, if he was a Hindu, and on Thursdays to the Rawal, so as to enable him to go in a happy frame of mind, shaved and with his clothes washed, to the mosque on Friday, which was a holiday. The presents in food were also double what they are now. The fee is now generally a pice per week; about 7 loaves per mensem for Muhammadan Pádahs, and certain quantities of flour, ghee, dál, salt, vegetables, called *sida*, for Brahmin Pádahs; a cash present on the commencement of each progressive step of instruction, on the occasion of a marriage, birth of a son in the pupil's family, on the completion of the course, on important festivals, &c.

I would again state that the language for which the Landé or Hindi characters are used in the business-composition which is taught to the student is *invariably the vernacular of the locality*, generally known as the Bhásha thereof, which it pleases enthusiastic memorialists in favour of Hindi to describe as that language, than which nothing can be more remote from fact or from the real wishes of the people, who are made to believe that the application is made on behalf of their own vernacular or Bhásha.

I would now beg to offer a few remarks on the subject of these schools, which I had originally written down in the form of notes, but which the short time at my disposal prevents my embodying in their proper places.

(*a*)—Teachers of Mahajani, Landé, Sarafi, Kaithi or Mundíá are often also called Bhai or Bhaya, as well as Guru and Pádah, thus affording another illustration of the spread of vernacular teaching beyond the limits of the Panjab on the rise of Sikhism.

(*b*)—Brahmin boys, of course, often attend the Pádha school, especially the younger brothers of a Pandit who wishes to follow the priestly or teaching profession of his ancestors. Muhammadan boys also often attend Pádah schools kept by Hindus.

(*c*)—In Landé schools, the Brahmin Pádha get flour, dál, ghi, salt, vegetables, pepper, on the 11th of each lunar fortnight "Ekádeshi," and a large present on the 4th of the light fortnight of *Bhadon*, in some places called "*Chauk Chaukri*" (because four boys forming a moving square, go along fencing with sticks). The teacher, accompanied by his pupils, goes to their parents' houses, outside of which the boys perform, for which they get sweetmeats and the master a turban and some cash, varying from 4 to 8 annas from poor families, and from 1 to 5 rupees from the well-to-do. The statement that has been made, of persons starting Landé schools just before this festival in order to get the presents, and then disappearing, does not seem to me to be founded on fact, or to have been confounded with teachers, who, in some places, are taken on for a fixed period, as the natives are quite sharp enough not to waste their presents on an itinerant or irresponsible teacher who, if not local, rarely gets any pupils at all. Before the boys set out on their Bhadon tour of collection of funds, sweetmeats, and turbans, they put each two or four sticks, according to their dexterity in fencing, before the god Ganésh, who is worshipped in the school-room as the patron of learning, together with offerings of ghi, flour, &c. The master then takes the food for himself, and then blesses the sticks, which are also worshipped by the boys. The disappearance of Landé teachers just after Bhadon, as alleged on the authority of some "educated" natives, is also unlikely, for the simple reason that most of the Banyas enter their sons on that day, so that they, at any rate, would not give the Bhadon present till a full year had elapsed.

(*d*)—In villages the accountant was often kept by a wealthy zemindar, in order to teach his children accounts; and there is no doubt that, side by side with the religious education given by the priest of each denomination, the ancient village system also occasionally included a teacher who instructed his pupils in mental arithmetic, just as the astrologer was a village servant, chiefly because he compiled the almanac of the year for the convenience of his fellow-villagers.

(*e*)—Gurmukhi and Landé are studied by both Hindu and Muhammadan merchants, by agriculturists and traders, and by officials in Native States, the condition of education in which may be taken to represent, to a smaller extent, the condition of education in the Panjab before annexation. In the last census, whilst only one in 39, including women, can read in British territory, at a yearly cost of from 13 to 16 lakhs to Government on education, one in 41 can read in the Native States, excluding women, as I will explain elsewhere. In Kashmir, *e.g.*, it is alleged that double the proportion of children of a school-going age than in British Panjab attend school. It must also be remembered that, whilst the percentage of 1 in 39 in British territory includes persons taught in indigenous schools, and who learnt to read before 1849 or annexation, the numbers in Native States are almost entirely those taught in indigenous schools.* Besides, it is well known that the education in Native States was always less extended than in the dominions of the native paramount power.

* Were all the women in Native States, who are able to read and write, included in the census returns, even the present alleged slight difference between British and Native territory, as regards education, would vanish. It is not to the credit of a respectable woman to have to admit that she is able to write, as caligraphy is often an accomplishment of superior *Hetairæ*. In British territory, girls who are *known* to attend female schools cannot help admitting their ability to write; but, as a rule, although little girls imitate their brothers, when writing, they are never supposed to be able to write a letter, which, *horribile dictu*, might be a love-letter. It is therefore certain that few women in the Native States admitted the soft impeachment of ability to *write*. As regards the census operations generally, it should not be forgotten that the enumerators were, as a rule, connected with offices, and had learnt the peculiar idioms which have been fostered by Anglo-Urdu. They would therefore often ask "*Can* you read and write?" which would elicit a larger number of affirmative replies (unless they were interested, as some bigoted Muhammadans or Hindus might be, in suppressing certain characters), than the more idiomatic enquiry in the Native States "*Are* you *read*?" which the person questioned would answer in the negative if he could only write his Landé, as he would suppose the question to refer to knowledge of Persian, Sanscrit or Arabic, or, at least, to that of Nagri or Gurmukhi. Thousands of people would thus be excluded. Indeed, the remarks to column 11 of the Census Forms *distinctly* excluded those who "can only read and not write or can only sign their names;" so that the pupils at Koran schools and women, who profess to be only able to *read*, were generally excluded, as were also the bulk of the shopkeeping class who, although able to *write* their *Landé* and to read that writing, would not profess to be able to *read*, unless asked in Anglo-Urdu. Again, the question in some tribes, "Do you know Persian?" or "What is your Persian?" would be supposed to refer to their *secret* dialect and not to the language known as such. One thing seems to me to be clear from the census returns, that they *underrate* the number of those "not under instruction" who "can read *and* write," as also that of those "under instruction;" but still the figures show that the number of those not under instruction who "can read and write" is far larger in proportion than that "under instruction" in a recently annexed province; whilst deducting from the latter head those reading in Government and aided schools, we still get the considerable number of about 60,000 pupils reading, no doubt, in acknowledged indigenous schools, *exclusive* of the large number throughout the province reading in private houses, which are not returned as being "under instruction." A great many persons also would profess to be illiterate, if they could only read or, in a sense, only write, *e.g.*, in Spiti all, and in Lahul nearly all can *read* (as in other Buddhist countries) but few can *write*. Many Sikhs can read their Granth who have not practised writing since they were at their indigenous school, and a large proportion of the trading community, although able to *write* their "Landé" would not be able to read books, as these are written in other characters. Finally, as already explained, although very many women can read, comparatively few would admit being able to write in the ordinary meaning of the term to them. In short, counting the large proportion of those who are able to read *or* write, and who are not under instruction, nor could have acquired that accomplishment in *our* schools, together with the number of those taught in indigenous schools, we find that, after 32 years of British rule, the province is still indebted to itself for such general culture as it may possess,—a sign that it is still possible to develop its education by withdrawing from all official interference in a matter that should be exclusively left to the people, represented by local Educational Boards and encouraged by Government aid given through their own "Hakims," and not doled out by the "*middlemen*," who, in education as in the arts of industry and trade of the country, have arrested genuine native progress.

(*f*)—If a boy learns arithmetic solely in our schools, he is of no use to the shop, because he finds there a different system of accounts, and that his "illiterate" father or brother can cast up the intricacies of, say, the grain trade accounts, by a mental process, far more rapidly and correctly than himself; whilst he also discovers that he has less staying power and patience than his uneducated kindred, and sells fewer things when he is in charge of the shop, as he is liable to get confused by a number of queries from customers, and by the haste in stating amounts to be paid for purchases. Besides, he is generally too proud to follow his father's vocation at all.

Various specimens of Mahajani, Kiráki (as called in the Multan district) of the multiplication-table, of several "Gurs" (formulæ), Dars (Rule of Three and rates) are added to this report in Appendix VII. (For a detailed account of Mahajani teaching texts see Part IV, Note 3.)

It will be noticed that the MAHAJANI characters are simpler than those of "LANDÉ", of which there are various kinds. Indeed, the "Mahajani" is called *Hindi* in the Karnal, Rohtak and Gurgaon districts, as well as in numerous other places; so that it is often doubtful, when a Hindu of the commercial class memorialises for Hindi, whether he does not, after all, mean his "Mahajani" character and his Panjabi or Bagri dialect.

LANDÉ, I have also seen confounded with MAHAJANI, but LANDÉ and SARÁFI are generally distinct.

To sum up, "Mahajani" is properly the character of merchants; "Landé" is properly the character of shopkeepers; and "Saráfi" is properly the character of bankers. One and all get occasionally confounded with one another, and with "*Hindi*," though (the word "*Hindi*" in the Panjab is generally used to denote the *Nagri character*, and never any of the *dialects* in the North-West Provinces, or, as is attempted to be shown now by a coterie of English-knowing Hindu nationalists, chiefly of Bengali extraction, *Urdu* written in the Nagri characters, though with a greater infusion of words derived from Sanscrit—an infusion which increases as the subject of the writing becomes more literary, declension and conjugation being the same as in Urdu. *No such dialect exists in the Panjab*, though whether it should be encouraged in order to assimilate the language of Pandits with that of Maulvis reading books on modern science and "general knowledge," is quite another question, which I would venture to answer in the negative, as it is PANJABI in the Nagri character that will naturally be developed for the Hindus in the Panjab, and no form of Hindi proper or equivalent to Urdu in the Nagri characters; Panjabi, in the Gurmukhi character, being similarly cultivated for Sikhs, and Urdu or Panjabi in the Urdu characters for Muhammadans.)

I have omitted all explanation of the THANKRI or THAKARI-LANDÉ character used in the Kangra hills with whatever be the vernacular of the writer employing it, or to the DOGRI and other characters used at Jammu and in the Kashmir territories. That books are written in the Dogri character is well known; that character is twofold: commercial and official. I also understand that it is an open question with the missionaries whether the New Testament should be circulated in Kulu in the Thakari character, or whether the bold step of introducing it in Urdu, the language of the schools, should be taken. The multiplicity of characters and languages should not be deterrent to our educational efforts; on the contrary, variety, provided it be based on *local* variety, is the very essence of local progress. To reduce all schools and systems to one monotony of returns, language, and course of study is to ignore the differences of human life, developments, and associations. Latin, and then French, have failed to remain the universal literary language of Europe, and no one now dreams of establishing one language and one character for the whole of Europe, as is the dream of superficial optimists for the more populated India, the linguistic sub-divisions of which are, after all, more extensive than the few millions of Spain, Portugal, Wallachia, Hungary, and other countries, which all insist on the preservation of their national language and characteristics, in spite of official, or other, convenience.

C.—QUASI-VERNACULAR INDIGENOUS EDUCATION IN THE PANJAB.

I have omitted an account of Lahul and Spiti, where, without any aid from an Educational Department, almost every man and woman is able to read, as the example offered of universal education by another Buddhist country, Burmah, under the guidance of its priesthood, is far more striking than any lesson that can be derived from these sparsely populated valleys. One thing, however, is clear—that unless we follow the lead taken by Burmah in identifying the priesthood with our educational measures, and in establishing an Educational Board (*vide* Appendix I), we shall never have mass-education in the full sense of the term. I have also excluded any reference to Pakhtu and Baluchi education, as what may claim that designation among the races speaking these languages is so connected with either Arabic or Persian as to be more suited for classification under the head of the semi-classical education which is given through the medium of Persian. Indeed, with the exception of Gurmukhi and Mahajani, there exists no vernacular indigenous education in the province.

III.—Quasi-Vernacular Schools (Urdu and Hindi).

Urdu, which we imported, did not boast of a single school on our advent. Hindi also had no special schools for its tuition. The Muhammadan vernacular, so to speak, was learnt incidentally, whilst it was also being improved, through the study of Persian and, similarly, the vernaculars of the Hindus, whatever they might be, were being developed through the study of Sanscrit. As Mr. Arnold states in the first Educational Report, paragraphs 17 and 21, "It will be seen that there are only ten Hindu indigenous schools, *and I rather doubt the actual existence*, as such, of these. To educate a boy by teaching him his native language is to the natives almost a contradiction in terms. *Persian is something, and Sanscrit is something; but what is Urdu?*" This is precisely what the Pathan or the Beluchi might be expected to say regarding his own language; and if there are now indigenous schools in the Panjab in which Urdu is taught, it is because it has become the recognised official language, and also because it is nearest to the vernacular spoken by Muhammadans in this province, in which, naturally, words from Persian and Arabic would abound. I would not for a moment depreciate the importance of Urdu as a literary language; on the contrary, inflectionally and in the *copia verborum* it stands higher than Persian, which is the easiest, as it is the most elegant, of all Oriental languages. Urdu also possesses a piquancy in poetry and epigram all its own; whilst its utility as the official language of Upper India and, practically, the *lingua franca* of this country, is beyond question. What I wish to point out is that its study, *as a separate language*, is contrary to the law of its natural development in this province, where many may yet be found, even in obscure villages, who can understand, if they cannot speak, classical Persian, but where rarely even a Government schoolmaster can be met who can perfectly explain the Urdu text-books of the Educational Department, which are written in the dialect of Delhi, spoilt by quaint idioms and an unsuccessful attempt at a misunderstood purism. For instance, whilst every Panjabi will understand the Persian for "greenish" or "mixed with green," *i.e.*, "sabzi-máil," he will not be able to understand the Urdu of the text-books, "sabzi-leita hua," which the Panjabi boy would translate as "he is taking vegetables." Besides, the jerkiness of the sentences in the educational text-books is opposed to the continuity and sobriety of thought of the Panjabi student. Urdu, with a strong element of Persian, is understood by all Muhammadans and the Amla class, as well as the educated Hindus generally throughout the Panjab; but an Urdu from which Persian and Arabic words are purposely eliminated, and their place is taken by local south-country Hindi, travestied in an Urdu garb, is simply unintelligible to the Perso-Panjabi-speaking population. The development of this vernacular would be a natural one if, as before annexation, the people were to study Urdu incidentally through Persian; and I, therefore, consider its *special* cultivation for several years at school to be a waste of time which could be more profitably employed in learning subjects of practical utility. The fact is that the direction of the Educational Department has long been in the hands of men, both European and Native, connected with Delhi, where alone it may be said to be less unpopular than throughout the rest of the province, which, in educational as also in other respects, has suffered from an administration whose sole sympathies are alleged to be with Delhi opinions, Delhi interests, and Delhi institutions, though I am not aware that the education of the once Imperial City of India has escaped the injurious influence of the Department, considering that portions of its district are now among the least educated in the whole province (see Director's No. 4S., dated 22nd September 1881, paragraph 10); whilst as regards primary schools the percentage of attendance on the whole population of the district, excluding towns, is only ·28, being actually below Gurgaon with ·34, Ludiana with ·36, Jalandhar ·51, Hushiarpur ·35, Amritsar ·40, Gurdaspur ·42, Sialkot ·31, Gujranwala ·39, Rawalpindi ·41, Jhelum ·44, Guzerat ·37, Shahpur ·30, Multan ·42, Muzaffargarh ·30, miserably small as even these higher numbers may be in a general estimate of the extent of Government and aided primary education throughout the Province. This hearth of Urdu, or rather Muhammadanised Hindi, is also one of the lowest in indigenous education, if we exclude the city, 400 pupils only studying Arabic, Sanscrit, Persian and Landé throughout the whole *district* of Delhi. As regards the *city*, it has ceased to be a seat of Muhammadan learning since the misapplication of the Nawab Itimad-ud-dowla Fund (see Appendix III to this Report), in spite of the protest of its natural trustees, the donor's relicts; whilst the Department has been unable to prevent the abolition of the Delhi College, once an ORIENTAL COLLEGE supported by Muhammadan subscriptions, and which, with better management, could have become self-supporting. Formerly, the best Arabic and Persian schools in India, as well as the purest Urdu literature, flourished at Delhi. In my own time, one of the greatest Sanscrit schools, from which the largest Sanscrit Explanatory Dictionary was sent to the Panjab University College, died from neglect, the Department apparently being unacquainted with its existence, although attention was drawn to it. Now it cannot be said, as implied in the Director's No. 4S., above quoted, that Delhi possesses almost the only, or the best, indigenous schools. On the contrary, my enquiries lead me to the conclusion that they are *below* the average of the better schools of the kind in the Panjab. Compare this state of things with the condition of Delhi described in Mr. A. Howell's remarks in page 19 of his Report on Education in British India in 1854, and in 1870-71 :—" Delhi had been the metropolis of a vast empire, the patroness of the arts and sciences, the nursery of Oriental literature, and the seat of schools and colleges, resorted to by the learned of the Eastern world. In 1792, an ORIENTAL COLLEGE, supported by voluntary contributions from Muhammadan gentlemen, had been founded at Delhi for *the encouragement of Persian and Arabic.* But this college and *other* academic institutions had long since fallen into deplorable neglect; their patrons had been reduced from affluence to poverty, and of the funds designed for their support, only a small remnant was left. Hence, on the constitution of the Committee of Public Instruction in 1823, Delhi had special claims, and it was resolved to found a college there. The college was opened in 1825, and in 1829 *it received a munificent bequest of Rs. 1,70,000 from Nawab Itimad-ud-dowla, the Prime Minister of the King of Oudh.* The application of the endowment was the subject of much discussion, especially after Lord William Bentinck's decision of 1835, which abolished stipendiary allowances to students in Oriental Colleges. The final resolve of the Committee, however, declared in 1839, was *to constitute the Delhi College " an efficient institution for Muhammadan learning.*" This resolution was *approved* by the Government, but *has not been maintained.* The last return of the Delhi College shows that " of 51 students, there are 49 Hindus to 1 Muhammadan." It is, indeed, sad that, generally, the lower Hindu *bourgeoisie* should dispense the patronage and almost monopolise the emoluments of the education and of the subscriptions which the liberality of Muhammadan nobles for several ages has handed down to the present generation.

As regards HINDI, I have already explained that, beyond Delhi, this language does not exist in the Panjab; that it is constantly confounded with Mahajani, and that it is used for purposes of party-warfare, as equivalent to the

"*Bhásha*" of the Panjab, its real vernacular, *i. e.*, Panjabi, written by educated Hindus in the Nagri characters. When Pandits advocate the extension of Hindi, they mean the extension of Sanscrit learning through the medium of *that* vernacular and in the described form; when Banyas wish for it, they think of the same vernacular in Nagri, Mahajani, or Landé, or merely wish for the cultivation of their sacred language, Sanscrit; when anglicised Hindus clamour for it, they have in view the unification of Hindus throughout India by the adoption of the departmental Urdu in Nagri characters. Wherever Hindi schools existed or exist in the Panjab, they were and are (with few exceptions) either Sanscrit schools in which the translation of the sacred writings is in the local vernacular and in the Nagri character, or else Mahajani or Landé schools. On this point the reports of the Educational Department from its commencement to the last year are almost conclusive. Paragraph 21 of 1856 says, " I do not quite understand the return of 289 Hindi schools. A *real* Hindi school is *very rare*, and I think a great majority of these 289, if strictly looked into, would have to be classed as Shastri (Sanscrit) or Landé." The Inspector of the Lahore Circle reports in 1871-72—" *Hindi schools are rare in the Panjab*; the considerable number entered in the returns as Hindi students probably include those of Gurmukhi. *I have no recollection* of having seen *any* private Hindi school, though small Gurmukhi schools are not uncommon." Mr. Pearson reports in 1872-73—" notwithstanding the newspaper cry for Hindi, raised by the Hindus, no serious effort is made to use the opportunities which exist. The NAGRI scholars are about a third of the whole of the primary schools in the Umbala circle, and there are many *Nagri* schools in Kangra and Hushiarpur." But the *Nagri character* is not the *Hindi language* of Delhi or of any part of the North-Western Provinces. It is useful as leading to Sanscrit, and I would be the last to discourage the use by all Hindus of *Nagri*, provided the language is Panjabi. DR. TRUMPP, than whom, probably, no greater authority exists on the subject of *Panjabi* and *Hindi*, distinctly states in his monumental translation of the Adi Grant, that Panjabi is nearer Sindhi than Hindi:—" Nának and his successors in the guruship were all Panjabis: but it is remarkable that their idiom does not differ so much from the *Hindui of those days in a grammatical point of view*, as the *modern Panjabi does from the Hindi*. But we must not rashly conclude from this fact that the Panjabi of those days was essentially the same as the Hindui, and that the peculiar grammatical forms of the Panjabi were developed in a later period, for such an assumption is disproved by the old Janam Sákhi of Bábá Nának, which is written in the *regular Panjabi*, a dialect which *differs considerably from the Hindui, as it uses pronominal suffixes and other grammatical forms, which are quite unknown in Hindui and only to be* FOUND IN THE COGNATE SINDHI, to which it approaches *far more than to the Hindui*." (Chapter V, on the language and the metres used in the Granth, page cxxv of his "Adi Granth"). Even Baluchi, not to speak of Multani and other dialects, has been strongly affected by Panjabi, which is as different from Hindi as Italian is from Provençal French; the Indian Latin or Sanscrit affecting, no doubt, both Panjabi and Hindi, just as Latin has influenced the various Romance languages in Europe, and being a link among its Catholic clergy, as Sanscrit is among Pandits all over India. But Italian is not French or Latin, as little as Panjabi is Hindi or Sanscrit.

As, however, URDU is *now* taught in several Persian indigenous schools, and HINDI text-books are now used in a few Hindu schools, it may be desirable to give a list of them, before proceeding to describe what has been erroneously called by the Educational Department " *the most genuine educational institutions in the country*," namely, the PERSIAN schools, which I have classed under the heading of SEMI-CLASSICAL INDIGENOUS EDUCATION."

(*a*)—URDU BOOKS USED IN SOME PERSIAN INDIGENOUS SCHOOLS—

1. Tashríb-ul-burúf . . . . (Alphabet of Urdu.)
2. Nasihatnamah . . . . (Admonitions in Urdu verse by Maulvi Qutbuddin of Delhi.)
3. Inshá Urdu . . . . (Letter-writer.)
4. Inshá Khird Afroz . . . . (Ditto.)

5. Hakáyat-i-Loqmán	(Æsop's Fables under the collective name of Lokmán.)
6. Guldastai-Akhláq	(On morals.)
7. Kissai-Shah Rúm	(A story, condemning pride, in verse.)
8. Bágh-o-Bahár	(The well-known story of the four dervishes.)
9. Fasána Ajáyeb	(Or " The wonderful story ".)
10. Dharm Singh ka Kissa . .	(A story moralising on the victory of Truth.)
11. Urdú-i-Moálla	(Letters of Ghálib, a specimen of the purest Urdu.)
12. Údi Hindi	(Another collection of the letters of Ghálib.)
13. Gulzár Nasím	(The two best poems in Urdu, the first by Pandit Dya Kishen Nasimand, the second by Mir Hassan.)
14. Sahrul Bayan	
15. Diwan-í-Zauq	(A collection of the poems of " Zauq ".)
16. Diwan-í-Ghálib	(Ditto ditto Ghálib.)
17. Indar Sabhá	(A drama of the Court of Indra.)
18 *Mirat-ul-urús (the bride's minor)	(Two novels on an English model to promote female education, by Maulvi Nazir Ahmed.)
19. Taubat-un-nasúh	
20. Mubádil-Hisab	(Arithmetic.)

(*b*)—Hindi books used in some Hindu schools—

1. Akhshar Dipika	Light of the alphabet.
2. Barn Mala	String of letters.
3. Pahare	Multiplication tables.
4. Bidhyarthe-ki-Pratham Pushtak	1st Book of the student—a treatise on the letters.
5. Charnavek.	
6. Baital Pachisi	The famous 25 stories of the Demon.
7. Prem Sagar	Ocean of love (the well-known story).
8. Dil Bahláo	Heart entertainments (stories).
9. Ganit Kirya	Arithmetic.
10. Ramayan	of Tulsi Das.
11. Ákhyan Manjri	A brief story.

I have also added (see Appendix V to this Report) a list of Urdu and Hindi works published under the auspices of the Panjab University College, or prescribed for its students up to the degrees in Arts Standards, in the hope that it may convince a candid mind that vernaculars, which can draw from languages and literatures so copious and extensive as Arabic and Sanscrit respectively, are quite capable of rendering the facts or scientific processes, if not the thoughts, recorded in the linguistic thesaurus of English, which has not yet found a translator of sufficient words and versatility to render the " Makámát of Hariri," and which is scarcely able to do full justice to Urdu poetry. Of course, in proportion as an European is less acquainted with Oriental languages, as well as with the subject-matter of the intended translation, will he deny the possibility of rendering facts and scientific processes (the property of the world), if not the poetry and literature (which are scarcely wanted) of his own country, into the vernaculars of India. True scholarship is inseparable from sympathy; but where both are absent, as, I deeply regret to say, is the case in the Panjab Educational Department, *non possumus* must become its motto, whenever any progress or reform is urged, and the result, after years of wasteful expenditure, has been that the province, inhabited by the most enterprising race in India, has retrograded; whilst Lower Bengal has increased its pupils to twenty times, and even the Central Provinces to five times, their original number, all three provinces starting, comparatively, on the same footing. It is also deplorable that, with the excessive leisure enjoyed by most of the higher educational officers, especially the Director and Inspectors, not a single original book of any merit should have been produced by any of them on the languages, education, history, ethnography, or antiquities of a province, which is a mine of all these treasures; nor has the Department enlisted the co-operation of the people in the foundation and liberal maintenance of a single Free Public Library, College, Society, Scholarship or Fellowship, or, in any way, identified the natives with the measures of Government. On the contrary, it has been by far the most active

* This book has been translated into Gurmukhi.

agency to disseminate discontent among the half-educated youths whom it has sent forth from schools and colleges paid by the State, and it has prepared a state of things which even the ablest Government will find it difficult to improve, instead of preparing its alumni for the duties of loyal citizenship and of public or private usefulness. Reverting to the subject of translations into Urdu and Hindi, which, although only quasi-vernaculars, none the less deserve cultivation, especially if, as originally intended by the Government of India, the Panjab University is established for the whole of Upper India, including the North-West Provinces, Oudh and Rajputana, into which its influence is already extending. The following extract from the preface to my "History of Muhammadanism" in Urdu (the *Sinin-ul-Islam*, 2nd Edition) may serve to show the direction which adaptations from European authors may take, however imperfectly I may have followed my own precepts :—

"I take this opportunity of pointing out that approved books on Science and Literature, written in any of the European languages, should not be translated, but 'ADAPTED' into Urdu. European writers, more specially perhaps those of our own times, appear to delight in generalising and in the abstract and impersonal, whilst the genius of almost all the 'Oriental Languages' is personal particular, concrete and dramatic. The ordinary difficulties of translation are sufficiently great even in the case of translation from one European language to another, to render it doubtful whether Shakespeare can be adequately translated into French, Béranger into English, or Dickens into Italian. In the case of Oriental Languages, the difficulties are increased to such an extent as almost to justify the assertion that most European books cannot be translated at all into them, but that they have to be *re-written.* Even in the translation of the New Testament, the language and spirit of which are so very 'Eastern,' into such Oriental languages as Arabic, Turkish and Urdu, the full meaning of the original (or *our* interpretation of it, or the association which has grown up with it) is rarely rendered. As an instance, I would refer to the 24th Chapter of the Gospel of St. Matthew, in the Turkish version of Turabi, which, I believe, contains 108 mistakes against grammar and sense.

"In Urdu we do not want translations; we want 'adaptations.' We do not, for instance, require Mill's Political Economy translated, but the *subject* of Political Economy introduced into Urdu in a popular form. The same view holds good with regard to History, Metaphysics and Literature generally, where we want the *subjects* treated in a simple and idiomatic manner, and not the translations of writers *on* these subjects.

"What I venture to propose is, I believe, a more useful task than mere translation. Translations, such as have hitherto appeared, seem, as a rule, only to require a Dictionary and a docile Munshi; versions, so intelligible that a lad of fourteen could thoroughly understand them, require the author to know the subject on, and the language in, which he writes, thoroughly.* Indeed, whenever words represent *thoughts*, as may be said to be the case with *Literature*, it is necessary to examine the associations with which either the one or the other are connected, and, if no exact equivalent can be found in the foreign language, then the translator should himself *narrate* these associations and, as it were, build up their history, in his version—his test being a satisfactory answer to the question: 'would a native, acquainted with the subject and desirous of teaching it in the most simple manner to those natives to whom it was quite new, express himself in this way?' Unless this is the adapter's practice, he will teach *sounds* but not *ideas*. Of course, in *scientific* terminology, the words of which represent *facts*, or *things*, it is practically immaterial by what combination of sounds the fact or thing is made known. Still, without some imagination and power of assimilation, no one, however great his purely linguistic attainments, can hope to write either 'science' or 'literature' for the native of India, so as to be really understood."

Whilst I, therefore, deprecate the *teaching* of Urdu, which can quite hold its own in the struggle for linguistic existence, as a waste of time in schools, where

* There is a common saying in the Panjab, derived from a Sanscrit source: "It is the speaker's fault, if he cannot influence the hearer."

it can be incidentally and far more improvingly learnt through the medium of Persian, wherever a class of the population desire to study that language, I am a strong advocate of the publication and dissemination of scientific books in Urdu and Hindi (the real vernacular of the North-Western Provinces) for the use, *inter alia*, of schools and colleges, believing that sound and advanced knowledge can only be obtained through the medium of one's own language (to which, till Panjabi is sufficiently developed, Urdu and Hindi are the nearest in this Province). Thinking in the medium of a foreign language does not aid reflection and, indeed, acts disastrously on both the intellect and the character. It is perfectly true that a knowledge of English is a key to an extensive literature and to much science and pseudo-science; but so also is German the key to a, probably, even more extended literature, and to certainly more profound scientific investigations; yet no one dreams of depriving an English graduate of his degree because he does not know German, and it is doubtful whether he would deserve the degree, if he knew German and little or no English. In spite of the comparative paucity, through perfect sufficiency, of scientific text-books, of our own prescription, in Urdu and Hindi, the first B. A. Graduate of this year is a Maulvi who does not know a word of English and who has beaten, among 15 candidates, 13 who were English scholars, including a "first man" of the Calcutta University.

D.—SEMI-CLASSICAL INDIGENOUS EDUCATION IN THE PANJAB.

IV.—PERSIAN SCHOOLS.

THE ease and elegance of Persian conquered most of the courts and offices of Asia, just as French was long the universal language of diplomatists and gentlemen in Europe. Its directness and absence of synthesis also, like French, encouraged the spread of popular scepticism in letters, morality, religion and politics, and Persian was the graceful garb in which the gay and the grave clothed falsehood or truth with impunity from a flippant world. It made a man a gentleman, with a delightful soupçon of being also a scholar, than which nothing was, as a rule, more undeserved. For Persian, like English, one of the most analytical of languages, soon competed in public estimation with the true scholarship of Arabic, from which it pirated with a charming candour that invited forgiveness. It then became the link between the man of letters and "the man of the world" till, at last, whoever wished to write for a larger public, wrote in Persian. The graver studies were left to Arabic, but it was agreed that no one could become a good Persian scholar without knowing, at any rate, the elements of the classical language of Muhammadanism. An Urdu poet, who knows Persian, still prefers the latter as the vehicle of his thoughts, partly because it is easier and partly, perhaps, also because he can command an admiring public, each member of which likes to be suspected of, at least, understanding Persian. This sentiment, however, does not apply to women, among whom the tendency to Persian poetry is considered an alarming symptom by male relatives. For them Arabic, which they do not understand, or Urdu, Hindi, Gurmukhi or Perso-Panjabi, which they do understand, and in which religious books for their use are written, are considered to be a sufficient literary accomplishment.

If I have called Persian "semi-classical," it is because it was the greatest element of culture, though not of mental discipline, to the East. Every one could learn Persian, whilst few had the courage to face Arabic or Sanscrit, to the former of which, however, it was often an introduction. In the words of Hafiz, it was the clay which derived its fragrance from proximity to, and association with, the rose. It is, however, no common clay. Its present decay, as the polite vernacular, or the "language of gentlemen" of the East, is as much to be regretted, as the elimination of the elements of Persian, Arabic and Sanscrit in Urdu or of Sanscrit in Hindi, does not, as is fondly imagined, purify these dialects, but simply reduces them to their pristine barbarism.

In the Panjab, Persian was the language of courts and of the court, though Ranjit Singh conversed by preference in Panjabi and recommended the study of Gurmukhi to those who came near him. Both Hindus and Muhammadans, who wished to have appointments under the State, studied Persian. The host of employés was enormous, as our first Administration Reports will indicate, and there was scarcely a family in the province which had not one or more of its members in Government service, chiefly military. The Muhammadans, moreover, read and taught Persian from religious and social pride, and the teacher's seat was almost entirely monopolised by them. The Hindu castes, especially the Khatris, to whom official employment was traditional, eagerly frequented the Persian schools, even when the Koran was also taught to their Muhammadan fellow-pupils; so strong was the Khatri feeling in favour of Persian, that they, till recently, spurned the study of Hindi or Urdu, for their caste-tradition is to learn whatever will give them official and political power. This is why they are now so eager for the cultivation of what they call "higher English education," if possible at the cost of the State, but, if necessary, at their own cost. Indeed, so deep-rooted is this feeling in the class, whether Muhammadan or Hindu, that aspires to official employment, that we need never to have started an Educational Department at all for the spread of English education, just as we need not maintain one at present for that or any other educational purpose, for the official demand for employés acquainted with English or any other language or subject that may be remunerative would have given us a more than sufficient supply for any grade of the administration in which only ability and attainments are required. The Hindu aspirants for office were ever of the persuasion of their masters. We find Hindu Persian writers prefixing their productions with praises of the Muhammadan prophet, or referring to the funerals of their distinguished fellow-countrymen as being "burials," and not the "burnings" abhorred to Muslim prejudice. By wealth chiefly can a Khatri indulge in the practice of the virtues of the Hindu religion, and to acquire wealth, most means were welcome. Therefore, in explaining the preponderance of Hindu over the Muhammadan pupils in the Persian schools of the Panjab, the question of the caste to which the pupils belonged must, in this *as in every other Indian enquiry* affecting the people, be constantly kept in view. Finally, we also find that all the religious books of the Hindus, *in current use*, were translated into Persian, and, subsequently, into Perso-Panjabi, in which form they are still to be met with.

Availing itself of a temporary prejudice of Government against Muhammadans, partly due to a misconception as regards the mutiny, which the Duke of Argyll has clearly proved to have been a Hindu rising, the Educational Department began its operations in the province by trying to oust the Muhammadans from the teacher's seat, and, finding that their schools were attended alike by their co-religionists and by Hindus, endeavoured to supplant them by the introduction of Hindu teachers, and by the absorption of the Persian schools. Of this endeavour, the "Précis and Conclusions" attached to this report, which are based on the reports of the Educational Department, afford ample and melancholy proof, even long after Government earnestly endeavoured to revive "Muhammadan education." So strongly, if erroneously, did the Muhammadan community believe itself under the disfavour of Government, that its most prominent members gave me their views regarding the appointment of Kazis and other matters, with the injunction not to mention their names. This was in 1872; but the Educational officer who officiated for me suppressed that document, and it does not appear in the collection of opinions then published by Government as regards "Muhammadan education;" but its recommendations have since been reported, and some of them are now carried out.

As regards, however, the absorption of the Persian schools into our educational system, it is a mistake to suppose that the best Maulvis came over to our schools, as is so constantly alleged in our reports. Some of them may have done so, as men will always be found who hope for improvement in a change of masters, but the most respectable, the best paid, and the, otherwise, well-to-do Maulvis stood aloof from our system, as they still do. Far more natural is it to suppose that those teachers only, who had fallen out with their *clientèle*, or who discovered signs of decreasing liberality on their part, or who preferred a fixed salary, however small, to a precarious income depending on their exertions or increasing reputation for learning, should have "come in" to form, much to their subsequent sorrow, the only basis on which an Educational Department of any pretensions could alone start in the Panjab. My own knowledge directly contradicts the allegation that the best indigenous teachers, whether Arabic, Sanscrit or Persian, joined the Government schools, certainly not as a body. The best Oriental scholars are still found presiding over indigenous schools, whilst few of any respectability or learning went over to the Government schools, as long, at least, as their own patrons lived, or their landed endowment was continued. It is absurd to suppose that men will give up incomes from Rs. 10 to Rs. 100 per mensem, or forfeit their reputation for sanctity and philanthropic teaching, in order to identify themselves with the Educational Department of the conqueror and the stranger, on salaries of from Rs. 5 to Rs. 10. What formed the basis of the educational operations—and a very sound one it was, considering its other elements—were (with some exceptions) the *flotsam and jetsam*, the *disjecta membra* of the existing indigenous teaching profession. That many of them were competent, only with a few weeks' preparation, to teach the new subjects of history and geography,* and sometimes even arithmetic, only shows that the mental training, elementary though it may have been in

* A list of names of places, often barbarously rendered in our text-books and unaccompanied by descriptions, has no educational value in the opinion of an indigenous teacher.

some cases, which they had received in Persian or Arabic, or both, was sufficient to enable them to be soon far ahead of their pupils in untried branches of knowledge, and is merely an encouragement for us at the present moment, to utilise the indigenous teachers that still remain, without obliging them to go to, what are, practically, Normal schools only in name.

Were England conquered by the kindred Prussians, not the most patriotic or the most respectable Englishmen would, especially at first, seek the favour of the conqueror. In India, where the difference in colour, creed, and customs is far greater between the European and the native than that existing between any two European races, all who were not *compelled* to meet members of the ruling race, avoided all intercourse with it, till time had shown the desirability of approximation. As a rule, those who flatter our preconceptions by imitating our manners, are those who, with some noble exceptions, have come into conflict with all that is respectable in their own community. It is for us, therefore, to take the first step to identify the interests of the chiefs, the wealthy, and the religious leaders of native society with the maintenance of our rule, by seeking them out in their seclusion with the profession and practice of good-will towards themselves, when, I believe, that the response will, in spite of persistent previous discouragements, exceed our expectations. I still know native scholars of the greatest merit who would as soon think of abandoning their religion or breaking their caste, as of calling on the officials of a Government erroneously deemed to be bent on the destruction of all that is revered in native traditions and associations.

The present returns of indigenous schools, imperfect as they obviously must be, when it is considered that I have had to collect them, without a staff, in three months, among a heterogeneous population, when three years were allotted for a similar purpose, among the more homogeneous people of Bengal, will show what remains of authorship or scholarship in the province. Not to speak of Arabic or Sanscrit, of which the Oriental College is the only seat of learning in any way connected with Government, and which is almost the exclusive monopoly of indigenous schools, even Persian is not taught satisfactorily in Government schools, and all those who wish to make practical use of it in composition, not to speak of the humbler penmanship, have still to engage either an indigenous teacher of Persian, or to attend an indigenous Persian school. Whilst I, therefore, fully admit that a great many Persian indigenous schools have been ruined by their absorption into the departmental schools, and by the cheaper, if greatly inferior, Persian teaching which is now given at the latter institutions, I contest the accuracy of the statement that the best Persian instruction, from humble caligraphy to the highest scholarship, is given in our schools. That education, as I have already stated, is imparted in private and indigenous schools. It is only lately that caligraphy has been raised, to any dignity in our primary schools, at the instance of Government and with the resistance, which still continues to be passive, of the department. Yet, without caligraphy, the sister to orthography, the courts and offices will continue to complain of the inelegance and inaccuracy of the papers written by pupils from our schools, and will prefer the nephews of Serishtadárs or Munshis, who, with less conceit, have greater clerical aptitude and patience—qualities which have been fostered by the extremely careful and artistic instruction in penmanship—which is the humble beginning, as it is the progressive accompaniment, of studies in Persian schools.

I myself owe a debt of gratitude to those who instructed a somewhat backward caligrapher in the mysteries and elegances of Muhammadan handwritings, which, even in their greatest involutions, preserve the quick and ready teaching of chiefly lineal letters, which the accustomed eye can embrace far more readily and accurately than a scrawl in one of the European characters. The proportions of letters in the Perso-Urdu character in themselves and to one another are determined by fixed and highly artistic rules. At the risk of digression, I would, in this place, desire the consideration of those interested in the subject to my papers, submitted to the Simla Text-book Committee, and to the Senate of the Panjab University College, on the advantages and disadvantages of the so-called Roman-Urdu characters, which only the superficial can imagine as likely or desirable to supplant, *in native use*, the characters of the various languages with which their associations are connected.

It is, however, not with writing, as in the Mahajani schools, that the course of instruction in Persian schools begins, but it is almost simultaneous with seeing, hearing and reading the letters of the alphabet which takes place in the morning, sometimes from 6 to 11, and the writing of the same letters from 1 to 4, when reading is again resumed till 6 or 7; boys who have not done this being kept sometimes till 9 o'clock. The letters are not taught in the confused and wasteful way that, I believe, has been held up to the admiration of the Education Commission, in which they are represented in four columns as "separate," "initial," "medial" and "final," as if the commonest sense could not tell the boy that when a letter is connected with another, it must be connected either on one or the other side of it, and that, if it stands alone, it has not to be so connected, but can even afford a flourish of its own. He is, therefore, only taught the letters as they stand unconnected, is told which letters may not have others added to them, and is then introduced to two letters in combination, and so forth. The writing is a matter of more difficulty, for the pupil has to measure, with certain number of prescribed dots, the distances between the proportions of a letter in length, height and breadth. Of course, the easiest plan for learning the letters of the alphabet in every possible combination would be to learn merely the principles which underlie the formation of certain groups of letters, as pointed out in my "Introduction to a Philosophical Grammar of Arabic," and which reduces the difficulty of learning the Urdu-Perso-Arabic characters separately or in combination to less than three hours' work, as I have tried with my students at King's College, London, but I doubt whether the plan would succeed with the teacher of a Persian or Arabic elementary school. As regards writing, however, I can only suggest the adoption of the native system.

The pupil is then introduced to the KHÁLIQ BÁRI, a triglot vocabulary in verse written in one night by the poet Khósro, during the reign of Muhammad Toghluk, it is said, for the son of the keeper of a Serái, where he was staying for the night. It is in Persian, Arabic and the Hindi of his age. The fact that this is the first reading-book (except, in the case of Muhammadan boys, books of religious devotion) in Persian, to which the pupil is introduced, disposes of the repeated allegations in the Educational Reports that the majority of Persian schools teach without giving the meaning of the text. The distinction of reading first without the translation "*bay-ma' ni*" and, then, with the translation, "*ba-ma-ni*" refers to a different stage, regarding which more further on. There can be no doubt that by the time the boy has mastered the "*Kháliq bári*" he already possesses a vocabulary, which is almost sufficient to give him the general meaning of what he reads, "*bay-ma-ni*" even if he had not been taught, as he is, to write short Persian sentences in the afternoons of the days on which he reads the *Kháliq bári*. A specimen of its mode of instruction, which reminds me of *Zumpt's* Latin rules in verse, much to the help of the memory, and of similar versifications adopted in some English schools, may give an indication of the educational value of the book: It begins thus :—

Kháliq, / A.*	Bári / A. P.	Surjan-hár / H.		= The Creator, as named by Arabs, Persians and Hindus respectively.
Wahid / one, A.	ék / one, H.	bidá / know	Kertá, / God, H.	= Know to be one God.
Rasúl / Prophet, A.	Peyghambar / Prophet, P.	ján / know, H.	Basit / Prophet, H.	= The prophet.
Yár / friend, P.	Dost / friend, P.	bole / say, H.	já Ith / go, H. Friend H.	= Go on saying "friend" (in the three languages).
Rah / road, P.	Tariq / road, A.	Sabil / road, A.	paitshán / discern, H.	= Know "the road" (of 3 Perso-Arabic words).
Art / meaning, H.	tehu-ka / three H. of H.	Marag / road, H.	ján / know, H.	= The meaning of the three know to be "road."
Sis hay / moon, H. is, H.	Máh / moon, P.	Neyer / sun (great star).	Khurshéd / sun, P.	= "Moon" in Hindi is "mah" in Persian; "sun" in Arabic is "Khurshed" in Persian.

* "A" stands for "Arabic;" "P" for "Persian;" "H" for "Hindi" now called "Urdu."

Kala	ujla	siáh	sufed	= Black, white (Hindi) is "siah,
black, H.	white, H.	black, P.	white, P.	sufed" in Persian.

Kháliq Bári, Surjan-hár.   *Rah. Tariq, Sabíl, paitshán.*
Wáhid, ék, bidá Kertár.   *Art, tehuka Marag Ján.*
Rasúl, Feyghambar ján Basit.   *Sis hay Mah Neyar Khurshéd.*
Yár Dost, bolo já ith.   *Kala, ujla, siáh, sufed.*

As the words are marked "A'in," "P" and "H" respectively, there can be little confusion, especially as the teacher explains them in every *second* lesson. The above Hemistichs are in one particular metre, those that follow in another, and so on, so that the boy, unconsciously, learns Prosody before, like Mr. Jourdain with his prose, he is aware of the accomplishment.

He then proceeds to the *Pandnama* of SÁDI, which is in verse, and was obviously intended by that great master for the use of children. In this little book, more commonly known as the KARÍMA (as its first line begins with that word) various vices are condemned, and the virtues are extolled. It is idle asserting, as is done in some Reports, even including that of the genial Mr. Adam, that no moral instruction is conveyed in Persian schools when the reading and writing of such maxims as are contained in the *Pandnama* are insisted on and tell their own tale, which, as many will be able to confirm, are the guiding stars of thousands of ex-pupils of these schools during their after-life and are constantly on their lips. For instance, how often when the advantages of education are pointed out in some Durbar, is there not a chorus of reciters of "an ignorant man cannot know God," or when some marvellous story is told of European inventiveness, the praise of a "Jehandída," is ironically given in tacit reference to the Hemistich "*Jehandída basiar goyed darógh*" = "A man who has seen the world tells many lies"; or "a miser, even if he should be an ascetic, will not enter paradise," &c.

The pupil then studies the "Dastur-us-sibián," an easy "letter-writer," followed by the "*Amadnamah*," exhibiting the forms of conjugating the Persian verbs which are read to the master, and by frequent repetition committed to memory, a far better plan, in learning languages, than beginning with the rules and exceptions of grammar, as the pupil has already a stock of phrases in his mind to which he can apply some of the rules.

He then reads the GULISTAN of Sádi, containing lessons on life and manners, in the morning, as an exercise chiefly in prose, whilst the afternoon is devoted to the drafting of letters, petitions, and, if more advanced, he may perhaps even compose verses for the criticism of his master. This he does long before he studies Prosody, when, after the preliminary experience, it becomes easier to him than had he begun with rules and examples. It is true that he first reads the "Gulistán," "*bey-máni*," "without translation"; but it does not follow that he is perfectly innocent of its meaning, as he certainly must understand the general drift, for it is precisely in the same way that he has read the "Karima" first, without, and then with, the translation, into his own Perso-Panjabi vernacular, of which Urdu is now taking the place.

The art of writing letters by merely resting on the palm of one's hand or on one's knee is acquired, first, by writing on boards, then on pieces of paper which are pasted together with starch, and, finally, on ordinary paper, so that the whole pomp and circumstance of the European method of requiring a chair, table, and inkstand and bending over one's seat are unnecessary to the native writer, who can carry all the paraphernalia of his profession in his waistband, and who can do his work standing or sitting on the ground.

The "Gulistan" is followed by the "BOSTAN," YUSUF and ZULEIKHA, JÁMI's version of the story of Potiphar's wife; the love of MAJNUN and LAILA; the exploits of Alexander the Great as in the SIKANDARNAMAH by the inimitable NIZÁMI, "the ANVAR-I-SUHILI" (the light of Canopus, the Persian version improved of KALILA-O-DAMNA), than which no work can be more replete with instructions of morality and prudence, far beyond the admirable lessons of the Hitopadesa on which it is partly based. The *Bahar-danish*, which is so emphatically condemned in the Educational Reports, is, no doubt, as many classical and semi-classical writings of Europe, of "a questionable morality," as stated by one

Inspector, or rather of "unquestionable immorality," if its *introduction* is referred to. Considering, however, that *this introduction* only forms 40 pages out of some 360, it seems rather hard to condemn a story of great merit and perfect innocence as of a "*highly immoral tendency*" (see Director's No. 48., dated 22nd September 1881, paragraph 5, section 3, fourth line from the bottom). Considering that the "introduction" has nothing *whatever to do with the main subject of the book*, and that it can be profitably printed or photo-zincographed without it, as the Department has done with expurgated editions of other Persian works, it seems rather hard to pass such a censure on a masterpiece of INAYATULLA, who presented it to the Emperor Shahjehan and whose tomb lies in ruins in front of the Railway station of Lahore, of which, together with Kashmir, he was the Governor. The introduction is called "the fifth Veda" in derision of those philosophers and students who learn "the four Vedas" and do not know the commonest things that are going on in the world around them. It is a Rabelaisian production, written in the best Persian style, but certainly, as Shahjehan remarked, dragging diamonds through the mire and not fit for the mental food of boys, which the body of the book, as certainly, is.

The letters of Abulfazl, addressed to provincial governors or foreign rulers on behalf of Emperor Akbar, as also to his friends and relatives, now finish the *ordinary* course in a good Persian school, and it cannot be doubted that, both as regards style and substance, these letters are an admirable introduction to further studies or to official employment. Arithmetic is greatly neglected in the ordinary Persian schools, but the Arabic numerals, often also the numerical value of the *Abjad* and the peculiar Persian official cyphering of numbers, called "Raqm" in a special sense, are taught to the great advantage of the future Munshi.

I subjoin a list of Persian books used in indigenous schools in the Panjab and, I believe, also the North-Western Provinces; some of these books are, of course, only studied in more advanced schools than I have described. It will be seen from it what an extensive literature is within the reach of most of these schools. I also would desire to draw attention to the model Persian Department of the indigenous Perso-Arabic school of Deoband, in which the system of classes is adopted, in supersession of the more usual course of giving the pupil his separate lesson in the evening, than hearing it next morning, and giving him another lesson to be again heard in the afternoon. The "Deoband" school's time-table and division of studies are, indeed, a model to those Persian and Arabic indigenous schools, which can afford to keep a staff of teachers.

The discipline in Persian schools is maintained by punishments which the master orders, and the pupil carries out; such as standing in a corner; pulling his own ears by passing his hands through his knees—a most uncomfortable position which, when protracted, may become a positive agony; having constantly to get up and sit down, an indoor exercise of some value; being kept beyond the usual school hours; being prevented from going to his meal at the usual time. The switch is also occasionally used, but I doubt whether any of these punishments can be called cruel, as even the ear-performance is, except in very bad cases, not unduly prolonged. Fines are not inflicted.

The teacher, who, according to his abilities, is called either Mian, or Ustád, and addressed by his pupils as "Mianji" or "Moulvi Sahib," is paid in cash and kind; the former by a weekly payment of one or two pice on Thursdays, or by a monthly payment which may range from 1 anna to 4 or 5 rupees; and the latter by subventions of food and presents on the occasion of a marriage in the pupil's family; a present, on commencing or finishing a new book; also one called *Idi* on every great festival, such as the Id-uz-Zuha, Holi, Salono, Id-ul-Baqr, Diwáli, Shab-berát. The competition with Government schools, which charge, comparatively speaking, a smaller fee to non-agriculturists, being chiefly supported by the Cess raised from the all-enduring and generally non-attending agricultural classes, has nearly ruined the Persian Maktabs, and has reduced most of their teachers from incomes of Rs. 25 to Rs. 30 per mensem to a pittance of Rs. 4 or 5, or even 2, supplemented by food. It is thus that, with the most benevolent intentions, we have destroyed one of the humbler professions of great utility to the cause of culture throughout the province.

The Maktabs are now generally held in the teacher's own house, or in the Baitaks and Diwankhanas of *Mahallas* of towns or Chaupáls of villages, the common *rendezvous* of the people. When attached to mosques, they also teach Arabic.

It is almost needless to observe that in such schools the majority of pupils would be Muhammadans, in which case certain religious books of tenets, such as the "Kanz-ul-Musalli," "Rah-i-Niját," "Ahkám-ul-Imám," "Masáil-Subhani" would be taught, though in most mosque schools, which are generally Koran schools, religious books in Arabic would be preferred. Hindus, however, for reasons which have been explained elsewhere, often attend Perso-Koran schools, and even at a purely Muhammadan institution, like Deoband, which makes the knowledge of the Koran obligatory on candidates seeking admission to it, a considerable number of Hindus attend. Nor has their religion ever been tampered with in the least, for the obvious reason that the Persian teacher depends on the good-will of his customers, and that he would forfeit it along with presents, sometimes during the whole pupil's life, if conversions were not of the rarest occurrence. I, therefore, see no evidence of the assertion made in the earliest Educational Report that "the steady growth of Muhammadanism in the Panjab may partly be traced to the advantage taken by the (Muhammadan) teachers of this confidence (of the Hindus)." Muhammadanism has not declined in numbers since annexation; on the contrary, it has largely increased, in spite of our deliberate supersession of Muhammadan teachers. It is natural that Islám should draw to itself all those who desire a simpler faith or greater domestic liberty than is allowed by the older creed of Hinduism which grows, in its turn, not by conversion, but, as already pointed out in my "Dardistan, 1867," by agglomeration of aboriginal tribes or by the restoration to the fold of Buddhists and Sikhs. Indeed, it may be asserted that the effect of the teaching in Government and aided schools is to recruit the ranks of Muhammadanism and of other monotheistic forms of belief, such as Brahmoism, by the accession of the minority, whose natural piety survives the inevitable result of secular teaching in Oriental countries: scepticism, unscrupulous immorality or mysticism. The teaching in Missionary schools, even where it is disliked, has been one of the agencies to maintain the respect of natives for their rulers, who, they saw, were not quite without religion (as the English, *e.g.*, are called in Turkey in consequence of the absence of demonstrativeness in Protestant worship) and who, therefore, might possess a sense of justice, although there can be no doubt that even Missionary schools unconsciously encourage the growth of Muhammadanism, as a list of Hindu converts to that faith from Government and Missionary schools will show. The subject of the effect of monotheistic preaching on, practically, polytheists, in a certain sense, is one of great interest and importance which, however, cannot be dealt with in this place. However, a few quotations in connection with the large attendance of Hindus at Muhammadan schoools (which incidentally disposes of the alleged intolerance of Islam to Hindus) may be relevant :—

Extracts from Educational Report of 6th July 1857.

"PARA. 8. But what had the people been doing for themselves in the way of education? *This is a v ry difficult question to answer. It is difficult to get accurate statistics, and it is difficult to interpret the statistics when we have them.* Certainly the idea of education is not new to the Panjabis. We find all the school phraseology ready made to our hand, and *chiefly supplied by the Muhammadans. As educators they are in possession of the field*; not only is the Koran taught in every mosque, but outside a great many mosques the standard Persian works are taught to all comers—to *more Hindus than Muhammadans.*"

"PARA. 12. The returns show a *very large preponderance of Muhammadan boys* at school. Every fact we meet proves beyond all dispute that *the teaching profession has been in their hands.* I cannot but think that the confiding attendance of so many Hindus at Muhammadan schools for the sake of learning the Persian language is a most remarkable fact. I cannot but think also that the steady growth of Muhammadanism in the Panjab may partly be traced to the advantage taken by the teachers of this confidence. *Certainly I find that the natural tendency of things, if left to themselves, is to throw the whole weight of Government in this matter of education on to the side of the Muhammadans—a tendency to be much resisted.*"

("PARA. 16. The *Persian schools are the most genuine educational institutions in the country.* They are attended largely by the Kuthries, *the Hindus forming a greater proportion than the Muhammadans.)* Writing is taught, but not with great energy, and certainly not with great success. The great object is to teach a boy to read the Gulistan and Bostan; and the lad who will read off a page of either in a fluent sing-song without understanding a word has received an education which fully satisfies both his teacher and parents. Little as the works of Sadi are understood by these boys, there is no doubt that they are much enjoyed. In one of the too frequent cases of child murder with robbery of ornaments, the victim, a lad of 13, was enticed out by his murderer, a youth of 18, on the pretext of having the Bostan read to him."

"PARA. 19. But *certainly the Hindus do not seem to be very sensitive or jealous as to the encroachments of Muhammadanism.* The Persian Koran schools are, of course, invariably kept by Muhammadan teachers, indeed, so are far the greater number of Persian schools. They are generally held in or just outside the mosque, to which the teacher is frequently attached. *Yet they are attended largely by Hindus,* more attracted by the Persian language than repelled by the Muhammadan religion."

"PARA. 20. It is in the *Sanscrit schools that the exclusive side of Hinduism comes out.* Like the Arabic schools, those called Sanscrit are largely attended by adults, and entirely by Bráhmans. We may be quite certain that a student attending a Shastri school will hardly be persuaded to undergo any other kind of instruction. *He would strongly object to learn the Persian character.*"

Although the above remarks cannot be deemed to be exhaustive of the subject with which they deal, they yet show an approximation to the life of the people and a desire to learn the truth about it, which is entirely absent from the latest reports. Indeed, the remarks of the Director, in paragraph 21 of his No. 48, dated 22nd September 1881, show that a stage of remoteness from all knowledge of Muhammadan feeling on a well-known subject had been reached, which makes all argument and experience useless. I refer to the subject of the injudiciousness of publishing text-books for Muhammadan boys with illustrations of men and animals, which the Nestor of schoolmasters in the Panjab, the Rev. Dr. Forman, pointed out even in places like Lahore, where civilisation or indifference to religion has made great strides, not to speak of the bigoted frontier with regard to which the paper referred to, as having been submitted at Simla, was specially directed. What knowledge of Muhammadanism, or what honest or competent agency can a department possess, the head of which "*is assured in every case that these drawings were very popular?*" "That the idea that there *could* be an objection, in consequence of conscientious scruples, did not *seem to occur to any one,*" when, as a matter of fact, there is scarcely a Muhammadan boy that does not disfigure or cut out the eyes or nose of the drawing of a man or animal in the Government text-book, in order to reduce it to the "inanimate," of which drawings *are* allowed. The Muhammadans, therefore, who send their children to schools where picture-books are used *waive* an objection, but that they entertain a great dislike to them, there can be no doubt. The fact, however, is that the picture-books are necessary to the trade in books which has been carried on by the Department and to the combination that supports it, much to the discouragement of literary activity throughout the province, and to the continued unpopularity of our schools with the mass of Muhammadans. A resolution of the Senate of the Panjab University College, arrived at after a special Sub-Committee's Report and protracted discussions will, no doubt, carry more weight than individual opinions. It is as follows:—" On the seventh point the Senate endorse the Simla Committee's recommendations as regards the desirability of schools throughout India being supplied with wall-maps, engravings, representing such natural phenomena as the Aurora Borealis, &c., &c. The native members deprecated the introduction of books depicting living objects, on the frontier, as it was desirable to attract these inhabitants and the populations in the Assigned Districts to our schools, and as the representation of living objects was prohibited by the Muhammadan religion. The Reverend Forman pointed out that, *even at Lahore*, he had found the *strongest aversion among the lower classes of Muhammadans to our schools in consequence of the extent to which pictures of living objects were depicted in our books*. The Senate recommended that books depicting living objects should not be introduced in frontier schools." (*Vide* Senate Proceedings of the 28th June 1879, paragraph 7.)

(I think, however, that it is only fair to the Educational Department that its account of the only kind of indigenous schools, regarding which it possesses an elementary knowledge, *viz.*, the Persian schools, should be compared with my own account of the same, and, with this view, its last utterance on the subject, (dated 22nd September 1881,) may be read with a melancholy interest:

"Before the introduction of the Government system of education, indigenous schools, in which the instruction imparted was confined to the Persian language, were scattered over the Province.) The system pursued was an indifferent one. Little boys were taught at first to read certain Persian books by rote, without *any* regard to meaning." (This is precisely the great fault which impartial Inspectors find with *our* schools, the only difference being that what they learn by rote in our schools is not explained by home associations, whereas what may be learnt by rote in indigenous schools has hundred opportunities of being explained.)

"Afterwards they went through these books a second time, and were now taught to translate them literally, word by word, into the vernacular, but there was no attempt at explanation. Such a system was little calculated to develop the intelligence of the pupil; nevertheless, the boys who attended the best of these schools for a sufficient time, devoting their attention to the study of one subject, obtained at last a *considerable knowledge of Persian* literature." (This is rather a startling result to be achieved by "rote" education; it is one that is not achieved by our system, so that natives who wish to become Persian scholars still go to the indigenous master.)

"Some of the books that were taught at that time in nearly all these schools, such for example as the *Bahár Dánesh*, were of a highly immoral tendency." (I should be glad to know the names of the other books referred to; in the case of the *Bahar Danesh* it has been shown that the accusation merely refers to some 40 pages of an introduction which is utterly unconnected with a story of about 320 pages.)

"Notwithstanding the defects of the system, there were amongst the teachers of indigenous Persian schools many men of considerable ability, well versed in Persian, and in some cases in Arabic." (This is again far more than can be said of our system, in spite of the "excellencies" which *we* find in it and the *defects* which we discover in a rival system, and which turns out "many men of considerable ability)".

The employment in Government vernacular schools of the ablest indigenous teachers.

"4. When Government vernacular schools were first established, we sought out *all the ablest Maulvis and Munshis* who were employed as teachers of Persian in the towns and villages throughout the Province, and placed them in charge of the new Government schools to which they generally brought their old pupils, whilst the improved organization that we introduced, and the *substitution of class teaching for the separate instruction of each scholar, enabled them to teach a much larger number than before*. Subsequently, when normal schools were established, the teachers were sent to these institutions to learn mathematics, history and geography; and *some of them, who were good Arabic and Persian scholars, acquired an elementary knowledge of such subjects in a remarkably short time*." (I think that it has been proved that the ablest Maulvis and Munshis were not, and, for obvious reasons, could not, have been employed by us; but this paragraph shows how, by the substitution of class teaching for separate teaching, we took the bread out of the mouths of a large number of teachers, without increasing the number of pupils under instruction in the Province. With what consistency, however, can it be alleged that a system, which, if mastered, enables a "good Arabic and Persian scholar" to acquire an elementary knowledge of mathematics, history and geography, "in a *remarkably short* time," is "little calculated to develop the intelligence of the pupil?" What other system has greater or even similar results? Certainly not *our* system, which so cripples the intelligence, that out of over 60 undergraduates and graduates that I have employed in various offices, presses, &c., under me, not one had the ability of a Babu of the old school or even of a Munshi of the present day, whilst none could obtain the grasp of any matter requiring administrative power, such as is possessed by the native trained in his own literature, for the obvious reason that thinking in a foreign language destroys reflection and ruins both the mind and character, however invaluable a foreign language may be as an attainment and opportunity for comparison, *after* the foundation has been laid in one's own religious and literary language.)

"5. So far our operations had no effect on the indigenous schools situated in large cities, where Government schools for instruction in English had been established. There was not then the same desire to learn English that there is at present; and the *teachers of indigenous Persian schools were naturally opposed to such an innovation*, which seemed calculated, if *successful*, to draw away their pupils." (A very natural instinctive apprehension, which the destruction of indigenous schools, even of those that could, admittedly, at once co-operate with the departmental system, such as the Persian schools, and without which there could never have been a department at all, has fully justified.)

Establishment of branch schools in Delhi.

"6. Under these circumstances, with the co-operation of native gentlemen, some of whom subscribed liberally for the purpose, I tried the experiment of establishing branch schools throughout the city of Delhi, in which the best of the indigenous teachers were employed." (Why, of all places, *Delhi*, in which education is at a low ebb, and why not Lahore, which had already become the centre of a great movement in aid of Oriental classical and vernacular literature, supported by subscriptions of princely munificence?) "The system was soon extended to all the cities where large Government or *Mission* schools existed; and branches were organized in connection with these institutions, which are maintained on the grant-in-aid system, and form the groundwork of higher education in the Province, as the majority of boys attending the large schools have received the rudiments of instruction in these branches." The above implies that all has been done that could have been done to utilize the indigenous schools, of which only those that taught Persian have any value, but the insinuation suggests a false conclusion, *viz.*, that really indigenous schools were aided *as such*, which is not the case, as branches were simply started to Government and Mission schools, in which some of the indigenous teachers were employed and their schools were destroyed.

"7. By these measures the *great majority of Persian schools* were absorbed in our educational system." (*Væ victis!* thus might the wolf say who had "absorbed" the lamb into his system.)

It may be well now to see what the instruction is in an indigenous school which is "not absorbed."

The DEOBAND Perso-Arabic School, which is supposed to be a model to indigenous schools of its kind throughout Upper India, the course of study in which is, more or less followed in the Panjab, extends to seven years. I quote it at length, partly because it is the only printed prospectus of a first-class indigenous school which has yet reached me. Before entering the Persian class, the Muhammadan applicant must have read the Koran. Not more than three lessons a day are allowed, and one day in every week is devoted exclusively to exercises in composition and translation (in the former of which attainments, the

Government schools are, admittedly, deficient). The following statement will show the complete scheme of study with the daily progress of the pupils :—

Year.	First daily Lesson.				Second daily Lesson.				Third daily Lesson.			
	Name of book.	No. of pages in the book.	Quantity of daily lesson.	Time of completing the book.	Name of book.	No. of pages in the book.	Quantity of daily lesson.	Time of completing the book.	Name of book.	No. of pages in the book.	Quantity of daily lesson.	Time of completing the book.
I	Kanzulmusalli .	16	3 lines	4 months	Risalá Benamázán	16	3 lines	2 months				
	Ahkám-ul-ímán .	12	¾ page	¾ month	Qayamat Namá .	30	½ page	3 "				
	Rah-niját .	22	½ "	4 months	Resala Tajhizo takfin . .	20	½ "	1½ month				
	Khazanatulilm .	24	1 "	1½ month	Janguama nafso rúh . . .	20	1 "	1 month				
					Safwatul masadir	27	½ "	2 months				
II	Paudnama of Sadi with translation	12	3 lines	3½ months	Qadir namá .	12	1 page	½ month				
	Paudnáma of Attár . . .	40	1 page	2 "	Mufidnamá .	26	6 lines	3½ months	Nami Haq .	12	1 page	½ month
	Dasturussibyan .	24	5 lines	5 "	Nadiruttartib .	40	6 "	2½ "	Badsé' Manzúm .	56	1 "	2½ months
					Nesabussibyan .	30	½ page	3 "	Malabuddá-minho	158	1 "	7½ "
					Nisab Musallas .	20	½ "	2 "				
III	Dasturulmaktubat . . .	27	½ page	2½ months	Nisab Badi-ul-ajayeb . .	10	½ page	1 month				
	Ruga'át Nizamia	16	½ "	1½ "	Tashrih-ul-huruf.	30	½ "	3 months				
	Insha Dilkusha .	37	½ "	3½ "	Masdar Fayyuz .	90	1 "	4 "				
	Insha fáyeq .	18	½ "	1½ "								
IV	Insha Bahári Ajam . .	32	½ page	3 months	Mufizi Farsi .	68	1½ pages	2½ months	Gulistan, Caps. 1, 4 & 7 . .	89	½ page	5 months
	Insha Khalifa .	35	½ "	2 "	Abdulwasá . .	84	2 "	3 "	Bostán, Caps. 1, to 4 . .	104	1 "	5 "
	Amanulla Hussini	30	1½ "	1 month	Jawahar-ul-húrúf	100	1 page	5 "	Yusuf Zulekhá .	180	3 pages	4½ "
	Ruga'át Alamgir	46	1 "	2 months					Anwari Suheli, Caps. 1 & 2 .	164	3 "	4 "
	Insha Munir .	40	1 "	2 "								
V	Insha Faiz Rasán	102	1 page	5 months	Nihrulfasáhat .	70	2 pages	1½ "	Naldaman .	128	3 "	3 "
	Hadayequlushsháq . .	138	4 pages	1½ "	Chahár Gulzár .	28	½ page	2 "	Shabnam-i-Shádáb	20	3 "	10 days
	Qiranussadain .	...	3 "	2½ "	Taskaratul Balaghat . .	102	2 pages	2 " and 11 days.	Waqaye Nimat Khán Ali .	154	4 "	2 months
	Tauqi áti kisra .	102	3 "	2 "					Mina Bazar .	44	3 "	1 month
					Hadayiq ul-balághat . .	100	1½ "	3 months	Seh Nasar Zahuri	92	2 "	3 months
VI	Sikandar námá .	208	2 lines	5 months	Panj Ruqá .	48	1 page	2 months	Diwan Nasir Ali	115	2 "	2 "
	Makhzan-i-Asrar.	154	3 "	2½ "	Husn-o-Ishq .	26	2 pages	13 days	Akláq-i-Nasiri .	500	5 "	5 "
	Qasayed Urfi .	128	2 "	3½ "	Saulat-i-Farúqi	100	2 "	2½ months	Akhláq-i-Jalali .	348	3 "	5 months and 16 days.
					Abul fazal, Vols. I and II . .	109	2 "	3½ "	Mizanuttib	208	2 "	5 months
VII	Rasáil Tughrá .	108	2 lines	2 months	Tahir-wahid .	95	2 pages	2½ months				
	Divan-i-Hafiz .	182	3 "	3 "	Kasáyed Badarchách . .	108	3 "	1½ "				
	Masnawi Mauláná Rúm, Vol. I .	92	1½ page	3 "	Ijázi Khusrawi .	150	2 "	3½ "				
					Rubáyat-i-Úsafi .	30	½ page	3 "				

The following is the list of text-books used in Persian indigenous schools.

(The books having asterisks before them are only read by Muhammadans.)

ELEMENTARY SCHOOLS—

The alphabet.

- * Kauzulmusalli . . . . .
- * Rahi nijat . . . . .
- * Ahkamuliman . . . . .
- * Risala Benamazan . . . .
- * Masáil Subhani or Hazár Masla .
- * Subhe-ka-Sitara . . . .
- * Resala Tajhizo takfin . . .
- * Jangnama nafso ruh . . .
- * Qayamatnama . . . .

} Books in Urdú containing the profession of the Muhammadan creed, prayers, funeral ceremonies, account of the resurrection day, and religious tenets generally.

Khaliq Bari . . . . A vocabulary in verse in Arabic, Persian and Hindi.

Karima . . . . . or Panduama of Sadi, admonitions to little boys in verse.

Amadnama (or Safwatul Masadir) Verbal roots and conjugations.

Paudnama of Attar . . . . Admonitions in verse.

Mahmúdnama . . . . . A collection of verses.

ELEMENTARY SCHOOLS—*concluded.*

Dusturussibian	An easy letter-writer with epistolary rules.
Qadirnama.	
Mufidnama	A book containing the names of ordinary things in Persian and also the first principles of arithmetic, &c.
· Nisabussibyan	A lexicon in verse in Arabic and Persian.
* Nami Hak	Religious tenets in Persian verse.
Mamu qiman	A famous Sufi poem.
* Málábuddaminho	Tenets concerning prayers, fasts, alms, pilgrimage, in Persian prose.
Dasturulmaktubat . . .	A letter-writer.
Ruqqaat Nizamia . . .	Ditto.
Insha Dilkush	Ditto.
Insha fayeq.	Ditto.
Masdar fayuz	Grammar of Persian language in Urdú.
Tashrihul huruf	Ditto.
Alif Kasrat.	Ditto.
Gulistan	
Bostan	
Insha Bahari Ajam . . .	Letter-writer.
Insha Khalifa	Ditto.
Aman-ulla-Husaini . . .	Ditto.
Ruqqaat-i-Alamgir . . .	Letters of Aurangzeb to his sons and courtiers.
Insha Munir	Letter-writer.
Insha Madho Ram . . .	Ditto.
Mufizi Farsi	Grammar.
Abdulwasa	Ditto.
Jawaharul huruf	Ditto.
Joharutlarkib	Ditto.
Yusuf Zuleikha by Jami . .	Poems. The story of Joseph and Potiphar's wife, in verse.
Masnavi Ghanimat . . .	Ditto.
Akhlaqi Muhsani . . .	On ethics, by the author of Anwari Suheli.
Anwari Suheli	The Persian version of Kalila Damna.

ADVANCED SCHOOLS—

Insha-i-Faizrasán . . .	Letter-writer.
Hadayequl-ushshaq.	
Qiranussa' dain of Khusru . .	A poem on the meeting of Kaikubad and his father (an historical incidence in poetry), by Khusrú.
Tauqiat Kisra.	
Bahari Danish	By Inayetulla Khan.
Chahari Gulzar	Grammar and Prosody.
Hadayequl balaghat . . .	Rhetoric and Prosody.
Naldamau	The story of Nal and Daman, an episode from the Mahabharat, by Faizi.
Shabnami Shadáb.	
Waqaye Nimat Khan Ali . .	A journal of the siege of Golconda by Aurangzeb.
Mina Bazar	An imaginary description of a "Female Bazar."
Zahuri	An introduction to a treatise on music by Ibrahim Adilshah (King of Bijapur.)
Ruqqaat-i-Bedil	Letters of Bedil.
Sikandarnama	An epic poem, by Nizami.
Tuhfatul Abrar	A masnavi, by Jámi.
Makhzan-i-Asear . . .	Treasury of secrets by Nizámi.
Laila Majnun	Story of Laila and Majnun, by Nizámi.
Kasáyed-i-Urfi	Odes of Urfi.
Panj Ruqqa	"Five Letters" by Iradat Khan, a courtier of Aurangzeb.
Husno ishq	"Beauty and Love."
Abulfazl	Letters of Abulfazl.
Insha Tahir Wahid.	
Divani Nasir Ali.	
Akhlaqi Nasiri	Moral Philosophy by the famous Philosopher "Tusi."
Me báyad Shanid	"It must be heard"—Admonitions.
Rasáyel Tughra.	
Diwan-i-Hafiz	Odes and Ghazals of Hafiz of Shiraz.
Badar Chach.	
Ajáz Khusrawi	Rhetoric.
Tuhfatul Iraqain	A description of Iraq Arab, and Iraq-i-Ajam, by Khaqani.
Kasayed-i-Khaqani.	
Diwan i-Anwari.	

ADVANCED SCHOOLS—*concluded.*

Shahnama of Firdausi (the Persian Homer).	
Hadiqa Hakim Sanai	A Masnawi, by Hakim Sanái.
Uruzi Saifi	Prosody.
Mantiquttair of Attár	"Discourse of Birds."
Akhlaqi Jaláli	Moral Philosophy of Dawwani.
Durre Nadira	History of Nadir Shah, by Munshi Mehdi Khan.
Masnawi Maulana Rúm	The famous Masnawi.
Majmá-ul-Mantiq	Logic.
Sughra	Do.
Kubra	Do.
Diwan-i-Ghani.	
Diwan-i-Sayeb.	

CONCLUDING REMARKS ON PERSIAN INDIGENOUS EDUCATION.

There are two more points in connexion with Persian indigenous education which deserve to be noticed. One is that, in addition to the teacher, a monitor or "Khalifa" is employed to assist him, a practice borrowed from "Koran schools," under which head more may be found regarding it; and the second point to which I would draw attention is that the Persian *instruction* received at school is not deemed to be complete without the *education* in *manners* which the life away from school should cultivate in co-operation with the school. It is, therefore, the practice in the better families to appoint an "*Ataliq*," "Governor" to the pupil sent to school, whose object it is to teach him how to behave towards friends, equals, superiors and inferiors, modes of address, manner of entering a house, making enquiries, and so forth. Some of these *Ataliqs* are senior confidential servants, or rather retainers of the family, keeping up its reminiscences and instilling self-respect in their charge. Others are specially appointed to the task. PERSIAN MAKES THE GENTLEMAN AND ARABIC THE SCHOLAR, but the Persian system would not be complete if it entirely depended on school instruction. Therefore, in this admirable system which we have so ruthlessly destroyed, instead of developing it in the interests of progress and of the State, the teacher co-operated with the parent and both with the "*Ataliq*." To Europe the "Ataliq" has become the "Attila," but my Yarkandi follower, Niaz Muhammad, whose ruler was also the ATALIQ Yakub Khush Begi of Forsyth and Shaw recollection, still spoke of me as his "Ataliq" "Governor," or rather "his Governorship" or "Fathership," from "Ata" father, to which "liq" is attached as "ric" is to "Bishop." How greatly our schools have brought about a deterioration of manners has been pointed out by Government without any effect on the department, whose Head merely persists in saying that the manners of youths educated under our system *are* good, just as for the last 16 years the text-books of the department *will* always be good, although every officer and native of respectability deplores the absence of good manners from our schools, as, indeed, how can they be taught where the teacher is independent of the parent and of the opinion of native society? A resolution, however, of the Senate of the Panjab University College, urged by the native members, and an extract from a "Review" by the Panjab Government, will show how far it is true that Government schools corrupt good native manners without giving any solid instruction, so that, as *educational* establishments, in the proper sense of the term, they are *far below* indigenous schools, where many boys, at any rate, pay their fee for "manners" and another fee "for learning." The unanimous voice of the public of the Panjab, as heard at the Education Commission, including the pupils which the department has itself trained, condemns its neglect of duty, its books, its want of sympathy and of scholarship, and yet the same stock phrases are repeated in report after report, possibly, on the chance that they may not be remembered, "that the books are good," or that they *will* be good, &c., as is now promised under the dread of the Commission. I will, therefore, also repeat a passage from my evidence, especially as I have been distinctly allowed to do so for the purposes of this Report:

"At a meeting of the Senate of the Panjab University College held on the 28th July 1879, the native members expressed their special satisfaction with the proposal regarding the contents of the vernacular primers which the Panjab representative had made to the Simla Text-book Committee, and which is now, more or less completely, carried out all over India, especially with subhead (*a*), which recommends that the series of vernacular readers for primary schools should convey instruction *inter alia* on the following subject:—'Reverence for God, parents, teachers, rulers, and the aged.' "

"The native members further, and with much force and complete unanimity, made a special representation on the importance of instilling lessons of reverence and of politeness in Government schools, the neglect of which had been a serious drawback to their popularity, and had identified civilisation, in the minds of many, with presumption, neglect of obligations, and the reverse of true wisdom. This was the reason why so many native gentlemen were unable to send their children to Government schools."

I would also repeat an important paragraph from the Parliamentary Report, which has already been referred to, and which embodies an admonition of the Lieutenant-Governor which the Educational Department of this province has not yet taken to heart, and which it never can do unless its entire present higher *personnel* is removed to some sphere of action in which it may be less injurious to the State than in the deterioration of national education.

"Native elegance and refinement, wherever they still linger, are evidently of Persian origin;) thorough mental discipline and scholarly habits exist with Pándits and Maulvís, whilst a smattering of various branches of 'instruction,' to be more or less offensively paraded, is what we have given to the natives with our so-called English education. That this is not an overcharged statement will appear upon reference to the official 'Remarks' published by order of the Lieutenant-Governor of the Panjab (Proceedings No. 606, dated 18th February 1873)—

"'Neither the English language nor literature is taught upon any scientific or intelligent system, and the success of English education, as a consequence, has not hitherto been marked in the Panjab. NOR HAS THE SYSTEM WHICH PRODUCES FEW SCHOLARS BEEN MORE SUCCESSFUL IN PRODUCING GENTLEMEN. *The Lieutenant-Governor desires that the department take especial care that the good manners natural to oriental youth are not lost at school. This matter has hitherto been neglected.* If the result of sending boys of good family to school is, *as is now often the case,* that they return pert, conceited, and studiously rude and familiar, it is no wonder that parents desire to educate their children at home. English education is not a desirable thing if it only signifies sufficient acquaintance with the English language to write and speak ungrammatically, sufficient acquaintance with English literature to be shallow, and with English history to be insolent. English education is to be penetrated with the spirit of the great English authors; to imbibe some portion of their strength and beauty, and nobility and gentleness, and wisdom; to mould the life and character upon the models they have furnished. This is the standard of education to which the department must endeavour to rise.'"

E.—CLASSICAL INDIGENOUS EDUCATION IN THE PANJAB.

V.—Koran Schools.

READ, in the name of thy Lord!
Who created man from congealed blood!
READ, for thy Lord is most generous!
Who taught the pen!
Taught man what he did not know!

"Read" was the very first word which the Angel Gabriel told to the Arabian prophet. It is the first word of the Korán, though the order of its chapters is now changed. The above five verses, taken from what is now the 96th Sûra delivered at Mecca, are generally allowed to have been the first that were revealed. It is the key-stone of the "Korán," the *book* that "pre-eminently deserves to be *read*," a word that may indeed be synonymous with "reading" generally, as in the 55th Sûra: "The All-merciful has taught man reading (or the Korán); He created man; He taught him discriminating speech (or Exegesis, "Beyan," interpretation). The sun and moon with their orbits, plants and trees, worship Him; He raised the heavens and appointed their balance, in order that you may not transgress in measure: therefore weigh justly and stint not the balance."

When a child, whether a boy or girl, is four years four months and four days old, the friends of the family assemble, and the child is dressed in its best clothes, which, as well as the board, books, writing material and the distributed sweetmeat, are provided by its maternal grandmother or maternal grandfather or uncle. The child is then seated on a cushion, and the Arabic alphabet (sometimes also the Arabic numerals), the present Introduction to the Korán (the Fátiha or opening chapter), the whole of the 96th Sûra, and the quoted verses of the 55th Sûra, are placed before it, and it is taught to repeat them after some relative or the respected tutor. Sometimes, also, the 87th Sûra is pronounced, which extols the teaching of the books of Abraham and Moses. If the child is self-willed, and refuses to repeat, it is made to pronounce the "Bismilla,"—"In the name of God, the All-compassionate, the Specially Merciful," which is accepted instead of the above *desiderata*, and from that day its education is deemed to have commenced. Among the lower classes this ceremony is dispensed with, and the child is sent straight to the Mulla with some sweetmeats. Sometimes the child sits in state for a day or two before the ceremony, during which also the tutor coaxes it to repeat the above series by putting sweet "laddus" into its hands. Indeed, everything is done to make the initiation of the child as impressive as possible on its mind, as also as to celebrate the event, wherever circumstances allow it, by invitations and presents to friends and relatives.

At school, which is generally attached to a mosque, or held in the Portico or one of the rooms in its quadrangle, the child is taught those Sûras of the Korán, beginning with the 78th, to the end of the volume, which were probably all given at Mecca, thus following the proper chronological order, which makes the Sûras delivered at Mecca precede those of Medina. The former Sûras are also much shorter, and are couched in the inspired language of a poet-prophet or teacher, whilst the lengthy Medina Sûras are more the production of a Legislator, dealing with more advanced subjects than the easy and eloquent admonitions to be impressed on a child's mind.

It is perfectly true that the teachers of these Koran schools are not good Arabic scholars; indeed, many of them have only a hazy understanding of what they teach the children (boys and girls up to a certain age read together; see my account of the "Races of Turkey, with special reference to Muhammadan Education," from which a passage is quoted in reply to Question 43 of the Education Commission, on the subject of mixed schools). At the same time, I cannot admit that "any of them are unable to sign their names," unless, indeed, he be a blind Háfiz (or one who has committed the whole Korán by heart), a member of a scholastic and priestly fraternity, among whom I have met men of the most astounding memory, which sometimes quite supplied the place of a very extensive reading of Arabic literature. For instance, the officiating 2nd Maulvi of the Oriental College, Lahore, began his career by standing first in an examination in the Arabic language, Law and Literature, among a considerable number of competing Maulvis. As for the statement that the humble teachers of the Korán schools disclaim altogether the ability to understand what they read or teach, they may, indeed, with the dignitary of Queen Candace, who was reading Isaias, the Prophet, reply to Philip's query—"Understandest thou what thou readest?" "How can I, except some man should guide me." But, like the Ethiopian in question, they generally do possess a very fair conception of the meaning of the Korán; for what Muhammadan, except the greatest scholar, can fully understand or altogether misunderstand that most remarkable of productions? Were a bishop to ask a village schoolmaster whether he understood the Bible, he might, perhaps, get a similar answer. Indeed, it is difficult for the teacher to be altogether ignorant of what he teaches, for the prayers and recitations are in daily practice, and everything, if not everybody, around him tells him, at one time or the other, what they mean.

Moreover, these Mullas, who are in some places called "Kat-Mullas or Nim-Mullas," = half-Mullas by their betters, besides teaching their pupils the formal reading of the Korán, perform marriage and funeral services, as well as other ceremonies in which readings from the Korán and certain prayers are necessary. Even the mere reading of the Korán accurately is no mean accomplishment, as it involves the greatest care in giving the correct vowel-points—a matter of the utmost importance, not only in disputed passages, but also in the general interpretation of the Korán. If all Englishmen could "merely" read their Bible in Hebrew, Latin or Greek, not to speak of their knowing their Sacred Scriptures by heart in these languages, and could apply suitable passages to every daily occurrence of their lives, they would, I submit, possess an accomplishment of which they might reasonably be proud. "MEMORY IS THE MOTHER OF THE MUSES," and I, for one, rejoice that in all native systems the soil is so well prepared for the ready reception of studies of every kind by the preliminary training of a faculty which is rather the healthy development of all faculties. There can be little doubt that the shallowness and self-complacency of modern students is largely due to the want of the sufficient cultivation of the memory in our schools; and it is probable that, with their further extension, the wonderful gift of memory, in which the native still stands first in the world, will also disappear along with his language, morals and religion.

Again, although the teachers may not explain the religious books in the elementary Korán schools, the parents to whom the boy repeats his lesson often does, and this they are enabled to do, even if they cannot write and read themselves, from their recollections and experiences of life and of religious exercises, so that there are scarcely many Muhammadans who do not understand the general drift of a passage from the Korán or many Hindus that of a Sanscrit devotional book in ordinary use. The consequence of the permeation of the Muhammadan population by Arabic words and phrases is that Arabic legal and other scientific words in Urdu translations are understood, to a certain extent, even by the vulgar. This is *less* the case with Persian words which are confined to the educated class and only filter to the classes below, whilst this is scarcely at all the case with newly-coined words, from English or even pure Hindi, unless, indeed, the latter are chosen or invented with more discrimination than has been displayed in departmental and other publications.

Even were the "Korán schools" as "educationally worthless" as they are described to be in our Official Reports, they would still deserve respect and tender treatment as the nurseries in which the bulk of our Muhammadan fellow-subjects derive, if only, the Shibboleths of their religion, but they do more, they give hope and comfort and resignation to millions of human beings, whom the irritation, false views of life and discontent taught by our system would render unhappy and drive into disaffection.

It should also be borne in mind that the Korán schools answer a double purpose, *first*, that of giving that amount of religious knowledge which is essential to a good Muhammadan and which was more intelligible, when Arabic was more spoken than it is now (a remark which also applies Sanscrit among Hindus as regards those Schools in which only Sanscrit religious books are taught) and, *secondly*, that of preparation for higher Korán schools or Arabic Schools, in which the Korán is explained with conscientious and scholarly minuteness. In their present humble and neglected condition they surely must incidentally also teach the *two* "r's," "reading and writing," and I can, therefore, not understand the remarks of Mr. Arnold, which other Directors have since repeated, in one form or another, that "attendance at Korán school does *not* necessarily involve a knowledge of *reading* and writing." Does this apply to the *blind* boys only, who learn the Korán from memory? If not, what *can* the statement mean? I quote one of the passages in which it occurs from the first Educational Report:—

"18. The number of Korán schools is given as 1,755; but I have no doubt that the number is *much greater*. In several districts *no such schools* are mentioned, *the fact being that probably every mosque is the site of what is elsewhere called a Korán school*. As attendance at these schools does *not necessarily involve a knowledge of reading* and writing, I have omitted the pupils of the Korán schools from my calculation of boys under instruction. Of course, strictly Korán schools are attended only by Muhammadans."

However, not to leave the matter of reading (and, *through* it, of writing) in Korán schools in doubt, it is impossible to learn to read the Korán with all the attention which its vowel-points and accentuation require, without that this *should necessarily* involve a knowledge of reading. The boy first learns the alphabet in the "Káida Baghdádi," said to have been compiled first for the son of a Baghdád Khalífa; then, as stated before, the last chapters of the Korán, as also the five "kálimas," in which the principal tenets of Islam are contained and which *are* explained to the pupils, whilst the *brochures* of these kálimas have also interlinear translations into Urdu or Perso-Panjabi. The boys also learn the Muhammadan profession of creed, beginning with "amantu billahi wa bil maláikati, wa kutubihi wa rasúlihi"= "I believe in God, his angels, his (revealed) books, *viz.*, the Korán, the Tóra (Old Testament), the Psalms, the Sahífa of the Jewish prophets and the New Testament, his apostles," the resurrection of the dead and the day of judgment, the existence of Paradise and Hell, &c. He is taught the practice of prayers, many of which were contained in his Korán reading. In most Korán schools also the following elementary religious books in Urdu, Persian or Panjabi are taught:—

Kanz-ul-Musalli (a book of prayers) in verse.

Rah-i-Niját (the road to salvation, containing religious tenets, in prose).

Risala Bey-namázan (threats to those who do not pray, chiefly compiled from the Korán) in verse.

Nasihat-náma (admonitions in verse, which, *inter alia*, contain the following advice:—

"Always remember God; make your heart glad with his name; cultivate (abád kar) this earth which is your temporary and deserthome, if you wish happiness in the next world." Also such practical, prudential advice as "Do not be a security, even for your father, or allow any one to be security for you, for such a course only encourages sin, &c.

Masáil Hindi (religious precepts regarding faith, prayer, fasting, almsgiving, and pilgrimage).

Subha-ka-sitára, the morning star (of a similar character as above).

Masáil Subháni (the same as above; very popular in the Punjab).

Kissas-ul-Arabia,—stories of prophets, both in prose and verse.

Many of these schools add Persian to their course, after the pupil has mastered his religious duties. There is no necessity for repeating an account of Persian elementary studies, which has already been given. The pupil may then take up the study of Arabic, to which Persian is always considered to be an introduction, when he will acquire a knowledge of the meaning of the Korán and of other books, of which more hereafter.

The Korán schools, which are very numerous, may be found in every mosque in the Punjab, even if they should only contain one or two pupils. They are also held in private houses, and it is not usual to have a large number of pupils in these schools, as each are supposed to require special attention, excepting in such large establishments as the "Bara Mian-ka Dars," the "lesson-house of Bara Mian," near "Mian Mir," where there are more than 200 boys preparing for the office of Háfiz by learning the Korán by heart. It will be remembered that the services of Hafizes are preferentially sought for in filling vacancies of priests and guides of prayer at mosques, and that they are essential to lead prayer at the "Terawih," supplications during the nights of Ramázán.

There are also innumerable Korán schools in the private houses of Moulvis and religious patrons, among whom widows hold an honoured place. The latter often teach the Korán themselves to boys and little girls.

The discipline in these schools is maintained more easily than in the more numerously attended Persian schools, but is otherwise much the same.* In the Korán, as also in the Persian schools, the senior boy or a special monitor (generally the teacher's son, if he is competent) assists in the instruction and supervision of the school, and takes the place of the head-teacher during his absence, thus qualifying to become his successor, or "Khalifah"—by which name, indeed, he is known, and which, as it were, puts the teacher in the seat of "the prophet," with his loyal assistant as the "Coming Khalifah." The income of the teacher of a school attached to a mosque is derived either from its landed or other endowment, or from a share in the offerings of the faithful. Some of the pupils may even pay fees, though this is not usually considered to be acceptable, as the instruction is given for the "sake of God," "Lillah," "fi sabil illah," "i'nd illah." On important occasions, however, in the pupil's family, a present may be offered to the teachers, and it is a gratifying circumstance that pupils who have left the school ever remember their religious teacher by sending him, say, a rupee on the 25th of Ramazan, or when a marriage or a male child's birth takes place in their family; such presents may be accepted as signs of the pupil's gratitude; but payment for instruction is not considered "the thing." Personal service, however, to the master, whilst in a state of pupilage (and even afterwards), is general, in order to relieve the teacher of petty household or other troubles. They bring his water, make his purchases in the bazar, look after his little children, and so forth. Food is also usually supplied to the teacher either by his pupils or his neighbours or fellow-villagers. The teacher of the Korán school is often the *Imám* of the mosque in which his school is held, when he derives his income from other sources, and, as a rule, teaches altogether gratuitously. It may, however, be mentioned that when a pupil finishes his reading of the Korán, a present, sometimes amounting to 100 rupees, a house, cattle, &c., according to the means of his parents, is not unusually given to the teacher. A holiday is given to the school when a pupil has finished the Korán; the boys, with the master and their relatives, assemble in the house of the "passed" student, when the present is given and the "*Amin*" is sung, which really means adding "Amens" to the blessings invoked by the master on the head of his little graduate. These "amins" are varied, and are in both Arabic and Urdu—at any rate, the *refrains* taken up by the audience are in Arabic, such as "Subhán man yaráni," "Praise be to Him who sees us," or *Chorus*, "Amin, ilahi, Amin," = "Amen, oh God, amen." The scene is one of great interest.

I have before me one of the excellent little books written for children in indigenous schools, of which the Curator's returns make no mention, as, indeed, of numerous original productions in which the Punjab is so prolific, and which still make this province of 19 millions the first in literary activity, and not *second* to Lower Bengal, in spite of its 68 millions, as has been stated.

---

* As stated in my cross-examination by the Education Commission, "discipline, so far as obedience and reverence are concerned, is superior in these schools to our own; and though the sight of little boys swaying backwards and forwards seems confusing to the English eye, it is, in fact, an accompaniment to the rhythm of the Korán. It also gives them some physical exercise."

This little book is "the present of the Amen on the completion of the sacred Korán." Indeed, it is one of the treatises which serves as a basis to the inauguration of the "passed" boy into practical life, and is varied according to circumstances. It narrates the birth of the child, the joys and hopes of the parents, his going to school, his first success in finishing the first quarter of the last section of the Korán, and the final triumph in completing that volume; the friendly teasing of the boys, the grand holiday, the necessity now for other secular studies, arts and sciences, which can all be acquired by *knowing their meaning;* the reaching of puberty and celebration of marriage, and the discharge of its responsibilities; the weeping of the bride's relatives on her leaving her home; the fellow-pupils invoke the blessings of the Almighty on the union, and wait not to be forgotten in the general rejoicings, in which a present to the tutor should have its place. Now comes one of the most touching incidents in the recitation, namely, the

CONTRACT BETWEEN THE CHILD AND ITS CREATOR,

the practice of which is first justified by reference to authorities, and which runs thus:—

"Oh God, Creator of the heavens and of earth; Thou who knowest all that is secret or manifest; Thou, who art all compassionate and specially merciful: I contract myself unto thee in this sublunary life, with that I testify that there is no God but Thou, who art ONE, and there is no partner with Thee. And I testify that Muhammad is your servant and prophet. Do not give me over to my own sinful self, for if thou abandon me to myself, I shall be caused to be near evil and be made far from good; for, indeed, I do not trust in aught but Thy mercy. Then place Thou to me a contract from before Thee, which Thou wilt fulfil unto the day of judgment, because Thou never ignorest Thy promise!

"Now may God, whose name be exalted, bless the best of his creatures, Muhammad and his posterity and companions, and all Muhammadan men and women, all of them! This I supplicate from Thy mercy, Thou who art the most merciful of those who have mercy."

This consecration of the child to the Creator, the objects of which had been explained in the preamble, is followed by the "Amen of birth," and the "Amen of marriage;" and thus the past and the future are combined in a ceremony which must leave a lasting impression for good on the mind of the "passed" pupil.

I may also mention that even the payment of a fee or present in Persian or Korán schools is accompanied by some act which raises it above vulgarity. For instance, before the *I'di* festival presents are offered, as explained elsewhere, the master gives the pupil a few original or borrowed verses, formerly in Persian and now generally in the vernacular, on red paper sprinkled with gold-dust, the contents of which vary according to the season or festival. I will quote a verse from one of them:—

"What flowers has Spring caused to bloom in the garden!
Every branch waves in the zephyr of Spring;
The nightingale whispers in the ear of the rose;
The joyful tidings of the advent of '*I'd*'," &c., &c.

(This refers to the alleged habit of the nightingale pressing his bill against the petals of the rose, which is neither the kiss of the lover nor the desire to inhale its fragrance, but a message of approaching joy in one of the *I'd* festivals.)

It is idle to assert, after such specimens as the above, which form a constant source of occupation to certain Maulvis and others of a poetic turn of mind, that Native poetry is exclusively erotic, and that it required the interposition of any Director to eliminate the element of love in the "Musháaras" alleged to have been originated in 1874-75. They are as old as the period when the beauties of nature, the heroism of man, the loveliness of woman, first inspired the native poets. I go so far as to allege that the bulk of poetry in the Panjab never was, and is not, more erotic than in any country in Europe. It is chiefly religious, provincial, narrative, and descriptive. I have already explained to what element the prominence of amorous poetry is now due,—indeed, it was the unfortunate assumption, which characterises European interference in so many matters, that they have all to teach and nothing to learn from natives, that led to the collapse of the Musháaras in 1875. The "irritabile genus" of poets did not want to be told by any one that they had, hitherto, debased their genius by celebrating love and they declined dictation in poetic inspiration, if, indeed, "*poeta fit, non nascitur.*" In 1865, weekly vernacular scientific lectures were organised by the Anjuman-i-Panjab, under Mr. H. D. Staines, at the conclusion of which disputations in Sanscrit took place among the Pandits, discussions on the lecture in the vernacular, and recitations of original poems on all subjects, in Urdu, Persian, Hindi, Arabic, and other Oriental languages. The effect of the mistake in 1874-75 lasted till 1879 when *public* Musháaras could again be revived at Lahore, which still continue; but they had never ceased in native society itself, as there is scarcely a gathering of friends or a family or popular rejoicing that is not accompanied by cataracts of poems. That they should now generally celebrate love is not only natural to youth and poetry, but is almost the only theme which we have left to the native Muse. What "patriotism" are they to sing whose country, religion, and old associations have been broken up? Perhaps, if the new scheme of "self-government" is honestly carried out, and the people are made to feel the dignity and responsibility of state-citizenship; if the ancient land-marks of language and literature are again set up, and if religion is again honored, the Panjabi poets may be more readily inspired to other strains than those of love and panegyrics in praise of officials, which are distasteful to Europeans, because they are either *admittedly* professional, conventional and insincere, or because they are felt to be undeserved. In the meanwhile, (provided no European or native presumes to dictate to poets,' or "attempts to promote a natural style of poetry and to discourage the artificial use of similes and expressions borrowed from Persian poets and imitations of Persian writings" (alleged to be) "unsuited to this country" (when they are the very source from which poetic genius is fed in the East), except by his own example, there will be ample scope for the celebration in poetry, of all subjects, left to the choice of the poets, in the Musháaras of Lahore or other places. (See Director's No. 4 S., dated 22nd September 1881, paragraph 22

When it is remembered how prosaic, far from God and the Muse, is the life of the bulk of the lower classes in Europe, one would fain express a hope that "Bible schools," really interwoven with the daily life and associations of the people, and rendered glorious by festivals and a consecration to duty, God, and country, might become as great an agency of real education in Europe as the Korán schools, however humble their appearance, are in the Panjab.

I have just received a letter from one of the lowliest of lowly teachers of a Korán village school, written in Perso-Panjabi and in the Urdu character, which may give some indication of the nature of the difficulties that these institutions have to contend with :—"Great sir! Read this petition with attention. Your worship desires that instruction be given in indigenous schools. How can this ever be, considering that the chief muharrirs (Educational officers), tahsildars, zaildars, lumberdars have rooted up their very foundations? If any one should go to an indigenous school, the chief muharrir, tahsildar, zaildar, lumberdar bully him and say: "Hear, thou wilt get no credit by going to this school." Indeed, the zaildars, lumberdars and Government schoolmasters say to the indigenous teacher "You are giving us a bad name; don't you stir." The schoolmaster then gets the boys away from the indigenous school, whether they go to his school or not. This is why the boys and *girls* of the unhappy Muhammadans have given up *even* reading their Korán. But God is in the whole Panjab. If the chief muharrir or zaildar sees a boy read in an indigenous school, he gets a burning in his body; and when the Government schoolmaster sees the boy, he abuses the teacher and tells the lumberdar: "*Will* you not obey the order of Government? Bring the teacher to his senses, or else I will complain against you." When the zaildar comes, he tells him—

"The chief muharrir is coming round; what glory will there be in my school if the *Mian* (teacher of the indigenous school) has again got the boys to go to him." Then let us suppose that the chief muharrir really comes; he will certainly abuse and put down the indigenous teacher, and tell him "What do *you* know? Tell me "where is God, and how do the heavens and the earth go round?" When the teacher *can* make some suitable reply, then the chief muharrir turns on the lumberdar and says: "You are not fit to be a lumberdar. I will report you." Then the chief muharrir speaks to the tahsildar. The result is that no indigenous school can continue to exist.

Hear; in D —, there was a Madrasa. The chief muharrir told the zaildar and wrote in all the visitors' books of the Government schools of the Zail that the indigenous schools in it were not flourishing. The helpless zaildar at once abolished the Madrasa of his village. In the same way, the Madrasas in other villages were also abolished, Sir! If indigenous schools are to be started, then let an order be issued to every lumberdar and zaildar, not to prevent any one who may wish to do so from reading in an indigenous school, and allow those who are already reading to go on doing so. Then, perhaps, will the Madrasas, the foundations of which have been rooted up by chief muharrirs, tahsildars and zaildars, be again re-established; but if such an order is not published, they will not continue."

The statements in this letter are far from being overdrawn. I have heard, on unquestionable authority, that worse persecutions than are here referred to were put in motion against those who ventured to maintain an indigenous or unaided school in competition, or even in the same place, with a Government school. Some indigenous teachers were driven out from villages in which their ancestors had taught for a century, if not longer. In other places, the jaghirdár, who wanted to restore a muáfi to an indigenous school, was prevented from doing so. In all places where the indigenous teacher left no heir, his muáfi, if any, was resumed, instead of maintaining it for the purpose of a school. In *all* cases where lands or other endowments were attached to mosques or other sacred edifices, there was an understanding that a school would form part of it; but the opportunity was not taken to insist on the fulfilment of a self-understood religious obligation on the part of the managers of these establishments, which would have maintained a network of schools in every town and village in the Panjab, capable of being developed up to the practical requirements of the community and in the truest interests of the State. That any indigenous education should continue to exist at all in the province, in spite of our steady efforts to discourage, if not to suppress it, and in the face of much official opposition, if not persecution, which those who know Indian life will understand to be easily practicable against what does not appear to enjoy the favour of the authorities, is a living protest of the people against our educational system, as well as its strongest condemnation.

VI.—Arabic Schools.

"Science is the knowledge of Arabic; Persian is sugar; Turkish (owing to its grammatical complications) is an art; Hindi (as non-Indians call the language of Hind) is salt" (owing to the pungency of its poetry).

This quotation from memory, the literalness of which I have no means of checking at Simla, seems to me to describe, not unhappily, the pre-eminence of Arabic among eastern languages and literature. The logic of its formations is unparalleled; its etymology is, in itself, a study of Arabian history and customs; the applications of its inexhaustible treasure of words, in their numerous forms, are graduated to the various domains of human thought and experience, and are simplicity itself when the key to them is found. What Europe owes to the labours of the Arabs in scientific research can never be sufficiently acknowledged. It is only in "Drama," and the appreciation of sculpture and music, that its puritanism repels the heathen mind. Taking almost everything in Greek philosophy and science, they rejected its worship of the human form, and its delineation of human passion on the stage. But in the rigid studies of history, philosophy, logic, mathematics. astronomy, medicine, including botany and zoology, the Arabs are masters of exactness, and it is to them that a sixth of the human race owes its civilization. No European can aspire to influence among any of the nations that Muhammadanism has strongly imbued without knowing Arabic. Unlike the Indo-Germanic group, it has not been materially affected by climatic and ethnic influences; but it stands forth, complete in itself, the perfection alike of power, profundity, and wealth, allied to a severe simplicity. Arabic, or its cognate Hebrew, is the fitting language of a creed that has ever held aloft the standard of the ONE and Jealous God.

The Panjab has ever been proverbial for the thoroughness with which Arabic grammar (etymology) was studied in it. This is alone a task of considerable magnitude, but it was worthy of a province which sent out conquerors, reformers and teachers to the south. My surprise can, therefore, be imagined when I heard an Inspector depose to the absence or poverty of grammatical studies in Panjab indigenous schools. He could not have referred to Urdu or Hindi, for these languages are not studied as such; he did not allude to Persian, which has scarcely a grammar; he could not have meant Sanscrit, for he professed to know a little of it, and would thus have ascertained that grammar is studied in Panjab Sanscrit schools in a manner which perhaps the greatest Sanscritist of this age has declared to be unrivalled; so he could only have referred to Arabic grammar, in which the Panjab has ever been pre-eminent, as acknowledged even by the jealous North-West. The productions on "Sarf" in the Panjab in one year exceed those of the North-West in ten, as, indeed, they also do in other branches, for the Panjabi is only stupid in the arts of intrigue, to which, when exercised by his other Indian fellow-countrymen, he falls an easy victim; but in anything that requires steady and hard mental work, he yields to no race in India, whilst in bravery and physical strength he is the master of most.

As stated in my cross-examination by the Education Commission, "The ARABIC SCHOOLS go from the most elementary knowledge of reading Arabic, up to the highest standard of Arabic Law and Literature, and the sciences contained in that literature, such as Medicine. They vary much, according to their grade. Grammar, Syntax and Rhetoric in the middle and higher schools are taught on a method which is considered by the highest European Arabic scholars to be far superior to our own. The exegesis of religion is taught in a most admirable way. *Aristotle* is taught in the higher *Arabic* indigenous schools, and his system and that of *Plato* are understood. In some. *Persian* is added and in some *Urdu*. The system of a '*running commentary*' between Professors and students is of considerable advantage. In some higher Arabic schools mathematics and astronomy are taught." Before, however, giving the time table and list of subjects studied at a model school like that of DEOBAND, I would briefly refer to the ordinary elementary course which is adopted in numerous schools and by private teachers, Maulvis and others.

The pupil begins his Arabic studies through the medium of Persian books or Arabic grammar, such as the "MIZAN-US-SARF" on Etymology "MUNSHAIB" on the same; followed by the well-known "SARF MIR," "PANJ-GANJ," "ZUBDA" (on permutations), "DASTUR-UL-MUBTADI"—all works on different branches of Arabic grammar—and, finally, so far as this portion of the course is concerned, the "NAHV-MIR" (a book on Syntax) and the "MIAT AMIL" of the famous poet Jámí in Persian verse, a hundred rules of Syntax originally in Arabic prose; then the pupil leaves the medium of Persian and addresses himself solely to the study of the Arabic language, Literature, Law and Science, as contained in the works of Arabian authors.

I cannot do better than refer to the scheme of studies at Deoband as a general indication of the course followed in the Arabic schools or colleges of various grades in the Panjab, with this difference that, whereas, at an institution like that of Deoband, all the grades are in one locality, in the majority of Arabic seminaries, the student has to travel to one place for logic, to another for mathematics, to a third for medicine, though, as a rule, in the better schools the following subjects are taught in one place, *viz.*, RHETORIC, LOGIC (Aristotle's), PHILOSOPHY (as in Avicenna's work on the subject—the Shifáa); Tusi's Shera isharát; Ghazálí's Abya-ul-ulúm or Vivification of learning—all more or less on an Aristotelian basis, though the Platonic system is understood, if insufficiently appreciated, and Ghazali attacks Aristotle himself with his Arabian school in the interests of orthodoxy (in his book called "Taháfat-ul-Filásifa"); LAW (including the "Usúl" or "Principles"); some books of literature, such as HARIRI and "Theology" or "Scholastic Philosophy" reconciling orthodoxy with reason. A polite Arabic letter-writer, the "Ajab-ul-Ajáib," is also commonly read, and a study of MEDICINE is the most accessible scientific subject in a considerable number of schools, as it is considered both in the light of a general accomplishment as also in that of a professional study, so that we find Nawábs, Maulvis and others, as well as Hakíms, acquiring a knowledge of Medicine in ordinary Arabic schools or from a private Maulvi. For this reason, a school like that of Deoband, would be deficient in a purely professional subject, when its literary and scientific course is sufficiently extensive; in other words, when it adds Mensuration and the Arabian works on Euclid, Algebra, the higher mathematics, including Astronomy, instead. (It is rather curious to find Europeans doubt the possibility of rendering mathematical and other scientific signs into Arabic, when our very numerals and the word "Algebra" itself are of Arabic origin.) It will, therefore, be necessary to subjoin the "medical course" of an Arabic school that makes this subject a speciality, of which the Yunáni class of the Oriental College (the members of which also go through a four years' course in European medicine) may be considered to be a model.

1. The Qanûncha (which also includes anatomy).
2. Mujáz.
3. Mizán-ut-tib, including treatises on the crises of diseases.
4. Kifáya Mansúri.
5. Mizán-ut-tib (use and doses of single and compound medicines).

The student of the Yunáni system then proceeds to the well-known works—

6. The Aqsarai.
7. Sadîdi.
8. Mufarah-ul-qulûb.
9. Tashrîh-ul-aflák.

And he concludes his medical studies with—

10. The Sharah Asbab;
11. The Nafîsi;
12. Avicenna's incomparable Kuliát-i-Qanûni;
13. The same author's Hummyat-i-Shaikh; and
14. The Jami-ush-Sharhîn;

altogether, about a six years' course, varied by attendance with his teacher on patients or, as is more usual, assisting him whilst dispensing medicine and medical advice, often gratuitously, equivalent to our out-door relief,—the practice and place, generally the tutor's house, being both called 'Matabb,' "place and act of dispensing medicine and medical advice."

It is unnecessary to add that many of the Arabic schools add Persian and some Urdu, arithmetic, and even, rarely, history and geography to their course, when, in proportion to the standards, the scheme of studies laid down under the head of "Persian schools" is more or less followed, to which I, therefore, must beg leave to refer the reader. As a rule, Arabic schools are chiefly, though not exclusively, attended by Muhammadans and their Persian or other departments indiscriminately by pupils from all communities, fees in cash or kind being generally obligatory in the latter case, whilst gratuitous instruction, as a religious duty, is often given, in the case of purely Arabic students, who are generally supported by the Muhammadan community when they are poor or come from a distance. Yet it is on such schools that the first Educational Report passes the following verdict:—

"*Para. 15. An Arabic school can hardly with propriety be called a school at all, the students being almost exclusively adults.*"—Well, then, we will, with greater propriety, call these schools, *Colleges*.

It must also be understood that the student of advanced Arabic learning is supposed to read everything bearing on the subject of his speciality, which only requires study, and not the master's interpretation, at his own house. A "*curriculum vitæ*" of a Panjabi Maulvi which I annex will give a very fair idea of the career of a Muhammadan who wishes to devote himself to learning or to become a Maulvi. Some of the highest works on Scholastic Theology, such as Ar-Razi's Great Commentary, the Tafsîri Kabîr, are not read at all in any Arabic College that I know of, and the same practice obtains with regard to other subjects also.

I need not add that all the professions, including that of priest, are open to the humblest Mussulman, though, as a rule, the hereditary professionals, priests, physicians and professors, take the lead or the larger share in emoluments and public consideration. Our educational system, by ignoring the native professions, has impoverished them, whilst it has closed the avenue to these professions by the introduction of "new men," from whom technical aptitude, rather than learning, is required. But India still resembles in many respects the middle ages, in which scholastic learning was the road to preferment or culture, and it is a very serious proceeding to have thrown out the hereditary guides of the people from professions which enabled them to live and to render learning honoured by the community. In the restoration of the highly-gifted Maulvi class to their hereditary dignity, I see a solution of the educational difficulty among Muhammadans, whether male or female, because it is their wives, as also widows, who are the most congenial material from which to supply female teachers, just as the utilisation of the Pandit class would place at our disposal the educational services both of the Pandits and of their wives among Hindus, and the similar employment of Bhais and their spouses would restore that teaching, under civilised auspices and more in accordance with the spirit of the age, which is so emphatically the characteristic of "Sikhism."

With regard to fees and discipline, the previous remarks on the subject of Persian or Korán schools will suffice, it being borne in mind that the teachers and students are of a higher calibre, and that the relations between them are those of friends, of whom the senior imparts his knowledge to the junior, generally for the love of God, or out of devotion to Arabic learning

If we wish to influence the many through the few, we should identify ourselves more closely with the Muhammadans, a once ruling race, than we have done hitherto. It is also time that the unnecessary antagonism, at any rate in India, between Christianity and Muhammadanism should cease. As a student of both systems of theology, I have been struck rather with their similarities, than with their differences, and it is the former, rather than the latter, that we should accentuate in our relations. As for Muhammadan fanaticism, this was chiefly stimulated and maintained in self-defence by the wanton expulsion and pauperisation of hundreds of thousands of the industrious Moors from Spain, by the crusades waged by Christians and by the domination of the Ottomans who accepted the sterner "Suras" of Madína, when Muhammad was under the pressure of his followers, in preference to the all-loving, if fiery, utterances of Mecca (see my pamphlet on Muhammadan education). My own long residence in Muhammadan countries has convinced me that it is earnestness in the few, rather than fanaticism, which characterises them, whilst the bulk of the people are too dreamy or apathetic to be bigoted. The Christians of various sects, as also the Jews, were allowed complete autonomy under Turkish rule, when all were a happy family, with occasional dissensions, till European interference, "constitutions" with the Code Napoleon and "foreign" education, which taught the "advanced" Turks the small-talk of infidelity, revolutionised the country. It is in various European countries that I have seen real bigotry, of sect against sect, class against class, and nation against nation, often fanned by those religious leaders whose fervour is a substitute for their real *raison d'étre*, learning. Indeed, I consider that the East is, and has ever been, characterised by tolerance, though European spies, emissaries, and unscrupulous merchants have often taxed its patience and roused an inevitable hostility. It is an encouraging sign of the liberality and far-sightedness of several of our Punjab missionaries that they would infinitely prefer instruction being given to, say, Muhammadans in their own religion than that the present "secular" system, which is destructive of the religious sense, should continue. The large-heartedness also of those missionaries who would pledge themselves not to make attendance at the Bible-class compulsory, wherever a Government institution is handed over to them, is deserving of the warmest appreciation and of the success with which it will certainly meet, though it is no more than what Maulvis and Mianjis in India have done for ages, *as a matter of course*, namely, allow Hindus who were desirous of studying Arabic or Persian, to attend only the purely literary classes of Muhammadan institutions, whilst positively discouraging their attendance at the religious or legal classes.

The following is the scheme of study of the Arabic Department of Deoband school with the daily progress of the student; the course of study extending to eight years :—

	1st Daily Lesson.				2nd Daily Lesson.				3rd Daily Lesson.			
Year.	Name of the text book.	Pages of the book.	Daily lesson.	Time of completing the book	Name of the text-book.	Pages of the book.	Daily lesson.	Time of completing the book.	Name of the text-book.	Pages of the book.	Daily lesson.	Time of completing the book.
			Pages.	Months.			Pages.	Months.			Pages	Months.
I	Mizan Ussarf (Etymology).	14	...	¾	......	...	...	...	......	...	...	...
	Munshaib (Etymology).	18	...	1	Panj Gunj (Etymology).	44	2	1	......	...	...	...
	Sarf Mir (Etymology).	48	1	2	Zubdá (Etymology).	16	1¼	½	......	...	...	...
	Sharah Miat Amil (Etymology).	51	1	2	Dasturulmubtadi (Etymology).	23	1	1	......	.	...	...
	Nahvi Mir (Syntax).	48	¾	3	Zarradi (Etymology).	23	1	1	......	...	...	...
	Hidayetunnahv (Syntax).	101	2	2	Mia Amil (in verse) (Etymology).	4	½	¼	Isagoge (Logic)	16	1	¾
					Sharah Mete Amil of Jami (Etymology).	10	¾	½	Qála Aqúlo (Logic).	60	1½	1¾
					Zariri (Etymology).	30	1	1¼	Mirqat (Logic)	32	¾	1¾
					Misbah (Etymology).	32	2	¾	Mizan-i-Mantiq (Logic).	28	1	1
					Marahularwah (Etymology).	64	2	1¼	Tahzíb (Logic)	20	1	1
					Fasúl-i-Akbari (Etymology).	93	2	2	Sharah Tahzíb (Logic)	85	1½	2¼
II	Sháfya (Etymology).	164	2	3½	Munyatuh Musalli (Law).	120	2	2¼	Qutbi (Logic)	172	3	2¼
	Káfya (Syntax)	100	2	2	Kadúri (Law)	234	3	3½	Mir Qutbi (Logic)	108	2	2¼
	Sharah Mulla Jami (Syntax).	400	2	8¼	Kanzud Daqayeq (Law).	420	4	4½	Maibuzi (Mental Science).	180	2	3¾
									Sullumululúm (Logic).	15	½	1
III	Mukhtasar Maani (Rhetoric).	340	3	4¾	Asul Shashi (Theol. Phil.).	56	1	2¼	Mulla Hasan (Logic).	251	3	3½
					Sharah Waqaya (Law).	227	2	4¾	Mir Záhid (Logic)	42	1	1¾
					Núr Ulanwár (Jurisprudence).	254	4	2¾	Ghulám Yahya (Logic).	52	2	1¼
									Abdulali (Logic).	66	2	1½
IV	Sharah Aqayed (Theol. Phil.)	128	3	2	Husámi (Jurisprudence).	184	4	2	Mir Záhid Jalalya (Logic) and	129	2	5½
	Khayali (Theol. Phil.)	104	2	2½	Tauzih Talwih (Jurisprudence).	211	1½	5¼	Mulla Jalal (Logic).	133		
	Nafhatul Yaman (Literature).	403	3	5	Musallam Ussabút (Jurisprudence).	66	...	2	Abdulali on above (Logic).	188	3	2¾
									Hamdulla (Logic)	232	3	3
									Qazi Mubarak (Logic).	128	2	2¾
V	Muqamat-i-Hariri (Literature).	412	2½	7	Mishkat (Tradition).	576	3	8	Khulasatulhisáb (Arithmetic).	84	...	2
					Jami Tirmazi (Tradition).	654	6	4½	Siráji (Law)	66	2	1¼
									Euclid	422	...	5
VI	Divan-i-Mutanabbi (Literature).	400	2	8¼	Sahih Múslim (Tradition).	917	6	6½	Sadrá (Natural Phil.).	249	4	2¾
	Tarikh-i-Yamini (Literature).	263	2	5½					Shamse Bazigha	164	2	3½
									Sharah Mawaqif (Theol. Phil).	69	2	1¼
VII	Dwan-i-Hamásá (Literature).	219	2	4½	Sahih Bukhari (Tradition).	1.128	6	7¾	Mirzahid (Amúr Amá) (Logic).	104	2	2¼
	Tafsír Jalálain (Kororis Exegeris)	510	4	5¼	Nisái (Tradition).	545	7	3	Abdulali (Amúr Amá) (Logic).	362	4	3¾
									Tashrih-ul-Aflak (Astronomy).	36	...	1½
									Saba Shidad (Astronomy),	...	...	1¼
VIII	Baizáwi (Kororis Exegeris).	120	1½	3¼	Abu Dáúd (Tradition).	718	7	4	Sharah Chaghmini (Astronomy)	138	1	5¾
	Hidáyá (Law)	578	8	8	Ibn-i-Maja (Tradition).	576	6	4	Jabr-o-Muqabila (Algebra).	372	...	8
					Muwatta (Tradition).	392	6	2¾	Masabat (Mensuration).	74	...	3

The following is a list of books taught in the Arabic indigenous schools:

I.—Arabic Grammar.

Mizan ussarf.	Nahv Mir.
Munshaib.	Mete Âmil.
Sarf Mir.	Sharah Meite Amil.
Sarfi Bahái.	Mete Amil (in verse) by Jami.
Panj Gunj.	Hidayetunnahv.
Zubdá.	Káfya.
Dasturulmubtadi.	Sharah Mullá.
Zarradi.	Alfia of Ibni Hajib.
Zariri.	Razi.
Sháfya.	Abdulghafúr.
Marah-ul-arwah.	

II.—Literature.

Alif Laila.	Qaliûbi.
Akhwánussafâ.	Saba' mua'llaqa.
Napfatulyaman.	Diwan-i-Hamasá.
Muqamat-i-Hariri.	Diwan Hassán.
Mutnabbi.	Diwani Hazrat Ali.
Tarikh Yamini.	Ajab-ul-Ajayeb (Letter-writer).
,, Timúri by Arabshah.	Munabbehat-i-Ibn Hajar.
,, Khulfá by Sayûti.	

III.—Logic and Philosophy.

Isagoge of Porphry.	Hamdullá.
Qála Agúlo.	Qazi Mubarak.
Mizan-i-Mantiq.	Hidayetulhikmat.
Tahzíb.	Maibuzi.
Sharah Tahzíb.	Rashidia (rules of argument).
Qutbi.	Sadra.
Mir Qutbi.	Shams-i-Bazighá.
Sullam.	Sharah Isharát.
Mulla Hasan.	Amúri Ammá.
Mulla Jalál.	Shifa of Avicenna.
Mir Zahíd.	

IV.—Muhammadan Law (fikah).

Munyatul-musalli.	Mukhtasir Vaqáya.
Kadúri.	Multaq-ul-abhár.
Kanzuddaqayeq.	Tanvir-ul-absár.
Sharah Waqáyá.	Ashbah wan-Nazáyer.
Hidáya.	
Sharifiâ.	
Sirájia.	
Fatawa Alamgiri.	
Fatavi Kazi Khan.	
Durre Mukhtár.	

V.—Jurisprudence.

Asul-i-Shashi.	Tauzih Talwih.
Núr ulanwár.	Musallam.
Husami.	

VI.—Rhetoric.

Mukhtasar Maani.	Mutawwal.

VII.—Theological Philosophy.

Sharah Aqáyed.	Sharah Muaqif.
Khayáli.	

VIII.—Hadîs (Traditions of the Prophet).

Mishkat.	Nisáí.
Tirmazi.	Abú Dáúd.
Sahih Muslim.	Ibn-i-Mája.
Sahih Bukhári.	Muwatta.

IX.—Exegesis and Commentaries of the Koran.

Jalálain.	Baidáwi.

X.—Astronomy.

Tashrihulaflák.	Sharah Chaghmini.
Sabá Shidád.	

XI.—Arithmetic.

Khulasatul hisáb.

XII.—Geometry.

Euclid. | Almajesta.

XIII.—Algebra, by Ibn Musa.

XIV.—The text books on Medicine have already been mentioned elsewhere.

The above list does not profess to be complete, but it is sufficient to show both the range and depth of the studies carried on in the Arabic schools and colleges of the Panjáb and Upper India.

Curriculum Vitæ

Of a Panjabi Maulvi (described in his own words).

"Up to the age of 20 years I studied grammar, logic, literature, arithmetic, and jurisprudence in my native town (Batala), and in different cities of the Panjáb, as Lahore, Hoshiarpur, &c., and finished the ordinary text-books in the above branches of learning, such as Mulla Hasan, a commentary on Sullum, Mirzahid, Maibuzi, Sadra, Mukhtasar Maani, Mutawwal, Hasami, Kanunchá, Khulasatulhisab, Kheyáli, Sharah Aqayed, Sharah Waqaya.

Then, as now, the natives of the Panjáb laid much stress on the study of Arabic grammar, and several commentaries on the Káfya, Sharah Mulla, Shafya and Mutawwal were generally taught in the Madrasas of the Panjáb. Khulasatulhisáb and logarithms were also taught.

Afterwards I travelled in India. On my way to Delhi, which was a seat of Arabic learning, I passed through Ludhiana, Malerkotla, Panipat, and Karnál, where I found regular and well-conducted Arabic schools.

I stayed at Delhi, and completed there the Hamdulla, Kazi, Tafsir Jalalain, Tauzih, Talvih, Hidáya, and the six books of *Hadís* (Bukhari, Muslim, Abú Daúd, Nisái and Ibn Maja) with Mishkat and Mawatta.

Then I went to *Aligarh*, and there I read the Sadra, Sharah Hedayet-ul-hikmat in philosophy and Sadidi, Nafisi and Kanún of Buali Sina (Avicenna) in medicine.

The next place where I went was *Kandhla* (a town in the district of Muzaffarnagar) and there I studied the most advanced books in philosophy and theological philosophy, such as Amur Amma of Mirzahid, Shams Bazgha, Sharah Mussalam and Sharah Mawaqif, and the first two books of Euclid in Arabic.

At Benares, which was my next halting place, lived Maulvi Muhammad Hasan, son of the far-famed Maulvi Gulshan Ali, who was famous all over India for his proficiency in mathematics. There I joined an immense class of Arabic scholars who had crowded there from all parts of India to study advanced astronomical and mathematical books, such as *Sharah Chaghmini, Bist báb Asturláb* (20 chapters of the Astrolabe), Almajesta and Euclid, and finished all these books. Then I went to Calcutta, passing through Jaunpur and Patna, and with the Maulvis of that metropolis I studied advanced books in Arabic literature, such as Diwani Hamasah, Diwan Mutanabbi, Sabá Muállaqa, and Hariri. At Jaunpur and Patna there were very well conducted and crowded Arabic schools, and these places were noted for philosophy and Arabic literature respectively. On my way to Benares I had stayed for a short period at Lakhnau also, and there one Maulvi Ni'matulla was famous for his proficiency in mathematics and philosophy, and there were some Maulvis in the Farangi Mahal (a quarter where the Sunni Maulvis lived, and which has become proverbial for a learned centre in Upper India), who did justly claim high proficiency in every branch of learning. Two of them, Maulvi Abdul Hai (now in the service of the Nizám) and Maulvi Abul Halim, father and son, held the first place among all of them.

On my way back home I found good schools in Saharanpur, Deoband and Rampur, and in Deoband I was struck by seeing the blind students learning mathematics and drawing geometrical drawings on boards.

Rampur and Murádábád also were, as they are now, seats of good Arabic schools in which literature, logic, mathematics, and philosophy were taught.

After completing my course of studies, I came back to the Panjáb and fixed my residence at Lahore, where I have been engaged since then in teaching students in different branches of learning. I made a journey to Arabia also, and in several towns of Arabia I had an opportunity to see schools.

Though the indigenous schools, whether Arabic, Persian, Sanscrit or Mahajani, have suffered very much by the improper competition and indirect repression of the Educational Departments in India, yet they are able to send out specialists in Persian, Arabic, mathematics, logic and other branches of learning far better than the graduates of the Departments.

These indigenous schools have been deprived of a great part of students on account of Government's ousting them from taking a share in the State patronage. These schools supplied at one time the majority of Sadr-ul-sudurs, Sadar Amins, and the ministers to the Native States. Even the first Deputy Inspector of Schools, the district visitors and professors in the Government colleges, were graduates of these schools, and many of them are still remarkable for their learning, honesty, uprightness, and the efficient discharge of their duties."

VII.—Sanscrit Teaching.

So much has been written on the influence of Sanscrit learning in Hindu polity that my remarks in a preceding chapter on "the religious and national foundations of indigenous education" may be deemed to be a sufficient introduction to the subject of Sanscrit teaching in the Panjáb. The information also given by Pandits Guru Prasad, Rishikesh Shastri, Kaka Ram and others in my Appendix II renders it unnecessary that I should do more than refer to its salient points. The eminent Pandit Rishikesh, however, who is a native of Bengal, has adopted the term "pátshálá" to include also the "padha" schools or "chatsálas" with which they have nothing in common, as he wishes to adopt *one* designation for all Hindu indigenous schools. The common acceptation of pátshálá is, chiefly, a religious one, and implies instruction in Sanscrit, however elementary. Whatever may be the origin of the name "pádha" and its proper application, it is clear that the teachers of Landé schools, as such, have only to do with mental arithmetic and various forms of commercial handwriting, correspondence and modes of transacting business. That the Landé, Mahajani and Sarrafi characters might have been adopted as a basis of elementary instruction for the masses in Upper India, just as Kaithi has been raised to the dignity of a character used in courts, there can be little doubt, but this has only been partially attempted by the development of the Gurmukhi character, as already explained. With far greater propriety could the term "pátshálá" be applied to Sikh schools, as they principally teach religion in it, but even such a use of the term would be misleading. Indeed, to a Hindu Panjábi "pátshálá" represents a school for, primarily, religious teaching and the study of Sanscrit.

In a typical pátshálá, the pupil begins with either the *Nagri* character (called Hindi), or even with the Gurmukhi character, and then proceeds to Sanscrit, the vernacular being generally Panjábi.) The spelling-books and readers once acquired, he goes on to Sanscrit grammar, poetry, rhetoric, the *puranas* and *itihás* (ancient history), jotish (astrology and astronomy), the vedant and nyaya (philosophy and logic), mantra, tantra, puja path (religious books) and may also finish with vaidik or the Hindu system of medicine. The books are detailed on page 7 of Appendix II, but it may also be useful to compare the separate list of Sanscrit text-books on grammar, poetry (including the drama), rhetoric, astronomy and astrology, medical science, logic, law, philosophy, religion and prose literature, which I have added to this chapter.

It is rare, however, that a pupil should find all these subjects taught in one school, though the renowned Pandit Kaka Ram of Bhin in the Ludhiana district, and Pandit Ram Lal of Ranika Raipur, the illustrious Pandit Ramdatta of the Amritsar district, Pandit Vedyadhar of Gujranwala, Pandit Girdhari of Sujanpur, Pandit Moniram of Kangra, Pandit Nikkeram and others teach "all the Shastras." The more common practice is to learn one or more subjects with one Pandit and the remaining subjects that the pupil wishes to acquire, with another Pandit, eminent in the particular speciality, of which the most famous teachers even adopt the name as their most honourable title, *e. g.*, Kaumudi, Chandrikí, Niáyik, or professors of the Kaumudi, Chandrikí, and Niáya system of Logic. Indeed, it was not without difficulty that Pandits were induced to give their services in colleges, where classes go from one teacher to another. This practice affects the parental relationship in which the master stands to his pupil and is considered to be injurious to the discipline which the Shastras enjoin. However, the poverty to which many Pandits now find themselves reduced compels them to waive this objection and to fall in with a system which, under present circumstances, is the best practicable one for giving young Hindus an extensive, rather than profound, knowledge of their literature. To teach law and philosophy to non-Brahmin Hindus still meets with opposition from some of the best Pandits, these being professional caste-subjects of study, which ensure Brahminical ascendancy over the rest of the community. As for grammar, lexicology, rhetoric, the drama and all other secular literature (not law or philosophy) the Sudras were ever allowed to study these subjects. In medicine, non-Brahmins have achieved a reputation which has raised the class of Baids far above their social rank, whilst, I believe, cases have also been known of non-Brahmins practising astrology, though I cannot speak from personal knowledge. Such a course would be a serious encroachment on a profitable source of income, which is, generally, the monopoly of Brahmins.* In the Punjáb also, it must be mentioned that instruction in the Vedant seems to have been mostly given by down-country Pandits, the study of grammar and of logic apparently forming the subjects in which Panjábi Pandits were *faciles principes* among their colleagues in India. The Kashmiri Pandits, it may be incidentally stated, also appear to have been, for a considerable time past, proficient in Persian.

The great aim, however, of a Pandit in teaching is to discharge a religious duty, and we therefore find larger numbers among them teaching gratuitously than even among Maulvis. For instance, Pandit Rishi Kesh Shastri gives a list of 86 famous Pandits, among many others, who maintain Sanscrit schools at their own expense, whilst many also feed and clothe their pupils. The largest number of pupils attending these schools seems to be 56 at Bhín, under Pandit Kaka Ram, for it is not considered conducive to careful study to instruct too many *elèves* at a time. Their ages vary from boyhood to old age, for Sanscrit is inexhaustible, and the capacities or occupations of students do not bring them to the same standard within fixed periods. The subjects studied in these "gratuitous" schools are generally "Grammar and Logic," "Grammar and Literature," the Puránas, Medicine and Astrology. The Vedant is more rarely taught.† The income of the Pandit is generally derived from his priestly avocations. In some places both students and teachers accept gifts from pious Hindus, but in most towns and villages the former alone are supported by the religious. Very rarely are *jaghirs*, granted by previous rulers to Pandits, now continued.‡

Whilst in many of these schools which are kept by Pandits in their own houses secular instruction is generally added to religious teaching, the study of languages, like Persian, would be considered to be a profanation, and it, therefore, seems to follow that if the subtle intellect of the Brahmin. which has

---

* Lala Chuni Lal reminds me that the founder of Jaipur was Jai Singh, who belonged to the Siwái Division of the Rajput caste.

† Many of the so-called Vedantis in the Panjáb are illiterate men, who obtain a smattering of that philosophy by attending the discussions (Shástrarth-Mubáhisas) of real Vedantists held in temples.

‡ Private persons, like Rai Kishn Chand of Batála, have endowed Sanscrit schools, where the pupils are also fed, in various parts of the province.

been developed by hereditary mental cultivation to the very highest standard, is to continue to lead in the present age, instruction in modern science can only be afforded to that class through the medium of Sanscrit, or through that of their Vernacular or of Hindi in the Nagri character. Books like Ballantyne's Synopsis of Sciences are invaluable for such a purpose; and although the old school of Oriental Educationists in India before 1835 erred in making *Arabic and Sanscrit* the *media* for the spread of Western Science in India, instead of the *Vernaculars*, it would by this time have succeeded in identifying the natural leaders of the people with the cause of progress, and a body of revered teachers from the priestly classes of both Hindus and Muhammadans would now be in existence, who would have been acceptable pioneers of advancing civilisation, maintained by their fellow-countrymen in the traditional manner and without any cost to the State, except in the form of rewards to successful teachers and authors. The Government would also have had the most intelligent body in the community identified with, instead of alienated from, the present system of administration. It is, perhaps, not too late to rescue the priestly classes from the degradation to which they have been consigned in the Panjáb. In Bombay the Brahmins have been allowed to maintain their educational ascendancy, to the advantage, I believe, of the rest of the community, and have adapted themselves somewhat to the altered state of things under British rule. In the meanwhile there is still some truth in the remarks on Sanscrit schools made by Mr. Arnold, in his first report, paragraph 20:

"It is in the Sanscrit schools that the exclusive side of Hinduism comes out. Like the Arabic schools, those called Sanscrit are largely attended by adults and entirely by Brahmins. We may be quite certain that a student attending a Shastri school will hardly be persuaded to undergo any other kind of instruction. *He would strongly object to learn the Persian character.*"

The success of the Oriental College at Lahore has already disproved the supposition that members of the practising priestly classes in the Panjáb are unwilling to undergo instruction in "general subjects" in addition to a more critical training, from our point of view, than is generally imparted in indigenous schools in their own literature. Several of the Pandits and Maulvis have read up to the degree standards; but the course to be pursued is one not of compulsion or interference with established systems, but persuasion and the adoption of the "comparative method." It would be absurd to refuse admission to a good Arabic or Sanscrit scholar because he did not come up to the Entrance or Middle or any Standard in "Arts." The great aim is to attract as many of these scholars as possible, and to train them to become enlightened leaders of their people. Thus alone can the learned professions be again revived in the province. To Maulvis and Pandits, combining Oriental learning with Western science, I look as the most suitable priests and teachers of the future; it is from them that alone the cultivation of literature as a profession can be expected. The Hakims and Baids of the Oriental College, who to a thorough study of their own systems of medicine and of the use of native drugs, a subject in which the most eminent European physicians admit that they have much to learn, add a course of instruction in European Medical science, are more likely to be welcome advocates of our system among the masses of the people as well as original enquirers, than persons *only* trained in our Medical schools. The valuable, if quaint, monographs in Sanscrit on the diseases of animals and other matters not usually studied in Europe, I have already referred to, and it is deeply to be deplored that steps are not taken to secure that the traditional explanation of these and other literary treasures in Sanscrit shall not perish in consequence of the want of encouragement to their exponents. In Law, also, those Pradhvivakas and Kazis who combine a thorough knowledge of their own Law with the principles of general Jurisprudence and those of our Administration, are more likely to aid the cause of justice and of scientific legal research and progress than the hundreds of pleaders whom we now turn out from our schools to the great promotion of litigation in this province. In fact, we seem to have touched no profession that we have not degraded, for even the appointment of Public Prosecutors in districts, as, indeed, was laid down in Section 235 of Act X of 1872 (Criminal Procedure Code), would have had the effect in the Panjáb of raising the respectability of the native Bar and its estimation by the people.

The fact that most of the higher Sanscrit studies are taught at the teachers' own houses, has induced me to give to this Chapter the heading of "Sanscrit teaching in the Panjáb," instead of that of "Sanscrit schools," which are, generally, of a more elementary character; and, although they sometimes add arithmetic to their course, are principally intended to instruct the sons of Brahmins, who form the majority of pupils, in the practice of ceremonial observances and rituals, which may enable them to gain a livelihood as family priests or incumbents of religious services at temples. The Pandits who teach at their houses may roughly be classed as follows :—

1. Profound Sanscrit scholars—who teach one or more, if not all, of the following subjects,—(Grammar, Logic, Law, Literature and Philosophy).
2. Teachers of Hindu Theology (the Shastras, &c., &c.).
3. Teachers of Hindu Astronomy and Astrology.
4. Teachers of the Vaidik system of Medicine (some of these are not Pandits, and accept some equivalent for their tuition —which leads to a remunerative profession—from their pupils, in the form of personal service, if not fees). In the case of the two first-named classes of teachers, no fee, in cash or kind, is taken; but, on the contrary, food is sometimes given by the teacher to the pupil, who, in return, performs such personal service as may be required from him by the teacher. It may also be noticed that Saddhus occasionally encroach on the teaching of Hindu theology, which is considered to be a function properly belonging to Brahmin Pandits. Baid teachers often give instruction in Medical books written in Hindi, such as translations of Charaka and Susruta.

As for the mode of instruction, nothing, in my humble opinion, can surpass the excellence of the system pursued in some of the best of these schools. The memory, the reverence for the teacher and for the subject he teaches, and the love for study are cultivated; the intellect is stimulated to original adaptations of the subject-matter read; Sanscrit is treated as a living language,—entering into all the thoughts and associations of the pupil who is encouraged to compose in it, if not to hold *extempore* discussions in it with fellow-pupils on subjects set by the teacher. The explanation of the meaning of the text in all its subtilties, and by constant re-examination, has rarely been neglected in the Panjáb, and is only now falling into disuse in those schools which merely prepare the pupil for ceremonial offices. It is on the Khatris and other wealthy classes that are patrons of Brahmins that the promotion of learning among Pandits to a great measure depends; and if they are satisfied with inferior attainments in their family priests, in consequence partly of the effect on them of the general disregard of Sanscrit learning by the authorities, the sons of the humbler Brahmins will not strive to attain excellence in their traditional Literature. The most learned of the present teachers also have not many pupils on whom their mantle can fall; but the race of Sanscrit scholars has not yet died out in the Panjáb, though it is undoubtedly fast disappearing.

The discouragement of the inferior castes to learn Law and Religion is based on the conception of the moral inferiority of those who are not "twice-born." To them the benefits of *secular education* have, however, ever been offered as alone suited to their spiritual development. This is why the middle and lower-middle classes of the Hindus have ever availed themselves of secular education, as afforded by Muhammadan or Hindu rulers or their own Pandits, and are strong partisans of the present Government system of secular education. Their incentive to study has been the acquisition of wealth or official power, and so slight is the hold of the Hindu moral code on the lower castes that Manu declares that "*A Sudra has no sin*, nor is he subject to any religious ordinance; neither has he any right to *Dharma*, but he is not *prohibited* to observe the Dharma" (or religious duties)—*Manu, Vol. X, p. 126.* What

Dharma is, is explained in the Yagnya-balkya, Vol. 3, p. 66.—"Truth, not to steal, not to be angry, modesty, purity, reason, patience, controlling one's passions and organs of sense and action, and *knowledge:* all these are called *Dharm.*" It seems to me to be clear from this that a Sudra, for instance, cannot be spiritually responsible for the neglect of religious, which include moral, duties, and that he is to be kept in check by the fear of punishment, if not to be stimulated to good actions by the hope of reward and praise in this world. In consequence of this view, which is borne out by history and experience, it has ever been the aim of the intelligent members of the lower castes to acquire toleration, if not social consideration, by deference to the higher castes, and, especially, by liberality to the priesthood. Unable to lead in religious matters, they often become the most ardent followers of religious discipline, whilst more independent minds embraced or originated reforms, which had the religious equality of all castes, if not the abolition of caste privileges, as one of their principal aims. This is also the reason why, under our rule, aspiring members of the inferior castes, as they become emancipated from social and spiritual thraldom, start Somajes and other religious associations, and in that sense it may be truly said that our system of secular education has given a religious and moral impetus to the Hindus of a certain class, which aspires to both intellectual and religious ascendancy. Of course, other motives also inspire some of the disciples, if not the leaders, of the new sects, but the main motive is the one to which I have referred. Religious convictions also not being traditional, and reflection not being aided by thinking in a foreign language, or adopting, as a revelation, the vague or incorrect impression of foreign religious ideas, render these classes peculiarly amenable to every wind of doctrine. Thus the pseudo-science of miscalled Theosophy, or the mistranslations from Sanscrit of the Arya, will lead them captive. They will, however, always seek a basis in the past, as, indeed, reformers of all creeds must do if they are to secure a popular following, and also because superior learning may even raise the Sudras to the highest spiritual, if not social, position, among their own fellow-countrymen, which is a powerful incentive, even more so than the hereditary caste-aim, say, of Khatris, for political power with the authorities, once Muhammadan or Sikh and now English. It is curious, for instance, to perceive how thoroughly Muhammadan is the spirit of some of the best Hindu writers in Persian, whilst Kayasthas long resisted the introduction of Hindi, their own vernacular, in supersession of Persian, which, up to a very recent date, was *the* language which they cultivated. The arts of success in life and an intellectual sharpness, though not profundity, being thus hereditary gifts in the middle or lower-middle Hindu castes, will, no doubt, bring them into power with the Government of a commercial nation; whilst the Brahmins, who have a heirloom of pure and profound intellect, applied to the higher efforts of reasoning, developed by centuries of culture, will fall behind in the race for ascendancy, unless they accept modern forms of ancient thought, when their natural superiority will re-assert itself. At the same time it must not be thought that debarring a Sudra from the study of Law and Religion in its pontifical sense was only due to a wish of the Brahmins to keep their professional monopoly in the true caste-spirit of India. It was also due to a study of the peculiarities of the nations, now castes, which were added to the general Hindu polity. If, however, a Sudra, by force of *character,* raised himself above his ethnic capabilities, he had everything open to him; though, if he raised himself merely by *intellect* or the practice of religious formulas, without their spirit, even the gods had reason to be afraid of his improved power for mischief, as is gradually becoming a fact at present. Manu (Vol. X, p. 127) says: "But those Sudras who desire to learn, who know *Dharma,* and those who follow the examples of good men, *except using the Mantras of the Vedas,* are not to be blamed; they should, on the contrary, be praised." Indeed, so long as knowledge is made an instrument for *good,* it is lawful to acquire it from the lowest caste or even outcaste. "Good knowledge may be acquired, with reverence, *from a man of low birth.* Higher religious laws may be learnt from an *autyag* (a man of a very low caste, such as a Chamár), and a good woman may be espoused from a low family.—(Manu, Vol. II, p. 238). Nór is the place of acquisition of what is good restricted as little as its source. "Women, jewels, knowledge, *Dharm,* purity, good speaking, different kinds of arts and sciences may be acquired *from everywhere.*"—(Manu, Vol. II, p. 240.) If the Brahmin, therefore, will swim with the stream, instead of waiting on its banks, in the proud consciousness of superiority, till it flows by, he will continue to be the "Ava" ξ Ἰνδῶν. So generous, however, to proved goodness and "knowledge," as explained, is the exclusive Brahmin, that, in the words of Manu (Vol. X, p. 65), he admits that "*A Sudra becomes a Brahmin and a Brahmin becomes a Sudra* (according to their respective merits and faults). Likewise, the offspring of a Kshathrya and of a Vaysya." Knowledge of what is good, to be used for good, is the key to the fortress of Brahmin exclusiveness. "Wealth, relationship, age, action and *knowledge*, these are the objects of honour; the last-named deserving greater honour than the first-named." Babu Navina Chandra Rai comments on the above passages as follows:—

"*Sudras*, or men of low caste, and women are, indeed, not allowed by the Shástras to use the *mantras* (prayer) of the Vedas, for these are specially intended for the twice-born castes (*i. e.*, Brahmins, Khettryas and Vysyas), but there is no prohibition in the Shástras to their acquiring general knowledge. There are several anecdotes in the Vedas and Purans of certain women and Sudras possessing the highest religious and philosophic knowledge, and being more learned than the best of the Brahmins; for instance, the anecdote of Gargi, in the Upanishad, and of a huntsman (called Vyádh) in the Mahabhárat, &c.

"I send you herewith some passages from the Hindu Law. From passage No. 1 you will observe that knowledge or learning is enumerated as one of the *Dharms* (religious duties). Passage No. 2 will show that a Sudra, although he has no right to Dharma, *is not even prohibited to observe the Dharma.* Indeed, in passage No. 3, he is praised if he observes the *Dharm* or acquires knowledge.

"Passage No. 4 shows that a man of low caste is not only entitled to learn, but also to teach.

"Passage No. 5 authorises a Hindu to acquire religious and scientific knowledge *from everywhere.* Is not the Hindu Law quite liberal?

"Passage No. 7 shows that knowledge deserves the highest honour.

"What more convincing proof can one require?"

The term "twice-born," like so many other Eastern expressions which are repugnant to the European when translated in all their literalness, have disguised parallels in the more artificial civilisation of the West. In Austria, as elsewhere, human beings are "geboren" = born; but respectable men are written to as "wohlgeboren" = well-born; a Knight, as "high-well born;" a Count as "high-born." Indeed, as a German nobleman remarked—"The human being begins with the Baron," or, as the Frenchman asked, who was introduced to a traveller who had seen the whole world (tout le monde), "quel monde?" with a "well-bred" sneer worthy of any member of "the Rag." In all countries men acquire knowledge in order to live, though there may be no necessity for the latter in a cynic's opinion; but this minimum condition once satisfied, there are great differences among nations, and classes of the same nation, as regards the incentives and aims of study. Even Englishmen and Germans are not quite on a par as regards acquiring knowledge for its own sake; whilst the Ministers of religion of all countries may be assumed to cultivate learning for, generally, less worldly aims than their respective laity. So it may be assumed in India that, whereas Khatris, Kayasts and Hindus generally value knowledge in proportion to its "loaves and fishes," Brahmins study for study's sake; Sikhs, in order to maintain the special characteristics which have raised them physically and nationally over their fellow-Hindus; and Muhammadans, in order to cultivate their intellects and to gain a passport to Paradise by means of their cherished learning which makes men equal. The question of Muhammadan, as of Brahmin and Sikh, education, can, therefore, not be solved, unless, especially as regards the first-named, an hour is set apart in all Government schools and colleges for instruction in their own religion by teachers accredited by their community and paid by the State, as Bhais are in the native army. This the "educated" Hindus will resist, as it will put Muhammadans on a level with themselves by removing the great Mussulman objection to availing themselves of our present system of education, whilst Brahmos, Aryas and the like will incline to "moral," as distinguished from "religious,' teaching, in order to attract the young generation to their own monotheistic fold, well knowing, perhaps, that mere moral teaching will not overcome the prejudice of Muhammadans against attending our schools.

After this lengthy apparent digression, which may have its use in showing the main-springs of Hindu educational movements, I cannot forbear, before resuming the subject of Sanscrit schools, from bearing my testimony to the great desire and appreciation of education among all *classes* of the Hindu, Muhammadan and Sikh communities, as also to the great talents which this "land of the sun" has so prodigally bestowed among its children. Mute inglorious Miltons are to be met with in almost every town or village, in almost every part of the "East." The early judgment of children often fills one with dismay, for it is too good to last; and certain habits – of which that of early marriage and the subsequent family cares which it entails is the least pernicious — are the almost inevitable grave of the higher intellect, the mental persistence and the moral keenness of natives, except, perhaps, of the Pandit, and, to some extent, of the Maulvi. The want of publicity also for the efforts of *indigenous* genius is also a cause of its decay. If I may be allowed to plagiarise from myself, "do what we may, our reforms, including the Roman character, will be considered by the masses as an insidious attempt to upset their religion. Learn to consult the natives, and you will strike a mine of intellect and a desire for reform, of the existence of which the half-trained European does not dream when he forces his crude notions on races that have long discussed and dismissed innovations in every branch of human thought and activity, because they had not the mechanical appliances for putting them into practice. Now, as 3,000 years ago, the East is the home of mental discipline, culture and repose, where genius is as universal as it is ignored, in consequence chiefly of the want of publicity and of easy communication. Without these advantages we should now be behind the Orientals, whom we despise. The one intelligent European among a thousand of his dull brethren is able to pass off his views and inventions as the embodiment of the civilisation of his Continent. When the whole East will have its cheap press and railways—provided always that it does not seek to slavishly imitate the West in its reforms—it must resume the position it once held, owing to the native genius of its peoples."

In the Panjáb, the Khatri must be re-associated with the Brahmin, if either are to be saved from degeneracy. I cannot do better than conclude this chapter with a list of books used in "Sanscrit teaching," as also with an account of Sanscrit schools in Bengal, as described by Mr. Adam in 1835, which applies, in many respects, to what still exists in the Panjáb, a province which, in most branches of indigenous education among Hindus and Muhammadans, in addition to the instruction imparted to its "very own" children, the Sikhs, has always stood foremost, at any rate, in Upper India, as will, I hope, be proved in another part of this Report.

List of Sanscrit Books.

Bálbodh.	Akshar dipika.

I.—Grammar.

Sáraswat.	Manoramá.
Chandriká.	Bháshya.
Laghú Kaumudi.	Pániniya Vyakarn.
Kaumudi.	Siddhánt Kaumudi.
Shekhar.	Prákrita Prákasa.

II.—Lexicology.

Amar Kosh.	Medini Kosh.
Haláyudh.	

III.—Poetry, the Drama and religious History.

Raghu Vans.
Megh Duta.
Mágh.
Kirát Árjuníya.
Ramayan.
Sri Mad Bhágwat and other Puránas.

Mahabharat.
Venisanhara.
Sakuntalá.
Naishádha Charita.
Mrichhakatika.
Kumara Sambhava.

IV.—Rhetoric.

Kavya Dipika.
Sáhitya Darpana.
Kuvlayanund.

Kavya Prakash.
Dasa Rupa.

V.—Mathematics, Astronomy, and Astrology.

Siddhant Shiromani.
Mahúrta Chintamaní.
Shighra Bodh.
Garbh Lagana.

Nil Kanthi.
Brihat Játak.
Parasariya.

VI.—Medical Science.

Sham Raj.
Susruta.
Charaka.
Madhava Nidan.

Nighant.
Shárang dhar.
Bháshya Parichchhed.
Vagbhat.

VII.—Logic.

Nyáya Sutra Vritti.
Vyutpattivád.
Tark Sangrah.

Gada dhari.
Tarkalankar.
Kari kávali.

VIII.—Vedant.

Atma Bodh.
Panch Dashi.

Sárírak.

IX.—Law.

Manu Smriti.
Yagya Valk.
Mitakshara.

Parasara Smriti.
Gautama.

X.—Philosophy.

Sankhya Tatwa Kaumudi.
Sankhya Pravachan Bhashya.
Yoga Sutra.
Vaiseshika, Siddhant Muktavali Sutra with a commentary.

Patanjali, Sutra Britti Sutra with Bhashya.
Vedanta, Vedantsár (see also above).
Mimánsa, Sutra with Bhashya. Artha Sangraha.

XI.—Prosody.

Srut Bodh.

Vritta Ratnákar.

XII.—Prose Literature.

Hitopadesa.
Dasa Kumára Charita.

Vásavadatta.

XIII.—Religion.

Rigveda Sanhita (rare).
Yajurveda, Shukla Yajur Vajasneyi Sanhita.

Samaveda, Mantra Bhága, Chhandasya Archika (very rare).

The suggestive extracts from Mr. Adam's Reports,* to be followed by an account of a Panjábi Sanscrit Model school, as also by a *curriculum vitæ* of a

* *Adam's Reports on Vernacular Education in Bengal and Behar, submitted to Government in 1835, 1836 and 1838, with a brief view of its past and present condition, by the Rev. J. Long. (Home Secretariat Press, Calcutta, 1868.)*

Extract from "Introduction" by the Rev. J. Long, 1st paragraph.

"Adam's Reports on Vernacular Education in Bengal have long been held in high esteem for their valuable statistics and researches on a subject of great social and political importance—the intellectual condition of the masses of Bengal. The investigations were conducted with great diligence, and extended over a space of three years, at an expense to Government of more than a lakh of rupees. In some points, as was to be expected from the difficulty of the enquiry, there are inaccuracies, but, on the whole, they afford a mass of information of great value."

Panjábi Pandit, may give some interest to an account of "Sanscrit teaching," which, writing against time, I have been unable to shorten.

The following extracts from Mr. Adam's report on Sanscrit learning in Bengal in 1835, apply to a considerable extent to the Panjáb :—

"The unendowed Hindu schools of learning in the Nattore thana are taught by 39 Pandits, of whom 37 are Brahmins, and 2 are of the Vaidya or medical caste.

"The two medical professors are brothers and jointly conduct a medical school at Vaidya Belghariya. There is no instance of two or more Brahmin Pandits in a similar way co-operating with each other, and uniting their talents and acquirements for their mutual advantage. Every one stands or falls by himself. *In this district, and even in a single thana, there are materials for a Hindu University in which all the branches of Sanscrit learning might be taught;* but instead of such a combination each Pandit teaches separately the branch or branches of learning which he has studied most, or for which there is the greatest demand, and the students make their selections and remove from one to another at their pleasure. * * *

The Pandits are of all ages, from 25 to 82, some just entering upon life, proud of their learning and panting for distinction; others of middle age, either enjoying a well-earned reputation and a moderate competence or disappointed in their expectations and anxious respecting the future; and some more advanced in years, possessing the heart-felt veneration of their countrymen, while others appear to be neglected and sinking to the grave under the pressure of poverty. All were willing to believe and desirous to be assured that Government intended to do something, as the fruit of the present inquiry, for the promotion of learning, *a duty which is in their minds constantly associated with the obligations attaching to the rulers of the country.* The humbleness and simplicity of their characters, their dwellings, and their apparel forcibly contrast with the extent of their acquirements and the refinement of their feelings. I saw men not only unpretending, but plain and simple in their manners, and although seldom, if ever, offensively coarse, yet reminding me of the very humblest classes of English and Scottish peasantry, living constantly half naked, and realising in this respect the descriptions of savage life; inhabiting huts which, if we connect moral consequences with physical causes, might be supposed to have the effect of stunting the growth of their minds, or in which only the most contracted minds might be supposed to have room to dwell, and yet several of these men are adepts in the subtleties of the profoundest grammar of what is probably the most philosophical language in existence; not only practically skilled in the niceties of its usage, but also in the principles of its structure, familiar with all the varieties and applications of their national laws and literature, and indulging in the abstrusest and most interesting disquisitions in logical and ethical philosophy. They are in general shrewd, discriminating, and mild in their demeanor. The modesty of their character does not consist in abjectness to a supposed or official superior; but is equally shown to each other. I have observed some of the worthiest speak with unaffected humility of their own pretensions to learning, with admiration of the learning of a stranger and countryman who was present, with high respect of the learning of a townsman who happened to be absent, and with just praise of the learning of another townsman after he had retired, although in his presence they were silent respecting his attainments.

The students are divided into two classes; one of which consists of those who are natives of the villages in which the schools are situated, and the other of the natives of other villages, the former called *natives* and the latter *foreigners*, corresponding respectively with the *externes* and *internes* of the Royal Colleges of France. The students of a school or college who are natives of the village in which it is situated are the *externes*, attending it daily for the purpose of receiving instruction, and daily returning home to their parents, relatives, or friends with whom they board and lodge, while the students who are natives of other villages than that in which the school is situated, are the *internes*, residing in the house of the teacher and receiving from him not only instruction, but also lodging and food. * * * The reasons that induce so many to leave the parental roof because there is no school of learning, or none of sufficient repute in their native villages; but in the great majority of instances they prefer to pursue the studies at some distance from home that they may be free from the daily distractions of domestic life, and from the requisitions often made by their fathers that they should perform some of the ceremonial observances of Hinduism in their stead in the family of some disciple at a distance; the large majority of students, although not wealthy, are above want, being the children of Brahmin-pandits, initiating or officiating priests, whose professional emoluments are comparatively considerable. In a majority of cases the apartments used as a school-house and as a place of accommodation for the students, are separate from the dwelling-house of the teacher, but built at his expense and often also applied to the purpose of hospitality to strangers. Sometimes the building is one that has descended from a deceased father or brother to its present possessor. The foreign students or those who have no house in the village, are lodged and fed and pursue their studies at night either in the building erected for a school-room in separate lodging apartments attached to it, or in the dwelling-house of the teacher, the last-mentioned course being adopted only when there is no other resource. * * * The period occupied by an entire course of scholastic studies is, in several instances, not less than twenty-two years, so that a student must often have passed his thirtieth year before he leaves college. This is a great deduction from the most valuable years of a man's life, but the period actually employed in collegiate study is lessened by the length of the vacations which the students receive or take. * * * The custom of inviting learned men on the occasion of funeral obsequies, marriages, festivals, &c., and at such times of bestowing gifts on them proportioned in value and amount to the estimation in which they are held as teachers, is general amongst those Hindus who are of sufficiently pure caste to be considered worthy of the association of Brahmins. The presents bestowed consist of two parts—first, articles of consumption, principally various sorts of food; and second, gifts of money. In the distribution of the latter at the conclusion of the celebration, a distinction is made between *Sabdikas*, philologers or teachers of general literature; *Smartas*, teachers of law; and *Naiyaiykas*, teachers of logic, of whom the first class ranks lowest, the second next, and the third highest. The value of the gifts bestowed rises not merely with the acquirements of the individual in his own department of learning, but with the dignity of the department to which he has devoted his chief labours, and in which he is most distinguished. It does not, however, follow that the professors of the most highly-honoured branch of learning are always, on the whole, the most highly rewarded; for in Rájsháhí logic which, by the admission of all, ranks highest, from whatever cause, is not extensively cultivated and has few professors, and these receive a small number of invitations and consequently of gifts in proportion to the limited number of their pupils and the practical disuse of the study. Their total receipts, therefore, are not superior, and even not equal to the emoluments enjoyed by learned men of an inferior grade, who have, moreover, a source of profit in the performance of ceremonial recitations on public occasions which the pride or self-respect of the logicians will not permit them to undertake. Whatever the amount, it is from the income thus obtained that the teachers of the different classes and grades are enabled to build school-houses and to provide food and lodging for their scholars, but several have assured me that to meet these expenses they have often incurred debt from which they are relieved only by the occasional and unexpected liberality of individual benefactors. When a teacher of learning receives such an invitation as above described, he generally takes one or two of his pupils with him, giving each pupil his turn of such an advantage in due course; and when the master of the feast bestows a gift of money on the teacher, it is always accompanied by a present to the pupil less in amount but proportioned to the respectability of the teacher's character and the extent of his attainments. The teacher sometimes takes a favourite pupil more frequently than others, the object being to give a practical proof of the success of his instructions as well as to accustom the pupil to the intercourse of learned and respectable society. As the student is furnished with instruction, food and lodging without cost, the only remaining sources of expense to him are his books, clothes, and minor personal expenses, all of which, exclusive of books, are estimated to cost him in no case more, and often less, than seven rupees per annum. His books he either inherits from some aged relative or at his own expense, and with his own hands he copies those works that are used in the college as text-books. In the latter case the expense of copying includes the expense of paper, pens, ink, ochre and oil. The ochre is mixed with the gum of the tamarind seed extracted by boiling, and the compound is rubbed over the paper which is thus made impervious to insects, and capable of bearing writing on both sides. The oil is for light, as most of the labour of copying is performed by night after the studies of the day have been brought to a close. An economical student is sometimes able, with the presents he receives when he accompanies his teacher to assemblies, both to defray these expenses and to relieve the straitened circumstances of his family at a distance. I have learned on good authority that ten and even twenty rupees per annum have been saved and remitted by a student to his family; but the majority of students require assistance from their families, although I am assured that what they receive probably never in any case exceeds four rupees per annum.

I have already mentioned that in this district, as in Bengal generally, there are three principal classes into which the teachers and schools of Hindu learning are divided, and which, therefore, may, with advantage, be separately considered. The acquirements of a teacher of logic in general pre-suppose those of a teacher of law, and the acquirements of the latter in general pre-suppose those of a teacher of general literature who, for the most part, has made very limited attainments beyond those of his immediate class. As these are popular and arbitrary designations, they are not always strictly applied.

Schools of general literature.—The age at which students enter on their studies varies from 7 to 14, and that at which they leave college varies from 20 to 32, the whole period of scholastic study thus varying from 11 to 22 years. All the students of a school of general literature receive throughout the year various sums, which average, the lowest four annas and the highest four rupees per month. The youths who commence the study of Sanscrit are expected to have acquired at home or in school merely a knowledge of writing and reading and a very slight acquaintance with the first rules of arithmetic, *viz.*, addition and subtraction, without a knowledge of their applications. Hence learned Hindus having entered with these superficial acquirements at an early age on the study of Sanscrit, and having devoted themselves almost exclusively to its literature, are ignorant of almost everything else. The studies embraced in a full course of instruction in general literature are grammar, lexicology, poetry and the drama, and rhetoric, the chief subject of the whole being the knowledge of language as an instrument for the communication of ideas. On entering a school of learning, a student is at once put to the study of Sanscrit grammar. Grammar is a favourite study in this district, and the most extensive and profound treatises on it in the Sanscrit language are those in most general use. In the 13 schools of this class there are four different grammars used. *Panini* being taught in 6, the *Kalapa* 2, the *Mugdhabodha* in 3, and the *Ratnamala* in 2. In teaching *Panini* the first work employed in the Bhasha Vritti, a commentary by Purusottama Deva on Panini's rules, omitting those which are peculiar to the dialect of the Vedas. This is followed by the study of the *Nyasa*, an exposition of the *Kasica Vritti*, which is a perpetual commentary on Panini's rules. The *Kasica Vritti* does not itself in any case appear to be used as a text-book, but references are occasionally made to it. The *Kalapa* grammar is taught first in the Daurga Sinhi, an exposition by Durga Singa of the Katantra Vritti, the latter being a brief and obscure commentary on the original aphorisms. This is followed by the *Katantra Parisista*, a supplement to the *Kalapa* by Sripatdatta; by the *Katantra Panjika*, a commentary on the Daurgi Sinhi by *Trilochandasa*; by the commentary of Sushena Kaviraja on the same; and by *Parisista Prabodha*, a commentary by Gobinatha on the supplement above mentioned. The original aphorisms of the *Panini* and *Kalapa* grammars are believed to possess divine authority, which is not attributed to any of the other works employed in this course of instruction. The Mugdhabodha of Vopadeva is studied without any commentary in the two schools where it is used; and the *Ratnamala*, a compilation by Purusottama from the *Panini* and *Kalapa* grammars, is studied with the commentaries called *Jiveshwari* and *Prabhava Prakasika*. A list of verbal roots with their meaning is also committed to memory in this part of the course.

Lexicology is the most appropriate name that has occurred to me for describing that branch of study by which, simultaneously with the study of grammar, a knowledge of the meanings of single words and of their synonyms is acquired. The only work employed for this purpose is the *Amara Kosha* by Amara Sinha, with the commentary of Raghunatha Chakravarttí. The names of objects, acts, qualities, &c., are classified and their synonyms given, which the students begin to commit to memory without the meaning; and they afterwards read the works and its commentary with the teacher who explains them. This gives the student a large command of words for future use either in reading or composition, and it is after some acquaintance with the grammar and the dictionary that the teacher usually encourages and assists the student to compose, verbally or in writing, short sentences in Sanskrit. The work in verse invariably read first is the *Bhatti Kavya* on the life and actions of Rám, so composed as to form a continued illustration of grammatical rules. This is followed without any fixed order by any of the following works or by others of the same class, viz., *Raghu Kavya*, also on the history of Rám. *Magha Kavya*, on the war between Sisupala and Krishna; *Naishadha Kavya*, on the loves of Nala and Damayanti; *Bhairavi Kavya*, on the war between Yudisthira and Durgodhana, &c., &c., &c. The poetry of the drama may be said to be almost wholly neglected here: in one college only I found that the *Mahanataka* is read.

In rhetoric the first work read is the *Chandomanjri* in prosody, and the only work by which this is followed here I found to be the *Kavya Prakassa* on the rules of poetical composition. All these branches of general literature are not taught by every teacher. Some teach only grammar, others grammar and lexicology, others add poetry with or without the drama, and others embrace rhetoric. But the whole of these are required to constitute a complete course of philology and general literature. The teacher of grammar only, the mere grammarian, ranks in the lowest scale of learned men; and in proportion to the number of the other branches of general literature which he adds to his acquirements, he raises his reputation and emoluments as a Sabdikar, philologer.

Hindu Law.—The age at which students enter on their studies varies from 9 to 15, and that at which they leave college varies from 18 to 32, the whole period of scholastic study varying from 8 to 23 years. Omitting one school in which the age of beginning and completing studies could not be satisfactorily ascertained, the average period of scholastic study in the remaining 18 institutions is between 16 and 17 years. The professors of law receive throughout the year various sums as presents which, according to their own statements, average the lowest Rs. 3 and the highest Rs. 35 per month.

The teachers of law are in all cases conversant with the grammar and lexicology of the Sanskrit language and can give instruction in them; some are also acquainted more or less familiarly with the poetical and dramatic writings: and a smaller number with the works on rhetoric. Every teacher of law receives students at the earliest age and instructs them according to the extent of his own acquirements in general literature, and when he has reached that limit, he carries them on to the study of law. His students sometimes object to this arrangement and leave him in order to complete with another teacher a course of study in general-literature. The majority of law-students, however, begin and end their studies in general literature to whatever extent they may desire to proceed with a professor of that branch of learning, and afterwards resort to a teacher of law for instruction in his peculiar department. On those occasions on which the study of the law is especially directed to be suspended, as on the first, eight, and thirtieth of the waxing and waning of the moon, when it thunders, &c., &c., the students most commonly revert to their studies in general literature, which at such times are not prohibited. The completion of *Raghunandana* on every branch of Hindu law, comprised in 28 books, is almost exclusively studied in this district. It consists, according to Mr. Colebrooke, of texts collected from the institutes attributed to ancient legislators, with a gloss explanatory of the sense, and reconciling seeming contradictions. Of the 28 books those are almost exclusively read which prescribe and explain the ritual of Hinduism. The first book invariably read is that on lunar days; and this is followed by the others without any fixed order of succession, such as those on marriage, on penance, on purification, on obsequies, on the intercalary month of the Hindu calendar, &c.; but the number of books read is seldom more than 10 and never exceeds 12, and is sometimes not more than 4, 3, and even 2. Raghunandana's treatises on inheritance, and Jimutavahan's on the same subject, are also taught by one or two Pandits.

Schools of Logic.—The age of commencing study is 10 or 12 and that of leaving college 24 or 32, the course of study taking up from 12 to 22 years, which must be understood, as in the preceding case of law schools, to include the preliminary study in grammar, &c. The course of instruction in logic embraces the reading and explanation of the following works, viz., *Bhasha Parichheda*, an introduction to the system of logic, with definitions of terms, qualities, and objects; *Vyapti Panchaka*, on the necessary or inherent qualities of objects; *Sinha Vyaghra*, a supplement to the preceding; *Vyaddhikarana-dharmabachinabhava*, on the same object; *Liddhanta Lakshana*, the same; *Abachhedoktanirukti*, the same; *Visesa Vyapti*, the same; *Paksata*, on inferential propositions; *Samanya Laksana*, on the definition of classes or genera; *Samanya Nirukti*, the same; *Avayava*, on syllogism; *Hetwabhash*, on fallacies; *Kusumanjali*, on the proofs of the divine existence, the attributes of the divine nature, and the means of absorption into it; and *Vyutpattivada*, a treatise on the derivation and meaning of the radical portions and of the suffixes and affixes of words. In one of the schools of logic, the second above mentioned, only a few of these works are superficially and partially read. The Vedantic school.—To teach the following branches of learning, *viz.*, general literature, law, the puranas, and the vedanta.

The *Pauranic school.*—The pandit gives instruction in general literature, in law, and in astrology; but as he also teaches the puranas, chiefly the *Mahabharata*, and derives a great part of his emoluments from the public recitation of them in wealthy families, the name given to his school is derived from that branch of his acquirements. In astrology, he teaches the *Joyatisa Tatwa* by Raghunandana, a summary of astrological knowledge; the *Jatak Chandrika*, on the calculation of nativities; and the *Satkritya Muktavali*, the *Dipika*, and *Samaya Pradipa*, on lucky and unlucky days. * * * *The Tantric School.*—The pandit teaches superficially grammar and the Vedant, but his distinctive name is derived from his professional instruction in the Tantra. The works classed under this name may be generally described to be employed in explaining the formulæ peculiar to the votaries of Siva and the female deities, by which they seek to attain supernatural power and accomplish objects either good or bad for themselves or others. The work taught by this pandit is the *Tantra Sar*, a compilation on those subjects. *The Medical School.*—The period of commencing the study of medical works is from twenty-two to twenty-five years of age, and that of discontinuing the study from twenty-five to thirty years of age, the whole period of study varying from 5 to 8 years. It is expected and required that medical students shall have previously acquired a knowledge of Sanscrit grammar and general literature, in some of the schools of learning taught by Brahman-pandits, after which they commence a course of medical reading in this institution. The period of study is shortened or prolonged according to the ability of the students for a shorter or a longer period to dispense with the emoluments f private practice. The school is taught by two aged brothers, Vaidyas in caste, most respectable men, and in high repute as medical practitioners. Neither Vaidya teachers nor Vaidya pupils receive invitations or presents, as Brahman-pandits and their pupils do, and the former are consequently dependent solely on their own means for the maintenance of their establishment. Vaidya teachers, however, like Brahman-pandits lodge and feed those pupils who have no home in the village in which the school is situated, and they also give their instruction to all gratuitously. The work first read is the *Nidana*, a standard medical work, after which the students of this school read *Chakradatta* by

Chakrapani; *Ratnamala*, by Rám Krisna; *Dravya Guna*, by Narayana Dása; a commentary by the same author on his own work *Madhamati ;* commentaries of Vijaya Raksita and Siddhant Chintamani on the *Nidana ;* a commentary on Chakradatta by Yasodhara; and *Patyapatya*, a work described as variously treating of the causes of disease, diagnosis, the practice of medicine, and materia medica. In a general view of the state of Hindu learning in this district, grammar appears to be the only department of study in which a considerable number of persons have a distinguished proficiency. * * * The medical professors who are venerable men and highly respected by all around them for their learning within their own peculiar range as well as for their general character might also be added. There are others who occupy a middle rank, but the majority of the pandits are superficial men, and I have reason to think would be so judged by competent persons amongst their own countrymen, that is, superficial compared with the highest existing standards of native learning, although all in general know well what they profess to know.

In some districts the poetry of the drama appears to be almost wholly neglected. I found only one instance in which the *Mahanataka* and that alone is read; whereas in some other districts dramatical literature is more generally and more fully studied, the *Mahanakata* being usually succeeded by *Sakuntala*, *Kautuka Sarvaswa*, *Hasyarnava*, *Venisanhar*, *Murari*, &c. In rhetoric, the *Srutabodha* and *Kavyachendrica*, the former on prosody and the latter on the rules of poetical composition and both in general use. * * * In law *Manu* and the *Mitaksara*. * * * I have already mentioned the comparatively refined tone of feeling and character which the cultivation of Hindu learning appears to give to its possessors; and the effect in the same measure extends to their families, for the children of Brahman-pandits are in general bright-looking and intelligent, modest and polite. The system of learned instruction also has a principle of diffusiveness in the gratuitousness with which the instruction is bestowed. * * *

The following are the different studies pursued in Sanscrit schools and the average age, at each period, of the students belonging to each branch of learning :—

Grammar	11·9	15·2	18·8
Lexicology	18·	19·2	20·2
Literature	16·	25·	26·5
Law	23·6	28·7	33·2
Logic	21·	26·5	34·6
Mythology	29·1	31·1	33·6

Grammar, lexicology, and literature, which includes poetical and dramatic productions, although begun in succession, are generally studied simultaneously, and the same remark is, in some measure, applicable to law and logic. Taking, however, each branch of learning separately, it would appear that the study of grammar occupies about seven years, lexicology about two, literature about ten, law about ten, logic about thirteen, and mythology about four.

In describing the works employed as text-books in each branch of learning all that can be attempted in this place is to give the names of the principal books. In grammar the *Mugdhabadha* with the Ramtarkavagisi commentary and the *Kalapa* with the commentary of Trilochana Dasa are chiefly used. In lexicology the *Amarakosha* is the only work employed. In general literature the *Hitopadesa* and *Bhatti Kavya* are read. In law, the following tatwas or treatises of Raghunandana, *viz.*, *Tithi*, *Prayaschitta*, *Udbaha*, *Suddhi*, *Sraddha*, *Ahnika*, *Ekadasi*, *Malamasa*, *Samayasuddhi* and *Jyotisha*, are first studied; and these are followed by the *Dayabhaga* and *Prayaschitta biveka*.

In logic, the works in use are the Mathuri commentary of *Vyapti Panchaka ;* the Tagadisi commentary of *Purva Paksha*, *Savyabhichara* and *Kevalanwaya ;* and the Galadhari commentary of *Avayava* and *Satpratipaksha*, all, of course, including their respective text: the *Sabdasaktiprakasika* by Gadadher is also read. In mythology the *Bhagavata Purana* and the *Bhagavad Gita*, a book of the Mahabaraita, are read. * * *

A most voluminous native author is Raghunandana Goswami, dwelling at Maro in the Patna thana, who is the author of 37 works. (Similar instances of prolific authorship are not unknown in the Punjab among Pandits, Maulvis and Bhais.)

Mr. Adam then offers the following general remarks on the state of Sanscrit instruction in Bengal, which, *mutatis mutandis*, largely apply to the Punjab :—

" *First.*—There is not, as far as I have been able to observe and judge, *any mutual connection or dependence between Vernacular and Sanscrit Schools.* The former are not considered preparatory to the other, nor do the latter profess to complete the course of study which has been begun elsewhere. They are two separate classes of institutions, each existing for distinct classes of society,—the one for the trading and agricultural, and the other for the religious and learned classes. They are so unconnected that the instruction in Bengali and Hindi reading and writing, which is necessary at the commencement of a course of Sanscrit study, is seldom acquired in the Vernacular schools, but generally under the domestic roof, and unless under peculiar circumstances, it is not extended to accounts, which are deemed the ultimate object of Vernacular school instruction. It has been already shewn that an unusually small number of Vernacular Schools is found in certain parts of the Beerbhoom district, which have no institutions of learning; and it now appears that in the Burdwan district, where Vernacular schools comparatively abound, there also schools of learning are most numerous. On the other hand, in that division of the Tirhoot district which contains the greatest number of schools of Hindu learning there are no Vernacular schools at all; and in the whole district the Vernacular schools are fewer, while the proportion of schools of learning is greater than in any other district. It seems to follow that the prosperity or depression of learning in any locality does not imply the prosperous or depressed condition of Vernacular instruction, and that the two systems of instruction are wholly unconnected with, and independent of, each other.

" *Second.—Sanscrit learning is, to a certain extent, open to all classes of native society* whom inclination, leisure, and the possession of adequate means may attract to its study, and beyond that limit it is confined to Brahmans. The inferior castes may study grammar and lexicology, poetical and dramatic literature, rhetoric, astrology and medicine; but law, the writings of the six schools of philosophy, and the sacred mythological poems, are the peculiar inheritance of the Brahman caste. This is the distinction recognized in the legal and religious economy of Hinduism, but practically Brahmans monopolize not only a part, but nearly the whole, of Sanscrit learning.

" *Third.—The teachers and students of Sanscrit schools constitute the cultivated intellect of the Hindu people,* and they command that respect and exert that influence which cultivated intellect always enjoys, and which in the present instance they peculiarly enjoy from the ignorance that surrounds them, the general purity of their personal character, the hereditary sacredness of the class to which most of them belong, the sacredness of the learning that distinguishes them, and the sacredness of the functions they discharge as spiritual guides and family priests. The only drawback on the influence they possess *is the general, not universal, poverty of their condition, increased by the frequent resumption of former endowments.* They are, notwithstanding this, a highly venerated and influential portion of native society; and although as a body their interests may be opposed to the spread of knowledge, yet their impoverished circumstances would make them ready instruments to carry into effect any plan that should not assail their religious faith or require from them a sacrifice of principle and character.

" *Fourth.*—The most favourable would probably not be a high estimate of the practical utility of the different branches of Sanscrit learning cultivated in these schools, *but neither is that learning to be wholly despised.* So long as the language shall exist, the literature it contains will constitute one of the most precious remains of antiquity connecting itself by links clearly perceptible, but not yet fully traced, with the history of almost every people of Western Asia and of Europe; and so long as the Hindus shall exist as a distinct people, they will derive some of their most inspiring associations and impulses from the great literary monuments which belong to their race, and which the progress of time will render more venerable, even when from the progress of improvement they may cease to be regarded as sacred. Viewed with reference to the present constitution and wants of native society, Sanscrit literature may be considered either as sacred, profane, or a mixed character. The Tantra scriptures, prescribing the ritual observances of Hinduism, are exclusively religious. Law includes not only the prescriptions of religion, but the rules of inheritance, contract, &c., which are recognized by the British Government and are essential to the working of civil society. The six Darshanas, of which I have found four taught in the schools, *viz.*, the Nyaya, Vedanta, Mimansa, and Sankhya, contain expositions not only of theological doctrine and ritual observance, but systems of philosophy on logic, on spirit and matter, and on moral and legal obligation. The mythological poems, the Mohabharath and the Bhagavat Purana, which are generally read, contain a system of metaphysical philosophy, disquisitions on political morality, and probably remnants of true history, mixed up with the fables of heroes and of gods. Astrology would be more correctly denominated *arithmology*, for it is the science of computation in the widest sense, and embraces not only divination and the casting of nativities by the situation and aspect of the stars, but also mathematical and astronomical science. The native medical writings may be worthy of much, but not of all, the contempt with which the native medical profession is regarded by Europeans at the present day, for to a calm observer the very supremacy of their authority, which is so absolute and undisputed as to have repressed all independent inquiry, observation, and experiment, would seem to imply no inconsiderable degree of merit in the works to which such an influence has been so long conceded. Finally, the works on grammar, general literature, and rhetorical composition, will be valued as long as the philosophy of language shall be studied, or the Sanscrit language itself employed as an instrument for the expression of thought and sentiment. These, and the collateral branches of learning constitute the national literature of the Hindus, a literature which needs not to be created, but which may be improved by the transfusion into it of those discoveries in art, on science, and in philosophy, that distinguish Europe, and that will help to awaken the native mind from the sleep of centuries.

" *Fifth.—The native mind of the present day, although it is asleep, is not dead.* It has a dreamy sort of existence in separating, combining, and recasting in various forms, the fables and speculations of past ages. The amount of authorship shown to exist in the different districts is a measure of the intellectual activity which, however now misdirected, might be employed for useful purposes. The same men who have wasted, and are still wasting their learning and their powers in weaving complicated alliterations, recompounding absurd and vicious fictions, and revolving on perpetual circles of metaphysical abstractions, never ending still beginning, have professed to me their readiness to engage in any sort of literary composition that would obtain the patronage of Government. It is true that they do not possess the knowledge which we desire should be communicated to their countrymen; but where the desire to bestow information exists on our part, and the desire to receive it on theirs, all intermediate obstacles will speedily disappear. Instead of regarding them as indocile, intractable, or bigoted in matters not connected with religion, I have often been surprised at the facility with which minds under the influence of habits of thought so different from my own have received and appreciated the ideas, which I have suggested. *Nor is it authors only who might be employed in promoting the cause of public instruction; it is probable that the whole body of the learned, both teachers and students, might be made to lend their willing aid towards the same object.*"

The following is a SKETCH OF A MODEL INDIGENOUS SANSCRIT SCHOOL by Pandit Bhagwan Das :—

SCHEME OF STUDY.

Lower School.

NOTE.—The course in each class should extend over one year.

CLASS I—(For beginners).

Alphabet . .	Varnmála (the rosary of letters).
Prose . .	Sanscrit Path ôpkárka (useful lessons, *viz.*, fables, &c.)

Poetry	. .	Riju Path, Parts I and II (easy lessons, *viz.*, abstracts from Purans, Hitôpadesa and other moral works).
Grammar	. .	Sár Kaumudi (essence of Grammar).

CLASS II—

Prose	. .	Hitôpadesa, Parts I and II.
Grammar	. .	Laghu Kaumudi, Part I (the smaller Kaumudi Grammar).
Poetry	. .	Raghuvans (I—VII) cantos (the poetical history of the family of Raghu, by Kalidása).
Prosody	. .	Srut Bodh (knowledge of verse).
Dictionary	. .	Amarkosh (vocabulary of synonyms).

CLASS III—

Prose	. .	Hitôpadesa, the whole.
Poetry	. .	Humar Sambhav (I—VI cantôs) (birth of Kartickeva).
Logic	. .	Karikávali or Tark-Sangraha.
Grammar	. .	Laghukaumudi, the whole.
Dictionary	. .	Amarkôsh, Part II.

CLASS IV—

Rhetoric	. .	Kavya Dipika and Sahitya Darpan.
Drama	. .	Venisanhara.
Dictionary	. .	Amarkôsh, the whole.

Middle School.

CLASS V—

Grammar	. .	Siddhant Kaumudi 1st half.
Poetry	. .	Magh, 10 cantos.
Drama	. .	Sakuntala, the whole.
Prosody	. .	Vritta Ratnakar, the whole.
Logic	. .	Muktavali, Parts I and II.
Philosophy	. .	Sankhya, Chandrika, and Vedantsar.

CLASS VI—

Grammar	. .	Siddhant Kaumudi, the whole, and Prakrit Prakash.
Poetry	. .	Bhatti Kavya, 10 cantos.

Higher School.

CLASS VII—

Rhetoric	. .	Kavya Prakash.
Logic	. .	Dinkari.
Philosophy	. .	Sankhya Pravachanabhoshya.

CLASS VIII—(the instruction in this class to extend over two years).

Grammar	. .	Manorama, Laghu Shabdender Shekhar, Paribhashendu Shekhar.

CLASS IX—(course extending over 2 years).

Grammar	. .	Shabd Ratna, Mohabhashya and Vyakarn-bhushan.
Logic	. .	Jagdishi, Vyut-patti-vad and Nyaya Sutra-vritti.

School hours—From 7 A.M. to 6 P.M.; 2 hours are allowed for recreation from 11 A.M. to 1 P.M.

Examination—No examination is held at the close of the year, but students completing one year's course are allowed to read in the next upper class. The teacher only tests their abilities by holding oral examinations in their respective courses on certain days of the month, on which the imparting of new lessons is prohibited.

The following is an account of Pandit Bhugwan Das's own educational career:—

"Pandit Bhagwan Das commenced studying Sanscrit at home with his grandfather Pandit Mehr Chand (whose abilities were considered to be equal to those of Pandit Maksudan, the noted Pandit of Maharaja Ranjit Singh's Court) when he was 10 years of age, and with him he read the following books:—

This course occupied him for a period of 5 years.

Alphabet	. .	Sanscrit Barnmala.
Prose	. .	Sanscrit Pathopkark.
Grammar	. .	Sar Kaumudi, Laghu Kaumudi, and Madh Kaumudi.
Poetry	. .	Raghuvans and Kumar Sambhav.
Prosody	. .	Srut Bodh.
Dictionary	. .	Amarkosh.
Logic	. .	Tark Sangraha
Vedant	. .	Vedantsar.

During the next four years he was put under Pandit Subhkarn, the Guru of Pandit Jalla of Raja Hera Singh, who lived in Lahore for a period of about 40 years, and with whom he read the following books :—

Grammar . .	Siddhant Kaumudi, Manorama, Tattwa Bodhini, Laghu Shabdendu Shekhar, Shabdkaustubh, Paribhashendu Shekhar and Mahabbashya.
Poetry . .	Magh, Kirat, and Naishad Charita.
Prosody . .	Vritta Ratnakar.

Subsequently he read one year with Pandit Udai Ram of Kaithal the following works on Logic :—

Muktavali, Siddhant Chandrodai and Dinkari.

The following works were read by him privately, without the aid of any teacher :—

Drama . .	Vasavdatta, Mrichha Katika, Vikramorvasi, Sakuntala and Meghduta.
Prose . . .	Dasa Kumar Charita.
Hindu Law . .	Manu Smriti; Parasari; Mitakshara, the key of Yagyavalk; Aprark; Prayaschit Muktavali; Praishchit Mayukh Sarbadinpratishtha.
Vedant . .	Panchdashi, Ashtavakra, Atmabôdh, Madhu Sudani and Sridhari.
Puran . . .	All the 18 Puranas.
Up Puran . .	Valmikya Ramayan and Mahabharat.
Astronomy . .	Shighrabôdh; Mahurt Chintamani, the key of Mahurt Chintamani; Piyjashidhara; Piyjashkanaka; Mahurt Darpan; Khat Panchashika, and many other books on various subjects.

No system of class instruction existed formerly in indigenous schools, but those desirous of studying Sanscrit were taught by Pandits at their own homes."

F.—FEMALE INDIGENOUS EDUCATION.

....en I was at the Imperial Assemblage at Delhi, I started a polyglot journal, in commemoration of a title which I had long advocated, in the hope that its adoption would mark an era of closer identification between the Imperial races of India and the now Imperial House of England. Among the contributions to the first number of the *Kaum-i-Kaisari*, the "Imperial nation," so named in honor of the "Kaisar-i-Hind," were some verses in Sanscrit from a Mahratta girl then wandering about with her brother, richer in intellect than in purse. Although education among Panjabi women of the higher castes of Hindus, the better Muhammadans and all orders of Sikhs is not so uncommon as would be supposed from the interested outcry of native reformers, in whose castes there are few educated women, and fewer still who will marry them, it is an accomplishment in India regarding which, to quote from memory the words of Pericles, "she is the noblest woman of whom least is heard either in praise or blame." After a period of liberty, to which Greek authors bear witness, the Hindu woman, always the tenderest and most respected of mothers and the man's temporal and spiritual wife, had, with her Muhammadan sister, found her greatest pride in retirement. Still, I felt sufficiently interested in the pair to take them to Lahore, where they lived in the compound of the Press, and where her brother, whiter than many Europeans, received a scholarship for more than a year, which was sufficient for their simple wants. Books were supplied to the young lady, who was anxious to be employed as a Hindi teacher in one of the Mission girls' schools, and who was reading English at the time; but the efforts of my wife to find her employment proved unavailing and, as her brother, a rolling-stone, had quarrelled with the Head Pandit of the Oriental College, to whom he was too proud to apologise, they resumed their travels, the brother leaving me an account of his wanderings previous to coming into port in the Panjab. In that interesting account I find no reference to Female Education. Just as Aberigh-Mackay among Englishmen, so Panditani Ramabai was ignored among natives at Lahore, till other provinces recognized the prophet that the Panjab had not noticed, though no one could help being struck with the unaffected modesty and love for learning of the young lady, whose emancipationist theories, if they existed at all, were then kept in the background.

Indigenous female education in the Panjab requires less development than revival. The girl who was ever taught to read Nagri or Gurmukhi or Arabic in her home or in a friend's house, conveniently situated, where other girls could also assemble, now has a brother at a Government School reading Urdu and becoming daily more dissociated from her in language and feeling. The mother also, for the same reason, cannot co-operate with the teacher, whilst the boys sneer at what they see at home in a speech which is almost unintelligible to her. For even the Hindustani-speaking mother has a dialect which is not that of her son: The spirit of disbelief also imported from the Government School is a source of great sorrow to her and adds to the deteriorating influences of a climate and of homes in which passions can only be restrained by the rigorous observance of conventionalities and the minute practice of religious ceremonies, which the Hindu lawgiver and native society in all Indian communities so wisely enforce. Though the Panjab has ever been more liberal in religion and manners, than the impenetrable North-Western Provinces, where Hindus and Muhammadans vie with one another in conservatism, yet the son or brother who would blaspheme the household god would pass a *mauvais quart d'heure* with his family, even if the Panjabi mother did not slap with her slipper the mouth of the young demagogue who, perhaps, an hour before had denounced the brutality of British rule and deplored the ignorance of his countrymen to a sympathetic audience. It is, therefore, not unnatural that he should desire to spread "female education" in a sense that will provide him with a more congenial home than he enjoys at present.

The Panjabi woman has, however, not only been always more or less educated herself, but she has also been an educator of others.* In Delhi, for instance, we find that, before the annexation of the Panjab, six *public* schools for girls were kept by Panjabi women, who had emigrated to the South for this purpose.

In other places, similarly, Panjabi women were to be found as teachers, just as the Guru or the Padha spread his instruction beyond the precincts of a province, where he was becoming a drug in the market. Among Muhammadans, very many widows considered it a sacred duty to teach girls to read the Koran, and though Delhi, like the rest of the North-Western Provinces, was far behind the Panjab in female education, we find that it had in 1845 numerous schools for girls kept in private houses.

For the native girl is even more intelligent and enquiring than her brother, and few were the families in which the father, brother or mother did not take a pride in teaching the younger female members to READ; there the education stopped short in theory, but the timid little girl would nestle up to her brother and imitate his writing, till she became fairly proficient in that accomplishment, though female self-respect forbids its being acknowledged. On the frontier, the superior class of *Hetairai* are known to have received an education in Persian poetry and in caligraphy, whilst even a lower class is said not to be deficient in the art of writing and in music, so that it will at once be understood why Persian poetry, which has an almost intoxicating effect on the native mind, is sternly prohibited to be heard or read by most respectable females. That nine-tenths of the educated natives are alleged to be averse to female education can only be true, if among educated natives both the old and the new schools are included. Even in the latter I doubt whether any one, whose power of reflection has not been destroyed by thinking in a foreign language, would willingly sanction a too sudden departure from the old lines on which indigenous female education has hitherto proceeded.

In the Hindu higher classes, both the parents were enjoined to instruct their children, including daughters, in their religious duties. The greatest respect to the mother and to the elder sister is distinctly laid down in the rules for the conduct of students. Among Muhammadans nearly all girls were taught the Koran; nor could a Sikh woman claim the title and privileges of a "learner" unless she was able to read the Granth. The knowledge, therefore, of her religious duties, imparted in numerous little treatises, and in some of the sacred texts and illustrated by stories of deities, saints and prophets, was deemed to be sufficient for one who had the duties of a household to learn, which, besides sewing and cooking, included the art of embroidery and the keeping of accounts in an elementary, and sometimes very primitive, form. Yet we find that there were many women, especially in the Panjab, whose influence in the State could not be ignored, whilst poetesses were by no means scarce, especially in the higher Muhammadan families. In Panjabi, the life, hopes, and disillusions of women are sung in numerous forms, of which the following, lately published in an English newspaper, gives an idea of independence allied to modest retirement:—

GIRLS' SPINNING SONG.	TRANSLATION.
Asán apná charkhá katná:	All day long my skeins I make;
Dúe dá munh nahín chatná.	Nor kisses give, nor kisses take.
Kyún dúe de káran róíye,	Why should I for another weep.
Bhed apne dil dá khóíye?	Nor in my heart my secrets keep?
Asán apne ghare de Rájá:	In my own home the Queen am I.
Dúe kane kujh nahín kájá.	Why should I for another's sigh?
Kyún jag mánas khúsh karná?	I that bow to my God alone,
Parná Málik diá charná.	Shall I a man for master own?
Kyún kusí de sang asán phasná?	Shall I fall into another's snare?
Kyún kusi de ghar já basná?	Pass my life in another's lair?
Asán ant same marjáná:	Will that other be ever true?
Dúe kusi sang nahín jáná.	When I go hence will he go too?

* The returns in Part II of this Report, incidentally, show the existence of several female indigenous schools, in some of which also boys of a tender age are admitted. Not to speak of the very numerous Koran schools for both boys and girls taught and supported by pious widows; there are the following schools, conducted by female teachers: Nawankôt and Moharwal in the Lahore District, Panipat has 6 schools so conducted, Wairowal and Fattahabad in the Amritsar District, Dhatrat and Asant in the Karnal District, &c., &c.

GIRLS' SPINNING SONG.	TRANSLATION.
Kyúṇ duniáṇ dá bájá bajáná ? Sukh chhorke dukh ko páná. Haiṇ mithí, mithí meṇ miljáná : Kyúṇ narm dusálá bichhnáná ?	And what is marriage here below ? What but barter of bliss for woe ? Dust turns to dust and dust am I. Why should my dust for marriage sigh ? R. C. T.

"When I go hence will he go too" is the wail of those who wish to be joined in death to those whom they love; but to whom this desire, which led to Sati and which explains the incurable grief of widowhood, has only a one-sided application. Still the mystic tie of marriage is not dissolved on the death of the husband, even if the wife does not join him on the funeral pyre, for whenever she dies, she is burned in a white shroud, so that her husband may receive her as still mourning for him. The law which enjoined a proper show of grief on widows, who, in all countries, assume to be "inconsolable," also protected her interests, and it is only among the mercenary classes of the once-born that widows suffer any show of indignity. Tearing off her ornaments is only an equivalent for wearing mourning, but on the 13th day after the death of the "dear departed" all the relatives gather and pour out rupees before her, with the view of making a provision for the widow *for life* which she often spends foolishly, unless it is entrusted to an elder male relative, especially after the year of sorrowing is over and she resumes most of her jewels and with them, perhaps, some of the gaiety of her blasted life.

Like the "Law of Celibacy" among Roman Catholic priests, that of widowhood, including the extravagance of Sati, was based on a conception of self-sacrifice to duty or affection, of which only the highest human nature is capable. Widows, as is indicated by the apostle of continence, are, in many cases, no doubt suffering from a hardship in not being allowed to re-marry with due regard to the *convenances*, and if certain reformers could only rehabilitate a widow that marries (and innumerable widows do so in the lower classes) in middle native society, they would not have the difficulty which they often encounter now of finding suitable wives in their own caste.

It must also not be forgotten that, if the 21 millions of alleged widows in India were allowed to be married without a social stigma, which deters most of them from the fatal step, an immense stimulus would be given to polygamy and that the peace of the majority of the better Hindu homes, which are chiefly monogamous, would be destroyed. The quarrels for inheritance would also be embittered, and we should have in numerous households a repetition of the scenes in the seraglio. How far the re-marriage of widows would lessen the solemnity of the marriage tie, the common sacrifices offered by husband and wife and the beauty, in spite of all that is said to the contrary, of Hindu married life as a centre of living affection for the poorer kindred, it is needless to enquire, but that 21 millions of widows cannot be married without some injurious effect on the chances of marriage of unmarried girls there can be little doubt. Finally, just as polyandria (confined to the brothers of the husband) in the respectable families, as in Tibet, is a check on overpopulation in a poor country, whilst it also gives a considerable power to women in some districts, so is the prohibition of widow-marriage a salutary precaution against an undue increase of the population in a crowded country like India, where already the supply of food is, in many parts, insufficient for the demand.*

---

* Dr. Hunter in his "England's work in India" under the head of "the hungry Residue of 40 millions" states:

"A square mile of land in England, says Mr. Caird, highly cultivated, gives employment to 50 persons, in the proportion, 25 men, young and old, and 25 women and boys, " or at the rate of 51 acres to 4 persons. France with its 180 persons to the square mile is considered a densely-peopled country, and ten acres of plough land would be reckoned a small holding. Well, *there is not a single district in India with only* 180 *persons to the square mile what is not exceedingly well off,*" compared with the unfortunate population in more crowded areas.

Dr W. H. Bellew informs me that the yearly rate of increase of the population in the Panjab is 0·6 per cent., whereas in England it is 1·27 per cent. The population in the Panjab (in British territory) enumerated in 1881 amounts to 18,850,437 (of whom only 8,015,210 are females) against 17,609,518 in 1868, so that during the interval of 13 years the population has increased by 1,240,919, or about 7 per cent.

Now the whole area of British possessions in the Panjab is 107,110 square miles, of which only 36,656 are cultivated, one-fourth culturable, and the rest unculturable waste; yet the census of the year 1881, which is under the mark, would give 514·3 persons to each square mile of cultivated land, so that it is easy to perceive to what straits for a livelihood the remarriage of the proportion of "the 21 millions of Indian widows" for the Panjab would reduce the population. It is far wiser for a Government to leave "well alone" or even to leave an ascertained ill alone, than fly to evils that it knows not of, by any encouragement to overpopulation or even to any form of female education that will make the women of the Panjab dissatisfied with their position. That position can only be improved with the increase of the general wealth of the country. Now the proportion of females to males in the Panjab is as 4·4 females to 5 males, which places women at a premium, and, therefore, obviously in the best possible position attainable under the present circumstances of the province.

There is a great deal of exaggeration about the hardships, if not cruelties, to which widows are subjected. As a rule, women in all countries can take care of themselves and interweave the interests of others with their own. The sight of a widow ready to burst into tears may grow to be trying to her surroundings, or, if poor, she may wish to make herself useful to the rest by working for them or rendering such other services as woman discharge in most native households. It may also be disagreeable to her to have to defer to the wishes, if not whims, of younger married women in her adopted family.

A portion of the male community is, however, pecuniarily interested in the widow question. Just as passing the Entrance, F.A., B.A. and M.A. Examinations raises the value of the bridegroom in certain castes in the matrimonial market, so would many an aspiring regenerator of his country wish to take care of the *peculium* of the widow, to which I have referred, by rescuing her from the cheerlessness of a home, no longer her own, even should she be staying with her parents. Probably, many widows would not object to re-marriage, but I doubt whether the signatures to a Memorial to Government, purporting to emanate from a number of widows, were genuine. If so, this circumstance would show that they could write and that they had, probably, also read the memorial, evidences of the extent of indigenous female education. It would be well to know to what caste these widows belong and whether they would object to marry a man of an inferior caste, or, indeed, of a superior one, for all castes are *now* jealous of intrusion from both above and below. It may be incidentally mentioned that certain crimes are more common in one caste than in another; for instance, forgery in the writer or Kayasth class, as would, indeed, be the natural tendency of the evilly disposed in that section of the community. If, therefore, a Kayeth were to accuse another of burglary or a Bengali another of actual assault (not mere abuse), there would be a *primâ facie* improbability of the charge and for the same reason, memorials from, *e.g.*, Brahmins, Rajputs or Jats, are more likely to be genuine than from some other castes.

Be that as it may, the lot of a poor widow is sad enough in all countries, to deserve sympathy, but it is minimized in India by the following considerations :—

1. The widows of Muhammadans, of Sikhs, of most of the hill tribes, and of nearly all the lower Hindu castes *do* marry, and the widows of Jats are *bound* to marry their deceased husband's brother, for the protection of the inheritance.
2. The widows who have grown-up sons or whose age entitles them to have a voice in the management of the household, practically, and, in numerous cases admittedly, rule it.
3. There, therefore, only remains a comparatively small number of widows in the higher and middle Hindu castes, and among them only those are to be pitied who are poor or who have unfeeling or no relatives, a rare circumstance.*
4. The misfortune of these, however, is alleviated—

(*a*) by the ideal of the sacredness of the marriage tie; the hope of rejoining the husband and being made worthy of his regard in proportion to her, generally, self-inflicted privations, such as sleeping on the floor instead of on a charpoy. It is here where religion strengthens and raises the character of a noble-minded Hindu widow;

(*b*) the social consideration which is given to a widow who, by her acts, shows her undying grief for her deceased husband;

(*c*) the sympathy of her own family to which she, in many instances, returns;

* According to the Census Returns, there were only 134,645 widows below 30 years of age, *viz.*, 1,208 child-widows between 0-9; 6,778 between 10 and 14; 19,346 between 15 and 19; 41,686 between 20-24; and 65,627 between 25-29 (of these, at least three-fourths can re-marry). There then remain those between 30 and 60 or upwards who have mostly grown-up children, and who, practically, preside over their households. The proportion, therefore, of marriageable widows is only 1 in 59·43 in a female population of 8,015,210, and, as not a fourth of these are condemned to celibacy, the hardship is not so universal as is alleged.

(*d*) the generally liberal provision for life that has been made for her on the 13th day, which relieves her, at any rate, from the most gnawing cares and allows her to address herself to the education of her children, if any.

"Laborare *et.* orare" is, therefore, the well-bred widow's remaining aim in a not ignoble life and, though she may have occasional misgivings, a high hope sustains her and is an example to her more restless or less religious sisters in misfortune.

That the lofty conception of matrimony among Hindus has not been without effect, may be inferred from the fact that most respectable and wealthy Muhammadans in India marry only *one* wife, whereas in other Muhammadan countries nearly all who can afford it exceed that number. Similarly, the Muhâmmadan system of the veil, curtain, or "purdah" has not altogether disadvantageously affected the Hindu wife, for if the statement of Greek authors be trusted, the women in the Panjáb enjoyed a liberty which sometimes bordered on license.

The case of child-widows, however, in the better castes, is pitiable, and it is for them that relief may be obtained by a judicious promulgation of certain relaxations allowed by their religion and tradition; but this can only be done by receiving the co-operation of Brahmins, though not for the marriage of the child-widows of their own caste, who may either be trained as teachers or represent the class of nuns in Tibet, Ladak, Spiti and other neighbouring countries, not to speak of nuns in Roman Catholic Europe. Indeed, it is doubtful whether the number of child-widows in India who cannot marry exceeds, in proportion, that of the nuns in the countries which I have mentioned.*

The cruelty of enforced widowhood may be educationally utilized by appointing widows, who can already read, as teachers of girls, visiting them in their own homes, or by training them for that profession. Among Muhammadans and Sikhs I do not apprehend that there will be much difficulty in securing a supply that will exceed the demand. Among Hindus also, with the co-operation of the Brahmins, objections against the above plan will also gradually disappear. The best means, however, for spreading female education in a manner welcome to native ideas is to employ the Maulvis, Pandits and Bhais for male teaching and their wives, or, sometimes, elder sisters, for female teaching. This will induce the priestly classes to attend more than they have hitherto to the education of their female relatives, an example which is sure to be followed by the other classes or castes. The present obstacles to female instruction will then disappear as if by magic, and a field will be prepared for the philanthropic labors of those who wish to impart a still higher education to the women of this country. That I have not overrated the influence of the priestly classes on the native community will be illustrated by some instances referred to by the Director of Public Instruction in his No. 4 S., dated 22nd September 1881:—"I have found, however, that in some cases *the people have no objection to the employment of a young man belonging to the hereditary priestly classes*, and to a family that is well-known and respected." When it is remembered how jealous all natives are as regards men, and especially young men, seeing their daughters, no greater testimony than the above could be adduced in support of the confidence of the people in their spiritual leaders, considering that it comes from a hostile witness, who is even opposed to the employment of an ORIENTAL teacher in a primary school, if he does not possess a Normal School certificate. If, in co-operation with the priestly classes, the wives of European and native officials would concert measures for imparting *secular* instruction to native girls, visiting them in their homes, they would, more than by the example of their domestic virtues, kindle the flame of sympathy between the rulers and the ruled, whilst providing themselves with an employ-

* There were only 675 Hindu child-widows between 0-9 years of age and 4,070 between 10 and 14. Of these, at least, two-thirds belong to the re-marrying castes. There were altogether 73,320 Hindu widows in 1881 below 30 years of age, of whom about a third are prevented from re-marrying. There were also 53,382 Muhammadan widows below thirty, most of whom will, no doubt, re-marry, and only 8,035 Sikh widows of corresponding ages. Where is the country in Europe in which, practically, *more* widows have a better chance of re-marrying than in India?

ment that would relieve the monotony of station-life, and that would be greatly conducive to the preservation of their health and spirits. Just as many missionary ladies assist their husbands in a noble task, I see no reason why the official's wife should not be a helpmeet to him in his great undertaking of identifying the interests and feelings of the people with the maintenance of a wise and liberal Government.

That native households are not invariably centres of frivolity or domestic tyranny, may be inferred from Mrs. Hossain Ali's spirited and detailed description of "Home rule" in Upper India, the sceptre of which is often wielded by the gentler sex. Household cares, the troubles of friends, embroidery, sewing, spinning, listening to the professional story-teller or songstress, or to the preaching of pious women, the recitations from sacred books, fill their time and supply the place of going to parties, to church or to a concert. The Reverend Lal Behari Dey, in an article just reprinted in the "Selections from the *Calcutta Review*" says: "People at home, ignorant of Hindu manners, have a notion that Hindu females, like negro slaves, are doomed to unrelenting servitude. That women in India do not attain to that state in society which they do in Europe, is unquestionable; but that they are viewed here in the light of slaves, cattle and household property is not true . . ." He then passingly refers to the juvenile plays of girls; their *Dolls, Bow-bows*, in which the mysteries of marriage are emblematically represented; *Hide and seek, Tilkuti*, in which the dexterity of fingers is exhibited; "that large class of plays in which the recitation of doggerel verses forms a principal part," and gives an account of the women's daily occupations of which we quote the following:—"The males are feasted first, on whom their wives and mother attend. Attendance at the table is not regarded by the Bengalis as a servile occupation, that office being usually performed by elderly matrons and Brahmins." He then mentions some of their games, such as *ashti-kusti*, not unlike backgammon, played by four persons; *Mongul Patan*, not unlike draughts, representing a mimic battle between the Moguls and the Patans; *Baghbundi*, or tiger hunt, not unlike the fortress game in Germany, &c., &c. Of course, amusements vary with the women of different castes, sects and classes, but few can have heard the light-hearted song over their work beyond the walls of a native house and imagine that its inmates were slaves. Women will also attend the recitations of a famous Pandit, though this is not often the case. On festivals and occasions of rejoicings, such as marriages and births, dancing-women are called in; but I think that enough has been said above to show that female life in the Punjab is not so hopeless and servile as it is perhaps imagined to be.

Some of the female schools, supported by Municipalities and entered as Government schools, teach the Korán, without doing which they would not be attended. Bawa Khem Singh once had 108 female schools under his superintendence and would, no doubt, have largely increased their number had he been encouraged by the Educational Department. I revived 50 of them in the Rawalpindi circle and opened them to inspection; but the spirit which had been inspired by Sir Robert Montgomery among the promoters of female education in the Punjab has died out in consequence of the disregard shown by the Department to the leaders of the movement. The following extract from my Report as Inspector of the Rawalpindi circle will show, when "read between the lines," the great injustice which the Department, and notably my predecessor, had inflicted on female, as also on indigenous, aided and unaided education in the Province, chiefly from want of sympathy with, and exact knowledge of, extra-departmental agencies:—

"When Bedi Khem Singh's schools were first established, at the inspiration of Sir Robert Montgomery, there was a sort of understanding or guarantee that these schools should not be inspected by officials, especially Europeans. I presume that it was for this reason that these schools have not been inspected, and that an amount of suspicion, both deserved and undeserved, has fallen on them. Without distinct orders from Government I should myself have hesitated to inspect them, although I received a sort of permission by the Bedi's agent to do so. The schools were closed a few days after I saw the agent—a course which was not calculated to strengthen the belief of the people in the permanence of our educational policy or to encourage Bedi Khem Singh in again offering us his services. After all the agitation that had taken place regarding 'female education,' it was certainly inconsistent to sweep away at one blow 108 schools, although the Department was perfectly justified in doing so, considering how very unfavourably both Major Urmston, D.C., and Mr. Frizelle have referred to these schools, that money was required for more important or less mysterious institutions, and that after all no Inspector can conscientiously support a grant about whose application he simply knows nothing. Whether an attempt might not have been made to inspect these schools in spite of what is, probably erroneously, considered to be the policy of Government in the matter, I will not discuss; but I have not the least doubt that the sensitiveness of the people on this subject is exaggerated."

Mr. Pearson truly remarks:—"I do not at all believe in the alleged scruples of the people about having their girls' schools inspected. They consist of little girls four or five years old, who may be seen playing in the streets with their writing boards. The only prejudice is against the system of payment by results. The simplest remedy would be to allow the grant in future only where the schools are open to the inspection of Government officers. I do not say that this plan is free from objections, but Bedi Khem Singh must be able to judge for himself whether he could accept the assistance of Government upon these terms." This view pre-supposes that Bedi Khem Singh profits by the arrangement, but the Bedi may be looking upon it as a great trouble and inconvenience which he has incurred merely to please the 'Sirkar.' I am glad that a letter of thanks at any rate has been sent to him, but I regret that once we had 108 female schools we should not have kept them up. A good deal is already gained by vesting the interests of a large body of teachers in the maintenance of "female education." We can afford to wait till the next generation for perfect "returns," which, after all, are no safeguard against fraud and jobbery.* In our hurry to build the edifice of an ideal Indian civilization "in one day," we risk a sudden collapse of what has already been raised. I have never been very sanguine about "female education" in this province, although the kindness of Native friends compelled me to become the first European president of the movement; but if female schools are to exist and to be inspected, there is no doubt that it can be done. In towns where greater temptations exist, Natives naturally take greater precautions regarding their daughters, and generally the higher and better families are averse to sending them any distance to school when they may be entrapped *en route*, as has occurred. Still numerous small schools conveniently situated, rather than a central school convenient for inspection, and inspected by educational Native officials of known respectability and a certain age, would not be objected to. The girls of the best families may be visited at their houses by female teachers of known piety. A certain amount of education has always been given to females, at any rate in Muhammadan families of standing. The 'purdah' is nowhere so strict as in Turkey, yet unmarried girls attend school up to the age of 14, as I have seen myself (*vide* my "Muhammadan Education in Turkey").

At the risk of repeating some of the suggestions or statements that I have already made, I venture to consider it to be necessary, for the further elucidation of the subject of female education in this province, to quote my evidence on this point before the Education Commission:

"*Q.* 41.—Is there indigenous instruction for girls in the Province with which you are acquainted; and, if so, what is its character?

"*A.* 41.—Yes; the wives of Maulvis and Bháis, for instance, are generally taught by their husbands and instruct their children up to a certain age in reading and religious duties. The wives also of the respectable Muhammadans generally can also read and write (though the latter attainment is not so much encouraged as the former for reasons into which it is not necessary to enter). Some of the ladies are good Persian scholars, and in a distinguished Muhammadan

* Many years ago I drew attention to a return in which 2,000 pupils were stated to be under instruction. On careful enquiry I found that 11 only had been in regular attendance.

family that I know, I have been given to understand that several of the ladies are excellent poets. The position of women is far higher among Muhammadans and Síkhs than is supposed, and there is no prejudice against their being educated, provided this can be done without interfering with the privacy of their domestic life. There are in proportion as many women that can read in Native States, where there has been no fuss made about female education, as there are in British territory, whilst in the latter also I have no doubt that many respectable women can read and write, who dare not say so. There have always been indigenous schools for Síkh females in the districts between the Chenab and the Attock. That the wives of priests should visit females of their community and teach them is right and proper, but that girls especially of a marriageable age, should cross bazars in order to assemble in a school, is, I think, objectionable. Much reading of elementary religious books, sewing, embroidery, cooking with extreme care for the household, great neatness, tenderness in trouble, and gentle mediation in family disputes, constitute the chief features of female home rule and education in the better classes, who regard their female relatives with a respect and a religious affection of which we have not even the outward profession in Europe.

"*Q.* 42.—What progress has been made by the Department in instituting schools for girls; and what is the character of the instruction imparted in them? What improvements can you suggest?

"*A.* 42.—The instruction nominally given in them and the number of pupils attending them are given in the educational reports; the reality is far below the returns. I have myself organised 50 female schools, and I consider it to be the least satisfactory portion of my work. At Lahore I was the first European President of the Female Education Society, but I resigned when I discovered that only 11 girls could really read and write out of over 1,100 that were returned as proficient in that attainment. On my expostulation, Mr. C. U. Aitchison interfered and started the present Female Normal School, which might have done well had only wives of priests been admitted to it, who would then have made house-to-house visitations to teach the girls in their own families; but the school is now managed in a denationalising spirit, whilst the Society's funds are disposed of by Government officers.

"The delicate question of female education requires reconsideration. It is premature in this country, so far as its parade is concerned, but it will grow, like all that is indigenous, if left to itself. When the state of Native society becomes such that men will require wives *à l' Européenne,* then our present system might be revived; in the meanwhile, domestic happiness and purity will be furthered by abolishing the present Female Schools, except wherever the local priesthood wish for their continuance, or where the management can be made over entirely to men like Baba Khem Singh and his relatives. I cannot understand what business it is of the Government to determine what the future relation of the sexes shall be among its subjects, for this is really what every innovation on indigenous female education comes to. It seems to me that Government is only bound to ascertain and to protect indigenous education. Instead of doing this, the truth about indigenous civilization was never ascertained, and its endowments as well as other forms of encouragement were destroyed. In the meanwhile, Government started this or that scheme, as if the country had been a *tabula rasa* before, thus reversing its function, which is to preserve what exists, and not to speculate in new forms of civilization or start creations of its own. As I have stated elsewhere, on the subject of education generally, at the first blush, 'it is not quite clear that it is a part of the *duties* of any Government to anticipate by the introduction of educational measures the *future* civilization of its subjects. As long as the attention of the rulers is directed to preserve security of life, intercourse, and property, Government has done all that can be expected from it, and it has even deserved well of the country. With the question of education it has apparently nothing further to do than not to arrest progress, and to be as completely as it can the exponent of the popular mind. When, however, a Government invokes all the sacred associations connected with the indefinite, but none of the less vivid, feeling of duty to do on a large and effective scale, within a short compass of time, what the best minds of a nation and the most happy combination of circumstances can only slowly and gradually accomplish, it furnishes us an example which is not easily paralleled in the history of any rule. It is therefore scarcely fair to quibble at the terms 'duty' and 'mission' in criticising the acts of Government, which is so single-minded and impartial in seeking the permanent good of its subjects.'

"A schoolmaster sends the following on the subject-matter of the above question:—

"'The progress made by the Educational Department in the matter of female education is very meagre. The character of instruction is in some schools Deva Nágari, in others Gurmukhi, and in others Persian.

"'Practical teaching in needle-work, lace-making, &c., &c., if introduced into our schools, is likely to make them more attractive and useful. Besides, a better class of teachers should be provided.'

"Another schoolmaster writes as follows:—

"'Some progress has, of course, been made by the Department instituting female schools, and the instruction given in them is the same as in the schools for boys. This kind of instruction, however, is not suited to female schools; there should not be any Persian in them and not so much of arithmetic. Female education in this country is purely and simply a forced thing, and almost a farce, because girls cannot stay long on account of early marriage; because some instruction in their own religion is of necessity to be given them in the school hours, otherwise they would not attend; and because efficient teachers (females) cannot be readily had for them.'

"*Q.* 43.—Have you any remarks to make on the subject of mixed schools?

"*A.* 43.—They would be an unmixed evil in the Panjáb, which is not ripe for them.* At the same time, it may be interesting to notice that in Turkey the Muhammadan boys are brought up with girls in schools attached to mosques, the latter remaining till they are 14 or till they are betrothed before that age. This I know as a fact, as I have studied Arabic and the Korán myself at such a school, being, probably, the only European, with the exception, perhaps, of Vambéry, who was allowed to do so, certainly at the time I speak of, about 1856. I think that the case of mixed schools in so orthodox a Musulmán country as Turkey serves to prove that there is no religious objection among Muhammadans to educate their girls up to a certain stage, and, as has been pointed out in the Parliamentary Report to which I have already referred, and from which I beg to be allowed to quote the following passage,— 'his treatise on the 'races of Turkey and the state of their education, with principal reference to Muhammadan education,' not only shows us the various methods adopted in the education of the numerous races of the Turkish Empire, but seems calculated to suggest the course which should be taken in dealing with our own Muhammadan subjects. The condition and progress of Turkey, to whose ruler the vast majority of Indian Musulmáns look with deference, affords an illustration of the compatibility of Western civilization with rigid orthodoxy; and it might be well to point out to our Musulmán subjects that many of the measures of our Indian Government are identical with those of Turkey.'

"*Q.* 44.—What is the best method of providing teachers for girls?

"*A.* 44.—If the wives of priests or of teachers of good caste, in Government and Aided schools were instructed by their husbands in the literary subjects which they are expected to teach, an indigenous method for the supply of female teachers would be ready at hand, the usefulness, economy, and early practicability of which would be a welcome substitute for the teachers now 'turned out' from female Normal schools, which I would either close or confine to the female relatives of priests or teachers.

---

* This remark does not apply to infant schools or to Koran schools, in which children of both sexes and of a tender age, often read together.

"*Q.* 45.—Are the grants to girls' schools larger in amount and given on less onerous terms than those to boys' schools; and is the distinction sufficiently marked?

"*A.* 45.—Article XV of the grant-in-aid rules puts girls' schools precisely on the same footing as schools for boys, except that their 'inspection by Government officers will not, *as a rule, be enforced.*' The latter provision I consider to be an indirect encouragement to Inspectors to insist on inspecting also female schools, a proceeding which is improper, except where asked for by the parents. I have myself opened 50 schools to official inspection, but I am not aware that I have done much good by it. At the same time, it is difficult not to sympathise with a Government Inspector, who has doubts as to the very existence of schools to which he is obliged to pay a grant without satisfying himself whether they deserve one by inspecting them himself or through one of his subordinates whom he can trust. As a matter of fact, female schools often receive grants on a larger scale and on less onerous terms than schools for boys; but it is in the nature of things that this should be so, and I cannot suggest any change in this practice, if the present female schools are to be continued. In the first flush also of the 'female education movement,' inspired by Sir Robert Montgomery, I have no doubt that thousands of rupees were spent, which could not be properly accounted for by the application of any rule. The distinction between schools for boys and those for girls are sufficiently marked in the Panjáb returns.

"*Q.* 46.—In the promotion of female education, what share has already been taken by European ladies; and how far would it be possible to increase the interest which ladies might take in this cause?

"*A.* 46.—The share taken by ladies belonging to missionary or, practically, secular bodies (such as the Association founded by Miss Carpenter) has been, comparatively speaking, both great and successful. Their schools, and even more, their visits to native households, have been both useful and interesting. As so many ladies engaged in the education of native females or in stimulating their interest in it by conversation are to be examined by the Commission, I must not tread on ground far more worthily occupied by them. They have, generally, more sense and tact in dealing with the question than men, though their usefulness may sometimes be impaired by religious over-zeal. It would, indeed, be well, if European ladies generally took a greater interest in their native sisters than they now do; but it is difficult to prescribe such interest, except under the pressure of clergymen or with the stimulus of publicity, when there is a danger of their motives being misconstrued. Ladies, like Mrs. Ross, Mrs. Steel, and others, have exerted themselves as volunteers in the cause of various forms of education, and I hope that the day will come when every official's wife will consider it to be her duty to study the vernacular and to cultivate friendly relations with the wives of Native gentlemen, which, in itself, will be an education to both, the political as well as civilising value of which cannot be overrated."

The Director, however, considers that the "Amritsar schools, under the management of the Committee, and the superintendence of the Lady Superintendent of the Normal School, are now taught chiefly by women, and are no doubt useful. I do not believe, however, that these or any other schools can be brought into a thoroughly satisfactory condition, till they are thrown open to regular and systematic inspection, and this I trust may be arranged shortly. The schools under the patronage of Bedi Khem Singh remain in the condition that has been frequently described in previous reports. They are maintained from public funds, though some *nominal* expenditure from other sources is entered in the returns. This is *supposed* to represent the value of presents in the shape of food given by parents to the teachers. There have always been serious irregularities in the management of the finances."

To reduce independent enterprise in education to a uniform level seems to be the great aim of the Educational Department, even where it is compelled to acknowledge the efficiency of missionary or other management.

It seems also strange that the department is unable to appreciate the value and opportunity of fostering female schools under the patronage of an eminent religious leader of the people. I consider that the treatment of Bedi Khem Singh during so many years is little short of persecution. In 1871-72, when accusations similar to those made in the above quotation led to the closing of his 108 female schools, I reported that this view presupposes that Bedi Khem Singh profits by the arrangement, but the Bedi may be looking upon it as a great trouble and inconvenience which he has incurred merely to please the "Sirkar" (Government). The statement that the expenditure is "*nominal*," and is "*supposed*" to represent the value of presents, in the shape of food, given by parents to the teachers is unjust, and shows that the best and most traditional manner of remunerating a teacher, namely by food, is not considered to be an equivalent to the money grant of Government, as if food could be purchased for nothing, and as if the teachers could live without such remuneration. At all events, the schools are cheap, numerous, and fairly popular. As purely Government institutions, they would be less so. Natives have had public indigenous female schools, *viz.*, at Delhi, but we cannot establish them without misgivings. Natives may start a "mixed school," but we could not do so, except for infants, without incurring the risk of popular dissatisfaction. Natives may put in a young Maulvi to teach their girls, but respectable "patrons" of *our* female schools will not send their daughters to a school where they may be seen by an official greybeard. As for "jobbery" in schools under native patronage, it is corrected by public criticism, whilst the misappropriations in an official department may go on for years with perfect impunity, if their disclosure is likely to affect a prestige in which no one believes. Indeed, I am not sure that a little nepotism would not be a sort of encouragement to honorary native patrons, provided the public interests did not suffer, and, *cæteris paribus*, I would myself rather appoint a relative of the patron or a man with local influence, than an outsider.

I have, in the course of my remarks in previous chapters, sufficiently indicated the course of reading adopted in indigenous female schools of the various communities. The story books for Muhammadan, Sikh, and even Hindu girls are, generally, a pleasant literature. The former read the Korán often together with little boys, and Urdu or Perso-Panjabi religious books, stories of prophets, &c.* The Sikh girls read the Granth and other books in Gurmukhi, and it is interesting to notice that in 1850 a book was already compiled by a Bhai for the use of girls in the form of a catechism on history, geography, natural phenomena, household duties, moral obligations, &c., telling them that they had a queen, and why should a woman not be a ruler, as some native states had one, and as such and such eminent women had existed in India, especially if she had able ministers. Now, if there had not been any female indigenous education among Sikhs, there would have been no object in publishing a book suited to the comprehension of the little girls of that community. The Hindu girls read Hindi prayer and religious story and other books, some of which are compiled in a superior style and yet suited to the readers. The instruction of females, whether given by Government, Societies or the indigenous teacher, should be adapted to the particular caste or class that is reading, and should preferentially be imparted by women making house to house visitations. At present, the Government system of female education differs little from that laid down for boys up to the Lower Primary standard, beyond which native females rarely study. I feel that, in order to give to this chapter an interest in which it would otherwise be wanting, I cannot do better than quote the opinions of some of the witnesses before the Education Commission, it being always borne in mind that an admirable suggestion may be suitable to one class of females and not to another. Miss Wauton, for instance, said :—

"I would suggest the opening of *industrial* schools where some light remunerative handicraft, such as *kasida*, *phulkári*, basket-making, knitting, lace-work, tape, weaving, &c., might be taught to many poor women in the large cities, who would thus be enabled to earn an honest livelihood."

---

* The Merát-ul-urus," or "bride's mirror," written by Moulvi Nazir Ahmad on the plan of an English novel, for the purpose of encouraging female education, has numerous female readers. It has been translated into Gurmukhi.

The following remarks of Mrs. Mary Chatterji are, of course, of more general application :—

"In the first instance it is always best to utilise the existing agencies. It is best to select a *pandit*, a *bhái*, or a *mulána* from the priestly class of the community for which the school is intended. The man must be of unimpeachable moral character, and possessed of social influence, and enjoying the confidence of the community. He should be, moreover, in full sympathy with the work himself, and, if not experienced in teaching, intelligent and teachable. A school commenced by such a teacher, with constant and intelligent direction, will have the best prospect of success. When the number of girls increases and becomes too large for him to manage alone, he should be supplied with an assistant. A young boy of good character and reputation, who has studied up to the entrance standard, may be employed for this purpose. He would be useful in teaching general knowledge and arithmetic. Pupil-teachers may be also made use of by the payment of small sums of money. This will train the upper class girls to teach, and also prove to them the practical value of learning. I have found this system successful in Hoshiárpur."

There are several schools in the Panjab in which women still teach the Korán, sometimes to both girls and boys. In other instances, both husband and wife teach the boys and girls together in the Korán schools; for instance, at Náwankot in the Lahore district, Thana Sarakpur, there are *three* such schools (see Returns annexed to this report), of which two are attached to mosques. At another school in the same district (Moharwal) a woman teaches 6 boys and 1 girl, for which she gets a chapatti from each pupil. At Paniput there are six Korán schools so conducted. At Wairowal, Amritsur district, the widow of a Government teacher gives gratuitous instruction to 20 girls in the Korán. At Dhátrat in the Karnal District Musammat Zainab instructs 10 girls in the Korán, the "Rah-i-Niját" (road of salvation), the "Masáil-Urdu" (another treatise on religious tenets), and other Urdu books gratuitously "for the sake of God." At Asant in the same District Musammat Manan, daughter of Khawája Bukhsh, teaches the Korán to 12 girls.

Among Sikhs there are also women-teachers. For instance, Bhani, mother of Ganda Singh, teaches Gurmukhi to 40 girls of the Ahluwalias in their own homes at Fattahabad in the Amritsar district. So Dr. Hunter is right in stating that there is some education among our Panjabi women, who, if left to teach on indigenous lines, improved, it may be, by wise and unobtrusive suggestion, may not become unworthy emulators of the Hindu lady, the Panditani Rama Bai Sanscrita. A Sikh lady the other day passed the "Buddhiman" or "ability" examination in the Panjabi language and literature of the Panjab University College, and others from the same community will no doubt follow her example. At Ropar, there is a female Hindu physician, Musammat Naraini Baidni, practising the Baidik system of medicine.

There has been a decline in female teaching since annexation, for the following reasons :—

(*a*.) Formerly the mother could teach the child Panjabi. Now, wherever the child learns Urdu, the teaching power of the mother is lost.

(*b*.) The weakening of the religious feeling has caused the decrease of all indigenous schools, including those conducted by women.

(*c*.) Formerly a woman guilty of misconduct was criminally punished, so that the safeguards against it were strong, and there could be less objection to granting women more education and greater freedom. Since the introduction of our law, adultery, for instance, can, comparatively speaking, be committed with impunity, and the necessary consequence is that the male population watches with greater jealousy any attempt towards emancipating the female sex.

(*d*.) The female education given by us was avoided by the more respectable, because it too closely resembled that enjoyed by a class, which, if not criminal, to which our system is now reducing it, was not reputable, although under the caste system which prevents society being gangrened, it confined vice and made it hereditary, if not respectable. By educating women on any but improved indigenous lines through their own priests, we run the risk of raising false ideals and ambitions which, by remaining unfulfilled, will cause the disappointed to fall in the social scale and create a class of unfortunates from the *disjecta membra* of the respectable castes, thus adding a most dangerous element to the further social *bouleversement* which our denationalising system has already created.

(*e.*) By keeping the female schools in public places, and by always attempting, in spite of any pledges that may have been given at the commencement of the "female education movement," to inspect them, thus preventing the very patrons of the schools from sending their own daughters to them.

Female education has, therefore, been brought into discredit with the respectable classes by official interference, which has already done so much mischief in the Panjab in various other respects, and which the boon of self-government given at the eleventh hour can alone remedy, provided all officials combine in a measure of temporary self-effacement for the sake of the common good. What there remains of female education will either be strangled or only have an artificial existence and temporary extension by the rewards or scholarships provided, if the Educational Department continues to interpose between the people and its natural progress. The recommendations of Bedi Khem are deserving of consideration—"The appointment of teachers should rest with the people, for they only can best know what kind of teacher they require. Unless the teacher possesses the confidence of the people, these latter will not send their girls to schools. The teachers must be men of thoroughly good principles, pious and God-fearing, and, at the same time, learned enough to discharge their work in an able manner. They may be either of the male or female sex, the chief requisite being that their conduct should be good;" and in another place—"Reading and writing in the vernacular, a little arithmetic and geography of the country in which they live, are quite sufficient. To attempt to introduce anything new might, instead of resulting in good, produce a quite contrary effect upon the schools. The little interest which people have begun to take in female education might receive a check, and the numbers, already small, might fall still lower."

Then as regards the efforts of European ladies—"The disinterested and unselfish efforts they make in this direction lose almost all their value when people consider that all this is done for the sake of the Christian religion."

"If these ladies were to exclude religion from their course of teaching, women would be attracted towards them in very large numbers, and would listen to all that is told them with greater attention, and learn all that is taught them with greater earnestness."

Pandit Ishar Pershad also notices that our bad system, bad mistresses, and occasional misconduct (of some of the teachers and pupils) have retarded the progress of female education in this province, which can only grow healthily with the largely increased number of educated men requiring educated wives.

The opinion of Miss W. N. Greenfield may fitly conclude this chapter:—

"In girls' schools, ordinary plain sewing, knitting and spinning should be taught as well as embroidery. The Panjabis are very fond of singing, but I fear Government school teachers could hardly be expected to teach that. The multiplication table might be sung, as is the practice in some 'bania' schools.

"Neither of the languages taught in the Government Female Schools in this district (Ludhiana) is the dialect of the people. *Both Urdu and Hindi are to them foreign tongues, though the latter has more affinity to Gurmukhi than the former.* I believe this to be one reason why the schools already established are not so useful or popular as they might be. The people ask 'are our daughters to become munshis and do 'naukri' that they should learn Urdu?' For most boys, education merely means Government or Railway employment, not increase of manliness and intelligence, or increased fitness for the ordinary duties of life. 'What then,' they naturally ask, 'do our girls want with such education?' Ignorant fathers and mothers naturally suspect something bad in what is wholly beyond their comprehension, and the wildest stories about the purpose of the Government in teaching the girls are circulated and believed.

"*Hindi, which is taught in five village schools in this district, is also unintelligible to the children* until they have made considerable progress; but on account of its being the character in which the Shastras are written, it is preferred by most Hindus, and we teach it largely in the city. But many of our Hindu pupils learn Gurmukhi also, and I should *always prefer beginning with the latter, and adding Hindi when the pupils have learned the use of reading.*

"*I find that Gurmukhi readers make most rapid progress, because as soon as they have learned the alphabet and begin to join the letters, they find that they make sounds familiar to them, and every sentence read has an intelligible meaning. Little tales are fully appreciated, and by the time the First Reader is finished, the child is able to read at sight and appreciate any simple Gurmukhi book, while the most ignorant parents listening to the lessons spelled out at home and recognising some of their own trite proverbs or witticisms encourage the little reader with a repeated "wah wah!'* Whereas our Hindi pupils labour through the first book, recognising only a few words here and there; the second, which contains short stories, is more comprehensible, but still ten per cent. of the words need explanation; and there are very few *native* teachers who ever pause to explain a word or see that the lesson is understood. Every book brings new difficulties, not only in the subject-matter, but in long compound words derived from the Sanscrit, the meaning of which might be recognised in Provinces where Hindi is spoken, but is far above the comprehension of our Panjabis. I strongly advocate, therefore, that in all *village schools* at least Gurmukhi should be taught *first*, in order to open the minds of the children, adding in the higher classes Urdu for Muhammadans and Hindi for the Hindus; and I feel sure that pupils so taught will be more intelligent and make far more rapid progress than those instructed on any other plan; while such as are early withdrawn from school will have gained a power of reading in their mother-tongue, which will enable them at any time to carry on their own education independently of any teacher.

"If the Indian Government purpose educating the masses of the people for their ordinary avocations, and not, as hitherto, only a handful of boys for Government service, this reasoning will apply with equal force to village boys' schools. 'One year out of the school course devoted to Gurmukhi would be quite sufficient to teach any boy of average ability to read and write it well, and if Urdu were then begun, side by side with Panjabi, the teacher would reap a great advantage from having an awakened intellect to deal with a mind to which words had begun to bear a meaning.

"The objection made by some that there is no literature in Gurmukhi seems to me a very superficial one. *If a large reading population be created, a literature suited to its wants will soon spring up.* What Urdu literature is there at the present time that is not more or less directly the fruit either of Government patronage or missionary effort? And what is the moral tone and intellectual status of the few native books of poetry and prose written independently of such influences?

"It must not be imagined that Panjabi is spoken in the villages only, and that Urdu is spoken and understood generally in the towns. Far from this being the case, all the lower classes, and the women of the higher, even including such foreigners as Kashmiris and Kabulis, use Panjabi as the medium for interchange of thought. Even the Government servants who talk high-flown Urdu in court often leave it at the door of their own homes and resume the familiar colloquial.'

"Primary schools for girls could no doubt be started without opposition in every village if it were the order of the Government, and the necessary funds were provided.

"(a.)—In a few places Sikh women will be found who can read and write Gurmukhi, and *these should first be utilised.* Where there is no suitable woman, any respectable man might be employed as teacher for a time, but to be replaced by a woman as soon as possible. Village schoolmasters might be encouraged to teach their own wives or daughters to fit them to take charge of the girls' schools.

"(b.)—The monitor system should be introduced. If, as soon as a girl can read and write moderately well, she were, while still under tuition, paid a small sum for teaching the younger classes, the parents would soon see the advantages of education.

"Certificates of qualification to teach up to the different standards should be given, and, by degrees, none but certificated female teachers should be employed.

"If at the yearly or half-yearly examination, pieces of cloth or some sweetmeats were given to the younger, and books to the elder, pupils, it would, I think, be a wiser way of rewarding progress, and the monetary rewards might be reserved for the teachers.

"The present Government series of Urdu Readers, while an improvement on the past, leaves much to be desired.

"The *kaida* still gives too much time to the letters and their various combinations, before beginning reading exercises.

"(The Christian Vernacular Education Society has just made a step in the right direction; and following the most modern improvements in English Primers, has published an Urdu First Book, in which the letters and their use in words are taught so gradually that the scholar knows many words, and can read whole sentences, before the whole alphabet is acquired. As far as we have tested this plan, the results are very satisfactory.)

"The Urdu First Reader, Government series, is too difficult to follow the *kaida* and provides no spelling exercises.

"The information given in the Urdu Readers (up to the fourth), though interesting, is not sufficiently useful or varied. For girls' schools especially, where the children are so early removed on account of marriage, it is most desirable that even the first books should contain lessons on sanitation, the preservation of health, simple remedies, and tales aimed at undermining popular superstitions.

"First lessons in geography, history, arithmetic, and letter-writing might all with advantage be combined in a very simple elementary series for the use of primary girls' schools.

"The 'Istri Shikshá' published by Government for the use of Hindu girls' schools is somewhat on this plan, but the lessons are not well graduated, the whole of the letter-writing and arithmetic being massed into the 4th, 5th and 6th parts, and the reading lessons have a very low moral tone. Indeed, it is difficult to conceive how such a lot of ridiculous stories, thickly interspersed with quotations from the Shástras, could ever have been published under the auspices of an enlightened Government pledged to religious neutrality."

"Perhaps a catechism founded on the Penal Code as the Government standard of morality might be approved by all parties.

"Amongst the higher classes, girls are so confined that the blessings of fresh air and exercise are unknown, whilst among the lower, they are the household drudges almost from babyhood, and are neither fed so well nor cared for as the boys. Should they be allowed to attend school in the morning, they must, on returning home, cook the food, grind, spin, and nurse the baby, while their more fortunate brothers have leisure for home preparation of lessons, and play. Add to all this the custom of early marriage, which takes the child from her lessons just when she is old enough to appreciate them, and it will be evident that a large amount of mental culture must not be expected from the girls of this generation. Should it be pressed upon them, it will be at the cost of injury to health and sacrifice of life.

"Our experience in the Christian Girls' Boarding School goes to show that much brain work cannot be done on ordinary native food; that a more generous diet with plenty of fresh air is necessary to keep school children in health. In institutions where this can be secured we may look for a higher standard of proficiency; but the standard for city and village day-schools should be much lower for girls than for boys.

"Both for girls' and boys' schools, especially in the younger classes, some drill exercise would be advantageous, but it should be given between classes, not for an hour at a time, the object being to relieve the muscles cramped by sitting, not to weary the children. Care will be needed in introducing this into girls' schools, lest a fear should be cherished that the girls are being taught to dance!

"Another point of extreme importance, which affects the physical well-being of every student, is that the type of all class-books should be *clear and large*. The ravages made by small-pox, ophthalmia and other diseases upon the eyes of the natives of this country are patent to all who live amongst them. I should think that fully 50 per cent. of the adult population have defective sight, and their sufferings from ophthalmia during certain seasons of the year are most pitiable. Home preparation for all the higher classes must be pursued at night, and the flickering light of an ordinary 'díva' is ruining to the students' eyes. It is therefore most important that no additional strain should be put on the eyes by the school-books being printed in a fine or defective type. No consideration of cheapness should weigh for a moment in comparison with the preservation of the blessing of good sight.

"If, instead of primers, the Government would have printed in each of the three languages taught in the Province a series of about twelve large sheets containing the alphabet, figures, and progressive spelling lessons up to the formation of short sentences, and have them hung up in a conspicuous position in every primary school, they would serve the double purpose of primers and writing copies, and be in the end not more expensive than books. This plan would have the additional advantage of correcting the position of the children during class time, as they would have to look *up* not *down* for their lesson. Stands for books in the higher classes are very desirable."

G.—OPINIONS OF WITNESSES BEFORE THE EDUCATION COMMISSION ON THE SUBJECT OF INDIGENOUS SCHOOLS IN THE PUNJAB.

I HAVE extracted the following opinions on indigenous schools in the Punjab from the answers of witnesses before the Education Commission in the hope that such a course would not only facilitate comparison, but also serve as a summary of the subject under enquiry:—

Pandit BHAGWAN DAS, the representative of HINDU indigenous schools in the Punjab, deposed to the following effect:—

"These schools have come down from time immemorial. In Lahore and Amritsar and many other small towns of the Punjab, native teachers called *Pándhas* give instruction in Hindi[1] and Landé; many *Sikh Bháis* teach Gurmukhi in their *dharmsálas;* and many *Pandits* teach Sanskrit in *mandirs* and in their own houses. The *Pándhas* maintain themselves by gifts and donations from their pupils, which are given on Sundays, or on religious occasions, or when any new book is begun, and they teach according to their own choice. There is no strict formal discipline in these schools; but what the boys learn here is far more strongly impressed on them than what they read in Government schools, for the boys learn all the day long and with great interest. There are no fixed hours of teaching in these schools, and *Pándhas* are generally Bráhmans. Some are good Sanskrit scholars; others have but moderate knowledge, and know only practical ordinary things. A University College has been established at Lahore to turn out competent teachers. If Hindi and Sanskrit scholars be encouraged by as good remunerations as the Urdu scholars are, there will be a great improvement in these schools. By the introduction of this foreign Urdu language, the people of the Punjab have not been benefited by the change of Muhammadan rule so far as education is concerned. These indigenous teachers would gladly accept grants-in-aid, provided that religious education were to be given along with secular instruction. Of all these indigenous schools, Government gives grants-in-aid only to a few of the *Pándhas*. If aid be extended to all kinds of schools, of *Pándits* as well as *Bháis* and *Pándhas*, there is every hope that primary education will be greatly extended."

And in another place—

"The people of the Punjab like that kind of primary education which may help in their religious education; and this religious instruction can only be given through Hindi and Sanskrit; and, as Hindi is not a subject of study in primary schools, a large number of the people of India do not avail themselves of this education. Only that class of people like the present system of primary education whose parents and relations are in Government service owing to their knowledge of Persian, or such persons who wish to prepare their children for Government service.

"Tradesmen and merchants and those who choose such professions do not care for the present system of education. They know that this education is of no use to them, and it is mere loss of time to acquire it."

Babu KHEM SINGH, the representative of SIKH indigenous education, was of opinion that—

"Indigenous schools still exist in the province. In the districts lying west of Jhelum they are to be found in large numbers. Their number has decreased with the advance of Government schools, and they are disappearing wherever these latter have been established to a large extent.

"They are a relic of an ancient village system, inasmuch as their maintenance depends upon the people. The teachers are paid not in cash, but in kind, by buying a certain proportion of the produce from the land cultivators.

[1] This means the "Nágari" character, never the Hindi *dialect*.—G. W. L.

"These schools are of various descriptions, and the course of instruction is different in each.

"Schools exist in Hindu places of worship, such as Thákurdwáras and Dharmsálas. Here instruction is given in Gurmukhi or Hindi reading and writing.

"*2nd.*—Schools in Masjids (Muhammadan places of worship). Here the Mulláh teaches the Korán and occasionally a little Persian. The Korán is merely learnt by rote without meaning.[1]

"*3rd.*—Schools at the private residence of men learned in Sanskrit or Persian whose fame has attracted scholars from different parts of the country. These men give a thorough instruction in Persian and Sanskrit literature. While the former is read by Hindus and Muhammadans, the priests and the laymen without distinction, the latter finds its lovers only among Bráhmans. Other classes among Hindus very seldom take to it.

"*4th.*—Máhájani schools, where a Pándha gives instruction to young boys below the age of 12 years in Hindi reading and writing, and the four simple rules of arithmetic. Mental arithmetic receives great attention in these schools, and those who have come out of them beat ignominiously the best boys of our public schools.

"*5th.*—Other schools in which the instruction given is similar to that imparted in Government schools have also been established, but these can be counted on the fingers. Religious and moral instruction is also given in the first four kinds of schools.

"Instruction given in the first kind of indigenous schools is mostly of a religious character, and hence is sought more for the comforts of the soul than the necessities of worldly life. The Bráhmans who read Sanskrit in Thákurdwáras or from ordinary pándits learn no more than is required for assisting in the performance of religious ceremonies, &c.: their learning is confined to a few *mantris*.

"In the 4th class of schools the Pándhas give an instruction which is of more practical use than any other which either private or public schools impart, and it is therefore seen that in villages *where a Pándha has started a school, students from the Government schools flock to him, notwithstanding all the efforts of the authorities and the teachers of the Government schools to prevent them from so doing*. The Pándha is a very cruel taskmaster. He makes use of corporal punishment in all cases of disobedience or neglect of duty. Wooden boards and canes are very liberally employed by him, and it rends one's heart to see how severely and inhumanely he beats his boys.[2]

"The fee is levied according to no fixed scale. A few pice at the end of every month, food and other necessaries of life, such as oil, soap, &c., a rupee or so in entering school, and subsequently at each change of class, or on occasion of marriages, births of sons, are what constitute the fee paid by pupils, or, in other words, the income of the teachers. In villages these men are also given a certain proportion of the produce at each harvest.

"The masters are not selected from any particular class. The profession of teaching has become hereditary, and it is more by succession than by selection that their places are filled up. Except in cases of men proficient in Arabic, Persian or Sanskrit, the teachers generally know no more than they impart to their pupils. No arrangements are made to train or provide masters in such schools.

"The masters would indeed very willingly accept aid from Government, and be ready to conform to the grant-in-aid rules. But the worst of it is there are

[1] Not quite.—G. W. L.

[2] I should like to know who translated Babu Khem Singh's evidence, as this statement is not consistent with what I know to be the fact.—G. W. L.

none among them who can impart any other education than that which they do at present. There are, however, two ways in which it may be done: 1*st*, other men, who should however play a subordinate part, should be added to these schools to teach geography, arithmetic and history; 2*nd*, these men or their sons might be induced to join Government and normal schools, to receive instruction in subjects of general knowledge, and modern methods of teaching. Assistance should be given to them when they return and supplement the teaching of their fathers by instruction in other subjects.

"The grant-in-aid system has not been extended to these schools; on the contrary, every effort is made to put them down wherever they become the formidable rivals of Government institutions."

In answer to the question—"Can you, from your experience, give the Commission any information respecting Sikh indigenous schools in your part of the Province?" this venerable spiritual leader of the Sikhs replied as follows:—

"There is a very large number of Dharmsálas in the Punjab, especially on the west side of the Jhelum, where Bháis give instruction in Gurmukhi reading and writing and the multiplication tables. The books used for reading are entirely religious, and these the boys learn by heart. Neither geography, nor history, nor arithmetic beyond the multiplication tables is taught in these schools.

"These schools can be made of very great use by proper means.

"Influential men of the districts might be induced to interest themselves in the improvement of these schools. The Bháis might be persuaded by offer of scholarships and rewards and otherwise through those who have authority over them to send their children to normal schools, to fit themselves for giving improved instruction to the boys who attend their Dharmsálas. The superior Bháis of towns and larger villages might be made Superintendents of the smaller village Dharmsálas in their neighbourhood.[1] Assistance might be given to these Bháis by Government, the Superintendent receiving something additional for his extra work.

"The four simple rules of arithmetic, more particularly mental arithmetic, a general acquaintance with the geography of India, with a minuter knowledge of that of the Punjab, and the history of their province during the Muhammadan, Sikh and Hindu periods could then be added to the subjects already taught."

Moulvi Faiz-ul-Hasan, the representative of Muhammadan indigenous education, thought that—

1. "For the purpose of ascertaining the exact number of the indigenous schools, a man should travel throughout the province.[2] The number of the indigenous schools has greatly decreased on account of the Government schools, and on account of the fact that the people pay much attention to the secular education. The people of this country used to study Arabic and Persian, and acquired proficiency in them; but now-a-days the education in the indigenous school is confined to a few parts of the *Korán* and a few elementary tracts (in Urdu or Persian) treating of Muhammadan Law and of religious tenets. There are very few who study Arabic for the sake of becoming accomplished scholars. The reason is obvious. The Muhammadans of this country being poor, cannot support or spare their sons so as to allow them to pursue learning. The foundation of the Oriental College has given a new stimulus to the study of Arabic, and scholars from every part of the country swarm to that institution in considerable numbers.

[1] See my evidence before the Commission on the subject of making Headmasters of High Schools periodically inspect the Middle Schools which are their natural feeders, Headmasters of Middle Schools similarly inspecting the Primary Schools.—G. W. L.

[2] If he belongs to the Educational Department, the effect of his visit will be the destruction of Indigenous Schools, *as such*, to judge from past experience.—G. W. L.

2. "In the mosques the Korán and religious tenets are taught, and in some schools Urdu and arithmetic are also added. In the Persian schools *Gulistan, Bostan, Zuleikha,* and *Sikandar Nama,* together with composition, are taught. In the Arabic schools, Arabic Grammar, Logic, Muhammadan Law, Hadís and Tafsír and Moral Philosophy are taught. Some teachers teach in mosques; others keep schools in their houses and live on fees, and some of them are employed by some rich men in the villages; and the Maulvis generally teaching Arabic teach gratis, without any compensation. The pupils attending these schools, when they are not natives of the village where the school is situated, live in mosques, or they are supported by their teachers.

3. "Those teachers whose profession is to teach, and the Mulláhs of the mosques, take some fees from the children of the rich men, but the amount of fees is not fixed—sometimes paid in cash, and sometimes in kind. The poor students are not compelled to pay fees, but, on the other hand, are supported in some cases by the well-to-do teachers.

4. "The teachers of these schools are—(1) Mulláhs of the mosques who conduct the prayers; (2) those whose hereditary profession is to keep schools; (3) Maulvis who know as a part of their duty to give instruction in Arabic Grammar, Muhammadan Law, Hadís and Tafsír. Their qualifications are sufficient for the standard up to which they are required to teach respectively.

5. "For training or providing masters for these schools no arrangements have been made.

6. "The teachers of these schools should be induced, by giving them some monthly allowance, to teach along with the Korán and Persian some useful subjects, such as arithmetic and geography, according to the Government educational scheme. But it is necessary for this step that the consent of the students and of their parents should be first obtained. The students who learn Arabic up to the high standard and want to become *Maulvis* do not pay attention to the sciences and arts taught in the Government schools and colleges.

7. "I am not sure that these teachers will readily accept the State aid, and conform to the rules under which such aid is given. The experiment should be tried on a more extensive scale than it has hitherto been done. Those teachers who teach without the expectation of any compensation, and those who teach religious books, will hardly like to lose their freedom and to conform to the grant-in-aid rules. They also fear that, with the acceptance of the Government grant, they will be compelled to teach some subjects which will interfere with religious education.

8. "Up to the present time the grant-in-aid system has been unknown to the people in general. The rules of the grant-in-aid system are unnecessarily strict, and do practically discourage the extension of that system."

These representatives of the Hindu, Sikh and Muhammadan learned classes and priests were followed by the Head of the Anglican Church in the Punjab, the Right Reverend T. V. French, D.D., Bishop of Lahore, who gave the following valuable testimony, which corroborates the statements of the preceding witnesses:—

"I have pretty often seen and visited Muhammadan schools in mosques, and Lálas' schools in the neighbourhood of temples and in bazaars.

"The former, especially in the Yusufzai country, had in many cases able and zealous teachers, industriously teaching theology and the Korán, logic, grammar, some little of law, history and mathematics, as also some poetry and moral philosophy. Between Múltán and Sakkar there seemed a number of fairly good indigenous Muhammadan schools; but in the Lálas' schools very little seemed learnt but a smattering of Hindu poetry and good arithmetic.

"It is, I fear, very doubtful whether the former would submit to inspection, unless there were great freedom allowed as to the particular books, a certain standard being required of reading and parsing, intelligent paraphrasing and rendering in the vernacular, dictation, arithmetic, principles of morals, elements of universal history, and the like.

"*A better class of Government books, becoming popular and accessible, and thoroughly idiomatic, ought to win confidence, and to be adopted (in the course of time) by pupils and teachers in indigenous schools.* At any rate, a scheme to this effect might be proposed, and would seem worth trying. Whether accepted or not, and whether successful or not, it would be something that might fairly be set against the large number of Mission Schools availing themselves of aid rendered by voluntary agencies.

"*Some of the best teachers in the world, I should think, are some of the Hindu fakirs (Sunyásis, Jogís, and the like, doing Guru's work*; but they teach nothing at present but their own philosophies and religious systems. I am afraid these travelling teachers could never be tamed and disciplined into any sort of order, or made to fall in with any Government system of education, unless it were in such large institutions as that three miles from Rohtak on the Delhi Road."

The Reverend C. W. FORMAN, D.D., the Nestor of Anglo-vernacular schools in the Punjab, is in favor of encouraging the Máhájani and Gurmukhi schools: "There are many Landé or Máhájani schools in the province, where the boys learn only arithmetic, account-keeping, and reading and writing bills in a character used for no other purposes. Reading the vernacular in the Devi Nágari, of which Máhájani is a modification, might be added to the instruction now given in these schools, if inducements were offered to the teachers to learn and teach it.[1] Again, I do not think Persian should form a part of primary education for the masses as is now the case. Nor that Gurmukhi and Hindi schools should be entirely ignored. I would teach the character and dialect which is most desired in each place. *The truth is, as yet we have no system of primary education, properly so-called, in the Punjab.* The scheme of studies in what are called Primary schools has been adopted with reference to its fitness to prepare boys for secondary education, rather than for the work of life."

Pandit ISHAR PARSHAD, the representative of UNAIDED Schools in the Punjab, who, for the last 11 years, has given more than a third of his salary as well as his time and the gratuitous teaching of his brother to an Anglo-Sanskrit school at Lahore, under every discouragement and even persecution by the Educational Department, as has been admitted by Government, gives the following singularly clear and concise account of indigenous education in the Punjab among the various communities:—

"Indigenous schools, though fast decaying under the (to them) baneful influence of the Government system of giving remunerative education almost gratis, still exist in large numbers in this province; though the number of pupils receiving instruction at these schools is, from various causes, far less than those at schools of the modern fashion.

"The following are the principal classes:—

"*Maktabs*; *Pándhas* (or Chatsáls); *Masjids*; *Pathshálas* (where *Sanskrit* or *Bhásha* is taught); *Pathshalás* and *Dharmsálas* for instruction in *Gurmukhi*; *Pándits*; *Bháis*; teachers of only Theology (Hindu and Muhammadan); teachers of the native medical science (*Hindi* and Persian, or *Yunani* as it is called); teachers of Astrology.

"Besides these, there are a number of private schools, not aided by Government, that are conducted (on a larger or smaller scale) after the modern fashion, *e. g.*, several in Lahore, one in Ludhiána, one in a village near Lahore, and several others here or there.

[1] This is already done in some of these schools.—G. W. L.

"The following is an abstract description of the subjects of their instruction, &c.:—

Class of institution.	Subjects of instruction; its character; and discipline in vogue.	Fees.	Classes from which teachers are selected.
Maktabs	These are places of instruction in Persian reading, writing, and composition, and a little of arithmetic; the pupils of superior schools (though these schools have now been closed in great many cases) are superior to those of Government schools in deepness and soundness of their knowledge of Persian, and are also generally more intelligent than the pupils of the present schools where cramming is in vogue. Attendance extends over the whole day; pupils are sent to call the absentees; misconduct and absence are corporally punished; special attention is paid to the pupils' conduct. I have personally known students of these old-fashioned schools (being teachers when I saw them), with whose depth of knowledge of Persian the present M. A.'s could bear no comparison. Arabic literature was also taught in some instances in the *Maktabs*, though higher instruction in Arabic literature, philosophy, logic, &c., was given by special teachers, some of whom still survive.	Ranging from a few annas to as many rupees. Before Government schools came into vogue, Persian teachers were sometimes paid as much as Rs. 25 or Rs. 30 per month for teaching the sons of wealthy men at their houses, where the teacher was allowed to teach other pupils for smaller fees. But even at the *Maktabs, i. e.,* the teacher's own house, a fee of Rs. 4 or Rs. 5 was not an uncommon thing. In the smaller Maktabs, food also forms part of the fee; also a small cash present and food on the occasion of a marriage in the pupil's family; a present on his commencing a new book; also one called *Ids*, on every great fair day.	The teachers were (and are) generally Muhammadans, though occasionally also Hindus. These teachers are not selected by any one, but open and conduct the school at their own option.
Pándhas	These are teachers of *Hindi*, or that form of writing which is used by traders. These teach *Hindi* or *Landí* or *Máhájani* characters, in which (in the respective vernaculars of the particular traders) all their correspondence is conducted and accounts kept; oral multiplication tables, ordinary (1 to 10) + (1 to 10); superior or called *baru gyarah* (11 to 30) + (11 to 30); fractional (1 to 50) + (1¼, 1½, 2½ 3½, 4½, and 5½, &c.); some fractions into fractions—*e. g.*, 1¼ + 1¼; 1½ + 2½; 2½ + 3½, &c.; account-keeping (and the most important of all) small petty sentences, resembling verses containing some very useful lessons of every-day life and morality; also *dars, gurs, &c.* The *pândha* goes round every morning to collect his pupils, and thus there are almost no absentees; attendance extends over the whole day, the pupils being allowed to go home at about mid-day for morning meal. Corporal punishment of several kinds is administered for absence and misconduct at school or at home, unlike our present schoolmaster, who has nothing to do with his pupils' conduct at home.	The fee is generally a pice (¼ anna) per week; 7 (or more or less) loaves per month in the case of Muhammadan *Pándhas*, and certain quantities of flour, &c., in the case of Bráhman *Pándhas*; a cash present on the commencement of each progressive step of instruction, on the occasion of a marriage, birth of a son, on the completion of the course, on the important fair days, &c.	The Pándhas were either Muhammadans of the *Rawal* class, or Hindu Bráhmans. The profession is almost hereditary.
Masjids or Mosques of the Muhammadans.	Most Masjids, which invariably exist in all larger Muhammadan villages and Muhammadan localities of towns and cities, are attended by Muhammadan boys, and occasionally girls. The pupils are generally taught here to recite the *Alkorán*; though in some exceptional cases Persian is also taught; in some Masjids higher Arabic literature, logic, philosophy, theology, &c., also form subjects of instruction. The majority of our old Arabic scholars have received instruction there.	The fee consists of loaves on particular days and small pecuniary presents on some occasions, which latter are much rarer than in the case of Maktabs. Those receiving higher Arabic instruction are generally those that have dedicated their life to knowledge, and as they are poor in the majority of instances, they pay no fee, but in some instances even get their food at the mosque.	The teacher is generally the Imám of the *Masjid*, though sometimes a separate person.

Class of institution.	Subjects of instruction; its character; and discipline in vogue.	Fees.	Classes from which teachers are selected.
Pathshálas *i. e.*, a place of reading) for Hindi (or Nágari) and Sanskrit.	At these small schools (which have very greatly decreased) the pupils were taught reading and writing in Hindi character, and recitations of Sanskrit religious books. They have sometimes turned out good scholars of Sanskrit and Hindi. A little of arithmetic was also occasionally taught. The sons of Bráhmans, who form the majority of pupils here, receive also instruction in the performance of religious ceremonies.	In these schools instruction used to be given gratis, the teachers receiving occasionally support from some charitable influential people.	Teachers in these used to be Bráhmans.
Pathshálas for *Punjabi* or Gurmukhi.	The pupils are here taught to read and write in the Gurmukhi characters; to recite the religious books of Sikhism, and occasionally of Hinduism. These are the only true places of primary instruction in the Punjab. The pupils learn to read and write a little of arithmetic, and receive some instruction in religion, without the least detriment to their worldly pursuits. Younger boys will attend for the whole day, while the elder ones will attend for some hours, and devote the rest of the day to learning (or doing the work of occupation to which they belong, or which their parents desire them to pursue in after-life). (These, too, have, however, suffered to a great extent from the *Munshi* and *Baboo*-making system of Government education.) Properly handled and fitly encouraged they could take an important place in a true system of national education.	A small cash fee and sometimes loaves are taken from the pupils.	Bháis or religious teachers of the Sikhs.
Dharmsálas, or religious places resembling monasteries.	Besides the fulfilment of the charitable purposes for which these institutions are designed by the founders, instruction is also given as in the last-mentioned case, religious instruction receiving more attention here than in the other.	Very small, if any, fee is charged here.	The keepers of the institution who are generally *Bháis* or *Granthis* and occasionally *Sadhus*.
Pándits .	Instruction, in what may be called classical Sanskrit, Grammar, Poetry, Logic, Hindu Law, and Metaphysics, is given by Pándits (who are themselves deep scholars) at their houses.	No fee; on the contrary food is sometimes given to the pupils who in return do every kind of service to the teacher.	Bráhmans.
Bháis . . .	Giving instruction as in the last-mentioned case to occasional students at their houses, in the higher subjects, which, however, are fewer than in the last case.	No fees . . .	Bháis.
Teachers of only Theology (Hindus).	In Sanskrit, Vedant, Shastras, &c., being the subjects of instruction.	No fees . . .	Pándits and *Sadhus*.
	In *Gurmukhi*, translation of the Sanskrit higher works of theology being the subjects.	No fees . . .	Bháis or Granthis and Sadhus (very generally).
	Of only Muhammadan Theology and Muhammadan Law.	No fees . . .	Maulvis or *Kazis*.
Teachers of the Native Medical Science.	Works of the *Hindi* or *Vaidik* system ... Works of the Persian or *Yunani* system ...	Service . . .	Hindi physicians. Hindu and Muhammadan physicians.
Teachers of— .	Native Astronomy and Astrology of the Hindu system.	Service	Hindu Astrologers (generally Bráhmans).
	Native Astronomy of the Muhammadan system (though comparatively with the last case very rare.).	Service	Hindu or Muhammadan Astrologers of that system.

"As these indigenous schools are private, and do not form any part of a system of national education (which itself does not exist at present), no arrangements have been made for training or providing teachers for them.

"These schools could be turned to the best account, if a true and solid basis could be established (in the face of opposition which proposals for it are certain to meet) for national education.

"The most important circumstances in which this could be achieved are these,—transfer of the entire management of education to the people; the substitution of friendly advice for official interference, in such a way that the advice might not be mistaken for interference; encouragement to the people to take interest in the improvement of education; laying down lines (but no more) which the people may be expected to carry out with the particular measures that they may think proper. Under the rules in force, very few masters of such schools could receive, or perhaps even would accept, Government aid. But, under a modified system of grant-in-aid rules, the masters of most of these schools would gladly accept such aid. But much in this matter depends upon the nature of the rules. For instance, native theology, philosophy, astrology, and medical science, are looked upon with disfavour, being supposed all of them as false and therefore deserving of every discouragement. Without going, however, into the question of their merit, in comparison with the western sciences, I do not think that many unbiassed reasoners would hold that a native theologian or physician is not far superior, and far more useful a man, than one utterly ignorant of God or a quack doctor; and thus I would consider that even instruction in such subjects (though distasteful to many Englishmen) should not be excluded by the rules from Government support, at least so long as people are not convinced of the superior merit of the western sciences.

"Properly speaking, the grant-in-aid system has not been extended at all to the indigenous schools; but many of the indigenous schools have in large towns been either merged into the departmental schools, or affiliated to them as branch schools, to swell the number of the pupils of such schools."

We now come to the evidence of Sikh Sirdars.

Sirdar ATAR SINGH, C.I.E., Chief of Bhadaur, says:

"A few indigenous schools do still exist as a relic of the past. Religious mendicants of the Udasi or Nirmála sects, Síkhs, Pandits, Pándhas and Bairagis, in some places teach Sanskrit or Gurmukhi. They give religious instruction, and teach reading and writing. The schools of Pándhas for teaching mental arithmetic and the Landé character, in which the Banias keep their accounts and correspondence, exist in greater numbers. The Banias and Khattris, whose sons generally attend these schools or those of Muhammadan Mulláhs, pay the Pándhas or Mulláhs a rupee on the occasions of marriage or birth of sons in their families, and one or two pice every week. Besides feasting them on festival days, each pupil in turn provides them with food daily. The Indigenous schools are of three sorts, *viz.* :—

"1. Those maintained by opulent people at their houses, for the education of their children.

"2. Those schools which are self-supporting by means of fees, &c., as detailed above.

"3. Charitable schools, in which Fakírs or religious men give religious instruction gratuitously.

"The Mulláhs generally teach *Karíma*, *Gulistan*, and *Bostan*, &c., besides the *Korán* to the Muhammadans. *Punishments of a light nature are awarded according to the desire of parents.* The Mulláhs of higher qualifications have generally become teachers in Government schools, and the few that are left are generally men of no superior attainments.[1] Among Hindus, men of inferior

---

[1] This, it will be remembered, is the statement of a Sikh Sirdar regarding Muhammadan teachers.—G. W. L.

castes can never become teachers; while among Muhammadans, religious mendicants, weavers,[1] barbers, oilmen, can and do become Mulláhs or teachers, if they have the requisite amount of learning.

"The qualifications generally of teachers of Indigenous schools have deteriorated, excepting of those Pándhas whose stock of knowledge has never been high, and consists of the multiplication-tables, a few arithmetical formulæ, and writing in the Landé character. Another class of Pándhas or Pándits teach astrology and religious observances to Bráhman lads. There are no arrangements for the training of these teachers. Whatever they have learnt from their teachers they teach in their schools; the system does not improve. *The Indigenous schools are capable of very great improvement and extension by means of grants-in-aid and proper inspection. Teachers would willingly take aid from the State and conform to the rules that may be prescribed. In my part of the country, I have not heard of any grant-in-aid being given to Indigenous schools.*"

Sirdar Kanwar BIKRAMA SINGH, Ahluwalia, C.S.I., states:

"There are not so many of these schools now as there used to be in former days. In these Indigenous schools, a little grammar is taught, and more attention is paid to reading and writing, in order that the student may become competent to read religious books and discharge his religious duties, to read and write letters, and peruse and understand books in general. The teachers are themselves deficient in arithmetic, and the students from these schools generally have to resort to the schools of the *Pándhas* to learn arithmetic, whose special work it is to teach arithmetic. The teachers are also ignorant of geography and the different arts and sciences. There is no system observed in these schools. The teachers manage them as they think best. There is no fixed rule about fees either. In the Persian schools the teachers arrange to realise fees, varying from one anna to one rupee per mensem, from the parents of the students. In some cases, they are satisfied with securing their meals only from the students. The fees are thus realised in various ways. Very few children are sent to the Hindu Pathshálas; such as wish to become Pándits generally go to a popular Pándit to prosecute their studies under him. Instead of paying fees, they render him services and go on studying. They sometimes support themselves by charitable donations to the Pathshálas; otherwise they go and beg *roti* and flour from Hindu houses, and thus support themselves. On occasions when Hindus give away money, clothes, &c., as religious offerings, these students have their share also. The fee in the schools of the *Pándhas*, where arithmetic is taught, is a pice a week, besides which the students have to provide the teacher with his daily meals by turn. When there is a marriage in a student's house, he has to pay a rupee to the teacher. They have also to pay a rupee when they are advanced enough to commence writing names, and a rupee when they commence rule-of-three in arithmetic.

"There is no rule for selecting teachers for the schools for Muhammadan children; any man possessed of competent knowledge can set himself up as a teacher. The Hindu Pathshálas are kept up by Bráhmans alone, such as are well versed in the subjects they are required to teach. The Pándhas are generally from the class of Muhammadans known as Rawals, or from Bráhmans. As far as I am aware, there is no system observed as regards the course of studies, or the selection of teachers, in these schools. If the teachers are allowed a grant-in-aid on the condition that they should teach in accordance with the Government rules and show good results at the examinations, and if they are allowed to retain the fees they realise, these schools can be placed on a satisfactory footing with very little expense. The teachers would be glad to accept aid from Government and bind themselves to comply with the rules issued by Government."[2]

[1] Quite so; there ought to be no caste or teaching monopoly among Muhammadans, but *weavers* received an impetus to teach the Korán and other books whilst at work, in consequence of Prince Aurangzeb, when a child, frequenting a school with a weaver.—G. W. L.

[2] It will be seen that *all* non-departmental witnesses agree as to the teachers of Indigenous schools availing themselves of Government aid, especially if the Grant-in-aid Rules were rendered less obstructive.—G. W. L.

Sodi HUKM SINGH's evidence is particularly valuable on the subject of Indigenous schools, to which he has evidently devoted attention:

"Indigenous schools *largely exist in the province*. They are of the following kinds :—

(1) Maktabs and Madrasas.
(2) Pathshálas.
(3) Pándhas' schools.
(4) Síkh Bháis' schools.

"In Maktabs and Madrasas, religious and other instruction is given to the Muhammadan students in Arabic and Persian. These schools are chiefly kept up by *Mulláhs* in mosques or in their own houses. A small fee is paid to the teachers by scholars. In Pathshálas, religious and other instruction is given to the Hindu students in Sanskrit and Hindi. These schools are chiefly kept up by *Pándits* in Pathshálas, Hindu temples, or in their own houses. No fee is generally charged to students, the teachers of such institutions being supported by private subscriptions in cash or kind. In Pándha schools, account-keeping is taught in Landé characters to the students, whose parents pay a small fee to the teacher. Such schools are generally kept up in the private residences of the Pándhas.

"In Gurmukhi schools religious and other instruction is given to the Síkh and other students. Such schools generally exist in *Dharmsalas*. A moderate fee is paid to the teacher, in cash or kind, &c., &c.

"No arrangements have been made for training or providing masters in such schools, by the Educational Department; but the Punjáb University College has of late turned its attention towards this subject.

"If these Indigenous schools be affiliated to the Punjab University and brought under the grant-in-aid system, they can be turned to good account as part of a system of national education.[1] I am sure the masters of these schools will be willing to accept State aid, and to conform to the rules under which such aid is given. The grant-in-aid system has hitherto been almost exclusively extended to the Christian Missionary schools, and to no others in this province as far as I know, except that Government pays a certain amount to the Punjab University College, as a sort of grant-in-aid.[2] There is great room to extend the grant-in-aid system to other Indigenous schools in this province."

And elsewhere: "The Pándits, Pándhas, Mulláhs, and Bháis are the private agencies which exist in this Province, and which can be utilised for primary instruction with very little cost to Government."

Sirdar GURDIAL SINGH, N. C. S., Assistant Commissioner, Hushiarpur, gives the following testimony :—

"It is very difficult to state exactly the extent to which indigenous schools exist; but in almost all the principal villages, where there is no Government school, there is some sort of indigenous private schools. They are generally of the following descriptions :—

"(*a*) Private teachers employed by some of the rich inhabitants of the place for the education of their sons, who, as a rule, are allowed to teach the sons of other people also. Generally, they teach Persian or Sanskrit. Such schools are very rare now, but they were very common before the Government Schools had been established all over the country, and are still to be found in Native States.

"(*b*) The arithmetic schools, where Pándhas teach arithmetic (mentally in most parts), and the Hindi or Landé alphabet, in which the boys make

---

[1] This duty should be entrusted to the Local Boards working with the Senate of the Punjab University in accordance with the principles of its foundation.—G. W. L.

[2] The Sodhi Sahib explained in his cross-examination how small, comparatively speaking, this grant was. Indeed, it has not hitherto amounted to a third of the annual expenditure, and a large portion of it has been devoted to Government institutions or objects.—G. W. L.

no further progress than writing names. Such schools are very common, and are largely attended by boys of the trading classes.

"(c) The Mulláhs of the mosques, the Pándits of Thákurdwáras, and the Sadhs and Bhéis of the Dharmsálas, who teach the village boys. They give them mostly religious instruction, but they also teach them to read and write in Persian, Sanskrit, or Gurmukhi characters, and in many instances give them a fair amount of instruction in these languages.

"(d) The schools of the higher orders, such as the Hindu schools of Ludhiána and the Mussulmán schools in some other parts of the country. With this class I am not personally well acquainted.

"The discipline is harder than in the Government schools, but not so regular. In many instances pupils are employed as servants. For slight mistakes they are occasionally severely beaten, whilst it is not an uncommon sight to see the boys employed in the menial service of the master, instead of in reading.

"The masters are supported by the community, by means of contributions paid mostly in kind; but no fixed fee from boys is demanded. Their parents, however, give presents to the teacher on the principal festivals and on occasions of marriages, births, &c. The masters are selected generally from the Mulláh, Pándit, and the Bhái class, and are as a rule of very moderate attainments; but occasionally good Arabic, Sanskrit, and Hindi scholars are met with in this class.

"There are no special arrangements for the selection and the training of the masters; but the education the Mulláh and the Pándit class is now receiving cannot fail to have its beneficial effect on the indigenous schools. The Punjab University College, through the Oriental College, is thus rendering a very good service to the cause of education in this way, as well as in many other ways. Only by giving grants-in-aid on liberal terms can these schools be turned to good account, and *not by absorbing them into the standard primary schools, as has been done in so many instances.* Most of the masters are very willing to accept State aid; and the extension of education will help the people in finding such masters as would be able to conform to rules laid down by Government. There is large room still for the grant-in-aid system being extended still further to such schools."

Sirdar DYAL SINGH deposes as follows :—

"It is not easy to say the exact extent of indigenous village schools in the Punjab. There are no statistics, so far as I am aware, on the subject, and the Director of Public Instruction in his Reports says: Now-a-days popular education in the Punjab does not take the indigenous schools into account. There were, however, 3,461 indigenous schools in 1857-58, as shown by the Report for that year, and there is every ground for believing that the number of indigenous schools now may not be less than what it was a quarter of a century ago. *In almost every large village which does not possess a Government or Aided primary school, there is one or more of these schools, and sometimes they are found to exist together with the primary schools.* These indigenous schools are to a great extent remnants of the ancient village system. They formed an essential part in the economy of every well-established village in olden times, and they have come down to us from those times. They may be divided into three classes.

1 the *Pándah* schools; 2, the *Mulláh* schools; and 3, the *Bhái* schools.

"The Pándah schools are attended by almost all classes of people, specially Hindus as well as Sikhs. The subjects of instruction are reading, writing, mental arithmetic, and a little book-keeping. The instruction given in these schools is of the utmost practical value to village merchants, patwaris, money-lenders and others, and consequently we see them attended in some instances by so many as 200 boys. These schools are held in some public place of the village, or in a shop, or at the houses of the teachers themselves.

(2) "The Mulláh schools are held in mosques. The subject taught is the Korán, which the boys are made to repeat without knowing the meaning. Sometimes a little Persian is also taught, and when the Mulláh is a learned man, as is seldom the case, he teaches the higher branches of Persian and Arabic learning.

(3) "The Bhái schools are held in Dharmsálas, where Gurmukhi books are read and taught to them. There is no regular system of fees. The teachers are paid both in cash and kind, according to the circumstances of the parents of the students. Small payments are also made on certain festivals, and on admissions and promotions. The system of discipline is very lax, save that in these schools great consideration is paid to the teacher who is held by the boys in the highest respect. There is no classification of students, and in one school the same book is often read by a dozen different boys in a dozen different places. There is consequently great waste of teaching power. The teachers in these schools are not selected, but are hereditary. Their qualifications are of a very inferior order, generally speaking, and they cannot travel beyond the subjects they teach. They belong to the sacred classes, and therefore, though their remuneration is not high, they are treated with respect. No arrangements, so far as I know, have yet been made for training or providing teachers for these schools. These schools can very well be turned into account if Government gives them a little encouragement. The best way to do so is to grant *muafis*, or aids, to the holders of these schools, according to the results they may show; also by giving a training to the teachers themselves; so that, besides the subjects they now teach, they may know a little mode of teaching, and a few of the subjects of general knowledge in use in our primary schools. Teachers who are so qualified would, in addition to the subjects they now teach, be able to teach other subjects, a knowledge of which cannot be dispensed with even in the most rudimentary form of education, and without which the training afforded in indigenous schools must always be regarded as highly defective and incomplete. If efficient schools, conducted by these men, were instituted or held in every village, that would solve the problem of primary education to a very great extent; the teaching would be imparted in a highly popular form, and the classes would soon be filled up with children from every section of the community.

"So far as the Punjab is concerned, the grant-in-aid system does not seem to have been extended to these indigenous schools. In some instances schools have been subsidized by Government; but in almost all these instances, they have ceased to retain their indigenous character, and have merged into ordinary Government or Aided schools, observing the system of instruction and the discipline in force in these schools, and controlled by the same agencies as they are. The three classes of indigenous schools above mentioned are, of course, quite independent of the Government controlling agencies, and they are hardly even subject to any kind of supervision. Any grants or aids made by Government to these schools should not be fettered with the condition that they shall in all respects be subject to the strict inspection of the Government controlling agency. Some kind of inspection may be introduced, but that simply for the purpose of testing the progress made in the schools and making suggestions how this condition might be improved. All officious interference should be avoided, and every freedom should be allowed to the teachers in selecting the books and in matters of internal discipline."

Among Muhammadan gentlemen, Kazi SAYAD AHMAD, Attaché to the Foreign Office, offers the following remarks:—

"Prior to the establishment of Mission and Government schools in the province, *there existed two or three indigenous schools in every quarter of an important city or town, and one in almost every large village*. These schools were of two descriptions—(1) those kept by private *mullahs*, who were paid fees, which varied according to the means and circumstances of the students; (2) schools which were kept by well-to-do people in their own houses for the instruction of their children, and into which sometimes the children of their neighbours and friends were also admitted. The teachers in such schools were only paid by those who originally engaged them. But since the establishment of Mission, Municipal and Government schools, both the number and status of these indigenous schools have gone down, because the people resort to Government, Municipal, and Mission Schools for the acquisition of secular subjects, religious instruction being confined to indigenous schools, in which *both* secular and religious instruction was in old days imparted. Indigenous schools of both descriptions are very defective as regards discipline. In the first place, no regularity and punctuality in attendance are observed by the students; secondly, they are not organised into classes, each pupil studying separately. The teacher thus cannot find time to teach all the scholars properly. As regards fees, they are paid as stated above; in the case of the first set of indigenous schools by students according to their own, or to the means of their fathers or guardians, as the case may be; and in the second, by their parents, who engage teachers for their instruction at home. The masters of such schools are generally selected from among the *mulláhs.* Their qualifications are not always the same; some can teach only up to the middle school standard of Persian literature, and others Arabic also to a certain extent. No arrangements exist up to the present for training and providing masters in such schools. Masters of these schools acquire their education from different quarters—Persian literature from one man, arithmetic from another, Arabic from a third, and so forth; and when they show themselves qualified to keep such schools, they either start schools on their own account, or are employed as teachers by private individuals for the instruction of their children. Masters of indigenous schools would accept State aid and conform to the rules under which such aid is given, if they are allowed to impart religious instruction to the boys, which in such schools takes precedence of all other subjects."

KHALIFA SYAD MUHAMMAD HUSAIN, Foreign Minister of the Patiala State gives the following important evidence :—

"It is difficult to give the statistics of indigenous schools, because no accurate enumeration has been made. In the part of the Punjab with which I am best acquainted, young boys, the sons of Banias, are sent to Pándhas' schools to learn mental arithmetic, &c., and to be kept out of mischief. One DR. RAHIM KHAN, KHAN BAHADUR, Honorary Surgeon, deposes as follows :—

"If by indigenous schools is meant the Muhammadan *maktabs* and the Hindu *pathshálas*, then every place of worship and every mohulla throughout the province has its own indigenous school. They are so far a relic of an ancient village system, as the subjects taught in them are religious, together with some *mental* arithmetic in the lower schools; the upper ones teaching morality, law, logic, grammar, and philosophy. But the last class of indigenous schools is now fast dying away. ***The system of discipline in force in these schools is far superior to what obtains in Government schools and colleges.***

"As the lower class of indigenous schools are generally managed by Mulláhs and Gurus, who are, as a rule, poor, a nominal fee of an anna or so is paid by the scholars. But, generally, the fees are not paid in cash, and the teachers receive their daily food and some clothing annually from the parents of the boys. In the higher indigenous schools, which are now fast disappearing, no fees are taken from the scholars; on the contrary, the latter receive food and clothing from the proprietors of such schools, who are generally well-to-do and of a religious turn of mind. The masters of such schools are generally selected from the sacerdotal class. Their literary qualifications for the lower schools are poor, being confined to mere religious subjects; but those who teach higher branches of science and ethics are generally men of very superior qualifications. Formerly, arrangements were made for training or providing masters for such schools. Thus, scholars of approved ability were selected from among the boys as monitors, and were made to teach the lower classes in the presence of their teachers.

"After acquiring sufficient experience in the art of teaching, these men used to open schools on their own account, and set themselves up as teachers.

"In order that the present indigenous schools be turned to good account, the Grants-in-aid Rules, as are promulgated by the Department of Education, should be relaxed and made liberal.

"The masters would be only too glad to accept State aid, provided that the rules for such aid be made less stringent.

"With the exception of the Missionary institutions, which are not indigenous in the literal sense of the term, so very few really *indigenous* schools receive aid from Government, that it might be justly said that the officers who are responsible for administering such aid are jealous of these schools, and do not like that other than their own schools should enjoy the loaves and fishes of the Department.

"A Pándha can teach a hundred boys, and they make from Rs. 10 to Rs. 30 a month. In the Korán schools attached to mosques, the teachers do not get more than from Rs. 6 to Rs. 10 a month owing to the poverty of the people. Muhammadan gentlemen often keep schools in their own houses to which any of the people in the neighbourhood are admitted without payment. There are schools of a higher class kept by respectable mulláhs, in which instruction is given in theology and literature. The mulláhs are sometimes assisted by rich men, or they maintain themselves from their private means. In the same way Sanskrit is taught by Pándits. These schools have ceased to flourish since the establishment of Government schools. *One reason of this is that educational officers look upon indigenous schools with jealousy, and do their best to supplant them.* The course of study is not the same as in Government schools, *but so far as literature is concerned it is superior. Most native officials have been educated in indigenous schools.* These schools may be aided advantageously upon the following conditions: There must be no interference with their scheme of studies. They should keep a register of attendance. They should be inspected occasionally by officers of the department. If the Government desires that subjects of general knowledge should be taught in addition to the usual course of study, the mulláh should be free to teach such subjects himself, or to find his own assistants. It must be understood, however, that indigenous schools of the higher class, both Arabic and Sanskrit, are not likely to accept grants-in-aid on any terms.[1]

"In the city of Ambala there are indigenous schools established in accordance with the scheme for Government schools, but which do not receive aid from Government, and have not applied for aid because of their dislike to interference.[2] These schools were established especially with a view to giving instruction in the Muhammadan religion, which is not allowed in the Government or Mission school. Another matter, which deserves mention here, is the need of an investigation into the circumstances of endowments made by native gentlemen for the benefit of education; for instance, the *Itimad-ud-daula* Fund, which was intended for the old Delhi College."[3]

Among Societies, the ANJUMAN-I-ISLAMIA of Amritsar states as follows:—

"The number of indigenous schools in this province is limited, and the instruction imparted in them is both religious and secular. Besides Persian, Arabic, and Sanskrit of high order, Landí and a system of Mahájáni accounts

---

[1] They would gladly do so, if their learning were duly honored, and if the Educational Department had nothing to do with them.

[2] This statement clearly shows that even where the Government scheme is taught, departmental interference is not welcomed.—G. W. L.

[3] The *whole* file of this case should be sent for and should be carefully examined by a Committee composed of Civilians, Lawyers, and the relicts of the Donor.—G. W. L.

are also taught in these schools. The fees taken vary according to the means of the parents of the pupils. Some of the masters teach as a religious duty, and consider it unlawful to take any remuneration. The teachers of these schools do not generally belong to one particular class, and they open schools to earn their livelihood in Persian and Arabic literature. *The attainments of some of these masters are very fair.* They will accept Government aid, but it is next to impossible that they will conform to the grant-in-aid rules."

The ANJUMAN-I-HAMDARDI-ISLAMIA of Lahore, however, points out that under "*the present grant-in-aid rules, which are generally useless indigenous schools will never improve*;" whilst they further assert that "some Mussulmán and Hindu priests, as well as strictly religious persons, keep aloof from the Government schools, because there is no moral and religious teaching. To deprive children of religious teaching for five years they think very wrong. In Europe, religious teaching in schools is given to those who desire it. In India, parents keep their children at home for religious teaching, and then send them to a Government school; but if religious teaching were allowed in Government schools, boys would be sent to school much earlier than they are."

On the subject of the indigenous schools, the Anjuman-i-Hamdardi-Islamia makes the following pertinent remarks :—

"In the Director's Report for 1878-79, the indigenous schools were said to be 4,662, and the number of scholars 53,027; but the actual numbers are considerably more, partly because the method of collecting the statistics is imperfect, and partly because the *people will not tell the truth, from fear of some new tax, or of compulsory education, which prejudices are due to the neglect of the educational officers in informing the people of the wishes of the Government.*

"Indigenous schools are of three kinds—

"(*a*) Those in which the founder and patron is the teacher himself, who instructs every one who comes to him, without remuneration, in Persian, Arabic, Sanskrit, religious books, or useful knowledge. —There are many schools of this kind, but the number has decreased owing to the negligence of the Education Department. For instance, between 1878 and 1879 the number of indigenous schools decreased by 719. In those schools of this kind in which fees are taken, there is no regular system, but payment is sometimes made in cash and sometimes in kind.

"(*b*) Schools in which people have their own children taught and to which they admit the children of their neighbours.—In these schools fees are not paid, but the teacher receives a salary from the patron. These schools are few in number, especially since the establishment of the Department.

"(*c*) High Schools for the study of Arabic and Sanskrit, which are either private or supported by subscriptions. In these schools mathematics are taught to as high a standard as in Government schools, and literature and philosophy to a higher standard. Fees are not taken. The students receive scholarships and rewards.

"In all these schools the primitive course of study is followed, but in the schools of a lower order the Government scheme has here and there been adopted. There is no one system of education in all these schools, but the teacher is guided by circumstances. The teachers are usually former scholars of the schools in which they teach, and their ability is examined at the time of their appointment, and their skill in teaching is always under observation. There are no training schools for their benefit. The indigenous schools may be benefited by being placed under Local Boards. Under each Local Board there should be a high school, to which all the indigenous schools should be attached as branches.

Of the three kinds of schools which have been described, the first,—*viz.*, those which are established by individuals,—may in large numbers be connected with the Department, the second sort in a less degree, and the third sort not at all. The best way of connecting the first sort of schools with the department is for the Government to give them grants-in-aid, and to encourage them to teach subjects of useful knowledge, but without laying down strict rules; and for this purpose to get the assistance of native gentlemen and *Maulvis*. On these conditions the managers of certain indigenous schools will be willing to accept grants-in-aid; and the reasons why they have not done so generally, is because of the strictness of the conditions and the negligence of the educational officers."

Q. 5.—What opinion have you of the extent and value of home instruction?

A. 5.—Boys brought up in indigenous schools and those who have studied at home, although few of them can compete with the pupils of Government schools in subjects of general knowledge, are for the most part superior in literature."

The Secretary of the SAT SABHA Society of Lahore gives similar evidence:

"The Report of the Director of Public Instruction for 1877-78 gives the number of indigenous schools to be 5,381, containing 61,818 pupils, *but in my opinion there are as many more*. These schools are of five sorts:

"(1) Schools kept by Pándhas, Bháis, and Mulláhs, who charge a pice a boy per week, and in addition receive food and something on festivals and other ceremonies.

"(2) Schools established by private subscriptions and endowments, where a number of teachers are employed, and the people are not only taught gratuitously, but some provision is often made for their food and clothing.

"(3) Schools established by respectable persons for the instruction of their own children, wherein a Hindi or Persian teacher is employed. In such schools, the boys from the neighbourhood are also admitted.

"(4) Self-supporting schools, where a teacher of some repute establishes or opens a school in a populous part of a city or town; his support rests altogether on fees charged on the boys.

"(5) Schools of private individuals, who devote themselves to teaching the pupils for the public benefit, or as a meritorious act.

"No. 1 and a few of the others follow the old village system of teaching the boys one by one, and have no fixed course for their guidance.

"The Pándhas teach in the Landí character and the multiplication-table as far as 30×10; the Bháis teach Gurmukhi; the Mulláhs, Persian. As the teachers depend on the pupils for their support, the discipline in such schools cannot be said to be good. The fees in schools of the last three or four classes do not exceed 8 annas. No fees are taken at the Sat Sabhá School at Lahore, where English, Urdu or Persian, Gurmukhi, drawing plans, and surveying with chain and compass or theodolite, &c., are taught gratuitously.

"The masters of such schools are not generally selected from any particular class: *some of them have excellent qualifications*, but some have only a poor education. Government has established Normal Schools for training masters for the schools. If they are well supervised, they may be turned to good account as part of the system of national education, provided the teachers allow such supervision. The masters are willing to accept State aid and to conform to the rules under which such aid is given. In my opinion the grant-in-aid system has not been extended to indigenous schools: *when applied for, the application was rejected.*"

The ANJUMAN-I-PUNJAB first points out that the following classes are practically excluded from primary education:—

"(a) Pious Muhammadans, because they do not get religious and moral instruction, which they consider desirable above everything.

"(b) Artizans, because they do not get instruction useful to them in their professions.

"(c) Bráhmans and Pándits, because neither is their religion taught nor is instruction given to them in Sanskrit or in the Deva Nágari characters. *These people study in their private houses, or in private schools, what is useful to them secularly and religiously.*

"(d) Hindu shop-keepers, because instruction is not given to them, such would be useful to them in their respective avocations, *e. g.*, book-keeping in the Máhájani and Hindi characters. These people receive their education from their *Pándhas.*

"(e) Sikhs, Bháis, Grunthees, Akalis and other Sikh artizans and cultivators, because they are not taught their sacred books and because Persian or Urdu is quite useless to them."

The Anjuman-i-Punjab then enters on the subject of indigenous schools: "There are many indigenous schools in our province, and the system followed in them is a relic of the ancient system. The subjects and the character of instruction generally given in them are as follows: *Hindus.*—Books on religion and devotion only in some institutions; and in other Purans, Jotish, Dharm-Shastras, Vedant. *Sikhs*—Grant, Janam Sakhi, Gurbelas, Bhagwat, Niáya (logic), Vedant and Hindi literature generally in the Gurmukhi character. *Muhammadans*—First, religious books, and then Persian reading and writing. In higher schools, Arabic and logic.

"*The system of discipline in vogue in the above institutions is very satisfactory.*

"In some institutions fees are taken, and in others not. Where they are taken, they are not always in cash, but often also in kind. The masters are selected from among the Pándits, Pándhas, Bháis, &c., among Hindus; and Mulláhs among Muhammadans.

"They are sufficiently competent to teach the subjects above-mentioned. No arrangements have been made for training or providing masters for these schools. These indigenous schools can be turned to good account as part of a system of national education, if Government aid were given to them, and if subjects imparting useful knowledge were taught in them; *but not under the restrictions of any scheme fixed by Government.*

"The best method to be adopted for this purpose is, that no payment should be made to them unless they submit a report of progress and a bill of expenditure, attested by the *local boards.* The report of progress should be attested by the District Inspectors when on inspection tour.

"Many masters of these indigenous schools are willing to accept State aid and to conform to the rules under which such aid is given, provided the rules are made more elastic and liberal.

"The grant-in-aid system has been extended to a very limited extent, and it should be further extended to the indigenous schools."

And again, "Government can expect nothing from private effort without a liberal aid to elementary instruction in rural districts.

The following are the private agencies (known to the Anjuman) for promoting primary instruction:—

Indigenous Schools.

In Mosques, Dharmsálas, private Sanskrit Schools (Pathshálas), Schools of Pándahs, Schools of the Anjuman-i-Islamia, Schools of the Anjuman-i-Hamdardi, the Anarkali School of Maulvi Rahim Bakhsh, the Schools of the Arya Samaj, Sat Sabhá School, Siri Guru Singh Sabhá School, Shia School.

The Anjuman Sanskrit School, the Hindu Schools at Lahore, Ludhiána, Jallandhar, and Amritsar: Sikhsha Sabhá Schools; Bhabra Schools of Gujranwalla, Jhelum and Rawal Pindi, Sanskrit School of Rai Múl Singh at Gujranwalla, &c."

And elsewhere, referring to the status of the present Government village schoolmasters, "their influence among the villagers is almost nothing compared to what Pândits of Pathshálas and Maulvis of Maktabs had in previous times."

The "Lahore Indian Association" says:

"The only practically useful classes among these Indigenous schools are those belonging to Pándhas. Those classes are sometimes attended by 200 or 250 boys, the boys coming from all sections of the community. No systematic attempt seems to have been yet made to utilize these schools by Government. The grant-in-aid system has hardly been extended to them. There are some schools which have been taken up and superseded by State schools. *But all such schools so superseded have ceased to be Indigenous schools, having been assimilated to the ordinary Government schools in all respects. The Indigenous schools are capable of being greatly utilized.* If the Government were to promise the more qualified holders of these schools certain bonuses or aids on condition of their teaching along with their ordinary subjects some branches of practical or general knowledge, they might prove a source of much benefit to the country. The Government might keep some control over these schools so subsidized by extending the supervision of its controlling agency over them; but it should not force its own scheme of instruction nor insist upon particular books being taught. The condition for the grant of bonuses or aids should reach subjects only and not books. Bonuses may also be given to passed Normal school students or other persons properly qualified who might open schools for primary instruction."

The "Delhi Literary Society" says:

"The existing indigenous schools may be divided into the following classes:—

"i.—Pathshálas, or, as they are more popularly called, Sáls.

"ii.—Maktabs, kept up by maulvis and munshis.

"iii.—Maktabs, kept up at private houses.

"iv.—Classes taught by eminent maulvis, pándits, and faqueers.

"v.—High schools of Arabic and Persian.

"vi.—Special classes in medicine, law, &c.

"vii.—Schools in connection with masjids and tombs.

"Classes (i), (iv), and (v) are so far relics of ancient village communities that some are supported from the proceeds of endowments and jageers made by former rulers and noblemen.

"It was not unfrequently the custom of the well-to-do classes, such as landholders and respectable officers of Government, to assign so much land, or such a part of their income, towards the maintenance of boys and teachers. Lands were granted revenue-free or on a quit-rent, and other similar indulgences were made to encourage the poor and the needy to reap all the advantages of a free education. Such liberality was looked upon as an act of virtue which would meet with its due reward on the life to come. Such grants still exist in districts bordering on the frontier, *e. g.*, Dera Ismail Khan, Dera Ghazi Khan, &c.

"And first as to pathshálas. Sir John Phear in his able work on Aryan villages thus describes a Bengali pathshála—'In passing along a village path one may come upon a group of ten or twenty almost naked children squatting under a pipul tree, and engaged in marking letters on a plantain leaf, or in doing sums on a broken piece of foreign slate, or even on the smoothed ground before them. The instruction is quite gratis. The instructor generally is an elderly Bráhman. Although there is no regular pay for the duty, the instructor does not, any more than other people, do his work for nothing. On the occurrence of special events in his family, the parents of his pupils make him a small present of rice or dâl, or even a piece of cloth; and when a child achieves a marked stage in its progress, a similar recognition of the occasion is made. A Bráhman guru (teacher) will, in addition, get his share of the gifts to Bráhmans made on festivals and ceremonies'

"The foregoing account of a Bengali pathshála is subject to numerous variations when applied to a Hindustani sál. As far as the caste of the teacher is concerned, the general rule in this part of the country is that none but Bráhmans carry on this work. Recently, however, an attempt, and a successful one, has been made by a Muhammadan in this city to carry on the same calling, and as he is possessed of a most agreeable disposition and is careful not to betray the least bigotry, Hindu parents are glad to send their boys to his school. Strict discipline and effective teaching have equally contributed to maintain the high reputation of this school. We suggest that it is this class of schools which the Government ought to encourage. In pathshálas the usual curriculum of study commences with teaching the numerals, goes on to the multiplication tables of integers and fractions, and ends with teaching how to read and write the Munda (Máhájani) and Hindi alphabets. The utmost qualification attained, but very rarely, is writing letters, accounts in discount and interest, and stories about Raja Parichat. The usual hours of tuition are from six or seven in the morning to eleven, and from two to sunset in the afternoon. There are generally no classes. Each boy learns his own lesson. The spirit of competition is thus absolutely wanting. In the evening all the boys, no matter to what extent they have advanced in their studies, have to repeat at the top of their voices after the guru or generally the monitor (barchatta), the senior boy in the school, the whole of the multiplication tables. Boys thus learn to repeat all the tables from sheer force of daily recitation, although, if examined in a way different from that in which they are taught, they at once fail to answer the question. They try to go back and recite from the beginning, and the joke is that sometimes the urchins pass over the answer required, simply because their intelligence had not been called into play, the whole being a mere matter of memory. The pernicious nature of such instruction needs no comment. Suffice it to remark that time and energy are equally wasted, and no appreciable result is obtained.

"Fees are collected both in cash and in kind. Every fortnight the boy takes a sidha, or offering of atta, dâl, salt and ghee to his teacher. In some houses the guru is given a feast on *mácash* monthly in honour of ancestors, on occasions of marriages and sradhs, and other festivals or jovial occasions, the guru's appetite is satisfied with victuals, cloth and money. Chauk chaknic is the grand gala day of the guru. The offerings made on this day go to maintain him or his family for several succeeding months. Cash is generally taken on the boys having learnt how to write his numerals, his multiplication tables one after the other, and the alphabets. On such occasions the patti is painted and polished, and the boy carries his writing in glee to his father, and receives the usual douceur for the guru, commensurate with the position in life of the boy's father. Presents in sweetmeats, &c., are also made to fellow-students. The day a boy is admitted into the school is observed as a closed holiday. The admission is also marked with a bountiful distribution of *laddus* (sweets). The attainments of gurus are generally very limited. Beyond reading and writing

Nágari and knowing a little Sanskrit, their attainments in literature are almost *nil*, while in arithmetic their qualifications do not comprise the more recondite rules of profit and loss, compound interest, proportion, partnership, square and cube roots, least common multiple, and decimals. No arrangements exist as regards the training of these teachers, for the simple reason that they have not yet been brought under Government supervision; and while Government has had anything to do with them, it has been in the way of taking over their boys, establishing a Government school, and leaving the guru to his own fate unconsoled and inconsolable. Natives would be happy if some change for the better were made in the status and position of these men. Up to this time they have been discouraged in every way. As, however, the system under which they exist has taken deep root in the soil, it would be wise to utilise them, to give them a small pay, to train them in normal classes, to teach them the subjects that would be most useful in villages and towns, and generally, after training, to send them to the village where their home is. Hereditary claims have always been acknowledged in India, and the influence of a hereditary schoolmaster is always very great in the community. These teachers would gratefully receive any support that the Government would vouchsafe, and the people of the village would be personally obliged for any favour shown to their hereditary guru. We have no doubt that these teachers would agree to conform to Government rules and discipline, in consideration of the aid granted by the State. At the same time we wish to submit that statements and naqshas should not be required from them in such numbers as is now the case. Under the present scheme perjury and false statements are resorted to, instead of being discouraged; and the aim of the teacher is more to prepare and submit a glossy naqsha than give a substantially good education to his boys; for the inspecting officers have more time to look at the naqshas and find fault with this thing and that in them than for actual inspection of tuition.

"The second class of schools are maktabs kept up by maulvis and munshis who have made teaching their profession and obtain their livelihood through it. These men usually levy small fees, say from 1 anna to 4 annas a month, from each boy, the amount of fees depending on the income of the father. The course of instruction is confined to reading and writing elementary books in Persian, and making calculations about pay and wages for so many days in a month, according to the old-fashioned practice which obtained in Muhammadan times. Some of the schools are fairly well attended, the income from fees being quite sufficient for the maintenance of a large family. Generally, however, the teachers are with difficulty able to keep body and soul together. The qualifications of these masters are also of a very limited character. On the principle, however, God helps those who help themselves, it is suggested these men should receive some encouragement. The men now in the service of Government in its Department of Public Instruction would be nowhere if Government dismissed them. These men, on the contrary, manage to earn a living without Government support, and are trusted by the people. Instead, therefore, of maintaining a large highly paid school establishment everywhere, would it not be wise and economical to utilise these men? The remarks about conformity to Government regulations and the grant-in-aid system made in connection with pathshálas, apply with equal force to this class of teachers.

"The third class of schools are transitory in their nature, and depend altogether on the whim or caprice of the individual who employs a maulvi or munshi to teach his children. These schools are in all cases liable to disruption on the boy's attaining the requisite knowledge to enable him to go to a Government school. Such maktabs are usually attended by boys from the neighbourhood who pay some small fees. The teacher in addition gets Rs. 4 or Rs. 5 per mensem from the master of the mansion. No State aid would be of any lasting benefit to such schools. Not being permanent, they don't deserve any grant-in-aid.

"The fourth class comes under the head of secondary education. Some learned maulvi, pándit or faqueer, employs his leisure hours in teaching the Korán, Hadis, the sacred books of Hindus or of religious sects, as the case may be; no fees are charged—nay, food is supplied to students in some cases. Sitting in a grove of trees, or by the side of a stream, or in public places, such as baghichas, dharmsálas or belas, pándits and faqueers devote themselves to religious instruction and meditation. Such places are usually held sacred, and offerings are made there in large quantities, which go to maintain the teachers and those taught.

"V. Traces of the 5th class are observable in the North-Western Provinces, at Deoband and other places, but nowhere in the Punjab. These schools teach to a high standard in Arabic and Persian, and are maintained by private munificence as well as by funded endowments. From their very nature they are incapable of conforming to Government rules, their great aim being to impart religious knowledge.

"VI. Some Muhammadan physicians and divines keep up classes for instruction in medicine and fiqa. The remarks made above apply to this class also.

"VII. This is a peculiarly Muhammadan institution. Boys and elderly men of poor parentage and slender means are fed and taught the Korán. Some in time grow to be imáms, and thus succeed in earning an income of Rs. 4 or Rs. 5 per mensem. For reasons recorded under the preceding heads, these schools also do not call for any State support.

"To sum up. We are of opinion that Government support be extended to schools coming under classes I and II; that half-yearly prizes be given to students attending them at times of examinations; that the masters be paid a fixed salary per mensem and rewarded every now and then in addition, when found deserving of further encouragement; that besides, subjecting these schools to inspection by Government officers, a scheme be devised of appointing a local board for a circle of 30 miles or less as suitable opportunities may offer; the members of these boards being selected from the influential classes of residents in the circle, entrusting to them the supervision of these schools, and looking to them for their proper management, rewarding and complimenting them whenever their efforts are successful, and for all these purposes bringing them under the influence of the district officer. We would also suggest that the grant-in-aid rules be relaxed to a certain extent in favour of these schools."

The Punjab Bráhmo Samáj is of opinion that—

"The whole of the Hindu and Sikh sacerdotal classes, the mercantile and the trading classes, the artizans and the agriculturists, are 'practically excluded from primary instruction' in this province, for neither the languages nor the subjects taught in the Government primary schools are of much practical use to them in the pursuit of their respective avocations. Such of them only as intend to train up their sons for service in Government offices avail themselves of the Government schools.

"Indigenous schools exist in this province to a large extent. Every principal village and town has its *Pándit, Pándha, Bhái* and *Maulvi* teachers in proportion to the different classes of population, *viz.*, Bráhmans, Khattris, Sikhs, and Mussulmáns. The instructions given by the *Pándits, Maulvis* and *Bháis*, are chiefly in religious books. The *Pándhas* teach mental arithmetic and Landé Máhájani writing. The Persian indigeneous schools have almost disappeared, as their place has been taken up by the Government primary and middle schools, contrary to the spirit of the Educational Despatch of 1854.

"The indigenous schools can be turned to good account as part of a system of national education by giving grants-in-aid to such teachers of these schools as may undertake and be able to teach the secular subjects that may be prescribed by Government. The best method to adopt for this purpose is to sanction the grant to each teacher annually, according to the *number* of students taught in the secular subjects (in addition to whatever else they may learn at their own desire or that of their parents or teachers) and the *amount of progress* made by each student. The progress may be reported by means of a monthly statement, and its accuracy tested by the periodical examinations of the District Inspectors of schools, or the members of the local board, if it be decided to entrust the management of primary schools to the local boards."

The Lahore " Arya Samáj " gives the following evidence :—

" Indigenous schools are to be found scattered all over the province, their numbers in those places where Government schools do not exist being larger. They are not now so numerous as they were before the advent of the English. One important class of Indigenous schools which used to give instruction in Persian to the sons of munshis and other such men as desired to get employment under the Mogul rulers, the court language in whose reigns was Persian, have to a great extent ceased to exist, there being no want for them owing to Government having made Urdu the court language and instituted schools of its own to teach it.

" The Indigenous schools are so far a relic of the ancient village system that they are presided over by hereditary teachers generally, who impart instruction in much the same fashion, and on about similar terms, only they do not supply the students with boarding and lodging as before. They also resemble the village system in the kind of instruction that is given and the discipline and system in vogue in them. Indigenous schools at present are of three kinds :—

" *1st.*—Those which impart purely religious instruction.

" *2nd.*—Those which give purely secular instruction.

" *3rd.*—Those which give instruction of both kinds.

" They are of the following descriptions :—

" *Religious.*

" 1. Gûrmukhi schools, held chiefly in Dharmsálas, where Gurmukhi characters and portions of Granth Sáhib are taught. In the religious houses of the different sects, young men of the order and outsiders are taught Gita, Vedant, the Upanishháds, and other philosophies and religious books. The teachers are generally of Udási, Nirmála, Bairági, and Sanyási sects.

" *Secular.*

" 2. Mâhájani schools, where multiplication-tables, bazaar accounts, and Landé or Saráfi characters are taught.

" 3. Private schools, in which teachers are engaged by private gentlemen to teach their own children, with whom they often allow other children also, sometimes gratuitously and sometimes on payment of fees, to read.

" 4. Persian *maktabs*, where Persian is taught by *Maulvis* and sometimes by Munshis.

" *Secular-Religious.*

" 5. Sanskrit Pathshálas, generally presided over by hereditary teachers and Pándits of reputation, where Sanskrit books in literature, religion, religious ceremonies, astrology, &c., are taught. In these schools students of a higher order are also sometimes to be met with. The schools are generally held at the residences of the Pándits, who, as a rule, teach gratis and earn their living by other means. Men learned in Arabic and Persian also teach students in this way at their houses.

" 6. Arabic and Persian schools, held generally in mosques, where books on religion and secular subjects are taught to Muhammadan lads and adults. Schools of class 2 are by far the most numerous, there being sometimes as many as five or six in a single town. In the cities their number is still larger. Those of classes 4, 5, 6, though not so numerous as of class 2, are also large; but the number of students attending them is comparatively small. Schools of the first class are to be found generally in villages, and are not very large in number ; while those of the third class are to be seen in cities and towns only. The system of discipline observed in these schools is quite dissimilar to that obtaining in Government schools. One principal feature of it is veneration for teachers, which in the religious schools is traditional, while in the secular schools it is often enforced by physical punishment.

"In the first and sixth classes no fees in money are given. The scholars supply their teachers with meals in turn and give some money each according to his means on occasions of festivals and marriages in the family. In the fourth class sometimes no food is supplied, but remuneration in the shape of fees, as well as at different stages of progress, is given in money.

"In the second class the pupils give something in kind twice a month and a pice every Sunday. Money is generally given at different stages of progress and on occasions of festivals. In some places a small quantity of oil is also given by the students in turn.

"The teachers in the second class of schools, who are both Hindus and Muhammadans, and those in the first class generally, succeed to the profession hereditarily. Their qualifications are very low. They do not know beyond what they teach, but they are generally very expert in imparting what they know. The range of instruction being very limited, the students often work sums mentally and without the aid of slates or any writing materials with wonderful rapidity. The same may be said to a very great extent of the qualifications of teachers in the third class; but the teachers in the fourth, fifth, and sixth classes are often men of good qualifications but want in practical experience. As no attempt at forming the boys into classes is made, the teacher is obliged to give lessons to each boy separately.

"No arrangements have yet been made to train teachers for these schools. The teachers that are trained in Normal schools, both aided and unaided, suit the requirements of the schools carried on on the Government system only.

"These schools are so numerous that many thousands of boys daily receive education in them; and some of them, especially of the second class, which are attended by the children of both Hindu and Muhammadan shop-keepers, are so popular that every effort should be made to utilise them. They can be turned to good account *by supplementing and not superseding* the course of instructions pursued in them. To set aside their present masters who have much local influence, or to tamper with the national way of teaching to any very serious exteut, will prevent any great use being made of them as part of a system of national education. The teachers, or their sons and relatives, in case they are themselves too old to go to school, must be induced by means of scholarships or bonuses to receive training in Normal schools established for the purpose in all those subjects which we have proposed in the course of instruction for Primary schools. The schools of the second and fifth classes, and especially of the former, can be very easily turned to good account by the above method. To utilise them to the fullest extent, it would be however necessary to make Hindi the medium of instruction in them. Those of the fourth class can also be to some extent utilised, but nowise the remaining classes.

"The masters, so far as we know, are not unwilling to receive State aid and conform to the rules under which that aid is given, only if changes setting aside their national ways of teaching are not very hastily but gradually introduced."

Lala Mulraj, the representative of the Bhashá Prachirni Sabhá, makes the following valuable statement:—

"Indigenous schools do not exist in the Punjab to the extent in which they existed before the introduction of Government and Grant-in-aid schools. As indigenous manufactures have died out on the introduction of foreign manufactures, so have the indigenous schools on the introduction of Government and Grant-in-aid schools. Those that exist are not as good as they used to be.

"The indigenous schools are of various kinds:

"(*a*) There are schools maintained by Pándhas, in which Landé or Hindi, or some other form of the same, is taught. These schools depend upon the Pándha, who is assisted sometimes by some member of his family or an advanced student. The fee is one pice a week, and bread (*roti*) on fixed days, and presents on holidays and marriage occasions. The subjects of tuition are reading and writing letters, *hundis*, &c., in Landé (or some form of the same), and arithmetical tables and mental arithmetic (*gur*), and the system of account-keeping. The pupils of such schools know mental arithmetic and account-keeping much better than those trained in Government schools. The boys have to come to school early in the morning and go home at the time of taking meals, before noon; and then they collect together again in the afternoon and sit till evening, when the school breaks up by singing tables and moral precepts. Boys of the schools who do not attend are forcibly dragged to school by the bigger boys, who are sent by the Pándha to collect the pupils. On occasions of marriages and other such ceremonies, the Pándha goes with his boys, singing the tables and moral precepts and auspicious songs, and gets his customary presents in cash and kind from the master of the family.

"The boys remain dirty, as they squat upon earth, and as they use wooden *phattis* or *tákhtis* colored black with lamp-black or soot, on which they write with *khariya mátti*, or chalk dissolved in water. Sometimes the boys write upon earth with fingers or sticks.

"(*b*) Schools maintained by Maulvis, in which only Persian literature and composition are taught. The Maulvi sometimes is paid by fees, like the Pándha, and at other times the parents of the boys make their separate terms with him. But these schools are not so largely attended as those of Pándhas generally.

"(*c*) There are small schools attached to Masjids, in which generally reading the Korán only, without its meaning, is taught. Sometimes in these schools Persian also is taught. Sometimes no fee is charged in these schools. There are small schools kept up by private persons here and there. I have seen schools kept up by weavers and other tradesmen, in which the master plies his trade, and goes on at the same time giving instruction to the boys in the Kurán and other religious books. Sometimes at such schools Persian also is taught.

"(*d*) There are in some places small *pathshálas* attached to *Shibdwálás* and *Thákurdwáras*, in which Sanskrit is taught. No fee is charged in these schools.

"(*e*) Here and there some enterprising Pándit, or a *Bráhmachari* or *Sanyasi*, gathers around him some lovers of Sanskrit, and gives instruction to them. No fee is charged in these schools. These schools, as well as those in *Thákurdwáras*, are maintained by the charity of the people.

"In indigenous schools generally, and especially in schools of the latter kind, the teacher is held in great reverence. In schools of the latter kind, students undergo great privations to acquire knowledge, and not unfrequently live by begging. The qualifications of the teachers are in some instances of a very high order. The Pándhas, however, generally do not know anything more than they teach. The work of Pándhas generally, and of Maulvis also in some instances, is hereditary.

"Most of the schools which were maintained by Pándhas and Maulvis have already become Government schools, and the masters of the few schools of the kind that remain are quite willing to accept State aid and to conform to rules. There can be very little doubt in this, that the masters of the other schools also would generally accept State aid, if they were allowed to teach what they liked, and were not required to conform to all the rules. Grants-in-aid are very seldom, if ever, given to indigenous schools. If grants-in-aid were given to indigenous schools they would spring up and flourish in every nook and corner of the country.

"No arrangements have been made specially by Government for training or providing masters in the indigenous schools; but if Government extended in practice also, and not in theory only, the principle of grant-in-aid and payment by results to indigenous schools, some of the men who now receive education in the Government and grant-in-aid institutions would set up private schools in different parts of the country.

"Indigenous schools can be turned to good account as part of a system of national education, by changing the policy of the Educational Department and of Government towards the indigenous schools. Hitherto these schools have not been encouraged; on the other hand, efforts have been made sometimes to put them down. When the master of an indigenous school is willing, it should be inspected by officers of Government. Pains should be taken to gather statistics about indigenous schools, and to publish these in the report on Education. The system of grants-in-aid should be extended to indigenous schools; but the best thing to do would be to offer rewards to the masters for the number of students that they succeed in passing from their schools in the different examinations of the Educational Department and of the University. The rewards should vary with the number of students and the difficulty of the examinations.

"It must be mentioned here that now-a-days societies are springing up in different parts of the country, as the Arya Samájes, the Anjumans, and the Sabhás, which also set up schools. Elementary education would be greatly diffused if these societies become part of the institutions of the country and are encouraged.

"Home instruction, independent altogether of school education, does not exist now to any very large extent except in the case of shop-keepers, who train up their sons in account-keeping in *Landé*, &c., and in the case of Maulvis and Pándits, who teach their children, at home, Arabic and Persian and Sanskrit. In the low educational test examination of candidates for employment or promotion in the public service, which nominally applies to all appointments of which the salaries exceed Rs. 15 per mensem, there is nothing to make it difficult for a boy educated at home to compete on equal terms with boys educated at school. Only those candidates are admitted into the examination who have not been studying in any Government or Aided school within six months from the date of examination (see *Punjab Gazette*, February 9th, 1882). There is no other special examination in general knowledge and literature fixed for qualifying for the public service; but if such examinations be fixed, they should be open also to persons educated at home.

"In former times it was only private effort which supplied elementary instruction in villages and in towns But with the advent of Government and grant-in-aid Mission schools, and owing to other causes also, private effort has greatly disappeared. But if Government made elementary instruction really elementary, and not classical as at present, and imparted it through the real vernacular of the people, or a language closely allied to the vernacular, and by the medium of Nágari characters, and also recognised the Nágari characters in its courts and aided private effort by grants-in-aid and payments by results where necessary, the diffusion of elementary instruction might be left to a great extent, if not wholly, to private effort.

"The private agencies which exist for promoting primary instruction are—

"(1) Schools of Pándhas, Maulvis, some of the schools in Masjids and Thákurdwáras.

"(2) Schools established by societies like the Arya Samájes, Sabhás, and Anjumans of Hindus (and Sikhs) and Muhammadans."

Now for the other side. I do not quote Lieutenant-Colonel Holroyd's evidence on the subject, as it is, practically, a transcript of what repeatedly appears in his reports, which I have quoted elsewhere; but Mr. J. Sime, B.A., the Inspector of Schools of the Lahore Circle, has the following impressions regarding indigenous schools:—"As far as I am aware, there are *no traces* of an old village school system in the Punjab. When the Government system was introduced, there was *here* and *there* in the villages indigenous schools, mostly Persian, which were gradually absorbed. The indigenous schools which now exist are mostly in the towns. The bulk of these are Kuráni, Shástri, and Granth Schools, all of a religious character. The instruction imparted is purely literary, and excepting in the Shástri schools, and *that rarely*, the attainments are of a very poor description. In the Kuráni schools Persian is sometimes added, occasionally also Urdu and Arithmetic. Besides these, there are Persian and Máhájani schools. In the former usually only Persian is taught, sometimes a little Arabic, occasionally Urdu, seldom anything else. The Máhájani schools are for the multiplication tables and shop-keeper's accounts, with elementary Nágari sometimes added.

"In none of these schools have I observed *any system whatever of discipline*. There is an understood, although unwritten, course of studies; but no class organisation; and rarely a register.

"Fees are levied in all the secular schools. Besides the monthly fees, presents in cash or kind are expected, and given on various occasions.

"As a rule, the masters of these schools are of inferior attainments. Sometimes a well-read man, on either the Sanskrit or Arabic side, will be met with; but even then the qualities *are not those required for a teacher of youth*. So far as I know, no attempt has been made to train the masters in those schools, so long as their schools have remained independent. When the schools have been taken over, the masters have generally been sent to the Normal School, but not always with success. *In many districts, these masters remain now the chief obstacle to instructional progress in the schools.*[1]

"Indigenous masters are, as a rule, willing to accept State aid; but by reason of their *poor* attainments, they would generally fail to fulfil the *easiest* conditions on which such aid could be given. It was on this account that the plan of incorporation was at first adopted. Grants-in-aid have occasionally been given to these schools, but, as far as my experience goes, not very successfully. On a careful review of the whole matter, I do not consider that in the circumstances the plan of incorporation was unwise; and I believe that this and the giving of grants-in-aid where the teachers are fairly fit, or where the grant would be likely to produce efficiency, are the only ways at present of turning the indigenous schools to good account. The offer of grants to new men setting up schools is another matter."—(The italics are mine.—G. W. L.)

Babu Hari Sing, Assistant Inspector of the same Circle, is, perhaps, even more emphatic. After pointing out a *sixth* class of indigenous schools, "schools set up by private individuals or by teachers dismissed from Government or Aided Schools in which a little of arithmetic and grammar are also taught, in addition to the ordinary Persian books," he says:—"The number of indigenous schools for secular education are very limited,[2] and the attendance more or less irregular in all. All are a relic of an ancient system, and no discipline worth the name is observed in any. The scholars pay no fixed rate of fees; but the teachers can make their subsistence, about Rs. 5 or 6 a month, partly in cash payment and partly in presents and other perquisites. They are mostly hereditary Mulláhs, Pándhas, Bháis or Pándits. The qualifications of teachers in schools of class 1, 3 and 6 are confined to Persian, Arabic, or Sanskrit literature,

[1] Here is a statement, which illustrates the unfriendly attitude of the Educational Officers towards Indigenous Schools.—G. W. L.

[2] They are even now, at least, five times the number of Government Schools, in spite of the attempts during 26 years to suppress them.—G. W. L.

as the case may be, in which some indeed are very proficient. Those in schools of class 2 are usually expert in the Native system of accounts, while those in classes 4 and 5 seldom go beyond the formal reading of their sacred books, the meanings of which they can in most cases neither explain nor understand. *Experience is the only training which the masters of such schools have acquired, and no other.* Such of these institutions as could be turned to good account have been already absorbed into Government and in larger towns into Mission schools also; *and there are few or none to be so utilised.* The best method, however, of turning them to any good account is to extend to them the system of payment-by-results. The masters will, of course, be glad to receive State aid; but I do not think that there will be many among them who will be able to conform to the rules under which such aid is at present given."

Strongest, however, is Babu JAIGOPAL, District Inspector of Schools at Amritsar:—

"In this province Indigenous schools exist *to a very limited extent now. Most of them have been replaced or absorbed by the Government Primary schools.* The subjects generally taught in them are the Korán and other sacred books for the Muhammadans only, and Persian literature, composition, and caligraphy for both Hindus and Muhammadans. The teaching is generally wanting in method, thoroughness, and intelligence, and is not much addressed to the understanding. If by discipline is meant regularity and punctuality of attendance, a fixed time-table and regular classification, then there is none of it at all. But the punishments inflicted upon the students are sometimes severe: they are similar to those described by Mr. Adam in his report on the Indigenous schools of Bengal and Behar. No regular fees are taken, but the teachers are remunerated by presents and daily meals; the latter are given in rotation by the pupils, and the former consist of cash payments. For instance, the boys have to pay *a pice each on every Friday.* A boy, when *commencing* a new book, has to give a present of one rupee. On the occasions of marriages in the families of the pupils, also presents of one rupee and upwards, according to the circumstances of the donors, are given. Payments in kind are also made by the agricultural class at harvest time. The masters of such schools generally belong to the Mullâh class, who are the hereditary priests and teachers of the village, and their qualifications are generally very moderate. No arrangements have, as far as I know, been made for training or providing masters in such schools.

"From what I know of the condition of Indigenous schools and of the qualifications of their masters, *I do not think that they can under any circumstances be turned to good account as a part of a system of national education,*[1] unless the teachers, before they are subsidized, can be induced to undergo a training in some Normal school—their places in their absence being supplied by men who have received a regular education in Normal or Secondary schools. They would, I dare say, be glad to accept State aid and to conform to the rules under which such aid is given. But I am afraid that *they will not be able to comply with the conditions required, and they are not competent to carry out the Government scheme of studies.* I do not think that the grant-in-aid system has been extended to them to any great extent, *or that it can be extended further with advantage. I am not sure if anything can be gained by doing so.*[1] The other Indigenous schools are those conducted by Pándhas, in which Máhájani writing and the Native system of accounts are taught. But these schools are few, and for the most part situated in towns."

Khan AḤMAD SHAH, Extra Assistant Commissioner of Hushiarpur, also, who was "employed in the Educational Department of the Punjab for eleven years," similarly contradicts the combined testimony of Societies and all other non-departmental witnesses as to the extent and character of Indigenous schools, but is more hopeful as regards their acceptance of State aid under the grant-in-aid rules.

---

[1] Here is another statement which illustrates the attitude of the Educational Officers towards Indigenous Schools.—G. W. L.

"*Indigenous schools may almost be said to have become extinct in this province.*[1] *The very few that survive* stick to the ancient village system. The instruction imparted is *restricted* to religious subjects and the requirements of the village community. There is no classification. The schools are open from morn till noon, and again in the afternoon. Mental arithmetic, Persian books and composition of the old Oriental style, are taught. Grammar is NOT included in the course of instruction. Corporal punishment is freely administered. There are no fixed rates of fees. In towns, small sums are paid weekly or monthly, according to the means of the parents or guardians; in villages, grain at harvest time and small sums on festivals are given. In addition to this, the schoolmaster is fed by turns by his pupils, and is rewarded on the occasion of particular subjects being begun or finished. The teachers are always chosen from a class that is held in special esteem from religious considerations; but *as a rule they are not men of any estimable qualifications.* No arrangements have been made for training or providing masters in such schools. To turn these schools to good account as part of a system of national education, it will be necessary to introduce into them the subjects generally taught in Government schools. They should also be made to conform to the system of discipline and classification in force in Government schools. This could be effected by the extension of State aid and supervision to such institutions and by training the village schoolmasters in the method of instruction imparted in Government schools. They will be found willing to accept such aid, and to conform to the rules under which it is given."

The following account of RAI SAHIB SINGH of Delhi, who has discussed the subject with "several kinsmen and relatives connected with the Educational Department," is interesting :—

"4. The number of indigenous schools in the Punjab is very small. It was considerably reduced on the introduction of the Government system of education. Many of them which then existed were from time to time taken in by the officers of the Education Department and incorporated in their own schools. Leaving out of consideration the Muhammadan schools held in mosques, of which I think nothing can be made,[2] the indigenous schools now existing may be divided into two classes, the *Pathshálas* and *Maktabs*. In the former, the children of the Hindus, especially those of the Banias, are instructed in the multiplication tables, and in most advanced of them to write letters and hundis in the Máhájani character. In the latter, the children of both the Hindus and Muhammadans are taught to read and write Persian and to do a little arithmetic. In both kinds of schools the use of the rod is in full play, and the chastisements the children receive at the hands of their masters are sometimes of the most merciless character.

"The boys are not divided into classes as in Government schools. Each reads his own lesson, but in the evening all the children have to repeat at the top of their voices the multiplication tables after the teacher or one of the most advanced pupils. No fees appear to be demanded by the teacher from his students; but from this it should not be understood he imparts instruction gratis. He is presented with the materials for a meal twice a month, and with some little cash on certain festive occasions. The fourth day of the light half of the moon in the month of *Bhadan* is for the teacher of a pathshála a day of great rejoicing. On that day Ganesh, the god of wisdom, is worshipped by the urchins, when presents in cash and sweetmeats are made to the teacher, who is sometimes invited by the parents of some of the pupils to their house with the whole school, when dresses of honour are presented to the master and his wife, and sweetmeats are distributed among the children. Presents are also made to the teacher on the completion by the pupil of each set of the multiplication tables. On the occasion of marriage of one of the pupils the master is not forgotten. The father of the bride is asked for a present in cash and clothes for the padha, which, I believe, is invariably made. In *maktabs* regular fees are taken by the teacher, according to the means of the parents of the pupils. Of course, he who pays the most receives the greatest attention. The padhas who teach at the *pathshálas* are a hereditary class of teachers. In this part of the country they invariably belong to the Bráhminical class, but in the Punjab there are Mussulmán padhas also, who, I believe, are the descendants of the Bráhmans forcibly converted to Muhammadanism during the Mussulmán regime. The qualification of the pathshála

[1] "Another friend of the Educational Department, MIRZA FATH MUHAMMAD BEG of Kasur, only deposes that "there are fewer indigenous schools than there used to be. The character of these schools is well known. When Government aid was offered to indigenous schools, very few were willing to accept it, and I do not think that they will be likely to do so now." (This is not consistent with the facts.) "There is no regular scheme of study in these schools."

[2] The feeling against Muhammadans is unmistakeable.

teachers are not of very high order, perhaps not much advanced beyond those of the best of their pupils. The teachers in *maktabs* are generally Mussulmáns possessing various degrees of qualification.

"No arrangements appear to have been made for training teachers for indigenous schools, which cannot be turned to much account. I know of no indigenous schools to which the grant-in-aid system has been applied in the Punjab. The few indigenous schools which receive grants-in-aid from the Punjab University are very inferior institutions, and incapable, I believe, of supplying candidates for any of its examinations."[1]

IKRAMULLA KHAN, a Magistrate of the same city, gives a more hopeful picture of indigenous Muhammadan schools, "*the wide-spread fame of many of these attracts students from the remotest parts of India.*" He states, *inter alia* :—

"4. The number of indigenous schools in the Punjab is very limited. The exact number of these schools cannot be known—the records on the point are not reliable; but it is certain that many such schools which existed before the introduction of the Government system of education have been absorbed in Government schools. In indigenous schools which still exist in cities, towns and villages, no change or improvement has been effected, either in the mode of teaching or the subjects taught. They are just what they were a hundred years ago, and may so far be called a relic of the ancient system.

"The indigenous schools are either low or high. The maktabs and pathshálas intended for the instruction of Mussulmán and Hindu youths in elementary knowledge are schools of a low order, the *Madrasas*, providing instruction in different branches of learning—religious and secular, for the advanced schools in Arabic and Persian—are schools of a high order.

"In maktabs the Korán is made the principal subject of teaching, while easy Persian and Urdu books, with a little writing, are often taught. Arithmetic, unfortunately, is much neglected. Pathshálas or Hindi primary schools do not give instruction either in classical or vernacular languages. There, the attention of the boys is solely confined to, the multiplication tables and to writing letters and hundis in the Mahájani character.

"In endowed Muhammadan schools no fees are taken, and not only instruction is given gratis, but such of the students who are unable to support themselves, are fed and clothed from the proceeds of the endowment. The Maulvis teaching in endowed Madrasas and giving gratuitous instruction at their own places of residence, are often men of very great learning, who have devoted their whole life acquiring a thorough knowledge of Muhammadan theology, law, philosophy, logic, and other abstruse branches of learning.

"The wide-spread fame of many of these attracts students from the remotest parts of India. The normal schools for training teachers is altogether an European idea.

"The maktabs and pathshálas may be made a part of the Government system of education by inducing the teachers to agree to accept the tuition of such subjects as arithmetic, history, geography (*if necessary, mensuration*) in addition to their own books (*which are always religious or moral*), and to open these schools to Government inspection.

"The teachers of these schools are at present unable to undertake this work; but I think they will not require much time to learn these additional subjects and make themselves equal to the task required of them, if they were only paid somewhat liberally till the system has been put in a working order and based on a reliable footing.

"The grant-in-aid system has not hitherto been extended to these schools in this province.

"I can think of no private agency existing for the promotion of primary education, except the Chaori school and the Fatahpuri Madrasa in Delhi, which receive no aid from Government. The former is a well-attended lower school and gives both religious and secular instruction; while the latter is a high school or college, teaching only religious books of a high standard, and allowing monthly stipends to such of the scholars who are unable to prosecute their studies without such support.

"There is indigenous instruction for girls among the Muhammadans, but it is to a great extent limited to the teacher classes and the old and respectable families. Parents who cannot afford to pay governesses teach their girls themselves.

"Ladies of high education are not generally found among the Hindus now-a-days. Books of a high standard in Arabic and Persian literature were taught formerly; but the instruction now given is limited to the Korán and sometimes a little book-reading and letter-writing is also taught in addition.

The opinions of European Civil Officers are in favor of encouraging the indigenous schools, with the exception, perhaps, of Mr. Baden-Powell, Addi-

[1] They constantly *pass* the University Examinations.

tional Commissioner of Lahore, who thinks "that the teachers would be quite incompetent to teach what Government would require." Mr. W. COLDSTREAM, Deputy Commissioner of Simla, however, has always been an advocate for the encouragement of these schools. Mr. E. O'BRIEN, Deputy Commissioner of Multan, finds in them his only hope for the spread of primary education; whilst Mr. J. G. CORDERY, Commissioner of Peshawar, has a generous sympathy for the priestly and learned classes of the province, and feels sorrow for their decay and neglect under our system, which are, indeed, worthy of his own scholarship.

As regards the Missionaries, they are too devoted to their noble aims, not to be able to appreciate the same feeling in the priests and teachers of opposing creeds, whom they naturally consider to be less destructive to the religious sense than the Government "secular" system, which is subversive alike of all religions.

In the evidence of "TEN MISSIONARIES IN THE NORTHERN PUNJAB," even the Korán or Mosque schools, which are so despised by the Educational Department, are referred to as follows:—

"Masjid schools might, where they do not conflict with existing schools, be made useful under the grant-in-aid system."

The liberality of these views in men held up by some officers as undeserving of grants (which the Educational Despatch of 1854 devised specially for them, few, if any, except Missionary institutions, being in existence at the time when it was framed),—because their funds are not subscribed locally (as if Government schools got *any* local subscription in most places), and because the Missionaries aim at the subversion of native creeds,—deserves, I submit, that the names of those who have shown such fairness to native religious schools, should be recorded. They are the Rev. H. David, B.A.; the Rev. J. W. Youngson, M.A.; the Rev. W. Harper, B.D.; the Rev. S. Martin, M.A.; the Rev. R. Stewart, D.D.; the Rev. A. Gordon, M.A.; the Rev. A. B. Caldwell, B.A.; the Rev. T. L. Scott, M.A.; the Rev. J. S. Barr, D.D., and the Rev. D. S. Sytle, the names being divided between the Church of Scotland and the American Presbyterian Church. Surely, if the testimony of high graduates and of experienced independent educationists is of any value, their preponderant condemnation of the Government education system is entitled to the greatest consideration.

The Rev. W. JUKES has the following observations on the indigenous schools in the Pesháwar District:—

"Indigenous schools in the Pesháwar District are comparatively few, for the village mosques can hardly be brought under that category; although some of the *Maulvis* or *Imáms* are sometimes persuaded to place their schools under Government supervision, it is *only in proportion as the Maulvi is a clever or somewhat ignorant man, that he will refuse or accept the Government pay.* In these mosque schools, the Korán is first taught, and after that Persian. The system of discipline is lax in the extreme, and no fees whatever are taken. *The remedy*, as I have endeavoured to describe in my answer to question 2, will *be to encourage the grant-in-aid system gradually.* There is another class of schools, called *maktabs*, which exist in fairly large numbers, in which the education is frequently non-religious, where the fees are very small. There are one or two instances of small schools in the Pesháwar City, which have been established on the individual responsibility of a Shiá Háji. As a rule, these kinds of schools exist for a few years, and then break up altogether."

The answer to which he refers is as follows:—

"*A.* 2.—The ONLY way to improve primary education is by *encouraging existing schools under purely native control*, whether in towns or villages, and rewarding the teachers, on the understanding that their scholars continue their education in higher schools.

"*Inspectors and Deputy Inspectors should not try to quash existing native schools, as is, or has been, so often the case, by swallowing them up in Government or Aided Schools. All such indigenous schools* should be under Government inspection, and the number of trained teachers should be indefinitely increased to meet the increasing need."

With singular liberality and farsightedness, Mr. Jukes makes the following suggestion :—

"In the examinations there should be purely optional papers on the various religions, Christianity included, It would give those an opportunity of taking a higher place who are interested in religion."

The experienced Rev. R. R. WINTER of Delhi (the only place for which the department may be said to have shown some consideration), says as follows :— "*In the villages,* the great majority of the landholding classes are neglected, and there is a general complaint, that though they pay the educational cess, they have in most places no power of educating their sons." As regards indigenous schools, Mr. Winter supplies the following important evidence :—

"Indigenous schools for the middle classes exist in considerable numbers in Delhi, but to a less extent in the villages. *They evidently supply a want that is felt*; for though from 16 to 20 years ago a large number of them were absorbed into Government or Aided schools of the ordinary type, *yet they have again sprung up* in greater numbers.

"Among Mussulmáns there are two large schools of a higher type, containing roughly about 100 and 200 boys, and a third is about to be opened ; in these teaching is given in Urdu, arithmetic, higher Persian and Arabic. There are also *innumerable* small "Maktabs" for teaching the simplest elements of Persian and the *Korán* by rote. They have no system of fees.

"The Hindus have many small "pathshálas" in which, for Banyás' accounts, they teach máhájani and multiplication tables of a highly complex kind ; also Hindi and occasionally a little Sanskrit. The master is rewarded by a *pice* a Sunday, by a little *atta*, &c., monthly, by a present as each boy finishes a certain part of a book, and by a mollifying feast given by the father on the admission of his son. These teachers, whether Maulvis or Pándits, have no previous training, being simply produced by the demand.

"I disfavour making these schools part of the Government system for very young boys ; the people prefer the liberty and variety allowed, and such schools must be indirectly influenced by the Government and Aided schools which the Hindu boys subsequently enter. As education steadily affects the minds of the people, they will themselves demand a higher standard in their indigenous schools. No such schools are found among the lowest orders."

The Reverend Dr. D'EREMAO, Roman Catholic Chaplain of Murree, gives evidence regarding indigenous schools, which, however disparaging to them, show that they could be utilized :

"Though what we would call a school does not exist indigenously, yet there are assemblages for teaching, connected principally with mosques and temples, which we may call indigenous schools. These are in fair number ; but I think the teaching is very poor and superficial, and the education is *nil.* Besides these, there are other so-called schools. An enterprising person starts as a schoolmaster, and gets a few pupils (he may be of any except the lowest caste), whom he teaches what he can. The first kind of indigenous schools is a relic of the village system. Reading, writing, a little grammar and arithmetic and religion are the subjects generally taught, but very superficially and perfunctorily. Discipline there is none, and is not dreamed of. Methodical teaching also is conspicuous by its absence. The old style of 'conning aloud,' which was a necessity when books were few, is still followed when each boy has a book of his own. Their qualifications are—first, a knowledge of religion ; and secondly, a certain proficiency in literature, which goes with it. They are usually narrow-minded, bigoted and ignorant of science. The Normal schools scarcely supply the want of teachers for such schools. These indigenous schools might be utilised for general education by exacting some kind of an examination previous to allowing a man to teach—a sort of licensing system. I dare say these indigenous schoolmasters would be glad of Government aid; but I am not aware that any yet receive it."

It will be clear from the above testimonies of leading members of the Hindu, Muhammadan and Sikh communities, as also from the priesthood of all denominations including representatives of various Christian bodies, of important societies and of the European and native civil service, that the indigenous schools have one only persistent and implacable enemy that denies either their existence or their usefulness or their capabilities for improvement and that enemy is the Educational Department. *Delenda*, therefore, *est Carthago* so far as the Punjab is concerned. Among the numerous scholars that may be mentioned in the educational departments of other provinces, which have nothing in common with the failure in the Punjab, Bengal has or had a Tawney, Hœrnle, or Croft; the North-Western Provinces, a Griffith, Ballantyne, Hall, Kern, and Thibaut; Bombay, its Buhler, Kielhoon, Haug, Grant, and Wordsworth; Madras, its Oppert and Porter; and even Burmah a Forchhammer—men who are either eminent orientalists, the first condition for educational success in an oriental country, or else distinguished scholars in other branches of learning. In the Punjab, however, circumstances have, I regret to say, brought together an educational staff which, whether as scholars or administrators, are, taken as a whole, much inferior to the same number of higher educational officers in any other part of India, if not in the scholastic world, even including such countries as Egypt which has a Dor and Rogers, and Wallachia with its Hazdeo and Constantineschu. The following pages will show not only that our educational officers have not left their mark on education, incentives to which are constantly given by their very profession and which abound, in every direction, in the Punjab, but that they have intentionally been the chief obstacles to the progress of education in a province that offers the most promising field, the most enterprising population, and a government of the most progressive traditions. They first started by abolishing a number of indigenous Persian schools in order to have a basis for their own existence, and they now continue it, not by the increased popularity of their own operations, but by the absorption of Máhájani schools, without which the small number of pupils in Government and aided schools would be even smaller than it is at present.

H.—THE PANJAB BEFORE, AND ON, ANNEXATION.

When I spoke about some of the moral and practical results of even the humblest indigenous instruction to one of the Secretaries of Government, who, along with Coloneis, seem to constitute the normal population of Simla, he said, in a tone of surprise, "well, then, we had better leave the country, as it seems we do not give the natives a better education than they already have." Without sharing this feeling, in which there is much to admire, I certainly think that our advent has not been an unmixed blessing to the Panjab, at least in education; and that we do not deserve to derive our income from its taxation, if we continue to treat education from a purely departmental or scholastic standpoint, instead of in a national spirit. We must cease to be foreigners in India, and even abandon every attempt to make its millions conform to the convenience of a handful in language, laws, administration or instruction. Assuming that the annual rate of increase in the population of the Panjab was the same between 1849 and 1868 as between the latter year and 1881 (the date of the last and most accurate census) or ·6 per cent., there were, on annexation, 15,697,598 human beings in the territories now included in the British possessions of this Province, of whom, roughly, 6 millions were Hindus, 8 millions Muhammadans and 1 million Sikhs. Including the since incorporated Delhi and Hisar Divisions, which now contain 4,476 towns and villages, there were, in 1854 (when an incomplete census was taken), 33, 355 towns and villages, and presumably the same number in 1849. Assuming, at least, the existence of 33,355 Mosques, Temples, Dharmsalas and other sacred edifices in which some teaching was carried on (not to count the 3,372 indigenous secular schools which were ascertained to exist in 1854, or to speak of the large number of schools held in the houses of teachers), and giving each "collegium" of pupils an average attendance of 10, we shall get, at least, 333,550 persons under instruction in a Province in which we have now about 113,000 assumed to attend Government and Aided schools, and a much smaller number in indigenous schools (according to the last census the total number "under instruction" of every kind would only be 157,623) What the state of education was in the time of Ranjit Singh may be inferred from the enumeration of Sikh authors in a previous Chapter. The list of men distinguished for learning in other denominations is even more lengthy; whilst the evidence of our own Administration and Settlement Reports (so far as I have been allowed to see them), is conclusive as to the general spread of the elements of education in the Province. Of course, people may differ as to what is a "school," just as the definition of "a village" seems to have risen from the day of Sir John Lawrence, when it contained about 450 persons, to being a town of 5,000 inhabitants for the purpose of Educational Reports on primary education. If a Koran school is not a school because only the Koran and prayer books are taught in it, or an Arabic school cannot be classed as such because it is frequented by adults; if a "collegium" held, according to Hindu tradition, in the teacher's own house, is not a school; if to read and write Gurmukhi and the "Paharas" is *not* to know the "three" or any "r's," then, of course, all discussion is at an end. If a Pandit is illiterate because he does not know the latitude of Timbuctoo, or cannot answer the question of Bishop Middleton as to where the English came from, and finally declares them to be descended from an alliance of cannibals with monkeys (a Darwinian solution of the Simian difficulty, not quite unworthy of notice), just as some Britons do not scruple to term the French a cross between the general ancestor and the tiger, then also there is nothing to be said in favour of indigenous education. The Russians call the Germans "Niemtzé," or unable to speak intelligibly, but there still exist intelligent speech and an extensive literature in the Fatherland. When, however, by school is meant an *indigenous* school; by a knowledge of reading or writing that of the *indigenous* characters; by learning or science, *oriental* learning or science, then, indeed, was education far more extended when we took the Panjab than it is at present. No man of *any* claim to erudition, no priest, no member of any of what we would call the learned professions, no poet of any merit, no clever artificer existed who did not enjoy the favour of Government, and *who did not teach*. In my own experience I have known a man who could burn encaustic tiles in colors, for which the trade would now pay thousands of pounds, apply in vain for rupees 20 per mensem, in order to teach his (now defunct) art to pupils, although attention was drawn to him by an International Jury of experts. By far the greater number of teachers and priests, who all taught, had grants of rent-free land, and *land given for such a purpose was never resumed*, whether there was or was not a school building, or the school was only held in the Chaupal, or village hall, or under a tree. It would have been a sacrilege, repugnant alike to Sikh, Muhammadan and Hindu, to resume such land, an d, even if its owner proved disloyal, the *object* of the grant was ever maintained; in other words, the school or teaching was continued, though, it may be, by a more loyal relative of the dispossessed grantee. A settlement report, quoted further on, will show that not only did successive Sikh, Muhammadan or Hindu chiefs respect their own religious endowments, but also that they respected those of *other* denominations. When we took the Panjab the country had gone through a period of internal discord, followed by war and annexation by foreigners, circumstances which everywhere are unfavourable to the maintenance of, or rather uninterupted attendance at, school. The period from 1849, the date of annexation, to 1852, shows the smallest number of charitable or religious endowments, for which, as a recent *Panjab Government Gazette* will show, there is still a noble emulation among natives, in no way stimulated by "a desire for personal distinction," but inspired solely by the religious feeling. Yet even in 1852, the report of the Hushiarpur District, a backward one, mentions one school to every 19·92 males (adult and non-adult), against 1 to every 20·69 in the Julundhar District and deplores that result. The schools were deserted; many of the priests had, of course, represented the Church militant against our invasion and feared to return to their lands, which were resumed without mercy, instead of continuing their object by making them over to other teachers. Still in the very year of annexation, 1849, Sir John and Sir Henry Lawrence were able to declare that there was one school to every 1,783 inhabitants in the most backward of the three Divisions of the Panjab, before the British Government had expended anything on education; whilst in the most advanced, there was one school to every 1,441 inhabitants. These statements of the Lawrences are *far below* the mark, as I believe has been shown. *Now*, in the words of the President of the Education Commission to the Director of Public Instruction, Panjab,—"there is one school of whatever sort, to every 9,028 inhabitants, and you leave the indigenous schools completely outside your Department, unaided, uninspected, unrecognised in any way. Does this strike you as a satisfactory fulfilment of Sir John Lawrence's plan for bringing a school within reach of every village?" Yet his enumeration, necessarily extremely defective, left out from calculation the great bulk of Koran and Landé, as well as the Sanscrit and Arabic, schools held in private houses, and was taken at a most unfavourable time for the collection of educational statistics. The minds of the religious were disturbed in witnessing the triumph of aliens, and the respectable and conservative elements of native society naturally kept aloof from intercourse with the invader, unless compelled to do so by political and other exigencies. They also feared to continue the tenor of their own ways, as they did not know what might give offence to the inexplicable stranger, who spoke of justice and yet did much which to them seemed unjust. Then it was that the presence of Missionaries, however hostile to the native creeds, and the strong religious convictions of the principal British administrators, had a somewhat reassuring effect on the people; for there was still hope for mercy, if not justice, when the rulers believed in God, though the absence of demonstrativeness in Protestant worship has often given the English the name of "creedless" in Eastern countries. Nor can it be denied that the personal benevolence of some of the European officers, or the inevitable influence of surroundings or the requirements of administration repeatedly gave a gentler interpretation to orders of the Government, which would be deemed Draconic in these days of liberal rule. Money had to be got out of the Panjab, by fair means if possible, but it had to be got. No way to get it was so effective as that of the resumption of rent-free lands, whether given for service to the State (which might indeed be resumed by an oriental conqueror), or for religious, which included educational, or for other purposes, which were inalienable in their very nature. The Board of Administration hoped to obtain, at least, a net profit out of the Province of fifty lakhs per annum to satisfy the Court of Directors, as will be seen from a quotation, further on, of one of its Administration Reports, but it wished to do so gradually by natural lapses of pensions and rent-free tenures. We had conquered the country, not always by the noblest means; and although we had fought with a chivalrous enemy, we asserted the widest rights of the conqueror. In our resumption of rent-free lands, we assumed that no one had any claim to his own holding, even if held for generations, except by our mercy for what we chose to leave him. It is difficult to speak of these matters without giving offence to men, who, judging from the narrow standpoint of what they deemed to be to the interest of their Government or nation, or their own advancement, did the best they could do for the unfortunate natives. I must, therefore, again appeal to the reader to place himself in the position of a native before he gives an opinion as to whether we did, or did not, deprive indigenous education of its endowments. A careful enquiry, in spite of the difficulties thrown in my way, has convinced me that we resumed by far its greater bulk, sometimes from ignorance of the actual state of the endowments, sometimes from carelessness, often in consequence of misrepresentations by underlings and Naboths, but more generally from the self-deception to which human nature is liable when dealing with the weak under the strong stimulus of official interest and in obedience to orders. Indeed, our Panjab officers deserve credit for the way in which they discharged an uncongenial duty.

I should have allowed the past to bury its dead, had I not been able to point out in my "Précis and conclusions" that the great wrong that has been committed in the Panjab (though greater wrongs may have been committed in other Provinces or countries) can be remedied, not noly without any cost to the State, but also to its pecuniary advantage, and that such remedy will eventually relieve it of all expenditure on primary education, besides, also, incidentally increasing the revenue. I was, moreover, bound to answer the questions of the Education Commission, which confronted me, in cross-examination, with two extracts from the Panjab Administration Report for 1849-51, which I will now proceed to quote:—

"Q. 4. You have alluded to the resumption of rent-free grants as a cause of the decline of indigenous schools. Are you conversant with the statements of Sir John and Sir Henry Lawrence on this point in their Administration Reports shortly after the annexation of the Panjab?

"A. 4. I should like those statements to be read out.

"Q. 5. Permit me to read to you the original documents. In the Panjab Administration Report for 1849-51, paragraph 377, it is stated: 'The Musalman schools are nearly all connected with the village mosque. In such a case the same endowment would support both institutions. It is superfluous to observe that wherever any land has been granted in rent-free tenure for such a purpose, either by the State and its representatives, or by the proprietary community, such foundations have been gladly maintained by the Board.' Paragraph 321 of the same Report (for 1849-51) runs as follows: 'The endowments mentioned in class No. 9 are both secular and religious, for the support of temples, mosques, schools, village-inns for the reception of travellers, paupers and strangers, generally of a monastic character. These institutions are ornaments to the villages. They have some architectural pretensions, and being embosomed in trees,' &c. * * * *. 'These endowments, *though occasionally reduced in amount*, have, *on the whole*, been regarded with liberality, and in confirming them, the officers have mainly regarded the utility of the institution,' &c., &c. Paragraph 497 of the Panjab Administration Report for 1851-53 tells us that 'The Sikh holy places have been respected,' &c., &c. Are these statements consistent with what you have toid us about the resumption of grants to indigenous schools?

"A. 5. These statements are not fully consistent with what I have said, but the facts are. These facts can only be ascertained by a reference to the resumption records; and these enquiries are, I understand, being made at my request in the Secretariat. I made my statement partly from information received when travelling in the Province, and partly from one of the earlier Educational Reports" (quoted at the end of the cross-examination).

That quotation is as follows—and, even if there had been no other, would have seemed to me to be conclusive as to the resumption of rent-free lands belonging to schools :—

"No. 335, 6th July, 1857.

Extract from Report of the Department of Public Instruction, Pànjab, for 1856-57.

PRIVATE SCHOOLS ENJOYING RENT-FREE LAND.

"*Para. 80.* You are aware that it was a common custom in former times to give grants of rent-free land to persons who were bound in return to teach youth. Most of these grants, the conditions of which were probably very little attended to, have been resumed, but I have been officially informed of their being allowed, on the condition above mentioned, at the places noted in the margin. In all such cases the school is now considered subject to Government inspection, and will be gradually made to conform to the rules laid down for one per cent. Tehsili Schools as each case may require."

District.	Locality.	Grant.
Amritsar	Sultanpur	One well.
Sialkot	Badánath	37 Gumaos.
Ludhiana	Jugraon	
Gugaira	Lashari	
Do.	Pakpattan	150 Rupees.

As, however, there still appears to be some doubt about the fact (which is an unpleasant one to admit), I will proceed to refer to a series of resumptions which have been brought to my knowledge. As stated on page 11 of my "Précis,"—"had I not feared to raise a storm of applications for the restoration of resumed land to schools, I should have been able to add numerous records in support of my assertion. As it is, a number of indigenous teachers have spontaneously submitted statements that their schools were, before annexation, supported by grants of land." I also so strongly rely on the earlier Administration Reports that I have quoted their allusions to this question at length, whilst I have taken the opportunity of republishing other matter which bears on my present enquiry, a course which I also hope will rescue from oblivion reports of considerable historical importance of which, in some cases, only one copy exists in the Secretariat. So closely was indigenous education interwoven with rent-free tenures of land, that it is impossible to give a history of the one, without an account of the other. Again, so distinctly was it avowed that the one per cent. village cess was raised for indigenous schools, that it is equally impossible to treat of indigenous schools, without referring to that cess. What I have to show is—

(1) That elementary, and sometimes high, oriental classical and vernacular education was more widely spread in the Panjab before annexation than it is now.

(2) That the Board of Administration in the Panjab was ordered to resume rent-free tenures of land, even in the case of schools and religious edifices when their endowments were large, thus following the example of the land resumptions in Bengal.

(3) That the Board of Administration, according to the lights available in a period of confusion, did so with as much tenderness as was compatible with the object in view.

(4) That in consequence most of the endowments of indigenous schools were gradually destroyed.

(5) That a Lieutenant-Governor of the North-West Provinces, whose educational policy we were supposed to follow in the Panjab, proposed to maintain indigenous schools with gifts of land.

(6) That the Court of Directors preferred to do so with money grants; that successive Secretaries of State, Viceroys and Lieutenant-Governors of the Panjab were unanimous in wishing to aid indigenous schools, and that the Village School Cess was primarily raised for this purpose, and also to provide Government village schools to serve as models to indigenous schools.

(7) That the action of the Educational Department of the Panjab, in spite of constant reminders, tended to destroy the indigenous schools whilst neglecting its own primary schools.

(8) That there is still an easy remedy to undo a great wrong, which is briefly indicated in the following quotation from my "Précis," and regarding which detailed proposals will be made elsewhere :—

"As for the resumptions of grants of rent-free land to persons who were bound in return to teach, my only ground, so far as this chapter is concerned, is the paragraph quoted from the Educational Report of 1856-57, and which, in the absence of evidence to the contrary, might have been deemed to be conclusive. But any evidence to the contrary only partially affects the question, for the assertion refers not only to religious schools attached to, or forming part of, religious buildings or endowments, most of which, though not all, were respected, and sometimes liberally treated, but also to semi-religious and secular schools granted either direct by the Governments that preceded us to persons from father to son on condition of teaching, or indirectly forming an obligation to jaghirdars or muafidars. The very circular of the North-Western Provinces, which formed the basis for the levying of the village cess in the Panjab, seems to imply this; but whatever be the case, the fact is notorious that numerous grants have been resumed. The resumption records and the documents for which I have applied to the Panjab Secretariat, but which have not been supplied, will prove a proceeding which it was perfectly natural for the Government to adopt at the time, and which, wherever any injustice may have been unintentionally caused, can be reversed, even now, with economy and future advantage to the State. Not to speak of reviving the obligation to maintain schools in all cases of jaghirs, the grant of waste land or an assignment of the value of, say, Rs. 2 per mensem on the village land, would establish in perpetuity and hereditary respectability the village teacher, whilst gradually tending to make him independent of the pecuniary aid from Government. In numerous parts of Europe a small free site and cottage form the only permanent remuneration of the village schoolmaster for the time being, and there is every reason why education should be replaced in India on its traditional and self-supporting basis.

The misconceptions under which these were resumed may be classified as follows :—

(*a*) In a number of instances the jaghirdars or muafidars were glad to get rid of their obligation to maintain the hereditary schools. This was an easy task under a new régime necessarily imperfectly acquainted with the previous state of things, and in the confusion following an annexation.

(*b*) When the enquiring officer was told that such and such land belonged to such and such a teacher, and the latter could produce no *personal* grant of the same,* it ran the risk of being resumed, whereby the school connected with it came to an end.

(*c*) The alarm of such resumption spreading, the teachers in professional possession alleged that these grants *were personal* to themselves. Even when their statement was believed and acted on, the course adopted ended in the resumption of the land after the death of the occupant at the time of the enquiry.

---

* An amount of legal proof was, often required in the case of such grants, which is rarely possessed in India even as regards one's own personal or ancestral property. See the remarks on the subject in Dr. Hunter's "Indian Musulmans," quoted elsewhere. The interest and avowed object of the Government were not to establish the genuineness of grants, but to resume them whenever a flaw could be discovered in them —(See orders of Government quoted further on.)

(*d*) Above all, was it impossible for European officers to ascertain and to appreciate whether the conditions of the grants were properly fulfilled. To many, the *laisser-aller* of oriental management of endowed schools seemed an abomination deserving their abolition, though the people were content to let them go on, and would have been grateful for any suggestion for their improvement or for their existence on the fulfilment of the conditions of their tenure. To others, schools teaching Gurmukhi seemed barbarous, and to teach Arabic seditious (see Reports). Others, again, thought that it was desirable to dispossess the Muhammadan from the teacher's seat which he was occupying at the time of annexation on political grounds. None had the leisure or sympathy to go into matters obscured by native diffidence of aliens, and by their own preconceptions. The consequence was that, throughout the country, by far the large majority of schools held on the grant of rent-free system were resumed. In my humble opinion, some compensation, as already mentioned, should be made in a manner which will be to the advantage of both agricultural progress and of the State; whilst, as regards the misapplied portion of the Village Cess, the relief from police charges to district and municipal bodies offers a convenient opportunity of increasing the allotment to primary and practical vernacular education among the agricultural population.

1.—THE STATE OF INDIGENOUS EDUCATION BEFORE ANNEXATION COMPARED WITH ITS PRESENT STATE.

So much has already been said by me on this subject that I need only quote a statement furnished to me by a Sirdar in further corroboration :—

(a) " *Gurmukhi Schools.*

"Formerly, in Maharaja Runjit Singh's time, there were many Gurmukhi Schools in Amritsar, which imparted instruction of a high order and enjoyed jagirs and stipends from the Maharaja. These have since been resumed. I proceed to give a description of a few of the more important ones :—

(1) Held in Bhai Juna Singh's (Granthi's house), was a large school, at which both the Granths, the Guru Bilas (history of the Gurus), and other religious books, with Arithmetic, Vyakarn and Puranas were taught. No fees were charged, while bread was supplied to the students.

(2) Bhai Lakhun Singh had a school in his house, teaching the same religious books. Though this school does not retain its former glory, the grandson of the Bhai still teaches a little. *The jagir*, the only means of subsistence, *has been resumed.*

(3) Bhai Ram Singh, a very learned man of former times, had a very flourishing school to which students from distant parts of the country flocked and took their lessons in all the higher departments of learning, such as, Vyakarn, Granth, Kavya, Alankar, Poetry, Pingal, Literature, History, Niti, Arithmetic, Astronomy, Lilavati, &c., and he enjoyed a subsistence allowance from the Government, which having now ceased, no one has succeeded him in his office.

(4) Bhai Khark Singh, Dhupia, enjoyed a similar grant and imparted similar instruction, being a man of great learning. No successor.

(5) Bawa Amir Das Udasi was a very learned man, and a splendid teacher of his time. He was the author of many important works. His Chela (disciple), Saut Singh, still lives, but has no source of income.

(6) Budh Singh was another learned man belonging to the same time. He brought out no less than five hundred works.

At present, there is only one learned man at Amritsar in the person of Bhai Gan Singh, who gives private tuition in all those higher branches of learning which have been given under the name of Bhai Ram Singh. He has not got his equal. He gets no aid from Government. His son, Sardul Singh, is also an author.

DAM-DAMA Sahib, a place of Gurus, in the Ferozepore District, used to send out scholars who had completed their education in all the branches of higher learning. Now there are very few learned people there, comparatively speaking.

(b) *Arabic and Persian Schools.*

In former times Arabic and Persian Schools of note existed in many places in which the higher Mathematics, Mechanics, Logic, Philosophy, Medicine, Astronomy, Grammar, Hadis, Fiqha, Poetry and Political Economy were taught; students from long distances flocked to the schools and were supplied with food and books. The teaching used to be splendid, a religious duty and merit being attached to teaching in the mind of teachers.

The teachers, besides enjoying jagirs from the Government, were respected throughout the lives of their students, who always contributed something towards their teacher's maintenance.

Primary instruction was given by Mullas in the mosques attached to villages and towns; this was shared by the Hindus on equal terms.

Besides these agencies for teaching, men of standing employed private tutors for their children; poor children were allowed to read with these teachers. Subsistence allowance was given by Government to the minor teachers as well. Some schools of the above description are described below :

At BATALA there was a large and widely-known school of Mean Saheb of the Qadiri family which drew its students from distant countries like Iran. Instruction was given in all the higher departments of learning, so much so that students of this school were famous for their attainments in mathematics. A Government jagir was enjoyed by this family *which has since been resumed.*

People of higher classes contributed liberally towards the support of this family, and though there is now no teaching, they still continue to send presents on occasions of marriage and rejoicing. Sahibzada Hussan Shah was the last teaching member of this family.

There was a similar school, with similar teaching and similarly drawn students at SIALKOT under the late Maulavi Shekh Ahmed, a very famous literary man of his time. This school has met with the same fate as above.

Mian Faiz had a school at GUJRANWALA, with splendid teaching in Persian and other subjects through the medium of Persian. This teacher was a great Persian scholar and *enjoyed a muafi.*

There was a grand school of BARA MIAN, at LAHORE. It may be called a college. It was liberally aided by the Government. It gave instruction in all branches of high and primary education. It still continues in a tottering state, void of its former glory. There was another similar institution in Moran's Mosque under Khalifa Sahib. Students from Persia and Arabia got splendid lessons in all branches of learning from this peerless man. Khalifa Hamiduddin, of the Lahore Government School, belongs to this family.

Maulavi Sultan Ahmed, of GUJRAT, and Nur Ahmed, of GUJRANWALA, were famous for their learning, and their teaching in mathematics and other branches of general knowledge was of the highest order. They were also aided by Government.

Khwaja Suleman had a flourishing school at SAINGROSA in the Dera Ghazi District. Men from Khorasan and Hindustan received high education here. The present state is not known.

There was a Persian School of a high order at MIRAN-WALI in the Gujranwala District. Mear Abdul Hakim of this family still gives instruction and food to students, resident and non-resident. Government does not afford him sufficient aid.

There were many other similar institutions which have not been equalled up to this time:

(c) Learned teachers of the present time.

I now proceed to give the names of certain learned teachers of the present time:

Amritsar.—Maulavi Abdul Ali Qari. He is a man of great learning and teaches a Muhammadan school; so do also Abu Abdulla and Maulavi Ghulam Ali.

Maulavi Sultan Mahmud is a very learned man; he is the Imam of Khair-uddin mosque, and a teacher in the Islamia school.

Gujranwala.—Maulavi Sarajuddin and Maulavi Mahbub-i-Alim are men of great learning and each of them teaches a school.

Maulavi Gulam Rasul, son of Mean Sher Din, practises medicine and teaches as well.

Ghulam Rasul, of Adilgarh, is a poet, a man of great learning, a caligrapher, and he also teaches in his village.

The Qari of Thoha in the Jhelum District is well-known for his ability in expounding the Quran. People from different parts of the Panjab come to him to learn Qiráat.

Begi-wal in the Hoshiarpur District has a Maulavi of great and unparalleled learning; he gives instruction in Galewala, District Gujrat. There is a similar Maulavi at Sial in the Shahpur District. Maulavi Abaidulla, of Multan, has not got his equal in learning.

(d) Hakims.

The well-known Lahore family of Faqirs had amongst its members many great Hakims. Faqir Saiyed Qamrruddin, Honorary Magistrate of Lahore, still practises medicine.

Hakim Hukum Rai was the hereditary family and Durbar Hakim of Maharaja Runjit Singh. He was a learned and successful medical practitioner. His son, Maya Das, was also a worthy son of a worthy father. Hakim Hiranand was a learned Hakim in Sialkot.

At Chatti, District Sialkot, Hakim Qutub-uddin's family is well-known; it has always produced eminent Hakims and still continues to do so.

Nathe Shah, of Gakkhar, in the Gujranwala District, is an excellent medical practitioner, and comes of a famous Hakim family.

Hakim Abdul Aziz, of Kot Udho, in the Muzuffergurh District is a great practical and experienced Hakim. His works on medicine have a wide fame, and are considered as authorities in India. His "Aksir Azim," and another work, "Zamurrad Akhzar" are the principal of these, and they were published in Maharaja Runjit Singh's time.

Hakim Udho Das, of Dera Ghazi Khan, is a very experienced and successful Hakim; people resort to him from all parts of the country.

Hakim Abdulla, senior, and Abdulla, junior, were once the two famous Hakims at Peshawar, who had very few equals. Hakim Vali Shah was one of Maharaja Runjit Singh's Hakims. He was well-known for his learning and ability in medical science. His family still has some Hakims among its members.

Hakim Bibe Rai was a very skilled Hakim in Lahore; his son, Jaigopal, still practises as a physician. The present well-known and able Hakims in Lahore are Muhammad Bukhsh, Alah Din and Ghulam Muhammad.

Hakim Hissam-uddin, of Amritsar, is an excellent physician. Gulab Rai used to be another, but he is dead.

Mirza Faqir-ulla Beg was a very famous Hakim in Kalanaur. His name has passed into a proverb as "the life-giver." In this town there was a family of Hakims of long standing; it still has an able Hakim in the person of Muhammad Sharif. He is a very learned Hakim and a thorough scholar in the necessary branches of medical science. This family had a medical school taught by its members. *A jagir of about Rs. 2,000 was enjoyed by it. On account of the resumption of the jagir, the regular school has ceased to exist,* though Muhammad Sharif teaches medicine to four or five private students. He possesses testimonials from the Kings of the Chugatta family, and traces his descent from the Abbaside Khalifas.

I have only mentioned the most famous Hakims that I know. There were many other families of hereditary Hakims. In conclusion, I may mention the name of the late Muhammad Bux, of Mukerian, in the Hoshiarpur District.

(e) *Hindi Baids.*

Pandit Madhsudan was the famous author and compiler of many Vaidic works. Pandit Dharni Dhar was an eminent Baid.

The Pandhas of Muradpur, in the Amritsar District, are celebrated Hakims in the Panjab. *Formerly they enjoyed jagirs,* but now no such means are at their disposal. Pandhas Gunga Ram and Kirpa Ram have now a dispensary of their own.

The Baids of the Datarpur District, Hoshiarpur, are a very famous family of Hindi physicians in the Panjab, and have a dispensary of their own.

(f) *Pathsháláa.*

Pandit Mela Ram formerly had, and his grandson, Kaushe Ram, now has, a pathshálá in Amritsar. Many students get instruction in this school and are given bread also.

The family of the Sindhanvalia Sardars always had their private tutors, and besides the sons of Sardars, others were also allowed to benefit by their teachers.

Among these teachers I may name Mean Mohsan Shah and Shabbaz Khan; the instruction given by these teachers was of the highest possible type in all departments of Arabic and Persian literature and science. Many members of this Sardar family distinguished themselves as the matchless literary men of their time, for instance, Sardars Attar Singh, Lehna Singh and Ajit Singh.

(g) *Artists.*

Ilahi Baksh was the principal architect in Maharaja Runjit Singh's days.

Saidu and Hyat were the famous gun-makers of Maharaja Runjit Singh.

The Ironsmiths of Dharmkot and Kotli were renowned. Muhammad Bakhsh, of Jastarwal, was very skilled in steel manufacturing, and was a noted sword-maker.

Allayar and his son were the architects employed in the Darbar Sahib."

Remarks on learning generally in the Panjab before annexation.

I can only add a few names to those above recorded:

Hashim Shah, the famous Arabic scholar and Punjabi novelist, whose scholarship procured his forgiveness for disloyalty by Runjit Singh, *more suo* with most rebels against his authority, has already been mentioned; so has also Akhwand Ali Ahmad, who came from the frontier to instruct Kaur Nao Nihal Singh, and Sirdars Ajit Singh and Lehna Singh in Mathematics and Astronomy.

In Sanscrit learning, Bhin near Jalandhar enjoyed, as now under Kaka Ram, a great reputation.

At BATALA, actually called "Batala Sharif," or the "illustrious Batala" in consequence of its fame for the cultivation of Arabic learning, and in imitation of "Bukhara Sharif," lived FAZIL SHAH and GHOLAM QADIR SHAH, who are said to have written 200 volumes each on various branches of Mathematics and Literature. The former wrote the famous "Taríkh-ul-wasûl" on Tasawwaf, a book on the Sûfi doctrine; the second wrote a similar Sûfi work, the "Sûfá-ul-mirat" in Persian which is equally known; also a volume of *Urdu* poetry, called the "Ramz-ul-íshq," in which the following quotation is still commonly referred to as an equivalent to the Muhammadan "La-allah-il-allah"—There is no God, but *the* God:

"Wohí, wohí, na dûja ko = It is He, it is He; no second to Him;
"Pargat hua Muhammad ko = who became manifest to Muhammad."

At BATALA also lived the famous Persian teacher, NARAIN DAS, a Puri Khatri (a high caste), who translated the Mahabharata into Persian under the name of "Gulistan Jinnat," or the "Garden of Paradise."

The book, however, had few purchasers, and was sold to waste-paper merchants under our rule. BATALA also had been the home of WAQIF (Shah Nur-ul-din), the illustrious Persian poet in the 17th century whose "Diwán" is still widely read.

GUJRAT also, as has been shown above, was famous, and kept alive the memory of GHANIMAT, who lived in the time of Aurangzeb, and whose Masnawi "Nairang Ishq" is said to have surpassed in beauty and purity some of the most famous Persian poety of *Irán*. He was a native of Kunja in the Gujrat District (famous for the beauty of its women), and as the teacher of Nawab Mukarram Khan, whose history he wrote.

At KAPURTHALA was Pandit Bullo Mal, called "Pandit" although a Khatri, who wrote on Geography, Mathematics and Astronomy, and whose "Astroláb" is still renowned; he died ten years ago.

The great Jalandhar Fakir and Physician, a Pûj, or Priest of the Jains, wrote on Astronomy and Astrology, or rather Arithmology, and is still known as "THE PUJ," a class among whom great native Physicians are as common as distinguished Sanscrit scholars.

MULTAN was proverbial for its "Mina" or inlaid work, and the textile manufactures of Lahore were said to be superior to those of Egypt.

The workmen of CHINIÔT, which gave a most successful minister, SAADULLAH KHAN, to Shah Jehan, constructed the Amritsar Temple; the tank being due to Guru Ram Das. Chiniôt itself possesses a mosque built by Saadulla with a moveable minaret in elastic stone. The famous Architect and Engineer, ALI MARDAN KHAN, constructed the Western Jumna Canal, besides numerous other works which have rendered his name immortal. He lived at DASKA, so called from being ten miles equidistant from Gujranwala, Sialkot and Wazirabad.

At SIALKOT the memory of one of the greatest Arabic scholars and authors MAULAVI ABDUL HAKIM, who lived in the days of Aurangzeb, was still religiously preserved in the Arabic schools of that city.

The Vedas were, comparatively speaking, little taught in the Panjab in Runjit Singh's time, the teachers chiefly coming from the Dekkan; but in Sanscrit, as in Arabic, Grammar, Panjab learning was proverbial throughout India, whilst Panjabi Pandits also excelled in Niaya (Logic), Mimánsa, the Dharmshastras, Vedant and Sankhya (six Shastras), Patidhant and Siddhant (Astronomy).

Among HAKIMS, MIRZA KALANAURI and SHEIKH AHMAD SIALKOTI founded a school in the days of Aurangzeb, whose traditions still survived; whilst at the Durbar of Runjit Singh, besides the amiable and accomplished Fakir Aziz-ud-din (to whose family the British owe so much), there were Hakim

Rai, styled the "Karm ferma," and Wali Shah; in the MUZAFFARGURH Zila, Kot Udda, Hakim Abdulaziz, already referred to, wrote in Arabic the "Aksîr Azîm" = or "Great Essence," and the "Zamurrad Akhzar," a book on drugs, containing the most successful prescriptions. His cures of ophthalmia were deemed to be almost miraculous, and he is said to have invented a paper glossed over by a substance which made the writing on it visible at night.

Among BAIDS, Pandit DHARNIDHAR was a famous author who resided at Lahore, and who divided with Pandit MATSUDAN, already named, a great reputation for knowledge of medicine. In the village of DATARPUR, in the Kangra District, there was (and is still) a famous family of Baid physicians who had a free dispensary.

It will be remembered that BABA AMAR DAS, already referred to, composed many works on the Waidak system of medicine. In the village of MURADPUR, in the Amritsur District, there similarly lived a family of Baids. Hakim HIRA NAND, a Khatri of Sialkot, was as famous in mathematics as he was in medicine; he was once Mir Munshi to Sirdar Lehna Singh, Sindhanwalia.

The names of eminent scholars in various parts of the Panjab, at or about the time of annexation, may be greatly multiplied, but I think enough has been said for the purpose of the present enquiry, which I am proud to think will, at any rate, rescue some names from the unmerited oblivion of a generation that does not know Joseph. Is it improbable that a Province in which the various Governments and creeds ever preserved a profound veneration for learning in spite of political vicissitudes, should have been barren of education in spite of the desolation caused by the disturbances which followed the rule of Sher Singh, and which must have accompanied annexation. Instances of fanaticism by which the education of any creed suffered were rare. It is true that the Sikhs destroyed the city of Sirhind, the head or limit of the Panjab towards India Proper, which had long been the seat of a Moghul Governor, and of the family of Aurangzeb's reputed Pîrs, because Guru Govind Singh's two younger boys had been killed there, but the tradition of the famous poet NASIR ALI of that family still survived. Oriental fanaticism is a temporary ebullition, and is certainly less thorough than the European intolerance, which, for instance, drove out an entire industrious population from Spain. The spirit of Sikhism is well exemplified in ADAN SHAH, a Fakîr who wrote the *Parsbhág* or "touchstone," in Gurmukhi (an adaptation of the "Kímia Saádat") in which Jesus, Nanak and other religious reformers are praised. It may be incidentally mentioned that this work has recently been printed by Jaggjodh Singh, son of Peshora Singh, and a grandson of Runjit Singh.

The Panjab, on annexation, was very much like Germany at the end of the Seven Years' War, and yet the earliest Administration and Settlement Reports written by the conquerors can give the following account of the state of its education, from which we shall quote, till the period when a patriarchal Government thought that it would fully discharge its duty to the people by handing over its education to a Department of Public Instruction :—

PANJAB ADMINISTRATION REPORT FOR 1849-51.

Popular Education.

"372. Popular education is a matter not easily to be studied and promoted under the pressure of urgent business, which has crowded on the Board ever since annexation. Some initiatory steps have however been taken. Last year a proposition regarding the establishment of a school at Umritsar emanated from the Deputy Commissioner of that district, and the Commissioner, Lahore Division, and this proposition was accompanied with a report on the general state of education throughout the division. The Board submitted for the consideration of Government the question as to whether a school, partaking of a collegiate character, should be founded at Lahore or Umritsar. The Government decided in favour of the latter city. At the same time, the Board called upon the several Commissioners to furnish educational reports for their several divisions. Reports have been received from all the divisions except Leia and Peshawar, in neither of which it is probable that education can be flourishing.

373. The high state to which educational statistics have been brought in the Agra Presidency will suggest a comparison on some of the leading points, and has supplied a standard by which our knowledge may be measured. The most important item of information may be gathered from the following figures :—

Division.	One school to every inhabitant.		One scholar to every inhabitant.	
Lahore	1,783	·98	214	·85
Jhelum	1,441	·90	193	·10
Mooltan	1,666	·66	210	·88
Agra Presidency	2,912	·20	326	·14

375. The schools are of three descriptions, namely, those resorted to by Hindus, Mussulman and Sikhs, respectively. At the Hindu schools, writing and the rudiments of arithmetic are generally taught in the Hindu characters; at the Mussulman schools, are read Koran in Arabic, and the didactic and poetical works of Sadi, in Persian (the Gulistan and Bostan); at the Sikh school, the Grunth in Goormukhi, or the repository of the faith, taught by Nanuck and Guroo Govind. In the Persian, Arabic and Goormukhi schools, which form the great majority, the studies being chiefly confined to sacred books written in a classical phraseology, unintelligible to both teacher and pupil, do not tend to develop the intellectual faculties of either.

376. It is remarkable that *female education is to be met with in all parts of the Panjab.* The girls, and the teachers (also females), belong to all of the three great tribes, namely, Hindu, Mussulman and Sikh. The number is not of course large, but the existence of such an education, almost unknown in other parts of India, is an encouraging circumstance.

377. The school-house is here, as elsewhere, primitive, such as a private dwelling, the village town-hall, the shade of a tree, a temporary shade, or the court-yard of a temple. The Mussulman schools are nearly all connected with the village mosque.* *In such a case* the same endowment would support both institutions. It is superfluous to observe that, wherever any land has been granted in rent-free tenure for such a purpose, either by the State and its representatives, or by the proprietary community, such foundations have been gladly maintained by the Board. The remuneration of the teachers is variable and precarious. It frequently consists of presents, grain and sweetmeats, given by the scholars and their parents. But, occasionally, the whole community subscribe for the support of the school, each member contributing so much per plough, which is considered to represent his means: not unfrequently also, cash payments are made, and sometimes regular salaries are allowed; cash allowances are perhaps more usual in the Panjab than in Hindustan.

378. In parts of Hindustan it is discouraging to observe how much education is circumscribed within certain castes, such as Brahmins, Bunyas, and Khyeths, who are exclusively devoted to learning, commerce or penmanship; while the great land-holding and agricultural tribes are wholly illiterate. A similar disproportion exists also in many parts of the Panjab. But, in other parts, education, such as it may be, is imparted *chiefly to the agricultural population.*† In most districts testimony is given that *all classes*, both agricultural and non-agricultural, manifest a desire for instruction. It has been ascertained that many old schools have increased, and many new schools have arisen, since annexation. In the cities especially, when it was seen that the Government were interested in the subject, numerous petitions were presented to the local authorities praying for the establishing of schools. Manifestation

* Indeed, *not* "nearly all."

† Now the agricultural population has been largely deprived both of the benefits of education and of the Village School Cess which was to pay for it.

of the popular will is rare in India, and the Board are unwilling it should be neglected, especially when indicative of such inspirations as these. The Commissioners and Deputy Commissioners concur in recommending the founding of a central school in most of our chief cities; and the Board will shortly submit a definite, proposition to Government, in the confidence that it will be favourably entertained, when the results which have attended the efforts of the Agra Government in this direction are considered.

379. It has been already intimated that the Board place much reliance on the new system of settlement as an engine for good, and a medium for the diffusion of knowledge. Not only will the village accountants receive a thorough training in mensuration and arithmetical calculation, but the landholders, being obliged to take a personal part in these operations, must acquire the rudiments of education, and must learn to exercise their faculties for the sake of preserving their most valued rights and dearest interests.*

380. A few words of special notice are due to the Umritsar school. The first annual report of this institution has been received. During the past year the average daily attendance has increased from 107 to 153, that is, 50 per. cent. Of these about one-fourth study English. The progress in this department is considerable, as might have been expected from the strong desire of learning English evinced by many parties at Umritsar previous to the establishment of the school. Reading, spelling, and writing; arithmetic, elementary Geometry, and Geography constitute the course of study. In Lahore, as well as Umritsar, the anxiety to acquire English is remarkable. Many Panjabee noblemen and gentlemen have their sons taught English privately, and many natives of Bengal, who possess a smattering of English, find employment as teachers of that language.

In the Umritsar school there are Hindi, Persian, Arabic, Sanscrit and Gurmukhi Departments.† The Sikh students of Gurmukhi are about one-fifth of the whole number. Among the Hindi scholars the prevailing castes are Khatris and Brahmins; among the Sikh scholars, Jats. The great majority are the residents of the city.

383. In order that the growing wants of the scientific establishment employed on surveys and public works may be supplied, the Board will encourage candidates to seek the education and training furnished by the Roorki College. It is also worthy of consideration whether an institution on similar plans might not be founded in the Panjab.

384. Connected with the subject of education is the employment of Panjabees in Government offices. It is rarely found that the Khatris, who usually seek appointments, possess sufficient qualifications for high employ; and as attainments of this nature were imperatively necessary, and were displayed only by natives of Hindustan, it was found necessary, after annexation, to place the latter in many of the best appointments.‡ The Board are however very anxious that the patronage should be enjoyed by natives of the country, and they doubt not that in the course of a few years numbers will become qualified. In the meantime by placing young Panjabees in subordinate posts, they hope that a body of men may become trained to rise to the highest position."

The following extracts from the Settlement Reports of 1852 may further illustrate the state of indigenous education in the Panjab from our point of view :—

AMBALA SETTLEMENT REPORT.

Page 87, para. 381. As an instance how *the followers of both the Mussulman and Hindu religion tolerate, nay protect, holy men of the other sects,* I may state that when Goroo Gobind was wandering in the Himalayas, he

---

* All this has *not* been done. † These have ceased. ‡ As they still are.

came to Sadhoura and was hidden by a Syud from the royal army. The Goroo gave him his comb, and some of his hair, which is still in possession of the Syuds, who can raise money from the Sikhs by showing this and the writing which accompanied it. The reverence paid to Googa Pir and Sudwar Lootteen by *both Hindus and Mussulmen* is also a curious fact connected with the religious habits of this people.

Page 89, para. 391. Educational institutions are of six kinds :—

(1) Muktabs, where Persian is taught.
(2) Chutsals, from Chutta, a school-boy, where Hindi is taught.
(3) Pathshala, from "path," reading, where Nagri or Shashtri is taught.
(4) Muktabs, where Arabic is taught.
(5) Schools in which Gurmukhi.
(6) Schools in which English is taught.

Para. 392. Persian schools are not much in vogue; they are only found in the Quasbahs, or large villages. They are generally set up in his own house by some individual who wants to teach his children and employs a teacher on 2 and 3 rupees a month; others who wish to have their sons educated too, send their boys and give the teacher from 2 to 8 annas a month according to their means. The income of the teacher is thus made up to 8 and 10 rupees a month. Boys come to school at from 5 to 6, some as late as 10; they read for 8 and 9 years; some as long as 12 or 18. Many then get paying employment of some kinds and discard their books. The parents are too lenient, and do not insist upon the attention of the children; some cannot pay the teacher and the boys are withdrawn,

Para. 393. The teachers are men of unfinished education; they are not examined previous to their appointment, and are many of them ignorant of everything but how to read and write. The teacher reads out the lessons which the children repeat after him; some few repeat from memory. *They have a repetition day once a week, generally Thursday, in the forenoons. In the afternoon of that day they learn poetry, and in the evening cap verses.* In some schools one of the boys is employed as an assistant to the master, and *hears every day the repetition of the previous day's lesson.* The course of reading is very low; works on ethics and morals are not read. *They are taught to read and write in all the schools,* and in some they are taught to cypher. The first attempts at writing are upon a chalked board with a pen made from the sunput grass. Then they come to paper doubled twice; a finished penman writes on a thin piece of paper, only supported by his hands.

Para. 394. Absence is punished by admonition, pulling the ears, and caning. If a boy does not come, another is always sent to bring him; *every boy is numbered* when he comes into school, and when they are dismissed are sent away in the order they came, the first with one pat on the hand, and the second with two, and so on. The last boy who comes into school and who is called a "phadee," gets the most pats, and these a trifle harder than the rest. Inattention and stupidity are punished as above, and by refusal of the indulgence of holidays. Boys are expelled for theft or any other serious misconduct. *Tutors are respected and looked up to, and the appointment is one much sought after.* Fridays are holidays, as are the Akheree Char Shumba, the last Wednesday in the month, Rujub and other feast days, and 'Teacher's' festivals. On the occasion of these festivals the children give small presents of 3 or 4 pies to their tutors, calling it "Eedee;" nothing of artizanship is taught by any respectable schoolmaster.

Para. 395. A Persian school and pathshálá were established in Umballa by Sir George Clerk; he got up a subscription of 11,000 rupees* from the Native Chiefs, the interest of which, 34 Rs. a month, was devoted to the instruction of children. I understand that the management of these schools is now

---

* Where is that money now?

entrusted to the American Missionaries at Umballa. In these the holiday is Sunday; a public yearly examination takes place in November; prizes are given to the best boy. The Bible, I believe, is not insisted upon, but read and explained to the boys once a week.

Page 93, para. 417. The Grunth is the holy book of the Sikhs, which they come to hear read by readers (Grunthees); it is considered advisable to hear the Grunth read at all times, but the most favourable dates are the holidays of Dewalee, Holee, Dasserah, and the 11th April, Shunkaryat, Makh, Bussunt, Punchamee, and the 5th and 10th evenings of the light half of the lunar months. The reason of the 5th and 10th being selected is that Guru Gobind Sing died on the 5th and Baba Nanak died on the 10th of the light half of the moon.

Ludhiana Settlement Report.

Page 29, para. 24. The native method of education, as it now exists, is very primitive in the district; there are some 60 schools where the children of the mercantile classes receive the education necessary to enable them to carry on their trade. These schools are very rude; the younger boys may be seen acquiring the rudiments of arithmetic with the finger for a pencil, and the sand on the ground at the doorway for a slate. Among the agricultural classes generally, there is no attempt at education. In some of the higher families, such as Jaghirdars, or others possessed of property exceeding the usual amount of an ancestral share in a village community, a reader of the Grunth may be found who imparts instruction to the extent of reading and writing Gurmukhi. *The young girls are likewise thus far instructed.* Such a teacher, if not permanently attached to the family, usually resides in it some 6 or 7 years, and the hildren of other neighbouring families are similarly admitted to share in the enstruction.

Page 30, para. 25. The *charitable institutions* throughout the district are *chiefly dependant upon grants of land* for their support. In the ordinary buildings devoted to these objects, whether small or large, they are all called Dharmsalas. Two or three religious mendicants are usually to be met with, *a reader of the Grunth*, the scriptures of the Sikhs, and a menial to prepare the food. *The volume of the Grunth*, written in "Gurmukhi" and resting upon a stand, covered with a showily embroidered covering, *is treated with universal respect*, and in Hans, of pergunna Jugraon, where the reader of the Grunth was a most diminutive dwarf, the adoration with which the ignorant rustics treated him, prostrating themselves to the ground in his presence, *was something ludicrous.** In the larger Dharmsalas a large kitchen establishment is supported, a pair of bullocks being required to grind the corn, and the supply of food daily meted out, not only to the poor and needy, but to the casual traveller, is very considerable.

Page 60, para. 50. *It has been only on the clearest proofs that the Muafidars have been recorded as proprietors of these rent-free lands*, or where the land has been resumed the settlement has been made with them; the *primâ facie* condition of such lands being, that they were the property in common either of the whole village or of that sub-division of the village in which the lands were situated.

Page 84, para. 74. The one per cent. road fund, and the commutation for service money are the only claims of Government upon the jaghirdars. Whatever rent-free plots of land are in these villages, excepting grants of the time of the Emperors, as regards resumption and continuance, they are under the observation of the jaghirdars.

From Settlement Report, Hoshiarpur District, 1852.

Educational Statistics, Appendix IV.

55. From the Educational Statistics given in Appendix N it will be seen that the state of learning is not very flourishing in this district. On comparing it with a similar return furnished by Mr. Temple for Julundhur, I per-

* Why.

ceive that in that district there is one school to every 4·87 mehals; in this district there is one only to every 10·01 mehals. But to every 9·48 inhabited mehals of the four pergunnahs exhibited, for Hoshiarpur there is one school. In the latter district there is one school to every 19·92 males (adults and non-adults); in Julundhur there is one to every 20·69. Here there are 7·79 boys to each school. Out of the 156 schools there are only 6 in which Gurmukhi is taught. Instruction in Persian seems to be most sought after.

Inferior character of the schools.

54. The paucity of educational institutions is doubtless very great; but what must be the character of such as there are, when the average monthly pay of each schoolmaster is only Rs. 2-7-4? This sum has been carefully enquired into; and, small as it may appear, it is, I believe, correct. It has been calculated from both money and grain payments. The class of schoolmasters is a very mean one. The teachers are generally old men, who derive but a partial support from their own exertions, the rest being made up by their near relatives, who often go out to service, and who, when they become too aged for the active duties of life, return and succeed in the school those to whom they have hitherto rendered pecuniary assistance. The schoolmasters generally eke out a further pittance by contributions of cooked food from their pupils; and they are further helped on by presents from the parents at marriage festivals.

Undecided cases.

247. The undecided cases involve lands to the annual amount of Rs. 36,070. Almost the whole of these, if taken up and determined, would be released, and some of them would be granted in perpetuity. All *doubtful* claims have been scrutinized and *resumed*, during the five or six years of our rule. It *is difficult, indeed, for any ambiguous title* to escape. The *Government officers of all grades pursue and relentlessly "attach" every tenure with a flaw in it,* and the people, though they respect and deprecate interference with prescriptive claims, are as ready to run down an iniquitous grant as the most zealous upholder of the public interest.

Value of resumed lands.

248. It may be worth while to record the amount of resumption which has occurred since the cession. The sums are set down according to the assessments fixed upon the confiscated holdings. *The large escheats in 1849-50 were owing to the rebellion.* The jaghir estate of Muhul Moree, belonging to the rebel Chief, Raja Purmood Chund, was alone valued at Rs. 33,000.

Sialkot.

The schools in the Sialkot District (excluding Bujwant) in 1852 (Prinsep's Report) were 149 in 129 villages (*so that several villages had more than one school*). Of these schools, all had been in existence *before annexation*, 61 above 30 years, 18 above 20 years, 16 above 10 years, 13 above 6 years, and 41 below 6 years. There were 150 teachers, one school possessing two teachers; 8 teachers taught gratuitously, 124 schools were held in Mosques or Dharmsálás, and 16 in miscellaneous places.

The remuneration was in 193 cases, Rs. 2,672, grain worth Rs. 452, total Rs. 3,511, so that the average pay of each teacher was Rs. 23 or about Rs. 2 per month. There were 1,922 pupils, of whom 889 were Muhammadans, 91 Sikhs, 45 , 291 Brahmins, 295 Katris, 24 Rajputs, 27 Jats, and 260 miscellaneous:—

963 were above 10 years of age.
557 " " 8 "
292 " " 6 "
110 " below 6 "

As regards the occupation of the parents of the pupils—

508 were agricultural.
261 in Trade.
1,153 miscellaneous.

The schools were—

1 for Gurmukhi.
7 „ Sanskrit.
15 „ Hindi (Lande?)
91 „ Persian.
35 „ Arabic.
None for Urdu.

The pupils read the following languages :—

12 Gurmukhi.
152 Sanskrit.
329 Hindi (Lande?)
993 Persian.
436 Arabic.

EXTRACT FROM ADMINISTRATION REPORT, PANJAB, 1851-52.

Proposal to extend system of the North-Western Provinces to the Panjab.

457. On the receipt of a report from the late Lieutenant-Governor, North-Western Provinces, on the results of the experimental scheme which had been carried into effect since 1849 in eight districts, with a recommendation to the effect that it might be extended throughout the North-Western Provinces, the Supreme Government were pleased to direct that the Panjab authorities should consider whether a similar plan might not be beneficially introduced into the Panjab. The subject immediately engaged the earnest attention which it demanded, and detailed projects have been submitted.

Educational wants of the Panjab.

458. It is believed that both the necessity and encouragement for the educational measure exist as much in the Panjab as in any province of this Presidency. There are less prejudices and fewer elements of passive hindrance or of active opposition here than elsewhere. The Sikh fanaticism and political fervour are dying out. The Hindus are less superstitious and less priest-ridden. The Muhummadans of the plains as contradistinguished from those of the hills and the frontier, though formidable in number, are less bigoted, less bound by traditionary practice, than their co-religionists in any part of India. The upper classes display a candid intelligence and inquisitiveness in respect to Asiatic learning and European science. The agricultural classes, though uncouth, are less apathetic and *less illiterate* in their tastes than might have been expected; *the village accountants display a skill* not surpassed, and often not equalled, in Hindustan. The ***working classes evince a considerable aptitude in mechanical art.*** On the whole, the Punjab is ripe for the introduction of an educational scheme.

Mode of establishing village schools.

459. There is ample scope for the establishment of Government schools at the revenue offices in the interior of the districts; for the appointment of district visitors, one to each district, aided by several assistants, who will not only preside over the Government schools, but also stimulate education by travelling about among the villages, explaining to the people the advantages of a school, to render aid by the procuring of schoolmasters and books. Such officers might induce the communities to set up one school, if not in every village, at least in every circle of villages, so that at length there shall be no village throughout the land in which the children do not attend some rudimentary school. The supervising officers should for the present be natives of Hindustan, but the schoolmasters must be Panjabis. Some special seminaries for the training of schoolmasters, such as Normal schools, should be established. The general system might be introduced to a greater or less extent, according as the civilization of particular tracts may vary, but all districts and divisions may be admitted to share in the benefits of education. The Persian and Urdu languages might be taught in all schools, under the patronage of Government. But other languages and characters, such as Hindi, Sanskrit, Gurmukhi, Pan-

Normal schools required.

Urdu language best adapted for Panjab schools.

jábi need not be used.* The simplification of language is a matter of importance, and the Panjab offers facilities in this respect. Gurmukhi, though of sacred origin, and in the days of Sikh supremacy *both a courtly and priestly tongue*, is now rapidly falling into desuetude. The Panjabi, as a spoken language, is also losing its currency, and *degenerating* into a mere provincial and rustic dialect, whereas the Urdu or Hindustani, as the prescribed language of the courts and of the public departments, is becoming familiar to the upper and middle classes, and the ruder population understand it nearly as well as their fellow-subjects of Hindustan

Social aspect of the Panjab.

496. During the period of the Board's report the country might still, though changes were everywhere being wrought, be recognized as the Panjab of the Sikh dynasty. The settlement of the country is by the present date assuming its solid and permanent proportions; the transition is well nigh complete, and the country is becoming the Panjab of the British power. *The feudal nobility* of Ranjit Singh, the pillars of his state, are *tending towards inevitable decay.* Their gaudy retinues have disappeared; their city residences are less gay with equipages and visitors; their country seats and villas are comparatively neglected. But the British Government has done all it consistently could to mitigate their reverses, and render their decadence gradual. They receive handsome pensions, or they retain for their lives a moiety of their landed grants. When any of them have been judged to possess hereditary claims, a fair share of their landed fiefs has been guaranteed to them and their posterity in perpetuity. They are treated with considerate respect by the servants of the Government; they swell public processions, and attend at ceremonial durbars.

Decay of the Sikh aristocracy.

The sons of this nobility and of the gentry generally are seeking Government employ, and acquiring a liberal education. Their retainers similarly enjoy the bounty of the Government. The numerous dependants of the late *régime* are also provided for. Not only are the royal widows and their attendants being cared for, but also the office-bearers of the court, the chamberlains, the mace-bearers, the soothsayers, *the physicians, the savans,* the musicians, the men-in-waiting, are all *borne on the pension rolls*† of the British State. *All these classes naturally sink into obscurity;* and though everything like splendour has vanished, yet it has not been succeeded by poverty; and the multitude, which surrounded and supported the throne of Ranjit Singh and his successors exist in substantial comfort.

Condition of the classes connected with the late court and nobility.

497. The priestly classes have also every reason to bless their new masters. The Sikh holy places have been respected. The shrines at Dera Nanuck, Umritsur, Turun Tarun, Anandpur, retain *a large portion*‡ of the endowments which a *Sikh Government had lavished on them.* Liberality has indeed been extended to all religious characters, even to mendicant friars and village ascetics. These people have been allowed by the thousand to *retain their petty landed grants on a life tenure.*‡ There is hardly a village mosque or a rustic temple, or a shaded tomb of which the service is not supported by a few fields of rent-free cultivation. These classes, though they will not become extinct, will yet greatly fall below their present numbers when the existing generation shall have passed away. *In the meantime they are kept contented,*§ and their indirect influence on the mass of the population is enlisted on the side of the Government. The early

The priestly castes and the religious classes.

The military class.

* This policy at once prevented the utilization of existing indigenous schools.

† The interests of indigenous education required the permanence of land tenures, not the personal solatium of pensions tenable for life.

‡ What becomes of the assertion that the endowments were respected, when either only a "portion" which in the conqueror's eye was, no doubt, "large" was maintained, or when the innumerable "petty landed grants" tenable in perpetuity, were reduced to "life-tenure?"

§ Here we have the secret of not taking away their all from the teaching "priestly castes and the religious classes."

absorption of the famous Sikh soldiery into the body of society will be a theme for future historians. The fiercer spirits have taken employment under their conquerors, and are serving on the Indus in the far West, and on the Irrawaddy in the far East. But the majority have returned to agriculture in their native Manjha and Mulmas, and anticipate the opening of the new canal. The staunch foot soldier has become the steady cultivator, and the brave officer is now the sturdy village elder.

Partial decline of the Sikh faith.

498. The Sikh faith and ecclesiastical polity is rapidly going where the Sikh political ascendancy has already gone. Of the two elements in the old Khalsa, namely, the followers of Nanuck, the first prophet, and the followers of Guru Govind, the second great religious leader, the former will hold their ground, and the latter will lose it. The Sikhs of Nanuck, a comparatively small body of peaceful habits and old family, will perhaps cling to the faith of their fathers; but the Sikhs of Govind, who are of more recent origin, who are more specially styled the Singhs or "lions," and who embraced the faith as being the religion of warfare and conquest, no longer regard the Khalsa now that the prestige has departed from it. These men joined in thousands, and they now desert in equal numbers. They rejoin the ranks of Hinduism whence they originally came, and they bring up their children as Hindus. The sacred tank at Umritsur is less thronged than formerly, and the attendance at the annual festivals is diminishing yearly. The initiatory ceremony for adult persons is now rarely performed.

Flourishing state of the agricultural classes.

The local Chiefs.

499. Among the agriculturists, the influence of the chowdries is on the decline. They are a species of local chiefs or principal resident gentry, who, under the Sikh *régime*, aided in collecting the revenue, and enjoyed many privileges and immunities. Many of their privileges are maintained to them, but, as their services are no longer required, their power is on the wane. The undue power of the headmen also over the village communities has been curtailed, but their legitimate position as representatives of the brotherhood, has been strengthened and defined. The numbers of these most useful coparcenaries are in every respect flourishing under British rule. Their tenures have been adjudicated, their rights recorded. The change from the appraisement of the standing crops, or division of the garnered grain, to a regular money taxation has protected these peasant proprietors from the interference of Government officials, from the frauds of their more intriguing brethren, and has given a real value to landed property previously unknown, while the harsher consequences of cash payments have been averted by reduced taxation. The class next below them, namely, the cultivators, are deriving equal benefit. never were their rights and the return for their labour so secure as now. The non-agricultural residents of villages are also living in increased comfort. They are no longer liable to tyranny and exaction on the part of their landlords. The cesses and manorial dues which they may have to pay are better regulated. The important class of village bankers are not likely to suffer materially under any *régime*; they are certainly well-to-do under British rule. They have enhanced facilities of recovering their loans from the landholders; in this respect they enjoy every possible advantage. On the other hand, the proprietary bodies are becoming less and less dependent on them, as frugality, prudence and good management increase under the influence of the money payment system.

The headmen.

The village yeomen.

The cultivators.

The village bankers.

The working classes.

500. The working classes and day labourers and artizans, owing to the progress of cantonments and gigantic public works, are prospering beyond all precedent. The mass of the poorer population in cities, the artizans and mechanics, are better off than they ever were. The miscellaneous classes, such as servants, camp-followers, strangers, emigrants from Hindustan, are all greatly benefiting by

the extraordinary cheapness of provisions.* Among the commercial classes *certain sections may be losers*, but the great majority are largely sharing in the general prosperity. In some places the ornamental manufactures that adorned the court and camp of Ranjit Singh and of his provincial governors are out of fashion, and *such branches of trade must suffer*. In other places the retail dealers must yield to the greater capital and enterprise of the wholesale traders; but the trading class who carry on the traffic between India and Central Asia, who conduct a commerce through the routes of Peshawar and Dehra Ismael Khan, in value at least half a million sterling per annum; who bring the furs and wool, the raw silk, the fruits, groceries, drugs, the leather, the chintzes, the horses from the far West, and send in return the British piece-goods, the European hardware, the Indian fabric, and the sugar of the Panjab; and the men who bring the wool and the iron from the Himalayan regions, and the shawls and blankets from Cashmere; and the parties engaged in the increasing export and import trade through Kurrachee in wool, indigo, saltpetre and European stores—all these people are thriving even beyond expectation. The great banking firms that have connexious ramifying all over India, and have even correspondents in Europe, are rising still higher, and will soon realize the description of "merchant princes."† According to the partial fluctuation of wealth among the mercantile classes, so is the rise and decline of cities. Some, such as Wazeerabad, Jullandhur, Loodiana, Buttala, and even Lahore to some extent, are falling off. Others again maintain their status, or else are rapidly growing in prosperity, such as Umritsur, Peshawar, Ferozepore, Mooltan. Others, again are rising up from villages to large towns, such as Sialkote, Jhelum, Rawul Pindee.

Manufacturers.

Traders.

Mercantile firms.

Rise and fall of cities.

501. In short, then, whilst the remnants of a bye-gone aristocracy are passing from the scene, *not with precipitate ruin, but in a gradual and mitigated decline*;‡ on the other hand, the hardy yeoman, the strong-handed peasant, the thrifty trader, the enterprising capitalist, are rising up in robust prosperity to be the durable and reliable bulwarks of the power which protects and befriends them. Among all classes there is a greater regard for vested right, for ancestral property, for established principle. There is also an improved social morality, many barbarous customs are being eradicated, and the position of the female sex is better secured and respected. *Among all ranks there is a thirst for knowledge and an admiration for the achievements of practical science.*§ But irrespective of the frame-work of society, the external face of the country is rapidly changing, from the advance of vast public works both for communication and irrigation; and *if the old palatial residences are decaying*, on the other hand *fine contonments are everywhere springing up*,‡ and the public buildings, both civil and military, as regards size and architecture are not surpassed at any station of Upper India. The alteration is apparent in town no less than in country. *The aspect of the streets is less gay and brillant than before*;‡ but the improvements in drainage, in

General prosperity of the agricultul and commercial classes.

Growing respect for right, property and principle.

Improved social morality.

Face of the country being changed by public works.

Progress of stations and cantonments.

* Surely two years of British rule (since annexation in 1849) cannot fairly be credited with "the extraordinary cheapness of provisions" from which a host of hungry Hindustani "camp-followers, strangers and emigrants" benefited, when they paid at all!

† This paragraph, in my humble opinion, rather describes the prosperous condition of the Panjab *before* annexation, than as a *consequence* of British rule, as is complacently implied. It is not likely that two years of a foreign rule, which caused the "ornamental manufactures" patronized by Ranjit Singh and his provincial governors to become "out of fashion," should have developed a trade which it requires centuries to foster and which is not, in proportion, more developed in 1882 than it was supposed to be in 1851-52, such as the extraordinary trade with Central Asia, the rise of great banking firms with "even correspondents in Europe, &c., &c." Of course, a certain stimulus was given to certain trades in places where we established cantonments or centres of our Government, but we no more caused the commercial prosperity, only *ascertained to exist in 1851*, than we were responsible for the hot weather of that year.

‡ This, however, *was* obviously the result of foreign rule

§ This, too, was due to the traditional reverence of the people for learning of every kind, as already described, which rendered them an admirable material for our educational operations, had they been wisely conducted, but this reverence for education was not *caused* by two years of British rule.

pavements, *in the laying out of bazars,* would prove to the commonest observer that an era of solid comfort and sanitary cleanliness had commenced.

Improved appearance of cities.

PANJAB ADMINISTRATION REPORT, *1854-55 and 1855-56.*

Lapses and resumption make up for reduction of assessment.

44. For this beneficent end there has been a considerable sacrifice of revenues; but this has been partially compensated for *by the resumption of jaghirs at annexation, and by the lapse of fiefs and jaghirs and petty tenures since that time.* These lapses have nearly sufficed to make up for the reductions subsequent to annexation, so that the land-tax has not materially fallen off since annexation. There has, however, after allowing for all these sets off, been a net sacrifice of at least half a million sterling, this sum being (at the least) the difference between the land-tax of the Sikhs and the land-tax of the British. But since annexation the lapses and resumptions have balanced the reductions of assessment; for, as regards actual realization, the tax yielded Rs. 1,59,40,722 or £1,594,072 for 1850-51, the highest year, and during the last year, 1855-56, it has still yielded Rs. 1,50,00,650 or £1,500,065. In this respect the policy of the Sikh Government was to tax heavily the agriculturists, and to make large assignments of revenue to the nobility as payment for service and support. But the policy of the British Government is to tax lightly the agriculturists, to pay its servants from its own treasury, to excuse the native nobility from service, and to gradually reduce their assignments of revenue.

First educational scheme.

70. In the last Panjab Report, written in July 1854, it was declared that the Panjab was ripe for the introduction of an educational measure. During that same year a scheme framed at Lahore was submitted to the Supreme Government, and the views therein enunciated have since been honoured with the approval of the Home Authorities. *But early in 1855 the despatch of the Hon'ble the Court of Directors, which initiated a new era for education in India, was received at Lahore.* This despatch was communicated with the Chief Commissioner's directions regarding the carrying out of its provisions to the Financial Commissioner to whose Department educational questions pertain. During 1855 the Financial Commissioner collected opinions from all the local authorities and thus prepared materials. Early in 1856 Mr. W. D. Arnold, son of the late Dr. Arnold, was appointed Director of Public Instruction. In February of the same year the Financial Commissioner, aided by the Director's suggestions, forwarded a complete scheme for future education in the Panjab, which has been duly submitted to the Supreme Government for sanction. Such is the preliminary history of what has been done in this Department.

Preliminary measures.

Statistics of existing schools.

71. The statistics of schools have been collected from all the districts. Though very tolerable in their way, they have yet to be subjected to that intelligent analysis which can only be secured by the aid of especially trained establishments. The next Annual Report will contain an exact classification of these statistics. At present it will suffice to state that the several divisions can show indigenous schools and scholars as follows :—

DIVISIONS.	Indigenous schools.	Scholars.	Population.	Proportion of schools to population.	Proportion of schools to population.
Cis-Sutlej States	332	3,506	2,282,111	1 to 6,873	1 to 650
Trans-Sutlej States	586	6,237	2,273,037	3,879	364
Lahore	1,270*	12,753*	2,117,894*	1,667	16[illegible]
Jhelum	774	5,782	1,762,488	2,277	304
Leia	No regular schools.				
Mooltan	212	2,186	971,175	4,581	404
Peshawar	198	1,128	296,364	1,496	262
TOTAL	3,372	31,692	9,110,341	2,701	288

* The Lahore Division has in 1882, 861 indigenous schools with 11,867 pupils, the population being 2,191,517, but it should be remembered that the statistics of 1854-55 were far less complete than those of the present year.

Besides the above there are schools of a superior kind established either by Government or under Government auspices, at Umballa, Ferozepore, Simla, Jullunder, Hooshiarpur, Kangra, Amritsar, Sialkot, Gujrat, Jhelum, Rawal Pindi, Shahpur. There is also some thirty-five schools scattered about in the interior of districts. The largest of the Government schools is that of Amritsar, which is endowed by a grant of Rs. 5,000 or £500 a year, and a yearly contribution of Rs. 500 or £50 per annum from Maharajah Dhuleep Singh, and has about 500 pupils, some of whom learn the English language and European science. It was explained in the last report that there are good Missionary schools at Lahore, Amritsar, Peshawar, Ludhiana, Umballa, Jullunder, Kangra and Kotegarh in the Hills. The indigenous, or village schools, are as yet of the rudest description. A lage proportion of the population being Muhammadans, the precincts of the village mosque are in many cases used as a school-house. For the same reason the Persian, Arabic and Urdu languages constitute the course of instruction in the western districts. In the eastern districts, however, there is some admixture of the Hindu and Sanskrit languages with the Nagri character, and other characters derived from the Nagri. In the central districts, and in a part of the Cis-Sutlej States, once the home of the Sikh nation, the Gurmukhi is not unfrequently taught The style of education is of course most primitive. The teachers derive a precarious subsistence from fees. Heretofore there have been no funds available for popular education; but the majority of the people, though ignorant, are yet not insensible to the blessings of knowledge, and are ready to make some small sacrifices for the education of their children.

Amritsar School.

Character of indigenous education.

72. As a leaven to operate upon this mass of ignorance, it is now proposed to found some thirty schools at the head-quarters of districts; about 100 schools in the interior of districts, four Normal schools, one Central College at Lahore with one Prinicpal and two Professors, all Europeans; the above schools are to be supported by the State. To encourage the people to establish or maintain schools for themselves in their own villages, it is proposed to appoint ten visitors and sixty assistant visitors. The whole would be supervised by one Director and two Inspectors. The cost of the above establishment and institutions will, if fully developed, amount to something less than three lakhs of rupees or £30,000 per annum. Besides the above it is proposed to allot Rs. 15,000 or £1,500 sterling per annum, as grants-in-aid to Missionary and other schools, an assistance of which it is already apparent that the Missionaries will readily avail themselves. In regard to local resources for the maintenance of *indigenous or village schools,* it is hoped that the landholders, as each new settlement of the revenue comes into operation, will engage to pay one per cent. upon their land-tax for education. For city schools we may rely on obtaining a share of the town duties levied for municipal improvements. *In many large villages also the proceeds of a similar cess may be available, which has been levied from time immemorial from non-agricultural residents.** A large portion of the existing fees paid to schoolmasters will also be maintained. On the whole, it is not improbable that the people themselves may be induced to devote, even at the present time, two or two and a half lakhs of rupees, or £25,000 sterling annually for education. This, added to the State contribution, will give an aggregate of not less than six or seven lakhs of rupees or £70,000 per annum, with which this great measure may be commenced and set on foot. When once a real impression shall have been made upon the popular mind, the amount may rise to ten lakhs of rupees or £100,000 and more annually. But even the latter sum, though large, would be hardly sufficient. For if the persons of school-going age were assumed to be one-eighth of the po-

Proposed establishment for native education in the Panjab.

Grants-in-aid.

Probable funds, public and private.

* This has never been continuously done under our rule. On the contrary, the cess levied from agriculturists has been largely, if not almost entirely, used to pay for the education of non-agriculturists by the Panjab Educational Department in opposition to the repeatedly declared policy of the Panjab Government.

pulation, *i. e.*, $1\frac{3}{4}$ millions out of $12\frac{3}{4}$, and if again half of these, or one-sixteenth, are to be educated, say 800,000 scholars, and if the cost of educating each were taken at Rs. 3 per annum (the very lowest possible amount), the aggregate expenditure would be 24 lakhs of rupees or £240,000 per annum. More than one generation must pass away before any such sum can be realized; and such is the difficulty of carrying out any really national education.*

Commencement of operations.

73. Provisional sanction has been received from the Government of India to commence the organization of the Educational Department on something approaching to the above status. Two months only have intervened between the framing of the scheme and the close of the period under report, *i. e.*, between February and May 1856. But something has been done even in this brief interval. A large portion of the educational staff has been organized; nearly all the visitors have been appointed and sent forth as emissaries and pioneers even to the wildest and most remote districts; more than half of the Government schools to be founded in the interior of districts, that is, about sixty in number, have been set on foot. At the head-quarters or central station of almost every district a school has either been founded or taken under management: one Normal school has been commenced; some 11,000 small text and school-books have been distributed. In fine, the Supreme Government may be confident that whatever degree of energy may have been desplayed in other Departments will be equally exerted in the cause of education, and we may hope that before another year shall have passed there may be a goodly array of results to show.

English education.

74. The Government have desired that this section of the report should be sub-divided into the headings of English, vernacular and industrial.† It is hoped that in future reports there will be the means of treating each of these important headings with proper fullness. At the present initiatory stage, however, the remarks upon each must be very brief. It would probably be premature to direct any very strenuous efforts at present upon English Education. The trials that have heretofore been made in the Panjab have not been very successful. It may be better to rest awhile, until a class of youths shall have arisen fit to receive the higher European learning by means of the English language. At present English education among Panjabis is little better than a forced exotic, ready to wither under the influences of practical life. The great and *immediate* object for attainment is the imparting of sound elementary knowledge in the vernacular form. Let the *mass of the people* be taught the plain elements of *our* knowledge *in their own language*. This is the first thing, and this, it is hoped, can be done in the present age of translating. No pains will be spared to establish depôts of vernacular books for the Panjab. The chief language to be used is the *Urdu* with the Persian character. The use of this tongue is rapidly spreading among all ranks, and is becoming more than a *lingua franca*. It is most fortunate that the Panjab presents such peculiar facilities for the simplification of language. As regards industrial education the only institution of this description is a school of Civil Engineering at Lahore, which has sixty scholars, all natives, and proves useful and popular. It is not probable that much can be done in the industrial branch for some time to come.

Vernacular.

Industrial.

---

* The difficulty would have been solved by utilizing the existing indigenous schools and preserving their rent-free tenures.

† There is no really industrial education in the Panjab in 1882.

186. The general result of the census for the Panjab territories may be thus epitomised :—

Divisions.	Square miles.	Villages.	Population.	Land Revenue, Rs. or £.	Persons to square miles.
			Souls.		
Cis-Sutlej States	8,090·11	4,962	2,282,111	Rs. 32,01,228 £ 320,112	28,208
Trans-Sutlej States	6,791·83	4,171	2,273,037	Rs. 33,91,296 £ 339,129	33,467
Lahore	11,627·88	8,188	3,458,694	Rs. 43,17,118 £ 441,711	29,741
Jhelum	16,761·22	4,647	1,762,488	Rs. 23,77,301 £ 237,730	10,535
Mooltan	15,494·00	2,489	971,175	Rs. 10,74,959 £ 107,495	6,268
Leia	15,271,70	2,531	1,122,621	Rs. 16,96,662 £ 169,666	7,350
Peshawar	7,588·50	1,891	847,695	Rs. 9,51,646 £ 95,164	11,170
GRAND TOTAL	81,625·24	28,879	12,717,821	Rs. 1,70,10,210 £ 1,701,021	15,580

Chief cities of the Panjab.

188. There are 36,210 villages in the Panjab, with an average of about 450 persons to each;* 2,124 small towns containing from 1,000 to 5,000 inhabitants; 76 containing from 5,000 to 10,000; 31 cities containing from 10,000 to 50,000; and four first class cities containing more than 50,000 inhabitants, *i. e.*, Amritsar with 122,184 souls, Lahore with 94,153, Peshawar with 53,294, Mooltan (including suburbs) with 55,999 souls.

Muhammadans and Hindus.

189. There are 7½ millions of Muhammadans to 5½ millions of Hindus. This numerical predominance of Muhammadans is remarkable and unusual in India. From the eastern boundary, that is from the River Jumna to the Chenab, the Hindus preponderate; from thence to the Trans-Indus frontier, and in the Southern districts, the population is almost entirely Muhammadan. But among these latter, while many are of pure Muhammadan extraction, yet many are of Hindu race converted to Muhammadanism under the Mogul Emperors. In the Lahore Division, which contains the Manjha or the original home of the Sikhs, a detail of the Sikhs was taken, and there were found only about 200,000 Sikhs to an aggregate population of about 3 millions. This circumstance strongly corroborates what is commonly believed, namely, that the Sikh tribe is losing its number rapidly. Modern Sikhism was little more than a political association (formed exclusively from among Hindus), which men would join or quit according to the circumstances of the day. A person is not born a Sikh, as he might be born a Muhammadan or born a Hindu; but he must be specially initiated into Sikhism.

Present paucity of Sikhs.

Now that the Sikh commonwealth is broken up, people cease to be initiated into Sikhism and revert to Hinduism. Such is the undoubted explanation of a statistical fact, which might otherwise appear to be hardly credible.†

Agricultural and non-agricultural classes.

190. More than half the population were returned as agricultural. The tendency in every Indian Census is to include among miscellaneous professions many persons who really derive their subsistence from the land.

* In how many, *if any*, of *such* villages is there a Government Primary Vernacular School in 1882 and is the Educational Cess levied from such a village or not? If the contribution of such a village is too small for an unnecessarily expensive Government school, why is the money not used to improve or aid an existing indigenous school?

† This fact, in my humble opinion, is to be deeply deplored, as destroying a bulwark of our rule.

It is probable, then, that two-thirds, if not three-fourths of the people are agricultural: again, somewhat more than half the population are returned as males. This slight disproportion of females, found to exist more or less everywhere in India, is believed to be not otherwise than correct.

PANJAB ADMINISTRATION REPORT, 1856-57 AND 1857-58.

Supervising establishment.

48. During 1856-57 the machinery of the Department was organized: a Director General was appointed on a salary of Rs. 1,200 per mensem; two Inspectors on Rs. 600 each for the Eastern and Western Circles, respectively; 11 Deputy Inspectors each to receive a salary from Rs. 80 to 150 per mensem, and to supervise two or more districts; and 17 Sub-Deputy Inspectors on salaries of Rs. 20 to 60; each district being divided into 3 or 4 tehseels or sub-divisions for administrative purposes. A Government school at the head-quarters of each tehseel was established; some 107 schools were thus founded. The principle of arranging with the landholders to pay for education a sum, calculated at one per cent. on the assessed land-tax was carried out everywhere in the Panjab (save in Lei and Hazara) without any objection being raised by the people; some Rs. 1,38,000 were collected on this account, and 456 village schools* were established from this resource. Each of these schools is placed in a central position, so as to be accessible to the children of three or four villages. Grants-in-aid to the amount of Rs. 6,970 were accepted on behalf of Mission schools in various parts of the Panjab. One Normal school was established; some four Government schools previously existing were taken by the new Department, and the statistics of the indigenous education throughout the Province were collected. Such was the commencement made during the first year.

Educational proceedings in 1856-57.

Education not affected by the troubles of 1857.

49. The second year, 1857-58, had scarcely commenced when the disturbances in Hindustan broke out with fury, and excitement arose more or less throughout the Panjab. The educational officers then resolved not to attempt the establishment of fresh village schools until the crisis should pass over, but to concentrate all efforts for the maintainance of the Government schools set on foot during the past year. The hope which had been entertained of establishing many hundreds of additional schools was thus deferred for some months. But the attendance at the Government schools was kept up undiminished. During the first quarter, May, June and July 1857, the first three months of trouble, there was actually a slight increase over the attendance of the preceding peaceful quarter.

During the next quarter of August, September and October, three months of awful crisis, when the fate of the Panjab really trembled in the balance, there was a diminution of only 97 pupils on an aggregate of 4,900, which, in fact, is no perceptible diminution at all. Even in the Cis-Sutlej States, which were disturbed extensively, the Government schools did not suffer. At Rawal Pindee only, near the Indus, were there any symptoms manifested of religious bigotry against the educational arrangements. In all other places, even on the fanatical frontier, there was no suspicion or prejudice raised on account of the schools. By November the crisis was overpast, and the establishing of additional village schools was immediately taken in hand. Nearly 700 new ones were founded by the end of December. During the two last quarters of the year perfect quiet had succeeded to excitement, consequently the system, laboriously sustained during a time of trouble has since been extended; the attendance of Government schools has increased month by month; the style of education has been improved and the village schools extended.

Recent progress.

---

* *Where* were these schools, and do they still exist in the same villages?

Educational expenditure.

50. The educational system thus started is, of course, still in robust infancy,* and a brief notice of some of its leading features will suffice at present.

Number of schools and scholars.

51. The expenditure for the two years may be thus set down :—

	1856-57.	1857-58.
	Rs. £.	Rs. £.
Expended by Government	1,05,392=10,539	1,44,868=14,487
Expended from the one per cent. fund collected from landholders.	23,472= 2,347	82,263= 8,226
TOTAL .	1,28,864=12,886	2,27,131=22,713

The actual collections for the one per cent. fund were:—In 1856-57 Rs. 1,38,044 or £13,804; in 1857-58 Rs. 1,51,544 or £15,154; so that there is a large unexpended balance at credit of the fund. In round numbers the educational income may be set down at three lakhs of rupees, or £30,000 per annum, of which half is paid by Government, and half contributed by the people.

The number of schools and scholars for the two years are :—

	1856-57.		1857-58.	
	Schools.	Pupils.	Schools.	Pupils.
Government "Tehseel" Schools	107	6,919	110	6,953
Special Institutions	15	2,254	16	1,714
One per cent. Village Schools	456	6,064	1,336	12,024
Indigenous Schools	5,024	30,196	3,461	26,317
TOTAL .	5,602	45,433	4,923	46,008

In round numbers, then, we have something less than 50,000 boys under instruction, which number gives the proportion of one pupil to 23 of the school-going population. The number of pupils may appear small to a population of 13 millions, but a considerable increase may be expected yearly, especially in the village schools.

Characteristics of Government schools.

52. In the Government schools the education consists only of the rudiments of history, geography, arithmetic and grammar. But even this much is imparted with difficulty, and is a vast stride in advance of the wretched education which previously existed. The class system, which is the distinguishing mark between the European and Native methods of teaching, is enforced. The Urdu language, with the Persian character, is used in the Government schools. The pupils are more than one half Hindu. The remainder are mainly Muhummadans. Sikh pupils are not numerous. *The pupils belong chiefly to the non-agricultural classes.*† There are even female schools, all Muhammadan. There is, of course, a great dearth of qualified teachers; but a Normal school has been established at Lahore with forty pupils, and another has been commenced at Rawal Pindi. Those teachers previously in office who may be found deficient are required to qualify at these institutions. The higher kinds of Government schools have yet to be founded, and the Lahore College is postponed till the general system shall be more advanced. A depôt for school-books has been set up, and during 1857-58 some 14,139 little books were sold to the people for about Rs. 3,000 or £300.

2. THE RESUMPTION OF RENT-FREE LANDS, INCLUDING THOSE BELONGING TO SCHOOLS OR CONNECTED WITH TEACHING.

We have already seen from the Hushiarpur Settlement Report that all "doubtful" claims had been resumed. How easily it was, under the circum-

* In 1882 it is in a state of weak second childhood, without an intervening period of healthy youth and manhood.

† Notice the diversion from the agricultural classes, previously described as imbued with an educational spirit, to the non-agriculturists.

stances, for a claim to be "doubtful" may be inferred from the stringent orders of the Government of India to the Bengal Board of Administration. In his No. 418 of 31st March 1849, the Secretary to the former Government urges the question of Rent-free tenures as "the very first object to which the Board should direct their attention, as the longer the investigation is delayed, so much the more do their tenures acquire the force of prescription and make resumption more unpopular and apparently unjust." He asserts the doctrine, which no liberal Government would probably maintain at the present day, at any rate in Europe, that "by our occupation of the country after the whole Sikh nation had been in arms against us, we have acquired the absolute right of conquerors and would be justified in declaring every acre of land liable to Government assessment." We had fought with a chivalrous enemy; we had not conquered the country merely by the sword, and, even if the whole Sikh nation had been in arms against us, which, it may be contended, was a patriotic duty, there was scarcely sufficient justification for resuming any portion of land belonging to the 14 times more numerous Hindus and Muhammadans that had not risen. The "right of conquerors" is really "might," and when once "might" was called "right" by the highest authority in the land, it was superfluous for the Secretary to add that "our officers should not allow their minds to be *exasperated* against claimants on this account." The statement further on, "that all grants were resumed by the Sikh rulers at will without reference to the terms of the grant, whenever State exigencies or even caprice dictated," is, no doubt, true as regards political and, sometimes, personal grants for services, but certainly *never* applied to religious and educational endowments as already explained. Again, "there is *not one* of the rent-free holders who would not look upon any concession as a matter of grace." This would, perhaps, be the case if the Sikhs had looked upon us as followers of Tamerlane, but not if they considered us in a more favourable light. Considering the enormous difficulties of investigating claims to rent-free tenures in a foreign and newly-conquered country, "the delay even of a single year" is deprecated "as" encouraging hopes which, "it was presumed," are not now entertained. It was "therefore particularly claimed that the officers will *set the minds of the people at rest* upon this most important particular at the earliest period." This "rest" reminds one, indeed, of a definition of peace in Tacitus.

Considering also that, as will be seen further on, the majority of grants were not confirmed in full, it was rather hard to force every holder of rent-free land, whether partially or fully confirmed, to "yield up every document in his possession," in order that the people should look on the restoration of "their own" as a *free-gift* of the British Government. "Disabuse them of the opinion that they have any *inherent rights* which attach to their tenures in virtue of *long possession*, and make them regard their new masters in the light of *personal benefactors*." How this was to be done by officers scarcely acquainted with the languages and usages of the Province, it is difficult to understand. "No rent-free tenure should be continued in favour of any man who has taken up arms against the British Government, whether by choice or *compulsion*." It is obvious how such a rule would encourage delation and intrigue against persons whom unscrupulous neighbours wished to dispossess. The patriotic and religious had fought against us; they were the very salt of the Province, and they were to be punished without mercy by the "right of conquest." The instances, however, are rare in civilized warfare when persons *forced* to bear arms against a foreigner are punished by the confiscation of their property, and it is to be hoped that this law remained a dead letter. I have, however, no doubt that many teachers so dispossessed joined the mutiny of 1857.

When such are the general principles laid down for the guidance of a subordinate Government, it is easy to perceive how the laudable exception made in favour of religious and charitable endowments would be interpreted. It runs thus:—

"All endowments, *boná fide* made for the maintenance of religious establishments or buildings for public accommodation, to be maintained, *as long as the establishments or buildings are kept up*, provided, as noticed beow, *they are not exorbitant*."

Who was to judge of the "*bona fides*" of endowments? Surely not the Government whose interest was to resume the land. Was it the interest of the Government to *keep up the buildings?* And how about the innumerable endowments for teaching that had *no building*, such as depended on the priest or secular teacher giving *instruction* in the village-hall, or under a tree, or in his private house? Why, finally, make exemption from resumption dependent on the *amount of the endowment?* It was for *the donor* to judge whether it was "*exorbitant*," but having once made it, no one had a right to reduce it, once the safety of a religious or charitable institution was guaranteed. Yes, from our point of view, the endowments *were* extravagantly liberal; but this was the glory of native rule of whatever denomination, and when such endowments were curtailed or neglected, the decline of the religious feeling and the pauperization of the professional or priestly classes, brought about the downfall of indigenous education, and of that national probity to which our Administration Reports bear abundant witness. "When grants of *great value* have been conferred for the maintenance of the State religion (which always included teaching), they should be *restricted to a smaller amount from obvious motives of political expediency*. On the other hand, should cases of *individual hardship* arise from a strict observance of these rules, whether from indigence, infirmity or sex, the Governor General, *on such being represented*, will be happy to relax the *severity of the rules*, or *confer a pension* upon the object," a course which might still consign his relicts to starvation. It is deserving of notice that the preservation of schools is not mentioned, though this was understood to be the case by the Panjab Board of Administration, the fact being, as shown in their own Reports, that the religious endowments included teaching.

What I have quoted is from the "Non-Regulation Law of the Panjab," by D. G. Barkley, C.S., and will be found at length further on. I have added a chapter on village boundaries, as it indirectly bears on my proposal to endow indigenous and primary schools in perpetuity out of the village lands or out of waste-lands.* I have also added other documents showing how "ecclesiastical and educational matters" were practically dealt with, even by the wisest and best of our rulers. What wonder that the hearts of some of our officers overflows with love and pity for natives, in spite of their many failings, so as to make up, in some degree, for the devastation caused by a foreign rule, which is only now beginning to introduce "self-government," with which its career in the Panjab ought to have *commenced*. Sir Donald McLeod could only "suggest" that "where the *resumption of an endowment held by a mosque or temple would lapse on the death of the present incumbent*" (so they *did* lapse in some cases) "it shall be competent to the district officer to refrain from carrying that decision into effect—if he shall be of opinion that the institution is valued by the people and that the resumption is likely to prove distasteful to them;" and he was also to *report* any case in which the resumption of a grant, hitherto appropriated to the support of a Dharmsálá, Takya or Khangah, is "*likely to create serious dissatisfaction*." I have further added documents showing that in the "investigations of claims to revenue-free tenures in the Trans-Sutlej States," numerous holdings were resumed or greatly reduced or made life-tenures according to certain rules on the often incorrect assumption that "grants in perpetuity by native Governments mean nothing," and how the local Courts were deprived of authority to open out questions of division or inheritance anterior to the register of "free gifts" by the Indo-British Government, for which register, as has already been stated, all documents showing their rights had to be given up by the owners.

How the resumptions were carried out will further be made clear by extracts from Administration and Settlement Reports, and by a list of schools and teachers who were formerly in possession of rent-free land which has been

* I believe that there will be no difficulty in inducing the village communities to give a few bigas of their common land to the permanent endowment of a school, appreciated by them. In some cases, waste lands would be available for the purpose; in others, the present Jaghirdars would gladly "release," for the sake of re-establishing an indigenous school, the "Muafi" land that they may have resumed. In every case, Government revenue would be an eventual gainer by the endowment with land of indigenous schools, whilst the cost of primary education would be reduced rather than increased in proportion to the contemplated extension of mass-instruction.

resumed. Were I permitted, or were it necessary or desirable to examine the resumption records, it would be easy to establish the fact that thousands of endowments intended for teaching were resumed either at once or at the death of the incumbent at the time of annexation, or at the expiration of a particular settlement, or at the decay of the building, or at the wish of the jagirdar or in consequence of other reasons, none of which justified our neglect to make provision for the perpetuation, under better auspices, of the foundation of indigenous education. What there is left of it is not a tenth of what existed, and may be principally classed as "unendowed indigenous education," its endowed form having been practically destroyed, as I think must be clear to any one who reads this Report without prejudice for a writer of unpleasant facts which it is not to his advantage to divulge, but which he is forced to communicate in the interests of truth and as a reluctant witness and reporter on this very subject, at the request of the Education Commission.

Worse, however, than any confiscation of educational endowments, often carried out under misrepresentations and generally with regret, is the gross breach of faith which, in defiance of the clearest orders of Government, was committed by the Educational Department in misapplying the village school cess which was raised for a distinct purpose. The consequence of this misapplication had been that we have replunged into barbarism the agricultural masses of this country, for which, before our advent, to quote from our own Reports, elementary and practical education had been provided by themselves. Trusting to us they paid the cess, which in most places would have been sufficient either to establish a new village school or to encourage an already existing one. We did neither. We applied the money of the agriculturists to defray the cost of the education of castes which had always been accustomed to pay for it themselves. Above all did our conduct spread a distrust of Government, a contempt for our system of education as well as a neglect of their own, as being no longer appreciated by the Government, among the masses of the community, the fruits of which will be seen when those whom we have trained to religious, social and polical scepticism become the leaders of growing disaffection.

As an instance of the general feeling as regards the resumption of rent-free land given to maintain schools, I beg to quote the last letter that I have received. It is signed by Lachman Das, a banker; Ganda Mal, Lambardar, Hazura Mal, Patwari, Sewa Ram, Bhai of a Dharmsálá, and Lala Nirunjan Das, a part proprietor of the village of Muradian, in the tahsil of Hafizabad in the Gujranwala District. The date of the letter is 24th September 1882:—

"Honoured Sir: We beg to represent that in our village (as above), Bhai Jay Singh used to teach Gurmukhi and attend to other duties of the Dharmsálá. In return for this he held a muáfi (rent-free tenure) of half the well, called Tirkhanawala, along with 25 gumaos of land, assessed at Rs. 13, situated in the above village. This Bhai *died two years ago* and the above-mentioned rent-free tenure has been confiscated by the Government, and the Gurmukhi school has been closed, from which injury has accrued to our children. Now we have ascertained that Government has appointed a Committee of Education for the benefit of our country, by which we have obtained an opportunity to express the griefs of our hearts, which are these: that we, the zamindars (agriculturists), in the Punjab are paying the larger portion of the expenditure on education, but are deprived of its benefits, because if we were to instruct our children in the language and characters of foreign countries, such as Persian, &c., there would be much waste of time, and not only so, but we should remain ignorant of our own agriculture and artizanships. Indeed, if our Government were to give instruction in our own language, which is Panjábi, and in the Gurmukhi characters, then we zamindars also would be able to derive benefit from education; otherwise not. This is why we have sent you this petition, so that the 'muáfi' above mentioned, which has been resumed, may be restored as before. Then will our children profit by instruction in Gurmukhi, and constantly offer up prayers for the welfare of the Sirkar." I need not add that the above letter, which is one of many of the same tenor, was neither directly nor indirectly suggested by any inquiries of my own. Indeed, it so happens that even the formal circular about indigenous schools was not sent to the village in question, and that it is not mentioned in any of the returns.

I have similarly received three more letters from different villages in the same tahsil, signed by the children of partially dispossessed holders of rent-free tenures. One of them runs as follows: "We are unable to be sufficiently grateful for all the blessings conferred on as by English rule. Under the Sikhs, 68 gumaos of land, assessed at 53 Rupees, were granted to Bhais Amîr Sing and Wazir Sing, the relicts of whom are now petitioners; this land was situated in the village of Kilá Murád Bakhsh, where there is a large dharmsálá in which Gurmukhi instruction has ever been given. To teach Gurmukhi was the conditions of the muáfi of our parents. Now, in consequence of the death of both muáfidárs, *two-thirds of the rent-free tenure have been resumed* and we are left with the remaining one-third. Having been deprived of the benefits which formerly accrued to us by that "muáfi," we are now in distress and tears. The dharmsálá, a fine building, has ever been considered to be a sacred edifice, where every traveller could get food, and where the children of the subjects of the powerful English Government were benefited by instruction in Gurmukhi, and, in consequence, offered up prayers for the welfare of the Sirkár "KAISAR-I-HIND." Now we beg Your Honour to exert yourself on behalf of the above muáfi so that it may be restored; that the edifice may remain in its previous splendour, where every traveller may obtain grain and water, and any one who chooses acquire sciences; and your petitioners will ever pray." A third letter, much to the same effect, states—"When we formerly held land free we had no anxiety for food, and therefore we could remain in our Dharmsálá and teach Gurmukhi sciences to the people, high and low, who all studied, with deep gratitude to Sirkár Queen VICTORIA, KAISAR, for giving them a share in the stream of Government generosity. Although the community has now been deprived of education *by the resumption of the muáfi* they have no means of redress except from the grace of the all-powerful Government. This is why we write at the request of the people, the morals of whose children will be improved by the alchemy of science, and who will ever pray God to bless our Government." Surely we might stretch a point, if this be needed, to maintain the educational or charitable endowments of those who, forgetful of their own subjugation, so loyally and chivalrously aided their new masters to put down the mutiny of 1857.

NON-REGULATION LAW OF THE PUNJAB, BY D. G. BARKLEY, M.A.

Extract from a letter, No. 418, dated 31st March 1849, from the Secretary to the Government of India, to the Board of Administration for the Affairs of the Punjab.

* * * * * * *

RENT-FREE LANDS AND PENSIONS.

39. The *very first object* to which the Board should direct their attention is the determination of all questions affecting the validity of grants to hold lands rent free. It is obvious to remark that *the longer the investigation is delayed, so much the more do these tenures acquire the force of prescription, and make resumption more unpopular and apparently unjust.* In our older provinces, notwithstanding the frequent declaratory enactments respecting the right and the intention of the Government, the investigations were delayed to so late a period as to give our proceedings a character of injustice and severity.

40. By our occupation of the country after the whole Sikh nation has been in arms against us, *we have acquired the absolute right of conquerors, and would be justified in declaring every acre of land liable to Government assessment;* and though our officers should not allow their minds to be *exasperated* against claimants on this account, yet it may instil into them *a wise caution against being too liberal and profuse in their concessions,* and against doing more for the grantees than their own Government would have done.

41. There is no reason, for instance, why we should maintain in perpetuity an alienation of the Government revenues which would have not been maintained by the power we have succeeded. The Governor General remarks that

all grants were resumed by the Sikh rulers at will, *without reference to the terms of grant*, whenever State exigencies or even caprice dictated. On the death of the grantee they lapsed as a matter of course,* and often were only *renewed on payment* of a large fine, equal in some instances to many years' collections. The Governor General further observes that the decision of the British Government on these claims will give a permanency, validity, and value to the tenure hitherto unknown. There is not one of the rent-free holders who would at this moment dispute this position, and who *would not look upon any concession as a matter of grace.* The delay even of a single year would encourage hopes which are not now entertained, and it is therefore particularly desired that the local officers will *set the minds of the people at rest* upon this most important particular at the earliest possible period.

42. Every holder of rent-free land, who is confirmed in his tenure by the Government, *must yield up every document* in his possession which entitles him to the exemption from revenue, and a grant must be given to him, under the Board's seal and Secretary's signature, declaring that the grant is a free gift of the British Government. The Governor General believes that this will have an important effect upon the native mind in disabusing them of the opinion that they have any *inherent rights* which attach to their tenures in virtue of *long possession*, and make them regard their new masters in the light of *personal benefactors*, from whom alone the indulgence with which they are treated may be considered to emanate.

43. No rent-free holder should be allowed to retain any police powers within his tenure, and the Government revenue should be assessed upon each village or tract which constitutes a separate tenure, so that the jaghirdar or other holder should not be allowed to rack-rent his tenants, or derive more from the land than would be taken by the Government whose place he occupies.

44. There may be particular instances in which it may be expedient to deviate from this rule, but these should all be considered special; and there may be instances in which it may be expedient to invest jaghidars with police powers, subordinate to the local civil authority; these should also be treated as special cases. The Governor General believes that in the Cis-Sutlej Province there are several States in which the assumption of police powers by the British Government has been quite unnecessary, and in one or two cases very inexpedient and much opposed to the interests and wishes of chiefs who have deserved well at our hands, and he will be glad to concur in a recommendation, which he understands has been for some time contemplated by some of the civil officers, to modify the stringency of these orders in cases to which they may not be considered applicable.

45. Where rent-free tenures are held under the condition of service, a scheme of commutation should be adopted on the scale for each horseman and footman authorized in the Sutlej Provinces. The *Governor General would merely caution the local officers against too strict an interpretation of the wording of the original grant:* in many cases the literal fulfilment of the terms of the original grant has not been exacted, and the actual demands for those contingencies for which the grantees have rendered themselves liable have fallen into abeyance, and to revive an obsolete claim now would be unfair and severe.

46. *No rent-free tenure should be continued in favour of any man who has taken up arms against the British Government, whether by choice or compulsion.* This will not exclude occupant cultivators from actual possession, but merely render them liable to revenue.

47. With these preliminaries, the Governor General proceeds to point out the rules which should guide the officers in their investigations of rent-free tenures.

---

* Not in the case of religious, which included educational, grants.

48. *1st.*—All grants for the provision or maintenance of former rulers deposed, or former proprietors dispossessed, to be maintained on their present terms, subject to future diminution after the death of the incumbents.

49. *2nd—All endowments, bonâ fide made for the maintenance* of religious establishments, or buildings for public accommodation, to be maintained *as long as the establishments or buildings are kept up*, provided, as noticed below, *they are not exorbitant.*

50. *3rd.*—All persons holding villages or portions of villages free of rent or money payment, and for which no service was to be rendered, by grants made by Maharajahs Runjit Sing, Khurruk Sing or Shere Sing, to be maintained in their holdings free of rent *during their lives.* Each case to be open to the consideration and orders of Government on the death of the holder, to be decided according to its merits. Long occupancy will of course receive the consideration of the Government.

51. *4th.*—All persons holding lands or grants as above, subject to a payment of fines in the shape of nuzzerana, peishcush, or the like, to hold for their lives, subject to the payment of quarter revenue, and *on the death of the holder the land to be resumed* and assessed at full revenue.

52. *5th.*—All persons holding land for which service of any kind was to be rendered to the Sikh rulers, including Badis and Sodhis, who were expected to perform religious services for the benefit of the donors, *to hold for life,* subject to a payment of *one-fourth revenue ;* the case of each such tenure to be reported for the consideration of Government on the death of the holder.

53. *6th.*—Grants made by persons *not having authority to alienate the Government revenues to be resumed.**

54. *7th.*—Where no deed of grant exists, *a holding of three generations to constitute a valid right, and entitle the holder to have his case adjudicated by the foregoing rules.*

55. *8th.*—Where chiefs or others hold lands rent-free which were not granted by Maharajah Runjit Sing, or any other ruler, but won by their own swords, they will deserve consideration, and their cases should be specially reported to Government with the Board's recommendation in each case : any particular cases not provided for in the foregoing rules, to be reported separately to Government for special orders.

56. When grants of *great value* have been conferred for the maintenance of the State religion, though they would be released under the rules above quoted, *they should be restricted to a smaller amount from obvious motives of political expediency.*† On the other hand, should cases of *individual hardship* arise from a strict observance of these rules, whether from indigence, infirmity, age or sex, the Governor General, *on such being represented,* will be happy to relax the severity of the rules, or *confer a pension upon the object.*

57. The State pensions should also form the subject of early scrutiny, and the same principles should be observed in investigating their validity.

VILLAGE BOUNDARIES.

59. The most essential preliminary is the adjustment and demarcation of boundaries. This should be commenced upon with the utmost vigour in every district, immediately the season admits of officers being under canvas, and be prosecuted till there is not a disputed claim left throughout the whole country. The mode of determining boundary questions in the North-Western Provinces is known to you, and as a fifteen years' practice has failed to suggest a better and more expeditious system, and as it is highly popular even amongst the litigants, it should be introduced into the Punjab without modification.

* This rule looks fair enough, but inevitably tended to deprive holders of "the benefit of the doubt."

† This rule necessarily led to the great curtailment of educational operations connected with religious endowments.

60. Care should, however, be taken in the uncultivated tracts not to insist rigidly that village boundaries should necessarily be conterminous. Many tracts will be found *to intervene* which should be marked off as *separate estates the property of the Government*, and either bestowed on the terms usually applicable to grants of waste land in the forests of the Dhoon and Sub-Himalaya, or be reserved till the spread of cultivation, which invariably follows our rule, enables us to dispose of them to advantage. Colonists may be invited from distant provinces to break up the soil and settle upon the land, though it is to be feared that the love of home which prevails among our agricultural classes will preclude the possibility of much advantage being derived from this source.

Extract from "Resolution of Government of India abolishing the Board of Administration, dated 4th February 1853."

* * * * * * *

7th. The local funds arising either from nazúl property, the one per cent. road fund, public ferries or otherwise, will be under the control of the Judicial Commissioner, and he will have authority to sanction any expenditure therefrom not exceeding (10,000) ten thousand rupees for any one work.

8th. Questions connected with *Ecclesiastical and Educational* matters will be decided by the Judicial Commissioner; the more important questions, in these and other departments, being referred to the Chief Commissioner for decision or submission to Government.

Revenue-free Holdings granted for the support of Religious Edifices.

Extract, paragraphs 2, 3 and 4, of a letter No. 917, dated 4th July 1860, from the Secretary to the Punjab Government, to the Officiating Financial Commissioner of the Punjab.

2. The Lieutenant-Governor sanctions the release of 12 ghumaos of land for the support of the temple in Mauza Bhopalwala of Samryal, Zillah Sialkot, so long as the building remains, on the usual condition of good behaviour.

3. His Honour further directs, as suggested by Mr. McLeod, that whenever, under the operation of a decision heretofore passed, the *endowment held by a mosque* or *temple would lapse on the death of the present incumbent*, it shall be competent to the district officer to refrain from carrying that decision into effect on his decease occurring, and *to report the case* for final instructions; and *if he shall be of opinion that the institution is valued by the people and that the resumption is likely to prove distasteful* to them, it will be incumbent on him to adopt this course.

4. The district officers may also be instructed to report any case in which they have reason to believe that the resumption of a grant, hitherto appropriated to the support of a dharamsalah, takya, or khangah *is likely to create serious dissatisfaction*, retaining the proceeds in deposit pending the receipt of final orders.

XVI.—Investigation of Claims to Revenue-free Tenures in the Trans-Sutlej States.

Copy of letter No. 78, from Secretary to Government of India, to Commissioner and Superintendent, Trans-Sutlej States, dated 23rd February 1874.

* * * * * * *

His Lordship observes that at present the recommendations of the officers, being in accordance with their individual views, are often contradictory and sometimes somewhat arbitrary, but that a principle having been once established, these and all future reports can be easily disposed of.

4. The Governor General remarks that all grants were resumed by the Sikh rulers at will, *without reference to the terms of the grant, whenever State exigencies or even caprice dictated ;* on the death of the grantor they lapsed as a matter of course, and were only renewed on payment of a large nazraná, equal, in some instances, to many years' collections. The Governor General further observes that the decision of the British Government on these claims will give a permanency, validity, and value to the tenures hitherto unknown, *notwithstanding sanads from Native Governments of perpetual release from all demands,* which the holders know *mean* nothing.

5. His Lordship therefore directs, with reference to the nature of the tenures in the Jallandhar Doab, that the following general principles and rules may be observed, thus rendering the adjustment of all claims easy and intelligible :—

1st.—All grants for the provision or maintenance of former rulers deposed, or former proprietors dispossessed, to be maintained on their present tenures in perpetuity.

2nd.—All endowments *boná fide* made for the maintenanec of religious establishments, or buildings for public accommodation, to be maintained as long as the establishments or buildings are kept up.

3rd.—All persons holding villages or portions of villages *free of rent or money payment,* and for which no service was to be rendered, by grants made by Maharajas Ranjit Singh, Kharak Singh, or Sher Singh, to be maintained in their holding free of rent *during their lives,* each case to be open to the consideration and orders of Government on the death of the holder, to be decided according to its merits.

4th.—All persons holding lands or grants as above, subject to a payment of nazraná, peshkash, or the like, to *hold for their lives, subject to the payment of quarter jama ;* and on the death of the holders, *the land to be resumed or assessed at full jama.*

5th.—All persons holding land for which service of any kind was to be rendered to the Sikh rulers, including Bedis and Sodhis, who were expected to perform religious services for the benefit of the donors, *to hold for life, subject to a payment of one-fourth jama.* The case of each such tenure to be reported for the consideration of Government on the death of the holder.

6. Grants made by persons not having authority to alienate the Government revenues to be resumed.

7. Where no sanad exists, a holding for three generations to constitute a title, and entitle the holder to have his case adjudicated by the foregoing rules.

8. In accordance with the above rules, the cases in the several statements have been ordered on, and the Right Honourable the Governor General directs that in future all cases in Trans-Sutlej territories may be decided by them, any particular cases being reported separately to Government for special orders.

XVII.—Rules for disposal of Rent-free Tenures.

Extract from para. 1 of No. 1119, dated 24th March 1853, from Secretary to Government of India, to Chief Commissioner, Punjab.

The Governor General in Council . . . . . is pleased . . . . to lay down the following rules for the future guidance in the disposal of rent-free tenures :—

I.—*Henceforth no cases where lands are resumed need be reported to Government,* whether donations in money are given or not, or whatever be the amount of the resumption.

II.—*Grants of land to village servants may be made* by Settlement Officers, under the authority of the Financial and Chief Commissioners.

III.—The Financial Commissioner shall have authority finally to dispose of all grants of land, *under 10 acres*, which *he may be* of opinion *should be released during the lives* of the occupants, or the term of settlement.

IV.—The Chief Commissioner shall have a similar authority, with a limit of *50 acres* for the lives of occupants, or the term of settlement.

V.—All other cases where it is proposed to release lands *above 50 acres* in extent, to the occupants for *their lives*, or to *release land of any amount to the second generation*, or *in perpetuity*, or *beyond the term of settlement*, or where it is proposed to release land forming a whole village, or the fractional part of a village, for any period of time, must be reported to Government.

Inheritance of Perpetual Grants.

I.—*No tenure descends to collateral heirs, but lapses to Government on* the failure of male legitimate issue in the line of the original grantees.

II.—The term of "original grantees" means the parties to whom the *British have confirmed* the grant.

The reason is simply this: When the Punjab was conquered it was ruled that in each case a grant must be given under the Board's seal and Secretary's signature declaring that the grant was a "free gift" of the British Government, and that the assignees must regard their new masters in the light of personal benefactors, from whom alone the indulgence with which they are treated may be considered to emanate. From this it clearly appears that the *local courts have no authority to open out questions of division or inheritance anterior to the register.* Any plea based on partition, descent, gift, which is *not supported by the registers, must at once be rejected.* As to questions subsequent to the register, the courts will decide according to the customary law of the country with regard to inheritance, subject to the limitations of the grant as shown in the register.

Extract from circular No. 2, dated 25th May 1860, from Secretary to Government, Punjab, to Commissioner and Superintendent,———Division.

* * * * * * *

It is the desire of the Lieutenant-Governor that the sons of the native aristocracy should when qualified obtain a fair share of the appointments in the gift of Government, and is happy to know that, of late, a great many have been provided for in the civil and military services. It is now a rule under this Government to select for the higher appointments men of rank and respectability, *experience having demonstrated the superiority of their weight and influence with the people. The great obstacle to their preferment has been their want of education.*

6. But an experiment is now in progress at Lahore of a promising character, which, if successful, will provide greater facilities for the education of the sons of the Sirdars than have hitherto been within their reach. The Government school is under the direction of competent teachers, *separate class rooms are devoted to the sons of the gentry* and to those of commonalty. *There are already 50 boys, the sons of Sirdars, who had not previously attended school, for their families shrunk from sending them to institutions in which they were liable to be associated with boys of a lower status** several of these boys have been sent from distant districts, and generally a desire for education has grown up.

* The subsequent abolition of class distinctions at the Lahore Government College and High School naturally led to the withdrawal of Sirdars' sons from an Institution on which they looked as one especially intended for their own order.

If the plan succeeds at Lahore, of which there is at present every hope, the Lieutenant-Governor will be glad to see a *similar* school established in *each division*. There is *no difficulty in procuring appointments for well-born cadets so long as they possess average qualifications*. They can be disposed of in the irregular force and in the civil department. The body to be provided for will probably not be numerous and fairly educated; they will have *preferential* claim from the Government, which has perhaps been *somewhat slow to improve* their condition and *elevate* their hopes.

7. In bringing the question of succession before the Chiefs, you will be careful to state the *favourable* intentions of Government towards the younger sons of *influential houses*.*

INSTANCES OF RESUMED "MUAFIS" BELONGING TO MAULVIS, PANDITS, AND BHAIS.

Kalúki, Gujranwala, Hafizabad tahsil—
22 ghumans.
4 kanals.

(1) Held by Bhai Bhagel Singh for the purpose of instructing boys. After the death of Bhai Bhagel Singh 17 ghumaos of the above land were resumed, and the rest was spared for the dharamsala. The applicants Kishen Singh, &c. (sons of Bhai Bhagel Singh), say that on account of the above resumption they closed their school. They add that if the resumption be cancelled and their muáfi be restored, they can open a school with several hundreds of pupils.

In the villages of *Buhlulpur, Chuharpur* and *Hasanpur*, tehsil *Samrala*, district *Ludhyana*—
7 bighas 14 biswas.
6 „ 17 „
2 „ 14 „

(2) The muáfis noted in the margin were held by Pandit Jaswant, son of Bhowani Dass, for the furtherance of Sanscrit instruction. The Pandit above named was allowed to hold the muáfis for the term of the settlement. The muáfidar died without issue, and the muáfis were resumed on 10th March 1867 by an order of the Deputy Commissioner. There was a fourth muáfi also which the Pandit held for ever, and it devolved after his death on his grandson (his daughter's son, named Mansa Ram, living in the village of Pawadat).

In the village of *Patti Maharsin*, district *Umbala*, tehsil *Umbala*—
15 bighas 5 biswas.

(3) The robkár dated 9th of May 1837 shows that the ancestors of Mufti Imam Bakhsh have held 40 bighas of (pukhta) land since the time of Aurangzeb. In the times of the Sikhs, Sardar Gurbakhsh took the half rent. When Umbala came into the possession of the Government an enquiry was made, and when it was proved that Mufti Imam Bakhsh, the then incumbent of the muáfi, taught pupils, 15 bigahs and 15 biswas of land were left to him, and the rest resumed. On the deaths of Mufti Muhammad Bakhsh and Mussamut Mihrunnissa, the then incumbents of the muáfi, it was resumed on the 22nd of November 1866.

Amritsar.
Jaghir of Rs. 1,200 per annum.

(4) Bhai Jewan Singh and Bhai Umra Singh represent that their grandfather Bhai Ram Singh had a jaghir of Rs. 1,200 per annum from the Sikh Government for the maintenance of a Gurmukhi school which he kept in his own Bunga. After the death of Bhai Ram Singh, Bhai Karam Singh and Bhai Beshan Singh, the fathers of the applicants, continued to teach the boys and a jaghir of Rs. 800 per annum was left to them. After their death the jaghir was resumed, and only Rs. 475 per annum is given to the applicants. As the sum was not sufficient to support their family they could not maintain the school, which was closed a short time after the reduction of the jaghir. The applicants request that if a suitable sum be given them (such as they used to draw formerly) they can open a very good Gurmukhi school in their Bunga.

* The admirable policy sketched out in this letter was never thoroughly carried out in practice. The Lahore Government College and School were opened to the commonalty, thus computing with the aided Mission College, and leading to the secession of the sons of the native nobility.

(5) **Maulvi Sirajuddin, of Gujranwala, in a private return furnished by him, says that the school which he now conducts had a muáfi of 60 ghumaos of land in the time of Maulvi Sultan Ahmad, deceased. On the death of the Maulvi, 35 ghumaos were resumed and 25 ghumaos were left for ever.**

Gujranwala.
85 ghumans.

The police returns say that the mosque of Qari in the village of Taizpur, which now contains three Koran schools, held a muáfi (details not given) which was resumed two years ago.

Taizpur, tahsil *Sharakpur*, district *Lahore.*

(6) A private return furnished by Maulvi Fatah Muhammad of Jalalpur mentions that the school in the grand mosque (which is conducted by Maulvi Fazil Muhammad, a distinguished Arabic scholar) held in the times of the Nawabs of Multan and the Sikhs a muáfi of the town duties, and the teachers attached to the school also received pensions.

Jalalpur, Perwala, district Multan.

Private information adds that the assignees of these pensions and muáfis still have documents.

(7) A private informant mentions that *Bhai Ki Darwajri*, a dharamsala in Raipur, held about 60 bighas (kham) of land as muáfi, but in the last settlement the land has been assessed.

In the village of *Raipur*, thana *Dalon*, district *Ludhyana.*
60 bighas
2 wells.

The Khankah of Pir Daulat Shah and the Dera of a Saniasi fakir had each a well as free-rent tenures, but they have also been assessed in the last settlement.

(8) All the muáfis noted in the margin, together with many others, were given to Pandit Tukta Sahai, of Rohtas, one of the most distinguished scholars in the Punjab, by Maharaja Runjit Singh, for the maintenance of a patshala which was the first of its kind in the province.

Rohtas fort, district *Jhelum.*
(1) 25 bighas in *Rampura.*
(2 15 bighas in the village of *Kotra Ahmad.*
(3) Village *Chak Mulan.*
(4) 2 ploughs, land in *Mirpur.*
(5) Land in the village of *Chhaharyan Gujran.*
(6) 2 0bighas land in *Manoharpur* village, 1 Guiya.

On the annexation of the Panjab, nearly all the muáfis were resumed. There is a patshala in Rohtas even now, but it has decayed to insignificance.

(9) An application signed by Lachman Hissedar, and Sahúkar Gunda Mal, Lumberdar, Hazura Mal, Patwari; Sewa Ram, Bhai; and Lala Niranjan Dass, residents of Muradyan, Tehsil Hafizabad, District Gujranwala, states that Bhai Jaising used to conduct a Gurmukhi school in the village dharamsala and lived on the produce of a muáfi of a half of tirkhanawala well and 25 ghumans which he held for the purpose of maintaining a Gurmukhi school and defray the expenses of the dharamsala. On his death, which occurred only two years ago, the muáfi was resumed. The school has been closed, and the applicants say that their children have consequently been deprived of education.

In the village of *Muradyan*, tehsil *Hafizabad*, district *Gujranwalla.* { 25 ghumaos of land, ½ portion of a well.

(10) Bava Ganga Dass, of Khitta Murad Bakhsh, states in his application that Bava Puran Dass (a spiritual brother of his, Gurbhai), held 31 ghumans of land attached to the Chuchakanwala well. He used to conduct a Gurmukhi school, but after his death half of the muáfi had been resumed, and what now remains is not sufficient to maintain the present incumbent, and therefore the school has much suffered.

Killa Murad Bakhsh, Tehsil *Hafizabad*, district *Gujranwala*, ½ of 31 ghumnas of land.

(11) The applicants Bija Singh, Gurdat Singh, sons of Amir Singh, and Uttan Singh and Kishen Singh, sons of Wazir Singh, state in their application that in the life-time of Amir Singh and Wazir Singh, their respective fathers, two-thirds of 68 ghumaos of land which they held as muáfi for the maintenance of a Gurmukhi school in the village dharamsala were resumed. The third portion which now remains is not sufficient for the maintenance of a school. The villagers have suffered much in thus being deprived of a means of their children's instruction.

Killa Murad Bukhsh, tehsil *Hafizabad*, district *Gujranwala*, ⅔ of 68 ghumnas of land.

(12) Surjan Dass and Santram state that their father used to hold a plot of muáfi amounting to 50 ghumans which was attached to the dharamsala. This dharamsala had a well-attended Gurmukhi school attached to it. Now, on the death of Nirmal Dass, the Gurbhai, 38 ghumaos were resumed and 12 ghumaos left. It is evident that they cannot maintain a school with the little which is left.

In the village of *Waniki*, tehsil *Hafizabad*, district *Gujranwala*, 38 ghumans of land.

Statement of Muáfis allowed to persons who were or are connected with education in the Sahansara Village.

No.	Mouza or Village.	Name of Muáfi holder.	Institution, Mosque or Dharamsala.	Annual Income.		Remarks.
				Land.	Cash.	
1	Sahansara .	Jamaiyta, son of Vazira, Mullana.	Mosque .	6 G. 7 K. 4 M.; assessed at 12 Rs.	*Nil*	Half released till death, and half during the pleasure of Government. Formerly the ancestors of this muáfidar taught the students, but since the establishment of Government schools, pupils have taken to them, and the muáfidar no longer teaches.
2	Ditto .	Phula, son of Gurmukh Padha.	...	2 G. 1 K. 10 M.; assessed at 3 Rs.	*Nil*	Gurmukhi, the father of the present muáfidar, taught Gurmukhi and Nagri. The work of teaching has been taken up by the village school. The Government muáfi has been resumed. His descendants now have a muáfi allowed by Sardar Thakur Singh.
3	Ditto .	Panjaba, son of Bhágú Pandha.	...	3 K. 14 M.; assessed at 1 Re.	*Nil*	The original muáfidar used to teach Nagri, but his descendants have ceased to do so since the establishment of Government schools. Government muáfi has been resumed; the present muáfi is allowed by the Sardar.
4	Ditto .	Thakur Dass, son of Gandar Mal, Brahmin.	...	1 G. 6 K. 4 M.; assessed at 4 Rs.	*Nil*	Used to teach Lunde before the establishment of schools. He does not teach now. The muáfi is, therefore, to be enjoyed only during the lifetime of the present holder.
5	Ditto .	Jawahir, son of Maharaj, Brahmin.	...	1 G. 5 K. 5 M.; assessed at 4 Rs.	*Nil*	Ditto.
6	Ditto .	Jas, son of Bhana Brahmin.	...	6 K. 12 M.; assessed at 1 Re.	...	The muáfidar used to teach Sanscrit, but since the establishment of schools Government has resumed the muáfi, though he enjoys some muáfi from the Sardar.
7	Ditto .	Sangat Dass, Mahant.	Gurudwara of Guru Arjan.	30 G.; assessed at 58 Rs. As. 7	*Nil*	This muáfi has been resumed, but some muáfi is allowed by the Sardar on account of a magnificent Gurudwara at which bread is given to the poor. Gurmukhi is still taught to Sadhus.
8	Ditto .	Guru Prasad, Chela of Sahao Narsing Dass.	Dharamsala	21 G. 6 K. 16 M.; assessed at 59 Rs.	*Nil*	This muáfi has been resumed by the Government, but is now allowed by the Sardar. Gurmukhi is taught here; passengers take rest.
9	Ditto .	Moti Ram, son of Rattan Chand, Brahmin.	...	3 G. 5 K. 11 M.; assessed at 9 Rs.	...	Used to teach Nagri, but since the establishment of Government schools the teacher's functions have ceased.
10	Ditto .	Nand Kaur, son of Gurbachan, Brahmin.	...	7 K. 9 M.; assessed at 1 Re.	...	Muáfi was resumed when the teaching functions were taken away by the schools. The muáfi now enjoyed is from the Sardar. Lunde was formerly taught.
11	Nand Ram, son of Bishen Dass.	Sahao .	Dharamsala .	17 G. 2 K. 9 M.; assessed at 24 Rs.	...	Gurmukhi used to be taught, but since the establishment of Government schools, teaching functions have ceased. The muáfi has taken the form of a muáfi for life.

In almost all the above eleven cases the teaching functions were monopolised by the schools established by Government, and the muáfis, which were enjoyed for the performance of teaching functions, were resumed.

Pupils attending these indigenous schools were, it is alleged, forcibly withdrawn by the Government village schools.

Statement of Muáfis connected with the instruction of Persian and Hindi in Mouza Raja Sánsi.

No.	Mouza.	Name of Muáfidar.	Institution, Mosque, &c.	Yearly Income.		Remarks.
				Land.	Cash.	
1	Rájá Sansi	Bava Prem Dass Sadhu.	Dharamsala Samahdan-wali.	12 G. 1 K. 18 M.; assessed at 29 Rs.	*Nil*	Gurmukhi was taught here, but when on the establishment of schools, pupils were forcibly withdrawn, Gurmukhi teaching ceased to exist, and the muáfi was resumed. The present muáfi is from the Sardars of Raja Sánsi.
2	Ditto	Ganesh Dass, Parohit.	Shivala	14 G. 6 K. 4 M.; assessed at 39 Rs.	...	Ditto.
3	Mustaq Singh	Dharamsala	...	21 G. 6 K. 2 M.; assessed at 43 Rs.	...	Ditto.
4	Ditto	Jawahir Singh, Brahmin.	Dharamsala of Amor Singh.	1 G. 4 K.	...	Ditto.
5	Ditto	Ishar Singh, Bhai.	Dharamsala Chaukwali.	...	...	Sirdars of Raja Sánsi and the other inhabitants used to support this institution for the sake of Gurmukhi teaching. Since the establishment of schools this support has been withdrawn. The Sardars alone now support this institution as a religious one.
6	Ditto	Hidayat Shah, son of Mehtab Shah, Faqir.	Takia	12 G. 6 K. 19 M.; assessed at 15 Rs.	...	This muáfidar used to teach Fiqa (Muhamadan law). Now the students have been taken into the village schools.
7	Ditto	Pir Bakhsh, Mullan.	Mosque	...	...	The villagers and the Sardar used to support this mosque as a place where Persian and religious books were taught, but now that the boys have been taken by force into the schools this support has been withdrawn. Sardar Thakur Singh gives some support.
8	Ditto	Raqim Shah, son of Husen Shah,	Ditto	...	...	Ditto.
9	Ditto	Jam Muhammad Mullan.	Ditto	...	...	Ditto.
10	Událá	Fateh Shah	Ditto	3 G. 5 K. 17 M.; assessed at 7 Rs.	...	This muáfi has been resumed by Government since the schools have forcibly assumed the teaching functions of indigenous schools. The present muáfi is allowed by Sardar Thakur Singh.

3.—Principles which were acted on in resuming Rent-free Tenures.

I now proceed to show that the Board of Administration for the affairs of the Punjab interpreted the orders received on the subject of the resumption of rent-free tenures in the most liberal spirit of which they were capable, with due regard to the welfare of the administration, and the thorough execution of the unpleasant task with which it was entrusted.

I must therefore be forgiven if I quote at length all the passages in the earlier administration reports which bear on the subject, and which explain the principles of action that guided the rulers of the Punjab.

Extracts from Punjab Administration Report for 1849-51.

Jaghirs and Pensions.

316. . . . . . . The grants held by the chief jaghirdari grantees who held one or more entire estates have been investigated under the Board's immediate supervision by a separate officer appointed for that purpose. The inquiry was commenced by Major Edwardes, and has since been prosecuted by Captain Becher till it has now nearly reached conclusion. The grants which comprised detached portions of estates have been partly investigated by the district authorities and by the settlement officers in those districts where a regular settlement might be in progress.

317. The pension investigations have been conducted in the same manner. The army pensions, and civil, and the important political pensions, have been disposed of by the special officer under the Board; the minor pensions, chiefly charitable and religious, by the district authorities.

318. Before particularising the method in which each class of grants has been dealt with, it may be well to recapitulate the principles enunciated by the Government in the letter last mentioned. These directions authorised the maintenance for life of incumbents of grants, *first* to former rulers and State pensioners; *second*, for endowment of religious and public institutions, as long as the object of endowment should be fulfilled; *third*, on the authority of Máhárájas Ranjit Singh, Khurruk Singh, and Sher Singh; *fourth*, on the payment of tribute to be charged with one-fourth revenue; *fifth*, for religious services.

Principles enunciated by the Government.

Grants not made on authority, nor for objects recognised in the above rules, were to be resumed, unless the party should have been in possession for three generations, in which case a prescriptive title was to be conferred for his lifetime.

* * * * * * *

320. . . . . . With regard to State pensions (class No. 5), the grants were maintained for life of incumbents subject to diminution after death. In the case of the royal ladies, mostly widows of Máhárájahs Ranjit Singh, Kharak Singh, and Sher Singh, the landed grants were not maintained; but a money computation for their lives was effected. * * * *

Grants to influential landholders.

Among the grants which come under the general denomination of personal may be noticed "the enams" (class No. 8). This term was under Sikh rule applied to certain deductions made from the revenue of an estate in favour of some village chief, called a chowdhry, who by local knowledge aided the revenue officers in ascertaining the resources of the village and in collecting the taxes, and also in the preservation of order and harmony. The agency thus secured, and the influence thus enlisted on the side of the local authorities, were important. The grants have been generally maintained during the life-time of the grantee upon the condition of general service. In the conducting of the new system of settlement, which chiefly works through popular agency, the chowdries have made themselves most useful, and their services may for the future be turned to good account in the detection and prevention of crime, in the management for the public convenience, such as the furnishing of supplies and carriage, repair of roads and the construction of useful works.

Secular and religious endowments.

321. The endowments mentioned in class No. 9 are both secular and religious for the support of temples, mosques, places of pilgrimage and devotion, *schools*, village inns for the reception of travellers and paupers, and strangers, generally of a monastic character. The institutions are ornaments to the villages; they have some architectural pretensions, and, being embosomed in trees, are often the only shady spots in the neighbourhood. They add much to the comfort of rustic life, and *keep alive a spirit of hospitality and piety among the agricultural people.* The endowments, though *occasionally reduced in amount, have, on the whole, been regarded with liberality,* and, in confirming them, the officers have mainly regarded the utility and efficiency of the institution. Such grants, *when insignificant in amount,* have been maintained, even though the original grantor might have been the headman of the village.

Classes 10 and 11, grants to objects of charity and to religious character.

The grants to objects of charity or to persons of sanctity have frequently been paid in cash, and in such cases have been brought under the denomination of pension. In regard to the charitable grants,—indeed with regard to all grants,—the tenor of para. 56 of the Government letter has been observed, and the rigour of the rule has been relaxed in favour of parties who, from "indigence, infirmity, age or sex, might be fitting objects of special indulgence."

* * * * * * *

237. The assessments were all fixed in money and included all payments in one aggregate sum. *They were unavoidably made with great expedition, and generally by officers who possessed but little previous knowledge of the subject, and who therefore committed many mistakes.* But in spite of such

defects, the settlements conferred a boon on the people by the fiscal relief they at once afforded, by the definition and consolidation of the public burthen, and by the cessasion of vexatious and inquisitorial processes.

PART III.—JAGHIRS AND PENSIONS.

* * * * * * *

Origin of landed grants in the Punjab.

313. Feudalism is known by enquirers to have prevailed in all Indian kingdoms, and, as developed in the Rajput principalities, it has obtained an European fame. *In no reign of the East did it prevail more than in the kingdom founded by Runjit Singh.* A large section of the Máhárájah's army consisted of cavalry contingents, furnished by chieftains holding grants on feudal tenures, and even a part of the regular troops received their pay in jaghirs instead of cash. In the same manner,—that is, by assignments on the revenue,—the civil officers of State and the royal household for the most part were paid; State pensioners, the families of military chiefs, and the old soldiers and the ladies of the royal palace were supported. Endowments for objects of sanctity, charitable donations and annuities to religious characters were granted; for the same objects pensions were conferred.

Pensions how granted.

314. The term "pension" has a wider significance than usual when applied to Sikh affairs. It meant not only an allowance granted to superannuated servants of the State, but also personal, charitable, and religious endowments.

In respect of intention and object, it is difficult to distinguish a pension from a jaghir, except that the one was paid from the treasury, and the other in the shape of assignment on the land revenue. Under the late Government a pension, however, was rarely beyond life; whereas a jaghir, after the death of the grantee, might be continued to his representatives.

Classification of grants both in land and cash.

315. From these preliminary remarks it will be seen that jaghirs and pensions may admit of the following classification:—

Section I.—Service grants	1. Military. 2. Civil. 3. Feudal. 4. Household.
„ II.—Personal grants . . .	5. State pensioners. 6. Royal ladies. 7. Family provision. 8. Allowances to influential land-holders.
„ III.—Religious grants . . .	9. Endowments. 10. Charitable. 11. Holy men.

The proceedings held with regard to these various classes of grants have been regulated by the principles laid down by the Most Noble the Governor General in the letter dated 31st March 1849. The word "grant" in the above classification is a general term, including both jaghirs and pensions, and both species will be considered together, there being no difference in their judicial treatment.

* * * * * * *

323. Of money pensions about 8,000 cases have been investigated and nearly 2,000 remain for decision; the latter cases are, however, all insignificant. It is believed that their aggregate value will amount to twelve lakhs per annum. But the lapses by demise will, year after year, operate as a sinking fund and cause a gradual but certain diminution. The jaghir inquiries cannot be numerically represented. It will be sufficient to state that the grants equivalent to nine lakhs of revenue either have been or are being investigated. *But there are doubtless many hundreds, even thousands, of petty rent-free tenures which cannot now be enumerated,* but which will be brought to light when the regular settlement comes on.

324. On the whole, the temporary alienation of the revenue under the two heads of "Jaghirs" and "Pensions" will amount to *upwards of thirty lakhs per annum*,—that is, to more than a fifth of the total revenue. The measure is justified by political expediency, and is the natural consequence of the liabilities which the British Government inherited from its predecessors. In such matters the policy of a Native and an European Government must differ. But it has been desired that *the revolution should take effect gradually and with as little asperity as possible.*

* * * * * * *

407. First, the receipts will be estimated. The land tax roll for 1851-52 exhibited a total of 106 lakhs; but, for reasons already given in the section devoted to revenue, there is reason to believe that this tax roll will not be maintained, and that a reduction of seven lakhs must ensue and the total lowered to 99 lakhs. On the other hand, *many rent-free tenures, great and small, are under enquiry, and many grants may be expected to lapse.* On these accounts 3 lakhs may be safely added to the 99. Thus the tax roll may be permanently assumed at 102 lakhs, being 3 lakhs less than the tax roll of the current year. An increase of nearly 2 lakhs over the amount of last year may be expected in the excise and stamps, and a considerable increase in the Post Office. Also 1 lakh may be anticipated as return from the Baree Doab Canal, for which, however, a heavy outlay must be entered on the debit side. On the other hand, a large decrease in the extra *are under enquiry, and many grants may be expected to lapse.* The 15 lakhs obtained from confiscation will fail in future, as also several minor items, such as the arrears, the sale of Mooltan property, &c., amounting to 2 lakhs. Thus 17 lakhs of extraordinary revenue will vanish, and instead of 151 lakhs, there will be precisely the same total as in the first year,—*viz.*, 134 lakhs.

411. . . . . . . By that time, also, the important items, *viz.*, the State grants to individuals, consisting partly of alienations of the revenue (jaghirs), and partly in cash payments (pensions), will have begun to diminish by demise and lapses. *The territorial grants, of which the aggregate valuation may be 25 lakhs, have either been confirmed for the lives of individuals or are under investigation.* Of these 25 lakhs it may be fairly supposed that 4 lakhs will have begun to lapse per annum and may be added to the tax roll. The 12 lakhs of pensions, of which the recipients are mostly advanced in life, will by this time begin to lapse at the rate of 3 lakhs per annum. . . . .
To recapitulate this. The revenue of 134 lakhs will have gained 10 lakhs by the canal, and 4 lakhs by jaghir-lapses, and will amount to 148 lakhs,– that is, 14 lakhs in excess. On the other hand, the ordinary expenditure will have gained 3 lakhs by the pension-lapses, and the extraordinary 10 by the completion of the public works and of the survey and settlement,—in all 13 lakhs.

412. Such, then, will the *net profit* of the annexed territory be ten years hence. But it is not likely to stop at that limit. *The jaghirs and pensions aggregate unquestionably 30 lakhs.* A large portion has been granted on life-tenure, and a large portion must lapse with one generation, and therefore the State resources must increase by nearly 30 lakhs. Of this, 8 lakhs (*viz.*, 4 lakhs for jaghir and 4 lakhs for pensions) have been anticipated in the foregoing accounts. But there are still about 20 lakhs, which year after year must go on lapsing, and must be added to the surplus of 50 lakhs just mentioned. **WITHIN FIFTEEN YEARS THE ANNEXED TERRITORIES WILL ASSUREDLY BE YIELDING A NET PROFIT OF 50 LAKHS, OR HALF A MILLION STERLING, PER ANNUM.**

* * * * * * *

416. Before concluding this section it may be well to offer a brief contrast

of the chief heads of revenue in the Punjab Proper as they stood during Ranjit Singh's reign and at the present time :—

	Land Tax.			Excise.	Grand Total.
	Khalsa.	Jaghir.	Total.		
Ranjit Singh	£1,050,000 0 0	600,000 0 0	1,650,000 0 0	200,000 0 0	1,850,000
Government	£1,050,000 0 0	200,000 0 0	1,250,000 0 0	200,000 0 0	1,450,000

It will have been understood from the section which treated on revenue that the "khalsa" represents the amount realised by the State, and the "jaghir" the amount temporarily alienated in favour of individuals. But in Ranjit Singh's time the jaghirs were feudal grants, for which a service equivalent was obtained, while in the present time they are chiefly political pensions. Nevertheless, in both cases they are a tax on the land. The total land tax, both khalsa and jaghir, under the British Government, is about 40 lakhs less than that of Ranjit Singh, and this represents the actual reduction in assessment.

But the relative proportion between the two headings has been changed.— By resumption and lapses many lakhs have recently been transferred from the jaghir to the khalsa heading. Thus, in this manner, the present khalsa has been made equal (in spite of reductions in assessment) to the former khalsa, while the present diminution in the aggregate of both headings has been thrown chiefly on the jaghir.

Extract from the Administration Report, Punjab, for the years 1851-52 and 1852-53.

Jaghirs and pensions.

Completion of all jaghir cases.

Inquiries into rent-free tenures.

359. In Part III, section 7 of the Board's report, the nature of the jaghirs and pensions under the Sikh regime, and the manner in which these grants and assignments had been treated under British rule, were detailed. It was stated that jaghirs and landed grants, equivalent to 9 lakhs of revenue, either have been or are being investigated. These inquiries have been completed during the years under report, the orders of Government have been obtained upon the cases, and in all those instances where the grants have been upheld, sanads or patents have been given to the grantees. In all the districts which have come under settlement, and in many districts not yet settled, the petty rent-free tenures have been investigated and disposed of by competent local authorities. *Probably some 90,000 cases in the old and new territory have been decided, and some thousands yet remain. There are also some thousands of cases of this description, in which the final sanction has been reserved by the Government, yet to be submitted.*

1852.

In Appendix No. XI to the Hushiarpur Settlement Report, there is a return of rent-free holdings in acres for the pargunnahs of Gurshunkêr, Hushiarpur, Hurrianna, and Onat, showing that out of a number of 6,705 disputed cases 3,875 were released and 2,830 resumed. Of the released the following are the headings :—

(1.)	Support of public buildings and institutions	528 cases.
(2.)	Support of *purohits* and *padahs*	430 ,,
(3.)	Support of schoolmasters	39 ,,
(4.)	For military service and hereditary nobility	161 ,,
(5.)	For chowdries, lumberdars, &c.	134 ,,
(6.)	As personal charity	1,991 ,,
(7.)	Long occupancy and miscellaneous	592 ,,

And in the Umballa Settlement Report there is a similar return for pargunnahs Roopur, Morinda, Khurur, Moburikpar, and Rotshah, showing that out of 3,587 disputed cases 2,350 were released and 1,237 resumed. Of the released the following are the headings :—

(1.)	Support of public buildings and institutions	498	cases.
(2.)	Support of *purohits, padhas*, &c.	473	,,
(3.)	Same schoolmasters	3	,,
(4.)	For military service and hereditary nobility	138	,,
(5.)	For chowdries, lumberdars, &c.	69	,,
(6.)	As personal charity	781	,,
(7.)	Long occupancy and miscellaneous	388	,,

Umballa Settlement Report for 1882.

Page 9, paragraph 47.—The almost universal system of the Sikhs was to collect their revenue in kind. Two-fifths of the gross produce was the ordinary proportion taken by them from the cultivators in these States. Where the soil was very poor, or in special cases where religionist castes were the occupants, this rate was lowered to one-third or even a fourth. But nowhere did the proportion exceed two-fifths in the Umballa District. In the Jullundar Doab a common rate was one-half—a convincing proof, if others were wanting, that the Trans-Sutlej soil is far more productive than the Cis-Sutlej. It was the usual practice for all Sikh jaghirdars of consideration to keep accounts of their revenues. Their records were often kept in detail. The name of the cultivator, the gross amount of produce, and the share derivable by the chief are all exhibited. Where, then, such papers could be procured without suspicion of fraud, they are manifestly valuable guides to an officer making his assessment.

Jaghirdars' revenue accounts.

Page 57, paragraph 265.—It may naturally be asked, Why, if the jammas were so high, did the people engage for them? There were conflicting interests to account for this. Rao Natho Singh, of Raipur, held pretensions to the malguzari of the whole tract in right of his ancient headship of the Chouhan clan, and the Aloo Chowdries, both Rajputs and Jats, held similar claims. The zamindars (residents) understood not the nature of our farming system, and thought that once deprived of the "theeka" they would lose their proprietary rights also. Accordingly the zamindars, rather than admit either of the above claimants, agreed to pay jummas which time has proved they could not pay; as it was, 7 villages out of the 111 were farmed.

Why the people engaged for excessive jummas.

Page 75, paragraph 329.—The treatment of the "*muáfi*" or *rent-free lands* prior to the division was a matter for consideration. Bitter feeling usually ran so high between the sharers that it would have been impossible to wait for the concurrence of both parties to either the resumption or release of such lands. It would have been a very unsatisfactory way of proceeding to leave the settlement of this question till after the partition, because the jumma of the villages assigned to the lessees Chuharunnee would thus have become subject to diminution, and a specious cause of complaint would have been given. By ascertaining or deciding what lands were *muáfi*, before working out the jumma, a degree of finality would be given to the partition which it would not otherwise have. Accordingly, with but very few and special exceptions, all lands were declared *muáfi* which either of the sharers asserted to be so. No evil has been found to attend this course. The Sikhs were too avaricious to over estimate the quantity of such holdings, and I do not believe that the suspicion which naturally might attach to the sovereign power of lowering the aggregate jumma of the villages by giving in false *muáfi* lists has been verified. But, even if such had been the case, a proviso was made that any lands in villages subsequently given to the weaker party declared rent-free by the superior sharer should be open to challenge by the former, and under such challenges a judicial enquiry was promised, but no such question has arisen, and I therefore conclude that the rent-free patches were accurately given.

Treatment of the rent-free lands.

Report on Umballa in the Cis-Sutlej States.

Page 64, paragraph 262.—This subject may well be divided into two classes: 1st, whole villages; 2nd, small patches held rent free. The enquiry into both these classes has been conducted, and with a few trifling exceptions completed in this office. All villages which have been found to be held rent free have been fully reported on; in most instances the orders of Government have been received on the recommendations which have been made by myself or the higher revenue authorities.

The Muáfi investigation.

Page 64, paragraph 264.—On the 2nd of April I sent my first batch of muáfi cases, 752 in number, and remarked on the orders of the district officers *who had resumed land held rent free for five or six generations*, because no *sunnud* was produced, because they were above 10 bighas, and for reasons even less sound than these.*

Paragraph 265.—The above remarks refer to the khalisah villages, those which pay revenue to the Government. During the settlement operations many villages held by jaghirdars have come under settlement, and a question arose, "Can a jaghirdar resume land which Government cannot or will not resume?" The question was proposed in my letter No. 631, dated 5th September 1854. I stated my opinion that a jaghirdar "should have no power for resumption more than the Government allows itself; but that with regard to the release of land, the reasonable wishes of the jaghirdar should be attended to." You were of a different opinion, and the Board concurred in your views. The rule which has been acted on is, *that the jaghirdar may resume at his pleasure rent-free holdings* (within the limits of his estate) the continuance of which has not been guaranteed by British officers; and that in cases where the jaghirdars are minors, the reasonable request of the jaghirdars, whether for resumption or release, shall be respected,—the settlement or district officer (as may be) being the judge as to the reasonableness or otherwise of the request.

Paragraph 266.—Thus the jaghirdars have had conferred on them a power which, if the British Government possess, they have never exercised. In such cases nearly absolute power has been put into the hands of the jaghirdars, nor have they been slow to use it. I mentioned in my memorandum on Chak Umballa that the *jaghirdars of Punjohra had resumed two-thirds of the villages of Junyatpoor which had been held free by the zamindar for 60 years*, which was given for political reasons at a time when it was an object to the Sikhs to secure the cordial assistance of the zamindars; "the Sikhs," I continued, "have availed themselves of *a power given them by the strength of our law, to carry out a resumption which, even when flushed with victory, they did not dare to attempt*†."

Page 86, paragraph 380.—With regard to the morals of the people, I would observe that they are ignorant and unimaginative, phlegmatic, unless their own interests are concerned, when they are very active and stickle at no means to attain their end; they are rather impetuous than brave; they are proud of their descent and devotedly attached to their homes, families, and lands. They are hospitable to strangers, and *have generally a rest-house in the villages for the accommodation of travellers.* They are humane and confiding to those they know and have been brought up with; peaceably disposed; have no feeling of patriotism further than the love of home above mentioned. They are industrious in their lazy way. They toil all day with a perseverance and slowness which astonishes the white man from the West, under a sun which would kill the more energetic and hot-blooded white. They are sober, not given to communication with strangers till they come to know them, when they give what information they have as accurately as they can, if it does not concern themselves. They are careful in the observance of their religious feasts, especially the women.

* How many officers objected to such improper resumptions, even according to the stringent rules that had been laid down!

† The decline of the religious feeling, as explained elsewhere, naturally led to jaghirdars becoming more grasping and less anxious to keep up the indigenous rent-free schools.

Page 87, paragraph 381.—Suttee was in vogue here until a very short time ago—1836. In that year, when Mr. Clerk wrote to Rao Nath Sing installing him as Sirdar, he mentions that he heard there had been a suttee in that family, and hoped that the practice would be discontinued.

Hushiarpur Settlement Report, 1852 (already quoted).

Paragraph 247.—All *doubtful* claims have been scrutinised and *resumed* during the five or six years of our rule. *It is difficult indeed for any ambiguous title to escape. The Government officers of all grades pursue and relentlessly "attach" every tenure with a flaw in it.*

Paragraph 248.—"*The large escheats in 1849-50* were owing to the rebellion."

Settlement Report, Jullundhur, 1852.

SECTION III.

FISCAL.

Rent-free tenures.

47. The first step in the fiscal operations, of course, was to decide what estates or detached patches of land were to be excluded from the rent-roll, and to be exempted from the payment of revenue. This extensive work was commenced, and in great part carried through, by the district authorities.

Jaghir estates.

48. This district, like most other parts of the Punjab, contains a number of jaghir estates, the relics of the feudal system pursued by our predecessors. It is superfluous to trace the history of these grants; suffice it to say, that here they were found to have been made either for military service or religious purposes, and were upheld by the Government, with certain modifications, during the life-time of the incumbents.

Feudal contingents disembursed.

49. The modification was this, that where a contingent had been formerly furnished by the grantee, and was no longer required, a portion of the estates, as a fourth, or a half, was resumed, as an equivalent for military pay which the grantee has no longer to disburse. In some cases where there had been no particular object, secular or religious, or where the object had ceased to exist, yet a life-tenure was allowed, as a special indulgence, on account of long occupancy.

Jaghir investigation commenced by district officer.

50. The investigation into the status of jaghir estates, and the resumption of spurious grants,—that is, grants made without due authority or for insufficient reasons,—was performed by the district authorities. The proportion which these jaghir mouzahs bear to the khalsa may be ascertained from the No. IV Statement, in which a separate division has been assigned to the jaghir villages in accordance with paragraph 6 of the Board's circular.

Detailed investigation conducted by Settlement Department.

51. The detailed lakhiraj enquiries regarding the patches of rent-free lands scattered amongst the khalsa villages was also set on foot by the district officers. In the year 1848, this branch of the enquiry was transferred to the Settlement Department by the Commissioner's orders: 2,233 cases have come under consideration; of these, 410 have been released and 2,233 resumed.

Grants of fiscal exemption.

52. In this, as in the first class of cases, fiscal immunity was allowed, either because the grant had been made for some specific purpose, or because the grantee had enjoyed long possession, or had otherwise become an object of personal charity. The claimants were called upon to produce their patents, but nevertheless they had to prove the existence of the conditions noticed above.

53. These lakhiraj proceedings were nearly brought to a close before annexation of the Punjab occurred and the new resumption laws were issued. A detailed register has been drawn up showing the cases of both parganas, and arranged in columns, with headings to denote the nature of the grant. It will be seen that, with exceptions, all the grants are held in life-tenure, and that the majority are maintained in consideration of long occupancy.

Lakhiraj register.

54. There is yet one class of subordinate and conditional grants bearing the name of "sonjee." They relate to lands exempted by the village community from the payment of "Dhal-Back," or subscription to defray the Government revenue, in favour of parties charged with the maintenance of religious houses, or the performance of municipal services. Whenever the fact of the service and its local importance was substantiated, *and the land in question was of small amount*, the grant was upheld for the term of the settlement, provided that the object of the exemption was strictly carried out, in pursuance of Commissioner's directions dated 30th August 1848.

Village service grant or sonjee.

Object of exemption.

55. The lands thus exempted were included in the "Minhie" area of the mahal. These grants stand on a different footing to Government grants, and have not been separately submitted for the sanction of higher authorities from this department. A "Sonjee" register has been prepared uniformly with the lakhiraj register.

Conditions of release.

---

149. The primary object in the mind of a Sikh financier was to extract the utmost from the land. Indian, indeed Asiatic, experience has usually shown that the occupant of the soil, be his rights what they may, can give up to the State half the gross produce without ruining himself or impairing the resources of cultivation.

Proportion of revenue demanded from the occupant of the soil;

150. This proportion the Sikhs resolved to demand. The justice or expediency of such a demand was another matter. It might possibly be enforced, and therefore it was to be made; to demand anything less than this was a sheer act of grace.

151. As I have before stated, the normal method of collecting this amount was the division of the garnered grain, or the appraisement of the standing crop; any money revenue which might be fixed would be based on the half-produce estimate.

And mode of its collection.

152. The rigour of the rule was relaxed only in favour of parties whom the Government used as an agency for collection. Over each circle of villages, locally denominated a tuppeh or talooqah, was placed a chowdry. In each village one or more persons were recognised as muquddums. The names of both these officers were borrowed from the imperial traditions. The chowdry was to aid in realising the revenues of his division, the muquddum of his village.

Chowdries and Muquddums;

153. In the lands or estates held by these parties, the Government demand was generally lowered from ½ to ⅖ (punchdoo), or ⅓ (tihara), or even to ¼. Various grants of land were also assigned under such titles as chowdrayut, muquddumee, &c. Gratuities were also allowed in cash or in kind under the general denomination of "enam." Similar favour was shown to the pargana qanoongoes who held their office upon an hereditary tenure, and were the official repositories of fiscal records; few, if any, cases could be named in which the favourable proportions had been accepted on any other consideration except actual service of some kind or other.

And the privileges enjoyed by them.

154. Under British rule, we have discarded the chowdries altogether in this district; we have dispensed with their services, and discontinued their remuneration. The muquddums we have retained as lumberdars, and the qanoongoes we have mostly taken into our service, but their hereditary perquisites have been abolished.

Chowdries discarded under British rule, but muquddums and qanoongoes retained.

155. But it was one thing to demand and another thing to collect half the gross assets of a harvest. The villagers, of course, corrupted the tax-gatherers and the "kuneas," or appraising officers. It may be safely affirmed that less than half was collected from the fields or granaries, and much less than half found its way to the kardar's treasury.

Difficulty of realising the Government share.

---

73. First and foremost, both in numbers and merit, are of course the Jats. It is needless to expatiate on the qualities of this renowned caste; sufficient to say that the Jullundhur Jats are in no way inferior to their brethren of Hindustan. The only difference is in religion, for under the Moghul sovereignty a great number of the Punjab Jats became proselytes to Islamism. This tribe flourished under the latter and (religiously speaking) corrupted Sikh Government, of which indeed they were the main bulwarks. As kardars and tax-gatherers, they served that State as faithfully in peace as they had ever served it in war, in return for which they were assiduously cherished, loaded with honour, and allowed to lord it with upstart pride over the Rajput and other proscribed classes. The statistics will show that the larger half of the district and its revenue is held and paid by them.

Jats—their prosperity.

APPENDIX No. XI.

SETTLEMENT REPORT, JULLUNDER, 1852.

Return on Rent-free Holdings, in Acres.

Name of Pargana.	Released.																						Resumed.		Total number of cases released and resumed.	Estimated jumma of released lands.	Estimated jumma of resumed lands.
	Total.		Term of release.						Object of grant.														Total.				
			In perpetuity.		For life.		Till expiry of present settlement.		Support of public buildings and institutions.		Support of purohits and pandas.		Support of school masters.		For military services.		For Chowdries, &c.		As personal charity.		Long occupancy and miscella.						
	No. of cases.	Quantity of land.	No. of cases.	Quantity of land.	No. of cases.	Quantity of land.	No. of cases.	Quantity of land.	No. of cases.	Quantity of land.	No. of cases.	Quantity of land.	No. of cases.	Quantity of land.	No. of cases.	Quantity of land.	No. of cases.	Quantity of land.	No. of cases.	Quantity of land.	No. of cases.	Quantity of land.	No. of cases.	Quantity of land.			
Garh Shunker .	744	3,338	86	521	225	2,330	433	487	111	474	189	104	9	19	10	444	3	34	303	2,094	119	169	275	1,937	1,019	5,1[illegible]	2,446
Hushiarpur . .	1,485	5,718	62	536	768	4,190	655	692	159	938	148	152	4	81	39	494	92	332	670	3,371	373	410	984	4,741	2,469	[illegible]	6,923
Hurriana . .	971	3,925	47	283	575	3,284	340	359	113	433	65	81	18	22	61	517	23	355	606	2,154	84	63	962	4,137	1,933	9,772	7,716
Oonah . . .	675	3,880	104	1,175	478	2,577	93	128	145	1,162	28	57	8	64	51	552	14	112	413	1,889	16	44	609	2,706	1,284	4,880	3,384
Total .	3,875	16,861	299	2,515	2,046	12,681	1,530	1,785	528	3,007	430	394	39	126	161	2,007	134	833	1,991	9,808	592	656	2,830	13,524	6,705	27,445	20,468

Hushiarpur Settlement Office,
30th June 1852.

P. SANDYS MELVILL,
Settlement Officer.

74. Next come the Mussulman Raens. They especially excel as market-gardeners. They cultivate more elaborately than the Jats, but they could not manage a large estate so well. In qualifications they much resemble the Ladhas and Kachies and Kurmies of the North-Western Provinces.

Raens.

75. Similar to them are the Sainees and Khumbos, but they are to be found in small numbers only. The Goojurs and their kindred tribe of Dogurs are generally to be found near the banks of the river. Here, as elsewhere, their habits are pastoral, but they are more industrious and less predatory than usual.

Sainees and Khumbos.

76. Lowest in the scale of prosperity are the Rajput gentry. In most parts of Upper India the tide of events has tended to submerge this class. But in Hindustan, though their superiority is fast waning, they are by no means considered as bad cultivators. Here, however, they have in a great measure brought this national ruin upon themselves by their inattention to agriculture, and their extinction has been hastened by the cruel and unfeeling treatment to which they were often subjected under the Sikh Government. They were over-taxed and ground down by Sikh priests and officials, and also by Jat kardars. Their villages were often destroyed and their mosques desecrated, and now they are a bye-word for idleness and destitution. There is hardly a Rajput estate in the whole district which is not in bad condition, however great its natural capacities and advantages may be.

Rajputs; their poverty.

75. While careful to avoid overloading the more industrious classes, I always endeavoured to lighten the fiscal burdens of these Rajputs. It would indeed be unfair to tax them at the same rates as Jats and Raens who cultivate every field with their own hands, or with the hands of their families, and consequently pocket the profits of both landlord and cultivator, while the others rarely touch a plough or yoke a bullock, but cultivate through the agency of servants, or lease out the land to tenants, and in either case receive only the landlord's profits. Not only motives of humanity and clemency point to moderate taxation for Rajputs, but also the experience of the summary settlement, which has evinced that none but light jummas can be steadily collected from them.

Relative amount of profit derived by Jats and Rajputs.

78. Similarly situated to the Rajputs are a few Syuds, Moguls, Pathans, and Shekhs, who may be styled genuine Mussulmans, in contradistinction to the other tribes of spurious Mussulmans.

Syuds, Pathans, Moguls, Shekhs.

79. There are other castes which do not need specification, as their numbers are very scarce. They have been included in the caste statistics under the heading of "Miscellaneous." Among them, however, I may notice that there are a few Khutrees. This tribe holds the same position as that held in Hindustan by the Bunneas and Kayeths. They are both the writers and the merchants of the Punjab. *They are sure to thrive and multiply under British rule.* As yet they possess but little land, and that little they have acquired by sales, mortgages, and such like transactions. The increasing landed occupancy of this class has proved an interesting subject of statistical comparison in the North-Western Provinces. Many years hence it will be instructive to note whether Khutree proprietorship has, or has not, increased in the Doab.

Khutrees.

Probability of their increase.

80. I will conclude this notice of the castes by observing that there are very few Brahmans to be found in the position of cultivators or proprietors.

Brahmans.

Extract from General Report on the Administration of the Punjab Territories, 1856-57 to 1857-58, inclusive.

SECTION II.

Part I.—Land-Tax.

Reasons of contentment of agriculturists.

39. The main cause of this fortunate result, no doubt, was that the people are always ready to pay revenue to the power that is, and that, despite our reverses, they still considered us to be that power. As already explained, the land-tax was light; there was no particular grievance to complain of in our revenue system; the tenures had been fairly adjusted; there was no class, among the landholders and cultivators at least, who had suffered by British rule; there were no dispossessed malcontents, no depressed village communities, no upstart usurpers over the heritage of others through the operation of our laws; there had been no wholesale or extensive transfers of estates or tracts from one set to another; *there had been some unfortunate transfers of individual properties*, but such cases were exceptional, among the agriculturists at least. Thus it befel that no one had reason to hope for benefit by a change of rulers; and so long as we were at all able to assert authority, most agriculturists were quite willing to pay tribute to Cæsar. It were vain from such facts to assume the existence of any active heart-felt loyalty.* But at all events there existed no feeling against us; there was a kind of passive sentiment in our favour among the masses. The best revenue administration will not secure much more than this; but recent events have shown that to secure even this much is great gain. Moreover, at that juncture there was an unusual degree of prosperity. The spring and autumn harvests of 1856 had not been abundant; there had been epidemic sickness among the people and murrain among the cattle; in many places there had been even a scarcity of grain and prices had generally risen—not indeed to the standard of former days, but much above the rates which had prevailed of late years. But in the spring of 1857 the harvest was excellent; sickness and murrain had abated; the markets, owing to previous deflection, were not overstocked, and prices did not fall greatly, so that generally the agriculturist had plenty of grain which he could sell at a tolerably good price. In some few places only was there a difficulty of exporting grain owing to the disturbed state of the times, which resulted in a slight glut of the markets, and a corresponding fall of prices. Thus, on the whole, agricultural prosperity told in our favour during the crisis.

Average prices of grain.

Reason why money is more plentiful among the agriculturists.

40. In former reports it was explained how the circumstance of so much money going out of the Punjab contributed to distress the agriculturist. The native army was Hindustani; to them was a large share of the Punjab revenue disbursed, of which a part only they spent on the spot and a part was remitted to their homes. Thus it was that, year after year, lakhs and lakhs of rupees were drained from the Punjab and enriched Oudh; but with the last year, the native army being Punjabi, all such sums have been paid to them and have been spent at home. Again, many thousands of Panjabi soldiers are serving abroad. These men not only remit their savings, but also have sent quantities of prize property and plunder, the spoils of Hindustan, to their native villages. The effect of all this is already perceptible in the increase of agricultural capital, a freer circulation of money, and a fresh impetus to cultivation. There has, indeed, been a diminution of labouring hands to till the ground, such large numbers of husbandmen having enlisted in the army; but this is more than compensated for by the augmentation of those means which are the sinews of agriculture as of everything else. Probably at no time since annexation have the agriculturists of the Punjab been in such easy circumstances as they are at the present time of writing.

---

* The Punjab remained loyal chiefly because it had been too recently subjugated to believe in the success of a rising, and because the Panjabis hoped to enrich themselves with the spoil of Hindustan.

Settlement Report of the Umritsur, Sowrian, and Turun Tarun Parganas, 1860.

16. Average of population to a square mile being 372.

Turun Tarun—Education 24.

Number of Schools.			Number of Students.							Number of teachers.	Pay Rs. 2,468-8 in money; 308 maunds in grain; 483 in ghass of land.
Number of towns.	Number of villages.	Total.	English.	Persian.	Arabic.	Nagri.	Gur-mukhi.	Lunde.	Total.		
99	160	259	47	1,028	460	267	353	1,487	3,742	259	

Page 135.—The proportion of village servants, such as *blacksmiths, carpenters, potters, kohars*, and *bhisties* over the whole population is 3 per cent., and from their number collectively 33 per cent. are given to agricultural pursuits. The remainder follow their more legitimate trades. *Choorahs*, the most useful and hard-working of all village servants, average 10 per cent., and 16 per cent. of their numbers are agriculturists. *Sadhs, Kashmiris, Faqirs, Mochis, Weavers, Shekhs*, and *Telees* average only one per cent. each, and from their aggregate number 23 per cent. devote their labours to the culture of land.

7th.— The Sub-division of Turun Tarun.

Page 131.—Mr. Blyth remarks that the cesses formerly levied from the non-agricultural residents have been disallowed. The Chief Commissioner, however, thinks that there is no reason why this class, already exempt almost entirely from taxation, should not continue to pay such cesses as may have been customary.

The income of the village watchman has been fixed at about three rupees per mensem.

Page 146, paragraph 22.—The additional cesses amount to no less than 21 per cent.,—that is, the jumma nominally of 100 rupees is a payment of 121 rupees by the zamindars: this is one of the features which I like least in modern settlements. It must always be remembered that only four-fifths of the burden on the people comes into the Government Treasury: it is made up in this way:—

Road Fund	1 per cent.
School Fund	1 ,,
Lumberdar's percentage	5 ,,
Mulbah	5 ,,
Putwari	3 to 3-8 per cent.
Chowkidars	6 per cent. about.
	21 per cent.

Page 147, paragraph 25.—Jussur comprised 27 villages formerly, but 37 were allowed at the settlement. It was held originally by one "Jussur," and then by one cosmanpudda, a convert from the Hindu to the Muhummadan religion, about 100 years ago.

Memorandum on the re-assessment of Pargana Narawal.

Page 166, paragraph 11.—The muáfidars have found great difficulty in realising their dues, owing to the Government demand having absorbed the entire outturn of the villages.

Page 166, paragraph 12.—The chowkidars have also been obliged to satisfy themselves with payment in kind, much below the amount they are entitled to receive.

Paragraph 13.—Such has been the fate of Narawal; the revenue has been realised. There have been but few balances, but the people have suffered many privations in meeting the heavy demands on them, and the condition of the pargana is now considerably impaired. Two-thirds of the cattle have disappeared. The landholders are in debt to the Shahs, and the Shahs are also ruined. They have mortgaged their property to pay the Government demand and have no prospect of redeeming it under the present state of things.

35, 36, 48, 53, 123, 124, 128, 132, 150, 153, 164, 169, 173, 187, 188, 198, 200, 205, 217, 218, 254, 273, 277, 278, 279, 281, 288, 290, 291, 307, 322, 334, 341.

Page 171, paragraph 38.—It is remarkable that those villages which have a large proportion of rent-free land were the most heavily assessed. *Vide* statistics in Statement V of the villages bearing the numbers noted in the margin. This had resulted from the adoption of the erroneous principle of excluding rent-free and inam lands from the village (cultivated) area at the time of assessment, the process having tended to exaggerate the percentage of ploughs and cultivation and induce heavy rates.

Extract from Mr. Blyth's *Report on Pargana Narawal.*

Page 184, paragraph 37.—The hereditary cultivators and tenants-at-will generally comprise the village servants, among whom the Jalaspa caste preponderate. They hold land on equally favourable terms with the proprietors, pay no proprietary rights, and are generally charged according to village rates.

Page 185, paragraph 46.—There are 168 schools. Of this number

124 teach Persian.
21 ,, Arabic.
9 ,, Shashtras.
9 ,, Gurmukhi.
5 ,, Lunde.

The pupils aggregate 1,245, of whom

819 learn Persian.
157 ,, Arabic.
106 ,, Shashtras.
77 ,, Gurmukhi.
86 ,, Lunde.

Paragraph 47.—The income of the teachers amounts to Rs. 2,024, averaging Rs. 12-4 per man per year, or one rupee per month, Rs. 3-4 of which is realised in cash and the remainder in grain.

Letter from R. H. Davies, Esq., *Secretary to the Government of the Punjab, to the Officiating Financial Commissioner.*

Page 196.—Owing to the original measurements made by the patwaris proving inaccurate, the area has been twice measured and the record of rights recast; and in consequence of the reduction of the jumma made by the assessing officer, Mr. Morris, having proved insufficient, a further remission, amounting to 21 per cent., has been granted, making the total abatement of demand on the summary assessment 31, and on the Sikh jumma 40 per cent. In other words, we get only Rs. 60,000 where the Sikhs got a lakh. .

Much, however, of this reduction is nominal as far as the zamindars are concerned. It is shown by the statistics furnished by Mr. Blyth that the price of the staple produce, wheat, has fallen by 35 per cent.; that the zamindar has now to part with 88 seers of wheat for one rupee, whereas at the time of the summary settlement he gave only 65 seers.

This excessive cheapness of produce which has now prevailed for several years, however beneficial to the urban population, must materially increase the difficulty of paying revenue in cash.

The diminution of demand on this score is therefore clearly just and necessary.

E. A. PRINSEP, ESQ., *to Commissioner, Umritsur,—No. 215, dated 31st January 1863.*

Page 26, paragraph 95.—The state of indigenous education is still at a very low ebb, no attention being paid to this till lately. During the Sikh rule the schools were supported by local effort, even such as drew out a precarious existence in connection with Hindu and Muhummadan places of worship. I took the statistics in A. D. 1852 and found that there were 149 localities where instruction of the most rudimentary character was being given to 1,922 boys, one-half of whom were young lads training to be made "Moollas" or priests of Islamism, and of the remainder the majority were Kuttrees and Brahmans learning account-keeping. Of the agricultural classes, there were only 500 boys, and under the age of 8 years only 400. Persian and Arabic (now both obsolete) were the popular languages. In two parganas, Zufferwall and Chahur, only 100 lads were receiving any instruction. Few could write their names, while teachers were indigent and illiterate in the extreme. In 1854 the district authorities introduced reform, which reduced the number of schools to 134. A return is annexed giving the statistics previous to the operations of the Educational Department, which may prove useful for future comparison.

Paragraph 96.—In every village of moderate dimensions places are set apart for religious worship; with the Muhummadans it is a mosque known by its three cupolas to distinguish it from the single-domed Shivala and Thakurdwara of the Hindus. They are generally built of pucca masonry and are enclosed with a low wall. Burial-grounds are attached to the former, in which are said to repose the ashes of holy men, sainted priests, or village progenitors. In many places enclosures are attached called "Dairas" by the Muhummadans and "Dharamsálás" by the Hindus, which contain accommodation for travellers and afford convenient rendezvous for rustic gatherings. Among the genuine Jats, or those who can look back to a Rajput origin, it is not uncommon to find a great veneration paid to the "Ibis," or mounds which in bygone days were the sites of their first location. They are marked by a few scattered tombs, or a grove of trees, or have since been selected by some shrivelled fakir as the place suitable for a solitary life.

With the Jats it is also curious to watch the reverence they pay to the Jund tree, which is often introduced into these places of worship. The Rajputs are more lofty in their religion and more rigorous in their discharge of it. Nothing can be done without consulting their Brahmans and Jaformans; no exercise complete unless attended with oblation, so that, as might be expected, the outward raised signs of religion are more numerous. Thakur is their god and temples are in his honour everywhere. Asceticism, too, is more openly encouraged in other parts of the district; monasteries are often attached to the larger Thakurdwaras situated in the Rajput tracts, the most noted of which are those at Biruntal and Lorne in Bujwant, Goddul and Chupras in Maharawall, and Tezu in Zufferwall.

Page 27, paragraph 97.—But there are three localities where the most prominent regard is paid to religious observances, *viz.*, at Rotlu Fuqueerchand Ber-Baba Nanak, close to Sialkot; and the tomb of Imam Shah, also at Sialkot. The two former are the strongholds of the Sikh faith and are popularly held to have been established by Babu Nanak himself. The first is situated on the road from Pusroo to Wuzeerabad in the centre of the Sikh villages, and is presided over by Baba Mehtab Sing Mohunt, who has some 200 disciples. Ber-Baba Nanak, close to Sialkot, containing the Samadh of Muttee Singh "Shaheed," has a temple with handsome cupola which was gilded at the expense of Maharajah Runjit Sing, by whom large endowments were granted for its support. Both institutions are above a century old and have been allowed a liberal jaghir by the British Government. The latter has a grant of Rs. 6,500 in perpetuity* and boasts of nearly 100 retainers. Here the first of the month Bysakee, the commencement of the new year, is always kept with festival rejoicings, to celebrate which sometimes 10,000 people are in attendance.

* We now have an instance of what was a "*liberal*" remnant, from *our* point of view, of an original endowment.

The mosque and tomb of Imam Shah occupies the southern suburbs of the city of Sialkot, and is supported by contributions from nearly every village in the district, possesses branch establishments in several places; and being one of the oldest and strongest positions of the Muhammadan religion, is held in great reverence throughout the Punjab. All the feast and fast days are rigorously kept, and during Mohurrum it is resorted to by large assemblages of the people.

V.—Judicial.

Page 85, paragraph 328.—But before any real evidence could be accepted to support the statement for or against claims, whether brought by occupants of individual holdings or by a number of co-partners, I very soon found that it was necessary to discover the past history and custom of villages. In the same way it was impossible to arrive at correct conclusions as to tenures: constant mistakes were made, which were found out too late, involving expense and delay. Several records, even when made up, were found to be faulty for this reason.

Page 89, paragraph 340.—Seeing how property is held almost universally by tribes, how much more readily understood is a share as the expression of a man's liability, and what reverence is paid by the descendants of a common ancestor to old usages as affecting each others rights, I am not surprised that there should be this adherence to the "pattidari" type of tenure.

Page 89, paragraph 341.—In a first settlement there can be no doubt to recognise generally that this tenure is tantamount to causing a great deal of additional trouble: it involves a comparison of possession with share, and this entails equalisation. Those who have more than their share (and they are generally the influential co-partners) resist. The settlement employés encourage them, for, if the internal assessment can only be thrown on the land in possession, the work is quicker done, and all parties in attendance are more quickly released. General assent, it is feared, is too often given to stereotyping a very evil form of creed in this way, and the mischief is not discovered till too late.

Page 109, paragraph 410.—On the whole, I am satisfied the records in the main are to be relied on. This is the general impression, and notwithstanding the trial they have had in a period of seven years, scarcely any complaint has been raised.

Paragraph 411.—One good proof may be adduced of this in the fact that, when all the records were destroyed by the mutineers burning down the cutcherry in 1857, and I was called upon, on my return from England, to replace them, though the putwaris had copies only of some of the principal papers, we were able to give in a new set and prepare many papers, such as the pedigree tables, agreeing with the former entries, without much trouble, in the space of one year.

From Charles Raikes, Esq., *to* D. F. McLeod, Esq.,—*No. 89 C. of 1856.*

Page 18, paragraph 38.—The following is an abstract of the schools in all three tahsils, Gurdaspur, Battala, and Pathankote:—

	Number of schools.		Number of students.
In towns .	76	Persian	1,285
,, villages	207	Arabic	417
		Nagri	89
Total	283	Gurmukhi	211
		Lunde	945
		Total	2,947

Pay, Rs. 791 in money.
3,361 maunds in grain.
274 ghumaos of land.
283 tahsils.

Four per cent. of the boys enumerated in the census are thus being taught. The excess of Persian and Lunde over other students indicates that the demand is for a practical education. The wits of the present generation certainly want sharpening. Until men can read, write, and cypher, they have few ideas, desire no more, and cannot communicate those which they have. Hence gross prejudices, blind dependence, easy credulity, and total absence of the means of power of forming a public opinion. It is only when their daily wants are abridged that the bulk of the people of this country have any opinion at all. Those who are instructed are not better men, but much more useful members of society. Only half the students are educated in the village, the town schools, though fewer, being more numerously attended.

Statement of Settlement Report of the Lahore District for 1860.

Paragraph 28.—There are 576 schools in the district, including those situated in the city of Lahore; 4,225 scholars are said to attend them. Of this number—

Schools A. No. I.—41·3	per cent. learn the	Koran.
37·0	,, ,, ,,	Persian and Urdu.
8·0	,, ,, ,,	Nagri.
6·7	,, ,, ,,	Gurmukhi.
7·0	,, ,, ,,	Hindi or debased Nagri.

The teachers are paid in cash, in grain, in assignments of land, and by daily rations. Grain and daily rations are the most common modes of payment in the villages.

Rights of hereditary cultivators newly created.

Paragraph 51.—The rights of hereditary cultivators have been entirely created under our rule. Under the Sikhs, the proprietor had always the right of ousting a tenant whenever he chose; but this was never done unless the cultivator made himself obnoxious, and the proprietor would have had to provide for the efficient cultivation of the land, or the removal of the cultivator would have been opposed by the kardar.

Lumbardars why numerous.

Paragraph 84.—The number of lumbardars in the whole district is 2,634, or one for every Rs. 214 of jumma, and 2¾ for each mahal. The reason for this large number is the difficulty of dismissing men who have formerly borne office without some proof of misconduct. No class of cases has been more perseveringly litigated, and I have generally found it more expedient to maintain the existing number of lumbardars, than to create a feud in the village by dismissing some and retaining others.

Muáfi land.

Paragraph 85.—There are 40,535 acres of rent-free land in the district, exclusive of entire villages or shares in villages held in jaghir. The revenue of these detached plots amounts to Rs. 32,642, and on this sum the ordinary village cesses are levied. Four thousand nine hundred and thirty muáfi cases have been investigated and reported in the Settlement Department.

Road Fund.

Paragraph 86.—The Road Fund Cess is charged on all lands, khulsa and muáfi.

Educational Cess.

Para. 87.—The schools fund cess of one per cent. has been entered in the Durkhwast Malguzari, in every instance, with the consent of the people. In pargana Chunian it was announced along with the jumma; in other parganas it was entered as a supplement.

Commissioner and Superintendent, Lahore Division, 1860.

Paragraph 20.—It is sufficient for me to remark that the causes which have led to over-assessment in the Punjab, namely, the former capacity of the people to bear taxation, owing to abundance of employment; the exaggerated ideas of fiscal resources obtained from the native fiscal records (which always over-estimate resources); the sudden plethora of grain caused by the turning of all hands to agriculture; the dearth of cash; the cessation of employment; the sudden transition from payment in kind to payment in cash,—all these causes operated powerfully in the Lahore district; some of them, indeed, operated peculiarly. From the description I have given in paragraph 4 of certain villages in the Manjha, you can imagine what must have been the state of Sobraon, or Vultoa,

or Burkee, when the flower of their youth were at annexation discharged from military service, and sent back to their villages to drive the plough. In the eastern or Kussur portion of the district, too, the people had misbehaved during the rebellion which preceded annexation, and this caused them to be regarded less leniently than many others*. Extensive reductions had afterwards to be granted in that neighbourhood.

Settlement Report of Ferozpur of 1859.

The village expenses.

Page 189.—Whenever I could do so with the consent of the people, I always gave a contract for the "Mulba," or village expenses, to the headmen. This would generally be at the rate of from 2 to 3 per cent. on the jumma, and the object was to prevent any disputes regarding the amount of it, or the manner in which it had been spent; but I by no means found that the people always approved of this arrangement. Many objected to it because it did not properly provide for the feeding of fakirs, in which they all wished to have a voice, and *without it they conceived that the village would never prosper*†.

Page 240.—The total value of the muafi plots in present possession of the different muáfidars is Rs. 16,829. Most of these cases were investigated soon after annexation by the district officer; but having no authority to resume any of the muáfis, he was only able to attach the proceeds of all those which he considered ought to be resumed, and the amount of the proceeds has been kept in the treasury deposits until the present time, very much to the annoyance of the accountant. *The principle adopted by this officer was to recommend the resumption of all muáfis granted by the zamindars.* The Government, however, in the rules subsequently promulgated for the guidance of officers employed in the investigation of muáfi cases, took a more liberal view of the subject, and *allowed all grants of an old date, however acquired, to be confirmed for the life-time at least of the present occupants*‡, *and reasonably so, for the grants made by the zamindars are generally those of all others which most deserve to be upheld, being often for some charitable purpose*, or else for the support of some religious devotee regarding whom, whatever we may think, yet the villagers are accustomed to trust much to his prayers, and would deeply feel any injury being done to him, *such as the resumption of the land which they had given him.*

The new rules.

Page 241.—Notwithstanding the investigation which had been previously made, I was obliged to summon the parties a second time in order to complete the proceedings in all details required by the new rules, and the grants were now invariably attributed to some ancient prince§. The existence of such a thing as a grant by the zamindars was altogether denied, notwithstanding the distinct assertions to the contrary in the former proceedings, and it was not without great difficulty that I succeeded in persuading the people that the principle formerly acted on had been renounced, and inducing them to give more truthful replies.

Different descriptions of rent-free grants.

Page 242.—It is impossible within reasonable limits to describe all the different kinds of grants that have been upheld. Those conferred in perpetuity are generally for the support of Hindu or Muhammadan places of worship, for the maintenance of tombs, for keeping up of "Dhurmsalas," or resting-places for travellers, for schools, for perpetual alms-giving, and such like purposes.

*** This treatment differed considerably from that of Ranjit Sing, who forgave the disloyalty of Kasur over and over again.**

† Practically they were right, as the presence of the holy men kept up the religious feeling in the community with its attendant advantages.

‡ And what was to become the endowment *after* the deaths of "present occupants"? I cannot conceive that a *deferred* appropriation of, say, an educational or religious grant, is an act of liberality.

§ It was thus we taught the villagers to invent excuses in order to protect the rent-free grants. See my account of the results of our first settlement enquiries as regards these grants in the "Précis and conclusions." The Ferozpur officer, however, confirmed in perpetuity *what there was left* of religious and educational endowments.

Settlement Report of the Gujranwalla District of 1860.

Page 18.—Sincerely endeavouring to show consideration to the people, the assessment of the Gujranwala and Ramnuggur sub-divisions was made by Mr. Morris, under my supervision, and the jummas of the villages were sanctioned by me, Mr. Morris having proceeded on sick leave to the hills. I myself announced these jummas in the summer of 1853. This assessment made a considerable abatement on the former revenue. But at that time prices of agricultural produce were in a transition state; difficulties were gathering round the agriculturists; and it was soon found that still further relief must be given. The assessment of the Hafizabad and Shekhopoorah sub-divisions was made by Mr. Morris independently of me. The summary settlement, though believed to be moderate at the time, and fixed at a deduction of ten per cent. on the average collections of five previous years, had proved severe, under the altered circumstances of the agriculturists. The regular assessment now made by Mr. Morris gave a further reduction of 17 per cent. Herein the intention certainly was to make a really moderate settlement, and the rate at which it fell, namely, one rupee two annas on the cultivated acre, with three-fourths of the cultivation artificially irrigated, is light as compared with those which prevail in highly-cultivated districts. The best part of the irrigated tract forms part of the well-known "Churkurree Mehal" (so called from the "churkur," or Persian wheel, by which the wells are worked). But although in these lands the soil is strong and the crops fine, still the water is deep below the surface; the masonry and the wooden machinery is expensive; the labour of men and bullocks is excessive day and night; the wear and tear of cattle is great; and whenever their fodder is poor, as is too often the case, they sicken or die, and then the irrigation is brought to a standstill. This of itself renders such estates unable to bear a high assessment. Then there is the liability to unequal competition in some seasons with the produce of unirrigated lands already mentioned. Then the husbandman is not well remunerated, after all this expenditure of labour and capital, unless his produce fetches a tolerably good price. Thus the general fall of prices throughout the Punjab peculiarly affected a district like this. Then, as already explained, the people were utterly careless and improvident—unaccustomed to the exercise of proprietary rights, and strangers to those habits of management which the possession of such rights would induce. Furthermore, unfavourable circumstances in the season had rendered money assessments distasteful to the people. When I announced the jummas in 1853, I could see that in their hearts the people were unwilling to enter into any engagements at all for cash payments. All these considerations rendered the Setttlement Officer anxious to fix a low assessment. Still, although Mr. Morris believed, and with apparent reason, when he made his final report, that the assessment was light, further experience proved that in some estates scattered over the district, pressure still existed. Time after time as the collections came to be made, here and there estates would show signs of distress. The masonry of a well would fall in, and the owner could not repair it; the machinery would break and he could not mend it; the oxen would die and he could not replace them; if a co-partner would die and his place could not be filled, a tenant would quit and a successor could not be found. Sometimes a man would dispose of his property in land in a manner which showed that he regarded it as worth less than nothing,—as a burden to be got rid of rather than as a possession to be cherished. The recurrence of these cases after a settlement which certainly appeared moderate was very discouraging.

20. There are processes which the Settlement Officer is by law empowered to use in the event of proprietors refusing to engage for the assessed revenue; but sale is not among those processes. In point of fact, however, these resignations were not technically refusals to engage. The people had once engaged in the usual form, therefore the Settlement Officer might have left them to be dealt with by the Collector according to law. As to the policy, the result has shown subsequently that when the assessment is so reduced as to render land really valuable, the people even in this district do never wish to resign their rights; and that when they become tolerably well-to-do they are content, and

cease to agitate for reduction. My own personal experience points to this conclusion. Still the difficulties with which Mr. Morris had to contend were great. No officer who had not seen these people from 1853 to 1855, would believe how provoking and contumacious they sometimes were. Some of them would even assemble in numbers and almost behave like a mob. Sometimes a circle of villages would combine to offer passive resistance to the progress of the settlement. Sometimes proprietors would desert their land, believing that no other occupant would be forthcoming, and that they would ultimately be re-admitted on reduced terms. Sometimes they would say that they would renounce their proprietorship rather than engage for any fixed assessment. And in this, as in all their other proceedings, they showed a strong tendency to combine. Such behaviour after the announcement of an assessment which reduced their burden by nearly one-fifth, induced the supposition that the more relief was granted, the more clamorous would they become for further relief. The fact is, they had not then learnt to appreciate, as they now do, the advantages of fixed money assessment, and were anxious to revert to the old system of collection. And considering the real difficulties which at that time beset agriculturists, and the past history and character of the people, this is not much to be wondered at. Thus it arose that Mr. Morris had, as he says, to search for fresh proprietors. Such a search was not indeed regular, but it was not without excuse. And there can be no doubt that firmness was at that time needed in dealing with these people. These cases were taken up by Mr. Cust in 1858, and reported to the Financial Commissioner and Chief Commissioner, who decided that they must be cancelled. The property was to be restored to the proprietors; and on restoring the property to the proprietors, the transferees were to have such compensation as might be practicable. This has been arranged in the same manner as in former cases. Most of these readjustments were effected in Mr. Cust's time and some in my own. No cases of this kind now remain pending. The people do, I believe, appreciate the just and liberal spirit which Government has shown in causing these restorations. One or two of the more remarkable cases I have heard cited as instances of British justice; while at the same time they have had their lesson, and remember that concession is not always made to contumacy, and that the fiscal interests of the State are not to be trifled with. Viewing, therefore, the peculiar difficulties with which Mr. Morris had to contend, I trust that these particular cases may not be allowed to detract from the general credit to which he is entitled for the settlement.

Education.

10. The state of education cannot be said to be very flourishing in this district.* I subjoin a statement, however, giving all the educational statistics, which I trust will prove interesting. In all cases where, under the former Government, land was declared rent-free for the support of schools, these grants have been upheld under the present settlement, and the various plots of land *proposed* for release.

Statement of schools, scholars, &c., in the Goojranwalah District with Purgana Shahdarah.

Name of Mouzah.			Number of schools.						Number of scholars.						Remuneration.		
With schools.	Without schools.	Total.	Arabic.	Persian.	Hindee.	Sashtree.	Gurmukhi.	Total.	Arabic.	Persian.	Hindee.	Shastree.	Gurmukhi.	Total.	Cash.	Grain.	Land.
413	1,289	1,702	345	119	36	20	40	560	1,743	1,609	633	244	376	4,006	240	297	113

Census statement of the Goojranwalah District with Parganah Shahdarah.

Number of Mehals.	Population.			Average number of people to each mehal.	Average number of people to each house.	Average number of people to each square mile.
	Men.	Women.	Total.			
1,702	300,876	299,013	599,889	352	4½	148

* True enough, but is it not worse now when there are only 266 indigenous schools instead of 560 which were still *ascertained* to exist in 1860, after most indigenous schools had ceased in consequence of our resumptions of rent-free land granted by zamindars of their own property?

PART II.

DETAILED REPORT

OF THE

Indigenous Schools in every district of the Panjab, with the names of the most distinguished Native Savans in each locality.

DELHI DIVISION.

DELHI DISTRICT.

GENERAL ABSTRACT.

District.	No. of Maktabs and Madrasas.	No. of pupils.	No. of Sanscrit and Nagri Schools.	No. of pupils.	No. of Gurmukhi Schools.	No of pupils.	No. of Hindi Mahajani Schools.	No. of pupils.	Total No. of Indigenous Schools.	Total No. of pupils.
Delhi .	141	2,073	19	177	...	...	56	1054	216*	3,304*

* The Police Returns only showed 116 schools and 1,778 pupils.

DELHI CITY.

AMONG the *Hakims*, Hakim Mahmud Khan, a physician of wide reputation in India, Hakim Shah Din, Hakim Abdulmajid Khan (son of Mahmud Khan), Hakim Nuruddin, Hakim Mazaffar Husain, Sayyid Ashraf Ali, Hakim Badruddin Khan, Hakim Ghulam Najaf Khan, Hakim Muhammad Husain Khan, Hakim Qeyámuddin, Hakim Latif Husain (oculist), Hakim Kutbuddin, Hakim Akbar Ali, and Hakim Serájuddin and *Binda Baid* deserve notice.

Among the *Maulvis*, Maulvi Nazir Husain (a Maulvi famous for his learning all over India and the present leader of the Muwahidin or Wahabis), Maulvi Hafizulla Khan, Maulvi Rahim Bakhsh, Maulvi Mansur Ali Khan, Maulvi Muhammad Shah and Maulvi Manzur Ali, are distinguished.

Pandits Radhi Misser, Goshain Benarsi Dass, Kishen Dat, Kesho Das, Balmukand, and Gobind Ram, are distinguished Sanscrit scholars.

Bhai Bhagat Singh, attached to the 15th Sikh Infantry, is a distinguished Bhai.

Abdulghani Arshad, the blind Hafiz Gholam Rasul Wiran, Nawab Ziauddin Khan Nayyir, Nawab Saiduddin Khan Talib, Maulvi Altáf Husain Háli, Maulvi Ammuján, Maulvi Mohammad Said, Nawwáb Bahauddin, Nawwáb Shujauddin, Mumtazuddin, Nawwáb Mirza, Suraj Narayen, Bihari Lal, Pandit Ramchander, Mirza Bakhtawar, Mirza Buland Akhtar, Mirza Beg Khan, Mirza Nasiruddin, Mir Shahjahan, Nawwáb Wahiduddin, Pir Kamruddin, Bismilla Beg, Yaqúb Beg, Sayyid Baqar Husain, Ramzan Ali, Badrul Islam, Fatahul Islam, Ghulam Mohumdi, Mirza Mahmud Shah, Umráo Mirza and Saifulhaq Adib are *Poets* of note.

Madrasas.—In Kuche Rahman quarter there is a Madrasa, in which Maulvi Abdulla, a distinguished Arabic scholar, teaches Arabic Grammar, Logic, Philosophy, Jurisprudence, Muhammadan Law, Hadis, Tafsir, Rhetoric and Astronomy. There are 40 boys, chiefly strangers. The school was established by Maulvi Abdurrabb, a preacher of great reputation, and the Head Maulvi receives Rs. 25 per month.

Maktabs.—Among the numerous maktabs which are shown in the table further on, the maktabs in (1) Chitla Darwaza (2) in Fatahpuri, and (3) in Deputy Gunj deserve special notice. The Chitla Darwaza maktab is conducted by Maulvi Abdulmajid with 10 assistant teachers under him, in which 235 pupils are taught Arabic, Persian, Urdu, the Koran, Arithmetic, &c. The whole income amounts to Rs. 150 per mensem, derived from subscriptions. This maktab is very well conducted, and the manager is to open another branch. The Fatahpuri maktab is supported by the managers of the Fatahpuri mosque from the income of the mosque. It has two departments—one a *school* in which Persian, Urdu and Arithmetic are taught to 60 pupils by Mirza Abdulghani, Allah Bakhsh and Mahmud Shah, receiving, respectively, Rs. 15, 9 and 7 per mensem; the other, a Koran school, in which Hafiz Rahim Bakhsh teaches the Koran to 60 pupils and is paid Rs. 5-12 by Hafiz Azizuddin, the well-known pleader and one of the managers of the Fatahpuri mosque. Another Hafiz, named Bahadur Ali, paid by Mahbub Buksh and Hafiz Azizuddin, teaches 7 pupils and gets Rs. 5 per mensem.

The Deputy Gunj maktab, under Mir Shahijahan, Muhammad Amir Khan, Abdurrazzak and Kari Kabiruddin has 42 pupils who learn Persian, English and the Koran, and pay Rs. 42 per mensem to the teachers.

The following more detailed account of the principal indigenous schools in the once "Imperial city" may be interesting :—

(1.)—Maulvi Abd-ur-rabb's Arabic Madrasa.

This Madrasa was established ten years ago by Maulvi Abd-ur-rabb, a Muhammadan preacher. The school is supported by *subscriptions* raised among the Muhammadans of the city and the adjoining towns, who pay the subscription monthly. The total expenses of this school amount to Rs. 70 per mensem.

The Head Maulvi, Maulvi Abdulla, a distinguished Arabic scholar, receives Rs. 25 per mensem. A Hafiz who teaches the Koran, and a Munshi who keeps the accounts, receive Rs. 5 and 7 per mensem, respectively. Seven scholarships, of the value each of Rs. 2-8 monthly, are given chiefly to outsiders. The remaining sum of Rs. 15 goes to defray the miscellaneous expenses, such as house-rent and the salaries of servants.

The boys of the city read the Koran, and those in the advanced classes are all outsiders with the exception of one who is a native of Delhi. The limited number of scholarships and of the teaching staff prevents the increase of pupils in this school, the number of pupils being now about forty.

Maulvi Abdulla does not teach the elementary books in Grammar, and those who enter his class must have finished their elementary course somewhere else.

The following books are taught in this school:—

Logic.—Qazi Mubarak, Hamdulla, Mulla Hasan.
Philosophy.—Shams Bázigha.
Rhetoric.—Mukhtasar.
Tafsir.—(Exegesis) Jalalain, Baidáwi.
Hadis.—Abú Daúd and Mishkát.
Theology.—Aqáyed Nasfi, Hashya Khiyáli.
Literature.—Sabá Muállaqá.
Law.—Hidáya.
Munázara.—Rashidía (mode of argumentation)
Jurisprudence.—Tauzih and Talwíh.
Inheritance.—Sirájia.

(2.)—Madrasa of Maulvi Nazeer Husain.

In this school, which is attached to the mosque of Nazeer Husain in the Hábash-Khán-ka-Phátak Street, Maulvi Nazeer Husain and his son Maulvi Sharif Husain teach only *Hadis*, *Tafsir* and *Law* to nearly 50 pupils. These pupils have come here from every part of India, for the purpose of obtaining a "certificate" from the Maulvi. The majority of the pupils live on their own means, the rest are supported by the Panjábi merchants of Delhi.

(3.)—Madrasa of Husain Bakhsh.

The building of this Madrasa, which is very spacious and beautiful, was erected by Husain Bakhsh, a merchant, in 1847. Before the mutiny of 1857 this school was well attended, and a great number of scholars read here religion and other branches of learning. After the mutiny the school remained closed for eighteen years. Seven years ago Maulvi Mansur Ali, of Rampur, re-established the school. About Rs. 40 a month are raised by subscription among the Muhammadans and expended in paying the salaries of two Maulvis (Maulvi Ismail receiving Rs. 12, and Maulvi Qadir Bakhsh getting Rs. 13 per mensem) a Hafiz and a Munshi. The number of pupils in this Madrasa is now about 20; *Maulvi Ismail* teaches Mishkát, Bukhári, Baizáwi, the *translation of the Koran*, Káfya, Hamdulla, Mulla Husan and Qála-Aqúla, and *Maulvi Qadir Ali* teaches Jalálain, Nasfi, Khayáli, Sharah Waqaya, Qadúri, Maibuzi, Qutbi, Mir Qutbi Mukhtasar Maáni and Nur-ul-anwar. (For explanation see list of Arabic text-books in the body of the report.)

Out of 20 pupils 3 receive scholarships.

The qualifications of the teachers are of a superior order. They are recognized as good Arabic scholars.

(4.)—Madrasatul-Kurán of Chitla Darwáza.

This school was opened in 1296 A. H. This school is supported by a subscription of Rs. 150 per mensem raised among the Muhammadans. The teaching staff consists of 14 teachers, with the following detail:—

(1) Maulvi *Abul Hosain*, on Rs. 15 per mensem, teaches the Urdu translation of the Koran and Hadis.
(2) Maulvi *Subhan Bukhsh* teaches Arabic Grammar on Rs. 10 per mensem.
(3) Maulvi Md. Husain
(4) Maulvi Ashiq Ali } prepare students for the Persian examinations of the Punjab University College, and receive Rs. 10 and 8 per mensem, respectively.
(5) A teacher getting Rs. 8 a month, teaches Arithmetic up to Double Rule of Three.
(6) Mahmud Ali teaches religious treatises in Urdu, and gets Rs. 6 per mensem.
(7) Hafiz Aziz Bakhsh
(8) Israrulla
(9) Mirza Ahmad Shah
(10) Hafiz Najmuddin
(11) Hafiz Abdurrahim
(12) Hafiz Hishmat Ali
(13) Hafiz
(14) Hafiz } teach the Koran, on Rs. 8, 6, 5, 5, 5, 5, 5 and 5 respectively.

The number of pupils attending the school is 235, out of which 40 pupils, who are all poor, are given scholarships ranging from four annas to one Rupee per month.

This school has a branch in the Chandni Chauk Bázár, and the expense of that branch, amounting to Rs. 20 per mensem, is defrayed by Myan Ali Jan, silk, merchant. Another branch is to be opened in the Habash-Khán-ka-Phatak where a house for the school is already being erected at a cost of Rs. 4,000, raised by subscription among the Muhammadan merchants. A sum is being raised by subscription for the maintenance of this branch. Maulvi Abdul Majid (a Muhammadan preacher) who is the real founder of this school, thinks that on opening the branch at Habash-Khán-ka-Phátak, the number of pupils will be nearly doubled.

The object of the founder of the school is to provide elementary religious education for Muhammadan boys and to prepare them for the higher Government schools, as also for the Oriental examinations of the Panjab University.

This school is very popular among the Muhammadans, and there is every hope that the school will make great progress

The system of "classification" has also been introduced; no tuition fees are taken in this school.

The founder, who is also the manager, seems very zealous in improving the school.

(5.)—Fatahpuri Mosque School.

The Fatahpuri mosque, which is situated on the northern end of the Chandni Chauk Bázár, had a large property in shops, houses, &c., attached to it.

After the mutiny this property was confiscated, but it was restored to the mosque on the occasion of the Imperial Assemblage by Lord Lytton. The property of the mosque gives an income of more than Rs. 300 per mensem.

A part of this income, about Rs. 150 per mensem, was set apart for the education of the Muhammadans.

In 1296 A.H. (1879) a school was opened in the Fatahpuri Mosque with two departments, one "upper" and the other "lower." The upper department is an advanced Arabic School, and the lower department consists of a Persian Maktab and a Koran School.

The present teaching staff is as follows :—

(1)	Maulvi Muhammad Shah .	Head Maulvi, teaching Hadis, Law and Tafsír, on Rs. 20 per mensem.
(2)	Maulvi Abdul Huq . .	2nd Maulvi, teaches Logic and Philosophy, on Rs. 20 per mensem.
(3)	Maulvi Bahauddin .	3rd Maulvi, teaches Arabic Grammar, on Rs. 8 per mensem.
(4)	Mirza Nasiruddin . .	1st Persian teacher, on Rs. 15.
(5)	Alla Bakhsh . .	2nd Persian teacher, on Rs. 7.
(6)	Moulvi Muhammad Shah .	3rd Persian teacher, on Rs. 7.
(7)	Hafiz Rahmun Bakhsh .	Koran teachers, getting each Rs. 5.
(8)	Hafiz Bahadur Ali . .	

Ten scholarships of Rs. 43 per mensem are given to poor pupils and outsiders.

Hafiz Abdul Karim, a dealer in skins, always gives a sum of Rs. 20 per mensem, which is distributed in scholarships to students who come from a distance.

The number of pupils in this school is about 186, with the following detail :—

Advanced Arabic	50
Koran	52
Persian, Urdu and Arithmetic	84
TOTAL	186

In the Arabic Department all books from the Mizán up to the most advanced books in Logic, Philosophy, Jurisprudence, Theology, Mathematics, Law, Hadis, Tafsír, &c., are taught.

The scheme of study of the Persian Department is given below :—

1st year.—Alphabet, Urdúki-pahli kitab, Rah-niját, Karima, numerals and multiplication tables.

2nd year.—Karima, Amadnama, Gulistan, Masdar Fayyúz, Rah-niját, Malabud in Urdú, compound division, dictation.

3rd year.—Bostan, Gulistan, Masdar Fayyúz, Malabud, decimal fractions.

4th year.—Bostan, Anwari Suheli, Masdar Fayyúz, Malabud, Rule of Three, dictation and translation.

The school is under the superintendence of the Fatahpuri Mosque Property Managing Committee, which consists of Prince Mirza Suleyman Jáh, as President, and Háfiz Azizuddin, pleader; Khan Bahadur, Shaikh Mahbub Bakhsh, Honorary Magistrate, Delhi; Hakim Muhammad Hosain Khan and Muhammad Ikramulla Khan, Honorary Magistrates of Delhi.

(6.)—Anglo-Arabic School, Delhi.

This school, which was opened in February 1872 for the purpose of promoting the study of the English language among the Muhammadans of Delhi, is maintained entirely from the proceeds of the endowment of Nawab I'timad-ud-daula. From the date of the endowment up to the opening of this school the interest (of Rs. 1,70,000) was expended on the old and new Delhi Colleges—(see Appendix III).

All the subjects up to the standard of the middle school examination are taught there with the addition of the Arabic language, which is an *optional* subject. In the distribution of scholarships preference is always given to those who study Arabic.

The scheme of study is the same as in the Government middle schools; and there seems to be no reason why religious education should have been excluded by the Education Department, under whose management the school is, from a school which is maintained purely from a private fund. Had the Department permitted the introduction of the Koran and of religious treatises in Urdu in the lower primary classes, the school would have become most popular among the Muhammadans of Delhi and would have attracted a thousand pupils instead of the 300 which it now has. The appointment of a Shia and a Sunni religious teacher in the lower school may *partly* fulfil the real wishes of the deceased Nawab.

Out of Rs. 600, the monthly income from the endowment, Rs. 230 are spent in paying the teachers of the middle school, Rs. 140 in paying the teachers of the primary school, Rs. 150 as stipends given to poor or distinguished pupils, and Rs. 42 for house-rent.

It may not be out of place to state here that the mausoleum of Nawab Ghaziuddin, which is situated just outside the Ajmeri Gate, was added to his endowment by the Nawab for a school-house. That building has been confiscated by the Government and is occupied by the police. The restoration of the building to the school would relieve the school funds of Rs. 42 a month, which might be utilized in giving scholarships to those Muhammadan pupils of this school who wish to prosecute their studies in the Upper School of Delhi or in the Lahore Government College, and which, being poor, they cannot now usually do.

The present teaching staff of this school is as follows:—

Middle School.

Khwájáh Shȧhuddín, Head Master	100	Rs. a month.
Maulvi Altáf Husain, Háli, Teacher of Oriental language	60	
Mírzá Ahmad Beg, 2nd Master	50	
Maulvi Najmuddin, Teacher of Arithmetic	40	

Primary School.

Master, Imtiyáz Husain, Officiating Head Master	20	not drawing full pay.
Maulvi Umar Ali, 1st Teacher of Persian	30	
„ Abdul Ali, 2nd Teacher of Oriental language	20	
„ Abdul Hakím, 3rd „ „	15	
„ Akbar Mirzá, 4th „ „	12	
„ Báqir Husain, 5th „ „	10	
„ Muzaffar Mirzá, 6th „ „	10	
„ Muhammad Ismail, 7th „ „	10	
Master, Muhammad Salim and Mir Nawáb Ali get their pay out of monthly fees income which amounts to	60	Rs. per mensem.

The school is open to both Hindus and Muhammadans, but the scholarships are only given to the Muhammadans. There is no Hindu teacher employed in the school, and the majority of the teachers are Shias, as the donor belonged to that persuasion.

Statement showing the minor Indigenous Schools in the City of Delhi.

Maktabs and Madrasas.

Quarter of the City.	Locality.	Names of the teachers.	Qualification of the teachers.	No. of pupils.	Subjects taught.	Income.
						Per mensem. Rs.
Billimaran	Munshi Gurdyal Sing's house.	Muhammad Ibrahim	Average	10	Persian, Urdu, & Arithmetic.	10
Pipal Mahadeo	Babú Brij Bhokan's.	Najaf Ali	Ditto	9	Persian & Urdu	5
Dasán	Babú Kidar Nauth's.	Muhammad Abdulla	Ditto	9	Ditto	5-8
Ditto	Munshi Sukhdyal's.	Amán Ullá	Ditto	5	Persian	5
Basar Sita Rám	Hari Shankar's	Maulvi Aladad Khán	Good	20	Persian, Arabic and Arithmetic.	8
Ditto	Rented-house	Bhairon Pershad	Ditto	18	Persian and Urdu.	4
Ditto	Ditto	Wasiruddin	Ditto	22	Ditto	7
Kúncha Pandit	Mosque	Muhammad Bakhsh	Average	4	Arabic and Religion.	3-8
Churi Walan	Akbar Khan's	Abdussamad Khan	Ditto	20	Persian and Arabic.	8
Matya Mahal	Mosque	Fazil Beg	Ditto	5	The Koran	Gratuitously.
Ditto	Ditto	Safdar Husain	Ditto	8	Persian	2
Kalyanpurá	Babú Sunderlal's	Muhammad Ashraf Ali	Ditto	14	Arabic, Persian, Urdu, Arithmetic & the Koran.	4
Haveli Bakhtawar-Khan.	Mosque	Karím Bakhsh	Ditto	25	The Koran	25
Gali Imám	Ditto of Maulvi Mahbúb Ali.	Husain Ashraf	Ditto	25	Ditto	3
Masjid Khhajár	Rented house	Khawaja Amir	Good	7	Persian and Urdu.	8
Baidwara	Ditto	Kanihya Lál	Average	30	Ditto	10
Gali Anár	Ditto	Mirza Alim Beg	Ditto	18	Persian, Urdu, & Arithmetic.	10
Ditto	Ditto	Manohar Lal	Ditto	10	Urdu and Persian.	5
Katra Níl	Ditto	Ilahi Bakhsh	Ditto	40	Ditto	Rs. 3 from Ramji Das.
Gali Pipal	Ditto	Sabir Ali	Ditto	8	Urdu	Rs. 4 from Sho Singh Rai, Gumashta.
Machhli Walán	Mosque	Hafiz Ali Khan	Ditto	35	The Koran	Gratuitously.
Kúncha Chelan	Private house	Mir Rahmat Ali	Ditto	2	Ditto	Rs. 3
Terahá Bairam Khan	Ditto	Ahmed Ali	Ditto	4	Ditto and Urdu	Rs. 2 & food.
Sadar Bázár	Ditto	Kabir Uddin	Ditto	7	The Koran.	
Ditto	Ditto	Abdur Rahman	Ditto	5	Ditto	Gratuitously.
Bangla Sayyid Firos	Mosque	Mir Sahib	Ditto	6	Ditto	About Rs. 1-6
Ditto	Ditto	Khuda Bakhsh	Ditto	5	Ditto	Ditto.
Gali Kanchni	Private house	Abdulla Shah	Ditto	2	Ditto	Ditto.
Mori Gate	Ditto	Abdullá	Ditto	6	Ditto	Ditto.
Dhobiwárá	Ditto	Bakhshi	Ditto	8	Ditto	Ditto.
Kishan Gunj	Ditto	Mussamát Hamidunnisa.	Ditto	10	Ditto	10 as.
						Per mensem. Rs.
Shish Mahal	Mosque	Amír Ali	Ditto	16	Ditto	2
Ditto	Ditto	Mir Naím	Ditto	12	Ditto	2
Ditto	Ditto	Mahbub	Ditto	22	Ditto	2-8
Sabzi Mandi	Ditto	Ali Bakhsh	Ditto	18	Ditto	2
Dtto	Ditto	Sheikh Abdulla	Ditto	8	Ditto	Gratuitously.
Bara Hindu Rao	Ditto	Sheikh Ali Bakhsh	Ditto	6	Ditto	2
Deputy Gunj	Ditto	Hafiz Abdulla	Ditto	10	Ditto	7
Khirki Ibrahim Ali Khan	Ditto	Maulvi Naimullah	. . .	8	The Koran	8 as.
Katrah Nil, Gali Nai Basti.	Private house	Maulvi Ilahi	. . .	8	Persian and Urdu.	5
Katrah Nil	Mosque	Maulvi Mazhar Ali	. . .	15	The Koran	5
Gali Saidanyan	Ditto	Maulvi Fateh Muhammad.	. . .	4	Persian	4
Kuncha' Qabil-Attár	Ditto	Muhammad Husain Ali.	. . .	18	The Koran	3
Zeri Diwari Bagh	Ditto	Muhammad Abdul Razaq.	. . .	6	The Koran and Persian.	3
Hamilton Road	Ditto	Khuda Bakhsh	. . .	5	The Koran	Gratuitously.
Badarrau Gate	Ditto	Abdulla	. . .	5	Ditto	Ditto.
Dor Walan	Ditto	Bakhshi	. . .	8	Ditto	Ditto.
						Per mensem. Rs.
Road Kabli Gate	Ditto	Muhammad Ali Khan	. . .	16	Ditto	3
Ditto	Ditto	Abdulla Khan	. . .	16	Ditto	5
Barahdari Nawab Wazir.	Ditto	Muhammad Asadgul	. . .	10	Ditto	Gratuitously.
Phatak Husain Khan.	Private house	Hafiz Ilahi Bukhsh	. . .	10	Ditto	Re. 1 per mensem and 3 annas at the beginning of every section of the Koran.
Gali M. Qadim	Mosque	Hafiz Abdurrahman	. . .	5	Ditto	Gratuitously.
						Per mensem. Rs.
Kuncha Bulaqi Begam.	Asimulla's house.	M. Muhammad Ahmad.	. . .	1	Arabic	4

Statement showing the minor Indigenous Schools in the City of Delhi—**continued.**

Maktabs and Madrasas—*contd.*

Quarter of the City.	Locality.	Names of the teachers.	Qualification of the teachers.	No. of pupils.	Subjects taught.	Income.
Bazar Dariba	Mosque	Karim Bakhsh	. . .	7	The Koran	Per mensem. Rs. Ditto.
Gali Anar	Ramji Das' house	Abdul Ghani	. . .	45	Ditto	15
Mosque Khajur	Raghnath Sahai's house.	Hafiz Najf Ali	. . .	6	The Koran	6
Haweli Jugal Kishor	Murli Dhar's house.	M. Muhayuddin	. . .	5	Ditto	4
Chira Khanah	Private house	Sham Lal	. . .	15	Persian	4
Ditto	Kashi Nath's house.	Mirza Muhammad	. . .	22	Ditto	Gratuitously.
Mosque Khajur	Bihari Lal's house.	Nasiruddin Ahmad	. . .	5	Ditto	Per mensem. Rs. 2-8
Katrah Khushal Rai	Ishari Parshad's house.	Qasim Ali Khan	. . .	12	Ditto	5
Kuncha Rahman	Mosque Pipal wali.	M. Abdul Ghafur	. . .	2	The Koran	1
Ditto	Tafazzal Husan's house.	Hafiz Muhammad Beg Khan.	. . .	2	Ditto	1
Maliwarah	House	Alah Bakhsh	. . .	4	Ditto	10 as.
Billimaran	Mosque	Khuda Bakhsh	. . .	2	Ditto	8 as.
Katrah Abbu	Muhammad Amir's house.	Muhammad Amir	. . .	2	Ditto	Rent-free tenure holder.
Billimaran	Mosque	Mir Qadir Ali	. . .	8	Ditto	As. 8 per mensem, and also rent-free tenure holder.
Ghattahwalan	Ditto	Maulvi	. . .	12	Ditto	Per mensem 12 as.
Katrah Bajwaryan	Ditto	Muhammad Umar	. . .	10	Ditto	As. 8 and rent-free tenure holder.
Gali Qasim Jan	Ditto	Master Hamidulla	. . .	2	English	Per mensem Rs. 7
Ditto	Ditto	Maulvi Alah Din	. . .	1	Persian	8
Ditto	Dy. Hadi Husain's house.	Muhammad Ali	. . .	2	Arabic and Persian.	5
Ditto	Ditto	Master Imtyaz Husain.	. . .	2	English	5
Katrah Alim Beg	House	Ahmad Husain	. . .	8	The Koran	1-8
Gali Qasim Ali	Dy. Hadi Husain's house.	Ahmad Ali	. . .	4	Urdu, Persian and Koran.	5
Billimaran	Hasan Khan's house.	Sayad Zaman	. . .	2	Arabic and Persian.	...
Barahdari Sher Afgan Khan	Hakumat Rai's house.	Abdul Karim	. . .	2	Urdu, Persian and English.	8
Ditto	House	Maulvi Barkat	. . .	4	The Koran	Rent-free tenure holder.
Pipal Mahadeo	Ramji Das's house	Chhajju Lal	. . .	1	Persian	Per mensem. Rs. 1
Sarak Jadid	Mosque	Habibullah	. . .	14	The Koran	1-8
Maktab Mir Jumla	Ditto	Hafiz Qadir Bakhsh	. . .	8	Ditto	8
Bazar Lal Chah	Ditto	Basharatullah	. . .	2	Ditto	Rent-free tenure holder.
Gali Chabuksawaran	Ditto	Abdul Mujid	. . .	5	Ditto	Per mensem. Rs. 1-8
Katrah Baryan	Latif Bakhsh's house.	Munshi Kulin Singh	. . .	5	Urdu and Persian.	2
Naya Bans	House	Mir Hassan	. . .	5	Urdu	7
Kuncha Sanjogi Ram	Siri Nawas' house	Khuda Bakhsh	. . .	1	Ditto	4
Katrah Adina Beg Khan.	Najf Khan's house.	Abul Razaq	. . .	5	Persian	4
Gali Mir Madari	Mosque	Hafiz Abdul Rahman	. . .	8	The Koran	...
Hauz Qazi	Ditto	Yaqub Ali	. . .	4	Arabic	...
Mosque Kalan	Ditto	Abdul Qadir	. . .	3	The Koran	...
Gali Imam	Ghulam Jilani's house.	Hafizuddin	. . .	8	Persian, Urdu and the Koran.	10
Kuncha Mir Ashiq	Mosque	Abdul Aziz	. . .	4	Ditto	...
Churiwalan	Janki Nath's house.	Jalaluddin	. . .	1	Persian	3
Chitli Qabar	Muhammad Ali's house.	Agha Mirza	. . .	7	The Koran	2-8
Gali Mufti (Tiraha Bairam Khan).	Ihsanul Haq's house.	Hafiz Ghulam Husai.	. . .	8	Persian and the Koran.	2
Ditto	Akhlaq Husain's house.	Wazir Muhammad Khan.	. . .	4	Ditto	2
Ditto	Bahauddin's house.	M. Qasim Raza Beg	. . .	2	Ditto	3
Zer Jama Masjid	Mosque	Hafiz Ali Khan	. . .	20	The Koran	...
Kuncha Chelan	House	Hafiz Haidar Ali	. . .	8	Ditto	2
Ditto	Murtaza Khan's house.	Abdurrashid and Amirul Shuja.	. . .	2	Persian and Urdu.	5
Ditto	Sharf Din's house	Mahammad Ishaq	. . .	10	Arabic	Gratuitously.
Haweli 'Azam Khan	Mosque	Nuruddin	. . .	1	Ditto	Ditto.
Aqabi Kalan Mahal	Ahmad Hasan's house.	Ahmad Hasan and Mukarram Hasan.	. . .	2	Ditto	Ditto.
Kuncha Baber Khan	Mosque	Inayet Husain	. . .	8	Ditto	Per mensem Rs. 4 annas
Mandi Kohnah	Muhammad Hasan's house.	Ilahi Bakhsh	. . .	14	The Koran	2

***Statement showing the minor Indigenous Schools in the City of Delhi*—concluded.**

MAKTABS AND MADRASAS—*concld.*

Quarter of the City.	Locality.	Names of the teachers.	Qualification of the teachers.	No. of pupils.	Subjects taught.	Income.
Lal Katra	Karim Bakhsh's house.	Ghulam Rasul		3	Persian	Per mensem. Rs. 3
Teliwara	Shish Mahall	Mir Alim Ali		9	The Koran	
Pull Bangash	Mosque	Mir Ahmad Ali		15	Ditto	
Shidipurah	Ditto	Ahmad Ali		3	Ditto	
Ditto	Ditto	Natthe Khan		3	Ditto	1-8
Qassabpurah	Ditto	Abdur Rahman		20	Ditto	...
Ditto	Ditto	Abdul Karim		8	Ditto	...
Sadarbazar	Maktab Bala Khanah.	Jan Muhammad		16	The Koran and Persian.	7
Sarak Bahadar Garh	Maktab	Amir Ali Khan		10	The Koran	7
Ditto	Mosque	Rahmatullah		2	Ditto	...
Bazar Kalan	Ditto	Rahimuddin.		15	Arabic, Persian and Urdu.	Rent-free tenure holder.
Chandiwalan	House	Ummaid Ali		10	Arabic	Ditto.
Haweli Bakhtawar Khan.	Mosque	Ismail Qadir Ali		25	The Koran	Per mensem. Rs. 15

LIST OF LANDE, SARAFI AND MAHAJANI SCHOOLS AT DELHI.

Quarter of the City.	Locality.	Names of the teachers.	Qualification of the teachers.	No. of pupils.	Subjects taught.	Income.
Nahar Sadat Khan		Bishamber		7	Lande	Re. 1 per mensem and 8 as. from each pupil when he has finished his course.
Gali Kuljas		Shiv Dyal		20	Arithmetic, Mahajani and Sarafi.	Gratuitously.
Kucha Lattu Shah		Maida Missar		3	Lande and Sarafi	Ditto.
Dharmpurah		Girdhari Lal		50	Ditto	Per mensem. Rs. 6
Kinari Bazar		Bishen Dass		12	Ditto	Gratuitously.
Baidwarah		Kanhiya Lal		30	Lande Nagri	Per mensem. Rs. 10
Ditto		Ganga Sahai		25	Nagri	10
Ditto		Badri Missar		15	Sarafi	3
Katrah Mahesh Dass		Baldeo		6	Ditto	Gratuitously.
Kúcha Khan Chand		Dovi Sahai		25	Ditto	Per mensem. Rs. 5
Chhatta Gosaín Makkhan Lal.		Lalji Parshad		20	Mahajani	Rs. 2 per mensem and flour, &c.
Basar Haus Qazí		Harna Lal		20	Ditto	Per mensem. Rs. 1
Katrah Baddú		Fateh Chand		20	Lande Nagrí	10
Pipal Mahadeo		Phirya Lal, Brahmin		40	Lande Mahajani Sarafi.	4 and kind.
Churi Walán		Dya Ram Misser		12	Ditto	4
Kocha Pati Rám		Mul Chand Misser		13	Ditto	5
Farrásh Khaná		Fatah Chand Misser		20	Ditto	10
Deputy Gunj		Pirag Dat		65	Ditto and Nagri	15
Sadar Bazár		Naththu Misser		20	Ditto	3
Khari Baoli		Mul Chand		20	Ditto	10
Naya Báns		Jawalá Misser		40	Ditto	5
Koncha Sanjogi Rám		Banai Misser		16	Ditto	3
Gandi Gali		Parshadi Misser		20	Ditto	4
Katra Mashrú		Jawala Pundit		50	Ditto	5
Koncha Seth		Kanhya Lál		7	Ditto	2
Dharampurá		Bainí Misser		20	Ditto	6
Chhipí Wara		Jagannanth		5	Ditto	0-8 as.
Naiwara		Ganga Pershád		8	Ditto	2
Baidwara		Keri Misser		10	Ditto	4
Maliwara		Harpershad		20	Ditto	4
Katra Níl		Madan Mohan		40	Ditto	5
Koncha Ghasi Rám		Chunni Lál		20	Ditto	3
Marand		Sarti Misser		13	Ditto	2
Dharampura		Janki Misser		60	Ditto	6

PÁTSHALAS.

Quarter of the City.	Locality.	Names of the teachers.	Qualification of the teachers.	No. of pupils.	Subjects taught.	Income.
Katra Mashru	Shop	Naththu Misser	Good	5	Sanscrit and Nagri.	Gratuitously.
Matya Mahal	Pandit Shankar Datt's house.	Shankar Dat	Do.	2	Sanscrit	Ditto.
Kucha Lalman	Private house	Badhi Misser	Do.	2	Ditto	Ditto.
Kucha Parmanand	Temple of Sanwal Das.	Balmukand	Do.	2	Ditto	Ditto.

The largest pátshala in Delhi is in the "koncha" of Mahi Dass, attached to the house of Lala Bhagwán Dass, Sahúkár. Pandit Gobind Ram, one of the most distinguished Sanscrit scholars in Delhi, instructs 30 pupils in Sanscrit Literature and is paid Rs. 10 per mensem with food and clothes by Lala Bhagwan Das, Sahúkár.

The largest *Mahajani* school is in the Billimarán quarter, conducted by Imam Ali who teaches Mahajani to 80 pupils, who pay him Rs. 25 per mensem.

THÁNA MOHNA.—Maulvi Haidar Ali is a distinguished Arabic scholar. Hatim Ali is the eminent Maulvi of this place; he is the teacher of the maktab at *Mohna* which is attached to Mir Barkat Ali Resaldar's house; 10 pupils attend and the subjects taught are the Koran and Persian. Hatim Ali gets Rs. 4 per mensem and his food and clothes.

Chandpur has a large pátshala, where Pandit Khyali Ram instructs 25 pupils in Nagri, Arithmetic, History and Geography and Religion. The Pandit gets Rs. 6 per mensem and his food.

THÁNA NANGLOI.—*Tingri* has a Mahajani school with 4 pupils; *Nolká* 1 with 6; *Shakurpur* 1 with 8; *Nagarwala* 1 with 10, and *Kanjawah* 1 with 12 pupils; in these five schools Mahajani and Hindi are taught.

Khor has a maktab with 8 pupils.

THÁNA BALAB GARH.—Ganga Balab *Baid* is mentioned as an eminent physician.

Shamápur has a maktab in the house of Rani Umrao Kour; a Brahmin, Radhakishen, teaches 5 boys Urdu and gets Rs. 5 per mensem from Rani Umrao Kour. *Balabgarh*, *Sooni* and *Karnera* have a pátshala each with 8, 14, and 2 pupils attending respectively. At *Sooni*, where there is the largest pátshala, Kedar Nath is the teacher and gets Rs. 3 per mensem.

THÁNA ALIPUR.—In the village *Holumbi* is the principal maktab, in charge of Sarfaraz Ali. It is attached to a private house; Persian, Urdu and Arithmetic are taught and 8 pupils attend; the teacher gets Rs. 4 per mensem and food from the Head Lambardar. *Naraila* has a small maktab, with only 4 pupils, in which Persian, Urdu and Arithmetic are taught.

Khera has a pátshala, where Murli Ram teaches 6 pupils Sanscrit; he gets corn at harvest time. There are the following Mahajani schools in this Thana:—1 at *Naraila* with 11 pupils; 1 at *Holumbi* with 9; 1 at *Jaute* with 13; 1 at *Bakhtawarpur* with 15; and 1 at *Halalpur* with 15 pupils. Mahajani and Sarafi are taught.

THÁNA FARIDABAD.—*Ajronda* has a maktab in the house of Kanwar Tej Singh; Ghulam Muhamad, of average qualifications, is the teacher and gets Rs. 3 per mensem and food; Police returns mentioned 4 and private returns 5 pupils. Persian and Urdu are taught. *Beroli* has a large pátshala with 30 pupils, Ganga Sahai teaches Nagri and Arithmetic and gets Rs. 7 per mensem (private returns state Rs. 5). At *Dosya* is another pátshala with 20 pupils, (private returns mention Gopal as the teacher, who gets Rs. 5 per mensem and teaches Nagri and Arithmetic); also that these schools are in the village halls (Chopal).

THÁNA MEHROLI.—At Mehroli itself is a maktab attached to a mosque, where Hafiz Nur Muhammad teaches the Koran to 15 boys. He gets only his food (the private return mentions Rs. 3 per mensem). In this place is also a Mahajani school where Kurya Ram, a Brahmin, teaches Hindi and Mahajani to 10 boys (private return states 15 boys). He gets Rs. 2-8 per mensem, (private return gives Rs. 4-8 cash and 8 annas in kind).

MAJHOLI.—There is 1 pátshala where Lakhi Ram teaches Sanscrit and Mahajani gratuitously to 3 boys; also a Mahajani school with 7 pupils.

Kabulpur (*Khurd*).—The maktab here is under Syed Ahsani Rasul, who is a well qualified man, teaches the Koran and Urdu, has 7 pupils, and gets Rs. 12 cash.

Kabulpur (*Kalan*) has a small maktab with 2 pupils only, in which Urdu is taught. It is stated in the return that owing to the poverty of the inhabitants they cannot support any teachers, and that if some schools for Persian and Nagri were provided for them, it would be a real boon to the people.

SOONIPAT.—Maulvi Imar Ali is well known here. The teacher of the best maktab is Inayet Khan, a man of average qualifications; he has 12 pupils, teaches Persian and the Koran and gets Rs. 3 per mensem. *Soonipat* has three other maktabs, 1 with 9, 1 with 13 and 1 with 8 pupils; in all three the Koran and Persian are taught. In the temple of the Saraogis at Soonipat is a pátshala in charge of Sabá Chand, who is a good scholar; the instruction is purely religious; he has 10 pupils and gets Rs. 4 per mensem. *Mohana* has a Mahajani school with 12 pupils; Kheman, their teacher, gets Rs. 4 per mensem. *Khubrá* and *Ratangarh* have each a Mahajani school with 10 and 2 pupils attending, respectively. Only Mahajani is taught.

Datoli has a Mahajani school with 8 pupils. *Biga* has the largest school of that description in this circle; Daleep, teacher, instructs 15 pupils in Mahajani. There is also a smaller one at *Supera* with 6 pupils. *Gadhi Lala* has a maktab attached to a private house where Persian is taught; Raziuddin is the teacher, he has 8 pupils, is a well qualified man and gets Rs. 4 per mensem and food. At *Gaúr* is a Koran school attached to the mosque, where Hafiz Habibullah has 12 pupils. He only gets his food.

THÁNA NAJAFGURH.—Pandit Ramji Lal, of the village *Dhasa*, is an eminent pandit, who gives instruction to 2 boys gratis in Sanscrit. There is a patshala at Dhasa, where Deodat teaches gratuitously Hindi and Nagri to 3 pupils and Mahajani and Arithmetic to 3 pupils. *Revalya* has a Mahajani school with 6 pupils. *Hastal* and *Ghuman Hera* have each a pátshala with 4 pupils attending at each.

HAVELI PALAM is added to the preceding thána returns in a "private return."

In the village at *Haveli Palam* itself is a pátshala, attached to the Village Hall, in which Uttum Chand, who knows Kaumudi very well, and has also a Normal school certificate, instructs 5 pupils in religious books and in the Kaumudi in Sanscrit, and has an income of about Rs. 2 per mensem.

There is a Mahajani school in the village of *Shahjahanpur Kotla*, under Harsewak, with 15 pupils, who learn Mahajani and religious books and pay Rs. 7 per mensem to the teacher.

DELHI DIVISION.

GURGAON DISTRICT.

GENERAL ABSTRACT.

District.	No. of Maktabs and Madrasas.	No. of pupils.	No. of Sanscrit and Nagri Schools.	No. of pupils.	No. of Gurmukhi Schools.	No. of pupils.	No. of Hindi Mahajani Schools	No. of pupils.	Total No. of Indigenous Schools.	Total No. of pupils.
Gurgaon	24	236	6	65	...	...	25	358	55	659

THÁNA HASANPUR.—The police returns mention no Maulvis, Pandits or Bhais of this thána.

In *Sultanpur* village there is a good Maulvi, Nabi Bakhsh, teaching Arabic and Persian to 12 pupils in Sayyad Nazir Ali's house, who receives his food and Rs. 2-8 per mensem. All the other important villages (?) of this thána have Government schools.

THÁNA NUH.—In *Shikarpur* in the chaupal or village hall, Ahmad Khan, of Ferozepore, teaches the two sons of Mattu Zaildar the Urdu Grammar and Primer, and receives food and Rs. 2-8 per mensem.

In *Taru* there is a good Sanscrit school conducted by Umrao Singh, who teaches the Amarkosh and Shikar Bodh gratuitously to 2 pupils.

THÁNA HATTÍN.—In *Hattin* as also *Jaffna* and *Mandraka*, there are schools teaching Sanscrit, Nagri, &c., of which the first is attached to a temple and the two latter are held in private houses; the names of the teachers being Munshi Nathu and Jumna Das, respectively. They are attended by 16, 5 and 10 pupils each. The income amounts to Rs. 30 per annum for each teacher, who also gets his food given him.

SOHNA.—Among the *Hakims*, Mirza Muhammed Beg and Dr. Sayyad Gholam Husain (who has retired and is practising as a private physician, using native drugs, as European drugs are not easily obtainable out of larger towns) deserve being noticed. The retired doctor is also an author. Among *Baids* Dhani Ram holds a good position.

Pandit Shadi Ram, a distinguished poet. is also *facile princeps* among his colleagues.

There are two good schools at Sohna; one situated in the Kaziwara quarter and the other in Kaitwara, both in private houses.

Haji Abdullah teaches (in Kazi Wahid-ud-din's house) Persian and the Koran, as also Arithmetic up to division to 12 boys (private returns have 14), and gets Rs. 3 per mensem (private returns only mention food and clothes from the Kazi). The other school (not mentioned by the police) is conducted by Pur Mal, who can teach English up to the Entrance Standard and who teaches that language, as also Persian and Arithmetic, to 4 pupils and gets Rs. 10 per mensem and food. He teaches the sons of Munshi Hardyal Sing. There is also a good Sanscrit school under *Pandit Shadi Ram*, a very good scholar, who teaches gratuitously the Puranas, Vedas (the Yajur Veda), Panini's Grammar, Prosody (Kavya Kosh Alankar and Chhand), as also Astrology, to 10 pupils gratuitously. The pupils attending his school come from distant villages, and *therefore*, as the Pandit explains, "no fees could be taken from them." The police returns state—"The wealthy students live on their own resources and the poor students are fed by the teacher."

There are two Mahajani schools in *Sohna* proper and *Sarmithla*, respectively, conducted, the former by Ganga Jiwan with 16 pupils paying Rs. 7 per mensem

(Rs. 2 by *siddha* explained elesewhere); the latter by Kedar Das teaching 5 pupils who pay him Rs. 2-8 in cash and 2-8 in siddha.

PUNAHANA.—Among *Baids*, Dula Ram and Zahiria are prominent, whilst among *Pandits* the names of Mohun Lall and Gudder are known.

At *Bisru* in the village hall *Baqar Ali* teaches the Koran and a little Persian to 8 boys and gets Rs. 4 per mensem. This circle is entirely inhabited by Meos, so more can scarcely be expected.

FARAKHNAGAR CIRCLE.—Maulvis Abdul Aziz and Abdul Hakim, good scholars, teach Arabic and Persian in the two Farakhnagar mosques to 27 pupils, receiving Rs. 5 per mensem each.

There are three Mahajani schools under Ramsaran, Ram Das and Ghasi respectively, teaching Nagri and Sarafi to 101 pupils and receiving Rs. 8 per mensem.

There is also a Mahajani school at Sultanpur under Ram Sahai with 7 pupils.

There is finally an Arabic school at Sultanpur under Muhammad Jan, but it appears that his pupils are included under the 27 first named.

The reporter says—"The pátshalas are really chatsalas, and they, as also the Madrasas, are of a middle standard."

PALWAL.—Two Hakims are mentioned as belonging to this place, Muhammad Ismail and Aminudin.

There are five maktabs in Palwal, which are in private houses; the names of the teachers, who have moderate qualifications, are Hafiz Bidha, Gholam Ali, Shujaet Ali and Hafiz Munna. These maktabs have an average attendance of about 37 boys, and they are taught the Koran and elementary Persian books. The teachers are paid in money and kind which amounts to about 6 annas per mensem for every boy. Palwal has also a Mahajani school attended by 20 boys.

The village *Chandant* has 1 maktab with 9 pupils; *Durgapore* also 1 maktab with only 3 pupils; whilst *Bagpore* has 1 Mahajani school with 7; *Dighot* 1 with 16; *Solrah* 1 with 6; *Ghori* 1 with 10; *Bilái* 1 with 6; *Mandkol* 1 with 5; and *Sohal* 1 Mahajani school with 5 pupils; in all of which Mahajani and Hindi are taught.

HODAL.—Hakim Shib Lal and Pandits Bhawani and Gangal are mentioned as distinguished in this place.

As for the schools, the police return says that there is no school there worthy of notice, and that the baniahs get their children taught Sarafi and shop-keeping either at their own shops or at those of their relatives.

FIROZPUR.—Pandit Polia Swami and Baids Amir Chand and Dil Sukh are mentioned in this place, which seems to have no maktab or Madrasa, but only a Mahajani school attended by 5 boys; but in *Sakurus* there is one maktab with 8 pupils reading Arabic and Persian, and also a Mahajani school with 5 or 6 boys; in *Marura* a Mahajani school with 5; at *Umarah* a maktab with 5; at *Nagina* a maktab with 12, and at *Biwan* a Mahajani school with 7 pupils.

RIWARI.—The following famous Hakims, Maulvis and Pandits reside in Riwari:—*Hakims* Najmuddin, Wahiduddin, Abdul Rahim, Matlub Husain, Basdeo, Ram Sahai, Ram Richpal Dhusar, Abdul Wahab, Ahsan Ali, Muhammad Ali, Fazl Mahmud, Harnarain and Shiv Sahai; *Maulvis* Nur Ali, Gholam Husain, Abdul Wási (also an author), Ilahi Baksh, Gholam Muhammad, Muhammaduddin Khan, Mulla Fazl Din, Mir Muhammad Husain and Nur Muhammed; *Pandits* Natha Singh and Dev Dat, both grammarians; Bishen Mitter and Ram Sahai, astrologers; Pandits Jaiturjee Swami, Sholoji, Ram Sewak Gujrati, Bhan Singh and Pandit Maha Singh.

The police do not return any maktab from Riwari; the private returns give four maktabs; *one* in the Lal Masjid, teacher Maulvi Nur Muhammad, eminent in theology, has 8 pupils, but no income. The *second* maktab is in the mosque of the Besatis, teacher Rahim Bakhsh, has read the Koran, has 20 boys, Rs.4 per mensem; the *third* school is in the Mahalla Palladaran, the teacher is Maulvi Muhammad Din, is a fair theologian, has 10 pupils to whom he teaches the Koran; the *fourth* is in the Maktari quarter, teacher Mulla Mahmud, teaches Koran to 20 boys and gets Rs. 3 per mensem.

There is a pátshala in Riwari in the Bauli Bazar, conducted gratuitously by an excellent Pandit, Deo Datt, and his brother Bishen; the Jotish, Viakarn, Bhagwat, Puran, &c., are taught, and the police return mentions 35 pupils, whilst the private retuins only name 22. There are two Mahajani schools at this place, one according to police returns with 30, though private returns name 40 pupils. Hindi and Mahajani are taught. The teachers' fees amount to Rs. 2-8 per mensem; private returns state "one anna to write a patti, and flour on the 12th of the Hindu month and two annas per boy on the Chauk Chandi festival which occurs twice a year." The other in the Bazar Bazazan where 20 boys are taught patti and slate writing by Kana. In *Chintwara* is also a school of exactly the same kind whose teacher is Umrao Singh and the number of pupils 15.

Gurganwa (Gurgaon).—Pandit Hira Lal is mentioned as a distinguished Pandit. In the Gurganwa Cantonments is a maktab which is attached to a private house; the teacher is Faiz 'Ali, who instructs about 13 pupils in Persian, and gets Rs. 6 per mensem and his food. There are also two smaller maktabs with 5 and 7 pupils, respectively, in which Persian and the Koran are taught.

The villages *Mauza Jharsa, Badshahpur* and *Mauza Gurganwa* have each one Mahajani school with 7, 20 and 10 pupils, respectively.

Shahjahanpur has only one Mahajani school where a Brahmin, named Ananda, teaches Mahajani to about 12 boys at a shop. He is paid at the rate of 2 annas a boy.

———

DELHI DIVISION.

KARNAL DISTRICT.

GENERAL ABSTRACT.

District.	No. of Maktabs and Madrasas.	No. of pupils.	No. of Sanscrit and Nagri schools.	No. of pupils.	No. of Gurmakhi schools.	No. of pupils.	No. of Mahajani schools.	No. of pupils.	Total No. of indigenous schools.	Total No. of pupils.
Karnal ...	43	538	11	111	1	8	22	385	77	1,042

PANIPAT.—Among the *Hakims* in Panipat, Haidar Husain, Muhammad Husain, Manjú Khan, and Barkat Ali, and among the *Baids*, Mulchand may be mentioned.

The place is famous for the number of its Hafizes (*i. e.* those who know the Koran by heart). Among the *Maulvis*, Maulvi Abdurrahman, Maulvi Rahim Bakhsh and Maulvi Raghibulla deserve notice. The last Maulvi conducts an Arabic Muhammadan school, located in the house of Kazi Sanaulla and teaches Arabic Grammar, Logic, Philosophy, Hadis, Tafsir (exegesis of the Koran) from Mizan-us-sarf to Shams Ba-zigha to 24 pupils. He receives Rs. 20 per mensem, raised by subscription among the Muhammadans of the town. Besides this school there are 20 Koran schools in the town, attended by 260 pupils, out of which 6 *are conducted by female teachers.*

Among the *Pandits*, Pandit Bhagwan Dass, Jainti Lal, Jawahar Lal and Badri Dass seem to deserve notice. There are 2 Mahajani schools in the town under Jog Dyan and Azimulla, respectively. The number of the pupils attending these schools is 25 and 30 respectively; the income of each teacher amounts to Rs. 6 per mensem.

The villages of *Kotani* and *Simla* of Gujars have each a Mahajani school, conducted by Ganga Ram Padha and Gulab Padha, with 8 and 4 pupils, and Rs. 2 and Rs. 4 as their monthly income respectively.

SAMÁLKA.—In this circle there is no indigenous *maktab* or *madrasa*, but there are *patshálas* in the villages of *Samálka, Manana* and *Jorási Khálsá.* The two patshálas in Samálka are conducted by Pandit Sita Ram and Pandit, Raja Ram, who are good Sanscrit scholars and teach Sanscrit, Astrology, Grammar and Dharm Shaster gratuitously. The other two pátshalas in Manana and Jorasi Khalsa are under Har Lal Guzrati and Pandit Sewag Ram respectively. The number of pupils attending the above pátshalas is 52.

Hakim Ghulam Rasúl, the teacher of the Government school, Samalka, practises as a native physician.

BATAṆA.—Among the Hakims, Qalandar Bakhsh, a native of Tiraori, may be noticed.

Madrasas.—In the village *Ranba* there are two Madrasas, one attached to the mosque of Mirdad, conducted by Ahmad Husain (*alias* Masita), son of Sheikh Qalandar Bakhsh, and Amir Husain as a monitor (*i.e.* Khalifa), teaching the Koran and Gulistan, Bostan and Bahar Danish to 28 pupils and receiving daily food, and 50 maunds of corn at harvest time and one rupee cash on every marriage in the village; the other is a maktab attached to the house of Mathra Mahajan, where Gharib, son of Hardwari, who was educated in the Government school of Kachhú, teaches the first and second books of Urdú and Persian up to Gulistan and Bostan to 8 pupils, each of whom gives him 4 annas a month and food once a week.

There is also a *Mahajani* school in Ranba under Kanihya Lál, son of Buddhú Jogi, who teaches Lande and Nagri to 13 boys, each of whom gives him 4 annas a month and food once a week.

ALUPUR.—In the village of *Korana* there is a maktab attached to the house of the Ziladar (a Government employé in the Irrigation Department) under Amanullah, a teacher of mediocre abilities, who teaches 8 pupils Persian (Gulistan and Bahar Danish) and receives Rs. 7 per mensem.

Korana has also 2 *pátshalas* conducted by Het Ram and Parmanand, who teach Sanscrit to 29 pupils gratuitously. *Alupur*, another village in the circle, has a Sanscrit pátshala, where Pandit Hardwari teaches Sanscrit to 10 pupils gratis.

There are Mahajani schools in the villages of *Bhalsi*, *Urlana* and *Qawi* under Salig Ram, Lodar Jogi and Shib Lal Rajpút, with 10, 15, 16 pupils, and Rs. 5, 4, 3-12 is the income of the teachers, respectively.

KUNJPURA.—There are 2 Madrasas attached to the houses of Nawab Jánbaz Khan and Nawab Ali Muhammad Khan, in which Abdulkarim and Abdulla teach the Koran to 15 and 6 boys, respectively, and are paid each Rs. 2 per mensem and food once a week.

SINK.—In this circle there is no eminent Hakim or Maulvi, but Dhendha and Ishq Lal, two barbers, practise as native physicians and surgeons.

In *Sink* proper there is a Koran school attached to the village mosque, in which Hafiz Abdulla "Ranghar" (the Muhammadan Rajputs are called so), teaches the Koran to 8 pupils gratuitously; he knows Persian also. He is ready to comply with any reasonable conditions of grant-in-aid.

The villages of *Balú* and *Agwand* have 2 Mahajani schools under *Nanda* and *Dilpat* Jogis, with 6 and 8 pupils who pay them 8 annas a month each.

INDREE.—Among the Hakims only Dindyal Brahman, a physician practising the Yunani system of medicine, is of some note. Pandits Tulsi Ram in the village of Kalsura and Dhami Dat in Pathan Kheri, who have been educated in Benares, deserve notice.

In the villages of *Janerun* and *Joro Majra* and *Gadhpur* are maktabs under Abdulla, Abdulkarim and Abdurrahman, respectively, in which the Koran and elementary books in Persian are taught. The number of the pupils in the above schools is 4, 1 and 8, respectively. Abdulkarim is given food, clothes and opium expenses, and Abdulla, who teaches gratis, can teach advanced books in Persian and arithmetic to decimal fractions.

In the village of *Badarpur*, Molar Brahmin teaches Sanscrit Grammar and Astrology to 5 pupils gratuitously.

In the villages of *Dhumsi*, *Jorpur*, *Fazilpur*, *Bhira*, *Oadhi Birbal* and *Kharya Darpanpur*, Mahajani is taught to 3, 2, 4, 12, 10 and 25 pupils, respectively, who pay their teachers an annual fee from 8 annas to 1 rupee, a pice once a week on Sunday (called Itwári), daily food and, in some cases, winter clothes also.

KARNAL.—Among the Hakims, Rahmatulla, and among the Pandits and Maulvis, Maulvi Ghulam Muhammad and Pandit Kashi Ram deserve notice. Maulvi Ghulam Muhammad conducts a *Madrasa* with Maulvi Salahuddin as his assistant. The Madrasa is situated in the Kalandar Gate quarter and has 25 pupils, who learn Arabic and Persian. The Head Maulvi and his assistant are paid Rs.15 and 6 per mensem out of the subscription raised for the purpose among the Muhammadans of the town. There is also a purely Persian maktab attached to the house of Nazir Kundan Lal with 12 pupils, and 6 Koran schools attached to the mosques with 67 pupils in them where only the Koran is taught.

Karnal has 3 *pátshalas* in which Sanscrit is taught gratuitously by Pandits Ram Saran Das, Pali Ram and Durga Das, in their private houses to 15 pupils.

Pádhás Umádat and Bihari teach Mahajani to 50 and 15 pupils, respectively.

KAITHAL.—In Kaithal, Sayed Barkat Ali, who can teach Persian up to Abulfazl, teaches Persian and the Koran to 15 pupils in his house and gets Rs. 3 per mensem.

Besides this there is a Mahajani school with 70 pupils, conducted by Imamuddin who gets Rs. 6 per mensem in cash and something also in kind.

GOHLA.—In the village of *Gohla*, Sayyid Shah Muhammad, who knows Arabic, Persian and Arithmetic, conducts a school in which 20 pupils, sons of agriculturists from the village and neighbouring villages, are taught Persian, Arithmetic, the Koran and religious books; is paid Rs. 4 per mensem with food and clothes by Muhammad Bakhsh, Lumberdar of the village.

PUNDRI.—Among the Pandits in Pundri, Pandit Daya Lal, and among the Hakims, Hakim Amanulla may be noted.

In this circle there is only one Mahajani school in *Pundri* under Shaikh Rahim Bakhsh, who teaches Lande to 22 pupils and has a monthly income of Re. 1-6 in cash.

DHATRAT.—A *maktab* under Alla Banda, a good Persian scholar, with 12 pupils, has no income from the school and lives on his pension of Rs. 10 per mensem.

A *Koran* school, conducted by a woman, Musammat Zainab, teaching the Koran, Rahnijat and other religious treatises in Urdu to 10 girls gratuitously.

A Hindi *Mahajani* school conducted by Lalji Brahmin with 27 boys, gets Rs. 10 per mensem.

Badladah.—Has a Gurmukhi school under Narain Das, an Udasi Fakir who has 8 *pupils.*

Asandh, has a female school, Mussamat Manan teaching the Koran gratuitously to 12 girls.

HISSAR DIVISION.

HISSAR DISTRICT.

GENERAL ABSTRACT.

District.	No. of Maktabs and Madrasas.	No. of Pupils.	No. of Sanscrit and Nagri Schools.	No. of Pupils.	No. of Gurmukhi Schools.	No. of Pupils.	No. of Lande and Mahajani Schools.	No. of Pupils.	Total No. of Indigenous Schools.	Total No. of Pupils.
Hissar .	46	592	12	133	...	...	8	386	66	1,111

HISSAR.—Among the Hakims of Hissar, Najaf Ali, Sadiq Ali and Sham Lal may be noticed. The Maulvis who deserve notice are Maulvis Ruknuddin, Khuda Bakhsh and Mubarakuddin. Among the Pandits, Hardeo, Ram Gopal, Shadi Ram, Shib Ram and Har Narayen may be mentioned.

In Hissar proper there are three Madrasas, conducted by Rahmatullah Azizuddin and Ghulam Rasul, respectively, who teach Persian and the Koran to 32 pupils. The first two have an income of Rs. 10 per mensem each, and the last one teaches gratuitously, but accepts what his pupils give him as *idi* on festival days.

There is a *patshala* in the village of *Shyam Sukh*, in which Nagri is taught by Jot Ram to 10 pupils, who pay him Rs. 10 per mensem.

In Hissar proper, Khairuddin, son of Abdulla, conducts a Mahajani school consisting of 30 pupils, and is paid Rs. 12 per mensem.

The Police returns say that there are some Pandits in the town, who teach their sons and also some pupils from the distant villages, but no details are given concerning them.

FATAHÁBÁD.—In the village of *Hanspur*, Maulvi Khuda Bakhsh, a good Arabic and Persian scholar, conducts a school which is attached to a mosque and contains 35 students who learn Arabic, Persian and the Koran. The teacher has no fixed income. The pupils, on finishing the Koran, give some donation corresponding to their means. Besides this there are Koran schools in the villages of *Bhirana*, *Eharwa*, *Bhirana*, *Hajrayún* and *Bighar*, with 20, 30, 25, 25, 35 pupils in them respectively. The teachers in these schools teach gratis, and accept what they are given on the finishing of the Koran in the form of *amin* (explained in the body of this Report), and as these donations are not enough to support them, they pursue other professions.

In Fatahábád proper, one Nabi Bakhsh teaches Lande and accounts to 20 boys, and is paid about Rs. 5 per mensem.

BHIWANI.—Among the Baids of Bhiwani, Mota Ram, disciple of Atma Ram Fakir (of the Dadu Panthi sect) and Sheo Narayen, Brahmin, seem to be distinguished.

Pandit Chokhraj, son of Durgadat, in Astrology, Pandit Ramjan in Mahabharat and preaching, and Sham Sukh Brahmin in Sanscrit Literature, have earned a reputation.

Though in every temple there are one or two pupils, a pátshala attached to the temple of Acharis is successfully conducted by a learned Pandit, named Sripat Brahmin (a blind man), who teaches Chandraka, Saraswat and Bhagwat to 15 pupils, and lives upon the income of the temple.

There is a Mahajani school also under Khairati, a Muhammadan of the Patiala State, who is a hereditary Pandha, and who teaches Mahajani to 100 pupils, and has an income of Rs. 100 per annum.

HANSI.—Among the Pandits in *Hansi*, Pandits Nath Mal, Sheo Narayen Kunj Lal and Sukhdeo are eminent, and among the *Hakims*, Ruldu Brahmin, Sheikh Masita aud Muniruddin deserve notice.

There are two maktabs in Hansi; one in the house of a mahajan, is conducted by Qadir Bakhsh, who teaches Persian and Urdu to 20 pupils on Rs. 5 a month, and the other is a Koran school attached to a mosque, where Gami Shah, a man of learning, teaches the Koran to 25 pupils and receives only food.

In Hansi there is also a pátshala in the house of Umadat Brahmin, the teacher, who teaches Sanscrit Grammar, Sarsat, Astrology, Shigar Bodh-Karam Kan, &c., to 8 pupils gratuitously.

Ram Narayen, son of Basto Ram, conducts a Mahajani school, attended by 90 pupils, and receives Rs. 20 per mensem.

RATYA has a pátshala; the teacher, Harjan, who has moderate qualifications, has 19 pupils and teaches Shastri. In the village *Muhamadki* is a maktab which is attached to a mosque, and where Sharfuddin, a blind man, teaches the Koran and Arabic to about 17 pupils. This place has also a Hakim, Mahmúd; another Hakim of repute lives in the village *Alika*. There are a good many "pachhadas" in this circle, who are Muhammadans and learn the Koran in the mosques of various other villages, amongst which the following are mentioned: the maktabs of *Baramdi*, of *Hanaspore* and *Bahmanwala*, with 20, 10 and 10 pupils respectively. The Police returns mention that there are some other villages also in addition to those named above, where from 2 to 4 boys learn the Koran in the mosques.

KAIRU.—In the villages of *Kairu* and *Leghan* there is a pátshala in each. In Kairu, Damodar Dass, disciple of Radhakishen Sadhu, who is a blind man, teaches Srimat Bhagwat, Chandraka, *Mahurat Chinta* Sarsut, Shigar Bodh and Puran to 12 pupils gratuitously, in the Paras (village-hall) of the Brahmins. The neighbouring village of *Hittampur*, which is the birth-place of the Sadhu, gives him one rupee on each marriage. The pátshala attached to the village temple of *Leghan* is under Pandit Gumani Ram, who teaches Sarsut and Arithmetic to 4 pupils, and lives upon the income of the temple.

NARNOND.— Pandit Raji Ram, son of Gogan Missar, a Sanscrit scholar, conducts a pátshala in his private house, and teaches Chandrika, Saraswat and Tark Sangraha to 4 pupils gratis. Among the Baids, Gogan Fakir may be mentioned.

SIWNI.—Among the Hakims, Sirajuddin and Jamaluddin should be named.

BAHAL.—There is a pátshala in the village of *Behal* under Pandit Ram Ruttan, a good Sanscrit scholar, who teaches Gita, Vishnu-Sahasra-Nam and Astrology to 12 boys in his private house, and receives Rs. 6 per mensem.

Bahal has a Mahajani school also under Bhonta Pandit, who teaches 20 pupils, who pay him Rs. 5 per month.

BALSAMAND.—In the villages of *Siswal* and *Kharya* there are two pátshalas, one in each, in which the Nagri alphabet and first book are taught. The Kharya pátshala is conducted by *Chetan* Brahmin of Sirsana, and that of Siswal by Baldeo Sahai, a Brahmin, native of the Jeypur State. The number of the pupils attending them is 7 and 12 respectively, and the income of the teachers consists of daily sidha (food) which each pupil gives in turn, and Re. 1 when a pupil finishes his course.

TUHANA.—Among the Maulvis in this circle, Maulvi *Abdulla*, a good Arabic scholar, teaches gratuitously the Koran, Persian, Arabic and Medicine to 14 pupils in a Madrasa attached to a mosque in Tuhanah, and Maulvi Rahmat Ali, a native of Musa Garh, deserve notice. Besides this Madrasa there are Koran schools in the villages of *Tuhana, Jamalpur, Hendanwala, Musá Garh, Diwana, Akkanwali, Chander, Daulat, Dhani Bawan* and *Anda Chhoi*, with 8, 9, 6, 16, 5, 12 21, 4, 12, and 3 pupils. In the Madrasas of *Diwana, Musá Garh* and *Anda Chhoi*, Arabic is also taught.

In the village of *Lehri* there is a Pandit, named Ram Narayen, who conducts a pátshala, in which Hora Chakra and Shigar Bodh are taught to 10 boys.

EXTRA.

The District Returns give the following additional particulars :—

Eminent persons.

HISSAR.—*Pandits* Rekbi Ram and Gobind Ram.

HANSI.—*Hakim* Naubat Rai.

BHIWANI.—*Pandit* Kali Das.

FATAHABAD.—*Hakim* Kazi Yusuf, and *Maulvi* Muharakuddin.

Indigenous Schools.

Name of place.	Number of schools.	Number of pupils.	Subjects taught.
Hissar	5	73	The Koran, Arabic and Persian.
Chandar (Major)	2	42	Ditto.
Bhatu	1	4	Ditto.
Mawad (Major)	1	7	Ditto.
Buddhakhera	1	4	Ditto.
Balyalwala	1	10	Ditto.
Alawalwas	1	17	Ditto.
Nagpur	1	8	Ditto.
Alika	2	6	Ditto.
Sardariwala	1	5	Ditto.
Nangal	1	7	Ditto.
Basti Bhima	1	5	Ditto.
Haroli	1	8	Ditto.
Bhiwani	2	81	Mahajani.
Hissar	1	45	Mahajani (under Chandu Lal).
Ditto	1	20	Sanscrit (under Rekhi Ram).

HISSAR DIVISION.

ROHTAK DISTRICT.

GENERAL ABSTRACT

District.	No. of Maktabs and Madrassas.	No. of pupils.	No. of Sanscrit and Nagri Schools.	No. of pupils.	No. of Gurmukhi Schools.	No. of pupils.	No. of Lande and Mahajani Schools.	No. of pupils.	No. of Indigenous Schools.	Total No. of pupils.
Rohtak .	45	452	33	351	...	...	21	381	99	1,184

MAHM.—Amongst Hakims, Hakims Alauddin, Amiruddin, Fazalhak are mentioned; the first-named is said to be a most famous Arabic and Persian scholar, who knows also European medicine. Mozuffar Ahmad Mahvi is said to be a poet.

Amongst Maulvis, the following are named: Hakim Alauddin, Mahomed Yakub and Mahomed Salamaddin. The maktab at *Mahm* is attached to the mosque of the masons and is conducted by Abdul Qadir, who is said to know the whole Koran by heart, which he teaches to 12 pupils. The only thing he gets is a present of sweetmeats from each pupil when they first begin the Koran. There is also a Mahajani school in this place, where one named Nuthoo teaches 12 boys. His income amounts to almost Rs. 15 per mensem from fees. Two other Koran schools under Shaikh Abdulali and Hafiz Jan Mohammad with 5 and 10 pupils are mentioned in a private return.

In *Farmaná* is a pátshala, attached to a temple, where 8 boys are taught Shastri.

BERI.—Gusain Futtan Lal (Hakim) and Pandits Ram Richhpal and Gunga Dut are named as distinguished in this place; Ram Richhpal teaches Sanscrit gratuitously to 30 pupils in a pátshala which is attached to a temple. *Beri* has also a smaller pátshala, where Sanscrit is the subject of tuition, and the number of pupils is 10.

SANPLA.—No school is named in the Police return as being in this place itself, but in the village *Mandohti* is a pátshala attached to the Lumberdar's house, where Parem Dut, who is a good Sanscrit scholar, teaches this language to 35 pupils. He is not paid as a teacher, but as a Brahmin. In *Dighal* is a Mahajani school, where a Brahmin, Sohun Lal, teaches Lande and Mahajani; he can also teach Sanscrit. He has 32 pupils who pay him each 4 annas a month.

JHAJJAR.—There is one Hakim, Agha Ali Khan; two Baids, Pursani Lal and Choranjee Lal; and two Pandits, Nagri Lal Biyas and Diakishen, the last educated at Benares, who are mentioned as eminent in the place. The best maktab is under Shaikh Muhammad Hassan, who is a good Arabic and Persian scholar, and teaches 7 pupils in those languages and Arithmetic. His income is Rs. 5 per mensem, and he gets besides 1 anna per boy on each festival. There are 4 other maktabs in the same place, in which Persian and Arabic are taught, 2 having 12 pupils and 2 only 6 pupils each.

There are besides 4 Mahajani schools in which Nagri is also taught, containing 30, 50, 5, and 21 pupils respectively. The teachers' names are: Har Narain, Lala and Ram Richpal, all three Brahmins; their monthly income amounts to Rs. 5, 10 and 4 respectively. To Gopinath's temple is attached a pátshala, where Birmha Nand teaches Sanscrit gratuitously to 8 pupils. In the villages of *Khodun* and *Silani* there is a Mahajani school in each, attended by 10 and 16 pupils respectively, and in *Kutani* is a maktab in which Shib Lal teaches Persian and English to 5 boys and gets Rs. 5 per mensem and his food.

KALANAUR.—In Kalanaur there is a native physician named Hidayet Ali Khan, who is a Government employé.

Among the Baids, Manak Dass Sádh (of the Dadupanthi sect) may be mentioned.

Lachhman and Chandan are Pandits of some reputation, and Kazi Qiyamuddin is an author.

In Kalanaur proper, besides the Government school, there are three Koran schools also, with 50 pupils; the largest of them is conducted by Hafiz Husnu and is attended by 20 pupils.

The villages of *Saipal, Kherri, Anwal, Kahnaur, Nigana* and *Lahli* have Koran schools, and the number of pupils in them is 20, 8, 22, 10, 6 and 8 respectively. The village of Kherri has a maktab also, attached to the house of Tahawwar Khan, Risaldar Major, in which Himayet Ali, a man of mediocre qualification, teaches the Koran, Karima, Khaliq Bari, Gulistan and Bostan to 10 boys and receives Rs. 6 per mensem and his food

There are two pátshalas in this circle, one at *Kalanaur* attached to the shop of Jaggan, Mahajan, in which Chandan, Brahmin, teaches the Ramayana, Bhagwat, &c., to 3 pupils gratuitously; the other is in the village of *Mokhra,* where 10 boys are taught Sanscrit, Bhagwat, &c.

Guhana.—Among the Hakims, Sayyed Amanat Ali in Guhana and Karim Bakhsh in Nagar, and among the Pandits, Desraj in Rera and Hansram in Ahmadpur Majra, may be mentioned; the latter, who has been educated at Benares, conducts a pátshala in his private house and teaches Sanscrit and the Bhagwat, &c., to 25 boys gratuitously. There is another pátshala in the same village conducted by Perbhu, Brahmin, who teaches Sanscrit to 15 pupils gratuitously and is a landholder. The villages of *Kathura, Khanpur,* and of *Gingana* have each a pátshala, in which Sanscrit is taught to 7, 4, and 2 pupils respectively.

In Guhana proper there is a maktab and a Koran school; the latter has 15 pupils under Hafiz Khuda Bakhsh, the blind, and is attached to the Khankah of Shah Walayat. The maktab is attached to the house of Chaudri Ghulam Muhuddin Khan, and is under Ghulam Muhammad, a good Persian scholar, who can teach up to Abulfazl, and is said to be an author also; he teaches the Koran and Persian to 12 pupils on Rs. 7 per mensem.

There are less important Koran schools in the villages of *Nagar* and *Kahni* and a Mahajani school in *Jhijhrana,* attended by 4, 4 and 8 pupils respectively.

Rohtak.—Among the Hakims in Rohtak, Háfizuddin, and among the Baids, Kanhia Lal and Bakhtawar Lal (the latter an oculist) are famous.

Maulvi Háfizuddin, who is now tutor to His Highness the Nawab of Dujána, is the most distinguished Arabic scholar in this part of the country.

Pandit Harparshad teaches Sanscrit to 10 pupils in a pátshala attached to the Ganga Mandar, and is paid Rs. 5 per mensem by Rai Bakhtawar Lal, Extra Assistant Commissioner. The other Pandit of some reputation is Harsaran Dass. Both Pandits are distinguished scholars of Sanscrit. (This pátshala is not mentioned in the Police returns.)

In Rohtak there is a maktab in a rented house, in which Persian, Arithmetic and Grammar are taught by Yusuf Khán, who receives Rs. 10 per mensem from Rai Bakhtawar Lal, Extra Assistant Commissioner. The number of pupils attending this maktab is 12 according to the Police returns, and 22 according to private information. The private return mentions also 6 Koran schools with 67 pupils, and one Mahajani school, under Lachman, with 7 pupils, and Rs. 3 per mensem as the income of the teacher, and another with 5 pupils.

The Police information returns a pátshala in *Tatoli,* conducted by *Nathu* Brahmin, who teaches Hindi and Sanscrit to 12 pupils in the *paras* (village-hall)

gratuitously, and a Mahajani school at Rohtak under Mehar Nath Jogi with 20 pupils and Rs. 5 per mensem as the income of the teacher.

KHARKHAUDA.—In this circle the largest *maktab* is in Hasan Garh, which is attached to a mosque, and is conducted by Sheikh Najibullah, a native of the town, who teaches Persian, Urdu and Koran to 22 pupils gratuitously, living on the produce of his lands in the town.

There is a *pátshala* in the village of *Badhlan*, attached to the Dharmsala of the village, with 6 pupils, who live on begging. The teacher Dya Rám, Brahmin, teaches Chandraka, Sarsut, Bhagwat and Shastras gratuitously, and he lives on what he earns in preaching in this and surrounding villages.

The village *Sahothi* has a Mahajani school under Bhagwana, Brahmin, a native of Beri, who teaches Mahajani, Nagri and Arithmetic to 20 pupils and receives Rs. 8 per mensem in cash.

BAHADURGARH.—Among the *Pandits*, Gobindat and Premdat, Brahmins, natives of the village *Asodá*, where each of them conducts gratuitously a pátshala with 12 and 10 pupils respectively, may be mentioned.

In the town of Bahadurgarh, Sham Lal, Pandit, who knows Sanscrit, Persian, English and Mathematics, teaches Persian and English to the two sons of Babu Bhagwan Dass, Sahukar, and receives Rs. 20 per mensem.

SALAWÁS.—In the villages of *Guryani* and *Jikhaná* there are 3 Koran schools, 2 in the former and 1 in the latter. The schools in *Guryani* are conducted by Shahamat Khan and Mussamat Rahiman (a *female* teacher), who teach 20 and 16 boys respectively; the *Jikhana* school is under Matlub Ali who teaches 4 boys and 6 girls. The income of the teachers consists in what is given them as a donation from Rs. 5 to 10 on a pupil finishing the Koran.

EXTRA.

The District Returns give the following eminent persons and schools, in addition to those which are already mentioned :—

ROHTAK.—*Hakim* Asghar Ali; *Baids* Gauri Sahai, Rudar Pershad and Layeg Ram, and *poet* Ramzan Ali.

JHÁJJAR.—*Hakim* Abdul Hakim; *Pandit* Parma Nand; *Maulvis* Abdar-rahim and Muhammad Husán, and Karim Bakhsh, *poet*.

SALAWAS.—*Hakim* Abdul Waháb of Guryani, and *Baid* Kishor Das of Dadla.

BAHADURGÁRH.—*Hakim* Zia Uddin.

Name of place.	Number of schools.	Number of pupils.	Subjects taught.
Rohtak	2	6	The Koran.
Kanhor	3	11	Ditto.
Guhana	3	26	Ditto.
Banyani	1	5	Ditto.
Gurawar	1	3	Ditto.
Bahu Akbarpur	1	4	Sanscrit.
Shuhdapur	1	4	Ditto.
Majea	1	15	Ditto.
Mokhra	1	20	Ditto.
Kharak	2	22	Ditto.
Jhájjar	2	9	Ditto.

Name of place.	Number of schools.	Number of pupils	Subjects taught.
Matan Hel	1	5	Sanscrit.
Bidhal	1	15	Ditto.
Nidana	1	4	Ditto.
Samchaha	1	10	Ditto.
Badelan	1	12	Ditto.
Matan	1	10	Ditto.
Asodha	1	6	Ditto.
Kiloi	1	25	Mahajani.
Nigana	1	20	Ditto.
Budher	1	6	Ditto.
Barsa	1	15	Ditto.
Rohna	1	30	Ditto.
Badelan	1	14	Ditto.
Khanda	1	12	Ditto.
Bahadurgarh	1	40	Ditto.

HISSAR DIVISION.

SIRSA DISTRICT.

GENERAL ABSTRACT.

District.	No. of Maktabs and Madrasas.	No. of pupils.	No. of Sanscrit and Nagri schools.	No. of pupils.	No. of Gurmukhi schools.	No. of pupils.	No. of Lande and Mahajani schools.	No. of pupils.	Total No. of Indigenous schools.	Total No of pupils.
Sirsa	101	703	5	23	10	65	6	173	122	1,014

FAZILKA.—Among the Pandits of Fazilka may be mentioned Pandits Sedhu Ram Narayan and Dialchand. Rupsi *Púj* (a learned Jain) is the *Baid* of the place. Among Maulvis, Sayad Muhammad Shah may be noticed.

In Fazilka there is a Madrasa attached to a mosque, taught by Maulvi Nuruddin, which seems to deserve notice. It is attended by 10 pupils who read Persian, Arabic and the Korán, and who pay their teacher, some in contributions of food and others in cash. A *Gurmukhi* school is also attached to a Dharmsala, attended by 8 pupils, who are taught gratis by Bhai Charat Singh. Another Gurmukhi school with 8 pupils and a pátshala with 6 pupils are mentioned in a private return. There is also a second Madrasa only attended by 5 pupils. (The returns are evidently incomplete.)

RANIA.—(No returns were furnished by the Police from this place.) There is a *Hakim* of some note in Rania called Mahomed Isa, and a *Baid* named Rakhjati. A private return gives 6 maktabs with 52 pupils, and a Mahajani school with 10 pupils in *Rania* itself.

DABWALI.—*Pipli* has a Hakim of some note, whose name is not given. At *Dabwáli* Bhai Tota Ram Sadh teaches 8 pupils at a Dharmsala; he gets one rupee on occasions of marriage, as also a supply of corn at harvest time, so that his income may be said to be about Rs. 4 per mensem. The schools in this thana are religious, the teachers being paid one rupee on marriages and 20 seers of wheat from every house during harvest. If the teachers be encouraged by grants, they seem willing to comply with any reasonable conditions that may be fixed by Government.

At *Pipli* there is a *maktab* with 4 pupils, whilst the villages *Khoyane Kakhanwali, Lohgadh, Pajawda, Anúpshar, Bhúrkhera* and *Salukhera* have each a *Koran* school attended by 8, 5, 5, 2, 7, 5 and 8 pupils respectively, and *Naurang* has a *Gurmukhi* school attended by 4 pupils.

ABUHAR.—Among *Maulvis*, Ahmaduddin, Mian Suleyman and Hafiz Fattehdin may be mentioned. The first-named, a good Arabic scholar, gratuitously conducts a school situated in the *Abuhar* mosque attended by 40 pupils, who read Persian and religious books. Throughout the thana these appear to be the subjects of instruction, and we find that *Balwana* has 2 schools with 13 pupils; *Kandwala* 1 with 20; *Khoyan* 1 with 12; *Diwankhera* 1 with 10; *Pajada* 1 with 12; *Ghallu* 1 with 7; and *Khoikhera* 1 with 5 pupils. *Abuhar* is said to have another maktab with 18 pupils.

SIRSA.—(The Police returns only give the name of one Hakim and none of the Baids, Bhais and Pandits of the place, for which see special list; they also give no maktab or Madrasa and only mention Hakim Abdulla of Sakandarpur; at Sirsa itself there appears, indeed, to be only one purely Koran school, attached to the mosque and attended by 6 pupils, the teacher Ibrahim having a very precarious subsistence).

There is one good *pátshala* at Sirsa, conducted by Kishor Chand *Jati* (a Jain priest who does not marry), who teaches the Baidak system of Medicine and Astrology to 4 pupils gratuitously. There are also two Mahajani schools, conducted by Pandit Ishar Das and Kishor Chand Jati respectively, the latter combining his Sanscrit school with a Lande school attended by 50 boys, who pay him nearly Rs. 4 per mensem. Pandit Ishar Das has 36 boys, paying one rupee per annum each and one pice per week, as also half a seer of flour. They are taught Hindi and Mahajani. The Police returns state a larger number of pupils than the private information, *viz.* 50 pupils.

Thána Behrajpur.—(also called *Dhaban*).—The *Maulvi* Rahmat Din, a very good scholar, conducts a school in connection with the *Behrajpur* mosque, attended by 7 pupils, who are taught the Koran, and Arabic Grammar and who pay about 9 maunds of grain at harvest time. At *Takhtmal* there is a good *pátshala*, in which both Sanscrit and Gurmukhi are taught, conducted by *Mangal Ram* Sadhu, a distinguished disciple of Fakir Sobha Ram. There are 6 pupils, of whom 3 are Brahmins and 3 Jats. He receives from 25 to 30 maunds of grain at harvest time. In this thana, which is inhabited by Jat Sikhs and Muhammadan Pachhhadas, who take no interest in education, Mahajani and Sarafi are nowhere taught.

Thána Sarawan.—Among *Maulvis*, Mian Rahmat and Fakir Kadir Bakhsh may be mentioned. At *Sarawan* itself, the latter, who is a good Arabic scholar, teaches 25 pupils the Koran and Arabic in a mosque, and receives 2 maunds of grain per annum per boy.

At **Rasulpur** also there is a *Madrasa* for Koran and Arabic with 15 pupils.

The following schools are added in a return furnished by Mr. Trafford, Deputy Commissioner of Sirsa :—

Tehsil.	Village.	No. of maktabs.	No. of pupils.	Subjects taught.
Sirsa	Bahauddin	1	12	Arabic Grammar and Koran.
	Jagmalera	1	7	Ditto ditto.
	Natar	1	3	Ditto ditto.
	Nakora	1	6	Ditto ditto.
	Harpi (lesser)	1	8	Ditto and Urdu.
	Neza Dalla (lesser)	1	10	Ditto ditto.
	,, ,, (major)	1	6	Koran.
	Kotli	1	12	Ditto.
	Shahpur (Begu)	1	9	Koran, Arabic Grammar and Urdu.
	Nago	1	5	Koran.
	Ferozabad	1	10	Koran and Urdu.
	Budhabana	1	8	Koran.
	Darbi	1	6	Ditto.
	Ahmadpur	1	6	Ditto.
	Kukarthána	1	4	Urdu.
	Sahanpal	1	6	Koran.
	Bukhara Khera	1	2	Ditto.
Darwali	Pinbari	1	8	Koran and Urdu religious books.
	Alika	1	8	Ditto ditto.
	Musahibwala	1	5	Ditto ditto.
	Renga	1	4	Ditto ditto.
	Báp	2	20	Ditto ditto.
	Panjuwana	1	8	Ditto ditto.
Fasilka	Ratanpur	1	5	Ditto ditto.
	Pakán	1	5	Ditto ditto.
	Jandwala	1	4	Ditto ditto.
	Mulanwali	1	4	Ditto ditto.
	Jambarwala	1	6	Ditto ditto.
	Arniwala	1	4	Koran and other religious books Urdu.
	Dabwala	1	5	Ditto ditto.
	Dalmir Khera	1	5	Ditto ditto.
	Baniwala	1	6	Ditto ditto.
	Battatiba	1	5	Ditto ditto.
	Midda	1	4	Ditto ditto.
	Malot	1	5	Ditto ditto.
	Bahk	3	18	Ditto ditto.
	Lakhukiutar	1	5	Ditto ditto.
	Jamalki	1	6	Ditto ditto.
	Chak Bahk	1	6	Ditto ditto.
	Bakyánwala	1	4	Ditto ditto.
	Pakki Tibbi	1	6	Ditto ditto.
	Amarkot	1	20	Ditto ditto.
	Jamálpur	1	6	Ditto ditto.
	Tutwala	1	6	Ditto ditto.
	Dara	1	18	Ditto ditto.
	Jhingar	1	12	Ditto ditto.
	Ganj Bakhsh	1	5	Persian and religious books.
	Arniwali		8	Urdu religious books.
	Azimabad	1	8	Ditto ditto.
	Panwarwala	1	10	Ditto ditto.

Tahsil.	Village.	No. of maktabs.	No. of pupils.	Subjects taught.
	Manzzam	1	8	Religious books.
	Salim Shah	1	7	Ditto.
	Hasta	1	5	Ditto.
	Ganjuwala	1	4	Ditto.
	Siddhuwana	1	6	Ditto.
	Nokeryan	1	5	Ditto.
	Mahar Sona	1	5	Ditto.
	Ráná	1	5	Ditto.
	Wali Shah	1	6	Ditto.
	Mohammad Pira	1	2	Ditto.
	Sedhuki	1	3	Ditto.
	Ghurka	1	2	Ditto.
	Usman Khera	1	7	Ditto.
	Pátshala.			
Sirsa	Kagdana	1	4	Sanscrit.
Ellenabad	Ellenabad	1	6	Sanscrit and Astrology.
	Gurmukhi Schools.			
Dabwalli	Meddu Khera	1	6	Religious books.
	Bám	1	5	Gurmukhi Garanth.
	Jhasár	1	8	Ditto.
Fazilka	Muazzam	1	6	Ditto.
	Mahajani Schools.			
Fazilka	Fazilka	1	6	Lunde.

EXTRA.

The *second* Police Return gives the following additional information regarding the eminent persons and the indigenous schools in the District.

Sirsa.—*Maulvi* Kadir Bakhsh, *Pandit* Kishaudat, *Bhai* Ishur Singg and *Poet* Karim Bakhsh.

Ranya.—*Moulvis* Saadulla of Ranya and Nabi Bakhsh of Nakar.

Thana.	Place.	No. of schools.	No. of pupils.	Subjects taught.	Remarks.
Sarawan	Koolanwali	1	7	The Koran.	
	Chhappanwali	1	9	Ditto.	
	Kabarwala	1	2	Ditto.	
Ranya	Utuar	1	8	Ditto.	
	Sathpal	1	3	Ditto.	
Fazilka	Balwana	1	10	Ditto.	
Sirsa	Sirsa	2	57	Mahajani	Under Azim Bakhsh and Badri, respectively.
Sarawan	Jhurrar	1	4	Gurmukhi.	

UMBALLA DIVISION.

UMBALLA DISTRICT.

GENERAL ABSTRACT.

District.	No. of Maktabs and Madrasas.	No of Pupils.	No. of Sanscrit and Nagri Schools.	No. of Pupils.	No. of Gurmukhi Schools.	No. of Pupils.	No. of Hindi and Mahajani Schools.	No. of Pupils.	Total No. of Indigenous Schools.	Total No. of Pupils.
Umballa	82	1,018	19	303	7	63	30	703	138	2,090

UMBALLA CITY.—Among the Hakims, Jafar Husain, Búali Bakhsh and Charan Singh deserve notice. Maulvi Mahmud Said, among the Maulvis, and Pandits Jamna Das, Parbhu Diyal and Salig Ram among the Pandits, may be mentioned. Bhai Luchman Singh is a Sikh priest and teacher, and Ahmad, Hasan is said to be an author.

There are two Madrasas in the city, one established by the Shias (called the Imamia School) and the other by the Sunnis, which is called the Islamia School. In the former Maulvis Ghulam Ali Khan, Sayyid Razi and Ibrahim, receiving Rs. 15, 20 and 4 per mensem, respectively, teach Arabic, Persian, the Koran and Arithmetic to 53 boys and prepare candidates for the Middle and Entrance, Munshi and Munshi Alim Examinations of the Punjab University College, and in the latter instruction is given to 30 boys in Arabic, Persian and the Koran by Moulvi Rafiq Ahmad, Nasiruddin and two Hafizes, who receive Rs. 15, 8, 2-8 and 1-8 per mensem respectively. The expenses are defrayed by subscriptions among the Muhammadans. The Head Maulvis in charge of the schools are good Arabic and Persian scholars.

Bhai Lachman teaches Gurmukhi to two boys in Manji Sahib.

Pandits Salig Ram and Jamna Das conduct each a pátshala, in which Sanscrit is taught gratuitously to 9 and 10 pupils (private returns mention 15 and 20) respectively.

Hirda Ram and Sheikh Ala Bakhsh conduct two Mahajani schools with 50 and 30 pupils respectively, and get food and a pice on every Sunday from each student. Private information adds two more Mahajani schools conducted by Allah Ditta and Ramjidas, with 40 and 20 pupils respectively.

Six Koran schools are also mentioned by the private returns, which contain about 80 pupils.

UMBALLA CANTONMENTS.—Among the Hakims, Hakim Murad Ali may be noticed. The Police returns mention three maktabs with 125 pupils, and one Mahajani school under Ali Bakhsh with 80 pupils, and Rs. 12 per mensem as the income of the teacher; but private information returns 10 *Koran schools* conducted by Kazi Khuda Baksh, Hafiz Abdul Majid, Barkat Ali, Abdulla, Ghulam Rasul, Amanatulla, Haidar Shah, Hafiz Abdulla, Hafiz Ramzan and Muhammad Newaz with 12, 30, 10, 8, 10, 13, 10, 8 and 15 pupils respectively, and one *Madrasa* conducted by Moulvi Kamaluddin teaching Arabic and Persian to 13 pupils on Rs. 20 per mensem; four schools, in which Urdu and English are taught, are conducted by Chura Mal, Madho, Mr. Andrews and Mr. Wilson, with 25, 10, 50 and 10 pupils and Rs. 8, 10, 40, and 10 as the teachers' monthly income; 4 Urdu maktabs with 107 pupils and one Mahajani school with 80 pupils.

POTUKI.—In *Moranda*, Subhanulla and Khalifa Makhkhan are Hakims of some reputation. Among the Bhais, Bhai Thakur Singh and Bhai Chatar Singh, natives of *Chamkaur*, may be mentioned.

In *Chaiwanta* (Khurd) there is a Koran school attached to a mosque, conducted by Mianji Sayyid Ali Shah, who teaches 10 boys, and receives 6 maunds of corn twice a year.

In the villages of *Bila* and *Mohan Majra* there are two Mahajani schools under Chunda and Nabi Bakhsh, with 25 and 9 pupils, the teachers' pay being Rs. 40 and 20 per annum respectively.

KHARAR.—In Kharar proper, among the Hakims. Hakim Ali Baksh and Ghulam Abbas, Pandit Nand Lal, Maulvi Akbar Ali deserve notice. Pandit Kapurya Rám in Rodyalá, Pandit Ganesha in Chauhatta and Pandit Kanhya Lal in Korali, and Hakims Najaf Ali and Ali Husain and Hakim Badan Singh in Korali are eminent Pandits and Hakims.

In this circle there are Koran schools in the villages of *Khanpur*, *Chircheari*, *Ghadera*, *Kheri*, *Majat*, *Persuhand*, *Manakpur*, *Khizrabad*, *Malanpur*, *Sil*, *Shukrullapur* and *Kharar* under Mehr Shah, Ghulam Rasul, Pir Mohamad, Amanat Ali, Mangti Shah, Alya, Qadir Baksh, Makhdum Jahan, Rahim Baksh, Nabi Baksh, Ata Muhammad and Gulab, with 5, 8, 15, 4, 6, 5, 6, 6, 4, 12, 12, and 4 pupils, the teachers' pay being 20 maunds of corn, 40 maunds of corn, Rs. 36, Rs. 84, 40 maunds of corn, ditto, the income of a Kaziship of the villages, ditto, ditto, 50 maunds of corn and Rs. 48 per annum with food, respectively. In Gadhera, Kheri, Malanpur and Sil, Persian is also taught.

There are two *pátshalas* in Kharar, conducted by Pandits Pirthi and Nand Lal, who teach Sanscrit to one and eight boys respectively in their private houses gratuitously.

In the villages of *Shukrullapur*, *Balwanki*, *Kaliwal* and *Kharar*, there are Gurmukhi schools attached to Gurudwaras and Dharmsalás, under Gulab Singh, Sobha Ram, Rikhi Rám and Birham Saran respectively. The number of the pupils attending these schools is 24.

RAIPUR.—Among the Hakims Mir Fasihuddin of *Gadhi*, and among the Pandits, Pandit Ram Lál may be mentioned

THANESWAR.—In the town of Thaneswar (the famous Kuruk Chattar of the Mahabharat), Pandits Búlchand, Atma Ram, Gangá Ram, Bhagwana, Chandu Lál and Murlidhar have the reputation of being good Sanscrit scholars, whilst among Hakims Ali Husain, Rahmatullá, Shadi and Moulvi Ishkulla, a good Arabic scholar, deserve notice.

In the villages of *Dhurálá* and *Mokhi* there are two maktabs, one attached to the house of the teacher and the other to the house of the Lumberdar of the village, in which Muhammad Ali and Karim Bakhsh teach Urdu, Persian, and the Koran (in the first Mathematics also) to 5 boys and 10 boys and 5 girls, and receive Rs. 2 per mensem and 40 maunds (khám) of corn per annum respectively. *Thaneswar* has also a Koran school attached to the mosque of weavers, where Dost Muhammad teaches the Koran to 7 pupils for daily food.

Pandits Atma Ram, Ganga Ram, Chandu Lál have, at their private houses, a *pátshala* each, and teach gratuitously 10, 5, and 6 pupils respectively, Shighar Bodh, Darpan Sandhia, Gita, Chandraka, &c. Pandit Búlchand also teaches 30 pupils Sanscrit.

RADAUR.—In the town of Radaur, Jaithu *Baid*, Ghulam Haidar *Hakim* and Harisaran *Pandit* are persons of local distinction.

In the village of *Bikana* there is a maktab attached to the house of Fatah Ali, Lumberdar, in which Nabi Bakhsh, a man of mediocre abilities, teaches Persian (Gulistan, &c.) to 5 boys, and receives 12 maunds of corn every six months. There are Koran schools in *Radaur* and *Rajbari*, both attached to mosques, where 15 boys in each are taught by Hafiz Raham Ali and Hafiz Ilahi Bakhsh, who receive 20 maunds of corn per annum each. Private information adds a maktab in *Gumthala* with 15 pupils.

In *Jutlana*, Rikhi Ram, a Pandit of good abilities, teaches the Hora Chakr Viwah Padhti, Durga pát to 12 pupils gratuitously.

The Mahajani schools in *Palawala*, *Gumthala Ráo*, *Dámla* and *Halahar* are conducted by Roli, Chandan, Roda and Pirdiya, who teach 9, 20, 10 and 32 pupils and receive Rs. 40 per annum, food, 15 maunds of corn every six months and Rs. 5 per mensem, respectively. *Gumthala Ráo* has also a pátshala with 10 pupils.

PIHOÁ.—In Pihoá, Mulha Ram and Bava Bishambar Dass among the *Baids*, and Jhaddá Lal, Haridat and Brahmanand among the *Pandits* are noted. *Hakim* Khair Muhammad of Gumthala (Gaddhú) is a physician of local reputation.

In *Gumthala*, attached to the grand mosque, there is a maktab under Hafiz Imamuddin, who is a man of good qualifications and who teaches Arabic, Persian and the Koran to 12 pupils, and is given corn at harvest time and daily food by the parents of the pupils. Besides this, the villages of *Usmanpur* and *Arnai* have each a Koran school attended each by 6 pupils. Urdú is also taught in these schools.

There are three pátshalas in *Pihoá*, attached to the Shivala, Gurudwara and to a private house, respectively, in which Pandits Hardat, Rura and Sita teach 35 pupils Sanscrit gratuitously.

The villages of *Sarsa*, *Kole* and *Barna* have each a Mahajani school, conducted by Tola Jogi, Jamna Dass and Nathu Jogi with 10, 12 and 8 pupils respectively. The income of the teacher consists only in corn, which the parents of the pupils give at harvest time; quantity not mentioned. A private return mentions a pátshala with 30 pupils in Kole.

JAGADHRI.—In Jagadhri proper there is a maktab and a pátshala; in the former 15 pupils are taught Persian by Maulvi Abdul Kadir on Rs. 5 per mensem, and in the latter Beli Ram, a good Sanscrit scholar, teaches Sanscrit to 15 pupils gratuitously, but he has an income of Rs. 10 per mensem from other sources.

In *Burya*, Bhai Tulsi instructs 25 boys in Gurmukhi gratuitously, but lives on an income from shop-keeping.

In Jagadhri there is a Mahajani school also, where 50 pupils are taught Mahajani, Sarrafi and Book-keeping by Pansari Jogi, with a monthly income of Rs. 10 per mensem. There are Mahajani schools in *Bulara* and *Burya* with 45 pupils each.

MUBARAKPUR.—In Mubarakpur, Hakim Daulut Ali and Pandit Umadat, Pandit Narayen Das and Pandit Jaidyal may be mentioned. Among the Baids, Rugghá Baid of Ramgarh deserves notice.

Pandit Narayen Dass, a good Sanscrit scholar, conducts a pátshala in Mubarakpur, where 25 pupils learn Sanscrit Grammar, the Vaidic system of Medicine, Astrology, Bhagwat, &c., gratuitously.

There are two Mahajani schools in *Mubarakpur* and *Manauli* under Sujan and Shib Ram Jogi, who teach 35 and 14 boys respectively. The former gets Rs. 2 per mensem and daily food, and the latter is given 2 maunds of flour monthly.

BILASPUR.—In Bilaspur among the *Baids*, Salig Ram, Brahmin, and among the *Hakims*, Chaudhri Bije Singh, are noted.

In the villages of *Khizrabad* (with two schools), *Deodhor*, *Khizri*, *Pirúwala*, *Shahpur*, *Lida*, there are maktabs, in which Urdu, elementary Persian, and the Koran are taught by Abdulaziz and Abdulwaháb, Abdulghani, Yaqub Ali, Ilahi Bakhsh, Abdurrahim and Imamuddin to 27, 5, 3, 3, 6 and 10 boys respectively. In Khizrabad the teacher of one school holds a muafi and the other is given

2 annas a month and a pice a week. The other teachers receive 20 or 22 maunds of corn every six months.

Mahajani schools in *Khizrabad, Ismailpur, Manakpur, Azizpur* are conducted by Kashmiri Padha, Bansi, Ajudhya and Ajudhya II., who teach Lande and multiplication tables to 15, 8, 4, and 2 boys respectively. Each of the above Padhás receives a pice every Sunday from each boy and daily food by turns.

CHAPPAR.—Among the Hakims, Qutbuddin and Farid Bakhsh in Mustafabad, and among the Moulvis, Faiz Muhammad and Abdul Khalik (in Chandura) are eminent. Narayna Brahmin Baid and Pandits Chuni Lal and Balmukand also deserve notice.

There is a Koran school in the village of *Fatahpur* attached to a mosque, in which Ala Bakhsh Myanji teaches Koran to 10 boys and gets 20 maunds (kham) of corn every six months.

In the village of *Talakur*, Partapa Jogi teaches Mahajani to 10 pupils on Rs. 3 per mensem.

MAZRA.—Among the *Hakims*, Mahtab Singh and Balmukand, among the *Baids*, Moti Rám, Dena Mal, and *Pandits* Berhma Nand and Ram Narayan are eminent men in Mazra. Among the *Bhais*, Kharak Singh may be noticed.

There are patshálas in the villages of *Luhána, Dúdmajra* and *Moolanpur*, where Sanscrit is taught to 20, 27 and 12 pupils by Pandits Berhma Nand, Ghansham and Pandit Shibsaran; the last one, teaching also Mahajani, receives Rs. 5 per mensem, and the rest teaching gratuitously. *Luhana* has also a Gurmukhi school under Bhai Kharak Singh with 15 pupils.

SINGHORE.—In this circle, Kazi Rahim Bakhsh and Muhammad Yasin, men of mediocre learning, conduct two maktabs in Babain and Majri respectively. The number of pupils attending these two schools is 15 and 10, who are taught Persian, Urdu and the Koran, and pay 18 and 10 maunds of corn per annum respectively.

SHAHABAD.—Bhai Kishen Granthi in Shahabad and Pandit Parmanand in Nalui may be mentioned.

In Shahabad, a maktab established by the Shaikhs is conducted by Myanji Ayyub Khan, a man of high qualifications, who teaches Persian to 12 pupils on Rs. 4 per mensem. Besides this there are four Koran schools attached to mosques containing 15 pupils. The village of Ratangarh has also a school, in which Myanji Abdullá teaches Arabic and Persian to 4 pupils, and receives Re. 1 a month in cash. Private information adds a maktab in Shahabad under Hafiz Imamuddin with 40 pupils.

Bhai Kishan Singh conducts a Gurmukhi school attached to the Gurudwará and instructs 15 pupils.

There is a Sanscrit patshála in Nalui, where 50 boys are taught Sanscrit (the Police returns give no details).

LADWA.—In Ladwa proper, Narayan Sing and Pandit Lachhmi Narayan, a distinguished Baid, and Hakim Rahim Baksh, may be mentioned.

Pandit Padam Nath, a good Sanscrit scholar, teaches Sanscrit to 15 boys in his private house; two other patshálas in *Ladwa* are added by private information having 15 pupils. The village of *Burkan* has a Mahajani school under Bansi Padha, who teaches Mahajani and Landé to 10 boys and receives Rs. 5 per mensem.

SODHI.—This village has a Koran school attached to the village mosque, in which Abdulhaq teaches the Koran to 8 boys, and receives 10 seers of corn from every plough in the village and something on marriages.

The only eminent person in the circle is Ramjidas of *Mithana*, who is a good Sanscrit scholar.

ROPAR.—Among the Hakims at Ropar, Kudratulla and Fazlkarim; among the Baids, Ramditta, Pohlu and *Narayani* (*a female Baid*); and among the Maulvis, Kutbuddin of Singah deserve notice. Bhai Bishan Singh, Granthi, and Saran Singh, poet, also are men of some reputation.

In Ropar there is a maktab and a Korán school, the former at a private house, and the latter attached to the mosque of the oilmen. Raja Lal, a certificate-holder of the middle school examination, teaches Persian, English, Arithmetic, and Urdu to 16 pupils (according to private information 20) on Rs. 7 per mensem.

The Korán school, of which the police returns give no particulars, is conducted by Hafiz Karim Bakhsh, and has 15 pupils.

In Ropar there is a patshála conducted by Chandu Lal Brahmin, teaching Sanscrit to 12 pupils.

Mangal Jogi Padha teaches Lande and accounts to 60 pupils in a Mahajani school, and receives Rs. 7 per mensem.

SADHORA.—Pandits Hiralal and Ganpat among the, Pandits, and Hakims Amanat Ali, Mansab Ali and Khadim Husain among the Hakims,deserve notice.

Sadhora has a maktab and 3 Korán schools; the latter 3 are attached to the mosques. Myanji Ataulla teaches Persian to 8 pupils on Rs. 6 per mensem. The Korán schools are under Hafiz Nuruddin, Bahadur Ali, Niyaz Ahmed, with 12 10, and 15 boys respectively, and receive only daily food.

MULLANA.—One Hakim, Rajab Ali, who lives in Sharukpur, may be mentioned.

In this circle there are only 4 Korán schools attached to the mosques of *Milk Shaikhan*, *Simla*, *Raju Kheri* and *Saha* with 10 ,6, 7, and 5 boys respectively (in the last three Persian is also taught), and 2 Mahajani schools in *Gaukalgarh* and *Kesri*, under Kashmiri and Masanya Padhas, with 25 and 23 pupils, and Rs. 6 and 4 as the incomes of the teachers respectively.

NARAYANGARH.—Pandit Kirpa Ram Bhagwati is a pandit of local reputation.

In the village of *Jatwar* there is a maktab attached to the house of Chaudhri Gopi Chand, attended by 9 pupils, in which Urdu, Persian, elementary books, such as Dasturussibyan, Dasturulmaktubat, Mufarruhulqulub and Gulistan, are taught by Sayyid Abid Husain of Sadhora, who receives Rs. 5 per mensem.

The village of *Lath* has a maktab attached to the Chaupal and supported by Rao Rahim Bakhsh Khán Rajput, in which Chand Khán Rajput teaches the Inshakhalifa, Mufidnama and the Korán to 7 boys, and gets Rs. 6 per mensem, daily food, ½ anna per boy a week, 2 annas per festival, and a few seers of cotton in winter.

The village of *Bhurawala* has a maktab attached to the house of Rao Najib Khan and Kunwar Khan Rajput, in which Urdu, elementary books of Persian, such as Insha Ghrib, Mufidnama, &c., and the Korán are taught by Ali Ahmed Shaikh to 14 pupils.

There is a Mahajani school in Khanpur of Brahmins, in which Paras Ram Padha teaches Lande to 15 boys, who give him each a maund of corn every six months.

A private return adds two more schools—a maktab in *Maherpur* with 10 pupils, and a Mahajani school at *Ghalore* with 10 pupils.

UMBALLA DIVISION.

LUDHIANA DISTRICT.

GENERAL ABSTRACT.

District.	No. of Maktabs and Madrasas.	No. of pupils.	No. of Sanscrit and Nagri schools.	No. of pupils.	No. of Gurmukhi schools.	No. of pupils.	No. of Lunde and Mahajani schools.	No. of pupils.	Total No. of of Indigenous schools.	Total No. of pupils.
Ludhiana	138	1,573	21	263	97	891	23	535	279	3,262

LUDHIANA.—Among *Hakims* of this town, Mir Muhammad Ali, Pir Jamayat Ali, Abdurrazzáq, Muhammad Ali and Nasir Khan, and among the *Baids*, Gangadin, are noted.

Among the *Moulvis*, Moulvi Abdulla, Abdulaziz, Ismail and Ismail II, Abdulwahid, Shah Din, Abdulqadir, Nizamuddin, Muhammad Musa, Husain Jan, Muhammad Husain, and Shihabuddin may be mentioned.

Pandits Chandi Pershad, Dhanpat, Dolu Ram and Gobind Dass Granthi are distinguished Sanscrit scholars.

Moulvi Abdulaziz, Ismail and Shah Din are said to be *authors*, and Mir Ghayasuddin, Mir Alma'i, Haider Ali, and Chiragh Din *poets*.

Moulvi Abdulla, a distinguished Arabic scholar, conducts a school attached to the grand mosque, where he teaches Arabic Literature, Logic, Philosophy, Muhammadan Law, Rhetoric, Hadis, and Persian to 30 pupils, and has no fixed income. Another madrasah, under Moulvi Abdulqadir, is attached to the sarai of Nawab Ali Muhammad Khan, in which he teaches 15 pupils Arabic and Persian, and gets Rs. 20 per mensem.

The other two schools, conducted by Moulvi Abdulaziz, a good Arabic scholar, and Rahmatulla, teaching Arabic and Persian, have 10 and 40 pupils respectively.

Besides these there are 44 minor maktabs and Korán schools, with 500 pupils, in Ludhiana, and Korán schools in the villages of *Rajuwal*, *Malikpur*, *Bermi*, *Bholiwal*, *Kharak*, *Jasyan*, *Kasaabad*, *Dheri* (Persian is also taught), *Sirah Ghaus*, *Garh*, *Hawas*, *Khasi*, with 6, 12, 8, 4, 10, 7, 6, 15, 7, 12, 4, and 30 pupils respectively.

The following statement shows the Maktabs and Korán schools at Ludhiana in full detail :—

LOCALITY.	Name of teacher.	No. of pupils.	Subjects taught.
Mosque of Muhammad Husain.	Muhammad Husain . .	9	Syntax, Prosody, Law and Hadis.
Mosque of Moulvi Abdullah.	Moulvi Abdullah . . .	5	Arabic and Persian.
„ Abdullah . .	Wife of Maulvi Abdullah .	15 girls.	The Korán.
„ at Badui .	Hafiz Abdullah . . .	8	Do.
„ of Raián .	Gámún Sháh	4	Do.
„ Gháti of Mewan	Hafiz Jhandu	9	Do.
„ Darbárú . .	Muhammad Saleh . . .	14	Do.
„ Imám Báráh .	Muhammad Afzal . . .	23	Syntax, Prosody and Persian.
„ Memárán .	Kamáluddin Hafiz . . .	5	The Korán.
„ Karmún .	Hafiz Iláhi Bakhsh . . .	11	Do.
„ Baghwáli .	„ Ghulám Rasul . .	32	Do.
„ Gujran . .	Ghulám Nabi	19	Do.

Locality.	Name of teacher.	No. of pupils.	Subjects taught.
Mosque Sarai Nawáb Ali Muhammad Khan.	Maulvi Abdulqadir	7	Syntax, Prosody, Law, &c.
„ Jumma	Abdullah	4	The Korán.
„ Thá Muhallah	Muhammad Sháh	5	Do.
„ Sulemán	Abdullah	5	Do.
„ Muchhipurah	Natihú Sháh	19	Do.
„ Hashim	Muhammad Khalil	22	Do.
„ Abdullah Sikhú	„ Sháh	4	Do.
„ Ali Najá	Umruddin	14	Do.
Muhalla Dhohwál	Abdul Ghání	11	Do.
Mosque of Bhaga rangrez.	Nur Muhammad	7	Do.
Mohalla Dholiwal	Hamadullah	15	Do.
Mosque of Jatán	Rahmatullah	5	Do.
„ „ Amkálú	Maulvi Nizamuddin	21	Do. and Persian.
„ „ Khudabakhsh	„ Shahabuddin	6	Do.
„ „ Kehwáli	Hafiz Amiruddin	13	Do.
„ „ Jamil Balia	„ Ahmad Shah	20	Do.
„ „ Jatan	„ Salám	9	Do.
Sarak cháuráh	„ Ibrahim	8	Do.
Ganji chhari	Muhammad Jan	8	Do.
Do.	Haji Abdurrazzáq	27	Do.
Phulwáli	Ghulám Husain	7	Do.
Mosque Abdul Wajeh	Hafiz Ali Bakhsh	9	Do.
„ of Jatan	Imamuddin	9	Do.
„ Lál	Muhammad Azim	27	Do. and Persian.
Muhalla Nál Bandan	Azim Khán	13	Do.
House of Din Muhammad.	Din Muhammad	4	Do.
Maqbaráh Fatah Jang	Hafiz Qadir Bakhsh	7	Do.
Mosque of Makotwah	Khairuddin	6	Do.
„ „ Urhah Khavat.	Abbas Ali	5	Do.
Náká chhaoni	Rahim Bakhsh	10	Do.
Muhalla Raián	Khairuddin	7	Do.
Do.	Ghulám Rasul	7	Do.
		500	

There is a patshala attached to the Thakurdwara of the wakils, in which Pandit Dolu Ram instructs 20 pupils in Sanscrit, gratuitously. The village of Dhandra also has a patshala with 12 pupils, who learn Sanscrit.

~~Bhai~~ Gobind Dass teaches Gurmukhi to 8 boys in his private house and lives upon alms. The other Gurmukhi schools in this circle are in Ludhiana, Lahara, Jaspalon and Dad, with 3, 5, 12 and 60 pupils.

Ludhiana has a Mahajani school also under Muhammad Bakhsh Jogi, who teaches Lande to 70 pupils (the private return mentions 100 pupils), and gets 1 seer of flour, 1 pice cash per week and daily food. The other Mahajani school in Ludhiana has 60 pupils. Lalton has a Mahajani school with 35 pupils.

SAMRALÁ.—Among the Hakims, Muhammad Bakhsh of Petrodi may be mentioned. A private return adds the names of Máidatta Baid, Pandits Chiranji Lal, Kanihya Lal, Devidyál Rámrikh, Badhawa and Bhais Bhagat Ram and Gurmukh Dass. Chiranji Lal and Devidyál are said to be poets.

The village of Samralá has a patshala attached to a shop, in which Chiranji Lal Brahmin, a Pandit of average qualifications, instructs 30 boys in Sanscrit Grammar, &c., on Rs. 4 per mensem and 12 pupils in Lande. There is another patshala with 10 pupils. The villages of *Bugli* and *Ghúngrali* have also patshalas, with 20 and 14 pupils in each.

There is a Gurmukhi school in the village of *Kotla Shamspur*, which is conducted by Bhagwan Dass Fakir, who teaches Gurmukhi to 11 boys, and lives on the income of a " muafi".

The villages of *Chahlan*, *Jatana* and *Dheloan* have a Lande school each with 8, 7 and 8 pupils.

DELON.—The villages of *Jarouhán*, *Dhulkot*, *Gujarwal* and *Rangyan* have 4 Korán schools (out of which the first 3 are attached to mosques and the last is held in the house of Nabi Bakhsh), conducted by Rahmatullah, Ahmaddin Hafiz, Khairuddin and Nizamuddin, with 11, 20, 10 and 9 pupils, respectively.

There are Gurmukhi schools in the villages of *Raipur* (3 schools), *Asi*, *Lohgadh*, *Bhamán*, *Singwala*, *Ballowál*, *Dhulkot*, *Kálak*, *Latala*, *Dhulmazra*, *Nigal*, attached to village dharamsalas, in which Ganda Singh, Panjab Singh, Manak Ram, Biran Dass, Ram Dass, Piram Dass, Prem Dass, Harparshad, Dya Ram, Jassa Singh, and Karam Dass teach 35, 20, 20, 3, 20, 28, 26, 22, 25, 1 and 5 pupils, respectively. Most of these teachers can only teach the Granth without interpretation, and a few of them know a little of Sanscrit also.

They get nothing for educating the boys, and live only on what the people give them as Fakirs and Sadhs.

Private information gives the following description of Raipúr, which was once the seat of Sikh learning:—

There are 5 " dehrás" in the village of *Raipur*, *Burj*, *Damdamá*, *Samádhwala Bhaiki Darwaji* (little gate) and *Dehra-panchayet*. In Burj, Nirmal Sadhus live, and there the sons of the villagers are taught Gurmukhi. There is a Gurmukhi library also. The inmates of the dehra and travellers are fed by the village. The pupils reading in the dehra collect bread from the village. One rupee on each marriage is also given to the dehra. Besides this, the Zemindars when they cause the Granth to be read give from Rs. 5 to 7. In Damdamá, which is held very sacred by the Sikhs as the refuge of Gurú Gobind, there lives Bhupsing, a Nirmal Sadh, a man of learning. The dehra is frequented by fakirs from distant places, who crowd here to be instructed by Sadh Bhupsing. The Samádhwala dehra has been repaired by Bhai Gandasing, and has a Gurmukhi school.

Bhaiki Darwaji had a well with *60 bighas of rent-free land, but in the present settlement the land has been assessed.* The houses belonging to this dehra are very extensive and splendid. There is no education given in this dehra *now*.

In the Dehra-panchayet instruction is now given. There is a dehra of Sanyasi fakirs also, which *had a well free of rent, but it is also assessed in the present settlement.*

There was one well attached to the Khánkah of Pir Daulat Sháh, which has *now been resumed* and assessed.

JUGRÁON.—In Jugráon among the *Moulvis*, Sharif Hasan and Sharif Husain, sons of Moulvi Rajab Ali Khan, deceased, and Moulvi Abdurrahim Gujar, may be mentioned.

Hakim Qamruddin and *Pandit* Bansidhar also deserve notice. Imdad Ali is said to be an author.

In the mosque of Agwar-i-Gujran, Abdullá, son of Moulvi Abdurrahim, a good Arabic scholar, who can teach up to Sharah Mulla (in Syntax) and Qutbi (in Logic) instructs 20 boys in Korán and Arabic Grammar, and has 51 bighas, 1 biswa and 13 biswasi of *land rent free from the Government, with the consent of the villagers.*

There are *Korán schools* in *Jugráon* (5 in number) *Bardiki, Gagra, Sidhwanbit, Salimpur, Abupura, Bhani Hakim, Sadarpur, Gorsiyan, Kotmáná, Bhundri, Aligarh, Tahara, Madarpúr,* with 138, 10, 23 (boys 7, girls 16 , 10, 34, 6, 5, 10, 5, 5, 6, 9, 16 and 7 pupils, respectively.

Jugráon has also a *patshala* attached to a Thakurdwara, in which Ganga Das Fakir Bairagi (a blind man) teaches Sarsut, Chandraka, Kavia-kosh to 20 pupils, and lives on alms.

There are two more minor patshalas having 17 pupils who learn Sanscrit Grammar, Logic and Hindu Law.

The village of *Dangyan* has a Gurmukhi school attached to the Dharamsala in which Sunder Das teaches 16 pupils. Besides, there are Gurmukhi schools in *Dangyan, Rasulpur, Dharka, Hans, Man, Tehara, Ghalib, Rumi, Manunka, Lamma* and *Kanunka,* with 9, 4, 3, 5, 4, 8, 10, 20, 5, 8, and 12 pupils, respectively.

There is a Mahajani school also in *Jugráon* under Jiwa Padha, instructing 75 pupils on Rs. 7 per mensem and another with 60 pupils. *Sidhwanbit* has also 2 Mahajani schools with 30 pupils.

This circle, consisting of 103 villages, is inhabited by Muhammadans (especially in villages on the bank of the river) and Jats. The mullas and fakirs teach and are given presents when a boy finishes his course.

RAIKOT.—In Raikot among the Moulvis, Moulvi Abdulkarim and Moulvi Asádullá (belonging to the same family, whose profession of instructing is hereditary) conduct a school and teach Arabic Grammar, Persian and the Korán to 30 pupils. They hold a muafi (rent-free) of 165 bighas land, and practise also as physicians.

Among the Baids, Durgadut, Ganda Ram and Gordhan, and among the Bhaís, Prem Das and Narsingh Das deserve notice.

Pandit Shib Ram is a good Sanscrit scholar. Mula Ram, another Pandit of average qualifications, conducts a patshala, in which Sanscrit is taught to 12 pupils. The Police returns mention two more patshalas conducted by Baldeo Kishen and Madsudhan with 6 and 7 pupils respectively.

In *Raikot* (9 schools), *Núrpúr, Saholi* and *Burj* there are Koran schools in which (Ismail, Kalu, Ismail, Ismail, Mangu, Ali Bakhsh, &c.,) Qadir Bakhsh, Shihabuddin, Sube Shah, with 98, 8, 4 and 1 pupils, respectively. Private information adds *Tajpur* with 20 pupils.

Munshi Gordhan, a good Persian scholar, who practises as a physician, also teaches Persian to 3 boys in Raikot.

The villages of *Saholi, Burji Hari Singh, Lakhkhá, Silwani, Jhorrán, Sedhar, Aychana* and *Ghumana* have each a Gurmukhi school attached to the village dharamsalas, in which Biram Dass, Mohar Singh, Paras Ram, Rakhi Ram, Sobhá Singh, Gurdat Singh, Gulab Das, Rámpershad, teach 2, 2, 12, 2, 6, 10, 4 and 10 pupils, respectively. There are Mahajani schools in Sakhana and Bopa-ka Kálán, with 12 pupils in each.

Private information adds a Gurmukhi school in *Raikot* conducted by Prem Das with 10 pupils, and another with 8 pupils, and Mahajani schools in *Bhauri Birgan* and *Tajpur* with 16 and 8 pupils.

DAKHAH.—In this circle there is only one patshala in the village of Khandour, with 3 pupils who learn Sanscrit.

There are Korán schools in the villages of *Hunbrán, Bhattao Dhuba, Banyawall, Walipur* (lesser), *Walipur* (major), *Ali Wál* (2 schools), *Ghumniwala, Barayeoh, Phagla* and *Pesaimi,* with 16, 7, 8, 9, 3, 24, 3, 4, 5, 2 pupils.

The villages of *Dakhah* (2 schools), *Bhatyan, Kilpur, Pindori, Dhat, Mandyani, Ragba, Mohi* (3 schools), *Chak, Dhapai, Isa Wal, Gohawar* and *Banuhar* have each a Gurmukhi school with 14, 8, 13, 5, 2, 2, 3, 27, 3, 4, 12, 15 and 12 pupils. There is a Mahajani school in *Purayen* with 9 pupils learning Lande.

The Mullás and Bhais in this circle receive corn at harvest time and one rupee on every marriage in the village.

SANEHWAL.—In this circle there are *Korán schools* in the villages of *Balyawal, Bhani Gahi, Koom* (*lesser*), *Koom* (major), *Fatahgarh, Kulani* (major), *Hadya, Maiwál, Dharawar*, with 14, 3, 4, 13, 9, 3, 7, 4 and 4 pupils. In *Balyawál, Fatahgarh* and *Koom* (major), Arabic and Persian are also taught.

The villages of *Umedpur* and *Jundyali* have a Gurmukhi school each, with 18 and 12 pupils respectively.

Sanehwal has a *patshala*, in which 3 pupils learn Sanscrit.

SHAHNA.—In this circle there are Gurmukhi schools in the villages of *Bhundar* with 3 schools and 20 pupils, *Jethuki* with 2 schools and 17 pupils, *Chunanwal* with 3 schools and 18 pupils, *Dhapali* with 3 schools and 34 boys, and *Alika, Bakhtgarh, Jodhpur, Chima, Chung, Raisar* and *Chaóki*, with a school each, and 2, 7, 2, 14, 3, 4 and 2 pupils, respectively. In all these schools the Granth is taught.

There is a *patshala* in the village of *Dhapáli*, with 10 pupils learning Gita, Sarsut and Bhagwat, with Ramkishen Brahmin, and a *Lande* school in *Chaoki* with 22 pupils.

The people, anxious to keep up their religious beliefs, get their boys taught Gurmukhi privately, because it is not taught in the Government schools, to which only those people send their boys, who wish to see them enter Government employment.

MACHHIWARA.—Among the Hakims, Shahnawáz, Wali Muhammad, Sayyid Shahnawáz, Kanahya Lal Qanungo, Sodhi Jaswant Sing and Pandit Kanahya Lal in the town of Machhiwara and Ala Rakha in Buhlulpur are distinguished.

Muhammad Ismail is a Moulvi of local reputation in *Chakki*.

Pandit Kanahya Lal conducts a patshala in the town of *Machhiwara*, in which he instructs 15 pupils in Sanscrit Grammar, and lives upon a muáfi which he holds.

There are Korán schools in *Máchhiwara, Mughliwal, Buhlolpur* and *Chakki*, with 17, 12, 4 and 16 pupils. The last school is attached to the village mosque and is conducted by Hafiz Qadir Bakhsh (a blind man), who teaches gratuitously and lives upon the produce of his lands.

KHANNA.—In Khanna, Alinawáz is an eminent Hakim. In the village of *Karodyan* there are 2 Korán schools attached to the mosques of the village, with 20 and 8 pupils respectively. Khairuddin Sayyid conducts the greater school gratuitously. *Khanna* has a patshala with 7 pupils.

There are Gurmukhi schools in the villages of *Bijah* and *Salodi* with 5 and 22 boys. The Salodi school is attached to a dharamsala under Odey Rám Fakir Udási, who has a muafi land and takes nothing for education.

The village of *Salodi* has also a Lande school under Ala Bakhsh *Jogi* (native of Rahawan), who teaches Mahajani and accounts to 20 pupils, who pay him daily food, one pice every week and one rupee on marriage, and a patshala with 20 pupils. There are minor Lande schools in *Kotla, Kheri, Alor, Bijah, Alero* and *Chikohi* with 10, 6, 10, 8, 7 and 6 pupils, respectively. *Salodi* and *Khanna* have each a patshala with 15 and 22 pupils.

LUDHIANA DISTRICT.

Extra.—A private informant adds to the Korán schools mentioned above, schools in *Jamalpur* with 30 pupils, *Nayadirki* 1 with 15 pupils, *Hebwan*

2 with 20 pupils, *Rajpura* 1 with 10 pupils, *Nurwata* 1 with 30, *Barwal* 2 with 40, *Fatahpur* 1 with 40, *Bhutghar* 1 with 5, *Kanbád* 1 with 10, *Gadh* 1 with 25, *Kakar* 1 with 10, *Lodhiwala* 1 with 10, *Bhatta Tahuwa* 1 with 10, *Talwandi Roi* 2 with 16, *Ahkuláhá* 1 with 8, *Chuharpur* 1 with 2, *Mirpur* 1 with 4, *Shiraz Majra* 1 with 6, *Purdat* 1 with 4, *Shahbázpur* 1 with 5, *Birhman* 1 with 14, *Lolori* 1 with 6, *Nanharkot* 1 with 30 pupils; to *patshalas* *Dyala* with 9, *Jaspalon* with 8 pupils; to Gurmukhi schools in *Utala* with 8 pupils, *Dhiru Majra* 2 with 6, *Manupur* 1 with 2, *Doheri* 1 with 4, *Todarpur* 1 with 12, *Lodhikhas* 1 with 12, *Bupa Rai* 1 with 10, *Akhara* 1 with 10, *Malla* 1 with 12, *Jechrari* 1 with 10, *Khundor* 2 with 9, *Sujapur* 1 with 6, *Rajwara* 1 with 5, *Jhachchawal* 1 with 12, *Dholan* 1 with 7; and Lande schools in Rajiwal with 30 and Jaspalon with 10 pupils may be added.

UMBALLA DIVISION.

DISTRICT SIMLA.

GENERAL ABSTRACT.

District.	No. of Maktabs and Madrasas.	No. of pupils.	No. of Sanscrit and Nagri Schools.	No. of pupils.	No. of Gurmukhi Schools.	No. of pupils.	No. of Lunde and Mahajani Schools.	No. of pupils.	Total No. of Indigenous Schools.	Total No. of pupils.
Simla .	9	129	...	...	...	...	2	47	11	176

Simla.—The name of the best known Moulvi is Abdussalam, and that of the best known Hakim, Mahbub Ali Sháh, who is also an author.

The largest maktab is attached to the Kashmiri Mosque; the teacher is Habibullah; there are 20 pupils, and the Korán, Persian and Urdu are taught: the teacher gets Rs. 10 per mensem in fees from the boys.

There are also 4 Korán schools: 1, in the Merchants' Mosque, with teacher Hafiz Abdul Majid; 2nd, in the Old Butcherkhana, with teacher Fakhruddín; 3rd, in the old Butchers' Mosque, with teacher Wali-ul-Husain; 4th, in the mosque of Kutub Khansama, with teacher Moulvi Abdussalam.

There are about 10 boys in each, and the only thing taught is the Korán.

Dagshai.—There is a maktab in a shop in which English, Urdu and Nagri are taught to 19 boys by Manru, who has fair qualifications. He gets Rs. 3 from his native pupils and Rs. 18 per mensem from the European pupils who read Urdu. The people are generally anxious to learn English and Persian, but a maktab, complete in all respects, is wanted. There is a second maktab in the Regimental Bazar, where the Korán and Urdu are taught, and 10 pupils attend.

Subathu.—The maktab in Subathu is attached to a mosque, the number of pupils attending is 30. The Korán, Urdu and Persian are taught gratuitously (*fi sabil Illah*) by Moulvi Kabir Shah and Hafiz Muhammad Husain. In the Patshala Pandit Shib Dyal teaches Sanscrit and Hindi gratuitously to 12 boys. There is also a Mahajani school where the same Pandit teaches Lande and Sanscrit to 12 pupils.

Kalka.—Hira Lal has a school with about 10 pupils, mostly sons of officials, to whom he teaches English. His qualifications are good; he was head-master at a Mission School for about 20 years. He gets Rs. 30 per mensem. At another school, a man named Allah Baksh teaches Mahajani to 35 boys.

JULLUNDHAR DIVISION.

JULLUNDHAR DISTRICT.

GENERAL ABSTRACT.

District.	No. of maktabs and Madrasas.	No. of pupils.	No. of Sanscrit and Nagri schools.	No. of pupils.	No. of Gurmukhi schools.	No. of pupils.	No. of Lande and Mahajani schools	No. of pupils.	Total No. of Indigenous Schools.	Total No. of pupils.
Jullundhar.	238	2,643	34	508	50	579	26	879	348	4,609

JULLUNDHAR.

Among the *Hakims* the most eminent are Ghulám Rasúl, Hakim Alamgir, Hakim Abdurrahman, in the town of Jullundhar, Hakim Muhammad Ahad Dad Khán in Basti Nau, Myanji Rahim Bakhsh, Hakim Shah Muhammad in Basti Shaikh, and Hakim Nur Ahmad and Hakim Muhammad Umar (the Government employé) in Basti Danishmandán. Among the *Baids* Gunpat Rai of Basti Ghuzan may be mentioned.

Moulvi Muhammad Hayat of Samipur, the most learned man in this circle, Moulvi Wali Muhammad, the famous preacher, and Moulvi Nur Muhammad deserve notice.

Among the *Pandits*, Pandit Ramdat, Honorary Magistrate, and Sripat Pandit in Basti Shaikh, educated in Benares and an hereditary scholar, are distinguished. Muhammad Salim of Basti Ghuzan and Barkat Ali Shaukat and Mirza Mawahid in Jullundhar are said to be *poets*.

There is a Korán school in *Basti Baba Khail* with 35 pupils (under Gamikhán), 8 in *Basti Shaikh* with 37 pupils, 2 in *Basti Dánishmandan* with 24, 4 in *Basti Ghuzan* with 57, 1 in *Basti Nau* with 80, 1 in *Basti Mattá Sahib* with 15 pupils, 1 in *Kollah* with 20, 1 in *Kalánpur* with 8, 1 in *Khurla* with 12, 1 in *Warana* with 22, 1 in *Dokoha* with 20, 1 in *Badala* with 19, and 20 in *Jullundhar* itself with 205 pupils.

There are 4 patshalas in Jullundhar, conducted by Pandit Gokal Chand, Grammarian, Banarsi Dass, Shiv Ram (certificate-holder of the Panjab University), and Deva Chand with 12, 16, 6 and 20 pupils, respectively, in which Logic, Grammar, Medicine, Dharam Shaster, and Prosody are taught.

There are 4 Mahajani schools in the city of Jullundhar and one in Basti Shaikh under Pir Bakhsh, Mayya Das, Jawala Parshad, Rám Sahai, and Surdhi Misser with 92, 60, 53, 50, 100 pupils, and Rs. 5, 5, 12, 1 pice a week per boy as the incomes of the teachers. There are two more Mahajani schools in *Basti, Ghuzan* and *Jamsher* under Qutbuddin and Karim Bakhsh with 40 and 26 pupils respectively.

There is one Gurmukhi school in *Lohár*, attached to a dharamsala, under Hari Das Faqir, instructing 6 boys, on Rs. 25 per annum.

Jullundhar Cantonments.—Among the *Hakims*, Naimulla Khán, a hereditary Hakim, and Ibrahim may be mentioned. *Moulvi* Qudrutullah and *Pandits* Parma Nand and Rám Narayan are also distinguished for their Arabic and Sanscrit learning respectively. A private return adds the name of *Bába Shivpuri* Baid Sanyasi.

Muhammad Siddik, a man of good qualifications, conducts a maktab with 40 pupils, who learn Arabic and Persian, and pay Rs. 15 per mensem to the teacher. There are besides 3 maktabs, with 27, 12, and 15 pupils; the best is conducted by Hafiz Qudrutullah gratuitously.

There are 5 Korán schools with 10, 5, 5, 5, and 5 pupils, respectively.

There are 2 patshalas in the Sadar Bazar, one of which is conducted by Gowardhan Dass, who teaches Sanscrit and Lande to 25 pupils, and the other has 14 pupils, who pay him 1 maund of flour, 6 seers of dal, salt and spices valued 10 annas, monthly, and Rs. 25 per annum; and the details about the other are not given.

KARTARPUR.—Among the *Pandits* in Kartarpur, Pandit Rám Chand, who conducts a patshala in which he instructs 3 pupils in Sanscrit and gets some corn at harvest time, and among the *Bhais*, Bába Hira Singh, and Bhai Ishur Singh, conducting 2 Gurmukhi schools attached to the dharamsalas, with 3 and 10 pupils respectively, are distinguished.

There are 2 maktabs in *Kartarpur*, one attached to a mosque and the other to a private house, conducted by Qutab Sháh and Ahmad Bakhsh (a man of good qualifications) with 5 and 6 pupils respectively. The former has an income of Rs. 4 monthly, and the latter is paid Rs. 5 per mensem by the Gurú of Kartarpur, to whose house the maktab is attached.

A Mahajani school in the town of Kartarpur is under Muhabbat Rawal, who gets Rs. 15 per mensem, and instructs 40 pupils in Mahajani, Lande, Sarrafi and Maharni (explained elsewhere).

BHOGPUR.—In this circle there are maktabs in the villages of *Chak Shakúr*, *Jamalpur*, *Sadachak*, *Ghori Wahi* (attached to the house of the Lumberdar), *Kharul*, *Dhadh Sanola*, *Chahirki* and *Rastgo*, attached to the village mosques and takyas under Ghulam Muhammad, Nabi Bakhsh, Ghulám Rasul, Khairati, Nizamuddin, Ruknuddin, Jhundu Sháh, and Abdulla, teaching the Korán Persian and Urdu to 2, 3, 4, 5, 3, 12, 4, and 5 pupils, respectively.

There is a Gurmukhi school in the village of *Sagran Wali*, in which Bahadur Singh Rámdasyá instructs 4 pupils in Gurmukhi, and lives on begging.

The maktab teachers receive nothing in cash, except what they receive by performing the marriage and funeral ceremonies.

ADÁMPUR.—Among the Hakims in Adámpur, Qutbuddin may be mentioned. A private informant adds Hakim Budruddin and Pandit Dala Rám also, as well-known.

In the village of *Kapurpind*, there is a maktab attached to the village mosque, in which Mulk Sháh, a man of average qualifications, teaches the Korán and Persian to 16 pupils gratuitously. Besides, there are maktabs in the villages of *Kalra* (attached to the Divankhaná of *Utam Singh*, under Ata Muhammad), *Jullowal*, *Lesriwala*, *Dhogri*, *Karyana*, *Sagran* and *Jalba*, with 8 (private information gives 9), 4, 3, 5, 14, 17, and 7 pupils respectively, in which the Korán, Persian and Urdu are taught.

Aláwalpur has a *patshala* in the house of Pandit Maya Rám, who instructs 8 pupils (private informant gives 10) in Sanscrit, and gets something as a present when a pupil finishes the Bhagwat. *Droli* (under Bhai Nandá Singh), *Domundha*, *Pandori* and *Mander* have Gurmukhi schools, with 49, 12, 8, and 7 pupils respectively, in which the Granth is taught.

There are Mahajani schools in *Ghuryal* and *Adámpur* under Miran Bakhsh, with 10 and 19 pupils respectively.

A private return adds Korán schools in *Adámpur* (2 schools), *Mehdipur*, *Chaman*, *Aláwalpur*, *Dhirowal*, *Nahlan*, *Chuharwali*, with 10, 10, 2, 10, 6, 8, and 5 pupils respectively, a Gurmukhi School in Ghuryal with 10 pupils, and another Mahajani school in Adámpur with 9 pupils.

The Lumberdars, influential Zemindars and Mahajans of Adámpur, send an application to the effect that they wish to encourage the Yunani system of medicine, and that accordingly some kind of support may be given to the physician of their town, Qutbuddin, by the Government.

BANGA.—In Banga, Nizamuddin, Puna Singh, Muhammad Bakhsh, Kishen Singh and Nur Muhammad are distinguished Hakims.

There are *maktabs* in *Bhin*, *Khankhanan*, *Mandhali* and *Palyan Unchyan*, conducted by Sháh Wali, Imam Sháh, Karim Bakhsh and Farzand Ali, with 12, 20, 30, and 11 pupils, respectively.

The maktabs in *Khankhanan* and *Mandhali* are attached to the houses of lumberdars, who pay the teachers Rs. 5 and 7 per mensem. Besides Arabic and Persian, which are taught in all these schools, in *Khankhanan* and *Mandhali*, Urdu and Arithmetic are also taught. *Mandhali* has also a Mahajani school with 20 pupils.

There are minor Korán schools and maktabs also in *Jandyala*, *Banga*, *Thandyan*, *Lodipur*, *Batoli* and *Anokharwál*, with 10, 4, 1, 2, 12, and 15 pupils, respectively.

Banga has 2 *patshalas*, and the village of *Bhin* (a seat of Sanscrit learning in the times of the Sikhs), *Khatkar*, *Phirala*, have a patshala each. Pandits Arjan, Gopal, Kaka Rám of Bhin, Ganga Rám and Gobind Rám, great Sanscrit scholars, conduct these patshalas and teach gratuitously Vyakaran, Chandraká, Logic and Dharam Shaster to 20, 20, 20, 20, and 15 pupils, respectively. In *Musápur*, *Phukri*, *Mukandpur* and *Gunachaur*, there are minor patshalas with 6, 5, 22, and 6 pupils, respectively.

There are two dharamsalas in the village of *Banga*, having a Gurmukhi school attached to each, conducted by Parma Nund Fakir and Bhai Jawahar Singh, teaching Gurmukhi gratuitously to 20 and 30 pupils respectively. The villages of *Phut*, *Khatkar*, *Musapur*, *Bains*, *Khankhana* and *Mehli* have each a Gurmukhi school, with 6, 10, 2, 2, 10, and 20 pupils, and the villages of *Rinda* and *Mehli* have Lande schools with 25 and 3 pupils respectively.

RÁHUN.—In *Ráhun* among the Hakims Myan Hasan Jahanyan, Ghulám Nabi, Walayet Ali, Moulvi Ghulám Muhiuddin, and among the Baids, Bava Sukhdeo Nauth and Pandit Bágh Rám Baid may be mentioned.

Pandits Dyal Rám, Maghi Rám, Khemraj, Jaggan Nauth, Amin Chand, Chajju Rám, and *Moulvis* Ghulám Muhiuddin, Maula Bakhsh and Akbar Sháh deserve notice. Bhai Rám Singh and Bhai Dasondha Singh (a washerman), and Pandit Khemraj are said to be eminent Bhais and a poet respectively.

There are very good *patshalas* in *Ráhun* and *Aur*, two in the former and one in the latter, conducted by Pandit Khemraj, Pandit Amin Chand (a certificate-holder of the Punjab University College), and Atra Brahmin, who teach Vedant, Astrology, Amarkosh, Bhagwat and Sanscrit Grammar to 10, 20, and 20 pupils, respectively. Pandits Amin Chand and Atra receive Rs. 60 and 50 per annum respectively. There are two patshalas in *Nawashehar* also, under Pandit Maha Rám and Bava Mangal Gir, with 7 and 12 pupils respectively, teaching Logic, Grammar, Astrology and Bhagwat.

There are Korán schools at *Ráhun* (7 in number) and the villages of *Aur*, *Kariam*, *Thatiala*, *Garhi Fateh Khan*, *Sawetah*, *Seikha Mazra'a* and *Mirpur Jattan*, under Ghulám Rasul, Muhkam Din, Abdulqadir, Sayyid Ali, Ahmad, Ghulám Nabi, Nizamuddin, Hafiz Sultan Bakhsh, Jewan Sháh and Khuda Bakhsh, a weaver (all men of limited qualifications), with 79, 6, 5, 10, 10, 15, 6, and 3 pupils, respectively. Abdulqadir, Sayyid Ali and Sultan Bakhsh receive Rs. 10, 15, 24 per annum respectively, the rest having no fixed income.

Gurmukhi schools in the villages of *Bhidana*, *Gurcha*, *Durgapur* and *Chuharpur*, attached to the dharamsalas, except in *Durgapur*, where the school is in a private house, are conducted by Partap Singh, Saudagar Singh Rámdasyá, Kánh Singh Kuka and Ganga Rám Udási, with 10, 7, 2, and 4 pupils, respectively.

In *Ráhun* Kanshi Rám Brahmin teaches Lande to 30 pupils, and receives Rs. 50 per annum in cash and kind. A private informant mentions another Mahajani school at *Ráhun* under Surjan Pandha with 40 pupils.

PHILLOUR.—Among the *Pandits* and Hakims, Pandit Hiranand and Hakim Bahadur Beg, of Phillour, are noted ones.

In the village of *Guhaar*, there is a maktab attached to the village mosque in which Ghulám Jabbár of Jullundhar teaches the Korán, and 1st and 2nd books of Persian, to 5 pupils, and gets about Rs. 5 per mensem.

Rurki has a school under Nabi Bakhsh (*alias* Nanak) Mirasi, who teaches to 28 pupils Gurmukhi, Lande and Sarrafi, getting about Rs. 8 per mensem.

NURMAHAL.—Among the *Hakims*, Hakim Khurshaid Ali, a Sayyad of Nurmahal, who formerly used to teach some pupils, and among the Pandits, Pandit Atma Rám and Madho Rám may be mentioned.

There is a patshala attached to a Thakurdwara, where Mast Rám, disciple of Mauju Rám Sadh Bairagi, teaches religious books to 25 pupils gratuitously, being himself supported by the owner of the Thakurdwara.

A private informant mentions 2 other patshalas in *Nurmahal*, one conducted by Pandit Atma Rám and the other by Pandit Rámdat, both being great Sanscrit Logicians and Grammarians, and teaching Logic and Grammar to 10 and 28 pupils respectively.

Nurmahal has also a Mahajani school under Faqir Bakhsh, son of Buta Jogi of the Malyar Kotla estate, with 40 pupils, and about Rs. 8 per mensem as the income of the teacher in kind and cash. Another Mahajani school is in the village of *Bilga*, conducted by Baga Jogi of the Malehr Kotla estate, with 70 pupils, and Rs. 7 per mensem in kind and cash.

There is a maktab in *Talwan* which is conducted by Núr Ali Sháh Sayyid of Nurmahal (who, except in mathematics, can teach to the middle school examination standard), teaching Gulistan, Bostan, Madho Rám, and Sikandarnama to 9 pupils on Rs. 4 per mensem, daily food and clothes.

NAKODAR.—Among the *Hakims* at Nakodar, Gulab Rai, Buddhú Rám and Karam Ilahi, and among the *Pandits* Pandit Nathu Rám may be mentioned.

In the villages of *Bupa Rai*, *Chak*, and *Nakodar*, Gurmukhi schools are conducted by Bhais Kharak Singh, Jhunda Singh, and Bava Sunder Dass (mentioned in the private returns only, teaching 20 pupils).

There is a maktab in *Mahatpur*, conducted by Kazi Jan Muhammad, with 40 pupils, and Rs. 4 per mensem as the emolument of the teacher.

There are Lande schools in *Nakodar* and *Sarih*, conducted by Nathu and Nurdin, with 40 and 20 pupils respectively. Nathu Rám teaches also Gurmukhi and Shastri, and has an income of Rs. 4 per mensem.

A private informant mentions one more Lande school at Nakodar, with 35 pupils under Amin Chand.

The second Police Return adds the following Indigenous Schools :—

Name of Place.	Name of Teacher.	No. of pupils	Subjects taught.
Nakodar	Amanat Ali	15	Law, Logic and Medicine.
Mahatpur	Hafiz Muhammad Bakhsh	7	The Korán.
Ditto	Pir Bakhsh	13	Ditto.
Khurrampur.	Ahmad Bakhsh	6	Ditto.
Gohar .		12	Ditto.
Ditto	Sirdar Ali	10	
Ditto	Jhundú Sháh	6	
Rasulpur	Idan Sháh	25	Persian and the Koran.
Talwandi	Ata-ullah	5	Ditto.
Ditto	Nabi Bakhsh	10	Ditto.
Ditto	Mahr Bakhsh	5	Ditto.

Name of Place.	Teacher.	No. of pupils.	Subjects taught.
Rogi	Bhole Sháh	8	The Korán
Ditto	Umruddin	10	Persian.
Sahna	Muhammad Sháh	3	The Korán.
Sahna Dedh	Ilahi Bakhsh	11	Ditto.
Wheryan	Mukham Din	15	Ditto.
Ditto	Nizamuddin	10	Ditto.
Ditto	Nizamuddin, II	10	Ditto.
Samankha	Azizuddin	9	Ditto.
Ditto	Muhammad Bakhsh	11	Ditto.
Ida	Najmuddin	5	Ditto.
Ditto	Jundi Sháh	3	Ditto.
Kabandran	Imamuddin	12	Ditto.
Mahúnwal	Azmat Ali	13	The Korán and Persian.
Chak Mughlani	Ghulám Muhammad	17	
Ditto	Imamuddin	7	The Korán.
Khurshaidpur	Shihabuddin	4	Ditto.
Malri	Ilahi Bakhsh	20	Ditto.
Sahari Wal	Dina	2	Ditto.
Sehu Wal	Ghulám Husain	4	
Alu Wal	Umar Bakhsh	12	Persian and the Korán.
Dhali Wal	Ganga Rám	3	Gurmukhi.
Sunkar	Sukh Khán	10	Sanscrit.
Ditto	Ganga Rám	5	Ditto.

SHAHKOT.—In Myanwali among the Moulvis, Moulvi Murid Ahmed, a good Arabic and Persian scholar, and among the Hakims and Pandits Hakim Jan Muhammad and Ata Muhammad, and Pandit Lachhmi Dhar of Shahkot and Pandit Anant Rám (both of them are poets also) deserve notice.

In Myanwali Afghanán, Moulvi Murid Ahmed instructs gratuitously 4 pupils (all outsiders) in advanced Arabic books, and feeds them also from his own pocket.

There is also a Lunde school in Shahkot with 11 pupils under Maula Bakhsh, who receives Re. 1-6 in cash and daily food.

In Shahkot there are 2 patshalas; the first is attached to the Thakurdwara of Bava Jiya Rám Dass Sádh, and the second is held in the house of the teacher They are conducted by Pandits Lachhmi Dhar and Anant Rám respectively, who teach Sanscrit, Grammar, Amarkosh, and Kavya to 15 and 4 pupils respectively.

EXTRA.*

A private return adds Maktabs in *Jadla* with 20, *Manjaur* with 20, *Padunatwali* with 15, *Barwa* with 15, *Khamachu* with 12, *Ladhana Uncha* with 12, *Bahadurpur* with 10, *Nimatpur* with 10, *Chakli Nabi Bakhsh* with 8, *Shamspur* with 7, *Ladhana Jaising* with 4, *Saiala* with 9, *Nagka* with 10, *Chaugatti* with 18, *Malsian* with 5, *Kanya Husaini* with 27, *Bhogyan* with 10, *Khairullahpur* with 20, *Jhungian* with 16, *Isewál* with 8, *Angi kiri* with 10, *Singowal* with 15, *Ismailpur* with 15, *Muhsampur* with 15, *Uggi* with 11, *Baloke* with 36, *Akbarpur* with 30, *Kili* with 10, *Budanwal* (2 schools) with 21, *Dheryan* with 9, *Kotli Gazian* (2 schools) with 18, *Guhir* with 26, *Paryan kalan* (2 schools) with 36, *Myanwal Rayan* with 20, *Aqilpur* with 30, *Bhin* with 12, *Phrala* with 15, *Nimatpur* with 10, *Tang* with 10, *Thala* with 10, *Phillour* with 12, *Garha* with 2, *Kang Rayan* with 2. *Sarhali* (2 schools) with 13, *Dadu wal* with 8, *Gulhaur* with 14, *Jandyali* with 6, *Raipur* (2 schools) with 24, *Kanyana* with 5, *Ashur* with 6, *Umarpur* (3 schools) with 44, *Kot Badal* (2

* 124 schools and 1,407 pupils have been added to the Jalandhar district in a District Return kindly sent by Mr. F. D'O. Ballock, the Deputy Commissioner, as also 5 schools and 136 pupils in the Kangra district. It came, however, too late for incorporation in Part III, which contains the "General Abstract" of the number of schools and pupils in the province.

schools) with 18, *Shamsabad* with 6, *Fatehpur Apra* with 15, *Dhamdev* with 6, *Khanbra* with 10, *Pholanwala* with 5, *Kadianwala* with 8, *Bareal* with 6, *Hamiri khera* with 5, *Udhopur* with 4, *Shahpur* with 2, *Kanyana* with 14, *Sagran* with 6, *Varana* with 15, *Talban* with 6, *Alipur* with 16, *Partappura* with 8, *Husainpur* with 2, *Bagra* with 4, *Bembeyanwali* with 8, *Sattarpur* with 2, *Jugral* with 9, *Khojpur* with 5, *Sattuwali* with 6, *Awardan* with 8, *Dhurjal* (2 schools) with 7, *Jibi* with 6, *Kandala* with 8, *Manko* with 8, *Alawalpur* with 12, *Badshahpur* with 10, *Chakonur* with 10, *Tirna* with 9, *Burjeyan kalan* (3) with 53, *Mondala* with 15, *Kalu mundi* with 10, *Salayeh* with 7, *Ranaut* (2) with 20, *Zahirpur* with 4, *Sand* with 12, *Kamalpur* with 8, *Taran kalan* with 1, *Nyadirki* with 5, *Naurangpur* with 6, *Sualehpur* with 12; Gurmukhi schools in *Rahya* with 12, *Mahal Khurd* with 15, and Mahajani schools in *Jádla* with 15, *Malyana* with 5, Bharú *Mazara* with 15, *Schidpur* with 15, *Bias Pind* with 20, *Jandu Singha* with 14, *Subhana* with 10, *Bholar* with 7, *Sher Singh Jul* with 10, *Thala* with 4, *Atti* with 6, *Tarkhan Muzare* with 7, *Laggar* with 6, *Bara Pind* (2) with 9, *Birh* with 12, *Dusang* (2) with 40, *Drulli* with 45, *Shahpur* with 11, *Dummanda* with 9, *Kalesian* with 6, *Lidra* with 7, *Kukarpind* with 10, *Khojpur* with 10, *Jundher* with 8, *Chitti* with 12, *Kandala* with 6; and Sanscrit schools in *Upra* with 10, *Bundali* (2 schools) with 32, *Lasara* with 10, and a Mahajani school in *Agilpur* with 16 pupils.

JULLUNDHAR DIVISION.

HOSHIARPUR DISTRICT.

GENERAL ABSTRACT.

District.	No. of Maktabs and Madrasas.	No. of pupils.	No. of Sanscrit and Nagri schools.	No of pupils.	No. of Gurmukhi schools.	No. of pupils.	No. of Lande and Mahajani schools.	No. of pupils.	Total No. of Indigenous Schools.	Total No. of pupils.
Hoshiarpur	123	1,395	34	435	36	332	18	252	211	2,414

HOSHIARPUR CITY.—*Hakims* Abdulla, Ali Sher, and *Maulvis* Mian Muhammad, Mahbub Alam, and Hadi Bukhtiyar and *Pandits* Narsing Das, Kanahia Lal, Sukhdyal, Sudama Rám, Rám Rattan, Gobind Rám, Gobind Rám Storia, Kaka Rám, Shivdyal and Kanahia Lal are the most eminent. The largest maktab in Hoshiarpur is attached to a private house. Hafiz Abdulla teaches the Korán to 25 pupils and gets Rs. 10 per mensem on an average; there are 3 other Korán schools with 20, 15 and 12 pupils, respectively; 5 patshalas, in which Pandit Narsingh Das Shastri, Pandit Lakhshmi Dhar, Kaka Rám, Shivdyal, and Kanahia Lal teach Shasters to 13, 7, 50, 20, and 15 pupils, respectively; 2 Gurmukhi schools attached to the dharamsalas of Gulab Singh and Hardas Singh with 14 pupils, in which the *Granth* is taught; and a large Mahajani school, with 50 pupils, in which Lande is taught. Ata Muhammad is the teacher of the latter and gets Rs. 6 per mensem. The village *Basi Moda* has two maktabs, the one attached to a mosque, in which Hafiz Qadir Bakhsh has 16 pupils, and the other 15. The Korán and "Fikah" (Muhammadan Law) are taught. A private information adds a Mahajani school under Lakkha Padha with 50 pupils.

Basi Daulat Khán has 2 maktabs, one under Sirajuddin, with 35 pupils, and the other under Amir Sháh, with 25 pupils, in which the Korán and "Fikah" are taught.

Patti 2 with 5; *Horkan* 2, attached to the village mosques with 4; *Badla* 1 with 4; *Kanaur* 1 with 18; *Pindori Kad* 1 with 10. In all these only the Korán is taught; whilst Persian and Urdu are added in the following maktabs :—

Basi Nau 2 maktabs with 34 pupils. *Ehrana* 2 with 16; *Bohan* 2 with 22; *Harta* 1 with 18; *Shamli* 1 with 20; *Phoglana* 1 with 20. *Hardokhanpur* 2 with 11; *Sisoli* 1 with 10; *Moukhliana* 1 with 9; *Khanora* 2 with 12; *Haidarwál* 1 with 14; *Bahala* 1 with 9; in this latter school no Urdu, but English and Persian, are taught; *Bahala* has also a patshala with 15 pupils, in which Shastri and Gurmukhi and Lande are taught. *Basi Kalan* has 1 patshala with 15; *Bijwara* 1 with 15; *Sahari* 1 with 15; *Nangal Shahidan* 1 with 6; in the former three, Shastri and the Vedas are taught; in the latter only Shastri.

Hardokhanpur, *Chagran* and *Bahadurpur* have each a Mahajani school with 7, 4 and 20 pupils respectively, in which Lande is taught.

The following are Gurmukhi schools: *Pur Hiran* 1 with 15; *Bhago Val* 1 with 4; *Chagran* 1 with 5; *Muna Kalan* 1 with 15; *Ajo Val* 1 with 4; *Pindori Rukman* 1 with 6; *Piyal* 1 with 10; *Rajpur* 1 with 16, in which the *Granth* and *Pothis* are taught.

Thana Mahilpur.—The following statement shows the number of Indigenous Schools in *Mahilpur.*

Name of Village.	Name of Teacher.	His qualifications.	No. of pupils.	Subjects taught.	Income of the Teacher.	Locality.
1. Baghnra	Hamira Fakir	Low	7	The Korán	Gratuitously	Attached to the takya.
2. Namolyan	Rangu Rawal	Ditto	5	Ditto	Ditto	In the teacher's house.
3. Taolyan	Dyal Shah Fakir.	Ditto	8	Urdu Persian.	Rs. 24 per annum in cash and 30 maunds of corn.	In the shop of Wazeru Brahmin.
4. Moju Muzara	Turab Ali	Ditto	10	Urdu and the Korán.	30 maunds of corn	Attached to a takya.
5. Bham	Rahmat	Ditto	10	Ditto	Rs. 40 per annum	Attached to the house of Qadir Bakhsh.
6. Hakumatpur	Imam Uddin	Ditto	8	The Korán	Re. 1-8 on each marriage occasion.	Attached to the takya of Gamu Shah.
7. Aima Jatan	Kamar Sháh	Ditto	16	Persian and the Korán.	Rs. 16 per annum in cash, 40 maunds of corn and daily food.	Attached to the house of Chajju Lumberdar.
8. Dihana	Jan Muhammad	Fair	10	Urdu, Persian, and the Koran.	8 annas per boy.	
9. Kot Fatohi	Farzand Ali Sayyad	Ditto	8	Urdu and Persian.	Rs. 4 per month paid by Narayen Dass Sowkar.	
10. Bholiwal Rathán	Mazhar Sháh Fakir.	Low	30	Urdu and the Korán.	20 maunds of corn and Re. 1-4 on each marriage occasion.	
11. Totú Mazrá	Bhai Budh Singh	Fair	7	The Granth	Gratuitously	Attached to the dharmsala of Nirmal Sadhu.
12. Lakhsihan	Munni Lal Brahmin.	Low	9	Gormukhi	Ditto	In his shop.
13. Pinjor	Kanihya Singh Nirmal.	Ditto	18	Ditto	Ditto	Attached to a dharamsala.
14. Ditto	Tara Singh Ramdasya.	Ditto	18	Ditto	Ditto.	
15. Jelwera	Ram Singh Sadh.	Ditto	2	Ditto	Ditto.	
16. Ditto	Natha Singh	Ditto	8	Ditto	Food.	
17. Khera	Sam Singh Sadh	Fair	15	Ditto	Gratuitously	Attached to a dharamsala.
18. Puchnangal	Didar Bakhsh Mirasi.	Low	12	Lande	Rs. 30 per annum and food.	
19. Dhada	Pir Bakhsh	Ditto	8	Ditto	Rs. 48 per annum.	
20. Thakarwal	Mayya Brahmin	Ditto	2	Ditto	Gratuitously.	
21. Jijun	Dhumar Jati	Good	4	Sanscrit	Ditto	Attached to a Thakurdwara.
22. Ditto	Hamira	Low	25	Sanscrit and Lande.	Ditto.	
23. Ditto	Jiva	Ditto	8	Sanscrit	Ditto.	
24. Baryán	Bhola Brahmin	Ditto	20	Sanscrit and Lande.	Ditto.	

Thana Mubarakpur.—Hakim Kazi Karm Karim in the village *Panjal*, Báid Tulsi Rám in the village Nari, and Pandit Ishar Das in Rajpur are the most eminent ones in the circle. The village *Koneran* has a maktab in a private house, in which 10 pupils are taught Urdu, Persian and Arithmetic by Imam Din, who gets Rs. 4 per mensem in cash and his daily food.

Thana Hariana.—The largest and best maktab of this Thana is in the village *Hezam*. It is situated in a private house, and its teacher is Rustam Ali, a man of first-rate ability in Arabic, Persian and Mathematics, having formerly also held a Government employment. There are 20 pupils, who are taught Arabic Grammar, Logic, and other mental science subjects, Persian, and subjects of general use as taught in Government schools. Several boys of the Government school, desirous of attaining higher knowledge, come over to this school; some even go up for the Departmental examination from this school. Rustam Ali takes no fees from his pupils; he has some land and lives on its produce, and gives food to the poorer boys. The town *Hariana* has two maktabs, 26 boys attending in both; Urdu, Persian and the Korán are taught. In the town of *Shám* are 5 maktabs, 31 boys and 6 girls attending; they are taught Urdu, Persian and the Korán. *Pindori Medo Mid* and *Badala Pukhta* have also each a *mixed* school; in the first named, 9 boys and 4 girls attend, and in the second 20 boys and 3 girls; the same subjects are taught as in the above. The following are *Korán schools*: *Basi Panj Bhan* 1 school with 10 pupils; *Sada Rain* 1 with 9; *Raowal* 1 with 3; *Talvandi Goni* 1 with 13; *Jandiala* 1 with 10 pupils; *Basi Babu* 1 with 10; *Nanda Chon* 1 with 5; *Birampur* 1 with 3; *Dadupur* 1 with 2; and *Basi Ballu* 1 with 27 pupils.

One large patshala is in *Hariana* with 20 pupils, in which Sanscrit grammar and classics are taught. *Jauri* and *Saida* have also patshalas with 15 and

6 pupils respectively. *Shám* has a small patshala where primary books are taught to 6 boys, and a Gurmukhi school with 3 boys, where reading and writing in Gurmukhi is taught, also a small Lande school with 4 boys. *Hariana*, however, has two larger Lande schools, with an attendance of 30 boys in the two. *Purajatan*, *Kang*, *Khanpur*, *Dhadhbawá*, *Gurganwal*, *Sus*, *Saidra*, *Mirzápur*, *Panjdeta* and *Khadiála* have a small Gurmukhi school each, in which reading and writing are taught, with 2, 4, 6, 5, 1, 7, 4, 4, 2, and 6 boys, respectively.

THANA TANDA.—The following Hakims of repute are mentioned: Hakim Muhammad Sháh in *Urmara*, Hakims Kasim, Akram, Shahabuddin, and Ghulám Muhammad, in *Miani*; M. Muhammad Bakhsh in *Raipind*; Abdulla Moulvi in *Talvandi Vadian*; M. M. Najmuddin in *Tanda*; Ganesha and Sandi in *Kotla*; and Hakims Akbar Khán and Jani Khán in Rasulpúr. The following places have maktabs: *Avan Kheura Sháh* 1 with 3; *Raipind* 1 with 2; *Jabria* 1 with 5; *Kotla* 1 with 5; *Zahura* 1 with 7; *Basi Jalal Khán* 1 with 5; in all these the Korán and Persian are taught; *Salimpur* and *Feroz* with a maktab and 3 pupils each, in which only the Korán is taught, as also at *Jalalpur* with 2; *Jebchak* with 5; *Bahadurpur* with 4; *Chakoya* with 6; *Jaja* with 8 pupils. *Karl Khurd*, *Alipur Madian*, and *Maghari* have each a maktab with 6, 7, and 9 pupils attending respectively, in which Persian and the Korán are taught, and finally a maktab or rather a madrasah at *Tilvandi Vadian* attended by 12 pupils, where Arabic, Classics, Logic, the Korán, &c., are taught. A private informant adds *maktabs* in *Ghilzian* with 15 and in *Kaluya* with 8 pupils, and a *patshala* in *Ghilzian* with 5 pupils.

THANA NURPUR.—The police return mentions one patshala at the village *Jatvahar*, which is attached to a very old temple; 10 pupils attend; Dittu Rám and Jai Dial teach *Jotish* (Astrology) *Vedant* (Pantheism), and *Viakarán* (Grammar). These Pandits have no income from the school, and one of them provides food for the pupils.

THANA ANANDPUR.—Hakim Ghulám Qadir, Hakims Atar Singh and Kali Nand, Baids Kirpu and Ganga Rám are the distinguished men of this Thana. *Anandpur* has three Gurmukhi schools, two in a private house and one in a temple. One has 20, the other 40, and the third 10 pupils; they are taught in Gurmukhi and Sanscrit by Hira Nand, Sukhrám and Bhai Puran Singh respectively; the first gets Rs. 6 per mensem, the second Rs. 7, and the third derives no income from his school. *Kiratpur* and *Daroli* have also each a Gurmukhi school with 15 and 4 pupils attending, respectively.

THANA GADH DEVALA.—Hakims Umar Bakhsh and Rahmat Ali, Baids Nathu and Mahant Jairám Das and Pandit Ruldú Rám are mentioned. *Gadh Devála* has a patshala in a private house, where Ruldú Rám instructs gratuitously 6 pupils in Sanscrit, Grammar, &c. At Dharián is a maktab attached to the mosque of the place with 6 pupils who are taught Persian and the Korán by Kamál Din.

THANA GADH SHANKAR.—Moulvi Muhammad Umar Din, Hakims Shah Nawáz (in Gadh Shankar), Muhammad Nawáz (in Panám), Baid Gokal Chand (in Saroá), Pandits Rikhi Kesh and Bishambar Das are named as the best known here. The largest maktab is in *Panam* attached to a private house, where Muhammad Nawáz, who is well up in Persian and Mathematics, fair in Arabic and good in Medicine, has 40 pupils; Urdu, Persian, Mathematics and the Korán are taught. The teacher gets Rs. 15 per mensem and 30 maunds of corn half-yearly.

GADH SHANKAR itself has also a maktab with 20 pupils, in which the Korán is taught; *Basiala* has 1 maktab with 15 pupils, *Raipur* 1 with 8, *Moila* 1 with 10, *Sejpur* 1 with 12, *Birampur* 1 with 12, and also *Parkhoval* 1 with 10 pupils. The only Gurmukhi school that is mentioned in this thana, is at *Moran Vali* attached to a dharamsala, where Natha Singh instructs 10 pupils in Gurmukhi and religious books; he gets some corn at harvest time. There are, however, three patshalas, one at *Sehwan* in the temple; Pandit Rikhi Kesh, educated at Benares, well up in *Jotish* and religious books, teaches these subjects to 10 pupils gratuitously and provides them also with food; the second at *Gadh Shankar* with 15 pupils; and the third at *Makand Dáni* with 7 pupils.

THANA MUKERIAN.—Ganga Rám, Fatih Muhammad, and Sandhi Sháh, Hakims in Mukerian; Ibrahim, Hakim in Khanpur; Palu Mal Brahmin, and Ata Muhammad Kazi in Bhangala, Roda *Barber* in Kali Bag and Tárá in *Chunyan* are named as well-known Hakims in the above thana. The largest maktab is at *Jandval* in a private house; Amir Ali teaches Persian to 7 boys and gets 30 maunds of corn once a year, and his daily food from Natha Sing, Zaildar. *Arthival, Sahrakval* and *Gahlarian* have each a small maktab, in which Persian is taught, and in the first two 5 pupils attend, whilst the last has only 3 pupils *Bhangala Nau* with 10 pupils; *Panj Dhira* with 3; *Panj Dhira Kulan* with. 3, and *Kamloh* with 2 pupils, are solely Korán schools.

Mansar has a patshala in which Shastri (Sanscrit) reading and writing is taught, with 5 pupils.

THANA BALACHOR.—Ali Bakhsh, Hakim in Garlún; Ahmad Sháh, Hakim in Khurd; Musaddi Rám, Hakim in Gadhí Kanúgoyan; Baja Mal, Hakim and Baid in Balachor; *Pandit* Rup Rám in Sahiba, are the distinguished men of above thana. The largest maktab is at *Mander*, attached to a mosque; Alah Bakhsh teaches Persian and the Korán to 25 boys; he gets 50 maunds of corn per annum, besides his daily food. *Paragpur* has a maktab in which the same subjects are taught to 12 boys; the teacher's name is Jhandú Sháh; he gets 24 maunds of corn and his food. *Mandiali* has exactly the same kind of school with 15 pupils, and teacher Namah Sháh.

Karaor has a madrasah in which Arabic and the Korán are taught, attended by 11 pupils. The following are Korán schools: *Hedun* with 10; *Chonkoya* with 8; *Ghamur* with 10 pupils. *Hasanpur* and *Rurki Mughlan* have each a maktab, in which Persian, the Korán, &c., &c., are taught; the first has 8, and the second 15 pupils. *Bachauri* has a patshala with 5 pupils, in which Sanscrit is taught; and a Gurmukhi school with 5 pupils, in which poetry, &c., in Gurmukhi are taught. *Sabha* has a patshala with 4 pupils reading Sanscrit.

THANA HAJIPUR.—Hakims Pandit Jaigopal (in Datarpur), Gokal (in Hajipur), Bhai Gyan Sing *Granthi* and Baids Kishn Sarn (in Rampur) and Shiv Lal (in Hajipur) are mentioned. *Bhahoval, Patti Hezam, Bhaboval, Kattoval,* and *Sahrak* have each a school at the first place with 4 pupils, where Arabic is taught; at the second place Arabic and Persian are taught, and 20 pupils attend; at the third the same subjects are taught, and the number of pupils it is 7; whilst at the fourth village Urdu is also added, the pupils attending being also 7. The teachers of the first three schools have no fixed income, but the fourth gets 5 maunds of corn per mensem.

Depur has a patshala with 5, *Bah Lakhan* with 14, and *Fatehpur* with 7 pupils; in these three patshalas Sanscrit and multiplication tables, &c., are taught.

Hajipur has a large Gurmukhi school with 18 pupils, where Gurmukhi, the multiplication tables, &c., are taught. *Dhar* and *Sheparian* have a Lande school with 7 pupils attending at each.

THANA UNÁ.—Eminent Pandits are Devi Ditta in *Kalgrano,* Duni Chand in *Sanoli,* Gobind Ram in *Panjawar,* Sukh Deo in *Santokh Gadh* and Maiva Rám in *Bhabor*.

The Police return mentions no maktab in this Thana, but 4 patshalas in which Sanscrit is taught, 2 at *Kalgrano,* 1 at *Meda Majra* and 1 at *Bhabur*. with 7, 20, and 40 pupils attending respectively.

The last-named place has also a Lande school with 10 pupils, and *Barhara* and *Panjawar* have each a Lande school with 6 and 15 pupils attending respectively, and *Uná* has another Lande school with 9 pupils.

THANA DOSÚYA.—At the town *Dosúya* are mentioned Pandits Bidya Dhar, Devi Dial and Gurditta Mal, also Hakim Búra Mal. The maktab of this place is attached to the mosque. The teacher Karim Bakhsh is said to be a man of poor qualifications; there are 25 pupils, and the subjects taught are Urdu, Persian and the Korán. *Kasba Kaithan* prides herself on Hakims Vilayat Sháh and Shamsdin; the largest maktab there has 25 pupils, and the 2 smaller maktabs have 27 pupils in both; the same subjects are taught as above

At *Alampur*, under the direction of the excellent Moulvi Ghulám Rasúl, is a large maktab with 40 pupils, where Persian and Urdu are very well taught by him gratuitously; the teacher at Dosúya gets Rs. 4 per mensem, and the one at Kasba Kaithan Rs. 2.

Thakur has also a large maktab with 40 pupils; it is attached to a *takya* (Muhammadan Fakir's place); Muhammad Bakhsh teaches Urdu, Persian and the Koran; he only gets about Rs. 2 per mensem. *Shangla* and *Usman Shahid* have each a maktab, in which Urdu and Persian are taught, with 25 and 20 pupils attending at each school. At *Phander*, *Dogbri*, *Fattu Barkat* and *Bhikowal* are maktabs, in which Persian and the Korán are taught to 20, 12, 10, and 5 pupils, respectively. The only Mahajani school in this circle seems to be at the town Dosúya with 11 pupils, in which Lande, Sanscrit and Arithmetic are taught.

On an inquiry being instituted by the Deputy Commissioner of Hoshiarpur, through the Tehsildars of that district, whether the teachers of indigenous schools in the district would accept the Government aid, on the condition of teaching up to the lower school standard of the Educational Department, and allowing their schools to be inspected by Government Officials, the result was as follows:—

(1) The Tehsildar of *Hoshiarpur* reports that there are 11 indigenous schools in the tehsil. The number of pupils attending these schools is not given. The teachers of the schools at Haryana and Basi Battu, of 3 schools in the Zaildárship of Medipur, of Biroti, and of 2 schools in the Zaildárship of Jahán Khelán, and all the teachers in the Zaildarship of Khanora, agree to the above condition, whilst the teachers of the school in Mahal and Mokdah (where the Lumberdar, Hera Singh, keeps a teacher for his daughter) does not agree with the conditions. The rest accept the Government aid, and will abide by the above conditions, if the aid given be not less than Rs. 3 per mensem. All the influential persons in this tehsil hail the proposal with great pleasure.

(2.) The Tehsildar of *Dosúya* reports that the teachers of all the indigenous schools in his tehsil agree to accept Government aid, and to abide by the conditions stated above, provided that no injury be done to the religious education which they are giving now, and the holiday in the school be given on *Friday*, as it is done now. The Tehsildar recommends that the teachers applying for the Government aid should be sure to receive it, as well as those who show an intention of starting new schools. The Lumberdar and Zaildar look upon the proposal with great satisfaction.

(3.) The Tehsildar of *Unú* reports that there are indigenous schools in the villages of Anandpur (2 schools) Mirpur, Chanpur, Roneran, Moda Majra, Kalgrano, Bhabúr, Pinjawar, Uná, (3 schools) Bila Ramgarh and Bibrera, altogether 14 schools. The number of the pupils attending 5 of these schools is not given, whilst the number of pupils attending the remaining 9 schools is 164. The teachers, Hiranand, teacher of Anandpur, Jawai Rám and Amin Chand of Uná, (who, at present, teach Nagri,) and Alladya of Núrpúr, who now teaches Persian, state that they can, and will teach up to the lower school standard, and abide with the conditions of inspection. The others cannot teach up to the required standard, but have no objection to their schools being inspected by the educational officers if they be given Government aid. All the members of Municipal Committees in the circle, and all Lumberdars and Sahukars approve of the proposal.

(4). It is reported by the Tehsildar of Gadh Shankar that there are 31 indigenous schools in his tehsil, 25 of which have 340 pupils: 19 teachers are Muhammadans and 12 Hindus. Two teachers being absent, 24 out of the remaining 29 agree to the conditions, and are ready to take Government aid, whilst 5 refuse to abide by them, some on account of old age, and some owing to inability to teach up to the required standard.

JULLUNDHAR DIVISION.

DISTRICT KANGRA.

GENERAL ABSTRACT.

District.	No. of Maktabs and Madrasas.	No. of pupils.	No. of Sanscrit and Nagri schools.	No. of pupils.	No. of Gurmukhi schools.	No. of pupils.	No. of Lande and Mahajani schools.	No. of pupils.	Total No. of Indigenous schools.	Total No. of pupils.
Kangra .	14	206	25	461	...	...	5	85	44	752

THANA BALACH.—There is a very respected Pandit, Pritam Deo, in *Tarjand*, and also a Baid of note, Bishn Deo. [The only school in this Thana is at *Tarjand*, which is supported by a missionary, who pays the teacher, Dhan Sukh, Rs. 10 per mensem, and who gets no other income from the boys. It has 30 pupils, and Persian, Urdu, Sanscrit and a little English are taught in it.]

SUJANPUR.—Jairam is the noted and experienced Baid of this circle. There is no maktab, but there is a Mahajani school. The teacher's name is Gota, and the pupils attending are 20; formerly there were over a hundred. Mahajani and Arithmetic, as used by shopkeepers, are taught. Gota teaches as a charity, as he is a Brahmin, and has therefore no settled income; if anything is voluntarily given him he accepts it. A private return adds a patshala under Girdhari Lal with 10 pupils learning Sanscrit.

THANA DERA.—In the village *Barun* Hakim Chartu Rajput is mentioned and in *Thor* Pandit Asa, a Brahmin, who teaches Sanscrit gratuitously in a patshala to 7 boys.

DHARMSAL.—Hafiz Umr Din, an eminent Moulvi, good Arabic scholar and Imam of the Masjid of the town, is the teacher of the madrasah of this place, which is attached to a mosque and where 15 pupils are taught Arabic gratuitously by him. In the village *Garda* Moulvi Sháh Din has a maktab, attended by 10 pupils, in which he teaches Urdu and Persian. He gets Rs. 5 per mensem and food.

JAVALAJI.—Pandits Saudagar, Narain and Raja Rám are noteworthy in this town, as also Baid Brij Lal and Bhai Kirpal Singh. In *Bairagpur* Pandit Balbhaddhar is mentioned. The Police returns have no schools for above places. But the town *Jwala Mukhi* has a good patshala, where Sanscrit Grammar and Poetry, &c., are taught by Raja Rám. He is paid in kind. This patshala is attached to a Thákurdwara and has 8 pupils. A private information adds another patshala in Javalaji under Narayen Dat with 50 pupils.

In *Garli* Lahna Singh teaches Lande and Urdu to 12 boys, and in *Nagrota* Sher Singh the same to 14 boys. They get about 3½ rupees each. Nagrota has also a patshala in which 19 boys are taught Sanscrit and Bhasha by Pandit Rám Kishen, who gets Rs. 5 per mensem.

NURPUR.—Moulvi Badruddin, Pandit Mani Rám and Hakim Rahman Bat are well known in the town of *Nurpur*, where the first-named is the teacher of a Madrasa which is attended by 10 boys and in which Arabic and Persian are taught. The teacher gets Rs. 10 per mensem in cash. There is also a patshala in Nurpur, a charitable institution. Pandit Roda Mal teaches 18 pupils in Sanscrit, Bhasha and Urdu. *Sulial*, *Nagrota* and *Landouri* have a patshala each, attended by 20, 19, and 15 boys, respectively. The teacher of the first is Pandit Rámkishen, and of that of the second and third Bhim Sen and Bawa Mohan Gir. Sanscrit, Bhasha and Urdu are taught. The teacher of the *Sulial* school holds 40 ghumaos of land granted by Government, and the teacher of the *Landouri* school holds 4 ghumaos of land given by the village proprietors.

In the village of *Gangna*, Nand Lal conducts gratuitously a Mahajani school and teaches to 14 boys Arithmetic, reading and writing, &c. In *Damtál* is a maktab attended by 16 pupils in which Gulám Muhammad teaches Persian and Urdu. He gets 5 maunds of corn worth Rs. 3 per mensem.

THANA KANGRA.—Baid Janti and Pandit Mani Rám are distinguished in this circle. In the village *Samloti* is a large maktab held in a private house. Beli Rám is the teacher, and the number of pupils attending 30. The subjects taught are Persian, Bostan, &c., Urdu, Arithmetic and translation into Urdu, and *vice versá*. The teacher gets Rs. 10 per mensem (cash Rs. 7 and kind Rs. 3). *Chatro* and *Gorkari* have each a small maktab attended by 5 and 2 pupils respectively; Gulab Din is the teacher of the first, and Aziz Din of the other one; they teach Persian and Urdu. Gulab Din gets Rs. 5 per mensem and *Rasad* (articles of food sufficient for one grown up man) from one person and 12 annas from 3 boys. Aziz Din gets Rs. 2 per mensem, food and clothing. Two patshalas under Pandits Mani Rám and Sobha Rám with 30 and 40 pupils respectively are added by a private informant.

THANA LOWAN.—Hakim Dhanpat Rai, Baid Kirpa Rám, Pandits Goka Chand, Jog Raj, Kirpa Rám, Dharm Das are the best known in this Thana. There is no other but a Government school. People teach their children themselves in their religion and Mahajani characters.

THANA PALAMPORE.—In the village *Perola* Moulvi Akbar Ali (also a physician) has a maktab supported by Hindoos and Muhammadans, in which Persian and the Korán are taught to 20 pupils. Akbar Ali gets Rs. 12 per mensem. Maulvi Rahmat Beg has exactly the same kind of school in *Darang*, gets the same pay, and has 18 pupils. The town of *Diwarua* has a patshala under Pandit Dhambeshur Rám, with 20 pupils learning Siddhant Kaumudi, Nyaya, &c.

THANA SARSAR.—The police returns mention no schools in this circle. Hakim Shib Rám (physician), Pandits Prabhu, Gopála and Sukhaman, Bhai Charn Das and Gouri Dat *Jotishi* (astrologer) are of repute in that place.

THANA KOTLA.—Har Bhaj is a well-known Baid in the town of *Kotla*, and Nabi Bakhsh a Moulvi in the town of *Tilokpur*. The maktab at Tilokpur is supported by the Rajas of Bhadú and Kishtwari, who allow the teacher, Nabi Bakhsh, Rs. 4 per mensem each. It is in a shop; 12 boys attend, and the subjects taught are Persian, Urdu and Arithmetic. The teacher gets also Re. 1-8 from 4 boys.

THANA HAMIRPUR.—The well-known Baids here are: Kahan Singh, Fateh Singh, Pir Singh Rajput of Dhamaraul, Jawáhar Singh. The Pandits, Kali Rám, Jawáhar and Barni Katouch, and Pandit Jaggan Nath of Tikkar (who teaches 2 pupils) are brought to notice. Pandit Taradat teaches Sanscrit to 25 pupils in the town of Hamirpur.

THANA KULLU.—Mohan Baid (a Government employé), Keso, Brahmin, are brought to notice.

Extra. Patshalas in *Haripur* 2 under Nitianand and Bholu with 20 and 25 pupils; in *Guler* under Shivdat with 20; *Dada* under Janardhan with 25, and in *Lowowal* under Nauranga with 20 pupils, are mentioned by a private informant. Maktabs in *Pirola, Kindor* and *Tilokpur* with 21, 10 and 7 pupils; patshalas in *Rugyulta, Indra, Fatahpur, Mahal Moryan,* and *Narmand* with 16, 12, 8, 25, 12 pupils, and a Lande school in Chinor with 25 pupils are added by another informant.

AMRITSAR DIVISION.

AMRITSAR DISTRICT.

GENERAL ABSTRACT.

District.	No. of Maktabs and Madrasas.	No. of pupils.	No. of Sanscrit and Nagri schools.	No. of pupils.	No. of Gurmukhi schools.	No. of pupils.	No. of Lande and Mahajani schools.	No. of pupils.	Total No. of Indigenous schools.	Total No. of pupils.
Amritsar	132	1,795	64	1,004	64	1,263	24	793	284	4,860

AMRITSAR.

The following *Hakims* are most distinguished in the city of Amritsar :—

Ganga Rám, Kirpa Rám, Pir Bakhsh, Azizuddin, Khairuddin, Dyal Singh, Rám Singh, Kishen Rikh, Mian Hisámuddin, Sharfuddin, Harji, Sarab Sukh Rám, Mangal Singh, Bhag Singh, Muhammad Sharif, Azimulla, Rámkishen, Rámji, Devi Dass, Sukh Rám, Naththa Singh, Moti Rám, Jíwan Singh, Dewa Singh, Hira Singh, Hakim Azimulla, Rám Misser and Shehabuddin. Hakims Mutiulla and Ilahi Bakhsh teach medicine.

Among the *Moulvis*, Moulvi Ruknuddin, Akbar Sháh I, Akbar Sháh II, Muhammad Fazl Karim, Rasul Baba, Moulvi Muhammad Shah, Moulvi Sultan Mahmud, Moulvi Khuda Bakhsh, Hafiz Ilmuddin, Moulvi Abdulla, Moulvi Ahmadulla, Ghulám Ahmad, Ahmad Bakhsh, Husain Sháh, Hamid Sháh and Moulvi Ghulám Ali Sahib are brought to notice in the police returns. A private informant adds the names of Abduljabbar, Muhammad Shafi, Ilahi Bakhsh, Ahmad Baba, Ghulám Rasul, Abdulali Qari, Abdussamad, Amiruddin, and Ashraf Ali.

Among the *Pandits* who deserve notice are Pandit Tulsi Rám, Pandit Balmukand, Baij Nauth, Parmanand, Rámdat, Gulab Rám, Kishen Dat, Kaushi Nauth, Aggaya Rám, Mulchand, Bhágmal Lachhman Dass, Kishen Chand, Rám Kishen, Kanihia, Kishen Chand II, Birj Lál, Shibsaran, Shibdyál Amar Singh, Naráyen, Rámdit, Shankar Dass, Har Bhagwan, Fatah Chand, Thakar Dass, Kishen Chand III, Gaupal, Beshen Dass and Pandit Devi Dass.

Among *Bhais*, the names of Bhai Hazará Singh, an author in Gurmukhi, Bhai Kishen Singh, Bhai Rám Singh, Bhai Prem Singh, Partap Singh, Atma Singh, Rupa Singh, Gopal Dass, Sadhu Rám, Mahesh Dass, Bhai Sudh Atma Singh, Bhai Rám Chand, and Bhai Partap Singh, are mentioned as most distinguished.

A private return adds the names of Pandits Achint Rám, Káká Rám I, Shiv Shankar, Káká Rám II, Gopi Nauth, Bhagat Rám, Madho Rám, Bansi Rám, Dhan Lál, Buta Rám II, Káká Rám, Ramdhan, Shambu Rám, and Dhari Lál, as most eminent scholars of Sanscrit.

The following are the largest indigenous schools in the city of Amritsar :—

I. *Madrasah*, attached to the mosque of Shaikh Khairuddin, in the Hall Bazar, in which 200 pupils are taught the Korán, Persian, and various branches of Arabic learning. The staff of the school consists of *Moulvi Sultan Mahmud*, Head Moulvi, getting Rs. 25 per mensem; Moulvi Khuda Bakhsh, getting Rs. 15 per mensem; Hafiz Ilmuddin, getting Rs. 21 per mensem; and Hafizes Alim Din, Maliki Alam, and Rahim Ali, getting Rs. 6, 5 and 4 per mensem, respectively. The school is established and supported by Shaikh Khairuddin, merchant and the Anjuman Islamia of Amritsar.

II. The largest *Patshala* in Amritsar is conducted by Pandits Achint Rám and others who teach Sanscrit Grammar and Poetry, Logic, Prosody &c., to 75 pupils, and prepare candidates for the Pragya and Visharad examinations of the Punjab University which gives a grant-in-aid of Rs. 40 per mensem to the school.

III. The *Gurmukhi school* attached to Akalbunga is the largest of its kind, where Bhai Atma Singh teaches Gurmukhi, the Granth, &c., to from 100 to 150 pupils.

The other indigenous schools at Amritsar will be shown in the following statements :—

A.—Statement showing the minor Korán, Persian, Arabic and Urdu schools in the town of Amritsar.

Locality.	Teacher.	No. of pupils.	Subjects taught.	Income.
				Rs.
1 Katra Bhangyan	Ruknuddin	10	The Korán and Persian	3
2 Mori Ganj	Akbar Shah	5	Ditto	3
3 Katra Ahluwalyan	Ahmad Bakhsh	15	Ditto	15
4 Private house	Husain Shah	15	Ditto.	
5 Katra Mahan Singh	Hamid Shah	10	Ditto.	
6 Katra Nihál Singh	Hafiz Imam Din	10	Ditto.	
7 Mosque	,, Pir Bakhsh	20	Ditto.	
8 Kila Bhangyan	Rahman Shah	8	Ditto.	
9 Katra Karani Singh	Ahmadullá	25	Ditto	10
10 Mosque	Karim Bakhsh	10	Ditto.	
11 Katra Khazana	Ghulám Rasúl	8	Ditto.	
12 Mosque	Fazal Din	8	Ditto.	
13 Bhai Sant Singh	Kayem Din	17	Ditto.	
14 Mosque	Roshan Din	9	Ditto.	
15 Katra Dúlú	Hamid Bábá	10		
16 Kucha Sai	Abdussamad	12	Ditto	51
17 Bagh Chanda Singh	Hafiz Said Ahmad	18	Ditto	41
18 Baghwala Mosque	Muhammad Hassan	18	Ditto.	
19 Katra Sher Singh	Ahmad Din	12	Ditto.	
20 Sultani Wind Gate	Muhammad Siddiq	8	Ditto.	
21 Katra Bhangyan	Pir Muhammad	12	Ditto.	
22 Katra Sant Singh	Nur Ahmad	25	Ditto.	
23 Do. Basant Singh	Abdul Majid	4	Ditto.	
24 Do. Sant Singh	Aziz Baba	5	Ditto.	
25 Do. Kuzgaran	Chiragh Din	5	Ditto.	
26 Do. Sagge Walan	Kazi Mihr Bakhsh	9	Ditto.	
27 Do. Khazana	Musammat Jan	2	Ditto.	
28 Ditto	Karim Bakhsh	13	Ditto.	
29 Do. Ramgaryan	Ghulam Mustafa	13	Ditto.	
30 Do. Karam Singh	Subhan Jiw	2	Ditto.	
31 Ditto	Per Muhammad	4	Ditto.	
32 Ditto	Ghani Shah	4	Ditto.	
33 Do. Karam Singh	Ghulam Din	8	Ditto.	
34 Do. Kalalan	Ghulam Rasul	13	Ditto.	
35 Do. Sirkibandan	Muhkam Din	12	Persian.	
36 Do. Bagh Singh	Rahmatulla	7	Ditto.	
37 Bazar Kafah Dozan	Nasrulla	...	Ditto.	
38 Mosque of Ghani	Fazal Ali	18	Ditto.	
39 Karmonki Deorhi	Khuda Bakhsh	10	Ditto.	
40 Kuche Hakiman	Ahmad Shaikh	6	The Koran and Arabic Grammar, &c.	

B.—Statement showing the higher Arabic, Persian and Urdu Schools in the town of Amritsar.

Locality.	Teacher.	No. of pupils.	Subjects taught.	Income.
41 Katra Safid	Moulvi Ghulam Ali	60	Translation of the Koran, Hadis, Law, Grammar and Logic.	
42 Katra Mahan Singh	Abdulla and Abduljabbar	33	Translation of Koran, Hadis, Law, Grammar, Persian and Urdu.	
43 Do. Ahlu Walyan	Ahmadulla	14	Ditto.	
44 Ditto	Muhammad Shafi	6	Ditto.	
45 Masjid Telian	Ilahi Bakhsh	4	Medicine and Persian.	
46 Katra Karam Singh	Ahmad Baba	23	Grammar, Hadis.	
47 Kotwali	Ghulam Rasul and Akbar Shah.	68	Grammar, Logic, Rhetoric, Translation of the Korán and Urdu.	
48 Katra Sultan Mir	M. Abdul Ali Kari	55	Arabic, Persian and Urdu.	
49 Jani Wind Gate	M. Abdussamad	10	The Koran, Persian, Urdu, Hadis and Law.	
50 Katra Ramgarhian	Ghulam Ahmad	12	Ditto.	
51 Ghauk Kirori	Amiruddin	31	Ditto.	
52 Katra Mahan Singh	Sayyid Ashraf Ali	21	Ditto.	
53 Kucha Safyan	Mutiulla	20	Persian, Arabic, Urdu, the Koran and Medicine.	

*C.—Statement showing the indigenous Gurmukhi schools in the town of Amritsar.**

Locality.	Attached to Dharamsala or a private house.	No. of pupils.	Teacher.	Income.
				Rs. A. P.
1 Katra Sher Singh	Dharamsala Addan Shahi	25	Kirpa Rám.	
2 Gali Nawaryan	„ Kumbarán	16	Permanand.	
3 Chauk Pasyan	„ Sarmukh Singh	10	Duman Singh.	
4 Gali Mudharyan	Dharamsala	10	Kanh Singh.	
5 Toba Bhai Salu	„ Bhai Shalu	125	Bhagwan Dass.	
6 Bunga Hukum Singh	Bunga Hukum Singh	50	Atma Singh.	
7 „ Nur Mahlayan		100	Kishen Singh.	
8 „ Ahluwalyan		8	Aya Singh.	
9 „ Anandpuryan		10	Atma Singh.	
10 Akhárá Birham Buta		44	Gopal Dass, Sadh Rám, Bishan Dass.	
11 Akhara Birham Nikka		10	Rám Singh.	
12 Katra Ramgarhyan	Dharamsala Bhai Saina	10	Prem Singh.	
13 Baba Atal	„ Bhai Binka Singh	12	Partap Singh.	
14 Katra Karam Singh	Shop	70	Sahib Singh	8 0 0
15 Kanak Mandi	„	45	Ramchand	2 12 0
16 Dhab Sati Rám	Dharamsala Bhai Sawaya Rám	25	Bhagwan Hari	1 4 0
17 Katra Nihál Singh	Dharamsala	50	Shib Dass.	4 0 0
18 Katra Karam Singh	Ditto	12	Hari Singh.	
19 Katra Khazána	Ditto	10	Anant Rám.	
20	Sirdal Singh-ka-Dharamsala	70 girls		

* A private informant states that there are 300 Dharamsalas in Amritsar, the names of which, however, he does not mention.

D.—Mahajani Schools in the city of Amritsar.

Locality.	Teacher.	No. of pupils.	Remarks.
			Rs. A. P.
1 Hatalí Sahib	Badha Nand Rám	25	1 9 0 per mensem income of the teacher.
2 Chaurasti Atari	Phaggú	40	2 8 0
3 Gurú-ki Mahal	Ali Bakhsh	80	5 0 0
4 Bazár Kanjran	Nabi Bakhsh	80	10 0 0
5 Ghanta Ghar	Kalá	50	6 0 0
6 Namak Mandí	Badri	50	3 4 0
7 Katra Dulú	Khuda Bakhsh	75	8 0 0
8 Ditto	Balak Rám	20	5 0 0
9 Chah Zargarán	Loknath	25	4 0 0
10 Katra Charat Singh	Harki Nandan	70	7 0 0
11 Ditto ditto	Shib Narayen	80	10 0 0
**12 Katra Karam Singh	Khuda Bakhsh	12	4 0 0

** Pandit Bhagwan Dass of Lahore, in his evidence before the Educational Commission mentions 35 mahajani schools with 800 pupils.

E.—Statement showing the Indigenous Sanscrit Schools in the city of Amritsar.

Locality.	Name of Teacher.	His qualifications.	No. of pupils.	Subjects taught.	Income.
1 Bazár Jaimal Singh	Tulsi Ram	Good	10		
2 Do. of Sher Singh	Harji	Do.	10		
3 Do. Ahluwalyan	Kishen Dat	Do.	30		
4 Do. do.	Kishen Chand	Do.	50		
5 Do. Ramgadyan	Shibdyal	Do.	20		
6 Bunga Hukum Singh	Agya Ram	Average	33		
7 Akhara Birham	Ram Kishen	Do.	35		Gratis.
8 Do. Malanand	Kishen Chand	Do.	15		
9 Bunga Mayanwala	Birj Lal	Do.	17		
10 Katra Challi Walyan	Shib Saran	Do.	20		
11 Patshala	Kaushi Nath	Good	35	Sanscrit.	
12 Katra Dal Singh	Bhagmal	Do.	19		
13 Bazar Shivdan	Kanihia	Do.	10		
14 Raughan Mandi	Mul Chand	Average	25		
15 Katra Nihal Singh	Tulsi Ram	Good	13		Rs. 2 per m.
16 Namak Mandi	Bhowani Dass	Do.	15		
17 Patshala	Ramdat	Do.	10		
18 Katra Ramgaryan	Basdeo	Do.	15		Gratis.
19 Katra Dúlú	Ram Saran	Do.	10		
20 Patshala	Kanah Chand	Average	12		
21 Ditto	Srab Dyal	Good	12		
22 Ditto	Sant Ram	Average	15		
23 Ditto	Vishnu Chand	Good	40	Sarsut and Chandraka.	
24 Ditto	Ramdat	Do.	20	Muktawli and Vedantsar, Tattwa.	
25 Ditto	Bhisham	Do.	5	Sanhita, Rudya Dundak.	
26 Ditto	Bali Ram	Average	9	Sarsut, Chandraka, Kavya and Kosh.	
27 Ditto	Bhoda Ram	Do.	15	Shradh Babek, Mahurat Ganpati.	
28 Ditto	Dhari Lal	Do.	4	Sanhita, &c.	
29 Ditto	Basheshur	Do.	4	Tajak.	

D (a).—A private return adds the following Sanscrit schools.

No. of schools.	(a) Locality.	(b) Names of teachers.	(c) No. of pupils.	(d) Subjects of instruction.	(e) Income of the teachers.
					Rs.
1	Namak Mandi	Achint Rám	75	Teaches Sanscrit up to the Vishárad standard of the P. U. College	
2	Katra Dal Singh	Gopi Nauth	20	Ditto ditto	80
3	Santoksar, Shivala	Krishn Chunder	30	Sanscrit Grammar, Poetry,	10
4	Sabienión-ka Bazar	Ram Dutt	15	Ditto ditto	10
5	Guru Singh-ka Bazar, Temple	Hari Narayan	10	Sanscrit Grammar and Puráns, &c.	20
6	Lahorí Gate, Ratan Singh's Temple	Swámí Anant Dass	10	Sanscrit Grammar, Vedánt, Poetry, &c.	8
7	Phullan Vála Chouk	Rám Dhan	7	Astrology	10
8	Gurú-ka Mahal	Rig Dev	15	Grammar and Medical books (Sanscrit)	8
9	Jamadár-ki Haveli (near to)	Bútá Rám	6	Grammar, &c.	15
10	Charat Singh's Katra	Shambhu Nath	16	Grammar, Poetry, Koosh; &c.	7
11	Churastí Atárí	Shoru Rám	10	Ditto ditto	10
12	Alú Valion-ka Bazár	Mádho Rám	10	Grammar, Logic, &c.	8
13	Sultan Vinde-ka Darvaza	Atá Rám	15	Grammar, Poetry, *Sáhitya*, &c.	8
14	Rám Gadhian-ki Dharamsala	Jai Rám	12	Grammar, Vedánt, &c.	10
15	Máí Sewan-ka Bazár	Bansí Dhar	15	Grammar, Logic, &c.	10
16	Kúcha Teli, Nimak Mandi	Fateh Chand	10	Grammar, *Puráns*, &c.	12
17	Charat Singh (Katra)	Káká Rám	15	Grammar, Logic, &c.	10
18	Mochion-ka Bazar, Temple	Thakár Dass	10	Grammar, *Vedánt*, &c.	10
19	Gandon-ka Bazar, Temple	Vishun Dass	8	Grammar, *Puráns*, &c.	15
20	Ditto ditto	Gopal	15	Grammar, *Vedánt*, &c.	10
21	Charat Singh-ka Katra	Káká Rám	8	Grammar, *Puráns*, &c.	10
22	Gurú-ka Bazar	Dhári Lál	15	Grammar, Logic, &c.	10
23	Jamadarki-Haveli (near)	Hari Narain	12	Grammar, Logic, &c.	10
24	Dúlo-ka (Katra)	Fakir Chand	10	Grammar, *Purans*, &c.	10
25	Phullan Vala Chouk	Kaka Rám	10	Astrology (*Jotish*)	8
26	Khazane-ka bazar	Pulastya	10	Grammar, *Purans*, &c.	15
27	Verbhan's School	Lakhsman Dass	15	Grammar, *Purans*, &c.	8
28	. . . .	Dhan Lal	20	Ditto Ditto	8
29	. . . .	Bhagat Ram	15	Ditto Ditto	

AMRITSAR CIRCLE.—Among the distinguished literary men in this circle is Pandit Jagan Nauth, of Morádpura, who is also a Hakim.

The following villages have Korán schools and maktabs :—

Fatahgarh, attached to the village mosque, under Rahmatullá, with 10 pupils.

Ruthyan, attached to a mosque under Mohammad Sharif, with 4 pupils.

Tangbála, attached to a mosque under Ghulám Mohammad, with 6 pupils.

Gumtála, attached to a mosque under Pirú, with 10 pupils.

Mundyala, attached to a mosque under Alayár, with 7 pupils.

The subjects of tuition are the Korán, Urdu and Persian.

The villages of *Dallá*, *Khápar Kheri*, *Khatanyan*, *Ghumanpura* have each a Gurmukhi school conducted by Hari Singh, Chandar Singh, Mangal Singh and Gopálá, with 8, 12, 5 and 6 pupils, respectively. The teachers are only given their daily food and corn at harvest.

VAIRU WÁL.—In Vairu Wál Pandit Maiya Dass and Pandit Mahábali are distinguished Sanscrit scholars; whilst among the Hakims Sultani Mal of Vairu Wál and Sayyad Barkat Ali of Jalalabad and Hakim Ibrahim of Fatahabad are brought to notice.

The widow of Myan Abdurrahim, late teacher of a Government school, Vairu Wál, teaches the Korán to 20 girls gratuitously. There are Korán schools also in the villages of *Vairu Wál Bava*, *Jalalabad* (4 schools), *Fatahabad* (2 schools), *Khawaspur*, *Dhunda*, *Bhel* and *Bhairu Wál*, with 8, 40, 22, 16, 3, 4 and 5 pupils, respectively. Persian is also taught in the last-named school.

In this circle there is one patshala in the village of *Fatahabad*, in which Pandit Raja Ram instructs 10 pupils in Sanscrit and Gurmukhi.

Bhani, a Sikh woman, mother of Gandá Singh, teaches Gurmukhi to 40 girls, the daughters of the Ahluwalia Sikhs, in their own homes in the village of Fatahabad and has a fair income. Ishur Singh, tehsildar of Fatahabad, has exerted himself much on behalf of female education. *Fatahabad* has two other Gurmukhi schools with 32 pupils.

Gurmukhi schools are mentioned in the villages of *Vairu Wál Bava*, one with 20 pupils, *Goyandal*, one with 16, *Dhunda*, two with 8, and *Sangar*, one with 8 pupils.

Fatahabad (under Raja Rám Pandit) and Goyandál have alse a Lande school each, with 20 and 4 pupils, respectively.

GHURANDA.—The distinguished Hakims in this circle who deserve notice are Hakim Ilahi Bakhsh of Sarai Amanat Khán, Hakims Sardár Ali and Nizámuddin in Rangar, Hira Jogi, and Mahamdi Jogi of Dhoi, and Mahamuddin of Gandiwand.

Among the Pandits, Pandit Hira of Ghuranda, Pandit Narsing Dass of Bhagná and Pandit Rámchand may be mentioned.

A private informant adds Moulvi Nizamuddin and Bhai Sahdú Singh.

There are maktabs in the villages of *Bhagná*, *Chanba*, *Dhuya* and *Burj*. The first maktab occupies the deserted house of the Government school, in which Maula Bakhsh teaches 9 pupils. Inayetulla, teacher of Dhuya maktab, teaches 5 pupils and receives Rs. 6 per mensem. The maktabs in Chamba and Burj, under Nizamuddin and Hafizulla respectively, are attached to mosques, have 4 (private informant gives 12) and 7 pupils, respectively. A private return adds two maktabs in *Sarai Amanat Khán*, with 15 and 6 pupils under Moulvi Nizamuddin and Hakim Ilahi Bakhsh, respectively. The subjects taught in all these schools are the Korán, Urdu, and Persian, and Arabic and Persian in the last two schools.

Bhai Sahdú Singh conducts a Gurmukhi school attached to a dharamsala in *Sarai Amanat Khán*, and teaches Gurmukhi to 14 pupils, who give him bread and clothes.

The other Gurmukhi schools in this circle are as follow :—

Place.	*Teachers.*	*Number of pupils.*
1. Dhund	Gobind Bakhsh . . .	30
2. Bhuchar	Harnám Singh . . .	12
3. Gandiwand	Sant Singh . . .	20
4. Atari	Dula Singh . . .	5
5. Daóki	Prem Singh . . .	3
6. Phusa	Bhai Rám Singh . . .	8

Bhai Sant Singh of Gandiwand teaches gratuitously and holds 100 bighas of land in the village of *Sukar Chak*, which he inherited from Gurú Hira Dass. His school is held in a Gurúdowarú which has a garden also with it. Bava Nihál Singh living in the Gúrudowarú practises Yunani medicine.

There are *Lande* schools in the villages of *Pul Kanjri* and *Bhagna Kalan* under Ali Bakhsh and Misri Dass with 11 and 9 pupils, and Rs. 6 and 5 per mensem as the incomes of the teachers, respectively.

SARHALI.—*Hakim* Aladiya, *alias* Chuhá, of Naushahra Panwan and *Pandit* Hemraj of Jama Rai deserve notice.

In the village of *Phakkupur*, attached to the dharamsala of the village, is a maktab in which Pir Sháh, a good Persian scholar, teaches Gulistan, Bostan, Urdu (and also arithmetic as in Zubdatulhisab) to 15 pupils, and receives 75 maunds of corn and Rs. 12 per mensem in cash.

An application from the teacher, signed also by all lumberdars and influential men of the village (all Hindus), asks for Government aid.

Kot Mohamad Khan has a patshala, attached to the Devidowará, where Bava Hira Dass of average qualification teaches Sanscrit to 8 pupils, on Rs. 4 per mensem. There are Gurmukhi schools in the villages of *Dhutyan* and *Murhana*, attached to the dharamsalas, in which Bhai Prem Singh and Bhai Shám Singh teach Pothi Panjgaranthi to 10 and 7 pupils, and receive Rs. 5 and 3 per mensem, respectively.

Sirdar Bakhsh conducts a *Lande* school in the village of *Munda* with 15 pupils, and Rs. 8 per mensem as the tuition fee.

JANDYALA.—*Muhassamura* and *Mannawala* have each a maktab, under Ghulám Husain and Guláb Ali Sháh, men of good qualifications, who teach Urdu and Persian to 8 and 9 pupils, and receive Rs. 4 and 6 per mensem as their income, respectively.

In *Jandyala* and *Mondala* there are Lande schools, one in each, with 25 and 30 pupils. Kishandyal of *Jandyala* and Hakim Ali of *Mondala*, who conduct these schools, receive one anna monthly per boy and Rs. 5 per mensem, respectively.

KHUNGAL.—In the town of *Majith*, Pandit Bhowani Dass, a good Sanscrit scholar and astrologer, who practises also in the Hindu system of medicine, and Pandit Mayya Das among the Pandits, and Gurdit Singh among the Bhais, are brought to notice.

There are two *patshalas* in the town of *Majith*, conducted by Pandits Bhowani Dass and Mayya Dass, alluded to above, who teach Sanscrit (Purans and Vyakaran) to 12 boys (each having 6 boys) gratuitously.

Majith has also three Gurmukhi schools, attached to dharamsalas, under Bhai Suchet Singh, Deva Singh, Gunda Singh, with 8, 6 and 5 pupils, respectively. *Maniwal* also has a Gurmukhi school under Jawahar Das Sádh with 18 pupils. Gurmukhi, Pothis and the Granth are taught in these schools.

There are 16 maktabs in this circle, the details of which are given in the following statement:—

PLACE.	Teacher.	No. of maktabs.	Subjects taught.	No. of pupils.	REMARKS.
1. Ajayebwali	Ibrahim	1	Urdu and the Koran	10	
2. Nag	Ata Muhammad	1	Do. and Persian	12	
3. Dudyan	Abdurrahman	1	Do. and the Koran	Boys 4, Girls 3	
4. Hamza	Mohkam Din	1	Do. do.	8	
5. Lurka	Imam Ali	1	Do. and Persian	15	5 mds. of corn monthly is the income.
6. Bhulluwal	1 Ishur Dass.	2	Urdu	12	3-12 per mensem.
	2 Akbar Shah		The Koran	6	1
7. Jajuwali	Mufti	1	Urdu	12	14 mds. of corn in six months.
8. Gosal	Shah Din	1	The Koran	Boys 6, Girls 3	
9. Bakurpur	Qutabshah	1	Do.	5	
10. Nanel	Rahimulla	1	Do.	12	
11. Sapariwand	Karim Bakhsh	1	Do.	5	
12. Bhuggewal	Shumsuddin	1	Do.	5	
13. Lohan Kalan	Charagh Ali	1	Do.	8	
14. Tarini	1 Muhammad Ashraf	2	Do.	10	4 per mensem.
	2 Ghulvm Muhammad			10	

TARANTÁRÁN.—Pandit Mayya Dass of Tarantárán is a distinguished Sanscrit scholar.

The largest maktab in this circle is in the village of *Bhular*, attached to the village mosque, where Shahabuddin, a man of average qualification, teaches Persian and the Korán to 19 pupils (a private informant gives 45 pupils, who learn the Korán, Persian, Urdu and Arithmetic), and pay the teacher Re. 1 per mensem with daily food.

In *Tarantárán* there is a Gurmukhi school, attached to a dharamsala conducted by Bhai Jiwan Singh, with 12 pupils learning Gurmukhi, and a *Lande* school, under Maula Bakhsh with 30 pupils, who pay their teacher

Rs. 10 per mensem. Another Lande school in *Kot Dharam Chand* has 5 pupils only.

The following statement will show the minor maktabs, Korán schools, and Gurmukhi schools in this circle :—

PLACE.	KORÁN SCHOOLS AND MAKTABS.			GURMUKHI SCHOOLS.		
	No. of maktabs.	No. of pupils.	Subject of tuition.	No. of maktabs.	No. of pupils.	Subjects taught.
Sheron	1	3	Reading and writing	2	5	Reading and writing.
Piddi	...	...	......	1	2	Ditto.
Bhujyan	1	8	Korán	...	...	Ditto.
Kalla	1	8	Do. and Persian	1	7	Ditto.
Lulpura	...	...	......	1	4	Ditto.
Wain Pain	...	...	......	1	2	Reading and writing and arithmetic.
Pedri	1	6	Persian	1	8	Ditto.
Pinjora	...	...	......	1	8	Ditto.
Jhabhal	...	...	......	1	5	Ditto.
Pindori Gola	1	12	Korán and Persian	...	...	
Gohlar	1	8	Korán	...	...	
Dev	1	8	Urdu	...	...	
Batol	...	...	......	1	6	Reading and writing.
Pindori Hasan	...	...	......	1	3	
Keronwal	...	...	......	1	6	
Shaikh Chak	1	4	Korán			

LOPOKI.—*Hakim* Zainulabidin, *Moulvi* Abdula of Suryan, *Pandits* Gunga Rám of *Kakar*, Amin Chand of *Phalluwal*, Chand of *Chauganwa*, Rámditta of *Sarangarh*, and Bhag of *Manj*, and *Baids* Basantman and Mula of Kohala, are distinguished among the Hakims, Baids, Moulvis and Pandits of this circle.

There are the following maktabs in this circle :—

1. *Manjh*, with 40 pupils under Karim Bakhsh (a good Persian scholar), who receives 25 maunds of corn per annum.

2. *Kamaski*, with 10 pupils under Haidar Sháh, who gets 20 maunds of corn per annum.

3. *Diniki*, with 15 pupils under Umar Din, on Rs. 3 per mensem.

4. *Phalluwal*, with 25 pupils under Imam Din, who gets corn at harvest as the tuition fee.

The subjects of tuition in these schools are—the Korán, Urdu-ki Pahli, Urdu-ki Dusri, Dusturussibyan, Insha Khadmi, Harkaran, Gulistan, Bostan, &c. A private informant mentions two more maktabs in *Lodi Gujar* and *Kakar*, under Mian Hanif and Muhkam Din with 10 and 35 pupils respectively.

The villages of *Diniki* and *Khyala* have each a Mahajani school with 15 and 12 pupils, under Umar Din and Karim Bakhsh, respectively. The monthly income of the teachers is Rs. 3 per mensem each. These Lande schools are only temporary. The teachers make a kind of contract with the parents to make the pupils go through a fixed course within a fixed period of time, after which they are at liberty to go to another place. *Manjh* has a Lande school under Sheikh Dit with 15 pupils.

WAZIR PIND.—Among the *Hakims*, Gada-áli Sháh of Divala, and among the *Baids*, Pandits Gauri Shankar of Piroman and Mayya Dass of Kalyar Ghuman, deserve notice.

Bhai Sukh Rám Dass and *Pandit* Gobind Rám, both of Mehta, are distinguished.

There are maktabs in the following villages :—

1. *Budhatha*, under Miran Bakhsh, with 6 pupils.

2. *Botala*, under Sayyid Imám Ali Sháh, with 6 pupils.

3. *Chima Bahta*, under Sayyid Amir Sháh, with 15 pupils.

The subjects of tuition in these schools are the Korán, Gulistan, Urdu-ki Pahli and Dusri Kitab. The teachers of the schools Nos. 1 and 3 have an income of Rs. 1 and Rs. 2-8 per mensem, respectively.

The villages of *Piroman* and *Mehta* have a patshala each, conducted by Pandit Gauri Shankar and Pandit Gobind Rám, both good Sanscrit scholars, teaching Vyakaran, Garar and Prem Sagar, &c., to 7 and 10 pupils, respectively.

There is a Gurmukhi school in the village of *Sithala* attached to the village dharamsala, in which Bhai Prem Dass Sádh instructs 6 pupils in the Panj Granthi, &c.

AJNÁLA.—Pandits *Gobind* of Ajnála, *Gunga Rám*, *Jawola Dass*, and *Jagan Nath* of Jastarwal, and *Atma Rám* and Thakar Dass of Ramdás, are distinguished for their Sanscrit learning. The Hakims who deserve notice are the following:—Sher Ali, Hakim of Bolian, Muhammad Bakhsh, Hakim of Raja Sansi, Hakim Nizamuddin and Buddruddin, both brothers, have the local reputation of being good physicians in this circle.

The following statements will show the number of the Korán schools, maktabs, Gurmukhi schools in this circle :—

PLACE.	Teacher.	No. of pupils.	Subjects taught.	Income of teacher.
1. Balbawa	Nayaz Ali	10	The Korán and Urdu-ki Pahli, &c.	1 maund of corn per annum per boy.
2. Baldarya	Qayamuddin	4	The Korán.	
3. Bhuggupura (Jastarwal)	Ghulam Husain	11	Do.	
4. Barwala	Ali Muhammad	8	Do.	4 maunds of corn per annum per boy.
5. Talwandi	Mir Hasan	9	Do.	
6. Jastarwal	Mus. Azis Bibi	15 Boys Girls. 2 13	Do.	Rs. 4 per mensem.
7. Jhadir	Faqirulla	6	Do.	Rs. 1 per annum per boy.
8. Dyali Ranghran	Karim Bakhsh	7	Do.	
9. Ramdas	Nizamuddin, Mustakim, Muhammad Bakhsh	34	Do.	
10. Singpura	Jiwan Shah	10	Do.	Daily food.
11. Shahpur	Kake Shah	2	Do.	12 maunds of corn per annum.
12. Sarangdi	Qutab Shah	15	Do.	
13. Sidhar	Badruddin	6	The Korán, Urdu, Persian	3 mds. of corn per annum.
14. Sahuwal	Amir Bakhsh	8	The Korán	Daily food and 6 mds. of corn per annum.
15. Adliwala	Muhammad Bakhsh	7	The Korán, Urdu, Persian	7 maunds of corn.
16. Kotli Zeb	Ghulam Din Charagh Shah	6	The Korán	1 loaf per boy every week.
17. Kot Rajadah	Said Shah	8	Do.	Daily food and 8 maunds of corn per annum.
18. Pachhi Nigal	Muhammad Bakhsh	11	The Korán and Urdu	Daily food and 11 maunds of corn per annum.

Gurmukhi Schools.

Sidhar	Kanh Singh	6	Gurmukhi	3 mds. of corn per annum.
Adliwala	Naurang Singh	9	Ditto	Daily food.
Fatahwal	Gurdyal Singh (Udasi)	6	Ditto	Ditto.
Lakhuwal	Dwan Singh (Nirmala)	5	Ditto	Ditto.

Teachers Nos. 5, 11, 12, 13 have muafis of 8, 3, 16 and 5 bighas of land, respectively. Teachers Nos. 8 and 9 (Mustakim) are weavers, and therefore live on their profession. The rest are mullas of the mosques and are given a marriage fee from As. 8 to Re. 1-8, and fees on occasion of death and birth, &c.

AMRITSAR DIVISION.

SIALKOT DISTRICT.

GENERAL ABSTRACT.

District.	No. of maktabs and Madrasas.	No. of pupils.	No. of Sanscrit and Nagri schools.	No. of pupils.	No. of Gurmukhi schools.	No. of pupils.	No. of Lande and Mahajani schools.	No. of pupils.	Total No. of Indigenous Schools.	Total No. of pupils.
Sialkot .	455	5,355	14	152	29	394	30	612	528	6,513

SIALKOT.—The names of the following Hakims, Moulvis, Pandits and Bhais are mentioned in the Police and District returns as deserving notice :—

HAKIMS.—*Sialkot.*—Muzaffar Sháh, Imamuddin, Sháh Muhammad, Sher Muhammad, Hakimuddin, Fatahdin, Gulab Singh, Hakim Bora, Hisamuddin and Muhammad Bakhsh.

Sialkot Cantonments.—Hakim Sirajuddin.

Chatti Shaikhán.—Mubinuddin, Karam Ilahi.

Pura Hiran.—Moulvi Abdulhakim.

Radas.—Hasan Din.

Phagwal.—Jauhar Sháh.

Hamza Ghaus.—Karam Bakhsh.

Butar.—Ghulám Muhammad.

Panchgrain.—Sháh Din.

Saulehpur.—Ismail.

Partanwali.—Devi Datta.

Kotli Luharán.—Ahmad Ali and Farzand Ali.

Richhara.—Mukanda, Prem Singh.

MOULVIS.—*Sialkot.*—Ghulám Husain, Karam Ilahi, Abdulla (who is a physician also), Ghaus, Haji Abdulla, Hafiz Sultan, Ataulla, Myan Husain, Karam Ilahi, Muhammad Alim, Abdul Hakim (son of Moulvi Muzammil), Muhammad Hasan, Mir Hasan (teacher of the Mission school).

Sialkot Cantonments.—Moulvi Fazli Ahmad, Moulvi Mubarak Ali.

Ballanwala.—Wahab Sháh.

Phagwal.—Muhammad Ali.

Butar.—Shahnawáz, Buta.

Adlakh.—Fazla, Nur Ahmad.

Lordhri.—Shahab Din.

Adálat Garh.—Ali Muhammad

Churyán.—Sháh Muhammad.

PANDITS.—*Sialkot.*—Hera Nand, Ganga Rám, Lekh Rám, Kaka Rám, Badri Nath, Damodar Dass, Mathura, Chakarbhan, Narsing Dass, Devi Dass, Mul Raj, Bhawania, Ganpat, Harya, Kashi Rám, Rámchand.

Sialkot Cantonments.—Jai Bhagwan.

Chatti Shaikán.—Rám Kishen, Gaukal.

Radas.—Rajrup.

Hiyal.—Mani Karan, Mathura.

Ajmalpur.—Gunda, Lalman, Jagat Rám.

BHAIS.—*Sialkot.*—Wazir Singh, Karam Singh, Ganga Rám, Bhag Singh, Mehtab Singh, Asa Singh, Sundar Singh, Nihal Singh, Gurdat Singh, Ittar Singh, Ganda Singh.

Partanwali.—Bhai Mul Singh.

Kotli Luharán.—Bhai Arjan Singh.

Hamza Ghaus.—Nihal Singh, Jagat Singh.

POET.—*Sialkot.*—Ishq Pecha.

The number of Madrasas, Maktabs and Koran schools in the Sialkot town and circle and particulars regarding them are given in the following statement :—

Locality.	Teacher.	No. of pupils.	Subjects taught.	Income of teacher.
Sialkot City.				Rs.
Mosque of Masons	Fatah Din	10	Persian and Arabic	20 per annum.
,, of Bhatta	Rahím Beg	20	Do. do.	25 ,,
,, of Pura	Nuruddin	20	Do. do.	30 ,,
,, of Sháh Ranjha	Muhammad Akbar	10	Do. do.	20 ,,
,, of Ghulam Ali	Quari Sahib	16	The Korán	...
Private house of the teacher	Núr Bakhsh	25	Persian and the Korán	50 per annum.
Mosque of Bena	Husain Bakhsh	18	Persian and Arabic	30 ,,
Old mosque	Karam Ilahi	30	Do. do.	20 ,,
Potters' mosque	Hafiz Sultan Ahmad	12	Do. do.	20 ,,
Afghans' mosque	Luqmán	12	Do. do.	20 ,,
Millers' mosque	Haji Abdulla	30	Do. do.	40 ,,
Carpenters' mosque	Hafiz Ilmuddin	10	Do. do.	15 ,,
Mosque of Sháh Chána	Ahmad Sháh	30	The Korán	50 ,,
Grand mosque	Hafiz Sultan	30	Do.	50 ,,
Mosque of Allalok	Hafiz Fazaldin	20	Do.	30 ,,
School of Bahár Khan	Moulvi Ghulám Husain	15	Persian and Arabic	96 ,,
Mosque of Afghans	Rahem-ulla	10	The Korán and Persian	20 ,,
,, of Kurhá Kashmiri	Karam Din	20	Do. do.	40 ,,
,, Kabutránwali	Moulvi Husain	14	Persian and Arabic	38 ,,
Tailors' mosque	Hafiz Hakim-ulla	10	The Korán	20 ,,
House of Deputy Wazir Ali	Moulvi Karam Ilahi	20	Arabic and Persian	60 ,,
,, of Mir Mazhar Ali	Rahim Bakhsh	16	Persian	144 ,,
Mosque Kunjriwáli	Myan Háji	20	The Korán and Persian	40 ,,
		Girls. Boys.		
Goldsmiths' mosque	Fazal Din	4 4	Persian and Arabic	Food.
Mosque of Kashmiris	Ghulám Muhammad	0 6	The Korán	Do.
Aráin's mosque	Sultan Shah	0 2	Do.	Do.
Molyan's mosque	Núr Hasan	5 0	Do.	Do.
Biba mosque	Husain Bakhsh	0 9	Do.	Do.
Yatím Shah's mosque	Amiruddin	0 5	Do.	Do.
Mosque of Chuna Sazan	Nizamuddin	1 2	Do.	Do.
,, of Kakki Zaiyán	Imamuddin	0 4	Do.	Do.
Mason's mosque	Nabi Bakhsh	0 7	The Korán and Persian	Do.
Madrasa Bahar Khan	Ghulám Husain	15	Arabic and Persian	96 per annum.
Sialkot Cantonments.				
Sadar Bazar	Ali Muhammad	16	The Koran	3 per mensem.
Lal Kurti	... ...	5	Do.	
Sialkot Circle.				
Surhali	Fatah Din	10	Arabic and Persian.	
Daluwali	Shah Muhammad	32	Do. do.	
Pitsar	Ghulám Husain	20	Do. do.	
Baoraná	Shahab Din	17	Do. do.	
Gulpár	Ramzan Ali	15	Do. do.	
Tepru[illegible]	Nur Din	35	Do. do.	
[illegible]húra	Barkat Ali	25	Do. do.	
[illegible]hagwal	Muhammad Ali	11	Do. do.	
[illegible]ohadpur	Zahúr Din	31	Do. do.	
Muzaffarpur	Ghulám Mustafa	12	Do. do.	
Channunmon	Nur Ahmad	14	Do. do.	
Panchgarain	Shah Sawár	22	Do. do.	
Larakhiwál	Pir Bakhsh	29	Do. do.	
Kharota	Muhammad Bakhsh	11	Do. do.	
Dholi Chand	Taj Din	12	Do. do.	
Laghwán	Guláb Shah	15	Do. do.	
Gondal	Hayat Ali	18	Persian	16 per annum.
Adlakh	Fazla	2	The Koran	4 ,,
Gadara	Nur Ahmad	4	Do.	8 ,,
Butar	Ghulám Muhammad	14	Do.	12 ,,
Partanwali	Amiruddin	13	Do.	16 ,,
Kotli Londi	Nizamuddin	11	Arabic and Persian	10 ,,
Waryám	Nazar Shah	5	The Koran	10 ,,
Tatti	Ilmuddin	5	Do.	10 ,,
Panunwál	Muhammad Bakhsh	39	Do.	8 ,,
Chaunkpur	Ilamddin	5	Do.	10 ,,
Malchhán	Laha	4	Do.	8 ,,
Kalá	Ramzan	6	Do.	8 ,,
Balianwala	Waháb Shah	5	Arabic	10 ,,
Wairam	Hasanuddin	10	Arabic and Persian	14 ,,
Radás	Dasondhi	6	The Korán	12 ,,
Adlakh	Abdulla	4	Do.	8 ,,
Kotli Laharán	Ahmad Din	3	Arabic Medicine	6 ,,

Name of place.	Teacher.	No. of pupils.	Subjects taught.	Income of teacher.
				Rs.
Kotli Luharan, western	Hasan Muhammad	22	The Korán	44 per annum.
Ditto ditto	Ghasia	10	Do.	20 ,,
Ditto ditto	Abdulla	10	Do.	20 ,,
Ditto ditto	Gulab Shah	16	Do.	82 ,,
Ditto ditto	Abdurrahim	8	... ...	32 ,,
Ditto ditto	Kanihea Singh	6	... ...	16 ,,
Urah	Ilahi Bakhsh	6	... ...	12 ,,
Langryal	Hasuruddin	9	... ...	22 ,,
Kaki Wali	Qadir Bakhsh	8	... ...	18 ,,
Chuman	Muhammad Shah	7	... ...	16 ,,
Saidan Wali	Addulla	10	... ...	14 ,,
Lakka Gadh	Qadir Bakhsh	6	... ...	16 ,,
Kotli Sura Singh	Ghulám Muhammad	7	... ...	16 ,,
Anjutar	Hasan Muhammad	4	... ...	14 ,,
Hamza Ghaus	Karam Bakhsh	7	Persian	8 ,,
Charar	Meran Bakhsh	5	Do.	15 ,,
Mandi Mandal	Rukauddin	6	Do.	10 ,,
Suslehpur	Ahmad Bakhsh	20	Do.	12 ,,
Rangpura	... ...	58	The Korán and Persian.	
Pura Nika (3 schools)	... ...	86	Ditto.	
Myanapura (2 schools)	... ...	50	Ditto.	
Pura Heran	... ...	5		

Gurmukhi, Shastri, Mahajani and Lande Schools in the Sialkot Circle.

Name of place.	Teacher.	No. of pupils.	Subjects taught.	Income of teacher.
Sialkot	Ali Muhammad and Nabi Bakhsh.	110	Lande	180 per annum.
Chatti Shaikhan	Ramkishen and Gaukal	18	Do.	
Rechhara	Radhi Shah	20	Do.	
Chatti Shaikhan	......	35	Do.	
Aguki	Moti Singh	12	Do.	12 ,,
Rechhara	......	40	Gurmukhi.	
Sialkot	Pandit Rámchand	5	Sanscrit and Gurmukhi.	
Ditto	Gobind Rám	12	Sanscrit Grammar, &c.	

A private return adds the following indigenous schools to those already mentioned :—

Name of Village.	Maktabs and Madrasas.	No. of pupils.	Subjects taught.	Pat-shalas.	No. of pupils.	Gurmukhi schools.	No. of pupils.	Mahajani schools.	No. of pupils.
Chirarbala	1	7	Arabic.	...	...	...	...	...	...
Hadali	1	5		...	...	...	...	...	...
Lagewal	1	12		...	...	...	...	...	...
Khanna	1	5	Arabic and Persian.	...	...	...	...	...	...
Muazzamabád	1	5	Ditto.	...	...	...	...	...	...
Moongar	1	13	Ditto.	...	...	...	...	...	...
Chak Sader	1	7	Ditto.	...	...	...	...	...	...
Khutiki	1	8	Ditto.	...	...	...	...	...	...
Kot Phokran	1	5	Ditto.	...	...	...	...	...	...
Kot Karam Bakhsh	1	7	Arabic.	...	...	...	...	...	...
Nagúr	1	5	Ditto.	...	...	...	...	...	...
Samail Awán	1	4	Ditto.	...	...	...	...	...	...
Raipur	1	5	Ditto.	...	...	...	...	...	...
Dhera Sindh	1	4	Ditto.	...	...	...	...	...	...
Kish	1	6	Ditto.	...	...	...	...	...	...
Phuni	1	11	Ditto.	...	...	...	...	...	...
Gujranwalá	1	8	Ditto.	...	...	...	...	...	...
Guna Kalán	1	12	Arabic and Persian.	...	...	...	...	...	...
Sahúwali	1	10	Ditto.	...	...	...	...	...	...
Lakra (Khurd)	1	5	Arabic.	...	...	...	...	...	...
Lakraburji	1	5	Ditto.	...	...	...	...	...	...
Kotli Koka	1	13	Ditto.	...	...	...	...	...	...
Mirza	1	26	Arabic and Persian.	...	...	...	...	...	...
Sayyùki	1	10	Ditto.	...	...	...	...	...	...
Daôki	1	8	Ditto.	...	...	...	...	...	...
Matoki	1	8	Ditto.	...	...	...	...	...	...
Mateli	1	6	Ditto.	...	...	...	...	...	...
Tirgari	1	5	Ditto.	...	...	...	...	...	...
Raipur	...	...	... ...	...	...	1	8	...	...
Peh Phanki	...	...	... ...	...	...	...	...	1	5
Sadh	1	17		...	...	...	...	...	...
Badryana	1	6		...	...	...	...	...	...
Phâth	1	11		...	...	...	...	...	...
Mahal Makra	1	6		...	...	...	...	...	...
Pindi Pinjoran	1	6	Persian.	...	...	...	...	...	...
Loti	1	12	Ditto.	...	...	...	...	...	...
Kapurâwali	1	10	Arabic and Persian.	...	...	...	...	...	...
Peroli	1	8	Arabic.	...	...	...	...	...	...
Bakarpur	1	8	Ditto.	...	...	...	...	...	...
Siri	1	11	Ditto.	...	...	...	...	...	...
Chakakhra	1	7	Ditto.	...	...	...	...	...	...

Name of Village.	Maktabs and Madrasas.	No. of pupils.	Subjects taught.	Patshalas.	No. of pupils.	Gurmukhi schools.	No. of pupils.	Mahajani schools.	No. of pupils.
Akbarabad	1	7	Arabic and Persian.	...	...	...	...	...	...
Chhrand	1	6	... ...	...	...	...	...	...	...
Kotla	1	9	... ...	...	...	...	...	...	...
Bhabryanwala	1	11	... ...	...	...	...	...	...	...
Nawal	1	8	... ...	...	...	...	...	...	...
Adalatgarh	1	17	... ...	...	...	...	...	...	...
Ajmalpur	1	12	... ...	...	...	...	...	...	...
Balluwal	1	16	... ...	...	...	...	...	...	...
Nakhkhuwal	1	8	... ...	...	...	...	...	...	...
Gujarkala	1	10	... ...	...	...	...	...	...	...
Adamdarag	1	10	... ...	...	...	...	...	...	...
Lakra (major)	1	5	... ...	...	...	...	...	...	...
Dholan	1	5	... ...	...	...	...	...	...	...
Kot Khamman	1	8	... ...	...	...	...	...	...	...
Piru Chak	1	19	... ...	...	...	...	...	...	...
Phalluwali	1	16	... ...	...	...	...	...	...	...
Richhara	1	14	... ...	...	...	...	...	...	...
Matiki	1	10	... ...	...	...	...	...	...	...
Tirga	1	24	... ...	...	...	...	...	...	...
Ladhar	1	8	... ...	...	...	...	...	...	...
Gangwal	1	12	... ...	1	8	...	...	...	...
Dhamanwale	...	...	... ...	...	...	...	1	1	12
Hiyal	1	8	... ...	...	...	...	...	...	...
Palbajwan	1	10	... ...	...	...	...	...	...	...

Falura.—The distinguished Hakims in this circle are Myan Ghulám Naqshband of Gudgor, Haidar Sháh of Sehni Wali, and *Moulvi* Sayyid Gulab Sháh (who is a good Arabic scholar) of Gudgor.

There are maktabs in *Gudgor*, *Wichhuki* and *Khananwali*, attached to the village mosques, under Sayyid Gulab Sháh, Usman, and Sháh Sawar, with 12, 6 and 14 pupils respectively. The subjects of tuition are the Korán, Arabic grammar, Muhammadan law, and Persian

Zafarwal.—Moulvi Qutbuddin and Ghulám Qadir Sháh are distinguished Arabic scholars in Zafarwal.

The following indigenous schools are mentioned in the Police returns :—

Place.	No. of maktabs.	No. of pupils.	Subjects taught.
Zafarwál	1	22	The Korán, Arabic and Persian.
Chhiwar	1	14	Ditto ditto.
Maráré	1	33	Persian, Urdu and Arabic.
Atharwá	1	15	The Korán.
Bhaniá	1	5	Do.
Hichli	1	3	Do.
Dhol	1	16	Do.
Nográn	1	25	The Korán and little Persian.
Sakror	1	24	The Korán.

The district return adds the following schools :—

Place.	Maktabs.		Patshalas.		Gurmukhi schools.		Lande schools.	
	No.	Pupils.		Pupils.		Pupils.		Pupils.
Zaparwal	...	...	1	18	...	...	...	...
Jalalpur	1	5	...	...	...	...	...	...
[illegible]dudh	1	12	...	...	...	...	...	...
[illegible]yala	1	10	...	...	...	...	...	...
Da[illegible]li	1	6	...	...	...	...	1	6
Jundyala	...	...	1	24	...	...	...	...
Dolum	1	6	...	...	...	...	...	...
Mehtabpur	1	6	...	...	...	...	...	...
Sayedpur	1	9	...	...	...	...	...	...
Chakkbokar	1	6	...	...	...	...	...	...

Place.	Maktabs. No.	Maktabs. Pupils.	Patshalas.	Patshalas. Pupils.	Gurmukhi schools.	Gurmukhi schools. Pupils.	Lande schools.	Lande schools. Pupils.
Kotli Chiwar	1	4	...	...	...	...	...	...
Chhiwar	...	...	1	4	...	...	...	...
Dogri	1	8	...	...	...	...	...	...
Charwa	1	26½	...	...	...	...	...	...
Majra	1	8	...	...	...	...	...	...
Joyan	1	10	...	...	...	...	...	...
Nerpal	1	6	...	...	...	...	...	...
Jamaljund	1	20	...	...	...	...	...	...
Salabiki	1	10	...	...	...	...	...	...
Maharajki	1	12	...	...	...	...	...	...
Mundeki	1	7	...	...	...	...	...	...
Kotli Khawaja	1	13	...	...	...	...	...	...
Lodhraki	1	8	...	...	...	...	...	...
Kalewali	1	7	...	...	...	...	...	...
Kotli Tirkhanan	1	8½	...	...	...	...	...	...
Khakhkhanwah	1	9	...	...	...	...	...	...
Chaunda	1	26	...	...	1	12	...	...
Alian Wali	1	15	...	...	...	...	...	...
Sangryala	1	8	...	...	...	...	...	...
Mehdiala	1	7	...	...	...	...	...	...
Sabuki	1	5	...	...	...	...	...	...
Depuki	...	...	...	...	...	...	1	25
Salora	1	6	...	...	...	...	...	...
Kot Bava	1	10	...	...	...	...	...	...
Changryan	1	6	...	...	...	...	...	...
Pendi Pahgu	1	20	...	...	...	...	...	...
Jetiwala Balla	1	6	...	...	...	...	...	...
Sabzpir	1	7	...	...	...	...	...	...
Jetiwala	1	18	...	...	...	...	...	...
Bhartal	1	6	...	...	...	...	...	...
Dholan	1	10	...	...	...	...	...	...
Saedanwali	1	12	...	...	...	...	...	...
Matyala	1	5	...	...	...	...	...	...
Sanktra	1	4	1	7	...	...	...	...

MYÁNI.—*Moulvi* Ghulám Husain of *Dudh* and *Hakim* Rahmatullah Sháh of *Basyan Wálá* are brought to notice.

In the villages of *Rampur* and *Kala Khatai*, there are Gurmukhi schools, one in each, conducted by Sital Dass and Hira Singh, and attended by 12 and 4 pupils respectively.

The following are the maktabs of Arabic and Persian in this circle:—

Place.	No. of Maktabs.	No. of pupils.	Subjects taught.	Teachers.
Dudh	1	14	Arabic and Persian	Ghulám Husain.
Kala Khatai	1	13	Ditto ditto	Ahmad Sháh.
Ditto	1	10	Ditto ditto	Ghulám Din.
Rajandiala	1	11	Ditto ditto	Nur Ahmad.
Ditto	1	10	Ditto ditto	Sháh Din.
Ditto	1	6	Ditto ditto	Júndú.
Nani	1	12	Arabic	Hashan.
Banduri	1	12	Arabic and Persian	Umar Din.
Karun	1	7	Ditto ditto	Imam Din.
Khond	1	12	Ditto ditto	...
Sada Nurli	1	13	Ditto ditto	Jani Sháh.

RÁYÁ.—The following Moulvis have been brought to notice as distinguished Moulvis:—*Nizamuddin Ulma* of Bhanyan, *Ghulám Muhammad* of Mari Kalan, *Nuruddin* of Ganguhar, *Muhammad Yar* of Badu Mali, *Hasan Muhammad* of Bhagyan, *Nur Ahmad* of Bhujh, *Umar Din* of Randhir,

Abdulhakim of Magula, and *Khán Muhammad* of Malakpur. All these Moulvis teach in the following indigenous schools :—

Place.	No. of Maktabs.	No. of pupils.	Subjects taught.	Income of the teacher.
Bhanán	1	21	Persian and Arabic	42 maunds of corn per annum.
Mári Kalán	1	13	Ditto ditto	26 " " "
Gangohar	1	12	Ditto ditto	24 " " "
Budh Mali	1	13	Ditto ditto	28 " " "
Bhágián	1	9	Ditto ditto	20 " " "
Bhhujh	1	10	Ditto ditto	18 " " "
Bandhir	1	15	Ditto ditto	30 " " "
Magulá	1	15	Ditto ditto	30 " " "
Malakpur	1	10	Ditto ditto	20 " " "

Baba Ram Dass and Pandha Utma Rám conduct a Gurmukhi and a Lande school, in the villages of Goyal Khurd and Malakpur respectively, the number of pupils attending being 11 and 25. The daily food, with 11 maunds of corn a year, constitute the income of the Gurmukhi teacher, whilst the Lande teacher receives Rs. 2-12 per monsem.

NARÚWAL—Rasmat Ali *Hakim*, Ilmuddin *Moulvi*, and Arura *Pandit*, of Narúwal, may be mentioned among the distinguished men in the circle.

There are maktabs in *Narúwal* and *Ra'yd Koraba*, one in each, conducted by Husain Sháh and Sayyid Abdul Hakim respectively, who teach the Korán, Bostan, Gulistan, Karima, &c., to 35 and 16 pupils respectively, and receive corn at harvest time as their tuition fees.

Narúwal has also a Lande school in which Pandit Arura teaches Lande and Sanscrit to 50 pupils.

The police officers say that the people of this circle feel inconvenienced by the fact that the schools are so few in number, and that therefore the people are almost excluded from education.

The district returns add the following schools to those mentioned by the police returns for the *Rayá* and *Narúwal* circles :—

Place.	No. of Maktabs.	No. of pupils.	Subjects taught.
Deryánwalá	1	12	Persian, Urdu and Arabic.
Dádú	1	13	Ditto ditto.
Unchí	1	7	Persian.
Dúngyán	1	16	The Korán.
Khan	1	4	Persian.
Shahálíwál	1	4	The Korán and Urdu.
Ladhar	1	4	Ditto ditto.
Chakrálí	1	7	Ditto ditto.
Kalkhánah	1	15	Persian, Urdu and the Korán.
Megah	1	14	Ditto ditto ditto.
Nadúkí	1	10	Persian and Urdu.
Gharyal Kalan	1	8	Arabic.
Jiun Koráyah	1	8	The Korán and Persian.
Mithá Sújá	1	1	Persian.
Marí Khurd	1	7	The Korán and Persian.
Kot Bhujh	1	3	Persian.
Tablá Kalán	1	3	The Korán and Persian.
Shamsherpur	1	4	The Korán and Urdu.

PASRÚR.—*Moulvi* Abdulla of *Pasrúr* is the only distinguished man in this circle, who teaches the Korán and advanced books in Arabic and Persian to 9 pupils in the mosque of Kakkazais.

The only Gurmukhi schools in this circle are in the villages of *Kalahwala*, where Mahan Singh teaches Gurmukhi to 10 pupils, *Kalbajwa* with 10 and *Koreki* with 6 pupils.

Pandit Gorianditta conducts a *Lande* school in *Pasrúr*, which is attended by 54 pupils. The other Mahajani schools are at *Budha Garuya* and *Paropi*, with 24 and 10 pupils.

The following are the Korán, Arabic and Persian schools :—

Place.	No. of Maktabs.	No. of pupils.	Subjects taught.
Pasrúr	4	56	Korán, Arabic.
Naglián	1	5	Persian and Urdu.
Nagal Rám Chand	1	9	Korán and Urdu.
Rasúlpur	1	6	Do.
Chuhan	1	12	Do.
Kalalwala	1	4	Do.
Bhag	1	4	Do.
Bhagut	1	12	Do.
Takhtpur	1	9	Persian.
Budha Dharga	1	6	Korán.
Panwana	1	15	Persian.
Kamalpur	1	18	Korán and Persian.
Khiva	1	8	Korán.
Kotli Mughlan	1	3	Do.
Malpur	1	25	Do.
Chida	1	12	Do.
Kal Bajwá	1	20	Korán and Persian.
Koriki	1	10	Korán.
Qazi Bhárang	1	12	Korán and Persian.
Jholki	1	5	Korán.
Shahti	1	6	Do.
Uncha Bharang	2	17	Do.
Kotli Fakir Chand	1	11	Do.
Mardana	1	2	Korán and Persian.
Kotli Wisakh Singh	1	3	Korán.
Kot Rae	1	9	Do.
Sangroli	1	8	Korán and Persian.
Tawaryanwala	1	6	Do.
Budha Guraya	1	20	Do.
Sarai	1	12	Korán, Arabic and Persian.
Siyan	1	8	Ditto ditto.
Lopri	1	6	Ditto ditto.
Thatthi	1	7	Ditto ditto.
Sikandarpur	1	1	Qaida Arabic.

Qala Sobha Singh.—Ghulám Hasan, Wazira, Babu Deviditta of Qala Sobha Singh, Sadig Ali of Lunar, and Muhammad Ali of Alipur (who is a Moulvi also) are said to be the most distinguished *Hakims* in this circle. Among *Moulvis*, Azizuddin, Hafiz Ali Akbar, of Qala Sobha Singh, and Imamuddin, of *Kot Arayan*, deserve notice. *Pandits* Kaushi Rám, Narayen Dat and Asanand and *Bhai* Hira Singh are also good scholars of Sanscrit and Gurmukhi respectively.

Place.	Income of the teacher.	No. of pupils.	Subjects taught.	Teacher.
Lala	Rs. 3 per mensem	25	Persian and the Korán	Nur Ahmad.
Kot Araián	Daily food	6	Do.	Imam Din.
Chahre	1 maund of corn per mensem.	16	Do.	Abdul Karim.
Ladhar	Food	5	The Korán	Buta Shah.
Kotli Muhammad Sadiq	7 maunds per mensem.	20	Persian and Arabic	Ismail.
Bhojú	Food	7	Do.	Maula Dád.
Panchgarain	2 maunds per mensem.	14	Do.	Hafiz Ismail.
Khairullapur	2½ maunds per mensem.	14	Do.	Tajuddin.
Alipur	Food	34	Do.	Ghulam Husain.
Chak Jagat Rai	1½ maunds per mensem.	5	Do.	Abdur Rashid.
Tanbu	1 maund of corn per mensem.	12	The Korán	Imam Din. Moali. Sher Muhammad. Shahamat Ali.
Bahki Ki	Ditto	6	Do.	Talebuddin.
Ropowali	2 maunds per mensem.	8	Do.	Hasan.
Qala Sobha Singh	Gratuitously	60	Persian and Arabic	Hafiz Ali Akbar.

Qala Sobha Singh has also a Mahajani school with 30 pupils and a Sanscrit school with 10.

Satráh.—Among the *Hakims* here Ilmuddin is distinguished. The villages of *Killa Suba Singh* and *Qahaarwali* have a Gurmukhi school under Bhai Sham Singh, with 25 pupils learning Gurmukhi and Lande, and a Lande school under Sirdar, with 11 pupils.

The Korán schools and maktabs in the *Satarâh* circle, as mentioned in the police returns, are as follow :—

PLACE.	No. of Maktabs.	No. of pupils.	Subjects taught.
Dhandal	1	8	The Korán.
Miánwáli	1	14	Persian and Arabic.
Fatehpur	1	12	" " "
Chángi	1	9	" " "
Sandráná	1	6	Urdu.
Mohanpur	1	4	The Korán.
Kotli Maqbará	1	8	Persian and Arabic
Dharang	2	12	" " "
Makhaná	1	5	The Korán.
Datárand	1	8	Persian and Arabic.
Kot Iman	1	3	Persian.
Lálá	1	6	"
Kotli Datá	1	4	Arabic.
Sarái	1	12	"
Verwálá	1	9	"

In the circles of *Pasrúr*, *Qala Sobha Singh* and *Satrâh* the following indigenous schools have been added by the District Return :—

PLACE.	Maktabs.		Patshalas.		Gurmukhi schools.		Mahajani and Lande schools.	
		Pupils.		Pupils.		Pupils.		Pupils.
Udofatta	1	20						
Lakkhanki	1	11	...	...	...	...	...	...
Ladi Jajja	1	9	...	...	...	...	...	...
Bhular	...	...	...	...	...	...	...	...
Jodhala	1	9	...	...	...	...	1	15
Saranwali	1	30	...	...	...	...	1	16
Changa	1	9	...	...	...	..	...	...
Kotli Hira	1	7	...	...	...	...	...	...
Kotli Maharan	1	16	...	...	...	...	...	...
Phakki	1	12	...	...	...	...	...	...
Dhirki	1	8	...	...	...	...	...	...
Nagal Ramchand	1	15	...	...	...	...	...	...
Mirza Bajwa	1	7	...	...	...	...	...	...
Tagipur	1	7	...	...	...	...	...	...
Kazi Pharang	1	16	...	...	...	...	...	...
Sohawa	2	10	...	...	...	...	...	...
Mangat	1	9	...	...	...	...	...	...
Gulúki	2	21	...	...	...	...	1	16
Chak Ogu	1	6	...	...	...	...	1	8
Data Zaidka	2	25	...	...	...	...	...	...
Gakkharwali	1	8	...	...	...	...	...	...
Manga	1	8	...	...	...	...	...	...
Gathyalian	1	18	...	...	...	...	...	...
Kotli Tarar	1	10	...	...	...	...	...	...
Bahlolpur	1	7	...	...	...	...	...	...
Malalu	1	8	...	...	...	...	...	...
Sukhana	3	18	...	...	...	...	1	10
Qaharwali	1	8	...	...	1	8	...	...
Thapnala	1	7	...	...	1	8	...	...
Thattha Gulab Singh	...	...	...	...	1	10	..	...
Bhupar	1	8	...	...	...	...	...	...
Saib	1	5	...	...	...	...	...	...
Sanopar	1	8	...	...	...	...	...	...
Shadi Khanwala	1	8	...	...	...	...	...	...
Rana	1	9	...	...	...	...	...	...
Wahiudu	2	14	...	...	1	8	...	...
Kila Suba Singh	1	14	...	...	...	...	1	8
Chhangi Shah Khak	1	6	...	...	...	...	...	...

DHARAMKOT.—There are schools in the following villages, in which Arabic, Persian and Urdu are taught :—

1. *Kotlihawah Sadlulla Khán*, attached to the police station, under Azizuddin, a man of average qualifications, teaching 13 pupils on Rs. 24 per annum.

2. *Rajawala*, attached to a mosque with 15 pupils under Bhawal Bakhsh, who gets Rs. 30 per annum.

3. *Ogá Rudar*, 2 maktabs under Hasandin, teaching 7 girls, and Ghulám Rasul teaching 25 boys. The income of each teacher being Rs. 20 per annum.

There is a Gurmukhi school in the village of *Chak Rám Dass*, in which Shibnath teaches Gurmukhi to 8 pupils.

DASKA.—Hakim Bute Khán, Hakim Barkhurdar and Hakim Sher Singh of *Goyandki*, Hakim Imam Din of *Mitranwali*, and Dwarka Dass and Zakir Sháh of *Jamki* are noticed as distinguished native physicians in this circle. Moulvi Abdulla Hamid of *Kot Banda* and Kazi Ghulám Muhammad of *Mitranwali* are the most eminent Arabic scholars, whilst Pandit Narayan of *Dhamouki* and Pandits Ishar Dass and Balrám of *Mitranwali* are brought to notice as noted Pandits.

The villages of *Jamki* and *Daska* have each a Sanscrit school with 18 and 4 pupils respectively. There are Gurmukhi schools in the villages of *Daska*, *Mitranwali* and *Galotyan*, with 86 and 20 pupils respectively.

The Lande schools in the villages of *Sandhanwala*, *Daska*, *Mitranwali*, *Phadiwala* and *Alumahar* have 7, 20, 6, 40, and 22 pupils respectively.

The following are the indigenous Korán and Perso-Arabic schools in this circle :—

Place.	No. of Maktabs.	No. of pupils.	Subjects taught.
Allumahar	2	20	The Korán.
Amawatra	1	10	Ditto.
Phadiwala	1	19	The Korán, Persian, and Urdu.
Thalyara	1	6	Ditto.
Thatta Goraya	1	4	Ditto.
Jamki	1	35	The Korán, Persian, and Urdu.
Jesarwala	1	7	The Korán.
Chak Mayana	1	4	Ditto.
Dhunduwali	1	8	Ditto.
Dholiwali	1	12	Ditto.
Rinjhay	1	5	Ditto.
Sakhkhuki	1	6	Ditto.
Sandhanwala	1	4	Ditto.
Kallarkot	1	3	Ditto.
Galutyan (minor)	1	14	Ditto.
Kotkhaman	1	10	The Korán, Persian, and Urdu.
Kotlikuka	1	8	Ditto.
Gujra	3	50	The Korán, Urdu, and Persian.
Maghukhaman	1	14	The Korán and Persian.
Murhana	1	4	The Korán.
Mahi Thakrai	1	10	Ditto.
Weruwala	1	6	Ditto.
Mitranwali	1	20	The Korán, Persian, and Urdu.
Behanwala	1	12	The Korán.
Kot Banda	1	16	The Korán, Persian, and Urdu.

Samryal.—*Moulvis* Nur Ahmad, Karam Ilahi, Nabi Bakhsh of Sahuwala, and *Hakims* Ghulám Husain and Roda of Samryal, are said to enjoy a reputation in this circle.

The villages of *Malkhanwala*, *Beguwal* and *Khartal* have each a Gurmukhi school under Bhais Ganda Singh, Karam Singh and Badhawa Singh, with 14, 40 and 12 pupils respectively. *Wan*, *Thanawali* and *Khartal* have Lande schools with 7, 10 and 11 pupils.

The Maktabs, Madrasas and Korán schools in this circle are as given below :—

Place.	No. of Maktabs.	No. of pupils.	Subjects taught.
Samryal	1	20	The Korán, Arabic, and Persian.
Wan	2	17	Ditto.
Jatteki	1	30	Ditto.
Majra (major)	1	16	Ditto.
Koluki	1	12	Ditto.
Kot Dina	1	5	Ditto.
Malkhanwala	1	20	Ditto.
Randhir	2	16	Ditto.
Chaoki	1	7	Ditto.
Kot Malyanwala	1	8	Ditto.
Badduki	1	12	Ditto.
Sahuwala	6	60	Ditto.
Beguwala	1	16	Ditto.
Kharuwala	1	10	Ditto.
Chakkopa	1	8	Ditto.
Nandgir	1	14	Ditto.
Chhalluki	1	12	Ditto.
Bhunawali	1	9	Ditto.
Herajamba	1	11	Ditto.
Sunderpur	1	13	Ditto.
Badar	1	6	Ditto.
Daduwali	1	7	Ditto.
Saruki	1	11	Ditto.
Thanawali	1	12	Ditto.
Chunki	2	15	Ditto.

Statement of the indigenous schools in the circles of *Daska* and *Samryal* which are not mentioned in the Police Returns :—

Place.	Maktabs.		Patshalas.		Gurmukhi schools.		Mahajani schools.	
		Pupils.		Pupils.		Pupils.		Pupils.
Dailam	1	45	...	...	...	...	...	...
Khartal	...	...	1	15	...	...	...	...
Phagguwala	1	40	...	...	...	...	...	...
Salwala	1	38	...	...	...	...	...	...
Shadiwala	...	...	...	...	1	30	...	...
Kot Daska	...	...	1	12	...	...	...	...
Rahanjuna	1	10	...	...	...	...	...	...
Killa Tek Singh	1	10	...	...	...	...	...	...
Bhartanwala	1	5	...	...	...	...	...	...
Dholiki	1	5	...	...	...	...	...	...
Lhouki	1	10	...	...	...	...	...	...
Dhamanki	1	3	...	...	...	...	...	...
Mundeki	...	...	...	...	1	10	1	5
Tatha	1	4	...	...	...	...	...	...
Sahuwala	...	...	...	...	1	7	1	20
Kamalpur	1	20	...	...	...	...	...	...
Manpur	1	5	...	...	...	...	...	...
Ballu Chak	1	10	...	...	...	...	...	...
Bhopalwala	1	7	1	5	...	...	...	...
Ghartal	1	45	...	...	1	12	...	...
Chakbhada	1	5	...	...	...	...	...	...
Bhallu Mahar	1	12	...	...	...	...	...	...
Kot Jundu	1	10	...	...	...	...	...	...
Adamki	1	12	...	...	...	...	...	...
Kandisian	1	10	...	...	...	...	...	...
Bhangat		8	...	...	...	...	...	...
Kamheawala	1	5	...	...	...	...	...	...
Bhakar Mali	1	30	...	...	...	...	...	...
Kotha Chishtiyan	2	30	...	...	...	...	...	...
Faranki	1	32	...	...	...	...	...	...
Itobela	1	14	...	...	...	...	...	...
Kopra	1	27	...	...	...	...	...	...
Ladli	1	8	...	...	...	...	...	...
Mundrawala	1	25	...	...	...	...	...	...
Jandu Shahi	1	5	...	...	...	...	...	...
Hardo-daska	1	40	1	10	2	25	1	50
Galotian	...	...	...	...	1	7	1	7

Phokalyan.—Among Pandits in this circle, Pandit ***Jagannath*** of Phokalyan, ***Lalman*** of Pitholi, ***Mayya Dass*** of Hayal, ***Ishar Dass*** of Kingwal, and among Hakims, Maya of Hayal, Ilmuddin of Phokalyan (who is also a distinguished Moulvi), ***Kaushi*** of Chak Sandal, and Mian Seraj Din of Kacchi Mand, deserve to be noticed.

There are maktabs in ***Phokalyan*** and ***Pal***, one in each, conducted by Moulvi Ilmuddin (referred to above), and Miran Bakhsh, with 18 and 22 pupils respectively. The subjects of tuition are Persian, Arabic and Urdu.

AMRITSAR DIVISION.

GURDASPUR DISTRICT.

GENERAL ABSTRACT.

District.	No. of Maktabs and Madrasas.	No. of pupils.	No. of Sanscrit and Nagri schools.	No of pupils.	No. of Gurmukhi schools.	No. of pupils.	No. of Lande and Mahajani schools.	No. of pupils.	Total No. of Indigenous Schools.	Total No. of pupils.
Gurdaspur.	131	1165	12	128	8	98	3	96	154	1,487

Fatahgarh.—Hakim Muhammad Sháh and Moulvis Muhammad Ali Sháh and Muhammad Usman Sháh are mentioned as the most eminent of this place; the latter is the teacher of the maktab which is attached to a mosque, and where the Korán, Hadis, and Muhammadan Law are taught. He gets about Rs. 30 a year, and the number of pupils attending is 20.

In the village *Tehjah* is a maktab with 10 pupils, where Persian and Urdu are taught. At the patshala in Tehjah, Narain, son of Sundar, teaches Sanscrit to 4 boys going through 8 books with them. His income from this source amounts only to Rs. 6 a year. In *Man* Urdu and Persian are taught in one maktab to 9 pupils, and the villages *Kathala, Lodi Nigal, Kharkyan* and *Rawal*, have each one maktab, where the Korán and Persian are taught, and where 3, 10, 10 and 16 pupils attend respectively.

Sri Govindpur.—Hakims Ghulám Nabi and Rám Chand and Bhai Jivan Kahar are the most learned of this circle. There is a Gurmukhi school in *Sri Govindpur* with 10 pupils.

Rajua has a maktab, which is held in a private house: 9 pupils attend, Arabic and Persian are taught, and the teacher Ibrahim, who is a man of good qualifications, is paid in kind, namely, 25 maunds of grain yearly. The villages *Mathola* and *Mari Buchyan* have a maktab with 5 pupils each in which Persian and Urdu are taught. *Mathola* has also a small Gurmukhi school with 4 pupils.

Lada Monda and *Ghari Afganan* have each a maktab, where only Urdu is taught with 6 and 7 pupils attending respectively. *Adlakh* has also a maktab, where Persian and Urdu are taught, 5 pupils attending: and *Bhanmari* has a Gurmukhi school with 6 pupils.

Pathankot.—The largest maktab of this circle is at *Haryál*, where 10 or 12 pupils are taught in Persian and Urdu by Fatah Din. They give him 60 maunds of grain yearly.

Shahr Chin has a maktab with 8 or 9 pupils where the Korán, Urdu and Persian, are taught; and *Kheré Basáu* and *Barwan* have each a maktab, where Urdu and Persian are the subjects of instruction, having 5 and 12 pupils respectively.

Sujanpur has a good Sanscrit school (*patshala*), where Piroo, a Brahmin, teaches gratuitously 25 pupils. In *Nirot Jaimal Singh* is a Mahajani school, where Balka Mahajan teaches Lande to 11 pupils gratuitously. It is remarked in the return that if any grant were to be given by Government to the *Sujanpur* and *Nirot* schools, their condition would improve. *Nirot Mahra* has a patshala under Shiv Rám Brahmin with 7 pupils.

Thana Chhamal and Shah Garib.—The *Hakims*, known best in this thana, are Nuru, Rajada, Mana, Akbar, Nizamuddin: the *Moulvis*, Didar Bakhsh in Mundyala, and Nimatulla. At *Mundyala* is a good maktab, attended by 18 pupils. Didar Bakhsh teaches them Arabic and Persian and gets 40 maunds of grain half-yearly.

Piali Afghanan, *Sultanpur* and *Khánpur* have each a maktab; in the first named Arabic and Urdu are taught, with 15 pupils attending; and in the two latter, Persian and Urdu are taught, with 14 pupils in attendance at each. *Bingra* has a large maktab with 20 pupils; Arabic and Urdu are taught. In *Gunah*, Persian, Arabic and Urdu, are taught, and the number of pupils is 18; and at *Sihari* the same subjects are taught to 14 pupils. The 5 following maktabs at *Chak Nihali*, *Chachwal*, *Nirpal*, *Biga* and *Shahpur Pagu*, have 12, 5, 6, 7 and 7 pupils respectively, and Urdu and Persian are the subjects of instruction. At *Naurangabad* only Urdu is taught to 8 boys; whilst at the villages *Shakar Garh*, *Chak Kazian*, *Moth*, *Bumbu*, *Isa*, and *Ádlakh*, Arabic and Persian are taught to 2, 8, 2, 8, 6 and 5 pupils respectively. The last place has also a Gurmukhi school with 8 pupils.

The following villages have also each a maktab in which Arabic or Urdu or both are taught. *Fatu Wal*, 1 maktab with 4 pupils; *Bibral*, 1 with 6; *Chikri*, 1 with 7; *Rambri*, 1 with 3; *Jichpur* 1 with 4; *Darman*, 1 with 7; *Bir*, 1 with 6; *Daudam kalan*, 1 with 5; *Saghal* 1 with 6; *Sakhkhuchak*, 1 with 8; *Piswal*, 1 with 7; *Kotli luli*, 1 with 8; *Phuri Chak*, 1 with 8; *Chak*, 1 with 5; *Rambra*, 1 with 5.

Sakhkhuchak and *Khanuwal* have each a Sanscrit school with 8 pupils in each.

PARMANAND.—*Pandits* Thakar Dass and Bhagwan Dass and Hakims Puran Rajadah and Rám Dass are noted. The largest maktab is at *Gharotah*, under teacher Miran. It is attached to a mosque; 10 pupils attend, and Arabic is taught. The villages *Chuhan* has 1 maktab with 8; *Biknor*, 1 with 8; *Sidipur*, 1 with 3; and *Narayenpur*, 1 with 3 pupils, in all of which only Arabic is taught. *Gharota* has another maktab with 5 pupils.

DINA NAGAR.—Maulvis Fatah Muhammad of *Jundi* and Hakim Muhammad Ali in *Pindori Bens* are the best men. The largest maktab is at *Thanba*; it is attached to a mosque, and Fazul Din, who is the mulla of the mosque, teaches Persian and the Korán to 7 boys. He gets 30 maunds of grain. *Ranwai* and *Chak Rám Shahai* have each a small maktab, in which only Urdu is taught with 2 and 3 pupils respectively.

Bhutia and *Uncha Bhangala* have each a maktab, with 3 pupils each, and the Karima and the Korán are taught.

A private return adds the following maktabs:—

Place.	Number of Maktabs.	Number of pupils.	Subjects taught.
Jotha	1	6	The Korán.
Chak Alya	1	8	Do.
Bhatuya	1	10	Do. and Muhammadan Law.
Haveli	1	7	Persian, Urdu and Arithmetic.
Dina Nagar	1	23	The Korán.
Do.	1	20	Do.
Do.	1	6	Do.

Dina Nagar has also a patshala with 8 pupils.

BATALA.—*Hakims*: Rahim Sháh, Ata Muhammad, Muhammad Husain, Bhawal Sher, Imamuddin, Devi Chand, Ghulám Ahmad, Lachman, Nabi Bakhsh and Ala-ud-Din; *Maulvis*: Sayad Zahur Hasan, Zahursháh and Zainulabedin; *Authors*: Mufti Imam Bakhsh and Mirza Sultan Ahmad; *Baids*: Mayadhari, Gopi Missar, Narayen, Dhonkalya, Raj Rup, Mela; *Pandits*: Purachand, Gaukal Chand, Arjan Dhulu and Kalu; *Bhai*: Kesra Singh. A private return adds the name of Pandit Ganga Bishen who teaches Sanscrit to 15 pupils.

The largest maktab in Batala has 63 pupils. It is attached to a mosque, and Hafiz Gauhar Sháh and Fazli Ahmad teach Arabic and Persian in it; there are, besides, nine other maktabs in which Arabic and Persian are taught, attended by 62 pupils. There are also 2 Lande schools with 85 pupils; Sangu and Arjan are the teachers, whose income from fees amounts to Rs. 18 per mensem. The following Korán schools are mentioned: *Galanwali*, 1 with 14 pupils; *Rangarmangal*, 1 with 2; *Longuwal*, 1 with 6; *Malakpur*, 1 with 5; *Balluwal* and *Aliwal*, each 1 with 2 pupils; *Talwandi Jhanglan*, 1 with 21; and *Jhora Singhian*, 1 with 6; in which, in addition to the Korán, also Urdu is taught. *Bhaluwal*, 1 maktab in which only Persian is taught to 5 pupils. *Nasirki* has a maktab in which Arabic and Persian are taught to 8 pupils.

KANHUWAN.—*Pandit* Shibdat and *Hakims* Ala Ditta and Rahim Bakhsh are named as the best known here. The patshala in Kanhuwan has 10 pupils, who are taught Sanscrit and Gurmukhi. Shibdat teaches them gratuitously.

Bhityan has 1 maktab with 8 pupils; *Santani*, 1 with 5; *Jalalpur*, 1 with 4; and *Sikwan*, 1 with 8 pupils; in all of which Persian is taught. *Jagwal Banger* and *Bhityan* has each a small Gurmukhi school with 8 pupils in each.

KOT NINAN.—Muhammad Sháh and Ahmad Ali are the best *Moulvis*; Hakims Ahmad Bakhsh, Kirpa Rám and Sunder Lal in Mulani Chak, are the distinguished *Hakims*; and Ganga Rám and Rodu, are the *Pandits* of repute.

The maktab at *Kot Ninan* has 6 pupils, and Persian and Arabic are taught.

Mingri has the largest maktab; 40 pupils attend; they are taught Persian and Urdu by Gauhar Sháh, who gets Rs. 5 per mensem.

Kot Bajina has the second best maktab; 15 pupils attend, and Persian and Urdu are taught. In the following villages, which have each a maktab, the Korán and Arabic are taught; *Jahidpur*, 1 maktab with 7 pupils; *Sukrangian*, 1 with 6; *Kasraj*, 1 with 7; *Bhabra*, 1 with 5; *Jirpal*, 1 with 4; *Danori*, 1 with 7; *Bhityan*, 1 maktab with 6 pupils, at which also Persian is taught.

DERA NANAK.—*Moulvi* Karim Bakhsh (who is a physician also), *Pandit* Dhanpat and *Bhai* Perag Dass are eminent men in this circle. To the mosque of this place is attached a maktab in which the Korán is taught to 10 pupils by Ata Muhammad, who gets his food and clothing. There is another maktab with 10 pupils.

There is also a Gurmukhi school which is attached to the dharamsala of Dya Chand, where Pirag Dass Udasi teaches 24 pupils (private informant gives 40), for which he gets his food and clothes. There is a patshala also with 21 pupils, who are taught Grammar and Logic by Pandit Dhanpat Rai. Another Gurmukhi school is attended by 25 pupils.

Dharamkot has a good maktab, in which the Korán, Arabic and Persian are taught to 31 pupils by Amanat Ali Sháh. There are 2 other maktabs with 37 pupils. *Dharamkot* has also a patshala with 12 pupils learning Sanscrit Grammar.

A private return adds the following maktabs in this circle:—

Place.	Maktabs.	Pupils.
Kotli Surat mali	2	12
Dera Afghanan	1	6
Shikar	2	23
Phugguki	1	9
Dihar	2	20
Meghan	1	19
Khwaja Wardak	1	6

Ranya.—The Police returns mention no school of any kind in this place, but they name the following men as distinguished in this circle:—Hakims

t

Bigamuddin and Chiraghuddin in Ghooman Khurd; Dasundhi Sháh, in Naushera, Nawab Sháh and Boolan Sháh in Ghooman Kalan, Jai Chand and Gurdyal.

Gurdaspur.—*Pandits* Ganesh Gir and Jit Rám, *Moulvi* Sher Muhammad, and *Hakims* Gulab Khatri and Kalu Barber are mentioned. The maktab at Gurdaspur is attached to a private house; there are 40 pupils, and Barkat Ali teaches them Persian, Arabic and Urdu. He gets 30 maunds of grain a year.

At one the patshalas, Pandits Jit Rám and Ganesh Gir teach Sanscrit gratuitously 7 pupils.

The following villages are put down as having each a maktab:—*Bahalpur Chura*, 1 with 6 pupils; *Migyan* also 1 with 6; *Shekhupura*, 1 with 4; *Birmar*, 1 with 8; *Tibur*, 1 with 5; *Myani Chelan*, 1 with 8; *Chandi*, 1 with 12; *Ghazikot*, 1 with 4; *Sahdu Chak*, 1 with 6; *Puruwal*, 1 with 4; *Rawalpindi* and *Phagwar*, each 1 with 6 pupils; and *Birnalah*, 1 with 8 pupils.

MOOLTAN DIVISION.

MOOLTAN DISTRICT.

GENERAL ABSTRACT.

District.	No. of Maktabs and Madrasas	No. of pupils.	No. of Sanscrit and Nagri schools.	No of pupils.	No. of Gurmukhi schools.	No of pupils.	No. of Lande and Mahajani schools.	No. of pupils.	Total No of Indigenous schools	Total No of pupils.
Mooltan.	71	1,118	10	109	11	203	8	686	100	2,116

THANA JALALPUR.—The Moulvis mentioned in this circle are Fateh Muhammad, Ghaus Bakhsh, Fazil Muhammad and Ala Bakhsh; Pandits Kishora Misser, Dida Misser and Kalu Misser. Ghaus Bakhsh is also an author and has written a treatise on inheritance according to Muhammadan Law. Among Hakims Jan Muhammad is mentioned. According to a private return, 2 maktabs are attached to the grand mosque, one with 16 pupils under Fazil Muhammad and the other with 4 pupils under Moulvi Ghaus Bakhsh; the subjects of tuition are Arabic Grammar, Logic, Muhammadan Law, "Tafsir" and "Hadis" (Commentaries and Exegesis of the Korán), "Hadis" (traditions of Muhammad). Above teachers have no fixed income at present. In the time of the Nawabs of Mooltan and the Sikhs they held pensions and rent-free land, the documents of which, they say, they have still in hand. The other maktabs at Jalalpur are under Moulvi Fateh Muhammad, Mian Ghulám Kadir, Mian Abdul Karim I, Mian Abdul Karim II, and Mian Jamal with 10, 8, 10, 7 and 4 pupils respectively. In the first-named Muhammadan Law, Persian and Commentaries on the Korán are the subjects of tuition, and in the rest the Korán and Persian only.

Basti Nonari and *Japurivalla* have each a Korán school under Sadik Muhammad and Abdul Khalik with 4 and 5 pupils respectively. There is a *Gurmukhi school* at Jalalpur attached to the temple of Kishora Misser, who teaches 15 to 20 pupils in Gurmukhi; he gets 16 seers of flour and six annas in cash per mensem. Also a patshala with 16 pupils under Dalla Misser, who is a good Sanscrit scholar. The boys learn the "Uttam Páth" and "Amarkosh." The teacher gets only 10 seers of flour and 4 annas per mensem.

Two Mahajani schools under Kishori Dass and Narsingh Dass with 15 and 20 pupils in which Hindi, Lande and multiplication table form the subjects of tuition.

MOOLTAN.—The distinguished *Moulvis* are Abdul Rahman, Rahim Bakhsh, Sultan Mahmud, Abdulla, Nur Muhammad, Nasiruddin, Khuda Bakhsh, Nizam Uddin, Qadir Bakhsh, Abdul Haq, Zain Ul-Abidin. The *Pandits* are Rám Bawa, Fateh Chand, Rikhi Kesh, Chandu Rám, Thakur Dass, Khalo Rám, Jhangi Rám, Kanihya Lal, Tharia Lal. *Bhais*: Jagat Singh, Damodar Das, Amar Singh, Salo, Paritam Das, Lalu Rám, Sant Dass, Saru Dass, Pokar Dass, Rám Dass, Kanihya Rám, Gulab Singh, Khem Dass, Dharma Dass, Utám Singh, Ganesh Dass, Daulat Rám, Sara Dass, Rám Dass, Dhian Singh, Ishar Parkesh. *Hakims*: Moulvi Nasir Uddin, Ghulám Rasa, Shah Bakhsh, Dildar Bakhsh, Qadir Bakhsh, Zaini-Ul-Abidin, Jand Vad, Alah Dad, Didar Bakhsh and Muhammad Hassan. *Baids*: Sukhkhu Lal, Machhar Bhagat, Dili Rám, Daulat Rai, Pyare Lal, Siddhu Rám, Kirpa Rám, Nemat Rai, Chela Rám, Takkan Lal.

The District Inspector of Schools has favoured me with the following lists of indigenous schools in the Mooltan district, which largely supplement the police return, but in some respects contradict them, which should invite further enquiry. One is as follows :—

EXTRA MAKTABS IN THE MOOLTAN CIRCLE.

Number.	Name of tehsil.	Name of town or village.	Locality.	Teacher's name.	His qualifications.	Number of pupils.	Subjects taught.	Income.	REMARKS.
								Rs.	
1	Mooltán .	Mooltan	Mosque .	Ghulám Mustafá	He knows Grammar, Arabic and Persian.	20	The Korán and Persian books, Gulistan and Bostán.	10	Is paid by Ghulum Kadir Khan Rais. He also gets some grain and bread on festivals.
2	Ditto	Ditto .	Ditto .	Abdul Rahim .	He knows Arabic Grammar.	25	The Koran, Gulistan, Bostán, Bahár Danish and Sikandar Namah.	10	Paid by Ghulam Kadir Khan Rais.
3	Ditto .	Ditto .	House .	Khudá Bakhsh	He knows the Korán by heart, and some Persian.	10	The Korán .	5	Ditto.
4	Ditto .	Ditto .	Mosque .	Dín Muhammad	Ditto .	17	Ditto . .	5	Ditto.
5	Ditto .	Ditto .	House .	Alah Wasáyá .	Knows a little Arabic and Persian.	30	The Korán, Gulistan, Bostán, and Sikandar Namah.	10	Ditto.
6	Ditto .	Ditto .	Shop .	Rahím Bakhsh.	Knows Arabic and Persian.	20	Ditto ditto .	5	Ditto.
7	Ditto .	Ditto .	House .	Ghulám Qádir .	Reads the Koran by rote and knows some Persian also.	14	Ditto ditto .	5	Ditto.
8	Ditto .	Ditto .	Ditto .	Mián Sálah .	Ditto .	20	Ditto ditto .	5	Ditto.
9	Ditto .	Ditto .	Mosque .	Abdul Rahmán	Good Arabic scholar	32	Grammar, Fiqah, Hadís, Tafsír.	...	Gets nothing from his pupils, but from his disciples.
10	Ditto .	Ditto .	Ditto .	Khudá Bakhsh	Ditto .	15	Ditto ditto .	...	Ditto.
11	Ditto .	Ghotá Sharífá.	Ditto .	Jamál Dín .	Ditto .	33	The Koran, Grammar, Hadís, and Persian books.		
12	Ditto .	Bahádurpur.	House .	Amir Sháh .	Knows Urdu and Persian.	30	The Korán, Urdú, Persian, and Arithmetic.	12	Gets also corn and bread on festivals.
13	Ditto .	Boch Khusroábád.	Garden .	Imám Bakhsh .	Ditto .	25	Ditto ditto .	12	Gets corn and also got prize of Rs. 20 in the last year from the Inspector of Schools, Mooltan Circle.
14	Ditto .	Mooltan.	Mosque .	Nizamuddin .	Knows Arabic and Persian.	25	Ditto ditto .	10	Paid by Ghulam Kadir Khan Rais.
15	Ditto .	Ditto .	Ditto .	Ghulám Haidar	Knows only the Koran.	25	Ditto ditto .	8	...

The number of patshalas in this city is 8. They are not attached to any temple. The names of the teachers are: Pandit Thakur Dass, Tharia Lal, Chandu Lal, Fateh Chand, Rám Bawa, Tirath Rám, Rikhi Kesh and Kholu Rám. The number of boys is 68 to whom Chandraka, Amarkosh, Bhagwat, Astronomy and Hindu Law are taught gratuitously. There are five Mahajani schools kept by Rata Misser, Gang Misser, Ude Bhan, Ganesha Misser, Bhubta Misser. The number of pupils attending is 636, who are taught Sarafi, Hindi and Sanscrit. The income of the teachers ranges from Rs. 5 to 10.

There are three Gurmukhi schools at Mooltan, 1 with 15, 1 with 7 and 1 with 8 pupils; the Granth and Vashisht Jog are studied.

DUGH MAL.—The largest maktab at Dugh Mal is attached to the mosque where Ghaus Bakhsh instructs 25 pupils in Arabic and Persian; he gets Rs. 10 yearly in cash. In *Sherpur* there is another maktab where 15 pupils learn the same subjects as at Dugh Mal.

SARAI SADDHU.—The most eminent Moulvis mentioned in this circle are: Ahmad-ud-Din, Qádir Bakhsh of Fazil Sháh, and Qádir Bakhsh of Haweli Mubárak

The largest maktab at *Haweli Mubárak Sháh* is attached to a private house; Qádir Bakhsh teaches 20 pupils Arabic and Persian; he gets eighteen maunds and twenty seers of corn at harvest. There is a maktab at *Chauki*

Mohán with 12 pupils, and at *Fasil Sháh* with 7 pupils, both being taught Arabic and Persian. There is also a maktab at *Bagar* where 7 pupils learn the Korán and Persian.

LADDAN.—Hakims Moti Rám, Shamsuddin, Yar Ali; Moulvi Nabi Bakhsh, and Bhais Santokh Sing and Amir Sing are mentioned in this thana.

Laddan itself has a large maktab with 26 pupils, in which Persian, the Korán and Arabic are taught. The teacher gets Rs. 4 per mensem and 12 maunds of wheat.

Lakhkha, Salayeah and *Sahuka* have each a Gurmukhi school with 6, 4 and 15 boys respectively; the last-named is the best and is under Santokh Singh.

SHUJA-ABAD.—As learned men of this circle, Hakim Din Muhammad, Bhai Dyal and Pandit Hemraj (astrologer) are named.

The following are the names of places which have maktabs: *Shuja-Abad* with 4 maktabs, 1 under Moulvi Muhammad with 20 pupils, 1 under Abdul Haq with 15, 1 under Nur Muhammad with 15, and 1 under Haider Ali with 10 pupils in which the Korán, Fiqah in Arabic and Persian, and the Gulistan and Bostán are studied. *Gajutha* with 30 pupils; *Rukan Hatti, Chak Kharji, Basti Denis, Basti Nasirpur* and *Basti Muhana* with 20 pupils each place, and *Basti Hattu* with 25 pupils, in all of which Arabic and Persian are taught. A *pat-shala* is at *Shuja-Abad*, where Pandit Hemraj, a man of very good qualifications, teaches Sanscrit to 25 boys. He gets about Rs. 5 per mensem in money and kind. There are three *Gurmukhi schools*, one at *Sikanderabad* with 15 pupils under Bhai Takni Rám, and two at *Shuja-Abad*, one attached to a dharmsala, with 25, where Fattu Rám teaches Hindi and Gurmukhi, and gets about Rs. 5 per mensem, and the other with 70 pupils taught by Pandit Karmu Lal in Gurmukhi and Sanscrit, who gets Rs. 8 per mensem.

NAWABPUR.—The following maktabs are in this circle: one at Sadarpur attached to a mosque where Hafiz Muhammad instructs 13 boys and 4 girls in the Korán; he gets food and corn at harvest; one at *Bakharwala* with 4 boys and 2 girls under teacher Alla Bakhsh; two at *Tahirpur* with 3 boys and 7 girls, teachers Imam Bakhsh and Ibrahim; one at *Bosan* in which 8 boys are taught the Korán and 5 Persian only, teacher Abdullah; one at *Sualeh-mehi* where 16 boys are taught Persian by Karim Bakhsh; one at *Nawabpur* where only 3 boys are taught the Korán; one at *Chúkwensparwali* where 8 boys read the Korán and Persian, teacher Ghulám Ahmed; and another small Korán school at *Chúhipur* under Allah Bakhsh with 3 boys.

Muhammadpur Ghotla has one good *madrasah* where Hafiz Muhammad Jamál, a good Arabic scholar, teaches Arabic to 15 pupils. He gets 16 maunds of wheat yearly and his daily food.

Nurbá has one Perso-Arabic school with 18 pupils where Alla Bakhsh, a good Arabic scholar, teaches Arabic and Persian. Above teacher is also the Imám of the village mosque, and he gets his food and clothing from the Lumberdar of the village.

THANA TALAMBA.—Baid Thakar Dass and Moulvi Abdulla deserve notice. There are five maktabs in this Thana, according to the police return; *Jarahin* with 20, *Ambab* with 7, *Panjkoha* with 9, *Ariwala* with 16, and *Faizpur* with 8 pupils, in all of which the Korán and Persian are taught; in the last place also Arabic.

There are no Gurmukhi or Mahajani schools, as the shop-keepers teach their sons in their shops.

THANA KAHROR.—Hakims Chetan Lal, Ahmad Bakhsh, and Moulvis Sualeh Muhammad and Ahmad Bakhsh are noted. There are two maktabs at Kahror, one attached to the house of Sualeh Muhammad, who teaches the Korán gratuitously to at least 15 pupils, and according to a private return another large Korán school attached to a mosque, where Hafiz Hamid teaches

47 boys gratuitously. The same source mentions a *Mahajani* school with 15 pupils, where Botu Rám teaches Lande and Mahajani gratuitously.

EXTRA.—The following schools* which are not mentioned in the Police Returns are found in the return furnished by the District Inspector of Schools:—

Name of tehsil.	Name of town or village.	Locality.	Name of teacher.	His qualifications.	Number of boys.	Subjects taught.	Income.	REMARKS.
* Shujá-Ábád.	Bangálah	Attached to a House.	Pir Bakhsh	Knows Urdu and Persian.	20	......	10	
Ditto	Shekhú-pur.	Ditto	Muhammad Amín.	Persian	20	Gulistán, Bostán, Zulikhá, Sikandar Namah and Sajjiutal Abrár.	5	
Ditto	Chutián.	Ditto	Alah Bakhsh	A well-known Arabic scholar.	20	Grammar, Fiqah, Asul-i-Hadís, and Tafsír.	10	
Ditto	Khánpur	Ditto	Imám Dín	Ditto	15	Ditto ditto and Persian.	10	He gets this from the owner of the mosque.
Lodhran	Jallah	Ditto	Ahmad Dín	Knows the Korán and Persian.	10	The Korán	7	
Ditto	Wahinaw	Attached to a Mosque.	Alah Bakhsh	Knows Urdú and Persian.	12	The Korán, Urdu, Persian and Arithmetic.	5	Got a prize of Rs. 5 last year from the Inspector of Schools, Mooltan.
Ditto	Chaukí Matí Khán.	Ditto	Imám Bakhsh	Ditto	10	Ditto ditto	5	Ditto ditto.

The following additional schools, which are neither in the police return nor in above lists, are extracted from another return:—

Ghauspur with 12 pupils
Bharjá with 5 „
Qasim Báti with 6 „
Makhdumpur with 8, „
} Persian and Arabic are taught.

A Gurmukhi school in Qasim Báti, attached to the dharamsala, under Bhai Simrán Dass, with 18 pupils.

* *Note.*—The Persian schools in this district are so numerous that there is not a village in which they do not exist. But as the number of pupils in them does not exceed 3 or 4, whilst during parts of the year they are entirely deserted, I have not given their names. Those which I have given in the above list are permanent schools.

MOOLTAN DIVISION.

JHANG

GENERAL ABSTRACT.

District.	No. of Maktabs and Madrasas.	No. of pupils.	No. of Sanscrit and Nagri schools.	No. of pupils.	No. of Gurmukhi schools.	No. of pupils.	No. of Lande and Mahajani schools.	No. of pupils.	Total No. of Indigenous schools.	Total No. of pupils.
Jhang .	122	1,423	. 14	197	55	770	5	116	196	2,506

JHANG PROPER.—The most eminent Hakims in this circle are—Mian Ján Muhammad, and Alla Bakhsh, at Jhang, and Mian Ahmed-ud-din, Mian Nur Muhammad, Nural Haq Afghan, Pandits Gurditta, Deviditta and Jagan Brahman, at Maghiáná. All of them practise the Yúnání system of medicine. A private informant adds Salámat, Sukh Rám and Muhalá, Baids, and Moulvis Ali Muhammad, Kazi Najafsháh, Ata Muhammad, Nur Muhammad, Hafiz Ala Bakhsh, and Obaidullah. *Pandits* Mayya Dass, Lorend Chand, Murli Dhar, Mohan Lal, Hardayal and Hargopal, and *Bhais* Lalsing, Gobind Dass Ramdiyal, Kahan Singh and Khán Chand are added by another informant. There is a maktab at Maghiáná, attached to a mosque, in which Mian Ján Muhammad teaches Arabic, Persian and religious books to 40 pupils, and gets Rs. 10 yearly with food from his pupils.

At Jhang Proper, there is also a maktab attached to a mosque, conducted by Mian Ghulám Muhammad, teaching the same subjects with the same emoluments as stated above, to 45 pupils. A private informant adds Korán schools with 15 and 26 pupils *in Jhang* and *Maghiáná* respectively.

There are patshalas at *Maghiáná* and *Jhang*, one in each. The former is under Chánan Dass Pandit, and the latter under Mayá Dass, who teach gratuitously 22 pupils (private return gives 35 and 15 pupils respectively) Sanscrit, Path Vishnú Sahansa nám, the 1,000 names of Vishnú, &c.

At *Maghiáná* there is a Gurmukhi school, in which Bhái Sain Dass Faqir teaches 90 pupils Gurmukhi, multiplication tables, Arithmetic, and the Granth. (A private return gives 6 Gurmukhi schools with 160 pupils.) There are also Gurmukhi schools at *Jhang* and *Gheore*, one in each, with 10 pupils in each. The subjects taught in these schools are the same as in the Maghiáná Gurmukhi school. The teachers have no fixed income, but get some flour weekly. There is no Mahajani school in this circle, but the shop-keepers teach their sons at their own shops.

WANUKA.—Among the Moulvis mentioned in the Police return is Ghulám Rasul, a learned man, who is also a most eminent Hakim. Among the Bháis, Panjab Singh at Langar Makhdum and Karm Singh at Lalián are distinguished.

There is a maktab at *Wanuka* attached to the mosque, under Moulvi Ghulám Rasul and Fazluddín who teach Syntax, Prosody, Logic, Persian, Medicine, religious books and the Korán to 15 or 20 pupils (faqirs), all outsiders. They have no income to support themselves, except what they earn in the practice of medicine and in agriculture.

There is a Gurmukhi school at *Lalián* and another at *Langar Makhdum*; both are attached to the dharamsalas. In the former, Bhái Karm Singh teaches Gurmukhi to 10 or 12 (private informant gives 20) pupils, and in the latter Bhái Panjab Singh teaches Gurmukhi, Lande, Saráfi and Mahajani to 15 or 18 pupils.

Lalián has also a Mahajani school, under Mularám, teacher, attended by 12 or 13 (a private return gives 25) pupils who learn Lande, &c. The teacher derives no fixed income from the school.

When a pupil finishes his study of Gurmukhi or Lande, he presents 2 to 3 Rupees to his teacher.

UCH.—The most eminent Pandit at Uch is Bhagwán Dass. Among the Moulvis, are Moulvi Nurullah and Muhammad Akram at Wasu and Astana. Among the Hakims, Muhammad Bakhsh is the distinguished one at Wasu and Astana, who practises Yúnání medicine.

The madrasas in this circle are, one at *Wasu* under Nurullah, with 12 pupils (a private return mentions 4 with 28 pupils), one at *Astana* under Muhammad Akram with 20 pupils, and one at *Lashari* under Fatah Muhammad with 12 pupils, two at *Kot-Shaar* with 14 pupils, and two at *Machhiwal* with 14 pupils. The subjects taught in all the above schools are Arabic, Persian and religious books. The annual income is Rs. 20 in kind with food.

Uch has a patshala attached to the temple, under Pandit Bhagwán Dass, who teaches gratuitously Sanscrit, Path Vishnú Sahasarnám, Gíta, &c., to 8 pupils.

There are 6 Gurmukhi schools :—

One at	Kot-Shakar	under Ganesh Dass,	with 10	pupils.
Two ..	Machhiwal	„ Sham Singh	„ 18	„
One	Rashidpur	Partab Singh	9	
One	Wasu		20	

The subjects taught in all the above schools are Gurmukhi, multiplication tables, Panch Granthi. The teachers have no income.

There is no Mahajani school at all, but the shop-keepers teach their sons at their own shops.

BALLU.—Among the *Bháis* Khazan Singh of Sháh Jiwna and among the *Moulvis* Sayyid Rusul of Ballu may be mentioned.

The largest maktab in this circle is in Ballu, attended by about 35 pupils, who learn Urdu and Persian and Arithmetic. The yearly income of Sayyid Rasul, the teacher, a good Persian scholar, is Rs. 43. He once also got a prize of Rs. 30 from the Government for the good organization of his school.

There are Gurmukhi schools in the villages of *Ballu* and *Shah Jiwna* attached to the dharamsalas, in which Bhái Gurmukh Singh and Bhái Khazan Singh instruct 45 and 20 pupils respectively in Gurmukhi and Lande, and each has a monthly income of Rs. 2.

CHINYOT.—In Chinyot (a place which has produced some historical personages, Saadulla, the famous minister of Shahjahan being one of them) *Hakims* Abdul Hakim, Khuda Bakhsh, Ghulám Haidar, Hafiz, Fatahuddín, Kazi Shaikh Ahmad and Girdhari Lal Baid; and among the *Pandits*, Gorandatta, Chander Bhan, Lachhman Dass, Sada Rám, and Shivdyal deserve notice. The *Moulvis* Ahmad Dín, Fakhruddín, and Abdul Halim, and *Bháis* Hira Singh and Bava Tirthdás may also be mentioned. A private return adds Kanshi Dass, Goshain Baid and Nizamuddín Fayez, a poet. Gorandatta, Lachhman Dass and Chander Bhan are said to be authors in Sanscrit and Hira Singh in Gurmukhi.

In *Chinyot* there is a *madrasa* attached to the Pukhta mosque, in which Moulvi Fakhruddín, a great Arabic scholar, teaches Muhammadan Law, Logic, Arabic Grammar and Persian to 50 boys, with an income of Rs. 10 per mensem. The Police returns mention only 20 pupils. According to the Police returns there are only 10 maktabs attached to the mosques in the town of *Chinyot*, under Abdul Hakim, Fakhruddín, Ahmaddín, Badruddín, Karumdin, Abdul Halim, Abdul Karim, Khudayar, Fazaldín and Khudayar II with 20, 20, 10, 8, 10, 7, 20, 20, 12 and 5 pupils respectively; but a private return gives 17 maktabs with only 127 pupils, whilst a third informant mentions 3 maktabs and 120 pupils.

Chinyot has a patshala also conducted by Pandit Gorandatta, a great Sanscrit scholar and astrologer, teaching Sanscrit Grammar, Prosody and Alankár

(Rhetoric) to 20 pupils. A private informant adds 3 more patshalas with 40 pupils.

There is a Gurmukhi school (attached to the dharamsala of Bhái Chamba) and 2 Mahajani schools, conducted by Bhái Hira Singh and Kishen Kaur and Panjab Singh respectively. The former is attended by 20 pupils and the latter by 25 pupils. A private return mentions 1 more Gurmukhi school with 25 pupils and 2 more Mahajani schools with 50 pupils. The village *Sheikhan* has a Gurmukhi school with 4 pupils.

BHORNA.—In this circle, Ghulám Husain (of Samandar) among the *Hakims*, Bakht Jamál, Abdul Wahab, Abdur Rahmán (of Mahamdi) among the *Moulvis*, and Amir Singh among the *Bháis*, deserve notice.

The villages of *Math Muhammad Sháh*, *Samandar*, *Mohamdi*, *Malakdi Bajuka*, *Adlana*, *Bhái* and *Bhorna*, have madrasas under Jewaya Sháh, Moulvi Bakht Jamál, Abdur Rahmán, Abdul Wahab, Din Muhammad, Amir Bakhsh, Imám Bakhsh, and Ghulám Muhammad, with 8, 6, 20, 6, 10, 12 and 6 pupils respectively. The subjects taught in these schools are the Korán, Arabic and Persian. A private informant mentions that the number of pupils in *Malakdi Rajuka* and *Mohamdi* is 20 and 25 respectively.

There is a Gurmukhi school at *Bhorna* with 6 pupils, under Amir Singh, who teaches Gurmukhi. The teacher has no income, but he is presented with some clothes, &c., when a pupil completes his studies.

MUSAN.—In this circle, Moulvi Fatah Sáhib, a famous Arabic scholar, among the Moulvis, and Muhammad Záhid, Jaláluddín, Saiyad Qutab Sháh, Saiyad Hasan Sháh, Moulvi Ghulám Murtzá, and Háfiz Jamáldín among the Hakims, deserve notice. Hakim Hasan Sháh also teaches Medicine.

The largest maktabs in this circle are—the first, at *Basti Pirkot*, attached to the mosque, under Moulvi Ghulám Nabi, who teaches Arabic, the Korán, Persian, Urdu, Arithmetic, Medicine, Letter-writing and Caligraphy to 30 pupils, and gets Rs. 10 yearly in money and kind, together with his income as a priest; the second, at *Salhiana*, attached to the mosque under Moulvi Muhammad Said, who teaches Arabic and Persian to 11 pupils and gets Rs. 30 annually; the third at *Qádirpur Khurd*, attached to the teacher Hafiz Ali Muhammad's house, who teaches the Korán by rote, Urdu and Persian to 15 pupils, and gets Rs. 10 per annum; and the fourth at *Udhwáná*, attached to the mosque, under Mián Mahmud, who teaches the Korán, and *Masáili Hindi* (religious tenets in Urdu) to 25 pupils, and gets Rs. 10 each year.

There are also small maktabs as under:—

Pirkot Sadháná	with	8	pupils	who	learn	the	Korán.
Malkhiáná	,,	8	,,	,,	,,	,,	Korán, Urdu and Persian.
Salhiáná	2 with	17	,,	,,	,,	,,	Korán.
Kot Sukhá	,,	7	,,	,,	,,	,,	Do.
Nijábat	,,	11	,,	,,	,,	,,	Do.
Khotiána	,,	7	,,	,,	,,	,,	Do.
Bhoráná	,,	5	,,	,,	,,	,,	Do.
Wásil Sháh	,,	6	,,	,,	,,	,,	Do. and Persian.
Musan	2 with	35	,,	,,	,,	,,	Do.
Kot Khán	,,	7	,,	,,	,,	,,	Do.
Láng	,,	6	,,	,,	,,	,,	Do.
Haweli Shaikh Ráju	,,	4	,,	,,	,,	,,	Do.
Debduáná	,,	4	,,	,,	,,	,,	Do.
Basti Chhidharán	,,	10	,,	,,	,,	,,	Do. and Urdu.

Mehpánwála	with	4 pupils who learn the	Korán and Urdu.
Sahjawál	,,	5 ,, ,, ,,	Persian and Urdu.
Talá Talwárá	,,	10 ,, ,, ,,	the Korán, reading and learning by rote.
Tháli Gadánwáli	,,	5 ,, ,, ,, ,,	Korán, Persian and Urdu.
Jahán Khán	,,	3 ,, ,, ,, ,,	Do. do. do.
Daduáná	,,	8 ,, ,, ,, ,,	Korán reading.
Siálánwálá	,,	9 ,, ,, ,, ,,	Do.
Hasan Khán	,,	3 ,, ,, ,, ,,	Do.
Rajiáná	,,	6 ,, ,, ,, ,,	Do.

The largest Gurmukhi school in this circle is at *Kotsáhib*, attached to the dharamsala, under Uttam Dáss, teacher, who teaches Gurmukhi, Arithmetic and Lande to 15 pupils, his annual income being Rs. 30. There are also the following small Gurmukhi schools in this circle :—

Pirkot Sadháná,	with	3 pupils learning	Gurmukhí.
Kot Sukhá	,,	8 ,, ,,	Do.
Musan	,,	9 ,, ,,	Do.
Kot Khán	,,	8 ,, ,,	Do.
Láng	,,	5 ,, ,,	Do.
Haweli Ghulám Jinat	,,	8 ,, ,,	Do.
Hasan Khán	,,	10 ,, ,,	Do.

General Remarks.—The inhabitants of this part of the country are not accustomed to serve their tutors. It is almost an ordinary custom for the pupils to give their teachers only a small loaf daily, called "handá" or "wadifa." When any pupil, after 3 or 4 years, finishes the study of the Korán or of the Granth, he presents, according to his parents' means, a present of from Rs. 5 to 10, cloth or cattle, to his teacher.

GHAR MAHARAJA.—Among the Hakims, Moulvi Mir Muhammad at *Bolá* and Moulvi Shaikh Muhammad at Mad Mahpál deserve notice.

The largest maktabs in this circle are at *Jhandir Nyaziwala* and *Mad Mahpál* attached to the mosques, under Moulvi Hafiz Diláwar and Muhammad Bakhsh, with 27 pupils (a private informant gives 30) and 16 pupils learning Arabic and Persian in the former, and Urdu and Persian in the latter. The first teacher gets 5 *kharwár* of grain (as much as an ass can carry on his back) annually, with food and clothing. The second gets corn of the value of Rs. 5 monthly.

There is no patshala or Mahajani school in this circle.

SHORKOT.—The most eminent Hakim in this circle is Mián Háji Mahmud Faqir of Hasu Wáli. There are 2 maktabs at *Shorkot* with 18 pupils.

The largest maktab is at *Khákí Lakhi*, attached to a private house and attended by 30 pupils, whom Asá Ram teaches Urdu. His income is precarious, the zemindars give him some corn half-yearly, the quantity of which is not fixed, but some give 1 or 1½ kharwár.

The Gurmukhi schools are at Shorkot and at *Dab Kalán*, attached to the dharamsala, with 10 or 20 pupils, the latter under Bhái Wasandá Faqir, Udasi, who teaches Gurmukhi and lives on alms.

BORÁNA.—Among the *Hakims*, Gahrá at Borána, Charagh at Pehal, and Ghulám at Tatta Umrá, and among the *Bháis*, Karm Singh at Buráná, Munná Singh at Tatta Umra, Karmchand at Tatti *Malaraja*, Kilián Singh at Deha, and Karpál Singh at Kot Sultan, are most eminent.

The largest maktabs attached to mosques are at *Shanman*, *Inayatpur*, *Tatti Malaraja* and *Sangra*, in this circle, with 8, 6, 18 and 5 pupils, under Karm, Imámuddín, and Ahmaduddín, who teach Arabic and Persian. The teachers have no income from the schools, but they get their daily bread from the Musalman community.

There are Gurmukhi schools at *Borána* and *Tatti Malaraja*, attached to the dharamsalas, with 20 and 8 pupils, under Bhái Karm Singh and Bhái Karmchand, who teach Gurmukhi gratuitously.

In all the above maktabs, Persian and Arabic are taught.

Additional List of Indigenous Schools in the Jhang District.

Place.	Madrasas or Maktabs.	No. of pupils.	Subjects taught.
Jhang	7 Maktabs	96	The Korán, Persian, Urdu and Arithmetic.
Jhokdaya	Korán school	10	The Korán.
Lurká	Madrasa	7	Arabic.
Jamalikhurd	Maktab	12	Urdu and Persian.
Diráj	Korán school	16	The Korán.
Pathanwala	Do.	5	Do.
Pirkot	Maktab	8	Urdu and Persian.
Kadirpur	Koran school	10	The Korán.
Abyana	3 Do.	10	Do.
Sajhar	2 Do.	14	Do.
Thatte said	Do.	8	Do.
Musli	Do.	9	Do.
Yakkawála	Do.	14	Do.
Khanana	Do.	5	Do.
Shaikh Chuhr	Do.	7	Do.
Chela	2 Do.	7	Do.
Dhillan	Do.	16	Do.
Ghari Shah	Do.	9	Do.
Kot Khaira	Do.	11	Do.
Raj leana	2 Do.	15	Do.
Sallara	Do.	28	Do.
Budhoana	Do.	8	Do.
Hassan Ali	Do.	6	Do.
Ranjit Kot	Do.	12	Do.
Pir Abdurrahman	Do.	9	Do.
Ahmadpur	Do.	12	Do.
Haveli Bahadur Sháh	Do.	4	Do.
Dale Kalán	Do.	9	Do.
Basti Nur Ahmad	Do.	25	Do.
Jandbir Wali Muhammad	Do.	25	...
Bagh	Do.	16	Do.
Leo	4 Do.	56	Do.
Mirniwala	10 Do.	...	...

Sanscrit Schools.

Place.	Schools.	No. of pupils.	Subjects taught.
Ahmadpur	1 Sanscrit school	22	Lande, Nagri and Sanscrit.
Jhang	3	33	Sanscrit.

Gurmukhi Schools.

Place.	Schools.	No. of pupils.	Subjects taught.
Kot Isa Sháh	3 Schools	27	
Kot Shakir	1 School	6	
Chatta	2 Schools	20	
Karan	1 School	8	
Mukhyana	1 Do.	6	
Sultanpur	1 Do.	6	
Khanana	1 Do.	12	
Mari	1 Do.	16	
Machhiwal	2 Schools	18	
Dhillan	1 School	24	
Gharishah	1 Do.	14	
Rajhana	1 Do.	10	
Budhoana	1 Do.	14	
Hasan Ali	1 Do.	10	
Kakúwala	1 Do.	10	
Pir Abdurrahman	1 Do.	25	
Haveli Bahadur Shah	1 Do.	16	
Kalin Bharwana	1 Do.	10	

Mahajani Schools.

Place.	Schools.	No. of pupils.	Subjects taught.
Rajoa	1	16	

MOOLTAN DIVISION.

MUZAFFARGARH DISTRICT.

GENERAL ABSTRACT.

District.	No. of maktabs and Madrasas.	No. of pupils.	No. of Sanscrit and Nagri schools.	No. of pupils.	No. of Gurmukhi schools.	No. of pupils.	No. of Lande and Mahajani schools.	No. of pupils.	Total No. of Indigenous Schools.	Total No. of pupils.
Muzaffargarh.	163	1,334	8	35	9	73	6	109	186	1,551

ALIPUR.—Shivlal Thakur, of Alipur (Baid), and Moulvi Jandwad deserve notice.

The town *Alipur* itself has (according to a private return) a maktab, in which the Korán is taught to 12 girls and 8 boys. The police return only mentions a Gurmukhi school with 8 pupils, in which religious books are taught, and a patshala with 2—3 pupils, where the instruction is also purely religious. At the village *Ghalwán* is a maktab attached to the mosque of Moulvi Muhammad, deceased, where 9 boys attend; the subjects taught are syntax, prosody, logic, and religious books. Moulvi Jandwad, a highly-educated man, teaches 4 pupils gratis.

At *Madvala* the same is taught as above to 5 pupils; whilst at the second maktab only Persian is taught by Ghaus Bakhsh to 8 pupils.

Bait-Nabi-Shah has a maktab with 14 pupils, under Fateh Muhammad, who teaches the Korán, Persian and Arithmetic. Above two teachers get a supply of grain occasionally, and a present on marriage and other festivals.

SYALWAN.—In the villages *Khaira*, *Thuth Gurmanee* and *Behrihook*, Moulvis Saleh Muhammad and Alla Bakhsh and Hakims Husain Sháh, Ahmadyar and Nihal Chund, and Malak Siddiq of Tatte Hamza deserve notice. The following table shows the maktabs in this circle:—

Names of towns and villages.	No. of maktabs.	No. of pupils.	Subjects taught.
Village Khairá	1	8	The Korán.
" Shaikh Umar	1	6	Do. and other books.
" Raobid Ghurbi	1	5	Do.
" Dúgur Killasarah	1	4	Do. and other books.
" Shadi Khán	1	7	Do.
" Bapah	1	6	Do. and other books.
" Ladhalungur	1	4	Do.
" Sohni	1	6	Do.
" Jhadhirdurejh	1	4	Do.
" Naun	1	7	Do. and other books.
" Jhujhanwali	1	11	Do.
" Lalmir	1	13	Do.
" Daryachokha	1	9	Do.
" Tattee Hamza	1	9	Do.

For the last four, the following details are given in the Police return:—They are all four attached to mosques. The teacher of the *Jhujhanwali* maktab is Hafiz Muhammad Azim; the one at *Lalmir*, Muhammad Bukhsh; the one at *Daryachokha*, Said; and the teacher at *Tattee Hamza*, Sháh Khuda Bakhsh.

This circle has small villages which contain no patshalas, nor Gurmukhi or Mahajani schools; where there are Government schools, the boys resort to them.

Dahaka.—In the town *Bait Isá*, only a small Persian school, with 6 pupils, is mentioned.

Khángarh.—Hakims Narain Dass Popli, Hira Nund and Tirath Mal are noteworthy in this circle; also Bhai Sarndas. Amongst the maktabs on the list, those of *Chuhrpur*, *Chamru Walá*, *Kot Dadun* and *Jhak* are the best. All these four are attached to mosques; some of the pupils attending are girls. The teachers of above are Muhammad Fazil, Karim, Hayat and Musa. They are paid in money and kind; besides fees, the students pay them 2 or 4 rupees at the conclusion of the *Korán*.

Maktabs of the Circle Khangarh.

Names of towns and villages.	Number of schools.	Number of pupils.	Subjects taught.
Khángarh	3	19	Korán.
Chuhrpur	2	17	Do.
Thatta Quraishi	1	3	Do.
Turf Massú	1	7	Do.
Monda	1	4	Do.
Gudpore	1	5	Do.
Kuchhi Saidu Khán	1	3	Do.
Chamrú Walá	1	4	Do.
Sulaimanpore	1	5	Do.
Kot Dadun	1	4	Do.
Bet-Mithai-Sháh	1	3	Do.
Kamalpore	2	11	Do.
Jhak	1	8	Do.
Shaikhpore	1	6	Do.
Paini	1	5	Do.
Ghazanfargarh	1	4	Do.

Khángarh itself has a Mahajani school with nearly 30 pupils, in which Ditta Misr teaches Landé. According to private information, besides Landé, Sanscrit and Gurmukhi, are also taught, and Brahmin Datrám is named as teacher. According to a third return, this school has 48 pupils, and in addition to the reading and writing of above characters, multiplication tables up to 30 × 10 are also taught.

The Police return has the following note*:—

From a private return from the Khangarh circle we extract the following which is not contained in the Police return:—"There are 3 good indigenous schools in this district, in *Panchmivala*, *Mustri Barai*, *Borman*. Besides religious books, they also teach the books which are taught in Government schools. With the recommendation of the Inspector of Schools of the Mooltan Circle, last year, every teacher is rewarded with Re. 1 per pupil yearly." Panchmivala or Basti Panchmivala is put down as having 27 pupils. The number of pupils of the other two is not mentioned. The same return mentions *Langar Sarai* with 18, and *Bosan* with 17, pupils.

Rangpur.—Moulvis Sultan Hamid and Shahabuddin; Pandit Nanuk Chand and Bhai Basant Dass, are distinguished in *Rangpur*. Rangpur itself seems to have no schools; at any rate, the police returns mention none. The following villages have maktabs:—

Names of towns and villages.	Number of maktabs.	Number of boys.	Subjects taught.
Khokhra Muhabbat	1	4 boys 6 girls	The Korán.
Basti Azim	2	1 boy 3 girls	The Korán.
Amirpur	1	5 boys 4 girls	Do.
Bulkana	1	7 boys 5 girls	Do.
Barahampur	1	5	Do.
Nikka Jamal	1	5	Do.
Arurpur	1	1 boy 2 girls	Do.
Ajmawanah	1	2 boys 2 girls	Do.

Amirpur has also a Gurmukhi school attached to a dharamsala and the Bhai lives in the same. *Six boys* learn Gurmukhi. Lande is taught at the shops.

*Note.—Throughout this circle there is no school which has a fixed monthly income. In some villages the Muhammadans have engaged the mullas of mosques to teach the *Korán* to their children. These mullas go every evening to the houses of the Muhammadan residents of the villages, and get one *chapati* (bread) from each house. They also receive presents on the occasion of students, beginning or finishing the *Korán*. Sometimes such presents consist of horses, buffaloes, &c.

Lande and Sarafi are often taught to the children at their relations' shops.

KIJAR.—The best Moulvis of this thana are: Ali Muhammad of Hujra, Ali Muhammad of Mihrpur, Salih Muhammad, Pir Muhammad, Din Muhammad, Mulla Yahya and Faizullah. The best Pandit is Sadanand. In the village of *Sharif Hujra* is a maktab, which is attached to a mosque, and where Ali Muhammad teaches to 8 boys Arabic and Persian. He gets Rs. 3 a month. In *Kijar* Sadanand teaches Sanscrit and Jotish (Astrology) to 5 pupils at the patshala there, which is attached to Gopi Nath's Mandir; he gets also only Rs. 3 per mensem. A great many Hindu boys learn Lande at the shops. The following villages in this thana have maktabs: *Mihrpur*, 1 with 5 boys, *Gauram*, 1 with 4, *Bugga-Ghulwan*, *Kijar* 1 with 4, *Bet Ali* 1 with 7 and 1 with 6, *Mianpur*, 1 with 8, and *Ahmed Mohana*, 1 with 12 pupils. They are all attached to mosques, and Persian is taught in them.

SITPUR.—Hakims Nur Bakhsh and Karim Bakhsh are mentioned. *Gahárám* and *Chandna* have each a maktab; they are attached to mosques. The first has 19 pupils and the second 21. The subjects taught are Persian and Urdu; the following books being read: "Gulistán, Bostán, Bahar Danish, Sikandernama, Tohfa Nasiha, Karima, &c." The teachers of above two schools are Allah Yar, Rahmat Ullah and two others. They get bread and money on specified occasions.

DAIRA DIN PANAH.—This town has a maktab, which is attached to the white mosque (Masjid Sufaid); Moulvi Abdullá, who is also preacher and Imám of the masjid, teaches gratuitously to about 11 boys Arabic, Syntax, &c., and Persian. The other distinguished persons are Moulvi Hidayat Ullah; Pandits Kali Chand and Khushi Rám; Hakims Mirza Ibrahim, Wali Rám, Alla Bakhsh, Mián Buddhan, Nazar Sháh, and Ghulám Rasul and Chhilkan Misser Baid.

Dín Panah has two patshalas attached to temples, with 4 and 7 pupils respectively; above Pandits teach Sanscrit, Poetry, *Purán* (mythology) and Astronomy; they teach gratuitously, and maintain themselves from the offerings that they receive from their *Jijmans* (those who pay them fees for performing marriage and other ceremonies).

It has a Lande school with 8 pupils, and a Gurmukhi school with 10 pupils attending them.

Ahsánpore has a Korán school with 4 pupils, a patshala with 5 pupils, in which Sanscrit and Lande are taught, and a small Gurmukhí school. According to a private return it has also a Mahajani school, in which Hindi and Mahájaní are taught, with 8 pupils.

Battáh has, according to a private return, 4 maktabs with 42 pupils, which is likely to be correct. *Jaunán* has a mixed school with 9 boys and 3 girls attending, in which the Korán and Persian are taught, *Khai* with 5 boys and 8 girls, *Khaimwala* with 4 boys and 4 girls; *Purhar Ghurbi*, 4 maktabs with 28 boys and only 3 girls; *Kot Údú*, 2 maktabs with 5 boys and 3 girls; has also a patshala with 2, a Gurmukhi school with 4, and a Lande school with 10 pupils.

Bhubpur, *Lunwala*, *Neel* and *Hingrai* have each a small maktab with 2, 8, 2 and 5 pupils attending respectively. *Mundah* has a large Gurmukhi school with 25 pupils (private return mentions only 10 pupils); the following Gurmukhi books are taught: *Jap*, *Sukhmani*, *Panchgranthi* and the Granth.

MUZAFFARGARH.—The distinguished *Moulvis* are: Barkat Ali, Akbar Ali, Kazi Yar Muhammad, Sultan Ahmad, Muhammad Afzul, Ghulám Muhammad, Abdul Hakim Ruknuddin, Sháh Muhammad, Abdulaziz and Qazi Muhammad Yar; *Hakims* Thakar Sant Lál, Kazi Muhammad Yar, Mián Abdul Hakim Mullan and Ghulám Rasul Khoja; *Bhais* Mutun Dhurmsalia and Ram Dhurmsalia.

Muzaffargarh itself has 2 maktabs with 11 pupils, according to a police return, in which the Korán, Persian Grammar and Syntax are taught; a patshal in which 5 boys are instructed in Sanscrit; a Gurmukhi school with 4 pupi and a Mahajani school in which the Mahajani and Lande characters and multip cation tables up to 30 × 10 are taught to 4 pupils; according to private information, however, the number of the pupils is 20, which probably is more correct. The teacher is Gopala Missar. *Lutkur* has a small maktab with 4 boys, in which Persian and the Korán are taught, a small patshala with 4, and a Gurmukhi school with 4 boys. *Tehree* has a Madrasah, in which Arabic Grammar, &c., is taught to 11 boys. The following are some more maktabs in this circle: *Bhootapur*, 2 maktabs with 8 boys, in which Urdu, Persian and the Korán are taught; *Jasseichan*, 1 with 5; *Duába*, 1 with 4; *Khánpur*, 1 with 3; *Chakrwari* 1 with 4; *Alipur*, 1 with 10; *Langar Sarai*, 1 with 6; *Ghagun*, 1 with 8; *Hajipur* 1 with 3, and *Taththa Syalan*, 1 with 5 pupils.

THANA JATOI.—Has the following maktabs:—

Names of villages.	Number of maktabs.	Number of pupils.	Subjects taught.
Village Phúlan	1	12	Persian and Arabic.
" Busan	1	15	Urdu and Persian.
" Bait Bagsha	1	20	Persian.
" Jhagiwalla	1	20	Persian and the Korán.
" Jatoi Janubi	1	10	Ditto.
" Sabiwalla	1	10	Ditto.
" Bustidanwar	1	12	The Korán and Persian.

All the above maktabs are attached to mosques; those at *Phúlan* and *Bait Bagsha* are said to be the best; the teacher at Phúlan is Moulvi Muslim, and at Bait Bagsha Moulvi Muhammad Yar.

THANA KURAISHI.—Hakim Khair Muhammad Quraishi and Fatah Muhammad Moulvi are distinguished men. The villages of *Karimdad Quraishi* and *Basti Ghulám Surhani* have a Madrasah each, attached to their mosque; the first has 7 pupils and as teacher Fatah Muhammad;* the second 20 and teacher Umar; the Korán, Arabic and Persian are taught. They get paid in kind—grain to the value of Rs. 5 and Rs. 8 per mensem.

THANA SHAHR SULTAN.—In this thana the following places have each a Perso-Arabic maktab with 10 pupils, which are attached to mosques: *Sháhr Sultan, Kotlah Sultan, Sháh Rupree*, and *Muslam Chuchra*. The names of the teachers of the first three are: Moulvi Allah Bakhsh, Allah Yar, Makbúl, and Lallú. They get occasionally some grain and their food and clothing.

THANA ROHILAWALLI—Contains the following schools: *Khanpur*, 1 with 10; *Barahmwali*, 1 with 15; *Aludwalli*, 1 with 20; *Dehrawuddú*, 1 with 7; *Galga* 1 with 11; *Jahdewalli*, 1 with 7; *Muhalkahakha*, 1 with 7; and *Mughunpala*, 1 with 5; they are all attached to mosques. Persian, Arabic and the Korán are taught in all, except in *Galga* and *Mughunpala*, where only the Korán is taught. At *Mahra*, in the house of Mohun Lal, is a Mahajani school where accounts in the Lande characters are taught to 15 boys.

EXTRA.

The following names of places, with schools, are taken from a Private Return: *Manna*, 1 with 18; *Khanam*, 1 with 13; *Aliwalli*, 1 with 11; *Nihalwalla*, 1 with 10; *Bakar Shar*, 1 with 8; *Allahdadi*, 1 with 6; and *Behli*, also 1 with 6; whilst *Leitkran* is mentioned as having a Gurmukhi school with 6 pupils.

* NOTE.—Besides the Moulvis mentioned above, there is a Moulvi, a native of the village Gulab Gurmani, who possesses good qualifications in Persian and Arabic, but he does not live there. He is a teacher in a Madrasah at Mooltan. In some villages there are Dharamsalas built for the Hindu travellers only. Lande is taught by Hindus to their children privately. There are no schools for them.

MOOLTAN DIVISION.

MONTGOMERY DISTRICT.

GENERAL ABSTRACT.

District.	No. of maktabs and madrasas.	No. of pupils.	No. of Sanscrit and Nagri schools.	No. of pupils.	No. of Gurmukhi schools.	No. of pupils.	No. of Lande and Mahajani schools.	No. of pupils.	Total No. of Indigenous schools.	Total No. of pupils.
Montgomery.	158	1,461	8	103	48	537	12	191	226	2,292

MONTGOMERY.—The Police Return mentions no maktab in this circle, but it gives the following dharamsalas: the largest at *Montgomery* itself with 30 pupils, teacher Jawahir Singh; *Koreshâh* 1 with 30 pupils, teacher Bhai Nihala; *Sidan Shâh* 1 with 5, teacher Nidhan Singh; *Mahomadpur* 1 with 10, teacher Malwal Singh; *Nurshâh* 3 with 24, teachers Hira Singh, Buta Singh and Kishan Singh. In all these dharamsalas Gurmukhi and Lande are the subjects of tuition. The teachers get their food, corn at harvest and a sum from 4 to 8 annas when a marriage takes place. *Dálá Bála* has a Mahajani school with 5 boys, where teacher Khanú teaches Mahajani and Lande. A private informant gives maktabs in *Montgomery* and *Nurshâh* with 5 and 10 pupils.

THANA DIBALPUR.—The largest maktab in this thana is at *Faridpur Jagir*, attached to a mosque where Ghulám Muhammad teaches to 13 pupils the Korán and Urdu. He has no fixed income. The other places that have maktabs are: *Basirpur* 1 with 13 pupils; *Windla* 1 with 9; *Retpur* 1 with 4; *Jammu-Wachhal* 1 with 9; *Pipli* 1 with 7; *Sualehwal* 1 with 6; *Shahniwáz* 1 with 16; *Kariwala* 1 with 6; *Koiki* 1 with 7; *Moda* 1 with 7; *Jamalki* 1 with 4; *Ainain* 1 with 7; *Somyan* 1 with 5; and *Pir Kasim* 1 with 4 pupils; 18 Korán schools, namely, *Kala Tara Singh* 1 with 12 pupils; *Phalron* and *Táláb* 1 each with 7 pupils; *Lalupur* 1 with 3; *Suaha* 1 with 13; *Ladhiwal* 1 with 23; *Mehtaki* 1 with 4; *Dibalpur* 1 with 8; *Harichandwala* and *Basti Sidan Sain* 1 with 5 pupils each; *Basanla* and *Balli Sada Singh* 1 with 6 pupils each; *Kundáwala* 1 with 4; *Bahripur* 1 with 9; *Faridkot* and *Bonga Sualeh* 1 with 8 pupils each; and *Mustafabad* 1 with 3 pupils, *Bakhshawala* with 5, and *Bunga Taláb* with 7 pupils.

Basirpur has a large *Gurmukhi* school attached to Baba Sampuran Singh's dharamsala, where Bhai Dya Singh teaches Gurmukhi and Lande to 35 pupils, and gets Rs. 12 per mensem. There are smaller schools of the same kind in the following places: *Manqulpur* has 1 with 7; *Muncharyan* 1 with 13; *Kahansingwala* 1 with 4; *Phalron* 1 with 6; *Kala Tara Singh* and *Bhawal Dass* 1 with 5 pupils each; *Bhuman Shák* 1 with 10; *Tanla* 1 with 6; *Nizam Din* 1 with 7; *Dibalpur* 1 with 12; and *Balli Sada Singh* 1 with 2 pupils; in all these Gurmukhi and Lando are taught.

Note.—The Police return has the following remark: "There is no patshala in this circle. In mosques the Korán is generally taught, and about 5 per cent. of the boys attend these mosques. In some Urdu is also taught. In the dharamsalas Gurmukhi and religious tenets are taught. The boys of Sikhs attending these dharamsalas are about 20 per cent., and those of other Hindus 5 per cent.

There is no fixed rate of payment in the *mosque* schools. Generally when a boy finishes the Korán, his parents give from Re. 1-4 to Rs. 5 to the teacher. But a mulla of a mosque, whether he teaches or not, receives a *chapati* (bread) from every house every night, and from 6 to 12 seers of corn at harvest time from *each well* (wells are attached to fields), as the remuneration of his duties of leading the prayers. In some villages beside the income above stated the landholders of the villages give a plot of land rent free, and the Government rent is defrayed by the villagers.

In *dharamsala* schools the following is in vogue: When a pupil attends the school, on the first day he buys an alphabet of Gurmukhi and multiplication tables from the teacher for one anna. When the pupil commences the Granth, a present of Re. 1-4 to Rs. 5 is made to the Bhai; the latter amount, however, is not always given. The Hindus give bread, &c., on festivals.

BAHLAK.—This circle has only three Gurmukhi schools: at *Thambra* and *Thattah Dhimak Salah* with 8 pupils in each and at *Masiki* with 6 pupils. *Pindi Shaikh Musa* and *Chhukmanga* have maktabs with 7 pupils, respectively.

THANA UKARA.—Only one Gurmukhi school is mentioned at *Satghara*, which is attached to a dharamsala; Gyan Singh, Bhai, teaches Gurmukhi to 10 boys.

KAMALYA.—Moulvi Khudayar, Hakim Alayar, Pandits Shib Dass and Sahib Ditta, and Bhai Nihal Dass are noteworthy. *Kamalya* itself has a dharamsala where Har Singh teaches the Granth to 25 boys, and also the first Gurmukhi reading book; each boy when finishing the latter, makes the teacher a present. The same place has a large Mahajani school, where Bhagwan Dass teaches Lande to 45 boys. The other Mahajani school is at *Chakar* with 12 pupils. The only maktabs mentioned in this circle are at *Chakar*, where 17 boys and 8 girls read the Korán, and at *Khairshah* where 10 boys read the Korán.

THANA ATARI.*—Moulvis Muhammad Yusuf, Abdurrahman, Shaikh Tahir, Ilahi Bakhsh, Sháh Sawar, Abdulla and Suleyman; Hakims Jawahar Singh Karamdin and Jamaldin; Bhais Kahan Singh, Chanan Singh Hira Singh, Mohan Shankar Dass and Singh are well known in above thana. The *maktabs* are: 1 at *Sandarki* might be called a *Madrasah*, as Arabic is taught there by Moulvi Abdurrahman. The number of pupils is 13. One at *Majahadki* with 7; *Gulab Singh* with 12; *Kalar Kalan* with 13; *Jaimal Bazidika* with 12 and *Kohela* with 7 pupils.

The *Gurmukhi* schools are: one in *Atari* itself (the best) which is attached to a dharamsala, and where Kahan Singh and Chanan Singh teach 25 boys Gurmukhi and Lande; each gets his food and a rupee on marriage occasions. The other Gurmukhi schools in this circle are at *Kalar Kalan* under Shankar Dass; at *Sodhi Wala* under Gopal Singh; at *Gulab Singh* under Hira Singh, and at *Killa Sada Singh*, under Mohna with 9, 10, 4 and 12 pupils attending respectively.

A revised second Police Return adds the following maktabs :—

Place.	Pupils.	Teachers.
Dogra	12	Ali Muhammad.
Gudar	12	Nizamudin.
Mamand Kalyar	13	Shamsuddin.
Jhogyan Hamun	9	
Amira Tejika	8	
Puran	9	
Lakhu Malkana	5	
Baggi Patni	4	
Parma Nand	4	
Rukanpura	6	
Khola Jaimal	5	
Khena	4	
Tahir Kalan	3	
Takril	5	
Bhuna-Sahiba-ka	3	
Jhogyan Ghulam Farid	6	
Shadi wala	5	
Tahli Bagar	7	

THANA PAKPATTAN.—Pandit Fatah Chand and Hakim Sirajuddin are mentioned; *Pakpattan* itself has a large *maktab* attached to a private house where Haji Ghulám Muhiuddin instructs 25 pupils in Persian. *Bunga Hayat* has a still larger maktab, in which 40 boys attend; this one is attached to a mosque and Muhammad Qamruddin teaches Persian as above. These teachers have no fixed income, but get now and then a present from the parents. There are three *Gurmukhi schools;* the largest at *Pakpattan* with 18 pupils; Tiku teaches Lande; he gets food on "Sankrat" (1st of the month) and "Amavas" (15th of the month), and presents when a pupil finishes his course. The other at *Pakl Sudhar* with 16, and the third at *Mulka Hans* with 15 pupils. Gurmukhi and Lande are taught in all.

THANA HUJRA itself has one large Perso-Arabic maktab with 16 pupils, and teacher Mian Hajee, who teaches gratuitously; there are besides two smaller maktabs at the same place (according to a private return) with 13 pupils in them. Tho other maktabs in this circle are: *Qadirabad* with 15; *Tilah* with 14; *Pir Hayat* with 10 (private return mentions only 7); *Paka Jojah* with 6, and *Jojakalan* with 12 pupils; *Dhalyana* with 10; *Kharal* and *Rámparsad* with 5 pupils each. *Sher Nagar* with 10, *Bahutta* with 8, *Jhogia misruk* with 6, and *Phalla chacher* with 8 pupils.

Gurmukhi schools are: one at *Hujra*, attached to a dharamsala, where Bhai Kapur Singh teaches Lande to 17 boys gratuitously; one at *Qadirabad* with 10; and one at *Shergarh* with 13 pupils. *Jethpur, Durgan, Sháhpur, Lalawala, Buhlulpur, Bhawan* and *Bhugan* have also Gurmukhi schools with 10, 5, 5, 6, 19, 8, and 5 pupils respectively.

SAYDWALA.—*Moulvis* Jamaluddin and Abdul Hamid; Pandits Shankar Dass, and Kaka Dass; *Hakims* Murad Bakhsh and Kesor Rám, and Bhai Labbhu are mentioned in above place. The Police return gives no maktab, and only one large Mahajani school with 35 boys in *Saydwala* itself, where Bhai Ralya Rám teaches Gurmukhi, Lande and Mahajani. A private return, however, gives the following maktabs: 1 in *Saydwala* with 12 or 16 pupils attending. The Korán and Persian are taught by Faqir Jamal Din gratuitously; *Porindah* 1 with 11; *Mukan Razi* 1 with 8; and *Jhoktor* 1 with 10 pupils; in these last ones the Korán and Urdu books are taught, *Mukan Sahi* with 15 and *Rajjab* with 5, in which only the Korán is taught, and *Mukan Sobha* with 4 pupils in which Persian is added.

The same private return mentions a patshala at *Saydwala*, and as teachers, Pandits Shanker Dass, Widia Dhar and Rám Kishan, who teach "Bhagwat," "Viyakarn," "Kaumudi" and other Sanscrit books to 12 pupils. At present, the above Pandits have no income, but in the time of Maharaja Ranjit Singh they had two wells rent-free and Rs. 100 in cash per annum.

BATTI.—Moulvi Ilahi Bakhsh, Hakim Moulvi Karimuddin, in Batti, and Bhai Rattan Singh, in Qabula, are well known.

The largest maktab is at *Batti*, attached to a mosque. Moulvi Ilahi Bakhsh, who is a good Arabic and Persian scholar, teaches 20 "Dervishes" (poor outsiders). He gets fees as a mulla and 4 bighas of land from the Lumberdar. There is a smaller maktab at Batti, with 10 pupils, where Karam Din teaches the Korán and Persian. The following villages have maktabs: in *Chichras* with 8 pupils, teacher Hasan; *Vali Muhammad* with 10, teacher Azizuddin; *Suman Sháh* with 13, teacher Ghulám Kadir; *Bhali* with 7, teacher Moulvi Nurdin; *Kota* with 14, teacher Abdus Satar; *Nura* with 4, teacher Sher Muhammad; *Shachok* with 10, teacher Ahmad Yar; *Tumúrát* with 13, teacher Sháh Muhammad; *Maluka* with 4, teacher Sherulla; *Marihazara* with 7, teacher Nabi Bakhsh, and *Tamlira* with 10 pupils. There are two *Gurmukhi schools*, 1 at *Batti* and 1 at Qabula, each having 12 pupils.

CHOCHAK.—Hakims Ghulám Nabi and Gul Muhammad and Bhai Jhanda Singh, in Kohla, are best known. *Lishari* has the largest maktab, attached to a mosque; 50 pupils attend, most of them strangers. Moulvis Myan Muhammad Qarí, Nizam Din, and Muhammad Bakhsh teach the Korán, Persian and Arabic. The zemindars of the village pay them about Rs. 200 per annum in cash and kind. They take no fees from the pupils. There are smaller maktabs, *Jandraka*, 1 with 15; *Kohla*, 1 with 7; *Kaman*, 1 with 5; *Migha* 1 with 4; *Joya* 1 with 16; *Baman Bala* 1 with 24; and *Islampur* 1 with 5 pupils. In all these only the Korán is taught, except in Baman Bala, where Arabic and Persian are added. There are two dharamsalas in which Gurmukhi is taught, at *Kohla* with 12 and at *Lishari* with 16 pupils, and two Lande schools, at *Jandraka* and *Kohla*, with 14 and 12 pupils respectively. Kanchia Bhagat, Hakim, and Madan Lall, Pandit, may be mentioned; *Magan* and *Kohla* have each a maktab with 20 pupils in each.

HARPA.—No maktabs are named here, and only the following schools: 1 patshala at *Muradki Katta*, with 4 pupils, where Moti Rám teaches Sanscrit, getting about 4 annas per mensem in kind; a Gurmukhi school at the same place, with 14, and another at *Bungha Bahawal* attached to a dharamsala, where Bhai Itar Singh teaches Lande and Gurmukhi to 20 boys, and gets Rs. 3 per mensem in kind, and a purely Lande school at *Dadra Bála*, with 12 pupils under Kanchia Rám.

BUCHIKI.—The following are the Korán schools belonging to this circle: *Badaghar* with 14, *Shahpur* with 5, *Chidpur* with 11, *Kot Tahir* with 6, *Bhaluana* with 10, *Baggi Dal* with 6, and *Ranya Baryarwala* with 12. The last is the best, and may be called a Madrasah, as Arabic, Muhammadan Law, and Persian are taught in it.

Buchhki itself has a patshala, where Bava Moti Rám has 6 pupils, whose tuition is only of a religious description. The teacher lives on alms. *Buchhki* has a Gurmukhi school with 20 pupils attending; *the teacher is a woman* named *Mussamat Rutno*; another Gurmukhi school is at *Chidpur* with 18 boys; teacher, Bhai Charan Dass; and another at *Dúpchi* with 7 boys under Bhai Jewan Singh. Above get no fees except corn at harvest.

GOGAIRA.—Muhkam Din of Fatahpur, Moulvi and Hakim, is mentioned. *Fatahpur* has the largest maktab in this circle, attached to a mosque, where Tajuddin, a good Arabic and Persian scholar teaches Gulistan, Bostan, Korán and Muhammadan Law to 17 pupils. He has no fixed income, but gets his daily bread and some donation on the completion of a pupil's course. The following are small Korán schools:—

Bhujyan with *Sadar* 4, *Gogera* with 7, *Burj Jivekhan* with 8, *Mardani* with 7 boys and 4 girls; *Tattah Ismael* with 6 and 4; *Tatteh Jiwan* with 5 and 3; *Miski* with 6 and 4; and *Jatana* with 4 boys and 4 girls; and *Alawalki* with 10 boys; and *Burj Jiwekhan* with 8 pupils. There are two dharamsalas in *Fatahpur* with 22 pupils, in which the Granth is taught, one in *Shadhan* with 4, and another in *Bhujyan* with also 4 pupils.*

KALYANWALA.—This circle has 5 Mahajani schools in which Mahajani and Lande are taught; *Kalyanwala* with 10; *Thatta Tirana* with 15; *Thatta Darbar Singh* with 5; *Godh* with 16, and *Alam Shah* with 10 pupils. Bava Krishngir is an eminent physician in this circle and also an author.

CHECHAWATNI.—Moulvi Murád, who is also a Hakim, Moulvi Nur Muhammad and Pandit Ramjas are mentioned.

Chechawatni has a maktab attached to a mosque, where Nur Muhamma[d] teaches the Korán and Arabic to 12 pupils and gets his food in return.

Bugge-ki-kathaya has a school of the same kind with 6 pupils.

EXTRA LIST.

The following list of schools is taken from a private return, which has been [...]ed in the Police returns of the Montgomery district:—

Rori, 1 maktab with 8 pupils; *Dograi* with 4; *Sher Nagar* with 4; *Dhalhánd* with 15; *Kotshah Mustan* with 8; *Jhang Abdalla Sháh* with 9; *Rajuwal* with 5; *Fanana* with 2, *Shahpur* with 11, *Shahuwal* with 5, *Phalwan Ladhuka* with 15; *Pholan Tolekalam* with 4; *Amliki Suhag* with 10; *Chishti Kutbuddin* with 7; *Lalkarki Jagwera* with 4; *Yawar Bhaldyanka* with 10; *Buchiki* with 8; *Muhilei Ali* with 7; *Manan Chandika* with 9; *Haneli* with 10; *Faridpur Suhag* with 5; *Mirzapur* with 2; *Dola pukhta* with 4; *Kot Sher Muhammad Khán* with 2; *Maruf* with 2; *Ardrewala Myanjan* with 4; *Buhlulpur* with 5, and *Awan Kalán* with 6, in which the Korán and Persian are taught.

* *Note.*—This circle is inhabited almost entirely by Jats who take very little interest in the education of their children.

LAHORE DIVISION.

LAHORE DISTRICT.

GENERAL ABSTRACT.

District.	No. of maktabs.	No. of pupils.	No. of Sanscrit and Nagri schools.	No. of pupils.	No. of Gurmukhi schools.	No. of pupils.	No. of Landé and Mahajani schools.	No. of pupils.	Total No. of indigenous schools.	Total No. of pupils.
Lahore .	295	4,247	32	377	43	571	28	902	398	6,097

LAHORE.—In the city of Lahore, among the HAKIMS, Hakim *Ala Din*, Hakim *Pir Bakhsh*, Hakim *Buzarg Shah*, Hakim *Najaf Shah*, Hakim *Jewan Khán*, Hakim *Mayya Dass*, Hakim *Bahadur Shah*, Hakim *Myan Gamún*, Hakim *Dost Muhammad*, Hakim *Shujáuddin*, Hakim *Ghulám Nabi*, (Zub-da-tul-hukamá and diploma-holder of the Panjab University College), Hakim *Ghulam Mustafá*, teacher of Yunani Medicine in the Oriental College, Lahore, Hafiz *Fakhruddin*, Zub-da-tul-hukamá, Hakim *Ameer Chand*, Hakim *Gulab Din*, Nawa *Abdulmajid Khán* Rais, Hakim *Wali Shah*, Hakim *Sharaf Shah*, Hakim *Khuda Bakhsh*, and Hakim Mehr Bakhsh; and among the BAIDS *Keshate Charan* Babu, *Narain Dass*, *Kalma Misser*, Pandit *Janardhan*, teacher of Vaidic in the Oriental College, Lahore, *Dahar Chand*, *Khushal Misser*, *Mehr Chand*, Pandit *Khanna Rám*, and *Beshan Baid*, deserve notice. *Hakims* Karim Bakhsh, of Baghvanpura, Lodhie Shah of Bhogewal, and Gul Muhammad of Koi Miran, may be added. The most noted of the MAULVIS in Lahore are, Khalifa *Hamiduddin*, Kazi of Lahore, Maulvi *Núr Ahmad* Sahib, Imam of the Anárkali Mosque, Maulvi *Ahmadali*, Bazár preacher, Anárkali, Maulvi *Ghulám Muhammad* Sahib, Buggewalá, Maulvi *Abu Said Muhammad Husain*, Secretary Anjunan Hamdardi Islamya, Maulvi *Ghulàmulla Kasúri*, Maulvi *Abdul Hakim*, Head Persian teacher in the Oriental College of Lahore, Maulvi *Muhammad Din*, Maulvi *Faizul Hasan*, Head Maulvi Oriental College, and the most distinguished Arabic Scholar in Upper India, Maulvis *Kazi Zafruddin*, Hafiz *Abdulaziz*, *Mir Abdulla* and *Momin Ali*, Arabic Teachers in the Oriental College, Maulvi *Ghazanfar*, Maulvi *Muhammad Jamál*, Maulvi *Abdul Aziz* of the Oriental College, and Maulvi *Abulqasim*, Mujtahid of the Shias; and Maulvis *Muhammad Din*, Maulvi *Zahúruddin*, and Maulvi *Ghulám Mustafá*, natives of Baghbanpura, and Maulvi *Sharf Ilahi*, of Bhagiwal, and Maulvi *Amar Din*, of Koi Mirán, are also good Arabic scholars.

Among PANDITS may be mentioned: *Rikhi Kesh*, *Misru*, *Bhagwán Dass*, Sanscrit Professor, Government College, Lahore; Pandit *Gauri Shankar Gushain*, Pandit *Lalu Lal*, Pandit *Godha*, Pandit *Sukhdyal*, Pandit *Guruper-shad*, Head Pandit of the Oriental College and one of the most distinguished scholars in India, *Balrám*, *Roopchand*, *Nund Lal*, *Kaushi Nath*, *Rugnath*, *Nageen Chand*, *Mahtab Ray*, *Hardat*, *Gobind Rám* and *Vaed Pathi*, of Hari Gayan Mandar, Pandits *Rikhi Kesh*, *Dya Rám*, *Sukhdyal*, of the Oriental College; Pandits *Pahad Chand*, *Mathradat* Shastri, *Dya Ram*, *Maharaj*, and *Ganpat*.

Among the BHAIS may be brought to notice the names of Bhai Bhagat Singh, Bhai Sant Singh, Níhál Singh, Partab Singh, Ganda Singh, and Naththa Singh, Bhai Ram Singh, Bhai Bhagwan Singh, and Prem Singh, Bhais Gurmukh Singh, Assistant Professor of Mathematics (in Hindi) in the Oriental College, Harsa Singh, Jogi Shivnath and Sadhu Dit Singh, teachers in the Oriental College, are distinguished Gurmukhi scholars.

The following are among the AUTHORS at Lahore:—

Dr. Rahim Khán, Dr. Amir Shah, Dr. Muhammad Husain, Rai Kanhia

Lal, Dr. Brij Lal, Mufti Ghulám Sarvar, Maulvi Faizulhasan, Maulvi Abdul-hakim, Pandit Guru Pershad, Pandit Rishi Kesh Shastri, Maulvi Ghulám Mustafá, Babu Novina Chandra, Pirzada Muhammad Hussain, Babu Shashi Bhushan Mukerji, Maulvi Muhammad Husain Azád, Pandit Sukhdyal, Dya Ram, Pandit Janardhan, Bhai Gurmukh Singh, Jogi Shiv Nath, Lala Ganga Rám, Maulvi Zafruddin, Maulvi Ghazanfar, Munshi Abdulaziz, Maulvi Muhammad Din, Hafiz Fakhruddin, Hakim Ahmad Ali, Gulab Singh, Munshi Karam Ilahi, Maulvi Abusaid Muhammad Husain, Maulvi Ghulám Ulla, Maulvi Ahmad Ali, Sayyed Amir Shah, Hafiz Umardaraz, Hakim Ghulám Nabi.

Maulvi Muhammad Husain, Tárá Chand, Charágh Uddín, Rám Sahái, Sarájuddín, Muhammad Yásín, Aláuddín, Maulvi Faizul Hassan, Kazi Fazl Husain, Maulvi Tájuddin, Muhammad Munir, Muzaffaruddin, Ganda Rám, Sháh Din, Pandit Mannath, Kazi Mahbúbálam, Jagír Singh, Habibulláh, Khádim Mohiyuddin, Háfiz Muhammad Din, Maulvi Abdul Hakim, Zahur-uddin, Hamid Ali Sháh, Gholámí, Ghulám Mahbúb Subhaní Nawáb, Muham-mad Din, Alaf Din, Zafruddin, Ghulám Kádir, Maulvi Atáulláh, Mufti Ghulám Sarwar, Mirzá Fatah Muhammad, Gurdás, Pandit Gurú Prashad, Pandit Rikhi Kesh, Pandit Sukhdyál, Pandit Hem Ráj, Pandit Rám Chand, Pandit Gangá Bishen, Bhái Gurmukh Singh, Bhái Uttam Singh and Lalla Kewal Kishen, Mufti Ghulám Safdar, Mufti Ghulám Akbar, Ahmad Husain, Shaukat, Firozuddin, Hafiz Umar Daraz, Abdulmajid, Mir Abdulla, Mirza Kháwar, Nisar Ali Shuhrat, and Mirza Ishrat, are *poets* at Lahore.

The most important of the indigenous schools in Lahore are the following:—

(1.) The Lahore Oriental College combines the functions of the Benares Sanscrit Government College, the Calcutta Arabic Madrasah, the Persian Department of the Lucknow Canning College, besides being an Arts College, both in Urdu and Hindi, having professional classes in Oriental Law, Oriental Medicine and in Engineering, a Department for the training of Munshis, Bhais, and of men beyond the frontier, and, finally, discharging the duties of a literary society in the compilation or translation of books into various Oriental languages (*vide* detailed report further on). This Institution was founded by the Anjuman-i-Panjab in 1865 and was held on its premises, where a Sanscrit School has now succeeded it. It now occupies one of the wings of the Lahore Government College.

(2.) The Imamia School of Nawab Nawazish Ali Khán, in which Arabic, Persian, Urdu, Mathematics, and the Korán are taught by Maulvi Abulqasim, the *Mujtahid* of the Shias, aided by four or five other teachers. The Nawab gives the Manager and head teacher, the said Maulvi, Rs. 150 per mensem. The Arabic teacher gets Rs. 12, and the Persian, Fikah, and Alcoran teachers Rs. 5, 7 and 9 respectively. The Head Maulvi gets Rs. 30 per mensem and the rest is spent in stipends and the other teachers' salaries.

(3.) The Islamia School, attached to the Padishahi Musjid, in which Maulvi Fazl Ahmed, assisted by some other teachers, teaches Arabic, the Korán, Persian, &c., to 54 pupils. The expenses of the school are defrayed by the Anjuman Islamya, Lahore, and nothing is taken from the pupils by way of fees.

(4.) The Guru Singh Sabha School, with 25 (the private return gives 30) pupils instructed in English and Gurmukhi by Bhai Partap Singh.

(5.) The Anjuman-i-Panjab Sanscrit School. The school was established on the 9th February 1882, and aims at becoming the "model Sanscrit school" of which a sketch has been given in Part I. It is, however, still in its infancy As a feeder to the Oriental College, it is partly taught by senior students from that institution. A number of shop-keepers have agreed to pay one anna per cent. on their gross income in support of the school.

Pandit Bhagwan Dass, Assistant Professor of Sanscrit in the Government College, Lahore, is in charge of the school. There are 3 classes: one studies *Lagu Kaumadi*, the other *Amarkosh*, and the third *Saraswat*. There is also a fourth class of beginners learning the alphabet.

Besides these, there are some advanced students who study special subjects connected with Sanscrit Literature, in accordance with the traditional custom of indigenous Sanscrit schools.

The school opens at 7 in the morning and closes at midday. The number of pupils fluctuates, but the average attendance is 50. The following is the teaching staff :—

Ganga Bishen
Sri Krishn } from the Oriental College.
Bullu Misser on Rs. 10 per mensem.
Nagin Chand on Rs. 8 per mensem.

There is a boarding-house (langar) also attached to the school in which 7 pupils live and are fed from the school funds. This *langar* is in charge of Pandit Sukhdyál, the teacher of Logic at the Oriental College where he has succeeded Pandit Ujaji, his father, a very eminent logician.

Up to the present time the school is maintained by the liberality of Rai Mela Rám, the contractor, and Lala Nihal Chand, who subscribe Rs. 50 and 27 per mensem, respectively, and by the one anna trade subscription.

I.—Statement showing the number of, and other particulars concerning, the Korán, Perso-Arabic Persian and Urdu schools in the town of Lahore.

Locality.	Teacher.	No. of pupils.	Subjects taught.	Income per mensem.
Káshmiri Bázár Mosque	Allah Jiwayá	3	The Korán and religious books in Arabic.	
Dabbi Bázár Golden Mosque	Hafiz Khair Din, a good Arabic and Persian scholar.	8	Ditto and Persian.	
Kuncho Kundi Grán Mosque	Mujibulla	6	The Korán & religious books.	
Káshmiri Darwaza Mosque	Fazal Din	11	Ditto.	
Police Lines Mosque	Ahmad Din	14	Ditto.	
Kucha Karim Naqqásh	Imam Din	3	Ditto.	
,, Sheikh Hussain	Hafizulla	22	Ditto.	
,, Prem Náth, Mosque	Badruddin	15	Ditto.	
,, Namad Malán ditto	Hafiz	15		
,, Vazir Khán ditto	Mohkam Din	8		
,, Mosque of Ghungrú Sazán.	Kalú	10		
,, Ghumarán Mosque	Muhammad Din	10		
,, Charkhgarán ditto	Karam Ilahi	6		
,, Vazír Khán ditto	Imam Din	6		
,, Hayát ditto	Núr Din	6		
,, Kasábán ditto	Hayát Shah	9		
Rang Mahal ditto	Fatah Din	12	Ditto	Rs. 4.
Kuche Chabuk Sawaran	Muhammad Abdul Aziz (well up in Arabic and Persian).	15	Persian and Arabic	,, 5.
Mosque of Faizulla, Eunuch	Mahmúd	10	The Koran	,, [illegible]
Takya Sadhwan, (Chini Waly Mosque).	Zahúr Ali (well up in Arabic and Persian).	30	Persian and Arabic	,, 6.
Kucha Gilányan	Ghulam Dastgír (well up in Arabic and Persian).	30	Ditto	Ditto.
,, Khátam Bandán	Ahmad Ali (ditto)	30	Ditto	Ditto.
Mahalla Lal Chah	Khair Din	5	Ditto	Rs. 2.
Kuncha Dhobyan	Chirágh Din	5	Ditto	Ditto.
,, Daryai bafán	Nabi	16	Ditto	Rs. 4.
Mahalla Chahl Bibyan	Muhammad Bakhsh (well up in Arabic and Persian).	30	Arabic and Persian	,, 6.
,, Lakarhárán Mosque	Nur Muhammad	15	Alcoran	,, 5.
,, Chábuk Sawaran	Muhammad Yar	6	Ditto	,, 2.
,, Sadhwán	Rasul Shah	20	Ditto	,, 5.
Haveli Miyan Khán Mosque	Din Muhammad	35	Ditto	,, 6.
Kucha Kalalan Mosque	Haidar Shah	25	Ditto	,, 6.
Mahalla Dhán Kuttan	Munir Shah	3	Ditto	,, [illegible]
,, Gheyan	Nezam Din	3	Ditto	,, [illegible]
,, Jarrahán	Abdul Aziz	[illegible]	Ditto	,, [illegible]
,, Sadhwan	Ghulam Rasúl	8	Ditto	,, [illegible]
,, Dhál	Ali Muhammad	4	Ditto	,, [illegible]
,, ,,	Mohamedyar	15	Persian	,, [illegible]
,, Bahr Wala	Kudratulla and Muhammad Bakhsh.	15	Persian and the Korán	,, [illegible]
,, Tirgarán	Miran Bakhsh	8	The Korán	,, 4.
,, Kamangaran	Hafiz Núr Din	13	Ditto	,, 6.
,, Tirgaran	Abdur Rahim	15	Persian	,, [illegible]

I.—*Statement showing the number of, and other particulars concerning, the Korán, Perso-Arabic, Persian and Urdu schools in the town of Lahore*—(concluded).

Locality.	Teacher.	No. of pupils.	Subjects taught.	Income per mensem.
Kuch Sirkibandán	Hasan Muhammad	17	The Koran.	
„ Dogran, Mosch	Abdul Ghafúr	7	Ditto.	
„ Mohlian	Said Ahmad	12	Ditto.	
„ „	Abdullá	8	Ditto.	
Vacho Wali	Rahmat Ali	23	Persian	Rs. 8.
Jouri Mori	Hasan Shah	15	Ditto	„ 4.
Chakla	Pandit Gopal	15	Persian and Sanscrit	„ 5.
Challa Kothi	Muhammad Din	30	The Koran	„ 7.
Barúd Khaná	Ghulam Muhammad	3	Ditto	Re. 1.
Said Miththa	Wazír	15	Religion, the Koran and Arabic.	Rs. 2.
Ditto	Fateh Din	20	Ditto	„ 8.
Sutar Mandi	Muhammad Yasin	8	Persian	„ 5.
Ditto	Shaháb Din	40	Religion, Arabic, Koran	„ 8.
Sathán	Shahám Din	16	Ditto	„ 8.
Ditto	Ghulám Muhammad	12	Ditto	„ 3.
Talwará	Hassan Din	10	Ditto	„ 2.
Bazár Hakiman	Jalál Din	15	Ditto Urdú	Re. 1.
Ditto	Abdulla Shah	20	Ditto	Rs. 8.
Kucha Kaghsian	Mohr Bakhsh	4	Religion, Koran	Re. 1.
Mohalla Jogyan	Zahúr Din	10	Ditto	Rs. 3.
Tatti Mallahán	Ghulám Yasin	7	Arabic and Persian	„ 2.
Ditto	Imam Din	2	Ditto.	
Bhati Darwazá	Mohr Pannu.	10	Persian and the Koran.	
Kucha Hajjamán	Jumma	9	The Koran.	
Ditto	Iláhyá	9	Ditto.	
Mosque of Lakarharán	Ali Muhammad	30	Ditto.	
Bhati Darwázá	Ghulám Husain	12	Ditto.	
Changar Muhallá	Chuni Shah	6	Urdu.	
Thata Myan Sultan	Jalál Sháh	6	The Koran.	
Kucha Prem Nath	Nurdín	8	Ditto.	
Chinyan Wali Mosque	Sayad Pír Shah	6	The Koran.	
Hamám Wali Maktab	Wasakha Singh	50	Sikandar Namá and other Persian books.	
Bhati Darwázá	Murad Bakhsh	5	Ditto.	
Mori Darwaza, Ibrahim's Mosque	Sayad Gauhar Ali	11	Zalikha, Gulistan, Bostan.	
Data Ganj Bakhsh	Hafiz Ahmad Din	7	Arabic and Persian.	
Panj Pirán	Sain Khudá Bakhsh	12	Ditto.	
Palace of Shaikh Waságwan	Hafiz Abdulla	20 boys & 5 girls.	The Koran	Is paid by a Rani of Maharaja Ranjit Singh.
Chohatta	Badruddin	15	The Koran and Persian.	
Near the house of Nawáb Nawazish Ali Khán.	Núr Ahmad	25	The Koran, Persian and Arabic.	
Lakar Mandi (Anarkali)	Maulvi Rahim Bakhsh	15	Grammar, translation of the Koran, and other religious books.	
Stable of Shah Nawáz	„ Muhammad	15	Translation of the Koran and other religious books.	
Chinyan Wali	Ghulám Nabi	22	The Korán, Urdu and Persian.	
Anarkali	Karim Bakhsh	25 }	The Koran, and elementary Persian and Urdu.	
Ditto	Nizamuddin	10 {	Koran.	
Sathán Mosque	Gul Muhammad, a teacher of 14 years' standing.	15 }		
Anarkali Mosque	Ghulám Muhammad	15	Koran and Persian.	
Said Mitha	Ilahi Bakhsh	30	The Koran.	

II.—*Statement showing the advanced Arabic schools in Lahore.*

Grand Mosque, Anarkali	Maulvi Núr Ahmad	80	Grammar, Logic, Muhammadan Law, Hadis and Mathematics.	
Lunge Mandi	Maulvi Rahim Ullá, also a physician.	40	Translation of Koran, Hadis, Grammar and religious books.	
Gumti Bazár	Hakims Ala Din and Ahmad Din.	8	Medicine in Arabic, Persian and Urdú.	
Havagarán, Shah Alami Darwáza	Maulvi Ghulám Hussain, assisted by Imam Din and Ahmad Din.	12	Grammar, Logic, Philosophy, Muhammadan Law, Jurisprudence, and Arithmetic, &c.	
Challe Kothi Mosque	Muhammad Din	15	Grammar, Logic and Medicine.	
Kamangrán	Ghulám Ulla and 2 monitors	12 stipend holders 8 free.	Grammar, Logic and Muhammadan Law.	Supported by Maulvi Fakhruddin Munsif, who gives Rs. 15 per mensem.
Pathran Wali Haveli	Mufti Salim Ullá	20	Grammar, Logic and Muhammadan Law, Medicine.	
Bhikhan Khan Mosque	Khalifa Kazi Hamiduddin	20	Grammar, Logic, Muhammadan Law, and all branches of the Arabian learning.	
Nawáb Sahibka-madrasa	Maulvi Abdul Qadir	. .	Grammar, Logic and Religion.	
Ghala Mandi Walá Madrasá	Ditto	. .	Grammar and Sciences.	
Maulvi Muhammad Hasan ka Madrasá.	Maulvi Abdullá	. .	Religious books.	
Maulvi Abdulaziz ka Madrá	Maulvi Abdulaziz	. .	Grammar, Logic, and religious books.	
Maulvi Ismail Ká	Maulvi Abdul Khalik	. .	Grammar.	

III.—Statement showing the Sanscrit schools in the city of Lahore.

Locality.	Teacher.	No. of pupils.	Subjects taught.	Income per mensem.
Akbari Mandi	Pt. Kanhia Lál	10	Sanscrit, Grammar, Nyaya and Vedant.	
Machhi Hatta	Pt. Kalyan	2	Ditto.	
Kucha Baiyan	Pt. Lalu Lál	4	Ditto.	
Pipal Vehra	Pt. Atma Ram	6	Ditto.	
Kucha Talwaran	Mishrá Pt.	6	Ditto.	
Sutar Mandi	Pt. Gauri Shankar	12	Ditto.	
Thakardwara Har Dass	Gurdatta	5		
" Shahiu	Sham Das	7		
Baghicha	Rudar Man	4		
Harsukh Rai's house	Rup Chand	10	Vyakaran.	
Private house	Khanna Misser	10		
Ditto	Uttam Chand	5		
Ditto	Daya Ram	12	Puran, Literature and Vyakaran.	
Ditto	Lok Nauth	5		
Ditto	Har Bhagwan	4		
Ditto	Raghu Nath	20	Logic and Medicine.	
Ditto	Pahad Chand	10	Vyakaran and Literature.	
Ditto	Bulram	15	Ditto.	
Ditto	Hardat	10	Ditto.	
Ditto	Mathra Dat Shastri	8	Puran, Literature, Vyakaran.	
Ditto	Maharaj	10	Ditto.	
Ditto	Ganpat	10	Puran, Literature, Astrology, Grammar.	
Ditto	Nand Lál	10	Sanscrit Grammar and Philosophy.	
Ditto	Govardhan	8	Astrology.	
Ditto	Jawar Lal	12	Ditto.	
Ditto	Bali Ram	10	Ditto.	

IV.—Statement showing the Mahajani schools at Lahore.

Locality.	Teacher.	No. of pupils.	Subjects taught.	Income per mensem.
Chauk Varnikhan	Niranjan Dass	10	Laude	Re. 1 nearly.
Pari Mahal	Ghulla and Bhagwat	20	Ditto	Rs. 8.
Pipal Vehra	Radha Kishen	7	Ditto	" 2.
Takeal	Rupidha	60	Ditto	" 15.
Sutar Mandi	Nala Bakhsh	25	Ditto	" 4.
Private house	Hari Kishen	60	Laude and Accounts.	
Ditto	Lunnkra	70	Ditto.	
Ditto	Balli	50	Ditto.	
Ditto	Nar Singh	50	Ditto.	
Ditto	Narayen	90	Ditto.	
Ditto	Pir Bakhsh	60	Ditto.	
Ditto	Sheelu	15	Ditto.	
Ditto	Dina	35	Ditto.	
Ditto	Bhagtu	50	Ditto.	
Ditto	Ghulam Hasan	25	Ditto.	

V.—Statement showing the Gurmukhi schools.

Locality.	Teacher.	No. of pupils.	Subjects taught.	Income per mensem.
Dharamsala of Sadhu Sing	Prem Singh	4	Gurmukhi.	
Chuni Mandi	Sher Singh	10	Ditto.	
Police Guard No. 4	Sham Singh	9	Ditto.	
Mohhan	Ram Singh	25	Ditto.	
Bhai Dya Sing's Dharmsala	Gopal Singh	9	Ditto.	
Ditto	Bhagwan Singh	15	Ditto.	
Baolisahib		10	Ditto.	
Kuncha Hanuman	Ganda Singh	5	Ditto.	
Niaz Beg		21	Ditto.	
Charar		6	Ditto.	
Kotli Abdur Rahman		22	Ditto.	

The following schools, although not, strictly speaking, "indigenous," may also be mentioned, as they are "unaided" by Government :—

(1). The Anglo-Vernacular School of Master Ishri Pershad, translator, Chief Court, Panjab, situated in the Vachhowali quarter, where instruction is given to 110 pupils up to the Matriculation Standard, in English, Persian, Urdu, Arithmetic, Geography, and History. The school is chiefly supported by fees amounting to Rs. 25 per mensem, and a contribution of Rs. 50 per mensem from Pandit Ishri Pershad, who also aids in teaching. The other two teachers are Safwat Ali, receiving Rs. 15, and Kanhia Lal, getting Rs. 10 a month. The rate of fees is only 4 annas a month. Besides the regular pupils mentioned above, the school has two extra classes consisting of the students of Government or Mission schools, who are weak in any subjects, and make up their deficiency in that subject here, and those young men that have got appointments, but wish to improve their attainments.

(2). The Anglo-Vernacular School of Master Ganga Din, in the Gumti bazar, conducted by Master Gunga Din himself, who teaches 40 pupils English,

Persian, Arithmetic and other Departmental books up to the middle school standard. The monthly income of the teacher from the monthly fees (of Re. 1 or annas 8 from each boy) amounts to Rs. 30.

(3). The Sat Sabhá Anglo-Vernacular School, conducted and supported by Lala Behari Lál, Secretary of the Sat Sabhá, with 22 pupils learning English, Persian, and other subjects of the middle school examination, with Gurmukhi, for the Buddhiman examination of the Panjab University College.

(4). The Anglo-Vernacular School situated in the Luhari Mandi, conducted by Perma Nand, who teaches English, Persian and Sanscrit, &c., to 20 pupils, and has an income of Rs. 8 only.

Lahore Circle.—The following statement will show the number of the indigenous schools in the rural portion of the Lahore and the Anarkali Police circles :—

Place.	No. of schools.	No. of pupils.	Subjects taught.	Remarks.
Dholi Wál, attached to the Mosque	1	80	Arabic, Persian, the Korán and Muhammadan Law.	Under Maulvi Muhammad Yasin, a good Arabic and Persian scholar.
Baghbánpura	4	60	Persian, the Korán, and Urdu	Nearly Rs. 7 per mensem in cash and kind is the income of the teacher.
Bhogiwal	3	80	Ditto	Ditto ditto.
Kot Khawaja Said	1	15	Ditto	Ditto ditto.
Mian Mir	1	5	The Korán	Ditto ditto.
Shahu	1	17	The Korán, Persian and Urdu	Ditto ditto.
Mahmud Bute	1	4	The Korán	Ditto ditto
Lakhudhar	1	9	Ditto	Ditto ditto.
Handu Gujar	1	10	Ditto	Ditto ditto.
Nat	1	12	Persian, the Koran, and Urdu	Ditto ditto.
Kotli Ghazi	1	10	The Koran	Ditto ditto.
Salamatpura	1	12	Persian, Korán, and Urdu	Ditto ditto.
Mauminpura	1	8	Ditto	Ditto ditto.
Fatahgarh	1	4	The Korán.	
Khoi Miran	2	80	Korán, Persian, and Urdu.	
Ichhra	2	16	The Korán.	
Pakki Tatti	2	21	Ditto.	
Ajudhiapur	1	11	Ditto and Persian.	
Sahuvari	1	4	Ditto.	
Sándhe	2	16	Ditto.	
Niaz Beg	1	26	Ditto.	
Bhikhewál	1	2	Ditto.	
Shahu Ghazi	2	27	Ditto and Persian.	
Tajpur	1	2	The Korán.	
Ganj	2	10	Ditto.	
Kotli Abdur Rahman	1	8	Arabic.	
Kila Gujar Singh	2	19	Ditto.	
Muzang	7	80	Ditto.	
Ditto	2	27	Persian.	

SHARAKPUR.—*Statement of indigenous schools in the circle of Sharakpur.*

	Name of town or village.	Attached to a mosque or kept in a house.	Names of teachers.	Qualifications.	Number of pupils.	Subjects of instruction.	Teachers' payment.
MAKTABS.	*Sharakpur*	Mosque in the town.	1, Maulvi Ahmad Din; 2, Maulvi Said Muhammad; 3, Nizam Din.	1, good; 2 and 3, average.	20	The Korán	Held a [illegible] formerly, but [illegible].
	Ditto	Mosque outside the town.	Kazi Muhammad Din and Kamal Din.	Ditto	20	The Korán and Urdu.	Bread, &c.
	Ditto	Mosque in the town.	Maulvi Ghulám Hasan and his son.	Ditto	40	The Korán	Ditto.
	Faizpur	Khaja Mosque	1, Myan Kadir Bakhsh, *Imam*; 2 Myan, Karim Bakhsh, *Hafiz*.	1, good; 2 Hafiz of Alcoran.	32	Ditto	Bread on every Thursday; some corn on festival days; and some slight cash income.
	Ditto	Kari Masjid	1, Kazi Ghulám Rasul; 2. Hafiz Pir Bakhsh; 3, Ilahi Bakhsh; 4. Ranjha.	1, average; 2, assistants to No. 1.	40	Ditto	Held a rent-free grant formerly; which has been resumed 2 years since.
	Ditto	Masjid of Mian Sahib.	Myan Muhammad Bakhsh.	Average	18	The Korán and Urdu.	(Bread, &c., as in No. 1.)
	Nawankot	Mosque	Khair Din *and his wife*.	Ditto	15 boys and 20 girls.	The Korán	Ditto.
	Ditto	In a private house	Maulvi Ilamulla *and his wife*.	Ditto	5 boys and 10 girls.	Ditto	Ditto.
	Ditto	Mosque	Maulvi Imamulla *and his wife*.	Ditto	15 boys and 14 girls.	Ditto	Ditto.
	Madadpur	Mosque	Maulvi Shah Din.	Average ability.	8	Ditto	Bread, &c.

	Name of town o village.	Attached to a mosque or kept in a house.	Name of teachers.	Qualifications.	Number of pupils.	Subjects of instruction.	Teachers' payment.
Dharmsalas.	*Nawánkot*	Dharamsala	Bhai Jawahar Singh.	Good.	10	Gurmukhi.	Bread; and holds some muafi ground.
	Sharakpur	Dharamsala outside the town.	Bhai Ranga Singh	Ditto.	10	Ditto	Bread, &c.
	Faizpur	Dharamsala	Bhai Rám Singh.	Ditto.	15	Ditto	One Hira Singh maintains the teachers. On occasions of marriages, there is a slight income.
	Banni	In a private house	Desá-ú-Fakir	Average	8	Gurmukhi and Landé.	Supported by his relations.
	Mirpur	Dharamsala	Bhai Kishen Dass	Good.	10	Gurmukhi.	Bread, &c.

In Nawánkot there is also the place of Bawa Chat Rám and a dharamsala of the Kuka Sikhs. *Fakirs* principally read there Gurmukhi religious books.

MANÁNWÁN.—Hakim Ismáil, in Phularwan, is mentioned as a superior man; no other names are given. There is a good school at *Mohammadpur*, or *Darogha Vala*. It is in a private house, under the superintendence of Munshi Khuda Bakhsh, Lumberdar. There are 30 boys, who are instructed in English, Persian, &c., as prescribed for middle schools, by Muhammad Qasim, who gets Rs. 20 a month in cash from the parents of the pupils. The other schools are at *Jandiála* with 10; *Padu* with 4; *Thehpura* with 5; *Jallo* with 10 pupils. They are all attached to mosques. In the first two, Urdu and the Korán are taught, and in the others only the Korán. There is a small Gurmukhi school, with only 8 pupils, at *Thehpura*.

VALTOHA.—There are 2 maktabs mentioned in this circle, 1 at *Talvandi Sobha Sing*, with 14 pupils, under Bahával Bakhsh, and 1 at *Bondána*, with 15 pupils, under Abdul Rahmán. Urdu, Persian, Arithmetic, &c., are taught. The first-named teacher gets Rs. 60 per annum, and food and clothes, and the other Rs. 5-8 per mensem, and also his food and clothes from the zamindars.

There are no other schools mentioned; but the remark is made that the shop-keepers teach their sons themselves in Landé, &c.

CHUNG.—Hakims Ghulám Farid and Mehr Ali are named as noteworthy. The largest maktab is the one at *Ali Abad*, supported by Nawab Nawazish Ali Khan; it contains 20 pupils, who are taught in Arabic and Persian by a good scholar, Maulvi Sayyad Muhammad. He is maintained by the Nawab, who also gives stipends to the boys. *Mohan Vál* has a maktab attached to a mosque under Abdulla *alias* Haji, with 12 boys and 3 girls, and another in a private house, where a woman, Musammat Saidan, teaches 6 boys and 1 girl. Arabic, the Korán, Persian and Urdu are the subjects of tuition. They get a loaf of bread each a day.

Bagarián has one maktab with 5 pupils; *Moráka* 1 with 8; *Rangilpur* 1 with 6; and Chung 1 with 8 pupils, in all of which the Korán and Persian are taught. The teachers of above schools have no fixed income; the one at *Maráka* gets Rs. 2 per mensem, besides bread; the others only bread.

THÁNA KANA KACHHA.—This Thána has a small maktab at *Kamanh*, attached to the mosque, under teacher Abdul Rahim, who teaches 5 boys Persian, &c., and a Gurmukhi school with 6 pupils, who are taught the Granth by Punjab Singh. *Ato Asal* has another small Gurmukhi school with only 3 pupils, and teacher Bhág Singh.

CLARKABAD.—There are five maktabs, in which Urdu and the Korán are taught: *Ladhe-ke-Unche* with 11; *Ladhe-ke-Niven* with 15; *Mir Muhammad* with 11; *Sheru kana* with 6; *Vatni* with 10, and *Rosa* with 6 pupils. *Báwaliana* has a Gurmukhi school with 12 boys.

KANGANPUR.—The following maktabs are given in the police return: 1 at *Mokal* with 18 pupils, under teacher Gulam Mohaiy-uddin; 1 at *Fateh Muhammad Kalan* with 20 pupils, under Mian Samandá; 1 at *Fateh Muhammad Khurd* with 18, under Mian Banda; 1 at *Landé*, with 25, under Maulvi Isa;

1 at *Kul* with 20, under Sayyad Muhammad Sháh; 1 at *Guri Vala* with 20, under Muhammad Yusaf; and 1 at *Shamkot* with 25 pupils, under Muhammad Sharf Din. In all these, Arabic, the Korán, &c., are taught; they are attached to mosques.

The teachers have no fixed income, but the parents, on the pupil's completion of his subject of study, give the teacher some remuneration according to their means.

Mokal has a large Gurmukhi school, attached to a dharamsala, with 65 pupils; Bhai Variam Singh and Hukum Chand teach them Sanscrit, Gurmukhi and Landé. *Landé Vala* has another with 15 pupils, under Vir Singh, and *Kul*, a third, with 25 boys under Bola Rám; the same subjects are taught as above; the teachers have no fixed income.

Thána Mángtawala.—Pandit Sukhá and Hakims Yár Muhammad, Imam Din, Barkhurdar and Sháh Muhammad, are mentioned as those most eminent in this circle. The maktabs are as follow: 1 at *Kariamwála*, with 6 pupils under teacher Jiwan; 1 at *Khuni*, with 12 pupils under Muhammad Fazil; and 1 at *Jamálpur*, with 14 pupils under Murád Bakhsh. The three maktabs are attached to mosques. In the first two Persian and Arabic are taught, and in the last only Arabic. They are paid Rs. 30, 20, and 10 per annum respectively. There are 5 Gurmukhi schools at the following places: At *Nankána Sahib*—attached to the Durbár Sahib, 1 with 12 pupils under Hukm Singh; at *Kila Dharm Singh*, 1 with 25 pupils under Parma Nand; at *Ásal*, 1 with 23 under Kalu Singh; at *Mangu Taru*, 1 with 13 under Sada Singh; and 1 at *Balo* with 15 pupils, under teacher Bhagat Rám. The subjects of tuition are Gurmukhi and religious books. The teacher of the first-named Gurmukhi school teaches gratuitously; the others get Rs. 30, 20, 10, and 18 per annum respectively.

Thána Bhai Pherú.—This Thána, according to the police return, seems to have only a Korán school with 17 boys in the village of *Lakhkhanki*, under Jiwan Ali; but there are several Gurmukhi schools, the largest at *Bhoya*, with 15 boys, attached to a dharamsala, under Megh Singh, who gets a pice from each boy every Sunday. The others at *Bhai Pherú* with 5, *Ular* with 6, and *Lakhkhanki* with 5 pupils.

Thána Luliáni.—There are the following maktabs in this Thána: 2 at the village *Santoki*; one attached to a mosque, with 10 or 12 pupils, under Maulvi Usmán, who teaches Arabic gratuitously; the other in a private house, with 6 pupils, under Maulvi Saidulla, who teaches Persian and gets Rs. 6 per mensem. *Vadánah* has one with 12 boys, and *Daftúh*, *Rukhánvála* and *Adrárah* with 2, 11 and 8 pupils, in all of which Arabic is taught. A private return adds one maktab with 9 pupils in *Lalliani* itself.

Thána Khudián.—*Khudián* and *Dhangke* have each a Landé school, with 12 pupils each, and *Ganja Kalán and Sunda* have a small maktab each with 5 and 11 pupils, in which the Korán and Persian are taught.

Thána Murídki with 3 maktabs, *Mari* with 8, *Léhdewala* with 6, and *Kol Sayadan* with 8 pupils; in the first and last the Korán is taught, and in *Léhdewala* Urdu.

Kasúr.—Among the names of distinguished Maulvis, Pandits, Hakims, &c., brought to notice, are found those of *Maulvis* Hakim Khuda Bakhsh, Hakim Welayet Sháh, Ghulám Dastgir (an author), Husain Sháh, Ghulám Dastgir II, and Ghulám Qadir II; *Hakims* Ghulám Qadir I, Sayyad Chiragh Sháh and Ghulám Ghaus; *Pandits* Kanhya Lal I, Kanhya Lal II, Durga Dass and Gobind Mal, and Bhai Hira Singh. There are 2 maktabs mentioned in the police return, 1 at *Kasúr* itself with 15 pupils, where Husain Bakhsh teaches Persian, according to the scheme of the Government schools; he gets Rs. 10 per mensem: 1 at *Khemkaran*, with 18 pupils, in which also Persian is taught. There are two large Landé schools at *Kasúr*, 1 with 40 boys, under Sharaf Din Ráwal, who gets Rs. 6 per mensem in cash and kind; and 1 with 30 boys. *Khemkaran* has also a Landé school with 20 boys in attendance.

A private return from Kasúr mentions a large maktab under Faiz Muhammed with 25 pupils, learning Korán and paying Rs. 6 per mensem to the teacher and 12 minor schools with 97 pupils learning the Korán, Persian and Urdu.

Pandit Murli and Bhai Rám Singh are also said to teach Sanscrit and Gurmukhi to 9 and 12 pupils respectively.

The village of *Khemkaran* has also 6 Korán schools with 58 pupils, a patshala with 8, and a Landé school with 16 pupils.

The other minor indigenous schools in this circle are given as below, in a private return :—

Kharyala	1	maktab with	7	learning	the Korán.	
Sehjra	1	,,	5	,,	,,	
Raja Jang	1	,,	10	,,	,,	
Loriwala	1	,,	7	,,	,,	
Shaikh Imad	1	,,	6	,,	,,	
Mahalam	1	,,	13	,,	,,	
Barj	1	,,	9	,,	,,	
Alyon	1	,,	7	,,	,,	
Jora	1	,,	11	,,	,,	
Warnala	2	,,	25	,,	,,	
Bedyan	1	,,	10	,,	,,	
Rajuki	1	,,	7	,,	,,	
Matta	1	,,	5	,,	,,	
Bhujki	1	,,	4	,,	,,	
Todipur	1	,,	15	,,	,,	and Persian.
Sahari Hatar	1	,,	8	,,	the Gurmukhi.	
Baba Thamman	1	,,	6	,,	the Sanscrit.	

THÁNA MUGHAL SÁRAI.—The eminent Hakim is Budhe Sháh, and the distinguished Maulvi is named Abdul Rahmán.

A maktab at *Jajjá* (*Major*) is attached to the mosque, in which Maulvi Abdul Rahmán teaches gratuitously Arabic, *Fikah, Alcorán,* and Persian to 14 pupils.

There is a Gurmukhi school at Sarái Mughal, attached to the dharamsala, in which Bhái Sangat Singh teaches Gurmukhi and Landé to 12 pupils. His income is nothing.

Jajjá has one Mahajani school, with 20 pupils, being taught in Landé, by Chánan, who gets about Rs. 2-8 and bread.

KHOLRA.—There is no eminent person in this circle.

The largest maktab at *Dal* is attached to the private house of Devi Datta Brahman, in which Karm Ilahi teaches Urdu and Arithmetic to 9 pupils and gets Rs. 5 per mensem in cash.

There are two small maktabs in this circle, as noted below, one at *Asal Guruki*, with 4, and *Mari Megh*, with 2 pupils; the subject taught in both is Urdu.

PATTI.—The eminent *Pandits* are named Uttamchand and Atma Rám and *Baid* Madho Rám, in this circle.

The maktabs at *Daweli, Kulla,* and *Satnu* are attended by 20, 16, and 7 pupils, being taught in Urdu, Persian, and Arithmetic. A private return mentions 8 maktabs, with 69 pupils in *Patti*.

Patti has one patshala, in which 23 pupils are being taught Sanscrit (literature) and Jotish (astrology) by Pandit Uttamchand gratuitously.

Maniálá and *Mari Gur Sing* have each of them one dharamsala; 10 pupils in each being taught in Gurmukhi.

There is a Mahajani school at *Patti*, with 18 pupils being instructed in Landé by *Kutab Din*.

Thána Shahdara.—The names of Maulvi Sultan Ahmad in Karaul, Bhai Mahtab Singh, and *Hakims* Maulvi Inayatulla, Abdulghani, Maulvi Sirajuddin, Hasan Muhammad Chiragh Din, and Imam Din at Shahdara, deserve to be mentioned. The largest maktab is at *Faizpur Khurd*, under teacher Mohkam Din, with 55 pupils; it is attached to a mosque, and the Korán, Persian, and Urdu are taught.

The following villages have each a maktab:—

Kot Begam with 10; *Faizpur* (Lesser) with 55; *Bhakhala* with 11; *Fateh Zaman* with 14; *Imangar Kalan* with 12; *Dal* with 14; *Kalor* with 7; *Mominpura* with 6; in all of which Persian, Urdu and the Korán are taught; whilst the following are merely Korán schools: *Sagian Kalan* with 6; *Mominpura* with 6; *Bholi Androu* with 6; *Awwal Khair* with 5; *Bhole Baniwal* with 4; *Goyal* with 3; *Lahanwala* with 4; *Imangarh* (Lesser) with 3; *Yarpura* with 20; *Karol* with 55; *Shahdra* with 21; and *Vandála* with 2 pupils. *Faizpur Khurd, Babakwal, Santpura, Ghazi Kakh* and *Imangar Kalan* have each a Gurmukhi school with 13, 13, 11, 4 and 12 pupils respectively; the last place has also a Landé school with 5 pupils.

At *Laban Vala* is a patshala attached to a temple where Har Bhaj teaches Sanscrit, reading, writing, and grammar to 8 boys; the teacher supports himself by the income from "muafi" land assigned to him by the proprietor of the temple.

Chunyan.—The police return mentions only 2 large Landé schools with 70 pupils; but from a private return we take the following: 5 maktabs at *Chunyan*: (1) attached to the safaid masjid with 15 boys under teacher Myan Naka; Persian books are taught; (2) attached to the Khajur Wali Masjid with 20 boys under Myan Phula; (3) attached to the Baharwali Masjid with 13 boys under Hafiz Bangha; and (4) attached to the Barukgaranvali Masjid with 11 boys under Chiragh Din: in these last three the Korán and Urdu books form the subjects of tuition; (5) attached to the Baharwal Wali Masjid under Hafiz Daud with 12 boys who are taught Persian; books like Gulistan, Bostan, Zuleikha, &c., being in use.

THE LAHORE ORIENTAL COLLEGE.

I subjoin the report for the year 1881-82 of the Oriental College, Lahore, as it is the model indigenous teaching University in the Panjab for all the indigenous educational elements of the province, Hindu, Muhammadan and Sikh. It combines modern requirements with the traditional learning of Maulvis, Pandits, Munshis and Bhais, which is imparted on a more critical system than is generally pursued in indigenous institutions.

Extract from Report of the Oriental College, Lahore, for the year 1881-82 (written by the Superintendent of Studies and Translations, Babu Navina Chandra Rai, Member of Senate of the Panjab University).

Character of the Oriental College.

The Oriental College is supported entirely from private subscriptions, fees, and the interest on endowments made by Native Chiefs. (*Vide* Report for 1880-81.)* Its annual expenditure is about Rs. 31,000 per annum, the detail of which (taking the

* It should not be forgotten that the Oriental College was first an Oriental School founded by the Anjuman-i-Panjab, in order to show, together with the Oriental Examinations which that society conducted, what it meant by its agitation for a "Bait-ul-u'lum" or "Mahavidyala" for the cultivation of Oriental Literature (a name still given to the College by the native public), or, as interpreted to the promoters by the, to them, at first, little known and less understood name of an "University" in the varying European uses of the term. It was only afterwards that the promoters learnt to connect *their* aspirations with the name and functions of a complete University, as a teaching body, a literary body, an examining body, and a body largely governed by themselves in all matters of education and of instruction, including the improved study of English, and a consulting voice in all questions connected with primary and secondary education.

Panjab University College Budget Estimate for 1882 as the basis) is as follows :—

	Rs.
Salaries of the College and School staff, contingencies and rent .	17,034
Endowed Fellowships, (half cost chargeable to Oriental College) .	2,544
Oriental Scholarships, General and Special	9,924
Engineering Scholarships	420
McLeod Kapurthalla Natural Science Fellow	1,000
Purchase of books for Oriental Library	150
TOTAL .	31,072

The above expenditure is defrayed from the following funds :—

	Rs.
Private subscriptions	16,000
Interest on endowments of Native Chiefs	15,300
Fees	72
TOTAL .	31,072

As the whole of the expenditure of the Oriental College is defrayed from private sources, the Oriental College cannot properly be classed as a Government institution, or even as a Government grant-in-aid institution, though it is managed by, and is subordinate to, a grant-in-aid institution, namely, the Panjab University College.

School Department of the Oriental College.

2. The total number of students on the rolls of the Oriental College was 222 on the 31st March 1882. The Oriental College has also a School Department attached to it for the instruction of such students as are preparing for the lower Oriental or the Arts (Entrance) Examination, though it cannot be said that all the students of the School Department belong entirely to it, for there are 57 who, so far as passing an Oriental Examination is concerned, belong to the College Department, in accordance with the rules fixed by Senate, while they are also borne on the roll of the School Department pending their passing the Entrance in Arts Examination; there are also 5 whose case is the reverse of this, for, although they have passed an Arts Examination, they have not passed one of the lower Oriental Examinations, and in that respect are returned as belonging to the *School*; while there are 125 who only belong to the School Department and 97 who belong entirely to the College.

Actual expenditure.

3. The actual expenditure during the official year 1881-82 on the two Departments, respectively, of the Oriental College, has been as follows :—

	College Dept.				School Dept.				Total.		
	Rs.	A.	P.		Rs.	A.	P.		Rs.	A.	P.
Salaries and Contingencies .	11,124	9	3	+	5,196	1	9	=	16,320	11	0
Endowed Fellowships . .	1,942	0	0	+	577	0	0	=	2,519	0	0
Oriental Scholarships . .	5,933	5	9	+	2,383	11	3	=	8,317	1	0
Engineering Scholarships .	208	1	6	+	20	0	0	=	228	1	6
Natural Science Fellow . .	666	10	9	+	333	5	3	=	1,000	0	0
Purchase of books for library .	150	0	0	+	0	0	0	=	150	0	0
TOTAL .	20,024	11	3	+	8,510	2	3	=	28,534	13	6

Number of students.

4. The following statement shows the number of students of each class, and the number prepared to go up for the next examinations to be held in this year.

Nature of Examination.	Borne on the roll.	Prepared to go up for the examination.
A.—College Department.		
Arts—		
Honours in Arts—Urdu	2	1
High Proficiency "	5	4
Ditto Hindi	3	3
Proficiency— Urdu	19	10
Ditto Hindi	7	3
Oriental—		
Arabic— Higher	10	5
" Middle	21	9
Sanscrit— Higher	9	4
" Middle	8	4
Persian— Higher	12	5
" Middle	11	4
Panjabi— Higher	3	2
" Middle	8	...
Professional—		
Medicine, Hindu, Senior Class	5	1
" " Junior "	9	6
" Yunani, Senior "	15	...
" " Junior "	19	10
Engineering, Senior Class	1	...
" Junior "	4	1
Law, Hindu, Senior "	6	...
" " Junior "	7	3
A.—College Department—*contd.*		
Law, Hindu, Muhammadan Senior Class	7	1
" " Junior "	19	3
B.—School Department.		
Arts Entrance—Urdu	79	11
" Hindi	39	9
" Panjabi	13	4
Oriental Arabic—Lower	27	10
Sanscrit "	24	8
Persian "	19	7
Panjabi "	7	4
Pushto "	16	11
Actual number of students.		
Sanscrit section	55	38
Gurmukhi section	17	11
Arabic "	82	46
Persian "	56	33
Yunani "	*8	...
Engineering "	4	1
Total	†222	129

The Lahore Oriental College, so far as can be ascertained, is the cheapest College, the average cost of a College student being Rs. 206 per annum, and Rs. 68 per annum for a student of its high school in India, *while it costs Government nothing*.

Character of instruction given in the Lahore Oriental College.

7. As regards the character or quality of instruction given in the Lahore Oriental College, it will be evident by making a comparison between the number of subjects studied in this College with those in other Oriental Colleges, and even with the English Colleges in the country, that the range of the former is much wider than that of any other College. For instance, taking first the higher Oriental Examination in Sanscrit, a Shastri title-holder of the Lahore Oriental College must pass through the following range of subjects:—

Sanscrit.—Grammar, Prosody, Rhetoric, Literature (prose, poetic and dramatic) two of the philosophies, and one of the ancient sciences;

Hindi.—A fair knowledge of the language;

General knowledge.—Arithmetic, Algebra, Geometry, History, and Geography;

whereas a Sanscrit title-holder of the Calcutta College has to pass *in any one branch* of Sanscrit learning only, *viz.*, Sanscrit literature, Hindu law (modern or ancient), or one of the philosophies. On the other hand, it may be said that the Sanscrit title-holder of the Calcutta Sanscrit College can acquire a knowledge of English up to the First Arts Standard. But in the Lahore Oriental College there is provision for a Shastri to learn all the subjects of the Bachelor of Arts degree, except the English language.

Next, comparing the qualifications of a degree-holder of the Government, or the English, College with that of an Oriental degree-holder of the Panjab University who can only be trained in the Lahore Oriental College, there is this difference, that while the latter has a great superiority over the former in his complete knowledge of one of the Oriental Classics and of the Literature, Law,

* These study in the Medical School as well as in the Yunani classes.

† There has been an increase of 31 students over the last year, when the number of the students on the roll was 191.

Science and Philosophy contained in it, he is equal to the English degree-holder in all other respects, except that he lacks a knowledge of a modern language (English) which he can easily acquire, if he wishes, in a couple of years.

The Government grant to the Panjab University College is very small in comparison to its grant in other provinces to inferior institutions.

It has already been stated that the Lahore Oriental College costs Government nothing, although the standard of this College is so high that no other Oriental College in the country, or in any country, can equal it; whereas the cost to Government on Oriental Colleges and Madrasahs in other provinces of a much inferior standard, and which together only represent a few of the Departments of the Lahore Oriental College, far exceeds the total contribution of Government to the *Panjab University College* as shown below:—

		Rs.	
Government assignment	to Calcutta Sanscrit College .	31,185	per mensem.
Ditto	to 6 Madrasahs in Bengal .	34,301	,,
Ditto	to Calcutta Madrasah . .	Unknown.	
Ditto	to Benares Sanscrit College .	11,896	,,
Ditto	to the Aided Oriental College of Lucknow	3,292	,,
	TOTAL .	80,674	,,
Total Government assignment to the Panjab University College, which also supports 34 students of the Government College with scholarships, as also the Law School, and conducts the Medical Examinations entirely in the interest of Government		21,000	,,

How many of the present students have passed the University examinations.

11. Of the students borne on the rolls of the Oriental College on 31st March 1882—

32	have passed the	Entrance Examination in Arts.
6	ditto	Proficiency in Arts Examination.
2	ditto	High Proficiency in Arts Examination.
14	ditto	Arabic Lower Examination.
4	ditto	,, Middle ,,
4	ditto	,, Higher ,,
8	ditto	Sanscrit Lower ,,
7	ditto	,, Middle ,,
2	ditto	,, Higher ,,
14	ditto	Persian Lower ,,
24	ditto	,, Middle ,,
14	ditto	,, Higher ,,
10	ditto	the Panjab Lower Examination.
4	ditto	,, Middle ,,
5	ditto	Hindu Medicine, Lower Examination.
15	ditto	Yunani Medicine ,, ,,
1	ditto	Engineering ,, ,,
4	ditto	Hindu Law, Junior ,,
7	ditto	Muhammadan Law, Junior ,,
1	ditto	,, Senior ,,

Every one of the College staff is an Author.

13. All the Professors, Assistant Professors and Teachers of the Oriental College are Authors, and almost every one of them has some work in hand of which detail will be given further on (see para. 15).

Passes in each year.

14. The following table shows the number of students of the Oriental College who have passed the University Examinations in each year :—

Years.	Arts.				Sanskrit.			Arabic.			Persian.			Panjabi.			Professional.						Total of passed students.	
	Entrance.	Proficiency.	High Proficiency.	Honors.	Lower.	Middle.	Higher.	Lower.	Middle.	Higher.	Lower.	Middle.	Higher.	Lower.	Middle.	Higher.	Medicine, Yunani.	Medicine, Hindi.	Engineering, First.	Engineering, Final.	Law, Hindu.	Law, Muhammadan.		
1871-72 . .	21	...	...	...	7	...	...	1	...	...	4	4	...	...	...	...	...	...	...	...	...	...	37	
1872-73 . .	5	...	...	...	13	10	...	9	7	...	8	2	...	...	...	...	...	...	...	...	...	...	54	
1873-74 . .	7	6	...	...	5	3	1	9	8	2	15	14	...	...	...	...	...	...	...	...	...	...	70	
1874-75 . .	3	...	...	...	2	4	2	4	5	5	13	4	4	...	...	...	...	...	...	...	...	...	46	
1875-76 . .	1	.	...	...	3	...	1	4	...	1	17	4	4	...	...	...	...	...	...	...	...	...	35	
1876-77 . .	6	1	...	...	1	3	1	5	4	...	5	12	...	...	...	...	...	...	...	...	...	...	38	
1878 (for two years) . .	24	2	...	...	3	5	2	7	5	2	19	8	2	10	...	...	...	...	...	...	...	...	86	
1879 . .	9	9	...	...	2	1	2	3	1	2	6	10	9	3	...	...	...	...	...	...	...	...	57	
1880 / 1881 — November 1880	13	3	2	1	2	1	1	2	1	3	4	11	7	...	4	...	1	...	...	...	...	...	56	122
to June 1881 (eight months)	2	...	...	...	4	...	...	8	...	...	5	...	...	6	...	...	16	5	6	1	4	9	66	
None of the higher Examinations in Arts and Oriental Languages were held in 1881.																								
Total .	91	31	2	1	42	27	10	52	31	15	96	69	26	19	4	...	17	5	6	1	4	9	546	

Progress of literary work.

15. The following table shows the amount of literary work done by the College staff to end of and during 1881-82 :—

No.	Name of Author or Translator.	Names of Books.	Subject.	No. of pages written to end of 1880-81.	Written during the year 1881-82.	Remarks.
1	Pandit Guruprasad.	Hindi translation of Parasar Smriti.	Hindu Law .	...	65	Complete.
		Hindi translation of Kal Madhava.	Ditto .	...	25	Ditto.
		Bhasha Vimarsh . .	Hindi Literature	100	...	Incomplete.
2	Pandit Rishi Kesh, Shastri.	Prakrit Viakaran . .	Prakrit Grammar	Part I	100	Completed and in press.
		Mimansa Paribhasha .	Vedic Literature .	...	50	In course of publication in the Vidyadai Critical Journal.
		Dattaka Chandrika .	Hindu Law .	...	75	Complete.
3	Pandit Sukhdyal, Shastri.	Kumar Shambhava, Hindi translation of—.	Sanscrit Literature.	5 Cantos	2 Cantos	
		Gautama Sutra Vritti, Hindi	Logic . . .	...	40	In progress.
		Nyaya Bodhni . .	Ditto . . .	...	339	Being printed.
4	Pandit Dyaram .	Commentary on Gautama Smriti.	Hindu Law .	...	22	
5	Pandit Janardun	Susrat	Hindu Medicine .	100	...	Could make no progress owing to illness.
6	Pandit Ramkrishna	History of England . .	History . .	...	50	In progress.
7	Pandit Hemraj .	Sami Karan Bhaskar .	A treatise on equations.	...	100	Ditto.
		Hindi translation of Srutabodha.	Sanscrit Prosody	...	12	Complete.
		Hindi translation of Bhasha Parichheda.	Do. Logic .	...	20	Ditto.
8	Pandit Harmukand.	History of India in Hindi	History . .	...	47	In progress.
9	Yogi Shiva Nath	Commentary on Hanuman Natak in Panjabi.	Drama . .	...	200	Ditto.
		Panjabi translation of Euclid.	Mathematics .	...	100	Ditto.
10	Maulvi Fyzul Hassan.	Faizia in Ilm Munazara in Urdu.	Dialectics . .	...	42	In the press.
11	Maulvi Abdul Hakim.	Qawaid Farsi . .	Persian Grammar	59	...	Incomplete.
12	Syad Shah Chiragh.	Urdu translation of Raisala Abdul Wasab.	Ditto	...	45	Ditto.

No.	Name of Author or Translator.	Names of Books.	Subject.	No. of pages written to end of 1880-81.	Written during the year 1881-82.	Remarks.
13	Dr. Amir Shah .	Revision of the translation (Urdu) of Roscoe's Chemistry.	Chemistry . .	...	50	In progress.
		Balfour Stewart's Physics (Urdu).	Physics . .	180	...	Will be printed shortly.
14	Lala Ganga Rám	Applied Mechanics by Major Brandreth, R. E., Urdu translation of—	Mixed Mathematics.	...	60	Ditto.
15	Pirzada Maulvi Muhammad Husain.	Fowler's Inductive Logic .	Logic . .	122	228	Complete.
		Ilm-i-Hayet . . .	Astronomy .	...	192	Complete; in the press.
16	Bhai Gurmukh Singh.	History of India by Elphinstone, Hindi translation of—	History . .	200	374	
		Parkinson's Optics, Hindi translation of—	......	...	15	In progress; complete.
		Physical Geography, Page's, Hindi translation of—	......	225	...	
17	Sheikh Umar Bakhsh.	Urdu translation of the Abstract of Hallam's Constitutional History of England.	History . .	...	230	
18	Syad Dilawar Ali Shah.	Page's Geology in Urdu .	Geology .	20	80	
		Wrigleys' examples in Urdu	Mathematics .	30	30	
		Page's Physical Geography in Urdu.	Geography .	30	...	
19	Babu Navina Chandra Rai.	Lectures in Urdu on Green's Larger History of England	History . .	...	100	With the assistance of Moulvie Ghulam Mustafa and Muhammaddin.
20	Ditto . .	Sthititattwa and Gati Tattwa.	Statics and Dynamics in Hindi.	...	...	Printed.
21	Ditto . .	Jalasthiti tattwa and Jalgita tattwa.	Hydrostatics, Hydraulics, and Pneumatics in Hindi.	...	...	Do.
22	Ditto . .	Nirman Videa . . .	A course of Engineering in Hindi.	...	...	In the press.
23	Maulvi Zafr-ud-din.	Alphabetical list of Arabic roots.	Arabic Grammar.	...	20	The letter Alif is nearly finished.
24	Pandit Muthra Das.	Rasain Vidia in Hindi .	Chemistry .	...	25	In progress.
25	Dr. Rahim Khán, Khán Bahadoor, (Medical Fellow of the Panjab University College.)	Amraz-ul-Hubela wal Milad (2nd edition).	Midwifery (in Urdu).	...	...	
		Medical Jurisprudence .	Medical Jurisprudence (in Urdu).	..	...	Printed.
		Amraz-ul-Sabian (2nd edition)	Diseases of children.			
		Do. Niswan (2nd edition)	Diseases of women			

Books completed.

16. It will be seen from the above statement that the following works have been completed during the year; the manuscripts are in hand for printing :—

Hindi translation of Parásar Smriti . . Hindu Law.
Prákrit Viákaran in Sanscrit and English . Prakrit Grammar
Hindi Dattaka Chandrika . . . . Hindu Law.
„ Kumár Sambhava, 7 Cantos . . . Sanscrit Literature.
„ Sruta bodha . . . . . „ Prosody.
„ Bhasha Parichheda . . . . . „ Logic (translation).
Urdu translation of Risalah Abdul Wasa . Persian Grammar.
„ „ Fowler's Inductive Logic . Logic.
„ „ Ilm-i-Hayet . . . Astronomy.
„ „ Balfour Stewart's Physics . Physics.

Books in the press.

17. The following books are in the press :—

Nyaya Bodhini . . . . Sanscrit Logic, an original work.
Kumár Sambhava . . . . „ Literature.
Weber's Sanscrit Literature in Hindi . . „ „
Nirmán Vidyá . . . . Civil Engineering.
Risálah Munázará . . . . Dialectics.
Ilm-i-Hayet . . . . Astronomy.

Books published during the year.

18. The following books and periodicals have been printed and published during the year :—

Statics and Dynamics in Hindi by Babu Navina Chandra Rai.
Hydrostatics, Hydraulics, and Pneumatics in Hindi by do.

Medical Jurisprudence in Urdu by Dr. Rahim Khán, Khán Bahadur.
Urdu Medical Gazette in Urdu.
The Arabic Critical Journal.
The Sanscrit ditto
Hydrostatics in Urdu, by Pirzada Muhammad Husain.
Key to Algebra by Maulvi Ghulám Mustafá.
Commentary on the Sabá Muallaqa by Maulvi Fayzul Hasan.
Translation of Kal Madho, a treatise on Hindu Law, by Pandit Guruprasád.

Books published or prepared up to date.

19. The following is the list of books published or prepared up to date for the Panjab University College which may be seen at the Senate Hall. (See Appendix V of this report.)

(As regards the text-books absolutely required in the Arts Course, it had been alleged that they had not been completed.)

21. Let us now see what the facts are. For the Proficiency Examination *three* subjects are compulsory; of these two may be languages, and for the third subject the candidate has to select one for himself from the following: Mathematics, History and Geography, a branch of Philosophy, and a branch of Natural Science. In Mathematics, the candidate is required to know Arithmetic, Algebra, and Euclid, Trigonometry to solution of triangles, and elements of Statics; and the following books exist on each of these branches of the subject:—

EXISTING BOOKS.

Arithmetic.—Turjuma, Barnard Smith's Arithmetic, in Urdu.
Zubdat-ul-Hisab in 4 parts, in Urdu.
Ganitsar in 4 parts, in Hindi.
Ganit Prakash in 4 parts, in Hindi.
Ganit Manjari in 4 parts, in Panjabi.
Algebra.—Jabro Muqabala in 3 parts, in Urdu.
Todhunter's Algebra by Zakaulla, in Urdu.
Bij Ganit by Yogi Shiva Nath, in Hindi.
Do. Pundit Kirpa Ram, do.
Do. Bapu Deva Shastri, do.
Sami Karana by Pandit Rám Kishan, in Hindi.
Key to Algebra, by Maulvi Ghulám Mustafá, in Urdu.
Euclid.—Tahrir Uqlaidas, in Urdu.
Todhunter's Euclid by Munshi Zakaulla, in Urdu.
Rekha Ganit in 2 parts, in Hindi.
Rekha Miti Tattwa (Tate's) in Hindi.
Ghana Jyamiti (Solid Geometry), in Hindi.
Trigonometry.—Plane Trigonometry, Roorkee edition, in Urdu.
Zakaula's Plane Trigonometry, in Urdu.
Ilmi Musallas, P. I. D., Panjab.
Solution of Trigonometrical problems, by Maulvi Ghulám Mustafá, in Urdu.
Plane Trigonometry, by Lakhsmi Shankara Misra, in Hindi.
Laghu Trikon Miti, in Hindi.
Sarala Trikon Miti-ki-Upakramanika, in Hindi.
Elements of Statics.—Todhunter's Statics, in Urdu, by Ayá Rám, B.A.
Statics by Zakaula.
Risala Ilmi Tabiyat, in Urdu.
Ditto by Pandit Kirpa Rám, in Hindi.
Statics by Lakhshmi Shankara Misra, in Hindi.
Sthiti Tattwa, by Babu Navina Chandra Rai, in Hindi.

The above proves beyond doubt that a complete course of text-books in both Urdu and Hindi, as far as is compulsory for the Proficiency Examination, *does exist.*

Now let us see what books exist in the alternative subjects of the Proficiency Examination:—

HISTORY AND GEOGRAPHY.

History, Ancient.—Taylor's Ancient History in Urdu.
Ditto ditto in Hindi.
Sairul Mutaqaddamin in 2 parts, in Urdu; or
History, Modern.—Nil.

Geography.—Jam-i-Jahán Numa in 4 parts, in Urdu.
Bhugol, by Pandit Rishi Kesh Shastri, in Hindi.
Bhugol Hastá Malak, in Hindi.
Jugrafia Tabai (Blandford's Physical Geography), in Urdu.

The above are sufficient for the alternative subjects of History and Geography.

The third alternative subject is a *branch of Philosophy* which includes—

Deductive Logic.—Fowler's Logic, in Urdu,
Tarka Vidya, in Hindi,

and *one* of the following:

(*a*) *Psychology.*—Atma Vidya, in Hindi.
(*b*) *Political Economy.*—Mrs. Fawcett's Political Economy, in Urdu.
Asul Siasut Madan, by J. S. Mill, Part I, in Urdu.
Siasat Madan, by E. A. Commr., Dharmanarain, in Urdu.
Political Economy, by Bhai Gurmukh Singh, in Hindi.
(*c*) *Moral Philosophy.*—Fleming's Moral Philosophy (under translation), in Hindi.

The above shows that there are a sufficient number of books to pass in this alternative subject also.

The fourth alternative subject is a *branch of Science* which consists of any of the following:—

(*1*) *Chemistry and Physics.*—Dr. Roscoe's Chemistry, in Urdu.
Balfour Stewart's Physics, in Urdu.
Rasáin Vidya, in Hindi.
Tattwa bodha (by Dr. Amir Sháh), in Hindi.
(*2*) *Zoology and Comparative Physiology.*—Nil.
(*3*) *Geology.*—Urdu translation, in hand.
(*4*) *Botany.*—Hindi translation, about to be commenced.

So one can take up this alternative subject also in its first branch.

Text-books in Vernacular for the High Proficiency Examination.

22. The text-books in the Vernacular for the High Proficiency Examination have been nearly completed, and arrangements have been made for the preparation of those few that are still wanting, as the following detailed account of them will show:—

For this Examination *three* subjects are compulsory; of these one should be a classical language. The remaining two subjects must be chosen from amongst the following four: (1) Mathematics, (2) a branch of Natural Science, (3) History and Political Economy, and (4) Philosophy. The first subject comprises the following branches:—

1st Paper.

Plane Trigonometry.—Sufficient number of text-books in Urdu and Hindi exist; see above.
Optics.—Lately prescribed; translation, in hand.
Descriptive Astronomy.—Maine's Astronomy in Urdu, by Pirzada Muhammad Husain.
Maine's Astronomy, by Gurmukh Singh, in Hindi.
Khagol Vidya, ditto, in do.
Kahgal Sar, ditto, in do.

2nd Paper.

Hydrostatics.—Besant's Hydrostatics, in Urdu.
Jalsthiti Tattwa, by Navina Chandra Rai.
Ilm-i-Harkat, in Urdu.
Dynamics.—Dynamics, by Lakshmi Shankara Misra, in Hindi.
Ditto by Shashi Bhusan Mukerji, in do.
Gati Tattwa, by Navina Chandra Rai, in do.
Plane Co-ordinate Geometry, by Zaka-ulla, in Urdu.
Taliya Krama Jyamiti, in Hindi.

The only book required in this subject is one on Optics, which is in hand.

The second alternative subject is a ***branch of Natural Science*** which may be any of the following collocations :—

1. *Mixed Mathematics.*—Books exist. See above.
   and Physics.— Ditto.
2. *Physics and Chemistry.*— Ditto.
3. *Chemistry and Mineralogy.*—Translation of a book on Mineralogy only is required.
4. *Ditto and Botany.*— Ditto on Botany only is required.
5. *Physiology and Zoology.*—Huxley's Physiology in Urdu. Translation of a book on Zoology only is required.
6. *Chemistry and Geology.*—Chemistry in Urdu. Geology in Urdu (in hand).

One can therefore take up this alternative subject in its first two branches.

The third alternative subject is ***History and Political Economy***, which comprises :—

Outlines of General History, both Ancient and Modern. { Taylor's Ancient History, in Urdu. Dr. Stülpnagel's Universal History (translation commenced).

History of England and India.—Green's History of England ; translation in Urdu in hand.
Tarikh Saltanat-i-Inglishi, in Urdu.
Elphinstone's History of India, in Urdu.
Itihas Timir Nash, in Hindi.
Bhárat Varsbka Itihas, by Bhandatt, in Hindi.
Lethbridge's History of India, in Hindi.

Political Economy.—Risala Ilim Intizam-i-Madan, by N. W. Senior, M.A., in Urdu.
Asul Siasat Madan, by Pandit Dharm Narain, in Urdu.

The fourth or the last alternative subject is **Philosophy**, which comprises the following branches :—

Psychology.—Atma Vidya, in Hindi.
Moral Philosophy.—Fleming's Moral Philosophy (under translation), in Hindi.
Logic, Deductive.—Books in Urdu and Hindi exist. See above.
Do. Inductive.—Fowler's Inductive Logic, by Pirzada Muhammad Husain, in Urdu.

The above detail shows that ***necessary*** text-books in vernacular ***do also exist*** for the High Proficiency or the Degree Examination, except the translation of a work on optics which is in hand, while considerable advance has been made in translation of works on optional subjects.

In addition to the books mentioned above, the Vernacular student has also access to numerous scientific periodicals, both in Urdu and Hindi, when issued from private presses,* and to many other scientific works published by natives which are not kept in Government Book Depôts or known libraries, and therefore omitted to be included in the above detail, as well as to the oral lectures of the Professors in the Oriental College. With such means of high education in hand there is no reason why a vernacular candidate should not be allowed to go up to the Degree Examination, and obtain, at least, the Vernacular Degree, especially when his knowledge of Oriental classics would always be far superior to that of Anglo-Vernacular candidates.

23. The Oriental College being a public institution is ***open to the inspection*** of every one who may wish to inspect it ; in fact, it is visited almost every week by new comers to the station, both Europeans and Natives. The following gentlemen have visited it among others :—

Mr. W. Baxter, M.P.
Mr. E. P. Blake, M.P.

---

* The ***Urdu Anjuman Journal*** contains scientific subjects in Urdu, the ***Hindi Critical Journal*** of Babu Navina Chandra Rai in Hindi ; while the ***Panjabi Journal*** of the Siri-Guru-Singh-Sabha will, in future, contain scientific subjects in Gurmukhi.

But, of course, the Oriental College is not *subject* to the inspection of the Inspectors of *Schools*, nor is it right that it should be so, when the Government College is not subject to their inspection, and when it is, practically, an Unaided Institution, or, if it be considered an Aided Institution, is placed directly under the Senate of the Panjab University College from which it derives a grant. Members of Senate and of the Executive Committee constantly visit it and even take part in the Committees of the Oriental College, whilst every matter of importance affecting the Oriental College is regularly discussed by the Committee.

24. The High Schools of the Educational Department have never succeeded in passing a single man for even the lowest Maulvi or Pandit Examination, for the obvious reason that they prepare for different examinations and have no appliances, at present, for teaching up to the Lowest Classical Standard of the Panjab University College. If, however, Vernacular High Schools are instituted for the purpose of passing the lowest and middle *Persian* or *Munshi* test, they can only be congratulated on their success, but this fact does not reduce the Munshi and Munshi Alim Examinations, especially as now raised, to the level of a Primary or the Middle School Examination. Again some native scholars, especially from beyond the frontier, whom it is so desirable to attract, have to be admitted, provisionally, without passing any of the University tests, on the examination of the Professors of the College, as is done at Benares and other Colleges, which no one thinks of reducing to the level of primary and middle schools on that account. Besides, even in some Government Arts Colleges, non-matriculated students are allowed to attend without any detriment to the general character of the Institution. These native scholars, however, as a rule, prepare for the Higher University Oriental Examinations, above the Oriental Entrance test. The annexed schemes of the lowest admission tests on the Oriental side (see Appendix B) will bear out what has been said above, whilst a passage in the last Oriental College Report may be quoted in further elucidation of this point:—

"No man can pass the lowest Maulvi or Pandit Examinations under seven years' study, and then only if he has had the advantage of access to books on Oriental Literature which are not common in India.

No one has ever passed these Examinations under 18 years, whilst the average age of successful candidates is much higher. To compare an Anglo-Vernacular Entrance student with a Maulvi or Pandit is indeed fallacious, but it is because the Maulvi or Pandit is, by far, the better man. Throughout all the Oriental Colleges in India, proficiency in either Arabic or Sanscrit, as tested by the professors of these subjects, is considered to be a sufficient qualification for admission. Nowhere has there yet been a public Oriental admission test, such as we have, and nowhere is any test so high as at the Lahore Oriental College. Nowhere is it expected from Maulvis or Pandits to have passed the Entrance Examination, though everywhere they are entered, as they deserve to be, as *College* students in the "Statistical Returns." Nowhere in India are there so many Maulvis or Pandits who have passed tests in 'branches of General Knowledge' as at our College, and nowhere have they reached to the same proficiency in these branches."

Prospects of the pupils of the Oriental College.

25. A few words as to the prospects of the students of the Oriental College will not be inappropriate in this Report. The services of the passed Munshis, who will generally be men of greater learning than those now employed in Government service, are likely to be utilised in the Judicial and Revenue Departments, and in various other posts as Vernacular Clerks. Many of the Maulvis who have also passed the Munshi Examinations may similarly be able to find employment. Such Maulvis as have not taken up Persian, and the Pandits and *Bhais* who canno at present look forward to any Government appointment, will necessarily fol low their old avocations pertaining to the sacerdotal class. They will, however, be more enlightened priests or indigenous teachers on account of having acquired a knowledge of Western sciences through the medium of their own vernacular than those who have not received any such education. They will, therefore, be a leaven of civilisation among their countrymen. Government might, however, utilise their services very advantageously in the Department of Public Instruction, as on account of their superior learning and position in Society they will command more respect from, and have greater influence for good among, the Native community than the class from which the teachers of vernacular schools are at present drawn. Some of the Maulvis who pass the Qazi Examinations in Muhammadan Law, and who, by attending the Law School, have also acquired a knowledge of Anglo-Indian Law, and of the principles of jurisprudence, will be admirably suited for the post of Qazi under the Qazi

Act. Similarly the Pandits who pass the *Pradvivak* Examinations in Hindu Law could be usefully employed as advisers in Civil Courts on questions connected with Hindu Law, if such posts were created by the Legislature. Of the six students of the Engineering Class who went up for the First Examination in Civil Engineering in 1881, all passed. Three have been appointed as Sub-Overseers in the Public Works Department of this Province, and two have joined the Roorkee College, of which one, named Harichand, obtained in the late Annual Examination of the First Year Upper Subordinate Class of that College *more than the maximum* number of total marks, *viz.*, 176 against 150 the maximum, and the other has since passed the Upper Subordinate Examination and is employed in the Public Works Department. Lala Ganga Rám, the teacher of the class has passed the Final Examination in Civil Engineering. He lately went up for examination in English of the Proficiency in Arts Standard which he has also passed. He has been employed as Apprentice Engineer in the Lahore Division of Public Works. Thus this class of the Oriental College has been eminently successful. It would be a great advantage to Government if it encouraged by a special grant-in-aid the training of trans-frontier natives, as also of selected Indian Sepoys in this class for the trigonometrical and other surveys. It is hoped that some of the men from Bokhara, Khokand, Gilgit, Chitral, Swat, Buner and the Kohistan generally, whom the Oriental College has succeeded in attracting to its Departments of Oriental Literature, Law or Medicine, will also be induced to learn Drawing and Surveying, whereby, on their return to their homes, they may become, in a general, as well as, perhaps, a more technical sense, "Pioneers" of civilisation. Of the 16 pupils of the Hakim Class who passed the First Examination in the Yunani system of medicine, 10 were admitted in the Lahore Medical School on scholarships of Rs. 6 each. The passed pupils of the Vaidya Class might also have been similarly admitted in the Medical School had books existed for teaching them the European Medical Science through the medium of Hindi. Such books are now being prepared in the Oriental College, and on their completion will be submitted to the Medical Faculty for approval. It is difficult, nay impracticable, to teach *perfectly* the European Science of Medicine *through the Vernaculars*, unless the students are acquainted with the technical terms of Medical Science already in use in Sanscrit and Arabic, and with the accounts of country drugs to be found in native medical works. For this purpose, at least, if not for that of comparative Medical Literature and Science it is desirable that the Vaidyak and the Yunani systems of medicine should be taught to the Vernacular candidates before they commence learning the Allopathic system.

The functions of the Natural Science Class.

26. The Natural Science Class, which is attended by both Pandits and Maulvis, is calculated to remove many of the scientific errors of the ancient systems which they may come across in studying the Eastern classics, just as a student in Europe studies the Western Classical Literature with advantage in spite of the scientific and other errors which are found in Latin and Greek. This class is now also attended by the fifty students who have joined the new Veterinary School lately opened at Lahore.

27. It is also due to the scientific instruction given in the Oriental High School that eight students from it have passed the so-called "Additional Title Examination" which is equivalent to the Entrance Standard, thus raising the number of passes during the last year from the already high number of 122 to 130 successful examinees.

ARTS.—[Oriental Section.]

The following extracts from the report of the Oriental College for 1880-81 are necessary in order to show the specifically Oriental Courses in Literature,

Law, and Medicine of that Institution :—

SCHEMES OF STUDY, TEXT-BOOKS AND EXAMINATIONS IN THE LAHORE ORIENTAL COLLEGE AND SCHOOL.

I.—PANDIT CLASSES OF THE LAHORE ORIENTAL COLLEGE.

Pragya or Proficiency Sanscrit Class—(18 Students).

Grammar—Sarala Vyakarana, or Laghu Kaumudi.
Prosody.—Srut Bodh.
Literature.—Poetry.—Raghuvans [I—VII cantos].
Poetry.—Kumara Sambhava [I—VII cantos].
Prose.—Hitopadesa.
Drama.—Venisambara.
Rhetoric.—Kavya Dipika.
Logic.—Karikavali or Tarka Sangraha.
Translation.—Hindi into Sanscrit and *vice versá.*
Reading and speaking Sanscrit.

The Pandits are also specially taught Hindi as a vernacular.

Visharad or High Proficiency Sanscrit Class—(6 Students).

Grammar.—First half of Siddhant Kaumudi.
Prosody.—Vritta Ratnakara.
Literature.—Prose.—Dasa Kumara Charita.
Poetry.—Magha [I—X cantos].
Drama.—Sakuntala.
Rhetoric.—Sahitya Darpana.
Hindu Law.—Manu, Yajnavalkya, Gautama or Parasara Smriti,—any one of these.
Philosophy.—*a.* Sankhya.—Tattwa Kaumudi
b. Vaiseshika.—Siddhant Muktavali
c. Patanjali.—Sutra Britti
d. Vedanta.—Vedantsar.
e. Mimansa.—Artha Sangraha
} any two of these.
Translation.—Sanskrit into Hindi and *vice versá.*
Composition in Sanscrit.—Reading and speaking fluently.

Shastrit or Highest Proficiency Sanscrit Class.—(7 Students).

Grammar.—Siddhant Kaumudi, the whole.
Pracrita Prakasa.
Prosody.—Vritta Ratnakara.
Rhetoric.—Kavya Prakasa and Dasa Rupa.
Literature.—Poetry.—Naishadha charita [first half].
Prose.—Vasavadatta.
Drama.—Mrichhakatika.
Philosophy.—*a.* Logic.—Vyaptivada by Jagadisa or Nyaya Sutra Vriti.
b. Vaiseshik.—Sutra with a commentary.
c. Sankhya.—Sutra with Pravachana-bhashya.
d. Patanjali.—Sutra with Bhashya.
e. Vedanta.—Sutra with Bhashya.
f. Purana.—Shanti Parb of Mahabharat or Valmikiya Ramayana.
Hindu Sciences.—Medicine.—Susruta, Charaka, or Bagbhatta.
Mathematics and Astronomy.—Sidhant Siromani.
Hindu Law.—Mitakshara.
Religion.—*a.* Rig Veda.—Sanhita, first four adhyayas of 1st Ashtak.
b. Yajur Veda.—Shukla Yajur Vajasaneyi Sanhita Madhyandini Sakha 10 adhyayas.
c. Sama Veda.—Mantra Bhaga, Chhandasya archika from 1st Prapathaka to Indra Parba in 5th Prapathaka.
Translation.—Hindi into Sanscrit and *vice versá.*
Composition in Sanscrit in an elegant style.
Reading, speaking, and discussion in Sanscrit.

The above classes and subjects are taught by Head Pandit Guru Prashad, Pandit Rishi Kesh Shastri, Pandit Daya Ram, and Pandit Sukh Dyal.

II. MAULVI CLASSES OF THE LAHORE ORIENTAL COLLEGE.

Maulvi or Proficiency Arabic Class.—(20 Students).

Grammar.—Hidayat-ul-Nahv ; Panj Ganj ; Kafia.

Literature.—Calcutta F. A. Course ; Sanin-ul-Islam, Parts I & II.
Alif Laila (first forty nights)—Tarikh-ul-Khulefa.
Logic.—Shara Tahzib.
Law.—Sirajia ; Kitab-ul-Muaris min Shara'-ul-Islam.
Translation.—Arabic into Urdu and *vice versá.*
Reading and speaking.

Maulvi 'Alim or High Proficiency Arabic Class—(14 Students).

Grammar.—Sharah Mullah ; Shafia.
Literature.—Tarikh Timuri (to death of Timur).
Calcutta B. A. Course ; Saba' Mual'laqa.
Rhetoric.—Mukhtasir Maa'ni.
Logic.—Kutbi, Sullam-ul-Alum.
Law.—Sharifia, Shara' Saraji or Kitab-ul-Muaris min Shara'-ul-Islam.
Mua'malat Kaduri.
Translation.—Arabic into Urdu and *vice versá.*
Composition.—Easy Essay.
Reading, speaking, and explanation.

Maulvi Fazil or Highest Proficiency Arabic Class—(7 Students).

Literature.—Maqamat-i-Hariri.
Diwan-i-Hamasa.
Diwan-i-Mutanabbi.
Logic.—Qazi Mubarak (Tasavurat) Hamd Ullah (Tasdiqat) Sharifia (ilm Munazarah).
Philosophy.—Sadra.
Law.—Mua'malat Hidaya.
Composition.—Essay in elegant Arabic.
Reading, conversation, and explanation.

These classes and subjects are taught by Maulvi Faiz-ul-Hasan, Mufti Ghulám Qadir and Hafiz Abdul Aziz.

MUNSHI CLASSES OF THE LAHORE ORIENTAL COLLEGE

Munshi or Proficiency Persian Class—(25 Students).

Grammar.—Abd-ul-wasi ; Miftah-ul-Adab (1st part).
Literature.—Calcutta F. A. Course ; Tohfat-ul-Ahrar.
Insha Munir ; Diwan Hafiz (Selections).
Moral Philosophy.—Akhlaq Jalali (Siyasat-ul-Madan).
Translation.—Persian into Urdu.
Urdu into Persian.
Reading and speaking.
Arabic.—(The Entrance course prescribed by the Panjab University College).
Urdu.—Entrance standard.
Caligraphy.—Native Book-keeping ; Landé and Sarafi ; Vernacular Office work as connected with Civil, Criminal and Revenue matters.

Arithmetic, the whole ; Mensuration of plane surfaces

Munshi 'Alm or High Proficiency Persian Class—(12 Students).

Grammar.—Chahar Ghulzar.
Miftah-ul-Adab.
Literature.—Qassaid Urfi, Calcutta B. A. Course.
Abul Fazl (1st Dafter).
Arabic Reader (Darait-ul-Adab).
Moral Philosophy.—Akhlaq-i-Nasiri.
Translation.—Persian into Urdu and *vice versá.*
Composition.—An easy Essay.
Reading and fluent conversation.
Arabic.—The Proficiency course laid down by the Panjab University College.

Munshi Fazil or Highest Proficiency Persian Class—(13 Students).

Rhetoric and Prosody.—Hadaiq-ul-Balaghat ; Ejaz Khusravi.
Literature.—Waqaya Niyamat Khan Ali ; Tughra.
Qassaid Badur Chach.
Durra Nadira.
Moral Philosophy.—Akhlaq Jalali.
Translation.—Persian into Urdu and *vice versá.*
Composition.—Writing an Essay on a given subject in elegant Persian.

These subjects are taught by Head Munshi Maulvi Abdul Hakim, by Maulvi Fazil Mahomed Din (H. P.) and by Sayyad Chirag Sháh.

PANJABI CLASSES OF THE LAHORE ORIENTAL COLLEGE AND SCHOOL. in 1880–81

There are three grades of the Gurmukhi (Panjabi) or Bhai Classes in the College.

I.—GYANI OR THE HIGHEST PROFICIENCY. II.—VIDWAN OR THE HIGH PROFICIENCY. III.—BUDHIMAN OR THE PROFICIENCY.

I.—GYANI CLASS*

- Vyakarn with Critical knowledge. } Grammar ... Whole, by Behari Lall.
- Granth Sahib ... / Janam sakhi ... } Literature.
- Prabodh Chandrodai Natak (Drama) by Gulab Singh.
- Laws applicable to the Panjab (lectures).
- Anek Darsana (History of Philosophy).
- Logic, Fowler's.
- Gurbilas 10th Padshahi (History of Guru Gobind Singh).

II.—VIDWAN* ...

- Vyakaran (Grammar) 3 parts ... Lalla Bihari Lall.
- Chhand Ratnawali (Prosody) Yogi Shiv Nath.
- Logic, Fowler's ... Lectures.
- Panj Granthi ... / Vidya Ratnakar } Lecture ... Lalla Bihari Lall.
- Hanuman Natak (Epic poem) whole.
- Yajnavalkas Dharm Shaster.
- Vyavahar adhyai (Hindu Law) ... By Bhai Harsa Singh.

III.—BUDHIMAN* ...

- Vyakaran (Grammar) 2 parts ... Lalla Bihari Lall.
- Pingal manjari (an elementary treatise on prosody) ... Do.
- Vidya Ratnakar / Jap Parmarth ... } Literature ... Do.
- Hanuman Natak (Drama) Acts 7.
- Tark Sangraha (an elementary treatise on logic) ... P. Bhan Dat.
- Atma Tattwa Vidya (an elementary treatise on philosophy) ... Lalla Bihari Lall.
- Vedant sar ditto ... ... P. Bhan Dat.

There are four students in the Gyani or the Highest Class, one in the second, and twelve in the third Class.

The present staff consists of—

I.—Bhai Harsa Singh, Head Bhai ... } in Languages.
II.—Bhai Dit Singh ... } in Languages.
III.—P. Yogi Shiv Nath, Teacher of General Knowledge.

There are two classes in the school; the upper one contains the students preparing for the Entrance Examination of 1882.

The following books are taught to those who take up Panjabi as an optional subject. (The scheme is likely to be revised.)

I.—Japji with Commentary . . . . . } By L. Behari Lall.
II.—Vidya Ratnakar . . . . . .
III.—Viyakaran sar (Grammar) . . .
IV.—Ratan Mala . . . .
V.—Manohar Varta . . . . . .

The following books on general knowledge are taught in the school Classes:—

I.—History of India, Lethbridge—by Harsa Singh (manuscript).
II.—History of England—lectures.
III.—Geography, Blochman's—by Bhai Harsa Singh.
IV.—Arithmetic—by L. Behari Lall and B. Gurdat Singh.
V.—Algebra for beginners—by Lala Behari Lall.
VI.—Euclid (under preparation).

* It should be remembered that the above-mentioned books are to be changed, and the scheme is under discussion for revision. The new scheme will include more difficult books than those on the list.

The subjects prescribed for the Entrance Examination in which books in Panjabi are still wanting are taught through Hindi or Urdu.

SPECIAL LAW CLASSES AT THE ORIENTAL COLLEGE, COMPOSED OF ORIENTAL GRADUATES (MAULVI 'ALIM, MAULVI FAZIL—VISHARAD AND SHASTRI), INTENDED TO TRAIN NATIVE JURISTS OR ASPIRANTS TO THE FUNCTIONS OF MUFTI OR QAZI, AND OF BYAVASTHA-BIT AND PRADVIVAKA RESPECTIVELY.

A.—Subjects for all the Special Law Classes.

Principles of General Jurisprudence (Manual by Professor Sashi Bhashan, M.A. & B.L., Pleader, High Court (Calcutta), Elements of Constitutional Law (Organisation and Powers of Government and Legislatures of India, the State Departments, and Laws relating to the economy of the country).

b.—Revenue Law rules, circulars, orders and procedure.
c.—Civil Law (of Personal Status, Property and Obligations) and Procedure.
d.—Criminal Law and Procedure.
e.—Evidence, Limitation, Stamps, &c.

} Lectures of the Law Lecturer of the Panjab University College.

B.—Subjects for Maulvis 'Alim aspiring to the title of Mufti Alim and the functions of Qazi Alim.

a.—Mukhtasir Vaqaya.
b.—Maltoq-ul-Abhar.
c.—Tanvir-ul-Absar.
d.—Sharifia* (Inheritance).
e.—Hisami, Principles of Muhammadan Law.

C.—Subjects for Maulvis Fazil aspiring to the title of Mufti Fazil and the functions of Qazi Fazil.

a.—Durre Mukhtar,
b.—Ashbah-wan-nazair.
c.—Fatawa Qazi Khán.
d.—Tauzih (Principles of Muhammadan Jurisprudence).

The Muamilat of Hidaya are studied as a portion of the Maulvi Fazil Course.

No subjects have yet been fixed for the titles of Allamat-ul-Qawanin (which, with Muhammadans, would be Qazi Fazil), suggested by the Government Committee appointed in 1871.

D.—Subjects for Visharads aspiring to the title of Smriti Ratna and the functions of Byavasthabit.

a.—Parasara Smriti.
b.—Manu Smriti.
c.—Vyavahara Tatwa.
d.—Daya Tatwa.
e.—Any Grihya Sutra.

"Manu," "Yajnavalkya," and "Gautama" are studied as a portion of the Visharad Course.

E.—Subjects for Shastris aspiring to the title of Smriti Ratnakar and the functions of Pradvivak.

a.—Mitakshara.
b.—Daya Bhaga (by Jimuta Vahana).
c.—Vira Mitrodaya (2nd Chapter).
d.—Kala Madhava.
e.—Dattaka Mimansa.
f.—Dattaka Chandrika.

The Mitakshara is studied as a portion of the Shastri Course.

The staff consists at present of the following teachers :—

Teacher	
Head Pandit Guru Prasad . . .	} For the Hindu Lawyers.
Pandit Rikhi Kesh	
Maulvi Ghulám Qadir	} ,, Muhammadan Lawyers.
Mir Abdulla	

* Already studied in part as a portion of the Maulvi 'Alim Course.

The students also attend the lectures given to Mukhtars and Pleaders. The lectures on the Principles of General Jurisprudence by Professor Sashi Bhushan Mukerjee will, it is hoped, be renewed at an early date.

The class for the study of Shiah Inheritance is improving, but, with the exception of its teacher, Maulvi Momin Ali, who has passed both the Maulvi 'Alim and Entrance in Arts Examinations, its members have not as yet acquired the preliminary liberal education which will entitle them to be enrolled as aspirants to the functions of Qazi.

NAME.	Full marks.	Minimum marks for passing.
(1)—Books for the Hakim-i-Hasiq Examination.		
1. Qanucha . . . . (Theoretical portion only, excluding anatomical part).	100	25
2. Mujaz	100	25
3. Mizan-ul-Tib, whole, including treatise on pulse, urine, and crisis of diseases (Buhran)	150	37
4. Anatomy of the Human Body; from Qanucha and Kifaya-i-Mansuri .	50	12
5. Well known simple and compound medicines, as in Mizan-ul-Tib* .	100	25
(2)—Vaidya Examination.		
1. Sarang Dhar.		
2. Nidan.		
3. Nirghant.		
4. Ajirn Manjari (Varap dish).		
5. Vaidya Jiwan.		
(3)—Umdat-ul-Hukma Examination.		
1. Aqsarai (scientific portion only)	150	37
2. Sadidi (practical portion, whole)	150	37
3. Mufarah-ul-qalub (whole, anatomical part excluded)	150	37
4. Tashrih-ul-Aflak	150	37
5. Human Anatomy from Mafarh-ul-qalub	150	37
(4)—Bhikhak Examination.		
1. Bung Sen	150	37
2. Chakra Datt	150	37
3. Bhao prakash	150	37
4. Jawar tamar Bhaskar	150	37
5. Sannipat Chandrika	150	37
(5)—Zubdat-ul-Hukma Examination.		
1. Sharah Asbab (whole)	200	50
2. Nafisi (theoretical portion only)	200	50
3. Kuliat-i-Qanuni Sheikh, Bu Ali Sena	200	50
4. Hummyat-i-Sheik, Bu Ali Sena	200	50
5. Jami-us-Sharhin	200	50
(6)—Vaidyaraj Examination.		
1. Charak Sangath	200	50
2. Shushrut	200	50
3. Bagbhut	200	50
4. Brahm Sangita (Ras Kam-Dhenu)	200	50
5. Hariti Sangita	200	50

* The questions will be confined only to the use and doses of the medicines.

The following are the *lowest* tests for admission into the Oriental *College* :—

Maulvi or Lower Arabic Examination.

	Papers.
Grammar, Syntax and Prosody.—Hidayat-un-Nahv ; Panj Ganj ; Kafia .	I
Literature and History.—Calcutta F. A. Course ; Sanin-ul-Islam, Parts I and II .	II
Alif Laila (first forty nights), Turikh-ul-Khulefa .	III
Logic.—Shara Tahzib .	IV
Law—.Sirajia ; Kitab-ul-Muaris min Shara-ul-Islam .	V
Translation.—Arabic into Urdu and *vice versâ* .	VI
Oral Examination.—Reading and speaking Arabic .	

The following are the details of the lowest Examination in Sanscrit :—

Pragnya or Lower Sanscrit Examination.

Grammar—Sarala Vyakarana or Laghu Kaumudi .	I
Prosody.—Srut Bodh .	II
Rhetoric.—Kavya Dipika .	II
Literature.—	
Poetry—Raghuvans (I—VII Cantos) .	III
" Kumara Sambhava (I—VII Cantos)	III
Prose—Hitopadesa .	IV
Drama—Venisanhara .	IV
Logic.—Karikavali or Tarka Sangraha .	V
Translation.—Hindi into Sanscrit and *vice versâ* .	VI
Oral Examination.—Reading and speaking Sanscrit.	

Lower Persian or Munshi Examination.

Grammar.—Abd-ul-wasi ; Miftah-ul-Adab (Arabic Grammar, 1st part) .	I
Literature.—Calcutta F. A. Course ; Tohfat-ul-Hara .	II
Insha Munir ; Diwan-i-Hafiz (Selection) .	III
Moral Philosophy—Aklaq-i-Jalali (Siyasat-ul-Madan) .	IV
Translation.—Persian into Urdu .	V
Urdu into Persian .	VI
Oral Examination.—Reading and speaking.	
Arabic.—Entrance Course of the Calcutta University (proposed from 1883).	

It is proposed to make the Examination in the whole of Arithmetic (which has hitherto been optional) a compulsory part of the Lowest Munshi Examination, as also the professional examination in Vernacular office work as connected with Civil, Criminal and Revenue matters and an Examination in Landé, Sarafi and Caligraphy, besides raising the standard of proficiency in *Arabic* to that of the Calcutta First Arts Course. As a matter of fact, the "Munshis" of the Oriental College have prepared the Arabic F. A. Course in addition to their other subjects.

The following are the *lowest* tests for admission into the Oriental *High School* :—

Sanscrit.—The standard of the Entrance Course in Sanscrit (see Calendar).
Arabic.—The standard of the Entrance Course in Arabic (ditto).
Persian.—The Entrance Course (see Calendar) and Sikandarnama, Zulekha and Insha.

The above admission tests will form the standard for the indigenous schools of all kinds throughout the province, after passing which their students will be enabled to prosecute their studies for the higher Oriental Certificates of the Panjab University in various branches, or else combine these studies with those in "general knowledge" at the Oriental College. The Assistant Professors, teachers, fellows, and senior students of this institution could also be utilised in inspecting the indigenous schools in the various districts to which they belong during the annual three months' vacation of that institution.—G. H. L.

Statement of the number of Students of the Oriental College who passed the various Examinations in May and June 1882.

Nature of Examination.	No. went up.	No. passed.	Remarks.
Arts—			
Entrance	22	2	These were sent up at their own request without any trial examination; hence the apparent large number of failures.
Proficiency	12	3	
High Proficiency, B.A.	4	1	One candidate has been plucked for a few marks in one subject.
Oriental—			
Sanscrit Lower	9	5	
Ditto Middle	3	3	
Ditto Higher	3	3	
Arabic Lower	14	9	
Ditto Middle	9	7	
Ditto Higher	6	3	
Persian Lower	14	2	
Ditto Middle	6	1	
Ditto Higher	9	4	
Gurmukhi Lower	5	3	
Ditto Middle	1	1	
Ditto Higher	3	1	
Pushto Lower	14	5	
Vernacular Office Work	6	1	
Arithmetical test for Munshis	13	3	
Professional—			
Hindu Law	5	5	Of these 2 only will get the certificate, the other 3 not having passed the Sanscrit Middle Examination yet.
Muhammadan Law, Higher	2	2	Will not get the certificates till they pass the Maulvi Fazil Examination.
Ditto Lower	2	2	Will not get the certificates till they pass the Maulvi Alim Examination.
Vaidyak System of Medicine	5	4	
Ditto Middle	2	2	
Yunani Ditto	11	7	

LAHORE DIVISION.

GUJRÁNWÁLÁ DISTRICT.

GENERAL ABSTRACT.

District.	No. of maktabs.	No. of pupils.	No. of Sanscrit and Nagri schools.	No. of pupils.	No. of Gurmukhi schools.	No. of pupils.	No. of Landé and Mahajani schools.	No. of pupils.	Total No. of indigenous schools.	Total No. of pupils.
Gujránwálá.	197	2,433	18	272	35	81	16	458	266	3,644

GUJRÁNWÁLÁ.—Among the *Hakims*, Ghulám Husain; among the *Baids*, Basant Rikh Púj and Pandit Kanshi Rám; among the *Maulvis*, Sirajuddin, Mahbúb Alam and Alauddin; among the *Pandits*, Vidyadhar, Sarasati Dass, Radha Kishen, Dila Rám, Chet Rám and Kanshi Rám; and among the *Bhais*, Gurdatta, Dharman, Nidhan Singh, and Shankar Singh, are the distinguished persons mentioned in the police return. A private informant mentions among the *Hakims*, Sarajuddin, Sultan Mahmud, Ghulám Muhiuddin, Shahabuddin and Chandar Bhan; among the *Baids*, Harirám and Devidial; among the *Bhais*, Lahora Singh, Fatah Singh, Múl Singh and Parem Singh; among the *Authors*, Ghulám Ghaus; and among the *Poets*, Ghulám Ghaus, Ahmad Hasan, Ghulám Qadir and Munshi Ahmad Ali, as the most eminent at Gujránwálá.

The two largest maktabs at Gujránwálá are one maktab attached to the Anjuman Islamia of Gujránwálá, under the superintendence of Maulvi Sarajuddin, with five teachers, namely, Maulvi Muhammaduddin for Arabic; Maulvi Muhammaduddin II for Persian; Nuruddin for Arithmetic; Ghulám Muhammad, 2nd Persian teacher; and Hafiz Fazl Din, Korán teacher, with 105 pupils being taught in Arabic up to Maulvi Fazil, Persian up to Munshi Fazil, Arithmetic up to middle and entrance standards, and the Korán. The teachers get their pay from the Anjuman fund, and an aid of Rs. 15 is given by the Panjab University.

The second maktab at Gujránwálá is attached to a mosque, with 36 pupils under Mahbub Alam, a municipal member, who teaches gratuitously Arabic and Persian.

But there are also the following maktabs at Gujránwálá mentioned in a private return:—

No. 1, at Gujránwálá, attached to the mosque, with 35 pupils, under Maulvi Sarajuddin, who teaches the Korán and Arabic. This school held a muafi of 60 ghumaos up to the death of Maulvi Sultan Ahmad, whom the present Maulvi has succeeded; but after his death 35 ghumaos were resumed and 25 ghumaos were left for the school in perpetuity.

„ 2, „ „ „ „ 40 pupils, under Muhammad Bakhsh, who teaches Persian.

„ 3, „ „ Shaikhanwali „ 15 pupils, being taught the Korán.

„ 4, „ „ Dairah Chandu Sháh, with 12 pupils, learning the Korán.

„ 5, „ „ mosque of Shaikh Ghulám Husain, with 20 pupils learning the Korán.

„ 6, „ „ mosque of Zarar, with 12 pupils learning the Korán.

„ 7, „ „ private house of Muhammaduddin Hafiz, with 9 pupils learning the Korán.

„ 8, „ „ private house of Sultan Ahmad Darvesh, with 12 pupils learning the Korán.

„ 9, „ „ private house of Shaikh Ahmad Hakim, with 20 pupils learning the Korán.

„ 10, „ „ mosque with 10 pupils learning the Korán.

There are two large patshalas at Gujránwálá, one attached to the Tomb (Samadh) of Raja Mahan Singh, father of Rajah Ranjit Sing, with 25 (private information gives 35) pupils, under Chetrám, who teaches Sanscrit up to the highest standard, and gets Rs. 15 per mensem from the Municipality. The second patshala is attached to the garden of Rai Múl Sing, Rais, with 40 (private information gives 25) pupils under Vidya Dhar, who teaches Sanscrit and astrology. Half the annual income of a well amounting to Rs. 100 is given by Rai Múl Singh for the support of the school. The pupils are given food also. In a private return a patshala with 15 pupils, under Dilarám, who teaches grammar, Hindi language and astrology, &c., is mentioned.

The following are the minor patshalas at Gujránwálá :—

No. 1,	attached to the private house of Pandit	Sarasati Nath, with 7 pupils learning Sanscrit, up to the highest standard.
„ 2,	„ „ „ „	Kanshi Rám, with 4 (private return gives 10) pupils learning Sanscrit, up to the middle standard.
„ 3,	„ „ „ „	Lakshmi Nath, with 10 do. do.
„ 4,	„ „ „ „	Amar Nath, with 4 do. do.

Another private informant adds 3 patshalas conducted by Mahesh Dass Jawaladat and Kirpa Rám with 10, 8, and 20 pupils respectively.

The important Gurmukhi schools at Gujránwálá are three in number. No. 1 is attached to the Dharamsala of Bhái Gurdatta, No. 2 to the Dharamsala of Bhái Dharmán, and No. 3 to the Dharamsala of Harbhajan Dass, with 20, 30, and 15 (according to another information 10, 15, and 22) pupils, under the teachers Gurdatta, Dharmán and Harbhajan, who all teach Gurmukhi and religious books. The teachers' income is not fixed but the pupils give them food, and when they finish a certain book, they present some cash. The offerings made to the Granth are taken by the teachers.

Besides the above, the following are smaller Gurmukhi schools at Gujránwálá, mentioned in a private return :—

No. 1,	attached to the Dharamsala	of Chanda Singh,	with 22	pupils learning	Gurmukhi
„ 2,	„ „ „	of Hatiyáránvali,	„ [illegible]	„	„
„ 3,	„ „ „	of Chávalmán,	„ 5	„	„
„ 4,	„ „ „	of Ishar Dass,	„ 3	„	„
„ 5,	„ „ „	of Tek Singh,	„ 5	„	„
„ 6,	„ „ „	of Múl Singh,	„ 2	„	„

The largest Mahajani school at Gujránwálá is attended by 50 pupils, whom Gokul Pádhá teaches Landé and arithmetic, and gets some bread, &c., from the pupils and Rs. 5 per mensem from the Mission School.

According to the police return, the rural part of the Gujránwálá circle has the following eminent persons: *Hakims*, Karm Iláhi, Núr Husain of Pirchok, and Saiyad Fazl Iláhi of Kot Bhawanidass; *Maulvis*, Muhammad Wahabi, Maulvi Musá of Manki, Ghulám Muhammad of Qillah Mán Singh, and Muhammad Alí of Puterhákhurd; and among the *Bháis*, Gurdat Singh of Maráliwálá is mentioned.

The largest maktab at *Tehwandi-Khajúrwáli* is attached to the village mosque, with 40 pupils under Maulvi Ghulám Muhammad, who instructs them in Arabic, in return for which he gets some corn at harvest time. There is one maktab, mentioned in the private return, at *Maráliwálá*, attached to a mosque, with 12 pupils under Charaghuddin, who teaches the Korán.

The following are the smaller maktabs in the above circle :—

No. 1	at Chak Pirn,	with 10	pupils learning	Arabic.
„ 2	„ Tatiá Dád,	„ 20	„ „	Persian.
„ 3	„ Jalál,	„ 25	„ „	Arabic and Persian.
„ 4	„ Mughalchak,	„ 9	„ „	„ „
„ 5	„ Botálá Sharam Singh,	„ 18	„ „	Arabic.

There is only one Gurmukhi school at Maráliwálá attached to the Dharamsala, with 10 pupils, whom Bhái Gurdat Singh teaches Gurmukhi, and receives in return some corn at the harvests of *rabi* and *kharif*.

HAFIZABAD.—Amongst the *Pandits*, Harnám Dass, son of Butárám Pádhá; among the *Maulvis*, Jaláluddin; and among the *Hakims*, Khudá Bakhsh, are the most eminent persons at Hafizábád mentioned in the police return:—

The following maktabs are mentioned in this circle:—

Bhawan Kohna, with 15 pupils learning Urdu and Persian.
Bhawan Khurd, 1 maktab, with 10 pupils learning the Korán.
Rám Ki, 1 maktab, with 15 pupils learning Persian.
Nikki, 1 maktab, with 15 pupils reading the Korán.
Ramki, 1 maktab, with 16 pupils learning the Korán.
Chak Kharai, 1 maktab, with 8 pupils ditto.
Chak Ghazi, 1 maktab, with 8 pupils ditto.
Shori, 1 maktab, with 8 pupils learning the Korán and Persian.
Sonánwála, 1 maktab, with 18 pupils learning the Korán.
Aláuddin Ki, 1 maktab, with 11 pupils ditto.
Kot Bakhshá, 1 maktab, with 11 pupils ditto.
Tattá Nának, 1 maktab, with 15 pupils learning Urdu, Persian and the Korán.
Aduki, 1 maktab, with 10 pupils learning Persian, the Korán and Urdu Primers.
Nánuana, 1 maktab, with 6 pupils learning the Korán.
Kasesi, 1 maktab, with 25 pupils studying the Korán and Persian.
Madhor, 1 maktab, with 12 pupils ditto.
Matiki, 1 maktab, with 12 pupils ditto.
Kot Khushal, 1 maktab, with 8 pupils reading the Korán.
Thatta Jaád Amiriwálá, 1 maktab, with 8 pupils ditto.

There is one patshala at Hafizabad, with 9 pupils studying Sanscrit. A private return mentions one patshala at the village *Porkhanda Jataiwla*, with 20 pupils under Pandit Devi Dial, who teaches *Saraswat*, *Chandrika*, and poetry.

Kuryala has one Gurmukhi school attached to the Dharamsala, with 10 pupils learning Gurmukhi.

There is only one Mahajani school in this circle, in the village of *Ramki*, attached to the Dharamsala, with 11 pupils learning Landé.

AIMANABAD.—Maulvis Ghulám Mustafá, Muhammad Umjar, Muhammad Din, Sultan Ahmad and Muhammad Din II, Pandit Ganda and Hakim Ghulámullah are brought to notice as distinguished in this circle. The important maktabs in this circle are at *Aimanabad*, *Baloki*, *Mangoki*, *Ratoli*, *Gharmola*, *Kharyal*, *Khanmusalman*, and *Jhandyala*, with 60, 8, 10, 14, 22, 10, 16. and 15 pupils respectively; the first four and the last are attached to mosques, and the rest to private houses under Hasan Muhammad and Fazl Muhammad at Baloki; Muhammad Umar at Ratali; Muhammaddin and Rahimulla at Mangoki; Rahimbakhsh at Gharmola; Karm Iláhi at Kharyal; Sultan Ahmad at Khanmusalman; Mustafá at *Aimanabad*; and Muhammaddin at Jandyala, who all teach Urdu, the Korán, and religious books. A private return adds 2 maktabs in *Aimanabad* with 22 pupils under Ibrahim and Ilmuddin, 2 in *Jandyala* under Ismail and Imamuddin with 22 pupils, and 2 in *Ratali* with 15 pupils.

There are two Gurmukhi schools at *Kharyal* and *Masanda*, attached to Dharamsalas, with 3 and 10 pupils, under Gurdatta Singh and Teja Singh respectively, who teach the Granth and get their food in return.

There is one Mahajani school at Aimanabad, with 50 pupils, under Ishar Dass, who teaches Landé and Sarafi, and gets Rs. 4.

WÁZIRABÁD CITY.—Among the *Maulvis*, Qadir Bakhsh and Muhammad Bakhsh, and among the *Hakims*, Karm Din and Mián Tipú Hakim, deserve notice.

The largest maktab at Wázirabád is attached to the mosque situated in the street of Daráb Khán, with 24 pupils, under Maulvi Sarajuddin, who teaches Arabic and Persian, and gets Rs. 2-8 per mensem.

In the general table of the police return the number of small maktabs is given,—13 at Wázirabád, with 181 pupils learning Arabic and Persian.

There is one patshala at Wázirabád, with 22 pupils, under Charanjit Brahman, who teaches Sanscrit, Landé, Sarafi and Gurmukhi, and gets Rs. 2 per mensem.

Wázirabád has a Gurmukhi school attached to the Guru Kothá, with 18 pupils, under Gandar Singh, who teaches Gurmukhi, and gets only 5 annas per mensem.

There is also a Mahajani school at Wázirabád, in the quarter of Kathra Thattiyaranwala, with 42 pupils, whom Nabi Bakhsh teaches Landé on Rs. 7 per mensem.

WÁZIRABÁD CIRCLE.—In this circle there are the following persons mentioned :—among the *Maulvis*, Fazldin and Ghulám Nabi ; and among the *Pandits*, Jamal Sing and Bishen Dass.

There are the following maktabs in this circle :—

Jagná,	with	5	pupils	learning	Arabic	and Persian.
Kot Khás	,,	18	,,	,,	,,	,,
Chak Rajab	,,	7	,,	,,	,,	,,
Mahadpur	,,	8	,,	,,	,,	,,
Kálhwálá	,,	7	,,	,,	,,	,,
Chak Bhattiyan	,,	5	,,	,,	,,	,,
Khánki	,,	4	,,	,,	Arabic.	
Márúf-ábád	,,	5	,,	,,	,,	
Ujlá Kalán	,,	6	,,	,,	,,	and Persian
Bahroki	,,	40	,,	,,	,,	,,
Chibáh Jimáh	,,	14	,,	,,	,,	,,
Ibnwálí (2 schools)	,,	55	,,	,,	,,	,,
Tattáh	,,	5	,,	,,	,,	
Churáh	,,	15	,,	,,	Persian.	
Kakkár Kolu (2 schools)	,,	25	,,	,,	,,	
Chak Galán	,,	7	,,	,,	,,	
Hiránwálá Kalán	,,	12	,,	,,	,,	
Futahgarh	,,	10	,,	,,	Arabic.	
Saranwáli	,,	25	,,	,,	,,	and Persian.
Událá	,,	6	,,	,,	Persian.	
Kot Qadir Bakhsh	,,	6	,,	,,	,,	
Dhonkal	,,	15	,,	,,	Arabic	and Persian.
Sidiwáli	,,	5	,,	,,	,,	,,
Pauchgaráin	,,	12	,,	,,	Persian.	
Khosar	,,	10	,,	,,	Arabic	and Persian.
Teh Hibá	,,	15	,,	,,	,,	,,
Nat (2 schools)	,,	22	,,	,,	Arabic.	
Bahgá	,,	4	,,	,,	,,	
Kot Nawáz	,,	5	,,	,,	,,	
Dudanwali Kalán	,,	5	,,	,,	,,	
Sohdrá (2 schools)	,,	15	,,	,,	Persian	and Arabic.
Pathánwáli	,,	20	,,	,,	,,	,,
Jorá	,,	20	,,	,,	,,	,,
Khakar (2 schools)	,,	20	,,	,,	,,	,,
{ Jandiyálá / Wahabwálá }	,,	15	,,	,,	,,	,,
Gulwálá	,,	15	,,	,,	,,	,,
Diláwar	,,	5	,,	,,	,,	,,
Alú Sadev	,,	16	,,	,,	,,	,,
Laheri Wálá	,,	25	,,	,,	,,	,,
Khakka Mitar	,,	6	,,	,,	,,	,,
Adil Nagar	,,	10	,,	,,	,,	,,
Dhárúwálá	,,	15	,,	,,	,,	,,
Widálá	,,	10	,,	,,	Arabic.	
Abeki	,,	20	,,	,,	,,	and Persian.
Teh Faqírulláh	,,	15	,,	,,	,,	,,
Dhuneki	,,	5	,,	,,	,,	,,
Bágaryán Nau	,,	10	,,	,,	,,	,,
Nizámuddin	,,	7	,,	,,	,,	
Pirkot	,,	8	,,	,,	,,	and Persian.
Khásar	,,	10	,,	,,	,,	,,
Kot Qadir Bakhsh	,,	8	,,	,,	,,	,,
Bahrám	,,	20	,,	,,	,,	,,
Chak Sudáh	,,	10	,,	,,	,,	,,
Hasanwálí	,,	5	,,	,,	,,	

There is a large patshala at *Báoki*, attached to the private house of Pandit Parasrám, who teaches *Sarsut* (a book on Sanscrit grammar), Devanagri books, and other books to 25 (private informant gives 18) pupils, and gets Rs. 3 in money and kind.

The largest Gurmukhi school in this circle is one at *Sohdarah*, attached to a Dharamsala, in which Báwá Jaimal Singh teaches Gurmukhi and Sanscrit to 21 pupils, and gets Rs. 12 in money and kind.

The following are smaller Gurmukhi schools in this circle :—

No. 1 at Chak Galán,	with 7 pupils being taught in Gurmukhi.
„ 2 „ Diláwár	„ 25 „ „ „ „
„ 3 „ Darveshki	„ 10 „ „ „ „
„ 4 „ Ladáhwálá	„ 8 „ „ „ „
„ 5 „ Kot Qadar Bakhsh	„ 15 „ „ „ „

The largest Mahajani school in this circle is at *Ahmad Nagar*, with 32 pupils, in which Thakur Brahman teaches Landé, and gets Rs. 2-8 in money and kind.

The following are small Mahajani schools in this circle :—

No. 1 at Begú Jammá,	with 4 pupils learning Landé.
„ 2 „ Jorá	„ 15 „ „ „
„ 3 „ Jandiálá Wahábwálá	„ 10 „ „ „
„ 4 „ Ladáhwálá	„ 5 „ „ „

QILLEH DIDÁR SINGH.—The most eminent persons in this circle are: among the *Hakims*, Fazl Iláhi, Government employé; Fazl Ahmad, native Hakim, who is able and well-experienced; Bhái Amar Singh at Qilleh Didár Singh; Hasan Muhammad, Government employé at Qilleh Chandá Singh; Devi Shái, Hakim at Badoki; Ibráhim at Butálá; Akbar Ali at Chéhal Kalán; Jiwan Sháh at Makiánvála; and Lal Chand at Chhattá Sindhwan; among the *Maulvis*, Maulvi Hasan Muhammad at Chandar, Maulvi Muhammad Gohar at Mukhar, and Maulvi Qásim Ali at Chéhal Nan; and among the Bháis, *Bhái* Jaswant Rái at Deodhi Kalán, deserve notice.

The important maktabs in this circle are in *Mákiánwáli*, *Udhowáli*, and *Badoki*, attached to the mosques, with 15, 14 (7 boys and 7 girls), and 9 pupils, under Jiwan Sháh, Ghulám Rasúl, and Ghulám Ali respectively, who teach religious books and Persian. Teacher No. 1 gets Rs. 5 in cash and Rs. 5 in kind, No. 2 teaches gratuitously, and No. 3 gets Rs. 6 in kind annually.

The following are smaller maktabs in this circle, mentioned in a private return :—

No. 1 at Qilleh Didár Singh, attached to the mosque of Mián Qawámuddin, with 12 pupils learning Persian and the Korán.

No. 2 at Qilleh Didár Singh, attached to the mosque of Mián Fazl Ahmed, with 10 pupils learning the Korán.

No. 3 at Qilleh Didár Singh, attached to the mosque of Shekhánwah, with 15 pupils learning the Korán.

There is no patshala in this circle.

There are 3 Gurmukhi schools in this circle, at *Kardo-Deodhi*, *Pahluki*, and *Badoki*, all attached to Dharamsalas, with 8, 21, and 6 pupils, under Jaswant Rái and Náth Singh, Jai Singh and Chanda Singh, respectively, who teach Gurmukhi. The first two teachers teach gratuitously, and the third and fourth receive half náli of corn annually.

A private return mentions also a Gurmukhi school at *Qilleh Didár Singh*, with 8 pupils learning Gurmukhi.

The Mahajani school is at *Olkhá*, with 15 pupils, under Thákur Dass, who teaches Landé and gets Rs. 2 monthly.

KHANGAH.—Among the *Bháis*, Bawá Sundar Dass, a Guláb Dasiá fakir, and among the *Pandits*, Naráin Dass Brahman, are distinguished.

There is no maktab in this circle.

There is a patshala at *Ajnia-wala*, attached to the Gurduárá of Báwá Surjan Dass, Mahant Guláb Dasiá, with 6 pupils, under Sundar Dass, who teaches gratuitously Multiplication Table to 4 pupils and Bál-updesh to 2 pupils.

Ajniá-wala has a Gurmukhi school, also attached to the Gurduárá of Báwá Surjan Dass, under Mahant Guláb Dasiá, who teaches gratuitously Shastri and Hindi to 24 pupils.

The important Mahajani schools in this circle are at *Ajnia-wala* and *Kot Hasan Khan*, with 24 and 15 pupils, under Bawá Sundar Dass and Naráin Dass Brahman respectively, who teach Landé to 15 and Gurmukhi to 24 pupils.

The teacher No. 1 has no income, but No. 2 gets Rs. 2 per mensem in money and kind.

PINDI BHATTYAN.—The most eminent persons in this circle among the *Pandits* are Pandit Nanak Chand and Sankardáss of Jalálpur, and Sukhrám of Jalalpur; among the *Bhais*, Ganesha Singh; among the *Hakims*, Juálá Sahái of Jalálpur, and Ghulám Hasan of Chak Bhatti; and among the *Maulvis*, Muhammad Husain at Jalálpur, and Ahmaddin at Chak Patti, deserve notice.

There are 2 maktabs in this circle, at *Jalálpur Bathyan* and at *Chak Patti*, attached to mosques, with 7 and 4 pupils, under Muhammad Husain and Ahmaduddin, who teach Arabic and Persian. Muhammad Husain gets Rs. 7 in money, and Ahmaduddin nothing.

There are 3 large Gurmukhi schools in this circle, at *Pindi Bhátián*, *Qilleh Murád Bakhsh*, and *Chak Patti*, attached to Dharamsalas, with 40, 20, and 28 pupils, under Gangá Dass and Ganesha Singh, Ishar Dass and Dasmal, respectively, who teach Gurmukhi and Landé. Gangá Dass has no income; Ganesha Singh gets Re. 1-8; Ishar Dass receives no pay; and Dasmal gets 4 annas. A small Gurmukhi school is at *Tatti Asáish Kálan*, with 10 pupils learning Gurmukhi.

There are 2 Mahajani schools at *Pindi Bhátián* and *Jalálpur Bhátián*, with 45 and 50 pupils, under Ganesh Dass and Balmukand, who teach Landé, Shastri and Gurmukhi. Ganesh Dás gets in cash Re. 1-8, and in kind 25 seers of flour; and Balmukand, in cash Rs. 2, and in kind 20 seers of flour.

AKÁL GARH.—Among the *Maulvis* at Akál Garh, Karm Bakhsh, and at Rám Nagar, Máulvi Ghulám Qadir, are distinguished in this circle.

The largest maktabs in this circle are in *Akál Garh* and *Rám Nagar*, both attached to private houses. The teachers are named Ahmad Bakhsh and Juálá Sahai, who teach Persian, and Urdu and Persian, to 10 and 13 pupils respectively. The former draws Rs. 2, and the latter Rs. 3 in cash per mensem.

The small maktabs in this circle are as under:

Akál Garb, with 10 pupils learning Persian.

Akál Garh,	attached	to a mosque,	with	12	pupils,	learning	Persian and Arabic.
Rám Nagar,	,,	,,	,,	13	,,	,,	,, and Urdu.
Rám Nagar,	,,	,,	,,	6	,,	,,	Persian.
Rám Nagar,	,,	,,	,,	9	,,	,,	Korán.
Zábarki,	,,	,,	,,	8	,,	,,	,,
Qachar,	,,	,,	,,	9	,,	,,	Persian and Korán.
Sahloki,	,,	,,	,,	10	,,	,,	,, ,,
Meraj,	,,	,,	,,	8	,,	,,	Korán.
Pujiá Chatta,	,,	,,	,,	8	,,	,,	,,
Kot Jan Bakhsh,	,,	,,	,,	20	,,	,,	Persian and Korán.
Unchá Chakkor,	,,	,,	,,	8	,,	,,	Korán.
Jokhian,	,,	,,	,,	10	,,	,,	,,
Borewali,	,,	,,	,,	10	,,	,,	,,
Kot Khallián,	,,	,,	,,	6	,,	,,	,,

Hazrat Khalyáulláh,	attached	to a mosque,	with	8	pupils	learning	the Korán.
Nonewálá,	,,	,,	,,	5	,,	,,	,,
Darpál Khurd,	,,	,,	,,	3	,,	,,	Urdu, Persian and the Korán.
Darpal Kalán,	,,	,,	,,	5	,,	,,	,, ,,
Fatahpur,	,,	,,	,,	3	,,	,,	Korán.
Pahroki,	,,	,,	,,	6	,,	,,	,,
Kot Bhágá,	,,	,,	,,	5	,,	,,	,,
Chámwálá,	,,	,,	,,	5	,,	,,	,,
Kot Ahár,	,,	,,	,,	5	,,	,,	,,
Sháh Ráhmán,	,,	,,	,,	9	,,	,,	,,
Bhadori Kalán,	,,	,,	,,	5	,,	,,	,,
Chakkar Teji,	,,	,,	,,	5	,,	,,	,,
Tánewálá,	,,	,,	,,	4	,,	,,	,,

The largest patshala in this circle is at *Akál Garh*, attached to a temple, with 20 pupils, under Káshirám, who teaches Shastri, and gets Re. 1-8. But the private return mentions one more patshala at Akál Garh, under Pandit Bhagwan Dass, with 6 pupils.

There are 2 large Gurmukhi schools at Akál Garh and Rám Nagar, attached to Dharamsalas, in which 13 and 35 pupils are being taught in Gurmukhi by Hirá Singh and Bishen Dass respectively. Each of the teachers gets Rs. 2 in cash monthly.

The small Gurmukhi schools as mentioned in the police return are—

No. 1 at Rám Nagar, attended by 5 pupils, and No. 2 at Jamki, attended by 9 pupils. Both schools are attached to Dharamsalas, and the subjects taught in them is Gurmukhi.

The Mahajani schools in this circle, mentioned in the police return, are 2 in number. One at *Akál Garh* and one at *Rám Nagar*, with 60 and 4 pupils, whom Sonhá Mal and Diwán Chand teach Landé (a private informant adds Hindi and arithmetic also). The former gets Re. 1-8 in cash, and the latter nothing.

There is also a Mahajani school at *Chakar Tejí*, attached to a Dharamsala, with 20 pupils, who are taught in Landé and shop-keeping.

SHEKHUPURA.—There is only one Hakim, named Atáulláh, deserving notice among the Hakims in this circle.

There are 6 maktabs mentioned in the police return as important ones in this circle, *viz.* :—

1st at Jivanpura Khurd, 2nd at Jandiálá, 3rd Tarolá, 4th Gurniánwálá, and 5th Mediálá; all attached to the mosques, in which 6, 15, 10, 6, and 7 pupils are being taught the Korán by Badruddin, Muhabbat, Shahábuddin, Sher and Wali Muhammad respectively.

The largest Gurmukhi school in this circle is at *Daran*, attached to the Dharamsala, in which Jamaiyat Singh *Kuká* teaches Gurmukhi to 8 pupils gratuitously.

EXTRA.—The private return received from Maulvi Sarájuddin, manager of the Islámia school at Gujránwálá, shows the following additional maktabs in the district of Gujránwálá :—

No. 1 at Kámonki, attached to the mosque of Mián Ghulám, with 6 pupils learning the Korán.

No. 2 at Mahluwálá, attached to the mosque of Shamsuddin, with 10 pupils learning Persian and the Korán.

No. 3 at Tattá Chiryá, attached to the mosque of Muhammaddin, with 10 pupils learning the Korán.

No. 4 at Hanjánváli, attached to the mosque of Háfiz Muhammaddin, with 30 pupils reading the Korán.

No. 5 at Shergarh Khurd, attached to the mosque of Mián Muhammad Husain, with 10 pupils learning Persian and the Korán.

No. 6 at Kot Qazi, attached to the mosque of Mián Sarájuddin, with 10 pupils learning Persian and the Korán.

No. 7 at Dahlánwáli, attached to the mosque of Mián Charágh Din, with 5 pupils studying the Korán.

No. 7 at Qilleh Noh Singh, attached to the mosque of Mián Ghulám Muhammad, with 5 pupils learning the Korán.

No. 8 at Atáwáh, attached to the mosque of Mián Nabi Bakhsh, with 8 pupils learning the Korán and elementary Persian.

No. 9 at Atáwáh, attached to the mosque of Mián Saiyad Muhammad, with 10 pupils learning the Korán and elementary Persian.

No. 10 at Atáwáh, attached to the mosque of Mián Abdulláh, with 10 pupils learning the Korán with translation.

No. 11 at Atáwáh, attached to the mosque of Mián Ismáil, with 4 pupils learning the Korán with translation.

No. 12 at Drop, attached to the mosque of Maulvi Ináitulláh, with 15 pupils learning the Korán and elementary Arabic and Persian.

No. 13 at Firozpur, attached to the mosque of Mián Muhammad Azim, with 10 pupils learning the Korán.

No. 14 at Firozpur, attached to the mosque of Muhammad Bakhsh, with 15 pupils learning the Korán.

No. 15 at Firozpur, attached to the mosque of Mián Muhammad Faiz, with 7 pupils learning the Korán.

No. 16 at Ladhwálá, attached to the mosque of Choudhri Hákim, with 15 pupils, under Najimuddin, who teaches the Korán and elementary Persian.

No. 17 at Kháli, attached to the mosque of Hisámuddin, teacher, who teaches the Korán to 10 pupils.

No. 18 at Kolnwála, attached to the mosque of Baháwal-uddin, teacher, who teaches the Korán and Persian to 8 pupils.

No. 19 at Burhá Gharát, attached to the mosque of Maulvi Ghulám Yásin, teacher, with 10 pupils learning the Korán.

No. 20 at Qilleh Nihál Singh, attached to the mosque of Maulvi Ghulám Muhammad, teacher, who teaches the Korán to 15 pupils.

No. 21 at Mán, attached to the mosque of Musá Wahábi, teacher, who teaches the Korán to 7 pupils.

No. 22 at Mán, attached to the mosque of Shamsuddin, teacher, who teaches the Korán to 8 pupils.

No. 23 at Kot Ladhá, attached to the mosque of Mián Karm Iláhi, teacher, who teaches the Korán to 10 pupils.

No. 24 at Kot Bhiwáni Dass, attached to the mosque of Ahmad Ali, in which Abdul Aziz teaches the Korán and Persian to 12 pupils.

No. 25 at Kot Bhiwáni Dass, attached to the mosque of Khunjáh Ahmad, teacher, who teaches Persian and the Korán to 7 pupils.

No. 26 at Kot Bhiwáni Dás, in which Mián Ahmad Ali teaches Arabic and Persian to 4 pupils.

No. 27 at Pinang, attached to the mosque of Jiwan, teacher, who teaches the Korán to 12 pupils.

No. 28 at Kharchåka, attached to the mosque of Hasan Muhammad, who teaches the Korán to 10 pupils.

No. 29 at Chharyálá, attached to the mosque of Sultán Ahmad, teacher, who teaches the Korán and elementary Persian to 10 pupils.

In the same return a patshala is mentioned at *Kot Bhiwáni Dass*, attached to the private house of Narain Dass, in which 5 pupils are being taught in elementary Sanscrit.

A Gurmukhi school at *Kamunki*, attached to the Dharamsala of Bhai Shám Singh, in which 7 pupils are being taught in Gurmukhi and the Panch Granthi.

LAHORE DIVISION.

FEROZEPUR DISTRICT.

GENERAL ABSTRACT.

District.	No. of maktabs.	No. of pupils.	No. of Sanscrit and Nagri schools.	No. of pupils.	No. of Gurmukhi schools.	No. of pupils.	No. of Landé and Mahajani schools.	No. of pupils.	Total No. of indigenous schools.	Total No. of pupils.
Ferozepur	137	1,345	11	144	35	311	14	326	197	2,126

FEROZEPUR CITY.—*Pandits* Kishen Chand, Rámji Dass, Maha Nand, and Hardwari; *Bhais* Hira Singh and Dial Singh; *Maulvis* Sharf Din, and Wali Ullah; *Hakims* Radha Kishen, Rahmat Ali, Surajbhan, Maya Dass, and Kishandat are mentioned as distinguished men in this circle by the police return. A private return adds Saiyid Mahtab Ali Sháh, Muhammad Ibrahim, and Khan Uddin to the Hakims; Hafiz Ghulám Muhammad, Maulvi Muhammad, and Ghulám Nabi to the Maulvis; Udham Singh to the Bhais. The same return names Muhammad Din as an author, Munshi Ahmed Ali as a poet.

There is a *Madrasah* attached to a mosque, with 20 pupils, where Ghulám Muhammad teaches Arabic. He gets bread only. But when a pupil finishes the Korán he pays his teacher Rs. 3 or 4, and when he gets married he gives him Re. 1-4, and at the birth of a child he gets 4 annas. There are three smaller schools in which Arabic and the Korán are taught, with 25 boys. A private return, however, informs us that there are 5 maktabs in Ferozepur City, which we presume is correct. There are 6 patshalas with 150 boys attending, with 57 pupils, the largest of which has 15 boys and belongs to Kashi Rám, pleader; Kishen Chand teaches Sanscrit grammar. There are 3 Gurmukhi schools with 12 pupils, and 2 Landé schools with 95 pupils.

In the FEROZEPUR CANTONMENT is also a patshala, with 20 pupils, in a private house, where Pandit Rámji Lal, a man of good qualifications, teaches Sanscrit Grammar, Arithmetic, Geography, &c., and gets Rs. 15 per mensem. There is also a large Mahajani school with 50 pupils, in which a Brahmin, Shadi Rám, teaches Devanagari.

NATHANA.*—This circle has, according to the police return, 1 patshala with 10 pupils in *Kalian Malki*; it is attached to a Shiv Duala, and Pandit Salig Rám teaches Sanscrit, in which he is well up, getting Rs. 10 per mensem. There are 6 Gurmukhi schools; the largest, at the village *Mehraj*, has 10 pupils; it is attached to a Dharamsala. Bava Atmarám teaches Gurmukhi. Each pupil brings him bread in turn; and when one finishes the Granth, a sum of Rs. 4 or more, according to his means, is paid by him to the teacher. The other five are: 1 in *Bahni*, with 7; 1 in *Mahraj Pati Sawal*, with 4; 3 in *Nathana Khas*, with 10; 1 in *Chak Ramsinghwala*, with 4; and 1 in *Mahraj Pati Karm Chand*, with 8 pupils. *Mahraj Pati Sawal* and *Lahra Mushabhal* have each a Landé school, the first with 10 and the second with 20 boys. The teachers of above get 8 annas per mensem from each pupil.

DHARAMKOT.—*Dharamkot* itself has a maktab, where the Korán and other books are taught, with 20 boys; *Jalalabad* 1, with 26; *Kishanpura Khurd* 1, with 17; and *Qadirwala* has the largest school in the circle of this kind, which is attached to a mosque, and has 50 pupils.

*In this police circle Persian and Arabic are nowhere taught except in the Government schools, the Muhammadan population being small. There are Gurmukhi schools, with chiefly religious instruction. The teachers of Landé and Mahajani (Pandhe) come from other parts, and often go from one place to another for the purpose of teaching, so that some of these schools cannot be considered as permanent establishments.

The other schools of the same kind: 1 at *Kishanpúra Khurd*, with 17. In *Dholewálá* is a small maktab with 4 pupils, in which Persian, Gulistan, Karima, &c., are taught, and one at *Indargarh* Madrasah, with 5 boys, where Arabic, Qaida, &c., are the subjects of tuition; whilst at the following: *Panduri* with 10, *Saiyad Muhammad* with 15, *Rajanwála* with 20, *Mandar Kanbo* with 8, *Bandar Kalán* with 13, *Bráhmki* with 5, *Mojgarh* with 3, *Kelá* with 10, *Kishenpurá Kalán* with 19, *Musawalá* with 4, *Talwandi Naubahár* with 6, *Baqirwálá* with 4, *Fatehpur Kinan* with 9, *Mirpur* with 6, and *Dulewálá*, 4 pupils only—the Korán and religious books generally are taught.

There is a *patshala* at *Dharamkot* with 15 pupils, which is attached to the Thákurduárá Kálan.* Pandit Bhopál, who is a good Sanscrit scholar, teaches Sanscrit Grammar, "Laghu Kaumudi," "Chandrika," "Saraswat," and other books. Besides these, 20 pupils are taught in other different places in the same subjects. The teacher maintains himself by reading (Kathá) and preaching. *Gurmukhi schools*: 1 at *Choga Kalan* with 7 boys, under Sain Dass, who teaches them gratuitously, 1 at *Indargarh* with 5, 1 at *Talwandi Malián* with 4, and 1 at *Melah Kankán* with only 2 pupils. In all these Gurmukhi characters, "Pothi," "Jap Saheb," &c., are taught. *Landé schools*: 1 at *Dharamkot*, where Landé characters and Hindi Arithmetic are taught to 40 pupils, and 1 at Kot *Isa Khán*, where Mahajani and Landé are taught, with 17 pupils.

There is the following remark with regard to this circle: In the maktabs religious teaching is predominant. The teachers get nothing fixed per mensem; but are paid at harvest in money or kind. At the patshalas the teachers receive nothing from their pupils, but maintain themselves by preaching sermons (kathás), &c. The pupils also maintain themselves from the alms given them from the Thákurduárá or Dharamsala. The Landé and Mahajani schoolmasters receive weekly from each student 3 pies and bread.

GHAL.—The *Madrasahs* of this circle are: 1 at *Misrivala*, with 6 pupils, under teacher Yásin; 1 at *Badhni*, with 5 pupils, under Hirá Singh of Badhni; 1 at Ván with 7, under Nabi Bakhsh; 1 at *Sháhzadi*, with 7, under Hafiz Varyám; 1 at *Kailas*, with 2, under Ruhuddin; and 1 at *Mohkamwala*, with 10 pupils, under Ibrahim. In the first-named Arabic and Persian are taught, in all the others only Arabic.

Patshalas there are two, 1 at *Mudki* with 10 pupils, under Pandits Jirám and Hazari, and 1 at *Bhángar* with 12 pupils, under Prabh Diál. They teach Sanscrit gratuitously. 3 Gurmukhi schools: 1 at *Bhángar*, with 5 pupils, under Atar Singh; 1 at *Patli*, with 19, under Jivan Singh; and 1 at *Shakúr*, with 10, under Bhúp Singh of Shakúr. Gurmukhi and the Granth are taught; they get no fixed fee from the pupils, but the villagers give them presents of money or grain by their own free will. One Mahajani school with 7 boys, at *Jhanjian* where Hindi Arithmetic is taught.

NEHAL SINGHWALA.—Three Perso-Arabic schools are mentioned, 1 at *Lopú* with 12 pupils, under teacher Jáni, to whose house it is attached; he is paid in kind; 1 at *Takhtupura* with 8 pupils, 1 at *Radki Kalan* with 2 pupils taught Persian by Kamruddin who is paid by Sirdar Sangat Singh. There are 3 Gurmukhi schools, the largest at *Saidoki* in the Dharamsala under Bhai Badan Singh, with 30 pupils, 1 at *Patoki* with 14, and 1 at *Burj Hamirá* with 12 pupils. One Gurmukhi school with 7 pupils is mentioned by a private informant in *Radki Kalan*.

NAWA KILLA.—In the village *Lakhoki*, Maulvi Hafiz Muhammad is considered a learned man; he is an author; also Maulvis Abdul Qadir and Muhiuddin and Hakim Ghulám Muhammad are renowned in that part. In *Kiryan* Maulvi Muhammad Salim and Maulvi Abdurrazzaq are named.

---

* Besides those at the Thákurduárá Kálan, there are pupils also who read at the houses of Pandits Asarám, Kali Rám and Rám Nath.

According to the Police return, the Madrasah at *Lakohki*, which is attached to a mosque, and in which Abdul Qadir, who is a good Arabic scholar, is the teacher, has 30 pupils; but a private return gives the number as about 100, and adds Hafiz Muhammad and Muhiuddin as teachers; the following subjects being taught: poetry and prose in Persian, Grammar and Syntax in Arabic, Logic, Law of the Hanifi sect, Tafsir and the Korán. The income of the school is about Rs. 300 per annum in cash and kind, derieved from 95 acres of land with 2 wells, assigned to it by the Panjab Government, for as long as it lasts, on the 5th July 1860.

The smaller maktabs in this thana are,—

Nasirá Khilji with 11, *Betú* with 6, *Johadpuráh* with 10, *Taur* with 12 *Hamadki* with 10, *Lakhá Háji* with 12, *Lohdari* with 5, *Bani Khurd* with 7, *Chak Rahmán* with 9, *Nawá Killeh* with 8. In all these the Korán and Panjabi books are taught, except at *Taur*, where, instead of Panjabi, they have Persian. The following are merely Korán schools: *Badal* with 9, *Mahma* with 15, *Karyan* with 16, and *Qalái* with 14 pupils. They are nearly all attached to mosques.

No patshalas or dharamsalas are mentioned, but 1 Landé school with 20 boys at *Bétu*, with Mothú teacher. He is paid in kind about Rs. 5 per mensem.

MAKHU.—This Thana has several good Maulvis; such as Fazluddin, Jalaluddin, Ismáil, Ghulám Ghaus, and Abdul Qadir, and one Hakim, Abdul Islam. There are 10 maktabs, as per following list:—

Names of towns and villages.	Number of schools.	Number of pupils.	Subjects taught.
Sidhya village	1	2	The Korán.
Rokniwálá	1	3	Ditto.
Talwandi Nepálán	1	16	Arabic and Persian.
Jhanda Baggá	1	3	Ditto.
Nizamuddin walá	1	6	Ditto.
Aminwala	1	2	Arabic, the Korán.
Amir Sháhwalá	1	5	Ditto.
Lalba	1	5	Ditto.
Mamsiwala	1	8	Arabic and Persian.
Shian Pári	1	3	Ditto.
Talwandi Moji Wali (under Fazl Ilahi)	1	12	The Korán.

Zira.—The following maktabs are mentioned without any further particulars:—

Names of towns and villages.	Number of schools.	Number of pupils.	Subjects taught.
Sháh Makir	1	16	Korán.
Ditto	1	4	Urdu.
Mondi Jamál	1	10	Korán & Muhammedan law.
Mandar	1	12	Korán.
Mahal	1	8	Ditto.
Máchhíwárá	1	8	Ditto.
Bundálá	1	20	Ditto.
Beri	1	4	Ditto.
Sháhwálá	1	5	Ditto.
Manuwálá	1	6	Korán and Persian.

MOGÁ.—Maulvi Pir Bakhsh in Kukre Kalán and Maulvi Ilahi Bakhsh in Dhaleki are mentioned as noteworthy. There is only one maktab mentioned, and that is at *Kukre Kalán*, under teacher Nizam, with 5 pupils, who are taught the Korán; the teacher gets no money, but some grain at harvest. *Ramúnwálá* has a small Gurmukhi school with 5 boys, and a Mahajani school with the same number of boys; *Madúki* and *Gehal Kalán* have each a Mahajani school with 12 pupils in each. In the above three schools Mahajani and Landé are taught.

BAGHPURANÁ.—This Thana has, according to the Police return, 2 maktabs, 1 at *Chotián*, under teacher Khair Sháh, with 11 pupils, and 1 at *Chandno*, under Muhammad Ali Khán, with 40; the subjects taught are Urdu and Persian. There are eight minor maktabs besides, with 116 pupils.

There are 8 Gurmukhi schools—1 at *Manoki*, with 22 pupils, under Dya Rám; 1 at *Kotlá Raká*, with 7, under Narayen Singh; 1 at *Hatráj*, with 6, under Rám Singh; 1 at *Chidáh*, with 26, under Hira Singh; *Sibian*, *Máhila Kalan*, *Nathúwálá* and *Gholia Khurd*, with 10, 8, 17 and 20 pupils, under Jai Parkash, Khuba Singh, Wasawa Singh, and Suhel Singh respectively: Gurmukhi, Pothi and Granth are taught

JALALABAD.—Maulvi Jamaluddin and Hakim Kamaluddin are mentioned in this circle. The only maktabs in this return are, at *Khubáya* with 27, at *Amir* with 10, and at *Chisti Nathúki* with 9 pupils, under Muhammad Sadik, Jamaluddin and Abdullah respectively, who are all three good Arabic scholars, and teach Arabic grammar and the Korán. They get their food and corn at harvest.

KOT BHAI.—No schools are mentioned in the villages of this Thana; only 1 Landé school at *Kot Bhai* itself, with 24 boys, under teacher Bholá, who gets Rs. 6 per mensem, besides a supply of bread from the boys by turns.

FEROZEPUR CIRCLE.—Among the names of distinguished Maulvis and Hakims brought to notice, are found Hakim and Maulvi Mir Muhammad in the village *Araf*, Hakim and Maulvi Sharafuddin at *Khai*, Maulvi Sháh Muhammad at *Boriwalá*, Maulvis Ibrahim, Qamruddin, and Sadaruddin at *Piruwala*. The largest Madrasah is at *Piruwala*, under Maulvi Qamruddin; it is attached to a mosque, and has 34 pupils (14 boys and 20 girls) who are taught Arabic. The teacher has no fixed pay; he gets 2 or 4 maunds of grain at harvest, Re. 1-4 when a student gets married, and 4 annas at the birth of a child, as also the teachers of all the other schools in this circle, they being all, except those who teach Landé, either Mullas or Qazis. The following list shows the smaller schools:—

Names of towns and villages.	Number of schools.	Number of pupils.	Subjects taught.
Ráwal	1	2	Arabic, the Korán.
Araf ki	1	12	Ditto.
Nizám wala	1	12	Ditto
Phála	1	4	Ditto.
Khái	2	14	Ditto.
Bahadurwalá	1	3	Ditto.
Sinahwalá	1	6	Ditto.
Madehra	1	8	Ditto.
Phallah	1	10	Ditto.
Sher Khán	1	8	Ditto.
Mushki	1	8	Ditto.
Katorá	1	7	Ditto.
Almiwalá	1	6	Ditto.
Chakiwalá	1	3	Ditto.
Husainiwalá	1	5	Ditto.
Nozang Kibli	1	5	Ditto & Urdu
Jagali Kalán	1	8	Ditto.
Sahe Aiman	1	3	Ditto.
Atari	1	2	Persian.
Yári Wala	1	5	Arabic.
Básidpur	1	1	Ditto.
Subah Kahn Chand	1	2	Ditto.
Dáhag Ki	1	12	Ditto.
Kirian Pehlwan	1	3	Ditto.
Lohriwalá	1	3	Ditto.
Allawalá	1	20 (12 boys and 8 girls.)	Ditto.
Dhohwalá	1	6	Ditto.
Sadh Singhwalá	1	3	Urdu & Arabic
Tut	1	2	Arabic.
Achhiwalá	1	3	Ditto.
Mahalam	1	14	Ditto.
Kerian Mehlo	1	2	Ditto.
Subah Usman	1	12	Ditto.

There is 1 *Gurmukhi* school, with 6 pupils at the village *Sandá* under Faqir Nihál Dass, to whose house it is attached, and who lives on the charity of the village.

Chhok Hari Har has a Landé school with 14 pupils, and teacher Dhamáli, who gets 1 pice a week and some bread from each of the boys, who also give him, when their studies are terminated, from Rs. 4 to 5 each.

MUKATSAR.—*Mukatsar* itself has a small Perso-Arabic school attached to a mosque, under Maulvi Nizamuddin, who is a well-qualified man and teaches Persian and Arabic to, at present, only 4 pupils. He has a "Muáfi" (Revenue-free) plot of 32 ghumans assigned to him, and gets bread and corn occasionally. The following are the other schools in this circle :—

Names of towns and villages.	Number of schools.	Number of pupils.	Subjects taught.
Budhi Már	1	8	Persian and Arabic.
Nihang Jhari	1	...	......
Bhagsár	1	5	Persian and Urdu.
Bhengiwálá	1	10	Ditto.
Rupáná	1	6	Persian and Arabic.
Sarái Nángá	1	6	Persian.
Sohniwálá	1	2	Arabic, and the Koran.
Kirpál Ki	1	5	Ditto.
Khapiánwáli	1	10	Ditto.
Gandar	1	3	Ditto.
Khángá Kalán	1	2	Ditto.
Qalerwálá	1	5	Ditto.
Madabar	1	10	Ditto.
Maha Badhar	1	2	Ditto.

* There are 3 Gurmukhi schools: 1 at *Nihang Jhari* with 3, 1 at *Bhagsar* with 3, and the largest at *Mukatsar* with 10 pupils, attached to the house of Gobind Sahai Suthra, who is the teacher. Lande and Gurmukhi are taught. Gobind Sahai gets about 4 annas per month from each boy.

* In this circle one may say that, on an average, 1 boy in each "Dehra" learns Gurmukhi from the "Dehrawala".

RAWALPINDI DIVISION.

RAWALPINDI DISTRICT.

GENERAL ABSTRACT.

District.	Number of Maktabs and Madrasas.	Number of pupils.	Number of Sanscrit Schools.	Number of pupils.	Number of Gurmukhi Schools.	Number of pupils.	Number of Lande and Mahajani Schools.	Number of pupils.	Total number of Indigenous schools.	Total number of pupils.	Remarks.
Rawalpindi . .	660	8,771	9	94	137	2,894	10	383	816	12,142	

Rawalpindi City.—Amongst men who deserve special mention are,—*Maulvis* Ahmad Bakhsh and Fazl Ahmad; *Hakims* Luchman Dass, Karam Chand, Qazi Muhammad Aman, Sobha Singh, Saudagar Sháh and Mathra Dass; *Bhais* Sher Singh and Rám Singh; *Pandits* Brij Lal, Lakshíaram, Vishmadatta, Bhagwan Dass and Bishen Dass.

The Police Returns mention the following maktabs and Gurmukhi schools :—

Maktabs.

Locality.	Teacher.	No. of pupils. Boys.	Girls.	Subjects.	Income.
Ahmad Wali Mosque . .	Fazal Shah . .	2	5		
Masjid Fazal . .	Faqir Shah . .	1	2	The Koran & Persian.	
„ Mian Saifu . .	*Mussammat Gohran* .	5	10	The Koran.	
„ Khojas . . .	Mian Sharaf Din .	2	5	„	
„ Saraiwali . . .	Sahibji . . .	8	8	„	
Shah Nazarka-mahalla . .	Qazi Ahmadji . .	12	0	„	
Private house . . .	Fazl Ahmad . .	10	0	Arabic and the Koran.	

Gurmukhi Schools.

Locality.	Teacher.	Boys.	Girls.	Subjects.	Income.
Dharamsala Tahal Singh .	Dharam Singh . .	0	4	Gurmukhi.	
„ of Mai Sukhi .	Amir Singh . .	25	0	„	
„ Bava Nikka .	Gurmukh Singh . .	6	8	„	
„ Panchayeti .	Bishen Singh . .	13	0		
„ Harsa Singh .	Uttum Singh . .	8	0		
„ of Pandits .	Arjan Singh . .	9	0		
„ Karam Chand .	Bishan Singh . .	4	0		
„ Mai Toti . .	Rum Singh . .	111	0		
„ SirdarNihalSingh	Arjan Singh . .	6	0		

A private informant adds a maktab conducted by Maulvi Muhammad Aman and Hafiz Muhammadji teaching the Koran, Gulistan, Sekandarnama, &c., to 12 pupils.

There are 3 pátshalas under Pandits Lakkhi, Thakurdass and Bhagwan Dass, with 7, 12, and 4 pupils learning Sanscrit grammar, &c., and two Lande schools, 1 with 90 pupils, under Didar Bakhsh, and 1 with 55 under Miran Bakhsh. The subjects taught are—Sarda unit-tens-hundreds, multiplication table, tables of 1¼, 1½, 2½, 3½, 4½, &c., Dárán, letter-writing and "Hundwi." The teachers get about Rs. 15 each per mensem, including food, &c.

In the *Rawalpindi Cantonments* there are 7 maktabs with 154 pupils, the largest being the one in the Sadr Bazar, attached to a mosque, under Ghulám-Muhammad, who teaches Arabic and Persian, and gets Rs. 5 per mensem. In the same Bazar is a small Gurmukhi school attached to a Dharamsala under Amir Singh with 6 pupils.

Rawalpindi Circle.—Baba Khempuri, of the village *Kirpa*, is a well-known Sanscrit and Hindi scholar. *Sidpur* has a large maktab attached to a mosque, with 30 pupils, under Hafiz Karam Bakhsh, who knows the Koran by heart; he gets food on every eighth day and a present from Rs. 5 to Rs. 6 from each boy on his finishing the Koran. There are 4 Gurmukhi schools: at *Gorukhpur* with 7, at *Adyala* with 12; *Dhala* with 8, and *Tirlahi* with 70 pupils; 5 Lande schools: *Kori* with 25, *Sidpur* with 30, *Kirpa* with 20, *Golra* with 25, and *Dhamyal* with 40 boys; and 10 maktabs: 2 at *Adyala* with 80, 1 in *Narala* with 8, 1 in *Lohi Bhir* with 18, 1 in *Jhangi* with 10, 1 in *Bangrel* with 8, 1 in *Rihara* with 9, 1 in *Shakarpuryan* with 25, and 2 in *Dahgal* with 12 pupils.

Jatali.—At *Jatali* or *Jatal* is a good maktab in which Urdu, Persian, arithmetic, &c., are taught to 50 pupils by Fazl Din; no other maktab is mentioned in this circle, but 6 Gurmukhi schools, the largest at *Sakhu*, with 83 pupils (28 girls and 55 boys); at *Sid* with 62 (32 girls and 30 boys); *Nerali* with 22 boys; *Kontrila* with 14 (6 girls and 8 boys); *Doltala* with 44 (24 girls and 20 boys); and *Kanet Khalil* with 35 boys; in all of which the Granth and Gurmukhi are taught.

Besides the schools mentioned above, there are the following maktabs and Gurmukhi schools in this circle:—

Maktabs.			Gurmukhi schools.
Dhok Dhab	with	25 pupils.	
Ráman		25 „	
Said (2 schools)	„	30 „	
Narali	„	8 „	1 school with 10 pupils.
Kak	„	6 „	
Rahdi (4 schools)	„	38 „	„ „ 15 „
Dhung	„	15 „	
Kartiyal	„	12 „	
Karkala (2 schools)	„	37 „	
Mangot (2 schools)	„	17 „	
Jatat (2 schools)	„	12 „	
Darkali Kalan	„	20 „	„ „ 16 „
„ Khurd	„	20 „	
Gursiyan	„	15 „	
Máchh	„	30 „	„ „ 30 „
Khali Khaggar	„	15 „	
Kurnali	„	8 „	„ „ 9 „
Kanet Khalil	„	12 „	
Partali Kalan	„	8 „	
Qatbal	„	8 „	
Hoshang	„	11 „	
Muradi Jamil	„	11 „	
Jachhi Bahadur	„	6 „	
Katyal	„	25 „	
Sanbral	„	12 „	
Lodi	„	12 „	
Jatli (2 schools)	„	30 „	
Sukhrela Sakhrota	„	30 „	
Tarkwal			1 „ „ 16 „

Pind Sultani.—*Hakims* Radha Kishen and Sher Mohamed, *Maulvis* Ahmad Din and Nùr Abdulla and *Bhai* Kalyan Singh may be mentioned. The following places have Koran, and Perso-Arabic schools in this circle. *Domel* with 60 pupils, and teacher Maulvi Nur Abdullá; *Galyal* with 40 pupils, under Maulvi Nur Ahmed; *Nara* with 48 under Maulvi Fazl Ahmed; *Sigri* also with 44, and teacher Mian Nék; *Thatha* with 37 pupils, teacher Maulvi Nizamuddin; *Dumal* with 23, teacher Ahmad Din; and *Khunda* with 40, teacher Rugnauth. *Domel* has a pátshala attached to a "Duara," where Bhai Kalyan Singh, who is a good Sanscrit scholar, teaches that subject gratuitously to 10 pupils, and holds a "muafi" of a well from Government. The same place has a Gurmukhi school, where the same Bhai as above teaches Sanskrit and Gurmukhi to 40 boys. *Nara*, *Sigri*, *Sial Thata* and *Jhund* have each a Gurmukhi school with teachers

Thakur Das, Gobind, Baba Ghaur Das and Bal Kishen, and pupils 24, 24, 17, 16 and 39, respectively.

The following maktabs are also added by another return: *Pindsultani* 3 with 38; *Milyal* 2 with 50, *Kahil* 1 with 6, *Jalwal* 2 with 23, *Marwal* with 6, *Thatta* 1 with 3, *Kamilpur* 1 with 7, *Kasran* 4 with 24, *Sial* 4 with 25, *Batut* 1 with 7, *Thatta* 3 with 25, *Rangabad* 1 with 10, and *Kot Jachi* 1 with 12 pupils.

KALLAR.—Pandit Bhagat Chand and Maulvis Mohammad Hasan and Mohammad Ahsan are respected men in this circle. Ten Perso-Arabic schools are mentioned in this circle,—1 at *Arazi*, attached to a mosque, with 12 pupils under Budruddin, who is a good Arabic scholar, and gets 4 annas per boy a month; 1 at *Duberan*, under Firman Ali with 25 boys; 2 at *Chuka* with 20, 1 at *Basandot* with 15, 1 at *Sahebdaniyal* with 10, 1 at *Takdi* with 20, 1 at *Kallar Saiyyadan* with 6, 1 at *Bhalkur* with 40 and 1 at *Mushat Badhal* with 25 pupils. *Duberan*, *Khalsa* and *Dhamali* have Gurmukhi schools with 19, 35 and 35 pupils respectively.

HIZRU.—Among the Hakims Dyal and among the Maulvis and Pandits Muhammadji and Wasakhi Ram may be mentioned. The largest maktab in this circle is at *Malak-Malya*, in which Persian and Muhammadan law are taught to 40 pupils. *Hizru* has a Perso-Arabic school, with 20 pupils, attached to a mosque; its teacher, Hafizulla, who is a very good Persian scholar, teaches gratuitously. The same place has two Dharmsalas, in which 60 and 30 boys are taught Gurmukhi and Takri by Bhais Ratna and Tulsi who get their food, and a Lande school with 70 pupils, and teacher Ala Baksh, who gets Rs. 15 per mensem. A pátshala under Pandit Wasakhi Ram with 8 pupils and maktabs in *Nartopa*, *Abdál*, *Shamsabad* and *Saman* are added with 32, 20, 15, and 25 pupils respectively.

FATAHJHANG.—The best known Maulvis, Pandits, and Hakims are,—Maulvis Ghulam Ghaus Kazi, Fazle Ilahi and Ghulam Yahya; Pandit Sukhraj, and Hakim Mathra Singh.

Fatahjhang itself has a Perso-Arabic school with 30 pupils, and a Gurmukhi school with 77 pupils; *Dhuk-Meke* a Perso-Arabic school, with 60 pupils, all outsiders, under Mohammad Ghalam Yahya, who is considered a distinguished scholar in those parts. Amongst the subjects taught are,—Arabic grammar, logic, philosophy, astronomy, arithmetic, jurisprudence, &c., &c. *Tandal* has a school in which the same subjects are taught, with 10 pupils. The other maktabs are *Thatti Gujar* with 15, *Dharnal* with 10, *Kot Fatah Khan* with 25, and *Bathar* with 12 pupils. *Fatahjhang* has also a pátshala under Sukhraj with 20 pupils.

RAWAT.—This circle has the following Madrasas:—

The largest at *Mankyala* with 30 pupils, and teacher Rukn Alam; 1 at *Sagri* with 12, *Nakrali* with 10, *Takhtpari* with 8, and at *Tanbir Reiyal* with 28 pupils; *Mughal* 5 with 76 and *Takala*, with 18 pupils. There are 4 Gurmukhi schools; the largest at *Basai*, attached to a Dharmsala, where Bhai Chanda Singh teaches 60 pupils gratuitously; *Takhtpari* and *Nakrali* with 40 pupils at each place and a smaller one at *Sagri* with 35 boys. The following maktabs are also said to be in this circle:—*Cheni* with 17, *Jawa* with 10, *Basai* with 17, *Awan* with 15, *Kalri* with 17, *Jabar-Darwesh* with 26, *Mari Danishmandan* with 22, *Mal Jamal* with 15, *Chimai* with 14, *Top Kalyal* with 14, and *Shadi Wimal* 1 with 15 pupils.

SUNGJANI.—Maktabs: *Dheri-Shahan* with 22, *Shah Alladitta* with 20, *Pidana* with 15, *Sangjani* with 4, *Weni* with 15, *Jatal* with 8, *Ghel Thebyan* with 10, and *Tatta Khail* with 8 pupils. In all these, Urdu, Persian and Arabic are taught.

At *Usman Khatar* is a Gurmukhi school with 38, and a Lande school with 15 pupils; at *Dheri-Shahan*, a Gurmukhi school with 10 and a Lande school with 13 pupils. *Sangjani* and *Weni* have each a Gurmukhi school with 20 and 9 pupils, respectively. *Kot Kalyan* and *Ghela* have also Gurmukhi schools with 10 pupils.

KAHUTA.—Among the Maulvis and Bhais, Maulvi Ghulam Nabi and Bhai Nihál Singh may be mentioned. The following maktabs and Gurmukhi schools are brought to notice:—

Names of towns and villages.	Maktabs.		Subjects taught.	Gurmukhi Schools.		
	Number of maktabs.	Number of pupils.		Number of schools.	Number of pupils.	Subjects taught.
Kahúta	4	35	Persian and the Koran	4	25	Gurmukhi.
Chuha Khalsa	2	56	Ditto	1	14	Ditto.
Chawbi	1	29	Ditto	...	...	
Biwar	1	54	Ditto	...	...	
Matur	1	18	Ditto	1	5	
Narah	1	20	Ditto	1	14	Ditto.
Balreta	1	7	Ditto	...	...	
Phun	1	10	Ditto	1	10	Ditto.
Sadiwat	...	...	Ditto	1	25	Ditto.
Phagwan	1	10		...	...	...
Sanbal	1	10	... ...	...	...	...
Kalyal	1	12	... ...	...	...	...
Asloha	1	15	... ...	...	...	...
Lari Musalmanan	1	12	... ...	...	...	...
Khalol	1	10	... ...	...	...	...
Duberan Rajgan	1	20	... ...	...	...	...
Jewra	1	14	... ...	...	...	...
Baghar Musalmanan	1	15	... ...	...	...	...
Pahar	1	10	... ...	...	...	...
Kot	1	13	... ...	...	...	...

The village of *Thua* has a pátshala under Bhai Nihal Singh teaching Shastri to 14 pupils, *Chuha khalsa* has also a patshala with 7 pupils.

ATTOCK.—The largest school in this circle is the Madrasa at *Sarwala*, attached to a mosque; Hafiz Ghulam Mohammad, a good Arabic scholar, teaches 30 boys gratuitously. *Hajishah* and *Mansar* have Perso-Arabic schools with 11 pupils each, under teachers Bahadur Khan and Abdulla, respectively, who get Rs. 4-5 per mensem and food and clothing. *Gondal* has two little schools; 1 with 5 pupils, in which Arabic is taught, and the other with 7 pupils, in which Persian is taught. This last place has also a Gurmukhi school with 8 boys attending, and taught by Ram Ditta, who gets Rs. 1 per mensem, food and clothing. Attock also has 2 Gurmukhi schools with 8 pupils. The villages of *Malahi Tola* (4 schools) *Wakner, Dher, Bagh Nilab, Shakardara, Nurpur, Londi, Mulla Mansur, Mandrota, Purmali* (2), *Mallah* (2), *Giri* have maktabs with 29, 24, 2, 8, 15, 6, 10, 5, 5, 5, 16 and 9 pupils respectively.

GUJAR KHAN.—The police returns state that *Maulvis* Nizam Din, Imam Din, Mohammad Baksh and Mohammad Hasan, *Hakims* Nawab Ali and Beli Ram, also *Bhais* Amir Singh, Dewa Singh and Jawand Singh, enjoy the highest respect in this circle. The largest school is at *Rahora*, under Maulvi Nizam Din, who teaches Persian and Arabic to 60 pupils. According to the general custom of the country, he has no fixed salary, but gets his food. The next best is the Madrasa at *Pidána*, in charge of Fazl Din, with 50 pupils. The other smaller ones are as follows:—

Arabic and Perso-Arabic Schools.

Names of towns or villages.	Number of schools.	Number of pupils.	Subjects taught.
Pindari	1	16	Arabic and Persian.
Bihan	1	8	Ditto.
Karoli	1	15	Ditto.
Dulmi	1	30	Ditto.
Bigam	1	10	Persian.
Rokyah	1	6	Arabic and Persian.
Sipyali	1	10	Ditto.
Jabar	1	10	Ditto.
Galini	1	12	Ditto.
Philot	1	20	Ditto.
Dauk	1	10	Ditto.
Nirali Jabar	1	12	Ditto.

***Arbaio and Perso-Arabic Schools*—(concluded).**

Names of towns or villages.	Number of schools.	Number of pupils.	Subjects taught.
Loi Hafiz	1	9	Arabic and Persian.
Pityan	1	30	Arabic.
Darhala	1	7	Ditto.
Batala	1	5	Ditto.
Mohri Bersal	1	6	Ditto.
Mohri Kenril	1	7	Ditto.
Bagyal	1	30	Ditto.
Chanda	1	20	Ditto.
Loi Champa	1	6	Ditto.
Chakrali	1	35	Ditto.
Valkhalsa	1	15	Ditto.
Binam	1	8	Ditto.
Gami	1	12	Ditto.
Nal	1	15	Ditto.
Kalyana	1	12	Ditto.
Marah Saman	1	20	Ditto.
Bhúl	2	16	Ditto.
Jundghár	1	5	Ditto.
Gujra	1	12	Ditto.
Charmut Kalán	2	9	Ditto.
Jund Bilú	2	14	Ditto.
Jabar Warnial	2	37	Ditto.
Sipiali Baghal	1	16	Ditto.
Dora Bedhal	1	13	Ditto.
Suhíwá Mirasian	1	18	Ditto.

There are 11 Gurmukhi schools—*Gujarkhan* and *Biblú* with each 15 boys, *Bigam* with 6, *Berki Bidhal* 2 with 28, *Kazian* 1 with 25, *Bhul* 2 with 17, *Bhagpur* 2 with 12 and *Dora Bedhal* 1 with 12 pupils.

CHAWANTRA.—Amongst the names of distinguished Maulvis, Mian Ahmed of Saroba and Mohammad Shah of Chikri are named; also Bhais Nihal Singh and Hera Singh. The best, although not the largest, school is the one of *Saroba*, attached to a mosque; the teacher, Mian Ahmed, a learned Maulvi with a college certificate, teaches the following subjects: Arabic Grammar, Logic, Muhammadan Law, Literature, Jurisprudence, Philosophy, Tafsir, &c. The number of pupils is 15. Mian Ahmed has no income in cash from his pupils but held once a muafi.

The following schools belong to this circle:—

Names of towns and villages.	Maktabs.			Gurmukhi Schools.		
	Number of schools.	Number of pupils.	Subjects taught.	Number of schools.	Number of pupils.	Subjects taught.
Dhulyal	1	22	Arabic Grammar, Logic, Tafsir, Hadis, Muhammadan Law, and Literature.	1	10	Pothi and Darbar Sahib.
Mandwal	1	20	Ditto	...	...	
Gangan	1	32	Muhammadan Law, Literature.	...	...	
Sihal	2	50	Grammar, Logic.	...	...	
Chakri	1	30	Muhammadan Law, Literature.	2	48	Gurmukhi, Darbar and Pothi.
Myana Mohra	1	17	Ditto	...	...	
Dheri	1	25	Ditto	...	...	
Balawal	1	15	Ditto	1	20	Ditto.
Dandi Gujran	1	5	Ditto	...	...	
Mahmuda	1	7	Ditto	...	...	
Bajar	2	25	Arabic Grammar, Jurisprudence and Muhammadan Law.	1	30	Ditto.
Chhan	1	20	Ditto	1	20	Ditto.
Sangral	...	...		1	15	Ditto.
Khallá	...	...		1	25	Ditto.
Ganganwala	...	...		1	25	Ditto.
Kolyan	...	...		1	17	Ditto.
Chawantra	...	...		1	27	Gurmukhi.
Adhwal	...	...		2	33	Ditto.
Myal	...	...		1	15	Ditto.
Chak Beli Khan	...	...		1	25	Ditto.
Mujahid	1	12		1	15	
Paryal	...	...		1	37	

PINDIGHEB.—Maulvis Fazal Ahmed and Mohammad Afzal, as also Bhai Sawan Singh, are mentioned as superior men. Another informant adds the names of Maulvis Gul Mohammad, Mian Ahmed and Mian Khurshaid, Pandits Sukhdyal and Radha Kishen and Bhai Gurda Singh. The best school is at *Kamalyal*, in charge of Kazi Fazal Ahmed; the Police return gives 18 as the number of pupils; a private informant, however, says 50. The subjects taught are Arabic Grammar, Urdu, Persian and Arithmetic, the Koran, &c. The teacher holds 10 ghumaos of rent-free land from the proprietors of the village. The same private return mentions 5 more maktabs in the above place with 52 pupils, in which the same subjects are taught. The following are the other schools in the Pindigheb circle :—

	MAKTABS.			GURMUKHI SCHOOLS.		
Names of towns or villages.	Number of schools.	Number of pupils.	Subjects taught.	Number of schools.	Number of pupils.	Subjects taught.
Pindi Gheb	6	45	Poetry and Muhámmadan Law.	3	208	Gurmukhi.
Gandakas	3	16	Ditto	1	12	Gurmukhi Mahajani and multiplication tables.
Khor	2	25	The Koran and Hadis.	...	...	
Kamalyal	1	12	Ditto	1	20	Ditto.
Noshera	1	16	Ditto	...	...	
Nikki Kalan	2	18	Ditto	...	...	
Tut	1	20	Ditto	...	...	
Tavin	1	10	Ditto	...	...	
Ikhlas	3	33	Arabic	1	14	Gurmukhi.
Langryal	1	21	Ditto	...	...	
Kharya	4	24	Persian	...	...	
Nauntha	1	10	Koran	...	...	
Dunal	1	10	Ditto	...	...	
Dhuk Gujar	1	7	Ditto	...	...	
Saltwál	1	13	Ditto	...	...	
Mulluwala	1	3	Ditto	...	...	
Gharibwal	1	8	Ditto	...	...	
Dholyan	1	7	Ditto	...	...	
Dandi	1	7	Ditto	...	...	
Sora	1	4	Ditto	...	...	
Sarvaya	1	16	Ditto	...	...	
Surgah	1	12	Ditto	...	...	
Ckakki	1	20	Ditto	...	...	
Nika Ghulam Shah	2	22	Ditto	...	...	
Dhok Dera	1	7	Ditto	...	...	
Tatti Kalra	1	4	Ditto	...	...	
Pherowali	1	6	Ditto	...	...	
Dhok Malyaran	1	5	Ditto	...	...	
Ahmadal	1	12	Ditto	1	5	

Pindigheb has also a pátshala which, according to the description in the Police return, seems to be of a superior kind. Pandit Rada Kishen conveys instruction in the following subjects to 12 pupils: Sanskrit Grammar, Logic, Astronomy, Vedant, &c.

HASSAN ABDAL.—Maulvi Kázi and Abdulaziz are named as good Arabic scholars.

There are 19 maktabs in this circle: *Tahdà* 1 with 18 pupils under Ubdullaziz, teaching Arabic literature and having a muafi of 4 ghumaos, *Burhan* 2 with 61, *Pevi* 1 with 16, *Garhi Afghanan* 1 with 15, *Hasan Abdal* 2 with 60, *Sultanpur* 1 with 15, *Samun* 1 with 7, *Wal* 2 with 30, *Budhu* 1 with 15, *Patsar Jogi* 1 with 10, *Bai* 1 with 15, *Fatahulla* 1 with 30, *Gutaryan* 1 with 20, *Koyala* 2 with 30, and *Purmiana*, 1 with 20 pupils. The villages of *Burhan*, *Hasan Abdal* and *Kot Fatah Khan* have each one Gurmukhi school with 32, 54 and 25 pupils respectively.

MAKHAD.—Maulvis Khurshed, Mian Ahmad and Mian Zaman; Hakims Gauhar Singh and Nonihal Singh are well-known in this circle. There are five Madrasas at Makhad itself, with 144 pupils (one with 112, one with 35, one with 22, one with 40, and one with 35 pupils). *Mèra* has a Madrasa with 50 and another with 60 boys, the latter is attached to a mosque, and its teacher Myan Ahmad, is considered a very learned man. Arabic Grammar, Muhammadan

Law are amongst the subjects of tuition; he only gets about Rs. 3 a month. There are two Gurmukhi schools; the largest at *Makhad*, attached to a Dharmsala with 25 boys, under teacher Bhai Sookhdyal Singh; the other at *Mehwali* with 25 pupils.

MANDRA.—Maulvi Kamruddin and Bhai Gulab Singh of Haryal are the distinguished men. Three maktabs are brought to notice only in this neighbourhood by the police, 1 at *Bijinyal* with 40, 1 at *Kori Dolal* with 30, and 1 at *Phuti* with 50 pupils; in the first Arabic and the Koran, and in the last two Urdu, the Koran, Arithmetic, &c., are the subjects of tuition. Three maktabs also in *Hakim Chathha* with 7, *Sosa* with 7, *Kalyal* with 20, *Baicha* with 8, *Dihar* with 20, *Tabkian* with 15, *Kameti* with 10, *Phata* with 20, *Nurwajhla* with 15, *Khakri* with 18, *Saug* 2 with 45, *Kajju* with 9, *Kurwada Malyaran* with 10, *Kurwada Sawan* with 8, *Dhara* with 8, *Charbial* with 7, *Chhari Bagyal* with 7, *Chhari Kalyal* with 12, and *Joryan* with 7 pupils. *Haryal* and *Ghonghrela* have small Gurmukhi schools with 30 and 40 pupils, respectively.

MURREE.—Maulvis Abdússamad, Chiragh Din and Bhai Bhagwan Singh are well known. There is only one maktab mentioned here, which is attached to a mosque, and where Abdulhack, a good Persian and Arabic scholar, teaches these subjects and arithmetic, &c., to 28 boys, and gets about Rs. 12 per mensem. According to a private return, this school is attended by 30 boys and 10 girls. There are other maktabs in the villages of *Arwari*, *Chharan*, *Potah*, *Dewal*, *Rawat*, *Methra*, *Sayyadan*, *Jadatar*, *Chichana* and *Masut* having 10, 10, 20, 20, 10, 14, 8, 20 and 10 pupils, respectively.

List of Indigenous Schools in the Rawalpindi District furnished by the District Officer, which are not contained in the Police Returns.

Name of Village or Town.	Maktabs.			Gurmukhi Schools.		
	Number of Maktabs.	Number of Pupils.	Subjects.	Number of schools.	Number of Pupils.	Subjects.
RAWALPINDI.						
Dhamál	2	18	Persian and Arabic	2	40	Gurmukhi and the Granth.
Kotah Khurd	1	15	Koran	...	...	
Mohri Ghuran	1	10	Ditto	...	...	
Mohra Jahar	1	10	Koran, Gulistan, Bostan, Sikandar Náma.	...	...	
Bandah Saughál	1	10	Koran	...	...	
Patkh	1	25	Ditto	...	...	
Orah	1	25	Ditto	...	...	
Dhok Lakkhan	1	25	Arabic and Persian	...	...	
Kalyam Telí	2	8	Koran and Persian	...	...	
Bagalyanah	1	2	Koran	...	...	
Kirpál	1	2	Ditto	...	...	
Kalyam Sayadán	1	6	Ditto	...	...	
Baggá Sagrál	1	10	Koran and Persian	...	...	
Bijnyál	3	36	Ditto ditto	...	...	
Chahán	1	10	Koran	...	...	
Rawát	2	16	Koran, Gulistan and Bostan.	1	22	Gurmukhi, the Granth and Sokhmeni.
Panjgaran	1	6	Ditto	...	...	
Sád Gangál	1	18	Koran and Gulistan	...	...	
Dhakálah	1	19	Ditto	...	...	
Lohadrah	1	5	Ditto	...	...	
Mohrah Jumah	1	3	Ditto	...	...	
Kobálah Kalán	1	4	Arabic	...	...	
Pagiar	1	6	Ditto	...	...	
Koliampur	1	2	Koran	...	...	
Mora Kalán	1	8	Sikandar Namá, Gulistan and Bostan.	...	...	
Malpur	1	25	Arabic, Persian and Urdu	...	...	
Sohán	1	30	Koran	...	...	
Kot Thál	1	8	Ditto	...	...	
Gorakhpur	1	20	Koran, Gulistan and Bostan.	...	...	

List of Schools furnished by the District Officer, which are not contained in the Police Returns,—(continued).

Name of Village or Town.	Maktabs. Number of Maktabs.	Maktabs. Number of Pupils.	Maktabs. Subjects.	Gurmukhi Schools. Number of Schools.	Gurmukhi Schools. Number of Pupils.	Gurmukhi Schools. Subjects.
Rawalpindi—*continued.*						
Derah	1	10	Koran	...	...	
Shahpur	1	5	Ditto	...	...	
Hafálah Kalán	1	7	Ditto	...	...	
Ditto Khurd	1	8	Ditto	...	...	
Sayadpur	1	15	Ditto	1	20	Panjgranthi and Granth.
Lomdah Mastál	1	10	Arabic and Persian	...	...	
Ghoerah	3	57	Arabic	2	40	Gurmukhi.
Korí	...	...	...	2	35	Ditto.
Nurpur	1	20	Persian and Urdu	...	...	
Samblol	1	6	Koran	...	...	
Janjál	1	6	Ditto	...	...	
Korí Malyárán	1	7	Ditto	...	...	
Safar	1	5	Koran	...	...	
Khetaryan	1	10	Arabic and Persian	...	...	
Telyán	1	12	Koran	...	...	
Kolyán Kot	1	9	Ditto	...	...	
Nún	1	22	Arabic and Persian	...	...	
Girjá Dhok	1	20	Koran	...	...	
Kotah	1	3	Ditto	...	...	
Sunbal	1	5	Ditto	...	...	
Jápah	1	4	Arabic and Persian	...	...	
Bányán Naunth	1	3	Koran	...	...	
Mohrá Amrá	1	8	Ditto	...	...	
Kothah Kalán	1	33	Arabic and Persian	...	...	
Hamak	2	14	Koran	...	...	
Rajwál	1	8	Ditto	...	...	
Bamla Kaut	1	6	Ditto	...	...	
Morgáh	1	7	Ditto	...	...	
Kalyál	1	5	Ditto	...	...	
Jarai	1	4	Ditto	...	...	
Khurtanah	1	50	Ditto	...	...	
Tolsoh Hirdá	1	3	Koran	...	...	
Malkah	1	8	Ditto	...	...	
Haidar Halím	1	12	Ditto	...	...	
Chak Chálú	1	3	Ditto	...	...	
Ojrí Kalán	1	20	Ditto	...	...	
Pind Naushírí	1	9	Persian and Urdu	1	6	Gurmukhi & Japji.
Dhok Sadar	1	3	Koran	...	...	
Pind Paiyán	1	2	Ditto	...	...	
Tarnol	1	5	Ditto	...	...	
Bandah	1	5	Ditto	...	...	
Dhok Sundar	1	6	Ditto	...	...	
Sarai Kolah	1	4	Ditto	...	...	
Do. Kharbozah	1	9	Persian and Arabic	...	...	
Chhokar	1	6	Koran	...	...	
Chuhar Barnál	1	15	Koran, Gulistan and Bostan	...	...	
Kattha Kák	1	4	Koran	...	...	
Tályán	...	...	...	1	8	Gurmukhi.
Rawat	...	...	...	1	40	Ditto.
Chappar	1	10	Ditto ditto	...	...	
Gangal	1	7	Koran	...	...	
Jabar Sánah	1	7	Koran	...	...	
Sírí Malana	1	5	...	...	...	
Tattah Gandpur	1	5	Ditto	...	...	
Katarian	1	8	Ditto	...	...	
Khakkar Khurd	1	10	Arabic and Persian	...	...	
Baudah	1	3	Ditto ditto	...	...	
Chorki	1	3	Figah and Poetry	...	...	
Dhok Himmat	1	4	Figah	...	...	
Piprah	1	6	Figah and Poetry	...	...	
Dhorí	1	8	Koran	...	...	
Baggá Shamál	1	38	Arabic and Persian	...	...	
Karkan	1	25	Ditto ditto	...	...	
Sangrah	1	10	Koran	...	...	
Mogu	...	...	...	...	...	
Chatroh	1	12	Koran	...	...	
Sihndú	1	12	Ditto	...	...	
Gharbaráo	1	7	Arabic and Persian	1	13	Gurmukhi.
Dharwalah	1	15	Ditto ditto	...	...	
Dhalyálah	1	10	Ditto ditto	...	...	
Pamtrár	1	9	Urdu and Persian	...	...	
Nogrí.	1	1	Persian	...	...	
Harnúh Sadánál.	1	2	Persian and Urdu	...	...	
Tarlái Kalán	1	40	Koran and Persian	...	...	
Jabar Murzál	1	7	Koran and Urdu	...	...	

List of Schools furnished by the District Officer, which are not contained in the Police Returns,— (continued).

Name of Village or Town.	Maktabs.			Gurmukhi Schools.		
	Number of Maktab.	Number of Pupils.	Subjects.	Number of Schools.	Number of Pupils.	Subjects.
Murree.						
Musiári	3	24	Koran and Urdu	...	...	
Bhan	1	3	Ditto	...	...	
Phatti	4	20	Ditto	...	...	
Hokrah Kir	1	15	Ditto	...	...	
Malot	1	12	Ditto	...	...	
Rawát	2	16	Ditto	...	...	
Sarmandal	1	14	Ditto	...	...	
Morí	1	1	Ditto	...	...	
Karor	1	5	Ditto	...	...	
Kilah Basand	1	30	Ditto	...	...	
Darlohi.	1	2	Ditto	...	...	
Salankharo	2	16	Koran	...	...	
Thab Bharámál	1	10	Ditto	...	...	
Lokot	1	7	Ditto	...	...	
Bagálí	2	25	Ditto	...	...	
Bojah	1	12	Ditto	...	...	
Phantí	1	4	Ditto	...	...	
Barhná	2	20	Ditto	...	...	
Bandhi	1	5	Ditto	...	...	
Káhyá	1	15	Ditto	...	...	
Malotwásyán	2	30	Ditto	...	...	
Murtazá Khán	1	22	Ditto	...	...	
Patar Mall	1	4	Ditto	...	...	
Osyáh	1	8	Ditto	...	...	
Ura	1	4	Ditto	...	...	
Ban Koyal	1	6	Ditto	...	...	
Sindhyá	1	12	Ditto	...	...	
Mádú	2	24	Ditto	...	...	
Kotli	2	12	Ditto	...	...	
Daliah	1	7	Ditto	...	...	
Tandkat	1	6	Koran	...	...	
Sánmlí	1	6	Ditto	...	...	
Mánkah	1	7	Ditto	...	...	
Baráhá	1	12	Ditto	...	...	
Alokas	1	2	Ditto	...	...	
Birkarán	2	30	Ditto	...	...	
Kotli	1	15	Ditto	...	...	
Ghoi	1	10	Ditto	...	...	
Daryá Gali	1	8	Ditto	...	...	
Khambramál	2	15	Ditto	...	...	
Dhílah	1	10	Ditto	...	...	
Phagwárí	1	8	Ditto	...	...	
Sahnah	1	8	Ditto	...	...	
Ghoti	1	10	Ditto	...	...	
Kakrá	1	4	Ditto	...	...	
Tarísái	1	6	Ditto	...	...	
Saamli	1	9	Ditto	...	...	
Ghorah Galí	1	6	Ditto	...	...	
Mangal	1	6	Ditto	...	...	
Sanbalbáh	1	4	Ditto	...	...	
Sáyan	2	9	Ditto	...	...	
Ghorah	1	8	Ditto	...	...	
Tahsil Fatahjang—						
Qatvál	1	12	Persian and Arabic	...	...	
Yáthar	...	...	...	1	15	
Attár	1	5	Ditto	...	...	
Malhúkál	1	12	Ditto	...	...	
Harn:ánwálá	1	13	Ditto	...	...	
Ghelákalán	1	15	Ditto	1	20	
Karar	1	20	Ditto	...	..	
Serobá	1	15	Ditto	2	16	
Tatrál Khurd	1	12	Ditto	...	...	
Chak Amrál	1	20	Ditto	...	...	
Jhangí Daim	2	28	Ditto	...	...	
Dhandhá	1	22	Ditto	...	...	
Thula Kalán	1	10	Ditto	...	...	
Kot	1	60	Ditto	1	60	
Paryál	1	10	Ditto	...	...	
Chawat	...	...	...	...	...	
Dhomel	...	...	...	1	15	
Jhánar	1	125	Ditto	1	15	
Ládiyán	1	22	Ditto	...	...	

Name of Village or Town.	Name of Teacher.	Maktabs. No. of Schools.	No. of Pupils.	Subjects.	Gurmukhi Schools. No. of Schools.	No. of Pupils.	Subjects.
Tahsil Attak—							
Hazru	...	3	69	Arabic and Persia	1	9	Sanscrit.
Musá	...	1	12	Ditto	...	...	
Ghaur Ghani	...	1	15	Ditto	...	...	
Kálú Khurd	...	1	11	Ditto	...	...	
Jalalá	...	1	10	Ditto	...	...	
Dasá	...	1	20	Ditto	...	...	
Tahsil Pindi Gheb—							
Sarurí	...	1	16	Ditto	...	...	
Nalbad	...	1	15	Ditto	...	...	
Rangli	...	2	30	Ditto	...	...	
Lasbál	...	2	8	Ditto	2	10	Panjgranthi and Granth.
Pindí Sarhál	...	2	40	Ditto	...	...	
Tharyálah	...	1	10	Ditto	...	...	
Farozdátá	...	1	6	Ditto	...	...	
Jábah	...	1	7	Ditto	...	...	
Chamat	...	1	10	Ditto	...	...	
Uchhrí	...	1	9	Ditto	...	...	
Losdral	...	2	12	Koran	...	...	
Chhaprí	...	1	7	Ditto	...	...	
Tahsil Gujar Khan—							
Charwáitál	...	2	45	Ditto	...	...	
Changábagyál	...	2	38	Ditto	...	...	
Kori Dalál	...	...	...	...	1	15	Ditto.
Játlí	...	1	20	Koran	2	24	Gurmukhi and the Granth.
Gujar Khán	...	...	...	...	...	...	
Bhatah Molyár	...	1	20	Koran and Persian	...	...	
Mhírah Shamas	...	1	20	Koran	...	...	
Biyol	...	2	16	Ditto	...	...	
Hichyárí Dalál	...	1	15	Koran	...	...	
Jand Melú	...	2	14	Ditto	1	16	Ditto.
Jand Najár	...	1	15	Ditto	...	...	
Kurtálí	...	...	...	...	1	6	Ditto.
Kautrila	...	1	7	Ditto	1	8	Ditto.
Mastalah	...	1	10	Ditto	...	...	
Dewi	...	1	10	Ditto	...	...	
Hartal	...	...	...	...	1	10	
Natah Gujar Mall	...	1	12	Koran	...	...	
Panjtol	...	1	30	Ditto	...	...	
Danahat	...	...	...	...	1	10	Ditto.
Tahsil Kahutah—							
Bivar	Bakhsh Mahomed and Meer Husain.	2	54	Koran and Persian.	...	...	
Theha	Nitál Singh.	...	...	...	1	14	Religious books.
Bishendatr	Lakhan Singh	...	...	...	1	25	
Bamali	Rám Singh	...	...	...	1	40	Ditto.
Kaithal	...	1	10	Ditto	...	...	
Salugran	...	2	9	Arabic	...	...	
Sapyalí Umar Khán	...	1	6	Koran	...	...	
Kandyári	...	1	4	Ditto	...	...	
Sithá	...	1	12	Ditto	...	...	
Nahesar	...	1	6	Ditto	...	...	
Thohá	...	5	56	Ditto	...	...	
Bedhá	...	1	12	Ditto	...	...	
Usmánpur	...	1	8	Ditto	...	...	
Sangaryán	...	1	12	Ditto	...	...	
Mirah Sagál	...	2	20	Ditto	...	...	
Chanor	...	1	12	Ditto	...	...	
Balhár	...	...	...	...	1	8	Gurmukhi.
Pind Bibá	...	1	8	Koran	...	...	
Sihar	...	1	5	Ditto	...	...	
Nalah Musálmánán	...	1	8	Ditto	...	...	
Nandnah Khyal	...	1	18	Arabic and Persian.	...	...	
Ditto	...	1	2	Koran	...	...	
Giddar Kallah	...	1	2	Ditto	...	...	

Name of Village or Town.	Name of Teacher.	Maktabs.			Gurmukhi Schools.		
		No. of Schools.	No. of Pupils.	Subjects.	No. of Schools.	No. of Pupils.	Subjects.
Tahsil Kahutah—*continued*.							
Munyádah	...	1	15	Arabic and Persian.	...	...	
Darkálí Mamurí	...	2	15	Koran	...	...	
Taryal	...	1	30	Ditto	...	...	
Derah Khalsah	...	4	20	Ditto	...	...	
Sakránah	...	1	25	Ditto	...	...	
Muregálah Magrál	...	1	12	Ditto	...	...	
Kanohá	...	1	15	Ditto	...	...	
Sadá Kamál	...	1	16	Ditto	...	...	
Samot	...	1	25	Ditto	...	...	
Chak Mirzán	...	1	11	Ditto	...	...	
Sodha	...	1	26	Ditto	...	...	
Kalar Badhal	...	1	16	Ditto	...	...	
Manglorah	...	1	24	Ditto	...	...	
Darkali Nia Shahí	...	1	17	Ditto	...	...	
Pindorah	...	1	14	Koran	...	...	
Muregalah Hyál	...	1	14	Arabic and Persian.	...	...	
Kalar Khás	...	1	18	Arabic	...	...	
Guff	...	1	14	Ditto	...	...	
Luní	...	1	7	Ditto	...	...	
Totah	...	1	5	Arabic and Persian	...	...	
Bohrateya	...	1	9	Ditto	...	...	
Kaithal Home	...	1	8	Ditto	...	...	
Súhí	...	1	4	Arabic and Koran	...	...	
Binjár	...	1	10	Ditto	...	...	
Kalitha	...	1	6	Ditto	...	...	
Sái	...	1	6	Arabic	...	...	
Phakhi	...	1	4	Ditto	...	...	
Kalarah	...	1	2	Ditto	...	...	
Batalah	...	1	8	Ditto	...	...	
Kam Kot	...	1	7	Arabic	...	...	
Bhangan	...	1	4	Ditto	...	...	

RAWAL PINDI DIVISION.

SHAHPUR DISTRICT.

GENERAL ABSTRACT.

District.	No. of maktabs.	No. of pupils.	No. of Sanscrit and Nagri schools.	No. of pupils.	No. of Gurmukhi schools.	No. of pupils.	No. of Lande and Mahajani schools.	No. of pupils.	Total No. of Indigenous schools.	Total No. of pupils.
Shahpur	435	5,287	28	460	63	1,249	14	286	540	7,282

SHAHPUR.—Among *Maulvis*, Maulvi Ghulám Murtezá holds a distinguished place at Birbal; he is an authority on religious matters in this village.

There are two large maktabs at Shahpur and Birbal in this circle, both attached to mosques, in which Mián Qáim Din and Maulvi Ghulám Murtezá teach the Koran in the first, and the Koran and Muhammadan law in the second maktab, to 55 and 50 pupils respectively. The former takes some bread as a stipend, and the latter teaches gratuitously.

The number of Gurmukhi schools is 2, one at Shahpur and the other at Bhakkar, both attached to Dharmsalas, in which Bhai Ásárám, disciple of Bhai Rám Kishen and Bhai Kishen Singh, teach Gurmukhi to 28 and 25 pupils respectively. They are supplied with bread.

NURPUR.—Among the names of distinguished *Maulvis*, *Bhais*, and *Pandits* brought to notice, are found those of Maulvi Ghulám Ali, son of Mián Razá Muhammad, and Maulvi Qáim Din, son of Fatah Din; Bhai Gharib Dás, disciple of Bhai Raliá Rám Mahant, Bhai Sobhá Rám, disciple of Bhai Átmá Rám, and Bhai Vishan Dás, disciple of Khem Chand, and Pandit Girdhári Rám, at Nurpur, Bhai Lakshmi Dás, disciple of Bhai Raliá Ram, at Rangpur, Ghulam Husain, son of Muhammad Yár, at Pilo Des, Jáná, son of Fakir Paoli at Buland, and Sultán, son of Kálú Páoli at Nawán Sagú.

The largest maktab at Núrpur is attached to the private house of the teacher Maulvi Ghulám Ali, son of Mián Razá Muhammad, of Núrpur, who teaches the Koran to 25 pupils. He teaches gratuitously.

The following are the smaller maktabs in this circle:—

1st—Núrpur,	with 47	pupils being	instructed in	the Koran.
2nd—Buland	„ 12	„	„	„
3rd—Pilo Des	„ 10	„	„	„
4th—Nawán Sagú	„ 8	„	„	„

Núrpur has 1 pátshala attached to the private house of the teacher, where Pandit Girdhári Rám teaches gratuitously Sanscrit grammar to 10 pupils.

The largest Gurmukhi school in this circle is the one at Núrpur, attached to the Dharmsala of Jagta, in which Bhai Gharib Dás, disciple of Bhai Raliá Rám Mohant. teaches gratuitously Gurmukhi to 28 pupils. There are two smaller Gurmukhi schools also mentioned, one under Sobha Ram with 24 pupils and the other under Vishen Das with 15 pupils. Another Gurmukhi school is at Rangpur with 15 pupils.

Núrpur has also a Mahajani school, attended by 20 pupils, being taught in Lande by Pandit Girdhári Rám. He teaches gratuitously, but takes what is offered.

MATÁ TIWÁNÁ.—The Police return states that Maulvi Qázi Shaikh Ahmad, his son Fazal Ahmad, and Maulvi Wali Muhammad at Matá Tiwáná, and Mián

Sharaf Din at Wárcháh, Maulvi Ghulám Muhiuddin at Utrá, are best known in this circle.

The largest maktabs in this circle are: **3 at Matá Tiwáná, 1 at Wárchhá, and 1 at** Utráh. The first 3 are attached to mosques, in which Maulvi Wali Muhammad, Qazi Shaikh Ahmad, with his son Fazal Ahmad, and Faiz Ahmad teach the Koran, Muhammadan law, Syntax, Prosody, and *Tafsir*, to 15, 10 and 10 pupils, respectively. Their income is not fixed; some give presents on marriage occasions and bread every Thursday. The fourth is attached to the mosque of Mián Sharf Din, in which Mián Sharf Din teaches gratuitously the Koran to 10 pupils. The fifth is attached to the *Khám*, mosque, attended with 15 pupils, whom Ghulám Mohiuddin teaches the Koran and derives his income in the same way as the first three.

There are 5 large Gurmukhi schools, 3 at Matána Tiwáná, of which 1 is attached to the Dharmsala Kalán, attended by 60 pupils, *viz.*, 25 under Bhai Vaisákhi, and 35 under Bhai Sant Sing, being taught in Gurmukhi. The teachers' income is not fixed, but people give what they please, when any pupil finishes his studies. The second and third ones are attached to the Dharmsalas of Kalián Singh and Mehr Singh, with 5 and 10 pupils, under Bhai Lachhman Dás and Hazúr Singh; the fourth and fifth are attached to the Dharmsalas Kalán and of Tulla, in which 20 and 8 pupils are being taught by Amar Singh and Chain Singh. Gurmukhi only is taught in all these schools, and the teachers have no certain income except what is presented to them from time to time.

Matá Tiwáná has one Mahajani school, with 8 pupils, under Uttam Arorá, who teaches Lande gratuitously.

A great number of Musulmans have left this neighbourhood on account of scanty rains, and gone elsewhere for labour, hence the number of pupils attending schools is very small; otherwise the schools under Qazi Ahmad, Fazl Ahmad, and his son, and Maulvi Wali Muhammad of Matá Tiwáná, are most remarkable.

HADLI.—Ghulám Yásin is mentioned as a superior Hakim.

The maktabs are at *Kattá Sangrál, Kattá Huzrál, Wahir, Jibbi* and *Nali*, attached to mosques, with 14, 16, 12, 42 and 21 pupils, under Ahmad Din Barkhurdar and Faqir Muhammad, Fazl Karim, Ghulám Nabi, and Karim Bakhsh, and Bahauddin Sultán, who teach Arabic, and get food and clothing only.

Jibbi has 2 Gurmukhi schools attached to the Dharmsalas, in which Báwá Lachman Dás and Bhai Mangal Singh teach Gurmukhi to 58 (24 girls and 34 boys) and 13 pupils, respectively, and get daily bread from each pupil.

Kattá has one Mahajani school, with 8 pupils, under Shankar Dás, who teaches Lande.

KHUSHÁB.—Among Maulvis, Ghulám Nabi holds a distinguished place.

Khusháb's largest maktab is attached to a mosque in which Ghulám Nabi teaches the Koran to 50 pupils gratuitously. There is also another maktab with 25 pupils.

The following are the other maktabs in this circle:—

Nos. 1 & 2	at Hamoká,	with 40	pupils,	being instructed	in the Koran.
No. 3	„ Muhibpur,	„ 20	„	„	„
„ 4	„ Meli Miánnur,	„ 17	„	„	„
„ 5	„ Tatti Kezá,	„ 8	„	„	„
„ 6	„ Joyá,	„ 10	„	„	„
„ 7	„ Joráh,	„ 14	„	„	„
„ 8	„ Kotlah,	„ 14	„	„	„
„ 9	„ Diwál	„ 14	„	„	„
„ 10	„ Dhák	„ 12	„	„	„
Nos. 11, 12 & 13	„ Rájar,	„ 12	„	„	„
„ 14	„ Nurdáná	„ 15	„	„	„

There are Gurmukhi schools at *Khusháb Hamoká, Joyá* and *Rájar* attended by 25, 17, 12 and 14 pupils.

MATÁ LAK.—The best Hakim and Maulvi is Mián Din Muhammad in this circle He is well up in medicine and has a sound khowledge of teaching; 15 or 16 *Hafizes* are sent out yearly from his school, where he instructs about 25 pupils in the Koran, Persian and Urdu.

NAUSHEHRA.—The best known Hakims are Mian Rajab at Wahdír, and Rajkor Brahman at Naushehra.

There are 7 maktabs:—at *Uchhala*, attached to the house of Alah Yar, Lambardar; at *Jahalar*, attached to the house of Fatah Khan, Lambardar; *Rohrar*, attached to the house of Bhím Saín; at *Sabhral*, attached to the mosque of Mian Muhammad; at *Kafri*, attached to the mosque of Ghulam Muhiuddin; at *Kurri*, attached to the village mosque; and at *Angha*, attached to the mosque of Bahá-uddin Lambardár; in which Kásim Sháh Saiyad, Sadárang, Bhímsaín, Ruk-nuddín, Ghulám Muhiuddin I, Qamruddin and Ghulám Muhiuddin II, teach Persian and Urdu in the first two maktabs, and Arabic in the rest, to 8, 8, 8, 31, 32, 30 and 25 pupils, respectively. The second teacher gets Rs. 5 and the third Rs. 4 per mensem, and the rest teach gratuitously.

There are 5 Gurmukhi schools at *Naushehrá, Khakki, Marúwal, Angá* and *Kafrí*, attached to the Dharmsalas in which Santokh Singh, Báwá Gulab Singh, Bawa Nand Parkash, Bhai Hari Singh and Anokha, teach Gurmukhi to 20, 6, 14, 24 and 15 pupils, respectively, without taking any pay.

The Police return states that the Gurmukhi instruction at Naushehrá, and the Arabic at Kurri are first-rate; but that Persian is nowhere well taught in this circle.

BEHRA.—The names of Hakims Shaikh Ahmad, Fazal Ahmad, Khuda Bakhsh, Diwan Duni Chand, and Parab Dial; Maulvis Ghulam Rasul, Amir Husain; Pandits Bhagwan Das, Parab Dial, Shiva Narain, Karam Chand, Jagan-Nath, Ram Narain and Shankar Das; and Bhais Juala Singh, Sukha Singh, and Bhai Kesho Das of Bhera, deserve to be mentioned.

There are 5 maktabs in this circle: four at *Bhera*, one attached to the mosque of Gondewala; the other attached to the mosque of Hafiz Mardan; the third attached to the private house of Uttam Singh; and the fourth attached to the mosque of Parachhánwali; one at Gondpur, attached to the village mosque in which Shamsuddin, Sharfuddin, Gulab Rai, Ghulam Rasul and Fazal Din teach, in the first two maktabs, the Koran, Muhammadan law, and Persian; in the third Persian, Urdu, Hindi and Sarafi; in the fourth, Muhammadan law, Hadis, Syntax and Prosody; and in the fifth, only the Koran to 35, 10, 25, 12 and 16 pupils, respectively. The first 3 teachers get Rs. 1 each in cash monthly, and the fourth and fifth have no income from their sohools.

There are 4 pátshalas at Behra: 1st at Muhalla Gusayanwala, attached to a private house; 2nd at Muhalla Chuharyan, attached to the temple of Sukha Missar; 3rd at Muhalla Sanhawála, attached to the house of Ratan Singh, Native Doctor; and 4th at Behra, attached to the Dharmsala of Bhai Ram Rat-tan; the last named has at present no pupils in attendance as it has only been started in August 1882 (the teachers will be supported from subscriptions raised amongst the Hindus of the town) in which 15, 12, and 10 pupils are being taught by Shankar Das, Shiva Narain and Jagan Nath; in the first, Grammar *Durga Path, Shigr Bodh*, and *Veds* are instructed; in the second, Grammar and six Shastras and *Sarasut Chandrika*; in the third, Grammar, and Astrology. The teachers get no fixed income.

A private informant gives the following list of Sanscrit schools in this district:—

No. 1, at BEHRA, under	Mothra Das,	with 15 pupils	learning Hindi and Sanscrit.
No. 2 „ „ „	G[illegible] ain Strut,	„ 50 „	„ „
No. 3 „ „ „	Prabhu Dial	„ 40 „	„ „

No. 4, at Behra, under Bahí Badho, with 30 pupils learning Hindi and Sanscrit.
No. 5 ,, ,, ,, Soharun Strut, ,, 36 ,, ,, ,,
No. 6 ,, ,, ,, Maya Das ,, 14 ,, ,, ,,
No. 7 ,, ,, ,, Jhangi ,, 20 ,, ,, ,,
No. 8 ,, ,, ,, Kashinam ,, 10 ,, ,, ,,
No. 9 ,, ,, ,, Waiddat ,, 12 ,, ,, ,,
No. 10 ,, ,, ,, Gulab Rai ,, 15 ,, ,, ,,

There are four Gurmukhi schools:—at *Behra*, attached to the Dharmsala of Bawa Juala Singh; at *Achron*, *Gondpur*, and *Hafizabad*, attached to the Dharmsalas; in which 10, 20, 25 and 10 pupils are being taught by Bava Juala Singh Bedi, Bhai Sota Singh, Bhai Sota Singh 2nd, and Gurdit Singh, respectively.

The subjects taught in the first school are Gurmukhi, *Japji* and *Sukhmani*, &c., and in the rest only Gurmukhi. The first and fourth teachers receive no pay, but the second and third get Rs. 1 each in kind monthly.

Behra has 2 Mahajani schools with 35 and 12 pupils, under Kesho Das and Hakim Parab Dial. In the first Lande and Sanscrit is taught, and in the second Persian and Sarafi Lande; the former gets Re. 1 in kind monthly, and the latter gets nothing.

Miani.—Among the names of distinguished Hakims and Pandits, are found that of Hasan Dín, Khudá Bakhsh, Ghulám Dastgir and Mián Núr Husain, Pandit Ladhá Rám and Pandit Káshi Rám.

There are three maktabs at *Miani*, attached to mosques, one at *Kotli Subhan* attached to a mausoleum (*Rozah*), and the 5th at *Chak Dadán*, attached to a mosque; they are attended by 110, 50 and 20 pupils respectively, in which Ghulám Dastgir, Hafiz Sultán, Mián Nur Hasan, Mohkam Din and Alim Din teach Arabic and Persian in the first and the Koran in the rest, without getting from the schools any income.

Miáni has two pátshalas with 10 and 15 pupils, under Pandit Kashi Ram and Thákur Dás, who teach in the first Grammar, *Shigr Bodh* and *Astrology*, and in the second, Grammar, *Garur*, *Magh* and *Katik*, without any income.

The Gurmukhi schools are 3; *viz.*, 2 at *Badshapur* and 1 at *Haryá*; the first is attached to a Dharmsálá, the second and third to shops, in which Shankar Das, Thakur Das and Pandit Atma Ram teach gratuitously Gurmukhi and Lande in the first two schools and only Gurmukhi in the third, to 20, 23 and 25 pupils, respectively.

Miáni has one Mahajani school with 35 pupils, who are taught in Gurmukhi and Lande, by Maya Das Ojha, gratuitously.

Chak Rám Das.—The Police return states that Hakim Ojha Devi Das of Chak Ram Das, who is a good scholar in Gurmukhi, Sanscrit and Lande, Maulvi Mian Gul Ahmad, who is distinguished for his knowledge of Arabic and Persian, and Karm Bakhsh, who is well up in Arabic and medicine, enjoy the highest reputation in this circle.

There are 3 maktabs in this circle; 1 at *Chak Ram Das*, 1 at *Chawah*, and 1 at *Sada Kamboh*, attached to mosques, in which Mian Gul Ahmad, Karm Bakhsh and Mián Roshan teach Arabic and Persian to 12, 12 and 16 pupils respectively. No fixed income is received by the teachers but they take presents.

Chak Ram Das has one pátshala attached to a private house in which 25 pupils are being taught in the Shastras, Gurmukhi and Lande, by Ojha Devi Das, who takes what people are pleased to offer him Some give Rs. 5, 10 or 15, when they finish their studies.

Jhawarya.—Pandit Hukam Chand and Maul [illegible] in Muhammad at *Jhawarya*, Pandit Hakim Rai and Hakim Ruku Hajam at *Kot Bahal; Khan*, Hakim Bhai Lorindra Ram at *Chak Musa*, and Hakim Sadhu Ram at *Gagwal*, and Maulvi Mian Muhammad Khalil are mentioned as superior men.

The largest maktab in this circle is at Bharat, in which Maulvi Muhammad Khalíl teaches Arabic and Persian, on Rs. 4 per mensem, in kind, to 14 pupils.

The following smaller maktabs are mentioned also in this circle :—

Nos. 1 and 2	at Kálrá,	with 16	pupils	learning	Arabic and Persian.
Nos. 3, 4 and 5	„ Kot Baháí Khán,	„ 48	„	„	The Koran.
No. 6	„ Jawarya,	„ 15	„	„	Arabic and Persian.
Nos. 7 and 8	„ Kot Kamú,	„ 12	„	„	The Koran.
No. 9	„ Kadalhti,	„ 7	„	„	„
No. 10	„ Kotti Awán,	„ 5	„	„	„
No. 11	„ Khurshed,	„ 15	„	„	„
Nos. 12 and 13	„ Ghaghwál,	„ 28	„	„	„
No. 14	„ Khanjar,	„ 6	„	„	„
No. 15	„ Khuájabad,	„ 10	„	„	„

Jhawarya has a large Gurmukhi school attached to the Dharmsala, in which Bhai Sant Ram and Bhai Ratan (blind) teach at Rs. 2 per mensem in money and kind, Gurmukhi to 30 pupils. The small Gurmukhi schools in this circle, are as under :—

No. 1, at Chak Musá,	with 25	pupils	learning	Gurmukhi.
„ 2, „ Kálráh,	„ 10	„	„	„
„ 3, „ Kot Baháí Khan	„ 6	„	„	„
„ 4, „ Kadlahti	„ 5	„	„	„

As there is no Mahajani school in this circle, the Hindus teach their sons in their shops themselves. The Hindus of Jhawarya and Chak Musa are very fond of learning Lande character, besides Gurmukhi. Many *Háfizes*, who are blind in this circle, and live in the mosques, teach the Koran by rote.

There is no pátshala in this cirle.

Kot Momin.—There are 4 maktabs in this circle : maktab No. 1 at *Kot Momin* is attached to the mosque of Maulvi Muhammad Sadíq, in which Ali Muhammad teaches 24 pupils gratuitously in the Koran ; No. 2 *Kot Kala* is attached to a private house, in which Faiz Muhammad teaches Arabic and Persian gratuitously to 12 pupils. The maktabs Nos. 3 *Taspal*, and 4 *Takmiana*, are attached to the village mosques, with 10 and 25 pupils, under Ghulám Nabi (2nd teacher's name is not mentioned in the Police return), who teach Persian and the Koran ; the former gets Rs. 5 per month.

The Gurmukhi schools are 2 in number : one at *Rám Rahán*, and the other at *Jalalpur*, the first attached to a private house and the second to a Dharmsala ; in which Thákur Dás and Charan Dás teach Gurmukhi and Lande in the former, and only Gurmukhi in the latter, to 20 and 12 pupils respectively, without having any income from the schools.

Sahiwal.—Hakim Abdul Karim, Baid Amir Chand, Maulvi Gulám Mustafa, and Pandit Sawan are well known in this circle. The maktabs mentioned in this circle are 8 :—at *Dinpur*, *Retri*, *Kot Gul*, two at *Garot*, *Haweli*, *Nathoká*, *Deráh*, and *Handwi* all attached to mosques except the last one, which is attached to a private house in which Fatah Darya, Mian Muhammad, Ghulám Muhiuddin, Abdulali, Sharf Din, Fazl Din, Ghulam Muhammad and Hafiz Karim Bakhsh, teach gratuitously the Koran, Persian and Arabic and Muhammadan law, to 27, 15, 7, 12, 30, 30, 13, and 20 pupils, respectively.

Farokha has one pátshala, with 40 pupils, under Pandit Rámkishen, who teaches gratuitously the Shastras and Hindi.

The 7 Gurmukhi schools are three at *Sahiwal*, one at Garot, one at *Farokha*, one at *Derah* and one *Wajha*, all attached to Dharmsalas, in which Bhai Jhandaram, Bhai Kanhaiyaram, Baba Gobindram, Bhai Gian Singh, Bhai Mata Singh, Baba Saín Das, and Baba Karm Das, teach gratuitously Gurmukhi to 60, 6, 30, 20, 10, 15, 20 pupils, respectively.

Farokha has also a Mahajani school, attended by 26 pupils, under Khallá, who teaches Hindi and Lande characters to 26 pupils. His pay is not fixed.

Madh.—Maulvi Ali Muhammad, Pandit Shib Dial, and Hakim Fazluddin may be referred to as the men supposed to be most eminent.

There are 3 maktabs:—at *Madh*, *Guana*, and *Nawankot*; the first and the third are attached to mosques, and the second to a private house, in which 5, 11 and 7 pupils are being taught; in the first maktab Arabic and Persian, and in the 2nd and 3rd only Persian by Maulvi Ali Muhammad, Muhammad Khán and Hasan Muhammad, respectively. The 1st and the 3rd teachers receive each Rs. 4 per mensem in kind, and the second Rs. 5 in kind.

There are 2 Gurmukhi schools at *Takht Hazara* and *Talibwala*, attached to the Dharmsala with 15 and 18 pupils, under Nanak Singh and Sher Singh who teach Gurmukhi, and receive in kind Rs. 2 and 3 per mensem.

Madh has one Mahajani school, with 25 pupils, under Lakhmidas Pandha, who teaches Lande, and gets Rs. 2 per mensem in cash.

Note.—The following list shows 383 schools and 4,399 pupils more than in the General Abstract of Part III; it was received at the last moment when the Abstract was already printed off.

EXTRA LIST.

The district return adds the following schools:—

Bhera.—Maktabs, 19 at *Bhera* with 260 pupils, 1 in *Alipur* with 12, 2 in *Hijka* with 20, 1 in *Zainpur* with 8, 1 in *Gaga* with 8, 1 in *Chhat* with 8, 1 in *Shaikhupur* with 5, 1 in *Duhan* with 20, in *Fatahgarh* with 8; Mahajani school, 1 in *Duhan* with 10 pupils.

Miani.—Maktabs, 1 in *Gawandpur* with 30, *Chak Saida* 2 with 20, *Kalyanpur* 2 with 27, *Kalas* 2 with 14, *Dhili* 1 with 8, *Kotli Gul Mahammad* 1 with 9, *Banna Mianwala* 1 with 5, *Bharat* 1 with 6, *Pind Rahim Shah* 1 with 22, *Kot Mukarram* 1 with 5, Burj 1 with 3, *Ghoghgat* 1 with 10, *Namtas* 1 with 8, *Raipur* 1 with 6, *Chillar* 1 with 5, *Achran* 1 with 10, *Ranshanpur* 1 with 6, *Duhan* 1 with 20, *Hazurpur* 2 with 15, *Awan* 1 with 7, *Wajki* 1 with 10, *Wairulwal* 1 with 20, *Kot Sanblanwala* 1 with 10, *Jiwanwal* 1 with 5, *Pind Makku* 1 with 10, *Khazar* 1 with 7, *Mona* 1 with 6, *Fakhuwal* 1 with 10, *Sagh* 2 with 13, *Kot Ahmad Khan* 1 with 3; Mahajani school 1 at *Miani* with 30 pupils, 1 in *Gawandpur* with 32.

Khushab.—Maktabs, 15 at *Khushab* with 182 pupils, *Kirpalka* 2 with 15, *Muhammad Shah* 2 with 9, *Jalalpur* 1 with 6, *Tibba Kayam Din* 1 with 4, *Meli Pir Bakhsh* 2 with 20, *Shaikwal* 1 with 4, and *Nami Wali* 2 with 6; Mahajani school at *Khushab* with 25 and in *Joya* with 6; a Gurmukhi school in *Hamuka* with 17, and 2 patshalas at *Khushab* with 24 pupils.

Sahiwal.—Maktabs, 13 at *Sahiwal* with 210 pupils, 2 in *Lakkhiwal* with 34, 2 in *Dhul Kadhewali* with 24, *Dinpur* 1 with 25, *Bhalliwala* 1 with 12, *Tatti Shahani* 2 with 30, *Handwi* 1 with 14, *Kela* 1 with 10, *Tatti Umar* 1 with 10, *Bura* 1 with 12, *Tatti Yaru* 1 with 7, *Pola* 1 with 32, *Badriwan* 1 with 7, *Shaikh Jalil* 2 with 25, *Nihang* 2 with 38, *Jahanyan Shah* 2 with 14.

Kot Nurbahar Shah 1 with 4, *Chawiki* 1 with 3, *Phuki* 2 with 8, *Aki* 1 with 3, *Saliga* 1 with 2, *Sial Sharif* 2 with 18, *Bugga* 1 with 5; 5 pátshalas at *Sahiwal* with 25; Gurmukhi schools 1 in *Sahiwal* with 60, 1 in *Shaik Jalil* with 5 and 1 with *Badarbhaun* with 26. There are Koran schools also in *Wattu*, *Dhupsari* and *Dhul* with 20, 12 and 8 pupils.

Hadali.—Maktabs in *Hadali*, *Kond*, *Chuha*, *Chinki* and *Basti Sher* with 18, 10, 8, 12 and 8 pupils; and Gurmukhi schools in *Hadali* and *Butala* with 40 and 6 pupils.

Matta Tiwana.—Maktabs in *Bindial*, *Khagli*, *Okhli*, *Monhla*, *Auli*, *Panja* with 60, 9, 10, 4 and 10 pupils.

Kattu.—Maktabs in *Karar*, *Tilokar*, *Daiwal*, *Pindi*, *Mallhuwal* and *Nari* with 7, 12, 13, 12, 2 and 8 pupils.

Nausharha.—Maktabs in *Nausharha* 1 with 25 pupils, *Sodhi* 2 with 16, *Surki* 1 with 7, *Khakki* 2 with 22, *Dahdar* 2 with 16, *Maruwal* 6 with 47, *Khotka* 1 with 12.

NURPUR.—Gurmukhi schools in *Roda* and *Rangpur* with 15 and 10 pupils respectively.

SHAHPUR.—Maktabs in *Shahpur Cantonments* 8 with 34, in *Akilshah* 8 with 28, in Jalalpur 1 with 20, in *Shahpur* 6 with 88, in *Chak Fatah Khan* 1 with 5, in *Chalpana* 1 with 7, in *Bhakkar* 3 with 49, and in *Nathuwala* 1 with 12. Gurmukhi schools in *Shahpur, Akilshah, Kotla Sayyidan* with 55, 5 and 15 pupils.

KANDAL.—Three maktabs in *Kandal Kalan* with 19 pupils, 8 in *Kandal Khurd* 3 with 14, 1 in *Tankiwala* with 20, 1 in *Khachki* with 7, 1 in *Gujranwala* with 7, 1 in *Tatti Sayyidan* with 22.

DHARIMA.—*Dharima, Bhakki, Jahanabad, Shah Yusuf, Manguwal Kalan Manguwal Khurd* and *Shahuwali* have maktabs in each with 15, 5, 5, 11, 45, 8 and 15 pupils. *Dharima* has also a Gurmukhi school with 30 pupils.

SAHUWAL.—There are maktabs in *Sahuwal, Sink, Mangeyab, Sultanpur, Tatti Muklim, Nizamabad, Bonga Billuchan Bonga Jhamahian, Bonga Saghwal, Chakrala, Gondal, Mochiwal, Tatti Hargan, Tatti Lamleni, Dhiruwal, Jalla Biluchan, Chandna, Mahkushan* with 14, 10, 8, 24, 5, 11, 9, 6, 6, 4, 12, 5, 3, 4, 5, 8, 8, 6 and 4 pupils. There is a Gurmukhi school also in *Tatti muklim* with 20 pupils.

DERA.—*Jarah* has 3 maktabs with 12 pupils, *Shaik* with 6, *Mubarikhan* 1 with 5, *Kamala* 1 with 17, *Rathana* 1 with 8, *Dehra* 1 with 8, *Gul Bibi* 1 with 11 and *Tatta Jhajjan* 1 with 7 pupils.

FARUKHA.—*Kalyar ,Sajjuka, Tatta Muhammad Panah, Tatti Jalal, Muradwalla, Wala, Boran, Tirkhanwala, Sahba, Mir Ahmad and Muhammad Aliwala* have a maktab each with 4, 22, 8, 7, 5, 16, 8, 3, 19, 6 and 7, pupils.

BIRHAL.—There are 3 maktabs in *Birhal* with 46, 1 in *Kot Maghrim* with 24 3 in *Chachar* with 63 and 1 in *Kot Pahalwan* with 5, and *Chachar* has also 8 Gurmukhi schools with 32 pupils.

JHAWARYA.—*Jhawarya* has 5 maktabs with 88 pupils, *Diwal* 1 with 6, *Jora* 1 with 4, *Chak Shekha* 1 with 4, and *Gangwal* 2 with 46 pupils.

CHAK RAM DAS.—*Bisrai* has 1 maktab with 20, *Dhodhi* 1 with 7 *Dhakwan* 2 with 5, *Aurkhaniwala* 1 with 20, *Bannah* 1 with 8, *Bonga Sukhra* 1 with 17, *Notha* 1 with 7, *Saydpur* 1 with 2, *Khan Muhammadwala* 3 with 18 *Ranjhawala* 1 with 10, *Dhal* 1 with 6, *Kot Malak Hakim Khan* 1 with 15 pupils.

MALKWAL.—*Chak Dadal* (3 maktabs), *Kothra, Malakwal Chak Nizam, Nasirpur, Chakrah, Bula* and *Kothala* have maktabs with 40, 30, 10, 14, 10, 12, 30 and 7 pupils.

HARYA.—There are maktabs in *Harya, Badshahpur* (3 maktabs), *Kartuwal, Shamari, Daira Alam Shah, Mal, Bhuluwal, Rukan* (2 maktabs), *Busal* (4 maktabs) and *Bhujuwal* with 6, 14, 10, 4, 27, 6, 3, 13 and 31 pupils.

KOT MOMIN.—*Bhahra* has 1 maktab with 8 pupils, *Sunda* 1 with 7, *Bhajan* 1 with 10, *Salim* 1 with 5, *Dhagrala* 1 with 6, *Kot Umrana* 1 with 8, *Buchkalam* 2 with 24, *Ad Rahman* 2 with 27, *Kot Sher Mohamad* 1 with 4, *Bhajuwal* 1 with 10, *Jajarur* 1 with 6, *Raharka* (both) 2 with 15, *Bhabra* and *Bhajan* have also Gurmukhi schools with 8 and 12 pupils.

MADH.—Maktabs in *Mohriwal, Ghaiwala, Tardianwala, Rahal, Dulliwala, Chak Suleman, Ramdyana, Ghaus Muhammadwala, Khambnan, Badin, Sidun, Chak Shojawal, Garhi Kala, Jalap, Kot Ghazi Khurd, Rahimpur, Kotla Panah* and *Tathla Baira* with 13, 2, 3, 14, 4, 5, 7, 2, 8, 3, 8, 14, 7, 3, 4, 2, 17 and 7 pupils. *Mianakot* has a pátshala with 20 and *Nawankot* a Mahajani school with 13 pupils.

DUDH.—*Jala, Makhsen Matila* and *Lalbani* have also maktabs with 4, 30, 10, 8 and 35 pupils. *Dudh* has a Mahajani school with 10 pupils.

MATH LAK.—There are maktabs in *Sidwana, Tanguwali, Chokra, Kot Changhatta, Samuranwali, Badar, Jalalpur* and *Mattalak* with 8, 10, 12, 8, 7, 19, 22 and 12 pupils.

RAWALPINDI DIVISION.

JHELUM DISTRICT.

GENERAL ABSTRACT.

District.	No. of Maktabs and Madrasas.	No. of pupils.	No. of Sanscrit Schools.	No. of pupils.	No. of Gurmukhi Schools.	No. of pupils.	No. of Mahajani Schools.	No. of pupils.	No. of Indigenous Schools.	No. of pupils in the Indigenous Schools.
Jhelum .	200	3,093	119	294	27	646	4	59	250	4,092

Jhelum.—The distinguished Maulvis in this circle mentioned in the Police returns, are Maulvi *Nur Ahmad* and Maulvi *Nur Alam* of *Khai Kotli*, and Maulvi *Barhánuddin* of Jhelum. The former two teach the Koran, Arabic Grammar, Muhammadan law, &c., to 10 pupils in the village mosque of *Khai Kotli*. Maulvi Barhánuddin, a good Arabic scholar, teaches all branches of Arabic learning to 10 pupils. The income of the Maulvi consists in 2 topas (a measure) of corn at harvest time from each house.

A private informant adds the names of the following Maulvis (who are said to be good Arabic scholars), with the particulars of the schools they conduct :—

Maulvi *Nur Alam*, teaching 10 pupils in the village of *Kari*.
,, *Ghulam Mahiuddin*, instructing 7 pupils in *Zahur*.
,, *Azimulla*, teaching 15 boys in *Chhanwat*.
,, *Ibrahim*, teaching 10 pupils in *Jahangir*.
,, *Shamsuddin*, instructing 8 pupils in *Phinbar*.

All these Maulvis teach Urdu, Persian, Arabic, Muhammadan law (Waqaya and Hedaya), Grammar, Logic, Tafsir and Hadis. They live on the produce of their lands. The number of their pupils is also fluctuating in different parts of the year. In the period of cultivation and famine the number decreases much.

The private return says that the Maulvis of this circle held rent-free tenures under the Mughals, but that these were resumed by the Sikhs.

The other indigenous Madrasas and maktabs given in a private return are the following :—

Place.	Teachers.	Subjects.	No. of Pupils.
Nogran	Ghulam Muhiuddin . . .	The Koran, Urdu & Persian	10
Suela	Ghulam Haidar	Do.	12
Kontrela	Mohammad Alim	Do.	10
Darhála	Murtazá	Do.	9
Janjil	Mohammad Hayat. . . .	Do.	8
Jaghta	Hafiz Mohammad . . .	Do.	11
Ghura Ahmad	Jan Mohammad	Do.	10
Ghai	Karam Din	Do.	12
Bhatya	Fazluddin	Do.	9
Bhunbli	Imamuddin	Do.	7
Bholula	Hafiz	Do.	9
Khengerpur	Karam Din	Do.	8
Muftiyan	Alam Sher	Do.	10
Jada	Kahi Bux and Nur Muhammed	Do.	20
Dinah	Nizamuddin	Do.	10

Pátshalas. The Police returns mention only 2 patshalas, *viz.*, (1) under *Mast Ram*, disciple of Har Bhajan Dass, with 30 pupils (private informant gives 40); (2) under *Pundit Suchanand* with 20 pupils (private informant gives 30), the same private return adding the names of *Arjan Das, Har Narayen, Barkat Ram, Sita Ram*, and *Mote Ram*, who teach Sanscrit to 12, 9, 14, 10 and 8 pupils, respectively.

AHMADABAD.—Among Maulvis and Hakims in this circle, Maulvi *Ghulám Nabi* of Lilla Behrwana, and Hakim *Qadir Bakhsh* of Ahmadabad are brought to notice by the Police returns, but a private return adds the names of Hakims *Sultan Bakhsh* and *Alim Din* of Lilla Behrwana, Maulvi *Baháuddin* of Ahmadabád, Maulvi *Ghulám Hasan* of Dhodhi, and Maulvi *Ghulam Muhammad* and *Jiwaya* of Lilla Behra. Hakim Qadir Bakhsh is said to be an author of some medical works, and *Tazál Husain* a poet in Persian and Urdu.

The Madrasas mentioned in the Police and private returns are as follow. (The Police mentions only 2) :—

PLACE.	Teachers.	No. of pupils.	Subjects taught.
Lilla Behrwana	Ghulám Nabi and Jiwaya	30	Arabic Grammar, Logic, Rhetoric, Philosopy, Mudammadan law, Tafsir and Hadis.
Ahmadabád	Baháuddin	6	Ditto ditto.
Ditto	Qadir Bakhsh	5	Ditto ditto.
Ditto	Karam Din	10	The Koran.
Lilla	Ghulam Muhammad	25	Arabic Grammar, Logic, Law, Rhetoric, &c.
Ditto	Séyyad Ghulám Sháh	4	Ditto ditto.
Ditto	Hafiz Shamsuddin (who takes 8 annas for each section of Koran).	20	The Koran.
Mundáhar Ditto	Hafiz Azam } 2 maktabs	22	Ditto.
Kotla	Khuda Bakhsh	12	Ditto.
Dhodi	Ghulám Hasan	10	Grammar, Logic, Law, Jurisprudence, Medicine, Tafsir, Hadis, &c.
Aththar	Mehdi Karam Din } 2 maktabs.	24	The Koran.
Saroba	......	20	Ditto.
Malvar	......	8	......

In *Ahmadabád*, Bhai Bishan Dás holds a free-rent tenure, but does not teach anybody.

TUMMAN.—Bhai Amar Das, Udási Fakir and Maulvi Mir Alam (son of Akhún Zada) both good Persian scholars of Tumman, and *Bhai* Amar Singh of Lada, and Sayyed Jalál, a distinguished Maulvi in Dholi, are brought to notice as eminent scholars.

In *Tumman*, Bhai Amar Dass and Maulvi Mir Alam have each a maktab, the former teaching Urdu, Persian and Arithmetic to 9 pupils, and the latter teaching Urdu, Persian and Arabic to 21 pupils gratuitously.

There are 5 more maktabs in *Tumman* with 25 pupils, and 3 maktabs with 47 pupils in *Lada*.

Lada has also a Gurmukhi school, in which Bhai Amir Sing teaches Gurmukhi to 16 pupils, and is paid Rs. 5 per mensem by Baba Khem Singh.

DUMMAN.—Hakims *Nihal Singh* of Bhin, and *Muhammad Shah* of Dharuki; Maulvis *Muhammad Hasan* of Galis, *Farman Ali* of Langáh, *Karam Din* of Mohra Mat, *Qazi Ghulam Muhammad* and *Ahmad Din* of Saba Mora are brought to notice as distinguished among the Hakims and Maulvis of this circle.

The Police returns mention only a maktab in the village of *Bhín*, conducted by Fatah Din, who teaches Urdu, Persian and Arithmetic to the primary examination standard to 26 boys, and receives 4 annas a month from each boy; and a Gurmukhi and a Lande school in the village of *Saidpur*, under Mussammat Lachhmi (wife of Sookhdyal Bráhman), and Ram Jiwaya respectively, with 16 girls in the former and 16 boys in the latter. Mussammat Lachhmi is paid by Baba Khem Singh of Rawalpindi.

A private return adds the following Koran and Perso-Arabic schools :—

Place.	Teachers.	Number of pupils.	Subjects taught.
Langáh	Farmán Ali (a good Arabic scholar).	45	The Koran and advanced books in Arabic and Persian.
Chikora	Muhammad Hasan . .		
Galas	Muhammad Husain . .		
Chawantryan	. . . . .	12	Ditto.
Juni	. . . . .	20	Ditto.
Mogla	. . . . .	12	Ditto and Persian.
Mondi	. . . . .	8	Ditto.
Júr	. . . . .	12	Ditto.
Bhubar	. . . . .	20	Ditto.
Kál	. . . . .	30	Ditto.
Lohir	. . . . .	8	Ditto.
Domali	. . . . .	30	Ditto.
Dura	. . . . .	10	Ditto.
Mohra Aluwala	. . . . .	12	The Koran, Arabic and Persian.

TALA GANG.—Among *Maulvis*, Maulvi Karim Bakhsh, of Tala Gang, and Maulvi Muhammad Hasan, of Mirjan; and among *Pandits* and *Bháis*, Pandit Ghani Shám and Bhai Dyál Singh of Tala Gang, may be mentioned.

Tala Gang has a *Gurmukhi* school attached to a Dharmsala and conducted by Bhai Dyál Sing, who teaches Gurmukhi to 60 pupils gratuitously.

Tala Gang has also a *pátshala* with 4 pupils, in which Sanscrit is taught.

The other Gurmukhi schools in this circle are in the villages of *Jatha*, *Dharali* and *Darwál* with 6, 30 and 13 pupils respectively.

The following statement will show the number of Koran schools and other particulars regarding them :—

PLACE.	Number of maktabs.	Number of pupils.	Subjects taught.
Tala Gang	1	35	The Koran, Arabic.
Nika Khot	1	18	Ditto.
Saghar	1	30	Ditto.
Chanji	1	16	Ditto.
Thohá Mom	1	30	Ditto.
Malakwál	1	17	Ditto.
Kot Sárang	1	38	Ditto.
Nargi	1	16	Ditto.
Dodial	1	25	Ditto.
Moglá	1	11	Ditto.
Dhular	1	25	Ditto.
Jathá	1	8	Ditto.
Perá Fatiál	1	18	Ditto.
Marján	1	47	Ditto.

Place.	Number of maktabs.	Number of pupils.	Subjects taught.
Bahlúmár	1	8	Koran, Arabic.
Mamdút	1	7	Ditto.
Tebi	1	30	Ditto.
Jasyál	1	19	Ditto.
Kufri	1	30	Ditto.
Chokhady	1	31	Ditto.
Laka Dhan	1	9	Ditto.
Maráli	1	8	Ditto.
Loteri	1	10	Ditto.
Kot Khalán	1	8	Ditto.
Diwál	1	12	Ditto.
Dhok Pathán	1	5	Ditto.
Ekwál	1	20	Ditto.
Dharáhi	1	10	Ditto.
Darwál		22	Ditto.

DINA.—*Munshi* Abdul Karim, Báwá Ram Das, and Pandit Kalyán Dás, of Rohtas, are mentioned in the police returns.

A private informant adds the names of the following Pandits of ROHTAS and schools of Sanscrit which they conduct there :—

Rohtas	Hardat Goshain, teacher	25	pupils.
Do.	Kalian Das ,,	20	,,
Do.	Ram Das ,,	50	,,
Do.	Baij Lal ,,	15	,,
Do.	Thakur Das ,,	10	,,

Pundit Hem Raj has furnished me with the following account of the pátshala at *Fort Rhotas* :—

"The subjects, taught in this pátshala are Astronomy, Astrology, Dharm Shastras, the science of Politics, Purans, Grammar, Geography (on the old lines and out of ancient books), and Literature in general.

"The institution is of very old standing, some of the lands were attached to it dating so far back as the time of Sher Shah Suri, when the grants made to it were more than at any other time except, perhaps, during the rule of Maharaja Runjit Singh. Most of these lands were confiscated by Aurungzeb, but they were more than made good by Maharaja Runjit Singh, who not only made grants of land for the support of the pátshala, but also fixed a percentage on the income of the people of its neighbourhood to be set apart for it. These lands were some of them resumed on the annexation of the Panjab by the British Government, and some on the death of Pandit Trikta Sahoy Goswami, father of the present incumbent. What remains still attached to the pátshala yields only an income of about Rs. 300 per annum. There is in addition another piece of land to the east of Fort Rhotas, called Choubutra, at present in the hands of the younger brother of Pandit Trikta Sahoy Goswami, although he has no right to it."

Pandit Tantram and Ditoo Gosai have also each a school in which Sanscrit, Hindi and Gurmukhi are taught; the number of pupils is not mentioned.

Rohtas has also a *Persian school*, conducted by Munshi Abdul Karim, a good Persian scholar, who teaches Persian to 12 pupils, and a *Gurmukhi* school under Bàwá Ram Das, who teaches Gurmukhi and Lande to 22 pupils.

There is a *Koran school* in the village of *Sagri*, in which Hafiz Karm Din teaches the Koran to 32 pupils.

SOHAWA.—In this circle *Pandit* Kanchiya, *Hakim* Muhammad Alam Qureshi, *Maulvi* Hayat Bakhsh and *Bhai* Nihal Singh, of *Bishandaur*, are referred to as distinguished scholars in their respective branches.

In *Bishand*, Maulvi Hayat Bakhsh and Bibi Shahzadi conduct a *male* and a *female* school respectively, the former teaching Persian and Arabic to 25 boys and the latter teaching the Koran to 20 girls. Their average income is Rs. 2 and Rs. 1 a month respectively.

There is a Gurmukhi school also in Bishandaur attached to a *Dharmsala*, with 20 pupils, who are taught Gurmukhi and Lande by Nihal Singh, whose average income is said to be Rs. 2 per mensem.

KALAR KAHAR.—The distinguished Hakims, Baids, Pandits, Bhais and Maulvis in this circle are *Hakims* Buta Mal and Ram Sahai of Bhon; *Pandits* Jawala Sahai (who is also a Baid), Kirpa Ram and Shankar Das; *Bhais* Arjan Singh and *Maulvis* Muhammad Shah of Bhon, Barhanuddin of Hitan, and Ahmaddin of Balaksar.

In the town of Bhon there are 2 *Koran schools* conducted by Muhammad Din and Jumma (weavers), who teach the Koran to 65 girls and boys. Maulvi Burhanuddin, of Hitar and Maulvi Ahmad Din of Bulaksar, conduct each an Arabic school. They teach Arabic Grammar, Logic, Law, Jurisprudence, &c., to 12 and 10 pupils respectively.

Bhon has also a Gurmukhi school, attached to a Dharmsala, under Bhai Arjan Singh, with 25 pupils, and a Gurmukhi, Lande and Sanscrit school, conducted by Pandit Kirpa Ram, who teaches Sanscrit to 15 pupils, Gurmukhi to 25 pupils, and Lande to 15 pupils, and has no fixed income.

A private informant mentions Gurmukhi schools in the villages of *Murid*, *Karyala*, *Pul Kasar* and Migan, under Sunder Singh, Ramji, Jawahar Singh and Asa Singh, teaching Gurmukhi and the Granth to 12, 20, 46 and 30 pupils respectively.

JELAPUR.—The village of Pannuwal has a Gurmukhi school, where Bhai Kandhara Singh teaches Gurmukhi to 10 pupils and receives 1½ pice a week from each boy.

There are maktabs and Koran schools in the following villages :—

Place.	No. of pupils.	Subjects taught.	Teachers.
Chak Majahid	15	The Koran.	Muhammad Din.
Ara	12	Do.	Mian Khuda Bakhsh.
Ara	20	Persian.	Nek Alam.
Baghanwala	8	Do.	Mian Abdulla.
Chakri Dohmenkhen	12	Do.	Muhammud Din.
Pannuwal	28	Do.	Ahmed Din.

DUMELI.—*Hakim* Bakshi Bishen Singh, *Maulvi* Mahtab Sheh, *Bhai* Narain Das, and Mian Mohammed, a *Poet*, are mentioned by a private informant as noteworthy. The police return mentions only two indigenous schools in this circle—

A maktab in *Phulara Sayadan*, attached to the Divankhana of Sayyad Myaz Ali Shah, Lambardar of the village, in which Mian Abdulla teaches Persian to 18 pupils and receives Rs. 4-8 per mensem and Re. 1-8 from each boy once in six months, and a Lande school in *Dumeli*, where Harnam Das, a Brahmin, teaches Lande to 14 pupils gratuitously. He is said to have taught the boys of the village for 44 years.

A private informant adds the following schools in this circle :—

Place.	Teachers.	Subjects taught.	Number of pupils.
Mohrá Kanál	Qutbuddín	The Koran	18
Bari Darohrá	Fatah dín	Do.	15
Husain Saiyedán	Magtáb Shah	Do. and Muhammadan law.	16
Jaji	Mir Mohammad	The Koran	14
Mahgot	Fatah Mohammad	Persian	10
Miána Mohrá	Mohammad Husain	The Koran and Persian	13
Jabál	Saiyad Ahmad	The Koran	16
Jandot	Imám Din	The Koran and Muhammadan law.	11
Dhok Vagh	Nizám Din	The Koran	12
Bulbul Kalán	Núr Alam	Do.	15
Banbi Saiyidan	Saiyad Rasúl	Do.	16
Sarng Dhan	Malik Mohammad	Do.	14
Sogbál	Abdulláh	Do.	8
Dhok Band (dakhli Sogbál).	. . . . .	Do.	6
Mohra Kanal (Dakhili Mohra Dheri).	. . . . .	Do.	8

Phuleri Sayaden has 1 Gurmukhi school with 12 pupils in which Arithmetic and Gurmukhi are taught.

CHAKWAL.—*Maulvis* Ghulam Husain and Burhanudin and *Pandit* Kahan Chand are said to be good scholars of Arabic and Sanscrit respectively.

The largest *Madrasa* in this circle is in the village of *Udharwál,* in which Maulvi Burhanuddin teaches the Koran, Persian, Muhammadan law and other religious books to 108 pupils.

In *Chakwal* there is a *pátskala* and a Lande school, conducted by Pandit Kahan Chand and Hakim Singh, teaching Sanscrit and Lande and Gurmukhi to 10 and 14 pupils respectively. Hakim Singh receives one pice weekly from each boy and from annas 2 to 4 from each boy when he commences the *pothi* (first reader). The other *Gurmukhi schools* are as follows :—

Bahla	with 16 pupils.		Mangwal	with 40 pupils.
Dewalyan	„ 16 „		Sankal Kaseer	„ 40 „
Chakral	„ 12 „		Latifal	„ 35 „
Tarid	„ 15 „		Mondi	„ 24 „
Dhodhial	„ 40 „		Megan	„ 40 „
Sang	„ 20 „			

The following statement shows the number of Koran and Perso-Arabic schools in this circle :—

Place.	No. of maktabs.	No. of pupils.	Subjects taught.
Didwal	1	16	Persian.
Diwalian	1	81	The Koran
Khewal	1	31	Ditto.
Khotian	1	20	Ditto.
Chakral	1	36	Ditto.
Chak Maluk	1	25	Ditto.
Chak Umra	1	15	Ditto.
Chak Norang	1	18	Ditto.
Farid	1	25	Ditto.
Dhab Kalan	1	25	Arabic and religious books.
Mari	1	25	
Lakhwal	1	22	Ditto.
Dhakkhu	1	16	Persian.
Thua Bahadar	1	40	Ditto.

Pind-Dadan-Khan.—*Maulvis* Muhammad Hasain and Sher Muhammad of *Kheora Namak*, who teach Arabic and Persian to 15 pupils in their native town, and *Hakims* Muhammad Yar of Mirzapur, Kasim Din of Jatipur, Ghulam Rasula Taj Din of Kalewal, Karam Chand of Lund, Jawahri Mal and Ramkor of Nitranpur deserve to be noticed.

The village of *Kasalyan* has a Gurmukhi and a Lande school with 8 pupils.

The following villages have Koran and Perso-Arabic schools :—

Place.	Subjects taught	Teacher.	No. of pupils.	
			Boys.	Girls.
Derá	Arabic	Sharaf Din	1	4
Lahri Panchgaram	Ditto	Kadir Din	10	5
Chandoi	Ditto	Rasmat Ali	15	7
Menwál	Ditto	Mean Jowan	1	2
Parerá	Urdu	Myan Fazal	1	1
Ghorá	Arabic	Imam Bakhsh	8	2
Makhyala	Urdu	Fazal Din	8	1
Salvi	Ditto	Pir Muhammad	1	...
Kask	Arabic	Myan Chirágh	8	5
Kureti	Ditto	Husain	4	...
Harnpur	Arabic, Koran,	Muhammad Ali	4	4
Keora Namak	Koran,	Muhammad Husain	6	...
Chak Ahmad	Koran, Arabic	Ahmed Din	12	...
Adowl	Ditto	Ahmed Bakhsh	3	...
Ditto	Ditto	Muhammad Bakhsh	2	...
Ditto	Ditto	Muhammad	2	...
Golpur	Ditto	Kher Muhammad	4	...
Koráh	Ditto	Fazal Muhammad	7	...
Ditto	Ditto	Kutbuddin	4	...
Dodh Dand	Ditto	Fakir Muhammad	4	...
Barahdi	Ditto	Muhkam Din	4	...
Khotrá	Ditto	Syed Umir Shah	18	...
Hatar	Ditto	Muhammad Din	12	...
Kotsáhib Khán Dákhili Pind.	Persian	Fazal Din	20	5
Pindadan Khán	Arabic	Roshan	20	10
Kotlá Dakhli Pind	Ditto	Alah Din	4	...
Shamanwal	Arabic	Khuda Bakhsh	8	...
Dafar	Ditto	Ditto	6	...
Kaslián (2 schools)	Arabic and Persian	Kadar Bakhsh and Hafez Mian.	25	...
Sidhwál	Ditto	Ainuddin	9	...
Darrah Paráh	Ditto	Cheragh Din	8	...
Sadhandi	Ditto	Kadir Bakhsh	16	...
Gharib wál	Ditto	Muhammad Bakhsh	10	...
Sádowal (2 schools)	Koran and Arabic	Hafez Sahib Din & Muhamad	25	...
Dhartálá (ditto)	Ditto	Khuda Bakhsh and Ghulam Muhamad	80	...
Kohtián Chálab	Ditto	Mian Abdulla	10	...
Karanpur	Ditto	Mian Ahmad	13	...
Dandot	Arabic, and Persian	Ghulam Husain	10	20
Bhaead	Arabic, Koran, &c.,	Nek Muhammad	10	11
Ratochhá	Ditto	Ghulam Husain	4	3
Minhálá	Arabic and Persian	Ghulam Din	3	5
Hawela Sad Sháh	Arabic, Koran, &c.	Mian Musahab	8	4
Khajolá	Ditto	Pir Bakhsh	8	4
Mel	Persian and Arabic, Koran, &c.	Ghulam Husain	5	4
Dabehri Jalsa	Arabic	Ditto	4	6
Chauni Makhdûm	Ditto	Ghulám Muhammad	9	7
Dháli Ballá	Ditto	Main Muhammad	4	2
Bisharat	Arabic and Persian	Syed Muhammad	14	5
Bari Kaláran	Arabic	Ghulám Shah	7	2
Bari Sháh Nawáz	Arabic, Koran	Muhammad Bakhsh	18	1
Lahr Sultanpur	Ditto	Jamil Muhammad	2	3
Mandi Dákhli Pind	Arabic	Ala Bakhsh	7	...
Pind-Dadan-Khán	Persian, Arabic, and Urdu	Ala Datta	12	...
Ditto	Arabic and Persian	Muhammad Sahib Din	40	18
Ditto	Arabic	Habebusrahman	4	4
Ditto	Ditto	Yusaf	12	...
Ditto	Ditto	Ghulám Ahmad	6	...
Ditto	Ditto	Ghulám Muheddin	3	2
Ditto	Ditto	Khuda Bakhsh	12	9
Ditto	Ditto	Samidudin	30	11
Ditto	Ditto	Zaida Alabudin	2	3
Ditto	Ditto	Husain Shah	7	...
Kot Sahib Khán Dakhili Pind	Ditto	Sualeh Muhammad	15	...
Ditto	Ditto	Fazal Muhammad	9	...

There are also two other schools in Pind-Dadan-Khan in which Sanscrit and Hindi are taught by Hakim and Maya Das to 22 and 15 pupils respectively.

RAWALPINDI DIVISION.

GUJRAT DISTRICT.

GENERAL ABSTRACT.

District.	No. of maktabs.	No. of pupils.	No. of Nagri and Sanskrit Schools.	No. of pupils.	No. of Gurmukhi Schools.	No. of pupils.	No. of Lande and Mahajani Schools.	No. of pupils.	Total No. of Indigenous Schools.	Total No. of pupils.
Gujrat .	274	3,828	20	318	53	879	19	393	366	5,418

GUJRAT.—Hakims Khuda Bakhsh and Masum Shah; Maulvi Hafiz Abdulla, Bhais Bhagwan Singh and Ishar Singh deserve to be mentioned; as also, according to reliable private information, Pandits Lakshmi Das, Gobind Ram, Jai Singh, Damodar Das, Chandu Das, Ganesh Das, Naraiyan Das and Nanda Lal, who are in charge of the following Sanscrit schools, in Gujrat City—1 with 10, 1 with 35, 1 with 25; 1 with 14; 1 with 6; 2 with 5 each and 1 with 10 pupils. The subjects taught are, in the first Sanscrit and Astrology; in the two following Hindi and Arithmetic; in the three following Sanscrit only, and in the two last schools Hindi and Sanscrit. According to a different source of information there is another large pátshala with 33 pupils who are taught Sanscrit and religious books by Pandit Ishar Das.

Gujrat proper, according to the Police returns, has only 2 maktabs, 1 under Hafiz Abdulla with 20 pupils, and 1 with 15 pupils, in both of which the Koran is taught.

KOTTALA SHEKHAN.—There is a maktab at *Sira* attached to a mosque under teacher Shamsuddin with 20 boys; one at *Phalya* in a private house under Muhammad Husain with 10 boys and 8 girls; one at *Shahdanwali*, and one at *Wasú*; the number of pupils in the last two is not mentioned. The subjects of tuition are Arabic, Persian and the Koran. There are 3 Gurmukhi schools at *Mangat*, at *Mikan* and at *Sira*, under teachers Mulla Singh, Atma Singh and Lakha Singh, with 40, 30 and 25 pupils respectively. At Mangat out of the 40 pupils 10 are girls; they are all three attached to Dharmsalas. The teachers are paid half an anna monthly by each pupil and get their food. The income of the teachers is not fixed. Besides the monthly fees, if any, they get some present at festivals such as one or two topas of corn. The food is supplied to them by turn from each boy. This system of paying the teachers was followed in the time of Maharaja Ranjit Singh.

LALA MUSA.—Amongst *Maulvis*, Abdulla, Muhammad Makhdúm, Ghulam Qadir, and Muhammad Alim Mian Nasrúlla are mentioned as noteworthy. The largest maktab in this circle is at *Chak Umar*, also called *Umar Chak*, under teacher Abdulla, who gives the following account of his school:—

"There are 14 boys in my school learning Arabic and Persian. The following subjects are taught:—

(1) *Sarf* from Sarf Báhai to Shafia.
(2) Syntax from Mita Amil to Sharah Mullá.
(3) Logic from Isagoge to Sullum and Hamdullá.
(4) Muhammadan law from Munya to Hidaya.
(5) Persian poetry from Karima to Sikandar Namah.
(6) Persian prose from Dusturussibyan to Abulfazl.
(7) Arabic literature from Alif Laila to Hamasah and Zahuri.

"Besides these, 40 boys learn the Koran by heart.

"In 1870 I appeared in the entrance examination of the Lahore University, and passed that examination in the 2nd division. Mr. Pearson, the Inspector of Schools, gave me Rs. 36 as a reward in recognition of my school."

The following are the smaller maktabs in this circle :—

Names of towns and villages.	Number of maktabs.	Number of pupils.	Subjects taught.
Shah Sarmast	1	30	Arabic, the Koran.
Dogah	1	50	Persian and Fiqah.
Buzargwal	2	10	Koran.
Kotla Qasim	1	18	Ditto.
Dhama	1	10	Urdu, Arabic Persian.
Biswal	1	9	Arabic, Persian.
Nosar	1	20	Arabic, Persian.
Kaliwal	1	15	Arabic, Persian.
Lala Musá	1	16	Arabic, Persian.
Khawajpur	1	20	Urdu, Persian.
Hanj	1	16	The Koran.
Bir Kharang	1	30	Arabic, Persian.
Ogawal	1	16	Arabic, Persian.
Kakrali	1	10	Arabic, Koran.
Kolta Arwalikhan	1	7	Ditto.
Dolta Nagar	1	10	Ditto.
Dhar Bakri	1	12	The Koran.
Jatrya (smaller)	1	12	Ditto.
Myana Chak	1	3	Ditto.

There are 2 Gurmukhi schools at *Buzargwal,* attached to Dharmsalas under Sunder Singh and Mohan Singh with 18 pupils ; 3 Lande schools – *Karali* with 4, *Kotla Arwalikhan* with 6, and the largest at *Dolya Nagar* with 25 pupils, under teacher Ala Baksh.

Note.—Religious education is asked for by the people, who are said to have forgotten whatever they knew of religion. The Government should establish schools for religious instruction as it has established schools for English and Urdu.

AURANGÁBÁD.—The distinguished Maulvis of this circle are—Maulvi Ghulám Rasúl and Maulvi Hyatulla. The largest maktab is at *Nirwal,* under Nizamuddín, with 35 pupils. The other maktabs are as follows :—*Chappar* with 20, *Shamsúbád* with 14, *Kotyan* with 27, *Pind Rahmanpur* with 10, *Bhagnagar* with 15, *Biveranja* with 20, *Mehi Kalan* with 18, and *Kumbi* with 23 pupils, in all of which the Korán only is taught. There are 5 Gurmukhi schools, three of which are at *Sarai Belani* and *Rhanwar* with 42 pupils, taught gratuitously by Gurdit Singh, Sahib Singh and Mul Singh ; 1 at *Pind Rahmanpur* with 5, and 1 at *Bhagnágar* with 10 pupils.

KUNJAH.—The names of Maulvis Khudá Bakhsh, Sher Ahmad, Ata Mohammad, Zainulabdin, Fazl Ahmad, Imám Alí, Kayem Dín, and Inayetulla, as also of Pandits Ramdat and Wasdeo deserve to be mentioned. The maktab at *Kunja* itself has 16 pupils, and Arabic and Persian is taught. There is a maktab at *Sahduki* having 32 pupils, in charge of Maulvi Inayetulla. According to a private return, *Shádiwál Kalan* has 3 Koran schools with 43 boys and 12 girls, and *Shádiwál Khurd* has 3 maktabs with 67 boys in which there is religious teaching, such as the Koran, &c., also Grammar. The other places in this circle that have maktabs are—*Adú Wál* with 25, *Machyana* with 24, *Madina* with 17, *Kiledar* and *Saman Pindi* with each 17, and *Phoguki* with 10 boys; with the exception of *Madina* and *Phaguki,* where only Arabic is taught, the above are Perso-Arabic schools. *Kunjah* has a school with 34 pupils, in which Sanscrit and Gurmukhi is taught by Shibcharan. A private return also mentions a Lande school with 18 boys. *Shádiwál* has a Sanscrit school with 20, and a Gurmukhi school with 20 pupils, and *Kiladar* has a Sanscrit school with 24 pupils.

JÁLALPUR (*Jattan*).—Amongst *Pandits,* Bhagwán Dass and Luchman Dass may be mentioned ; there are also several Maulvis of note, whose names, however, are not mentioned. The Police return is evidently wrong in bringing to notice only 2 maktabs with 44 pupils at Jalalpur, as a very reliable private return mentions 6 maktabs with 93 pupils, and another even 8 maktabs and 119 pupils, in which the Koran and Persian, or only the Koran is taught. There are further 2 pátshalas with 35 pupils, in which Sanscrit, moral books and astronomy are taught, and 2 Lande schools, 1 with 50 pupils under teacher

Ghulám Nabí, and 1 with 20 pupils under Ghasitá, in which Lande and account-keeping are taught. The first teacher gets Rs. 7 per month and the second Rs. 3.

KHÁRIÁN.—Maulvi Sadruddin of Mulka is mentioned as a distinguished man. The largest maktab is at *Jund* with 75 pupils under Hafiz Ilmuddin, who teaches the Koran and Persian gratuitously. Hafiz Ilmuddin, the teacher of the maktab at Jund, gives the following description of his school:—

"My school is attended by 75 pupils, and this number is subject to decrease and increase. Out of these 75, 12 are natives of the village, and 18 pupils come from the neighbouring villages and return to their homes at night. The remaining 45 pupils are strangers, who live upon alms and reside in the mosque. I teach gratuitously, and have no fixed income. I teach only the Koran, Qirát and Muhammadan law. In other branches of learning I am not so proficient as to be able to teach. I am now 46 years old, and have been teaching for the last 26 years. I subsist only on agriculture. My land is cultivated by a mercenary "kashtkar," who takes half of the produce of my land. Some of the pupils are taught by me and others are taught by more advanced scholars."

The other places in this circle with maktabs are as follows:—

Names of towns and villages.	Number of maktabs.	Number of pupils.	Subjects taught.	Number of Gurmukhi schools.	Number of pupils.	Subjects taught.
Havel	3	55	The Koran	...	...	
Mulka	1	30	The Koran and Arabic Grammar, Syntax and Logic.	...	...	
Mohri	2	25	The Koran	...	...	
Boryanwali	2	19	Ditto	1	5	Gurmukhi and Lande.
Gotaryala	...	...	......	1	15	Ditto ditto.
Kharyan	3	28	The Koran	...	...	
Dhurya	2	27	Ditto	1	7	Gurmukhi.
Mehayek	1	18	Ditto	...	...	
Dogah*	2	72	The Koran, Persian Grammar and Syntax.	...	...	
Samantpur	1	7	Ditto ditto	1	6	Ditto.
Marala	1	9	Ditto ditto	1	13	Ditto.
Dhuni	1	12	Ditto ditto	...	...	
Piyagú	1	6	Ditto ditto	...	...	
Utam	1	8	The Koran	...	...	
Rasulpur	1	5	Ditto	...	...	
Jachyan	1	18	Ditto	1	4	
Pindi Khakh	1	4	Ditto	...	...	
Baharwal	1	12	Ditto	1	5	
Sidhwal	1	19	Ditto	...	...	
Chak Sikander	1	12	Ditto	...	...	
Thuth Rai Bahadar	1	12	Ditto	...	...	
Dhar	1	35	Ditto	...	...	
Baruali	1	15	Ditto	1	8	
Big	...	...	......	1	20	
Ramgarh	...	...	......	1	30	

* A private return remarks that at Dogah all the Arabic knowledge to be found in the Punjab is imparted at this school.

LANGA.—The names of Hakims Ganda Singh, Ali Ahmad, Jalal, Hayat, Sayid Mustafa and Imamdin; Maulvis Shaik Ahmad, Kutab Din, Sirajuddin, and Amir Shah; Pandit Rupa; Bhais Jawala Singh, Phela Singh and Purbhu Singh, are brought to notice in the Police return.

Langa itself has, according to one source of information, a large maktab with 90 boys; whilst, according to another source, it has 2 maktabs, 1 attached to a mosque under Ghulam Ahmad and Nurdin (assistant) with 92 boys, who read Arabic and the Koran; the other in a private house with 32 boys and 9 girls under Fazl Ilahi, who learn Arabic, Persian and the Koran. The teachers have no fixed income from the pupils. In the Dharmsala Langa, Gurmukhi and Lande are taught to 20 boys by teacher Mohra; another school of the same kind is at *Pindi Kalu*, with 16 boys and 20 girls; whilst *Gagra* and *Lhori* have each a school with 12 and 8 boys respectively, in which only Gurmukhi is taught; *Keryan Wala* and *Bahrian wali*, have each a Madrasa with 25 and

16 pupils respectively where Arabic is read; *Helan* has a Mahajani school with 12 boys who learn Hindi and Shastri.

DINGAH.—The largest school in this circle is at *Chikori Phallawal*, attached to a mosque, under Maulvi Nuruddin and his son-in-law Mohammad Alim, who are both superior men; there are 105 pupils (90 boys and 15 girls), according to the private return,; the Police return says only 80. The subjects taught are Urdu, Persian, Arithmetic, the Koran, Muhammadan law, "Hadis and Tafsir" (Tradition and Commentaries) Grammar, Logic, Philosophy and Jurisprudence. *Dingah* itself has a maktab with 15 boys and 16 girls; 2 Gurmukhi schools 1 at Dingah with 35 pupils under Sant Singh and 1 at *Bhaogalpur* with 20 pupils: 3 Lande schools at *Kot Biloch, Chak Fatah Shah* and *Dingah* with 10, 8, and 17 pupils respectively.

QADIRABAD.—The Police return mentions 2 Perso-Arabic schools, 1 at Qudirabad, attached to the mosque, in charge of Shaik Ahmad, with 18 pupils; and 1 at *Bhuta (old)*, with 10 boys; 2 Persian schools at *Sidar* and at *Dhuni*; with 13 and 10 pupils respectively; 1 Arabic shool, (Madrasa) with 6 pupils.

There is 1 pátshala attached to a temple under Pandit Ganpat Rai, a good Sanscrit scholar, who teaches "Vedant" (philosophy) to 10 boys gratuitously; 2 Gurmukhi schools, 1 at Qadirabad, attached to a Dharmsala under Gulab Singh, who gets Rs. 2 per mensem in cash or kind, and has 12 pupils, and 1 at Sidar, with 16 pupils; 2 Lande schools, in which also Gurmukhi is taught, at Qadirbad and Bhuta (new) with 20 and 16 pupils respectively.

KARYALWALA.—Amongst eminent men, Maulvi Shaikh Ahmad, Qaz Mahmud, Bhai Sant Singh, and Gobind Sahai Bhagat, are named. There are 4 maktabs or Madrasas: (1) *Hajiwala*, with 13 pupils, and teacher Shaikh Ahmad, who teaches gratuitously; and 2 more schools with 9 pupils. (2) *Awan*, with 7 pupils, and teacher the Mohamad Qazi, who gets 5 bighas of rent-free land. (3) *Hazara*, with 25 pupils, and teacher Rukunddin (a blind man), who gets nothing. *Naushera*, with 60 pupils, and teacher Ibrahim, who gets Rs. 25 per annum. They are all attached to mosques: in the first two Arabic, in the third the Koran, and in the fourth Persian, form the subject of tuition. Gurmukhi schools there are 3; the largest at *Tanda*, attached to the temple of Devi Duara: it has two departments, in the one Sanscrit is taught to 26 pupils by Bhagat Govind Sahai, and in the other Gurmukhi and Lande to 70 pupils by Lajpul. They get Rs. 56 in cash per annum; 1 at *Naushera* and 1 at *Lakhi Wal* with 12 and 14 pupils respectively, in both of which Gurmukhi and Lande is taught. *Karyalwala* has a Lande school, where accounts are taught to 14 boys.

The following additional List, *which is not contained in the Police Returns*, has been supplied by *Lala Bhagwan Das*, the painstaking District Inspector of Gujrat:—

NAME OF VILLAGE OR TOWN.	MAKTABS.		
	Number of maktabs.	Number of pupils.	Subjects.
Chako	1	...	Principles of Law, Logic, Philosophy, Medicine and Grammar, Urdu, Persian, Arithmetic, Fiqah, Hadis, Tafsir, and the Koran.
Khuáspur	1	40	The Koran and Persian.
Ditto	1	21	Ditto.
Darekri	1	35	The Koran, Persian and religious books.
Ditto	1	14	The Koran.
Ditto	1	12	Ditto.
Kunjáh	1	15	Ditto.
Saroki	1	5	Ditto.

Name of Village or Town.	Maktabs.		
	Number of maktabs.	Number of pupils.	Subjects.
Dharkí Kalán	1	30	The Koran.
Ditto Khurd	1	8	Ditto.
Mohlá	1	25	Ditto.
Chewaránwálí	1	22	The Koran and Persian.
Ditto	1	13	Ditto.
Ditto	1	12	Ditto.
Chewaránwàli	1	10	Persian and the Koran.
Majrah	1	21	Persian, the Koran, & Medicine.
Tarkah	1	18	Koran.
Nágaryánwálah	1	14	Ditto.
Manghuwál	1	14	The Koran and Persian.
Ditto	1	20	Ditto.
Khojujánwáli	1	14	Ditto.
Ditto	1	3	Ditto.
Golekí	1	12	Ditto.
Ditto	1	6	Ditto.
Golekí	1	3	Ditto.
Alí Shahr	1	13	Ditto.
Magghowál	1	5	Ditto.
Kalachor	1	21	Ditto.
Ditto	1	7	Ditto.
Ditto	1	8	Ditto.
Islám Garh	1	5	Ditto.
Miáuípindí	1	25	The Koran, Persian, & religious books.
Ditto	1	3	The Koran.
Ditto	1	8	Ditto.
Givewanjal	1	7	Ditto.
Majrah	1	8	The Koran and Persian.
Sháhjahání	1	16	The Koran.
Sondotah	1	10	Ditto.
Dhammá Malkah	1	25	The Koran and Persian.
Sher Garh	1	8	The Koran.
Máchhí Wál	1	9	Ditto.
Ditto	1	8	Ditto.
Bhatí	1	6	Ditto.
Soanbrí	1	20	Ditto.
Bhotáh	1	12	Ditto.
Nír	1	15	Ditto.
Sarai	1	8	Ditto.
Sarai	1	10	Ditto.
Lánbrí	1	8	Ditto.
Chakoráh	1	4	Ditto.
Chhokar Kalán	1	15	The Koran and Persian.
Chhokar Khurd	1	20	Ditto.
Mahesí	1	5	Ditto.
Kapránwalah	1	10	Ditto.
Manián	1	12	Ditto.
Ditto	1	12	Arabic.
Baágowál	1	10	Ditto.
Tánadah	1	...	
Motá	1	15	The Koran.
Baddhan	1	8	Ditto.
Chopalah	1	20	Ditto.
Sheikh Chokání	1	40	Urdu and Persian.
Sháhjahání	1	9	The Koran.
Manjúki	1	13	Persian.
Kissuki	1	15	Ditto.
Nat	1	6	Ditto.
Jam	1	20	The Koran.
Nanjunwal	1	25	Persian.
Málowál	1	10	Persian and Arabic.
Jedar	1	13	The Koran.
Bharmán	1	10	Ditto.
Dhamnal	1	10	Ditto.
Sarhadri	1	15	The Koran and Fiqah.

Name of Village or Town.	Maktabs.		
	Number of maktabs.	Number of pupils.	Subjects.
Bhagrádwálah	1	14	The Koran.
Kharián	1	6	Ditto.
Jhaddar Kalán	1	13	Ditto.
Jatáláh	1	7	Ditto.
Baddar	1	1	Ditto.
Chak Shjáwal	1	10	Religious books.
Arah	1	9	The Koran.
Panjauriyáán	1	15	Koran, Hqah and Hadis.
Nasirah	1	16	The Koran.
Naurang	1	10	Ditto.
Jandánwalah	1	10	Ditto.
Maralah	...	...	
Dallo	1	8	The Koran.
Ghakká	1	4	Ditto.
Pindí Rámpur	1	4	Ditto.
Mahí Khurd	1	8	Ditto.
Chak Nath	1	4	Ditto.
Khánpur	1	1	Ditto.
Dhok	1	4	Ditto.
Gadí Gurao	1	1	Ditto.
Sarái	1	5	Ditto.
Noth	1	10	Ditto.
Kakrot	1	5	Ditto.
Qázi Báqar	1	7	The Koran and Persian.
Dhok Murid	1	5	The Koran.
Marhí	1	3	Ditto.
Ghanyán	1	8	Ditto.
Kasbah	1	3	Ditto.
Nung	1	5	Ditto.
Pindi Baháuddin	...	...	
Rasul	1	13	The Koran.
Warah Balyán	1	6	Ditto.
Borah	1	7	Ditto.
Kotly Afghánán	1	4	Ditto.
Mangat	1	4	Ditto.
Ditto	1	4	Ditto.
Madhra	1	8	The Koran, Persian & Lande.
Pakkowal	1	2	The Koran.
Rattowal	...	...	
Kadhar	1	9	The Koran.
Khab Joru	1	4	Ditto.
Miánwál	1	10	Persian.
Khiwah	1	9	Ditto.
Khiwah	1	15	Ditto.
Garhi, Gakhar Khán	1	6	Ditto.
Gauhar	1	5	Koran.
Kot Jálpán	1	7	Ditto.
Noth	1	12	Ditto.
Kalu Wáli	1	11	Ditto.
Mahabbatpur	1	11	Ditto.
Ditto	1	11	Ditto.
Dittu Chuhar	1	12	Ditto.
Karl Mahabbatpur	1	6	Ditto.
Kot Jaránah	...	...	......
Mánjhi	1	12	The Koran.
Ditto	1	10	Ditto.
Mekin	1	10	Ditto.
Ditto	1	7	Ditto.
Pindi Lalah	1	8	Urdu and Persian.
Bagh	1	25	Ditto.
Dogal	1	12	The Koran.
Phaliah Kolan	1	2	Ditto.
Jokalyan	...	...	......
Thatta Aliah	...	...	....
Thatta Garhiwala	1	8	The Koran and Persian.
Chak Mittha	1	6	The Koran.

Name of Village or Town.	Maktabs.		
	Number of maktabs.	Number of pupils.	Subjects taught.
Chak Mittha	1	4	The Koran.
Ranmal	1	6 boys and 9 girls.	Ditto.
Chak Tahir	1	5	Ditto.
Higarwala	1	10	Ditto.
Kot Phulle Shah	1	6	Ditto.
Rám Sahki	1	10	Ditto.
Pindi Dhothar	1	7	Persian.
Gadho	1	8	Ditto.
Narang	1	8 boys 5 girls.	The Koran.
Khosar	1	4	Ditto.
Chabarki	1	6	Ditto.
Ditto	1	4	Ditto.
Pindi Ratti	1	5	Ditto.
Paharyanwali	1	16	Ditto.
Kot Machu	1	6	Ditto.
Ghakkoki	1	5	Ditto.
Gotaryalah	1	12	Persian.
Kalyanah	1	8	Ditto.
Bhagwal	1	5	Ditto.
Waraichanwalah	1	15	Ditto.
Ditto	1	13	Ditto.
Haslanwalah	1	20	Ditto.
Khori	1	12	Ditto.
Kolian	1	4	Ditto.
Matiol Walah	1	12	Ditto.
Sikarwali	1	15	Ditto.
Hil	1	32	Ditto.
Dhakranwali	1	10	The Koran and Hadis.
Thikaryan	1	10	The Koran.
Begah	1	4	Ditto.
Banyan	1	7	Ditto.
Barnauli	1	10	The Koran and Religious teaching generally.

Name of Village or Town.	Pathsalas.		Gurmukhi Schools.		Mahajani Schools.	
	Number of Páthsalas.	Number of pupils.	Number of Gurmukhi Schools.	Number of pupils.	Number of Mahajani Schools.	Number of pupils.
Kunyáh	1	8	...	...	1	15
Taroki	...	...	1	10	...	...
Shadiwal Kalan	...	...	...	...	1	30
Khalan	1	10	...	...	...	...
Tándah	...	...	1	9	1	10
Karyanwalah	...	...	...	...	1	13
Arah	1	6	1	9	...	—
Tandanwalah	...	...	1	9	...	...
Baryanwali	...	...	1	7	...	...
Múng	...	...	1	16	...	...
Pindi Baháuddin	...	...	1	35	...	...
Madhrá	...	...	1	12	...	...
Rattowál	...	...	1	12	...	...
Miánwál	...	...	1	40	...	...
Kadhar	...	...	...	...	1	15
Tokályán	1	2	...	...	...	...
Ganhar	...	...	1	5	...	...
Náth	...	...	1	19	...	...
Kot Taránah	...	...	1	19	...	...
Mánghi	...	...	1	17	...	...
Pindi Kálú	...	...	1	20	...	...
Thatta Aliáh	...	...	1	15	...	...
Ranmal	...	...	1	9	...	...
Higárwalah	...	...	1	12	...	...
Gotaryalah	...	...	1	25	...	...
Ghachyan	...	...	1	11	...	...

PESHAWAR DIVISION.

KOHAT DISTRICT.

GENERAL ABSTRACT.

District.	No. of Maktabs and Madrasas.	No. of pupils.	No. of Patshalas.	No. of pupils.	No. of Gurmukhi schools.	No. of pupils.	No. of Mahajani schools.	No. of pupils.	Total No. of schools.	Total No. of pupils.
Kohat .	39	679	...	...	3	41	...	...	42	720

KOHAT.—Mohammad Amin, Kazi Hissam Uddin, and Rustum Gul are the three well-known Moulvis in this circle.

There is a large Maktab, attached to a mosque, with 200 pupils, who are taught Arabic and Persian. Kazi Hissam Uddin, a good scholar, assisted by six minor teachers, is in charge of the pupils and teaches them gratuitously. There are also 9 minor Perso-Arabic Schools attended by 220 students, and also a Gurmukhi School, attached to a Dharmsala with 7 pupils taught by Karm Singh, who gets his income from fees. Gurmukhi is the subject taught.

TERI has six mosque schools kept by Ali Gul, Muhammad Yasin, Abdul Hakim, Ghulam, Saiyad, and Akhir Sher. The first is a learned Mulla; the others too possess a fair knowledge. Altogether, 65 students attend these schools, who read the Koran and Arabic Grammar. The teachers get some income from the zemindars.

Teri has also a Gurmukhi School kept at the house of the teachers, Rup Lal and Brij Lal. The pupils attending this school are 21 in number. The subjects taught are Gurmukhi and Hindi. Each pupil pays a pice every Sunday.

LACHI has one Maktab held in a shop which is attended by 18 pupils. Saiyad Ali Muhammad is the teacher; he can teach up to the 4th Class of the Middle School. Persian, Urdu and Arithmetic are the subjects taught. There is also a Gurmukhi School here, attached to a Dharmsala, with 13 pupils, who pay 13 annas a month in all. Karm Singh is the teacher's name.

SUKH TALAO.—Mian Majid Gul, of the village *Ziarat Shekh Ala Dad*, is the eminent Hakim who practises in this Thana. At Jabar, Moulvi Ata Ullah is a noteworthy Moulvi.

SHAKARDARRAH has one Pandit in Mehta Hemraj. In this Police station there is a Maktab with 18 pupils reading Persian, Gulistán and Bostán and the Koran. Mian Yar Muhammad and Mian Muhammad are the teachers, the former being a good Persian and Arabic scholar, and the latter a Mulla in Arabic and Persian. The Teachers' half-yearly income comes up to about 10 maunds of grain each.

NIZAMPUR.—There are three Maktabs, attached to mosques, in this Thana. One in *Manduri*, with 12 pupils reading Arabic, Persian and Muhammadan Law and Grammar under Muhi Uddin, teacher. One at *Jabbi*, with six pupils, and teacher Mulla Golab, and one at Nimal, with 12 pupils under Mir Husain; they read the same subjects as above. The first gets Rs. 3 per mensem and bread and clothing from the mosque's proprietor, and the other two loaves of bread only.

GUMBAT has one Maktab with 7 pupils reading Arabic and Persian. *Kothri*, with 4 pupils reading the same subjects; *Parshi*, with 8 pupils and

* My returns from the Peshawar Division are incomplete, as the Peshawar *District* itself has furnished no information regarding its indigenous schools, in spite of constant applications to the Police and Civil Authorities.

Persian the subject of study; *Gurzai*, with 7 pupils reading Persian; *Tulanj*, with 14 pupils and Persian the subject of study; *Gandhali*, *Marchangi* and *Rasti* each one, with 6, 2, and 10 pupils respectively, learning Arabic; *Nakband*, *Mahah*, *Katta Kani*, *Yerushalam*, *Taharlabahar*, *Kunda*, and *Talkan*, each one, with 22, 2, 1, 4, 8, 3 and 5 pupils, respectively, who are taught Arabic, and *Khushagarh*, one Maktab with 15 students, who are instructed in Arabic and Persian.

HANGU.—Maulvi Muhammad Atûf is a learned *Maulvi* in this circle. *Hángú* itself has 2 Koran Schools, attached to mosques with 15 pupils.

PESHAWAR DIVISION.

HAZARA DISTRICT.

GENERAL ABSTRACT.

District.	No. of Maktabs and Madrasas.	No. of pupils.	No. of Patabálas.	No. of pupils.	No. of Gurmukhi schools.	No. of pupils.	No. of Mahájani schools.	No. of pupils.	Total No. of schools.	Total No. of pupils.
Hazárá .	80	1,026	3	85	15	163	1	25	99	1,299

SHIKÁRI.—Moulvi Hamíd Ali *alias* Mullán Táyá may be referred to as the man supposed to be most eminent.

There is one large Maktab in this circle attached to the mosque, in which the teacher (name not mentioned) teaches Persian, Arabic, Syntax, Prosody and Logic, to 40 pupils; and gets 22 maunds of corn at each harvest time. The small Maktabs are as under :—

2 at Shikári attached to mosques, with 19 pupils learning Persian and Arabic, and
1 ,, Dhodhiyál, ,, ,, 12 ,, ,, Muhammadan law.

Baffá has one large Gurmukhi School, in which Bhái Rám Kishen teaches Gurmukhi to 22 pupils, and gets 8 annas as a fee from each pupil.

Shikári and *Dodhwál* have 2 Gurmukhi Schools, with 20 and 12 pupils, respectively, learning Gurmukhi and Hindi in the first and only Gurmukhi in the second.

GHAZI.—Among the names of distinguished Moulvis, Hakims, and Bháis, are found that of Hakim Ghulam Qádir of Dheri, Bhái Parem Singh Dharmsáliá of Srikot, and Moulvi Háji Muhammad Núr of Srikot.

Srikot has a Maktab attached to a mosque, with 15 pupils, under Moulvi Háji Muhammad Núr, who teaches Arabic and Persian religious books. The teacher has no fixed income, but gets something from the pupils, at harvests and festivals.

There is also a Gurmukhi School at Srikot, in which Bhái Parem Singh teaches Gurmukhi to 4 pupils. He gets his daily food and some corr

KHANPUR.—Qázi Ghulám Husain of Khánpur is the eminent Moulvi mentioned in this circle.

There is a Maktab in Khánpur attached to a mosque, in which Mián Ahmad teaches the Koran, Persian and Arabic books, to 25 pupils. When a pupil finishes the Koran or some other book, he then presents something to the teacher.

There is also a Gurmukhi School at Khánpur attached to the Dharamsálá, in which Bhái Ganeshá and Bhái Pujárá teach Lande to 20 pupils. The teachers receive their daily bread, and also a present when a pupil finishes the Granth.

The two smaller Gurmukhi Schools, at Jáwalyá and Chhijián, are attended by 10 and 16 pupils, who are taught Gurmukhi, Lande and Multiplication tables.

OGI.—Moulvi Núr Hasan may be referred to as the man supposed to be most eminent in this place.

The largest Maktab, in this circle, is at Shamdahráh, attached to the mosque, in which Moulvi Núr Hasan teaches Arabic and Persian religious books to 39 pupils. The teacher gets no monthly pay, but the people give him something at harvest time.

The following are the smaller Maktabs, in this circle :—

No. 1, at Ganyan,	attached to a mosque, with	28	pupils, learning Arabic and Persian religious books.
No. 2, at Arboráh,	ditto	24	ditto.
No. 3, at Báhndi,	ditto	12	ditto.
No. 4, at Dehrá,	ditto	28	ditto.
No. 5, at Sufedáh,	ditto	5	ditto.
No. 6, at Malugá,	ditto	10	ditto.
No. 7, at Bázár,	ditto	5	ditto.
No. 8, at Ogi,	ditto	29	ditto.
No. 9. at Pánjúráh,	ditto	7	ditto.
No. 10, at Rashidáh,	ditto	11	ditto.
No. 11, at Kot,	ditto	4	ditto.
No. 12, at Malukráh,	ditto	16	ditto.
No. 13, at Bhág Bhánda,	ditto	10	ditto.
No. 14, at Masir Máhndi,	ditto	12	ditto.
No. 15, at Kathiáí,	ditto	23	ditto.
No. 16, at Chhichár Bála,	ditto	14	ditto.
No. 17, at Kabál Bálá,	ditto	10	ditto.
No. 18, at Kabál Páin,	ditto	7	ditto.
No. 19, at Kondráh,	ditto	4	ditto.
No. 20, at Chalandaryán,	ditto	10	ditto.
No. 21, at Sháhkot,	ditto	11	ditto.
No. 22, at Taráoráh,	ditto	16	ditto.
No. 23, at Dindwár,	ditto	4	ditto.
No. 24, at Dhatoli,	ditto	7	ditto.
No. 25, at Tarwái,	ditto	4	ditto.
No. 26, at Bágaryán,	ditto	22	ditto.
No. 27, at Dilbori,	ditto	14	ditto.
No. 28, at Kángú,	ditto	4	ditto.
No. 29, at Chov Kalán,	ditto	5	ditto.
No. 30, at Jaskot,	ditto	14	ditto.
No. 31, at Chhichrí,	ditto	7	ditto.
No. 32, at Samalbot,	ditto	7	ditto.
No. 33, at Japet	ditto	5	ditto.
No. 34, at Manyol,	ditto	6	ditto.
No. 35, at Kewal,	ditto	16	ditto.
No. 36, at Dewal,	ditto	14	ditto.
No. 37, at Belián,	ditto	32	ditto.
No. 38, at Kilká,	ditto	8	ditto.
No. 39, at Kotláh,	ditto	7	ditto.

KARÉLIÁN.—Moulvi Jalál-uddin of Anuráh is the most eminent man, mentioned in the Police return, of this circle.

The largest Maktab in this circle is at *Anuráh*, attached to a mosque, in which Moulvi Jalál-uddin teaches Arabic and Persian religious books to 10 pupils; he gets 10 seers of corn at harvest time from each pupil; and the villagers have given him land for two ploughs.

The following are the smaller Maktabs :—

No. 1, at Jagrán Bálá,	attached to a mosque, with	7	pupils being taught in Arabic and Persian religious books.
No. 2, at Jhokhan,	ditto	5	ditto.
No. 3, at Hál Jaddál	ditto	4	ditto.
No. 4, at Dáltari,	ditto	9	ditto.
No. 5, at Bhaduráh,	ditto	5	ditto.
No. 6, at Ladar Malag,	ditto	9	ditto.

NÁRÁH.—Moulvi Mián Abdulláh of Chhaprí is well known in this circle.

The best Maktab in this circle is at Chhaprí, attached to the mosque, in which Abdulláh, Bedulláh, and Musá teach gratuitously Arabic and Persian to 7 pupils.

The following are the other Maktabs in this circle :—

No. 1 at Satoráh, attached to a mosque, with	3 pupils, learning the Korán and Persian.		
No. 2 at Sajkot,	ditto	15	ditto.
No. 3 at do.	ditto	12	ditto.
No. 4 at Kayáláh,	ditto	15	ditto.
No. 5 at Manhál,	ditto	3	ditto.
No. 6 at Karchhá,	ditto	10	ditto.

Sajkot has a Gurmukhi School attached to the teacher's house, with 7 pupils, under Mussammát Mullo (widow of Manglá), who teaches Gurmukhi and gets 6 pies per mensem from each pupil.

Satoráh, Sajkot, Mohvi, Bari Behan, Mohábri and Dhanak have Gurmukhi Schools each, with 8, 7, 3, 10, 5 and 5 pupils respectively, being taught Gurmukhi.

SHERWÁN.—Sherwán Kalán has a large Maktab attached to the mosque, in which Muhammad Hayát and Qází Faiz Talab teach religious and other books to 20 pupils. They get 20 maunds of corn annually; besides this they take what is offered to them by anybody. The small Maktabs in this circle are at Tháthi, Gághút, Kangar Bálá, Júthá, and Ber, with 23, 17, 17, 17 and 11 pupils, respectively. Persian and Arabic are taught in all these Maktabs except the last one, in which Arabic religious teaching is only conducted.

Sherwán Khurd has a Gurmukhi School, attached to a Dharamsálá, where Tulsá Singh teaches Gurmukhi to 14 pupils, and gets 6 maunds of corn per annum.

MÁNSEHRA.—Among the names of distinguished Moulvis brought to notice is found that of Moulvi Muhammad Saiyad of Dib Garán.

Pakhwál has the largest Maktab in this circle, attached to the mosque, in which Muhammad Jí (who is a distinguished scholar of Arabic, Persian, Syntax, and Prosody) teaches Arabic, Persian, religious and other books to 88 pupils, on an income of Rs. 20 per annum in money and kind. There is also a smaller Maktab in the same village with 22 pupils. Dátáh, Hansheryán and Jalo have Maktabs, each, with 30, 30 and 32 pupils respectively. Arabic and Persian religious and other books are taught in them.

HARIPUR.—There is a large Maktab at Sikandarpur, attached to a mosque, in which Moulvi Abdulláh teaches, gratuitously Logic and the Korán, &c., to 20 pupils. There are besides 4 Korán Schools with 30 pupils.

Haripur has a large Pathshálá, attached to a temple where Lál Dás, disciple of Tin Rám Bairági, teaches gratuitously Sanskrit and Hindi to 40 pupils, and a Mahájani School, under Gurdattá, where Lande is taught to 25 pupils.

The following Maktabs belong also to this circle :—

Names of Teachers.	Number of Pupils.
Amirgul	6
Fateh Muhammad	10
Abdullá	8
Ghulám Hosain	6

MÁLÁKOT.—Hakim Lakhmi Dás of Málákot is a man of high position in this circle.

Málákot has only a Gurmukhi School attached to a Dharamsálá where Bhái Shám Singh and Bhái Juáhir Singh teach Gurmukhi to 16 pupils, and get a fee of one anna per mensem from each pupil.

ABBOTTÁBÁD.—Khán Akhonzádáh of Nawáshahr may be referred to as an eminent man.

Nawáshahr has a Gurmukhi School, attached to the Dharamsálá, in which Mahán Singh teaches Gurmukhi and Lande to 30 pupils. He gets a fee of 7½ annas per mensem from each pupil.

A private return mentions a Maktab at Abbottabad itself, which is conducted by Mian Saifulla, a good Persian scholar, who teaches the Koran and elementary books in Persian to 14 boys and 6 girls and receives about Rs. 7 per mensem in kind and cash.

DERAJAT DIVISION.

DERA GHÁZÍ KHAN DISTRICT.

GENERAL ABSTRACT.

District.	No. of Maktabs and Madrasas.	No. of pupils.	No. of Patshalas.	No. of pupils.	No. of Gurmukhi schools.	No. of pupils.	No. of Mahájani Schools.	No. of pupils.	Total No. of Schools.	Total No. of pupils.
D. G. Khan .	179	1,645	5	42	5	32	7	144	196	1,863

DERA GHAZI KHAN.—Among the names of distinguished Hakims, Baids, Moulvis, Pandits, and Bháis, brought to notice, are found those of Hakim Udho Dás, Baid Múlchand, Moulvi Shákir Muhammad, Pandits Parmánand and Bihari Lal of Dera Ghází Khan, and Bháis Sidhu Ram and Santok Dás of Roghá.

The principal Maktab here is attached to a mosque. The number of students in this Maktab is 28. They are taught the Koran by Hafiz Abdulmajid, a good reader of the Koran, who only gets alms as a mullah of the mosque. There are nine smaller Maktabs also, attended by 172 pupils, reading the Koran and Persian. Dera Ghazi Khan has also a Gurmukhi and a Mahajani School, with 2 and 50 pupils, respectively. Pobhú Rám conducts the Mahajani School and gets about Rs. 5 per mensem.

The Maktabs in the suburbs of this Thana are at *Khákí*, with 20 pupils reading the Koran, Persian and Arabic; *Gaggu*, with 19 pupils, reading the Koran and Persian; *Jhak Otra*, with 12 pupils, studying the Koran; *Rekra*, with 8 Perso-Arabic students; *Núrpur*, with 10 Persian and Koran-reading pupils; *Samina* with 8 Arabic and Persian-reading pupils; *Basti Haji Muhammad Akram*, with 9 students taught in Arabic Grammar, Persian and the Koran, and *Ráwin*, with 7 pupils reading the Koran.

There is a Pathshálá in a private house at *Dera Ghází Khan*, in which Pandit Bihari Lal, with fair abilities in Sanskrit, teaches Sanskrit to 8 pupils. He has no fixed income. There is also another Pathshálá under Kahan Dás, with 25 pupils. Bhái Sidhu Ram has a Gurmukhi School at his own house, where 10 pupils are taught gratuitously by him. Sohu Ram Ojha teaches gratuitously in a Hindi School, where there are 28 pupils.

Maktabs here are not prosperous, owing to a want of interest for education on the part of the people. There is no Mahájani School. Boys generally read Mahajani with some of their relations.

AHMED ADI has a Maktab with 7 pupils reading the Koran. Moulvi Fateh Muhammad of Kala is the eminent Hakim, and Darvesh Muhammad, the famous Moulvi, in this Thana.

The best Maktab in this Thana is at *Ghumman*. It is attached to a mosque. Qázi Darvesh Muhammad, a fair scholar, teaches books in Persian, general knowledge and also the Koran, to 12 pupils. His income in cash and kind comes to Rs. 20 yearly. This income consists of daily bread and something in cash paid on marriages and deaths and on the finishing of the Koran, also some corn at harvest. There are some other Maktabs situated at *Land*, *Kedalwala*, *Band*, *Phiphrár*, *Biti Mukul* and *Kala*. There are 34 pupils in all attending these Maktabs. The subject of study is the Koran.

KOT CHHATTA.—The most famous literary men in this locality are, Moulvi Hafiz Din Muhammad and Saujad Rahmat Ulla Shah.

The two principal Maktabs in this Thana are one at *Lakh Sawar* and the other at *Mana*, both attached to mosques. Hafiz Khuda Bakhsh and Ahmed Shah are the teachers, who teach the Koran and Persian. The number of pupils attending each school is 39 and 24. The teachers have no income but what they get as alms.

The minor schools, with their details, are given below:—

Each with one school attached to a mosque.		No. of Pupils.	Subjects taught.
	Basti Malana	4	The Koran.
	Basti Bakiani	5	Ditto.
	Lotak	13	The Koran, Persian and Muhmadan Law.
	Shah Jamal	15	The Koran and Persian
	Arain	14	Ditto.
	Jakhhar	6	Ditto.
	Shero	7	Ditto.
	Haji Kamana	8	Ditto.
	Riasat Choli	27	Ditto.

The Maktabs in this Thana are not in a flourishing condition. People take little interest. Teachers don't get anything either in cash or kind. Hindi and Mahájani are taught at home by the relatives of the pupils, no such school being in existence.

RAJANPUR.—Moulvi Mahamad Ali, an author, of *Rajanpur*, and Moulvi Musa, also an author, of *Kotla Isan*, are the famous Moulvis, and the latter with Khuda Baksh of *Kotla Nasir*, are the well-known Hakims. The Pandits are Khushi Ram and Joya Ram.

There are three Maktabs in *Rajanpur* with 15 pupils; one of these with 4 pupils is attached to a mosque, where Moulvi Ghulam Husan, a good scholar teaches poetry. He has no income but what he gets as a Mullah. This city has also a Pathshála, where Khushi Ram and Joya Ram teach 10 pupils in Nágri, Sanskrit and Hindi gratuitously. There are also 2 Gurmukhi schools here, attached to Dharmsálas, one with 3 pupils and the other with 5. They derive their income from the followers of Sikhism. The other maktabs in this Thana are—one at *Kotla Isan* with 4 pupils, and one at *Kotla Nasir* with 5 pupils In both poetry is taught.

FAZILPUR.—There are no noteworthy schools of any description in this Thana. Boys in their nonage read a little with the Mullas attached to mosques, and when they grow up a little are called to help their parents. Small Maktabs exist in certain villages as shown by the statement below:—

Name of place.		Teacher's name and Qualifications	No. of pupils.	Teacher's income.	Subjects taught.
Attached to Mosques.	1 *Rangpur*	Ghulam Mahammad; knows Persian and the Kóran	6	Corn as a mullah and not as a teacher.	The Kóran and Persian.
	2 *Bekh*	Nabi Bakhsh; knows Arabic and Persian well.	7	Ditto.	Arabic and Persian.
	3 *Sukhániwálá*	Alla Bakhsh; knows Persian up to Sikundarnámá.	10	6 boras of wheat and Rs. 24 yearly.	Persian.
	4 *Shikarpur*	Chandu Ram; passed middle school examination.	8	Rs. 15 per month.	English, Persian and Urdu.
Attached to Mosques.	5 *Qasimpur*	Mahammad Bakhsh; knows little Persian and the Kóran.	8	As No. 1	The Kóran.
	6 *Kotla Rabnyat*	Inayat Ulla; knows Arabic and Persian well.	2	Ditto	Ditto.
	7 *Gujjar Wali*	Alla Dilla; knows the Kóran and a little Persian.	2	Ditto	Ditto.
	8 *Kotli Khudai*	Ahmed Ali; knows Arabic and Persian well.	3	Ditto	Ditto.
	9 *Mehriwala*	Ghaus Bakhsh; knows the Kóran and Persian.	4	Ditto	The Kóran and Persian poetry.
	10 *Noshehra*	Ali Muhammad; knows Arabic and Persian.	4	6 chonas of wheat yearly and a suit of clothes, six monthly.	Persian.

In the three Maktabs, where the teachers have a fixed income, they teach persons of rank, and get their pay from them. In fact, as a rule, the teachers teach at the houses of their employers.

JAMPUR—*Statement of Schools, &c., with the details connected with them in Thana* JAMPUR.

MAKTABS.

Names of places.	Teacher's name and his qualifications.	Income of the teacher.	No. of students.	Subjects taught.	REMARKS.
Kotla Diwan	Hafiz Samana, knows the Kóran only.	Daily bread	5	The Kóran	Here there is a Hakim of the name of Mir Muhammad Pashu.
Basti Dukar	Fateh Muhammad, moderate ability in Persian.	Do.	5	Persian	
Muhammadpur	Qazi Ali Muhammad, moderate Persian scholar.	Do.	4	Do.	
Boliwála	Mian Hyat, moderate Persian and Arabic scholar.	Do.	8	The Kóran.	
Basti Ahdiwála	Mian Khan Shah	Do.	8	Do.	
Qasiwála	Mian Ahmed, moderate Arabic and Persian scholar.	Do.	4	Persian	
Basti Muhammad Bukhsh Amdani	Hafiz Dosh Muhammad Hafiz-i-Kóran.	Do.	4	The Kóran.	
Basti Muhammad Khan Amdani	Ghulam Mohammad, Hafiz-i-Kóran.	Gratuitously	6	Do.	
Hiro	Hafiz Abdul Majid, moderate Arabic and Persian scholar.	Daily bread	30	Arabic and Persian.	
Adam Ghar Kohna	Khan Muhammad, knows the Kóran and a little Persian.	Do.	6	The Kóran and Persian.	
Chah Bhabhiwala within the limits of *Adam Ghar Nau.*	Moulvi Bahawal Uddin, a good scholar in Arabic and Persian.	Do.	25	Persian and Arabic.	This teacher is the famous Moulvi of this place.
Basti Kaagri	Alla Bakhsh, a reader of the Kóran.	Do.	12	The Kóran.	
Landi Pataf	Mian Ali Muhammad, moderate in Persian.	Do.	7	The Kóran. and Persian	
Basti Rana	Muhammad Yar, knows the Kóran.	Do.	5	The Kóran.	
Dangara	Nasir knows the Kóran	Do.	7	Do.	
Khanwah	Sohanra, moderate ability in Persian and Arabic.	Do.	7	Persian	
Kotla Shah Mir Alim	Nur Muhammad, moderate in Arabic and Persian.	Do.	12	Arabic and Persian.	
asti Shah Ali	Hassan, moderate in Persian.	Do.	4	Persian	
Wahgana	Imam Bakhsh, knows the Kóran.	Do.	6	The Kóran.	
JÁMPÚR	Ghulam Mohammad Shah, knows the Kóran.	Do.	7	Do.	Sharf Din and Chotar Mal are the noteworthy Hakims.
Do.	Ramzan, knows the Kóran.	Do.	8	Do.	
Do.	Abdul Rahim, knows the Kóran.	Do.	6	Do.	
Do.	Ghulam Muhammad, knows the Kóran.	Do.	8	Do.	
Do.	Kazi Karim Bakhsh, knows the Kóran and Persian.	Do.	5	The Kóran and Persian.	
Do.	Hafiz Taj Muhammad, knows the Kóran.	Do.	6	The Kóran.	
Kotla Mughlán	......	...	...	...	Here lives Dost Ali, Hakim.

PATHSHALAS.

Names of places.	Teacher's name and his qualifications.	Income of the teacher.	No. of students.	Subjects taught.	REMARKS.
Kotla Mughlan	Pandit Shib Dyal, *fair ability in Sanskrit.*	Do.	6	Sanskrit.	Has also a Gurmukhi School attached to a Dharamsala, with 3 pupils. The teacher's name is Hurnam Das. He gets his daily bread.
Kot Táhir	Anand Puri, fair ability in Sanskrit.	Do.	3	Do.	
JAMPÚR	Megha Ram, fair ability for Sanskrit	Do.	15	Do.	

KOT MITTHAN—Moulvi Nur Muhammad is the famous hereditary Hakim in this city.

In this city there is one Maktab attached to a mosque having 19 pupils learning the Kóran and Poetry. Moulvi Nur Muhammad, an excellent scholar, and Nabi Bakhsh, are the teachers. They have no fixed income but live on alms.

The other minor schools in the suburbs are at *Nurpur*, with 10 pupils reading the Kóran; *Dera Bhai*, with 10 reading Poetry and the Kóran; *Bhágsar*, with 7 reading the Kóran; *Murghai*, with 6 reading the Kóran; *Kotla Gedishah*, with 6 pupils being instructed in the Kóran and Poetry; *Kotla Hasan Jamra* with 6 Kóran-reading pupils; *Madgola* 1 with 4 Kóran and Poetry-reading pupils; *Bámanka* with 3 Kóran-reading students; *Basti Saddiq* with 4 Poetry-reading boys; *Basti Sonattra*, with one Kóran-reading pupil; *Bangálá*, with 2 Kóran-reading pupils; *Basti Dhagar*, with 3 pupils reading the Kóran and Poetry; *Basti Pahli* with 2 Kóran-reading pupils. All these, with the exception of three are attached to mosques.

TAUNSA.—In this circle Maulvi Muhammad Husain and Maulvi Muhammad Yar of *Tonsa* and Maulvi Muhammad Shah Alam of *Sokar* and Maulvi Muhammad Husain of *Domar* are distinguished Arabic scholars and experienced physicians, Khair Shah Sayyid of *Ghani* is an illiterate poet. Maulvi Musa of *Tonsa* is an eminent Maulvi.

The principal maktabs in this circle are: 3 in *Tonsa* under Maulvi Musá, Myan Havút and Hafiz Ahmad Ali, respectively; 1 in *Sokar* under Maulvi Muhammad Shah Alam; 2 in *Mangrota* under Hafiz Chandan and Myan Jandu and 1 at *Kot Kasram* under Myan Jan Muhammad. The number of pupils attending all these schools is 184 (out of which 10 are girls), and the subjects of tuition are Arabic, Persian and the Kóran.

The other Maktabs and Kóran schools in the circle are as follow:—

Place.	No. of pupils. Boys.	Girls.	Subjects taught.
Hairse (Western)	3	5	The Kóran.
Ditto (Eastern)	5	16	Ditto.
Makúl (Majoo) 2 maktabs	7	...	Ditto.
Cholani	2	...	Ditto.
Basti Usman Shah	1	...	Ditto.
Sanjar	15	...	Persian.
Matto	6	...	The Kóran.
Darahi	6	6	Ditto.
Bichhra	5	...	Ditto.
Bindi	6	...	Arabic Grammar.
Daera Dinpanah	3	...	The Kóran.
Jhang (Northern)	4	...	Ditto.
Ditto (Southern)	7	...	Persian and the Kóran.
Dona (2 maktabs)	23	...	Ditto.
Bolani	2	3	Ditto.
Morjhingi	5	...	Ditto.
Mari	5	..	Ditto.
Manjhota	9	8	Ditto.
Tibbi Kasrani	4	2	Ditto.
Kazi Wali	3	1	Ditto.
Ratira	9	...	Ditto.
Basti Buzdar	17	...	Ditto.
Binda	6	...	Ditto.
Mundrani (2 maktabs)	23	...	Ditto.
Bughlani	7	...	Arabic Grammar.

HARAND.—Myan Aqil Muhammad Rais of Harand is a most distinguished scholar and author in this circle.

There are Maktabs in *Harand* with 15, *Basti Panch Ali* with 3, *Lundi* with 6, *Lalgarh* with 10, *Miranpur* with 8, *Bhakkarpur* with 7, *Tibbi Lundan* with 10, *Judrindan* with 10 and *Banbli* with 4 pupils.

The subjects of tuition are the Kóran and Persian.

YÁRU.—Ghulam Muhammad Kuraishi is the famous Moulvi in this Thana.

There are no schools in this Thana with the exception of the following minor Maktabs at *Bátil*, with 16 pupils reading Hadis and Fiqa; *Yáru* with 15 pupils reading Persian and the Koran; *Basti Hot*, with 26 pupils reading the Koran and Persian; *Sadar Dui*, with 13 Koran-reading students; *Jarwar*, with 9 Koran-reading students; *Chhabri Wálá*, with 10 pupils reading the Koran; *Sandela*, with 20 Perso-Arabic students. All these Maktabs are attached to mosques.

OJHAN has a Moulvi of the name of Musa, and a Bhai of the name of Santokh Das.

This Thana has a Maktab, attached to a mosque, at which 25 students attend. Moulvi Musa, a good Arabic and Persian scholar, teaches Arabic, Persian and the Koran to these pupils. He gets 10 Rs. per month from the Nawab of the place. There is also a Gurmukhi School, attached to a Dharamsala. In this school Bhai Santokh Das instructs 12 pupils in the Granth. He gets Rs. 15 monthly from the city *panches*. There is a minor Maktab at *Kotla Jáfir*, attended by 14 Koran-reading pupils.

DÁJAL.—There is one Moulvi mentioned in this Thana, whose name is Murid Ghaus and who lives at *Nushehra*.

Bhatti Sulgyan in this Thana has a Maktab with 6 pupils, attached to a mosque. The teachers are Moulvi Ghulam Haidar and Moulvi Usman, men of moderate abilities. Their income amounts to about Rs. 60, in kind, yearly.

*EXTRA LIST.

Lala Aya Ram, District Inspector of Schools of Dehra Gházi Khan, sends the following list of schools:—

Names of towns and villages.	No. of Maktabs.	Locality.	Number of pupils.	Subjects taught.
TAHSIL SANGHAR.				
Basti Nasir	1	Attached to Mosque	5	The Korán, and Persian (Gulistán and Bostán.
Barri Shah	1	Ditto	6	Ditto.
Chandarawálá	1	Ditto	6	Ditto and Persian (Gulistán and Bostán).
Fanjá	1	Ditto	5	Ditto ditto (ditto ditto).
Aliwálá	1	Ditto	5	Ditto.
Haji Hamand	1	Ditto	5	Ditto ditto (ditto ditto).
Basti Maláná, Yaki, Jam, Aisam, Naták, Hássú	6	Ditto	20	The Korán. There are only one or two pupils in each of these places. Therefore the total number for all is only stated.
Horá	1	Ditto	7	The Koran.
Dájal	4	Ditto	26	Ditto and Persian.
Basti Massú	1	Ditto	5	Ditto.
Danwar	1	Ditto	7	Ditto.
Hájipur	1	Ditto	6	Ditto.
Basti Punar, Hajo, Kot Jánu	4	Ditto	10	The Koran.
Akilpur	4	Ditto	10	Ditto.
Dhaggo	1	Ditto	10	Ditto.
Basti Kotla Molá, Kotlá Ahmad, Basti Ismáil, Gabol, Basti Rindán, Kotla Sher Muhammad	6	Ditto	20	Ditto

Towsa, *Mangrotá*, *Sokar*, *Dera Gházi Khan*, and *Kotlá Nasir* have each a Mahájani School (the first four attached to shops), attended by 11, 10, 30, 30, and 5 pupils respectively. The subjects taught in the first four are Lande and Multiplication tables, and in the fifth only Lande.

* Besides the principal schools attached to mosques, there are one or two boys found reading in almost every other mosque.

DERAJAT DIVISION.

BANNU DISTRICT.

GENERAL ABSTRACT.

Districts.	No. of Maktabs and Madrasas.	No. of Pupils.	No. of Sanskrit Schools.	No. of Pupils.	No. of Gurmukhi Schools.	No. of Pupils.	No. of Landa or Mahajani Schools.	No. of Pupils.	Total number of Indigenous Schools.	Total number of Pupils.
Bannu ...	105	1,340	...	...	14	281	3	75	122	1,636

Bannu.—Ghulam Jan, Mansa Ram, Chhotu Ram, Bahawal Khan, Kura Ram, Tika Ram, Beli Ram, Vazir Khan, Najaf Ali are the noteworthy Hakims; Qutub Uddin, Amir Ulla, Saleh Din, Khair Ulla, Haji Gul, Muhamad Alim, Golam Yusaf, Ruh Ulla, Badar Din, Mir Riza, Alim Khan, Nur Ulla, Shah Jahan, Gulab Din, are the well known Moulvis; Lekh Raj, Kahar Singh, Ram Das, Kanhya Singh, Bara Singh, Niranjan Singh, Gurdial Singh, Nihal Singh and Sant Singh are the Bháis.

Edwardesabad.—There is an Urdu and a Persian School at Edwardesabad, held in a Shivala, attended by 25 Urdu and Persian-reading pupils. This Maktab is conducted by Kabli Mal, who has a fair knowledge of the subjects taught. No Patshála exists here.

There is one Gurmukhi School connected with a Dharamsala. The numerical strength of this school is 25. In this school only Gurmukhi is taught by Bawa Ram Das, who gets Rs. 2 per mensem.

There are two smaller Gurmukhi Schools besides this, attended by 36 pupils, This thana has one Mahájani School. Forty students attend this school. The teacher's name is Duni Chand, who teaches Lande and Nágri. His income from the students amounts to about Rs. 10 per mensem.

Mianwali.—Dost Ali is the eminent Moulvi in this Thana, and Asa Singh the noteworthy Bhái. The other well-known Hakims in this Thana are Devi Das and Jasvant at Vatta Khel and Abdul Rasul at Chak Dala.

There are two Maktabs, attached to mosques, in this place, attended by 20 students reading the Koran.

The other Maktabs in this Thana are, one at *Van Majhran*, with 12 pupils, *Vatta Khail*, with 12, *Billu Khail* has three with 40, *Kundian* 2 with 20, *Shahbas Khail* 1 with 12, *Selhwan* 4 with 53, *Phakra* 3 with 51, *Musa Khail* 1 with 50, *Chakrala* 1 with 15, and *Mouza Gil* 1 with 18. All these Maktabs are attached to mosques, and in all of them the Koran and Muhammadan Law is taught, with the exception of *Selhwan* and *Phakra*, where Arabic and Persian are taught. They have no fixed income. Some teachers get something in cash and others in kind up to Rs. 2 or 3 a month. The teachers possess moderate abilities. Pathshálas there are none in this circle. There is a Gurmukhi School in each of the following villages: *Vatta Khail*, *Kundian*, *Billu Khail*, and *Musa Khail*; the number of pupils attending are 5, 8, 10 and 20, respectively, the subjects taught being Gurmukhi, Hindi, and Vyakarn; all are attached to Dharamsalas.

The well-known Moulvis of this Thana are Ahmed Din in *Vatta Khail*, Syed Rasul in *Van Majhran*, Ali Muhamad in *Selhawan*, Chan Pir in *Gil*, Syed Ahmed in *Musa Khail*, and Qazi Ghulam Nabi in *Chakrala*.

The Pandits are Jassu Lal in *Billu Khail*, Lal Chand in *Kundian*, and Devi Dyal in *Musa Khail*.

The Bháis in the suburbs are Gyan Singh and Gauhra Ram in *Vatta Khail*, Kahar Singh in *Billu Khail*, and Bhagat Singh in *Kundian*.

MOJHA.—Qazi Ghulam Mustafa of *Shakarpari* is the famous Hakim in this Thana. He is in medical attendance on the Malaks of *Kala Bágh*. The well-known Moulvi is Ghulam Husain of *Vahe Váli*. Múl Sant Sukh is the eminent Bhái of *Mojha*.

There are no Schools, Maktabs or Pathsháls in this Thana. The Imams attached to the mosques teach the Koran to a few boys and get in return bread, corn at harvest and some cash on the occasion of the pupil finishing his Koran.

KÁLÁ BÁGH.—Has one Maktab held in a mosque, in which only the Koran is taught to 70 boys by Hafizes, Ahmed Mahmud and Ghulam Husain, and Sharaf Din, who are all of them indifferent scholars. The teachers get bread and nothing more.

ISÁ KHAIL.—Mian Muluk Ali of *Kulur* is the eminent Maulvi in this Thana, the well-known Hakims being Rochi Ram of *Kamru*, Ghulam Muhammad Shaikh of *Isa Khail*, Qazi Abdulla and Ghulam Ali of *Kanglanwala*. Ram Rakkha is the noteworthy Pandit and Gurmukh Singh the first Bhái.

Isa Khail has six Maktabs, attached to mosques, with 118 pupils. In these the Koran, Hadis, Urdu and Persian are taught by the following teachers:—Qazi Nur Kamal, Mian Haji, Ghulam Haidar, Mian Ahmed Ali, Fateh Sher Ali and Mussummat Bakhtan, wife of Ali.

Kalur has 3 Maktabs and a Gurmukhi School, attended by 21 and 5 students respectively; the Maktabs being kept by Mian Maluk Ali, Sultan Ahmed and Zaman Ali, and the Gurmukhi School by Pokhar Ram. The subjects taught in the Maktabs are the Koran, story books and Hadis.

Turg has 4 Maktabs, with 23 pupils, taught by Mian Ghulam Muhammad Nur Alim, Ghulam Ali and Hafiz Khoja. There is also a Gurmukhi School here, with 6 pupils, taught by Bhái Khem Chand. The Koran is taught in the Maktab and Gurmukhi in the Gurmukhi School.

KAMAR MASHAFI.—At this place there are 3 Maktabs with 20 pupils who read the Koran and books on poetry. The teachers' names are Muhammad Azim, Alí Muhammad, Muhammad Shafi. They get no fixed salary.

Mubda Khel has one Maktab, containing 7 pupils, who are taught poetry and the Kóran by Imamuddin. The teacher has no fixed income.

PILAN.—Here there is a Maktab held in a mosque. In this Mian Hamand, a great Arabic and Persian scholar, teaches the Kóran to 60 pupils gratuitously. There is a Mahájani School with 8 pupils, who are taught Lande gratuitously by Makand Ram.

Harnoli has one Maktab, in a mosque, in which Khwaja Umar, a man of learning, gives lessons in Arabic to 18 pupils gratuitously. There is a Gurmukhi School also, attended by 80 pupils who read Gurmukhi with Bawa Amar Das, an Udási Faqir. This school is attached to a Dharamsálá. Instruction is given gratuitously.

LAKKI.—In this Police station Gopal Ram, Dwara, Abdul Rahman and Thala are the famous Hakims; Ali Muhammad, Muhammad Husain, Jauhar Shah, Duráná, and Abdul Wahab are the Moulvis.

There are two Maktabs here attached to mosques, with 40 students reading Persian and Arabic. Moulvi Ali Muhammad and Muhammad Hassan, good scholars in Arabic and Persian, are the teachers. This Thana has also two Gurmukhi Schools, with 12 boys, attached to Dharamsalas. Kalu Shah and Hardit Shah are the teachers.

Langar Khail of Hathi Khan, Ghulam Moman Khail, Ahmad Khail, Baggu Khel, Kamal Khail have each got a Maktab, with 16, 8, 9, 60 and 12 pupils. In these the Kóran and Arabic are taught. The first is attached to a mosque.

GHOR LAWANA.—In this Thana there are four Maktabs, one in *Ghor Lawana* with 10 pupils, one at *Ismail Khail* with 11 pupils, one at *Muzaffar Khan* with 5 pupils, and one at *Hardanu Shah*, with 5 pupils. The first three are attached to mosques and have for their subjects of study Arabic, Persian and Pashtu, the fourth is not so attached, and Persian and Urdu are the subjects of tuition. Muhammad Akbar Shah, Moulvi Ahmed, Gul Muhammad and Gul Hasan are the teachers. They know little Urdu, but are good scholars in Pashtu and Arabic. Their average monthly income, in kind, is Rs. 6 each.

The famous Maulvis in this Thana are, Maulvis Muhammad and Muhammad Akbar Shah.

MARBAN.—In this Thana, there is a Madrassa at *Hawid*, with 14 pupils taught by Abdul Majid, of moderate abilities. The subjects taught are Urdu and Persian. Teacher's income Rs. 5 a month with daily bread. There is a Mahájani School at *Náwár*, in which Lande and a little Gurmukhi is taught to 27 pupils. This school is held in a Dharamsala. Teacher's name is Lekhraj, who gets daily bread from the guardians of his pupils.

Additional List of Schools received from a private Informant.

MAKTABS.

Name of Village or Town.	Name of Teacher.	Number of Schools.	Number of pupils.	Subjects taught.
Abá Khail	...	1	8	The Kóran and Fiqa.
Páindah Nichan Khail	...	1	8	Fiqa and Poetry.
Khoedád Khail	...	2	12	Fiqa, the Kóran and Poetry.
Daddewála	...	1	6	The Koran.
Deo Khail	...	1	6	Do.
Zangi Khail	...	1	8	Grammar and Fiqa.
Sayad Khail	...	1	6	The Kóran, Poetry, Books of Medicine.
Ibak Khail	...	3	40	The Kóran, Poetry, Books of Medicine.
Mandrah Khail	...	1	12	The Kóran.
Mir Azam Michan Khail	...	1	8	Grammar, Poetry and Fiqa.
Miná Khail	Muhammad Hussain.	1	15 or 25	Fiqa, Grammar, Syntax, Mantiq, Natural Sciences, Mathematics, Hadis, Tafsir, Persian.
Ditto	Ali Muhammad	1	10	Fiqa, Grammar, Syntax, Mantiq, Natural Sciences, Mathematics, Hadis, Tafsir, Persian.
Ditto	Jawahir Sháh	1	20	Fqa, Grammar, Syntax, Mantiq, Natural Sciences, Mathematics, Hadis, Tafsir, Persian.
Ditto	...	3	11	Fiqa, Grammar, Syntax, Mantiq, Natural Sciences, Mathematics, Hadis, Tafsir, Persian.
Nádir Khail	...	1	4	The Kóran.
Baijist Khail	...	1	3	Do.
Titar Khail Gató Khan	...	1	8	Grammar, Fiqa and Poetry.
Jang Khail	...	1	9	The Kóran.
Daulat Tojah Zái	...	1	4	Fiqa.
Shemún Khail	...	1	6	Do.
Ghazni Khail	...	1	8	Grammar, Poetry and the Kóran.
Gandi Umar Chak	...	1	4	Poetry and Fiqa.
Landewah	...	1	15	Fiqa.
Marmandi	...	1	16	Do.
Záfar Khail	...	1	5	Poetry, Fiqa and the Kóran.
Adam Zái	...	1	12	Poetry and Fiqa.
Ahmad Zái	...	1	8	Do. Do.
Titri Khail	...	1	4	Fiqa.
Tajori	...	1	12	Do.
Takhti Khail	...	1	4	Do.
Darka	...	1	8	Do.
Kot Kashmir	Khair Muhammad	3	22	Fiqa, Grammar and Syntax.
Warli	...	1	6	Fiqa.
Garbi Barkharádr Faqir	...	1	8	The Kóran.
Garbi Sultan Mahmud Khán	...	1	5	Poetry.
Sahibdád Khán Maidád Khail	...	1	4	Do.
Alim Shah Khail	...	1	12	The Kóran.
Mudni Khail	...	1	8	Do.
Basti	...	1	5	The Kóran, Fiqa and Persian.
Nár Hardeo Shah	...	1	6	

Gurmukhi Schools.

Name of Village or Town.	Name of Teacher.	Number of Schools.	Number of pupils.	Subjects taught.
Miná Khel	Hardit Shah	1	6	Gurmukhi.
Nár Hardeo Shah	Hardeo Shah's son or grandson.	1	8	Do.

Another private informant adds the following names of eminent persons and of indigenous schools in this district:—

BANNU.—*Pandit* Totta Ram; *Maulvis* Faizullah, Muhammad Hayat, Ghulam Kadim; *Bhai* Tek Singh and Dara Shah, a famous Pashtu *poet*.

ISA KHAIL.—*Hakims* Amirchand, Lalchand, Dasondha Ram, Núr Muhammad, Shaikh Najaf, Nur Muhammad second, Dost Ali, Ghulam, Husain, Ali, Fazal and Haidar (an oculist and surgeon famous for his skill in lithotomy); *Maulvis* Kazi Núr Kamal, Ghulam Rasúl, Muhammad Husain, Jan Muhammad, Imam Din, Muhammad Azam and Bahauddin; *Pandits* Ganesh Das, Basdeo Ram, Ruchi Ram, Topan Lal and Ramdyal and *Bhais* Narayan Singh, Wasewa Singh, Ram Singh, Shivdyal Singh, Perdhan Singh, Khem Singh and Bhagat Pohkar Das.

MIAN WALI.—*Hakim* Shamgir; *Pandits* Ramchand, Behari Lal, Chhail Das, Sham Das; *Maulvis* Ali Muhammad, Sayyid Rasul, Muhammad Hayat, Nur-i-Mustafa, Hafiz Ghulam Husain, Ghulàm Mustafa and Kamruddin and *Bhais* Gulab Singh, Bava Amar Das, Kalyan Singh and Asa Singh.

LAKKI.—*Maulvis* Khair Muhammad, Qul Ahmad, Sualeh Din, Tahir Din, Jan Muhammad, Ibrahim, Jan Muhammad second, Zaafran and Umargul, *Bhai* Sarup Singh.

The following are the schools to be added to those already recorded:—

Place.	No. of schools.	No. of pupils.	Subjects taught.
Salima . . .	1	12	The Korán.
Bazar Ahmad Khan .	1	20	Ditto.
Jandu Khail . .	1	20	Ditto.
Katti Sádát . .	1	20	Ditto.
Marban . . .	1	12	Ditto.
Akbar Khan . .	1	10	Ditto.
Multan . . .	1	6	Ditto.

N.B.—The above return reached too late to enable me to enter the names of the above scholars in the list of Maulvis, &c., in Part V.

DERAJAT DIVISION.

DERA ISMAEL KHAN.

GENERAL ABSTRACT.

District.	No. of Maktabs.	No. of pupils.	No. of Sanscrit Schools.	No. of pupils.	No. of Gurmukhi Schools.	No. of pupils.	No. of Mahajani.	No. of pupils.	Total number of Schools.	Total number of pupils.
Dera Ismail Khan	190	1,755	15	220	17	192	24	487	246	2,664

There are very few indigenous schools in this district. The number of all kinds of such schools, the pupils attending them, and other particulars connected therewith are given in detail in the accompanying statement:

1. MADRASAS.—When a Mulla in a village or town takes up the task of giving religious instruction, he goes and sits in a mosque and in a few days 4 or 5 little boys collect round him to learn to read. These are often sent to the school by the parents to keep them out of mischief rather than receive useful lessons. The method of imparting instruction is very defective. Boys are required to learn by rote each word of their lessons, and the consequence is that very few of them ever succeed in finishing the Koran. As soon as the boys get older they leave the school to assist their parents in their respective callings: so that after having spent 4 or 5 years or even more in the Madrasa the boys are as ignorant as those who have never seen the school. The income of village Mullas is not fixed, but a fee called "Bismalla" is paid them by the agricultural classes on the occasion of collecting their grain heaps. The people of the village also give "Wazifa" or baked bread to the Mulla every night. On the occasion of a festival also the "Mulla" obtains food and other presents from the villagers. When the pupil finishes a chapter of the Koran, he must give some "Hadia" or present to his teacher before commencing the next. But all these presents are considered to be alms, and it is always understood that he teaches the boys gratis.

2. OTHER RELIGIOUS BOOKS.—Religious instruction other than lessons in the Koran is limited only to a small number of Talib-ul-ilms. These generally quit their homes and attend such Madrasas, the teachers of which are noted for their knowledge in Arabic literature. They mostly subsist on "Wazifas" sent to the mosque by the people. In some instances they beg their own bread. The most eminent schools of this class are in Dera. They are two in number, and the names of head Maulvis are Salih Muhammad and Abdul Ghafur. Religious books, logic and Arabic grammar are taught in them. They finish their course by about 30 years of age, but after they leave the school, they become highly bigotted Mussulmans, looking down upon the whole world as kafirs or infidels. With all their knowledge they are practically unable to compose a letter.*

3. PERSIAN.—Persian is usually commenced after the boy has finished his Koran. The following text books are used in all the Persian indigenous schools:—

1. Amad Nama.
2. Karima.
3. Nisab Zaruri.
4. Gulistan.
5. Bostan.
6. Yusuf Zulaikha.
7. Sikandar Nama.
8. A few inshas or letter-writers.

No method or system is observed in teaching, and the consequence is that the work of 2 or 3 years is rendered a tedious task of from 7 to 10 years.

4. PATHSHALAS.—Only the Brahmins give their sons instruction in Sanscrit reading and writing. The teachers get no remuneration for their pains, the work of imparting "vidia" or knowledge being considered by them the most

* It must be noticed that this Report has been supplied by the District Inspector of Schools, Ghulam Muhammad Khan, and by Daiza Ram, Deputy Superintendent of the Vernacular District Office of Debra Ismail Khan, formerly a Government School teacher, and now a leading Member of the Sabha Society of that place.

sublime and noble. Most of the boys leave off the school when they have finished a few elementary books relating to funeral and conjugal rites and ceremonies. Dera has the most eminent Sanscrit scholars in the district. They teach Vyakaran or Grammar, Jotash or Astronomy and Vedant Shastras.

5. GURMUKHI.—Gurmukhi is taught in some of the temples. The pupils pay a small weekly fee either in atta or copper coin. The course is considered to be finished when the boy can read the "Granth." He then leaves the school and pays a small sum as present to the teacher. Gurmukhi reading being easy to learn, the more advanced men read with their relatives or even neighbours.

6. MAHAJANI.—The Hindus invariably know the elements of Mahajani. Boys are sent to read, to write and repeat multiplication tables to a venerable Hindu who, it may be noticed, is unable to do any other work. In fact, the teacher has nothing to do but to keep an eye on the pupils. They teach each other and when the account-keeping is finished, the boys leave the school and join their father's or relative's shops, and it is there that they are trained in the native mode of account keeping. If in a village no teacher is available to teach the boys, they are taught by their own father and brothers.

The multiplication tables curren' are as follows:—

1. Ikki or 1×10 to 5×10
2. Chbakki or 6×10 to 10×10
3. Giyárí (yárí) or 11×10 to 15×10
4. Solhi or 16×10 to 20×10
5. Ikwíhír or 21×10 to 25×10
6. Chhawíhir or 26×10 to 30×10
7. Ikatríhir or 31×10 to 35×10
8. Chhatríhir or 36×10 to 40×10
9. Sawáyá or $1 \times 1\frac{1}{4}$ to $50 \times 1\frac{1}{4}$
10. Deara or $1 \times 1\frac{1}{2}$ to $50 \times 1\frac{1}{2}$
11. Adháe or $1 \times 2\frac{1}{2}$ to $50 \times 2\frac{1}{2}$
12. Tak Paisa or table of money.
13. Path Paropi or table of measurement.

The Mahajani teachers are paid as in the case of Gurmukhi teachers.

Among the names of distinguished Maulvis, Hakims, Pandits, &c., are brought to notice:—

Maulvis.—Saleh Muhammad, Abdul Ghafur, Alla Dad and Mulla Miskin, Hakims.—Fazal Ali, Zind Ali and Tikam Ram. *Pandits.*—Mohun Lal, Kishan Das and Riki Kesh. *Bhais.*—Kirpal Singh and Bawa Khem Das.

The largest maktab in this district is at the town of Dera Ismail Khan, attached to a mosque under two teachers, Saleh Muhammad and Abdul Ghafur with 40 pupils under each; they are both good Arabic scholars and instruct their pupils in Persian, Arabic, Theology and Logic. They have no fixed income.

The largest Patshala is also in Dera Ismail Khan. It is held in a private house in charge of Gundo Lal, who is well versed in Sanscrit and teaches to 35 boys Viyakaran and Jotash, and has also no fixed income. The best Gurmukhi school is at *Kalachi* attached to a Dharamsala under Ganga Ram with 12 pupils who learn, read and write in Gurmukhi.

Dera has the three largest Mahajani schools of the district under Jugal Das, Ditta and Ramaiya with 50, 40 and 10 pupils respectively, who each pay some small monthly fee to their teacher. The Mahajani system of account-keeping is the principal subject of tuition. Annexed table gives the total of indigenous schools and their number of pupils in this district:—

NAMES OF TAHSILS.	Number of Maktabs and Madrasas.	Number of Pupils.	Subjects taught.	Number of Patshalas.	Number of Pupils.	Subjects taught.	Number of Gurmukhi Schools.	Number of Pupils.	Subjects taught.	Number of Mahajani Schools.	Number of Pupils.	Subjects taught.
Tahsil Dera Ismael Khan	8	314	Koran. Religious Books. Persian.	6	145	Viyakaran. Jotash. Sanscrit.	...	...	...	3	100	Account-keeping.
Kalachi	61	676	Ditto.	3	11	Ditto.	3	29	Religious Books.	4	99	Ditto.
Tank	23	135	Ditto.	...	...	...	1	10	Ditto.	2	26	Ditto.
Leiah	60	560	Ditto.	4	48	Ditto.	3	45	Ditto.	4	102	Ditto.
Bhakkar	38	271	Ditto.	2	16	Ditto.	10	109	Ditto.	11	170	Ditto.
TOTAL	190	1,755		15	220		17	192		24	497	

Part III.

A.—General Statement showing the number of pupils in indigenous schools in the Panjab, as also the number of persons "under instruction" according to the Census of 1881 and the number of pupils in Government and Aided schools (see pages 14 to 16 of the Preface to this report).

District.	I. Number of pupils in Government and aided schools.	II. Number of persons "under instruction" according to Census.	III. Balance, i.e., number of pupils in indigenous schools after deducting numbers in column I from column II.	IV. Number of pupils in indigenous schools according to Police, District and private Returns.	V. Higher number in each district taken to represent the actual number.*	Remarks.
Delhi	4,317	6,736	2,419	3,304	3,304	
Karnal	1,922	2,778	856	659	1,042	
Gurgaon	3,148	3,392	240	1,042	659	
Hissar	1,412	1,737	295	1,111	1,111	
Rohtak	2,378	2,897	519	1,184	1,184	
Sirsa	622	1,689	1,067	1,014	1,014	
Amballa	5,229	6,365	1,136	2,090	2,090	
Ludhiana	3,574	5,258	1,679	3,262	3,262	
Simla	470	1,213	734	176	176†	
Jalandhar	6,120	7,762	1,642	3,242	3,242	
Hoshiarpur	4,720	8,177	3,457	2,414	3,457	
Kangra	2,400	5,132	2,732	616	2,732	
Amritsar	5,792	9,106	3,314	4,860	4,860	
Sialkot	4,483	9,980	5,497	6,513	6,513	
Gurdaspur	5,259	7,615	2,356	1,487	2,355	
Lahore	5,279	10,472	5,193	6,097	6,097	
Ferozepur	2,475	3,523	1,048	2,126	2,126	
Gujranwala	3,335	7,572	3,237	3,644	3,644	
Rawalpindi	4,302	9,416	5,113	12,142	12,142	
Jhelum	3,493	4,660	1,167	4,092	4,092	
Gujrat	3,737	5,994	2,258	5,418	5,418	
Shahpur	2,105	3,659	1,554	2,853	2,853	
Multan	3,546	7,241	3,695	2,116	3,695	
Jhang	1,958	3,778	1,820	2,506	2,506	
Montgomery	1,142	3,156	2,014	2,292	2,292	
Muzaffargarh	1,612	3,401	1,789	1,551	1,789	
Dehra Ismail Khan	1,958	3,080	1,122	2,664	2,664	
Dehra Ghazi Khan	1,895	3,434	1,539	1,863	1,863	
Bannu	1,183	2,116	934	1,636	1,636	
Peshawar	1,814	8,183	6,369	...	6,369‡	
Kohat	375	1,276	901	720	901	
Hazara	986	2,274	1,288	1,299	1,299	
Total ...	94,379	1,63,362	68,983	86,023	98,318	

* If the number of pupils ascertained to be in indigenous schools is higher than the number stated to be "under instruction" in the census returns (after deducting the pupils in Government and aided schools), then the former number is taken. If, however, the balance of the census is larger than the number, as yet, ascertained to be in indigenous schools, the census return is accepted.

† The reason for taking the lower number has been already explained.

‡ In spite of every effort and both telegraphing and writing to the various Authorities, no returns of that District have yet been received. The "balance," however, under column III may well be assumed to represent the lowest number of pupils in indigenous schools.

B.—Statement showing the number of (a) Maktabs and Madrasas, (b) Patshálas, (c) Gurmukhi schools, (d) Mahajani schools and of their respective pupils on 30th October 1882 throughout the Panjab.

District.	Number of Maktabs and Madrasas.	Number of Pupils.	Patshalas.	Number of Pupils.	Number of Gurmukhi schools.	Number of Pupils in the Gurmukhi schools.	Number of Mahajani schools.	Number of Pupils in the Mahajani schools.	Total number of indigenous schools.	Total number of pupils in the indigenous schools.
Delhi	141	2,073	19	177	...	...	56	1,054	216	3,304
Gurgaon	24	236	6	65	...	...	25	358	55	659
Karnal	43	538	11	111	1	8	22	385	77	1,042
Hissar	46	592	12	133	...	...	8	386	66	1,111
Rohtak	45	452	33	351	...	...	21	381	99	1,184
Sirsa	101	763	5	23	10	55	6	173	122	1,014
Amballa	82	1,018	19	303	7	66	30	703	138	2,090
Ludhiana	138	1,573	21	263	97	891	23	535	279	3,262
Simla	9	129	...	...	...	...	2	47	11	176
Jullundhur	143	1,613	30	456	26	310	25	863	224	3,242
Hushiarpur	123	1,395	34	435	36	332	18	252	211	2,414
Kangra	11	168	20	388	...	...	4	60	35	616
Amritsar	132	1,795	65	1,074	63	1,193	24	798	281	4,860
Gurdaspur	131	1,165	12	128	8	98	3	96	154	1,487
Sialkot	455	5,365	14	152	29	384	30	612	528	6,513
Lahore	295	4,247	33	377	43	571	28	902	398	6,097
Gujranwala	197	2,433	18	272	35	461	16	468	266	3,644
Ferozepore	137	1,345	11	141	35	311	14	326	197	2,126
Rawalpindi	660	8,771	9	94	137	2,394	10	883	816	12,142
Jhelum	200	3,003	19	294	27	646	4	59	250	4,092
Gujrat	274	3,628	20	318	53	879	19	593	366	5,418
Shahpur	85	1,447	19	373	45	893	8	170	157	2,853
Multan	71	1,118	10	109	11	208	8	686	100	2,118
Jhang	122	1,423	14	197	55	770	5	116	196	2,506
Montgomery	158	1,461	8	103	48	587	12	191	226	2,292
Muzaffargarh	163	1,384	8	35	9	78	6	109	186	1,551
Dera Ismail Khan	190	1,755	15	220	17	192	24	497	246	2,664
Dera Ghazi Khan	179	1,645	5	43	5	32	7	144	196	1,863
Bannu	105	1,340	...	...	14	221	3	75	122	1,636
Peshawar	...	...	...	...	...	...	...	...	...	...
Kohat	39	679	...	...	3	41	...	...	42	720
Hazara	80	1,028	3	85	15	163	1	24	99	1,299
	4,079	56,610	492	6,729	889	12,354	468	11,297	6,868	86,023

C.

A general abstract of the Indigenous Schools in the Punjab.

Name of place or Thana	Number of Maktabs and Madrasas.	Number of Pupils.	Number of Patshalas, i.e., Sanskrit and Nagri Schools.	Number of Pupils.	Number of Gurmukhi Schools.	Number of Pupils in Gurmukhi Schools.	Number of Lande Schools.	Number of Pupils in Lande Schools.	Total number of Indigenous Schools.	Total number of pupils attending Indigenous Schools.
DELHI DIVISION.										
I.—Delhi District.										
Najafgarh	...	...	4	13	...	...	2	9	6	22
Datoli	2	20	...	...	...	...	3	29	5	49
Soonipat	4	42	1	10	...	...	3	24	8	86
Mehroli	3	24	1	3	...	...	2	22	6	49
Faridabad	1	5	2	50	...	...	...	...	3	55
Alipur	2	12	1	6	...	...	5	63	8	81
Balabgarh	1	5	3	24	...	...	...	...	4	29
Haveli Palam	...	...	1	5	...	...	1	15	2	20
Nangloi	1	8	...	...	...	...	5	40	6	48
Mohna	1	10	1	25	...	...	...	...	2	35
Delhi	126	1,947	5	41	...	...	35	852	166	2,840
Total ...	141	2,078	19	177	...	...	56	1,054	216	3,304
II.—Gurgaon District.										
Shahjehanpur	...	..	...	...	...	...	1	12	1	12
Gurgaon	3	45	...	...	...	...	3	37	6	82
Rewari	4	58	1	22	...	...	3	75	8	155
Ferozepur	2	17	...	...	...	...	3	23	5	40
Palwal	7	49	...	...	...	...	8	75	15	124
Farrukhnagar	3	27	...	...	...	...	4	108	7	135
Punahana	1	8	...	...	...	...	...	...	1	8
Sohna	2	18	1	10	...	...	2	21	5	49
Hittan	...	...	3	31	...	...	...	...	3	31
Nuh	1	2	1	2	...	...	...	...	2	4
Hasanpur	1	12	...	...	...	...	1	7	2	19
Total ...	24	236	6	65	...	...	25	358	55	659
III.—Karnal District.										
Samalka	...	...	4	52	...	...	...	...	4	52
Batana	2	36	...	...	...	...	1	13	3	49
Indri	3	13	1	5	...	...	6	66	10	84
Alupur	1	3	3	39	...	...	4	41	8	83
Kunjpura	2	21	...	...	...	...	...	...	2	21
Siuk	1	8	...	...	...	...	2	14	3	22
Karnal	8	104	3	15	...	...	2	65	13	184
Kaithal	1	15	...	...	...	...	1	70	2	85
Gohla	1	20	...	...	...	...	...	...	1	20
Pundri	...	...	...	...	...	...	1	22	1	22
Panipat	21	284	...	...	...	...	4	67	25	351
Dhatrat	2	22	...	...	...	...	1	27	3	49
Budladah	...	...	...	...	1	8	...	...	1	8
Asandh	1	12	...	...	...	...	...	...	1	12
Total ...	43	538	11	111	1	8	22	385	77	1,043

A general abstract of the Indigenous Schools in the Punjab—(continued).

HISSAR DIVISION.

IV.—Hissar District.

Name of place or Thana.	Number of Maktabs and Madrasas.	Number of Pupils.	Number of Patshalas, i.e., Sanscrit and Nagri Schools.	Number of Pupils.	Number of Gurmukhi Schools.	Number of Pupils in Gurmukhi Schools.	Number of Lande Schools.	Number of Pupils in Lande Schools.	Total number of Indigenous Schools.	Total number of pupils attending Indigenous Schools.
Fatahabad	6	170	...	...	...	...	1	20	7	190
Bhivani	...	...	1	15	...	...	1	100	2	115
Hansi	2	45	1	8	...	...	1	90	4	143
Kairu	...	...	2	16	...	...	...	...	2	16
Barnond	...	...	1	4	...	...	...	...	1	4
Behal	...	...	1	12	...	...	1	20	2	32
Balsamand	...	...	2	19	...	...	...	...	2	19
Tohana	12	110	1	10	...	...	...	...	13	120
Hissar	3	32	1	10	...	...	1	30	5	72
Hatya	4	57	1	19	...	...	...	...	5	76
Extra	19	178	1	20	...	...	3	126	23	324
Total ...	46	592	12	133	...	...	8	386	66	1,111

V.—Rohtak District.

Name of place or Thana.	Number of Maktabs and Madrasas.	Number of Pupils.	Number of Patshalas, i.e., Sanscrit and Nagri Schools.	Number of Pupils.	Number of Gurmukhi Schools.	Number of Pupils in Gurmukhi Schools.	Number of Lande Schools.	Number of Pupils in Lande Schools.	Total number of Indigenous Schools.	Total number of pupils attending Indigenous Schools.
Saupla	...	...	1	35	...	...	1	32	2	67
Kalanaur	10	132	2	13	...	...	...	...	12	145
Gohana	4	35	5	53	...	...	1	8	10	96
Rohtak	7	89	3	22	...	...	2	32	12	143
Kharkhauda	1	22	1	6	...	...	1	20	3	48
Mahm	3	27	1	8	...	...	1	12	5	47
Bahadargarh	1	2	2	22	...	...	...	...	3	24
Beri	...	...	2	40	...	...	...	...	2	40
Salawas	3	46	...	...	...	...	...	...	3	46
Jhajjar	6	48	1	8	...	...	6	132	13	188
Extra	10	51	16	144	...	...	8	145	34	340
Total ...	45	452	33	361	...	...	21	381	99	1,184

VI.—Sirsa.

Name of place or Thana.	Number of Maktabs and Madrasas.	Number of Pupils.	Number of Patshalas, i.e., Sanscrit and Nagri Schools.	Number of Pupils.	Number of Gurmukhi Schools.	Number of Pupils in Gurmukhi Schools.	Number of Lande Schools.	Number of Pupils in Lande Schools.	Total number of Indigenous Schools.	Total number of pupils attending Indigenous Schools.
Sirsa ... ... / Rania	23	173	3	14	...	...	3	110	29	296
Dabwali ... ... / Bahrajpur	15	94	1	3	6	29	...	...	23	126
Abuhar ... ... / Sarawan ... ... / Fazilka	56	453	1	6	3	22	1	6	61	487
Extra	6	44	...	...	1	4	2	57	9	105
Total ...	101	763	5	23	10	55	6	173	122	1,014

A general abstract of the Indigenous Schools in the Punjab—(continued).

UMBALLA DIVISION.

VII.—Umballa District.

Name of place or Thana.	Number of Maktabs and Madrasas.	Number of Pupils.	Number of Patshalas, i.e., Sanskrit and Nagri Schools.	Number of Pupils.	Number of Gurmukhi Schools.	Number of Pupils in Gurmukhi Schools.	Number of Lunde Schools.	Number of Pupils in Lunde Schools.	Total number of Indigenous Schools.	Total number of pupils attending Indigenous Schools.
Umballa Cantonment	19	346	...	...	...	...	1	80	20	426
Kharar	12	87	3	9	4	24	...	...	18	120
Potuki	1	10	...	...	...	...	2	34	3	44
Thaneswar	3	27	3	21	...	...	...	...	6	48
Badaur	3	35	1	12	...	...	4	79	8	126
Pehoa	3	24	3	35	...	...	3	30	9	89
Bilaspur	7	54	...	...	...	...	4	28	11	82
Chappar	1	10	...	...	...	...	1	10	2	20
Mullana	4	28	...	...	...	...	2	48	6	76
Sadhora	4	45	...	...	...	...	...	...	4	45
Ropar	2	35	1	12	...	...	1	60	4	107
Sodhi	1	8	...	...	...	...	...	...	1	8
Ludwa	...	...	1	30	...	...	1	10	2	40
Singhore	2	25	...	...	...	...	...	...	2	25
Shahabad	6	71	1	50	1	16	...	...	8	138
Narayengarh	3	30	...	...	...	...	1	15	4	45
Mazra	...	...	3	59	...	...	1	15	4	74
Mubarakpur	...	...	1	25	...	...	1	49	2	74
Jagadhri	2	15	1	15	1	25	3	95	7	150
Umballa City	8	163	2	35	1	2	4	140	15	340
Naherpur	1	10	...	...	...	...	...	...	2	20
Ghalore	...	...	...	...	...	...	1	10		
Total ...	82	1,018	19	303	7	66	30	703	138	2,090

VIII.—Ludhiana District.

Name of place or Thana.	Number of Maktabs and Madrasas.	Number of Pupils.	Number of Patshalas, i.e., Sanskrit and Nagri Schools.	Number of Pupils.	Number of Gurmukhi Schools.	Number of Pupils in Gurmukhi Schools.	Number of Lunde Schools.	Number of Pupils in Lunde Schools.	Total number of Indigenous Schools.	Total number of pupils attending Indigenous Schools.
Raikot	15	164	3	28	10	66	4	48	33	303
Dakha	11	81	1	8	16	120	1	9	29	218
Sanewal	9	61	1	3	3	30	...	...	13	94
Shahna	...	...	1	10	20	123	1	22	22	155
Ludhiana	60	716	2	32	6	88	2	195	70	1,031
Machiwara	4	40	2	15	...	...	...	...	6	55
Samrala	...	...	4	71	1	11	3	23	8	105
Jugraon	19	304	3	27	12	104	4	171	38	616
Delon	4	50	...	...	13	206	...	...	17	256
Khanna	3	37	4	64	2	27	7	67	15	195
Miscellaneous	14	120	...	...	16	117	...	...	30	237
Total ...	138	1,573	21	268	97	891	23	535	270	3,263

***A general abstract of the Indigenous Schools in the Punjab*—(continued).**

Name of place or Thana.	Number of Maktabs and Madrasas.	Number of Pupils.	Number of Patshalas, i.e., Sanskrit and Nagri Schools.	Number of Pupils.	Number of Gurmukhi Schools.	Number of Pupils in Gurmukhi Schools.	Number of Lande Schools.	Number of Pupils in Lande Schools.	Total number of Indigenous Schools.	Total number of pupils attending Indigenous Schools.
IX.—Simla District.										
Sabatu	1	30	...	...	...	...	1	12	2	42
Simla	5	60	...	...	...	...	...	...	5	60
Dagshai	2	29	...	...	...	...	...	...	2	29
Kalka	1	10	...	...	...	...	1	35	2	45
Total ...	9	129	...	...	...	...	2	47	11	176
JULLUNDAR DIVISION.										
X.—Jullundar District.										
Jullundar	38	593	4	51	1	6	7	421	50	1,074
Do. Cantonment*	9	124	2	39	...	...	...	...	11	163
Kartarpur	2	11	1	3	2	13	1	40	6	67
Bhogpur	8	38	...	...	1	4	...	...	9	42
Adampur	16	125	1	10	5	86	3	38	25	259
Bangah	10	107	0	134	8	100	2	28	29	369
Rahun	14	134	5	69	4	23	2	70	25	296
Phillour	1	5	...	...	1	28	...	...	2	33
Nurmahal	1	9	3	63	...	...	2	110	6	182
Nakodar	32	330	3	65	2	23	3	95	40	513
Shahkot	1	4	2	19	...	...	1	11	4	34
Miscellaneous	11	133	...	...	2	27	4	50	17	210
Total ...	143	1,613	80	456	26	310	25	863	221	3,242
XI.—Hoshiarpur District.										
Tanda	18	112	1	5	...	...	...		19	117
Nurpur	...	...	1	10	...	...	...		1	10
Anandpur	...	...	...	...	5	89	...		5	89
Gadhdewala	1	6	1	6	...	...	...	...	2	12
Gadh Shankar	8	127	3	32	1	10	...	...	12	169
Mukerian	8	38	1	5	...	...	...	...	9	43
Balachor	0	114	2	9	1	5	...	...	12	128
Hajipur	4	38	3	26	1	18	2	14	10	96
Una	...	...	4	67	...	...	4	40	8	107
Dasuya	12	249	...	...	...	...	1	11	13	260
Mubarikpur	1	10	...	...	...	...	...	...	1	10
Hariana	20	179 (33 girls)	4	47	11	44	3	34	38	317
Mahilpur	10	112	4	57	7	77	3	22	24	268
Hoshiarpur	32	397	10	171	10	89	5	181	57	788
Total ...	129	1,395	34	435	36	332	18	252	211	2,414

A general abstract of the Indigenous Schools in the Punjab—(continued).

Name of place or Thana.	Number of Maktabs and Madrasas.	Number of Pupils.	Number of Patshalas, i.e., Sanskrit and Nagri Schools.	Number of Pupils.	Number of Gurmukhi Schools.	Number of Pupils in Gurmukhi Schools.	Number of Landé Schools.	Number of Pupils in Landé Schools.	Total number of Indigenous Schools.	Total number of pupils attending Indigenous Schools.
XII.—Kangra District.										
Balach	1	30	...	...	...	...	...	...	1	30
Sujanpur	...	...	1	...	...	...	1	20	2	36
Dera	...	...	1	10	...	...	...	...	1	7
Dharamsal	2	25	...	...	...	...	...	...	2	25
Jowalaji	...	...	3	77	...	...	2	26	5	103
Nurpur	2	26	4	67	...	...	1	14	7	107
Kangra	3	37	2	70	...	...	...	...	5	107
Hamirpur	...	...	1	25	...	...	...	...	1	25
Palampur	2	38	1	20	...	...	...	...	3	58
Kotla	1	12	1	2	...	...	...	...	2	14
Kullu	...	...	...	...	...	...	...	...	...	...
Miscellaneous	...	...	6	110	...	...	...	...	6	110
Total ...	11	168	20	356	...	...	4	60	35	816
MULTAN DIVISION.										
XIII.—Multan District.										
Kahror	2	62	...	...	...	...	1	15	3	77
Talamba	6	60	...	...	...	...	...	...	6	60
Ghotla	1	15	...	...	...	...	...	...	1	15
Nawabpur	10	107	...	...	...	...	...	...	10	107
Shujabad	11	215	1	25	3	110	...	...	15	350
Ladan	1	26	...	...	3	25	...	...	4	51
Sarai Saddhu	4	46	...	...	...	...	...	...	4	46
Dugh Mal	2	40	...	...	...	...	...	...	2	40
Multan	15	341	8	68	3	30	5	636	31	1,075
Jalalpur	9	68	1	16	1	20	2	35	13	139
Miscellaneous	11	138	...	...	1	18	...	...	12	156
Total ...	71	1,118	10	109	11	203	8	686	100	2,116
XIV.—Jhang District.										
Jhang	11	222	7	103	8	180	...	...	26	505
Wanuka	1	20	...	...	2	38	1	25	4	83
Uch	10	88	1	8	6	67	...	...	17	163
Ballu	1	35	...	...	2	65	...	...	3	100
Chiniyot	11	182	4	60	2	45	3	75	20	362
Bhurna	7	68	...	...	1	6	...	...	8	74
Musan	30	269	...	...	8	66	...	...	38	335
Ghar Maharaja	2	46	...	...	...	...	...	...	2	46
Shorkot	3	48	...	...	2	30	...	...	5	78
Boráná	5	37	...	...	2	28	...	...	7	65
Miscellaneous	41	413	2	26	23	255	1	16	66	710
Total	122	1,423	14	197	55	770	5	116	196	2,506

A general abstract of the Indigenous Schools in the Punjab—(concluded).

Name of place or Thana.	Number of Maktabs and Madrasas.	Number of Pupils.	Number of Patshalas, i.e., Sanskrit and Nagri Schools.	Number of Pupils.	Number of Gurmukhi Schools.	Number of Pupils in Gurmukhi Schools.	Number of Lande Schools.	Number of Pupils in Lande Schools.	Total number of Indigenous Schools.	Total number of pupils attending Indigenous Schools.
XV.—Muzaffargarh District.										
Rohilanwallee	8	82	...	...	...	...	1	15	9	97
Shahr Sultan	4	40	...	...	...	...	...	...	4	40
Karimdad Qureshi	3	27	...	...	...	...	...	...	3	27
Jatoi	22	269	...	...	...	...	...	...	22	269
Muzaffargarh	15	77	2	9	2	8	1	20	20	114
Alipur	22	166	1	3	1	8	...	...	24	177
Sinlwan	14	99	...	...	...	...	...	...	14	99
Dhaka	1	6	...	...	...	...	...	...	1	6
Khangarh	25	170	...	...	...	...	1	48	26	218
Rangpur	9	52	...	...	1	6	...	...	10	58
Kijar	8	54	1	5	...	...	...	...	9	59
Sitpur	5	64	...	...	...	...	...	...	5	64
Dera Din Panah	19	146	4	18	3	39	3	26	29	229
Miscellaneous	8	82	...	...	2	12	...	...	10	94
Total	163	1,334	8	35	9	73	6	109	186	1,551
XVI.—Montgomery District.										
Montgomery	4	51	5	81	...	...	1	5	10	137
Thana Dibalpur	31	242	...	...	12	112	...	...	43	354
Babiak	2	12	...	...	3	22	...	...	5	34
Thana Ukara	...	...	...	...	1	10	...	...	1	10
Kamalya	2	35	...	...	1	25	2	57	5	117
Thana Atari	24	184	...	...	5	60	...	...	29	244
Thana Pakpattan	2	65	...	...	3	49	...	...	5	114
Hujra	15	138	...	...	10	98	...	...	25	244
Saydwala	7	69	1	12	...	...	1	35	9	116
Batti	13	130	...	...	2	24	...	...	15	154
Chochak	10	167	...	...	2	17	2	26	14	210
Harpa	...	...	1	4	2	34	1	12	4	50
Buchhki	7	64	1	6	3	56	...	...	11	126
Gogera	11	101	...	...	4	30	...	...	15	131
Kalyanwala	...	...	...	...	...	...	5	56	5	56
Chechawatni	2	18	...	...	...	...	...	...	2	18
Miscellaneous	28	185	...	...	...	...	...	...	28	185
Total	158	1,461	8	103	48	587	12	191	226	2,393

A general abstract of the Indigenous Schools in the Panjab—(continued).

Names of place or Thana.	Number of Maktabs and Madrasas.	Number of Pupils.	Number of Patshalas, i.e., Sanskrit and Nagri schools.	Number of Pupils.	Number of Gurmukhi Schools.	Number of Pupils in Gurmukhi Schools.	Number of Lande Schools.	Number of Pupils in the Lande Schools.	Total number of Indigenous Schools.	Total number of pupils attending Indigenous Schools.
AMRITSAR DIVISION.										
XVII.—Amritsar.										
Jandyala	2	17	...	...	...	...	2	55	4	72
Sarhali	1	15	1	8	2	17	1	15	6	55
Ghusanda	6	54	...	...	7	92	2	20	15	166
Wazerpind	3	27	2	17	1	6	...	...	6	50
Amritsar Circle	5	37	...	...	4	31	...	...	9	68
Khungal	16	146	2	12	4	37	...	...	22	195
Vairowal	12	118	1	10	8	124	2	24	23	276
Lopoki	6	135	...	...	...	...	3	42	9	177
Tarantaran	9	102	...	...	13	68	2	35	24	205
Ajnala	18	177	...	...	4	26	...	...	22	203
Amritsar City	54	967	59	1,027	20	792	12	607	145	3,393
Total	132	1,795	63	1,074	64	1,193	24	798	284	4,860
XVIII.—Gurdaspur.										
Futah Garh	7	78	1	4	...	...	...	...	8	82
Sri Govindpur	6	38	...	...	3	19	...	...	9	57
Pathankot	4	38	2	32	...	...	1	11	7	81
Chhamal	34	274	2	16	1	8	...	...	37	293
Parmanand	6	37	...	...	...	...	...	...	6	37
Dina Nagar	12	98	1	8	...	...	...	...	13	106
Batala	20	196	1	15	...	...	2	85	23	296
Kanhuwan	4	15	1	10	2	6	...	...	7	31
K? Hinan	10	104	...	...	...	...	...	...	10	104
Dera Nanak	15	182	2	36	2	65	...	...	19	283
Gurdaspur	13	105	2	7	...	...	...	...	15	112
Total	131	1,165	12	128	8	98	3	96	151	1,187
XIX.—Sialkot District.										
Sialkot City }	152	1,920	3	25	2	48	7	212	164	2,205
" Circle }										
" Cantonments }										
Falora }	52	576	4	53	1	12	2	31	59	672
Zafarwal }										
Raiya }	29	298	...	...	...	...	1	50	30	348
Naruwal }										
Pasrúr }	111	1,137	1	10	10	119	8	114	130	1,380
Kala Sobha Singh }										
Satrah }										
Dharamkot	4	60	...	...	1	8	...	...	5	68
Daska }	94	1,204	6	64	13	191	12	205	125	1,664
Samryal }										
Meani	11	120	...	...	2	16	...	...	13	136
Pahukalyan	2	40	...	...	...	...	...	...	2	40
Total	455	5,355	14	152	29	394	30	612	528	6,513

A general abstract of the Indigenous Schools in the Panjab—(continued).

LAHORE DIVISION.

XX.—Lahore District.

Names of places or Thana.	Number of Maktabs and Madrasas.	Number of Pupils.	Number of Patshalas, i.e., Sanskrit and Nagri Schools.	Number of Pupils.	Number of Gurmukhi Schools.	Number of Pupils in Gurmukhi Schools.	Number of Lande Schools.	Number of Pupils in Lande Schools.	Total number of Indigenous Schools.	Total number of pupils attending Indigenous Schools.
Patti	11	112	1	23	2	20	1	18	15	173
Moghal Sarai	1	14	...	...	1	12	1	20	3	46
Shahdara	28	281	...	...	5	53	2	13	35	347
Khudian	2	10	...	...	...	...	2	24	4	34
Lulliani	7	60	...	...	...	...	...	...	7	60
Bhai Pheru	1	17	...	...	4	31	...	...	5	48
Mangtawala	3	32	...	...	5	88	...	...	8	120
Kanganpur	7	146	...	...	3	105	...	...	10	251
Clarkabad	6	59	...	...	1	12	...	...	7	71
Kana Kachha	1	5	...	...	2	9	...	...	3	14
Chung	7	64	...	...	...	...	...	...	7	64
Valtoha	2	29	...	...	...	...	...	...	2	29
Mananwan	5	59	...	...	1	3	...	...	6	62
Sharakpur	4	257	...	...	5	47	1	4	10	308
Kasur	39	367	3	24	...	...	4	106	46	497
Chunyan	5	71	...	...	...	...	2	70	7	141
Kehalra	3	15	...	...	...	...	...	...	3	15
Muridki	3	22	...	...	1	8	...	...	4	30
Lahore	160	2,627	28	330	13	183	15	647	216	3,787
Total ...	295	4,247	32	377	43	571	28	902	398	6,097

XXI.—Gujranwala District.

Names of places or Thana.	Number of Maktabs and Madrasas.	Number of Pupils.	Number of Patshalas, i.e., Sanskrit and Nagri Schools.	Number of Pupils.	Number of Gurmukhi Schools.	Number of Pupils in Gurmukhi Schools.	Number of Lande Schools.	Number of Pupils in Lande Schools.	Total number of Indigenous Schools.	Total number of pupils attending Indigenous Schools.
Gujranwala	19	450	10	159	10	117	1	80	40	806
Hafizabad	19	230	2	29	1	10	1	11	23	280
Aimanabad	14	204	...	...	2	13	1	50	17	267
Wazirabad	72	878	2	47	7	104	6	108	87	1,137
Killa Didar Singh	6	75	...	...	4	38	1	15	11	128
Khangah	...	...	1	6	1	24	1	15	3	45
Pindi Bhattyan	2	11	...	...	4	98	2	95	8	204
Akalgarh	30	288	2	26	4	62	3	84	39	410
Shaikhupur	6	44	...	...	1	8	...	...	7	52
Miscellaneous	29	303	1	5	1	7	...	...	31	315
Total ...	197	2,493	18	272	35	481	16	458	266	3,614

A general abstract of the Indigenous Schools in the Panjab—(continued).

Names of places or Thana.	Number of Maktabs and Madrasas.	Number of Pupils.	Number of Patshalas, i.e., Sanskrit and Nagri schools.	Number of Pupils.	Number of Gurmukhi Schools.	Number of Pupils in Gurmukhi Schools.	Number of Lunde Schools.	Number of pupils in Lunde Schools.	Total number of Indigenous Schools.	Total number of pupils attending Indigenous Schools.
XXII.—Ferozepur District.										
Nathana	...	...	1	10	8	41	2	30	11	81
Muktasar	14	74	...	...	3	16	...	...	17	90
Ferozepur	35	243	...	...	1	6	1	14	37	263
Kot Bhai	...	...	...	...	...	...	1	24	1	24
Jellalabad	3	46	...	...	...	...	...	...	3	46
Bagahpurana	10	167	...	...	8	116	...	...	18	283
Moga	1	5	...	...	1	5	3	29	5	39
Zira	11	105	...	...	...	...	...	...	11	105
Makhu	10	53	...	...	...	...	...	...	10	53
Ferozepur Cantonment	...	...	1	20	...	...	1	50	2	70
Ferozepur City	4	45	6	57	3	12	2	95	15	209
Nawakilla	14	244	...	...	...	...	1	20	15	264
Dharamkot	23	275	1	35	4	18	2	57	29	385
Ghal	6	87	2	23	3	34	1	7	12	100
Nihal Singhwala	3	22	...	...	4	63	...	...	7	85
Extra	4	29	...	...	...	...	...	...	4	29
Total ...	137	1,345	11	144	35	311	14	326	197	2,126

RAWALPINDI DIVISION.

XXIII.—Rawalpindi District.

Names of places or Thana.	Number of Maktabs and Madrasas.	Number of Pupils.	Number of Patshalas, i.e., Sanskrit and Nagri schools.	Number of Pupils.	Number of Gurmukhi Schools.	Number of Pupils in Gurmukhi Schools.	Number of Lunde Schools.	Number of pupils in Lunde Schools.	Total number of Indigenous Schools.	Total number of pupils attending Indigenous Schools.
Rawalpindi	25	377	3	23	14	247	7	285	49	932
Jatali	34	548	...	...	12	347	...	...	46	895
Pind Sultani	32	533	1	10	6	150	...	...	39	693
Kallar	10	173	...	...	3	89	...	...	13	262
Hisru	6	152	1	8	2	90	1	70	10	320
Fatahjang	8	62	1	20	1	77	...	...	10	159
Rawat	24	262	...	...	4	135	...	...	28	397
Sangjani	5	105	...	...	6	87	2	25	13	217
Kahuta	25	370	2	21	9	93	...	...	36	484
Attock	23	198	...	...	3	16	...	...	26	214
Gujar Khan	43	583	...	...	11	180	...	...	54	763
Chawantra	17	275	...	...	17	352	...	...	34	627
Pindi Gheb	50	514	1	13	7	259	...	...	58	786
Hasan Abdal	19	362	...	...	8	111	...	...	27	473
Makhad	7	254	...	...	2	50	...	...	9	304
Mundra	23	373	...	...	3	76	...	...	26	449
Murree	10	162	...	...	...	...	...	...	10	162
Miscellaneous	297	3,481	...	...	35	535	...	...	332	4,016
Total ...	680	8,771	9	94	137	2,894	10	385	816	12,144

***A general abstract of the Indigenous Schools in the Panjab*—(continued).**

Names of places or Thanas.	Number of Maktabs and Madrasas.	Number of Pupils.	Number of Patshalas, i.e., Sanskrit and Nagri Schools.	Number of Pupils.	Number of Gurmukhi Schools.	Number of Pupils in Gurmukhi Schools.	Number of Lande Schools.	Number of Pupils in Lande Schools.	Total number of Indigenous Schools.	Total number of pupils attending Indigenous Schools.
XXIV.—Jhelum.										
Pindadan Khan	64	846	3	37	...	...	...	...	67	882
Sohawa	2	45	...	...	1	20	...	...	3	65
Jhelum	21	215	7	123	1	20	...	...	29	358
Ahmadabad	16	196	...	...	...	...	...	...	16	196
Damman	15	245	...	...	1	16	1	16	17	277
Dina	2	44	7	120	1	22	...	...	10	186
Tamman	10	102	...	...	1	16	...	...	11	118
Tala Gung	29	556	1	4	4*	109	...	...	34	669
Kalar Kahar	4	87	...	...	5	123	1	15	10	225
Jalalpur	6	95	...	...	1	10	...	...	7	105
Chakwal	15	453	1	10	11	298	1	14	28	775
Dumeli	16	210	...	...	1	12	1	14	18	236
Total ...	203	3,063	19	294	27	646	4	59	250	4,002
XXV.—Gujrat District.										
Gujrat	2	35	9	143	...	...	...	...	11	178
Kotiala Shekhan	4	38	...	...	3	95	...	...	7	133
Lala Musa	21	368	...	...	2	18	3	35	26	421
Aurangabad	9	182	...	...	5	57	...	...	14	239
Kunja	14	276	3	78	1	20	1	18	19	392
Jalalpur (Jattan)	8	119	2	85	...	...	2	70	12	274
Kharian	31	523	...	...	10	113	...	...	41	636
Langa	5	264	...	...	4	76	1	12	10	352
Dinga	2	136	...	...	2	55	3	35	7	226
Qadirabad	5	67	1	10	2	28	2	36	10	131
Karyalwala	4	105	1	26	3	96	1	14	9	241
Miscellaneous	169	1,725	4	26	21	321	6	173	200	2,245
Total ...	274	3,828	20	318	53	879	19	393	306	5,418
XXVI.—Shahpur District.										
Shahpur	2	50	...	...	2	55	...	...	4	105
Nurp	5	77	1	10	4	88	1	20	11	189
... ...	5	60	...	...	5	103	1	8*	11	171
Kand	5	105	...	...	2	71	1	8*	8	184
Khushab	16	281	...	...	4	68	...	...	20	349
Mota Lak	1	25	...	...	...	...	...	...	1	25
Naushehra	7	142	...	...	5	79	...	...	12	221
Bhera	5	98	14	273	4	65	2	48	25	484
Miani	5	146	2	26	3	68	1	35	11	273
Chak Ram Das	3	40	1	25	...	...	...	...	4	65
Jhawarya	16	176	...	...	5	76	...	...	21	252
Kot Momin	4	71	...	...	2	32	...	...	6	103
Sahiwal	8	164	1	40	7	161	1	26	17	391
Madh	3	23	...	...	2	33	1	25	6	81
Total ...	65	1,447	19	373	45	898	8	170	157	2,888

Name of place Thana or Tahsil.	Number of Maktabs and Madrasas.	Number of Pupils.	Number of Patshalas, i.e., Sanscrit and Nagri Schools.	Number of Pupils.	Number of Gurmukhi Schools.	Number of Pupils.	Number of Lande Schools.	Number of Pupils.	Total number of Indigenous Schools.	Total number of Pupils.
DERAJAT DIVISION.										
XXVII.—Dera Ghazi Khan District.										
Dera Ghazi Khan	18	293	1	8	2	12	2	58	23	371
Ahmed Ani	8	53	...	...	...	...	...	...	8	53
Kot Chhatta	11	162	...	...	...	...	...	...	11	162
Rajanpur	5	21	1	10	2	8	...	...	8	43
Fasilpur	10	44	...	...	...	...	...	...	10	44
Jampur	25	203	3	24	...	...	...	...	28	227
Kot Mithan	14	83	...	...	...	...	...	...	14	83
Yaru	7	109	...	...	...	...	...	...	7	109
Ojhan	2	39	...	...	1	12	...	...	3	51
Doyil	1	6	...	...	...	...	...	...	1	6
Miscellaneous	35	153	...	...	...	..	5	86	45	239
Harand	0	73	...	...	...	...	...	...	9	73
Tonsa	34	403	...	...	...	...	...	...	34	403
Total ...	179	1,645	5	42	5	32	7	144	196	1,863
XXVIII.—Bannu District.										
Edwardesabad	1	25	...	...	3	61	1	40	5	126
Mianwali	20	303	...	...	4	43	...	...	24	346
Kala Bagh...	1	70	...	...	...	...	...	...	1	70
Isa Khail	13	162	...	...	2	11	...	...	15	173
Kumar Mashfi	6	105	...	...	1	80	1	8	8	193
Lakki	7	145	...	...	2	12	...	...	9	157
Ghoriwala	4	31	...	...	...	...	...	...	4	31
Marban	1	14	...	...	...	...	1	27	2	41
Miscellaneous	52	485	...	...	2	14	...	...	54	499
Total ...	105	1,340	...	...	14	221	3	75	122	1,636
XXIX—Dera Ismail Khan.										
Tahsil Dera Ismail khan	8	214	6	145	...	...	3	100	17	459
„ Kulachi	61	576	3	11	3	29	4	99	71	715
„ Tank	23	135	...	...	1	10	2	26	26	171
„ Leiah	60	559	4	48	3	45	4	102	71	754
„ Bhakkar	38	271	2	16	10	108	11	170	61	565
Total ...	190	1,755	15	220	17	192	24	497	246	2,664

A general abstract of the Indigenous Schools in the Panjab—(continued)

PESHAWAR DIVISION.

XXX.—Hazara District.

Name of place or thana.	Number of Maktabs and Madrasas.	Number of Pupils.	Number of Patshalas, i.e., Sanskrit and Nagri Schools.	Number of Pupils.	Number of Gurmukhi Schools.	Number of pupils in Gurmukhi Schools.	Number of Lande Schools.	Number of Pupils in Lande Schools.	Number of Indigenous Schools.	Total number of pupils attending Indigenous Schools.
Shikári	4	71	...	...	3	54	...	...	7	125
Ghagi	1	15	...	...	1	4	...	...	2	19
Khanpur	1	25	...	...	3	46	...	...	4	71
Ogi	39	444	...	...	...	...	...	...	39	444
Karólian	7	49	...	...	...	...	...	...	7	49
Náráh	7	65	...	...	7	45	...	...	14	110
Sherwán	6	105	...	...	1	14	...	...	7	119
Mánsehra	5	152	...	...	...	...	...	...	5	152
Haripur	9	80	1	40	...	...	1	25	11	145
Máldkot	...	...	1	15	...	...	...	...	1	15
Abbottábád	1	20	1	30	...	...	...	...	2	50
Total ...	80	1,026	3	85	15	163	1	25	99	1,299

XXXI.—Kohat.

Name of place or thana.	Number of Maktabs and Madrasas.	Number of Pupils.	Number of Patshalas, i.e., Sanskrit and Nagri Schools.	Number of Pupils.	Number of Gurmukhi Schools.	Number of pupils in Gurmukhi Schools.	Number of Lande Schools.	Number of Pupils in Lande Schools.	Number of Indigenous Schools.	Total number of pupils attending Indigenous Schools.
Kohat...	10	420	...	...	1	7	...	...	11	427
Teri	6	65	...	...	1	21	...	...	7	86
Lachi	1	18	...	...	1	13	...	...	2	31
Shakardara	1	18	...	...	...	...	...	...	1	18
Nizampur	3	30	...	...	...	...	...	...	3	30
Gumbat	16	113	...	...	...	...	...	...	16	113
Hangu	2	15	...	...	...	...	...	...	2	15
Total ...	39	679	...	...	3	41	...	...	42	720

PART IV.

NOTES.

1.—THE SIKHS AND THEIR EDUCATION.

(*a*).—THE "PÁHUL" (POHOL).

The process of Sikh initiation, as originated by Guru Govind Singh, is described as follows in Dr. Trumpp's Adi-Granth, page xc. It succeeded an act of voluntary self-sacrifice among five disciples, who thus cemented the unity of Sikhs by "blood and iron" [1] :—

"He made them bathe and seated them side by side; he dissolved purified sugar in water and stirred it with a two-edged dagger, and having recited over it some verses, which are written in the *Akalustut*,[2] he made them drink some of this sherbet, some part of it he poured on their head and the rest he sprinkled on their body; then patting them with his hand, he cried with a loud voice: "say the Khalsá of the Váh-Guru! victory of the (to) the holy Váh-Guru." After he had given the Páhul to these five in thi manner, he took it likewise from them, and in this way all the rest of his disciples were initiated, to whom he gave the name of the *Khalsá*, adding to the name of each of them the epithet of *Singh* (lion). Then he gave the order that whoever desired to be his disciple, he must always have five things with him which all commence with the letter *kakka* (*i e.*, *k.*), viz., *the hair* (kês) which must not be cut, a *comb* (kangha), a *knife* (karad), a *sword* (kirpán), and *breeches reaching to the knee* (kachh), otherwise he would not consider him as his disciple."

(*b*).—As regards the obligation of every Sikh to read, Dr. Trumpp states as follows: "Every Sikh is enjoined to read the Granth for his devotion, especially the Japjí of Nanak and the Japjí of Govind Singh; these two he should always read when taking his meals" (Prahlad-sai, v. 10).

---

[1] There can hardly be any doubt that this bloody human sacrifice was really offered, as all reports agree on this point. The Sikhs, who felt very much the atrocity of such an act, would never have ascribed anything of this kind to their Guru, if it had not really taken place. At the same time, we may learn from this fact, that the Brahmans, even as late as the seventeenth century, did not scruple to offer up a human sacrifice.—(*Note by Dr. Trumpp*).

[2] The praise of the Timeless one follows immediately after the Jâpjí in Govind's Granth. It commences with the words:—

The protection of the Timeless divine male is to us.
The protection of ALL IRON is to us.
The protection of the all-time is to us.
The protection of the all-iron is to us.

The all-time (*i. e.*, he who comprehends all time) and the all-iron (*i. e.*, he who is all-iron) are epithets for the Supreme Being.

(c).—Gurmukhi Text-Books.

The following text-books at present are taught in Gurmukhi Schools :—

I.—*Literature.*

Bálopadesha; Panj Granthi; the tenth Guru's Panj Granthi; Janam Sakhí; Hanu Natak; Bhái Gurdás dián Bárán; the Granth; Mahadarsha Amrita.

II.—*Vedanta.*

Ekadash Bhagwat; Tulsi Ramayana; Vishnu Purán: Pingal (10 parts); Ashwa Medha; Adhyatam Ramayan; Vichár Ságar; Moksha Pantha; Surya Prakásha; the sixth Guru's Guru Vilás; Vashishtha Purán; Daswán Askandha.

It may be noted that of these Class I are studied by elementary students, while Class II is meant for advanced students.

(d).—Discipline in Gurmukhi Schools.

The school-time is from 6 to 10 A.M. and from 12 A.M. to 6 P.M., the intermediate time being allowed to the students for refreshment, &c. In case of a boy being absent, his school-fellows are sent to summon him. In case of the boy's resistance, his fellows use force against him. If the excuse for absence is not sufficient, he is given some task. The only punishment used is to make the offender seize his ears under the legs.

(e).—Remuneration of the Teacher.

The teacher gets food from each boy once a week. When the boy begins to write names, or whenever he begins a new book, he has to pay a rupee, or something less according to his means, to the teacher on each of the occasions. The teacher also gets half-yearly a rupee or two according to the circumstances of the parents of the pupil, and sometimes clothes also.

(f).—Account of Gurmukhi Education by Bhai Gurmukh Singh.

Bhai Gurmukh Singh has taken pains in collecting information concerning Gurmukhi teaching in some of the Panjab districts, such as Ferozpur, Hoshiarpur, and Sialkot. From what he has gathered from these quarters, it is clear that by the establishment of Government village and town schools, and the procedure adopted by them, a deathblow has been dealt to the indigenous Gurmukhi and Nagri schools. A solicitude for obtaining employment for their children induced the parents of many pupils attending the indigenous schools to withdraw them from those institutions of combined religious and secular education and to send them to the purely secular schools established by Government. The love for Gurmukhi learning, especially of a religious nature, had, however, taken so strong a root in the minds of the Sikh village community, that notwithstanding the subversive forces applied by Government by means of its secular schools, Dharmsálás still exist in the majority of villages, at which a few boys of the better class still attend, the number being very small compared with that before the all-absorbing institutions of Government came into existence. Among other things of importance, Bhai Gurmukh Singh has shewn, beyond the possibility of doubt, that there is a universal desire of learning and teaching the Gurmukhi religious books among Sikhs of all classes. It is not a conjecture of his own on which he bases this conclusion, but figures have been given in support of his assertions. He further shews that the disparity between the number of the Gurmukhi-knowing people of the old school and that of the same class of the present time is out of all proportion, the former being many times more than the latter.

The following are the towns and villages which our informant has taken as specimens of the general state of things :—

Ferozpur District.

Kasur—With a population of 21,000, has some persons of the former generation only who know Gurmukhi, but none of the present one, yet it has six Dharmsálás. There is a desire for Gurmukhi instruction. Three Native gentlemen have given their signatures in favour of introducing Gurmukhi, as representatives of others.

Khem Karn—With more Gurmukhi than Persian or Urdu-knowing people—has 4 Dharmsálás with 90 Gurmukhi-reading pupils. Here there is a general wish for Gurmukhi. Four lambardars have signed for Gurmukhi on behalf of the community.

Mukatsur.—Fourteen Pujaris bear testimony to the general desire for Gurmukhi schools.

Sialkot District.

Babe di Ber.—Population 250. Fifteen boys and 11 girls learn Gurmukhi. There is 1 Gurudwara here. A preference for Gurmukhi instruction is testified by the signatures of 88 persons.

Sialkot, Mahalla Seedi Vasi.—Five Dharmsálás with 40 Gurmukhi-reading pupils; 111 lambardars and gentlemen of the city have offered to thank Government if Gurmukhi instruction were extended.

Cantonment Sudder Bazar.—Population 5,000. The number knowing Gurmukhi equal the number knowing Urdu. One hundred lambardars and other gentlemen bear testimony to the general desire for Gurmukhi.

Cavalry lines, 10th Bengal Lancers.—One Dharmsálá with 7 Gurmukhi students; 128 native officers and sowars wish for the extension of Gurmukhi teaching.

Nine smaller villages—With five Dharmsálás and a population of about 8,000—have all expressed a desire for Gurmukhi teaching through 180 representatives of all classes. This is the class of villages which has especially suffered by the introduction of Government village and town schools.

Eighty-four smaller villages and towns are given in this district, with a similar falling-off in the number of Gurmukhi schools and pupils and a similar desire on the part of lambardars and Raïses.

District Hoshiarpur.

Six small Towns and Villages—Have been taken as examples. In these there are 13 Dharmsálás and Thakurduaras, with about 70 Gurmukhi and Nagri-reading pupils. A desire for the extension of Gurmukhi and Sanskrit teaching has been testified by 17 Raïses and lambardars on behalf of the community.

Ludhiana District.

The instances of *12 different villages and towns* have been given. The population of these is numbered at 1,700; the Dharmsálás are 7 in number, with only about 20 Gurmukhi-reading pupils. Seventeen lambardars have borne testimony to a general desire for Gurmukhi teaching in these villages by their signatures.

Twenty-four smaller villages, chiefly composed of a Sikh population, living in 3,800 houses, have 13 Dharmsálás with only 115 Gurmukhi-reading pupils. Forty-two lambardars and pattidars have signed in favour of the establishment of Gurmukhi schools.

Twenty-six still smaller villages have been mentioned with a similar falling-off in the number of Gurmukhi and Hindi-reading pupils, and a similar general desire for the extension of this beloved instruction.

The Manjha Country, between Attari, Taran Táran and Kasur.

Eighty-four villages are mentioned in this part of the country with 96 Dharmsálás, with a number of Gurmukhi-reading pupils, so small as 140. The decay of Gurmukhi indigenous education in its most striking aspect is shewn in this part of the country, where, in spite of the existence of an average of 1·2 Dharmsálás per village, the average of Gurmukhi-reading pupils does not come up to even 2 per village. Nothing could be more typical of the killing influence of Government village schools on indigenous moral and religious Gurmukhi and Nagri education. But, in spite of all this, there is still visible that love for religious Gurmukhi education of which mention has been made above. For the last assertion there is an ample proof in the expression of popular desire for that education through the mouthpieces of village communities, the Lambardars, Pattidars, Sardars and Raises, &c. The number of these Lambardars, Pattidars, Raïses, &c., petitioning for Gurmukhi in this part of the country is no less than 115.

(The details regarding each of the villages and towns in which there is a desire for Gurmukhi education will be incorporated, it is hoped, in my second volume on "the History of Indigenous Education in the Punjab.")

2.—An Account of Mahajani Text-books.

The following is a brief account of two of the treatises in use in Mahajani schools. One is lithographed, a process by which information can be conveyed to the masses at a fifth of the cost of printing,[1] which, whether in the Urdu or the Roman characters, is also wasteful of space. Its illustrated frontispiece represents Ganesh, the god of learning, seated under a vignette of the radiant moon, having on one side the Tortoise and Fish incarnations of Vishnu. Below Ganesh is seated the Pádha, before whom one boy standing up is reciting his lesson, whilst the rest of the boys are seated in a listening attitude. The little book begins with the Nagri characters, simple and in combination, which are, logically, followed by their abbreviated (tailless) Landé equivalents, each letter of that alphabet being represented several times in a row, so as to impress its form on the learner. The alphabet is divided into "Kaka-mundás" or consonants (the first letter of which is K) and "Nam-mundás" or vowels. Then comes a table of enumeration which is accompanied, progressively with each row of numerals, by simple addition, followed by the addition of fractions, an invaluable exercise. Then follows a table showing how annas and pies should be written in accounts, as also "seers," "chataks," "damris" and "ratis," rupees and maunds, taking care of themselves as they are written in ordinary letters and numerals. This is succeeded by a letter to an equal on business in the Nagri character giving an account of rates in the market. The treatise concludes with the forms of addressing and beginning a letter, and also gives a specimen of an addressed envelope. It will be seen that this commercial primer is mainly intended for Banyas, and that it endeavours to supersede or explain the Landé by the Nagri characters. The multiplication table (which is often sung to any tune that may be popular at the time, such as, for instance, some of the melodies of the itinerant Parsi Dramatic Company from their "Indra Sabha," "the Court of Indra,") is given, generally, in manuscript, to the pupils or merely committed to memory. The more advanced student is then taught book-keeping, as already explained.

Another treatise, in manuscript, I have translated at some length in order to give a more vivid idea of the course pursued in the Mahajani schools.

---

[1] The following Resolution of the Senate of the Panjab University College may illustrate this assertion :—

"*Rendering of Scientific Terms in the Vernacular.*—As regards the subject of translation, adaptation or transliteration of technical terms, the Senate were of opinion that 'where no term already exists or can be easily adapted in the vernacular from any of the classical oriental sources or otherwise, so as to be intelligible to the native mind, a careful system of transliteration should be adopted, if into Urdu, for instance, with all the vowel points given.' Dr. Leitner's suggestion that the equivalent of the scientific term should, in such a case only, also be given in the Roman character in brackets, was rejected, owing to the incongruousness and wastefulness of that character, even in the lithographed form in which the addition was suggested, it having been shown that the promotion of knowledge among the masses in the vernacular characters, by means of lithography, in which improvements should be made, was infinitely cheaper and quicker than in the Roman character, a book in the vernacular character costing about one-fifth of the same book in the Roman character, and, with the great existing scope for improvement in lithography, might be reduced to even less than one-fifth."

The following is one of the **pahárás** (multiplication table) taught in down-country Hindi schools under the name of **Mahárni** ("Mahárni" merely means "repetition"):—

Pauna Multiplication of ¾.			Saváyá Multiplication of 1¼.			Deorá Multiplication of 1½.			Dhaiyá Multiplication of 2½.			Unṭá Multiplication of 3½.			Dháuṇchá Multiplication of 4½.			Páuṇchá Multiplication of 5½.		
1	¾	¾	1	1¼	1¼	1	1½	1½	1	2½	2½	1	3½	3½	1	4½	4½	1	5½	5½
2	¾	1½	2	...	2½	2	...	3	2	2	5	2	...	7	2	...	9	2	...	11
3	...	2¼	3	...	3¾	3	...	4½	3	2½	7½	3	...	10½	3	...	13½	3	...	16½
4	...	3	4	...	5	4	...	6	4	...	10	4	...	14	4	...	18	4	...	22
5	...	3¾	5	...	6¼	5	...	7½	5	...	12½	5	...	17½	5	...	22½	5	...	27½
6	...	4½	6	...	7½	6	...	9	6	...	15	6	...	21	6	...	27	6	—	33
7	...	5¼	7	...	8¾	7	...	10½	7	...	17½	7	...	24½	7	..	31½	7	...	38½
8	...	6	8	...	10	8	...	12	8	...	20	8	...	28	8	...	36	8	...	44
9	...	6¾	9	...	11¼	9	...	13½	9	...	22½	9	...	31½	9	...	40½	9	...	49½
10	...	7½	10	...	12½	10	...	15	10	...	25	10	...	35	10	.	45	10	...	55

The method of the Hindi "Gu-," by means of which calculations are **easily made, may be somewhat illustrated by the following:—**

As the number of seers for a rupee, the same number of maunds for **Rs. 40.**

As the number of seers for the rupee, the same number of chataks for one anna.

As the number of rupees for the maund, the same number of annas for 2½ seers.

The calling out of each letter of the Landé alphabet is accompanied, first by a word in common use beginning with that letter, and then by a phrase or proverb impressing it on the memory, which similarly begins with the letter to be learnt.

Name of letter.	Word illustrating name of letter.	Meaning.
Kakká.	Kubrá.	Hump-backed.
Khak-ká.	Khatrí.	A Khatri.
Gag-ga.	Guáliyá.	Cowherd.
Ghag-gá.	Ghí-ká-Ghará.	Pitcher full of ghi.
Nan-ná.	Náí kí Arsí.	Barber's looking glass.
Chach-chá.	Chúchalyá.	Beaked.
Chhachh-chhá.	Chhábaryá.	Confectioner's tray.
Jajja.	Janbú.	Jammu.
Jhajjá.	Jhár kí Bérí.	Shrub.
Taṭṭá.	* Adhí púrí.	Half a loaf of bread.
Thaṭṭá.	* Sawái púrí.	One and a quarter of bread.
Daddá.	Doli Gánth.	Double-Knot.
Dhaddá.	Dhóngar Bójhrá.	
Ane.	Tin lakír kó kahiyé. *	Say 3 lines.
Tattá.	Tuní.	
That-thá.	Thálí.	Plate.
Dad-dá.	Dál.	Half a grain.
Dhad-dá.	Dhurí-kamán.	Double bow.
Pap pá.	Páwaryá.	
Phapphá.	Phati kharí.	
Babbá.	Bindá.	
Bhabbhá.	Bhár ká konchá.	
Mammá.	Muchh-marorná.	To twist moustaches.
Rárá.	Rám katárá.	Dagger.
Lal-lá.	Lákhrá.	
Bab-ba.	Bindí wáwá.	Dotted.
Sussá.	* Teran.	A spool.
Há-Há.	Hiran.	
Bhabh-bhá.	Bindí Rárá.	
I, é.	* Ulti Sáth kí ái.	
Ú.	* Munh-móré ú.	The mouth-rounding "u"?
Á.	* Derh lakír kí á.	

* The name refers to the form of the letter, for which see Appendix VII.

The above letters are first taught; in the villages, many Pádhás teach only these letters, but not the words added to them.

This is followed by the "*Sar-harfi-Chaupái.*"—Alphabet taught by means of a Chaupái Poem (which seems to combine Hindu with Muhammadan religious notions and terms) :—

Name of *letter.*		
Kak-ká.	*Kakká* kar kartá kí pújá,* Wahí Niranjan aur nahín dúja.	K. Worship the Creator. He is the pure one and no one else.
Khakh-khá.	*Khakh-khá* khá-pí mat ná phúló, Is Dunyá kó dekh ná bhúló.	Kh. Do not fatten on eating and drinking, Do not be misled by worldly things.
Gaggá.	*Gaggá* gun apná mat cháhó, Gun chhór tum Wákó páó.	G. Do not seek your own interest, Ignore your interest and find Him.
Ghagghá.	*Ghagghá* ghat men rahe tumháre, Dekh yahán jin liyé utáré.	Gh. The (name of the Deity) must be always in your heart, Look at the example of those who were incarnations.
Nanná.	*Nanná* nit Wákí kar sewá, Jaldí terá pár ho khéwá.	N. Always (only) worship Him, So that your boat may soon reach the shore.
Chach-chá.	*Chhach-che* jó tum chatar kaháó, Prem piyá se† nih-lagáo.	Ch. If you wish to be called a wise man, Fix your love upon the beloved (Father).
Chhachh-chá.	*Chhachh-chhe* chhin ká nahín bharosá, Suno kán kar pakar bharosá.	Chh. We cannot be sure of living even for one moment, Lend, therefore, your ear to this warning.
Jajja.	*Jajje* jin par kirpa kini, Bahut Barái jag men díní.	J. Those whom God favours, Get great honor in this world.
Jhájjá.	*Jháje* Jhuth túfán‡ ko tyago, Sach bóló tum pyáre lágo.	Jh. Renounce falsehood and scandal; Speak the truth and you will be loved.
Nanna.	*Nanna* nam usíká líje, Hardam uski Bandagí kíje.	N. Take His name alone. Worship Him in every breath.
Tattá.	*Tattá* tándá koí din terá, Thik thik nahin chale savéra.	T. Your temporary sojourn (in this world) is for a few days, and yet you don't take early steps to go quite straight (to obey the will of God).
Thathhé.	*Thatte* Thát pát jo hainge, Rakh chaukas, nahín tágo lenge.	Th. Whatever be your property keep with care; otherwise thieves will take it.
Daddá.	*Daddá* Darná chit mat ho tú, Báhút jág kar, thorá so tú.	D. Do not be of a timid heart, Wake much and sleep little.
Dhaddé.	*Dhadde,* Dhúnde phirté ho, Pachhtawe jab nahin de koí.	Dh. You go about asking for gifts, but you will repent when nobody gives.
Náne.	*Náné,* Ran-par raho tú qaim, Rahe mál terá nit dáim.	N. Be steady in the field§ and your wealth will be secure for ever.
Tatte.	*Tatte,* Tum lo meré bhái, Thári karí tumhárí áge ái.	T. Take (my advice) oh brother; your works will come before you (find you out).
Thatte.	*Thatte,* thárí yé-bí máyá, Din imán ki karó saháyá.	Th. All this is your capital: "Defend religion and faith."
Daddá.	*Daddá,* Dunya takia haigá, Chale áye, phir chalna haigá.	D. This world is a temporary halting-place. We have come, and will have to go.
Dhaddá.	*Dhaddá,* Dháve Dhanraj nám tumhárá, Qazá ka chor Shaitán tumhárá.	Dh. Your name may be that of a wealthy person (?), but your fated thief is Satan.
Nanna.	*Nanne,* Nisdin jágo piyárá, Chale nahin hai kisika chárá.	N. The day that you will have to go (to die) oh dear, no one's help will be of avail.
Pappá.	*Pappá,* Pap karo mat koí, Har ko bhaje, so Har ka hoí.	P. Don't commit any sin. Whoever remembers God will be His (own).
Babbá.	*Babba,* Behtar isko jáno, Yád rabb kí dil se máno.	B. Know this to be best, "remember your Lord and obey Him from your heart."
Bhabba.	*Bhábba,* Bhúl gayá, kyá Sáko, Jín chhin men paidá kyá báko.	Bh. Have you forgotten Him who created you in one moment ?
Mammá.	*Mamme,* Mat jánwar sáre, Rahe yád uski ko pyáre.	M. All the animal creation is dear to His memory.
Jajja.	*Jajjé,* jiskí yeh hai báni, Rachí shisht búnd ik páni.	J. He whom I praise is the Being who created the Universe out of a drop of water (?).

* The language seems to be a pure down-country Hindi. The manuscript was obtained from Panipat.

† When a woman addresses her husband in song, she calls him "*Piyá*" or "beloved"; here it is used to the Deity.

‡ Originally a "storm," then the "confusion caused by falsehood."

§ Battle-field of life.

Chaupái read by pupils, in the evenings, in the Hindi School.

1. Pahle samrún, sachchá sáin, Jin ne sagrí dhúm machái.	I first count the bead (of the names) of the True Master who is the cause of all this bustle (busy Universe).*
2. Dújé samrún Saraswatí mái, Ab vidyá de mujhé sawái.	In the second place I invoke Mother Saraswati and ask her to give me an increased knowledge.
3. Tíje sunó kal-jug ká hál, Zaráh nahíṇ dunyá ká khiyál.	In the third place hear an account of Kali-jug. There is not the least solicitude for the interests of the world.
4. Paráí istri par dálé jál, Takté phiré begánáṇ mál.	Man goes about entrapping another's wife, and watching dishonestly another's property.
5. Zará nahíṇ aurat kó dar, Báráh baras kí mángé bar.	Females have banished all fear, and ask for a husband when only 12 years old.
6. Is samaṇ kí bát jo kahúṇ, Ghar meṇ lare sás aur bahú.	To tell you how it fares in this age, The mother-in-law fights with the daughter-in-law in the house.
7. Ghar meṇ lare daráni jitháni, Unke áge sás nimáni.	A similar quarrel goes on at home between the wives of younger and elder brothers, and in their presence the mother-in-law is cowed.
8. Ghar meṇ kyá jorú ne shor, Unke áge piyá kamzor.	The wife makes a row at home and the husband has no power to check her.
9. Jab bahú kháné ko kháwé, Sás bahú kí jhút úthawé.	When the bride has taken her food, the mother-in-law has to eat what she has left.
10. Yeh waqt ultá gayá hó, Háre kahná jite jo.	The times have taken a perverse course, because people call him a loser, who is (really) the winner.
11. Is Kali-Yug ko aisá ján, Kisí kisí meṇ rahá Imán.	Know the Kali-Yug to be an age when very few have any faith.
12. Baré baré páp lagé karné, Báp lagé betóṇ se darné.	Big and respectable people are beginning to commit sins, and fathers are afraid of their sons.
13. Rabb kí pujá man se tiyágen, Búre kám meṇ rátó jágeṇ.	They have given up God's worship from their hearts, and spend whole nights in sinful actions.
14. Dekho bhái Dunyá ká hál, Zará nahíṇ marne ká khiyál.	Look, brother! at the ways of the world —people have no thought of death.
15. Hál suno dunyá ká sárá, Yeh dunyá hai dhúnd basárá.	Hear the whole state of this world—this world is all a dark abode.
16. Thorá hai zindgi ká phál, Jo chhin meṇ jáné dam nikál.	This life bears little fruit, if the breath goes out in a moment.
17. Rabb apne se chit do lá, Jo chahó tum apná bhalá.	Fix your mind upon your Creator if you have a desire for your own good.
18. Áyá basant suno ré lógó. Jaisá karo waisá tum bhógó.	The Basant (spring) is come; hear, oh people; as you act, so you will enjoy.

The translation is a rapid and incomplete reading of the original, which seems to me to be not an unfaithful picture of the Panjab, as it is after 32 years of the reign of "law" and 26 years of "education." The province in which, according to our earliest Administration Reports, forgery, perjury, adultery and swindling were almost unknown, is now becoming rapidly proficient in these arts. The peace of families has fled with the rise of young Panjab; "fathers are beginning to fear their sons," the religious sense is dying out and litigation is wasting the energies of the people, whilst the "educated" are driven to pleasure and disaffection by a system of education which unfits them for anything except posts under Government, the number of which must always continue to be limited.

The following extracts from Mr. A. P. Howell's "State of Education in India during 1866-67" may be quoted as bearing on the questions of Mahajani Schools, of Urdu *versus* Hindi and of the difficulty of ascertaining the exist-

* Compare this with the first line of the celebrated Urdu Masnawi of Mir Hasan: "Let me write first the profession of the Unity of God, before whom first bowed in adoration the pen."—"Karún pahle tauhíde Yezdán raqam, Jhuka jiske sijda-ganya awwal Qalam."

ence of indigenous schools, even in such a province as Oudh, where there was no wish to destroy them :—

"33. From the first considerable practical difficulty has arisen from the fact of there being in Oudh two entirely distinct vernacular characters—Urdu and Nagri—each having claims of its own not to be lightly neglected. The common-spoken language of the province is Hindi, with a large admixture of Persian words, the proportion of the latter varying from a maximum in our law courts to a minimum in remote country villages. The written characters in actual use are Urdu and Nagri, with its corruptions, Kaithi and Mahajani. Urdu is easier than Nagri to write, and, being the character used in our courts, and a kind of *lingua franca* understood all over India, is most useful to boys in after-life. On the other hand, Nagri has the more perfect alphabet, is far easier to read, and is the native dress of the vernacular of the province. Kaithi and Mahajani are merely forms of Nagri, the tops of the letters being omitted, the vowels wholly or partly left out, and the letters themselves mutilated. I believe no such thing as a printed book in Kaithi or Mahajani exists ; but bankers, shop-keepers, and patwaris (village accountants) keep their accounts in these characters, and use them in their business correspondence. As a general rule, the persons just named cannot read the printed Nagri at all, and look upon it as rather a useless accomplishment. In attempting, then, to judge from present usage what vernacular characters should be taught in schools, the case stood thus : all persons connected with courts and offices, all candidates for Government employment, all Muhammadans, and nearly all educated Hindus, use Urdu (the character introduced by the Muhammadan rulers) ; Pandits and other Sanscrit scholars write pure Nagri, whilst the whole trading community adopt the corrupted forms mentioned above.

"34. From the outset Kaithi and Mahajani have been excluded from the course of studies, there being no books, and it being well known that a Nagri scholar can master the two written characters in a few weeks. As regards Urdu and Nagri, no favour was shown. A pupil, on entering a zillah or tehsili school, was allowed to choose either, and confine his attention to that exclusively. This proved to be practically very inconvenient, for, though the Urdu element preponderated largely, each class was broken up into an Urdu and Nagri section, requiring separate tuition, which, with the number of teachers available for each school, it was impossible to supply. Under the new scheme all pupils in zillah schools are taught Urdu, experience having shown that this, though essentially foreign, is, under present circumstances, far more popular than Nagri. Each class, however, from the fourth to the seventh, unless specially exempted, is sent for one or two hours a day to the pandit, *to learn to read and write the Nagri character*.

"Native scholars are unanimous in the opinion that elegance in Urdu composition can be attained only by reading Persian, and they regard time spent in reading Urdu as thrown away. These views are no doubt exaggerated ; but, as there are a large number of Persian words and phrases in the current language of the province, a knowledge of Persian is doubtless useful, and as it is moreover a very favourite subject among respectable natives, Hindu scarcely less than Muhammadan, the change is likely to be popular.

"98. Indigenous schools are not included in the statements accompanying this report, as no reliable statements regarding them are available. Deputy Inspectors are directed to find out where such schools exist, and to visit the most important of them if they have time, the object being (1) to collect information, and (2) to endeavour to improve them.

"99. Very few indigenous schools of any kind exist in villages ; but in towns they are more or less numerous. They are either Persian or Hindi. In the former boys learn to read *Karima*, *Amad Nama*, *Gulistan*, *Bostan*, and other Persian works, and to write Persian and Urdu letters. They read no Urdu books, and do not attempt arithmetic, grammar, geography, or any of the subjects usually taught in Government schools. The number of pupils is generally very small. In Rai Bareilli the Deputy Inspector reports 36 schools, whose aggregate attendance is only 172. The teacher is usually a private servant of the patron of the school, from whom he receives food and two or three rupees per mensem in cash. Hindi schools are patronised by bunnias and other shop-keepers, and are often attended by 20 or 30 boys each. The curriculum of studies consists of the Kaithi-written character, the multiplication-table, and a mechanical kind of arithmetic, enabling the pupil to work out rapidly questions of a certain type in proportion and interest. No books of any kind are used; neither teacher nor pupil being able to read any printed character whatever.

"100. It does not appear that any great improvement in schools of this description can be made at present. The Persian teachers are, as stated above, generally private servants, and, so long as patrons are to be found who consider Persian all that is necessary, the course will remain what it is. The Hindi *Guru* is paid to teach what the Banya considers necessary, and, if he ceased to do this, pupils would cease to come. Moreover, his inability to read printed books prevents his adopting ours even if he wished. In some instances Hindi schools have been converted into Government institutions, and a trained teacher sent to give instruction in Nagri, whilst the *guru* continues to impart his own peculiar lore for a portion of the day. If he learns to read and write Nagri himself, he is promised admission to the Normal School."

3.—Appendix to the Memoirs of Statistics on Indigenous Education in the North-Western Provinces, printed 1850.

The following extracts are in support of the assertion that a Lieutenant-Governor of the North-Western Provinces proposed to maintain indigenous schools with gifts of land, but that the Court of Directors preferred to do so by money grants:—

Note to No. 1089 of 1846, of Secretary, North-Western Provinces, to Secretary, Government of India, dated 18th November 1864.

"The views of the Honourable Court of Directors on the peculiar features of Mr. Adams' proposal are explained in the following paragraph of their letter No. 3, dated February 23rd, 1842:—

"Mr. Adams expresses his opinion that existing native institutions are the fittest means to be employed for raising and improving the character of the people, and that to employ those institutions for such a purpose is the simplest, the safest, the most popular, the most economical, and the most effectual plan for giving that stimulus to the native mind which it needs on the subject of education, and for eliciting the exertions of the natives themselves for their own improvement, without which all other means must be unavailing. Government should do nothing to supersede those exertions, but should rather endeavour to supply the means for making them more effectual. In this principle we most fully concur.

* * * * * * * *

"8. The proposed scheme contemplates the endowment of a school in every village of a certain size, the Government giving up its revenue from the land, which constitutes the endowment, on assurance that the zemindars have appropriated the land for the purpose of maintaining a schoolmaster.

"9. This system is most in consonance with the customs and feelings of the people. The schoolmaster will become a recognised village servant, elected and supported in a manner consonant with the usage of the village community.

"10. An endowment in land is preferable to a money payment, because it gives greater respectability of station than a pecuniary stipend much exceeding the rent of the land, and because it connects the schoolmaster with the community in a way which renders his services more acceptable to them than if he were the paid servant of the Government.

"11. A jagheer of from 5 to 10 acres of land will give a rental varying from Rs. 20 to 40 per annum. This is in itself small, but for the jagheer of a village servant it is handsome. In 47 villages of one pergunnah of zillah Agra the average holding of each proprietor is less than 15 acres, and on this they have to pay the Government assessment. Besides this, it is not desired that the endowment should constitute the sole means of support for the village schoolmaster. He will still receive presents and fees in money, food and clothes, as is now usual, even if he do not receive a regular fixed payment from some of his scholars. All the statistical returns of the emoluments of schoolmasters show that their present emoluments are very small, so much that the addition of an endowment of 5 acres would place them in a state of comparative wealth.

" 12. It is not probable that endowments will be made on the proposed plan to the full extent for many years, but it may be well to enquire what is the utmost amount which this measure may finally subtract from the income of the State.

* * * * * * * *

" 17. It is the standing reproach of the British Government that whilst it continually resumes the endowments of former sovereigns, it abstains from making any even for those purposes which it considers most laudable. The present measure will in some degree remove this reproach, and that in a manner most acceptable to the people at large."

Scheme for founding village schools.

1. Whenever the zemindars and majority of the respectable inhabitants in any mouzah which contains houses shall wish to establish a school in their village, and permanently to endow it with a jagheer for the schoolmaster, containing not less than 5 acres of land, they shall state their wishes in a written representation to the Collector of the District, and shall specify the lands which they wish to set apart as an endowment.

2. The Collector, on receiving this application, shall satisfy himself of the sincerity of the desire on the part of the applicants, and of the reality of the proposed endowment, and shall then recommend to Government through the usual channel the remission of the public demand on the lands so appropriated, calculated* on the mode specified in paragraph 29, Circular Order of Sudder Board of Revenue, No. IV.

3. The nomination of a schoolmaster shall rest with the zemindars and principal residents of the mouzah, but no person shall be appointed schoolmaster unless he fully understand, and is able to explain and give instructions in Ram Surrun Doss' four elementary books, both Urdu and Hindi. The Collector shall satisfy himself to the extent of these acquirements before he sanctions the appointment.

4. The Collector, or his Deputy, or Assistant, or any other person specially appointed by the Government for the purpose by public notification in the *Gazette*, shall be empowered to visit these schools, and to ascertain that the endowment is faithfully appropriated to the support of the schoolmaster, and that the schoolmaster appointed continues in the active and efficient discharge of his duties.

5. If the visitor consider the schoolmaster to have become inefficient or neglectful of his duties, he shall call on the zemindars and other respectable residents to discharge him, and to nominate another qualified person. If the villagers will not accede to this requisition, he shall be competent, with the concurrence of the Commissioner, to resume the land for Government, and to levy from the village the amount of the original assessment.

Extract from a despatch from the Honourable the Court of Directors in the Public Department, No. 20 of 1847, dated the 25th August.

Proposed establishment of village schools in the North-Western Provinces.

9. The plan proposed by the Lieutenant-Governor of the North-Western Provinces, which is supported by the recommendation of the Governor General, is the endowment of a school for instruction in the vernacular language, through the medium of elementary books prepared for the purpose, in every village of a sufficient extent. The endowment to consist of the relinquishment of the Government demand of revenue on a given extent of land, on assurance that the zemindars appropriate the land to the maintenance of a school. The amount of the grant is computed at from 5 to 10 acres, which would yield an annual income to the proprietor of from Rs. 20 to 40 a year. This, though small, is considered to be sufficient, as in many villages the holding of each proprietor is less than 15 acres, from which he has to pay the Government revenue. The schoolmaster is also to be permitted to receive the fees, which it has hitherto been customary for the scholars to pay him.

10. It appears that in the Regulation Provinces under consideration there are 79,033 villages. Of these 18,000 contain 100 houses and upwards, and 5,440 contain 200 houses and upwards. The jumma is rated at 2 rupees per acre, and the amount of the revenue proposed to be alienated, supposing the endowment to be restricted to the large villages, would be therefore from Rs. 54,400 to Rs. 1,08,800 per annum. If extended to the smaller villages, it would be from Rs. 1,80,000 to Rs. 3,60,000, according as the endowment should include 5 or 10 acres. The smaller sum would be from 2 to 4 annas per 100 rupees on the revenue of the province (4 crores of rupees); the larger sum would be from 7 to 14 annas per 100 rupees. The amount of this alienation, in the opinion of the Lieutenant-Governor, will not be felt, and will be more than replaced by the annual increase of the rent-roll from causes constantly in operation, and strengthened as those causes would be by the extension of useful information among the agricultural population.

---

* At the average rate of the Government jumma and 10 per cent. additional.

11. The advantages of this plan over a money grant to the schoolmaster are represented to be its harmonising with the feelings and practices of the people, its conferring upon the schoolmaster a higher degree of respectability and influence, its connecting him with the community in a way likely to render his services more acceptable to them, and its tendency to efface the reproach, to which the British Government is exposed, of continually resuming the endowments of former sovereigns, without making any itself, even for purposes which it considers most laudable.

* * * * * * *

13. We are not satisfied, however, of the expediency of the particular plan proposed by the Lieutenant-Governor of the North-Western Provinces. It has no doubt the advantages ascribed to it, and is apparently the most economical arrangement for effecting the object proposed. Endowments of land are, however, open to obvious objection. They have an inherent tendency to assume the character of permanent and hereditary property independent of any reference to the tenure by which they were originally held. An actual occupant, even should he prove inefficient, would think himself deprived of a right if he was removed, and a son would claim to succeed to his father, whether he were competent or not to discharge similar duties. The evil would be aggravated by the extreme difficulty of exercising a vigilant control over such numerous establishments, and in one or two generations it might happen that the alienation of revenue would be of little avail in securing the education of the people. A money-payment cannot be so perverted; it is given for a definite duty, and when that duty is negligently or inadequately discharged, it is easily withdrawn or transferred to a more competent individual. We are disposed to prefer, therefore, the grant of a monthly stipend to such schoolmasters as may be appointed to the larger villages, or to those, if properly qualified, who may be already employed in them, making them responsible to the local Government, through the constituted authorities, for the proper discharge of their duties. We shall be prepared to give our favourable consideration to any measure which may be suggested upon these views.

Extract of a letter from J. THORNTON, Esq., Secretary to Government, North-Western Provinces, to the Secretary to the Government of India, Home Department,—No. 507, dated the 19th April 1848.

9. The objections to money-payments to village schoolmasters are these :—

First—They must consist of money-payments, the faithful disbursement of which in remote parts of the district it will be difficult to ensure.

Second—They lead the schoolmaster to look exclusively to the Government, and to neglect the conciliation of the people. The schoolmasters are considered the servants of the Government, and not of the people, and are therefore viewed with less of cordiality and more of distrust than if they were remunerated by an endowment of land.

Third—There will always be danger lest the actual appointment of a village schoolmaster, or his apprehended introduction into a village without the wish of the people, will discourage others from coming forward to meet the voluntary exertions of the people. The Government schools may sometimes supersede and discharge the natural efforts of the people to supply their own wants.

4.—A FEW ROUGH NOTES AND PROPOSALS ON THE SUBJECT OF INDIGENOUS SCHOOLS, CHIEFLY BASED ON A PERUSAL OF REPORTS ON INDIGENOUS SCHOOLS IN THE NORTH-WESTERN PROVINCES.

The following rough notes and proposals, regarding indigenous schools generally, may illustrate some of the statements and suggestions in Part I of this report:—

Indigenous schools are not necessarily religious, either in the Punjab or in the North-Western Provinces. For instance in the district of Fatehpur there are two Hindu religious schools attended by 7 pupils, against 151 secular schools attended by 881 pupils. In 13 o these no fees are paid. Muhammadans have 18 religious schools with 85 pupils, and 50 secular schools with 386 pupils.

In the Mozaffarnagar districs, out of 264 indigenous schools, only 58 are religious.

To have the poor classes looked after, religion must be taught.

Indigenous teachers are not interested in giving their schools a higher position than they deserve. Their reports, therefore, are *under*, rather than *over*, the mark.

Government returns are only approximate, so are indigenous.

The people should appoint their own masters, and to some extent fix the subject of tuition.

Indigenous books are often childish—Government books too dry.

Government schools should become more like indigenous schools, and indigenous schools more like Government schools, so as to avoid a conflict in a common cause.

Indigenous schools are as much a relic of an ancient village system as they are the result of modern requirements, which are not met by the Government system of education.

Although the teachers do not explain the religious books in the elementary schools, the parents to whom the boy repeats his lesson often do, even when they cannot themselves write and read, from their practical experience of life and of religious exercises; so there is no one who does not understand the general drift of a passage from the Kuran and Sanskrit devotional books. The consequence of which is that the introduction of Arabic and Sanskrit words into translations is understood to a certain extent even by the vulgar. This is less the case with Persian, which is confined to a more educated class.

In Hindi schools, Sanskrit Grammar, Sarrafi, and the Native method of accounts and book-keeping are taught, but never Hindi as a language, the Sanskrit Grammar being explained in the vernacular of the district, through which, if Hindi is the vernacular, that vernacular is not only incidentally learnt, but also improved by the study of Sanskrit Grammar. Similarly, in Muhammadan schools, Persian literature and polite letter-writing are taught, by which, incidentally, Urdu is acquired. Were elementary land-surveying and patwari accounts taught in indigenous schools, they would almost completely answer the requirements of agriculturists.

If a boy learns arithmetic in our schools, he is of little use for the shop, because he finds there a different system of accounts and the meanest Banya can cast up the intricacies of the grain-trade accounts by a mental process far more rapidly than if he had taken honors in Mathematics at the Calcutta University.

The sons of the present indigenous teachers who wish to follow the profession of their fathers might be trained at the Lahore Oriental College in their own learning as well as in general branches of knowledge, to which a course of instruction in the science and practice of teaching, on European as well as Oriental methods, may be added. In every case, the village schoolmaster ought to be one of the people, and not a Government official anxious to exercise his little brief authority.

That presents should be made to a teacher by a boy on the completion of a book or part of a book may certainly be called a "payment by results."

One of the *most* indigenous forms of Urdu education is for a wealthy man to employ a teacher for his sons and those of his relatives, and to allow him to teach those of his friends, also on some payment. It was thus that Aurangzeb himself read with the son of a weaver.

The officers of the Educational Department look on indigenous schools as competing with them, and therefore either neglect or suppress them; but there is no reason why there should not be co-operation, as their aim is the same or ought to be so.

The average attendance in indigenous schools, except in those of the Pádhás is 10; the lowest attendance in a Government village school is 20; the consequence is that the Government school can never reach the small villages.

Besides, far greater personal attention to each boy can be given in an indigenous school than in a Government school, especially as it is the practice for each boy to bring his lesson separately to the teacher, whilst the remainder are conning over what they have learnt from the teacher and what they are preparing; although both in elementary and advanced Muhammadan schools it will often be found that the same text-books are used, yet the mode of instruction, even in such books as Abul Fazl, Akhlaqi-i-Muhsiri, Gulzar Dabistan, Ruqat Nizami, Safwat-ul-Mesader, Karima, Khalik Bari, Amadnama, Gúlistan and Bostan are taught far more perfectly in the advanced schools (*Mozaffarnagar*); also Namkina, Sikandarnama, Masdar Fayúz, Tahirwáhid, Minabazár, Panj-rukha.*

The *Halkabandi* system *alone* can successfully compete with indigenous schools.

Punishments are lenient where teachers depend on their pupils, such as standing in the corner and beating with a slight switch, retention after school-hours or at meal-times, pulling the ear.

Fees vary according to the wealth of the pupils. They are given either on Sundays or on Thursdays, as Friday is often a holiday. The *I'di* is a fee from six pies to one anna which the pupil presents with a composition in honour of the festival. Sometimes there is a contract rate for food between parent and teacher.

Pandits are often supported by "*Jajmanee*" or "*Katha*," the contribution of the families to whom they act as religious advisers, and they often feed the sons of their clients during teaching hours.

One of the results of the establishment of Government village schools has been that the people have not started Persian or other schools at their own expense, which they otherwise would have done.

Masters of Persian schools are also supplied with food by the owner of the house where the school is held, while the Hindu teachers get a *sidha* (atta dal and salt, &c., &c.) twice a month from each pupil.

The object of indigenous schools is education for its own sake or preparation for the work of life; that of Government schools is examination and employment under Government.

The books commonly read in Sanskrit schools are "Beharsat," "Kaumudi," and "Amarkosh." "Akshardipika," "Saraswat," "Chandrika," "Kirmit-shraddha" and "Vyakaran" are also taught, also Astronomy, Nyaya.

The extension of the present Government system of education depends on the extension of Government employment and no further.

In secular Hindu schools the text-books are "Pathi" (really "a board") "Charan Jika" and "Ramchandrika" for reading, and "Lilawati," for arithmetic.

In Arabic schools, after the completion of the grammatical course, literature, logic and law are taught, the Kuran schools being chiefly confined to the middle classes, (*a*) by rote, (*b*) by heart for the Hafizship.

The cultivation of the memory is one of the best results of indigenous schools.

The absence of classification in schools is not wholly a disadvantage, as it enables each boy to get on in accordance with his talent and industry, and the clever boy is not kept back in consequence of the dull boy.

The great object of natives in starting schools is to enable *gratuitous* education to be given.

Pice paid on Saturday are called "Sandina." Many Padha schools exist in out-districts, but only a few months in the year (during rainy season).

In the highest indigenous schools even our entrance course could be introduced.

The object of the grant-in-aid should be publicly explained in every village.

---

* In Hindu schools the Balbodh, Shighr-bodh, Saraswat, Mahúr.-Chintamani Chandrika, Amarkosh, Bhagwat, Ramayan Adhiatm, Lilawati, Manorama and Haribans are used; also Akshar Dipika, and Suraj-pur-ki-Kahani, Bidya-ankur, Baranmala and arithmetical tables.

Gurmukhi or Landé are studied by both Hindu and Muhammadan agriculturists or traders, officials of Native States, the state of education in which may be taken to represent to a certain extent the state of education in the Panjáb before annexation

Many teachers in private employ cannot, of course, accept the grant except when their employers permit them to do so, which would rarely happen, as they would lose their liberty, get their schools crowded, *i.e.*, except where they wish to stand well with the authorities.

In many districts three-fourths of the schools have been closed owing to the existence of Government schools and the general depression of the people.

In Goruckpore one boy in every three attends a school, and one boy in 28 in the country.

A custom of travelling Landé teachers also prevails in the country.

It is in proportion as one is oneself in favour of indigenous schools that one believes in their accepting aid.

The ancient indigenous village system is oral instruction and learning arithmetic by heart.

Attendance registers are not kept, but boys' names are called out from time to time which keeps order even in a Padha school of a hundred boys, and ensures attendance, as the absentees are sent for from their homes.

No fines are levied. Instruction lasts from morning till evening, with a recess of two hours for food, from 11 to 1. Teachers generally never leave the school-houses.

In *Etah* aid is given to six schools from halkabandi allotments, and are to a great extent the remnants of private schools preparatory of the younger boys for Government schools, or to keep them under supervision, and of the older boys for Persian education beyond the school course.

If the Lahore Government College could be called a college when it had only four students, there is no reason why an indigenous school should not be called a school when it has less than ten pupils.

District officers when on tour should receive applications for new schools.

In Hindu schools, which are both secular and religious, the following books are taught: Saraswat, Chandrika, Sidhant Kaumudi, Bhagwat, Ramayan, Laghu Kumudi, Balmik Ramayan, Mahurath Chintamani, Sarb Sangrah, Satya Narain, Srimad Bhagwat, Durgapath, Shankarbodh, Gulistan, Bostan, Bahardanish, Insha Khalifa, Abul Fazl, Sikandarnama, Yusuf Zuleikha, Mufidnama, and Panjrukha.

In Persian and Arabic schools, which are both secular and religious, the following books are in use: in schools I—Sipárá-ám, Karima and Mamokima, Gulistan and Bostan, guide to praying and fasting, and Kuran; in schools II—Sikandarnama, Bahardanish, Abul Fazl, Yusuf Zaleikha, and the Kuran.

The school, if only a secular one: the following subjects are generally taught in the advanced schools in the Urdu, Persian and English languages: Karima, Mamokima, Dastur-us-sibyan, Gulistan and Bostan, English, First Book, Second Book, Third Book, Fourth Book, Grammatical Primer, Arithmetic, Geography, History of India.

The native system is that a man shall first commit his book to memory and then learn the meaning. The consequence is that they at any rate keep the prayers required for different ceremonies in mind, whilst others derive a livelihood from this attainment, *e.g.*, Brahmins among Hindus, who are family priests, and Hafizes amongst Muhammadans, who are preferentially elected as Imams of mosques, and who at any rate must lead the prayers at night during the Ramazan (called *Taravih*). (This also applies to the Punjab.)

Sometimes boys are allowed leave before the end of the school when they have learned their lesson thoroughly.

The advantage of the private school kept by a wealthy man is that his poorer neighbours can learn gratis along with his own children.

Even when teachers who have been taught in Government schools are employed in indigenous schools, which is very rare, they fall into the traditional method of teaching. People consider the style of education in indigenous schools as better than in Government schools.

Grants from Government will only be accepted if the parents on whom the teachers depend agree to the condition of such grants

Rajputs do not care for learning;

Khatris give their children an education suited to their position and no more; and

Muhammadans consider that Persian is taught better in indigenous schools than in Government schools.

The continuance of indigenous schools is practically a protest against the Government system, and seems to be a survival of the *fittest* in native opinion.

The multiplication-table is taught in Hindu schools, and in addition the product of the various numbers and $1\frac{1}{4}$ and $2\frac{1}{2}$, &c.

Sometimes the indigenous teacher is a man whom a villager has brought up to keep his accounts and teach his children.

Care should be taken to make the teaching of poor children a condition of giving a grant from the cess or otherwise to an indigenous school.

If regular returns had been kept of the indigenous schools in the Panjáb by the Educational Department, as is, I believe, done in the North-Western Provinces, there would not now be this difficulty of ascertaining the number and subjects of study of these schools.

In Hindu schools boys learn arithmetic in the morning, and writing in the afternoon.

The latter is first done with a piece of wood on a powdered board (if not on the ground), and then on paper.

On the Ashtmi festival, twice a month, the Brahmin master gets flour and dál and a pice from each pupil.

Once a year, on the 12th Bhadon, the master accompanied by his pupils goes round their houses with a salver into which each puts from 4 annas to a rupee.

In Muhammadan schools the teachers similarly get a gratuity from 2 annas to a rupee on the Ed-ul-Fitr, Ed-uz-zuhá, and Shab-i-barat, as well as a pice on Thursdays to have themselves shaved and their clothes washed in order to appear decently on Friday at the mosque.

Where the whole family are teachers, some of them may have other occupations, but they can always be obtained for teaching purposes.

Often, even now, new indigenous schools are started, and Sanskrit schools teaching grammar up to Siddhant Kaumudi and Kavya, as also schools to teach the multiplication-table up to Bikat-pahara.

There are Pandits who accept neither presents nor fees; they teach the Nyaya, Vedanta, Mimansa and Sanskrit grammar to the advanced students, and to the rest Kathas (recitation of religious or Puranic legends), such as Sata Narayana, Ekadashi Mahatma, Bhagwata Saptah, Gita, &c., in Sanskrit, and to explain them in Hindi; also the outlines of astrology, the rules for explaining the Hindi calendar, and the method of performing the ceremonies observed on births, marriages, and deaths.

In Landé schools they get flour, dál, ghi on the 11th of each lunar fortnight, Ikadashi, and a large present on the 4th of the light fortnight of *Bhadaun*, usually called Chauk Chaukri (because four boys go along playing with sticks). This fee is 4 to 8 annas from poor parents, and 1 to 5 rupees from the well-to-do, and sweetmeats are also distributed to the pupils, and a pagri, sometimes, to the teacher. It, however, is said to have happened in the southern part of the Punjab and in the North-Western Provinces that Landé schools are started just before this festival, and then disappear.

Competition between Indigenous and Government schools should be encouraged, and district and municipal scholarships be thrown open to them as well as to others, and the successful indigenous student be allowed to remain in his school if he chooses.

Grants should not be given so as to make the teacher independent of his pupils.

Indigenous schools in the Punjab are not so ephemeral as in many parts of Oudh and the North-Western Provinces.

The attachment to old text-books of those who have themselves been taught in indigenous schools should not be lost sight of.

Teachers of Indigenous schools who have been taught in Government schools are often not allowed by the parents of the pupils to teach History and Geography, Arithmetic being most valued.

If the Indigenous teachers themselves were to be sent to Normal schools, their own schools might be broken up during their absence

Indigenous schools are often in close proximity to Government schools.

Indigenous schools are often deserted, as instruction in Government schools, especially in Arabic and Sanskrit, is cheaper.

Private tuition in the Panjáb is often as ephemeral as in Europe.

Patwaris have been known to prefer sending their children to an Indigenous school, though they are warned that they are, thereby, disqualified for office.

The best way to aid Indigenous schools is :—

(1) Public scholarships obtainable at the "public service" and other examinations, the number of *optional* subjects in which should be increased.

(2) The liberal supply of text-books, without on any account prescribing their exclusive use.

(3) Prizes to pupils passing in any *one* subject of general knowledge at public examinations, and khilats to the teachers for every three pupils so passing.

If Indigenous schools are to be assisted, no further increase of Government Primary schools shoul take place, but the present Government schools should be converted into model Indigenous schools.

Pupils in Persian schools learn by rote moral precepts, aphorisms and verbal conceits, which are generally explained to them by their parents or friends. Shikasta writing is taught in the Persian schools.

If a pupil read silently he is supposed to neglect his work.

The Collector of Ballia says that the Indigenous schools are looked on with jealousy by the Educational Department.

Pathi is a piece of ground rubbed over with coal or mud.

The explanations given by the teacher must also be remembered by the pupils.

Every boy is taught separately.

Teachers of Mahajani, Landé, Sarafi, Kaithi or Mundia schools in the North-Western Provinces are often called Bhai, Guru, Padha, &c., &c., which seems to illustrate the fact that many of them came from the Panjáb.

Night schools might be opened with advantage, both for boys and adults, in towns and the larger villages wherever agreeable to the people and the teacher.

[*Note.*—See Hoskins' complaint against Educational Department, Budaun.]

The teacher might register his school with the Deputy Commissioner. Some boys read the Ramayana in Hindi; sometimes the Kuran is also taught in mixed schools.

No grant should ever be given when its effect would be to lessen the parents' outlay on the education of their children.

When the crops are good there are more Indigenous schools.

Indigenous schools are often started by rich zemindars and mahajans, who do not like to send their children to a public school.

Proposals.—Taking the cost of each student in Panjab Government and aided schools a Rs. 13-4-4 per annum, which includes pupils, whether they have passed examinations or not, (see page 6 of Report), it would certainly not be expensive to pay the following rewards to teachers and pupils for *passing* the following tests :—

(1) For passing "the public service examination," three rupees to the teacher for each student so passed; the pupil requires nothing, as he is sufficiently compensated by obtaining a certificate qualifying for the public service.

(2) For passing in all the subjects of the Indigenous course, to be indicated for each kind of schools by the Panjáb University, a certificate should be given, as also prize books of the value of two rupees, according to the standard which he has passed, which is to be of three grades. For each three students so passed the teacher to get five rupees, as also a khilat and certificate at a public annual meeting. The examination of Indigenous schools to be conducted directly or through local examiners appointed by the Panjáb University.

(3) To each pupil passing in any one *or more* subjects of general knowledge by the lower primary standard, provided the scheme is improved, one rupee.

(4) For passing the Maulvi and Pandit examinations of the Panjáb University, Rs. 5, 10 and 15 for each successful candidate according to the grade of these standards, and Rs. 2, 5 and 10 respectively according to the three Munshi grades, and Rs. 2, 4 and 8 according to the three Bhai grades. Considering that only 1,006 candidates have passed the Oriental examinations of all kinds of the Panjáb University College since 1871, there is no reason to apprehend an excessive increase of the public or local expenditure on rewards for such successful candidates at the various Maulvi, Pandit, Munshi and Bhai examinations, whilst the beneficial effect of such expenditure will far outweigh the outlay, in the revival of letters and in the favourable reception of subjects of general knowledge by indigenous teachers.

5.—The Condition of Indigenous Education in Districts of the North-Western Provinces before their Incorporation in the Panjáb.

It is necessary for the completion of the Report on what is now the Panjáb to contrast the state of Indigenous education in certain districts before their annexation from the North-Western Provinces with their present condition.

From Report of A. Roberts, Esq., *for 1849.*

Panipat.—Panipat district in 1849 had 105 schools. It was composed of the parganas of Sanipat and Panipat, and Karnal. Of 105 schools, 13 were Persian, 15 Arabic, 27 Hindi or rather Mahajani, and Sanskrit 32. All the teachers of the Hindu schools were Brahmin, except two who were Banyas. One Muhammadan taught a Hindu school, and two Brahmins taught Persian schools. Mr. Johnson, the Deputy Collector, estimated the proportion of school-taught children to the whole population 1·8 per cent., but thought it should be doubled to include girls that were under instruction and boys taught at home, thus showing the existence of considerable female and intramural instruction. The proportion of school-taught children is now 25 at Paripat(?); Sanipat 8, Karnal 13.

Delhi.—Delhi district had 321 schools, of which 270 were in the city, 8 in suburbs, and 43 in the interior district. The Delhi district has now 216 schools.

The proportion of Persian to Hindu schools was 5 to 1; considering that that city contained more Hindus than Muhammadans, this is remarkable. Of the Persian teachers 256 were Muhammadans, 8 Kayasts, 2 Brahmins, 2 Khatris, 1 Banya.

Of these teachers 24 had been in that profession over 27 or nearly 28 years. In these Persian schools the Hindu boys very nearly, if not quite, equalled the Muhammadan boys in number. Of the teachers of Hindu schools, 52 were Brahmins and 1 a Kayast.

Of these, 14 teachers had taught nearly 35 years.

There were six public girls' schools, conducted by Panjábi women, and attended by the daughters of the wealthy Panjábi merchants of that city.

Rohtak had 46 schools. It has now 99 Indigenous schools.

Gurgaon had 100 schools. It has now 55 Indigenous schools.

It may be mentioned that of the 46 Arabic and Persian schools in Panipat 24 were held in mosques. Of the 28 in Haryana (Hissar) 21 were held in mosques; and of 268 in Delhi, 80 were held in mosques.

The grand total of male pupils under instruction in the North-Western Provinces, in a population of 21,630,167 (exclusive of the districts now annexed to the Panjáb), was 64,333 in 7,361 schools, thus showing that the indigenous education in the North-Western Provinces was far below that in the Panjáb, with its much smaller population, whilst the districts annexed from the North-Western Provinces are still below the average of the real Panjábi districts as regards indigenous education.

6—Terms used in Indigenous Schools.

The following are a few of the terms used in the Indigenous schools:—

School—*Chátsal* (from *chát*, a teacher, and *sál*-hall, place [the teacher's house]).

Páthshal (from *páth*, a lesson [reading house]).

Dharmsálás.

Madrasa.

Maktab.

Teachers—of Chátsalas, Pándhas.

of Páthshalas, Pandits.

of Dharmsálás, Bhais.

of Madrasas, Maulvis } terms interchangeable and varying ac-
of Maktabs, Mians } cording to the office of the teacher.

Pupils—of Chátsalas, Munde, Chatya.

of Páthshalas, Vidhiartis

of Dharmsálás, Sikh.

of Madrasas, Talib-ilm.

of Maktabs, Shagird (also of Kuran schools).

Monitor—In Muhammadan schools generally the *Khalifa*.

Lesson—In Hindu schools, *páth*.

In Muhammadan schools, *Sabaq*.

Holidays—In Hindu schools *chhutti* (festival-teonhar).

In Muhammadan schools, *tatil* and *chhutti*.

Revising—"*Amokhta Parhna*" in Muhammadan schools.

In Hindu schools the repetition of multiplication-tables is called *Maharni*.

Writing Board—(Hind.) *patti*, (Persian schools) *takhti*.

Rod—(H.) *santi*, (Pers.) *chhari* and also *kamchi*.

Pen—(H.) *lekhni*, (Pers.) *kalam*.

Inkstand—(H.) *bhoka, buddhka, kuliya*. (Pers.) *dáwát*.

Polisher—(H.) *ghota*, (P.) *mohra* and also *ghota*.

Ruling lines—(H.) *samas karma*, (Pers.) *jadwal, mistar*.

Book— (Sans.) *pushtak*, (H.) *pothi*, (P. and A.) *kitab*.

Sheet of Paper—(H.) *táo, pathra*, (P.) *takhta*.

Leaf—(H.) *panna*, (S.) *patra*, (Pers.) *wáraq*, and *page* is called *sufha*.

Pasteboard—(Pers.) *wasli*.

Satchel (H.) *bandhna*, (P.) *basta, juzdan*.

Correction—(H.) *shodhna*, (Pers.) *isláh*.

Dictation—(P.) *imlá*.

Handwriting—(H.) *lekh*, (P.) *khat*.

To read by rote—(H.) *maukik path*, (P.) *rawán parhna, nazira parhna*.

To learn by heart—(H.) *kanth karna*, (P.) *barzaban az-bar kerna, yad kerna, nokzabán karna, hifz karna*.

To look over the day's lesson previously to learning it—(H.) *bechárna*, (P.) *mutáala karna*.

File of old letters—(Pers.) *maktúb* (used to practise the pupil in reading Shikasta and other running hands).

PART V.

LIST OF MAULVIS, PANDITS, BHAIS, PANDHAS, HAKIMS, BAIDS, AUTHORS AND POETS IN THE PANJAB.

N.B.—THOSE IN ITALICS ARE IN CHARGE OF SCHOOLS.

Places.	Maulvis.	Pandits.	Bhais.	Pandhas.	Hakims.	Baids.	Authors.	Poets.
				I.—DELHI DISTRICT.				
Delhi ...	*Nazir Husain*, Hafizullah Khan, *Rahim Bakhsh*, Mansur Ali Khan, *Muhammad Shah*, Manzur Ali, *Abdulla*, Abdurrab, Abdulkadir, Zea-ud-din, Nazir Ahmad, *Sharif Hussain*, *Abul Hasan*, *Abdulmajid* *Abdulhaq*.	*Gobind Ram*, *Pandit Radhe Misser*, *Gosain Banarsi Das*.	Bhagat Singh ...	*Imam Ali*, *Piragdat*.	Mahmud Khan, Abdul Majid, Ghulam Riza, Saraj-ud-din, Badr-ud-din, Qeyam-ud-din, Latif Husain, Qutb-ud-din, Ghulam Najaf, Zahir-ud-din, Akbar Ali, Mohammad Hussain, Nur-ud-din, Muzaffar Hussain.	Binda ...	Maulvi Nusrat Ali, Maulvi Najm-ud-din, Munshi Altaf Husain, Maulvi Abdulmunsur, Maulvi Nazir Husain, Maulvi Mohammad Shah, Maulvi Nazir Ahmad, Maulvi Zea-ud-din, Munshi Sayyid Ahmad, Munshi Ambeparshad, Munshi Zakaulla, Munshi Umrao Singh, Munshi Uggar Sain, Munshi Ummaid Singh, Mirza Beg, Abdulla Beg, Rukn-uddin, Ghazanfarali, Ulfat Husain, Maulvi Abdurrab, Lala Sagar Chand.	Adib, Arshad, Hali, Talib, Nayyir, Nawab Mirza, Hafiz Ghulam Rasul, Wiran, Maulvi Ammujan, Nawab Baha-ud-din, Nawab Shuja-ud-din, Nawab Mumtaz-ud-din, Sheikh Nur Ilahi, Badrul Islam, Fatah-ul-Islam, Umrao Mirza, Amir Mirza, Maulvi Muhammad Said, Sayyed Bakar, Nawab Saraj-ud-din, Mirza Muhammad Ashraf, Yakub Beg, Shaikh Ramzan Ali, Pandit Ram Chander, Lala Suraj Narayen, Maulvi Jamal Urrahman, Ahmad Ali, Mirza Mahmud Shah, Mirza Ghulam Muhammad, Mirza Bakhtawar Shah, Mirza Buland Akhtar, Mirza Beg Khan, Nasir-ud-din, Mir Shah Jahan, Nawab Wahid-ud-din, Peer Qamr-ud-din, Bismilla Beg, Behari Lal.

List of Maulvis, Pandits, &c., &c., in the Panjab—(continued).

Places.	Maulvis.	Pandits.	Bhais.	Pandhas.	Hakims.	Baids.	Authors.	Poets.
				I.—DELHI DISTRICT.—continued.				
Mohna ...	*Muhammad Hatim Ali, Haidar Ali.*	*Khiali Ram* ...	......	......	......	......	Haidar Ali.	......
Balabgarh ...	......	*Kidar Nath* ...	......	......	......	Gunga Balab ...	......	......
Majholi ...	......	......	......	......	......	Jas Ram ...	......	......
Sunipat ...	Imar Ali (Shia) ...	Sabachand ...	......	......	......	......	......	......
Najafgarh ...	......	*Ramji Lal, Deodat* ...	......	......	......	......	......	......
				II.—GURGAON DISTRICT.				
Hathin	......	Pandit Mavashi, Hittu Missar, Jamna Dass.	......	......	......	......	......	......
Hasanpur	*Nabi Bakhsh* ...	......	......	......	......	......	......	......
Nuh	......	Umrao Singh ...	......	......	......	......	......	......
Sohna	*Haji Abdulla* ...	*Shadi Ram* ...	......	......	Mirza Muhammad Beg, Syed Ghulam Husain.	Dhani Ram ...	Syyid Ghulam Husain.	Pandat Shadi Ram.
Punahana	......	*Mohan Lal, Giddar*	......	......	......	Dula Ram, Zaharya...	......	......
Furrukhnagar	*Abdulaziz,* Abdul Hakim.	......	......	*Ramjiwan* ...	......		......	......
Palwal	......	......	......	*Radha Kishen* ...	Muhammad Ismail, Amin-uddin.	......	......	......
Hodal	......	Bhawani, Gangal ...	......	......	Shib Lal ...	......	......	......
Ferozepur	......	Polia	......	......	......	Amar Chund, Dilsukh	......	......
Biwari	Maulvi Nur Ali, Ghulam Husain, Abdulwasa, Ilahi Buksh, Mohammad Din Khan, Mulla Fazluddin, Mir Muhammad Husain, Nur Muhammad.	Bhan Singh, *Bishan Mitter, Deodat,* Ram Sahai, Sholoji, Jetarji, Maha Singh, Ram Sewak Gujrati.	......	*Amra, Kanhia Ganeshi*	Najmuddin, Matlub, Husain, Wahid-uddin, Abdurrahim, Abdulwahab, Ahsan Ali, Mohamad Ali, Fazli Mohamad, Abdulwasa.	Bas Deo, Ram Sahai, Ram Richpal, Harnarayen, Shib Sahai.	Abdul Wasa ...	......
Shahjahanpur	......	......	......	*Ananda* ...	......	......	......	......
Gurgaon	......	Hira Lal ...	......	......	......	......	......	......

III.—KARNAL DISTRICT.

Famalka	......	*Raja Ram, Sita Ram, Har Lal, Sewag Ram.*	......	......	Ghulam Rasul ...	......	Mr. Abdulla Athim ...	......
Butana	......	......	......	......	Kalandar Bakhsh ...	......	......	......
Indri	......	Tulsi Ram, Dharni Dut.	......	......	Diadial ...	......	......	......
Alupur	......	*Hardawari, Hait Ram, Permanand.*	......	......	......	......	......	......
Siuk	......	......	......	......	Dhindha, Ishk Lal ...	......	......	......
Asandh	Ghulam Nabi ...	......	......	......	Ghulam Nabi ...	......	......	......
Salwan	......	Dya Ram ...	......	......	......	......	......	......
Karnal	*Ghulam Muhammad, Salah-uddin.*	Kanshi Ram, *Ram Saran.*	......	......	Rahmatullah ...	......	......	......
Kaithal	Sayyad Barkat Ali ...	......	......	*Imam Din* ...	......	......	......	......
Gohla	*Shah Muhammad* ...	......	......	......	......	......	......	......
Pundri	......	*Dya Lal* ...	......	*Rahim Bakhsh* ...	Aman-ullah ...	......	......	......
Badlada	......	......	......	......	Muhammad Bakhsh...	Hira Lal ...	......	......
Panipat	Abdurrahman, *Raghik Ullah*, Rahim Bakhsh.	Bhagwan Das, Jainti Lal, Jawahar Lal, Badri Dass.	......	*Jogdhyan, Azimulla*	Haidar Husain, Muhammad Husain, Manju Khan, Barkat Ali.	Mulchaud.	......	......

IV.—HISSAR DISTRICT.

Fatahabad ...	*Mohamad Khuda Baksh, Abdurrahman*, Mubarakuddin.	......	......	*Nabi Bakhsh* ...	Kazi Yusuf ...	......	......	......
Bhiwani ...	......	Chokharaj, Ramjas, Shamsukh, *Basdeo, Sripat*, Kali Das.	......	*Khairati* ...	......	Mota Ram, Shiv Narayen.	......	......
Hansi ...	*Gami Shah* ...	Nath Mal, Sheo Narayen, Kunj Lal, Sukhdeo, *Umadat.*	......	*Ram Narayen* ...	Ruldo, Shaikh Masita, Munir-ud-din, Naubat Rai.	......	......	......
Sairo ...	......	*Damodar Dass*	......	......	......	......	......	......

List of *Maulvis*, *Pandits*, &c., &c., *in the Panjab*.—(continued).

Places.	Maulvis.	Pandits.	Bhais.	Pandhas.	Hakims.	Baids.	Authors.	Poets.
IV.—HISSAR DISTRICT—continued.								
Narnond ...	......	*Raje Ram* ...	....	......	......	Gugan ...	......	......
Siwani ...	......	....	......	......	Siraj-ud-din, Jamal-ud-din.	......	......	......
Bahal ...	......	*Ram Ratan* ...	......	*Bhonta* ...	......	......	......	......
Tuhana ...	*Abdulla*, Rahmat Ali	Ram Narayen ...	...	......	......	......	......	......
Hissar ...	Rukn-ud-din, Mubarkuddin, Khuda Bakhsh.	Hardeo Ram Gopal, Shadi Ram, Shib Ram, Har Narayen, Rikhi Ram, Gobind Ram.	......	*Khair-ud-din* ...	Najaf Ali, Sadiq Ali, Sham Lal.	......	......	......
Ratya ...	......	......	......	......	Alim-ud-din, Mahmud.	......	......	......
V.—ROHTAK DISTRICT.								
Mahm	Hakim Alauddin, Muhammad Yakub, Muhammad Salamuddin, Muhammad Abdul Ghani, Muhammad Wali.	Birhamdat (in Farmana), Ganga Ram, Narayen Dat.	......	*Santu*	Hakim Alauddin, Fazalhak, Amir-ud-din, Ala Bakhsh.	Pirbhu ...	......	Muzaffar Ahmad Mahvi, an Urdu and Persian poet.
Kalanaur	......	*Chandan*, *Lachhman*.	......	......	Hidayat Ali Khan (in Government employment).	*Manak Dass* ...	......	Qiyamuddin.
Gohana	Muhammad Amanat Ali.	*Hans Ram* ...	......	......	Hakim Amanat Ali, Mazhar Ali, Karim Bakhsh.	Des Raj ...	Ghulam Ahmad ...	......
Rohtak ...	Muhammad Hafizuddin, Haji Amir Ali, Rafiuddin.	*Harparshad Harsaran*.	......	*Mehar Nath Jogi* ...	Hafiz-ud-din, Asghar Ali.	Bakhtawar (oculist) .. Kanahiya Lal ... Gauri Sahai, Layeq Ram Rudarparshad	Hafiz Anwar Ali ...	......
Kharkhoda	*Najibulla* ...	*Dya Ram* ...	......	......	......	......	......	......
Bahadurghar	......	*Gobinddat*, *Premdat*	......	......	Zai-uddin ...	......	......	......

Jhajjar ...	Abdurrahim, *Muhammad Hasan*	Dia Kishen ... Hardat ... Nagri Lal ... Choranji Lal ... Bermahnand ...	....	*Harnarayen*	Agha Ali, Abdul Hakim, Abdulwahab, (of Guryani.)	Parsani Lal, Chi·anji Lal.	....	Karim Bakhsh. ......
Sanpla	......	*Birhamdat* ...	......	*Sohan Lal* ...	......	......	......	......
Beri	......	*Ram Richhpal*, Ganga Dat, Shivpershad.	......	......	Fattan Lal, Gulab Dass	......	......	......
				VI.—SIRSA DISTRICT.				
Ranya ...	Saadulla, Nabi Bakhsh	......	......	......	Muhammad Isa ...	Rakh Jati ...	......	......
Dabwali ...	......	......	Tota Ram Sádh ...	......	Shaikh Qureshi ...	......	......	......
Sirsa ...	Kadir Bakhsh ...	Pundit Ram Krishen, Ishar Dass.	Ishur Singh ...	......	Abdulla (of Sikandarpur).	Keshore Chand Jati...	......	Karim Bakhsh.
Abuhar ...	*Muhammad Ahmed Din*, Mian Suleymán Hafiz Fatah Din.	......	......	......	Ahmad Din ...	Varyam ...	Ahmad Din ...	Muhammad Akram.
Behrajpur ...	*Rahmat Din* ...	......	*Mangal Ram Sádhú*...	......	......	......	......	......
Sarawan ...	Fakir Kadir Bukhsh	......	......	......	......	......	......	......
Rasulpura ...	Rahmat ...	......	......	......	......	......	......	......
Fázalka ...	Sayyid Muhammad Shah, Ghulam Rasul of (Hasta).	Sedhu, Ram Narayan, Dyalchand.	......	......	......	Rupsee-puj ...	......	......
				VII.—UMBALLA DISTRICT.				
Mazra's	......	*Birmha Nand* Ram Narayen.	Kharak Singh ...	......	Mahtab Singh, Balmukand.	Moti Ram, Diva Mal.	......	......
Singhore	Kazi Rahim Bakhsh (in Babain), Muhammad Yasin	......	......	......	......	......	......	......
Shahabad	......	Perma Nand (in Nalwa), *Padam Nath*.	Bhai Kishen ...	......	Hakim Bahar Khan	......	......	......
Ladwa	......	......	......	*Bansi*	Rahim Bakhsh ...	Lachhmi Narayan, Narayan Singh.	......	......

List of Maulvies, Pandits, &c., &c., in the Panjab.—(continued).

Places.	Maulvis.	Pandits.	Bhais.	Pandhas.	Hakims.	Baids.	Authors.	Poets.
			UMBALLA DISTRICT—(continued).					
Sadhi	......	Ramji Dass ...	......	......	......	......	......	......
Ropar	M. Qutb-ud-din (in Sanga).	*Chandu Lal* ...	Bishan Singh ...	*Mangal* ...	Fazl-i-Karim, Qudrat-ullah.	Ram Ditta, Pulu, Narayani (a woman)	......	Saran Singh
Sadhora	*Myanji Ataulla* ...	Hira Lal, Ganpat, Shankarya.	*Kank Singh* ...	......	Khadim Husain, Amanat Ali, Mansib Ali.	Husain Bakhsh ...	......	......
Mullana	......	......	......	......	Rajab Ali ...	......	......	......
Chappar	Faiz Muhammad, Abdul Khalik.	Chuni Lal, Balmukand.	......		Qutb-ud-din, Farid Bakhsh.	Narayana ...	......	......
Bilaspur	......	......	......	......	Bije Singh ...	Salig Ram ...	......	......
Mubarakpur	......	Uma Dat, Narain Das, Jai Dayal.	......	*Sajan Jogi* ...	Hakim Daulat Ali ...	Rugha Baid ...	......	......
Jagadhri	*Abdul Qadir* ...	*Beli Ram* ...	*Tulsi* (of Burga) ...	*Pansari* ...	......	......	......	......
Umbala	Muhammed Said, *Ghulam Ali Khan, Rafiq Ahmad, Sayyid Razi.*	*Jamna Das, Salig Ram, Parbhudyal, Hari Saran.*	*Lachhman Singh* ...	*Hirda Ram, Shaikh Ala Bakhsh.*	Jafar Husain, Buali Bakhsh, Charan Singh.	......	Ahmad Husan ...	......
Pihoa	Hafiz Imam-ud-din ...	*Rura, Jhuddu Lal, Hardat, Sina.*	Tola ...	......	H. Khair Muhammad.	Mulla Ram, Bishambar Das.	......	......
Radaur			......	......	......	......	......	......
	....	Hari Saran ...	......	......	Ghulam Haidar ...	Jethu ...	......	......
Thanesar	Ishq ulla ...	*Bulchand*, Atma Ram, Ganga Ram, Bhagwana, Chandu Lal, Murli Dhar.	......	......	Rahmat-ulla, Shadi, Ali Husain, Ramji Das, Nanak Chand.	......	......	......
Babyal	......	Gobind Ram ...						
Raipur	......	Ram Lal ...	......	......	Fasih-ud-din ...	......	......	......
Murinda	......	......	......	......	Subhan-ulla, Khalifa, Makkhan.	......	......	......

......	......	......	Thakur Singh, Chatar-Singh.	......	......	......	......	......
Kharar	Akbar Ali ...	Nand Lal, Pundit Ganesha (Chauhatta), Kapurya Ram (Rudyala), Kanahia Lal (Korali).	......	......	Ali Bakhsh, Ghulam Abbas, Najaf Ali, Ali Husain, Badan Singh.	......	......	......
Umballa Cantonments ...	......	......	......	......	Murad Ali ...	......	......	......
Narayanpur	......	Pundit Kirpa Ram ...	......	......	......	......	......	......
				VIII.—LUDHIANA.				
LUDHIANA.								
Raikot	*Asadulla, Abdul Karim.*	*Madsudhan, Baldeo Kishen.* Shiv Ram, *Mula Ram.*	*Prem Dass, Narsing Das. Paras Ram.*	*Fatah Din* ...	*Pandit Gurdhan*, Abdul Karim.	Durgadat, Ganda Ram.	......	......
Bhup Rai Kalan ...	......	......	......	......	......	......	......	......
Khanna	......	*Ganga Ram* ...	*Ude Ram* ...	*Ala Bakhsh Jogi* ...	Ali Nawáz ...	......	......	......
Machhiwara	Muhammad Ismail (of Chakki).	*Kanahia Lal* ...	......	......	Shah Nawaz, Wali Muhammad, Sayyid Shah Nawaz Kanahia Lal Kanungo, Alla Rakha.	Sodhi Jaswant Sing...	......	......
Samrala	......	*Chiranji Lal* ...	Bhagwan Dass Faki	......	Muhammad Bakhsh...	......	......	......
Ludhiana	*Abdul Aziz,* Abdul Qadir, *Abdulla,* Shihab-ud-din, *Muhamad Hasan,* Husain Ján, Ismail (1), Ismail (2), Abdul-wahid, Shah Din, Nizam-ud-din, Muhammad Musa.	Chandi Pershad, Dhanpat, *Dolu Ram.*	*Gobind Dass* ...	*Muhammad Bakhsh Jogi.*	Muhammad Ali, Ahmad Ali, Ganga Din, Jamniyat Ali, Abdur-razzáq, Mohammad Ali, Nasir Khan.	Ganga Din ...	Muhammad Abdulaziz Shah Din, Ismail (1).	Ghaiás-ud-din, Haida. Ali, Chiragh Din.
Shahna	......	*Ram Kishen* ...	......	......	......	......	......	......
Jagraon	Sharif Hasan, Sharif Husain, Abdurrahim, *Abdulla.*	Banshi Dar, *Ganga Dass.*	*Sunder Dass* ...	*Jiwa*	Qamruddin ...	......	Imdad Ali ...	......
Delon	......	......	*Bhup Singh, Ganda Singh.*	......	......	......	......	......

List of Maulvis, Pandits, &c., &c., in the Panjab—(continued.)

Places.	Moulvies.	Pandits.	Bhais.	Pandhas.	Hakims.	Baids.	Authors.	Poets.
IX.—SIMLA.								
Simla ...	*Abdussalam, Mahbub Ali Shah, Habibulla.*	......	......	......	Mahbub Ali, Amir-ud-din.	......	Mahbub Ali ...	Jamal-ud-din Jamali.
Subatu ...	*Kabir Shah*, Hafiz Muhammad Hasan.	*Shib Diyal* ...	......	......	......	......	......	......
X.—JALLANDHAR DISTRICT.								
Jallundhar ...	Wali Muhammad, Nur Muhammad, Muhammad Hayat.	Ramdat, Sripat, *Gaukal Chand, Banarsi Dass; Shio Ram*, Tulsi Ram, Devi Chand.	Bhai Man Singh, Hari Dass.	*Pir Bakhsh, Mayya Dass, Jowala Pershad.*	Alamgir, Ghulam Rasul, Abdurrahman, Muhammad Allad Dad Khan, Rahim Baksh, Shah Muhammad, Nur Ahmad, Muhammad Umar.	Gunpat Rai ..	......	Barkat Ali, Shaukat, Mirza Muwahid, Muhammad Salim.
Jallundhar Cantonments ...	Qudratullah, *Muhammad Siddiq.*	Ram Narayen, Parma Nand.	......	......	Naimullah, Ibrahim	......	......	......
Kirtarpur	......	*Ram Chand* ...	*Hira Singh, Ishar Singh.*	*Muhabbat Rawal* ...	......	......	......	......
Adampur	......	Dala Ram ...	*Nanda Singh* ...	*Miran Buksh* ...	Qutbuddin, Budruddin	......	......	......
Bunga	......	*Arjan, Ganpat, Kaka Ram of Bhin, Ganga Ram, Gobind Ram.*	*Parma Nand, Jawahar Singh.*	......	Nizamuddin, Puna Singh, Muhammad Bakhsh, Kishen Singh, Nur Muhammad.	......	......	......
Rahun	Ghulam Muhi-ud-din, Maula Bakhsh, Akbar Shah.	Dyal Ram, Baghi Ram, Khemraj, Jagan Nauth, Amin Chand, Chhajju Ram, Maghar Ram.	Ram Singh, Dasundha Singh (washerman).	......	Hasan Jahanyan, Ghulam Nabi, Walayat Ali, M. Ghulam Muhiuddin.	Bava Sukhdeo Nath, Pandit Bagh Ram.	......	Khemraj (Kabeshur).
Phillaur	......	Hira Nand ...	......	......	Bahadur Beg ...	......	......	......
Nur Mahal	......	*Atma Ram*, Madho Ram, *Mast Ram, Ramdat.*	......	......	Khurshaid Ali ...	......	......	......
Nawa Shahr	......	*Mala Ram, Jaidyal, Shio Dyal, Kaka Ram, Ram Chand.*	......	......	......	......	......	......

Nakodar ...	......	*Nathu Ram* ...	*Kharak Singh,* Jhunda Singh, Bava Sundar Dass.	*Nur din, Amir Chand*	Gulab Rai, Budhu Ram, Karam Ilahi.	......	......	......
Shahkot ...	*Murid Ahmad of Mianwala.*	*Lachmi Dhar, Anant Ram.*	......	*Maula Bakhsh* ...	Jan Muhammad, Ata Muhammad.	......	......	Lachmidhar, Anant Ram.
				XI.—HUSHIARPUR DISTRICT.				
Hushiarpur ...	Mian Muhammad, Mahbub Alam, Hadi Bakhteyar.	*Narsing Das, Kanhia Lall Sukdial, Sudama Ram, Ram Rattan, Gobind Ram Joshi, Gobind Ram Sioua, Kaka Ram, Shibdial.*	*Gulab Singh, Hardass Singh.*	*Atta Muhammad* ...	Abdulla, Ali Sher ...	......	......	......
Haryana ...	*Rustam Ali* ...	Thakur Dass, Canda Ram.	......	......	......	......	......	......
Mubarakpur ...	......	Ishar Dass ...	......	......	Karam Karim ...	Tulsi Ram. ...	......	......
Dasuha ...	*Ghulam Rasul* ...	Bidya Dhar, Devi Dyal, Gurditta Mul.	......	......	Burn Mal, Ghulam Rasul, Wilayat Shah Shamsuddin.	......	......	......
Una ...	......	Devi Ditta, Dunichand, Gobind Ram Sukhdeo, Maiyya Ram.	......	......	......	......	......	......
Hajipur ...	......	......	Gyan Singh ...	......	Jai Gopal, Gaukal ...	Kishen Saru, Shiv Lal.	......	......
Balachor ...	......	Rup Ram ...	......	......	Ali Bakhsh, Ahmad Shah, Mussadi Ram.	Baga Mal. ...	......	......
Mukeryan ...	......	......	......	......	Ganga Ram, Fatah Muhammad, Sandhi Shah, Ibrahim, Ata Muhammad, Puhlu Mal.	Pohlu Mal ...	......	......
Gadh Shankar ...	Umar-ud-din, *Muhammad Nawaz.*	*Rikhi Kesh,* Bishambar Dass, Tilok Chand.	*Naththa Singh* ...	......	Shah Nawaz, Gaukal Chand, Umar din *Muhammad Nawaz.*	......	......	......
Gadh Dewala ...	......	*Ruldu Ram* ...	......	......	Umar Bakhsh, Rahmat Ali.	Nathu, Jai Ram ...	......	......
Anandpur ...	......	......	*Hira Nand, Sukh Ram, Puran Singh.*	......	Ghulam Kadir, Atar Singh, Kali Nand.	Kirpu, Gunga Ram...	......	......

List of Maulvis, Pandits, &c., &c., in the Panjab.—(continued).

Places.	Maulvis.	Pandits.	Bhais.	Pandhas.	Hakims.	Baids.	Authors.	Poets.
			XI—HUSHIARPUR DISTRICT—continued.					
Nurpur ...	......	*Ditta Ram*, Jaidial ...	......	......	......	......	......	......
Tandá ...	Muhammad Bakhs, Naju-ud-din, Abdulla.	......	......	......	Mohamad Shah, Kasim, Akram, Ganeshu, Sandi.	......	......	......
Barabasi ...	......	Kesho Nand, Polo Ram, Mayya Ram.	......	......	......	......	......	......
			XII.—KANGRA DISTRICT.					
Kallu ...	......	Kesho ...	......	......	......	Mohan Baid ...	......	......
Hamirpur ...	......	Jawahar, Kali Ram, Barfi Katoch, *Taradat*	Jawahir Singh ...	......	......	Kahan Singh, Fatah Singh, Bir Singh, Jawahar Singh.	......	......
Kotla ...	*Nabi Bakhsh* ...	......	......	......	......	Harbaj ...	......	......
Sarsar ...	......	Parbhu, Gopala, Sukhman, Gauridat.	Charan Das ...	......	Shib Ram ...	......	......	......
Palampur ...	*Rahmat Beg, Akbar Ali.*	Chet Ram, *Dimbeshwar*, Chatar bhuj.	......	......	Akbar Ali ...	......	......	......
Lowan ...	......	Gaukal Chand, Jograj, Kirpa Ram, Dharam Dass, Rudardat shastri.	......	......	Dhanpat Rai ...	Kirpa Ram ...	......	......
Kangra ...	......	Mani Ram, Sobha Ram.	......	......	......	Jainti ...	......	......
Nurpur ...	*Mir Badruddin, Ghulam Muhammad.*	Mani Ram ...	......	......	Rahman Bat ...	......	......	......
Jawalaji ...	......	*Saudagar, Narayandat, Roja Ram,* Balbhaddhar.	Kirpal Singh ...	......	......	Brij Lall ...	......	......

Dharmsal ...	Muhammad Umardin, Shah Din.	......	......	......	......	......	......	......
Dera ...	......	Asá ...	......	......	Chartu Rajput ...	......	......	......
Balách ...	......	......	......	......	......	Bisher Deo ...	......	......
Sujanpur ...	......	Girdhari ...	......	......	Jai Gota ...	Ram ...	......	......

XIII.—AMRITSAR DISTRICT.

Amritsar ...	Muhammad Buknuddin, Akbar Shah, Akbar Shah 2nd, Fazli Karim, Rasul Baba, Muhammad Shah, Sultan Mamud, Abdulla, Ahmadulla, Ghulam Ahmad, Ahmad Bukhsh, Hussain Shah, Hamed Shah, Maulvi Ghulam Ali, Khuda Bakhsh, Imam Din, Hafiz Pir Bakhsh.	Tulsi Ram, Balmukand, Baij Nath Parma Nand, Ramdat, Gulab Ram, Thakar Dass, Dhari Lall, Kishendat, Kashi Nath, Agya Ram, Mul Chand, Bhag Mal, Lachman Dass, Kanihia. Kishen Chand, Ram Kishen, Birj Lal, Shib Saran, Shibdyal. Amar Sing, Narayan, Ramdat, Shankar Dass, Har Bhagwan, Fatah Chand, Thakur Dass, Sanwan, Kishen Chand, Gopal, Bishen Dass, Achint Ram, Kaka Ram, Shib Shankar, Gopi Nath, Bhagat Ram, Madho Ram, Bansi Ram, Dhan Lal, Bula Ram, Kaka Ram II. Ramdhan, Shambu Ram, Harji, Bhawani Dass, Basdeo, Ram Saran, Kahan Chand, Sarabdyal.	Hazara Singh, Bishan Singh, Ram Singh, Birham Partap Singh, Atma Singh, Rupa Singh, Gopal Dass, Sadho Ram, Mahesh Das, Atma Singh, Ram Chand, Partap Singh, Perma Nand, Kanh Singh, Bhagwan Dass, Daya Singh, Bishan Dass, Prem Singh, Sahib Singh, Ram Chand, Bhagwan Hari, Shib Dass, Hari Singh, Anant Ram.	Kala, Nabi Bakhsh, Ali Bakhsh, Badri, Khuda Bakhsh, Harki Nandan, Shiv Narayen.	Ganga Ram, Kirpa Ram, Pir Bukhsh, Azizuddin, Khairuddin, Dyal Singh, Ram Singh, Kishan Rikh, Hisam-ud-din, Sharaf Din, Harji, Sarabsukh Ram, Mangal Singh, Muhammad Sharif, Azimulla, Bhag Singh, Ram Kishen. Shahabdin, Ramji, Devidass, Sukh Ram, Naththa Singh, Ram Misser. Jiwan Singh, Deva Singh, Hira Singh, Pandit Jagan Nath (of Muradpura). Ilahi Bakhsh, Mutiulla.	......	Hazara Singh. Dr. Sahibditta, Anwar Shah, Habibulla, Yunas Singh, Ghulam Ali, Babu John Hari, Sirdar Thakar Singh.	......

List of Maulvis, Pandits, &c., &c., in the Panjab.—(continued).

Places.	Maulvis.	Pandits.	Bhais.	Pandhas.	Hakims.	Baids.	Authors.	Poets.
XIII.—AMRITSAR DISTRICT—continued.								
Wairowal	......	Mayya Dass, Mahabli,	......	......	Sultani Mal, Sayyed Barkat Ali Hakim Ibrahim.	......	......	......
Lopoki	Muhammad Abdulla...	*Bhag*, Amin Chand, Ganga Ram, Ramditta, Chand.	......	......	Hakim Zainul Abdin	Mula, Basant Man ...	......	......
Tarantaran	......	Mayya Dass ...	*Jiwan Singh* ...	*Maula Bakhsh* ...	......	......	......	......
Kathu Nangal	......	*Bhiwani Das (Pt. and Astrologer) Mayya Dass.*	*Gurdat Singh* ...	......	......	Bhiwani Das ...	......	......
Ajnala	......	Gobind, Ganga, Ram Jawala Das, Atma Ram, Thakur Das, Jagan Nath.	Gurdyal Singh, Naurang Singh, Divan Singh.	......	Sher Ali, Mohamad Bakhsh, Sadanand, Mohamad Bakhsh II, Nizam-uddin, Badruddin.	......	......	......
Wazirpind	......	Gobind Ram ...	Sukhram Dass ...	......	Gada Ali Shah ...	Gauri Shankar, Mayya Dass.	......	......
Sirhali	......	Hem Raj ...	Prem Singh, Sham Singh.	......	Allahdiya ...	......	......	......
Gharinda	Inayatullah, Nizam uddin.	Ram Chand, Pt. Narsing Dass, Hira.	*Sant Singh, Madho Singh, Harnam Singh, Dula Singh, Prem Singh, Gobind Bakhsh.*	......	Ilahi Bakhsh, Sardar Ali, Nizam uddin, Hira Jogi, Mohamdi Jogi, Muhammaddin.	Ram Lal, Nihal Singh, Bhagrit Ram, Buddha.	......	......
XIV.—GURDASPUR DISTRICT.								
Sri Govindpur	*Ida, Nizam-ud-din, Sher Ali, Nur-ud-din, Ghulam Qadir, Ibrahim.*	......	*Hira Singh, Surma Singh, Jiwan.*	......	Ghulam Nabi, Ramchand.	......	......	......

Banya	......	......	......	......	Nizam-ud-din, Chiragh Din, Dasondhi Shah, Bholan Shah, Mahtab Shah.	Jaichand, Gurdiyal ...	......	......
Gurdaspur	Sher Muhammad ...	Ganesh, Girgast Ram	......	......	Gulab, Kalu ...	......	......	......
Pathankot	......	*Pirs, Shib Ram* ...	......	......	......	......	......	......
Chhaunal ...	*Ghulam Ali, Muhamad Hanif, Didar Bakhsh, Hayat Ali.*	......	......	......	Nizamuddin, Mana, Nuru, Rajada, Akbar.	......	......	......
Parmanand ...	......	Thakur Dass, Bhagwan Das.	......	......	Puran, Ram Das ...	......	......	......
Dina Nagar ...	Fatah Muhammad ...	......	......	......	Muhammad Ali ...	......	......	......
Fathagarh ...	Muhammad Ali Shah, Muhammad Usman.	*Narayan* ...	......	......	Muhammad Shah ...	......	......	......
Batala ...	Zahur Husain, Zahur Shah, Zain-ul-abdin.	Puranchand, Arjan, Gokalchand, Dhulu, Kalu, *Ganga Bishan.*	*Keshra Singh* ...	*Sangu* ...	Muhammad Husain, Bahawal Sher, Imam-ud-din, Ata Muhammad, Devi, Chand, Mirza, Ghulam Ahmad, Lachhman, Nabi Bakhsh, Ala Din.	Mayya Dhas, Gopi Missar, Narayan, Dhaunkalya, Raj Rúp, Mela.	Mufti Imam Bakhsh, Mirza Sultan Ahmad, Mirza Ghulam Ahmad.	Mufti Imam Bakhsh.
Dera Baba Nanak ...	Karim Bakhsh ...	*Dhanpat* ...	Pirag Dass ...	......	Karim Bakhsh ...	......	Karim Bakhsh ...	......
Kanhuwan ...	......	*Shibdat* ...	......	......	Alla Ditta, Rahim Bakhsh.	......	......	......
Kot Nainan ...	*Muhammad Shah,* Ahmad Ali.	Rodu, Ganga Ram ...	......	......	Ahmad Bakhsh, Kirpa Ram, Sunder Lal.	......	......	......

XV.—SIALKOT DISTRICT.

Sialkot City	*Ghulam Husain Karam Ilahi,* Abdulla, Ghaus, *Haji Abdulla, Hafiz Sultan,* Ata Ulla, *Mian Husain,* Karam Ilahi, Muhammad Alim.	Hira Nand, Gunga Ram, Lekh Ram, Kaka Ram, Badri Nath, Damodar Das, Mathra, Narsing Das, Devi Das, Mulraj, Gunpat, Harya, Kashi Ram, Ram Chand, Chakarbhán.	Ganga Ram, Phag Singh, Mehtab Singh, Karam Singh, Asa Singh, Sunder Singh, Nihal Singh, Gurdut Singh, Atar Singh, Gunda Singh.	*Ali Muhammad, Nabi Bakhsh.*	Muzaffar Shah, Imam-ud-din, Shah Muhammad, Sher Muhammad, Hakim-ud-din, Fatahdin, Gulab Singh.	......	Munshi Diwan Chand.	......

List of Maulvis Pandits, &c., &c., in the Panjab.—(continued).

Places.	Maulvis.	Pandits.	Bhais.	Pandhas.	Hakims.	Baids.	Authors.	Poets.
XV.—SIALKOT DISTRICT—continued.								
Sialkot Circle	*Habibullah*, Wahab Shah, Muhammad Ali, Shah Nawaz, Nur Ahmad, Ghulam Kadir, Shihab Din.	Ram Kishen (Astrologer), Raj Rup, Gokal, Lalman.	Ram Singh, Mul Singh, Arjan Singh.	......	Mubin-ud-din, Karam Ilahi, Ahmad Din Farzand Ali, Karam Bakhsh, Hasan Din, Jawahar Shah.	......	......	......
Samryal	Nur Ahmad, Karam Ilahi, Nabi Bakhsh (in Sahuwala).	......	......	......	Ghulam Husain, Ruda, Chunda.	......	......	......
Daska	Abdulla, Ghulam Muhammad Qazi, Mir Ahmad.	Narayen, Ishur Das, Balram, Musaddi, Janki Abhe Ram, Duni Chund.	......	......	Bute Khan, Barkhurdar, Sher Singh, Imam Din, Abdulla, Dwarka Das Juni Shah, Abdul Hakim.	......	......	Firozdin.
Satrah	......	......	Sham Singh ...	......	Ilmuddin ...	......	......	......
Pasrúr	*M. Abdulla* ...	......	*Mahan Singh* ...	......	......	......	......	......
Kila Sobha Singh ...	*Azizdin, Hafiz Ali Akbar, Muhammad Ali*, Imamuddin.	Kashi Ram ...	Hera Singh ...	......	Ghulam Husain, Sadiq Ali, Muhammad Ali, Wazira, Devi Datta.	......	......	......
Naru Wal ...	Ilmuddin ...	Arura ...	......	......	Rasmat Ali ...	......	......	......
Ra'iya ...	*Nizam uddin, Hasan Muhammad.*	......	Ram Dass ...	*Atama Ram* ...	......	......	......	......
Dudh	Ghulam Hasain ...	......	......	......	Rahmatulla Shah ...	......	......	......
Zafarwal	Qutbuddin, Ghulam Qaidr.	......	......	......	......	......	......	......
Falora	Sayad Gulab Shah ...	......	......	......	Ghulam Nakshband, Haidar Shah.	......	......	......
Sialkot Cantonment ...	Fazel Ahmad, Mubarak Ali.	Jai Bhagwan ...	......	......	Sirajuddin	......	......	......
Palm Ralyan ...	Ilmuddin, Miran Bakhsh	......	......	......	......	......	......	......
Phoklyan ...	Sirajuddin ...	Jagan Nath, Lalman, Mayya Das, Lahur Das.	......	......	Mayya, Ilmuddin, Kashi, Sirajuddin.	......	......	......

List of eminent men added by the district returns.

SIALKOT DISTRICT.

Tahsil Raya	Shah Dia ...	Birj Lal, Ganesh Dass, Shankar Dass, Thakur Dass, Radha Kishan.	Amar Singh, Deva Singh, Dyal Singh.	......	......	Shankar Dass, Neraiyan Dass.	......	......
" Zafar Wall ...	......	Amir Chand ...	......	......	Mehman ...	Jodha Mal ...	......	......
" Pasrur	Ali Akbar, Azizuddin	Mahtaba, Hira, Jiwan Mal, Jawahar, Narayan Dat, Asa Nand.	Kanh Singh, Harnam Dass, Jawahar Singh.	......	Qadir Pir, Badruddin, Bhagat Singh, Alim Din, Abdul Karim, Faiz Rasul, Hamid Ali, Sher Shah, Zaman Shah, Khadim Ali, Abdul Azim, Gulab, Wasawa Singh, Karam Shah.	......	......	Sant Singh, Sher Ali.
" Daska	Imam Din, Ghulam Ahmad, Mohamad Din, Sultan Ahmad, Kayem Din.	Jawala Sahai, Radha Kishen, Ram Dass, Kanhia Lal, Raghu Vans, Debi Chand, Bura, Naththa, Devi Dyal, Ganesha Mal, Devidatta Mal, Ganpat Rai, Ramgopal, Mukand Ram, Gobind Ram.	Gehna Singh, Bhup Singh, Bhag Singh, Sher Singh, Surjan Singh, Chet Singh, Gurmukh Dass, Sobha Singh, Charan Singh.	......	Shihabdin, Akbar Shah, Alam Shah, Abdul Hakim, Sher Muhammad, Nur Muhammad, Jhunda Mal, Fazal Din, Karam Ilahi, Husain Bakhsh, Muhammad Bakhsh, Ghulam Muhammad, Nabi Pakhsh, Bishan Dass, Khuda Yar, Kayem Din.	Shankar Dass, Jaina, Mohkam Shah, Ganpat Rai.	......	Kayem Din.

XVI.—LAHORE DISTRICT.

Shahdara	Inayetullah, Siraj-ud-din.	*Harbhaj* ...	Mahtab Singh, Gurdat Singh.	......	Inayet-ulla, Abdul Ghani, Imam Din, Sultan Ahmad, Saraj Din, Hasan Muhammad, Cheragh Din.	......	......	......
Dholi Wal	*Ghulam Yasin* ...	......	......	......	Ilahi Buksh Zaildar	......	......	......
Niyaz Beg	......	......	......	Buta Ram ...	......	......	......	......
Chunyan	......	Balkishan ...	......	......	......	......	......	......
Bhatti	......	*Uttum Chand*, Atma Ram.	......	......	......	Madho Ram ...	......	......

List of Moulvis, Pandits, &c., &c., in the Panjab—(continued).

Places.	Maulvis.	Pandits.	Bhais.	Pandhas.	Hakims.	Baids.	Authors.	Poets.
				XVI.—LAHORE DISTRICT—(continued).				
Sattu-ki	Muhammad Usman ...	......	......	......	......	......	......	......
Mangta Wala	......	Sukha ...	*Parmanad*, Hukm Singh.	......	Yar Muhammad, Imamuddin, Barkhurdar, Shah Muhammad.	......	......	......
Mughal Sarai ...	*Abdurrahman* ...	......	Sangat Singh ...	*Chanan* ...	Buldu Shah ...	......	......	......
Kana Kachha	......	......	Varyam Singh ...	......	......	......	......	......
Aliabad	*Sayyid Muhammad*...	......	......	......	......	......	......	......
Mohlan Wal	*Abdulla* ...	......	......	......	......	......	......	......
Shahpur	......	......	......	......	Ghulam Farid, Mehr Ali.	......	......	......
Manawan	......	......	......	......	Ismail ...	......	......	......
Kasur	Khuda Bakhsh, Wilayat Shah, Ghulam Dastgir I, Ghulam Dastgir II, Hasan Shah, Ghulam Kadir I, Ghulam Kadir II, Ghulam Ghaus.	Kanihiya Lal I, Kanihiya Lal II, Durga Dass, Gobind Mul.	*Hira Singh*, *Ram Singh.*	......	Khuda Bakhsh, Wilayat Shah, Ghulam Kadir I, Ghulam Kadir II, Ghulam Ghaus, Sayyid Chirag Shah.	......	Ghulam Dastgir ...	......
Nawakot	......	......	Bhai Jawala Singh ...	......	......	......	......	......
Lahore	*Hamidadin*, *Muhammad Husain*, *Ghulam*, *Muhammad*, Nur Ahmad, Ahmad Ali, Ghulam Muhammad, Muhammad Husain, Ghulamulla, Abdul Hakim, Muhammad Din, Abul Kasim, Muhammad Din, Zafruddin, Abdulla, Ghulam Mustafa, Sharaf Ilahi (of	Misru, Bhagwan Dass, Lalu Lal, Godha, Gausi, Sukhdiyal, *Kanihia Lal*, Rikhi Kesh, Gauri Shankar, Balram, Rup Chand, Nand Lal, Kashi Nauth, Rug Nauth, Nagin Chand, Mehtab Rai, Hardat, Gobind Ram, Vaidpato, Pahar Chand, Muthradat, Dya Ram,	Bhagat Singh, Sant Singh, Nihal Singh, Partap Singh, Ganga Singh, Naththa Singh, Ram Singh, Bhagwan Singh, Prem Singh.	*Rajada*, *Hari Kishan*, *Launkra*, *Narayan*, *Pir Bakhsh*, *Sharfu*, *Bhagtu*, *Balla.*	Ala Din, Pir Bakhsh Bazurg Shah, Najaf Khan, Jiwan Khan, Mayya Dass, Buhadur Shah, Gumán, Dost Mohamad, Shujauddin, Ghulam Nabi, Ghulam Mustafa, Amir Chand, Hafiz Fukhruddin, Gulab Din, *Nawab Abdulmajid Khan*, Wali Shah, Sharaf	Khushal, Janardhan, Narayen Dass, Kalwa, Dahar Chand, Mihr Chand, Khanna Ram, Bishan Baid.	Mufti Ghulam Sarvar, Muhammad Husain Azad, Rai Kanihia Lal, Dr. Rahim Khan, Dr. Muhammad Hussain, Shashi Bhushan, Pirzada Muhammad Husain, Novin Chander Rai. Kirpa Ram, Shiv Nath Yogi, Maulvi Abdul Hakim.	Maulvi Mahammad Husain Azad, Tara Chand, Cheraghuddin, Ram Sahai, Kewal Kishen, Uttam Singh, Ilhai Bakhsh, Nisar Ali, Sirajuddin, Muhammad Yasin, Alauddin, Maulvi Faizul Hasan, Fazal Hasan, Muhammad Tajuddin, Muhammad Munir, Mohzaffar Din, Ganda Ram.

	Bhugguwal), Ghulam Mustafa (of Bhagwanpura), Muhammad Zahuruddin, (of Bhagwanpura), Maumin Ali, Rahim Bakhsh, Muhammad Jamal, Abdulmajid.	Maha Raj, Ganpat. (All these pandits teach Sanscrit.			Shah, Khuda Bakhsh, Mir Bakhsh, Karim Bakhsh (of Bhugwanpura), Lodhi Shah, (of Bhugguwal), Gul Mohamad (of Koi Miran).		Moulvi Faizul Hasan, Ghulam Mustafa, Babu Amolak Ram, Gand Ram, Ganga Ram, Lala Behari Lal, Dr. Amir Shah, Dr. Brij Lal, Bhai Gurmukh Singh, Pandit Bhandat, Mumtaz Ali, Abdul Aziz, Bishi Kesh, Pandit Sukh Dyal, Ghulam Kadir, Muhammad Din, Hafiz Ahmad Ali, Ghulam Nabi, Sayyid Amir Shah, Fazli Ilahi, Mayya Dass, Hafiz Fakhruddin, Gulab Singh, Hemraj Gusain, Rahim Bakhsh.	Shah Din, Pandit Man Nath, Mahbub Alam, Jagir Singh, Habibulla, Khadim Muhinddin, Hafiz Muhammad Din, Abdul Hakim, Zahuruddin, Hamid Ali, Ghulam Ali Shah, Nawab Ghulam Mahbub Subhani, Muhammad Din, Imam Bakhsh, Alaf Din, Zafruddin, Ghulam Kadir, Ata Ulla, Ghulam Sarvar, Ghulam Akbar, Mirza Fatah Muhammad, Gurdas, Guru Parshad, Rikhi Kesh, Sukh Dyal, Hem Raj, Pandit Ram Chand, Ganga Bishan.

XVII.—GUJRANWALA DISTRICT.

Gujranwala ...	*Sarajuddin*, Mahbub Alam, *Muhammad Din* I, *Muhammad Musa*, *Muhammad Din* II, *Nur Din*, Alauddin, Gulam Husain.	*Widyadhar*, Dala Ram, Radha Kishan, Kashi Ram, *Surasti Das*, *Chet Ram*.	Lahaura Singh, Fatah Singh, Mul Singh, Parem Singh, *Gurdit Singh*, Nadhan Singh.	......	Ghulam Husain, Sarajuddin, Sultan Mahmud, Ghulam Karam Ilahi, Muhiuddin, Shahab, Nur Husain, Chandar Bhan, Fazli Ilahi.	Hari Ram, Kashi Ram, Davi Dyal, Basant Rikh Puj, Kashi Ram.	Gulam Ghaus, Gyan Chand, Brij Lal.	Ghulam Ghaus, Ahmad Hasan, Ghulam Qadir, Ahmad Ali
Shekhupur ...	*Muhabbat* ...	......	*Jumayat Singh* ...	......	Ataulla ...	......	......	......
Akal Garh ...	Karim Bakhsh, Gulam Qadir, *Ahmad Bakhsh*.	*Kashi Ram* ...	Hira Singh, Bishan Das ...	*Sobha Mal* ...	......	......	......	......
Hafizabad ...	Jalaluddin ...	Harnam Das ...	......	......	Khuda Bakhsh ...	......	......	......
Kaluki .	*Mustafa*, *Muhammad Umar*, *Muhammad Din* I, *Sultan Ahmad*, *Muhammad Din* II.	Ganda ...	*Gurdat Singh*, *Teja Singh*	*Ishar Das* ...	Ghulamulla ...	......	......	......
Wazirabad ...	Fazal Din, Qadir Bakhsh, Ghulam Nabi, Muhammad Bakhsh.	Bishan Das, *Lakshamidat*.	*Jaimal Singh*, *Ganda Singh*	*Thakur*, *Nabi Bakhsh*,	Karam Din, Nathu...	Kosalya Das ...	......	......

List of *Maulvis, Pandits, &c., &c., in the Panjab*—(continued).

Places.	Maulvis.	Pandits.	Bhais.	Pandhas.	Hakims.	Baids.	Authors.	Poets.
XVII.—GUJRANWALA DISTRICT—(continued).								
Kilah Didar Singh ...	Hasan Muhammad, Muhammad Gauhar, Qasim Ali.	......	*Jaswant Rai*, Amar Singh	Thakur Das ...	Fazli Ilahi, Fazli Ahmad, Hasan Muhammad, Devi Sahai, Ibrahim, Akbar Ali, Jaian Shah, Lal Chand.	......	......	......
Khanqah-i-Dogran ...	......	*Narayan Das* ...	*Sundar Das* ...	......	......	......	......	......
Pindi Bathyan ...	*Muhammad Husain, Ahmad Din.*	Nanak Chand, Shankar Das, Sukh Ram.	*Ganesha Singh, Ganga Das, Ishar Das*	*Ganesh Das, Bal Mukand*	Juwala Sahai, Muhammad Hasan.	......	......	......
XVIII.—FEROZEPUR DISTRICT.								
Ferozepur Thana ...	Nur Muhammad, Sharfuddin, Shah Muhammad, Ibrahim, *Qamrud-din*, Sadruddin.	......	......	......	The first five Moulvis given in No. 2 practice medicine also.	......	......	......
Jalalabad	*Jamal-ud-din, Muhammad Siddiq.*	......	......	......	Kamiluddin ...	......	......	......
Bagahpurana	......	Rup Lal ...	......	......	Wazir Singh, Narayan Das Patwari.	......	......	......
Moga	Maulvi Pir Bakhsh, Ilahi Bakhsh.	......	......	......	Nihal Chand ...	......	......	......
Makkhu	Fazluddin (of Talwandi), Jalaluddin, Ismail, Ghulam Ghaus, Abdul Qadir.	......	......	......	Abdul-islam ...	......	......	......
Ferozepur Cantonments ...	Abdurrahman, Ghulam Nabi.	*Ramji Dass* ...	......	*Shadi Ram* ...	Abdurrahman, Panna Lal.	......	......	......
Ferozepur City	Sharaf Din, Walilulah.	*Kishan Chand, Ramji Das, Mahanand, Hardowari*, Balkishan, Perbhu dyal.	*Hira Singh, Dyal Singh.*	*Maula Bakhsh* ...	Rahmut Ali, Radha Kishan, Suraj Bhan, Mayya Das, Kishan Dat.	......	......	......

Nawa Qila ...	Muhammad Fazil, Muhi-ud-din, *Abdul Qadir*, Muhammad Salim, *Abdurrazaq*.	......	......	......	Ghulam Muhammad	......	Muhammad Fazil ...	......
Dharamkot ...	Maulvi Shadi Shah, Moulvi Abdurrahman (of Jalalabad).	*Bhuyal*, Ratta Ram ...	Bishen Singh ...	*Karim Bakhsh* ...	Bindraban, Muhammad Abdurrahman.	......	......	......
Nihal Singhwala ...	......	......	Bhai Badan Singh (of Sidaki).	......	......	......	......	......
Nathana ...	......	Prem Singh, *Salig Ram*	......	......	......	......	......	......
Mukatsar ...	*Nizamuddin* ...	......	Govind Shah ...	......	......	......	......	......
XIX.—RAWALPINDI DISTRICT.									
Marree ...	*Abdussamad*, Abdulhaq, Chiragh Din.	......	*Bughan Singh* ...	......	......	......	......	......
Kallar ...	Muhammad Hasan, Muhammad Ahsan.	......	*Dasondha Singh* ...	......	......	......	......	......
Kahuta ...	Ghulam Nabi ...	......	*Jagat Singh*, Nihal Singh.	......	......	......	......	......
Hizru ...	Muhamadji ...	*Baisakki Ram* ...	*Ratna* ...	*Ala Bakhsh* ...	......	......	......	......
Saydpur ...	......	......	Khempuri Singh ...	......	......	......	......	......
Rawalpindi (Cantonments) ...	......	......	*Amar Singh* ...	......		......	......	......
Pind Sultani ...	*Ahmad Din*, *Abdulla*	......	*Kalyan Singh* ...	......	Mirza Karim Beg, Ibrahim.	......	......	......
Chawantra ...	Myan Ahmad, Myan Muhammad Shah.	......	Nihal Dass, Hira Singh.	......	Radha Kishan, Sher Muhammad.	......	......	......
Gujar Khan ...	*Nizam Din*, *Imam Din*, Muhammad Bakhsh, Muhammad Hasan, *Fazaldin*.	......	Amir Singh, Deva Singh, Jawanda Singh, *Buta Singh*.	......	Nawab Ali, Beli Ram	Jai Singh ...	......	......
Fatah Jang ...	*Ghulam Ghaus*, *Ghulam Yahya*, *Fazl Ilahi*.	*Sukh Raj* ...	......	......	Mathra Singh ...	......	......	......
Chuha Khalsa ...	......	Bagat Chand ...	......	......	......	......	......	......

List of Maulvis, Pandits, &c., &c., in the Panjab—(continued).

Places.	Maulvis.	Pandits.	Bhais.	Pandhas.	Hakims.	Baids.	Authors.	Poets.
XIX.—RAWALPINDI DISTRICT.—continued.								
Jakhad ...	*Abdulhakim, Muhammad Khurshaid, Myan Ahmad, Myan Aman.*	......	Gurmukh Singh ...	......	Gauhar Singh, Nonihal.	......	......	......
Mundra ...	*Kamar Din* ...	......	*Gulab Singh* ...	......	......	......	......	......
Rawalpindi City ...	Ahmad Baksh, *Fazli Ahmad.*	Brij Lal, Bhagwan Das, *Bishen Dass Lakkhi.*	*Ram Singh, Amar Singh.*	*Didar Shah, Miran Bakhsh.*	Lachhman Das, Karam Chand, Saudagar Shah, Mathra Das, Suba Singh, Motha Singh, Karam Singh.	Bhai Sher Singh ...	......	......
Rawalpindi Circle ...	*Shaikh Ahmad* ...	......	*Jai Singh* ...	......	......	......	......	......
Sangjani ...	*Fazl Din* ...	......	*Mula Singh, Mangal Singh, Bishan Dass, Mohar Singh, Lachhman Singh, Sham Singh.*	......	Jiwan Singh ...	......	......	......
Jatli ...	*Muhammad Husain*	......	......	......	......	......	......	......
Rawat ...	*Rukn Alam, Fatah Muhammad.*	......	*Chanda Singh, Jawahar Singh.*	......	......	......	......	......
Attock ...	*Hafiz Gulam Muhammad.*	......	......	......	......	......	......	......
Pindi Gheb ...	Fazli Ahmad, Gul Muhammad, Myan Ahmad, Myan Khurshaid.	Sukhdyal, *Radha Kishan.*	*Gurdit Singh* ...	......	Dyal ...	......	......	......
Hasan Abdal ...	Kazi ...	......	Gopal Singh ...	......	......	......	......	......
XX.—GUJRAT DISTRICT.								
Kharyan ...	*Ilmuddin, Sadruddin*	......	*Bava Sunder* ...	*Fakir Muhammad* ...	......	......	......	......
Khori ...	*Muhammad Alim, Muhammad Ghulam Ghaus, Abdul Malik.*	......	......	......	......	......	......	......

Menhu Wal	Muhammad Baksh, Chiragh Din.	......	......	......	......	......	......	......
Dinga	Muhammad Nurdin (of Chikori).	*Vasdeo*, Ram Narayan	*Sant Singh*	*Datta*	Hafiz Nurdin, Masum Shah, Nurdin.	......	......	......
Langa	*Nur Din*, Shaikh Ahmad, Kutbuddin, Sarajuddin, Amir Shah.	......	*Phela Singh, Jawala Singh, Prbhu Singh.*	*Rupa*	Imam Din, Mustafa, Hayat, Jalal, Ali Ahmad.	Ganda Singh	......	......
Aurangabad	Hayat-ullah *Nizam-uddin*, Ghulam Rasul.	......	*Gurdat Singh*	......	......	......	Hayat-ullah	......
Lala Musa	*Muhammad Abdulla, Muhammad Makhdum Ghulam Qadir, Muhammad Alim, Nasrullah.*	......	......	......	Abdulla	......	......	......
Jalalpur, Jattan	*Sadruddin, Jiwan*	Pandit Bhagwan Dass, *Lachhmi Dass.*	......	*Ghulam Nabi*	......	......	......	......
Kadirabad	*Shaikh Ahmad*	*Ganpat Rai*	*Gulab Singh*	*Devi Dass*	......	......	......	......
Kunjah	Maulvi Khuda Bakhsh, *Sher Ahmad, Ata Muhammad, Fazli Ahmad, Zainulabidin, Kalim-ullah, Fazl Ahmad, Inayat-ullah, Imam Ali, Kayam Din*	*Ram Ditta, Vasdeo, Shibcharn.*	......	......	......	......	......	......
Gujrat	*Hafiz Abdulla*	*Ishur Dass*	Bhagwan Singh, Ishur Singh.	......	Khuda Bakah	......	......	......
Karyalwala	*Shaikh Ahmad, Kazi Muhammad, Rukn-ud-Din.*	*Gobind Sahai, Lajpat, Ram Saru, Detwar*	......	......	Masum Shah	......	......	......

XXI.—JHELUM DISTRICT.

Jalalpur	......	......	*Kandhara Singh*	......	......	......	......	......
Tila Gung	Karim Bakhsh, Muhammad Hasan.	Ghansham	*Dyal Singh*	......	......	......	......	......

List of Maulvis, Pandits, &c., &c., in the Panjab—(continued).

XXI.—JHELUM DISTRICT—(*Continued*).

Place.	Maulvis.	Pandits.	Bhais.	Pandhas.	Hakims.	Baids.	Authors.	Poets.
Damman ...	... Muhammad Hasan, Farman Ali, Karim Din, Ghulam Muhammad, Ahmad Din.	......	*Lachhmi* (a female teacher.)	*Ram Jiwaya* ...	Muhammad Shah, Nihal Singh, Ghulam Muhammad.	......	......	......
Dinah ...	... *Abdul Karim, Karm Din.*	*Kalyan Das,* Jant Ram, Dittu Gosahin } Rohtas	*Ram Das* ...	......	......	......	......	......
Sohawa ...	... *Hayat Bakhsh* ...	......	*Nihal Singh* ...	......	Muhammad Alim, Kanhiya.	......	......	......
Kalar Kahar ...	... Hayat Ali ...	Jawala Sahai, *Kirpa Ram*, Shankar Das.	*Arjan Singh*, Hira Singh.	*Kirpa Ram* ..	Buta Mall, Ram Sahai.	Jawala Sahai ...	......	......
Jhelum ...	... *Nur Ahmad, Nur Alim, Burhanuddin.*	*Harimin Das, Parem Singh*, Barkat Ram.	......	......	......	......	......	......
Ahmadabad ...	... Qadir Bakhsh, *Ghulam Ali, Jiwaya.*	......	......	......	Qadir Bakhsh, Sultan Bakhsh, Alim Din.	......	Qadir Bakhsh ...	Fazal Husain.
Pind Dadan Khan ...	*Muhammad Hasan, Sher Muhammad.*	......	......	......	Muhammad Yar, Hashim Din, Ghulam Rasul, Taj Din, Karm Chand, Jawahri Mal, Ramkaur.	......	......	......
Tamman ...	... *Mir Alam, Jalal* ...	......	*Amar Das, Amir Singh.*	......	..	......	......	......
Chakwal ...	... Ghulam Husain ...	*Kahan Chand* ...	*Sant Das* ...	......	......	......	......	......
Dumeli ...	... *Abdulla* ...	......	......	Harnam Das ...	......	......	......	......

XXII.—SHAHPUR DISTRICT.

Madh ...	*Ali Muhammad, Muhammad Khan, Hasan Muhammad*	Shib Dyal ...	*Nanak Singh, Sher Singh.*	*Lakhmi Das* ...	Fazal Din ...	......	......	......
Kot Momin ...	*Ali Muhammad, Faiz Muhammad.*	......	*Thakur Das, Charan Das.*	......	......	......	......	......
Jhawaryan ...	*Din Muhammad, Muhammad Khalil.*	Hukm Chand, Hakim Rai.	*Sant Ram* ...	......	Larenda Ram, Sodhu Ram, Rukna Barber.	......	......	......
Chak Ram Das ...	*Gul Ahmad, Karm Bakhsh.*	......	......	*Uja Devi Das* ...	Gul Ahmad, Karm Bakhsh.	Uja Devi Das ...	......	......
Miani ...	*Nur Husain, Ghulam Dastgir.*	Laddha Ram, *Kashi Ram.*	Shankar Das ...	*Maya Das Ujha* ...	Hasan Din, Khuda Bakhsh, Ghulam Dastgir.	......	......	......
Bhera ...	*Ghulam Rasul,* Amir Husain.	*Bhagwan Das,* Parabu Dyal, Mohia, *Shiv Narayan Mohla,* Karm Chand, *Jagan, Nath,* Ram Narayan *Shankar Das.*	Jawala Singh, Sukhkha Singh, *Kesho Das*	*Parabh Dyal* ...	Shaikh Ahmad, Fazal Ahmad, Khuda Bakhsh, Dani Chand, Parabhu Dyal.	......	......	......
Naushahra ...	*Ruknuddin, Ghulam Muhiuddin.*	......	*Santokh Singh, Hari Singh.*	......	Rajjab, Rajkaur ...	......	......	......
Mota Lak ...	*Din Muhammad* ...	......	......	......	Din Muhammad ...	......	......	......
Khushab ...	*Ghulam Nabi* ...	......	......	......	......	......	......	......
Kond ...	*Ahmad Din, Faqir Muhammad.*	......	*Lachhman Das, Mangal Singh.*	*Shanker Das* ..	Ghulam Yasin ...	......	......	......
Shahpur ...	*Ghulam Murtaza* ...	......	*Kishan Singh* ...	......	......	......	......	......
Nurpur ...	*Ghulam Ali,* Qayam Din, Ghulam Husain, Jana, Sultan.	*Girdhari Ram* ...	*Gharib Das,* Sobha Ram, Bishan Das, Lakhmi Das.	......	......	......	......	......
Mitha Tiwana ...	*Shaikh Ahmad, Faiz Ahmad, Sharaf Din, Ghulam Muhiuddin, Wali Muhammad.*	......	*Baisakhi, Sant Singh, Amar Singh, Chatan Singh,* Roda.	......	......	......	......	......

List of Maulvis, Pandits, &c., &c., in the Panjab—(continued).

Places.	Maulvis.	Pandits.	Bhais.	Pandhas.	Hakims.	Baids.	authors.	Poets.
				XXIII.—MULTAN.				
Jalalpur ...	Fatah Muhammad, Ghaus Bakhsh, Fazl Muhammad, Ala Bakhsh.	Kishora, Dida, Kallu	Dhyan Singh ...	...	Jan Muhammad ...	......	Ghaus Bakhsh ...	......
Multan City ...	Maulvi Nasir-ud-din, Jandwad, Sultan Muhammad, Nur Muhammad, Abdulla Ghulam Sarvar, Khuda Bakhsh, Nizam-uddin, Kadir Bakhsh, Abdulhaq, Zainulabidin.	Fakir Makhhan Mal, Malik Jhangi Ram, Kanihya Lal, Kura Mall, Chundu Lal, Ram Bava, Fatah Chand, Rikhi Kesh, Thakur Das, Kallu Ram, Pharya Lal.	Ishur Das, Uttam Prakash, Jagat Singh, Damodar Das, Amar Singh, Shalu, Pritam Das, Lalu Ram, Sant Das, Saru Das, Pomar Das, Ram Das, Kanihya Ram, Gulab Singh, Khem Das, Dharma Singh, Ganesh Das, Daulat Ram, Sara Das.	......	Nasir-ud-din, Alladad Saifulla, Shah Bakhsh, Didar Bakhsh, Muhammad Hasan.	Sukkhu Lal, Machhar Bhagat, Deli Ram, Daulat Rai, Pyare Lal, Kirpa Ram, Nimat Rai, Chela Ram, Takkan Lal.	......	......
Ditto. (circle) ...	Hafiz Muhammad Jamál.	.....						
Sarai Saddhu Circle ...	Ahmad-ud-din, Kadir Bakhsh, Kadir Bakhsh (of Haveli Mubarak).	....	......	......	......	......	......	......
Nawabpur ...	.....	......	......	......	Abdul Kadir, Bhana Kirar, Muhammad Bakhsh.	......	......	......
Shujabad ...	....	Hemraj (Astrologer).	......	Bhai Dyal Singh ...	Din Muhammad ...	......	......	......
Ladan (Circle) ...	Nabi Bakhsh ...	......	Santokh Singh, Amir Singh.	.....	Motti Ram, Shams-ud-din, Yar Ali.	......	......	......
Kharor ...	Ahmad Bakhsh, Suleh Muhammad.	.....	......	......	Chittan Lal, Ahmad Bakhsh, Rahim Bakhsh, Abdul Hakim.	......	......	......
Talamba ...	*Abderrahman* ...	......	......	......	......	Thakar Dass ...	......	......
Jelu ...	*Ala Bakhsh* ...	......	.....	......	......		......	......

XXIV.—JHANG DISTRICT.

Jhang ...	... Ali Muhammad	Kurif Dhar Gusain, Maya Dass.	Sain Das ...	......	*Jan Muhammad* Ahmad Din, Nur Muhammad, Nurulhuq, Pandit Gurditta, Devi Ditta, Jagan.	Salamat, Mohla ...	Dr. Chetun Shah ...	......
Ballu ...	... .	......	*Bhai Khazan Singh*, Gurmukh Singh.	...	......	......	......	......
Chiniot ..	... Ahmad Din, Fakhruddin, Abdul Alim.	......	Hira Singh, Bava Tirith Das	......	Abdulhakim, Ghulam Haidar, Kalmuddin, Shaikh Ahmad, Girdhari Ram.	Gurandatta, Chandar Bhan, Lachhman Das, Shivdyal, Kanshi Das.	Chandar Bhan, Goranditta, Lachhman Das.	Nizamuddin, Fayez.
Bhorna ...	... Bakht Jamal, Abdul Wahab, Abdurrahman.	......	*Amir Sing* ...	......	Ghulam Husain ...	......	......	......
Uch ...	... *Nurulh.., Muhamad Akram.*	Pandit Bhagwan Das	......	......	Muhammad Bakhsh	......	......	......
Musan ...	... Maulvi Fazah, Ghulam Murtaza; *Ghulam Nabi, Muhammad Said*	......	Uttam Dass ...	......	Muhammad Zahid, *Jamaldin* Sayyid Qutab Shah, *Sayyid Hasan Shah*, Hafiz Jamal Din, Ghulam Murtaza.	......	......	......
Ghar Maharaja	... Moulvi Nur Muhammad Shaikh Muhammad, *Hafiz Dilawar.*	......	......	..	Nur Muhammad, Shaikh Muhammad.	......	......	......
Shorkot ...	... .	......	Wasanda Udasi ...	......	Myan Haji Mahmud	......	......	
Birana ...	... .	......	Kar m Singh, Munna Singh, Karam Chand, Kalyan Singh, Khaayal Singh.	......	Ghahra, Chiragh, Ghulam.	......	......	......
Wanuka ...	... *Ghulam Rasul, Fazluddin.*	... .	Panjab Singh, Karam Singh.	......	Ghulam Rasul ...	......	......	......

XXV.—MONTGOMERY DISTRICT.

Kamalya ...	Muhammad Khudayar	Shib Das ...	Bhai Nihal ...	Bhagwan Dass ...	Alayar ...	Sahibditta ...	......	......
Checha Watni ...	Muhammad Murad ...	......	Jawand Singh ...	......	Muhammad Murad	......	......	......
Gogera ...	Muhkam Din ...	......	......	......	Muhkam Din ...	......	......	......

List of Maulvis, Pandits, &c., &c., in the Panjab—(continued.)

Places.	Maulvis.	Pandits.	Bhais.	Pandhas.	Hakims.	Baids.	Authors.	Poets.
XXV.—MONTGOMERY DISTRICT—(continued).								
Kalyanwala ...	......	......	Bhai Narayan ...	......	......	Bava Kishangir ...	......	......
Atari ...	Muhammad Yusuf, Abdulla, Abdurrahman, Muhammad Ilahi Bukhsh, Shaikh Tahir, Muhammad Suleyman.	......	Kahan Singh, Hira Singh, Shankar Dass, Chanan Singh.	......	Baba Jawahar Singh, Jamal Din.	......	......	......
Buchiki ...	*Manj* ...	......	Bhai Charan Dass ...	......	......	......	......	......
Harpa ..	......	Madan Lal ...	Atar Singh ...	......	......	Kanihya ...	......	......
Chuchak ...	*Myan Muhammad, Qari, Nizamuddin,* Muhammed Bakhsh.	......	Jhhunda Singh ...	......	Ghulam Nabi ...	......	......	......
Batt ...	*Ilahi Bakhsh* ...	......	Ratan Singh ...	......	Karimuddin ...	......	......	......
Sayd Wala ...	Jamaluddin, Abdulhamid.	Imrat Phal, Shankar Dass, Kakka Dass.	Jassa Singh ...	......	Chandi Ram, Kishora Ram, Murad Bakhsh.	......	......	......
Hujra ...	*Myan Haji* ...	......	*Kapur Singh* ...	......	Alayar ...	......	......	......
Satghara ...	......	......	*Gyan Singh* ...	......	......	......	......	......
Pakpattan ...	*Ghulam Muhiuddin, Kamruddin* ...	Fatah Chand ...	Narayan Singh ...	......	Sarajuddin ...	......	......	......
Dipalpur ...	*Chaughatta, Ghulam Muhammad.*	......	Sampuran Sing, Deva Singh.	......	......	......	......	......
XXVI.—MUZAFFARGARH.								
Daera Din Panah	*Mian Ibrahim, Maulvi Abdulla, Hideyet Ullah.*	Kalichand, Khushi Ram.	Jassa Singh ...	......	Ibrahim, Rala Ram, Wali Ram, Ala Bakhsh, Buddhan, Nazar Shah, Pohkar Dass, Ghulam Rasul, Sukh Ram. ...	Chilka Missar, Magha Ram.	......	......

Sitpur	Maulvi Nur Bakhsh,	......	......	......	Muaivi Nur Bakhsh, Karim Bakhsh.	......	......	......
Hujra Sharif	*Ali Muhammad, Sualeh Muhammad, Pir Muhammad, Dua Muhammad, Faiz Ullah, Muhammad Yakya.*	*Sadanand* ...	......	......	Din Muhammad.	......	......	......
Rangpur	Sultan Hamid, Shihab-ud-din.	Nanakchand ...	Sant Dass ...	......	......	......	......	......
Khangarh	......	......	......	......	......	Narayen Dass, Hiranand, Tirath Mal.	......	......
Dhaka	Ali Muhammad ...	......	......	......	......	......	......	......
Sayalwar	Sualeh Muhammad, Ala Bakhsh, *Shah Khuda Bakhsh.*	......	......	......	Hosain Shah, Ahmad Yar, Nihal Chand, Malak Siddiq.	......	......	......
Alipur	Maulvi Jandwad, Ghaus Bakhsh.	......	......	......	Muhammad Yar ...	Sant Lal.	......	......
Muzaffargarh	Barket Ali, Akbar Ali, Yar Muhammad, Sultan Muhammad, Ghulam Muhammad, Muhammad Afzal, Rukn-ud-din, Abdul Hakim, Shah Muhammad, Abdul Aziz, Muhammad Yar.	Gopalla Lal ...	Mattu Bar, Beru Ram	......	Ghulam Rasul, Mulla Abdul Hakim, Sant Lal, Megraj, Muhammad Yar.	Megraj.	......	......
Sayyid Sultan	Maulvi Ala Bakhsh ...	......	......	......	......	......	......	......
Quraishi	Fatah Muhammad, Maulvi Umar, Muhammad Bakhsh.	......	......	......	Khair Muhammad.	......	......	......
Muchwali	......	......	......	......	Ala Yar.	......	......	......
			XXVIII.—DERA	I KHAN DISTRICT.				
Dera Ghazi Khan ...	Shakir Muhammad ...	Bihari Lal ...	Sadhoram ...	......	Udho Das ...	Mul Chand ...	Lala Aya Ram B.A. ...	......
Ghamman ...	Ruhadat Nila, Darvesh Muhammad, Din Muhammad, Fakir Muhammad ...	Sarati Lal, Purna Nand Missar, Bhagwan Das	Kewal Ram, Santokh Dass, Gurdit Singh ...	......	Fatah Muhammad, Dost Ali, Muhammad Hassan (of Tonsa.)	Missar Thanbu Lal ...	......	......
Sakhi Sarwar ...	Hafiz Din, Muhammad Rahmatullah Shah.	......	......	......	......	......	......	......

List of Maulvis, Pandits, &c., &c., in the Panjab—(continued).

Places.	Maulvis.	Pandits.	Bhais.	Pandhas.	Hakims.	Baids.	Authors.	Poets.
XXVIII.—DERA GHAZI KHAN DISTRICT.—(continued).								
Rajanpur ...	Muhammad Ali ...	Khusi Ram, Jasa Ram ...	......	......	Musa, Khuda Bakhsh	......	Muhammad Ali, Musa.	......
Jampur ...	Bahauddin ...	......	......	......	Nur Muhammad, Sharf uddin, Chetan Mal, Myan Dost Ali.	......	......	......
Ujhan ...	Musa ...	......	Santokh Das	......	......	......	......	......
Yaru	Ghulam Muhammad Quraishi.	......	......	......	......	......	......	......
Wajhal ...	Murid Ghaus ...	......	......	......	......	......	......	......
XXIX.—DERA ISMAIL KHAN.								
Dera Ismail Khan ...	*Sualeh Muhammad*, *Abdulghafar*, Abdul Kadir.	Mohan Lal, Kishan Das, Rikhi Kesh, *Gobind Lal*.	Kirpal Singh, Bava Khem Dass, *Ganga Ram*.	Jugal Das Maksudan Lal, Suraj Bhan.	Fasli Ali, Zind Ali, Takan Mal, Chimman Lal, Ghulamuddin.	......	......	......
Biharpur ...	Aladad, Ahmad Yar	......	Ratna Ram ...	Chautha Ram.	Aladad ...	......	......	......
Kalanchi ...	Ghulam Rasul, Sadr-uddin, Mulla Miskan	Tula Ram, Thaku Lal, Ram Chander, Lal Chand.	......	......	......	......	......	......
Gil ...	Maulvi Ghulam Muhammad ...	......	......	......	......	......	......	......
Ranwal ...	Jan Muhammad ...	......	......	......	......	......	......	......
Daraban ...	Ata Muhammad ...	Radha Kishan ...	......	......	Radha Kishan ...	......	......	......
Chodhwan ...	Fatah Muhammad, Abdulhak ...	......	......	......	......	......	......	......

Kari Shammuzai ...	Muhammad Abdul Karim ...	......	......	......	......	......	......	......
Layya ...	Zaid Ali, Nur Muhammad, Ghulam Hasan, Abdulhakim ...	Jhangi R ...	......	......	Zaid Ali, Ghulam Hasan, Sheikh Muslim, Ghulam Hasan Khan ...	......	......	......
Basti Kasi ...	Faqir Mohamad ...	......	......	......	Faqir Muhammad, Wali Muhammad	......	......	......
Kot Sultan ...	Abdulazis ...	......	......	......	Abdulazis ...	......	......	......
Nawankot ...	......	Thakur Das ...	Tika Ram ...	......	......	Gurdiyal ...	......	......
Chaubhara ...	......	......	Bhai Sarn Dass ...	......	......	......	......	......
Karor ...	......	Pandit Fatah Chand.	Udho Das ...	......	......	......	......	......
Mamkera ...	Ata Muhammad ...	Uttam Chand, Parsotam Lal, Ranjit Ram, Bhagwan Dass.	Hardyal ...	......	......	......	......	......
Darya Khan ...	......	Chela Ram ...	......	......	......	......	......	......
Mebal ...	Jan Mohamad, Veryam ...	......	......	......	......	Dwarka Ram ...	......	......
Kaujan Fazal ...	Nur Mohamad Ahir	......	......	......	......	Thakur Dass ...	......	......

XXX.—BANNU DISTRICT.

Bannu ...	Sikandar, Ghulam Haidar, Faizulla, Abdul Karim, Muhammed Hubab, Ghulam Kadim.	Totla Ram ...	Meghraj, Kahan Singh, Ram Das, Kanhaiya Singh, Tara Singh, Niranjan Singh, Gurdyal Singh, Tek Singh, Sant Singh.	......	Ghulam Jan, Mansa Ram, Jothu Ram, Bahawal Khan, Kura Ram, Tika Ram, Beli Ram, Wazir Khan, Najaf Ali, Bolu, Qutab din, Amzala, Saleh-din, Khair Ullah, Haji Gul, Muhammad Alim, Ghulam Yusuf, Ruh-ullah, Badrud-din, Mirazar, Alam Khan, Nur Ullah, Shah Jahan, Gulab Din.	......	......	Darashah, a Pushtu poet.

List of Maulvis, Pandits, &c., &c., in the Panjab—(continued).

Place.	Maulvis.	Pandits.	Bhais.	Pandhas.	Hakims.	Baids.	Authors.	Poets.
XXX.—BANNU DISTRICT—(continued).								
Ghoriwalah ...	Muhammad, Muhammad Akbarshah.	......	......	......	......	......	......	......
Laki ...	Ali Muhammad, Muhammad Hasan, Johar Shah, Mulk Duran, Abdul Wahab, Khair Muhammad, Qul Muhammad, Jan Muhammad, Saheb Din, Taher Din, Jan Muhammad, Ibrahim, Zaafran, Umargul.	......	Bhai Sarup Singh ...	......	Gopal Ram, Duara, Abdul Rahman, Shain, Harkishan, Hemraj, Sadiq, Qazi Abdulla, Shaikh Ghulam Muhammad, Amir Shah, Lal Chand, Shaikh Najaf, Nur Muhammad.	......		
Pilan ...	Muhammad Yar ...	......	......	......	Mian Hamid ...	......	......	......
Shakarpari ...	Ghulam Husain ...	......	Sant Singh ...	......	Qazi Ghulam Mustafa	......	......	......
Mian Wali ...	Ahmad Din, Dost Ali, Sayyad Rasul, Ali Muhammad, Chanpir, Sayyad Ahmad, Qazi Ghulam Nabi.	Jassu Lal, Lal Chand, Devi Dial, Bihari Lal, Chhaildas Sham Das, Ram Chand.	Gyan Singh, Gohra Rai, Kahn Singh, Asa Singh, Bhagat Singh, Gulab Singh, Amar Das, Golim Ram.	......	Devi, Das Jaswant, Abdul Rasul, Shamgir.	......	......	......
Isa Khail ...	Maluk Ali, Nur Kamal, Ghulam Rasul, Muhammad Hasan, Khan Muhammad, Imam Din, Muhammad Azam, Bahauddin.	Ram Rikha, Gurmukh Singh, Ganesh Das, Vasева Ram, Ruchi Ram, Topan Lal, Ramdyal.	Narayen Singh, Ram Singh, Pohkar Das, Pirdhan Singh.	......	Ruchi Ram Singh, Gulam Muhammad, Ghulam Ali, Fazal, Haidar Dost Ali.	......	......	......
XXXI.—KOHAT DISTRICT—(continued).								
Kohat ...	Muhammad Amin, Qazi Hisam Uddin, Rustam Gul.	......	......	......	......	......	......	......
Shakardarrah ...	......	Mehta Hemraj ...	......	......	......	......	......	......
Sukh Talso ...	Moulvi Ataullah ...	......	......	......	Shaikhulla, Majid Gul.	......	......	......
Lachhi ...	Zinulabidin. ...	Daulat Rai ...	Karm Shah ...	......		......	......	......

XXXII.—HAZARA DISTRICT.

Shikari ...	Hamid, Ali Alias Mullan Taya.	......	......	......	......	......	......	......
Ghazi ...	Haji Muhammad Nur	......	Parem Singh ...	......	Ghulam Qadir ...	......	......	......
Khanpur ...	Ghulam Husain ...	......	......	......	......	......	......	......
Og ...	Nur Hasan ...	......	......	......	......	......	......	......
Karelian ...	Jalaluddin ...	......	......	......	......	......	......	......
Narah ...	Abdullah ...	......	......	......	......	......	......	......
Mansehra ...	Muhammad Said ...	......	......	......	......	......	......	......

ADDITIONAL LIST OF AUTHORS AND POETS IN THE PANJAB.

Ragu Nath Das.
Ahmad Shafi.
Nihal Chand.
Pandit Pran Kishn.
Chet Ram.
Mahmud Hasan.
Maulvi Ghulam Rasul.
Maulvi Maula Baksh.
Kewal Kishen.
Hazara Singh.
Chandu Lall.
Sada Sukh Lall.
Paudit Ganeshi Lal.
Munshi Ghulam Muhiuddin.
Pandit Hanwant Ram.
Munshi Munni Lal.
Maulvi Muhammad Muslim.
Munshi Gauga Sahai.
Jaidyal Singh.
Maulvi Abdulla.
Imam Hosain.
Sheikh Muhayuddin.
Maulvi Mihr Naththu.

Narayen Das.
Faqir Chand.
Rajab
Shri Gopal.
Sayyid Fazal Shah.
Arura Rai.
Ghazi-uddin.
Jaimal Das.
Ata Ahmad.
Hasan Din.
Muhammad Khalil.
Abduljabbar.
Chunni Lal.
Shah Abdulla.
SayyidAhmed Ali.
Narayen Kishen.
Maulvi Gholam Akbar Khan
Ghulams.
Abdul Basit.
Makhkhan Lall.
Hafiz Fazal Din.
Shah Walaya.
Munshi Rajab Ali.

Munshi Jowahir Lal.
Maulvi Muhammad Husein.
Abdul Wahab.
Mufti Muhammad.
Maulvi Amjad Ali.
Pandit Munni Lal.
Asir Uddin.
Sad Uddin.
Munshi Kanhya Lal.
Muhammad Lutf Ali Khan.
Munshi Nihal Chand.
Hirde Ram.
Nawab Fateh Ali Khan.
Brahma Nand.
Mir Ul Hasan Khan.
Maulvi Abdul Kabir.
Mulla Nazr Muhammad.
Munshi Ali Muhammad.
Babu Kuljus Rai.
" Murli Dhar.
Imam Uddin.
Muni Megh Raj.
Mir Abbas.

Ram Rai.
Khaira Shah.
Shambhu Rai.
Bhawani.
Chuha Mall.
Amar Singh.
Nagar Ram.
Nand Lal.
Shah Wali.
Muhib Ulla.
Raushan.
Mir Hasan.
Mihr Das.
Imam Bakhsh.
Ganga Ram.
Barda.
Ahmed Baksh.
Kashi Ram.
Munshi Ghulam Rasul.
Nizam Uddin.
Muhammad Abdush Shakur.
Shiv Narain.
Ghasita.

Ghulam Husain.
Muhammad Yusuf.
Pandit Bhan Dutt.
Jiya Lal.
Maulvi Muhammad Fakhir Husain.
Munshi Dhanpat Rai.
Daulat Ram.
Munshi Hasib Uddin Ahmad.
Haji Munshi Muhammad Masih Ulla.
Munshi Muhamed Bilal.
Munshi Wazir Singh.
Hafiz Abdurrahman.
Mir Panah Ali.
Debi Sahai.
Jai Krishan.
Muhammad Nur Uddin.
Hafiz Muhammad.
Muhammad Abdul Mansur.
Umrao Singh.
Kishan Singh.
Abdul Rasul Khan.
Akbar Ali.
Dyal Singh.
Shah Din Shadan.
Ghulam Nabi.
Munshi Kidar Nath.

Munshi Muhammad Abdul Ghafur.
Abul Hasan.
Jaimal Singh.
Ahmadyar.
Jamal Uddin.
Mian Jan Muhammad.
Chiragh Uddin.
Maulvi Din Muhammad.
Umr Din.
Muhammad Husain Shah.
Ghulam Kibirya.
Khuldi.
Maulvi Saiyid Ahmed.
Muhammad Isa.
Munshi Mul Chand.
„ Khuda Bakhsh.
Fakhhr uddin.
Maulvi Talattuf Husen.
Moulvi Ghulam Nabi.
Khushi Ram.
Siraj Uddin.
Bihari Lal.
Bishan Singh.
Moti Ram.
Seona Ram.
Mussammat Zainab Bibi, Mahbub.

Nattha Singh.
Badri Das.
Maulvi Rahim Bakhsh.
Babu Nanak Chand.
Ambe Prashad.
Muhammad Amir Ulla.
Ram Singh of 25th Panjab Infantry.
Jai Dyal Singh.
Maulvi Muhammad Ali.
„ Mirza Muhammad Ali.
Muhammad Ibrahim.
Shigopal.
Nain Sukh.
Munshi Daya Ram.
„ Sada Sukhlal.
Pandit Maharaj Kishen.
Munshi Amir Bakhsh.
Abu Hamid Muhammad.
Abdul Haq.
Abdul Aziz.
Pandit Bansi Dhar.
Muhammad Yasin Shah.
Munshi Ganpat Rai.
Raza Hasan.
Muhammad Hussain.
Rai Chiranjit Rai.

Shiv Ram.
Jugal.
Abdul Jabbar.
Ram Bakhsh.
Fard Faqir.
Khushdil.
Muhammad Shams-ul-Haq.
Faiyaz-ul-Haq.
Prem Chand.
Ahmad Jami.
Madho Narain.
Kunj Bihari Lal
Pandit Kashi Nath.
Munshi Husain Bukhsh.
Muhammad Husain Khan.
Thakur Lal Singh.
Saiyid Aulad Hasan.
Muhammad Abdul Rahim.
Maulvi Abdulla.
Maula Bakhsh.
Pandit Mohan Lal.
Fazl Shah.
Dr. Khubdad Khan.
Muhammad Asad-Ulla Khan.

PRÉCIS OF,

AND CONCLUSIONS FROM,

THE RECORDS OF THE PANJAB GOVERNMENT AND OF THE PANJAB EDUCATIONAL DEPARTMENT, BEARING ON THE SUBJECTS OF THE VILLAGE SCHOOL CESS AND OF INDIGENOUS SCHOOLS.

CONTENTS.

Chapter A.

PAGE.

Précis of, and Notes on, the contents of the "Extracts from the Reports of the Panjab Educational Department, and from the Reviews thereon by the Government of the Panjab between the years 1856-57 and 1880-81." (See Chapters C, D and E.) 1

Chapter B.

Conclusions from above, and statements regarding the income and expenditure from the Village School Cess since 1856-57, the statistics of Indigenous Schools, the misapplications from the Village School Cess from 1856 to 1881, and the principal items of expenditure in 1881-82 10

Chapter C.

Introduction to the "Extracts" as above, consisting of a summary of the Breaches of the Educational Despatches of 1854 and 1859 of the Secretary of State, and of an Extract from the Proceedings of the Supreme Government forwarding the Despatch of 1859, by the Panjab Educational Department... 23

Chapter D.

Official documents connected with the raising of the Village School Cess 26

Chapter E.

"Extracts" (above alluded to) from the Panjab Educational Reports and from the "Reviews" thereon by the Panjáb Government between 1856-57 and 1880-81 34

CHAPTER A.

Precis of, and Notes on, the contents of the "Extracts from the Reports of the Panjab Educational Department, and from the Reviews thereon by the Government of the Panjab between 1856-57 and 1880-81."

The "Extracts" begin with an enumeration of the alleged breaches by the Panjab Educational Department of the orders and instructions contained in the Despatches of 1854 and 1855 of the Secretary of State for India. (See Chapter C.) Pages 23 & 24.

This is followed by an extract from the Proceedings of the Government of India, communicating the Despatch of 1859 to the Local Governments, drawing their attention to the example of various provinces, and making a distinction between the application of grants-in-aid and that of local rates for primary education.

Pages 24 & 25.

The "Extracts" begin with letters between the Financial Commissioner of the Panjab and the Secretary to that Government regarding engagements to be taken on all future occasions of a new settlement or revision of settlement for the payment of *one per cent. upon the juma as a cess for village schools* in accordance with the circular received from the Government of the North-Western Provinces which is quoted, and which also makes provision for the payment of that cess in Muafi estates, and in the settlement of detached parcels lapsed or *resumed.* (See Chapter D.)

Page 26.

Circular from Financial Commissioner to all Commissioners ordering the extension of the cess not only to future settlements, but also to existing settlements wherever the people are willing to pay it.

Pages 26 & 27.

The Deputy Commissioner, Ferozepur, proposing to *deduct* the one per cent. cess from the juma, the Commissioner, Cis-Sutlej States, forwarding the objection to Financial Commissioner, does not support it, although he admits that the cess would not be universally popular if the people had an idea that it was optional.

Financial Commissioner, whilst objecting to the *deduction* of the cess from the revenue as proposed, considers that it would perhaps be impolitic to enforce the additional payment; requests that every effort should be made to induce the zemindars to accede to it, as it is for the benefit of *their* offspring.

Pages 27 & 28.

Commissioner, Cis-Sutlej, reports that the people generally are averse to the introduction of any new tax, but proposes that the cess be immediately levied from the people *without going through the formality* of asking their consent.

Page 28.

Financial Commissioner replies that the cess is one so essentially and manifestly for the benefit of the people themselves and their progeny that *much fastidiousness in regard to its introduction would be out of place.*

Page 28.

Director reports that the definite information regarding the cess is small. In Jhelum there exist 157 indigenous schools, and the cess in that district being Rs. 7,075, this would give Rs. 45 a year to each school to which Government adding 3 rupees per annum from the grant given in each district, the sum of Rs. 4 per mensem could be given to each indigenous school, being nearly double the usual pay of teachers in village schools. In Rawalpindi the case is the same, but in Gujrat there are more schools, though the cess is less; whilst in Shahpur the cess is Rs. 2,901, and only 19 indigenous schools, giving Rs. 12 per mensem to each. The remedy for this disproportioned state of things is for the people or Government to start *more* schools, except in Gujrat, where the schools may be sifted from mosques and the cess only applied to really useful schools. Both the state of indigenous schools and the prospects of the one per cent. tax are considered together.

Pages 28 & 29.

Secretary to Government, Panjab, reports to Government of India that a clause is usually inserted in the fiscal engagements with landholders, with their consent, that they will pay one per cent. on their land tax for the education of their children. The total balance at close of the official year 1857-58 to the credit of the fund was Rs. 1,83,853, intended to be spent on village education on the *Halqabandi* system—namely, one school *to each little circle of three to five villages.* As these schools increase, the indigenous schools diminish. The statistics of these indigenous schools are still being collected, but are still far from perfect. From these statistics the Landi and Arabic schools are properly excluded. In 1856-57 there were 456 one per cent. and 5,024 indigenous schools; in 1857-58 there were 1,336 one per cent. schools and 3,461 indigenous schools, so that there were altogether fewer schools of both kinds in the latter than in the former year.

Page 29.

The Government of India, replying to Panjab on the 23rd January 1860, considers that the alleged voluntary contribution of the cess is not altogether free from injustice, seeing that it falls entirely on the agricultural population, whilst the village cess schools are equally open to other classes who do not pay fees. No more ought to be taken from the people than will suffice for the expenditure on village schools for the year. His Excellency objects to the accumulation of a fund from this source, and desires that for the future the demand of sums in excess of what is required for the current expenses of the village schools as well as any accumulation may be avoided. Including indigenous schools at the end of 1857-58 there were 4,923 schools attended by 46,008 scholars, which is little; but His Excellency observes that considerable increase is looked for in the one per cent. or village school [cess]. (The word in brackets is omitted by oversight in the letter.)

Page 29.

Director's Memorandum of 13th February 1868 gives an account of the origin and extension of the cess, which is described as being levied for the maintenance of village schools, as was already fully the case in a district like Gurgaon made over from the North-Western Provinces. He then gives an estimate of the income of that cess from 1856-57 to 1868-69, but regrets that his office has no record of the amount actually realized, but it will have one in future. (The estimate does not correspond with the figures recorded in the Educational Report of the years referred to, except on the understanding that additional sums were taken from accumulations of the cess from previous years, which had been prohibited by the Government of India.)

The balance in hand on 30th September 1867 was Rs. 1,91,231. Director states that originally the amount of cess raised in each *pargana* was, as a rule, expended in that pargana, but that in 1860 the old system was swept away, and the cess annually collected, together with the accumulations thereon, formed into a general fund, to be spent as follows: 1st, on tahsili (town) and female schools; 10 per cent. for salaries of school muharrirs; 5 per cent. for the Sirkari Akhbar; 4 per cent. for contingencies of *all* vernacular schools; 6 per cent. for teachers at normal schools, and the remainder to village schools in the direct ratio of its annual income from the cess. Subsequently, the Supreme Government paid salaries of chief muharrirs and for the "Akhbar," as also Rs. 40,740 per annum for the maintenance of one model school for each tahsil. It also ordered that female schools, not intended principally for agriculturists, shall be no longer maintained from the cess. Vernacular schools are now classed as town or village schools according to the standard to which they attain and without reference to their locality; *not a few schools situated in large towns consequently appear in the return as "village schools."* The Imperial grant for model schools is chiefly expended on existing town schools, which often cost more than the grant, *when the difference is paid from the village cess.* Thus, in 1866-67 Government spent Rs. 21,566, and the cess Rs. 15,125 for town schools. On village schools Government spent Rs. 24,702 and the cess Rs. 1,39,326. It is pointed out that Government contributes more to vernacular than to town schools. Major Fuller's original proposition, however, being that all town schools should be entirely supported by Government and all village schools by the cess. An account is then given, showing the expenditure from the cess for the current year as Rs. 17,152 per mensem on various heads, of which Rs. 13,016 were spent on "*male schools, town and village,*" and Rs. 862 on female village schools. (This statement does not seem to correspond with the previous estimate of the cess or with the sum spent from cess according to the report—*vide* my detailed Statement I). Formerly the cess bore the expense of *various* kinds of educational buildings, exclusive of village school-houses. The *halqabandi* system is abandoned, because boys from one village cannot be easily induced to attend a school in a neighbouring village, and because *more good could be effected by fixing the rates of vernacular schools in the larger villages, or where the people showed some desire for education.*

In practice, the principle of distributing the remainder of the cess in proportion to the income of each district was also not observed.

Cheques on the one per cent. fund for the budget accounts, and signed by Director, are remitted monthly to Deputy Commissioners, by whom they are cashed (so that an account of the expenditure of the cess is, or may be, kept in Director's office). *The effect of the cess has been to supersede many of the old "maktabs" and "patshalas."* Urdu and Arithmetic have been widely diffused, and Persian is taught better than in the "maktabs." The indigenous schools were said to be 6,309 in 1859-60 and 5,434 in 1866-67, which was not *altogether* due to the operation of the *one per cent. cess. Arrangements, however, having been made for encouraging indigenous schools by grants-in-aid, it may be hoped that an improved class of such schools will come into existence.* In 1858-59 many vernacular schools were first established, and the effect on the manners of the boys since is remarkable, *as they are ready to come any distance for an examination, and are often neat and orderly; but the old idea still prevails that if a boy goes to school he is of no use for the plough. There are no means of ascertaining the number of boys who have received an education in cess schools.* Pages 30 to 33.

II.—Precis of Extracts from Educational Reports and Reviews of Government thereon.

(*See Chapter E.*)

The first educational report enquires what had the people been doing for themselves in the way of education. This is a very difficult question to answer. It is difficult to get accurate statistics and to interpret them when obtained. School phraseology is ready to hand, and Muhammadans are in possession of the field as educators. The Koran schools are worthless; and outside the mosques the Persian Koran schools attract even more Hindus than Muhammadans. The number of indigenous schools is *under* and not *over*stated, but show that a very large preponderance of Muhammadan boys are at school. The growth of Muhammadanism in the Panjab may greatly be traced to the advantage taken by Muhammadan teachers of the confiding attendance of so many Hindus at their schools for the sake of learning Persian. The natural tendency of things is to give Muhammadans a preponderance in the conduct of education which should be much resisted. Koran and Landi schools do not deserve the name of schools, and are not included in the statistics. Of the 24 schools returned as Arabic schools the great majority were purely secular, but they can hardly *be called schools at all, as the students are almost all adults*. The Persian schools are the most genuine institutions in the country, and are attended more largely by Hindus than Muhammadans, the Gulistan and Bostan forming their great attraction. There are *only ten Urdu indigenous schools*, if, indeed, there are any. The people believe Persian and Sanscrit to be something, but not Urdu. Every mosque is probably the site of a Koran school, but the boys attending such schools do not necessarily learn reading and writing, and are, therefore, not included in the education of boys under instruction. Hindus attending *Persian* schools are not jealous as to the encroachments of Muhammadanism, but those attending Sanscrit schools, who are largely adults, would strongly object to learn the Persian character. *Hindi* schools (289 in number) are probably Shastri or Landi schools, *a real Hindi school being rare*. The return of Gurmukhi schools is incomplete, but will be, it is hoped, supplied next year. A really accurate list of these schools, which are chiefly religious and attended by Sikhs, would be interesting. In *Landi* schools the children of shopkeepers are taught book-keeping, and the *various systems of accounts deprecated by our courts*. A few can perform feats in Multiplication and Rule of Three in their heads, but are often unable to do so on paper. The power of writing a character which *neither they nor anybody else can read an hour afterwards* is not an accomplishment. The average income of a village school teacher is Rs. 2-5-2; but he makes money by the practice of his religion, the presents of parents on certain festivals, a quantity of grain at harvest, or the boys give the master in turn daily two meals. In a few cases, Mr. Montgomery reports, *grants of land have been given to the individuals on condition of teaching*, when nothing is charged to the pupils, or they are supported by the masters. Occasionally each plough is assessed at the rate of 5 seers, &c. Director agrees with Mr. Reid of the North-Western Provinces that, rude and imperfect as our tahsil schools are, far greater good can be effected through one of them than through a large number of village schools. The value of these indigenous schools is probably great as harmonizing institutions to which the people are much attached, but educationally they can hardly be voted too low. The Government village school, which costs double an indigenous school, is worth a trial; but still it is a question whether the one per cent. would not be more profitably returned to the contributors, and thirty teachers on a district on Rs. 15 per mensem be better than 100 village school teachers on Rs. 5.

The cess was generally voluntarily given. Director had only to spend it, for which there were two courses: first, on existing indigenous village schools, which would have been cheapest, as half the expenditure would already have been provided by the village, and reasonably to select the best of these schools or to found new ones in central situations, the only course possible for a central department. In the former case, the schools would have had to be left to the district officer, who can, perhaps, induce the people to support schools besides paying the cess, which the educational officers cannot do, at least till the people see some return for the payment already made. Cess was ordered by Supreme Government to be spent *locally*. The total of Government village schools was 450, which cost Rs. 23,472 out of the cess, amounting to Rs. 1,38,034, leaving a balance of Rs. 1,14,562, which should be expended on building village school-houses and the establishment of more village schools.

The number of pupils reading respectively Persian and Hindi cannot be accurately stated. Muhammadans are beginning to teach Urdu reluctantly, a language which it is most desirable to teach, except where teaching Hindi would make us more popular, as there is a danger of throwing too much into the hands of Muhammadans. No *European* Inspector should visit female schools, but Native Inspectors should see whether we are not paying some hundreds of rupees per mensem to enable Muhammadan girls to read the Koran, which they do without such payment. The proportion of boys under instruction, omitting the Landi and Koran schools and to the school-going population is 1 to 36, which is probably below the mark, Jhelum and Lahore yielding more satisfactory, because more accurately ascertained, returns, though there is no reason to suppose that these divisions are really better off than others. Had "Landi and Koran schools" been included, which form by far the greater proportion of indigenous schools, the proportion would have been better, but the representation would have been false!

As regards the resumption of rent-free lands to schools, it was a *common custom* in former times to give grants of rent-free land to persons who were in return bound to teach youth. *Most* of these grants have been resumed, but they have been allowed in five places, that are mentioned, subject to Government inspection. Tables then follow showing amount of cess and number of schools (more accurately and completely dealt with elsewhere). Pages 34 to 37.

The Financial Commissioner forwarding the above report to Secretary, Panjab, recapitulates the statements made therein, supporting Director's resistance to throwing the weight of Government in education into the hands of Muhammadans. It has been found unavoidable to transfer the village cess schools to the Educational Department; the disinclination on the part of some of the district officers to do so has retarded their establishment, which since the transfer has proceeded with greater vigour. The *halqabandi* system has been introduced, much pains being taken in the determination of the central localities. Urdu is the language which must predominate (conclusions are drawn by Financial Commissioner which are only suggested, not actually stated, by Director as facts). Pages 37 to 39.

(The extracts from subsequent educational reports, quoted in the body of the "Report of Indigenous Education since Annexation," even more strongly than above, show that the first object of the cess was to support "existing indigenous village schools," and, secondly, to establish Government village schools in central localities as models to indigenous schools.)

In 1863-64 the Director reports that no trustworthy statistics of indigenous schools are procurable, and that the European Inspector never has the time to examine them himself.

Page 39.

In 1864-65 he further considers that the collection of statistics from purely indigenous schools would not be worth the trouble and expense which it would entail. Many of the best have been amalgamated with Government schools, and grants will be made to them under the simplest possible mode of examination in the Draft of revised grant-in-aid rules submitted to the Supreme Government. (This Draft was too technical to embody the spirit of the Educational despatches of 1854 and 1859, even if they had been translated to the people, as ordered, in their vernaculars.)

Page 39.

In 1865-66 the revised Grant-in-aid Code specially provides for Government aid being extended to good indigenous schools, and district officers and Inspectors have been expressly requested to bring forward all deserving schools. (How could they do so when they had "never time to inspect these schools," when "statistics regarding them were not procurable," and when "the collection of these statistics was not worth the trouble and expense?") Director trusts that he will bring many of these schools under inspection, if the necessary funds are assigned next year, when endeavours will be made to obtain *some approximately correct statistics* and to show them in the returns.

Page 39.

1866-67. These statistics having been at last supplied to a certain extent, it is found that, whereas there were 63,090 pupils in indigenous schools in 1859-60, there were only 32,607 pupils in 1866-67. The Panjab Government much regret this result, "and His Honour trusts that the system of making grants-in-aid to indigenous schools of merit, under Article XIV of the Grant-in-aid Rules, commenced during the year under report, will *arrest the further decline of these institutions, which are doubtless in many respects more suited to the tastes and wishes of the people, than schools established through direct Government agency.*"

On this the Director asks for *an addition to the number of Deputy Inspectors* (or an increase of expense instead of a re-allotment or curtailment of existing expenditure) "*now* that the Government desires indigenous vernacular schools to be visited (as if the educational despatches had not all along insisted on an inspecting agency for these schools). He then proposes the *amalgamation* of the cess with "the above sums," and with the increased amount thus available proposes to open an "elementary *English* school at Rajanpur," to *raise* the salaries of *existing* Government teachers, *particularly* (not exclusively, as intended) at the best vernacular schools. He looks to cess, local revenues and Government grants as a means to meet the requirements of existing schools (but not as an obligation to increase the number of schools, *especially* if unconnected with the department). Pages 39 & 40.

In 1867-68 Captain Holroyd reports that few teachers of indigenous schools appear anxious to avail themselves of Government aid, and considers that the school at Fateegurh is the only *bonâ fide* indigenous school where an education equal to that of a Government town school can be obtained. According to statistics of district officers, on which no great reliance can be placed, there were 4,888 indigenous schools with an attendance of 46,947 pupils not under Government inspection (although this had been insisted on by Government). (This number *now* includes the Koran and Landi schools, which were *not* included in 1860, when the number of pupils in indigenous schools was reported to be over 82,000 by the Panjab Government.)

Page 40.

In 1868-69 Captain Holroyd again reports that there are only three indigenous schools in the Panjab where any attempt is made to impart "general knowledge" through the vernacular, and again reports that the schools are unwilling to avail themselves of the conditions of Government aid.

Page 40.

In 1869-70 Captain Holroyd reports that, according to the statistics supplied by district officers, which are by no means reliable, there were 3,995 indigenous schools, receiving no aid from Government, and supposed to contain 52,479 students. He considers there is no machinery in existence by means of which reliable information regarding these schools can be obtained. Urdu is seldom taught in them, as the boys trust to learning it incidentally through their Persian studies.

Page 40.

In 1870-71 there were 4,133 indigenous schools, supposed to contain 50,551 boys. The remarks of the previous year are repeated.

Page 40.

In 1871-72 Mr. Cordery, Officiating as Director, Dr. Leitner makes an effort to excite an interest in primary and indigenous education in the Rawalpindi Circle. The Lieutenant-Governor in his Review on the Educational Report of that year "*is somewhat doubtful of the policy which has diminished the number of primary and lower class schools.*"

He is not unwilling to give effect to Dr. Leitner's view of *supplementing deficiencies* in the educational cess by the private subscriptions of the people, "*utilizing whatever teaching element is indigenous or popular in the village.*" "*This consideration should never be lost sight of, and its importance is increasing with the growth of the demand for education.*"

"During his tour in the cold weather the Lieutenant-Governor has been much struck by the absence—*in some districts the almost entire absence—of the sons of agriculturists from the village schools supported by the agricultural population from the percentage on land-revenue*, but which are filled by the children of munshis and shop-keepers, the men who, under the present Government, are rapidly increasing in wealth, and who hope to give their sons such an education as will enable them to rise above the position in life in which they were born. It is not, however, desired by Government that any such sentiments should be felt by the agriculturists; what they require is the simple education which is found in the 1st class only of the primary schools—Urdu reading and writing, and the simplest rules of Arithmetic. Nothing more than this is necessary. But this it is impossible to acquire in one year, which forms the term during which each boy remains ordinarily in the lowest class. He is then promoted to a higher class in which the *study of Persian, Geography, and the higher rules of Arithmetic are required. The Lieutenant-Governor sees in the educational course of the schools in Panjab villages no provision made for teaching Hindi, Gurmukhi, or the reading of village account books, all of which would be useful in some parts of the country to the classes for which these schools are primarily intended. Boys of every grade and class in life are forced into the same mould, and have to pass through the same educational course, the consequence being that all those to whom it is unsuited (and these form a majority of the people) often decline to attend the Government schools.*"

His Honour remarks, further on, that "*the object of the Government is rather to impart elementary instruction to the masses than complete education to the few. The improvement of the vernacular system of education, the increase in the number of primary schools,* the development, or rather the creation, of a vernacular literature, and the translation into languages known by the people of approved works—these are the aims which the Government should set before it as the most useful and important."

Pages 41 & 42.

Mr. Cordery in his report urges that the desire of the people for the fusion of secular instruction into their religious schools affords an opportunity for the application of the grant-in-aid system. He hopes that this policy will be gradually adopted, not only on the frontier, but throughout the Province, in which case the better class of indigenous schools may assume a more prominent position in the education of the country. He supports Dr. Leitner's proposal regarding the relation into which they may be brought towards the Panjab University College, which Dr. Leitner thinks may exercise a most beneficial influence on the thousands of indigenous schools in the Province, if it carries out the original principles on which it was founded. *Exact information* regarding these schools Mr. Cordery considers to be *impossible*, but they may be roughly divided into four classes: 1st, the Patshala schools of Arithmetic; 2nd, the Arabic schools, which would not object to the incorporation of secular instruction; 3rd, the Sanscrit schools, which are of a character very similar to the Arabic schools; 4th, the Persian schools, which only teach badly what is better taught in Government schools.

Page 42.

The Inspector of the Amballa Circle reports that the only indigenous schools of any importance are the schools in the City of Delhi, superintended by the Reverend Mr. Smith. These schools received a Government aid of Rs. 250 last year (these schools were mission schools, and not indigenous schools at all; they were chiefly frequented by converted Chamars and Mehtars, to whom, at no period, really indigenous education was ever allowed to be extended).

This Inspector states that he has taken every opportunity of seeing indigenous schools, but that he has been unable to select *any* as worthy of Government support. Yet, he offered a grant-in-aid in *many* cases, but the teacher declined to accede to the conditions proposed. The Inspector finally admits that in the returns of indigenous schools a number of aided schools are included which cannot properly be called indigenous.

Page 43.

The Inspector of the Lahore Circle reports that the school of Fateegurh, whose manager receives a grant of land and a money grant, is excellent. That of Jullunder was once an excellent indigenous Persian school, and most of the amlas of the neighbouring districts were educated in it. Its proprietor resolved to introduce subjects of general knowledge, and receives an annual grant of Rs. 180. The returns of purely indigenous schools are very unreliable, but may be taken as an approximation to their actual number; so must also their expenditure, which is a rough valuation of the cost of the presents made to the teachers. The most numerous of these schools are those of the Pandahs, in which an ingenious, though rude, system of mental arithmetic is taught, as also a sort of phonetic writing of names and Hindi notation, subjects which are just sufficient to enable the baniah to carry on all the intricacies of his trade. These schools are popular.

The Arabic schools come next in point of number, and are held nearly always in mosques; most of them only teach the Koran by rote, but a few proceed to Grammar and Logic. The ages of the students extend from 8 to 60. The Persian and Urdu schools are numerous, but not so much as before Government vernacular schools were started. The students learn the Kerima by heart, first without the meaning, and then with the meaning; they then go on to the Gulistan, Bahardanish, and other Persian books. The ages of students vary from 6 or 7 to 20 or 22. *Hindi* schools are rare in the Panjab; the considerable number entered in the return as Hindi students probably include those of *Gurmukhi*. The Inspector has no recollection of having seen any private *Hindi* schools, and does not know what books are read in the Gurmukhi schools. There are *very few* Sanscrit schools in the Lahore Circle, which generally teach the Shasters, and, rarely, general literature, metaphysics, &c. The so-called indigenous schools teaching English are generally established by Bengalis for their own children.

Pages 43 & 44.

The temporary Inspector of the Rawalpindi Circle, Dr. Leitner, reports that the only means exerting a lasting influence on the people is to establish semi-secular schools. The difficulties in dealing with the question must be met soon, but are not insuperable. He further states that:

"6. *In the extension and liberal interpretation of the grant-in-aid rules to all classes without distinction will, as he has represented for years, be alone found the solution of educational problems (including the question of "Muhammadan Education") and the fulfilment of the Educational Despatch of* 1854. *It alone will gain the confidence of the people and their co-operation with us for the general aims of the Educational Department.*" Had the grant-in-aid system not existed, the circle would have been without high education of any kind, which is now given by Missionary Institutions, to which a debt of gratitude is due.

Our educational system has no great hold on the masses. "Whilst at a cost of Rs. 1,74,802-12-8 we instruct, and inspect in this circle 216 schools, containing 13,988 pupils, the people *educate*—to feelings not of loyalty—21,632 pupils in 774 unaided indigenous schools maintained at an annual cost of Rs. 31,099-6. In reality it will be found that there are more than double that number of schools (containing nearly 40,000 pupils) unaided by Government. *It has been denied by an Inspector of long standing that there were any such schools, but this is merely another proof of how little we, who ought to know most of the inner life of the people, are acquainted with what is going on.* But, even if double the number of pupils supposed to be under instruction in both aided and unaided schools were actually and properly educated, we should not have fully discharged our duty to the masses. We are bound to take more notice in a national and representative spirit of the indigenous schools. *Yet in the face of the appalling ignorance of the country, and knowing that the Supreme Government would strongly support any measure for the extension of education*, we have *abolished* numerous village schools in order to feed a few central places convenient for our inspection, instead of endeavouring to have a *school in every village* in the circle. There can be no doubt that unless we strengthen and improve University education, "primary" and "secondary" education have no standard to look to; but this can never be an excuse for neglecting the masses. The Panjab University, which is established on a national basis, is the most effective organization for giving life to education and reality to our department. The "resolution" of the Senate of that institution to help schools in which efficient secular instruction is imparted in addition to any religious teaching there may be given in them, is a solution of the "Muhammadan question," whilst it enunciates a principle of the widest application to all denominations. The effect of the "resolution," so far as it has been carried out, has been to promote toleration and to create a feeling of genuine attachment to a "truly paternal" Government; for not only have Hindu, Muhammadan, English, Anglo-vernacular and vernacular schools been started or projected, but even in the purely Muhammadan school at Bal Bikari the majority of the pupils are Hindus, who read the secular subjects only. The effect on the Native priesthood will be to induce it to study its own classics critically and to add to them a knowledge of Western sciences. The ignorant members, whose only learning has been disloyalty, will lose their influence, and those who are anxious for the propagation of still higher truths and learning will find a field ready prepared for their labors, whilst Government, having the interest of the priesthood on its side, instead of against it, will have at its disposal a powerful agency. Anyhow, whatever be the nature of the schools established, it is to be wished that the melancholy sight of ranges of 12 miles and upwards being without any educational appliances will no longer be tolerated by a civilised and wise Government.

Inspection should be more thorough, and should interest the teachers, children and parents, as well as the Moulvis and Pandits and the local notables, in the progress of education and in rendering it practical, which is not now believed to be the case. Committees of local instruction and the educational work of tahsildars should not be treated in a disparaging tone, as it is not the duty of educational officers to put down, but to develope, Native agency. In spite of the drawback of holding the Inspectorship only temporarily, no great difficulty was found to obtain advice, co-operation and subscriptions in starting a considerable number of schools, indigenous, aided and Government, as well as in making arrangements for further support (which fell through owing to the unfriendly attitude of his successor to private enterprise).

Inspectors and district officers should make their tours coincide. The status of educational subordinates should be improved, and they, as well as *head masters, those of the larger schools especially, should be encouraged to communicate freely with the Inspector on every subject connected with their administration; for nothing can be a greater advantage to a superior officer and to the cause of education than to be able to elicit the whole truth, however destructive to preconceptions this may be.*

The substance and reality of education is now sacrificed to returns and classifications, which are a mere office convenience; the numerous, and not always clearly worded, departmental circulars should be codified in brief and intelligible language, and each circle should have an immediate and complete grasp over its own statistical figures, and not, as now, be obliged to obtain them from the Director's office.

We have an education machinery, but we have no educational government. Everything of importance should be translated into the vernacular for the information of the majority of our subordinates. That this is not systematically done may be inferred from the circumstance that the grant-in-aid rules devised to encourage Native enterprise, and the very soul of our educational policy, do not exist in a translated form in this circle.

The female schools, however imperfectly worked, have been one of the aims of the Panjab Government, and should not be hastily abolished, as was proposed repeatedly regarding Bedi Kem Singh's numerous schools, which should be improved, and wherever there is no objection, opened to the inspection of educational Native officials and others of known respectability and a certain age. After all the agitation that had taken place regarding "female education," it was certainly inconsistent to sweep away at one blow 108 schools, a course which was not calculated to strengthen the belief of the people in the permanence of our educational policy or to encourage Bedi Kem Singh in again offering his services in its support (the temporary Inspector revived and re-organized fifty of these schools, and found no difficulty in opening them to inspection). In this, as well as other instances, the policy of reducing or abolishing grants is injurious to the interest of the circle. "Improve the schools, but do not reduce or abolish them." As regards Government village schools, people are applying for their restoration where they had been abolished. Some applicants even offer to subscribe towards them, but *the general feeling is that they are entitled to them as they pay the "Educational Cess."*

Pages 44 to 47.

The Inspector of the Multan Circle reports that there are said to be 554 indigenous schools containing 7,329 scholars, of whom 4,438 learn Arabic, 30 Sanscrit, 1,431 Persian, and 76 Urdu.

Page 47.

In the Report for 1872-73 the Officiating Director (Mr. C. Pearson), reporting at length on the difficulty of applying the grant-in-aid system to indigenous schools, the great untrustworthiness of their statistics, the impracticability of laying a foundation upon them, as in Bengal, where the Government education is a progressive improvement upon them, the almost insurmountable difficulty of introducing any kind of education in the frontier districts, that, notwithstanding the newspaper cry for Hindi raised by the Hindus, no serious effort is made to use the opportunities for acquiring Hindi which already exist, and that our village schools should be made as cheap and as numerous as possible by constant efforts, and by diverting a portion of the funds which are now spent in sustentation allowances, in a too liberal scale of salaries and in diffusing a smattering of English.

The Panjab Government, however, in their review on this Report distinctly re-iterates its support of indigenous schools as follows:—

"*Review by Government, paragraph* 9.—His Honour has considered the observations contained in paragraph 54 of the Report regarding the difficulty of applying the grant-in-aid system to indigenous schools in the Panjab. It may be difficult, but His Honour is not convinced of its impracticability in all cases, and adheres to the views expressed in the review of last year's Report, that the policy should *never be lost sight of.*"

In 1873-74 and in 1874-75, as well as in 1875-76, Major Holroyd being Director, the Panjab Government again and again urged the necessity of aiding indigenous schools in spite of the constant objections of the Educational Department and of the Inspector of the Rawalpindi Circle (Mr. Pearson.)

Pages 48 & 49.

1873-74.—*Review by Government, paragraph* 22.—In the indigenous schools of the Peshawar District, out of 2,570 pupils 2,016 are under instruction in Arabic, a proof, otherwise abundantly corroborated, of the general reverence accorded to the teaching and literature of Islam. In the

Government schools of the lower class the number of pupils is only 752, and among these there are very few Pathans, Sayads or Mullazadas. There is, indeed, a strong *religious prejudice against the Government scheme of education.* On other grounds, the Khans object to their tenants going to school, and parents of the agricultural class desire no instruction of children already useful in the fields. In the presence of such obstacles the most cautious and conciliatory action is required. *But enquiries personally instituted by the Lieutenant-Governor lead him to believe that some of the existing teachers are willing to accept grants-in-aid on the departmental* terms. To those—and there are several—who teach Persian well rewards might be given, and by others presents of Persian and Arabic school-books would be willingly received. The exertions of leading men in the promotion of education should always be liberally acknowledged. Page 49.

1874-75.—*Review by Government, paragraph 10.*—The Inspector (Mr. Pearson) of that Division (Rawalpindi) observes that the question of aiding good indigenous schools has not been lost sight of, but that there seem to be obstacles to the carrying out of the suggestions which were made in the last Report. His Honour would be glad to be informed by further report of the nature of these obstacles, as he considers *that judicious aid given to indigenous schools is a very important part of the work of the Educational Department.* Too little is done in the frontier districts in this direction, and the *department should, as far as possible, utilize existing agency and improve indigenous schools by giving grants-in-aid on reasonable conditions of efficiency and permission for inspection.*

The people of the frontier districts are in many cases suspicious and bigoted, and will far more readily send their children to private schools than to Government schools, where they are taught, no doubt better, but less in accordance with their wishes and prejudices.

Page 49.

1875-76.—*Review by Government, paragraph 12.*—It is observed that the difficulty of aiding indigenous schools, specially in frontier districts, *the desirability of which has been so often impressed in reviews of Educational Reports,* is found, as indeed was anticipated, chiefly to lie in the absence of eligible schools to aid ; but *the Lieutenant-Governor trusts that this important point may not be lost sight of, and that the Department will, in consultation with the civil authorities, continue to endeavour to utilize and develop, so far as may be possible, the existing educational institutions of the country, and enlist on the side of the Government, and an improved form of education, the teachers of indigenous schools, whether attached to Hindu or Muhammadan religious institutions or separate from them. The Panjab University, furnishing through the Oriental College attached to it, teachers for these indigenous schools, may well assist in this important work.* Pages 49 & 50.

In 1876-77 the Director, Major Holroyd, after reporting favourably on three vernacular aided schools, of which two also taught religion, recapitulates at considerable length all his previous objections to the encouragement of indigenous schools by pointing out, first, that the great majority of Maktabs had already been absorbed into our system, that their instruction was practically valueless, and that there was scarcely any indigenous schools in the Peshawur district which it was possible to influence in the manner desired by the Lieutenant-Governor.

As a *general rule, no useful influence can be exerted by the Department on the majority of existing indigenous schools.*

Signs, however, are not wanting that indigenous schools of a different kind may be expected to spring into existence. The people have in some cases appointed English teachers, and have in others established Anglo-vernacular schools for themselves, in the hope generally that a grant-in-aid may be obtained from Government. Pages 50 & 51.

(However satisfactory this might be, it is clear that the above course would not be the same as to develop indigenous schools *as such,* and to discourage a smattering of English, as intended by the Local Government.)

In 1877-78 the Director reports that both the Muhammadan schools in Amritsar have reverted to their purely religious character, one of them having already relinquished the grant-in-aid. There were 5,381 indigenous schools containing 61,818 pupils as compared with 4,803 schools and 56,642 boys of the previous year. The Inspector of the Amballa Circle cannot understand how in the Amballa district with 1,539 boys the fees only amount to Rs. 19-13-0, whilst 500 boys in the Hissar district pay 1,132-8-0 for the year. (The former was probably the mere cash amount; the latter also included the valuation of presents given to the teacher.) The Hindu school at Ludhiana, which teaches English, is also returned as an indigenous school.

Mr. Pearson reports on the enormous increase of Arabic students in the indigenous schools of Gujrat, but considers that this is probably due to somewhat better returns. He considers that a census of educated persons taken once in ten years would be far more instructive than this attempt to count indigenous schools, which, in nine cases out of ten, are not schools at all in any educational sense. Probably more learning is acquired privately than at school. Pages 51 & 52.

In 1878-79 the Panjab Government held that the district funds are as much a portion of the provincial taxation as any other branch of the revenue, and from this point of view the entire cost of agriculturists is borne by Government. The "Review" then goes on to say (paragraph 7) :—

"It must be remembered at the same time that the agriculturalists themselves consider that they pay for the education received: Though the cost of educating agriculturalists is defrayed from District Funds, it was paid, until within the last few years, from the educational cess which has now been merged in these funds; and the educational cess was raised for the *express* purpose of maintaining schools for the Agricultural population, and was at, first, in theory at least, a voluntary contribution." Page 52.

The Director reports that the plan of creating indigenous schools in the Peshawar District, as His Honour contemplated, may have been worth trying, but was not very likely to succeed, and has led to some waste of money. At present 10 of these schools are maintained.
Page 52.

In 1879-80 Lieutenant-Colonel Holroyd reports that there is a Hindi school at Lahore and also a Muhammadan school in which English is taught, and repeats that, on the establishment of Government schools in the Panjab, the indigenous Persian schools were gradually absorbed in the Government system. The Panjab Government in its Review remark on the absence of comparative statistics under the head of Primary Vernacular Education, and again lays down that it *is the chief duty of the State to provide for primary schools as follows* :—

Review by Panjab Government, paragraph 11.—"The absence of comparative statistics under this head (primary vernacular education) is the more to be regretted, as it is from primary schools that all others are recruited; and it is, therefore, the chief duty of the State in educational matters to provide for primary schools and to see that the instruction given in them is good and sound; and with regard to this duty the Lieutenant-Governor would earnestly direct the attention of all district officers to the necessity of inducing their subordinates to take an active interest in the cause of education."

Again, in the "Review" by the Panjab Government on the Educational Report of 1880-81 (*Lieutenant-Colonel Holroyd*) the Government re-iterates the principles which it has already mentioned—

Review by Government, paragraph 12.—"The results of primary teaching in aided schools are far from favourable as compared with those in Government schools; and this is the more unsatisfactory as grants-in-aid should be given only under very special circumstances to primary schools, which, as a rule, must be supported from local resources.

"This principle has been repeatedly laid down by Government, and cannot be too strongly enforced; and it is already under consideration in connection with the further decentralization scheme to relieve district and local funds of some of their present charges, *so as to enable them to devote more of their income to the cause of primary education.*

"*There is a constant tendency to overlook the duties of the State with regard to primary education* and to turn greater attention to the more showy results of higher education, and this tendency requires to be steadily watched. *Signs of it are not wanting in the present report;* but it would appear from the review of educational progress during the past decade that a somewhat larger proportion of the total expenditure is now spent on primary education than in 1870-71; and if it be found possible to carry out the financial arrangements above-mentioned, a still greater increase will take place in the future. Meanwhile, the Lieutenant-Governor would once more direct the earnest attention of all officers to the duties of District and Municipal Committees in the matter of primary education."

CHAPTER B.

Conclusion arrived at from "Extracts from Official Documents referring to Education between 1854 and 1881."

The following references to the despatches of the Secretary of State of 1854 and 1859, which are the foundation of our educational policy in India, and the extracts from orders of the Government of India, and from the reviews of the Panjab Government on the Educational reports, will, I believe, suffice to show, when compared with the reports of the Educational Department—

1. That the village school cess, which was introduced into the Panjab from the North-Western Provinces, was primarily intended for existing indigenous village schools, and secondly, for the creation of new village schools to serve as models to indigenous schools.

2. That the Educational Department practically frustrated this object by professing that these schools were useless, or that it was impossible to collect accurate statistics regarding them, or that they were not schools in the proper sense of the term, or that district officers alone could attend to them, or that their teachers were unwillingly to receive Government aid, and to comply with any conditions, however lenient, to secure such aid, or that the languages taught in the indigenous schools were either barbarous or purely religious (which affected all the Gurmukhi, Arabic and Sanscrit schools), or that it had already absorbed into its system the Persian maktabs which were the only indigenous schools of any value.

3. The consequence of this attitude of the Educational Department was that practically only new village schools were established, which, however, did *not* serve as models to indigenous schools, but rather tended to destroy them, and which were not sufficiently numerous to represent the total outlay from the village school cess, except perhaps in the years 1858-59 and 1859-60 (after which the cess was persistently applied in a great part to non-agriculturists and to town schools up to the present date), even by providing only one school for a cluster of villages, not to speak of one village school to every radius of 2 miles, as in the North-Western Provinces, the consequence of which is that there are now barely one school to every 26 villages in the Panjab, and that there are only 1,284 Government vernacular primary schools for the 34,324 towns and villages in British territory in the Panjab, according to the last Census.

4. The statistics of the village school cess conclusively prove that, had the intention of Government been carried out, the amount of the cess at the disposal of the Educational Department would have been sufficient for about 5,000 indigenous schools, to be aided by a monthly grant of from 2 to 5 rupees per mensem, as these schools already derive a fair, and sometimes a lucrative, income in their respective localities, and as, in the majority of cases, they would gratefully have been both able and willing to avail themselves of the conditions on which such aid could have been offered to them. It is alleged that the villagers would have discontinued their own support of these schools had Government offered aid; but this result was unlikely to happen, for religious and other reasons, especially if the aid had been afforded *as a favour* to deserving schools and been contingent on the applications of the villagers themselves, who would thus have retained an interest in the progress of their traditional schools.

5. Be that as it may, the amount of the cess would have been sufficient to give nearly 2,000 new village model schools situated in convenient village centres, supported at from Rs. 8 to Rs. 10 per mensem, and by the fees of the pupils, whilst the effect on the contributing villages of seeing that their money was spent on the purpose for which it was raised would have stimulated their further liberality.

6. The statistics show that there was an accumulation of at least Rs. 4,74,947 from the village cess, which was not spent on establishing new village schools.

7. The statistics further show that the number of agriculturists attending school was comparatively larger in 1859-60, when the total expenditure on education was Rs. 2,15,789, than at present, when it is nearly 16 lakhs.

8. Out of an income from the cess of over 56 lakhs, from 1856-57 to 1880-81, at least 15 lakhs have been spent on purposes other than village schools, whilst the remainder has also not been entirely applied to village schools situated in villages.

9. Out of a total expenditure on education of nearly 227 lakhs since 1858-59, barely Rs. 30,000 have been spent by Government on indigenous schools so-called, the majority of which were really mission or branch schools, *i.e.*, scarcely a seven-thousandth part.

10. As it would have been impossible for the Educational Department to make any start at all, had it not absorbed many of the existing Persian maktabs, the schools so re-constituted cannot be called "indigenous." It, therefore, seems to follow that, as no help was afforded to indigenous schools out of the village school cess, its primary charge, the entire sum of 56 lakhs raised from that source since the beginning of the Department has been levied under an understanding that has not been fulfilled.

11. The elimination of the term "village cess" for "educational cess," of "village school" for "lower school" or "primary school," of accounts showing the actual expenditure

from the educational cess for accounts from "districts funds" or "local rates,", and the reluctance of the Educational Department to carry out the principles of the Despatches of 1854 and 1859, especially as regards indigenous education, would seem to show that the amalgamation of the cess with district funds, and the apparent or real difficulty of ascertaining how much of the former is spent on village schools situated in villages, has brought about a confusion in the accounts and statements which does not appear to be altogether unwelcome to the Department. In connection with this assumed attitude on the above points, the Educational Report of 1872-73 may be consulted with advantage, and the repeated attempts, several times successful, of omitting the returns of the indigenous schools from the educational statistics may be borne in mind.

12. In spite of these perplexing circumstances, the Panjab Government has constantly urged the fulfilment of the Educational despatch of 1854. When induced, on departmental representations, which it was difficult to set aside, to allow the reduction of village or primary schools, it invariably retraced its steps and re-iterated the principles on which alone our educational policy can be founded. This assertion is fully borne out by the accompanying extracts, whilst the special attention of the Department was drawn by Sir Donald McLeod to the fulfilment of the despatch of 1854 in his Circular No. 296, dated 10th June 1865, end of paragraph 2.

13. The non-promulgation to the people in their vernacular of the grant-in-aid rules which were primarily intended for Anglo-Vernacular and higher schools, but from which, under certain circumstances, village and indigenous schools were not excluded, if the amount from the cess or other local tax was insufficient for the discharge of the admittedly "first duty of Government," must, I regret to say, be deemed to be intentional, because attention was repeatedly drawn to their not being translated, and because, to the best of my knowledge, they are not yet translated, nor are they even now communicated to the people in a style which they can understand and in the spirit of the Educational despatches. The spirit of educational enterprise is great in the Panjab, but instances are numerous, as at Amballa, where private native effort has been discouraged on the avowed ground of the existence of a Government school.

14. As for the resumptions of grants of rent-free land to persons who were bound in return to teach, my only ground, so far as this chapter is concerned, is the paragraph quoted from the Educational Report of 1856-57, and which, in the absence of evidence to the contrary, might have been deemed to be conclusive. But any evidence to the contrary only partially affects the question, for the assertion refers not only to religious schools attached to, or forming part of, religious buildings or endowments, most of which, though not all, were respected, and, sometimes, liberally treated, but also to semi-religious and secular schools granted either direct by the Governments that preceded us to persons from father to son on condition of teaching, or indirectly forming an obligation to jaghirdars or muafidars. The very circular of the North-Western Provinces, which formed the basis for the levying of the village cess in the Panjab, seems to imply this; but whatever be the case, the fact is notorious that numerous grants have been resumed. The resumption records and the documents for which I have applied to the Panjab Secretariat, but which have not been supplied, will prove a proceeding which it was perfectly natural for the Government to adopt at the time, and which, wherever any injustice may have been unintentionally caused, can be reversed even now with economy and future advantage to the State. Not to speak of reviving the obligation to maintain schools in all cases of jaghirs, the grant of waste land or an assignment of the value of, say, Rs. 2 per mensem on the village land, would establish in perpetuity and hereditary respectability the village teacher, whilst gradually tending to make him independent of the pecuniary aid from Government. In numerous parts of Europe a small free site and cottage form the only permanent remuneration of the village schoolmaster for the time being, and there is every reason why education should be replaced in India on its traditional and self-supporting basis. Had I not feared to raise a storm of applications for the restoration of resumed land to schools, I should have been able to add numerous records in support of my assertion. As it is, a number of indigenous teachers have spontaneously submitted statements which will be found elsewhere, that their schools were, before annexation, supported by grants of land. The misconceptions under which these were resumed may be classified as follows :—

(*a*) In a number of instances the jaghirdars or muafidars were glad to get rid of their obligation to maintain the hereditary schools. This was an easy task under a new régime necessarily imperfectly acquainted with the previous state of things, and in the confusion following on annexation.

(*b*) When the enquiring officer was told that such and such land belonged to such and such a teacher, and the latter could produce no *personal* grant of the same, it ran the risk of being resumed, whereby the school connected with it came to an end.

(*c*) The alarm of such resumptions spreading, the teachers in professional possession alleged that these grants *were personal* to themselves. Even when their statement was believed and acted on, the course adopted ended in the resumption of the land after the death of the occupant at the time of the enquiry.

(*d*) Above all, was it impossible for European officers to ascertain and to appreciate whether the conditions of the grants were properly fulfilled. To many, the *laisser-aller* of Oriental management of endowed schools seemed an abomination

tion deserving their abolition, though the people were content to let them go on, and would have been grateful for any suggestion for their improvement or for their existence on the fulfilment of the conditions of their tenure. To others schools teaching Gurmukhi seemed barbarous and to teach Arabic seditious (see Reports). Others again thought that it was desirable to dispossess the Muhammadan from the teacher's seat which he was occupying at the time of annexation on political grounds. None had the leisure or sympathy to go into matters obscured by native diffidence of aliens, and by their own preconceptions. The consequence was that, throughout the country, by far the large majority of schools held on the grant of rent-free system were resumed. In my humble opinion, some compensation, as already mentioned, should be made in a manner which will be to the advantage of both agricultural progress and of the State; whilst as regards the misapplied portion of the village cess, the relief from police charges to district and municipal bodies offers a convenient opportunity of increasing the allotment to primary and practical vernacular education among the agricultural population.

15. The following documents deserve special attention :—

A.

Extract from Report of the Director of Public Instruction, Panjab, for 1856-57,—No. 186, *dated 6th July* 1857.

PRIVATE SCHOOLS ENJOYING RENT-FREE LAND.

"PARA. 80. You are aware that it was a common custom in former times to give grants of rent-free land to persons who were bound in return to teach youth. Most of these grants, the conditions of which were probably very little attended to, have been resumed, but I have been officially informed of their being allowed, on the condition above mentioned, at the places noted in the margin. In all such cases the school is now considered subject to Government inspection, and will be gradually made to conform to the rules laid down for one per cent. tahsili schools, as each case may require."

District.	Locality.	Grant.
		Rs.
Amritsar...	Sultanpur ...	One well.
Sialkot ...	Badanath ...	37 gumaos.
Ludiana ...	Sugraon.	
Gugaira ...	Lashari.	
Ditto ...	Pakputtan ...	150 rupees.

B.

Extract from paragraph 2 of Panjab Government letter No. 296, *dated* 10*th June* 1865, *to Director of Public Instruction, Panjab.*

"Attention is drawn to paragraph 65 of the despatch of the Right Honorable the Secretary of State for India. 'The Government schools and colleges, whether high or low, should be regarded, not as permanent institutions, but only as means for generating a desire and demand for education, and as models meanwhile for imitation by private institutions. In proportion as the demand for education, in any given locality is generated, and as private institutions spring up and flourish, all possible aid and encouragement should be afforded to them; and the Government, in place of using its power and resources to compete with private parties, should rather contract and circumscribe its own measures of direct education, and so shape its measures as to pave the way for the ultimate abolition of its own schools."

STATEMENT I.

Income and expenditure from Village School Cess and number of Village Schools since 1856-57.

Years.	Income.	Expenditure.	Surplus.	No. of Cess Schools.	No. of pupils.	Total expenditure on Department.	Remarks.
		Rs.	Rs.			Rs.	
1856-57 ...	1,38,034	23,472	1,14,562*	456	6,064	......	* Apparently largely spent in building school-houses when the schools were removed from mosques, temples, &c., &c.
1857-58 ...	1,51,544	82,263	69,281*	1,336	12,024	......	
1858-59 ...	1,92,002†	1,92,002	......	2,029	26,377	......	† This is the only year in which the income of the cess was almost wholly spent on its avowed purpose.
1859-60 ...	1,75,226	......	......	1,704	37,000	2,57,482	
1860-61 ...	2,29,101‡	1,24,772	1,06,743	1,686	32,165	2,85,789(?) 3,77,953	‡ This probably includes a sum from the accumulation, as elsewhere the income of the year from the cess is only estimated at Rs. 1,89,970. However, as the grossest misapplications of the cess began with 1860-61, the separate statement from that year to 1880-81 may now be referred to, which shows the expenditure from the cess as annually levied *plus* the accumulated balance drawn upon by the Department.
Actual income for that year only.	(1,89,970)						
1861-62 ...	2,84,979	1,81,300	1,03,676	1,750	38,849	5,11,287	
Actual income for that year only.	(2,04,943)						
1862-63 ...	3,25,867	1,52,494	1,73,373	1,807	46,559	7,23,077	
Actual income for that year only.	(2,08,908)						
1863-64 ...	3,01,089	1,62,087	1,39,000	1,807	51,753	6,52,578	
Actual income for that year only.	(2,10,000)						
1864-65 ...	2,75,513	1,62,004	1,13,508	1,745	52,917	7,88,988	
(Actuals) ...	(2,10,000)						
1865-66 ...	2,31,491	1,43,977	78,494	1,746	55,593	8,66,766	
(Actuals) ...	(2,10,000)						
1866-67 ...	2,50,813	1,39,326	1,10,484	1,660	53,757	9,49,065	
(Actuals) ...	(2,12,710)						
1867-68 ...	2,16,618	1,40,742	75,876	1,555	51,326	9,49,176	
(Actuals) ...	(2,07,422)						
1868-69 ...	2,23,512	1,37,790	85,722	1,462	51,100	9,84,685	
(Actuals) ...	(2,10,083)						
1869-70 ...	2,03,002	1,41,133	61,869	1,128	43,486	9,98,818	
1870-71 ...	2,21,048	1,40,605	80,443	1,087	43,080	10,18,640	
1871-72 ...	2,11,454	1,42,816	68,638	1,057	44,429	10,60,525	
1872-73 ...	2,19,776	1,58,205	61,571	1,042	45,178§	12,56,919	§ Number of agriculturists reduced to 39,293.
1873-74 ...	2,12,906	1,61,814	51,092	1,148	52,511	11,41,606‖	‖ Next year stated as Rs. 12,77,435.
1874-75 ...	(doubtful) 2,58,829	1,89,937	69,092	1,218	59,984	14,07,286	
1875-76 ...	2,15,359	2,15,359	See detailed statt.	1,218	61,131	14,51,161	
1876-77 ...	2,08,222	See statement	,,	1,264	57,972	14,57,552	
1877-78 ...	2,11,140	,,	,,	1,215	57,829	14,44,512	
1878-79 ...	2,15,046	,,	,,	1,210	54,065	13,69,146	
1879-80 ...	2,33,479	,,	,,	1,295	62,649	13,41,118	
1880-81 ...	2,25,716	,,	,,	1,284	64,564	13,92,534	
Total ...	56,37,136(a)	27,92,098	15,62,424	......	......	2,26,96,663	

(a) From the total income of Rs. 56,37,136 (all of which was spent) it, therefore, appears that Rs. 4,74,947 represented the difference between the yearly income of the cess and the amount spent from previous accumulations during nine years, *viz.*, from 1860-61 to 1868-69, after which no accumulation was left from the cess, the yearly income from which, however, continued in a large measure to be applied to purposes for which it had not been raised.

The following table may give an indication of the manner in which the above amount has been arrived at :—

	Rs.
1860-61.	
Amount spent from cess as per report	2,29,101
Amount derived from the cess of that year, as per Director's memorandum of February 1868	1,89,970
Difference	39,131
1861-62.	
Amount spent from cess	2,84,979
Amount raised that year	2,04,943
Difference	80,036
1862-63.	
Amount spent from cess	3,25,867
Amount raised that year	2,08,908
Difference	1,16,959
1863-64.	
Amount spent from cess	3,01,089
Amount raised that year	2,10,000
Difference	91,089
1864-65.	
Amount spent from cess	2,75,513
Amount raised that year	2,10,000
Difference	65,513
1865-66.	
Amount spent from cess	2,31,491
Amount raised that year	2,10,000
Difference	21,491
1866-67.	
Amount spent from cess	2,50,813
Amount raised that year	2,12,710
Difference	38,103
1867-68.	
Amount spent from cess	2,16,618
Amount raised that year	2,07,422
Difference	9,196
1868-69.	
Amount spent from cess	2,23,512
Amount raised that year	2,10,083
Difference	13,429
Total difference between amount spent and amount raised from cess from 1860-61 to 1868-69	4,74,947

The difference in each year is as follows :—

	Rs.	
1860-61	39,131	as above.
1861-62	80,036	„
1862-63	1,16,959	„
1863-64	91,089	„
1864-65	65,513	„
1865-66	21,491	„
1 66-67	38,103	„
1867-68	9,196	„
1868-69	13,429	„
Total ...	4,74,974	

STATEMENT II (*a*)—*Indigenous Schools.*

In 1866-67 " indigenous schools " re-appear in the statements annexed to reports. Rs. 400 if so much, were spent that year by Government on 5,434 ascertained indigenous schools having 41,619 pupils, alleged to have been brought under inspection.

In 1867-68, 4,955 indigenous schools, containing 48,653 pupils, were alleged to have been brought under inspection, on which Government was alleged to have spent Rs. 3,596, the probability being that at least 1,898 Rs. of that sum were spent on Mission branch and female schools, as in the previous year.

1868-69.—83 indigenous schools out of 5,222 are shown to be "aided" that year at a cost to Government of Rs. 7,981. Enquiry will show how few of these "aided" schools were really indigenous : 58,454 pupils are alleged to have attended these 5,222 indigenous schools.

1869-70.—60 indigenous schools, out of 4,055, were shown as aided, at a cost to Government of Rs. 7,184. Enquiry will show that very few out of these 60 schools were really indigenous schools : 54,309 pupils are stated to have attended the indigenous schools in the Panjab that year. Between 1866-67 and 1878-79 the following sums were spent by Government on so-called indigenous schools, by far the larger proportion of which were Mission and branch schools.

	Rs.
1866-67	2,298
1867-68	3,596
1868-69	7,981
1869-70	7,184
1870-71	1,010
1871-72	987
1872-73	0
1873-74	40
1874-75	9
1875-76	179
1876-77	2,327
1877-78	608
1878-79	1,625
1879-80 (No returns)	...
Total ...	29,835

Considering that nothing was spent on independent indigenous schools from almost the commencement of the Educational Department in 1856-57 (the schools that were absorbed into the Department and deprived of their characteristic features obviously not counting, or, if counted, being a charge on the village school cess), it appears that, from a total expenditure on education of nearly 227 lakhs of rupees, Government (or rather the Department) only spent Rs. 29,835 on indigenous schools, of which the great majority were not indigenous schools at all. Out of an expenditure from the village cess on all sorts of purposes of over 56 lakhs scarcely a seven-thousandth part was spent on indigenous schools, even in name.

STATEMENT II (*b*)—*Statistics regarding Indigenous Schools compared with Government vernacular Primary schools*

Years.	Number of indigenous schools.	Number of "indigenous" pupils.	No. of Government "village" or "lower" or "primary" vernacular schools and number of their pupils.
1856-57	5,024	30,196	456 schools with 6,064 pupils.
1857-58	3,461	26,317	1,336 „ 12,024 „
1858-59	6,173	82,023	2,029 „ 26,377 „
1859-60	6,309	63,090	1,704 „ 37,000 „
1860-61	6,559	82,267	1,686 „ 32,165 „
1861-62	...	...	1,750 „ 38,849 „
1862-63	...	...	1,807 „ 46,559 „
1863-64	...	...	1,807 „ 51,753 „
1864-65	...	...	1,745 „ 52,917 „
1865-66	...	...	1,746 „ 55,593 „
1866-67	5,434	33,063	1,660 „ 53,757 „
1867-68	4,888	46,947	1,555 „ 51,326 „
1868-69	5,222	55,454	1,462 „ 51,100 „
1869-70	3,995	52,479	1,128 „ 43,486 „
1870-71	4,133	50,551	1,087 „ 43,080 „
1871-72	4,292	54,612	1,057 „ 44,429 „
1872-73	4,154	48,771	1,042 „ 45,178 „
1873-74	4,463	54,445	1,148 „ 52,511 „
1874-75	...	No returns	1,218 „ 59,984 „
1875-76	4,406	48,697	1,218 „ 61,131 „
1876-77	4,803	56,642	1,264 „ 57,972 „
1877-78	5,381	61,818	1,285 „ 57,829 „
1878-79	4,662	53,027	1,210 „ 54,065 „
1897-80	...	No returns	1,295 „ 62,649 „
1880-81	...	...	1,284 „ 64,564 „
1881-82	...	...	...
1882-83	...	...	...

STATEMENT II (*c*) (from 1870-71 to 1881-82).

***Showing** the admitted number of pupils in Indigenous Schools since 1870-71, and their expenditure, together with the amount of the Village School Cess and the contribution from the Provincial Revenues to the Educational Department of the Panjab, as also the amount contributed by that Department to Indigenous Schools.*

Year.	Number of pupils in admitted indigenous schools.	Private expenditure of admitted indigenous schools.	Contribution of Government to indigenous schools.	Village school cess.	Contribution to education from imperial or provincial revenues.	Remarks.
		Rs.	Rs A. P.	Rs.	Rs.	
1870-71 ...	50,551	63,004	1,010 0 0	1,84,054	6,27,641	
1871-72 ...	54,612	66,614	987 6 4*	1,86,391, elsewhere 2,11,454	6,16,854	* The table gives the impression that 25 of these schools were aided; but it appears that this aid, amounting to Rs. 1,233-7-9, was from "*private*" sources.
1872-73 ...	48,771	59,123	The expenditure from both educational cess and local rate is given as Rs 2,11,454.†	Not separately entered.	8,23,716	† This corresponds with educational cess of 1871-72.
1873-74 ...	54,445	65,218	40 0 0	2,66,293‡	6,12,157	‡ This is now entered under the heads of Local Rates or Cesses, although there can be no doubt that by far the greater bulk of this amount was received from the village school cess.
1874-75 ...	No statement to be found in this year's report, except in Form B2 under the head of Unaided Institutions under Inspection, under which no entry is made.	...	...	3,50,085§	7,67,825	§ Ditto ditto ditto.
1875-76 ...	48,697	49,317	179 0 0	4,12,772	7,34,989	Ditto ditto ditto.
1876-77 ...	56,642	49,157	2,327 0 0	4,33,898	7,18,301	Ditto ditto ditto.
1877-78 ...	61,818	42,022	608 0 0	4,17,209	6,86,558	Ditto ditto ditto.
1878-79 ...	53,027	40,160	1,625 0 0	3,45,038	6,91,153	Ditto ditto ditto.
1879-80 ...	No statement furnished ...	...	...	3,86,993 To this should be added Rs. 2,718, spent on aided schools.	5,58,522 Elsewhere entered as Rs. 5,59,964.	Ditto ditto ditto. Colonel Holroyd has carried his proposal with the Government of India as regards statistical returns which excluded indigenous schools, and also tended to exclude oriental colleges, although both kinds of institutions exist in other provinces, *e.g.*, Bengal and the North-Western Provinces.
1880-81 ...	No returns ...	...	...	3,83,482 To this should be added Rs. 2,545, spent on aided schools from that source.	5,84,417	It would be well to ascertain how much of the amount of Rs. 3,86,027 levied under the head of Local Rates or Cesses belongs to the village school cess, and how much of that amount has been spent on village schools and indigenous schools.
1881-82(*a*) ...	? ...	? ...	? ...	...	...	

(*a*) A detailed statement of the expenditure of this year, amounting to nearly 16 lakhs, is separately annexed.

STATEMENT III (from 1860-61 to 1880-1881).

Instances of the misapplication of the Village School Cess.

(A portion of this Statement up to the year 1869-70 has already been printe Lei tner's evidence before the Commission.)

In 1860-61 (see Review of Government on Educational Report) the total expenditure for the year was Rs. 4,18,510, "of which Rs. 2,29,101 were derived from the one per cent. cess on the land revenue paid by the agriculturists, and only Rs. 1,48,510 from the general revenues of Government." Of Rs. 2,29,101 levied by the one per cent. village school cess, only Rs. 1,24,772 were spent on village schools, and over a lakh of rupees was misapplied to the following purposes:—

Rs. 8,544 were spent on zillah school-houses. Seven tahsili or town schools were built from the village school cess.

Rs. 32,764 were spent on tahsili schools, Rs. 605 on female schools (quite a special expenditure), Rs. 20,059 on normal schools, whilst as large a sum as Rs. 39,624 were spent on the general establishment and other charges of the Educational Department.

In spite of this improper expenditure there was still an excess of Rs. 13,691 of receipts from the cess, over charges emphatically payable from general funds.

This unfortunate cess had also to bear *Rs. 5,925 gratuities to dismissed officials, Rs. 1,815 cost of tents purchased for Director's and Inspector's offices, and Rs. 26,505 for contingencies and books, of which Rs. 10,500 were paid as an advance for their purchase* (*vide* Statement No. 17, and paragraph 52 of Director's Report of that year). Major Fuller was then the Director of Public Instruction, Panjab. See Secretary of State's despatch of 1859 excluding, for the future, military men and civilians from such appointments *practically* reserved for purely educational officers.

In 1861-62 *Rs. 2,84,979* were derived from the village cess fund in a total expenditure for that year of Rs. 5,11,287. Of this sum Rs. 20,848 were spent on the salaries and contingencies of the general establishment of the Educational Department (*vide* Table 17 of that Report).

Rs. 2,801 were given to superior zillah schools, Rs. 54,977 to tahsili schools. Rs. 3,170 to female schools, chiefly in cities, and Rs. 21,880 to normal schools, thus leaving Rs. 1,81,300 for village schools, leaving again over a lakh of rupees misapplied to other purposes. But even of the amount spent on village schools a large portion was wasted, for Rs. 73,864 were spent on building tahsili and village school-houses. Formerly the village schools were attached to, or held in the courtyards of, mosques and other sacred edifices, whereby the reverence of the pupils for education was increased, and the very best buildings which, as a rule, the various localities could offer were already devoted to the accommodation of schools, not to speak of the importance of not ruining these indigenous schools by taking away their pupils to other buildings in the same places.

The above strictures appear all the more deserved when it is remembered that Rs. 20,848 were taken from the one per cent. village school cess to pay the office establishment and travelling allowance of Directors and Inspectors, the Curator's Office and the book depôt (*vide* paragraphs 8 and 42 of Director's Report for the above year).

1862-63.—The village school cess fund of that year amounted to Rs. 3,25,867, out of a total expenditure of Rs. 7,23,077. Of the village cess Rs. 20,933 were spent on the general establishment as already detailed; 991 vernacular school-houses were built at a cost of Rs. 1,38,753* from the cess; Rs. 2,012 were spent on zillah schools; Rs. 19,402 on normal schools; Rs. 17,088 on town schools; Rs. 5,866 on female schools—(*vide* paragraph 9 of the Report of that year).

1863-64.—The village school cess fund of that year amounted to Rs. 301,089, of which Rs. 23,497 were given to the general establishment; Rs. 19,720 to normal schools; Rs. 20,676 to town schools; Rs. 14,709 to female schools; Rs. 67 to jail schools; and Rs. 60,335 for buildings. Only Rs. 1,62,087 were spent on village schools, leaving Rs. 1,39,000 misappropriated (*vide* paragraph 12 of Report).

1864-65 (see paragraph 12 of Report and paragraph 3 of Panjab Government Review thereon).—The village school cess fund amounted to Rs. 2,75,513, of which Rs. 19,636 were paid to the general establishment; Rs. 7,849 were paid to town schools; Rs. 5,465 to zillah schools; Rs. 18,761 to female schools; Rs. 75 to jail schools; Rs. 19,884 to Government normal schools; and Rs. 41,838 on educational buildings generally†. The Panjab Government remark on the complaint of the Director that "the educational cess fund is burdened with charges which do not properly belong to it," that the application of that fund to objects not strictly appertaining to it is a matter for which the Supreme Government was not responsible.

1865-66.—The village school cess fund amounted to Rs. 2,31,491. Of this only Rs. 11,514 were spent on the general establishment, as the fund was gradually getting exhausted, and Government had to come to the rescue with Rs. 24,000 for the Book Depôt, and Rs. 17,220 for chief school muharrirs. However, Rs. 7,658 were still spent on zillah

* Of which Rs. 1,08,077 were from the village cess. Only Rs. 1,52,494 were spent on village schools, thus leaving a balance of Rs. 1,73,373 misapplied from that cess during that year.

† Only Rs. 1,62,004 were spent on village schools that year, and Rs. 1,13,508 were misapplied.

schools; Rs. 10,750 on town schools; Rs. 13,619 on Government female schools, as well as Rs. 2,889 actually on *aided* female schools—an application which surely was never contemplated as a part of the grant-in-aid itself; Rs. 16,071 were spent on Government normal schools; and Rs. 25,000 on educational buildings. It must, however, be noted that Rs. 10,000 spent from the cess on Government female schools were subsequently refunded from Imperial revenues, a precedent which might well be followed as regards all sums improperly taken from that fund. Only Rs. 1,43,977 were spent that year on village schools, or about Rs. 18,000 less than the previous year, leaving for the first time a sum below one lakh of rupees misapplied to other purchases, namely, Rs. 78,494 (*vide* paragraph 6 of Director's Report of that year). It also deserves notice that the returns only show three small *indigenous* village schools, one of which was abolished, although by article 14 of the revised Code of the Grant-in-Aid Regulation it was hoped that Government aid would in future be extended to good indigenous schools, of which hundreds existed, and had the very first claim to the educational cess.

1866-67.—The village school cess fund rose to Rs. 2,50,813 from the amount of the previous year. Of this Rs. 11,413 were spent on the general establishment; Rs. 8,523 on zillah schools; Rs. 15,125 on town schools; Rs. 13,035 on Government female schools; Rs. 16,775 on Government normal schools; Rs. 46,602 on educational buildings generally; and *nothing* to indigenous schools. As only Rs. 1,39,326 were spent on village schools, Rs. 1,10,484 were again misapplied that year. Government desiring the collection of statistics regarding indigenous schools, the opportunity is taken to suggest an addition to the number of Deputy Inspectors as a pressing necessity. But the indigenous schools are practically still as unknown as they are uninspected. However, we find that the preliminary attempt of collecting statistics that year regarding indigenous schools gave a total of Rs. 41,619 pupils taught at an expenditure of Rs. 81,093. I believe it is on these admittedly imperfect statistics of the year 1866-67 that all subsequent statistics have been practically based. The grant to them by Government is shown as Rs. 2,298; but on enquiry it appears that only Rs. 400, if so much, were really given to indigenous schools and female schools.

1867-68.—Captain Holroyd now becomes Director of Public Instruction, and indigenous schools are quietly dropped out of the Reports with the remark that few teachers of indigenous schools appear anxious to avail themselves of Government schools in the Panjab, where an education equal to that of a Government town school can be obtained. The number of pupils is reported to be 48,653, instructed at a cost of Rs. 1,05,033, which is alone sufficient to show how untrustworthy the returns, either of this year or of the previous year, must be. Government gave Rs. 3,586 to 67 of these schools. How far these schools were indigenous is explained further on. The village school cess that year had fallen to Rs. 2,16,618, or to over Rs. 34,000 less than the previous year—a circumstance which, as the Panjab Government remarks, is not explained in the Report. Rs. 3,622 were spent on the higher class of Government zillah schools, and Rs. 4,790 on Government middle zillah schools; Rs. 11,998 on Government town schools; Rs. 10,322 on female schools; Rs. 85 on jail schools; Rs. 5,164 on *aided* schools of the lower class; Rs. 17,665 on Government normal schools; Rs. 11,406 to the general establishment; and Rs. 10,824 on educational buildings. On village schools Rs. 1,40,742 were spent, leaving a misapplied balance of only Rs. 75,876.

1868-69.—Table 17, showing the proportioned expenditure from provincial and cess funds, respectively, is now omitted. In the table of indigenous schools we find the total of 58,454 pupils, educated at a cost of Rs. 1,04,759, of which Government paid Rs. 7,931, Rs. 3,550 of which were spent on Delhi alone. It is stated that 83 indigenous schools had been inspected, but it appears that among these were counted the lower departments of Government schools at Delhi and Lahore and the Mufidi-Am mission schools at Delhi. The Director now states that there are only two *bonâ fide* indigenous schools in the Panjab, where any attempt is made in imparting instruction in general knowledge through the vernacular, and that a very few teachers of indigenous schools desire to avail themselves of Government assistance (*vide* paragraphs 154-160 of the Report for that year).

The village school cess in 1868-69 amounted to Rs. 2,23,512, being a slight increase over the previous year. The Director applies for more money for a supervising agency when all that was required was to devote the whole of the cess to supporting more village schools, or rather indigenous schools. That year the total number of village schools was reduced by 93.

Of the educational cess, Rs. 4,487 were spent on high schools; Rs. 15,622 on middle schools; Rs. 9,454 on female schools; Rs. 15,410 on normal schools; Rs. 154 on jail schools; Rs. 245 on middle *aided* schools; Rs. 4,260 on lower *aided* schools; Rs. 12,129 to the general establishment; Rs. 23,962 on buildings; nothing from the cess, as in the previous year, on indigenous schools, which ought to be supported from that source, and not by special grants-in-aid. On *lower* schools a very unfortunate substitution for the previously unmistakeable designation of *village* schools, even less than in the previous year, was spent, namely, Rs. 1,37,790, leaving a misapplied balance of Rs. 85,722 for that year; the Government expenditure on education being Rs. 5,96,802. and 2,02,215 being paid from private sources and *local* funds—a very important addition, which will make it necessary in future returns to investigate accurately how much is derived from the village school cess and how much from other rates.

1869-70 begins with a statement (paragraph 3 of the Review by Government) referring to "the exhaustion of the savings from the education cess fund, out of which many village schools had been supported;" whereas in reality about half of the money received from the educational cess had never been applied to village schools in any sense of the word, and not at all to indigenous schools. Fortunately, Government did not comply with the Director's proposal "to force sensational results by the imposition of an additional education cess." Probably the results, considering the irritation already felt by the agricultural classes, would have been sensational in another than merely an educational sense. However, even in that year, Rs. 16,784 were spent on middle schools out of the cess; Rs. 7,038 on female schools; 16,081 on normal schools; Rs. 24 on jail schools; Rs. 298 on aided high schools; Rs. 108 on middle aided schools; whilst the general establishment could only get Rs. 5,084 out of the cess, and only Rs. 16,450 were spent on buildings; so that Rs. 1,41,133 could still be spent on the *lower* class schools, which probably included *other* than *purely* village schools, leaving a misapplied balance of only Rs. 61,869 for that year. As regards indigenous schools, the Director observes in paragraph 194 of his Report that there is no machinery in existence by means of which reliable information regarding the statistics of indigenous schools could be obtained. However, the table, at the end of this Report, No. 38, shows a total of 54,309 pupils in indigenous schools, educated at a cost of Rs. 92,256, of which Government paid Rs. 7,184. On enquiry, however, it is found that of this amount Rs. 3,340 were paid to the Delhi schools, the nature of which has already been explained, whilst I very much doubt whether more than Rs. 1,546 were paid that year to really indigenous schools, if, indeed, even that amount was devoted to that purpose.

1870-71.—There were 1,087 Government village schools (so called), the income from the educational cess was Rs. 2,21,048, of which Rs. 1,40,605 were spent on so-called village schools. Of the balance of Rs. 80,443, Rs. 3,000 were paid as half the salary of the Assistant Inspector and Inspectress of Female Schools of the Lahore Circle (Mr. and Mrs. Mackintosh). Rs. 1,591 were spent on high schools, Rs. 17,820 on middle schools, Rs. 6,624 on female schools, Rs. 17,411 on normal schools, of which only Rs. 4,619 seem to represent the cost on villagers sent to these schools. Nothing was spent on indigenous schools from the cess, Rs. 5,211 on general establishment, and Rs. 10,676 on buildings. There was actually a saving of over Rs. 18,000 from the cess, but this was not spent, even after satisfying a number of improper charges, on increasing the number of village schools in accordance with the "despatch." On the contrary, the number of village schools which had been so largely decreased in the previous year was still further reduced from 1,132 to 1,087, whilst the opportunity was taken to introduce the graded system from 1st April 1870 to the immediate advantage of the Inspectors and of the Director with retrospective effect.

1871-72.—The educational cess provided Rs. 2,11,454 to the expenditure of the Educational Department out of Rs. 2,16,337, there being thus an unexpended balance of the cess of nearly Rs. 5,000, which was not used in increasing the number of village schools. The Lieutenant-Governor was somewhat doubtful of the policy which had diminished the number of primary and lower class schools, and stated in his Review that:—

"*the object of the Government is rather to impart elementary instruction to the masses than complete education to a few.* The improvement of the *vernacular system* of education; *the increase in the number of primary schools*; the development, or rather the creation, of a vernacular literature; and the translation into languages known by the people of approved works,—these are the aims which the Government should set before it as the most useful and important."

Rs. 1,42,816 were spent on schools of the lower class, of which 1,057 were in towns and villages. Nearly Rs. 69,000, therefore, were spent that year on the usual items of misapplication, for which see paragraphs 3 and 4 of the Report for 1871-72. The Director, in addition to his annual increment in the grade in which he had been placed from 1st April 1870, also drew an excess of Rs. 3,437, as if he had been in that grade since his appointment. As usual, half the salary of the Inspectress of Female Schools and of the Assistant Inspector of Lahore was paid from the cess.

1872-73.—In this Report the confusion between the educational cess and the local rate begins; and it is, moreover, distinctly stated, in the first paragraph of Director's Report (Mr. Pearson), that the *distinction between local and provincial revenue was not maintained in the account of expenditure.* This is accordingly done in the 2nd paragraph, where the amount of expenditure on vernacular schools is stated to be Rs. 2,19,776, which is precisely the same amount as the educational cess for that year; thus leaving it to be implied that the educational cess was almost wholly spent on the object of the village cess. This is, however, not at all the case, for, in the first paragraph of the Review of Government on the Report, we find that the amount spent on Government schools of "lower class," which included English as well as vernacular schools, was only Rs. 17,164, thus leaving about Rs. 48,000 out of the cess practically unaccounted for. In tables 18 and 19 annexed to the Report, we find the total of primary Government schools put down as 1,042, on which Rs. 1,58,205 is shown as having been expended from what is rather comprehensively called the *"public funds," whilst the column from the educational cess is left a complete blank,* although, as shown elsewhere, some sort of account was still kept up of that cess—see also paragraph 25 of the same report. It seems to me to be clear from an investigation of the accounts as submitted for that year that the amount of misapplication from the village cess was over Rs. 60,000, and not Rs. 48,000, as would appear at first glance. We now get the number of agriculturists attending schools (*vide* paragraph 26 of Report), but we are not told how many of them belong to towns, so that one is unable to ascertain the number of schools and of scholars in villages paying the educational cess, and thus to ascertain exactly how much of the village cess is really spent on schools situated in villages. Considering that there are 329 towns possessing more than 5,000 inhabitants, there would seem to be little more than 700 schools in villages and towns possessing less than 5,000 inhabitants. The number of agriculturists, however, attending school is returned at 39,293, and as the educational cess was Rs. 2,21,592, the cost of education of each was about Rs. 5·8 per annum, which, as it was paid by the villagers' cess, was practically a fee to that amount, no inconsiderable sum, if the poverty of these tax-payers is considered. In contrast to this excessive expenditure Table 38 appended to the report shows 4,154 indigenous schools attended by 48,771 pupils and costing only Rs. 59,123, or little more than a rupee on each student.

1873-74.—The designation "educational cess" which had supplanted the more correct appellation "village cess," now vanishes from the Report altogether, just as the term "village schools" had to make way for the more comprehensive term "schools of a lower class" or "primary schools," making it difficult to ascertain the amount of the educational cess and what is spent from it on its own legitimate purpose. We have now a division in expenditure between "general local fund" and "district funds," and under the head of District Funds we find an expenditure of Rs. 1,61,814 from district funds spent on 1,148 primary Government schools, a petty increase on which the Director congratulates himself in paragraph 21 of the Report, stating that "amongst the agricultural class our schools steadily advance in popularity." As, however, the educational cess of that year amounted to Rs. 2,12,906, over Rs. 50,000 at least must have been misapplied, even if all the primary schools had been village schools.

1874-75.—There were 1,218 "primary schools," on which Rs. 1,80,937 were spent from "district funds" (and nothing, of course, from "general local funds," and only Rs. 6,600 from provincial services). It seems, however, that the educational cess amounted to Rs. 2,58,829, but this is doubtful. All we know is that an assignment of Rs. 3,29,397 was made from "district funds," into which the educational cess had been merged.

1875-76.—There were 1,218 primary Government schools. In another place we have the number of "lower and primary schools" put down at 1,298. The classification changes for the worse, as the tables are no longer as comprehensive as they were before or show the same things in the same places. However, in Table B, Education Form 3, we have the cost of Government primary schools put down as Rs. 2,15,359 as "from local rates or cesses," being probably the exact amount of the educational or village cess for that year. The entry "district funds" has also vanished. Thus, the "village cess" became "educational cess," and the expenditure from it was shown; then, the expenditure from it was not shown; then, the name was dropped and we had "district funds." Finally, this was also discontinued, and we now have "local rates or cesses."

1876-77.—The number of Government primary schools is returned at 1,264 (elsewhere at 1,217) costing from district funds Rs. 2,08,222 (a term again revived), whilst the "general local funds" only give 5,110 for the same purpose). The object is now to show that, if anything, the whole of the village cess is spent on village schools; but this cannot be the case, as, even if there were a thousand village schools and each cost Rs. 15 per mensem, whereas the bulk only receive Rs. 10, the annual cost could not be more than Rs. 1,80,000, as I believe the cess is returned at Rs. 2,25,000. It is clear that the whole cess is not spent on village schools, even including every town under 5,000 inhabitants, an amplification of the term "village," which, I submit, the orders of the Government regarding the application of the village cess never contemplated. As, however, there are scarcely 20 "village schools" in the province at Rs. 20 per mensem, and the bulk is at Rs. 10, an average of Rs. 12 per mensem would be nearer the mark for the supposed maximum of 1,000 village schools, so that not more than Rs. 1,44,000 can be annually expended from the cess on village schools, leaving about Rs. 81,000 still spent on other purposes. I submit, however, that it is not satisfactory to be given accounts regarding the expenditure on primary education in which one is compelled to have recourse to calculations which are not furnished by the returns themselves.

1877-78.—On pages 24 and 25 of the Appendices to the Report for that year we have the number of Government primary schools put down at 1,215, at a cost to the "district funds" of Rs. 2,11,140.

1878-79.—The total of "Government primary schools" is put down at 1,210, costing Rs. 2,15,046 from "district funds;" notice that the schools slightly decrease and that the cost is somewhat greater.

1879-80.—The statistical tables again change, but in subsidiary Form No. 4 we find the grand total of "primary Government vernacular schools" to be 1,295. The heading "district funds" is again omitted, and these schools are supposed to be supported from the former, occasionally meagre, heading of Local Rates and Cesses, which now give these schools Rs. 2,33,479, or rather *more* than the educational cess, which cannot be the case, as I have shown in my remarks regarding the returns of the year 1876-77, and which also apply to subsequent years.

1880-81.—The total number of "Government vernacular primary schools" is returned at 1,284, costing Rs. 2,25,716 from the convenient heading of "Local Rates or Cesses" and receiving the magnificent contribution of Rs. 991 from the provincial revenues, whilst municipalities contribute Rs. 22,335. This latter item seems to me to be significant, because, as municipalities spend Rs. 51,660 per annum on their schools, and as, at least, 195 primary schools are situated in municipalities, the difference between the above sum of Rs. 51,060 and the sum of Rs. 22,335, supposed to be contributed to primary schools, namely, Rs. 28,725, seems to me to represent the sum taken by these municipalities out of the village cess for their own schools.

STATEMENT IV.

Showing some of the principal items of expenditure in the year 1881-82.

	Rs.	A.	P.
(*a*) Government College ... (exclusive of Rs. 12,655 for scholarships).	47,902	0	0
(*b*) Training College* ... (this is not required at all, as shown elsewhere).	24,236	0	0
(*c*) Direction ...	42,452	0	0
(*d*) Inspection ... (of this sum Rs. 42,000 are spent on four Inspectors, three of whom are rising to higher grades).	1,27,186	0	0
(*e*) Scholarships in colleges ...	12,655	0	0
(*f*) " " schools ... (of which Rs. 49,256 are spent on *Government* schools and Rs. 7,375 are supposed to be spent on *aided* schools).	56,631	0	0
(*g*) The total expenditure on *English high* schools is ...	2,53,196	0	0
(*h*) And on *Vernacular high* schools ... (these are not required at all, as there is the Oriental College).	57,238	0	0
Primary English schools ... (the number of these schools ought to have been given in an extra column in the same table).	1,72,537	0	0
(*i*) On schools for Europeans ...	26,016	0	0
(*j*) Primary vernacular schools of all kinds ... (of which Rs. 2,32,801 are supplied by local rates and cesses, and only Rs. 24,058 by municipal grants, although the majority of these schools are in towns and are tahsili schools) (the number of town and village schools, respectively, ought to have been mentioned), whilst from provincial revenues only Rs. 1,733 are given to primary vernacular schools).	2,78,833	0	0
(*k*) Of the scholarships in aided institutions, only Rs. 1,562 are given from provincial revenues, Rs. 988 from local rates, and Rs. 391 from municipal grants. Enquire whether the balance of Rs. 7,375, shown as "scholarships in aided schools," is a portion of their grant.			
The average cost—			
Of educating a Government college student is nearly per annum ... (exclusive of Rs. 12,655 per annum for scholarships on 103 students.)	499	0	0
Of a training college student ...	449	0	0
Of an English high school student ...	70	0	0
Of a vernacular high school student ...	19	14	7
Of a primary English student ...	7	13	6
Of a primary vernacular student... (which, in the form of a grant-in-aid, would be nearly enough to keep a whole *school*).	4	2	2
(*l*) Under *Miscellaneous* we find a cost of Rs. 77,105; this is rather a large item to put under this head. Does this include the unnecessary Book Depôt, which *one* bookseller, assisted by a clerk, would gladly undertake on commission?			
A pupil in the School of Art, which is a mere school of carpentry and drawing, costs the relatively enormous sum of ... per annum, whilst if that school merely worked in connection with existing trades the cost per pupil could not exceed *one-tenth* of that amount.	322	14	10
The total expenditure from provincial revenues on education is ...	6,41,701	0	0
The total expenditure on education is ...	15,95,665	0	0

(This does not include Rs. 41,880 spent by the Panjab University out of its own funds on education, in addition to the Government grant of Rs. 28,000 during the calendar year 1881.)

---

* See Report for 1880-81 as regards the work which this institution is intended to do, and which can easily be done in the existing normal schools for the lower standards, and in the Government College, Lahore, for the higher standards, without any extra cost whatever, or in the Oriental College if the Lahore College is not to be maintained.

CHAPTER C.

Branches of the Educational Despatches of the Secretary of State and of the forwarding orders of the Supreme Government, by the Punjab Educational Department.

THE Educational despatches of the Secretary of State of 1854 and 1859 have not been carried out in the following particulars :—

DESPATCH OF *1854, paragraph 9.*—The Department has *not* secured the assistance of the learned classes of India who pay hereditary veneration to the ancient classical languages in the spread of education which is considered to be so valuable from the honourable and influential position which they occupy among their fellow-countrymen. (See also paragraphs 49 and 51.)

21. In the selection of educational officers sufficient regard has *not* been paid to the requirement that they should possess the confidence of the Natives of India. (*Vide* also paragraph 56.)

41. Useful and practical knowledge, suited to every station in life, has *not* been conveyed to the great mass of people, for which purpose Government was prepared to sanction a considerable increase of expenditure, making no difference between vernacular and anglo-vernacular schools of the same class (paragraph 44).

46. Indigenous schools have *not* been made capable of imparting correct elementary knowledge to the great mass of the people, nor have their most promising pupils been rewarded by scholarships, nor have they been placed under efficient inspection (paragraph 47).

57. The principles of the grant-in-aid have *not* been clearly and publicly placed before the Natives of India, nor has it been distinctly stated that schools of all denominations would be admissible to the grant irrespective of their religious teaching. (See also paragraphs 34 and 28.)

60. A more minute and constant local supervision than for the general system of grant-in-aid has *not* been given to indigenous schools.

61. Government colleges or schools *have* been founded in districts where institutions exist capable, with the aid of Government, of supplying the local demand for education.

62. The opportunities of transferring Government to grant-in-aid institutions have *not* been taken.

63. Scholarships have *not* been given to both Government aided and indigenous schools.

64 & 65. The existing Government scholarships have *not* been reduced in colleges, nor have they been devoted till quite recently to young men preparing for the scholastic profession. (*Vide* also paragraph 68.)

69. The indigenous schools have *not* been encouraged, the teachers in possession have *not* been improved, the hostility of this class of persons whose influence is so great over the minds of the lower classes *has* been provoked, and they *have* been superseded where it was possible to avoid it.

70. Vernacular primers and readers have *not* been advertised for public competition, and have *not* been liberally rewarded, but the Department has *written, approved, printed, published, sold* and *introduced* its own books in its own schools, this being the only great market for them in the province.

71. The oriental colleges have *not* been encouraged by the Department in this work of translation.

72 to 76. (See Index to Despatch). University degrees are *not* the passport to employment.

77 to 78. (See Index). The Native mind has *not* been directed beyond mere Government employ to wider and more important spheres of usefulness among their countrymen.

89, 92 and 93. The example of other Provinces has been admittedly *not* studied, and it is doubtful whether any officer on his appointment was ever directed to read the despatches as an indication of the policy which he was bound to carry out. The end of paragraph 93 distinctly refers to some such system, "as the model by which the efforts of other presidencies for the same object should be guided."

DESPATCH OF *1859, paragraph 3.*—Increased attention has *not* been paid to the indigenous schools already existing throughout the country, and Muhammadan and Hindu religions schools giving a good secular education have *not* been encouraged.

5 & 41. The Directors of Public Instruction, if military men, have *not* retired from the Army immediately on their appointment, but have, on the contrary, risen from the grade of Lieutenant to that of Colonel,—to the great confusion of their speciality.

16. Masters of indigenous schools have *not* been encouraged to adopt improved methods of teaching. See also paragraph 15, in which vernacular education is placed on a level, in point of importance, with that of the instruction to be afforded through the medium of English.

19. The existing schools are generally more than two miles apart. The Government has *not* paid half of the 1 per cent. educational cess, nor has it been levied in part abatement of other demands, nor has the whole of the village school cess been devoted to schools situated in villages, as appears to have been done in the North-Western Provinces.

21. The principle of encouraging indigenous schools by periodical inspection and rewards, as in the North-West, nor that of an itinerant teacher to instruct village schoolmasters, as in Bengal, has *not* been followed in the Punjab.

34. The notifications regarding grants to all denominations were again *not* promulgated as intended to the people concerned.

40. The cost on managing the Department *is* properly susceptible of reduction, as it still bears 35 per cent. on the provincial allotment to education.

41. The *preferential* nomination for the higher officers in the Department of professional educationists has *not* always been carried out in practice.

49, 50, 51, 52 and 53. The support of vernacular schools is made a charge to Government, and not to the grant-in-aid, which in paragraph 54 is specially applied to English and anglo-vernacular schools.

64. No "report, as far as practical," has been given regarding the number and character of schools unconnected with Government control. (*Vide* Extracts from Reports of the Department of Public Instruction, Panjab, and the reviews thereon by Government during 1856-57 to 1880-81.)

48. "It is most important to make the greatest possible use of existing schools and of the masters to whom, however inefficient as teachers, the people have been accustomed to look up with respect." This has *not* been done.

50. "The means of elementary education should be provided by the direct instrumentality of the officers of education." This has *not* been done in the sense of the despatch. The work has been done by District Officers. That the Government of India and the Local Governments understood these despatches in the sense which I have mentioned may be inferred from the reports on education which accompanied the despatches, *vide* paragraphs 3 to 16 of Bengal Report of the 19th October 1860 on the grant-in-aid question, and paragraphs 4, 5, 6, 7, 8, 9, 10, 11, 12 and 16, and other Reports, too numerous to mention, which were all supplied to the Education Officers of the Panjab, but which appear not to have been read, and certainly not to have been attended to, whilst some of its main principles have been opposed by some of the higher officers of the Department. In the Panjab report acknowledging the despatch, the number of indigenous schools is stated to be 6,559, said to be attended by 82,267 pupils, whilst "*for the inspection of village schools only,*" there were 38 extra Sub-Deputy Inspectors, an arrangement which, if given a proper chance, would have been more beneficial than a smaller number of better paid chief maharrirs.

Extract from the Proceedings of the Right Hon'ble the Governor General of India in Council, in the Home Department (Educational), under date 11*th June* 1859 *(communicating the Despatch of* 1859 *to the Local Governments).*

6. General approval is expressed of the present English and anglo-vernacular schools, but it is intimated that the extension and maintenance of schools of this class ought, as a general rule, to be effected under the grant-in-aid system. The Governor General in Council desires that this intimation may be at once acted upon in the Lower Provinces of Bengal, so far as that no fresh schools of this class shall be founded unless supported in part by local subscription in conformity with the requirements of the grant-in-aid rules for the time being, and His Excellency in Council also desires that the other Local Governments may be called upon to report whether a similar rule may not be introduced in their several jurisdictions.

Paragraphs 48 to 53.

7. It is remarked by the Secretary of State that no general plan of popular education has been definitively adopted in any part of India, except in the North-Western Provinces, and a decisive opinion is expressed, in which the Governor General in Council entirely concurs, that this important branch of education must be effected by means altogether independent of the grant-in-aid rules, and it is added that "the means of elementary education should be provided by the direct instrumentality of the officers of Government according to some one of the plans in operation in Bengal or the North-Western Provinces, or by such a modification of those schemes as may commend itself to the several Local Governments as best suited to the circumstances of different localities."

To provide means for the measures to be thus undertaken for the education of the people, the expediency of imposing a special rate to defray the expense of schools for the rural population is suggested.

His Excellency the Governor General in Council commends this most important question to the careful consideration of the Local Governments, and desires that each Government will report definitively the measures which it desires to adopt for the elementary education of the people, and the means by which it is considered that the requisite funds may be obtained.

CHAPTER D.

Official Documents connected with the raising of the Village School Cess.

[NOTE.—The italics throughout these documents are almost always mine.—G. W. L.]

(*A*).—*From the Financial Commissioner of the Punjab, to the Secretary to the Chief Commissioner of the Punjab, No.* 384, *dated* 18*th December* 1854.

With reference to the circular of the Sudder Board of Revenue, North-Western Provinces, No. 15, dated 5th current, and published in the *Agra Government Gazette* of the 12th idem, in which it is directed, in conformity with the instructions received from the Government, North-Western Provinces, that on all future occasions of a new settlement or revision of settlement engagements be taken for the payment of 1 per cent. upon the *juma* as a cess *for village schools,* in the same manner as has been hitherto the practice in the case of the road fund, I have the honor to solicit permission to issue corresponding instructions for these Provinces.

From the Secretary to the Chief Commissioner of the Punjab, to the Financial Commissioner, Punjab, No. 1084, *dated* 28*th December* 1854.

I am directed to acknowledge the receipt of your letter No. 384, dated the 18th instant, and in reply to convey the sanction of the Chief Commissioner to your proposal to issue instructions similar to those promulgated by the Sudder Board of Revenue, North-Western Provinces, in their Circular No. 15, dated the 5th current, that on all future occasions of a new settlement or revision of settlement engagements be taken for the payment of 1 *per cent. upon the juma as a cess for village schools.*

Order by the Sudder Board of Revenue, North-Western Provinces, dated Agra, 5th December 1854.

CIRCULAR No. 15.

To all Revenue Authorities.

The following instructions received from Government, on the subject of the levy of the road fund, and *village* school cess, of one per cent. for each, are promulgated for the information and guidance of all settlement and revenue officers.

2. On the occasion of every new settlement, a revision of settlement engagements will be taken for the payment of one per cent. on the jama, *as a cess for village schools,* in the same manner as has hitherto been the practice with the road fund.

3. In muafi estates, of which a sub-settlement may be made with proprietors in behalf of the muafidar, *the payment of these cesses should be a condition* of the engagement taken from the proprietors.

4. The levy of the cesses should be made through the Tahsildar from proprietors; the amount being carefully entered in the engagement as additional land revenue, payable separately to the Tahsildar, and leviable under the ordinary rules applicable to arrears of such revenue, though to be appropriated by the Government, on receipt, to specific beneficial purposes. The muafidar, becoming proprietor, will, of course, succeed to the same obligations as the former proprietor when sub-lessee.

5. In the settlement of detached parcels lapsed or *resumed,* the jamas of which are incorporated with those of the estates to which they belong, these cesses should be paid by the parcel-holder to the proprietor, and by the proprietor to the Government, and the engagements taken accordingly from each of the parties.

6. Where a mukurrareedar or an obareedar holds direct, the percentage will be calculated only by the amount of his quit rent or mukarraree or obaree jama. Where a sub-settlement is made with proprietors on behalf of a mukarrareedar or an obareedar, they will come under the same rule as proprietors in sub-settlements on behalf of a muafidar.

(*B*).—*Circular from the Financial Commissioner of the Punjab to all Commissioners, No.* 4, *dated* 18*th January* 1855.

I have the honour to forward, for your information and guidance, and that of the District and Settlement Officers who are, or may be, employed in your Division, copies of the letters noted in the margin, from which you will perceive that, on all future occasions of renewal or revision of settlement, engagements are to be taken for the payment of 1 per cent. upon the jama *as a cess for village schools.*

2. The measure is so desirable a one and so well calculated to benefit the people themselves, that it seems of very great importance to render its introduction as general as possible; and I accordingly authorise you to extend it to existing settlements *wherever you may find that the people themselves are willing to agree to it.*

From the Commissioner and Superintendent, Cis-Sutlej States, to Financial Commissioner, No. 62, dated 19th March 1855.

With reference to your circular No. 4, dated 18th January, I have the honour to enclose copy of a letter No. 66, dated 12th instant, from the Deputy Commissioner, Ferozepore, proposing to deduct the one per cent. education fund from the jama.

2. I presume this arrangement cannot be allowed. If Government is to pay the charge, the simplest way is to pay the sum out of the General Treasury, instead of deducting it from the land revenue. Mr. Brandreth also proposes a reform in the manner of shewing the accounts; this would involve a radical change, which must be universal, if effected at all, and is a distinct question altogether.

3. I understand the drift of his letter. He has taken a large increase on the summary settlement, and is unwilling, even for so laudable purpose as education, to add more to the village burdens. Yet he is anxious to establish an education fund, and *proposes to deduct it from the jama raised already some twelve per cent. beyond the former demand.* This measure is exceptional and opposed to the principle of the scheme. I cannot recommend its adoption.

From Deputy Commissioner, Ferozepore, to Commissioner and Superintendent, Cis-Sutlej States, No. 66, dated 12th March 1855.

I have the honour to acknowledge the receipt of your circular No. 24, dated 30th ultimo, enquiring whether the zemindars of this district would generally agree to the introduction of a one per cent. fund for the provision of village schools. About a year ago several zemindars of Budnee and Maree spoke to me about the establishment of a dispensary at some convenient and central spot in the Moza Tahsil. They were evidently anxious for it and were prepared to contribute something towards it. A few months back the Tahsildar sent me a paper signed by all lumberdars of Talooquas Budnee and Maree, in which they proposed to contribute 1½ per cent. on the jamas of their respective villages for the establishment of a dispensary and schools. I have no doubt, therefore, though it is impossible to suppose, that an arrangement of this sort would be universally popular, yet that the proposed percentage would be generally agreed to and paid without grumbling. In the other tahsils, however, where the agriculturists are principally Mussulmans, I do not think, if they had an idea it was *optional* with them to refuse it, that they would give their consent to any such arrangement.

2. I should be unwilling, however, for my part, to take any increase on the jama of the Jut villages in the Moga Tahsil, which is already much higher than that of the summary settlement. I would propose to deduct the education fund from the jama of the whole district. It would not be necessary to alter the jama of each village. In my opinion it would be very advantageous, and save a great deal of needless detail in the village and tahsil accounts, if the jama of each village was made to include both the road and education funds, and this jama should be shewn in all the mouzawar statements of every description, but the Tahsildar in his urz-irsal would give the detail on account of land revenue, road funds and education fund, it would only be necessary to show the former amount in the accountant's touzis, but in the settlement statement and annual revenue statements this detail should be given below the total of each pergunnah in order to make it correspond with the touzis.

3. The revised jama of this district has not yet been submitted to the superior authorities; there would consequently be no difficulty to making the reduction on the total jama; therefore, if you and the Financial Commissioner would sanction my preparing the yearly statements in the manner which I have proposed, I should like to carry this arrangement into effect from the commencement of the next financial year.

From the Financial Commissioner, to the Commissioner and Superintendent, Cis-Sutlej States, No. 880, *dated 4th April* 1855.

I have the honor to acknowledge the receipt of your letter No. 62, dated 19th ultimo, and quite agree with you in considering that a deduction from the revenue assessed upon villages in the Ferozepore District to meet the charge of one per cent. on account of village schools is inadmissible.

2. Where the assessment has been determined on and given out with your consent, and still more where it has been acted upon, it would *perhaps be impolitic* to enforce even this additional payment; but every practicable effort should be made in a district, of which the settlement is not yet reported, to *induce the zemindars everywhere to accede to it.*

3. There cannot, I think, be any valid objection on the part of the assessing officer to allow the additional item to be required from the agricultural proprietary, as the education to

their offspring is a social duty more or less incumbent upon all holding that position, though hitherto much neglected by them, and they could hardly have this effected more economically than under the auspices of Government.

From the Commissioner and Superintendent, Cis-Sutlej States, to the Financial Commissioner, No. 141, *dated* 4*th June* 1855.

With reference to your letter No. 4, dated 18th January, regarding the introduction of a cess for village schools, I have the honor to state that in this division all the settlements had been completed before your circular arrived.

2. *The people generally are averse to the introduction of any new tax*; first they do not know what good will result from it; and, secondly, they are suspicious that the precedent may lead to the establishment of other cesses. At the same time, the Deputy Commissioners generally are of opinion that if Government order the tax of one per cent. it will be paid without demur.

3. In Thaneisur great reductions have been made in Mr. Wynyard's and Captain Abbott's settlements. I would, therefore, take the opportunity of introducing this cess, which should be readily agreed to, in return for the abatements allowed in the Government land revenue.

4. So in Simla the settlements are being revised, although they have once been completed, for the reason that they have been found unequal and heavy. Here also I would introduce the cess.

5. In Umballa, Ludhiana and Ferozepore, I propose, directly that the educational establishments sanctioned by Government are distributed over this division, *a cess of one per cent. be immediately levied from the people without going through the formality of asking their consent.*

From the Financial Commissioner of the Punjab, to the Commissioner and Superintendent, Cis-Sutlej States, No. 1946, *dated* 12*th June* 1855.

I have the honour to acknowledge the receipt of your letter No. 141, dated 4th current, regarding the introduction of the educational cess into the several districts of your Division, and entirely approve of the arrangement proposed by you.

2. The cess is one so essentially and manifestly for the benefit of the people themselves and their progeny, that *much fastidiousness in regard to its introduction would be out of place*, while the anomaly of some parganas paying, and others not paying, would be apparent, and might be inconvenient. I gladly, therefore, authorise you to carry out the measures you propose in the manner, and at the times, indicated in your letter under acknowledgment.

(*C.*)—*Memorandum by the Director of Public Instruction, Panjáb, dated* 28*th January* 1856.

It will be seen from the accompanying table that the amount of definite information received as to this cess is extremely small. Most officers, however, write encouragingly, and it is reasonable to expect that in the course of a few years the sum so realised will amount to one per cent. on the whole land revenue of the country.

2. At present, however, we are in possession of complete practical information from one Division only, *viz.*, Jhelum. In the Jhelum District there are already known to *exist* 175 indigenous schools, and the amount *derived from the one per cent. cess is Rs. 7,075, which give Rs. 45 a year to each school.* Three rupees a year may be added as the share which each school would have in the grant given by the Government to each district, and we have at once a sum of Rs. 4 a month, being nearly double the usual pay of teachers in the village schools. If it be true that an increased number of schools would diminish this rate, it must also be remembered that Mr. Thornton considers Rs. 12,000 yearly available for his Division, or Rs. 3,000, to each district, from sources which have not yet been taken into account.

3. Rawalpindi would show almost exactly the same results, the cess yielding Rs. 7,073, the number of village schools being 151.

4. In Gujrát the revenue, and consequently the cess, is less, and the number of schools much greater, so that for the 457 schools said to exist the one per cent. tax of Rs. 5,614 would not furnish more than a rupee a month.

5. Lastly, Shahpur yields Rs. 2,901 to the educational funds, but has only 19 indigenous schools, each one of which, therefore, would receive Rs. 12 a month.

6. Of course, the remedy for this last disproportional state of things is either to induce the people to establish more schools, or, if they hold back, for Government itself to do so, and support them with the superfluous proceeds of the tax. It is more difficult to decide how such a case as that of Gujrát is to be dealt with, where schools so greatly exceed the means of supporting them. Perhaps when schools may begin to be sifted and carefully discriminated from mosques, their numbers may diminish. At any rate, we shall probably retain sufficient control over the expenditure of the one per cent cess as to take care that it is appropriated for the support of really useful schools, and not squandered indiscriminately on good, bad, and indifferent.

7. But these discussions before experience has been had are little worth. My only object is to state broadly the salient facts which the best information we yet possess regarding *both the state of indigenous education and the prospects of the one per cent. tax would* seem to suggest for future consideration.

Extract of a letter from the Secretary to the Chief Commissioner of the Punjab, to the Secretary to the Government of India with the Governor General, No. 200, *dated* 14*th August* 1858.

PARA. 7. But besides the above expenditure on the part of Government, there is the one per cent. fund for the fiscal engagements entered into with the landholders. *A clause is usually inserted, with their consent, to the effect that they will pay at the rate of one per cent. on their assessed land tax for the education of* THEIR *children.* Generally the people assent willingly enough to this payment. There are only two districts, Leia and Hazara, where it is not levied. On this account there were collected during 1856-57 Rs. 1,38,044, and during 1857-58 Rs. 1,51,544; but as the schools can only be gradually established, the whole of the sums collected have not been expended within the year. In 1856-57 only Rs 23,472 were spent, leaving a balance in hand of Rs. 1,14,572, and during 1857-58 Rs. 82,263, leaving a balance of Rs. 69,281. *The total balance at close of the year standing to the credit of the fund amounts to Rs.* 1,83,853—a very satisfactory sum indeed—which may enable us to impart a great impulse to *this* branch of education as opportunity may arise. The one per cent. fund schools are established upon what is called the *Hulqa bundee* system, which means that the villages of a district are divided into so many little circles (containing, say, from 3 to 5 villages each), and that a school is set up at some central site in each circle so that all the children within that circle may be conveniently able to attend it, if so minded. These schools, though supported by the people, are yet under Government inspection and control, and our efforts must be largely directed to the improvement of them.

8. As might be expected, the indigenous schools previously existing *became considerably absorbed into the one per cent. schools; a sthe latter increase, the former diminish.* The fact is, that gradually the men who teach, and the boys who learn, in inefficient indigenous schools are gradually transferred to efficient village schools under an improved Government system. *The statistics of these indigenous schools are still diligently collected.* They are, still, however, far from perfect. From these statistics a large number of so-called schools are excluded, as being unworthy the appellation—such are the Lunde schools, where boys learn nothing but a barbarous character which is so obscure that *what is written can seldom be read clearly even by the writer himself,* and the Arabic schools where boys only learn to repeat a few verses of the Quran in Arabic which they cannot understand. If these were admitted, the return of schools would be considerably swelled, but they are properly excluded. It must be confessed that the education even in those village schools which are reckoned is extremely meagre and defective—

14.	1856-57, one per cent. schools	...	...	456
	„ indigenous „	...	...	5,024
	1857-58, one per cent. schools	...	...	1,336
	„ indigenous „	...	...	3,461

Extract of a letter from C. BEADON, Esq., *Secretary to the Government of India with the Governor General, to the Secretary to the Government of the Punjab and its Dependencies,— No.* 192, *dated Camp Ughana, the* 23*rd January* 1860.

PARA. 6. It is stated in Mr. Temple's letter that the entire expenditure on the part of Government will hereafter be Rs. 2,12,484, but, in addition to this, there is a cess at the rate of one per cent. in the land revenue throughout all the districts of the Punjab, except Leia and Hazara. In 1856-57 this cess yielded Rs. 1,38,044; and in 1857-58, Rs. 15,15,544; and when the year 1857-58 closed, there was a balance in hand of Rs. 1,83,853. This cess is said to have been contributed by the people voluntarily, and it may be so; but His Excellency thinks the contribution to be not altogether free from injustice, seeing that it falls *entirely* on the agricultural population, while the village schools which are maintained from the funds so provided are equally open to the commercial and the non-agricultural classes, and as yet *none* of the scholars are required to pay fees for tuitions. It is said to be in contemplation to levy fees from the non-agricultural classes, and it would be but just that this should be done as soon as the system of public education is sufficiently firmly established to carry out the measures without making the schools unpopular. I am further desired to remark, in respect to the education cess, that no more ought to be taken from the people than will suffice to meet the expenditure on village schools for the year. The demand of sums in *excess of what is required* for the current expenses of the schools, and the *accumulation of a fund* from this source, are *open to serious objection;* and His Excellency desires that, for the future, such demand and accumulation may be avoided.

* * * * * * *

10. Including indigenous schools, there were, in the Punjab, at the end of 1857-58, 4,923 schools, attended by 46,008 scholars, yielding a proportion of 1 to 23 of the school-going population. The proportion is low, but *His Excellency observes that considerable increase is looked for in the one per cent.,* or village school (cess). [The latter word seems to have been omitted by an oversight in the letter in question.—G. W. L]

Memorandum on Educational Cess,—dated Lahore, 13th February 1868.

Before the formation of the Panjáb Educational Department, the agriculturists of several zilas were induced by district officers to contribute a small percentage on the land revenue for the support of schools. On the appointment of a Director of Public Instruction in 1856, and the organization of a separate department, it was thought desirable that the educational cess should be extended to the whole Province, and an order was issued that where the settlement had not been completed *one per cent. on the revenue should be levied for the maintenance of village schools*, and that in other cases district officers should endeavour to induce the people voluntarily to subscribe to the cess. In July 1857, Mr. Arnold, the Director, was able to report that the cess was then being levied in for the greater portion of the Panjáb. It was long, however, before the full amount was raised throughout the Panjáb. Thus, it was not till 1864 that the people of the Hoshiarpore District, who were amongst the first to raise a cess, agreed to contribute at the rate of one per cent., and the cess in this district must still be viewed in the light of a voluntary contribution, as it has not yet been included in the settlement. Origin of the Cess.

2. In the districts made over from the North-Western Provinces after the mutiny, the cess had already been introduced, but not on one uniform plan for every district. Thus, in the Gurgaon District the people in the villages contained in each 'halqa' contributed amongst them sufficient to pay the salary of the village teacher of that particular 'halqa.' Districts made over from North-Western Provinces.

3. The cess is now raised in every district of the Panjáb at the rate of one per cent., with the exception of Hazara, where it is taken in one village only. Cess now levied in every district, except Hazara.

4. The table given below will show the annual estimated income from 1856-57 to 1868-69. I regret to state that there is in this office no record of the amount actually realised, and I have been unable to procure the desired information in Lahore. It is doubtless very essential that the actual income should be known, and it will accordingly in future years be ascertained and recorded in this office. [This does not appear to have been done yet—July 1882.—G.W.L.] Income from 1856 to 1867.

Memorandum of the estimated income of the one per cent. Educational Cess Fund.

Years.	Amounts.	Remarks.
	Rs.	
1856-57	1,38,034	Balance in hand on 30th September 1867 as per statement of Accountant General, Rs. 1,91,231-13-5.
1857-58	1,51,544	
1858-59	1,92,002	
1859-60	1,75,226	
1860-61	1,89,970	
1861-62	2,04,943	
1862-63	2,08,908	
1863-64	2,10,000	
1864-65	2,10,000	
1865-66	2,10,000	
1866-67	2,12,710	
1867-68	2,07,422	
1868-69	2,10,083	

5. The one per cent. cess was originally contributed for the support of village schools, and the amount raised in each pargana was, as a rule, expended in that pargana. A small proportion also of the cost of the supervising agency was borne by this fund. Object on which cess at first expended.

6. In 1860 the Department was thoroughly re-organized, *the old system was swept away*, and an entirely new order of things was introduced. It was then ruled that the cess collected annually in all districts, together with the accumulated balances of the same, should be formed into one *general* fund, which was to be expended in the following proportion :— System introduced in 1860.

The first charge was to be the cost of tahsili and female schools, after that 10 per cent. of the balance of each year's income was to be set aside for the salaries and contingent expenses of school muhurrirs * ; 5 per cent. for the publication of the Sarkari Akhbar ; 4 per cent. for contingent expenses of *all* vernacular schools, including cost of prizes given by district officers ; 6 per cent. for stipends of teachers studying at the normal school, and the remainder was to be devoted to the maintenance of village schools, the number allowed for each district being, as a rule, in the direct ratio of its *annual* income from the educational cess, any small savings that might accrue from month to month might be expended by district officers in prizes, &c.

Charges transferred to Imperial revenue.

7. Subsequently, the Supreme Government consented to pay the salaries of chief muhurrirs and the cost of the Sarkari Akhbar, and to allow Rs. 40,740 per annum for the maintenance of one "model school" in each tahsil of the Panjáb, and it has been ordered that female schools not intended principally for the daughters of agriculturists shall be no longer maintained from the fund.

Town and village schools.

8. Vernacular schools for boys are classed as town or village schools according to the standard to which they attain, and *without reference to the locality where they may be situated.* As a matter of fact, however, those that come up to the standard fixed for town schools are generally situated in towns, though *there are not a few schools situated in large towns that do not come up to this standard, and consequently appear in the returns as village schools.* Of course, there may be two or more town schools, or there may be none whatever, in any particular tahsil.

Grant from Imperial revenue for model schools expended partly on town and partly on village schools.

9. The grant from the Imperial revenue for "model schools" is expended on town schools in tahsils where such schools exist. Where they do not exist, it is expended on the best village school in the tahsil. A town school often costs more than the grant made for a model school, and *the difference is then paid from the one per cent. cess.* During 1866-67 Government contributed Rs. 21,566-7-2, and Rs. 15,125 were paid from the one per cent. cess for town schools. For village schools the cost to Government was Rs. 24,702-12-2 and to the cess Rs. 1,39,326-10-7.†

Objects on which cess now expended.

10. The objects on which the cess is now expended and the distribution of expenditure for the current year are as follows :—

	Rs.	A.	
Assistant School Muhurrirs	502	0	Per mensem.
Travelling allowance to Chief Muhurrirs ...	435	0	"
Cost of male schools, town and village ...	13,016	7	"
Cost of female schools, village	862	0	"
Stipends to normal school students	1,155	0	"
Stipends to vernacular scholars selected from vernaculars schools and sent to zila schools by district officers ...	352	0	"
Part cost of normal schools	500	0	"
Scholarships to students of vernacular schools sent to zila schools by Inspectors	330	0	"
Total ...	17,152	7	"
Expenditure on educational buildings during 1867-68 ...	10,824	0	"

The salaries of teachers employed in male schools, town and village, vary from Rs. 5 per mensem to Rs. 30 per mensem. As shown in the last paragraph a large portion of the cost of town schools and by far the greater part of the expenditure on village schools is paid from the cess. The cost of erecting and repairing village schools is paid from the cess, *which formerly bore the expenditure on various other kinds of educational buildings.*

Halqabandi system does not now exist in the Punjab.

11. Originally the whole country was divided into "Halqas," and one school was established in each. It was intended that this school should meet the requirements of all the villages contained in the halqa. The system did not answer and was soon abandoned. Boys from one village cannot easily be induced to attend a school in a neighbouring village, and it was found that *more good could be effected by fixing the sites of vernacular schools in the larger villages or in those where the people showed some desire for education.*

* The Chief Muhurrir was to be under the Deputy Commissioner of the District, and was to visit schools, to accompany the Inspector and the District Officers on their tours, &c. The Assistant Muhurrir was to keep the accounts, make out returns, &c., &c.

† From this it will be seen that the amount contributed by Government for vernacular schools is greater than the cost of town schools, though, of course, it would not be greater if any considerable number of village schools should come up to the higher standard. Major Fuller's original proposition was that all town schools should be entirely supported by Government, and all village schools by the one per cent. cess.

Originally the cess was to be expended as far as possible where raised. Then, after meeting certain charges the number of schools maintained from balance was to be in proportion to the income of each district.

12. It has already been stated (paragraphs 5 and 6) that the cess raised in each tahsil was originally expended as far as possible in that tahsil, and that in 1860, when the Department was re-organized, the cess was formed into one general fund, of which a certain portion was set apart for the cost of *tahsili* (afterwards town) and female schools and for school muhurrirs for Sarkari Akhbar and for *contingent expenses*, and for stipends to teachers at the normal schools; and it was ruled that the number of village schools in each district supported from the balance that remained after providing for these charges should, as a rule, be in the "direct ratio of the income" of the district. *The various changes, however, that have occurred in the items of expenditure chargeable to the cess have probably made it difficult, if not* IMPOSSIBLE, *to observe this rule*, as any fresh charge must have altered the proportion of the expenditure from the fund in every district. Formerly there was a large unexpended balance, and for some years the expenditure was allowed to exceed the income; of late, however, district officers have been invited to reduce the expenditure where possible, and every proposed increase has been disallowed.

At present expenditure or number of schools not in proportion to income.

13. At the present time the expenditure in some districts much exceeds and in others falls far short of the income, and though *the above rule has not been formally rescinded, it has been allowed to fall into abeyance.* To restore the proper proportion of schools will entail considerable reductions in some districts, but the present distribution of expenditure requires careful revision, as it appears to be regulated on no fixed principle, but to have resulted from the changes that have been made in the charges payable from the cess, and from a dislike to enforce the reduction of schools in localities where the income is small.

Fund, general fund; but originally intended that expenditure should be, as far as possible, in proportion to income. This is not the case now.

14. To sum up, the fund is a general fund, but it was intended that, after providing for certain general charges, the balance should, as a rule, be distributed in proportion to the income of each district. *In practice, this principle has not been observed, and in some localities* the expenditure is much greater than the income, in others much less. A redistribution of expenditure is necessary, but must be carried out with great care.

Machinery controlling expenditure.

15. Expenditure in each district is sanctioned in accordance with the provisions made in the budget submitted by Deputy Commissioners to the Director, and passed by the Local Government. Cheques on the one per cent. cess fund for the full amount sanctioned in the budget and signed by the Director are remitted monthly to Deputy Commissioners, by whom they are cashed. All appointments are made by Deputy Commissioners, who submit to this office monthly, in the vernacular, copies of the pay bills of establishments, and statements showing the balance in hand at the commencement of the month, the savings, if any, during the month, and the balance in hand at its close, also the amount expended on prizes, scholarships, &c. The original bills are retained in the district offices, and the money is disbursed by the Deputy Commissioners through their tahsildars. The expenditure from this fund is shown in the annual returns of the Department.

The amount sanctioned for erection and repair of buildings is remitted to district officers in advance at the commencement of the year, by the Director of Public Instruction, Panjab, by means of cheques on the educational cess fund. At the close of the year the district officers render an account of the advances to the Director of Public Instruction, Panjáb.

Effects of the cess.

16. The effect of the one per cent. cess has been to *supersede many of the old "maktabs" and "patshalas," or to convert them into Government schools*, and to extend education to numerous localities where no schools formerly existed. Amongst the rural population of the Panjáb a knowledge of the Urdu language and of arithmetic has been widely diffused, and in many of our schools Persian is taught very much better than it could be learnt in the old "maktabs."

Reduction of indigenous schools.

17. The number of students attending vernacular schools had increased from 42,038 in 1859-60 to 62,355 in 1866-67. The statistics of indigenous schools are hardly to be depended on; for 1859-60 the returns gave 6,309 schools with 63,090 pupils; in 1866-67 there were said to be 5,434 schools containing 59,750 pupils. *That the number of indigenous schools has greatly decreased, there can be no doubt: this*, however, is not to be attributed *altogether* to the operation of the *one per cent. cess*, as very many have been absorbed by the introduction of the branch school system in connection more especially with zila schools.

Character of indigenous schools.

18. Indigenous schools not of a purely religious character consist for the most part of maktabs where various Persian books are learnt by rote, or of "patshalas" where the boys learn Landi or "Mahajani," and the Native system of keeping accounts. In the latter, however, the principal subject of instruction is the multiplication table to 30 × 30 and from ¾ to 2½ × 30. There are, of course, some schools where Persian is well taught, but this is by no means the case in the great majority, and it may be safely affirmed that *all the boys who would have attended the schools that have now disappeared receive a much better education* than they could have obtained under the old system, and *arrangements having been made for encouraging indigenous schools by grants-in-aid, it may be hoped that an improved class of such schools will come into existence.*

Effects of schools on habits of boys.

19. In some districts the effect of the Government vernacular schools on the manner and habits of the boys is very remarkable. In 1858-59, when many of these schools were first established, the wildest reports were circulated, and it was asserted that Government after collecting all the little boys, intended to send them down to Calcutta with some ulterior object

that was not clearly explained, but in a short time the scholars were ready to *come in any distance for an examination.* When the discipline maintained in a district is good, all the boys who appear at an examination are neat and clean in their persons, and are provided with every requisite, such as paper, pens, ink, &c., &c. This is particularly the case in the Ludhiana District (where the standard of education in village schools also is unusually high), and is to be attributed to the active supervision of the chief muharrir. The effect produced by many of our village schools in teaching habits of neatness, order and cleanliness to the rural population is of great importance.

No general desire for education amongst agriculturists.

20. It cannot be said, however, there is any general desire for education amongst the agricultural population, and though there are many places where the lamberdars do take a genuine interest in the schools, the proportion of such places is small. *The old idea still prevails very extensively that if a boy goes to school he is of no use for the plough.*

Progress made in education.

21. There are *no* means of ascertaining the number of boys who have received an education in schools *supported from the one per cent. cess.*

CHAPTER E.

(A).—Extracts from Educational Reports and from the Government "Reviews" thereon, regarding Indigenous Schools and the Village School Cess.

Extract from a Report, No. 33, dated 6th July 1857, from the Director of Public Instruction, Panjab, to the Financial Commissioner, Panjab.

PARA. 8. But what had the people been doing for themselves in the way of education? *This is a very difficult question to answer. It is difficult to get accurate statistics, and it is difficult to interpret the statistics when we have them.* Certainly the idea of education is not new to the Panjábis. We find all the school phraseology ready made to our hand, and *chiefly supplied by the Muhammadans. As educators they are in possession of the field;* not only is the Kurán taught in every mosque, but outside a great many mosques the standard Persian works are taught to all comers—to more Hindus than Muhammadans. In the documents appended to this report a place where the Kurán only is taught is called a Kurán school; a place where the Kurán forms the staple, where the whole thing would fall to the ground, were it not for the Kurán, but where secular Persian is taught besides, is called a Persian Kurán school. The former institutions are educationally worthless, which would be too harsh a sentence to pass upon the latter.

9. I greatly regret that the state of the returns from the western districts of the Panjáb is such as to prevent my vouching for the accuracy of the statistics of indigenous schools. Those of the Eastern Districts *have been carefully tested.* I think the most striking fact which they present is this, that out of 29,000 boys said to be attending indigenous schools nearly 18,000 (of whom nearly half are Hindus) are learning Persian.

10. I regret that the return of indigenous schools given in Table C is, on the whole, very far from complete. As regards the cis-Sutlej and trans-Sutlej Divisions, I believe, indeed, that the extent of error is indicated by the marginal remarks, and that, as far as they go, the returns are correct. I have compared them with those collected by the tahsildars, in obedience to orders issued by the Board of Administration in 1853, and find in every case a great increase. But the returns from the Western Circle are quite worthless—indeed, for the most part blank; and I have been only able to avail myself of the very imperfect statistics collected in previous years.

11. I am quite sure, however, that the facts as regarding indigenous schools are *under* and not *over* stated.

12. The returns show a *very large preponderance of Muhammadan boys* at school. Every fact we meet proves beyond all dispute that *the teaching profession has been in their hands.* I cannot but think that the confiding attendance of so many Hindus at Muhammadan schools for the sake of learning the Persian language is a most remarkable fact. I cannot but think also that the steady growth of Muhammadanism in the Panjáb may partly be traced to the advantage taken by the teachers of this confidence. *Certainly I find that the natural tendency of things, if left to themselves, is to throw the whole weight of government in this matter of education on to the side of the Muhammadans—a tendency to be much resisted.*

13. In giving the number of boys actually under instruction in indigenous schools, I deduct those attending "Quran" and "Landé" schools, because, as a rule, the instruction given at these two classes of institutions does not deserve to be taken into account. With this abatement the number of boys under instruction at indigenous schools, according to returns confessedly imperfect is 24,968. The numbers given in the Panjáb Report from 1854-55 to 1855-56 are 31,592, but therein are included the two classes of schools not taken into my account.

14. The relation of scholars to population will be found in paragraph 91 of this report.

15. Of the 24 schools returned as Arabic, it is possible that some should have been entered as Kurán, though pains have been taken to avoid this error. *An Arabic school can hardly with propriety be called a school at all, the students being almost exclusively adults.* They are, I believe, quite exclusively Muhammadans.

16. The Persian schools are the most genuine educational institutions in the country. They are attended largely by the Kuthries, *the Hindus forming a greater proportion than the Muhammadans.* Writing is taught, but not with great energy, and certainly not with great success. The great object is to teach a boy to read the Gulistan and Bostan; and the lad who will read off a page of either in a fluent sing-song without understanding a word has received an education which fully satisfies both his teacher and parents. Little as the works of Sadi are understood by these boys, there is no doubt that they are much enjoyed. In one of the too frequent cases of child murder with robbery of ornaments, the victim, a lad of 13, was enticed out by his murderer, a youth of 18, on the pretext of having the Bostan read to him.

17. It will be seen that there are only *ten Urdu indigenous schools, and I rather doubt the actual existence, as such, of these. To educate a boy by teaching him his native language is to the natives almost a contradiction in terms. Persian is something, and Sanskrit is something, but what is Urdu ?*

18. The number of Kurán schools is given as 1,775 ; but I have no doubt that the number is much greater. In several districts no such schools are mentioned, *the fact being that probably every mosque is the site of what is elsewhere called a Kurán school.* As attendance at these schools does *not necessarily involve a knowledge of reading* and writing, I have omitted the pupils of the Kurán schools from my calculation of boys under instruction. Of course, strictly Kurán schools are attended only by Muhammadans.

19. But *certainly the Hindus do not seem to be very sensitive or jealous as to the encroachments of Muhammadanism.* The Persian Kurán schools are, of course, invariably kept by Muhammadan teachers; indeed, so are far the greater number of Persian schools. They are generally held in or just outside the mosque, to which the teacher is frequently attached. Yet they are attended largely by Hindus, more attracted by the Persian language than repelled by the Muhammadan religion.

20. It is in the *Sanskrit schools that the exclusive side of Hinduism comes out.* Like the Arabic schools, those called Sanskrit are largely attended by adults, and entirely by Bráhmans. We may be quite certain that a student attending a Shastri school will hardly be persuaded to undergo any other kind of instruction. *He would strongly object to learn the Persian character.*

21. I do not quite understand the return of 289 *Hindi* schools. A real Hindi school is very rare ; and I think a great majority of these 289, if strictly looked into, would have to be classified as Shastri or Landé.

22. The return of Gurmukhi schools is very incomplete. There must be several in Gurdáspur, though none are recorded. I am surprised to find 41 in Ráwalpindi. If this is correct, it is not likely that there are none in Gujrát and Jhelum. A really accurate list of these schools would be interesting, and in my next report I hope to be able to supply one. These schools are chiefly of a religious character, attended only by Sikhs.

23. The Landé schools are those in which the children of shopkeepers are taught the mysteries of book-keeping, and in which *that vicious system of accounts which is daily deprecated in our Civil Courts* is perpetuated. I have seen several of these schools, and, considering the tales we have all heard of the marvellous arithmetical quickness of Hindi boys, have been rather disappointed. One or two boys in each school can, indeed, perform wonderful feats in the multiplication table up to limits far beyond the orthodox twelve times twelve, and can work Rule of Three problems quickly in their heads ; often, at the same time, quite unable to work them on paper. But the majority do not seem to me to acquire any great quickness at figures ; and certainly if they do not gain this they gain nothing, for the power of writing a character which *neither they themselves nor anybody else can decipher an hour after it has been written cannot be called an accomplishment.*

24. The average income of each village school teacher per mensem is found to be Rs. 2-5-2. As regards his income from teaching only, I believe this is very near the mark ; but the village teacher generally *makes money in other ways*, in connection with the mosque, or, if a Bráhman, by the rites and ceremonies which constitute so large a portion of Hindu life.

25. As regards the mode of remuneration common in the Panjáb, I have nothing material to add to the following statement made by Mr. Montgomery in the 5th paragraph of his letter No. 567 of 8th November 1850 to the Secretary to the Board of Administration :—

"The mode by which the teachers are remunerated is as varied as it is in other parts of India. When the pupils pay money the average salaries of the master run from Re. 1-2-0 in Pargana Tulwandi to Rs. 7-8 and Rs. 8-8 per mensem in the city of Lahore and Pargana Kussoor. In a few schools the boys pay a small weekly sum in money, to which are added donations by the parents of the children on particular festivals. In other schools at harvest time the boys of the parents give a certain quantity of grain, or sometimes the boys in turn give the master daily two meals. In two schools in the Demanuggur District the landholders give 50 maunds of grain to the schoolmasters to remunerate him for instructing their children. In a few cases grants of land have been given to individuals on the condition of teaching. Where this is done nothing is charged ; and in some instances the masters support pupils at their own expense. *Occasionally each plough is assessed at the rate of 5 seers for the instruction of the village children*, and, in addition to this, the children once a week bring a certain quantity of food for the master."

26. Mr. Reid, in one of his valuable reports on Public Instruction in the North-Western Provinces, remarks on the far greater good which can be effected through one tahsili than a large number of village schools. Rude and imperfect as our tahsili schools are, it is impossible not to feel the same even now. *The value of these indigenous schools, as harmonizing institutions to which the people are much attached, is probably great, and certainly I for one would deal very tenderly with them ;* but educationally, as promoting intellectual improvement, they can hardly be rated too low. Even in India Rs. 2-5 per mensem is very

poor pay. *In one per cent. schools we cannot afford to pay more than Rs. 5.* It remains to be seen whether we shall do much more for Rs. 5 than has hitherto been done for less than half the money. Certainly the village school system is well worth, and is destined, I trust, to receive a fair and patient trial. But it must, I think, be for some time to come regarded as on its trial. *It must still be considered an open question whether the 1 per cent. cess would not be more profitably returned to the contributors,* whether education would not really be more effectually disseminated by establishing thirty teachers in a district on Rs. 15 than a hundred on Rs. 5.

* * * * * *

50. When it was determined, however, to establish a separate Educational Department in the Panjáb, it was thought that the educational cess should also, if possible, be extended to all districts of the territory. *Accordingly it was ordered* that in all cases where settlement had not been completed, *1 per cent. on the revenue should be levied for the maintenance of village schools;* and wherever a settlement existed, the District Officer was instructed to induce the people voluntarily to consent to the introduction of the cess. This consent was, as may be supposed, very generally given, and in far the greater portion of the Panjáb the cess is being levied, as will appear from the Table H appended to this Report.

Cess introduced prior to establishment of Educational Department.

51. It is not for me to express any opinion on the policy of the 1 per cent. cess. I found it authorized when I joined my appointment, and had nothing whatever to do with recommending it. All that remained for me to do was to spend the money.

52. *It was not easy to determine how this should be done. Two courses were open to us: first to administer the cess in small grants-in-aid of* existing *village schools; secondly, to select certain of the best of these schools, or to found new ones in central situations, and to pay the teachers as regular Government servants.*

In grants to indigenous schools.

53. In favour of the first course it was obvious that the money so spent would go much further. Taking 5 rupees as the very lowest monthly stipend on which the village schoolmaster could be maintained, it might be reckoned, on the first plan of aiding indigenous teachers, that half this sum would be derived from the village, while on the second plan the whole must be paid out of the cess. Thus, we could aid twice as many schools as we could maintain.

* * * * * *

56. Altogether I am of opinion that if the education scheme had been left to district officers to carry out, the first course would have been the best, but that with a central department the second is the most efficient, if, indeed, it be not the only one practicable.

57. The district officer can perhaps induce the people to support schools besides paying the 1 per cent. cess, but certainly nobody except the District Officer is able to do this. We soon found that the zemindars regarded the 1 per cent. cess as a quittance in full of all claims on them for the education of their children; and though it might fairly have been said that they could not expect to gain this end by so trifling an expenditure, yet I do not think it would have been prudent to urge the matter of further payments, at least till the people could see some returns for the payment already made.

* * * * * *

60. It was from the first resolved, *and has now been expressly ordered by the Supreme Government, that the* 1 per cent. cess should be spent locally, *that is, that the amount raised in each pargana shall not, without the express permission of the Financial Commissioner of the Panjáb, be spent out of that pargana. The amount of the cess in each pargana formed, therefore, the limit of the village school organization.*

* * * * * *

Number of village schools established.

67. The total number of Government village schools existing in the Panjáb at the end of the year under review was 456, whereof 170 had been established prior to the institution of this Department. The total annual cost of these schools is Rs. 23,472, whereas the annual amount of the cess levied in the Panjáb is not less than Rs. 1,38,034, leaving an unexpended balance of Rs. 14,562. Of course, this balance will be devoted to educational uses, and will probably be found very useful in the erection of village school-houses. Still, it is very desirable that the establishment of the schools should be proceeded with as soon as possible.

* * * * * *

Language and character to be used in village schools.

69. I regret that the incomplete condition of the original returns prevents my stating exactly the number of pupils reading respectively Persian and Hindi. With the exception, however, of Síalkot, where the Hindi teachers form a larger, and of Kangra, where they form an overpowering, proportion, the majority of the teachers are certainly Muhammadans, teaching Persian, and beginning not very willingly to teach Urdu. I have no doubt that in the village no less than in the tahsili schools Urdu is the language which, so far as instruction is concerned, it is most desirable for us to teach. Still there is a great danger, if we exclude Hindi, of throwing the whole matter too much into the hands of the Muhammadans; and in the institution of village schools for some time to come, it will be of comparatively little consequence what is taught, and of much consequence that the people should learn to regard the schools with a friendly eye. (For paragraph 80 on the resumption of grants of rent-free lands to schools see below.—G. W. L.)

* * * * * *

Inspection of female schools.

84. A question has arisen as to the nature of the inspection to which these schools are to submit. Both the Inspectors (and this entire movement has taken place subsequent

to their appointment) have judiciously exempted the schools from visitation by any European officer. On the other hand, it is distinctly understood that every school is open to the Native Sub-Deputy Inspector, or at least the Deputy Inspector. Without this we have no security that we are not paying some hundred rupees a month to enable little Muhammadan girls to sit behind a curtain and recite the Kurán, which they will do readily enough without any such encouragement. The Deputy Inspector, however, is to be accompanied in his visits to such schools by the respectable inhabitants of the place.

1 to 36. The total proportion of boys under instruction (omitting Landé and Kurán schools, and also the districts of Simla, Leiah, Dera Ghazi Khan, Dera Ismael Khan, Peshawar and Kohat, from which no returns of indigenous schools have been received) to the school-going population of the Panjáb is 1 to 36.

*　　*　　*　　*　　*　　*

Why the proportion is so low. 93. These figures will appear very unfavourable. In that laborious and valuable record, the "Statistics of Education, North-Western Provinces," it is made a subject of regret that, "whereas in Russia, the most barbarous of European empires, the proportion of boys at school is one to nine, in India it is one to twenty-five." In the Panjáb the ascertained proportion is 1 in 36.

94. I must repeat, however, that the figures, which are the best I can give, err exclusively on the side of incompleteness. The divisions in which the most accurate returns have been obtained are those of Jhelum and Lahore, having been prepared in the former by the local authorities some years ago; in the latter both by the local authorities, by Mr. Montgomery, when Commissioner, and by this Department. I have no reason to suppose that these divisions are really better off than others, but the facts have been more carefully ascertained.

95. I may also repeat, in explanation of the unfavourable proportion, that I have exclued "Landé and Kurán schools," the latter forming by far the greater proportion of indigenous schools so-called. If these had been included, I could have represented a far greater proportion of the population as under instruction, but the representation would have been practically false.

RESUMPTION OF RENT-FREE LANDS TO SCHOOLS.

PRIVATE SCHOOLS ENJOYING RENT-FREE LAND.

Extract from Report of the Director of Public Instruction, Panjáb, to Financial Commissioner, Panjáb,—No. 33, dated 6th July 1857.

"PARA. 80. You are aware that it was a *common custom* in former times to give grants of rent-free land to persons who were bound in return to teach youth. *Most* of these grants, the conditions of which were probably very little attended to, have been resumed, but I have been officially informed of their being allowed on the condition above mentioned, at the places noted in the margin. In all such cases the school is now considered subject to Government inspection, and will be gradually made to conform to the rules laid down for one per cent. tahsili schools, as each case may require."

District.	Locality.	Grant.
		Rs.
Amritsar ...	Sultanpur ...	One well.
Sialkot ...	Badanath ...	37 gumas.
Ludiana ...	Ingraou ...	*
Gugaira ...	Lashari ...	
Ditto ...	Pakputtan ...	150

TABLE B.—*showing*—

Total annual 1 per cent. cess.	Total number of 1 per cent. schools.
Rs. 1,57,051.	456.

TABLE C.

Statement showing indigenous schools in the Panjáb in the year 1856-57.

Numbering 4,252.

Table showing number of existing indigenous schools, dated 28*th January* 1856.

Total number *shown* 2,695.

TABLE H.

Showing the state of the one per cent. village school fund in the Panjáb for the year 1856-57, amounting to Rs. 1,15,151-9-3.

Extract from a letter No. 328-2609, *dated* 28*th June* 1858, *from the Financial Commissioner, to the Secretary to the Chief Commissioner, Panjáb.*

PARA. 5. Under the first of the above headings Mr. Arnold justly commends the exertions of Mr. Inglis in Siálkot, Mr. Temple in Gujrát, Colonel Abbott in Hoshiárpur

* To this there is a note in Mr. Arnold's, the Director's, own handwriting in the original report to the following effect: "Fill up; it can be ascertained in Persian Office."—G. W. L.

Mr. Brandreth and Lieutenant Mercer in Ferozepore, Lieutenant Edward Paske in Shahpur and Lieutenant Reid in Gugairah; and he states that *previous* to his appointment there existed 34 schools directly or indirectly supported by Government.

6. Of indigenous schools during the year under review he supplies a return (marked C), but observes that the returns for the Western or 2nd Circle are not to be relied on, while those of the 1st Circle he believes to be tolerably correct. The entire returns show 24,968 boys attending the schools, of whom considerably more than half were Muhammadans, and about three-fifths were reading Persian. The average rate of remuneration to teachers he shows to have but little exceeded Rs. 2 per mensem, and the greater number of these, as shown by the return, were Muhammadans. The general character of the instruction communicated he describes as being of the humblest kind. Those schools in which the "Landé" or provincial character of the Hindu community was alone taught *he excludes entirely* from his returns, as well as those in which the *Kurán only is taught*; and he considers the *only indigenous schools worthy of the name* to be these in which the chief or only subject of study is Persian.

7. The returns of Gurmukhi schools he considers to be very incomplete and erroneous. They are chiefly of a religious character, and attended only by the Sikhs, and as he considers that correct returns of them would be interesting, he hopes to report more fully in regard to them in his next report.

8. In connection with this branch of the subject, he remarks (paragraphs 12 and 19) that every fact we meet proves that hitherto education has virtually been in the hands of the Muhammadans; and he is disposed to attribute the steady growth of Muhammadanism in the Panjáb in part to advantage taken by teachers of the confidence reposed in them—the Hindus largely attending schools of which the spirit is essentially Muhammadan, and evincing little or no jealousy in this particular. He adds that he finds the natural tendency of things, if left to themselves, is to throw the whole weight of Government in this matter into the hands of the Muhammadans—a *tendency which, he justly observes, should be strenuously resisted.*

* * * * * *

16. The third branch of the subject taken up by Mr. Arnold is the *village school cess*, and the establishments entertained from it. As independent efforts had been previously made by local officers in some districts by local contributions, considerable difficulty was experienced, in the first instance, in determining the position to be held by the district and divisional authorities in relation to these schools in particular, and, indeed, to the Educational Department generally. But in the end it has been found unavoidable to transfer to the educational establishments virtually the entire control of these as well as all other schools, although the most friendly relations have throughout been maintained with the district authorities.

17. *At first some of the latter wished to retain the expenditure of the school cess entirely in their own hands, and the difference of views existing on this and other points had the effect of retarding considerably, in some parts, the establishment of village schools. But by the close of the year nearly all had consented to transfer the Fund and its management to the officers of the Educational Department; and since then the establishment of village schools has proceeded with greater vigour.*

18. By the end of the year under review 456 schools in all had been established, of which 170 previously existed; and the number of scholars attending them was 7,296,* of whom 2,736 were Muhammadans, 4,104 Hindus, and 456 Sikhs. The expense incurred has been Rs. 23,472, *while an unexpended balance still remained of no less than Rs.* 1,14,562. Efforts have been made to introduce something of system and efficiency into these schools, and some progress has been attained; but so much attention as could be desired is not as yet generally paid to the few simple rules which alone it has been possible to lay down.

19. *It was at first a question how the proceeds of the fund might be best applied—whether by merely giving grants-in-aid to a large number of indigenous institutions, or by establishing a limited number of* bonâ fide *Government schools supported entirely by the fund. It was speedily found, however, that the creation of the fund led the people generally to consider their contributions thereto as an acquittance in full for all claims upon them on account of the education of their children*; and this consideration, as well as the desire to establish institutions capable of giving a really sound, though humble, order of education has led the adoption generally of what is termed in the North-Western Provinces the *Halqabundee* system—that is, the selection of central localities, and the establishment at these of schools more or less efficiently organised and superintended, which shall supply the wants of the villages adjoining.

20. Much pains have been taken in the determination of these central localities; maps have been prepared; reports furnished by the Deputy and Sub-Deputy Inspector, after careful personal inspection, showing population, revenue, and other statistical datas. These have been submitted for the opinions and suggestions of district officers; the wishes and inclination of the people have been, as much as possible, consulted; and it is believed that as good a distribution has been made as was attainable.

21. The language to be taught and the general character of the school was determined in conformity with the wishes of the majority, and the result has been that while in Kangra Hindi schools greatly predominate, and in Siálkot partially so, Urdu and

* These numbers are given by Mr. Arnold in the 68th paragraph of his Report, but they differ materially from those entered in table B, in which there appears to be some error.

Persian schools chiefly prevail elsewhere, in many parts, to the entire exclusion of every other. Muhammadanising tendency is generally apparent, which it will be right not unduly to encourage; but there can be no doubt that, as a rule, the Urdu is the language which must predominate, and which may be taught with the greatest advantage.

(B.)—Extracts from Reports of the Department of Public Instruction, and Reviews of Government thereon.

1863-64 (*Captain Fuller*).

Trustworthy statistics of indigenous village schools not procurable.

REPORT, PARA. 53.—There are only two male schools of this class, one of which has been abolished. Indigenous village schools are visited *occasionally*, and encouraged by the grant of small rewards in cash and books; but *no regular returns of them are kept*, as even with a very large staff of Deputy and Sub-Deputy Inspectors, trustworthy statistics regarding them can scarcely be procured. To obtain regular returns every month, or to insist on a proper register of attendance being kept up by the teacher, is not attempted, I think, in the provinces where they make the greatest show. The statistics of an indigenous school obtained at any visit by an inspecting officer are supposed to remain unattested until that school happens to be visited again, which may not be for 6 or even 12 months. As these schools are of a very fluctuating character, and little or no control can be exercised over them (*the European Inspector never having time to examine them himself*), the statistics that are obtained depend greatly on the season of the year at which the schools are visited by the native inspecting staff, and on the credence given by the latter to the teachers' statements regarding the attendance at their schools. As a rule, I should say, the latter always took the most favourable view of the circumstances of all indigenous schools, in order to keep up their credit with their superiors.

1864-65 (*Major Fuller*).

Indigenous village schools.
General statistics and progress.

REPORT, PARA. 68.—There is only one small school left of this class of schools and, as I explained in paragraph 53 of my last report for 1863-64, *I do not consider the collection of statistics from purely indigenous schools worth the trouble and expense it would entail*—that, when obtained, any satisfactory reliance can be placed on them. But such schools are visited and encouraged from time to time by the Educational and Civil Officers of various grades, and many of the best have been amalgamated as branches with the superior Government and aided schools in their neighbourhood. Special provision, too, has been made for grants to this class of schools under the simplest possible mode of examination and distribution in the draft of revised grant-in-aid rules submitted to the Supreme Government.

1865-66 (*Major Fuller*).

General statistics, &c., proposed to assist these schools and good indigenous vernacular schools generally under Act XIV of the revised Code of Grant-in-aid Regulations.

REPORT, PARA. 61.—There are only three small schools of this class in the returns, which are scarcely worth noticing. One of them has been abolished. Act XIV of the revised Code of Grant-in-aid Regulations specially provides for Government aid being extended to good indigenous schools; and district officers and inspectors of schools have been expressly requested to bring forward all deserving schools that they can recommend for support under the terms of that article. If the necessary funds, therefore, are assigned during 1866-67 for meeting grants to schools of this class, I trust we may be able to bring a considerable number of them under Government inspection; and endeavours will then be made to obtain some *approximately correct statistics* of them, and to show the same in the returns for the future.

1866-67 (*Lieutenant-Colonel Fuller*).

Indigenous schools.

REVIEW BY GOVERNMENT, PARA 18.—From the statistics contained in Statement VIC it would appear that there are 5,434 indigenous schools in the Panjáb, with an average daily attendance of 32,667 pupils, of whom—

10,454 study Persian,
1,266 study Urdu,
3,234 study Hindi, and
3,960 study Sanskrit.

If these statistics are at all reliable, they show a large falling off since the year 1859-60, when the number of such scholars was reported as 63,090.

This result is much to be regretted, and His Honour trusts that the system of making grants-in-aid to indigenous schools of merit, under Article XIV of the Grant-in-aid Rules, commenced during the year under report, will arrest the further decline of these institutions, *which are doubtless in many respects more suited to the taste and wishes of the people than schools established through direct Government agency.*

REPORT, PARA. 6.—*Now* that Government desires indigenous vernacular schools to be visited by educational officers and encouraged by Government grants, and stricter professional supervision over Government schools, under the immediate control of district officers, is found by Inspectors to be much needed, *an addition to the number of the Deputy Inspectors has become a pressing necessity*; but hitherto I have refrained from urging the point, as it involves extra expenditure.

The ordinary assignment from the Educational Cess Fund for support of vernacular schools is to be amalgamated with the above sums, and the whole to form a fund under the

Deputy Commissioner's immediate management for the maintenance of schools, generally throughout the district, of a lower grade than the zillah school. With the increased amount thus available, it is intended to open an *Elementary English School at Rajanpore;* to raise the salaries of teachers, particularly at the best vernacular schools, and so secure the services of really competent teachers even for village schools; and to carry out such other measures as may appear to the Educational and Civil Officers most calculated to render education popular and efficient. The amount available from the Educational Cess Fund is fixed and invariable, but that raised from local sources will, it is hoped, in time become larger, and in time the Government grant-in-aid will also be proportionally augmented; and, thus, as the requirements of the schools naturally increase with the expansion of education, so will the pecuniary means of meeting them probably become to a larger extent available.

1867-68 (*Captain W. R. M. Holroyd*).

REPORT, PARA. 142.—Few teachers of indigenous schools appear anxious to avail themselves of Government aid. The school at Fatehgarh in the Amritsar District deserves special mention, as it is reported by the Inspector to be equal to a Government town school, and it is probably the only *boná fide* indigenous school in the Panjáb where an education of this description can be obtained. **Indigenous school at Fattehgarh in the Amritsar District.**

PARA. 143.—According to the statistics supplied by District Officers, on which, however, I fear no great reliance can be placed, there are 4,888 schools with an average attendance of 46,947 not under Government inspection. The number of students reading Persian is 9,914, Urdu 2,517, Hindi (Nagri) 4,333, and Sanskrit 3,935. No less than 37,413 are returned as studying miscellaneous subjects, and in this number are comprised boys who read the Qurán, and students of patshalas, where "Landé" and the multiplication tables only are taught. **General statistics of indigenous schools.**

1868-69 (*Captain W. R. M. Holroyd*).

REPORT, PARA 157.—The Fatehgarh school and the school of Khalifa Ibrahim at Jalandhar are making satisfactory progress. The former is equal to a Government town school. These and a vernacular school at Ludhiana are, I believe, the only *boná fide* indigenous schools in the Panjáb, where any attempt is made at imparting instruction in general knowledge through the medium of the vernacular. *Indigenous schools in the Jalandhar and Gurdaspur Districts.*

158. Very few teachers of indigenous schools desire to avail themselves of Government assistance, as they are unwilling to introduce the study of Mathematics, History or Geography.

1869-70 (*Captain W. R. M. Holroyd*).

REPORT, PARA. 144.—According to the statistics supplied by District Officers, which are however, as I have remarked, by no means reliable, there are 3,995 indigenous schools which receive no aid from Government. These are supposed to contain 52,479 students, of whom 31,981 are Muhammadans, 156 are returned as reading English, 7,929 Urdu, 2,641 Hindi in the Nagri character, 8,804 Hindi (Landé Mahajani, &c.), 22,511 Arabic, 9,162 Persian, 2,528 Sanskrit. Of the students said to be learning Urdu, no less than 6,297 belong to the Rawal Pindi District, where 14 were entered as studying this language last year. This serves to show the very careless manner in which these returns are made up. There is, however, *no machinery in existence by means of which reliable information regarding the statistics of indigenous schools could be obtained.* It appears, as I remarked last year, that a very large proportion of the boys attending indigenous schools learn Arabic, *i.e.*, to read the Qurán by rote. A considerable number learn the multiplication table and banyas' accounts. Many study Persian, which is generally taught in a most unintelligent manner, though there are, of course, a considerable number of schools where a thorough knowledge of the language can be obtained. *Urdu is very seldom learnt at all in indigenous schools, as the students trust to obtaining a sufficient knowledge of the vernacular by means of their Persian studies.* *Reluctance of indigenous schools to avail themselves of Government assistance.*

1870-71 (*Captain W. R. M. Holroyd*).

REPORT, PARA. 145.—According to the statistics supplied by District Officers, on which, however, very little reliance can be placed, there are 4,133 indigenous schools which receive no aid from Government. They are supposed to contain 50,551 boys, of whom 29,084 are Muhammadans. As I have reported on former occasions, there is no machinery in existence by means of which reliable information regarding the statistics of indigenous schools can be obtained. A very large proportion of the boys learn the Qurán by rote, a considerable number learn the multiplication table and banyas' accounts, and many study Persian, which is generally taught in a most unintelligent manner, though there are, of course, some schools where a sound knowledge of the language can be obtained. *Urdu is very seldom learnt in indigenous schools, as the boys trust to obtaining a sufficient knowledge of the vernacular by means of their Persian studies.* *Indigenous schools.*

(The above is practically a copy of paragraph 144 of the Report of 1869-70, and an amplification of the statements made in previous reports, thus showing how little further information had been gained after several years of supposed experience in apparently carrying out the instructions of Government on the subject. *Indigenous schools.*

1871-72 (*J. G. Cordery, Esq., C.S., Officiating Director*).

REVIEW BY GOVERNMENT, PARA. 2.—In the districts of the Rawal Pindi Circle, the inhabitants of which have been hitherto averse to education, Dr. Leitner made strenuous endeavours to excite a real interest in the subject. But whatever the exertions of individual officers of the Department, the Lieutenant-Governor agrees with the Director that the active interest of District officers and their personal superintendence is necessary to ensure the co-operation of Educational Committees in the Panjáb and the *success of village schools.*

* * * * * *

Primary schools. 7. The Lieutenant-Governor is somewhat *doubtful of the policy which has diminished the number of primary and lower class schools.* It was no doubt desirable to raise the status of the teacher by giving him more pay, and thus securing greater efficiency; and the fact that the number of students was increased, although the number of schools has diminished, is a strong point in favour of the change. But the Lieutenant-Governor is not unwilling to see effect tentatively given to the view of Dr. Leitner, Inspector of the Rawal Pindi Circle, that a better mode of obtaining increased efficiency in primary schools is by inducing (so far as this can fairly be done) the people themselves to contribute to their support, *supplementing deficiencies in the Educational Cess* by their private subscriptions, and placing as many primary and village schools as possible on the grant-in-aid principle, thereby *utilising whatever teaching element is indigenous or popular in the village.* This consideration, His Honour believes, should never be lost sight of, and its importance is increasing with the growth of the demand for education; while the resources of the Government, available for educational purposes, have reached their utmost limit, at any rate under the existing financial system, by which the means at the disposal of the Local Government for educational purposes consist of a fixed assignment from Imperial revenue, and a percentage upon the land revenue of the province, which has shown little tendency to increase.

* * * * * *

Study of Persian. 10. Not only are the text-books in need of revision, but the general scheme of studies for vernacular schools also appears to require re-consideration. More especially would the Lieutenant-Governor refer to the study of Persian, which is taught in every primary school in the Panjáb, the pupils in which should naturally belong to the agricultural classes. Persian is a language nowhere spoken in the Panjáb, except perhaps in the city of Peshawar itself. It is the vernacular of no class of the people. Its use is confined to men of rank or Munshis of Government offices, and by devoting so much attention in its schools to its study the Government has embarked on a policy of questionable wisdom. The beauty of the Persian language, its richness in ornament, and its copious literature, will prevent its study ever being neglected by Natives of position; but to the great mass of the people its acquisition is a pure waste of time. During his tour this cold weather, the Lieutenant-Governor has been much struck by *the absence—in some districts the almost entire absence—of the sons of agriculturists from the village schools supported by the agricultural population from the percentage on land revenue,* but which are filled by the children of munshis and shopkeepers, the men who, under the present Government, are rapidly increasing in wealth, and who hope to give their sons such an education as will enable them to rise above the position in life in which they were born. It is not, however, desired by Government that any such sentiments should be felt by the agriculturists. What they require is the simple education which is found in the 1st class only of the primary schools—Urdu reading and writing, and the simplest rules of Arithmetic. Nothing more than this is necessary. But this it is impossible to acquire in one year, which forms the term during which each boy remains ordinarily in the lowest class. He is then promoted to a higher class in which the *study of Persian, Geography and the higher rules of Arithmetic are required. The Lieutenant-Governor sees in the educational course of the schools in Panjáb villages no provision made for teaching Hindi, Gurmukhi, or the reading of village account books, all of which would be useful in some parts of the country to the classes for which these schools are primarily intended. Boys of every grade and class in life are forced into the same mould and have to pass through the same educational course, the consequence being that all those to whom it is unsuited (and these form a majority of the people) often decline to attend the Government schools.*

* * * * * *

Study of English. 11. Eight thousand nine hundred and fifty scholars, almost exactly 10 per cent. of the school-going population of the Panjáb, receive instruction in English. This is a large decrease in numbers compared with the years of 1865, 1863, 1867 and 1868, when the number of English students averaged about 12,000.

The Lieutenant-Governor considers that the reduction in the number is due to a rational policy of abolishing altogether the study of English in those schools where it cannot be efficiently taught. Even now, English is taught by many masters who are quite incompetent for the work; and there is no advantage in throwing upon the country a class of men with a mere smattering of the English language, literature, or the sciences which are taught through the medium of English. The only result is to create a class of scholars of the most superficial acquirements, and yet filled with a sense of their own importance, and discontented unless they receive salaries which can only justly be asked by accomplished English scholars. *There is no danger whatever that the study of English will be neglected in the Panjáb.* The anxiety to acquire it is each day becoming more marked; and while the Government has no desire to discourage its study, it should yet take care that it is not taught in any schools where the agency at command is insufficient to teach it properly. It is no doubt true that at the present day in India the highest education cannot be given, except through the medium of

English ; but the great mass of the people do not require the highest education. *The object of the Government is rather to impart elementary instruction to the masses than complete education to the few.* The improvement of the vernacular system of education, the *increase in the number of primary schools,* the development, or rather the creation, of a vernacular literature, and the translation into languages known by the people of approved works—these are the aims which the Government should set *before* it as the most useful and important.

Possibility of a great extension of primary schools by placing them on the grant-in-aid principle.

PARA. 80 OF REPORT.—The present gratuitous occupation of our agricultural schools by the banya class has been already alluded to, and affords a just basis on which local committees might take action in this direction. On the frontier, again, the desire of the people for the fusion of some secular instruction into their religious schools affords a similar opportunity for grants-in-aid upon the conditions sanctioned by the Imperial rules. It is my hope that a gradual adoption of this policy will meet the approval of Government throughout the province.

Indigenous schools; their relations to the Panjáb University College.

81. If so, the better class of indigenous schools may possibly assume a more prominent position in the education of the country than can be at present assigned to them. Dr. Leitner has the following suggestive paragraph regarding the relation into which such schools may be brought towards the Panjáb University College. :—

"The Panjáb University College will, I am sure, exercise a most beneficial influence on the thousands of indigenous schools in the province if it carries out the original principles on which it was founded, and faithfully fulfils the promises on the strength of which subscriptions are given Although, owing to some mistake, the announcement of its last oriental examination was only made a few weeks previous to its being held, 23 Maulvis, teachers of schools, came to Rawal Pindi from various parts of the circle, and some from considerable distances. Fourteen returned when they saw the circular of that institution, stating that by the next year they hoped to be able to reach the standard of oriental attainments laid down in it. The desire to obtain diplomas will also stimulate the study of Western science, which is already becoming popular."

Indefinite character of these schools; but they may be roughly divided into four classes.

82. But at present no trustworthy figures with respect either to the number or to the attendance of these schools have been obtained. *Exact information is impossible* when the character of the thing itself is indefinite and shifting. A few children sitting together in a shop and learning the multiplication table, or half a dozen middle-aged men meeting occasionally in a musjid to read the Kurán, are, in some districts, alike held to constitute an indigenous school. There is no attempt at discipline or at any enforcement of regularity. And the teachers are paid by allowances of grain in kind supplemented by presents often of some value and given on such occasions as the marriage of one of their scholars. But the schools may be roughly divided into four classes, with two of which *it is quite possible that we may establish some connection.*

The patshala class schools of arithmetic.

83. The first class is the most numerous, being known as the patshala schools, and being kept by Pandas. The instruction given consists solely in an elaborate system of mental arithmetic, commencing with the multiplication table as high as 20 times 20, and going as far as a rapid calculation of profit and loss. No reading or writing is taught beyond the Hindi system of notation and a phonetic mode of spelling names. But these schools supply the poorer banya with all the information absolutely necessary for his trade, and will continue to flourish in towns, side by side with better education, and quite unaffected by it. They are generally left at the age of thirteen.

The Arabic class. Schools of Muhammadan religion would not object to the incorporation of secular instruction.

84. The Arabic schools are next, both in number and attendance, the ages of the students attending them varying from 6 to 60. Their object is mainly religious, and much of the instruction imparted consists in the repetition of the Kurán and other devotional forms by rote. But the elder students frequently advance to the study of Arabic logic and grammar.

Sanskrit class of a character very similar to the Arabic.

85. The Sanskrit schools are not so numerous, but where they exist, are more favourably reported on than any other schools of this description. Mr. Alexander, Dr. Leitner and Mr. Cooke all concur in specifying some of them as doing good work.* Both the Arabic and Sanskrit schools may certainly be encouraged by the Lahore University College in the manner suggested by Dr. Leitner, and be converted into most useful and popular institutions, if they can be brought to accept the conditions attached to Government grants-in-aid.

Persian class; these schools only teach badly what is better taught in Government schools.

86. The fourth and last class consist of Persian schools, and a very interesting account of the unscientific and laborious system pursued in these schools will be found in the 142nd paragraph of Mr. Alexander's report. It is gratifying to learn that this is being *frequently* abandoned in favour of a scheme and study closely approximating that laid down in our own vernacular schools. But I see no object in offering much encouragement to institutions which, while they in no way make up for other deficiencies by any special appeal to the sympathies of the people, are not so good intrinsically as our own. The adoption of the Government courses is, in their case, the best point to which we can guide them.

---

* But the method pursued by these untrained teachers has, in nearly all cases, the great drawback of imparting a knowledge of particular books almost by rote, rather than any power to use the language. A curious illustration of this is reported to have occurred last year even at Benares. Three hundred such Sanskrit students on being examined before Sir W. Muir and the Raja, however well-acquainted with certain works, were found unable to write a grammatical sentence themselves.

Indigenous schools.

The Inspector of Schools of the Ambala Circle reports as follows :—

PARA. 78 (section III) (*Report*).—The only indigenous schools that I can report of as being of any importance are the schools in the city of Delhi, under the superintendence of the Rev. Mr. Smith. These schools, 11 in number, were established by Mr. Smith before his departure for England, and having been closed during his absence, he has now reopened them. They contain about 250 boys, with an average daily attendance of 200. In the Central School alone is any fee taken, and about Rs. 2 a month are realised. I have visited these schools and examined some of the classes cursorily, but have held no regular examination, as Mr. Smith was obliged to leave Delhi at the time I was appointed to see them. I hope to visit them again when I return to Delhi in June. These schools received a Government aid of Rs. 250 for last year.

I have taken every opportunity, while on tour, of seeing indigenous schools, but have not been able to select any as worthy of Government support. In many cases where I have offered a grant-in-aid the teachers have declined to accede to the conditions proposed.

* * * * * * * *

135. *In the return of indigenous schools is entered a number of aided schools, which cannot properly be called indigenous.*

The Inspector of schools of the Lahore Circle reports as follows :—

Vernacular school Fatehgarh.

136. The school at Fatehgarh, in the Gurdaspur District, is under the management of Maulvi Muhammad Ali Shah, *who receives a grant of land* and a money grant of Rs. 120 per annum for its support. The Maulvi has had his son and younger brothers educated in the Lahore Normal School, with a view to make them efficient teachers of his schools. The attendance is large, and the instruction good. The Government scheme of studies for vernacular schools is strictly followed, and the second will probably be able to rank in the middle class.

137. The Jalandhar school originally belonged to Khalifa Ibrahim, who died during the year. It existed for very many years as an indigenous Persian school, and an excellent Persian education was given in it. Most of the amla of the Jalandhar neighbouring districts have been educated at this school, which is also attended by the children of all the more respectable Muhammadan inhabitants of Jhalandar. The proprietor of the school, appreciating the growing value of instruction in subjects of general knowledge, resolved to introduce the teaching of Arithmetic, Geography, &c., into his school, and applied for a grant under Act XIX to enable him to engage the services of a competent teacher. The death of Khalifa Ibrahim last year was a great loss to the school, which is now kept by his nephew, Baha-ul-din, a young man of 20 years of age. The school has latterly somewhat fallen off in efficiency, but it will be carefully looked after by the local authorities, and will doubtless recover itself. An annual grant of Rs. 180 is given to the school.

* * * * * * * *

140. The returns of the purely indigenous schools are very unreliable, but I suppose we may take them as giving an approximation to the actual number of these schools and their pupils. In the majority of cases the teachers of these schools are paid in kind. At harvest time the zemindars are often in the habit of giving the teachers of their villages a present of grain. Parents of the boys frequently send a daily supply of cooked food from their own kitchens, presents occasionally made of cloth, jewels, or household articles. And on occasions of a marriage or of other private or public festivals an offering of a few rupees is made to the teacher. The expenditure, therefore, from private sources, as stated in the return, must be looked on chiefly as a rough valuation of the cost of the occasional presents made to the teachers.

Panda schools.

141. The most numerous of the private schools, and the most largely attended, are the schools of the Pandas. In these the sole subject taught is a rude system of bazar accounts. The boys learn first the multiplication table in integrals as high as 20 times 20, or even higher. Then they are put through fractional tables, are taught to add and subtract large figures without writing them down, and, finally, to calculate profit and loss, interest and discount. The whole is done by an ingenious, though rude, system of mental arithmetic, the only writing taught being a sort of phonetic writing of names, and of course the Hindi system of notation. The education given in these schools is all that is obtained or cared for by the ordinary banya or mahajan, and, indeed, it is just sufficient to enable him to carry on all the intricacies of his petty trade. These schools are liked too by the people, because they are useful in keeping their children out of mischief. They serve as infant schools to which children of the most tender years can be sent to be taken care of from morning to night, while the parents are engaged in their daily avocations. The ages of the boys in these schools range from 2 or 3 to 13 or 14.

Arabic schools.

142. The Arabic schools come next in point of number. These are purely religious schools, held nearly always in a mosque. The course of study in almost all of them consists in learning portions of the Kurán by heart, and acquiring familiarity with forms of prayer and religious observance. In a few schools a wider range is taken, and after the Kurán and some commentaries have been mastered, the study is extended to works on grammar and logic. The ages of the students in the Arabic schools extend from 8 or 9 to 60 years.

143. The Persian and Urdu schools are not so frequent now, as before the Government vernacular schools were started, but there is still a large number of these scattered all over the country. The old system of instruction was as follows :—The boys first learnt the alphabet, and then were at once put to the Karima, a collection of Persian aphorisms in verse by

Shekh Sadi. This book they were made to learn by heart from beginning to end, without spelling or understanding a single word. When by patient labour of several months, passing over their books with their fingers running along each line as they repeated it, they had committed the whole to memory, the letters and words had become so familiar to their eye that they were able to read with some facility. They were then put through the book again, this time learning the meaning of the couplets also by heart. They then went to the Gulistan, Bahar Danish and other Persian books of questionable morality. Very little grammar beyond the conjugations of the verbs was taught. The course was a most laborious one, and it required many years of hard labour to make a lad a good scholar; at the same time the system, though admirably calculated to strengthen the memory, was equally calculated to weaken and crush the faculty of independent thought. This course of instruction is still followed in many schools, but I am happy to say that in many also the more logical system employed in Government schools is being adopted, and with it many or most of the Government school-books. The ages of the students vary from 6 or 7 to 20 or 22 years.

144. Hindi schools are rare in the Panjáb, and though I see in the return of indigenous schools a considerable number entered as *Hindi students,* I imagine that these are intended to include the students of *Gurmukhi, who are more numerous.* I have no recollection of having seen any private Hindi school, though small Gurmukhi schools are not uncommon. The books read I am not acquainted with, but I fancy few boys learn more than just to read and write. **Hindi and Gurmukhi schools.**

145. There are a few Sanskrit schools in this circle, but very few. In such as these the books chiefly studied are the Shastras. General literature, metaphysics, &c., are seldom touched. The best school of the kind perhaps is the one maintained by Rai Mull Singh at Gujranwala. **Sanskrit schools.**

146. Amongst indigenous schools I see that 345 boys in the Lahore District are entered as learning English. These boys are entered in two or three schools, established by Bengalis for their own children, or by benevolent Native gentlemen for the children of the poorer classes, who cannot afford to enter the Government school, or object to entering the mission school. It is some time now since I have seen any of them, but when last I did so they were doing fairly. **English schools.**

The temporary Inspector of Schools of the Rawal Pindi Circle reports as follows:—

PARA. 4 (*Dr. Leitner's Report*). Indeed, the only means, in my humble opinion, of exerting a lasting influence on the people of this circle, especially those of the frontier, is by the establishment, under proper guidance, of semi-secular schools. A permanent change in the character of the people of the frontier can only be effected by educating the rising generation. In order to carry out this object the parents must take a real interest in the matter, but they will never do this unless their sacred studies are to some extent recognized by Government. I admit that there are difficulties in dealing with the question, but they will have to be met soon, and they are not insuperable to officers intimately acquainted with the feelings, the language and the religion of the Natives. In whatever way, however, the interest of the people may be sought to be awakened in education, the co-operation of the district officers and the raising of the status of the higher Native educational officials are the essential conditions of success in this circle.

* * * * * * * *

6. *In the extension and liberal interpretation of the grant-in-aid rules to all classes without distinction will, as I have represented for years, be alone found the solution of educational problem (including the question of "Muhammadan Education") and the fulfilment of the Educational Despatch of 1854. It alone will gain the confidence of the people and their co-operation with us for the general aims of the Educational Department.*

7.(*a*) What can be done by grant-in-aid institutions has been shown by the success of the mission school at Rawal Pindi, which secured for this circle the highest position gained by the Panjáb at the late Entrance Examination of the Calcutta University. Indeed, were it not for missionary institutions, this circle would be without higher education of any kind. This debt of gratitude which we owe to them should be borne in mind when considering the subject-matter of the next paragraph to which I solicit your earnest attention.

* * * * * * * *

13. It is, however, no use deceiving ourselves into the belief that our educational system has a great hold on the masses. Whilst at a cost of Rs. 1,74,892-12-8 we instruct and inspect in this circle 216 schools, containing 13,988 pupils, the people *educate*—to feelings not of loyalty—21,632 pupils in 774 unaided indigenous schools maintained at an annual cost of Rs. 31,099-6. In reality it will be found that there are more than double that number of schools (containing nearly 40,000 pupils) unaided by Government. I have heard it denied by an Inspector of long standing that there were any such schools, but this is merely another proof of how little we, who ought to know most of the inner life of the people, are acquainted with what is going on. But even if double the number of pupils supposed to be under instruction in both aided and unaided schools were actually and properly educated, we should not have fully discharged our duty to the masses. We are bound to take more notice in a national and representative spirit of the indigenous schools. (I need scarcely say that I have examined several of those schools.) Yet in the face of the appalling ignorance of the country, and *knowing* that the Supreme Government would strongly support any measure for the *extension* of education, we have *abolished* numerous village schools in order to feed a few central places convenient for our inspection, instead of endeavouring to have a *school in every village* in the circle. There can be no doubt that, unless we strengthen and improve university education, "primary" and "secondary" education have no standard to look to; but this can never be an excuse for neglecting the masses. The Panjáb University, which is established on a national basis, is the most effective organisation for giving life to education and reality to our depart-

ment. I therefore look with much favour on the proposals of districts in this and the Multan Circle to send men on scholarships to that University, or to strengthen its general work for the country by means of subscriptions and schools attached to one or the other of its departments. The "resolution" of the Senate of that institution to help schools in which efficient secular instruction is imparted, in addition to any religious teaching there may be given in them, is a solution of the "Muhammadan question," whilst it enunciates a principle of the widest application to all denominations. The effect of the "resolution," so far as it has been carried out, has been to promote toleration and to create a feeling of genuine attachment to a "truly paternal" Government; for not only have Hindu, Muhammadan, English, Anglo-vernacular and vernacular schools been started or projected, but even in the purely Muhammadan school at Bal Bikari the majority of the pupils are Hindus, who read the secular subjects only. The effect on the Native priesthood will be to induce it to study its own classics critically and to add to them a knowledge of western sciences. The ignorant members, whose only learning has been disloyalty, will lose their influence, and those who are anxious for the propagation of still higher truth and learning will find a field ready prepared for their labours, whilst Government, having the interest of the priesthood on its side instead of against it, will have at its disposal a powerful agency. Anyhow, whatever be the nature of the schools established, it is to be wished that the melancholy sight of ranges of 12 miles and upwards being without any educational appliances will no longer be tolerated by a civilised and wise Government.

20. The method of examination which I adopted somewhat differed from the one in vogue. The aim being how most to influence teachers, children and parents, it became necessary to show (1) that every subject taught had a practical bearing—a fact most parents in the agricultural districts doubt; (2) that "individual" as well as "class" excellence was recognised; (3) that the subjects prescribed had been really taught. With this view I put questions in every subject having a reference to "common things," examined each pupil individually, and went through the course laid down. To "written" I added "oral" examinations. Successful boys were put in the 1st, 2nd and 3rd divisions respectively, those in the first division being brought to special notice. Results of examination and instructions to teachers were left at most places. I conversed with the masters on their work, and ascertained their attainments, wishes and local information, and publicly stated my reasons for the praise I gave to those who had done well. Native notables, the parents of the pupils, Maulvis and Pandits, and sometimes the whole of their schools, were invited to attend the examination and distribution of prizes, sweetmeats, &c.

21 (4) *and* (5). I greatly regret the disparaging tone in which the committees of local instruction and the educational work of Tahsildars are treated in previous reports. It is not the duty of educational officers to "put down" but to "develope" Native agency. In spite of the difficulty in my way of holding my office only temporarily, I found the Native gentry and officials only too glad to help me, if they could, and to discuss proposals for their improvement. I held meetings at Gujrat, Jelalpur, Jhelum, Pind Dadan Khan, Chakwal, Talagang, Bal Bikari, Danala, Rawal Pindi and other places. I made the acquaintance of almost every Native of any influence in the places I visited, and met many friends of the Department, among whom I would mention Raja Zeman Mehdi of Darapur. The Tahsildars everywhere, but especially those of Jhelum, Talagang and Chakwal, exerted themselves on behalf of the Department. Learned Maulvis and Pandits emerged from their obscurity to meet the Educational Inspector. As a proof that these Committees are not so useless as was supposed, I beg to annex a statement of their subscriptions and proposals:

I.—Gujrat: (*a*) Rs. 2,900 have been raised to promote some village schools to the status of middle schools, and to provide an upper school for the City of Gujrat. Parents have been willing to sacrifice the scholarships received by their sons at Lahore if this boon were conceded to Gujrat; (*b*) discussions regarding the establishment of female schools, of an Anjuman, and of semi-secular schools for the two leading creeds are taking place among them.

II.—Jhelum: Rs. 750 subscribed for a Muhammadan school.
Talagang: „ 850 „ „
Chakwal: „ 500 and land, subscribed for a *Hindu-Muhammadan school.*
Bal Bikari: „ 200 „ „ „
And applications reach me from different places in the Jhelum and Rawal Pindi districts for English, Anglo-vernacular and oriental schools, the applicants often professing a readiness to subscribe half the amount required for the maintenance of these schools.

III.—The Local Committee of Chakwal proposed to help education in addition to what is already given in the following way:—

		Rs. Per annum.
(1.)	*For a Government school in every unprovided village* ...	1,800
(2.)	To provide assistant masters for existing schools ...	750
(3.)	For a Hindu-Muhammadan school	800
(4.)	To help the Panjáb University in examining and inspecting these schools, and in rewarding oriental scholars, publishing oriental books, &c., &c.	750
(5.)	To provide scholarships for promising youths anxious to prosecute higher studies of a professional or educational character at Lahore	400
	Total of additional help to education ...	4,500

IV.—Talagang was equally liberal and circumspect. Pind Dadan Khan would only propose an additional Rs. 1,500 per annum and Jhelum followed the lead of Chakwal. The Municipal Committee of Rawal Pindi offered Rs. 100 to the best man from their district in the Panjáb University Entrance Examination, and other offers from that district have reached me.

22. I think it of great importance to our Department that Inspectors and District Officers should make their tours coincide, provided always that the tour is distinctly understood to be an educational one, otherwise the Natives gather round their own "Hákim," and the Inspector may find himself more neglected than if he had gone alone. Major Harrington of Gujrat made his tour, principally an educational one, and to this fact the success of my visit to that district is to be attributed. The most practical plan in my opinion would be for the Tahsildar, who can almost always spare the time, to accompany the Inspector through his tahsil. This would be sufficient in the eyes of the Natives to establish "education" as one of the most favoured operations of Government. The position of the Chief Mohurrir should also be improved, and he should certainly not rank below a Naib Tahsildar. What respect can be expected to be shown for the person and the work of an official who sits on the ground in the presence, say, of a Naib Tahsildar drawing less pay, and who has not even a chaprassie allowed him in his circle? If his work is to be efficient, he should hold a high position in the district office.

23. The "moral influence" of an Inspector has no doubt its advantage, but it should be supplemented by the exercise of a *direct educational* influence in the schools he visits. At present the only record of his inspections consists of a few notes for his own information, and a few remarks—generally of a barren nature—which he puts down in the Visitors' Book, *in English!* The village schoolmasters cannot read them, and the chances against their being seen by any one except the Inspector himself on his next tour are very great. I consider that the results of the examination and the remarks on every subject connected with the school should be written at the time in the Visitors' Book and translated into Urdu, and that the master should be required to furnish both the Mohurrir and Inspector with a copy of these "results and remarks" for record in their offices. I also consider that subordinate officials and head masters, those of the larger schools especially, should be encouraged to communicate freely with the Inspector on every subject connected with their administration; for nothing can be a greater advantage to a superior officer, and to the cause of education, than to be able to elicit the whole truth, however destructive to preconceptions this may be.

25. The change in the classification of schools, a mere office convenience, will be perplexing in village schools, especially for a time. *I have pointed out before how large a space compared with their intrinsic value educational forms occupy in our scheme; and that to them substance and reality are frequently sacrificed.* But these "forms" even are far from being perfect or business-like. The numerous and not always clearly worded circulars in this office require to be codified in brief and intelligible language, if they are to be thoroughly understood and vigorously carried out.

We have an education machinery, but we have no educational government. Everything of importance should be translated into the vernacular for the information of the majority of our subordinates. That this is not systematically done may be inferred from the circumstance that the grant-in-aid rules devised to encourage Native enterprise, and the very soul of our educational policy, do not exist in a translated form in this circle.

26. Finally, I venture to doubt the advantage of having to obtain any statistical information regarding my own circle from the Director's Office. It appears to me to be more natural and more conducive to the despatch of business and to the general efficiency of local administration for me to supply you with that information. At present annual returns, *e.g.*, which could be prepared here, if all local information were sent to me direct, reach me from your office by the end of April. This alone must delay the early submission of reports. Again, there is no very strong reason why establishment bills for the whole of this circle should not be countersigned by the Inspector. This would enable him to know immediately and accurately when and how certain expenditure has been incurred, &c. My proposal would tend to lighten the labours of your office whilst securing the more efficient working of my own.

63. When Bedi Khem Singh's schools were first established, at the inspiration of Sir Robert Montgomery, there was a sort of understanding or guarantee that these schools should not be inspected by officials, especially Europeans. I presume that it was for this reason that these schools have not been inspected, and that an amount of suspicion, both deserved and undeserved, has fallen on them. Without distinct orders from Government I should myself have hesitated to inspect them, although I received a sort of permission by the Bedi's Agent to do so. The schools were closed a few days after I saw the Agent—a course which was not calculated to strengthen the belief of the people in the permanence of our educational policy or to encourage Bedi Khem Singh in again offering us his services. After all the agitation that had taken place regarding "female education," it was certainly inconsistent to sweep away at one blow 108 schools, although the Department was perfectly justified in doing so, considering how very unfavourably both Major Urmston, D.C., and Mr. Frizelle has referred to these schools, that money was required for more important or less mysterious institutions, and that after all no Inspector can conscientiously support a grant about whose application he simply knows nothing. Whether an attempt might not have been made to inspect these schools in spite of what is, probably erroneously, considered to be the policy of Government in the matter, I will not discuss, but I have not the least doubt that the sensitiveness of the people on this subject is exaggerated.

Mr. Pearson truly remarks :—"I do not at all believe in the alleged scruples of the people about having their girls' schools inspected. They consist of little girls four or five years old, who may be seen playing in the streets with their writing boards. The only prejudice is against the system of payment by results. The simplest remedy would be to allow the grant in future only where the schools are open to the inspection of Government officers. I do not say that this plan is free from objections, but Bedi Khem Singh must be able to judge for himself whether he could accept the assistance of Government upon these terms." This view pre-supposes that Bedi Khem Singh profits by the arrangement, but the Bedi may be looking upon it as a great trouble and inconvenience which he has incurred merely to please the "Sirkar." I am glad that a letter of thanks at any rate has been sent to him, but I regret that once we had 108 female schools we should not have kept them up. A good deal is already gained by vesting the interests of a large body of teachers in the maintenance of "female education." We can afford to wait till the next generation for perfect "returns," which, after all, are no safeguard against fraud and jobbery.* In our hurry to build the edifice of an ideal Indian civilization "in one day" we risk a sudden collapse of what has already been raised. I have never been very sanguine about "female education" in this province, although the kindness of Native friends compelled me to become the first European president of the movement; but if female schools are to exist and to be inspected, there is no doubt that it can be done. In towns where greater temptations exist, Natives naturally take greater precautions regarding their daughters, and generally the higher and better families are averse to send them any distance to school when they may be entrapped *en route*, as has occurred. Still numerous small schools conveniently situated rather than a central school convenient for inspection, and inspected by educational native officials of known respectability and a certain age, would not be objected to. The girls of the best families may be visited at their houses by female teachers of known piety. A certain amount of education has always been given to females, at any rate in Muhammadan families of standing. The "purdah" is nowhere so strict as in Turkey, yet unmarried girls attend school up to the age of 14, as I have seen myself (*vide* my "Muhammadan Education in Turkey").

64. There is an aided vernacular school at Peshawar supported by the Municipality and a grant. I am not aware that there is any private subscription for this school, and do not think that it substantially differs from a Government vernacular school. Mr. Pearson has recommended a reduction of the grant—*a policy which I consider injurious to the interests of this circle. Improve the schools, but do not reduce or abolish them.* The Peshawar school has 203 names on the rolls, with an average daily attendance of 112 and Rs. 48-9-9 in fees. I have quoted Mr. Pearson's views on this school in his report on the Peshawar District.

65. At Gujrat, Jhelum, Pind Dadan Khan and Chakwal I took the opportunity of calling in the neighbouring indigenous schools. With one or two of them I was pleased, but, of course, they all suffer from want of controlling or rather encouraging and guiding agency. At Sahawal, near Pind Dadan Khan, we had abolished a school, but a zemindar continued to maintain it very generously from his own resources. The teaching of the school has, however, very much fallen off. Applications for the restoration of Government schools have reached me from several places. Some applicants offer to subscribe towards them, but *the general feeling is that they are entitled to them, as they pay the "educational cess."* There are some very fair oriental schools throughout this circle. There is a large Sanskrit school at Jhelum, and a very good Sanskrit school at Rawal Pindi. Superior oriental schools have been started at Chakwal and Bal Bikari, and others are in course of formation at Jhelum, Rawal Pindi and Talagang. From other places also liberal offers for the establishment of semi-secular schools have reached me.

These schools are entitled to a grant-in-aid if they are well managed, as the subscriptions are *literally* local.

66. The Panjáb University College will, I am sure, exercise a most beneficial influence on the thousands of indigenous schools in the province, if it carries out the original principles on which it was founded and faithfully fulfils promises on the strength of which subscriptions were given. Although owing to some mistake the announcement of its last oriental examination was only made a few weeks previous to its being held, 23 Maulvis, teachers of schools, came to Rawal Pindi from different parts of the circle, and some from considerable distances; 15 returned when they saw the circular of that institution stating that by the next year they hoped to be able to reach the standard of oriental attainments laid down in it. Their desire to obtain diplomas will also stimulate the study of "Western Science," which is already becoming popular.

D. W. Thompson, Esq., Inspector of Schools, Multan Circle, writes as follows :—

PARA. 74.—The usual statement of indigenous schools for this year accompanies this report. It will be seen from it that there are said to be 554 schools of this class, containing an aggregate of 7,329 scholars; 4,438 learning Arabic, 30 Sanskrit, 1,431 Persian, and 76 Urdu, besides a number of others learning arithmetic *and* accounts.

* Many years ago I drew attention to a return in which 2,000 pupils were stated to be under instruction On careful enquiry I foundthat 11 only had been in regular attendance.

1872-73 (C. Pearson, Esq.).

Review by Government, para. 9.—His Honour has considered the observations contained in paragraph 54 of the Report regarding the difficulty of applying the grant-in-aid system to indigenous schools in the Panjáb. It may be difficult, but His Honour is not convinced of its impracticability in all cases, and adheres to the views expressed in the Review of last year's Report, that the policy should *never be lost sight of.*

Report, para. 54.—No question is of more importance than the best means of increasing the number of cheap but efficient primary schools. The system of grants-in-aid has been found unsuited to the case of indigenous village schools.

The experience of the North-Western Provinces is thus stated in the Review of the last Report by His Honour the Lieutenant-Governor:—

"The intention of Mr. Thomson's government at that time was to establish a standard Government school at each tahsil, and to subsidise and improve by inspection the indigenous village schools, *not to supplant them by Government schools.* Before long, however, it was found that the indigenous schools did not possess in themselves any elements which were capable of development into useful schools, imparting even a primary education, and by degrees the principle of establishing Government schools in the villages was accepted."

I believe that similar attempts to improve the indigenous school *without annexing it* have been equally unsuccessful in the Panjáb. On the other hand, we learn that in Bengal the patshalas have readily adapted themselves to the requirements of a sound elementary system of education, and apparently good primary schools have been established at much less expense than in Northern India. The question is whether the difference is in the character of the indigenous schools or in the system applied to them.

55. Mr. Woodrow, Officiating Director in Bengal, in his report for 1871-72 (page 56), sums up the work of patshalas thus:—

"Patshalas are practically Government schools. On the 31st March they were 1,801 in number, and contained 45,702 pupils and cost Government Rs. 92,115, out of a total of Rs. 1,49,445. Hence the average cost to Government of each patshala was Rs. 51-0-6. On every rupee of expenditure on these schools Government pays 10 annas, and the people 6 annas. Probably something is given in the shape of food and clothing, which is not regularly brought to account; but yet there is reason to fear that whenever Government takes up a village school, the people diminish their contributions."

The average payments of fees were Rs. 31 in each school and Re. 1-4 for each boy. The average number of scholars is 25 in a Government patshala, and 11 in an indigenous school. The Guru of the former has generally gone through a course of instruction in the Government normal school, and his school, though of a more humble character than our own primary schools, is equally under the control of the officers of Government.

56. The unimproved patshala is described by Babu Bhudeb Mukerji, Inspector of Schools in the Rajshahi Division (pages 141-43). The course consists of—

(1) the elements of reading and writing;
(2) addition and subtraction, the multiplication table;
(3) agricultural and commercial accounts;
(4) the composition of business letters, petitions, grants, leases, &c.

But most Gurus want the capacity to carry their pupils beyond the second stage of progress. The pupils of the improved patshalas are said to be better in all respects excepting handwriting.

In Northern India the Mahajani school, which corresponds most nearly to the Bengal patshala cannot furnish the nucleus of a good primary school.

57. Now it appears to me that there is one important difference between the indigenous schools of Bengal and of Northern India. The Bengal patshala takes its pupils in the right direction, and the Government system of education is merely an improvement upon this. With us the schools in which banyas' accounts are taught correspond most nearly to the Bengal patshalas, but the written characters which they use are not uniform, every commercial centre having its own alphabet; and, consequently, the course of study in the improved school must commence from the beginning. It is even more impracticable to attempt to lay a foundation upon those schools, if they may be so called, in which little children learn to read by rote a few pages of the Kurán.

The Persian *Maktab* is the foundation of the Government primary school in Northern India.

58. The Persian *Maktabs* have been extensively absorbed into our vernacular schools. It is only within the last few years that pupils taught in our own schools have been available for teacherships, and there is some danger in exchanging the hereditary Mulla, who can always be retained, for a young man who is looking out to better himself, and will be off at any moment if he does not get as much pay as he thinks he deserves.

But where the chief difficulty of getting the people to accept education exists, there the Persian *Maktab* is not found. Two or three boys may be seen reading Persian in the mosque, but there is nothing which might form the nucleus of a school; and hence the almost insurmountable difficulty of introducing any kind of education in the frontier districts.

Hindi and Gurmukhi in primary schools.

59. Of 49,997 boys in primary schools, 4,103 study Hindi (Nagri) and 1,522 Mahajani. The latter, as I have explained, is useful only for the shop; but it is curious that, notwithstanding the newspaper cry for Hindi raised by the Hindus, no serious effort is made to use the opportunities which exist. The Nagri scholars are about a third of the whole in the

primary schools of the Amballa Circle, and there are many Nagri schools in Kangra and Hoshiarpur. But Hindi does not lead to employment, and no one cares to go beyond the elements of reading and writing.

Primary education how to be extended.

60. The extension of primary education will not, I believe, be effected by the adoption of any new system, but by constant efforts to make our village schools as cheap and as numerous as possible, and by diverting a portion of the funds which are now spent in sustentation allowances, in a too liberal scale of salaries and in diffusing a smattering of English.

Indigenous schools.

The Inspector of Schools of the Rawalpindi Circle (Mr. Pearson) also reports as follows:—

35. The question of aiding indigenous schools was discussed in the first paragraph of this Report, and I have now only to give some account of the statistics. These are collected by the Tahsildars from the reports of patwaris and others, and are evidently very inaccurate. I am glad to see that the very large numbers formerly reported from Jhelum District have this year been reduced to a more moderate computation ; but the estimated cost of indigenous education, Rs. 18,979 in that District, is preposterous, although Rs. 9,000 less than it used to be. No returns have been received from Hazara. The other Districts of the Circle are reported to number 15,713 indigenous scholars. Of every 100 of these 2 read Urdu, 7 Hindi (Nagri), 10 Lande and Mahajani, 45 Arabic, 30 Persian, 6 Sanskrit. A true idea of what actually goes on may be gathered from the reports of the School Mohurrirs, which concur with my own observations. In the great majority of indigenous schools Mussulman boys read the Kurán by rote only ; next to these come the Mahajani schools, and in connection with both are students learning Persian and Urdu, Sanskrit, or Arabic, with a view to their future occupation.

The School Mohurrir of Jhelum recently inspected 41 indigenous schools in which Persian is taught. He found on an average three or four who could read and write in each, and in one case only as many as eight. The School Mohurrirs of Rawal Pindi reported upon 15 selected schools, in which on an average from 8 to 15 boys could read and write. The School Mohurrir of Peshawar reported that he was able to find only one indigenous school in which more than two or three boys could read and write Persian, and that is in the city. On the frontier, where it is suggested that the people may have less prejudice to indigenous schools than to those set up by Government, it should be remembered that there is hardly any material to work upon.

1873-74 (*Major Holroyd*).

REVIEW BY GOVERNMENT, PARA. 22.—In the indigenous schools of the Peshawar District out of 2,570 pupils, 2016 are under instruction in Arabic, a proof, otherwise abundantly corroborated, of the general reverence accorded to the teaching and literature of Islam. In the Government schools of the lower class the number of pupils is only 752, and among these there are very few Pathans, Sayad or Mullazadas. There is, indeed, a strong religious prejudice against the Government scheme of education. On other grounds, the Khans object to their tenants going to school, and parents of the agricultural class desire no instruction of children already useful in the fields. In the presence of such obstacles the most cautious and conciliatory action is required. *But enquiries personally instituted by the Lieutenant-Governor lead him to believe that some of the existing teachers are willing to accept grants-in-aid on the departmental terms.* To those—and there are several who teach Persian well—rewards might be given, and by others presents of Persian and Arabic school-books would be willingly received. The exertions of leading men in the promotion of education should always be liberally acknowledged.

1874-75 (*Major Holroyd*).

REVIEW BY GOVERNMENT, PARA. 10.—The Inspector of that Division (Rawal Pindi) observes that the question of aiding good indigenous schools has not been lost sight of, but that there seem to be obstacles to the carrying out of the suggestions which were made in the last report. His Honour would be glad to be informed by further report of the nature of these obstacles, as he considers that *judicious aid given to indigenous schools is a very important part of the work of the Educational Department.* Too little is done in the frontier districts in the direction, and *the department should, as far as possible, utilize existing agency and improve indigenous schools* by giving grants-in-aid on reasonable conditions of efficiency and permission for inspection.

The people of the frontier districts are in many cases suspicious and bigotted, and will far more readily send their children to private schools to be taught by priests or mullas than to Government institutions, where the education is no doubt better, but less in accordance with their wishes and prejudices.

1875-76 (*Major Holroyd*).

REVIEW BY GOVERNMENT, PARA. 12.—It is observed that the difficulty of aiding indigenous schools, specially in frontier districts, *the desirability of which has been so often impressed in reviews of Educational Reports,* is found, as, indeed, was anticipated, chiefly to lie in the absence of eligible schools to aid ; but the Lieutenant-Governor trusts that this important point may not be lost sight of, and that the Department will, in consultation with the civil authorities, continue to endeavour to utilise and develop, so far as may be possible, the existing educational institutions of the country, and *enlist on the side of the Government* and an improved form of education *the teachers of indigenous schools,* whether attached to Hindu or

Muhammadan religious institutions or separate from them? The Panjáb University, furnishing through the Oriental College attached to it teachers for these indigenous schools, may well assist in this important work.

1876-77 (Major Holroyd).

REPORT, PARA. 99. The school of Khalifa Ibrahim in the Jalandhar District has passed under the management of the Deputy Commissioner, and does not virtually differ from the Government vernacular schools of the district. The two Muhammadan schools at Amritsar, maintained, the one by Mean Muhammad Jan, the other by Maulvi Abdul Qari, are said to fulfil very fairly the purpose for which they were founded, as they give a fair oriental education, including religious teaching, combined with instruction in Arithmetic, Geography, &c. **Aided lower schools, Lahore Circle.**

100. It will be convenient here to notice the returns of the indigenous schools of the province. According to the returns furnished by District Officers there were at the close of the year 4,803 schools containing 56,642 boys. This shows an increase of about 8,000 over the previous year. The increase is confined to the Districts of Hazara and Kohat, for which returns were not supplied last year and to Gujrat. The increase in the latter district, however, is evidently due to an error in the returns either for the year under report or the previous year. In the remaining districts there has been, on the whole, a slight falling off. **Statistics of indigenous schools.**

Considerably more than half the boys attending indigenous schools are returned as learning Arabic; and of those returned as learning Arabic about three-fifths are in the Rawal Pindi Circle; 518 are shown as learning English, 2,805 Urdu, 7,887 Persian, 1,228 Sanskrit, 8,307 Hindi, in the Nagri character, and 9,285 banyas' accounts, &c. **Notice of indigenous schools.**

Formerly there was a considerable number of Maktabs or indigenous schools in which Persian was taught, but the great majority of these have been gradually absorbed in our system. When primary schools were first established throughout the province we employed all the indigenous teachers we could find who possessed sufficient ability and were willing to accept appointments. Such men generally brought with them their own pupils, and the numbers were, of course, swelled by new boys. Amongst the teachers thus employed were many men who were good Arabic and Persian scholars, but they were ignorant of mathematics, history and geography, and were subsequently sent to study these subjects in normal schools. In many of the large towns Government and Aided schools were set on foot in which English was taught. *At first, there was considerable rivalry between these and the indigenous Maktabs, and this continued for some years.* I then tried the experiment of organising branch schools in various quarters of the City of Delhi, and the system was soon extended throughout the larger towns and cities of the province. Where indigenous schools of a suitable character existed, these formed the nucleus of the branches which are now maintained on the grant-in-aid system, and constitute the basis of higher education.

The indigenous schools thus taken over by the Department were for the most part Persian Maktabs. Some of the teachers in these Maktabs were, as I have already stated, good Persian scholars, while the attainments of others were of a much lower order.

The system of instruction that prevailed in most of these schools was of a very indifferent character. The boy began with the Karima which they were required to learn by heart, first *be-m'ane, i.e.*, without the meaning, and then *ba-m'ane, i.e.*, with the literal translation, but without any comprehension of the subject-matter. The same process was then gone through with other Persian books The pupil, if told to read from the beginning of a chapter, could repeat what he had learnt by heart with fluency, and follow the text in his book. If put on the middle of a sentence he was generally unable to read a word. His memory was certainly strengthened by this system, but there was no attempt to cultivate his intelligence or to exercise his reasoning power. When Urdu books were introduced by the Department they were taught at first in the same way, and it was only by slow degrees that we were able to suppress entirely the former practice.

In indigenous schools, where banyas' accounts are taught, the boys receive no literary education whatever. Constant efforts have been made, however, to bring as many of these schools as possible under the influence of the Department. Of course, nothing can be done in cases where the teacher and parents will allow the boys to learn nothing beyond the multiplication table, banyas' account, and hundi-writing; but a considerable number of schools have been absorbed into our branch school system, the boys being taught the element of Urdu in addition to accounts and hundi-writing, and being drafted eventually into the main school.

It must not be supposed that the boys returned as reading Arabic really learn that language. The great majority merely learn certain portions of the Kurán by heart. The teacher is generally himself incapable of translating what he teaches into the vernacular. Sometimes he is blind. He rarely possesses the will or the ability to teach anything beyond that which custom requires. Over these schools the Department can exercise no influence, but it does not follow that no influence is exercised over the boys, and, as a matter of fact, many of the latter enter Government schools after having learnt what is considered necessary in the mosque.

It was observed in the review by Government, see my last Annual Report, that the difficulty of aiding indigenous schools in frontier districts lay, as had been anticipated, chiefly in the absence of eligible schools to aid, but that the Lieutenant-Governor trusted to the Department, in consultation with local authorities, to continue its endeavours for the development of existing educational institutions, and the enlistment on the side of Government and an improved form of education of the teachers of indigenous schools, whether attached to religious institutions or separate from them. This matter has received constant attention for some years past in the Peshawar District; and as there were scarcely any indigenous schools already in existence which it was possible to influence in the matter desired, the experiment has been tried of promoting the establishment of new schools of this class. On this subject Mr. Pearson writes as follows :—

"In compliance with the orders of His Honour the Lieutenant-Governor, for some years past efforts have been made to encourage indigenous schools by grants-in-aid. In the City of Peshawar there are a few such schools which have been attached to the Municipal aided schools or to the Mission school, but in neither case have the results been very satisfactory. In the district, however, there is only one Persian school of any reputation, *viz.*, that at Prowg, which has been in receipt of an allowance from the District Fund for the last two years. Since my last inspection four indigenous schools have been established under Mullas who have some experience of the Government school system. The plan which has been adopted is to place one of these men under the patronage of a Khan, who provides his food and other advantages. The Mulla receives in addition an allowance of Rs. 5 or Rs. 3 from the District Funds.

"He sits in the village mosque, teaches the Kurán in the usual manner, and besides instructs some of his pupils in the subjects of the Government course. Only those who read something besides the Kurán are included in the returns. The system, which is, in fact, a creation of indigenous schools, was not contemplated by the Lieutenant-Governor, and it is too early to say whether it will turn out well; but the cost is trifling, and the experiment seems worth trying."

It has been shown that the majority of the indigenous schools in which in former days any kind of literary education was given have been actually absorbed in our system, and that we have assimilated also a considerable number of schools in which formerly the multiplication table, elementary accounts, and hundi-writing were the sole object of study. It has been explained also that, as a general rule, no useful influence can be exerted by the Department on the majority of existing indigenous schools, where the boys learn portions of a religious book by rote in a foreign language under the superintendence of a teacher who is incapable of imparting any other instruction. Signs, however, are not wanting that indigenous schools of a different kind may be expected to spring into existence. The people have in some cases appointed English teachers, and have in others established Anglo-vernacular schools for themselves, in the hope generally that a grant-in-aid may be obtained from Government.

1877-1878 (Major Holroyd).

REPORT, PARA. 112.—The Muhammadan school in Amritsar has not proved very successful, and at the end of the year, the Manager, Mian Muhammad Jan, relinquished the grant-in-aid and determined to maintain the school merely as a religious institution.

Maulvi Abdul Ali Qasi's school in the same town will probably come to the same end before long, as those boys who wish to learn subjects of general knowledge prefer to go to the Government or mission schools, and will not remain in the Muhammadan institution after they have gone through the ordinary religious course.

Statistics of indigenous schools.

113. There were, according to the returns, 5,381 indigenous schools at the close of the year, containing 61,818 pupils as compared with 4,803 schools, with 56,642 boys. Of these boys 406 were in the Umballa Circle, 1,201 in the Lahore Circle, 3,156 in the Rawal Pindi Circle, and 618 in the Mooltan Circle. The general character of these schools is described in the extract given from the report of Mr. Pearson, the Inspector of the Rawal Pindi Circle, which will be found of interest.

Inspector's report on indigenous schools, Umballa Circle.

114. Regarding those in the Umballa Circle Mr. Cooke writes as follows :—

"According to the annual returns, there are 406 private schools in this circle, giving instruction, such as it is, to 5,816 boys. The annual expenditure is Rs. 5,119 or about 14 annas for each pupil. Seven-tenths of the cost are paid from fees, and the rest from private sources. I do not look upon these returns as by any means trustworthy. In the matter of fees, for instance, it is difficult to understand how it happens that when in the Umballa District, with 1,532 boys, the fees amount to Rs. 19-13-0 for the year, 500 boys in the Hissar District pay comparatively the enormous sum of Rs. 1,132-8-0. The largest number of pupils are in the Umballa and Ludhiana districts, and in these the fees and the total annual expenditure are the smallest. I shall attempt to discover on what information, and in what manner, these returns are prepared.

"With regard to instruction, there are 67 boys learning English. Most of these are probably the pupils of the Hindi school at Ludhiana, which receives a grant from the Panjáb University College: 200 learn Urdu, 411 Nagri, 2,118 Mahajani, 2,177 Arabic, 740 Persian; and 268 Sanskrit."

Inspection Report on indigenous schools, Rawal Pindi Circle.

The following extract is from Mr. Pearson's report :—

"The chief difference in the return of indigenous schools is an enormous increase in the number of Arabic students in the district of Gujrat. Formerly these statistics were collected by the patwaris, but for the last two years the lists have in this district been made up by school teachers and lambardars, under the direction of the District Inspector. The latter returns are more likely to be correct than those of former years, but anyhow they are useful as an indication of the various forms in which literature is cultivated. The facts have often been explained in these reports, and fluctuations in the numbers are to be accounted for by different modes of compilation rather than by actual changes.

"In every village there is a mosque, and the little boys at one time or another read by rote some portion of the Kurán. Something more than this is learnt by those who are brought up to the office of priest, and there are besides itinerant students who go wherever they can most easily beg their living. The list of students of Gurmukhi and Sanskrit is made up in the same way. Every banya learns the system of accounts which is in use, and wherever the trading class is sufficiently numerous to support a schoolmaster, the little boys learn the elements of their future business to the extent of getting by heart the multiplication table, and writing names, figures, &c.

"The education of the banya is rarely completed in school. He learns there as much as can be taught mechanically, and the more intellectual part is acquired afterwards in his father's shop.

"It appears to me that a census of educated persons taken once in ten years would be far more instructive than this attempt to count indigenous schools, which in nine cases out of ten are not schools at all in any educational sense. Certainly, if the object is to ascertain the means of education available for the people, *it is a mistake to neglect the fact that, apart from the Government schools, probably more learning is acquired privately than at school.* In Europe people are too busy to spend their time as teachers without remuneration, but in India a brother or a friend will generally be found to do the work of a tutor. In Europe, however, the girls are not usually sent to school in the families of gentlemen, and it would be fallacious to judge of the education of women in that class by the number maintained on their account. The same objection lies against an educational census in India based upon the statistics of schools."

1878-79 (*Major Holroyd*).

Review by Government, para. 7. The entire cost of the education of genuine agriculturists is paid from the Local or District Funds. These funds are considered by Government to be as much a portion of the provincial taxation as any other branch of the Government revenue, and from this point of view the entire cost of the education of agriculturists is borne by Government. It must be remembered at the same time that the agriculturists themselves consider that they pay for the education received. Though the cost of educating agriculturists is defrayed from District Funds, it was paid, until within the last few years, from the educational cess, which has now been merged in these funds; and the educational cess was raised for the express purpose of maintaining schools for the agricultural population, and was at first, in theory at least, a voluntary contribution.

Report, para. 120. A few years ago His Honour the Lieutenant-Governor desired that the District Committee should aid the Mullas who maintain private schools or maktabs. In every village the young boys read the Kurán in the mosque and occasionally some of them learn a little Persian. They do not learn to translate the kurán, and this, indeed, is often beyond the power of the teacher. It was found that hardly any of these schools could be made efficient by grant-in-aid; but Mr. Christie, District Superintendent of Police, who was at one time in charge of the educational business of the district, hit upon the plan of creating such schools as His Honour contemplated. As observed by the Inspector, the experiment may have been worth trying, but was not very likely to succeed. and has led to some waste of money. At present 10 of these schools are maintained.

1879-80 (*Major Holroyd*).

Report, para. 149. There is a Hindi school in Lahore, which receives, I believe, some aid from the Maharajah of Kashmir. There is also a Muhammadan school in which English is taught, but the income is insufficient to teach that language successfully. The instruction given is, I believe, gratuitous.

150. The great majority of boys learning Persian are in the Rawal Pindi Circle. On the establishment of Government schools in the Panjáb the indigenous Persian schools or maktabs, formerly very numerous, were gradually absorbed in the Government system, all the best teachers obtaining employment in the Department. Those who have still retained an independent existence are naturally more numerous in the Rawal Pindi Circle.

Review by Government, para. 11. The absence of comparative statistics under this head (Primary Vernacular Education) is the more to be regretted as it is from primary schools that all others are recruited; and *it is therefore the chief duty of the State in educational matters to provide for primary schools,* and to see that the instruction given in them is good and sound; and with regard to this duty the Lieutenant-Governor would earnestly direct the attention of all district officers to the necessity of inducing their subordinates to take an active interest in the cause of education.

1880-81 (*Lieutenant-Colonel Holroyd*).

Review by Government, para. 12.—The results of primary teaching in aided schools are far from favourable as compared with those in Government schools; and this is the more unsatisfactory as grants-in-aid should be given only under very special circumstances to primary schools, which, as a rule, must be supported from local resources.

This principle has been repeatedly laid down by Government, and cannot be too strongly enforced; and it is already under consideration in connection with the further decentralization scheme to relieve District and Local Funds of some of their present charges, *so as to enable them to devote more of their income to the cause of primary education.*

There is a constant tendency to overlook the duties of the State with regard to primary education and to turn greater attention to the more showy results of higher education, and this tendency requires to be steadily watched. *Signs of it are not wanting in the present report*; but it would appear from the review of educational progress during the past decade that a somewhat larger proportion of the total expenditure is now spent on primary education than in 1870-71; and if it be found possible to carry out the financial arrangements above-mentioned, a still greater increase will take place in the future. Meanwhile, the Lieutenant-Governor would once more direct the earnest attention of all officers to the duties of District and Municipal Committees in the matter of primary education.

APPENDIX I.

Appointment of an Educational Syndicate for British Burma.

Extract of a letter from E. S. Symes, Esquire, C.S., Officiating Secretary to the Chief Commissioner, British Burma, to the Secretary to the Government of India, Home Department, No. 6125-24E., dated Rangoon, 5th September 1881.

I am directed to submit copy of a notification, which was published in the *British Burma Gazette* of the 27th August 1881, regarding the appointment of an Educational Syndicate for British Burma. I am to explain that the gentlemen named in the margin have been appointed to be members of the Syndicate, and I am now to solicit sanction to the payment of a salary of Rs. 150 a month to the Registrar, who will ordinarily be an officer of the Educational Department with other duties.

EDUCATIONAL SYNDICATE.

Mr. John Jardine, Judicial Commissioner ..	*President.*
Mr. C. F. E. Allen, Government Advocate ...	*Members.*
Ba One, Esq , Assistant Commissioner ...	
Rev. Dr. Bennett, American Baptist Mission ...	
Right Rev. Dr. P. Bigandet, Bishop of Ramatha and Vicar-Apostolic ...	
Dr. E. Forchhammer, Professor of Pali ...	
G. S. T. Harris, Esq., Executive Engineer, Rangoon	
W. de Courcy Ireland, Esq., LL.D., Officiating Inspector General of Police	
Surgeon-Major Hugh Johnstone, Junior Civil Surgeon, Rangoon	
Rev. Dr. Marks, Principal, St. John's College, Rangoon	
Major Scott-Moncrieff, C.S I., R.E., Officiating Chief Engineer	
Rev. C. A. Nichols, American Baptist Mission ...	
Moung Po, Merchant	
P. Hordern, Esq., Director of Public Instruction	*Ex-officio.*
Pe Moung, Esq., Officiating Junior Inspector ...	
R. G. Hodson, Esq., Offg., Principal High School	

2. I am to explain that the establishment of some representative body of this kind to promote discussion and furtherance of educational objects, was suggested some time ago by Mr. Jardine, who had been Fellow and Examiner of the Bombay University. There was some complaint regarding the results of the provincial examinations last year; and the staff of, at any rate, one aided school represented that the examinations were too much of a departmental affair. Then, when the revised grant-in-aid rules were sanctioned, it became more than ever necessary to have some representative body to conduct and control the provincial examinations. Accordingly, such a body was constituted, and the enclosed rules were drawn up for their guidance. Possibly the scope of the duties of the Syndicate may hereafter become wider.

3. There will be a great deal of heavy and important work in connection with the provincial examinations. This duty has hitherto been done by the Director of Public Instruction himself. It took him away too much from his own proper duty; moreover, the arrangement was open to the twofold objection that, under it, the Department examined its own work, and that outside institutions had no voice in the conduct or manner of the examinations. This work will now devolve on the Registrar of the Syndicate. I am accordingly to solicit permission to pay a salary of Rs. 150 a month to the Government officer who may be appointed to be the Registrar of the Syndicate.

Extract from the "Rangoon Government Gazette."

GENERAL DEPARTMENT.

Notification dated Rangoon, 25th August 1881.

No. 298.—For the purpose of directing and controlling the public examinations to be held under the grant-in aid rules, and for the purpose of promoting the study of medicine, engineering, law, and technical arts, the Chief Commissioner has decided to establish, under the Presidentship of Mr. John Jardine. Judicial Commissioner, a body to be called "The Educational Syndicate of British Burma."

The body will be constituted under the following rules, namely,—

Educational Syndicate, British Burma.

Constitution of the Syndicate.

The members of the Educational Syndicate, British Burma, shall be appointed by the Chief Commissioner, and shall consist of not more than 20 members inclusive of a President and Vice-President.

2. As far as possible all educational interests shall be represented on the Syndicate.

The following Government officers will be *ex-officio* members :—

(1) the Director of Public Instruction ;

(2) one Inspector of Schools ;

(3) the Principal, Government High School, Rangoon ;

and the Syndicate shall include the following :—

(4) one Burman Inspector or Deputy Inspector of Schools ;
(5) one European officer of the Commission ;
(6) one Burman officer of the Commission ;
(7) one officer of the Survey or Public Works Department ;
(8) one Barrister-at-law ;
(9) one Medical officer.

3. The President shall be appointed for two years ; and some member resident in Rangoon will be appointed permanent Vice-President.

4. All appointments to the Syndicate will be honorary.

Duties of the Syndicate.

5. The Syndicate will be responsible for the conduct of all provincial examinations including :—

the middle school examination ;
the upper primary school examination ;
the lower primary school ditto ;
the survey school ditto ;
the teacher's certificate ditto.

They will frame detailed regulations for the superintendence of examinations (both written and oral), at local centres by the District Committees of Public Instruction.

They will annually appoint examiners in all subjects and determine, subject to such money limits as the Chief Commissioner may from time to time prescribe, the rate of fees payable in each case.

They will regulate the conduct of examinations of aided schools held by Inspectors of Schools in accordance with the grant-in-aid rules.

Examiners will be appointed as early in the year as possible, and their appointments will be notified in the *British Burma Gazette* under the signature of the Registrar to the Syndicate.

The Syndicate will fix the dates of the several examinations.

They will also regulate the percentage of marks required to qualify in each examination for a pass and for honors.

It will be within the province of the Syndicate to recommend to the Local Government modifications in the provincial standards for schools of all grades and to frame proposals for imparting instruction in—

Medicine and surgery ;
Engineering ;
Law ;
Technical arts.

Expenditure.

6. All expenditure of the Syndicate will be met from provincial funds ; and bills on account of the Syndicate will be payable on the signature of the Registrar and countersignature of the President or Vice-President.

Conduct of business.

7. Resolutions of the Syndicate will be determined by a majority of votes ; and the President, or, in the absence of the President, the Vice-President, will have a casting vote.

Five members will constitute a quorum.

Ordinary meetings will be held quarterly ; but any meeting may be adjourned or special meeting called by the President of his own accord or on the requisition of five members : the place and time of meeting to be notified by the Registrar to each member.

Duties of Registrar.

8. The duties of the Registrar will be—

(i) to conduct and keep all correspondence of the Syndicate regarding provincial examinations ;

(ii) to be responsible for secret printing of question-papers, for their despatch to local centres of examination, and for the receipt and distribution to examiners of the answer-papers ;

(iii) to supply all necessary forms and stationery required for the use of examiners, superintendents, and candidates ;

(iv) to notify to members the time and place of meetings, and to attend every meeting and take minutes of the proceedings,

(v) the Registrar will be a salaried officer of the Board, and will not be entitled to a vote or to any share in the deliberations.

APPENDIX II.

A.—Hindu Indigenous Schools.
B.—Sikh Indigenous Schools.
C.—Muhammadan Indigenous Schools.

A.—HINDU INDIGENOUS SCHOOLS.

By PANDIT RISHI KESH, *Shastri.*

I.—In the Panjáb indigenous schools exist to a large extent. Almost every village has at least one of such schools, while in large villages and towns every mahálla or part of such villages and towns does contain such a school in its centre. Thus, in Lahore the number of such schools is not less than fifty.

The inhabitants of the Panjáb, being chiefly divided into three communities—*viz.*, the Muhammadans, Sikhs, and the Hindus,—we find three kinds of indigenous schools, such as *maktab*, *dharmsála*, and *pathsalá*, and the teachers of such schools are called *mullás*, *bháis*, and *pándhas* or *pándits* respectively. The character of instruction given in the indigenous schools of Sikhs is entirely religious. It is the *pathsalá* or the indigenous schools of Hindus only in which some secular instruction is given. I will notice here some special characteristic of these schools.

The *pathsalás* may be divided into four classes :—

(i) *Private schools.*—These schools are kept up by private individuals at their own houses. A person engages a teacher primarily for the instruction of his own children and gives him a place in his own premises. Children of his relatives and neighbours are gradually admitted, each paying a trifling fee to the teacher. Thus, a pathsalá or a little school is formed.

(ii) *Self-supporting schools.*—This class of schools is abundantly found in the Panjáb. A teacher of some reputation selects a quarter in a village, city or town, fixes his residence there, and opens a school in which the children of all classes are admitted, each paying a trifling fee.

These two classes of indigenous schools are of the lowest order. *Lundé* and Deva Nágari alphabets, along with the *pahara* (a kind of mental arithmetic), are the only subjects generally taught in these schools. The teachers of such schools are called *pándhas.* The word *pándha* means a *purohita* or priest. Mention of this system may be found in the *Dharmshastras* and the Puranas. Among the Hindus the office of teachers was held by family priests from time immemorial. This custom was observed in the Panjáb up to recent time. Not many years ago none but the family priests of the villages could establish a *pathsala* in their precincts, and when such a priest happened to be ignorant or unable to perform his priestly duty, he appointed a substitute who held the double office of a village teacher and a priest. Thus, in those days the *pándhas* were invariably selected from the Bráhmana class, and such custom still prevails in many villages. Owing to divers causes, the practice has undergone a thorough alteration throughout the Province. In these days, not only Muhammadan students are allowed to read in such schools, but many of the *pándhas* themselves belong to the Muhammadan religion. In many schools the Persian alphabet is also taught along with *Lundé* or Deva Nágari.

The Muhammadan *pándhas* are generally foreigners to the villages in which they establish schools, and always shift their scene of labours with the least inconvenience. But the Hindu *pándhas* are regular fixtures, transmitting their office for generations sometimes. The discipline in such schools cannot be called good, although they may be more congenial to the habits and notion of the people themselves.

The fee taken in these schools is generally one pice per boy every Sunday and on other different holidays. In most rural villages the fees are taken in kind. Besides regular fees, when a student finishes his education as imparted in such schools, or makes some remarkable progress, the teachers are rewarded by his parents or guardians as far as their means allow. The *pándhas* have also a regular share in the gifts generally collected when a marriage or like ceremonies take place in his village.

The qualifications of these teachers are very low, and their education is generally very poor. In the Panjáb no one insists upon, nor does any machinery, exist for, the training of *pándhas.* With an improved method of teaching and the introduction of useful subjects like arithmetic, Indian geography, mensuration, and the elementary principles of agriculture and sanitation, the *pándha* schools may be turned to good account as part of national education. The following suggestions are submitted for best effecting this purpose :—

(1) The villages shall be thrown into circles, each being subject to the frequent inspection of a competent inspector.

(2) The *pándhas* should not be hampered by rules and conditions, but should be allowed to teach in the language that the villagers prefer. Text-books may be recommended, but not enforced.

(3) A system of bonuses and prizes such as obtain in the Guru training system of Bengal should be established in a large scale. A liberal and impartial system of bonuses and prizes would, I believe, soon induce the *pándhas* to qualify themselves for their new duties.

(4) One or more central institutions for training *pándhas* should be founded.

There is no difficulty in getting competent teachers for the proposed institutions, for the passed students of the Oriental College may very conveniently be appointed not only to teach the *pándhas* on the subjects above alluded to, but also to extend their reformed Oriental knowledge among the community.

(iii) There is another class of Hindu indigenous schools, namely, the private schools of pándits, who devote themselves to gratuitous Sanskrit instruction simply for the sake of public benefit. In these schools the higher branches of Hindu philosophy and literature are taught. The pándits are invariably Bráhmanas; their character is very simple, and mode of living very decent. They have generally a high education, though in most cases confined to one subject only, *viz.*, philosophy, grammar, Dharmshastras, Puranas or the Vedas. Every pándit considers it a religious duty to instruct a number of pupils.

The number of these schools is not inconsiderable in the Panjáb; every renowned town or city has a number of such schools. The students at such schools are of advanced age and belong to the Bráhmana class. No fees are taken in such schools, but, on the other hand, the students are supported partly by the pándits themselves, and partly by the Hindu community of the places in which such schools exist.

These schools have done wonderful work in their way. But for them Sanskrit knowledge would have been nowhere in India. If India has anything still to boast of, it is her pándits only, the relics of her old civilization, and the treasure home of her unrivalled wisdom. But, in these days, a universal misfortune has befallen the pándits, not only in this Province, but throughout the country. English-educated natives in general, in the conceit of their wordly wisdom, view a man of deep Sanskrit learning with contempt and regard him as no better than a common fool; but it would be a pity if our enlightened Government fails to see the claims of Sanskrit and of the pándits in a better light.

Recently, some move in the right direction has been made by the founders of the Panjáb University College, and successively followed by the learned Principals of the Calcutta and Benares Colleges to rescue the pándits from oblivion. A system of Title Examination has been instituted with regard to pándits and pupils. But in the Panjáb owing to the apathy of the Government, no sign of progress is apparent.

I give below a list of some famous pándits of the Panjáb who, at their own expense, maintain Sanskrit schools.

List of the Pándits holding Sanskrit Schools of their own.

Number.	Names of the Pándits.	Subjects taught in the school.	Number of students.	Residence.
1	Raghunath	Naya, Vedant and Bhagbata	About 20	Lahore District, Lahore.
2	Pabadchand	Naya and Vaidya (Medicine)	10	Ditto ditto.
3	Rúpachand	Vyakarana	10	Ditto ditto.
4	Balarama	Vyakarana and Literature ...	15	Ditto ditto.
5	Haradatta	Ditto ditto ...	10	Ditto ditto.
6	Mathuradatta Sastri ...	Ditto ditto ...	8	Ditto ditto.
7	Dayaram	Purana, Literature, Vyakarana.	12	Ditto ditto.
8	Maharaj	Ditto ditto ...	10	Ditto ditto.
9	Ganapat	Purana, Literature, Astrology, Grammar.	10	Ditto ditto.
10	Fatechand	Siddhanta Kankudi Puran ...	15	District Amritsár, Amritsár.
11	Thakurdass	Vedant	10	Ditto ditto.
12	Gopal	Naya and other Philosophers	15	Ditto ditto.
13	Bhakatram	Chandika (Grammar) ...	30	Ditto ditto.
14	Ramdatta	All branches of Sanskrit literature.	25	Ditto ditto.
15	Krishnadatta	Naya and Vyakarana ...	20	Ditto ditto.
16	Kashinath	Naya ...	10	Ditto ditto.
17	Krishnadatta	Chandika (Grammar) ...	15	Ditto ditto.
18	Dharilall	Grammar and Naya ...	12	Ditto ditto.
19	Devachand	Naya and other Sastras ...	20	District Jalándhar, Jalándhar.
20	Bhishma	Grammar ...	20	District Hoshiárpur, Hoshiárpur.
21	Rishikesh	Vyakarana and astrology ...	15	Jajon.
22	Balamukanda	Ditto ...	20	Ditto. ditto.
23	Gangaram	Grammar and Literature ...	20	Pandwadi.
24	Tulasiram	Saraswata (Grammar) ...	30	Kundat.
25	Balaram	Saraswata ...	25	District Hoshiárpur, Kundat.
26	Nathuram	Naya and Vyakarana ...	20	Datarpur.
27	Duna	Astrology, &c. ...	12	Keldá.
28	Radhakrishna	Grammar ...	25	Hajipur.
29	Govindaram	Vyakarana and Naya ...	30	Sunda.
30	Kakaram	All Sastras ...	50	District Ludhiána Bhin.
31	Prabhudoyal	Naya ...	10	District Umballa, Umballa.
32	Yamunadass	Grammar and Literature ...	15	Ditto ditto.
33	Harisarana	Grammar ...	15	Ditto ditto.
34	Ram Lal	All Sastras ...	40	Ranika Raipore.
35	Brahmananda	Grammar, Literature ...	20	Nalbi.
36	Bulchand	Literature, Astrology ...	20	Jhaneswar.
37	Brahmanand	Grammar, Literature ...	10	Ditto.
38	Govindram	Grammar ...	10	Bibyal.
39	Padmanath	Grammar, Naya ...	10	Ladua.
40	Mukandaram	Grammar ...	10	Ditto.
41	Haradatta	Naya, Literature ...	15	Pahoya.
42	Brahmananda	Naya ...	15	Ditto.

Number.	Names of the Pándits.	Subjects taught in the school.	Number of students.	Residence.
43	Hariram	Grammar Purana ...	10	Kaul.
44	Haribhakla	Grammar ...	10	Ditto.
45	Ramjidass	Vaidya, Grammar ...	10	Boh.
46	Hariram	Grammar, Puran ...	10	Sirsa.
47	Ramsarna	Grammar, Ramal ...	10	District Karnal, Karnal.
48	Tulsiram, Sastri ...	All Sastras ...	20	Nissang. ...
49	Ramji Lal	Grammar ...	...	Sambhali.
50	Rishiram	Grammar ...	30	Pai.
51	Dayalal	Grammar, Naya, Vedanta ...	20	Pundari. ...
52	Basudeva	Naya, Vedanta ...	10	Fatehpur District, Delhi.
53	Sreedhar	All Sastras	20	Dasana.
54	Harayasa Rai	Naya	20	Bhahana.
55	Hetram	Vyakarana	20	Karana.
56	Hansaram	Ditto	20	District Hansi, Majra.
57	Hetram	Ditto	20	Karana.
58	Bhairavadatta	Naya	20	Nabha District Nabha.
59	Lakshmidhar	Grammar, Dharmasastra ...	20	Nabhá.
60	Bansilal	Grammar, Literature ...	20	Ditto.
61	Sriram	Vyakarana	15	Ditto.
62	Dharanidhar	Ditto	15	Ditto.
63	Vidyadhar	All Sastras	20	Gujránwála District, Gujránwála.
64	Barkatram	Jyotisha	10	Jhelum District, Jhelum.
65	Natthu	Seddhanta Kaumude ...	15	Kala.
66	Brijlal	Saraswata, astrology ...	12	Ditto.
67	Lakshmidatta	Literature	15	Wazirabad.
68	Vishmadatta	Saraswata Purana ...	40	Ráwalpindi District, Ráwalpindi.
69	Lakshiram	Purana Grammar ...	10	Ditto.
70	Brijlal	Grammar (Chandrika) ...	15	Ditto.
71	Muralidhara	Naya Saraswata ...	10	Peshàwar District, Peshàwar.
72	Narayanadatta ...	General Sastras ...	20	Jwala Muki, Tahsil Dehara.
73	Taradatta	Unknown	15	Tahsil Wadaun, Hamirpur.
74	Girdhari	All Sastras	20	Sujanpur Tahsil, Sujanpur.
75	Dimbheswar	Ditto	30	Palampur Tahsil, Palampur.
76	Nityanada	Grammar, &c. ...	20	Haripur Tahsil, Haripur.
77	Bholanath	Literature, &c., &c. ...	20	Ditto.
78	Narada	Panma Grammar ...	15	Dada Tahsil.
79	Rudradatta Sastriya ...	Vedanta, &c.	10	Kangra Tahsil, Nagrata.
80	Maniram	All Sastras	20	Kangra Tahsil, Kangra.
81	Nikkeram	All Sastras	30	Unknown.
82	Chetram	Astrology	15	Palampur Tahsil, Palampur.
83	Chaturbhuja	Astrology	10	Palampur Tahsil, Dhodhauli.
84	Sobharam	Grammar, &c. ...	12	Kangra Tahsil, Kangra.
85	Kalidas	Grammar, &c. ...	15	Bheri Tahsil, Bheri.
86	Liladhar	Literature, &c. ...	15	Sulha Tahsil, Sulha.

II.—Schools established by Rájás or Mahárájás in their own territory or in some holy places. These schools are also of a high order. In these schools, both the pándits and students are supported by the Rájás and Mahárájás themselves; but, being of a strictly private nature, they cannot be brought under the influence of the authorities.

II.—List of Sanscrit Indigenous Schools in the Panjáb (furnished by Head Pandit Guru Parshad, Pandit Kaka Ram, and others).

ANSWER 1.

I have drawn up a list of indigenous schools which I have handed over to Pandit Bhagwandass. I will name a few of these schools now.

Lahore and Amritsar.—(1) The Lahore Sanscrit School, established in the Anjuman premises; (2) Pandit Kashinath's Sanscrit School at *Nai Chhatri*, Amritsar; (3) Sanscrit School in the Mandir of Raja Teja Singh at Amritsar; (4) Sanscrit School of Pandit Krishna Datta, of Bhoa, at Amritsar; (5) Pandit Ram Dat's Sanscrit School, in Mahalla *Sabuni*, at Amritsar; (6) Pandit Krishna Datt's Sanscrit School, in Aluvale-ka-Katra, Amritsar; (7) Pandit Gopi Nath's Sanscrit School, in Dal Singh's Katra, at Amritsar—(This Pandit was brought up in the Lahore Oriental College, and has passed the Vishárad Examination); (8) Pandit Tulsi Ram's Sanscrit School, in *Kanhya-ka-Kattra, Karmo-ki-Deorhi*, Amritsar; (9) Pandit Kakaram's Hindi School at Sakri Kooi, Mohalla Nihal Singh, Amritsar; (10) Pandit Krishna Datt's Hindi School at Nihal Singh-ka-Katra, near the Darbar Sahib, Amritsar; (11) Pandit Gopi Nath's Hindi School in *Pasion-ka-Chowk*, Amritsar; (12) Pandit Mulchand's Hindi School in Pasion-ka-Chowk; (13) Pandit Thakur Dass' Sanscrit School, Mochion-ka-Bazár, Darana Mul-ka-Thakurduara, Amritsar; (14) Pundit Mul Chand's Son's Sanscrit School in Chitta Katra, Amritsar; (15) Pandit Lukshman Datt's Sanscrit School, Topewala Darwaza, Amritsar; (16) Pandit Harbhagwan's Hindi School in Namak Mandi, Amritsar; (17) Pandit Fateh Chand's Sanscrit School, Telion-ki-Gali, Amritsar; (18) Pandit Tretaram's Hindi School, Khatikan-ki-Dhab, Amritsar; (19) Pandit Bhodaram's Hindi School, Khatikon-ki-Dhab, in front of Mashki's Gali, Amritsar; (20) Pandit Sarb Sukhson's two Hindi Schools in Guru-ke-Mahal, Amritsar; (21) Pandit Kakaram's Hindi School in Charhat Singh's Kattra, Amritsar; (22) Pandit Kakara Bhumbwala's Hindi School in Charhat Singh's Kattra, Amritsar, and several other Sanscrit and Hindi Schools; (23) Pandha Chhibba's Hindi School at *Gopale-ma-ka-Thakurdwara*, Dal Singh-ka-Mahalla, Amritsar; (24) Bhai Hojuris' Hindi and Gurmukhi School for boys and girls near Kowlsar, *Dal Singh-ka-Katra*, Amritsar; (25) Badda Pandha's Hindi School at Charhat Singh's Katra, in front of Shahr-ki-Gali, Amritsar, and many others.

Gujranwala.—(1) Pandit Vidya Dhar's Sanscrit School, under the patronage of Rai Mul Singh; (2) Saraswati Nath's Sanscrit School; (3) Pandit Chetram's Sanscrit School—(has passed the Visharad Examination); (4) Many Pandhas' Schools. *Gujrat District.*—The famous Sanscrit School of Kiladar, taught by a Cashmiri Pandit. The school enjoys a *jagir*, *Ram Nagar*. *Gujranwala District.*—Pandit Kanhya Lall's Sanscrit School. *Wazirabad.*—Pandit Lakhshmi Nath's Sanscrit School. *Sialkot.*—Pandit Mukand Lall's Sanscrit School, in village Daska of Pushkarná Brahmins; Pandit Gobind Rám's Sanscrit School in Daska. *Umballa District.*—Pandit Brahma Nand's famous Sanscrit School at Thaneshar; Pandit Bal Chand's Sanscrit School at Thaneshar; Pandit Brahmanand of Bhoa's Sanscrit School; Pandit Bhyron Dat's Sanscrit School at *Ladwa*; Pandit Ram Lall's Sanscrit School at Ram Raipur; Pandit Brahmanand's Sanscrit School at Nahir; Pandit Harinam's Sanscrit School at village Kowl; Pandit Hari Bhakta's Sanscrit School at village Kowl; Pandit Padma Nábha's Sanscrit School at *Ladwa*; Pandit Mukandrams' Sanscrit School at Ladwa.

Delhi District.—Pandit Sri Dhar's Sanscrit School at Dasna; Pandit Harjas Rai's Sanscrit School at Bhatana.

Hansi District.—Pandit Hans Rám's famous Sanscrit School in village Magra.

Karnal District.—Pandit Ramjidass' Sanscrit School at Tambli; Pandit Rikhiram's Sanscrit School at Pái Gáon; Pandit Tahiram's Sanscrit School at village Nisang; Pandit Dya Lall's Sanscrit School at village Pundri; Basudun Pandit's Sanscrit School at *Fatehpur*; Pandit Mahában's Sanscrit School at Fatehpur.

Jhind.—Pandit Sriram's Sanscrit School, also Pandit Jugal Kishore's Sanscrit School.

Rawalpindi.—Pandit Vishundass' Sanscrit School.

Jhelum District.—Pandit Kalyandass' Sanscrit School in Rohtas; Pandit Jantram's Sanscrit, Hindi and Gurmukhi School at Rohtas; Pandit Dittoo Gosai's Sanscrit, Hindi and Gurmukhi School at Rohtas; Báun Mastram's Sanscrit School in Jhelum *City*.

Kangra District.—Pandit Sobharam's Sanscrit School in City of Kangra; Pandit Bholanath's Sanscrit School at Haripur; Pandit Nityanand's Sanscrit School at Haripur; Pandit Nágar's Sanscrit School at Haripur; Pandit Girdhari's Sanscrit School at Sujánpur; Pandit Krishna Datt's Sanscrit School at Sujánpur, Tahsil Hamirpur; Pandit Brahmánand's Sanscrit School in village Ghasowta; Pandit Sohan's Sanscrit School in village Bijapur; Pandit Nikkram's Sanscrit School in village Khyrariasat, Lambagaon; Pandit Narain Datt's Sanscrit School at Jwala Mukhi; Pandit Satyagar's Sanscrit School at Jawala Mukhi; Pandit Rudia Datta's Sanscrit School at Nagrota, Tahsil Kangra; Pandit Maniram's Sanscrit School in Kangra; *Mandi* Sanscrit School; Pandit Jograj's School in Bijapur, Tahsil Hamirpur; Pandit Urbidhor's School in village Bhubharna, Tahsil Pálampur; Pandit Gowri Datt's School in village Dhameta, Tahsil Hamirpur; Pandit Guttoram's School in village Sujánpur, Tahsil Hamirpur, &c., &c.

Answer 2.

In all the above schools the students begin generally with *Hindi*, and in some places Gurmukhi also, and then proceed to the study of Sanscrit. The subjects taught are—in *Hindi* and *Gurmukhi*, spelling books and readers; in *Sanscrit*—grammar, poetry, rhetoric, *purani* and *itihas* (ancient history), jyotish (astrology and astronomy), vedánt and nyaya (philosophy and logic), mantra, tantra, puja, path (religious books), *vaidyak* (Hindu medicine).

Books.—In Sanscrit grammar.—Sáraswat and Chandrika; Loghu Kaumudi; Siddhant Kaumudi; Panini's Grammar up to Mahábháshya (The Great Commentary). *In Nyaya (Logic).*—Tark Sangraha; Kárikamli up to Jágdishi, and Gádadhari.—*In Jyotish*; Shighrabodha; Maharta Chintamani; Graha Lághava; Bháswati; and Siddhant Siromani. *In Poetry.*—Raghubans, Meghaduta, Kumar Sumbhava (Káli Dás' works); Mágh; Bhatti; Naishada, &c. *In Rhetoric.*—Kuvalyánand; Kávyaprakash; Bágbhatta. *In Vedánt.*—Vedántsar; Vedánt Paribhásha; Panchdashi; Chitsukhi. *Vedánt in Hindi.*—Vichár Ságar; Panchdashi; Mokhshopáya; Kéhár, Mála, and many others. *In Purans.*—Srimad Bhágavat and Mahabharat, &c. *In Váidyak* (Hindu Medicine).—Sárangdhar; Nighanta: Modho Nidan; Bháen Prakash Charak; Susruta; Bágbhatta; Lolambaráj; Ras Manjari; Agirna Manjari; Chikitsa Sar; and Bang Sen, &c.

Answer 3.

In most of the schools the teachers teach *gratis*, as their religious duty and for the maintenance of their national knowledge—nay, many of the teachers give food and clothing to the students, as well as books, &c., out of the income derived from their priestly avocation and hereditary property. In a very few schools the teachers have *jagirs* granted to them by the Hindu kings, and continued by the British Government. In some schools the pious Hindus of the village give alms to the students, but the teachers receive nothing. In some places both the students and teachers receive gifts from pious Hindus.

Answer 4.

The attendance generally is from 10 to 60 students in each school. In Hindi and Gurmukhi schools the number of students often reaches to a hundred.

Supplementary List of Indigenous Schools supplied by Pandit Guruprasad.

Jullundur District.—Sanscrit School of Pandit Málárám Sari, in village Nowa Shahar; of Pandit Jay Dyál Nárad, in the same village; of Pandit Sheodyal Bábá, in the same village; of Pandit Kákárám Nárad, in the same village; of Pandit Rám Chand, in the same village.

Hoshiarpur District.—Sanscrit School of Pandit Nandrám, in village of Amota; of Pandit Thákurdáss, in village Hariana; of Pandit Gaindorám, in village Hariana; of Pandit Vidyadhar, in village Shám Chourasi; of Pandit Amba Parshád, in village Baribasi; of Pandit Keshavanand, in the same village; of Pandit Polorám, in the same village; and Pandit Myarám, in the same village; of Pandit Tilok Chand, in village Gurh Shankar; of Pandit Hakorám, in the same village; of Pandit Uttam Chand, in the same village; of Pandit Bishambharrám, in the same village; of Pandit Gandárám, in village Dagaon; of Pandit Kanhya Lall, in city Hoshiarpur; of Pandit Kákárám, in the same city.

Ferozepore District.—Pandit Balkishen, in City Ferozepore; Pandit Prabhudyál, in the same city.

Jullundur District.—Pandit Amir Chand, in town Ráhun; Pandit Kshemráj, in the same; Pandit Bhogorám, in the same; Pandit Jagan Nath, Pandit Maghiram, Pandit Chujjurám.

Multan District.—Pandit Gangabihan *Vishárad*, in City Multan; Pandit Thákur Dáss, in the same city; Gosain Khillurám, in the same city; Joshi Rishi Kesh, in the same city.

Gurdaspur.—Pandit Anup Dás, in village Sri Hargobindpur; Pandit Janki Prasad, in the same village.

Batala School,—in Bhandári-ka-Thákurdwárá—30 students, *two teachers*.

All students are fed by Bhandári Rai Bhág Singh. The school hours are eight hours daily.

Supplementary List of Indigenous Schools.

Umballa District.—Pandit Ramjidass' Sanscrit School in village Bôh; Pandit Gobindram's Sanscrit School in village Babyal; Pandit Rám Narain's Sanscrit School in village Sahana, in City Umballa; Pandits Jamnadass, Prabhu Dyal, and Saligram's Schools.

Nabha.—Pandit Bansi Lall's School; Pandit Dharnidhar's School; Pandit Bhyron Dutta, Pandit Srirám, Pandit Lakshmi Dhor—about 500 students in these schools.

Ludhiana.—Pandit Dhanpat's School; Pandit Gangaram's School in village Khanna.

Jullundur.—Pandit Devi Chand's School; Pandit Tulsirám's School.

Hoshiarpur District.—Pandit Rikhi Kesh's School in village *Jego*, Tahsil Una; Pandit Gobindrám's School in Una; Pandit Gobindram's School in Sandahgarh; Pandit Byragiram's School in village Bhalana; Pandit Parmanand's School in village Sukhsál, Tahsil Una; Pandit Tulsidass' School in village Kumrat, Tahsil Una; Pandit Dunna Pándha's Hindi School in village Kasera; Pandit Kákárám's famous school in village *Bhine*, Tahsi Garh Shankar—*This Pandit feeds about 80 students* from his private income. Even during the famine time he continued to feed his pupils: *A story is related of him that he made his wife attend on his pupils when she remonstrated against his spending a large sum of money on them.* Pandit Magarrám's Sanscrit School in village Taksál; Pandit Shivarám's School in village Paloha.

B.—LIST OF SIKH INDIGENOUS SCHOOLS.

Bhai Dit Singh's account of Indigenous Schools in the Panjáb.

As I was a *Sadhu* (wandering mendicant), I have travelled over a great part of the Panjáb, my occupation being learning and teaching. I have travelled from Umballa to Rawalpindi through Main Doab, Dhaba, Malwa, Majha, Pothohar districts. The information gained by me during the course of my travel is, that in Muhammadan villages the Mullahs teach generally the Arabic alphabet and the Qurán.

In Hindu villages, inhabited principally by Brahmins, the children are taught Deva Nágari or Hindi characters. The books taught in their schools are *Bálbodh* (Primer) Sarasant (Sanscrit Grammar), Prem Ságar (a Hindi standard book), Tulsi Ramayan (the epic poem in Hindi), Viah Paddhati (marriage rituals). The Brahmins' income is derived from the voluntary gifts of the villagers.

It is the general feature of this province that, wherever there are ten houses of Hindus or Sikhs there is sure to be a *Dharmsálá* (Sikh religious place). There is a *Bhái* and a copy of the Granth Saheb (Sikh religious scripture) in every Dharmsálá. The *Bhái* teaches the children of the village the following books :—the Bálbodh (Primer) to the Granth, and the sayings of Guru Gobind Singh; both Sikh and Hindu boys read these books. *In Pothuhar many of the Muhammadans also read Gurmukhi.* In the schools taught by the *Sadhus* (mendicants) the following subjects and books are also taught :—Vedant (a particular Hindu philosophy the principle of which is idealism), Nyaya (logic), Vaidak (medicine), Rajviti (elements of polity), *sahitya* (rhetoric), &c., all these books are written in the Gurmukhi characters. For instance, the school of Sádh Tilokrám (who teaches the *wandering* Sádhs, who follow the teacher wherever he goes). There is scarcely a village in which one or two men conversant with Gurmukhi learning is not to be found.

The income of the Bháis is derived from the villagers.

List of Dharmsálás (some of them only).

Lahore.—Mohallá thá Mohallan Bhái Rám Singh, 25 students learning Gurmukhi. Mái Rupán di Dharmsálá, Bhái Bhagwán Singh, 10 to 15 students. Baba Ishwar Dás-di-Dharmsálá, Bhái Prem Singh, 5 to 10 students. Baoli Saheb, 10 to 15 students. Sri Guru Singh Sabha School, 30 students. Sat Sabha School, 50 students.

Amritsar.—Akálboonga, Bhái Atma Singh, 100 to 150 students. Sardal Singh-ki-Dharmsálá teaches 60 to 70 girls. There are 20 Mission schools for girls. There are 15 Government schools for girls. There are altogether *three hundred* Dharmsálás in Amritsar in which Gurmukhi is taught.

Village Gandiwind, at the Dera of Sádh Hira Dáss, 40 to 50 students of Gurmukhi.

Village Bhái ka Mának, Bhái Gurmukh Singh teaches Hindi books on Vedant, &c., written in Gurmukhi characters.

Village Nandipur, Dharmsálá, 10 to 15 students.

In *Gujranwala,* there are many Dharmsálás in which boys read Gurmukhi.

In *Tarantáran* (Amritsar district), there are many Dharmsálás in which boys read Gurmukhi.

In *Anandpur* (Hoshiarpur district), there are many Dharmsálás in which boys read Gurmukhi, &c.

The *Bháis* get loaves every day from the houses of their students. On marriage occasions they get a fee of Re. 1. At the crop seasons they get 5 to 10 seers of grain.

B.(*b*) Bhai GURMUKH SINGH sends me the following account of indigenous schools :—

"The origin of the indigenous Hindu schools can be traced back to the earlier times of their civilization, or even to the still earlier times of the Hindu village system. But the sphere of instruction seems to have been confined in those days even to the children of Bráhmans, for we read that in the second part of their age they used to read Sanskrit.

A relic of that old system is, although quite changed in principle, now seen among such Bráhmans who take interest in teaching gratis in their homes or in native pathsalás.

The present system of home or pathsalá instruction is undefined and indeterminate. Much depends upon the will of a tutor, or upon the choice of their pupils to select subjects of instruction; but much more depends upon the usage of times, for we see that this private educational system extends to a little of grammar or Viyá Karn, to a little of *path*, púja (tuition to perform religious, marriage and other ceremonies) Ramayana, Bhagavat, Mahabharata or astrology, but the four latter are deemed most difficult, and therefore sought by few.

But the great wonder is that from time immemorial the study of Sanskrit has been monopolized by Bráhmans alone, for we seldom see Khatris reading that language for wordly affairs.

Sanskrit and Deva Nágari characters were deemed sacred and fit for the study appropriated for the next world, and therefore Khatris and others (besides Bráhmans) never learnt them for wordly affairs. It seems, therefore, probable that the Lundí characters were invented to carry on the workings of worldly affairs. The *Lundí* was, as it appears, first used by *Váisas* or the commercial class of people; but when the Khatris, being obliged by the Muhammadan rule to abandon their military profession, mixed with their Váisa brethren, they adopted *Lundí* characters for their trade purposes; and, thus, we see *Lundí* used all over India by the commercial classes of the people, and Sanskrit characters confined to the Bráhmans.

But all the Khatris and other Hindus did not become shopkeepers; these men began to learn Persian (as they do now learn English) for the sake of obtaining some employment. Thus, we see that most of the Khatris become Múnshís during the Muhammandan rule, and they forget Sanskrit so far as to learn their religious books written in Persian characters. Therefore we find the Gita, Mahábharat, &c., written in Persian characters, and there is a testimony of Nanak which bears on this. Nanuk says: *Khatriyán apná dharm shadiya malesh bhaká gahí.*

As the number of Muhammadans increased in India, Persian private schools were opened side by side with the Sanskrit Bráhmanic schools or Lundí commercial institutions. But, as the intercourse between the two nations increased, the Hindus opened out Persian schools, and the Muhammadans called Rawals opened Lundí schools. These three sorts of indigenous schools have continued down to the present time, although great reduction has occurred in Persian or Sanskrit school attendance, for people of all classes have begun to learn English or Urdu, not so much to receive instruction as for sake of obtaining Government employment.

The birth of Nanak introduced another change. Up to this time, the Hindus or Muhammadans, used to learn Panjábi and Persian, or both; and there were two sorts of characters, Lundí and Persian—used for public business. Gurú Agand, the second Gurú, is said to have invented the Gurmukhi character; but this is doubtful. In my opinion they existed before Nanak.

The Gurmukhi characters are simplified Deva Nágari characters and are derived through Lundí, the difference being that Lundí has got no more vowels than three (like Persian alphabet), the Gurmukhi has got as many as the Deva Nágari. But the Gurmukhi characters were made to supply the wants of the age, for we see letters in the Sanskrit alphabet that are difficult for pronunciation to a Panjábi villager. No one speaks "khshá" but "kh," and no one speaks "stri" but "istrí." There is no "rh" in Deva Nágari, and we read "gur" instead of "gurh." Nanak travelled in all parts of India, and udási fakírs, the followers of his son, Sai Chand, have spread his doctrines over the whole of India.

Thus, dharmsálas arose everywhere, and there is hardly any district or city in which one or more dharmsálas are not found.

I have received applications for the Gurmukhi Journal from Khandes, Deccan-Hyderabad, various parts of Southern India, Dacca in Bengal, &c.

But the great spread of Gurmukhi took place in the Panjáb, for the victories of the Sikhs extended their sway from the borders of Biluchistan to the confines of Oudh. Between these limits, the Gurmukhi was firmly established, and thus we see from Umballa down to the foot of Suleiman range, every village (provided it may not be of the Muhammadans entirely) has got a dharmsála in which a Bhai reads the Granth, teaches Gurmukhi and other things.

The lads of the villagers when very young are sent to these dharmsálas, but no sooner they are able to read Granth they leave their study.

But the cities also in the Panjáb are not destitute of dharmsálas, and we see that in each city in which Hindus mostly reside a dharmsála is established and the Granth is read.

These dharmsálas are in most places (even those that are beyond the limits of the Panjáb), supported by the grant of some piece of land.

Dharmsálas are in *Malwa* known by the name *Deodis*.

As these dharmsálas increased (particularly in Pothahár even in very Deraját), the Hindus (leaving Bráhmanism) become half Sikhs, for they become followers of Nanak, but do not receive the Panhál.

Thus, we see that in Pathahar almost all Khatris and Aroras worship the Granth, learn Gurmukhi and call themselves Sikh (in contradiction to Singh).

The first book that occurs in Panjábi is the Janam Sakhi of Nanak, and it is older than any Urdu or Hindi book.

As the Sikhs increased Gurmukhi literature increased, and in the end of the latter part of the eighteenth century, most of the Nirmalá fakírs, having studied Sanskrit, succeeded in translating many books in Gurmukhi; therefore we find hundreds of books in Gurmukhi (on all subjects, such as philosophy, logic, prosody, rhetoric, &c.,) most of which can be seen in the Ludhiána Bhadhour House Library.

Gurmukhi literature far exceeds that of Urdu or Hindi.

There are, therefore, four kinds of indigenous schools in the province—

(i) Sanskrit confined chiefly to the Bráhman.

(ii) Lundí (Panjábi is written in these characters) for the shopkeepers.

(iii) Persian schools.

(iv) Gurmukhi dharmsálas.

Urdu is added now to such indigenous schools as have become aided.

Sanskrit and Persian indigenous schools have greatly decreased, for the people in cities like to read in the Government schools for the sake of employment.

C.—STATEMENT OF MUHAMMADAN INDIGENOUS SCHOOLS.

(*a*) *List of Indigenous Schools, with other particulars, in Lahore submitted by* MOULVI FAIZ-UL-HASAN.

No.	Name of School.	Name of Teacher.	Name of books taught in the School.	Number of boys.	REMARKS.
		I.—Perso-Arabic	*Schools.*		
1	Masjid-i-Hakiman	Sayad Abdulla Shah	Alcoran, Urdu *ki pahli* and *Dusri kitab*	20	
2	Lál Masjid	Jalál-ud-din	Alcoran and different books in Persian and Urdu.	15	
3	Masjidi Mulla Khan Kalán	......	Ditto ditto	20	
4	" Khurd	Imám Dín	Ditto ditto	10	
5	Chinian wáli Masjid	Sayad Pir Shah	Alcoran	8	
6	Rahmat Rájwáli Masjid	Shekh Ahmad	Ditto	11	
7	Chiraghdin wáli Masjid	Hafiz Muhammad Din	Persian and Arabic books	10	
8	Uchi Masjid	Khalifa Ali Muhammad	Alcoran	9	
9	Mir Hassan wáli Masjid	......	Ditto	12	
10	Sathán Kalán	Hisám-ud-Din	Ditto and other Persian and Urdu books	11	
11	Chiraghdin wáli Masjid	Háfiz Jalal-ud-Din	Alcoran	20	
12	Patolian wáli Masjid	Háfiz Shaháb-ud-Din	Ditto	6	
13	Phulon wáli Gali	Háfiz Imám-ud-Din	Ditto	9	
14	Daroghe wáli Masjid	Sayad Ramzán Ali	Alcoran and Persian books	6	
15	Said Mitha wala Maktab	Sayad Ahmad Ali	Persian books	8	
16	Barútgarán wáli Masjid	Háfiz Fateh Dín	Alcoran	21	
17	Hamám wáli Maktab	Wasákha Singh	Sikandarnama and other Persian books	50	
18	Bháti darwaze wála Maktab	Monar Murád Bakhsh	Ditto ditto	5	
19	Masjid Hafiz	Maihr	Alcoran and Persian books	9	
20	Ibrahim Mori Gate	Punmin Sayad Gauhar Ali	Zuleikha, Gulistan, Bostan, &c.	11	
21	Maktab Maulvi Said-ud-din	Maulvi Ghulámulla	Arabic and Persian books and religious books	8	
22	Haweli Mián Khán	Háfiz Nur-ud-Din	Alcoran	15	
23	" "	Háfiz Abdul Hak	Ditto and Arabic and Persian books	10	
24	Jogián wáli Masjid	Mián Zahur-ud-Din	Ditto	7	
25	Dáta Ganj Bakhsh	Hafiz Ahmad Din	Ditto	7	
26	Masjid Anarkalli	Maulvi Nur Ahmad	Ditto and Arabic and Persian books	25	

C.—*List of Indigenous Schools, with other particulars, in Lahore*—(continued).

No.	Name of School.	Name of Teacher.	Name of books taught in the School.	Number of boys.	Remarks.
1	Said Masjid	Mian Nika	Persian books	15	In Chunian, town of the Lahore District.
2	Khajur-wali Masjid	Mian Phula	Alcoran and Urdu books	20	
3	Baharwali Masjid	Háfiz Raugha	Ditto	13	
4	Barutgaranwali Masjid ...	Chiragh Din	Ditto ...	11	
5	Baharwal wali Masjid ...	Hafiz Daud	Gulistan, Zuleikha, &c.	12	
		II.—Arabic Schools.			
1	Nawab Sahib ka Madrasah ...	Maulvi Abdul Kader	Grammar, logic, religious subjects.		Supported by Mian Ahsan Shah, Honorary Magistrate.
2	Ghala Mandi wala Madrasah ...	Maulvi Abdul Kader	Grammar and other sciences	...	
3	Maulvi Muhammad Hassan ka Madrasah.	Maulvi Abdulla	Religious books.		
4	Maulvi Abdul Aziz ka Madrasah ...	Maulvi Abdul Aziz	Grammar, logic, religious books.		
5	Maulvi Ismail	Abdul Khalik	Grammar, &c.		
		*III.—Persian Schools.**			* Besides No. 1, Mir Muhammad, Mir Ghizas-ud-Din, and Ibn Muhammad Kasam teach people on remuneration. Shahzadas Shahpur and Nadir engage two teachers to teach Persian to their children.
1	Masjid Imámbára	Muhammad Afzal	Alcoran, Persian and Urdu books.		
		IV.—Pandhon ke Madaris (Mahajani Schools).			
		Naugarh, Goli Maroak ka Muhalla, and Purane bazar schools.			

There is also one Hindu school in which Persian, Urdu and English are taught. It is aided by the Panjáb University, and is established by subscriptions.

C.—(*b*) *List of Schools submitted by Mufti Zafar Din.*

No.	District.	Situation.	Tahsil.	Name of the Managing Teacher of the School.	Description of knowledge given.	Remarks.
				I—Arabic Schools.		
1	Amritsar ...	Amritsar ...	Amritsar ...	M. Ghulam Ali ...	Religious instructions of all kinds ...	People support the students.
2	Do. ...	Do. ...	Do. ...	M. Abdul Ali ...	Arabic, logic and religious instructions...	Ditto.
3	Do. ...	Lahore ...	Lahore ...	M. Sultan Ahmad ...	Arabic knowledge of every description ...	Khair Din, merchant, supports the school.
1	Lahore ...	Do. ...	Do. ...	K. Hamedud-Din ...	Ditto ditto	Students supported by people.
2	Do. ...	Do. ...	Do. ...	Nur Ahmad ...	Grammar and religious instructions ...	Ditto.
3	Do. ...	Do. ...	Do. ...	Mufti Salimullah ...	Medicine, Arabic books, &c. ...	Ditto.
1	Gujrát ...	Khori ...	......	M. Muhammad Alam ...	Logic and other religious traditional subjects.	Students supported by the teacher himself.
2	Do. ...	Chakori ...	......	M. Mír Din ...	Ditto ditto ...	Villagers support the students.
3	Do. ...	Machháná ...	......	......	Ditto ditto ...	Ditto.
1	Jhelam ...	Kadhate ...	Chakwal ...	M. Ghulám Muhammad ...	Grammar and religious subjects ...	Ditto.
2	Do. ...	Karsal ...	Do. ...	M. Ghulám Nabi ...	Ditto ditto ...	Teacher is the proprietor of the school, but students are supported by people.
3	Do. ...	Attar ...	Do. ...	M. Burhan Din ...	Grammar and logic ...	Ditto.
4	Do. ...	Do. ...	Do. ...	M. Ghulám Ali ...	Ditto ...	Ditto.
5	Do. ...	Ballanwálá ...	Do. ...	M. Ahmad Din ...	Ditto ...	Ditto.
6	Do. ...	Dhabwálá ...	Do. ...	M. Abdul Halim ...	Grammar and logic and religious instructions	Students supported by the villagers.
7	Do. ...	Sar ...	Do. ...	M. Ahmad Din ...	Grammar	Ditto.
8	Do. ...	Khiwalanwálá ...	Do. ...	M. Khan Mulk ...	Grammar and logic ...	Ditto.
9	Do. ...	Chak ...	Do. ...	M. Fazl Ahmad ...	Ditto ...	Ditto.
10	Do. ...	Bazid Lilli ...	Do. ...	M. Ghulám Nabi ...	Ditto ...	Ditto.
11	Do. ...	Meki Dhok ...	Do. ...	Ghulám Yahya ...	Ditto ...	Ditto and by Fatteh Khan Malik.
12	Do. ...	Ahmadabád ...	Do. ...	Kádar Bakhsh ...	Medicine ...	Supported by the villagers.
13	Do. ...	Pharlanwálá ...	Gujar Khan ...	Abdul Hak ...	Grammar and logic ...	Ditto.
14	Do. ...	Chakora ...	Do. ...	Muhmmad Ju ...	Ditto ...	Ditto.
15	Do. ...	Katwal ...	Do. ...	Ghulám Rasúl ...	Ditto ...	Ditto.
16	Do. ...	Chakwal ...	Chakwal ...	Ghulám Hasain ...	Ditto ...	Ditto.
1	Lahore ...	Lahore ...	Lahore ...	Islámia Anjuman	Grammar, Persian	Barkat Ali Khan is manager of the institution. It is maintained by subscriptions by Muhammadans.
2	Do.	Do.	Do.	Several teachers (names not given) ...	Do. logic	This has been established and supported by Nawab Nawazish Ali Khan.

C.—(b.) *List of Schools submitted by Mufti Zafar Din*—(continued).

No.	District.	Situation.	Tahsil.	Name of the Managing Teacher of the school.	Description of knowledge given.	Remarks.
				II.—Perso-Arabic Schools.		
1	Gujránwala ...	Gujránwala ...	Gujránwala ...	Muhammadan and others	Grammar, logic	Established in 1874 by Ali Khan, Fakír Jamál Din, and aided by other Muhammadans and the Government.
2	Do. ...	Do. ...	Do. ...	Muhammad Bakhsh	Do. Do	......
3	Do. ...	Jandiála ...	Do. ...	Muhammad Imám Din	Grammar, logic, and religious books ...	The boys are supported by the people.
1	Jullundhur ...	Jullundhur ...	Jullundhur ...	Wali Muhammad	Ditto ...	Ditto.
1	Saharanpur ...	Saharanpur ...	Saharanpur ...	......	Ditto ...	Ditto.
1	Gurdáspur ...	Batala ...	Batala ...	Muhammad Abdulla	Ditto ...	Ditto.
1	Gujránwala ...	Gujránwala ...	Gujránwala ...	Muhammad Alaud Din ...	Ditto ...	Ditto.
1	Saharanpur ...	Daoband ...	......	......	Ditto ...	Maintained on subscriptions.
1	Hoshiarpur ...	Awán ...	Dasuya ...	Ghulam Rasúl	Medicine	Pupils are supported by the villagers.
1	Gujranwala ...	Dilawar ...	......	" Muhammad	Grammar, Arabic	Ditto.
2	Do. ...	Rasúlnagar ...	Hafizabad ...	" Kader	Ditto	Ditto.
3	Do. ...	Jalálpur ...	Ditto ...	Muhammad Hasain	Ditto and Medicine ...	Ditto.
4	Do. ...	Gujranwala ...	Gujranwala ...	Mahbúb Alám	Arabic and Persian	Ditto.
5	Do. ...	Alipur ...	Ditto ...	Karim Bakhsh	Grammar, logic	Ditto.
6	Do. ...	Kot Máre Khan ...	Ditto ...	Muzaffar Din	Medicine	Ditto.
7	Do. ...	Chak Sáda ...	Ditto ...	Nizam-ud-din	Ditto	Ditto.
8	Do. ...	Kot Kazi ...	Ditto ...	Zia-ud-din	Religious books	Ditto.
9	Do. ...	Mangoki ...	Ditto ...	Muhammad Din	Ditto	Ditto.

Note.—There is scarcely a village with a Muhammadan population which does not contain a *Mulla* (teacher), or an institution where boys are at least given religious instruction.

C.—(*b*) *List of Schools submitted by Mufti Zafr-ud-din.*

No.	District.	Station.	Name of School.	Name of Teacher.	Subjects taught.	Remarks.
1	Jullundhur ...	Jullundhur ...	Masjid-i-Gulab Shah	Nur Muhammad ...	Alcoran and Persian ...	Is supported by the parents of the pupils.
2	Do. ...	Do. ...	" Bakir ...	Shah Muhammad ...	Vernacular, &c. ...	This is an aided school. Is also aided by Panjáb University College.
3	Do. ...	Do. ...	" Hanzwali	Hafiz Haji ...	Alcoran ...	Parents of the students support the teacher.
4	Do. ...	Do. ...	" " ...	Abdul Karim ...	Grammar, religious subjects ...	Ditto.
5	Do. ...	Do. ...	Unchi Masjid	Ghulam Muhammad ...	Persian and Arabic ...	Is maintained by fees realised from boys.
6	Do. ...	Do. ...	Imbliwali "	Ghulam Jilani ...	Persian ...	Is maintained by fees collected from boys.
7	Do. ...	Do. ...	Kazian "	Muhkam Din ...	Do. ...	Is supported by parents of the boys.
8	Do. ...	Do. ...	Purani Kotwali "	Nur Muhammad ...	Arabic and Persian ...	Education is given gratis.
9	Do. ...	Do. ...	Kila "	Do. ...	Do. ...	Ditto.
10	Do. ...	Do. ...	Ali "	Sultan Din ...	Alcoran and Persian ...	Is supported by the parents of the boys.
11	Do. ...	Do. ...	Jamid "	Muhammad Yusaf ...	Do. ...	Ditto.
12	Do. ...	Do. ...	Saidan "	Ahmad Shah ...	Persian ...	Education is given gratis.
13	Do. ...	Do. ...	Koli "	Hafizulla ...	Alcoran and Persian ...	Is supported by parents of the boys.
14	Do. ...	Do. ...	Karadgaran "	Nathe Khan ...	Alcoran ...	Ditto.
15	Do. ...	Do. ...	Muftian "	Wali Muhammad ...	Arabic and Persian ...	His livelihood depends on preaching.
16	Do. ...	Do. ...	Alamgir "	Jahangir ...	Alcoran ...	Supported by parents of the boys.
17	Do. ...	Dokoha ...	Dokoha "	Najam-ud-din ...	Arabic, Persian and religious instructions.	Gratis.
				Sialkot District.		
1	Sialkot ...	Sialkot ...	Kabutranwali Masjid	Hassan ...	Persian ...	Supported by parents of the boys.
2	Do. ...	Do. ...	Masjid ...	Ghulam Ali ...	Alcoran ...	Supported by subscription from the gentry of the city.
4	Do. ...	Bambawalla ...	" Bambawala ...	Haider Ali ...	Do. and other religious books ...	Is aided by the lambardars of the village.
3	Do. ...	Kotli Loharan ...	" Kotli Loharan	Ahmad Ali ...	Alcoran ...	Supported by the parents of the boys.
5	Do. ...	Orah ...	" Orah ...	Wahab Shah ...	Do. and other religious books ...	Maintained by the zemindars.

C.(*a*)—*List of indigenous schools, with other particulars, in Lahore submitted by two other Moulvis.*

No.	Name of teacher.	Name of school.	Names of the books taught in the school.	Income of the teacher.	Average attendance of students.
1	Moulvi Núr Ahmad ...	Janu Masjid, Anarkali ...	Grammar, logic, literature, divinity, all branches of religion, law, mathematics	By voluntary, but insufficient, subscriptions of Muhammadans ...	20
2	Ghulam Muhammad, son of Meer Ahmad ...	Ditto	Kurán and other Persian books	Re. 1 for teaching each "Sêpára" of the Kurán and for every other book is paid to the teacher as remuneration ...	15
3	Shahabuddin ...	Masjid, Patolian ...	Ditto	Lives on the income of the mosque	40
4	Sain Khuda Baksh ...	Mosque near tomb Panj-piran ...	Ditto	Ditto	12
5	Fateh Din ...	Said Nitha mosque ...	Kurán	Receives As. 8 or Re. 1 for teaching each "Sêpára" of Kurán ...	20 boys and 2 girls.
6	Ahmad Din ...	Chhalle Kotal mosque ...	Ditto	Lives on fees paid by students	30
7	Mohammad Din ...	Ditto	Grammar, logic, and medicines	Ditto	15
8	Ghulamulla ...	Mosque of Kamangaran	Ditto ditto ditto and religious law	Lives on the income of the mosque	10
9	Abdur Rahim ...	Haji's Mosque, Tergran Street ...	Ditto ditto ditto ditto and Urdu ...	Lives on the fees paid by students	25
10	Miran Bakhsh ...	Imamshah mosque ...	Kurán	Lives on the income of the mosque	25
11	Hafiz Mohammad Bakhsh and Kudratulla ...	Bahrwali mosque ...	Ditto	Lives on the fees paid by students	30
12	Hafiz Abdulla ...	A school near the palace of Shekh Wasawam ...	Kurán	Is paid by the Rani of Mahárájá Ranjit Singh ...	20 boys and 5 girls.
13	Khalifa Badar-ud-din ...	Mufti Bakar's mosque in Chohatta Street ...	Kurán and other Persian books	Lives on fees paid by students	15
14	Núr Ahmad ...	School near the house of Nawab Nawazish Ali Khan ...	Kurán and other Arabic and Persian books	Ditto	25

15	Mohammad Bakhsh ...	Mullán Masjid mosque ...	Ditto	Ditto	25
16	Ghulam Dastgir ...	Gilamian mosque ...	Kurán	Paid fees to the teacher	25
17	Mufti Salimulla ...	Near Pathranwali Hawali	Grammar, logic, mathematics, and medicines	Lives on fees paid by students	20
18	Khalifa Kazi Hamudud-din ...	Near Bukkan Khan mosque ...	Grammar, logic, and all branches of religious law	Is a Government employé, and this is his private school ...	20
19	Ghulam Nabi ...	Chinyan mosque ...	Kuárn, Urdu and Persian language	Lives on the income of the mosque	22
20	Maulvi Mohammad ...	Near stable of Shah Nawaz ...	Translation of Kurán and other religious books	Some Muhammadans assist him inadequately towards his subsistence	15
21	Maulvi Haider ...	Ditto.	Grammar and other books read in villages	Receives remuneration for the books he teaches	10
22	Maulvi Rahim Bakhsh ...	A mosque in Anarkali near Lakarmandi ...	Grammar, translation of Kurán, and other religious books ...	The teacher is an employé; the school is (not adequately) supported by some people	15

Lahore;
The 13th June 1882.

(Sd.) GHULAM MUSTAFA,
2nd Teacher of Mathematics and Lecturer in Medicine, Oriental College.

(Sd.) MOHAMMAD DIN,
2nd Teacher of Oriental Languages, Oriental College.

D.—ACCOUNT OF SHIAH INDIGENOUS SCHOOLS AT LAHORE.

Dated 13th June 1882.

From—MAULVI MOMAN ALI, Teacher, Imámia Class, Oriental College, Lahore.

I GIVE the following brief account of Shiah indigenous schools :—

I.—There is one Imámia school at Nawazishabad supported by Nawáb Nawazish Ali Khan. It contains 15 pupils, who are taught. Arabic, Persian, Urdu and *Ilm-i-Fikah* (ecclesiastical law).

The first teacher, a resident of Karbala, getting Rs. 30 per mensem, teaches Arabic and *Fikah,* and the second imparts education in Persian and Urdu. The boys are given stipends according to their merits.

II.—There is another Imámia school at Lahore, eatablished by the Nawáb. Arabic, Persian, Urdu, mathematics, and Alcoran are taught in it.

The institution has one Arabic teacher on a pay of Rs. 12, and one Persian teacher on Rs. 5, per mensem. One who teaches *Fikah* gets Rs. 7, and one who teaches Alcoran receives Rs. 9 a month.

Maulvi Abdul Qásim is Superintendent of the School, and gets Rs. 30 a month. The average number of boys taught in the school in former times was 40, but it is now not known. The boys are given stipends according to their merits.

III.—There is also a Maktab with 35 boys in Lahore Mochi Gate. Persian, Urdu and Alcoran are taught in it.

IV.—There is one more *Maktab* in the same locality, with 18 or 20 boys.

V.—A female school exists in the same locality, and instruction in Urdu and Alcoran is given in it.

Govt. C. B. Press, Simla.—No. 32 E. C.—6-7-82.—125.

APPENDIX III.

Papers connected with the origin of the Itimad-ud-Dowla Fund.

A.—Extract from a letter No. 1035, dated Fort William, the 30th October 1840, from the General Committee, P. I., to the Right Honorable the Governor General of India.

[*This letter is signed by 16 Members, such as* EDWARD RYAN, W. W. BIRD, H. T. PRINSEP, *&c., &c.*]

DELHI COLLEGE.

PARA. 7. We have deferred stating our sentiments on this important Institution, in order to have the opinions of our President and of Mr. Colvin, who had both carefully examined the state of this College at our request.

8. The following are the changes we propose for placing the Delhi Oriental College in an efficient state, and at the same time for perpetuating the memory of its generous and philanthropic Benefactor, the late Nawab Fazal Ali Khan, Itimad-ud-Dowla.

I.—With this view the College has been dedicated to him and a slate of marble has been fixed in a conspicuous part of the College upon which the name and magnificence of the donor are engraved.

II.—We propose that the following pecuniary scholarships be instituted and called the scholarships of Nawab Itimad-ud-Dowla. The scholarships will be in addition to those allowed to all our Oriental Colleges :—

	Rs.
3 at Rs. 8	24
2 at „ 30	60
1 at „ 40	40
Total ...	124

III.—From local inquiries we think it probable that the services of an able Maulvi may be procured for a salary of Rs. 100 a month, and we recommend that a second of the Shiah Sect, of approved respectability and learning, be appointed by Nawab Hamid Ali, the representative of the late Nawab Itimad-ud-Dowla. We beg leave also to propose the Nawab as a permanent Member of the Local Committee for conducting the affairs of the Delhi College.

IV.—We propose an increased rate of allowance for the Arabic and Persian teachers, so as to insure a superior class of instructors, with such additions as are necessary to constitute the Delhi College *an efficient Institution for Muhammadan learning.*

	MONTHLY INCOME.			Particulars.	MONTHLY EXPENSE.					
					Present.			Proposed.		
	Rs.	A.	P.		Rs.	A.	P.	Rs.	A.	P.
Expense from Fund ...	250	0	0	Head Arabic Teacher, Shiah ...	...			100	0	0
Interest in 1,70,000 ...	604	0	0	Ditto, Sunni ...	50	0	0	100	0	0
				2nd ...	40	0	0	80	0	0
				3rd ...	30	0	0	60	0	0
				4th ...	...			50	0	0
				5th ...	...			45	0	0
				Head Persian Teacher ...	30	0	0	60	0	0
				2nd ...	30	0	0	30	0	0
				3rd ...	20	0	0	20	0	0
				Head Sanskrit Teacher ...	50	0	0	80	0	0
				Assistant ...	...			16	0	0
				Arithmetician ...	10	0	0	16	0	0
				Writing Master ...	20	0	0	16	0	0
				Establishment ...	87	0	0	70	0	0
				Stipends ...	240	0	0	...		
				Prizes ...	33	0	0	12	8	0
				Books and contingencies ...	16	0	0	16	0	0
				Scholarships ...	...			328	0	0
				Nawab Itimad-ud-Dowla scholarship ...	...			124	0	0
	854	0	0		661	0	0	1,223	0	0

V.—We consider it necessary to appoint a Principal who shall exercise a general supervision over the Muhammadan College, as well as to direct the English Institution; and that there be one set of accounts kept for both the College and Institution and that the Principal act as Secretary.

VI.—We are of opinion, after a careful examination of the different candidates, that Mr. Botras, at present a Deputy Collector in Behar, possesses the character and acquirements necessary for our purpose, by his intimate knowledge of European literature and science together with a competent knowledge of the Oriental languages.

VII.—After a careful consideration of the subject, we are of opinion that it is unnecessary to retain the services of Mr. Taylor. Whether we think fit to recommend him to the favorable consideration of Government for the services he has rendered, will much depend on the answers we receive to enquiries we are now making.

VIII.—We have much pleasure in proposing Mr. J. Thomason of the Civil Service as a gentleman peculiarly well qualified to superintend the Oriental College of the North-Western Province, and we have communicated with the Honorable the Lieutenant-Governor of the North-Western Provinces on the subject, in order to give full effect to the Resolution of Your Lordship in Council communicated in Mr. Busbhoy's letter dated 15th July last.

B.—Extract from the "Bengal and Agra Gazette" for 1842, Vol. I, p. 88.

DELHI ORIENTAL COLLEGE OR INSTITUTION.

Members.

T. F. Metcalf, Esq.	J. L. Mowatt, Esq.
E. Colvin, Esq.	Dr. Ross.

Syad Hamid Ali Khan.

			Rs. A.P.
Head Arabic Teacher,	(Shiah)	Maulvi Jafir Ali	100 0 0
" Do.,	(Sunni)	Mamluk Ali	60 0 0
2nd Do.,		Syed Muhammad	50 0 0
3rd Do.,		Saiduddin	35 0 0
4th Do.,		Subhan Bukhsh	30 0 0
Head Persian Teacher,		Emam Bukhsh	40 0 0
2nd Do.,		Hasan Ali	35 0 0
3rd Do.,		Ahmad Ali	20 0 0
Head Sanscrit Teacher,		Thakar Das Pandit	60 0 0
Assistant,		Kidar Nath	20 0 0
Writing Master,		Syed Muhammad	20 0 0
Arithmetic Teacher,		Faiz Parsa	20 0 0
English Writer,		Babu Bansi Dhar Bose	12 0 0

The Delhi Oriental College was founded in 1792. It appears to have received its first aid from the General Committee of Public Instruction by an appropriation of Rs. 600 a month from Parliamentary Grant in 1824, and in 1826 a further appropriation of Rs. 400 a month was made from the General Fund for the Oriental Institution at Delhi. In 1827 an English class was added to this institution and a third item of receipt amounting to Rs. 250 a month called the Escheat Fund was allowed as a fixed contribution for the purpose of education. The resources of the Delhi Institution accordingly at this period were Rs. 1,250 a month. The Delhi College acquired a large accession of income in 1829 by the magnificent grant of the late Nawab Itimad-ud-dowla, formerly Minister at Lucknow, who endowed the Institution with a sum 170,000 of Company's paper, in return for which Donation the ORIENTAL COLLEGE was thenceforth dedicated to that nobleman.

With the interest of 5 per cent. Company's paper received from the Nawab (Rs. 708 a month) a monthly sum of about Rs. 2,000 became available for education purposes at Delhi, but the grant having been subsequently re-invested in the 4 per cent. loan, it produces at present only 604 Company's rupees a month, and consequently Rs. 1,854 a month, is the aggregate of the items referred to composing the existing assignment for education at Delhi.

It would appear that in 1829, when the large accession of Fund was obtained through the Nawab's grant, the English Class was separated from the Muhammadan or Oriental College, and a distinct institution or English Seminary was established under the control of the Original College Committee with the same Superintendent and Secretary.

The Nawab died in 1830, before the Delhi Institution, as it is now called, was finally established, so that he had not the opportunity of offering remarks upon any part of the arrangements which were contemplated by the Government and the General Committee.

The College will, in future, be likewise designated the College of Nawab Itimad-ud-Dowla, and to do further honor to the memory of the Nawab, the Government have directed a certain number of extra scholarships beyond the general rates to be allowed at other Institutions to be assigned to this College, and to be designated as the scholarships of the Nawab.

In 1835 the total number of pupils was 197, consisting of 61 in the Arabic Department; 80 in the Persian and 56 in the Sanscrit. In 1836 there was a considerable diminution of 56 students, which was attributed to the order of 7th March 1835, forbidding a stipendiary allowance; in the subsequent year there was a still further decrease of 18 pupils, and in 1838-39 the number was reduced to 100, but the progress of pupils has been both creditable and satisfactory.

The receipts for 1839-40 were equal to the disbursement, *viz.*, Rs. 11,482-12-6. Of this sum Rs. 10,248 were obtained from the General Fund of the Committee and the balance as charges of tuition.

C.—Quotations from the General Report on Public Instruction in the North-Western Provinces of the Bengal Presidency for 1853-54.

Local Committee (page 28).

Nawab Hamid Ali Khan.

Establishment (page 29).

Name.	Designation.	Amount of salary.	Date of appointment.
Jafir Alli.	Shiah Teacher,	Rs. 100.	1st April 1841.

Remarks (page 36).

"Shiah classes under Maulvi Jafir Alli.

"All these classes passed an excellent examination, as far as the literary portion of their studies was concerned. They, in general, failed decidedly in Mathematics—a failure which occurs in the Shiah classes year by year. In Nagri, on the contrary, they distinguished themselves highly."

Detail of Receipts (page 48).

	Rs.	A.	P.
From Nawab Itimad-ud-Dowla	7,253	5	4

I.—Letter from Master Ram Chandra, late Director of Public Instruction, Patiala.

As a student and a teacher I was connected with the Delhi College for about thirty years (1833-1863).

Among other things regarding this College, I know that Nawab Fazal Alli Khan—a noble of the Court of Lucknow— had invested rupees one hundred and seventy thousand for educational purposes, and that out of the annual interest of this Fund a part of the expenses of the College were defrayed.

At the end of 1839, the late Mr. Thomason, then Secretary to the Government, North-Western Provinces, was sent by Government to improve the state of the College, composed of an English and an Oriental Department. It was then that the late Nawab Hamid Alli Khan of Delhi, son-in-law of the Nawab Fazal Alli Khan—was made a member of the Local Committee of Public Instruction at Delhi; and at the request of this Hamid Alli Khan, a Shiah Moulvi named *Jafir Alli* was appointed as Head Arabic Teacher of the Shiah class, in order that, along with literature and science, he may also teach the Muhammadan law according to the creed of the Shiah Sect. This arrangement was evidently made by Mr. Thomason in consideration of the munificent gift of the orignal donor, whose son-in-law Hamid Alli Khan was, both being of the Shiah persuasion.

This shews that the object of the donation of one hundred and seventy thousand rupees—as understood by the English Government—was to advance Oriental education, and that too accordingly to the Shiah Religion. I have no doubt that till 1857, when the Mutinies broke out and the College was destroyed, the money from the Nawab Fund was expended in the Oriental Department according to the wishes of the donor.

PATIALA;
The 13th November 1871.

(Sd.) RAM CHANDRA.

D.—References to other papers connected with the Itimad-ud-Dowla Fund.

Letter from the Secretary to Government, Punjab, to Financial Commissioner, Punjab, No. 2451, dated 16th November 1859, regarding transfer of Promissory Notes, detailed below to the Director of Public Instruction, Punjab.

Note No. 5149 of 1832, 33—in favor of Director and Commissioner of Delhi. Value Rs. 2,700.

Note No. 16658, ditto for Rs. 1,000.

From Punjab Government letter dated 14th October 1862, No. 1332, to the address of the Director of Public Instruction, it appears that the Deputy Commissioner of Delhi has procured from Calcutta a copy of the Will.

Major Fuller in his No. 54A., dated 12th July 1864, to the address of the Secretary to Government, Punjab, states that the Nawab Fazal Ali Khan has endowed this amount for the spread of education, but has left no instructions for any special kind of education.

E.—Remonstrances against present application of the Nawab Itimad-ud-Dowla Fund.

1.—*Translation of Mukhtarnama by Haji Begum, daughter of Nawab Fazal Ali Khan Itimad-ud-Dowla, appointing Moulvi Syed Jafir Ali as her Agent.*

Register No. 37 of 1866—Revenue Department, Delhi.

KNOW ALL MEN BY THESE PRESENTS THAT

I, Haji Begum, daughter of the late Nawab Itimad-ud-Dowla Syed Fazal Ali Khan Sahib, and wife of Nawab Itimad-ud-Dowla Syed Hamad Ali Khan, inhabitant of Delhi, seeing that the sum of Rupees one lakh and seventy thousand (1,70,000) entrusted to Government by my father Nawab Itimad-ud-Dowla Syed Fazal Ali Khan, for the purpose of instruction consistent with the religion professed by himself, is not applied properly in accordance with our wishes, appoint Moulvi Syed Jafir Ali as my Agent holding general powers-of-attorney from me to conduct this case, and declare myself responsible for the actions and pleadings of the said Moulvi in courts where necessary, and for any documents presented by him. I further assert myself willing to accept any decision of the case assented to by the said Moulvi Jafir Ali.

Seal of Haji Begum.

Dated 5th April 1866.

Witnesses

Seal of Mir Kulu, son of Syed Rasul Buksh of Badl Bhang Khan.

Seal of Sheikh Imam Buksh, son of Khoda Buksh, of ditto.

This Mukhtarnama has this day been authenticated with the evidence on oath of witnesses entered in the margin in the Court of Mr. Thomson William Neil, Extra Assistant Commissioner, Delhi.

Dated 5th April 1866.

2.—*Translation of declaration witnessing to the fact that the deed of the Will of Nawab Itimad-ud-Dowla said that the sum of Rupees one lakh seventy thousand (1,70,000), if not spent by Government in imparting religious instruction, would at the option of Syed Hamad Ali Khan be demanded back from Government.*

Haji Begum, daughter of Nawab Itimad-ud-Dowla Syed Fazal Ali Khan, and wife of Nawab Itimad-ud-Dowla, Syed Hamad Ali Khan declares that her father the late Nawab Itimad-ud-Dowla Syed Fazal Ali Khan entrusted to Government in A. D. 1829 the sum of Rupees one lakh and seventy thousand (1,70,000) for imparting religious instruction, and again a written deed of Will to her husband Nawab Syed Hamad Ali Khan purporting that if Government did not spend this money in accordance with his wishes, he was authorized to take the amount back from it. It was in obedience to this portion of the Will that a few years previous to 1841 A. D. when Syed Hamad Ali Khan saw that the money was not applied to religious instruction as required by the donor he tried to get it back. The Government then set aside the sum of Rs. 250 per mensem, out of the monthly interest of the principal sum which amounted to about Rs. 700, for the particular purpose of religious instruction. Moulvi Hafiz Syed Jafer Ali was appointed Head Shiah Teacher on Rs. 100 per mensem. The remaining sum of 150, one hundred and fifty rupees, was allotted to Shiah students. The surplus of the interest money about Rs. 450 [four hundred and fifty rupees only] was spent in general instruction in Arabic, Persian and Sanskrit. This continued from 1841 to the time of the mutiny, when the teachers and students both went away to their respective homes. All this can be clearly gathered from the letters of Members of the Local Committee, and that of the Court of Directors and other papers, deposited with Government; and as it is not unknown to the Raeses, and Ahlkars, and other respectable persons, we are desirous that this declaration may also be filed with other Government papers, as forming part of the grounds of the case.

Seeing that since the mutiny the entrusted sum is being wholly spent upon general education, against the expressed wishes of the donor, and the arrangement of Government which continued from 1841 to the time of the mutiny, there being no Shiah class for whose instruction the sum was originally given in the school at Delhi as previously, we are desirous that the amount may either be transferred to the Unversity for Oriental languages, or spent in the Delhi school according to the original arrangement of Government. *Dated 12th April 1866 according to 25th Zi-qad 1282 Hijiri.*

(1) Seal of Mirza Mohammad Hidayet, known as Mirza Elahi Bakhsh.

(2) Seal of Ziauddin Ahmad.

(3) Seal and signature of Shahabuddin Ahmad.

(4) I subscribe to all that is said in the above declaration (Seal of Raja Sabz Ram).

(5) Seal of Raja Debi Sing.

(6) The above is a statement of what I also have heard. The contents are true to my

belief (signature of Mahesh Das).

(7) Seal of Sheikh Mahbub Bakhsh, Honorary Magistrate.

(8) The above corresponds to what I have heard (signed), Juvan Lal, Honorary Magistrate.

(9) Seal and signature of Itzad-ud-Dowla Umdat-ul-Mulk, Willayat Husein Khan.

3.—Translation of order passed on the application of Haji Begum and other heirs of the deceased Nawab Itmad-ud-Dowla, originally presented to Government of India, but sent by it to the Punjab Government. It requested the Government to apply the proceeds of the money deposited by the father of Haji Begum with Government for the purpose of instruction, to teach Muhammedan Jurisprudence to Shiahs in accordance with their religious belief.

THE GOVERNMENT OF THE PUNJAB ORDERED—

That the applicants be informed that the expenses of the school established in Delhi which gives instruction in Arabic and English will be paid out of the income arising from the said deposited sum. As a token of respect to the deceased Nawab Itimad-ud-Dowla a majority of Shiah teachers have been employed in the School. But it cannot be supposed that instruction to the Shiahs will be conducted strictly in accordance with the line marked out by them. If the applicants can bring sufficient proof to show that the money was originally entrusted to Government for this particular purpose, or if they can produce the original Deed of Will, or a certified copy of it, every attention will be paid to their assertions.

SIMLA: (Signed) PANDIT MOTI LAL,

Dated 24th August 1872. *Mir Munshi.*

4.—Translation of application presented by the heirs of Nawab Itimad-ud-Dowla to the Registrar, Punjab University College, desiring the transfer of the sum of one lakh and seventy thousand rupees, 1,70,000, from Government to the Punjab University College.

The deceased Nawab Itimad-ud-Dowla Fazal Ali Khan, of whom we are the heirs, had entrusted to Government the sum of one lakh and seventy thousand rupees for religious instruction to Muhammadans of the Shiah Sect, to which he himself belonged. For (17) seventeen years ending with the mutiny year, the arrangements continued in accordance with his wishes. After that time the whole thing fell to the ground, and although some time ago a new scheme* has been set on foot, which we anxiously hoped would revive the original institution, this has proved in the end to be quite in opposition to the wishes of the donor; the person who has been appointed the head teacher of the school being professedly of a different sect from ours. We are hopeful that the Government will take measures to give religious instruction in accordance with Shiah principles, as required by the deceased Nawab. For this purpose a sum of Rs. 250 per mensem may be entrusted to us as the salary of the teacher and student; so that we might be able to appoint Syed Jafer Ali (who originally held this post under orders from the deceased Nawab, and is looked upon with respect by all Shiahs) as head teacher of the school. We are willing and pleased to have the remaining sum transferred to the Punjab University. In connection with this, Nawab Sultan Mirza might be appointed as our Secretary, and Nawab Muhammed Mirza Sayad Hadi Husein Khan, Moulvi Sayad Abbass Husein and Sayad Mohammed be appointed as Members.

Signed for the heirs of the deceased Nawab Itimad-ud-Dowla.

Sayad Fazal Ali Khan Sehrab Jang.

Seal of Morad Begum, daughter of the Nawab.

,, of Haji Begum.

Signature of Mahammed Mirza.

Do. of Sayad Abbass Mirza.

Do. of Sayad Yusuf Mirza.

Do. of Sayad Wazir Mirza.

Do. of Sayad Sultan Mirza.

5.—Translation of letter dated 8th February 1877, from Sayed Fazal Ali Khan and heirs of the deceased Nawab Itimad-ud-Dowla, to Dr. G. W. Leitner, Registrar, Panjab University.

DEAR SIR,

We must first express our deep thanks for the assistance you so kindly give us.

We are in receipt of your letter for which we were eagerly waiting. We have read over the contents, and in reply beg to say that the purport of the application we gave you in Delhi was that a sum of Rs. 250 per mensem be entirely entrusted to us; and that in connection with the remainder to be deposited with the Punjab University, the persons mentioned in that application be selected as Members. If this cannot be done, we also agree to the appointment of Nawab Sayed Sultan Mirza as a Member of the Executive Committee to act and vote as other Members of the same.

---

* The Anglo-Oriental School.

6.—*Translation of application of the heirs of Nawab Itimad-ud-Dowla, presented to Mr. Lepel Griffin, Secretary to the Government of Punjab.*

The end and aim of this our application which has already been brought to the notice of Government is: that the sum of Rs. one lakh and seventy thousand, entrusted to Government by Nawab Itimad-ud-Dowla Sayed Fazal Ali Khan, the deceased, for the instruction of Shiahs, continued to be spent properly, in accordance with the arrangements, sanctioned by the late Nawab Hamad Ali Khan, from 1841 to 1857, after which period, notwithstanding our requests, the plan accepted by Nawab Hamad Ali Khan and sanctioned by Government was not received. We have therefore the honor most respectfully to request that the proceeds of the fund be now transferred to the Punjab University, and that a sum of Rs. 250 per mensem, out of the income, be entirely left at our disposal, as heirs of the deceased Nawab, to be spent in the instruction of Shiahs, as the pay of teachers, students, &c., so that by this means a Shiah school, as before, be supported and continued in Delhi. The remaining Rs. 450 per mensem might be spent in the teaching of other sciences to which the Shiah students of the said Delhi School may also have access.

We also request that Sayed Sultan Mirza, descendant of the Nawab Itimad-ud-Dowla Mirza Fazal Ali Khan, the deceased, be appointed a Member of the Senate of the Punjab University and his votes taken in connection with the expenses out of this sum.

We have sent a similar application to the Punjab University.

We, the heirs of the Nawab, and the heads of the Shiah sect, have now brought the above to the notice of our gracious Government, and hope that due consideration will be paid to it.

7.—*Copy of letter No. 163, dated 17th March 1877, from Dr. G. W. Leitner,* M. A., *Registrar, Punjab University College, Lahore, to Lepel Griffin, Esquire,* C. S., *Officiating Secretary to Government, Punjab.*

Has the honor to submit herewith certain extracts from the proceedings of the Executive Committee of the Punjab University College, relative to the application of the Itimad-ud-Dowla Fund of Delhi in accordance with the wishes of the Shiah community and the original practice, together with a Mukhtarnama and a petition of the relicts of the late Nawab Fazal Ali Khan, the donor of the fund, begging for its absorption in the funds of the Punjab University College on certain conditions. This matter has come before the Committee at various times since 1871, and is one in which the Shiah community generally take an interest. The renewed instance, however, of the relicts during the recent visit of the Registrar to Delhi on the occasion of the Imperial Assemblage, induces the undersigned to submit the matter, with the sanction of the Executive Committee, to Government for decision in accordance with the wishes of the Shiah community and the interests of the Punjab University College, as a national Institution.

Extract from the Proceedings of a meeting of the Executive Committee held on the 13th May 1871.

"A letter from the representatives of the Delhi Nawab Fund was read requesting that the endowment be given to the University on condition of its setting apart Rs. 250 per mensem for the support of a Shiah class at Delhi. The Committee approved of the general principles of the application, and requested Registrar to make further enquiries."

Extract from the Proceedings of the Executive Committee, dated 1st June 1876.

Para. 11.—"Dr. Leitner then gave an account of the origin of the Itimad-ud-Dowla Fund and of the steps that the relicts and friends of the late Nawab Sayad Fazal Ali Khan had taken to place its administration under the University College. Certain steps had been taken some time ago to place the matter before the late Lord Mayo, the consequence of which was that Government founded an Anglo-Arabic School at Delhi. This was however not exactly what the relicts of the donor wished, and they appeared to carry with them the wishes of the Mahommadan community generally in desiring to have the funds added to those of the Punjab University College on certain conditions. It now appeared that Government did not consider it to be a Government Institution, as pensions had been refused to its teachers, and it was also not a grant-in-aid Institution.

"The committee then desired to place the management of this matter in the hands of the Registrar, who mentioned that the originator of the idea was Nawab Nawazish Ali Khan and suggested that a Sub-committee be formed with the Nawab as President and himself and Faqir Sayad Qamar-ud-Din and Nawab Abdul Majid Khan as Members, to take such steps as may commend themselves to their judgment in order to bring the matter to a successful conclusion. This was agreed to."

The following proposal was decided by the Members of the Executive Committee during the summer vacation on a notice being circulated to them, dated the 6th September 1876, paragraph 12. "That Government be applied to make over to the Panjab University College the Nawab Itimad-ud-dowla Fund, in accordance with the wishes of the relicts and for the better fulfilment of the conditions of the gift."

In January 1877, whilst at Delhi, the Registrar received a renewed application from the relicts of the late Nawab Fazal Ali Khan, who with other Shiah gentlemen called upon him to settle the question. They stated that the Arabic learning imparted in the Anglo-Arabic School was not worthy of the name; that they had sent up representations to the Deputy Commissioner who seemed to be favourable to the justice of a Shiah gift being applied in accordance with the wishes of the Shiah community; they asked that Rs. 250 per mensem, as formerly, be devoted to a pure Shiah class (*vide* enclosed), and that the rest be given to the Panjab University College, in which they requested that there should be three Members on behalf of the relicts of the late Nawab Fazal Ali Khan. The Registrar was of opinion that two-thirds of the balance also should be devoted to Delhi men studying Arts, Law, Medicine or Engineering at Lahore, whilst only the small balance of one-third of the income left might go to the general purposes of the University College and for the supervision of the trust, added to its General Funds. With this view the relicts expressed their greatest satisfaction, being far more than they had any right to expect, but they only wished Rs. 250 to be set apart for Shiah purposes and the rest to be absorbed by the University College."

Translation of a letter to Registrar, Panjab University College, from Syed Sultan Mirza, giving information of a memorial signed by the people of Delhi protesting against the resolution of Government, with reference to the Nawab fund, published in the Government Gazette.

The teachers of the (Anglo-Oriental) school of Delhi have read over the resolution of Government, with reference to the Nawab fund, published in the Government Gazette. They have accordingly drawn up a memorial praying Government to continue the arrangements at present in force, and not to transfer the amount to the Panjab University. The citizens of Delhi have signed the memorial, some of them through avarice, others through fear. We believe the memorial will be sent to the Panjab Government, and therefore take this opportunity of previously informing you of it. None of us, the heirs of the deceased Nawab, have signed the memorial, nor ever will. On the contrary, we beg to know what measure in your opinion should be adopted in opposition to this.

We are grateful to you for the kindness shewn towards us, and the trouble taken by you for our sake.

Translation of the second letter to Registrar, Panjab University, from Syed Sultan Mirza, in reply to a letter from this Office.

I am in receipt of your docket No. 737, dated 12th September 1877, and in reply beg to say that the resolution of Government referred to in my last letter is contained in the Government Gazette No. 34 of the 23rd August 1877. You will find it in the Supplement to the Gazette of that date. It is stated therein that the income from the Nawab fund will be entirely spent in Lahore, and this is not what I and yourself had agreed to. A sum of Rs. 250 out of the income is required by us in Delhi for the support of the Shiah school. We hope you will try for the fulfilment of your promise with us. The citizens of Delhi are drawing up a memorial opposing the transfer of the amount to Lahore, and this is very soon expected to be sent to Government. I write this to you by way of information, and want to know if any measure is to be adopted against this.

Translation of a third letter to Registrar, Panjab University, from Syed Sultan Mirza, received on the 20th December 1877.

This is in reply to your docket No. 829. I convey to you hereby the sincere thanks of the whole nation to which I belong for the trouble you take for our sake. A copy of the inscription on the stone fixed upon the gate of the late Ghazi-ud-din Khan's School is sent herewith. You will kindly acknowledge the receipt of it. The words (ba-yad-i-hasanat-i-Nawab Itimad-ud-dowla) "in memory of the good qualities of Nawab Itimad-ud-Dowla" have particular reference to the Muhammadans and their religion; for the word *hasanat* can have no connection with any other than religious instruction. The Bible, for instance, is taught in the Mission Schools for *hasanat*, improving the morals, and other sciences as the means of subsistence. Men of your qualifications and vast abilities can draw important conclusions from this one word. But the peculiar right of Muhammadans and of religious instruction to the money deposited by the late Nawab is not to be drawn from this one word alone. No, the fact has been recognized by Government itself. Is it not a matter of regret then that although we, the heirs of the late Nawab, are willing to accept a sum of Rs. 250, per mensem only, out of the total proceeds of the amount, as the fulfilment of the condition on which the money was entrusted, the Government does not yet pay attention to our requests, and that we are, up to date, deprived of our rights?

The inscription also shows that the money was intended for Delhi alone. Should the Government be bent upon following this hint of the inscription, you would do well to establish a branch of the University in Dehli, FOR WE WISH IT, FROM THE BOTTOM OF OUR HEARTS, THAT THE MONEY BE TRANSFERRED FROM THE DEPARTMENT OF EDUCATION TO THE PUNJAB UNIVERSITY. At present some evils have crept into the school in Delhi. It was at first situated in Qaem Jan's lane, the centre of the most populous part of the city. The students from all sides of the city had therefore to walk equal distances. The ease with which boys could come to the school had led to an increase in the daily attendance. The removal of the school, as at present, to Chandni Mahal near the Delhi Gate, situated in a corner of a less populous part of the city, will, on account of its greater distance from this part, oblige young boys to leave the school, and thus prove an obstacle to its progress.

There are many other evils which I do not think fit to note down here.

The inscription reads as follows :—

"In memory of the pious deeds [Hasnat] of Nawab Itimad-ud-dowla Zia-ul-mulk Syed Fazal Ali Khan Bahadur, Sehrab Jang, who entrusted to the British Government [the Sahibs of the English Company] the sum of one lakh and seventy thousand rupees for the encouragement of learning [u'lum] in this school situated in Delhi proper, the place of his birth and residence. Inscribed in the year 1829 A.D.

(Engraved by Syed Amir Razwe.)

NOTE ON ABOVE BY DR. LEITNER.

1. The Kitab-ul-Vaqf or Chapter on Endowments in the Lama't Damashqia (the accepted Shiah authority) composed by Sheikh Abi Abdulla Shahid Muhammad bin Makki says :—

"An endowment to adulterers, sinners, seceders (Khawarij) and the deifiers of Ali is unlawful."

Whoever gives anything as a gift, or in a will, or as Vaqf (endowment), the same will not be accounted in his "Hasnat" "good deeds," if it be not spent in religious acts, with the exception of *one* kind of gift, namely alms, (sadaqa) which it is allowable to give to the enemy of one's religion.

2. As regards disposal by will.

"A will 'on behalf of the poor' should be applied to the poor of the testator's nation (sect)."

3. In the Chapter on Alms it is said :—

"Alms to the opponent of right (the true faith) is allowable."

Again the author says "Tafwiz" or "Transfer" this is applied to property, being in the responsibility (or belonging to) of the transferor which is made over to the responsibility of the transferee.

"Will" cannot extend to more than a third of the property.

"It is the condition on any amount exceeding the third that it depends on the permission of the relict (or inheritor), and if not, (such a provision) is void."

Extract from No 2244, dated 23rd May 1877, referring to the Itimad-ud-Dowla Fund. From Lepel Griffin, Esq., Officiating Secretary to Government, Punjab, to the Secretary to the Government of India, Home Department.

"Your endorsement No. 65, of the 20th March last, forwarded to the Government of the Punjab a memorial from the inhabitants of the city of Delhi, on the subject of the recent removal of the college classes of the Delhi College from that city to Lahore, for early report, with especial reference to the Nawab Itimad-ud-Dowla endowment.

With the Delhi College as originally constituted and as it existed up to the mutiny, the Punjab Government has in no way interfered. It was then known as a College, but was in reality no more than an exceedingly good town school, aided by an endowment due to the liberality of Nawab Itimad-ud-Dowla. The institution thus constituted and thus endowed has not been touched. All that has been done has been to withdraw, for financial reasons, those college classes which were experimentally added to the Delhi School by the Punjab Government in 1864.

With reference to the above-named endowment, regarding which you call for especial notice, I am directed to observe that the middle class school formed out of the Anglo-Vernacular Department of the District School is entirely supported by this endowment at a monthly cost of Rs. 607. The endowment was originally intended for Muhammadan education exclusively; but, subsequently, at the suggestion of the Government of India, it was granted by Nawab Itimad-ud-Dowla for the general advancement of education at Delhi. The original papers regarding the grant and the will of the Nawab appear to have been destroyed during the mutiny, and copies have been vainly applied for to the offices of the Administrator General, the North-Western Provinces, and the Government of India. That the wish of the founder in favor of Muhammadan education had been, however, insufficiently considered was admitted by the Punjab Government in 1872, when the school was reorganized in such a manner as to satisfy the trustees of the endowment and the Muhammadan community, and provision was especially made for the teaching of students of the Shia sect to which the founder of the endowment belonged. That the action taken by the Punjab Government was approved by the Government of India is clear from the following extract from a demi-official letter from the Secretary to the Government of India, in the Home Department, to my address, dated 3rd August 1872.

"I herewith return, with many thanks, the file of papers belonging to your office about the creation of a Shia Department in the Delhi College."

"From a perusal of the papers it appears that the Punjab Government has quite anticipated the wishes of the Government of India as to the management of this school."

In the arrangement then made with reference to the Itimad-ud-Dowla endowment, no change has been as yet made, though there is, at the present moment, a proposal on the part of the trustees of the fund, supported by the most important members of the Shia community in the Punjab, a copy of which is herewith forwarded, from which it will appear that, so far from the amalgamation of the Delhi and Lahore Colleges being in opposition to the wishes of the trustees of the Itimad-ud-Dowla endowment, they wish to go further than has been proposed by Government, and retaining at Delhi Rs. 250 a month for the especial training of Shia students, to make over the balance of Rs 450 per mensem to the Panjab University for the general promotion of education. This memorial has not yet been disposed of, and were it favorably considered, the Lieutenant-Governor would wish to go further in the interests of Delhi than is proposed by the petitioners, and to apply the whole of the available portion of the endowment to the support, at the Lahore University, of Delhi students. This would, he considers, be only equitable in accordance with the terms of the original grant by the Nawab, who desired the money to be spent on the education of students of his Native city of Delhi."

To this the following reply was sent by the Government of India, No. 199, dated Simla, 15th August 1877.—From Arthur Howell, Esquire, Officiating Secretary to the Government of India, Home Department, to the Secretary to Government, Punjab. [*Extract.*]

"With regard to the Itimad-ud-Dowla endowment and the views of the Delhi community generally, the explanation is equally satisfactory. You say that—(here the above views of the Punjab Goverment are quoted at length).

"6. There being no question of misapplied endowments or breaking of pledges, direct or implied, the Government of India cannot but admit that there is much force in the above arguments."

APPENDIX IV.

List of Books in the Gurmukhi Characters.

(Incomplete.)

1	Nuskhe Baidak Bhasha	...	A Treatise on Medicine.
2	Salôtri Taswiran San-jugat	...	Ditto on Veterinary Art.
3	Darb Darpan	...	Ditto on Substances.
4	Yūsafi Vaidak	...	A Medical Treatise by Yūsafi.
5	Pathyā Pathya	...	A Treatise on Medicine.
6	Nirghant	...	A Vocabulary.
7	Hashim Shahi Nuskhe	...	A Medical Treatise by Hashim Shah.
8	Baid Mano tsawa	...	A Treatise on Medicine.
9	Chikista Sar	...	An Elementary Practice of Medicine.
10	Saririk Baidak, Saririk Birtant	...	A Treatise on Medicine and Anatomy.
11	Pran Sukh Darvesi	...	On bodily ease.
12	Safatak Nuskhe	...	Prescriptions.
13	Khair-ul Tajar-ab Baidak	...	A Treatise on Medicine.
14	Fil Nama Akbari	...	Ditto on Elephants by Akbar.
15	Fil Nama	...	Ditto on Elephants.
16	Rognas	...	Ditto on Diseases.
17	Ria zul Adviya	...	Garden of Medicine.
18	Tib Sihabi	...	A Medical Treatise by Sahib.
19	Tib Akbari	...	Ditto by Akbar.
20	Karaba Din Safai	...	Ditto on Health.
21	Karaba Din Kadri	...	A Practical Treatise on Medicine.
22	Fawaid-ul Jowahar	...	A Treatise on Gems.
23	Salutri Gutka	...	A Manual of Veterinary Art.
24	Madan Chandrodaya.		
25	Nidan	...	A Treatise on the Symptoms of Diseases.
26	Nirghant Bhasa	...	A Vocabulary of the Hindi Vernacular.
27	Baid Ratan	...	A Treatise on Medicine.
28	Rasoi-Nama	...	Cookery, a Treatise on.
29	Riyaz-ul Favaid.		
30	Nirghant Madanpal	...	A Vocabulary.
31	Dil Lagan	...	A Tale of Love.
32	Asp Nama, Bhagwan Das	...	A Treatise on Horses by Bhagwan Das.
33	Baj Nama	...	Ditto on Hawks.
34	Ikhtyarat Badi	...	A Law Book.
35	Tib Akbari	...	A Medical Treatise by Akbar.
36	Hamla ke Ilaj	...	Treatment of Pregnancy.
37	Khabira Ijat	...	On Leavening.
38	Danish Nama	...	A Treatise on Wisdom.
39	Bhakha Ramal	...	Mode of Divination from Birds.
40	Ramal Sar	...	An Astrological system.
41	Zubda Hikmat	...	Elements of Medical Science.
42	Radha Govind Sangit	...	On Music.
43	Sangit Sar Utrardh	...	Ditto.
44	Par Sitar Sangit	...	Playing on the Sitara.
45	Sangit Bhakha	...	A Treatise on Musical Language.
46	Tala Dhyaya.		
47	Budh Parkas Darpan	...	On the Culture of the Faculties.
48	Raga Mala Sangit	...	On the Modes of Music.
49	Narindar, Mirgaindar Natak	...	A Drama.
50	Sirkari Kharrhe	...	Official Letters.
51	Sabha Parkas Bava Niranjan	...	On Society, by Niranjan.
52	Sabha Parkas Bhai Bahal Singh	...	Ditto, by Bahal Singh.
53	Ras Rahs.		
54	Kavi Priya	...	Prosody.
55	Kavi Ballabh Chotta	...	Prosody Manual.
56	Fateh Parkas.		
57	Ras Bilas	...	On Enjoyment.
58	Bhav Bilas.		
59	Alankar Darpan	...	Rhetoric.
60	Sabha Mandal	...	Circle of Assemblage.
61	Ras Ratnakar.		
62	Bihari Satsayia.		
63	Kabya Nirne	...	Prosody.
64	Lalit Lalam	...	Music.
65	Kabya Sindhata	...	Prosody.

No.	Title	Subject
66	Tark Sangreh	... Compilation of Criticisms against different sects.
67	Habir Hathi.	
68	Kabya Narain	... Prosody.
69	Man Rakhan Pingal	... Rules of Poetry.
70	Ratan Hajara	... Selections from standard Bhasha poets of the later period.
71	Ras Parbodh	... A Manual of Philosophy.
72	Sundar Singai	... Beautiful Ornaments.
73	Rask Priya Ti ka Jorawar.	
74	Kavya Swar Vaisar	... Prosody.
75	Prabha Kar Parstar Stik.	
76	Sangarah mala.	
77	Ast Bajee Bidh	... On Fireworks.
78	Chitra Bilas	... Decoration.
79	Rajnit	... Rules for the Guidance of Kings.
80	Kavi Bilas	... Prosody.
81	Naval Ras Chandrodaya.	
82	Jagat Binod	... About the World.
83	Singar Sangreh.	
84	Bodh Khorsi	... A Philosophical Work.
85	Bhav Panchasaka.	
86	Ras Kalol	... Amusements.
87	Karna Bharn.	
88	Krishan Chandraka	... A Religious Book.
89	Roop Basant ki Katha	... A Fable.
90	Ritu Bilas	... Enjoyment of the Seasons.
91	Ras Raj.	
92	Madhawa Nal	... Fable.
93	Kusam Vatka.	
94	Badan Kala Nidh Pingal	... Prosody.
95	Parbin Rai Krit Pingal	... Ditto.
96	Chinta Mani Krit Pingal	... Ditto.
97	Kavi Bhookhan Pingal	... Ditto.
98	Amar Chandraka Bihari di Tika	... A Grammar.
99	Ras Payukh.	
100	Bihari ki Tika Kab Krishen Krit	... A Poem.
101	Alankar Kala Nidh.	
102	Laghu Pingal	.. Prosody.
103	Amrit Saraswti	... Literature.
104	Rup Dip Pingal	... Prosody.
105	Kut Kabit	... Ditto.
106	Chhando Malka	... Rules of Poetry.
107	Astajam.	
108	Kavi Priya Tika	... Prosody.
109	Wahid Bari.	
110	Amad Nama.	
111	Ful Mala.	
112	Krishen Sahitya Sindhu.	
113	Sudha Sagar	... Philosophy.
114	Alankar Sudha Sagar	... Ditto.
115	Lal Chandraka Satsaistika	... A Grammar.
116	Bal Bhadar Sikhan	... A Book on Religion.
117	Kok Panj Saik.	
118	Ram Kabitavali	... Prosody.
119	Kavi Ballabh Vadda	... A Poem.
120	Bakha Bhukhan Satik.	
121	Singhasan Batisi	... Fables.
122	Baital Pachisi	... Ditto.
123	Chhand Ratnavali	... On Prosody.
124	Rabrath Chintka.	
125	Chhand Bodhni	... Rules of Prosody.
126	Kabitta Narain	... On Prosody.
127	Ras Ratna Kar.	
128	Raghu Raj Bilas	... Ramayan.
129	Anek Arthi.	
130	Tantar Sungreh	... Mechanics.
131	Adbhut Bilas.	
132	Indar Jal	... Juggling.
133	Janam Sakhi Guru Nanuk	... Guru Nanak's Life.
134	Sarb Loh Uttrrádh	... Sikh Religious Book.
135	Sukh Manee Bani	... Ditto.

136	Sau Sakhi Guru Govind Singh ...	Sikh Religious Book.
137	Sakhian Panjah	Ditto.
138	Sakhi Suhove Sahib wali ...	Ditto.
139	Panth Parkas Chhand-o-band ...	Ditto.
140	Prem Sumarg	Ditto.
141	Tika Hakaitan	Ditto.
142	Bai Baran Puratan.	
143	Muntkhib Jakhira.	
144	Ilag Masturat	A Book on the Treatment of Diseases of Women.
145	Jamli Fawaid.	
146	Sarahim Sabab.	
147	Amrajul Shafa	A Medical Treatise.
148	Tarikh Muhammad Pagambar ...	Life of Muhammad.
149	Ad Guru Granth Sahib ...	Sikh Scriptures.
150	Deswen Padshah i da Granth Sahib ...	Ditto.
151	Gurblas Chhi Padshahi ...	Life of the sixth Guru.
152	Suraj Parkas Daswan Padshah ...	Ditto tenth ditto
153	Bar Bhai Gurdas ki ...	A Sikh Religious Book.
154	Tika Baran Gur Ratan Mala ...	A Commentary.
155	Baran Mani Singh ki Tika ...	Commentary by Mani Singh.
156	Kitab Sakhian Guru Angad ki ...	A Sikh Religious Book.
157	Raht Nama, Mazhabi Shara ...	Ditto
158	Maha Bharth (Nasar) ...	Maha Bharath in prose.
159	Maha Bharth (Nazmi) ...	Ditto in verse.
160	Ranjit, Devi Das	Rules for the Kings by Davi Das.
161	Bhagwat (Nazam).	
162	Bishan Puran, Dhru Katha ...	Story of Dhrov (Vishnu Puran).
163	Manu Simriti (Nazam).	
164	Ranjit Budh Sagar.	
165	Raj Ratan Chandrodaya.	
166	Sangit Darpan	On Music.
167	Hanuman Natik	War between Rama and Rawana.
168	Adhiyatam Ramayana.	
169	Asmedh Jaimni	Great Horse Festival of the Aryans.
170	Asmedh Ramain	Ditto Feast by Rama.
171	Kosh Santokh Singh.	
172	Vichar Mala.	
173	Panch Dasi Vedant Dyal Nemi Kirit ...	The Vedant Philosophy.
174	Mokh Panth	Philosophy.
175	Amritdhara.	
176	Avagad Hulas.	
177	Vedant Sar.	
178	Vedant Rahas.	
179	Sur Sagar, Sur Das Jika ...	Exploits of Krishna by Sur Das.
180	Tulsi Ramayan	Life of Rama, by Tulsi Das.
181	Bhugol	A Geography.
182	Kavi Tarangni	Prosody.
183	Lilavati	Mathematics.
184	Ilam Hait.	
185	Akbar Nama.	
186	Ain Akbari ...	Laws of Akbar.
187	Surodai Harcharan Das ...	Observations on the "nostril air."
188	Surodai Sukh Singh.	
189	Darvesi.	
190	Alankar Ratna Kar	Decoration with Jewels (Rhetoric).
191	Alankar Kalanidh.	
192	Ganga Lahri.	
193	Alankar Dipak.	
194	Mohan Lila	Exploits of Krishna.
195	Pran Sangli Gohst Sidhan di ...	Sikh Religious Book.
196	Bihangam Bani	A Sikh Religious Book.
197	Ghost Atme Parmatme ki ...	A Philosophical Discourse.
198	Sakhi Raje Janak ki	Life of Janak.
199	Tika Japji, Bhai Santokh Singh ...	A Commentary on the Japji.
200	Tika Japji, Anand Ghan ...	Ditto.
201	Tika Japji, Guru Angadji ki ...	Ditto.
202	Gurbilas Daswin Padshahi ...	Life of the tenth Guru.
203	Gosht Makke ke Kazi Rukan Din ke Sath	A Sikh Religious Book.
204	Bhai Nand Lal ki Gajlan ...	Ditto.
205	Siri Nanak Chandraka ...	Ditto.
206	Khalsa Satak	Ditto.

207	Balmik Ramayan.	
208	Siri Vishisht ji ka Updesh ...	Vishisht's Advice to Rama.
209	Adbhut Narain (Ramayan).	
210	Atharon Dhiyai Gita ...	18 Chapters of "Gita," a Hindu Religious Book.
211	Guru Miharban Ramayan ...	A Book on the Hindu Religion.
212	Govind Gita	Ditto.
213	Sar Gita O-ankar Mahatam ...	Ditto.
214	Pandav Gita	Conversation between Pandav and Krishna.
215	Ram Gita	Ditto Ram and his brother Lachman.
216	Garbh Gita	Philosophy.
217	Sapat Shloki Gita	Hindu Religious Work.
218	Vishnu Gita	Ditto.
219	Ribhu Gita	Ditto.
220	Krishnarjun Sambad	Conversation between Krishna and Arjan.
221	Ajap Parkas-o-unkar Vichar ...	Philosophy.
222	Adwait Kousaw Devta ...	Philosophical Works.
223	Aduait Mirtu Devta	Philosophical Works.
224	Jagutiya Devta	Philosophical Works.
225	Prashan Uttar Suk Dev Krit ...	Questions and Answers by Sukh Dev.
226	Khat Prahali.	
227	Gian Churan Pustak	Philosophy.
228	Amritsagar Vedant	Ditto.
229	Manak Bodh, Manak, Krit Vedant ...	Philosophical Books.
230	Bavanja Up Nikadan Vedant ...	Philosophical Books.
231	Chid Vilas Vedant.	
232	Dig Vije	By Sankra Charj (Vedant).
233	Sidhant Katash Vedant	Philosophy
234	Gian Samundar Vedant	Philosophy
235	Ram Ride Vedant (Philosophy) ...	By Gulab Singh.
236	Vedant (Ditto)	By Astavakar.
237	Mokh Panth Vedant (ditto) ...	By Gulab Singh.
238	Prashan Uttri Vedant ditto ...	Questions and Answers.
239	Anbhav Parkas Vedant ditto.	
240	Ekadas Vedant (ditto).	
241	Adhiatam Parkas Vedant (ditto).	
242	Vichar Sagar Vedant ditto ...	By Nihal.
243	Sar Sangreh Vedant ditto.	
244	Nāri Prikhiya	Medical Treatise on the beating of the Pulse.
245	Sudh Darpan Vartik	A Medical Treatise.
246	Meghbilas Vaidak	Treatise on Medicine.
247	Amir Parkas (Philosophy) ...	By Amir Das.
248	Vaid Sar (by Arjun Das) ...	A Medical Book.
249	Budh Parkas Darpan ...	On Music.
250	Rag Sagar Rag kirit ...	Ditto.
251	Dharm Prabodh by Dharm Singh.	
252	Manu Simriti.	
253	Mahma Parkas.	
254	Sadh Suman Chandraka.	
255	Panj Granthi Bani	Sikh Religious Book.
256	Chakkar dhar chitra Chandraka.	
257	Jagat Jai Kari.	
258	Prem Parkas.	
259	Soor Kirt Kavitawali.	
260	Bandi Basotam Sahassar Nam.	
261	Prem Prabha Kar.	
262	Prem Sudha Kar.	
263	Gur Kavita Manik Piyukh.	
264	Bar bar Dohawali.	
265	Samer Bhukhan.	
266	Sarvar Bharn.	
267	Kavi Rhidaya Sudhakar ...	Prosody.
268	Bhagti Lata.	
269	Budh Bardh by Budh Singh.	
270	Padmakar Kavya	Prosody
271	Daduji ki Bani.	Doctrines of Dadu.
272	Sundarji ki Bani.	
273	Bakhnaji ki Bani.	
274	Chain Dasji ki Bani.	
275	Jagjiwan Dasji ki Bani.	
276	Sarbang ki Bani.	
277	Panj sai Sakhi Rajab ...	Stories by Rajab.

278 Baisakh Mahine ka Mahatam.
279 Katik ditto.
280 Magh ditto.
281 Ikadsi Mahatam.
282 Dasam by Krishen Das.
283 Dohawali by Tulsi Das.
284 Bine Patraka by Tulsi Das.
285 Katha Suk Dev ki Churasi Jun ki.
286 Amar Katha ... Story told by Shiva to Parwati.
287 Bha Mirt Sa Mirt by Gulab Singh.
288 Bhagat Mala, Prameswar Darshan ... Lives of Saints.
289 Bhagat Nabha di ... Ditto by Nabha.
290 Bhagat Mala Parachian ... Ditto separate pieces.
291 Mala, Kirat Singh ... Ditto by Kirát Singh.
292 Bhagat Mala by Maluk Das.
293 Prastat Prabhakar by Keso Das.
294 Ras Raj Moti Ram Naika Bhed.
295 Narindhar Bal by Maluk Das.
296 Bighan Harn Saphatak, *i. e.*, by different Poets.
297 Bhav Panchaska.
298 Khat Panchaska by Atam Ram.
299 Ras Kalap Sangreh, Murari.
300 Darpan, Chándon ke Nam.
301 Bijya Binod Padmakar krit.
302 Jahan Gir Chandraka ... Biography of the Mogul Emperor, Jehangir.
303 Anvar Chanderka.
304 Kumad kala nidh by Sahib Singh.
305 Ram Kaleu by Ram Lall.
306 Ras Manjri by Agar Das.
307 Dhihan Manjri by Agar Das.
308 Rask Raj Nit.
309 Sunit Panth by Nihal.
310 Raj Nit Chanaka.
311 Sabha Jit Hardyālkrit.
312 Niti Satak.
313 Pingal Prabhakar ... Rules of Poetry by Girdhar.
314 Pingal Sar.
315 Ganga Dhar Pingal.
316 Madhwa Bilas Raj Nit.
317 Gorakh Kundli ... ... Observation on the passing of the nostril air.
318 Nanak Sarodha ... ... Observation by Nanak.
319 Shiv Surodaya Kal Gian.
320 Surodya by Charn Das.
321 Sar Surodaya.
322 Saganti Sagan Vichar ... ... Observations of Omens.
323 Nujum Alam Krit ... Astrology by Alim.
324 Moharram Sal da phal dekhna ... Guide to predictions about the coming year.
325 Janwaron ki Vichar ... Observations of Omens from the sounds of Birds.
326 Kak Bhasa ... ... Observations of Omens from the sounds of the Crow.
327 Chugharia ka Mahurat.
328 Phahi ka Vichar ... ... Predicting Omens from the sound of Phahi or Phawi, a foreboding bird which generally comes out during the night.
329 Chinta Man Jotash ... ... Astrology.
330 Siyal ka Vichar.
331 Gadhe ke bolne ka Vichar ... Omens connected with the braying of the Ass.
332 Jatka Alunkar ... ... Astrological Treatise.
333 Khat Phanchaska Jotash ... Ditto.
334 Maharaj Parkas Jotash ... ... Astrology.
335 Megh Mala Jotash.
336 Sath Sambti.
337 Kundi Dak Bhadhli ki ... ... Predictions from natural phenomena.
338 Ang Bhurne ka Vichar ... ... Omens from the beatings of some pulse on the body.
339 Swapan Vichar ... ... Explanation of dreams.
340 Samundri ka Vichar ... ... Divinations from the marks on the palms of hands and the soles of feet.
341 Girdhar Kian Kundlia

342 Vairag Satak Bharthariji ka.
343 Amar Kosh ... ... Vocabulary.
344 Dropadi Charitar ... ... Miraculous covering of Daropti.
345 Sudama Charitar ... ... Miraculous building of the golden house of Sudama by Hirdi Ram.
346 Tahkan Asmedh ... ...
347 Ram Asmedh ... ... } Great Horse Sacrifices of the Ancients.
348 Jaiman Asmedh ... ...
349 Nurd Puran.
350 Garar Puran ki Katha ... ... The story of Nasketn going alive to the city of the God of Death and his return, generally read after the death of a person.
351 Nas Ket ki Katha ... ... A fabulous being supposed to have been born from the nose of a princess who smelt a flower.
352 Tehkan Krit Sahaosar Nama.
353 Rajjab ke Chhape.
354 Parsbhag Adan Shahi.
355 Suthre ki Bani Jhegar Shahi.
356 Bani Bhangar Dasdi.
357 Fakar Nama by Bhanger Das.
358 Bani Jallandi.
359 Bani Sheikh Chilidi.
360 Sadhu Jan ki Bani ... ... Precepts.
361 Faridji ki Bani.
362 Kabirji ki Bani.
363 Git Govind Jai Devji ka ... Songs.
364 Ram Lalam Git by Balmike.
365 Ram Rahas Gita.
366 Sukh Sastar Sangit.
367 Pad Ratnawali ... ... Treatise on the use of words.
368 Chamak Damak Duhawali.
369 Sat Narain ki Katha ... ... Story.
370 Gau Singh ki Katha ... ... Story of a Cow and a Lion.
371 Tulsi Satsaya.
372 Ram Kalaiu by Tulsi Das.
373 Bhakha Kosh. ... A Hindi Dictionary.
374 Hitu Updes ... ... The Hitopadesh (translation of).
375 Tarikh Kur Khetar ji ki ... The events of the Mahabbharath.
376 Anjil ... ... The New Testament.
377 Tavarikh Durabe di ... ... History of Duraba (?)
378 Chahar Khani Baidak ... ... A Medical Book.
379 Tark Bhakha ... ...
380 Adbhut Ramain.
381 Ramain Sar.
382 Kusam Nam Mala.
383 Badri Munir ... ... Punjabi Romance.
384 Nal Damyanti ki Katha.
385 Kabit Bhai Gurdas de.
386 Hakait Dasme Pad Shahi.
387 Hastamal Vedant ... ...
388 Astawakra Vedant ... ... } Philosophical Works.
389 Sat Mat Nirupan.

(See also Panjabi series by Lala Behari Lal; Panjabi books compiled under the auspices of the Punjab University College and of the Ludhiana Mission.)

APPENDIX V.

LIST OF VERNACULAR SCIENTIFIC BOOKS PUBLISHED BY THE PUNJAB UNIVERSITY COLLEGE, OR USED BY CANDIDATES FOR THE DEGREE STANDARDS IN ARTS.

MATHEMATICS.

Ilm-i-Sakun.—Translation of Todhunter's Statics, into Urdu, by Aya Ram, B. A.

Ilm-i-Harkat.—A treatise on Dynamics, in Urdu, by Babu Shashi Bhushan Mukarji, M.A., B.L.

Sakun Syalat.—Translation of Besant's Hydrostatics, into Urdu, by Pirzada Muhammad Husain, McLeod Arabic Fellow of the Punjab University College.

Gati Viggyan.—A treatise, in Hindi, on Dynamics, by Babu Shashi Bhushan Mukarji, M.A., B.L. (Manuscript.)

Jalasthiti tattwa, Jalgati tattwa and *Buyuk tattwa.*—Hydrostatics, Hydraulics and Pneumatics, in Hindi, with diagrams, by Babu Navina Chandra Rai.

Tailya-krama-Jyamiti.—A treatise on Plane Co-ordinate Geometry, in Hindi, by Pandit Kirpa Ram, late Professor of Mathematics in the Oriental College.

Ghan Jya Miti.—A treatise on Solid Geometry, in Hindi, by Pandit Kirpa Ram, together with a Vocabulary of Mathematical terms in Sanskrit and English.

Bij Ganit.—A Hindi treatise on Algebra, by Yogi Shiva Nath, Assistant Teacher of General Knowledge in the Punjabi Department of the Oriental College, in two parts. This contains a large number of exercises, and is the largest work on the subject yet published in Hindi.

Hall Jabar Muqabila.—Key to Algebra, in Urdu, by Maulvi Ghulam Mustafa of the Oriental College.

Man tattwa.—Translation of Todhunter's Mensuration, into Hindi, by Babu Panchanan Mukarji of the Oriental College.

Urdu translation of Maine's Astronomy, by Pirzada Muhammad Husain.

Sthiti tattwa, Gati tattwa.—Elements of Statics and Dynamics, in Hindi, by Navina Chandra Rai.

Mensuration, by Babu Kura Mal.

Todhunter's Algebra, in Urdu, by Professor Zaka-ulla (Muir College).

Plane Trigonometry (by Educational Department), in Urdu.

Todhunter's Mensuration, in Urdu, by Professor Zaka-ulla.

Barnard Smith's Arithmetic, in Urdu, by ditto.

Todhunter's Theory of Equations, in Urdu, by ditto.

Ditto Plane Co-ordinate Geometry, by ditto, in Urdu.

Elementary Plane Trigonometry, in Hindi, by Professor Lakshmi Shankar, M.A.

Khagol Vidya.—Elements of Astronomy, in Hindi.

Do. Sar.—Another treatise on the same subject in Hindi.

Elements of Astronomy, in Urdu (principally from Lockyar).

Elements of Algebra, by Bapu Deva Shastri, C.S.I., Professor of Mathematics, Benares College.

Cape's Trigonometry, in Urdu (Rurki Text-book).

Statics, in Urdu, by Professor Zaka-ulla.

Arithmetical Exercise, in Urdu, by Najm-ud-din.

A History of Arithmetic, in Urdu, by Durga Pershad.

Solutions of Equations, in Hindi, by Pandit Ram Krishn.

Analysis of Barnard Smith's Arithmetic, in Urdu, by Babu Amolak Ram.

Practical Geometry, in Urdu, by Ganda Ram.

Maine's Astronomy, in Hindi.	*	By Bhai Gurmukh Singh, who has passed the M. A. or Honors in Arts Standard in Mathematics, in Hindi.
Besant's Hydrostatics, do.	*	
Todhunter's Dynamics, do.	*	
Do. Plane Co-ordinate Geometry, in Hindi.	*	
Optics, in Hindi (in progress).		

* These are in manuscript, and are the basis of Lectures in the High Proficiency Class.

Ilm-i-Tabai.—Natural Philosophy, Part I.

Kshetra Chandrika, Parts I & II, Mensuration and Surveying.

Barnard Smith's Arithmetic, in Hindi.

Risala-i-usul.—Steam Engine.

Risala-Ilm-i-Hisab (Translation of Fitche's Science).

Kitab Ilm-i-Riyazi Bil Amal or Practical Mathematics.

Natija-i-Tahrir Uqlaidas.—Exercises on the first two books of Euclid, Part I.

Do. do. on the 4th and 6th Books, Part II.

Phailawat.—Practical Arithmetic.

Bij Ganit, Bhag Pahla.—Translation of Todhunter's Algebra.

Laghu Trikonmiti.—A treatise on Plane Trigonometry, in Hindi.

Rekha Ganit.—Elements of Euclid, Parts I and II.

Rekha miti tattwa.—Tate's Geometry, in Hindi.

Vyakta Ganit.—Elements of Arithmetic, Part II.

Misbah-ul-masahat, Parts I and II.

Tahriri-i-uqlaidas.—Euclid in Urdu, Books I to VI and IX.

Risalah Ilm-i-Tabiyat.—Natural Philosophy, Dynamics, Statics, Mechanics, &c.

Ganit Prakash.—Arithmetic in 4 Parts, in Hindi.

Ganit Sar.— Ditto ditto ditto.

Hindi bij ganit.—Algebra, by Pandit Mohan Lal, in 2 Parts.

Risalah Ilm-i-Masakt.—Mensuration by Behari Lal.

Geometrical Problems and Solutions in Urdu.

Asul Ilmi-i-Hindsa.—Tate's Geometry, ditto.

Haddon's Algebra, in Urdu.

Tate's Exercise in Mechanics, in Urdu.

Ditto Elements of Mechanism, ditto.

Treatise on Logarithms, in Urdu.

Siddha Padartha Vigyan.—Natural Philosophy, in Hindi.

Jabr-o-Muqabla.—Algebra, in 3 Parts (P. I. Department, Punjab).

Zubdat-ul-Hisab.—Arithmetic, in Urdu, in 4 Parts.

Rekha Ganit Prasnavali.—Geometrical problems, in Hindi.

Arithmetic in Gurmukhi, by Lala Bihari Lal.

Algebra ditto ditto ditto.

Euclid ditto ditto ditto. (Manuscript.)

The Literature of Mathematics in Arabic and Sanskrit is very extensive, whilst there is also a large number of Vernacular books bearing on various branches of that subject, and not mentioned in the above list, which comprises more than an ordinary Mathematical student, is likely to require, either in Europe or India. Abdulla, a student from Bokhara, had from Arabic Mathematical Works alone acquired a proficiency in that subject, which Professor Lindsay, M. A. (Cambridge), considered to be so great that he had nothing further to teach him.

Natural Science.

Ilm-i-Kimia.—Translation of Roscoe's Chemistry, into Urdu, by Assistant Surgeon Syad Amir Shah. The work is now under revision for the second edition.

Tadrisati-i-Ilm-i-Tabai.—Lectures on Physics, in Urdu, by Assistant Surgeon Syad Amir Shah, delivered in the Oriental College.

Tattwa Bodha.—The same in Hindi.

This work, a review of which lately appeared in a Home Paper, has been much appreciated by scholars in England.

Ilm-i-Tabi.—Translation of Balfour Stewart's Physics, into Urdu, by Assistant Surgeon Syad Amir Shah.

Barqi Maqnatisi.—A treatise on Electricity and Magnetism, in Urdu, by Raghu Nath Das.

Bhu Tattwa Vidya.—Translation of Cook's Geology, into Hindi, by Pandit Ganga Bishan, Shashtri of the Oriental College.

Elements of Chemistry, by Professor Zakaulla, in Urdu.

Rudiments of Physical Geography, in Urdu } By Professor Lakshmi Sankar, M. A.
Ditto ditto in Hindi }

Ilm-i-Tabiat.—Rudiments of Physical Geography, by Richard (Urdu).

Mushadat-ul-Makhluq.—Natural History.

Nizam-i-Haiwanat.—Natural History of Mammalia.

Astanai-Ilm Mausam.—The Threshold of Meteorology.

Bahar Hawa.—Easy Lessons on the Origin of the Atmosphere.

Jama-ul-Nafais, Part III.—A Treatise on the Ocean and its Products.

Ditto Part IV.—A Description of Equatorial Countries.

Ditto Part V.—A Treatise on Entology.

Risalia Mujarribab Kimia, or Experimental Chemistry.

Bijli Dipika.—A Treatise on Electricity and Galvanism, in Hindi.

Vayu Sagar.—A Treatise on the Atmosphere and Chemistry.

Outlines of Modern Farming,—by Robert Scott Burn, translated into Urdu, by *The Scientific Society.*

Electricity—by Sir William Snow Harris, F.R.S., translated, into Urdu, by the above Society.

Jaghrafia Tabai.—Translation of Blandford's Physical Geography in Urdu.

Charu Path in 3 Parts.—Entertaining Lessons on Science and Literature in Hindi.

Vahya Prapancha Darpan.—Natural Science, in Hindi.

Works on Zoology, Botany, Chemistry, Geology, and Mineralogy, for the Vernacular students of Medical Schools.

HISTORY.

Tarikh Mutaqaddamin.—Ancient History, in Urdu, by Maulvi Gulam Mustafa, of the Oriental College, based on Taylor's Ancient History.

Sanin-ul-Islam.—A Sketch of the History and Literature of Muhammadanism, in Urdu, by Dr. G. W. Leitner.—Parts I and II.

Umdut-ul-Tawarikh.—A Diary in Persian of Maharajah Ranjit Sing, by Lala Sohan Lal, his own diarist, in 4 volumes.

Selections from the 2nd Volume of the above.

Raja Tarangini.—An English translation of the first three books of this famous Sanskrit History of Cashmere by Mr. Buchanan, of the Department of Public Instruction, Punjab.

Prachin Itihas, Part I.—A Manual of Ancient History, in Hindi, by Bhai Gurmukh Sing, Assistant Professor of General Knowledge in the Oriental College, translated chiefly from Taylor's Manual of Ancient History up to the end of the Greek period.

Sikhanda Itihas.—A History of the Sikhs in Punjabi, by Pandit Bhanu Datta.

Tarikh Timuri.—Translation of the "History of Timur, by Arab Shah," into Urdu, by Moulvi Ghulam Qadir, late 2nd Teacher of Arabic in the Oriental College.

Hume's History of England, in Hindi—(Manuscript).

Green's Longer History of the English People.—In Urdu—(Manuscript) in progress.

Collier's History of England, in Urdu, 2 volumes.

Epitome of Indian History (Lethbridge), in Urdu.

Universal History, by Dr. Stülpnagel (in course of translation, into Urdu)—Manuscript.

Hallam's Constitutional History, in Urdu (Manuscript), in progress.

Itihas Timir Nasak.—History of India in 3 parts, in Hindi, by Raja Siva Prasad, C.S.I.

History of India, in Hindi, by Pandit Bhanu Datta.

Rollins' History of Egypt, translated into Urdu, by the Aligarh Society, and other Special Histories.

Tarikh-i-Panjáb.

Aina-i-Tarikh Numa, in 3 parts.

Mukhtasar Sair Inglistan.

Sair-ul-Mutaqaddamin.—Translation of Landmarks of Ancient History, Parts I and II.

Tarikh Alam.—Translation of Wilson's Ancient History.

History of India.—Part I, Hindu Period, Vol. I by the same author.

Ditto Vols. II and III, from 1786—1856 A.D., by the same author.

History of India (in Urdu), Part III, *English Period,* Vol. I from 1612—1878 A.D., by Munshi Muhammad Zaka-ulla, Professor of Vernacular Sciences and Literature, Muir College, Allahabad.

History of India—Vol. IV from 1858 to 1876 A. D., by the same author.

The Muhammadan Period of the History of India compiled from several Arabic, Persian and English Histories, by Professor Zaka-ulla, 2 vols. in Urdu.

The History of Persia,—by Major-General Sir John Malcolm, translated and published into Urdu, by *The Scientific Society*, Parts I, II, III and IV.

Ancient History of Egypt—with additions, translated into Urdu, by *The Scientific Society.*

Compilation from Rollins' Ancient History of Greece in 3 Parts, translated into Urdu, by *The Scientific Society.*

There exists a large number of Histories in Arabic and Persian, and Historical Monographs, in Urdu and Hindi.

See also Elliot's Translations of Native Historians.

Do. List of Punjabi books in Simla Text-book proceedings.

Geography.

Geography—compiled from various English Works, in 4 parts (in Urdu), published by *The Aligarh Scientific Society.*

Bhugal Sar of Pandit Rishi Kesh, Shastri, in Hindi.

Blochman's Geography, in Urdu.

Jagat Bhugol, in 2 parts.

Bhugol Chandrika.

Do. Vidya.

Jam-i-Jahan Numa, Urdu translation of *Bhugal Hastamalak,* in 4 parts.

Jugrafia-i-Jahan.

Gulprakash.—A treatise on the use of globes.

Jagat Bhugol.—Geography of the World, in 2 parts.

Bhugol Hasta Malak, by Raja Siva Prasad, C.S.I., in 4 parts.

Hughes's Geography, in Urdu, Rurki Edition.

Geography, in Urdu, by Professor Zakha-ulla.

N.B.—The Physical Geographies have been entered under head "Natural Science."

Political Economy.

Risalah Ilm Intizami-i-Madan.—Political Economy, by N. W. Senior, M. A., in Urdu.

Mrs. Fawcett's Political Economy, in Urdu.

Asul Siasat Madan.—Elements of ditto by J. S. Mill, Part I, in Urdu.

Siasat Madan, by E. A. Commr. Dharamanarain, in Urdu.

Fawcett's Political Economy, by Bhai Gurmukh Singh, in Hindi (Manuscript).

There are also other Vernacular treatises on this subject which seems to have a great attraction for natives.

Mental Science.

Mantiq Qyasi.—Translation of Fowler's Deductive Logic, into Urdu, by Madan Gopal, M.A., edited by Aya Ram, B.A.

Inglandiya Tarka Vidya.—Translation of the same, into Hindi, by Lala Baij Nath, B. A.

A'tma Tattwa Vidya.—Translation of Bain's Mental Science, into Hindi, by Pandit Kamaladatta (Manuscript).

Nyaya Bodhini.—A treatise on the Sanskrit System of Logic, in Hindi, by Pandit Sukhdyal, Shahstri, Professor of Sanskrit Logic in the Oriental College. This is the first work of the kind in Hindi.

Lakshanavali.—Definitions of the technicalities of Sanskrit Logic. An oriental work in Sanskrit, by Pandit Sukhdyal, Shahstri.

Turjuma Sullum.—Translation into Urdu of Sullum, an Arabic treatise on Logic, by Maulvi Ghulam Qadir, Assistant Professor of Arabic in the Oriental College.

Rashidia.—A treatise in Urdu on the rules and modes of dialectics, by Maulvi Fyzal Hasan, Professor of Arabic in the Oriental College.

Muntakhabat-i-Akhlaq-i-Nasari.—An Epitome of Tusi's Moral Philosophy, in Urdu.

Substance of Hamilton's Lectures on Metaphysics.—Volume I in Urdu, by Maulvi Muhammad Din of the Oriental College (Manuscript).

Principles of Inductive Logic, in Urdu (compiled from Fowler, Jevons and Mill), by Pirzadr Muhammad Hasain, H.A.

Mubadi-ul-Hikmat.—A treatise on Logic.

Elements of Mental Science, in Urdu, by Hafiz Ahmed.

An extensive and profound Philosophical Literature exists in Arabic, Sanskrit and Persian, of which much has been translated into Urdu, Hindi and even Punjabi.

PROFESSIONAL SUBJECTS.

Civil Engineering.

Nirman Vidya.—A Hindi Series on Civil Engineering, by Babu Navina Chandra Rai, comprising Principles of Statics, Dynamics, General Construction, Roads, Bridges and Irrigation Works based on the Weal's Series and Rurki treatises.

Masalah Tamirat.—Translation of Lang's Building Materials, into Urdu, by Lala Ganga Lam, Mayo Patiala Fellow, Panjab University College. This is a much larger work than the Rurki treatise, in Urdu now extant (manuscript).

Risalah dar bab Ashiya-i-Saman Imarat.—Rurki treatise on Building Materials.

Risalah-i-Ilm Usul Naqashi.—Translation of elements of drawing, Parts I and II.

Chitra kari sar.—An elementary treatise on drawing, Part II.

Risalah bayan banane sarkon ke.—Rurki treatise on Road making.

Risalah Mazbuti Ashiyai Saman-i-Imarat.—Strength of Materials.

Risalah Pulon ka.—Rurki treatise on Bridges.

Risalah-i-Ilm-i-Abpashi.—Ditto on Irrigation Works.

Risalah Darbab Fane Najjari.—Ditto on Carpentry.

Risalah Traverse tables, in Urdu.

Risalah Tamir Imarat.—Rurki treatise on construction of Bridges.

Risalah khudai matti.—Ditto on Earthwork.

Imsal Takhmine Imarat.—Ditto on Estimating.

Byan Nakhshah Khechna Mahrabon ka.—Ditto on drawing Arches.

Risalah Paimaish.—Ditto on Surveying.

Tarkib Paimaish.—Ditto on Surveying by Chain and Plane table.

Treatise on laying out Curves, in Urdu.

Ditto on adjustment of instrument in ditto

Mashq Naqsha Kashi.—Exercises in Drawing by Kura Mal.

Medical.

Medical Jurisprudence, in Urdu, by Dr. Rahim Khan, Khan Bahadur, Honorary Surgeon and Medical Fellow of the Punjab University College. Divided into two Parts—Part I treating of :—Personal identity, impotence, rape, pregnancy, delivery, infanticide, feigned diseases, unsoundness of mind, death, real and apparent, drowning, hanging, strangulation, suffocation, wound and mechanical injuries ; death by fire, lightning, cold or starvation, and Part II treating of :—Toxicology.

Urjuza Sanaya.—A treatise on Yunani Medicine, in Urdu, by Maulvi Ghulam Qadir.

Aushadavali.—Native Materia Medica, in Sanskrit, Hindi, Urdu and English, by Pandit Janardan, Teacher of Vaidyak System of Medicine in the Oriental College.

Amrit Sagar.—Translation of a famous work of that name in Hindi on Vaidyak System of Therapeutics, into Sanskrit, by Pandit Dya Ram, 4th Teacher of Sanskrit in the Oriental College.

Hindi Series of Medical Works, complete (in progress).

The works of Charaka and Susruta are also being translated into Hindi, as also the great Arabic and Persian Medical Text-books, which are contrasted and compared with books on Modern Medical Science, the students attending also the Lahore Medical Schools.

The Theory and Practice of Medicine by Dr. Rahim Khan in Urdu.

The Theory and Practice of Surgery, by Dr. Brij Lal Ghose, in Urdu.

The Disease of Children, in Urdu, by Dr. Rahim Khan.

Ditto Women, ditto ditto.

An Urdu Medical Monthly, embodying recent research, is published and widely circulated, under the auspices of the Punjab University College. It is edited by the Medical Fellow of the University College. There are also other Medical and Sanitary Journals subscribed for or otherwise assisted by the Institution.

There are numerous translations in the Vernacular of European Medical Works for the Vernacular Students of Indian Medical Schools.

Law.

Elements of jurisprudence.—An abstract from Austin, &c., in English and Urdu, by Babu Shashi Bhusan Mukarji, M.A., B.L.

Constitution of Law.—Constitutional History of India, in Urdu, by Syad Amir Shah.

Qaduri.—Translation of an Arabic treatise on Muhammadan Law, into Urdu, by Maulvi Ghulam Qadir.

Yajnya balkya-Sanhita.—Text of the famous work *Mitakshara* on Hindu Law with Hindi translation, by Pandit Guru Prasad, Professor of Sanskrit in the Oriental College.

Daya bhag.—Selections from *Mitakshara* containing that portion of Hindu Law, which treats of the distribution of the estate of a deceased person, in Hindi, by Pandit Guru Prasad.

Dattaka Chandrika.—Hindu Law on the adoption of a son, in Sanskrit and Hindi, by Pandit Rishi Kesh, Shastri.

Markby's Elements of Jurisprudence, in Urdu (translated by Pirzada Muhammad Husain).

The same book is also being translated, into Urdu and Hindi, by others.

Blackstone's Commentaries on the English Laws, first six chapters and a part of the seventh, as much as required for the Final Examination in Law, (lithographed).

Principles of Jurisprudence, by E. W. Parker, Esq. (in progress).

Mayne's Commentaries on the Penal Code (in progress).

There is an extensive series of Vernacular translations of the Codes, the Acts of the Legislature, &c., &c.

As regards the Sanskrit and Arabic Legal Literature there is no necessity to point out its extent and erudition.

Numerous Commentaries have been translated into the Vernaculars.

Miscellaneous.

A Vocabulary of Technical Terms—in Hindustani-English.

The Hindi Scientific and Critical Journal as also the Urdu and Gurmukhi Journals, published under the auspices of the Anjuman-i-Punjab or of the University College keep up a stimulus to scientific study and communicate current scientific progress, just as the Arabic and Sanskrit Critical Journals (to which a Persian Critical Journal has lately been added by the Punjab University College) are intended to foster research into these Literatures on the comparative method, as also to encourage enquiries into subjects connected with the History, Ethnology, Antiquities, &c., &c., of India in the modern critical spirit.

APPENDIX VI.

PANJAB ADMINISTRATION REPORT FOR 1849-50.

(See passages in italics or notes on pages 12, 15, 17, 18, 19, 20, 21, 22, 23, 24 and 25).

10. The flower of the population is Jat; they form the majority of converts to the religion of Nanuk. They are the core and nucleus of the Seikh commonwealth and armies. Equally great in peace and war, they have spread agriculture and wealth from the Jumna to the Jhelum, and have established a political supremacy from Bhurtpore and Delhi to Peshawar. Essentially yeomen by lineage and habit, they can yet boast of two regal families at Lahore and Bhurtpore, who in their days have stood in the first rank of Indian powers. In the Panjab they display all their wonted aptitude for stirring war and peaceful agriculture, and the feudal polity of the Khalsa has imparted to them a tinge of chivalry and nobility. Their chief home is in the Manjha, or centre portion of the Baree Doab, and their capital is Umritsur. But they have also extensive colonies at Gujranwalla, in the Rechnah Doab; Guzerat, in the Chuj; and about Rawul-Pindee in the Sind Saugor. For centuries they have peopled the southern Punjab, of which the capital is Mooltan; but there they are held in different repute, and their importance is merely agricutural. In many localities the Jats profess the Muhammadan creed, having been converted chiefly during the Emperor Arungzeb's reign. In the south they mainly belong to this persuasion.

Population.

Jats.

13. Among the pure sects of Mussulmans, the Pathans alone acquired social importance. They are scattered throughout the country, but their central localities are Mooltan and Kussoor in the Baree Doab. At the former place, indeed, they have won for themselves historical distinction. They originally obtained a grant from the Emperor Shah Jehan, and with this acquisition they thoroughly identified themselves; they excavated canals, they improved the condition of the peasantry, and they raised the province from barrenness to wealth. They defended their heritage with the utmost gallantry against the aggression of Runjeet Singh, and in the last war they furnished the best portion of Major Edwardes' levies.

Pathans.

14. There is one race of spurious Mussulmans, named Raens, who, politically insignificant, are yet to be found in the vicinity of all great cities. Unrivalled as market-gardeners, they are the men who carry on that elaborate and perfect cultivation which must strike the observer in all our chief suburbs. There is a race of Dogras (not to be confounded with Dogurs, an important tribe on the banks of the Sutlej); they are Misser Rajpoots of the Jummoo Hills (resembling the Kunaet of the Simla Hills), descended from a Rajpoot father and an inferior mother. Maharaja Golab Singh is a Dogra, and with his clan calls himself the true Rajpoot of a particular line of country.

Dogras.

15. Such are the tribes who furnish two estates of the primitive realm, the soldiers and husbandmen. The third estate, of the merchant and the penmen, consists of a tribe named Khutries; their profession in India is looked upon as effeminate, but these writers and traders are not much inferior in courage and firmness to the ruder tribes, while they are superior in civilisation, refinement and capacity for affairs. Some of Runjeet Singh's best governors and ministers were Khutries. The Brahmins are not numerous, but they usurped many political functions; learning and science of course centre in them.

Khutries.

16. From the Beas to the Chenab the Hindu race predominates, but in all parts of this region the Muhammadans are numerously interspersed, and in the south they actually form the majority; but of the Muhammadans a large portion are of Hindu origin. From the Chenab to the Indus the population chiefly consists of Hindu converts to Muhammadanism; beyond the Indus the pure Muhammadan race prevails. Of the whole population two-thirds are Mussulmans (both spurious and genuine), the remaining one-third are chiefly Hindus, and of these half are Seikhs. Now, with the single exception of Seikhs, it is remarkable that the Hindu races, whether converts to a foreign creed or professors of their ancestral faith, consider themselves as subjects by nature and born to obedience. They are disposed to regard each successive dynasty with equal favour or equal indifference, whereas the pure Mussulman races, descendants of the Arab conquerors of Asia, retain much of the ferocity, bigotry and independence of ancient days. They look upon empire as their heritage, and consider themselves as foreigners settled in the land for the purpose of ruling it.

17. They hate every dynasty except their own, and regard the British as the worst, because the most powerful, of usurpers; up to the Indus, then, the vast majority of the population are our natural subjects; beyond that river they are our natural antagonists.

Elements of social antagonism.

19. **Of agricultural products, sugarcane is grown everywhere, and indigo in the southern regions; both are exported towards Sind and Cabul.** Cotton is produced, but the uncertainty of seasons which prevails in the Panjab will probably prevent its becoming a cotton-growing country. Wheat and maize are two great staples of excellent quality; they fully supply the home consumption, and are often carried to foreign markets. The general agriculture and tillage are good; manure is used, and rotation of crops is known. Canals are not unfrequent, and the well irrigation, carried on by means of Persian wheels, is everywhere first-rate. The country is unfortunately bare of trees, timber is almost unprocurable, and even firewood is scarce, and can only be obtained in large quantities from the central wastes. But the province of Mooltan is in one respect a bright exception; there the date and palm-trees are clustered into dense groves, or extend into stately avenues for miles.

Agriculture.

20. The chief seats of art and commerce are Umritsur in the north, and Mooltan in the south. The indigenous manufactures are chiefly silk, carpets, and wool. There are also good artificers in carpentry, ironmongery and armoury; articles of all these description are more or less exported. The imports consist chiefly of British cotton and piece goods, of the shawls and woollens of Cashmere, and of the dried fruits and furs of Afghanistan.

Manufactures and commerce.

23. Besides these, however, one subject of course rivetted the attention of the monarch, namely, the gathering of the taxes. To this important department all other branches of the civil administration were subordinate appendages. Men of wealth and influence, who had distinguished themselves by their courage and capacity, were deputed to the remote provinces as farmers of the revenue, and were armed with pretorial and pro-consular power. So long as their remittances to the royal treasury were regular, they might exercise plenary authority over life and property. Of these Provincial Governors the most able and the most celebrated was Sawun Mull, of Mooltan; next after him stood Golab Singh, the present Sovereign of Cashmere. The best were Desha Singh and his son Sona Singh, who ruled Umritsur and the Mangha with a mild sway. The sternest were General Avitabile, who held down Peshawur with an iron hand, and Hurree Singh, whose prowess and cruelties kept Hazara in unwilling submission. The military chiefs who held feudal demesnes (jaghirs) on the condition of sending contingents into the field, had also unlimited authority within their jurisdiction.

Fiscal Department paramount.

Provincial Governors.

24. In those districts which were neither granted nor leased out, the local tax-gatherers were called Kardars, or agents. The powers enjoyed by these individuals varied greatly according to their personal influence at Court; but they all were directly responsible to the King and Council, whereas the Kardars in the provincial governorships were responsible to the Governor, who must, in his turn, account to the central authority. It would be unsafe to say that the Kardars never acted in the plenitude of power, but, as a rule, their most important proceedings were subject to review by the Lahore ministry.

Local tax-gatherers.

25. In the whole State there were only two classes of functionaries—the military and the fiscal. In the latter were combined all civil functions whatever. There were no special officers for the dispensing of civil justice or the execution of criminal law. To this rule there was an exception at the city of Lahore, where an officer of justice styled Adalutee was stationed. But there was no such functionary at the commercial capital of Umritsur. The police officers (thanadars) occasionally were political and military officers, rather than civil. Their business was to check disturbance, and to arrange for the marching of troops.

Two classes of State functionaries—military and fiscal.

No special ministers of justice.

26. The military commandants, with detachments of the army in the interior, were usually independent of the civil authorities, but this independence was gradually expanded into the power of active interference; many commandants thus situated committed great excesses; much license was permitted to the army, and indeed to all servants of the State. The line of march was often marked by plunder, and impressment and compulsory labour were dreaded by the peasantry.

Detached military commanders.

27. The pay of Kardars, and other secondary officials, was uncertain and precarious. It seemed to be tacitly understood that they must live by the perquisites of their appointments. The arrangements of the exchequer and the auditing of accounts were for many years notoriously defective. It was only towards the close of the Maharaja's reign that financial order was introduced. Up to that period no office of account had been established. For the record of what he gave and took, Runjeet Singh had trusted to his tenacious memory, aided by such primitive devices as the notches of a stick. The rude complication of accounts in the district treasuries facilitated embezzlement. Money was taken from the people in one shape and restored in another, till the items, after balancing and counterbalancing, became so confused, that a dishonest official might cloak any amount of fraud. There can be no doubt that all this laxity encouraged the officers to cheat the State and over-tax the people. Nobody seemed better aware of this than the Maharaja himself, who,

Salaried officials how paid.

Laxity and confusion of accounts.

whenever caprice or exigency might dictate, would call upon his old servants to pay fees or "aids," and if they refused to disgorge, would plunder both them and their families.

Justice how dispensed.

28. Written law there was none; still rude justice was dealt out. Private property in land, the relative rights of land-holders and cultivators, the corporate capacities of village communities, were all recognised under the direction of the local authorities; private arbitration was extensively resorted to; the most difficult questions of real and personal property were adjudicated by these tribunals. The adjustment of affairs in a commercial emporium like Umritsur required no further interposition than this. The arbitrators would, according to their respective faiths, consult the Mussulman Shureh or the Hindu Shasters; the Kazees and Kanoongoes exercised privately and indirectly those functions which had descended to them since the imperial times. The former continued to ordain marriage ceremonies, to register last testaments and attest deeds; the latter to declare recorded facts, and expound local customs. The Maharaja constantly made tours through his dominions; he would listen to complaints during his rides, and he would become angered with any Governor in whose province complaints were numerous. At Court also he would receive individual appeals.

Criminal penalties how inflicted.

29. The unwritten Penal Code contained but two penalties—fine and mutilation. There was scarcely any crime from larceny up to murder for which impunity might not be purchased by the payment of a fine.* Mutilation was reserved for such offences as adultery and seduction, and also for violent theft and robbery. Imprisonment was almost unknown, and capital punishment rare; it was never ordered by Runjeet Singh, or inflicted by his permission. But in distant and disturbed districts, such as Peshawar and Hazara, he did not interfere when Avitabile enforced a Draconic code in which hanging was decreed for every crime from larceny to murder; or with Hurree Singh, who summarily decapitated criminals, or blew them from the cannon's mouth.

Fine, mutilation and capital punishment.

Fiscal system.

30. The fiscal system will be noticed more exactly in the section which treats of revenue; suffice it now to say that Runjeet Singh availed himself of all known sources of taxation. He seems to have overlooked few taxes which have been levied in any country, civilised or uncivilised. Taxes, direct and indirect, upon land, houses, people; upon manufacturers, foreign or domestic; upon commerce internal or external, upon imports;—all found their place in his fiscal régime. Property in land was fully recognised and upheld, and the agriculturists were not unnecessarily oppressed as long as they paid their revenue. The village communities lived on in their full integrity.

General results of Runjeet Singh's Government.

31. That the resources of the country were not strained by this taxation can hardly be supposed. But in some respects the Government gave back with one hand what it had taken with the other. The employés of the State were most numerous; every Jat village sent recruits for the army, who again remitted their savings to their homes. Many a highly-taxed village paid half its revenue from its military earnings. Thus money circulated freely. Again, the presence of vast bodies of consumers created an immense demand for manufactures and commodities. Prices were quoted high, the market was brisk, and thus the commercial interests bore up against their load of taxation. Whatever faults may be found with their commercial regulations, the Seikh Khalsa may well vaunt of having raised up the city of Umritsur. Moreover, it is well known that nations will cheerfully pay enormous taxes when the Government is popular and when the public mind is kept excited by martial triumphs. The rule of Runjeet Singh was eminently suited to the genius of the people, and the spirit of the Seikhs mounted high when they saw province after province added to the dominions of their mystic commonwealth.

Its fame and popularity.

Constitution of the regency.

The conservative policy.

32. The events of 1845, which obliged the British Government to assume a share in the management of the kingdom, require no mention here. The policy of the British representatives was strictly conservative; their object was to interfere only to preserve, never to destroy. It was desired to reconstruct shattered institutions, to carry out the spirit of the constitution, as it would have been carried out by a benevolent native ruler. But to give effect to this view, it was necessary that many grave abuses which had grown up since the death of Runjeet Singh should be reformed. The army being irregularly paid was ill-disposed and idle. The civil Governors, great and small, were unbridled in embezzlement; violent crime was increasing; justice between man and man was more and more hard of attainment.

Nevertheless numerous reforms effected.

33. For all these evils remedies were attempted; the overgrown army was reduced; the discharged soldiers were paid up; the troops were paid, disciplined, and worked with regularity; the finances were scrutinised; the arrears justly due from the tax-gatherers were demanded with rigor; efforts were made by the enforcement of economy to free the exchequer from its long

* One thousand rupees was the fixed fine for a man's life, but Rs. 10,000 was sometimes taken. Occasionally a robber was enlisted on high pay as a cavalier or foot soldier or officer.

accruing liabilities. In the fiscal department arrangements were made to fix and limit both the demand on the people and the remuneration of the revenue officers. Summary settlements of the land revenue were made, and a liberal salary was allowed to the Kardars. It was hoped that by these means the people would have to pay less, while the State received more. The multiplicity of indirect and miscellaneous taxes was simplified, and the budget was so framed that the revenue, while restricted to a few fixed duties, should not be diminished. Here, again, it was believed that a relief would be afforded to the people, without any sacrifice to the State interests. Individuals of character and repute were appointed as separate administrators of civil and criminal justice. The Penal Code was reduced to writing, and rendered more severe and just, and yet more humane. Heinous crimes were referred to the Council of Regency, and appeals from all the local rulers were regularly heard.

Deputation of European officers.

Official misfeasance was systematically prosecuted. European officers were deputed to visit the outlying districts. All the chiefs who might be considered to represent the intelligence, the honesty, and influential interests of the country were summoned to Lahore for the purpose of framing rules and regulations for the future; and an assembly of 50 Seikh elders, heads of villages under the guidance of Sirdar Lena Singh, sat for some months at Lahore, in the autumn of 1847, to frame a code of simple law for the guidance of the Seikh people. The resources of the kingdom were examined, and their development was studied. Plans were formed for the construction of new canals, the repair of old ones, the re-opening of ruined wells, and the re-peopling of deserted villages. An engineer of rank and experience was appointed from the British service, and three lakhs from the revenue were set apart by the Council for public improvements.

Legislative arrangements.

Detectives—1. Regular police.
2. City Watchmen.
3. Rural constabulary.

163. The detective civil police may be thus detailed:—The regular establishment paid by the State; the city watchmen, and the rural constabulary, paid by the people.

Tehsildar's control.

165. For the control of these establishments an important machinery has been provided. The Board are anxious that the local influence and knowledge of the native collectors of land revenue (tehsildars) should be used for this purpose. Each tehsildar has been accordingly invested with police powers within his jurisdiction. The police are subordinate to him, but he is not to supersede them. He is to animate them when negligent, to overawe them when corrupt; he is responsible that they are faithful to the State, and unoppressive to its subjects. He is to infuse vigour and honesty into their functions, without usurping them. He is not to concern himself, as a rule, with individual cases, unless they be of a heinous nature, or unless an affray be anticipated, especially if the dispute relates to land. Our fiscal arrangements will eventually strike at the root of these disputes. In the meantime the tehsildar, with his revenue experience, is the fittest man to handle them.

Rules for their guidance.

The Board have promulgated a code defining the mutual relations of the tehsildar and the police, and distinguishing the tehsildar's police capacity from his other capacities, fiscal and judicial.

Town duties introduced.

176. The house-tax was at first introduced into our great cities; but to pacify discontent, the Board have permitted the watch and ward funds to be raised by town duties. This plan is now extensively in vogue, but it has never been introduced, except at the urgent request of the townsmen; care has been taken that, as much as possible, the articles taxed should be luxuries and not necessaries. The measure has been carried out with eminent facility and success. It is surprising to see how a tax, not the most equitable that could be devised for this particular purpose, and repugnant to our system, may yet be made to work admirably through the power of popular sympathy.

Dhurut, Wazun Kushee, and Choonghee cesses.

178. There are three cesses which, being sometimes confounded together, require a precise definition. The Dhurut was a tax paid by the merchant who brought grain from small villages to sell it in a large one. It amounted to something less than one per cent. on the market price, and fell upon the consumer. But the grain of the village in which the market might be situated was exempt from taxation. The proceeds of the cess were received by the landholders when there were no merchants of influence, and by the mercantile community when their number and strength was considerable. The Wazun-Kushee, or weighment cess, was levied indiscriminately on grain, which might be weighed at the shop or in the market, if there was one. It amounted to about two per cent. on the grain, and was the personal remuneration of the weighman. Where the landholders had full command of the Dhurut collections, they frequently farmed the cess to this functionary. Both these taxes, then, were levied on grain, and were customary in villages. Now the Choonghee was levied on all articles of merchandise, both in transit and in the market, and was current in towns or cities. The English equivalent for the expression is town duties, it was included in a long category of taxes collected by the Seikh Government. Its abolition as an item of the public income formed a part of the fiscal reform introduced under the regency. It has now been resuscitated for Municipal purposes. With regard to the two other taxes, the Board would maintain the weighment cess, it being the remuneration of one of the village office-bearers, but the Dhurut they would discontinue. If a tax of this nature be needed for village municipality,

The three cesses how to be regulated.

they would prefer to introduce the Choonghee, which is more capable of adaptation to the various grades of rustic society.

Rural constabulary.

179. The rural constabulary form the lowest, but perhaps the most important, grade. They are the rank and file of the police force. Here, as in most regions of Upper India, their office is coeval with the institution of the village society. Under the late Government their functions were often nominal; their remuneration often scanty and precarious. One of the earliest measures after annexation was the organisation of this important body throughout the villages. The arrangements then made have been generally retained, but in places modified. It has been found that, like the townsmen, the villagers are often on this head sensitive and jealous. The Board, however, are fully alive to the importance of conciliation; measures of this kind, however good in themselves, will not succeed unless they are made acceptable to the people.

Principles regarding village watchmen.

180. There are several principles which the Board wish to see carried into effect. The office of watchman forming a portion of the village community, there should be at least one such officer to every collection of houses. The number may be exceeded when the size of the village may require it. The remuneration of the watchmen must be adequate to support them without recourse to any other mode of livelihood. The situation should be worth not less than three rupees per mensem. It is better that the salary should be paid in cash, but if the villagers prefer it may be paid in kind. In small villages, where regular payment in cash or kind might be burdensome to the establishment, the Board do not object to assignments of land. On the occurrence of vacancies the nomination should rest with the landholders, the confirmation with the Magistrate. The watchmen are of the people and should continue to mingle with them, while they look up to the regular police, and obey the behests of the European superiors. They should be sufficiently under the control of the police so as to become trusty servants of the State, and sufficiently under the control of the landholders so as not to become rustic despots.

Investigation of rent-free tenures.

92. In the fiscal department the first object of attention was to be the inquiry into rent-free tenures, that is, what lands were to be exempt from taxation, and on what terms; at the same time a set of rules for release and resumption were laid down. Existing settlements of the revenue, made during the Resident's regency, were to be upheld as a temporary measure. In tracts not previously settled, a quinquennial settlement was to be made. But all summary settlements were liable to such modifications as might be introduced when the regular settlement should come on. The confirmation of settlements was to rest with the Board. In the management of the revenue, the maintenance of village communities, and the demarcation of boundaries, the rules in force throughout the North-Western Provinces were to be observed. The arrangements regarding the abolition of the customs and of the transit duties, and the establishment of an excise on the single article of salt, were to be upheld.

Fiscal system.

SECTION VI.

Administration of Civil Justice.

Cases connected with landed property referred to the Settlement Courts.

217. Soon after annexation this department was relieved of its most difficult branch by the Board's order of January 1850, which practically interdicted the hearing of cases relating to landed property, and transferred them to the Settlement Courts. It is presumed that these Revenue Officers who are brought most in contact with the agricultural classes, who must necessarily acquire much local experience and great familiarity with tenures, will decide suits regarding landed property in a manner accordant with the wants and sympathies of the people. The Board believe that the union of fiscal and judicial functions in the same set of officers is calculated to confer many benefits on the landed community. But as Settlement Officers have not as yet crossed the Chenab, this injunction has been followed in the Lahore division only; and it being found that landed disputes were in some places accumulating to the inconvenience of individuals, the complication of tenures, and the disarrangement of village communities, and as the prospects of a regular settlement seemed remote, the Board resolved to vest the ordinary Civil Courts with power to entertain all such cases relating to real property as might require immediate decision. At the same time provisions were made to secure strict control on the part of Commissioners over the exercise of this power. However, during the period under review, no cases of this nature came under trial, and it may be considered that the civil returns now under review comprise cases relating to personal debts, contracts, and such like transactions.

But under certain conditions may be entertained by the ordinary civil tribunals.

Private arbitration.

223. Private arbitration is a potent means of popular justice. The attribute of divine discernment, which the people of India fondly ascribe to their cherished institution is no less associated with arbitration in the minds of the Punjabees.

From the first the Board have been anxious that public disputes should be referred to that rude tribunal, whose voice is all-powerful in the regulation of private affairs, where individuals are most vitally concerned, and of those social and family interests which are dearest to mankind. These native assessors are especially useful in ascertaining the truth in questions relating to intricate accounts, local usages, and social practice. But it has been found that, unless vigilance and discrimination be exercised, abuses will arise in the working even of this institution. The selection and appointment of the arbitrators, the conduct of the inquiry and the mode of recording the award must be scrupulously and jealously guarded.

In England, from the time that a jury is empannelled and sworn, their every movement is observed; their place of sitting and of consulting, the delivery of their verdict, are all matters of the strictest rule. So must it be with these Indian juries; otherwise the very thing which should have been our guidance, will become an occasion of stumbling and a bye-word; and if discredit should be thrown on the system of Punchayets, and the faith of the people in this, their best, institution should be broken, their morality will thereby be weakened. Impressed with these convictions, the Board have drawn up a detailed code of rules to regulate the proceedings of arbitrators.

Abstract of Punjab revenues prior to annexation.

236. In September 1847, Raja Dena Nath, Chancellor of the Lahore Exchequer, furnished the following abstract of the mode in which he considered the land revenue of the Punjab to have been collected:—

No. of District.	Mode of collecting the revenue.	Rs. Amount of revenue.
8	Farmed out by Kardars	25,49,873
8	Assessed, the engagements being made with the heads of the villages	18,23,556
43	The revenue collected by division and appraisement of the crop	89,44,658
	Total Estimate of Land Revenue	1,33,18,087

Summary settlement of the revenue under the Regency.

During the winter of 1847 a general money assessment was commenced of all the districts immediately under the Durbar. During that season it was completed in the four Doabs and Hazara, and some portion of Peshawur. There was no survey or measurement. The officers entrusted with this duty were aided by the production of Durbar accounts of past collections, and by the local knowledge of the Kardars. But the papers did not furnish a clue to all the additional items which may have been levied. Our officers took rapid tours through the districts about to be assessed, thus gaining a general idea of the country and the condition of the people. Finally, they assembled at central spots, the headmen and accountants of villages, and tested the accuracy of the Durbar returns by their accounts. The payments of 3, 5, and 10 years were assumed as data for the new assessment; but the calculations formed on this basis were modified by the general aspect and condition of each district.

Derangement of taxation from sudden increase of production.

268. The effect of a very large and sudden increase of production, even where prices do not fall in a greater ratio, must have a tendency to derange money assessments. Rich and highly irrigated soils produce no more in a favourable season than in one of actual drought. In the great famines of 1834 and 1838 the agriculturists in the villages along the canal of the Delhi territory made enormous profits. Their produce in a year when grain was selling at 7 seers for the rupee, was equal to what their lands yielded when it averaged 30 seers, and the revenue paid by them was the same. Exactly the reverse has occurred in the Punjab. Villages with great capabilities of soil and irrigation are proportionately highly assessed; and with the average amount of produce, prices have fallen a half. To those villages a season of abundance and low prices is manifestly an evil.

Relief ordered wherever distress proved to exist.

270. The cry of over-assessment has been very general throughout the country, but more particularly so in the Rawal Pindi and Jhelum districts of the Sind Saugor Doab, Dera Ghazi Khan beyond the Indus, and in Mooltan. There has been a very general demand among the agriculturists for a return to grain payments, to a division or appraisement of the crops, every season. The Board have resisted this call, but have directed the suspension of revenue wherever it appeared desirable, and have urged on local officers the necessity for a new settlement where the old one had expired, or the current one was manifestly excessive. The reduction and equalisation of revenue, it is hoped, will afford the necessary relief.

Miscellaneous Extracts from Administration Report for 1849-50.

Gang robbery is associated with historical remembrances. Capital punishment was awarded to it. Many of the great thoroughfares passed through desolate localities.

Infanticide.—Bedis practised infanticide, also some of the Mussulman sects and some subdivisions of Khatris, but not Punjab Rajputs.

Influential classes have been partially thrown out from employ, but the public works have given occupation to the class which is most inclined to petty crimes.

Slavery in the Panjab was domestic.

Adultery was regarded with great vindictiveness, and therefore the Board made it criminal, to avoid worse crimes.

Forgery has been increased by the investigation of titles and rights, and *perjury* by the establishment of Courts.

Union of fiscal and judicial in the same officer conferred benefit upon the landed community.

Justice should be dealt without intricacies, and *pleaders* should *not* be encouraged.

Board do not believe that *our system* should ever be *successful.*

Seikh Government levied half of land produce, sometimes 60 per cent., but not often. Fifteen per cent. must be deducted for fraud. The practice was from two-fifths to one-third of the gross produce, wherever Seikhs had fully conquered and land was fairly cultivated. In some districts Government share never exceeded one-third, and the average was one-third, one-fourth, one-fifth, and one-eighth.

Collection was sometimes in money in Seikh times.

Dena Nath's assessment was as follows :

Farmed out to Kardars 25 lakhs.

Engagement with heads of villages 18 lakhs.

Revenue by division of crops 98 lakhs.

British Government *reduced* the revenue, throughout, below the assessment of Dena Nath from 24 to 19 lakhs.

The first year Government collected 98 lakhs against 133 lakhs of Dena Nath.

Army cost 63 lakhs.

Occupancy and *conquest* were declared the real *titles* in land. Occupancy was rarely referred to any distant period.

Under Seikhs, tenants displaced the descendants of ancient proprietors whose rights were limited to one seer in a maund.

Hindus had chiefly coparcenary communities.

Hereditary cultivator almost undistinguishable from proprietor, except that he cannot sink wells and sell the land, but he can sub-rent it. Free tenures by jaghirdars and other privileged classes.

Salt was prejudicial to the revenue, but not to the consumers. Duties were abolished on 27 articles.

Quotations from the Administration Report, Punjab, for the Years 1851-52 and 1852-53.

Domestic morality in the Punjab.

250. Domestic morality in the Punjab is somewhat low; indeed many customs sanctioned and enforced previous to British rule had a sure tendency to make it so. Among many classes with some pretension to respectability, and more or less throughout the province generally, *especially in the hill districts,* there prevails a system of exchanging girls, which (aggravated by the intrigues of professional agents who earn a livelihood by the traffic) ultimately produces the most mischievous effects. These exchanges, concerning as they do many families and involving many couples, and thus ramifying into a great variety of complications present the strongest temptations to fraud, cause women to be regarded as negotiable commodities, and are in fact quite as objectionable as regular money sales.

Vicious system of betrothals.

Pecuniary consideration.

251. Among other classes, again, the indirect giving and receiving of valuable consideration (though not of actual cash) on account of marriages and betrothals introduce dishonest dealing and sordid mendacity into these transactions, which of all others should, if possible, be kept free from such taint.

Extract from para 350.—They enquired into, or otherwise disposed of, at least 80,000 petty rent-free tenures.

Administration Report, 1856-57 and 1857-58.

Section III.

Education.

47. The last Report mentioned the inauguration into the Panjab of the new system of national education prescribed for all India by the Home authorities. The present Report will describe the first two years of progress with that system, that is, the years 1856-57 and 1857-58.

48. During 1856-57 the machinery of the Department was organised; a Director General was appointed on a salary of Rs. 1,200 per mensem; two Inspectors on Rs. 600 each for the eastern and western circles respectively; 11 Deputy Inspectors, each to receive a salary from Rs. 80 to 150 per mensem, and to supervise two or more districts; and 17 Sub-Deputy Inspectors on salaries of Rs. 20 to 60, each district being divided into three or four tehsils or sub-divisions for administrative purposes. A Government school at the head-quarters of each tehsil was established; some 107 schools were thus founded. The principle of arranging with the landholders to pay for education a sum calculated at one per cent. on the assessed land tax was carried out everywhere in the Panjab (save in Leia and Huzara) without any objection being raised by the people; some Rs. 1,38,000 were collected on this account, and 456 village schools were established from this resource. Each of these schools is placed in a centrical position, so as to be accessible to the children of three or four villages. Grants-in-aid, to the amount of Rs. 6,970, were accepted on behalf of Mission schools in various parts of the Panjab. One normal school was established; some four Government schools, previously existing, were taken by the new Department, and statistics of the indigenous education throughout the province were collected. Such was the commencement made during the first year.

Supervising establishment.

Educational proceedings in 1856-57.

49. The second year, 1857-58, had scarcely commenced when the disturbances in Hindustan broke out with fury, and excitement arose more or less throughout the Panjab. The educational officers then resolved not to attempt the establishment of fresh village schools until the crisis should pass over, but to concentrate all efforts for the maintenance of the Government schools set on foot during the past year. The hope which had been entertained of establishing many hundreds of additional schools was thus deferred for some months, but the attendance at the Government schools was kept up undiminished. During the first quarter—May, June, and July 1857,—the first three months of the trouble, there was actually a slight increase over the attendance of the preceding peaceful quarter. During the next quarter of August, September, and October,—three months of awful crisis, when the fate of the Panjab really trembled in the balance,—there was a diminution of only 97 pupils on the aggregate of 4,900, which, in fact, is no perceptible diminution at all. Even in the Cis-Sutlej States, which were disturbed extensively, the Government schools did not suffer. At Rawal Pindee only, near the Indus, were there any symptoms manifested of religious bigotry against the educational arrangements. In all other places, even on the fanatical frontier, there was no suspicion or prejudice raised on account of the schools. By November the crisis was over past, and the establishing of additional village schools was immediately taken in hand. Nearly 700 new ones were founded by end of December. During the two last quarters of the year perfect quiet has succeeded to excitement; consequently the system, laboriously sustained during a time of trouble, has since been expanded; the attendance at Government schools has increased month by month, the style of education has been improved, and the village schools extended.

Education not affected by the troubles of 1857.

Recent progress.

50. The educational system thus started is, of course, still in robust infancy, and a brief notice of some educational expenditure of its leading features will suffice at present.

Educational expenditure.

51. The expenditure for the two years may be thus set down—

	1856-57.		1857-58.	
	Rs.	£	Rs.	£
Expenditure by Government	1,05,392 =	10,539	1,44,868 =	14,487
Expended from the one per cent. fund collected from land-holders	23,472 =	2,347	82,263 =	8,226
Total	1,28,864 =	12,886	2,27,131 =	22,713

The actual collections for the one per cent. fund were: in 1856-57, Rs. 1,38,044, or £13,804; in 1857-58, Rs. 1,51,544, or £15,154; so that there is a large unexpended balance at credit of the fund. In round numbers, the educational income may be set down at three lakhs of rupees, or £30,000 per annum, of which half is paid by Government, and half contributed by the people.

Numbers of schools and scholars.

The number of schools and scholars for the two years are :—

	1856-57.		1857-58.	
	Schools.	Pupils.	Schools.	Pupils.
Government "tehsil schools"	107	6,919	110	6,953
Special institutions	15	2,251	16	1,714
One per cent. village schools	456	6,064	1,336	12,024
Indigenous schools	5,024	30,196	3,461	26,317
TOTAL	5,602	45,433	4,923	40,008

In round numbers, then, we have something less than 50,000 boys under instruction, which number gives the proportion of 1 pupil to 23 of the school-going population. The number of pupils may appear small to a population of 13 millions; but a considerable increase may be expected yearly, especially in the village schools.

52. In the Government schools the education consists only of the rudiments of history, geography, arithmetic, and grammar. But even this much is imparted with difficulty, and is a vast stride in advance of the wretched education which previously existed. The class system, which is the distinguishing mark between European and Native method of teaching, is enforced. The Urdu language, with the Persian character, is used in the Government schools. The pupils are more than one-half Hindus. The remainder are mainly Muhammadans. Seikh pupils are not numerous. The pupils belong chiefly to the non-agricultural classes. There are even female schools—all Muhammadans. There is, of course, a great dearth of qualified teachers; but a normal school has been established at Lahore with forty pupils, and another has been commenced at Rawal-Pindee. Those teachers, previously in office, who may be found deficient, are required to qualify at these institutions. The higher kinds of Government schools have yet to be founded, and the Lahore College is postponed till the general system shall be more advanced. A depôt for school books has been set up, and during 1857-58 some 14,130 little books were sold to the people for about Rs. 3,000, or £300.

Characteristics of Government schools.

In conclusion it may be said that the fact that popular education did not fall off during a season of danger, trouble, and excitement, goes far to prove that through it all the people preserved an even mind, and that British rule still kept a hold upon its subjects.

Administration Report, 1858-59.

Section III.

Education

31. In this department much must depend on the normal schools at Lahore and Rawal-Pindee, and the one more recently established at Delhi. At these institutions are trained the teachers for what may be called the country and parochial schools. Many of these teachers are unqualified for their duties, and their acquirements, therefore, are tested by their being obliged to go through a certain course of training previous to being confirmed as Government teachers.

Normal schools.

32. The principal zillah or country schools are at Umritsur, Ferozepore, Simla, and Gujerat. In addition, a school at Delhi, formerly known as the Delhi College, and maintained by a bequest made by the late Nawab Fazl Ali, has lately been established. The course of study at these superior schools may be pursued through the medium of the English or the vernacular languages, at the option of the pupils. It comprises history, geography, and mathematics, together with the rudiments of science and natural philosophy; and is similar to that required from candidates for entrance into the Calcutta University.

District schools.

33. Inferior to these are three classes of schools, in which the medium of instruction is the vernacular only. These are the Government tehsil schools, the village schools, maintained by the cess of one per cent. on the land-revenue, and the indigenous schools, which are independent of Government control, unless supported by grants-in-aid. In the last-mentioned class the plan of study is purely native, and the instruction generally rude and vicious. But the machinery of the Educational Department is systematically employed in the creation and improvement of the "tehsil" and "one per cent." village schools.

Tehsil schools.

Village schools.

Indigenous schools.

As regards the Panjab Provinces, exclusive of the Delhi territory (where the organisation is still incomplete), the following figures will exhibit the progress made during the past year:—

Progress.

	1857-58.		1858-59.	
	Schools.	Pupils.	Schools.	Pupils.
Government tehsil schools	110	6,953	116	8,812
One per cent. village schools	1,336	12,024	1,844	24,072
Indigenous schools	3,461	26,317	6,173	32,023
TOTAL	4,923	47,006	8,193	64,907

In the Delhi territory the number of pupils in the schools under Government control is reported to be about 3,500, but the next returns will probably show a large increase. It will be observed that whilst there has been a slight increase in the number of pupils at the tehsil schools, the attendance at the one per cent. schools has been doubled. Still the latter are far from being in a satisfactory condition. Until lately many have been confined to mosques, and have been mere seminaries for the propagation of Islamism. Many of the teachers are ill-paid and incompetent, and it will take time to mature the reforms which are indispensable. There has been no opposition on the part of the people to the spread of education. In some instances it has been eagerly sought, though generally its progress is suffered with the apathy of ignorance.

Character of village schools.

34. During the past year the Local Government has enjoined upon the divisional and district authorities a more active visitation and inspection of the schools, which are certain to draw encouragement from their influence.

Visitation and inspection of schools.

Cost of education.

35. The expenditure for 1858-59 is as follows:—

	Rs.
Expended by Government	1,69,100
Expended from the one per cent. fund	1,16,691
TOTAL	2,85,791

Of the Government expenditure, Rs. 8,054 went in grants-in-aid of Mission schools which are usually in a very efficient state.

Mission schools.

36. Books to the number of nearly 40,000, realising some Rs. 6,100, have been sold. About the same sum is to be devoted to the gratuitous distribution of books.

Books.

Female education.

37. Female education has yet scarcely begun in these provinces.

38. The Department has recently sustained a severe loss by the death of the Director Mr. W. D. Arnold, under whom it was first organised, and from whose ability and character its future development might have been confidently expected.

Mr. Arnold.

ADMINISTRATION REPORT, 1859-60.

SECTION III.

EDUCATION.

55. It was intimated last year that the Lieutenant-Governor was not satisfied with the working of the Educational Department in these provinces.

Organic defects in previous system.

Organic defects existed, which neutralised the exertions of the superintending officers. Reports on the subject were accordingly called for, as well from the Civil authorities, as the departmental funtionaries. A very elaborate commentary on the past operations and their tendency was also submitted by Mr. Roberts, the Officiating Financial Commissioner, under whose general control, up to that time, they had been carried on. In the several accounts submitted there was a very general agreement as to the unsatisfactory results of the efforts which had been made, during the three years foregoing, to diffuse education amongst the people. Those efforts had been vigorous and comprehensive. But in the endeavours to establish a uniform system and a pervading machinery, sufficient regard had not been had to the means, without which these could not be successful. After a careful review of the information collected, the Lieutenant-Governor was inclined to trace the acknowledged imperfections of the system mainly to the following causes :—

Their causes.

Inferiority of the native superintendents.

1st.—The inferiority of the native superintendents. *These were mostly foreigners from Hindustan.* A similar class has not yet arisen in the Panjab, and only third-rate men found it worth while to take service so far from their houses. Notwithstanding which the supervision of the tahsili and village schools was committed to these incompetent men in preference to delaying the operations.

2nd.—The excessive extent of the circles superintended by the European Inspectors. Each included some 600 schools, which the Inspector was supposed to visit and examine yearly. In each division was a Native Deputy Inspector, and in each district a Sub-Deputy Inspector, whose reports and accounts came before the European Inspector, and took up a great part of his time. It was physically impossible for him to exert that searching control, and initiate that wholesome impulse, without which the whole machinery became inactive and mischievous.

3rd.—The dissociation of the Educational Department from the Civil authorities. The people seldom bestir themselves, even in matters of which they approve, without an impulse from above, whilst they will often strenuously exert themselves to accomplish the purposes of the powers that be. Now, although individuals amongst them occasionally display an extraordinary desire for learning in general, as might be expected amongst an uneducated people—there is very great apathy on the subject. It is true that the Department is a State institution, but the people are accustomed to learn the will of the Government through the district officer, whom alone they regard as its representative. And they inferred that the spread of education was a secondary matter, because he had nothing to do with it.

4th.—The incapacity of the schoolmasters. For the tehsili schools only *inferior men from Hindustan* were procurable. The village schools were taught by the old masters, who were loath and incompetent to enforce the new-fangled curriculum of study. *It would have been better had these village schools not been interfered with*, until fit masters had been trained for them in the normal schools.

56. Such were the leading defects ascertained to exist. The following are the measures, devised by the Lieutenant-Governor for their correction. They came into operation at the commencement of the current official year :—

Measures devised for their correction.

1st.—The Native Deputy Inspectors and Sub-Deputy Inspectors—many of them foreigners—have been dismissed with gratuities, and their appointments abrogated. Such as are fit will probably obtain employment as schoolmasters. By their dismissal, considerable funds become capable of more advantageous appropriation.

2ndly.—The general superintendence of the vernacular schools, tehsili and village, has been transferred to the district officers.

3rdly.—The expense of the tehsili schools, heretofore paid from the general revenues has been transferred to the one per cent. fund.

4thly.—Arrangements have been made for increasing the number and efficiency of the normal schools for training vernacular masters. The character of the education imparted will greatly depend upon the efficiency of these schoolmasters.

5thly.—A commencement has been made in the establishment of high schools at the chief towns of the principal districts, where the study of English may be pursued under competent masters, without excluding vernacular instruction. The saving effected by the dismissal of the Native Superintendents, and by defraying the expense of the tehsili schools from the one per cent. fund, will be devoted to the improvement and multiplication of these superior schools.

6thly.—The aid given to good private institutions for secular instruction, whether under the direction of Missionaries or not, has been increased in amount.

7thly.—The Director of Public Instruction has been placed in direct communication with the Local Government.

Great improvements anticipated from the change.

57. These measures have been at work for too short a time as yet to render their effects apparent, but there is every reason to anticipate, from their introduction, a great improvement in the character of the educational institutions, and an increase to their popularity.

Review of the past year's operations.

58. A rapid review of the progress of the Department during the year must close this section.

59. In consequence of the discovery of serious irregularities in the management of his office, it became necessary to remove the Inspector of the Rawal-Pindee Circle.

Zillah schools.

60. In the attendance at the four principal zillah schools there was a decline from 783 to 723.

Tehsili schools.

61. At the 140 tehsili schools the number of pupils was 10,353, being an increase of 1,200 on the former year.

Village schools.

62. The number of one per cent. village schools decreased from 2,029 to 1,704 ; but in the average daily attendance, amounting to 27,264, there was a slight improvement.

Private institutions.

63. At private institutions the attendance rose from 1,025 to 1,424.

64. English students increased from 860 to 1,725.

Additional normal schools established.

65. Six additional normal schools for the training of vernacular teachers were established and the students increased from 75 to 792.

Grants-in-aid increased.

66. The money granted in aid of private institutions was augmented from Rs. 6,812 to Rs. 8,960.

Indigenous schools.

67. The number of pupils at indigenous schools exempt from Government instruction is stated at 63,090 ; but it is admitted that the returns are doubtful.

Comparative statement of students and daily attendance.

68. Excluding these, therefore, the following figures will show, comparatively with the preceding year, the aggregate number of students :—

YEAR.	Hindus.	Mahomedans.	Others.	TOTAL.	Average daily attendance.
1858-59	21,653	13,521	2,780	37,954	34,713
1859-60	24,493	17,016	4,177	45,686	42,388

69. The total expenditure from all sources has been a little short of 3½ lakhs, as will be seen from the following figures :—

	Rs.	A.	P.
Cost of supervising establishment	93,642	10	6
Cost of Government schools	65,521	3	3
Schools in receipt of aid	26,861	6	9
Cost of one per cent. schools	1,56,442	5	1
TOTAL	3,42,468	9	7

The amount contributed by the State was Rs. 1,62,622-8-6, and of this Rs. 68,978 were spent on schools, not on provision.

Book department.

70. The number of books sold increased from 29,579 to 53,235.

Normal schools.

71. There are only two schools at present in which the range of instruction is sufficiently extensive to qualify students for the University examination. One is at Delhi, the other at Umritsur.

At Delhi.

The Delhi school is supported by a bequest of Nawab Fazl Ali. There are eight classes, and in all but one English is taught as well as the vernacular. The subjects are English reading and translation, history, geography, arithmetic, natural philosophy, Euclid, and Algebra. But the Inspector complains that the knowledge of the boys is, too generally, superficial. He has endeavoured to introduce a better system, by appointing fixed hours for the study of each subject, and by paying some of the students to act as teachers. Two peculiarities are noted : *the pupils greatly dislike being made to study their own language as well as English,* and they all desire to begin geometry before they have mastered arithmetic. Altogether there are 234 statents. Two scholarships have lately been founded by native gentlemen.

At Umritsur.

72. At the Umritsur school there are 219 names on the register. Of these students, only 43 learn English. *Classes in which Gurmukhi and Sanskrit were taught, and which have hitherto been largely attended, have recently been abolished.* The services of an English head-master have now been procured, and the appropriation of State funds has been enlarged. There is also a good Missionary school at Umritsur, but it is found that in large towns there is room for both.

Establishment of a first class school at Lahore as a nucleus for a college.

73. On the visit of the Governor General to Lahore, *the Sirdars made an express request that a college might be founded at Lahore.* The Lieutenant Governor therefore took immediate measures for the creation of a first class school. *At Lahore and in its neighbourhood many of the chiefs and courtiers of the Seikh monarchy reside. They retain all their aristocratic exclusiveness, whilst they are sufficiently alive to the exigencies of the future to desire education for their sons. To meet their wishes, two departments have been made in the school. Into the higher, none but the sons of persons who are eligible for the Governor General's Durbar are admissible ; in the lower there is no distinction of rank. This arrangement is extremely agreeable to the upper class, and without it they would not have sent their sons ; as it is, there are now about 60 boys in the higher department, and 140 altogether. The change which may be hoped for in the Seikh*

Two departments formed for the upper and lower classes.

aristocracy may be measured by the fact that Runjeet Singh used to keep his royal accounts by cutting notches on a stick. In this school an entrance donation and tuition fees have been made leviable, these dues will generally be collected in Government schools for the future.

Donation and tuition fees levied.

Expected advantages from the recent reforms.

74. With the Director of Public Instruction in direct communication with Government; with the attention of the Inspectors concentrated on the development of the higher class of schools, on the dissemination of European learning, on the training of vernacular school masters, and on the provision of suitable books; with the urban and village vernacular schools under the inspection and encouragement of the District Officers and their subordinates, acting in communication with the departmental officers; with the elevation and increase of high schools and training institutions, and the new impulse given to private seminaries; with the facilities for education afforded to the higher classes; the Lieutenant-Governor indulges in the hope that, in the present year, the diffusion both of western science and of vernacular rudimental instruction, may be permanently promoted.

Administration Report for 1860-61.

Section III.

Education.

Cause of changes explained last year.

68. In the last report the causes which led to the superintendence of the tahsili and village vernacular schools being imposed on the district officers, whilst the direction of the training schools for vernacular teachers, and of the zillah anglo-vernacular schools was reserved to the Inspectors of Public Instruction, were explained at length. The results by which, during the past year, the change has been followed, will now be briefly noted.

Causes of diminished attendance.

69. Several circumstances combined have tended to diminish the attendance in the vernacular schools. The famine, and the dearness of provisions would, at any time, have had this effect; but during the past year, the levy of tuition fees has been strictly enforced, and the expenses of living and education have thus simultaneously increased new rules; striking off from the register the names of scholars absent for a certain period, have also been introduced. Many of the best teachers have been temporarily withdrawn from their own schools to pass through a course of instruction in the training institutions, and some of the tahsili have become zillah schools.

Reduced number of tahsili schools, and of scholars.

70. Under these circumstances it is not surprising to find that the number of pupils at the vernacular schools is less than at the end of 1859-60. There are now only 123 instead of 140 tahsili schools, with 6,437 instead of 10,353 scholars, and an average daily attendance of 4,564 instead of 7,636.

Number of village schools also reduced.

71. The village schools, also, have been reduced from 1,704 to 1,686, the number of scholars has fallen from 37,000 to 32,165, and the daily attendance from about 30,000 to 26,867.

Expected improvement.

72. It is believed, however, that the decline of these schools will not long endure. The causes from which it has occurred are, for the most part, fortuitous; and, in more prosperous years the attendance may be expected to increase, under a stricter system, and improved tuition.

Incompetency of tahsildars to supervise, and appointment of a qualified native.

73. The management of the civil authorities has been found to be defective in one respect. Many of the tahsildars are not competent to conduct any searching examination even of these elementary schools. A qualified native drawing a salary (varying with the number of schools) and travelling allowance, has, therefore, been placed at the disposal of each district officer, for the purpose of supervising the educational details of the schools, in a manner less superficial than that in which the visitation of the tahsildar is necessarily conducted.

Deficiency of the present teacher, and difficulty of setting him aside.

74. No more elaborate inspection is as yet required, nor would it repay the cost. In general these schools are in the lowest stage of development. To expend large sums on their supervision before infusing some principle of improvement would be useless. The true means of unfolding their powers must be inward, not external, and can be attained only by educating the teachers. But the work is one of time. The incumbent teachers cannot be set aside without alienating the people. They are averse, too, to quit their homes for any length of time, and it has been found necessary to limit their first attendance at the normal school to six months. But it has been proved that this training, slight as it must be, is sufficient to create a marked difference in the management of village schools. The trained master, though he may not much increase his knowledge, acquires a better method of communicating it, and a clearer idea of his own deficiencies.

Normal Schools.

75. The Normal schools are eight in number, and are placed at Delhi, Umballa, Jullunder, Lahore, Mooltan, Rawal-Pindee, Dehra Ismael Khan and Peshawur. The number of teachers receiving instruction increased during the year from 325 to 431, and the daily attendance from 292 to 352. *Of the teachers, 334 were Muhammadans, and only 111 Hindus.* Altogether 273 received certificates of proficiency.

A manual of directions has been furnished to the teachers in training, relating to their attendance, conduct, and studies. No striking improvement in vernacular education can be looked for until the present generation of teachers has passed away. In the meantime the vain fears of the people on the subject are being rapidly dispersed.

Zilla Schools.

76. In accordance with the scheme initiated in 1859-60, the number of *superior* zilla schools has been raised from 6 to 20; and the number of *inferior*, reduced from 6 to 3. The number of scholars at the close of the year was 2,309, and the average daily attendance throughout the twelvemonth 2,018.

77. The following extract from the Report of the Director of Public Instruction for 1860-61 will explain the general character of these important schools:—

"The curriculum for zilla schools has been framed on the basis of that adopted after long experience in the school classes of the Government colleges and high schools of the North-Western Provinces. The main principles observed in it are that classification must depend on the English attainments of pupils. Nothing but confusion and failure results from attempting to preserve a separate classification for English and vernacular studies. Distinct departments in each language, with the boys arranged in classes according to their attainments in each, was tried for many years; but, with the concurrence of every educational officer of experience, that system has been superseded of late years by that which I have adopted. It will be some time before it can work smoothly, for many boys who are now mere beginners of the English language, have made considerable progress in the vernacular, and by the new classification being in a lower class, are required to read very simple Urdu works.

"These, however, they can master very quickly, and by applying the spare hours of their vernacular studies to pushing on in English, they will be able to qualify themselves before their class-fellows for promotion to a higher class. The greater intelligence, too, they have gained by their vernacular studies will assist them considerably in conquering the difficulties of English, so that their rise will doubtless be rapid, until they reach the class for which they are fitted both by their acquirements in English and in the vernacular.

"Another principle is that English shall be taught simply as a language during the first few years of a boy's education. General knowledge he must acquire through the medium of his own tongue until he is sufficiently conversant with English to understand an English work on any subject like arithmetic, history, or geography with tolerable ease. Having acquired some proficiency in these subjects by his previous course of reading, he will in the higher classes be able to revise his knowledge with the aid of more advanced English treatises.

"The curriculum being designed theoretically for boys who are supposed to have no knowledge either of English or the vernacular on entering a Government school, the greater time in the lower classes is prescribed for the study of the latter, which is of the first importance Practically, most boys entering zilla schools have some knowledge of their own tongue, and so more time can be given by them to the acquisition of English. As the pupil advances to the upper classes, the time for studying English is gradually increased, and that allowed for the vernacular appears rather short in consequence,—it must be remembered that a pupil of that standing has acquired such a mastery of his own language as to be able to carry on his vernacular studies, to a great extent out of school hours, and almost without the aid of a master.

"The object aimed at in this curriculum is to educate a pupil up to the standard of the Calcutta University, and all the studies lead gradually up to that point.

"For this purpose the text books in the first or highest vernacular class will be those ordained by the University for candidates for matriculation at the next December's matriculation."

Progress of the Zilla schools, why retarded.

78. The progress of the zillah schools has been retarded by the difficulty experienced in procuring efficient English masters, and a supply of the requisite books.

Delhi Zillah School.

79. The following description of the Delhi zillah school which is one of the best, will give a clear idea of the actual condition of these institutions at the present time:—

"The number of scholars has increased from 277 to 434 at the close of the year; the average daily attendance from 208 to 339. No less than 289 boys are learning English. The number of Hindus is greatly in excess of Muhammadans, there being 324 of the former and 17 of the latter. I held a very strict examination of this school in December last, chiefly by written papers, and was well satisfied by the progress of the classes, since the previous annual examination. Lalla Ramchundro, the head master, had evidently exerted himself to improve the institution, and had been ably assisted by Wazir Ali, and the rest of his educational staff. At the same time, many defects were brought to light, which the masters are now endeavouring to rectify. Translation and composition in English were found, as might have been expected, the weakest point in the study of the upper classes. The lower classes struck me as very promising indeed. Great attention had been paid to English writing, and marked improvement in this respect was visible. The English pronunciation of the pupils struck His Honour the Lieutenant-Governor as decidedly faulty, when he briefly inspected the institution in February last. The public distribution of prizes and scholarships took place in the middle of March, and owing to circumstances, was not so well attended as it usually has been. The native gentlemen who gave scholarships last year continue them for this, and another was added."

Satisfactory progress of the Lahore zillah school.

80. The Lahore zillah school, in which there is a class exclusively for the sons of the native chiefs and gentry, has made satisfactory progress under Mr. Beddy, the head master.

Zillah schools established in certain districts.

81. Zillah schools in various stages of advancement are now established at the following places :—

UMBALA CIRCLE,—Delhi, Goorgaon, Ferozepore, Thanesur, Simla, Rohtuck, Hissar, Jhujjur, and Kurnal.

There are also excellent anglo-vernacular schools under the direction of missionaries at Delhi, Umballa and Loodhiana.

LAHORE CIRCLE.—Rahon, Hoshiarpore, Umritsur, Buttala, Lahore, Goojranwalla, Mooltan, Jhung and Sealkot.

82. In this circle also are very good missionary schools. That at Lahore, under the able and experienced superintendence of the Revd. Mr. Forman, is considered the best in the Punjab Provinces. The others are at Umritsur, Mooltan and Sealkot.

RAWUL-PINDEE CIRCLE.—Goojrat, Shahpore, Jhelum, Dera Ghazee Khan and Abottabad.

Missionary Schools.

83. There is also a missionary school at Rawul-Pindee, and a smaller one at Khairabad, attended chiefly by the sepoys of the 24th Punjab Infantry, which is composed of Muzhubee Seikhs. The school at Peshawar, under the direction of the Reverend J. McCartby, is, with reference to the character of the population, a remarkable institution. It contains 135 boys, and there is a branch school in the cantonments which contains 45. It is a promising sign that some of the Muhammadan Khans of the frontier have sent their sons to this school.

School houses.

84. During the year many zilla and village school-houses have been erected.

Grants-in-aid to missionary and private schools.

85. The sums granted in aid of missionary and private institutions amount to Rs. 2,337 per mensem, or Rs. 2,800 per annum.

Girls' Schools.

86. There are now 38 schools for females, containing 812 girls, with an average daily attendance of 671; of these schools, 29 are in the Jullundhur District, and have been established through the personal influence of Captain Elphinstone, and Deputy Commissioner.

"He commenced by impressing on the people the importance of educating their daughters as well as their sons. This being admitted, he encouraged those who showed the greatest readiness to support his views to open a school, and promised pecuniary aid on the part of Government. *Several of the old indigenous tutors, who were in the habit of teaching the Koran by rote have been induced, by the offer of regular salaries, to agree that they will give up teaching the Koran during school hours and steadily pursue the Government scheme of studies.* The attendance has been enlarged by the liberal distribution of books, and presents in cash and clothes."

Statistics of cost.

87. The following table exhibits the cost of the several classes of schools, and the aggregate expenditure on Education during the year :—

Present number of Schools.	Description of School.	Aggregate expenditure from the sources.	Chargeable to imperial revenue.	Chargeable to one per cent. Educational cess fund.	Cost of Educating each Pupil.			
					Total cost, 1859-60.	Total cost, 1860-61.	Cost to Government, 1859-60.	Cost to Government 1860-61.
		Rs.	Rs.	Rs.	Rs. A. P.	Rs. A. P.	Rs. A. P.	Rs. A. P
30	Superior zillah schools	55,306	43,025	...	24 14 0	35 5 1	13 1 0	24 5 10
3	Inferior zillah schools	2,610	2,520	...	...	10 5 9	...	10 0 0
128	Tahsili schools	35,470	958	32,764	5 14 0	6 7 10	5 9 0	0 2 9
1686	Village schools	1,24,778	1,620	1,22,358	4 8 4	4 10 3	...	0 1 0
38	Female schools	1,426	2	605	8 1 11	3 3 0	8 1 11	...
10	Private schools (superior)	35,395	16,220	...	11 8 0	22 15 3	3 3 0	10 0 11
10	" " (inferior)	9,299	3,709	...	22 1 0	25 10 11	7 10 0	8 9 7
8	Normal schools	29,996	9,931	20,059	52 3 0	85 3 6	53 3 0	26 1 1
	General establishment and other charges	1,07,501	67,877	39,624	...	...	...	...
	Excess of receipts over charges	16,632	2,941	13,691	...	...	...	...
	TOTAL	4,18,510	1,46,858	2,29,101	...	...	...	...

88. It will be observed that the sum granted by the State has not exceeded £15,000. But the state of the imperial revenues has not admitted of a larger grant being made. The total population of the ten commissionerships of the Panjab Provinces is 14,794,611 souls. If it be assumed that one-eighth is formed of children of a school-going age, then, at the cheapest rate of education, or Rs. 4-8-0, a sum of Rs. 83,21,967 or £832,196, is required for the general diffusion of the most elementary learning. It will be long before funds so large can be provided, but with improved finances it is hoped that a liberal support of the institutions, which during the past year have been placed on firm foundations, will not be denied by a Government, the safety as well as the duty of which consists in the dissipation of ignorance and error.

Inadequacy of present means for the general diffusion of learning.

89. Copies of the Holy Scriptures in English, the vernacular and romanized Urdu, have been placed in the libraries of all Government schools; *and to pupils desiring it, instruction may be given in the Bible out of school hours by Christian teachers, whether Native or English.*

The Bible.

Administration Report for 1861-62.

Section III.

Education.

Progress of education.

70. The progress of education will be gathered from a review of the several classes of schools.

Zillah schools.

Zillah schools are 23 in number, 21 of the superior and two of the lower grade. The number of students on the rolls has fallen from 2,309 to 2,283, and the average attendance from 2,018 to 1,814. But the students of English have risen from 1,523 to 2,016.

Tahsili schools.

Four of these schools have been reduced since last year; the number is now 119. Notwithstanding this the students have increased from 6,437 to 6,765; the average attendance from 4,564 to 5,452.

Village schools.

Village schools have increased in number from 1,686 to 1,750; the students from 32,165 to 38,849; the attendance from 26,867 to 31,016.

Female schools.

Female schools have increased in number from 38 to 52; the pupils from 812 to 1,312; the average attendance from 671 to 1,168.

Normal schools.

Normal schools are 8 in number. The average attendance increased from 352 to 377. The preponderance of Muhammadans over Hindus has slightly diminished, but still remains as 289 to 104. During the year 398 teachers obtained certificates on examination.

Private educational institutions.

Private institutions aided by Government and subject to official inspection are 30 in number. The 15 higher class schools contain 2,290 scholars, and have an average attendance of 1,925; the lower 623, with an average of 484. The large schools under the superintendence of missionary clergymen at Lahore, Peshawur, Umritsar Delhi, Rawal-Pindee and elsewhere, contribute most efficiently towards the education of the people.

Aggregate results.

71. In all there are 1,982 schools either maintained or aided by Government, having 52,480 scholars on their rolls, and an average daily attendance of 42,192.

Expenditure on education.

72. The aggregate expenditure has amounted to Rs. 5,11,284, of which 1,75,758 are from imperial revenues, Rs. 2,84,976 from the proceeds of the educational cess, and the balance from private sources. A tabular analysis of the expenditure is subjoined.

Description of schools.	No. of schools.	No. of scholars on the rolls at close of 1861-62.	No. of scholars attending daily on an average during 1861-62.	Average expenditure from all sources.	Chargeable to Imperial Revenue.	Chargeable to one per cent Educational Cess Fund.	Cost of educating each pupil. Total Cost. 1860-61.			Total Cost. 1861-62.			Cost to Government. 1860-61.			Cost to Government. 1861-62.		
							Rs.	A.	P.	Rs.	A.	P.	Rs.	A.	P.	Rs.	A.	P.
(Superior) zillah	21	2,146	1,714	81,102	63,698	2,801	31	5	1	45	11	1	24	5	10	37	2	6
(Inferior) "	2	125	100	2,202	2,721	...	10	5	9	23	0	5	10	0	0	23	2	5
Tahsili	119	6,765	5,452	59,186	1,278	54,977*	6	7	10	6	11	9	0	2	9	0	2	9
Village	1,750	38,849	31,016	1,57,174	2,195	1,81,300*	4	10	3	4	7	2	0	1	0	0	1	0
Female	52	1,312	1,168	3,170	...	3,170	2	2	0	2	11	6	0	0	1	...		
Private (superior)	16	1,729	1,485	36,760	19,160	...	22	15	8	24	12	0	10	0	11	12	14	11
" (inferior)	20	1,137	860	23,656	10,518	...	25	10	11	23	14	1	8	9	7	11	15	8
Normal	8	495	377	36,920	14,957	21,880	85	8	6	97	14	10	38	1	1	39	10	9
General establishments and other charges	...	...	...	81,064	60,216	20,848												
Total	1,982	52,480	42,192	5,11,284	1,75,758	2,84,976												

* Of this Rs. 73,864 on building tahsili and village school-houses.

Increased appreciation of education by natives.

73. There have been some hopeful indications of an increasing appreciation of the advantages of education on the part of people.

Candidates for entrance to Calcutta University.

Spread of English language in vernacular schools.

Adult classes for study of English.

Four candidates educated in the Panjab were successful in passing the entrance examination for the Calcutta University. In fifteen schools a teacher of elementary English is now maintained, partly by voluntary subscriptions contributed by the students. Adult classes for the study of English have been formed at some principal stations at the request of the inhabitants, bankers, traders attending amongst others.

Review of progress in Umbala circle.

74. In the Umbala circle there was some retrogression, in consequence of the famine and sickness, from which the tract suffered severely. The attendance at the zillah schools (excepting Delhi) fell from 574 to 446. Still the students of English rose from 407 to 458. In 39 tahsili schools the average attendance fell from 45 to 43 per school. On the other hand, the number of the village schools increased from 482 to 550, the average daily attendance from 6,547 to 7,408. The average of each school is 13 students. The increased attendance is very visible in Goorgaon, Rohtuk, and Sirsa, though these districts all suffered from famine. The education in these schools is of course very rudimental. The Inspector, Captain Holroyd, observes :—"It should be borne in mind that the majority of these schools have not yet been in existence for four years ; that in most cases the village schoolmasters were originally teachers in indigenous schools ; that they were totally ignorant of cyphering, had never heard of geography, and had never seen a map of their own or of any other country ; and that they had not the slightest idea of cultivating the understanding of their pupils, to whom they taught Persian after the old traditional method."

Review of progress in Lahore circle.

75. The statistics of the Lahore circle show improvement. In the eight superior zillah schools the average attendance rose from 748 to 779, and the number of pupils learning English from 705 to 899. In the tahsili schools the average daily attendance increased from 2,128 to 2,227. In the village schools the names on the rolls rose from 17,407 to 21,455, and the average daily attendance from 15,607 to 17,280.

School established at Kurtarpoor.

76. A significant incident is mentioned by the Deputy Commissioner of Juliundhur—"There is now a school at Kurtarpoor. The late Guru Sadha Singh had paramount influence there, and objected to a Government school being established in the town. Since his death the people themselves have come forward and petitioned for one ; and there is now a small school of fifty boys, *in which the young guru professes* to take great interest."

School founded by Sirdar Jhundu Singh, Bootalah.

77. *But the old Seikh Noblesse are not all opposed to education.* Sirdar Jhundu Singh of Bootalah, in the Goojranwalla District, has procured the foundation of a school at that place, of which he pays half the expense.

Hours of attendance limited.

78. It is stated that the zemindars complain that when their children learn to read and write they will not plough but require a servant, and that, practically, the hours of attendance are limited to three hours a day.

Government system re-acting on indigenous schools.

79. The Inspector was solicited by the teachers and pupils of one of the indigenous schools (not in connection with Government) to assist them in studying Arithmetic and Geography. Some of the students of the Normal School were accordingly deputed for the purpose. The circumstance *shows that the Government system is causing a re-action on schools not within its direct influence.*

Review of progress in Rawal-Pindi Circle.

80. In the four zillah schools of the Rawal-Pindi circle the average attendance declined from 262 to 238. The number of tahsili schools has been reduced to 37, with an attendance of 1,867, of whom 665 are agriculturists. The Inspector reports favourably of the progress of the schools in the frontier district of Bunnoo.

Interest taken in education by the Lughari Chief, Jumal Khan, in Dera Gazee Khan.

81. The village schools have increased from 340 to 359, the pupils from 6,047 to 7,253. Of the district of Dera Gazee Khan it is remarked : "The increase of 44 village schools is chiefly owing to the great interest shown by the Lughari Chief, Jumal Khan, in the cause of education, as he himself supports the greater number of pupils attending the school at Choti, a village almost entirely inhabited by Biluchis.

Female education in Jullundur District.

82. Of the female schools 34, attended by 1,052, are in the Jullundur District. The best of these schools has been thus reported on by a lady who inspected it :

"*The native lady in charge, Hyat Bibi, was greatly deserving of commendation.* She was a well-mannered, intelligent person, and appeared to have perfect control over her scholars. The elder girls read several Persian and Hindustani books, among others the Gulistan. The little pupils were all clean and well dressed. Most of the schools have been provided with an instructress in needle work, and the girls have begun to learn writing. This was an innovation, the general opinion being that there *might not be much harm in women learning to read books, but that they could not possibly make a good use of writing.*" An instance is mentioned of the effects of the inspection made: "My visits and the little presents I made them, seemed to create a great excitement, and immediately after my departure some 30 or 40 girls enrolled themselves as scholars."

Exertions of Captain Elphinstone, in the cause of female education.

83. These schools owe their origin to the exertions of Captain Elphinstone, the Deputy Commissioner. If they shall contribute in any effectual degree to dissipate the existing prejudice against the education of girls, their usefulness can hardly be overrated. When once the social restriction is removed, it will not be difficult to direct the course of female learning.

Erection of school-houses.

84. During the year great progress has been made in the erection of school-houses throughout the province. The supply of books and maps has also been much increased.

Advantage of placing village schools under superintendence of district officers.

85. Advantage has certainly attended the superintendence exercised over the vernacular schools by the district authorities. By holding public examinations, and distributing prizes, by countenancing the schoolmasters, and occasionally selecting the pupils for public employment, the civil officers have it in their power to stimulate the progress of learning. And in several districts the effects of their influence are perceptible

---

EDUCATIONAL REPORTS.

No. 12, dated Lahore, the 25th June 1858.

From—Director of Public Instruction, Panjab,

To—The Financial Commissioner, Panjab.

2. At the close of 1856-57 there were 456 village or 1 per cent. schools, attended by 6,064, scholars; at the close of 1857-58 there are 1,336 1 per cent. schools, attended by 12,024 scholars. The main efforts of the year have been directed, first, to improving and methodising the existing tehsili schools; secondly, to *extending* the operations of the village schools.

Progress of organisation in the 1st circle.

4. Of the 1,336 village schools, 940 are in the 1st circle; of the 12,024 boys attending these schools, 9,400 belong to the 1st circle; of these 940 schools, 633 have been established during the year under review. Nor would there have been anything under ordinary circumstances to prevent the establishment of a *far larger number*, of the whole number indeed which the village school fund is capable of maintaining, of which number we may be considered as *falling short in the 1st circle by about 600*. But I need not say that the circumstances of the year have been extraordinary. In June 1857 Lieutenant Paske very properly, in my opinion, and with my full sanction, suspended the development of the village school system. Several schools already established, especially in Umbala and Thaneysar, gave way and we thought it better to avoid a repetition of failures. Even in the Panjab men were thinking of other things than the establishment of village schools. We were always reluctant to close a school once opened, and this we must have done very frequently had we gone on opening new schools during the hot season of 1857. Accordingly we waited till the autumn; soon after the fall of Delhi, the restriction was taken off, and nearly the great majority of 633 village schools established within the year date from that period.

Extra Sub-Deputy Inspectors.

5. We soon found that the schools were outgrowing the means of inspection and control. Every district has a Sub-Deputy Inspector, but this officer, while managing and inspecting the tahsili schools and collecting data and carrying out orders in connection with the establishment of village schools, has little leisure to inspect the latter class of schools when established. A village school left to itself *is not an institution which we have any great interest in maintaining.*

Organisation, 2nd circle.

6. And in each of these schools the progress so far as it has been made at all, is genuine. The boys are *not* reading the Koran, and they *are* reading Urdú and Arithmetic.

Organisation, 2nd circle, village schools.

7. The number remaining to be established with reference to the present state of income and of sanctioned expenditure from the village school fund of the circle, may be estimated at 360.

Organisation, 2nd circle, zillah schools.

9. That the establishment of a zillah school was to be larger than that of a tahsili school, that the course of instruction was to be higher, and that *although the main business of the school was always to be conducted in and through the medium of Urdú, yet in a Zillah school English was always to be taught as an accomplishment to those who were willing to pay for learning it.*

11. It is easier to establish a new than to improve an old school. Improvement of existing schools is not a fact easily ascertained or established. Examination marks do not prove much. Examination papers are too voluminous evidence.

Progress of school as regards the quality of instruction.

We must consider what we found on the one hand, and what we aim at on the other. We found a whole population agreed together that to read fluently, and, if possible, to say by heart a series of Persian works of which the meaning was not understood by the vast majority, and of which the meaning when understood was for the most part little calculated to edify the minority, constituted education. I do not wish to speak too contemptuously of the Persian school of instruction. I have no right to do so. A man must understand the Persian language, and know the Persian literature far better than I do, before he presumes to pass on either any very harsh sentence of condemnation. But we should not be establishing schools, if we did not regard some elementary educational principles at least as settled. And among these principles is this: first, that what a boy learns as a fact shall be a true fact, and the Sikhandarnama is a narrative of facts which are not true; secondly, that a boy shall understand what he reads, and nine boys out of ten do not understand the Bostan. We found then a whole people wedded to a system diametrically opposed to that which we wish to introduce, to whom the Urdú language, which we properly wish to make the medium of popular instruction, because it is the nearest approach that exists to a common vernacular, is utterly inconsistent with, and indeed opposed to, the idea of erudition or learning. Urdú is as offensive to a learned Arabic scholar as vernacular English in connection with learned subjects would have been to a scholar of the age of Erasmus. We found a people ignorant of the geography of their own province; ignorant that there was such a science as geography, and therefore prepared to reject geography, as men are inclined to reject whatever is strange to them. We found them in the matter of arithmetic divided into two main classes: the Katthries trained by long diligent practice to great skill and quickness in mental arithmetic, but at a loss directly they got beyond their accustomed problems, because unacquainted with scientific methods; and the Muhammadans scorning the whole business as quite unworthy of a scholar and a gentleman, to say nothing of a true believer. I have said nothing of the religion of the Koran taught in so many schools, even schools attended by Hindus, and which tended to make so-called education a popular or rather an *essential* institution with the Muhammadans. But in short we found a population with their own idea of the meaning of education, and to that idea thoroughly attached, and to whom our idea of education, being inconsistent with their own, was thoroughly distasteful, as to an Asiatic everything is distasteful which is new. Well, I am not going to say that in two years our idea has taken them out of the field. It would be preposterous to say, or for anybody, if it was said, to believe, anything so improbable. We have not rudely discarded all the old Persian books. I should think it very unwise, and worse than unwise to do so. But we have greatly limited their number, prohibiting everything which is grossly indecent on one ground, and everything which pertains to religion on another ground, and limiting altogether the time allowed for Persian as distinguished from Urdu studies. The progress made is this, that in every tahsili school certainly, and in far the greater number of village schools, I believe, all boys have learnt, or are learning (what before they were frequently when their education was finished most ignorant of), the art of reading and writing their native language; that in every tehsili school there are boys, Muhammadans as well as Hindus, acquainted with the first four rules of arithmetic, with the rule of three, and generally with vulgar fractions,—a knowledge which two years ago might have been sought in vain in most districts of the Panjab; that in every tahsili school there are boys able to give an intelligent account of the early Muhammadan invasions of India, and to pass a good examination (I have heard boys on the banks of the Indus pass what would be called in an English village school a *very* good examination) in the geography of their own country, of India, of Asia, and of the Globe. This is the extent of the course at an average tahsili school: at some of the best they know decimal fractions, and have read the 1st, or as far as the first four books of Euclid. Now I am not saying that this is a very great amount of knowledge, but I think it is fair progress for two years from the state of things I have described.

12. I have inspected a school in 1856 57 before the teacher went to the Normal school, and I have inspected the same school in 1857-58 after the teacher returns, and have found a very sensible improvement. Of course six months' tuition will not work wonders, but after all the simple rules of arithmetic and the leading facts of geography are not very difficult, and an intelligent teacher soon learns enough to teach his boys on his return a great deal which they did not know before.

The effect of the Normal schools.

24. In my last report I stated that the return of indigenous schools given in Table C was confessedly inaccurate; but that the statements contained in it were under, not over the mark; that it was erroneous by reason of imperfect investigation, not by reason of exaggeration. I cannot say that I regard the return now submitted (Table C) as complete. *In fact, to compile a perfect statistical record of indigenous schools in the Panjab would require a larger establishment than ours, and one occupied only with that particular business.* It is not to be supposed that there are 304 more schools in Jalandhar than there were a year ago, but that *a more minute enquiry has brought that greater number to light,* and the same remark applies to the districts of Sialkot, Ludhiana Rawal-Pindee, Jhelum, and Shahpur. Again, it is not be supposed that there are no Koran schools in Kohat. *I have no doubt that every mosque is what may be called a Koran school.* On

Indigenous schools.

the other hand the decrease of indigenous schools in districts Amritsar, Hoshiarpur, Gujerat, Mooltan, Jhang, and Khángarh is probably genuine, *and represents the effect produced by the introduction of the 1 per cent. village schools.* The average attendance at each of these schools is 7, which gives an aggregate average of 43,736 boys attending indigenous schools of all sorts, instead of 40,192 of last year.

Modifications in the making of village schools.

16. In *modification of this* system the yield of the 1 per cent. cess of each district was afterwards expended locally on the establishment of new schools. The most populous villages, and those in which, from their centrical position the schools would supply the wants of the largest number of the surrounding villages, were situated as the sites for those new village schools. The teachers were appointed on a fixed salary of Rs. 5 per mensem. Simple rules were drawn up for their guidance, and a course of study of the most rudimentary character was prescribed for introduction in the schools.

State of village schools at the commencement.

17. On assuming charge of this office in February last I found that this modified system was not working successfully. Native subordinates had been careless and injudicious in their selection of teachers. Many were selected only for this reason—that they were of the same creed as the parties appointing them; men were nominated at the instigation of the people; in short, almost all bad men selected for any other reasons than their aptitude for the employment. It must, moreover, be admitted that good men could scarcely be obtained on so small a pittance as Rs. 5 per mensem with no prospect of advancement. I found that for the most part the teachers of the old indigenous schools had been selected; that they were allowed to work upon their own system, to impart religious in preference to secular instruction, and to conduct their schools heretofore as in mosques and temples, and as I found that we revived and upheld the old indigenous schools, increased the funds of these schools without improving their character; and, moreover, that while proclaiming our principle of religious neutrality, and our desire to spread secular education, we did in effect aid to a great extent in propagating Muhammadanism; for we paid the priestly attendants of mosques for teaching the Koran. It may be urged that the funds expended were not from the treasury of the State, but were collected from the people for the purpose of education, and should be spent in the form of education most desired by themselves. But the cess was collected for establishing secular schools, and on secular schools only it should be expended. Moreover, to establish and control schools of a religious character, through the agency of this Department, would be in direct contravention of the neutrality policy proclaimed by Government.

Reformatory measure adopted for village schools.

18. Accordingly, with the sanction of your predecessor, I immediately adopted the following reformatory measure:—

I ordered all village schools to be removed from the precincts of mosques and other buildings of a religious character. Native subordinates assured me that no other buildings were available. *I then ordered that the schools should be closed rather than be held in such buildings.* On the issue of this order I found that the buildings were not only available, but had been procured.

I directed the disuse of all books of a religious character in the schools, and in order to leave no room for the pretext that secular books were not procurable, I distributed a supply of school-books, maps, gratuitously, among the village schools in every district.

I took measures to secure the removal of old and inefficient teachers who had been selected solely for their priestly merits; and in order to secure the services of efficient teachers, I divided the village school teachers into three grades on Rs. 10, 7 and 5 per mensem, respectively. Thus, while provision has been made for raising the salaries of the most efficient beyond the small pittance they have heretofore received, *a spirit of emulation has been created among this class of teachers.*

In most districts there are large balances to the credit of the 1 per cent. school fund being the unexpended collection of former years. *These balances are now being expended in defraying the cost of village school-houses.* Then, while by this measure we are removing any difficulty that may exist for want of school buildings, we give the people an earnest of our intention to spend the yield of the cess solely in fulfilment of the purpose for which it was intended.

Prospects of success in the working of the new scheme for village schools.

19. Such are the measures that have been adopted for improving the village school system in the Panjab. These measures have only been introduced within the last few months. They have therefore scarcely had as yet sufficient trial to admit of an opinion being formed with regard to their efficacy. That they are popular may be inferred from the readiness with which teachers attend the normal school, from the increased attendance at schools, and from the numerous applications for the establishment of new schools. The progressive increase in the number of these schools will be seen in reference to Statement 2. There are now 2,029 village schools in the Panjab attended by 26,377 pupils. The amount expended from the yield of the cess during the year 1858-59 is Rs. 1,92,002, which would show the average cost of each school to amount to Rs. 94. It must, however, be borne in mind that *village schools do not absorb the entire yield of the 1 per cent. cess;* certain fixed quotas are paid for office establishment, maintenance of normal schools salaries of extra Sub-Deputy Inspectors and supervisors of village schools,

and also towards defraying the cost of publishing the *Sirkari Akhbar*. Deducting these charges from the fund, the average cost of each school is about Rs. 80 per annum.

* * * * *

Progress in the establishment of zilla schools.

21. In addition to these is the large school in the city of Delhi, which is fast approaching the standard of a collegiate institution, but as this school, though organised and controlled by the officers of this Department, is maintained from private sources, it has not been included in the returns of Government institutions.

* * * * *

Suggestions with regard to retrenchments in the art of controlling establishments.

28. Government desires to know what retrenchments can be made in the controlling establishments of this Department. On reference to the Statement No. 1 it would at first sight appear that the cost of controlling establishments is disproportionately great as compared with the cost of instruction establishment, the outlay on the former being almost twice the amount expended on the latter. It must, however, be considered that the scheme of education is yet in its infancy in this province ; scarcely three years have elapsed since the Department was organised, and while it was necessary at starting to constitute the controlling establishments on a complete footing, the establishments for direct instruction are of a slower growth, and must expand gradually and progressively.

I would here express my belief that more is to be expected for the cause of education by seconding private efforts than by the direct action of Government. A lack of rupees judiciously expended on grants-in-aid to private schools will do more for the spread of knowledge than twice that amount spent directly by the State for the same purpose.* Government schemes are ever the most costly, and Government agencies are always the most extensive. I do not see how, in carrying out the Government scheme of education in the Panjab, any very great or tangible retrenchment can be made in the controlling establishment.

Persons unconnected with the service may be secured on smaller emoluments. Doubtless there are now in England hundreds of gentlemen, trained educationists and scholars who have had the best college education, who are now experiencing the reality that talent in England is a drug in the market, and who, earning a scanty pittance by undertaking private tutorage and such like occupations, would readily accept the higher situations in this Department on half the salaries now paid to the Inspectors. If the proposal to employ persons unconnected with the service be adopted, I venture to suggest that gentlemen with tastes indicative, and aptitude for the special work of the Department be secured from England.

* * * * *

Remark on introduction of a general plan of popular education.

30. In connection with the adoption of a general plan of popular education the Supreme Government desires to know what measure it is proposed to introduce for the elementary education of the people, and the means by which it is considered that the requisite funds may be obtained on this point. I would observe that the village school system, as modified according to the detailed plan sketched in paragraph 17 of this report, is now in force, and making rapid and successful progress. It provides for the education of the mass of the people in the three great elements of science—reading, writing and arithmetic ; the instruction imparted is of the most rudimentary character, and one adapted to the requirements of the people. This system is very similar to the system of schools established in the North-Western Provinces. This system does in all essentials differ little from the Halqua bandee system established in the North-Western Provinces. I am unable to suggest any improvement or modification. If the system is only allowed a fair trial, I am confident of its success.

With deference and due respect to higher authority, I venture to deprecate the introduction of the measure above alluded to, which will tend to create diversity in a system the uniformity of which does at present constitute one of its greatest elements of success. The expediency of enforcing this special rate of 1 per cent. cess appears to me that undoubtedly the cess is light, and scarcely felt. The advantages given in return for it are great. Nor do I think that the cess is unpopular, where the people have *not* been consulted, that is, where they have been told they must pay it, and it is collected from them. It is unpopular in localities where the people are promised option in the matter of paying the tax, but when tehsildars with that amount of gentle persuasion they know so well how to exercise put in the forcible *must* in collecting the cess it would be free-will offerings.†

Appointment of Extra Sub-Deputy Inspectors.

41. It may have been mentioned that during the past year Extra Sub-Deputy Inspectors were appointed to organise village schools. As schools of this class increased in number, it was found that the control and supervision of these as well as of Government schools could not be undertaken by Deputy and Sub-Deputy Inspectors in addition to their other duties ; hence it was determined to employ another or lower grade of subordinates to be styled Extra Sub-Deputy Inspectors, who were to be paid from the yield of the 1 per cent. cess, and

* From this principle the Educational Department has persistently departed, till with an expenditure of nearly 16 lakhs in 1882, there are scarcely 114,000 pupils under instruction in Government and Aided Schools in the Panjab.

† What greater condemnation of our educational system can be expressed than in the cynical remarks of the Director of Public Instruction himself ?

to be employed exclusively in the establishment and management of village schools. Subordinates of this class have been entertained and appointed to districts where the number of existing village schools rendered their employment desirable. Thus, the expansion and development of the machinery has been gradual and progressive, proved increasing in proportion with the extension of the operations of the Department.

43. It has been shown that *the scheme of organising village schools was based upon the principles of supporting and fostering existing indigenous schools, that it was proposed to search out these schools and to assist them with pecuniary aid from the yield of the 1 per cent. cess, that thus, partially supported by the State, they would be in a measure amenable to Government rules and Government supervision, and might become institutions, where the mass of the people could receive instruction of an elementary but useful character. This scheme, sound in theory, has failed practically after a trial for a period of two years after the first introduction of the scheme.** The yield of the 1 per cent. cess in such district was expended in affording aid to the indigenous school of that district, on the understanding that those schools were still to be mainly maintained by those who had established them. In many localities, however, it was found that the people tried to rid themselves of the responsibility of maintaing their own school, and to throw the entire burden of their support on the State. In other localities it was found that the additional funds supplied led to no improvement of the school. The teachers readily accepted the increase of pay, but they did not fulfil the conditions on which such increase was allowed; they did not adhere to the rules prescribed by the Department, nor did they attempt to adopt the plan of instruction laid down for their schools. Thus all efforts to develop the standard of indigenous schools failed; they continued what they were at starting—schools in which the boys were taught the Korán or the Shastur (according as the teachers were Musulmans or Hindus), and in some of which a certain amount of secular instruction of a fantastic, desultory character was also imparted.

44. *Attempts to raise the standard of indigenous schools having proved unsuccessful, efforts were made to establish new village schools supported entirely from the yield of the 1 per cent. cess.*† In villages where it was considered desirable to establish these schools, teachers were appointed by the subordinate officers of the Department on fixed salaries of Rs. 5 each; a few simple rules were drawn up for the guidance of the teachers; and a plan of an elementary course of instruction was prescribed for adoption in the schools. But this modified plan did not succeed; subordinate officers made bad selections. Instead of appointing the best qualified teachers, they selected for the most part the old teachers of the indigenous schools, with a view of meeting the wishes of the people. These old teachers, with small pay and no prospect of advancement, did not find the inducement sufficient to make them follow the scheme prescribed by Government, they fell back upon their old time-honoured but useless system; so the new schools became a revival of the old indigenous schools. Moreover, in contravention of the neutrality principle upon which the operations of the Department are based, these schools became in too many instances of a religious character. Subordinate officers, especially those of the Muhammadan creed, zealous for their faith, and in direct opposition to the rules of the Department, appointed as teachers men whose fanatic character rendered them unsuitable as secular teachers. Thus it was found that a large proportion of the village schools were no more or less than religious institutions, presided over by the village peers or their disciples, conducted within the threshold of mosques, and in which reading the Korán formed the principal course of study.

45. Within the last few months the system has been changed, and a different policy is now pursued. At starting too great concessions were made for the sake of popularity in order to win the people. The schools were made not what they ought to have been, nor what it was desired they should be, but what the people wished them to be, and in effect they became neither useful nor popular. Now, however, the schools have been remodelled upon the system it is desired to introduce. The change was at first unpopular, but any people, however ignorant, if not deterred by a timorous policy and half measures, will learn to appreciate what is really for their good, and the scheme is now becoming popular. All schools have been removed from mosques and other buildings of a religious character; old and inefficient teachers, and those, too, who were selected solely for their priestly merits, have been removed. Provision has been made for securing the services of efficient teachers by ensuring prospects of advancement; village school teachers have been divided into three grades on salaries of Rs. 5, 7 and 10 per mensem, respectively. Thus, while provision has been made for raising the salaries of the most efficient beyond the small pittance they have heretofore received, a spirit of emulation has been created among this class of teachers. Normal schools have been established for the special instruction of village school teachers, and no teacher who has been promoted to the 1st grade will be confirmed in that grade until he has gone through the prescribed course of study in the normal school. As every teacher must go through a course of instruction in one of the normal schools, and as these normal schools will be periodically examined by the

* Scarcely a sufficient time for the fair trial of the policy of the Despatch of 1854.

† It seems to me that the points for which I contend have been proved by the Director himself, namely, that the Cess was, primarily, raised for the support of indigenous schools; secondly, that it was applied to the formation of Government village schools, for which the best indigenous masters were *not* forthcoming, as has since been alleged by the Educational Department and, thirdly, that the Cess was applied to more showy purposes than the maintenance of the humble village schools for which it was raised.

Inspector and Director of Public Instruction, the qualifications of every teacher will become known to the superior officers of the Department. A useful and rudimentary course of study has been prescribed for, *and will be strictly enforced*, in village schools. Now that Extra Sub-Deputy Inspectors have been generally appointed, a stricter supervision will be exercised over the working of village schools. The unexpended balances of former years, now lying in district treasuries to the credit of the village school fund, are being expended in defraying the cost of erecting school-houses and in the purchase of school-books for gratuitous distribution. It is hoped that before the close of the year village school-houses will have been erected in numerous localities in every district, and before the expiry of two months a map of the world and rudimentary books on history, geography, and arithmetic will be studied in each of nearly two thousand village schools in the Panjáb. The present system promises well; it is popular with the teachers, and through them will ere long become popular with the people. There are now existing in the Panjáb upwards of 2,000 village schools, attended by 26,377 scholars, in all of which schools the boys are taught the three great elements of science—reading, writing and arithmetic. The number of pupils attending these schools is steadily on the increase, a sure sign of their growing popularity.

No. 182, dated Lahore, the 7th September 1859.

From—Director of Public Instruction, Panjáb.

To—The Financial Commissioner, Panjáb.

* * * * * * * *

Object of the report.

2. I propose in the first instance to review the measures that have been adopted and the results that have been achieved in the operation of the orders issued by the Honourable Court of Directors in their despatch No. 49 of 1854. I shall then proceed to notice the specific points to which attention has been drawn and upon which information is required by the Supreme Government.

Plan of operations of the Department.

3. I have already, both in my annual report and in my memorandum on the constitution and development of this Department, entered into a full recital of points connected with the introduction and progress of the scheme of education in the Panjáb. In both those documents, and more especially in the latter, I have sketched the plan of operations, have traced the course of action, and have pourtrayed the results that have been achieved during the brief existence of this Department. To recapitulate what has thus been lately brought in ample detail before the notice of the Local Government appears to me superfluous. I propose, therefore, in this first function of my present report, to show in brief outline only what it was proposed to do, what scheme it was desired to introduce, what has been done, and with what success. The scheme has worked on furthering the cause of education in this province. I will enter into details only when necessary in order to elucidate the statistics appended to this report.

First step in the formation of the Department.

4. The first step in the formation of the Department was the appointment of the late Mr. D. W. Arnold to the post of Director of Public Instruction at the commencement of 1856. That officer immediately drew up a scheme which provided for the introduction of a system of education suitable to the requirements of the Panjab.

Object and plan of village school system.

5. *The scheme was based upon the principle of making existing indigenous village schools the nucleus of a new improved and organised system. These schools were to be searched out and fostered; they were to be aided by contributions from the yield of the 1 per cent. school cess, and thus, partly supported by a system of grants-in-aid, they would become in some degree amenable to Government supervision.* The aim was to be, to secure the introduction and substitution of useful and systematic instruction of an elementary character in place of the desultory impracticable course of study then existing.

Scheme for the establishment of Government schools.

6. At the same time it was proposed to open out new sources for the provision of instruction, and to set up a higher standard than the village school could be expected to attain by the establishment of district Government institutions supported wholly by the State.

* * * * * * * *

Grants-in-aid.

11. Under the provision of the Honourable Court's despatch the scheme contemplated also the introduction of the system of grants-in-aid, that is, the affording pecuniary aid assistance to mission and other private schools unconnected with Government institutions.

* * * * * * * *

Results attending the introduction of grants-in-aid of indigenous village schools.

15. It has been shown above that the scheme of education was based upon the principle of making the *existing indigenous schools the nucleus of a new and improved system.* Practically this part of the scheme has failed. These schools, as they then existed, scarcely deserved the name; for the most part they consisted of assemblies of lads collected at the thresholds of mosques and temples, and taught by the priestly attendants to repeat passages from the Korán or Shasturs. In a few instances this course of study may have been varied by a little secular

instruction of a desultory and fantastic character. It was found impossible to elevate the standard of these schools. The teachers were firmly wedded to their old time-honoured but useless system, and they adhered to it in all its integrity, readily accepting the additional aid afforded them from the yield of the 1 per cent. school cess, but quite ignoring the fulfilment of the conditions on which such aid was granted. They neglected to adhere to the simple rules furnished for their guidance, and they failed to introduce the scheme of secular studies proposed by the officers of this Department. Moreover, those who had originated these schools, as soon as they observed a prospect of obtaining aid from the yield of the cess, attempted to withhold their own contributions, and to throw the whole burden of support on the village school fund.*

Popular feeling with regard to the system of grants-in-aid to mission schools.

31. The Supreme Government desires the expression of an opinion as to the feeling of the natives towards the system of grants-in-aid to schools conducted by missionaries....It appears to me that natives generally, in this part of India at least, never give the subject a thought. Those few who have noticed the system have never raised the least objection; indeed, some have expressed their astonishment at the moderation of Government.† I do not think that the natives are jealous of missionary efforts. They know that the avowed object and end of missionary labour is to evangelize, but they associate the idea of missionary teaching with that of persuasion and argument, and therefore do not fear it; on the other hand, they would dread any departure from its neutral policy on the part of Government....The action of the insurgents, while passing through Ludiana in June 1857, in the destruction of the mission premises in that city, may perhaps be instanced in proof of hatred of missionaries and missionary establishments. I am not, however, of opinion that this circumstance can be adduced as showing special animosity against missionaries. The mission premises were unprotected and the insurgents destroyed wherever they felt that destruction was sure. Their desire was to be rid of us and to destroy the landmarks of our dominion. They had a general hatred, and a will for general destruction.

* * * * * * * * * * * * * * * *

The introduction of measures for educating the people, how far connected with the disturbances of 1857.

33. The spread of education may have been one among other predisposing causes that led to the calamitous events of 1857. If it was so, its primary influence for evil was limited, except upon the minds of the few whose interests were directly opposed to its introduction. Any apprehension or alarm that may have been excited in the minds of the mass of the people was superficial, and was awakened not before, but after, the breaking-out of the flame of rebellion....The priesthood fear that popular education will dispel popular ignorance and superstition, free the people from the thraldom of priestcraft, and so remove the guiles of the priesthood. Thus, therefore, the priests, wilfully misconstruing the intentions of the Government, have found, in the introduction of education, a weapon which they have skilfully used to fan the flame of rebellion, and excite popular fears, by propagating the delusion that the introduction of education was a design on the part of the British Government forcibly to convert the people‡. The delusion was readily seized and turned to account by rebel chiefs whose proclamations teemed with appeals to religious feelings. In several of these proclamations it has been declared that the Government measures for the spread of education were direct attempts to convert the youths of the land. The measures adopted by Government are strictly neutral, and are not in themselves in any way calculated to excite suspicion or to cause alarm. If there is cause for alarm, it is, in my opinion, in the too oft reiterated assurance of the neutral policy of the Government. I think that on this subject there cannot be too much reliance on its actions only; let the Government prove the neutrality of its policy. The people will judge by their own sad experience and by the traditions of native dynasties; in spite of all we may say to the contrary, the people will never believe that it is not our intention to interfere with their religion, and our attempts to assure them by the most direct declaration of neutrality only excites suspicion, and the doubt that mere assertion is the mask under which we hide contrary purposes. I repeat that nothing need be said, but everything should be done, to prove our neutrality.

I have already observed that the few natives who trouble themselves to think about the system of grants-in-aid for mission schools are astonished at the extreme moderation of Government in affording such really nominal assistance to this class of schools. I have shown that the sum expended by Government in grants-in-aid to mission schools is under 4 per cent. of the whole outlay incurred by the State in furthering the cause of education in the Panjáb. I do think that, without any controversion of the principles of neutrality, and without disturbing the confidence that may be felt in the non-aggressive spirit of the Government, much more might be done, and ought to be done, by the State in the way of supporting mission

* Of course, they did so, as they saw that the Educational Department interfered with the religious instruction given in these schools, in contravention to the declared policy of Government, and as secular subjects of instruction were forced on these schools, the usefulness of which was not then, and is not now, clear to the agricultural, the trading and the "learned" classes of the community and is, even now, only appreciated by those anxious for Government employment.

† Moderate indeed, is the aid afforded to mission schools in the Panjáb. The aggregate of these grants is within 4 per cent. of the whole annual outlay incurred by the State for the spread of education.

‡ This accusation is really opposed to fact, though there can be no doubt that the action of the Educational Department as regards indigenous schools might have given a plausible weapon into the hands of agitators, and also that some "dispossessed" teachers joined the ranks of the mutineers.

schools by the increase of grants-in-aid. It is surely the prerogative of the ruling race to countenance and support its own religion. While we are undoing (endorsing?) the acts of natives by largely upholding in popularity the alienations they have in this kind made from the revenue of the State for the support of their own religion, we do little or nothing to further the cause of our own faith. I advocate a large *increase to existing grants given in aid of mission schools*, and the *extension* of the system wherever *practicable*. The ostensible object of the missionary student is to evangelize, but, setting aside this consideration, it must be acknowledged that they do much towards raising the moral, intellectual and physical condition of the people, and on this account therefore they deserve additional support from the State. It has been urged that while by the spread of education and the introduction of Western science and learning into India, we lead its people to throw off their own faith, we are bound to give them facilities for acquiring a knowledge of the true faith. Yes, but we ought not to thrust these facilities upon them against their will, and in contravention of the oft-proclaimed principle of neutrality, by the introduction of religious teaching into our secular schools as it has been proposed that we should do. Rather place these within their reach, and leave to them the option of their acceptance; and this we can do, and ought to do, by rendering increased aid to the missionary institutions. Such a course is not opposed to the principles of neutrality; nor is it calculated to excite the least apprehension or create any doubt in the minds of the people. It is the prerogative of the dominant power; it conforms with the usages of natives, and it is the duty of a Christian Government.

To conclude, it has been said that in the neutrality of the Government lies the hope of the missionaries, and it may be added that to the labour of the missionaries must we look for evangelical success. Attempts, therefore, to depart from the terms of our neutrality would obstruct, rather than promote, Christianity. The introduction of the Bibles into Government schools would be opposed to the principles of strict neutrality, and opposed also to the terms of the proclamation issued by Her Majesty the Queen on her assumption of the direct Government of India. I am of opinion, therefore, that those who recommend the introduction of the Bible into Government schools would render the least effectual service to the cause that every Christian must have at heart. If they would cease to urge the adoption of a measure that the Government cannot, neither on the grounds of justice or expediency, carry into effect, and that they would turn their attention to aiding more vigorously the labour of missionaries. Let the people of England establish new missions, and let the Government countenance and support missionary efforts more effectually than it has hitherto done, and then the cause of Christianity will progress more rapidly, more surely, and with less offence than would be the case if even we continue fully to discuss measures which are opposed to the principle of neutrality.

• • • • • • • • • • • • • • • • • • •

APPENDIX VII.

A COLLECTION OF SPECIMENS OF COMMERCIAL AND OTHER ALPHABETS AND HANDWRITINGS AS ALSO OF MULTIPLICATION TABLES CURRENT IN VARIOUS PARTS OF THE PANJAB, SIND AND THE NORTH WEST PROVINCES.

PART A.

LIST OF CONTENTS.*

INTRODUCTORY.

SET 1.—I.—Names of letters of the Thakari Alphabet, II. Thakari of Mandi, III. Numerals in Thakari, Lande, Nagri and Arabic.

IV.—Thakari and Sarafi compared with Kaithi, Landé, Nagari and Gurmukhi.

SET 2.—Roman, Gurmukhi and Nagri alphabets compared with three kinds of ordinary Landé, Kangra-Landé, Patiala-Lande, Lande-Sarafi, Delhi-Sarafi, Thakari and Dogri.

SET 3.—Hindi Numerals and Letters comparing various kinds of Lande with Sarafi and Kaithi.

SET 4.— I.—Table of Interest in Rawalpindi Lande.

II.—Pahara or Multiplication Table of Rawalpindi.

III.—Letter in the Rawalpindi Mahajani (?) character, called the Local Panjabi character.

IV.—Table of Land measurement.

V.—Letter in the Rawalpindi Banya character

VI.—Specimen of a Hundi.

VII.—Multiplication Table by 1, $1\frac{1}{4}$, $1\frac{1}{2}$, $2\frac{1}{2}$, $3\frac{1}{2}$, $4\frac{1}{2}$.

VIII.—Rate Table.

IX.—Fractional Multiplication Table.

X.—Substraction.

XI.—Division.

XII.—Addition.

XIII.—Multiplication.

XIV.—Letters in Local "Panjabi."

XV.—Banya letters.

XVI.—Names in Banya letters.

SET 5.—Multiplication Table from 1 to 40 (from Shahpur) Fractional Multiplication Table.

CONTENTS OF PART A.

	PAGE.
Arora Lande used in Sind	1
Banya Lande used in Sirsa, Hissar, &c.	2
Bhawalpuri used in Bhawalpur	3
Bisati Lande, used by Muhammadan merchants in the North West Provinces	4
Kaithi used in Oudh, the North-Western Provinces and Upper Bengal	5
Karabi Lande used by Banyas in Sind	6
Khoja Lande used by eunuchs in the service of Native States	7
Lamawasi Lande used in Findi Bhatian, Chunia, &c.	8
Lande used in Sealkot, Wazirabad, &c.	9
Marwari used in Rajputana by Marwaries and traders generally	10
Marwari mixed with Sarafi, used in Ajmir, Jeypur, &c.	11
Mudia (Lande) used in Oudh, Garhwal, and Towns in the North-Western Provinces, below Allahabad	12
Multani Lande used in Multan and adjoining Towns	13
Muria used by merchants in Behar and Benares, &c.	14
Parachi used in Bhera Khoshab, &c.	15
Rori Lande used by Bankers in the Panjab and Sind	16
Sarafi used by Bankers in the North-West Provinces and Oudh	17
Sarika used in the Derajat of the Panjab	18
Shikarpuri used in Upper Sind	19
Sindi used in Sind	20
Tbul used in the Derajat of the Panjab	21
Thakari or Thankri used in Kangra and (with some modifications) in Kulu, Mandi and Sukeyt	22—23
Mahajani as used in Jalandhar	24
Mahajani of Ambala	25
Kyunthali Thakari with the signature of the Raja of Kyunthal (Simla)	26
Lande of Jalandhar	27
Lande letter from Jalandhar	28
Jalandhar Lande Alphabet (two kinds); Sarafi Alphabet and Mahajani Alphabet ...	29
Malehr Kotla Lande, Mahajani (little used) and Sarafi	30
Lande of Dehra Ghazi Khan	31
Lande used by Native Mahajans of Sirsa and by Oswal Mahajans of Sirsa	32
Names and meanings of the letters of the Lande Alphabet	33
Table showing the various alphabets used in Mithila	34

* For a history of Lande, Maháјani and Saráfi, together with an account of Mahajani and Landé Schools, see page iii of the "Introduction" to Dr. Leitner's "History of Indigenous Education in the Panjab;" also pages 37 to 45 of Part I. of that History. See also a detailed account of Mahajani text books in Part IV. of the same work.

PART B.

SET 1.—Comparison of different kinds of Lande with official Dogri.
SET 2.—Specimens of I. Gurmukhi, II. Nagri and III. Sanscrit.
SET 3.—I. Sialkot Mahajani-Lande, II. Mahajani-Dogre, III. Amritsar Lande, IV. Amritsar Banya characters, V. characters used by the Bikaniris in Amritsar, VI. specimen of Landes, VII. differs from Karnal Mahajani, VIII. Tarn Taran (District Amritsar), specimen of Lande, Sarafi, Lande-Thakari, &c.
SET 4.—Mahajani used in Rohtak, I. Rohtak Sarafi.
SET 5.—Mahajani and Sarafi used in the Delhi, Karnal and Gurgaon Districts, I. Delhi Mahajani, II. Delhi Sarafi, III. Gurgaon, IV. Gurgaon Current Mahajani writing, V. Gurgaon Mahajani ; VI. Karnal ; VII Karnal Mahajani.
SET 6.—Landes used in the Multan, Jhang, Montgomery and Musaffargarh Districts.
I.—Massan Thana (Jhang District).
II.—Jhang District.
III.—Lande Uch (Jhang District).
IV.—Montgomery.
V.—Multan Lande.
VI.—Lande letters used in Multan.
VII.—Lande.
VIII.—Sarafi.
SET 7.—Landes used in the Simla and Ludhiana Districts.
I.—Thakari or Tankri characters used in Simla.
SET 8.—Mercantile characters used in the Lahore, Gujranwala and Firozpur Districts, I. Gujranwala, II. another kind used at Gujranwala, III. Lande, IV. Lahore, V. Lahore, (another kind), VI. Lahore (another kind) VII. Lahore (another kind). VIII Lahore (another kind).
SET 9.—Lande-Thakari and Sarafi characters used in the Hushiarpur and Kangra Districts, I. Thakari used in Kangra, II. Hushiarpur-Landes, Sarafi and Thakari, III. Lande used in Jejun, District Hushiarpur, IV. Lande, II. used in Jejun, V. Lande, III. used in Jejun village, Mahilpur Thana.
SET 10.—Multiplication Table and different kinds of Landes used in the Gujrat, Shahpur and Rawalpindi Districts. I. Rawalpindi, II. Rawalpindi, III. Lande of Bhera, Shahpur, IV. Lande of Gujrat, V. Multiplication Table, VI. Gujrati-Mahajani, VII. Dinga, Gujrat District.

Set No. 1

1 Names of letters of the Thakari Alphabet

نام حروف ٹھاکری علاقہ کانگڑہ

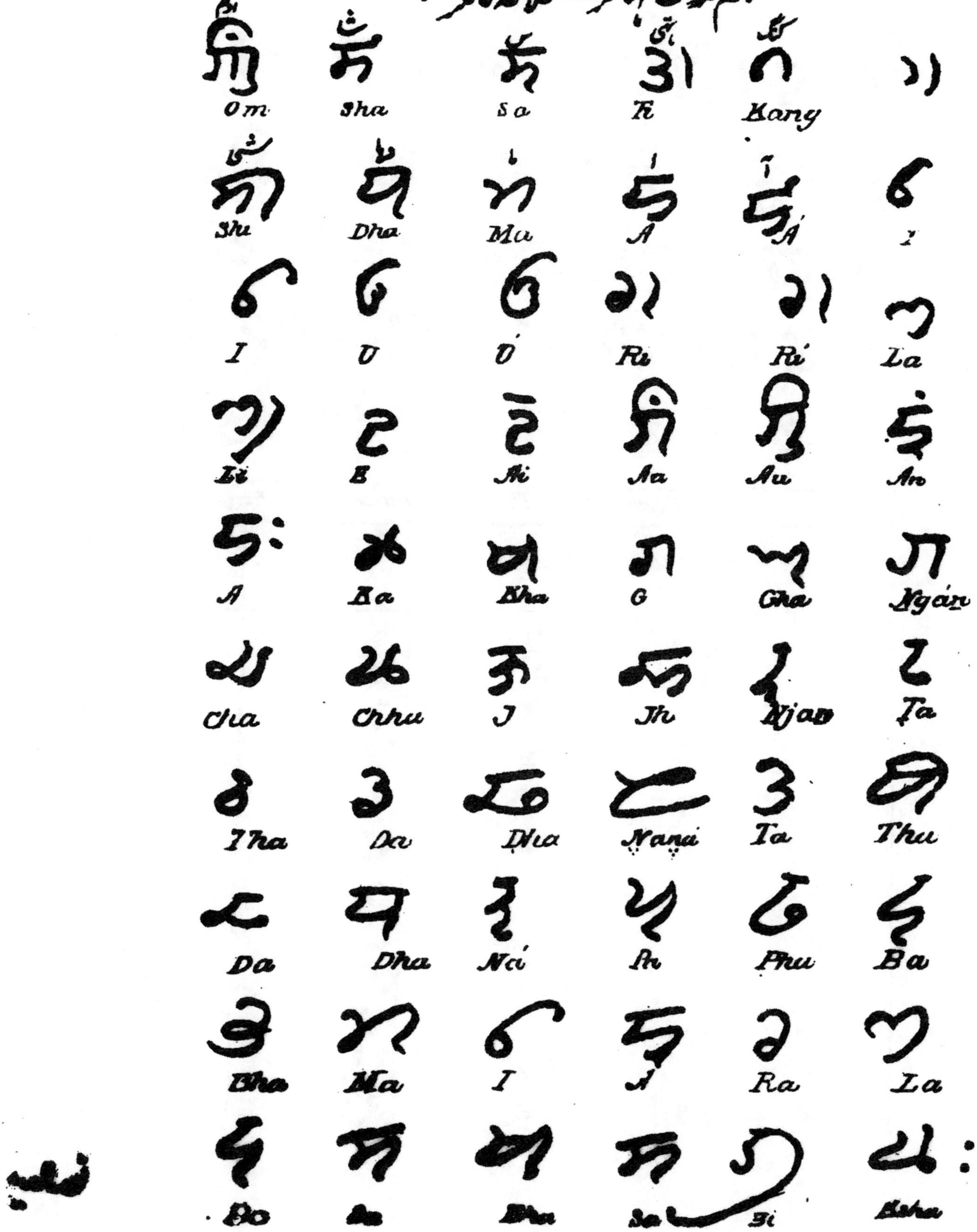

II. Thakari of Mandi

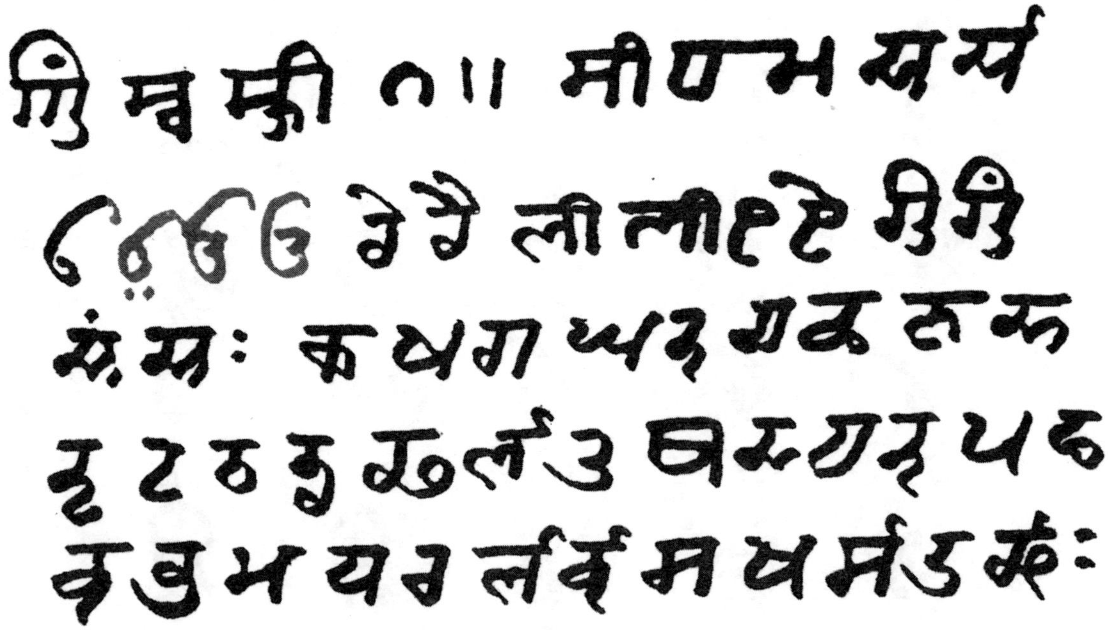

III Numerals of Thakari Lande and Nagri				
	Thakkari	Lande	Nagri	Arabia
1	𑛁	੧	१	١
2	𑛂	੨	२	٢
3	𑛃	੩	३	٣
4	𑛄	੪	४	٤
5	𑛅	੫	५	٥
6	𑛆	੬	६	٦
7	𑛇	੭	७	٧
8	𑛈	੮	८	٨
9	𑛉	੯	९	٩
10	𑛁𑛀	੧੦	१०	١٠
11	𑛁𑛁	੧੧	११	١١
12	𑛁𑛂	੧੨	१२	١٢

13	[illegible]	[illegible]	[illegible]	١٣
14	[illegible]	[illegible]	[illegible]	١٤
15	[illegible]	[illegible]	[illegible]	١٥
16	[illegible]	[illegible]	[illegible]	١٦
17	[illegible]	[illegible]	[illegible]	١٧
18	[illegible]	[illegible]	[illegible]	١٨
19	[illegible]	[illegible]	[illegible]	١٩
20	[illegible]	[illegible]	[illegible]	٢٠
21	[illegible]	[illegible]	[illegible]	٢١
30	[illegible]	[illegible]	[illegible]	٣٠
31	[illegible]	[illegible]	[illegible]	٣١
40	[illegible]	[illegible]	[illegible]	٤٠
50	[illegible]	[illegible]	[illegible]	٥٠
60	[illegible]	[illegible]	[illegible]	٦٠
70	[illegible]	[illegible]	[illegible]	٧٠
80	[illegible]	[illegible]	[illegible]	٨٠
90	[illegible]	[illegible]	[illegible]	٩٠
100	[illegible]	[illegible]	[illegible]	١٠٠
1000	[illegible]	[illegible]	[illegible]	١٠٠٠
1001	[illegible]	[illegible]	[illegible]	١٠٠١
1100	[illegible]	[illegible]	[illegible]	١١٠٠
10000	[illegible]	[illegible]	[illegible]	١٠٠٠٠

نوٹ:

IV. Alphabets of Nagri Gurmukhi

Sarah	Kaithi	Lande	Thakari	Gurmukhi	Nagri	Urdu
صراف	کائیتھی	لنڈے	ٹاکرے	گورمکھی	ناگری	فارسی

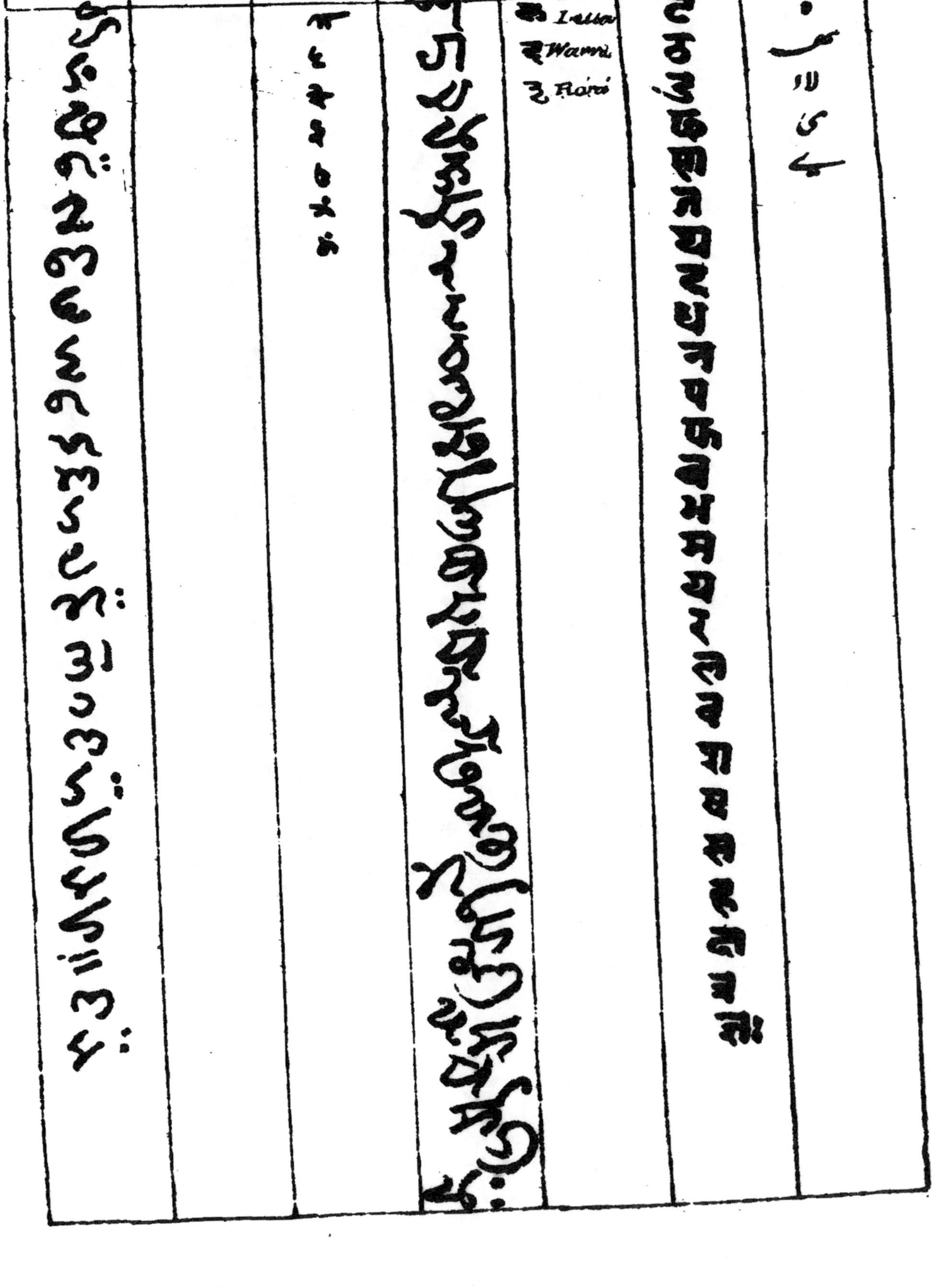

Thakari and sarrafi compound

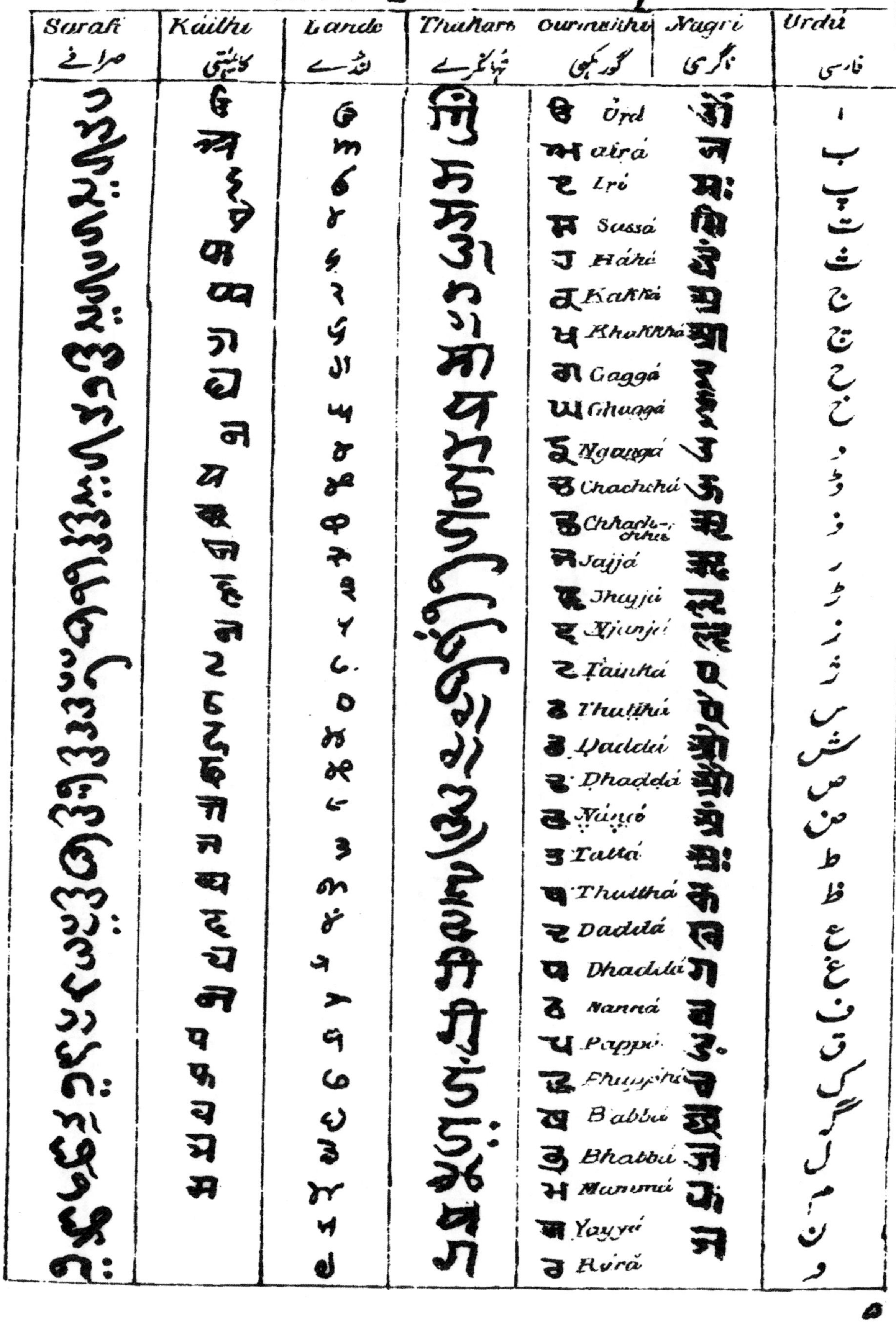

Set No. 2

Comparison of the alphabets of Nagri Gurumukhi with Differed kinds of Lande Sarafi & with Thakuri and Dogri

Roman equivalent	گورمکھی Gurmukhi	ناگری Nagri	Lande I	Lande II	Lande III	Kangra Lande	لنڈے پٹیالہ Patiala Lande	Lande Sarafi	صرافی دہلی Dehli Sarafi	فارسی Urdu equivalent letters	ٹاکری Takri	ڈوگرے Dogri	کراکی Karaki
u	ੳ ura	उ	[illegible]	[illegible]	[illegible]	[illegible]	[illegible]	[illegible]	[illegible]	و	[illegible]	[illegible]	
a	ਅ aira	अ	[illegible]	[illegible]	[illegible]	[illegible]	[illegible]	[illegible]	[illegible]	ا	[illegible]	[illegible]	
i	ੲ iri	इ=ए	[illegible]	[illegible]	[illegible]	[illegible]	[illegible]	[illegible]	[illegible]	ی	[illegible]	[illegible]	
s	ਸ sassa	स=श	[illegible]	[illegible]	[illegible]	[illegible]	[illegible]	[illegible]	[illegible]	س	[illegible]	[illegible]	
h	ਹ haha	ह	[illegible]	[illegible]	[illegible]	[illegible]	[illegible]	[illegible]	[illegible]	ح	[illegible]	[illegible]	
k	ਕ Kakka	क	[illegible]	[illegible]	[illegible]	[illegible]	[illegible]	[illegible]	[illegible]	ک	[illegible]	[illegible]	
kh	ਖ Khakkha	ष=ख	[illegible]	[illegible]	[illegible]	[illegible]	[illegible]	[illegible]	[illegible]	کھ	[illegible]	[illegible]	

g gagga
gh ghagha
ngaṅga
ch chachha
chh chhachhha
j jajja
jh jhaja
ñyañja
ṭ ṭainka

th thatthà
d dadda
th dhadda
ṇaṇa
t tatta
th thattha
d dadda
d dhadda
N nanna

p	ਪ	pappá	प	
ph	ਫ	phuppha	फ	
b	ਬ	babba	ब	
bh	ਭ	bhabba	भ	
m	ਮ	mamma	म	
y	ਯ	yayya	य	
r	ਰ	rara	र	
l	ਲ	lalla	ल	
w	ਵ	wawa	व	
ṛ	ੜ	ṛaṛa		

Set No 3

Comparison of different kinds of Lande with Kaithi Gurmukhi & Sanscrit

Numerals	نمبر Number	گورمکھی Gurmukhi	شاستری Lande I	صرافی Sarrafi	لنڈہ Lande I	لنڈہ دیگر Lande II	انڈہ دیگر Lande III	لنڈہ دیگر Lande IV	لنڈہ دیگر Lande V	کایتی Kaithi	رومن Roman Letters
1	੧	ੳ	उ	[illegible]	[illegible]	[illegible]	[illegible]	[illegible]	[illegible]	उ	u
2	੨	ਅ	अ	[illegible]	[illegible]	[illegible]	[illegible]	[illegible]	[illegible]	अ	a
3	੩	ੲ	इ	[illegible]	[illegible]	[illegible]	[illegible]	[illegible]	[illegible]	इ	i
4	੪	ਸ	स	[illegible]	[illegible]	[illegible]	[illegible]	[illegible]	[illegible]	स	s
5	੫	ਹ	ह	[illegible]	[illegible]	[illegible]	[illegible]	[illegible]	[illegible]	ह	h
6	੬	ਕ	क	[illegible]	[illegible]	[illegible]	[illegible]	[illegible]	[illegible]	क	k

عبداللہ

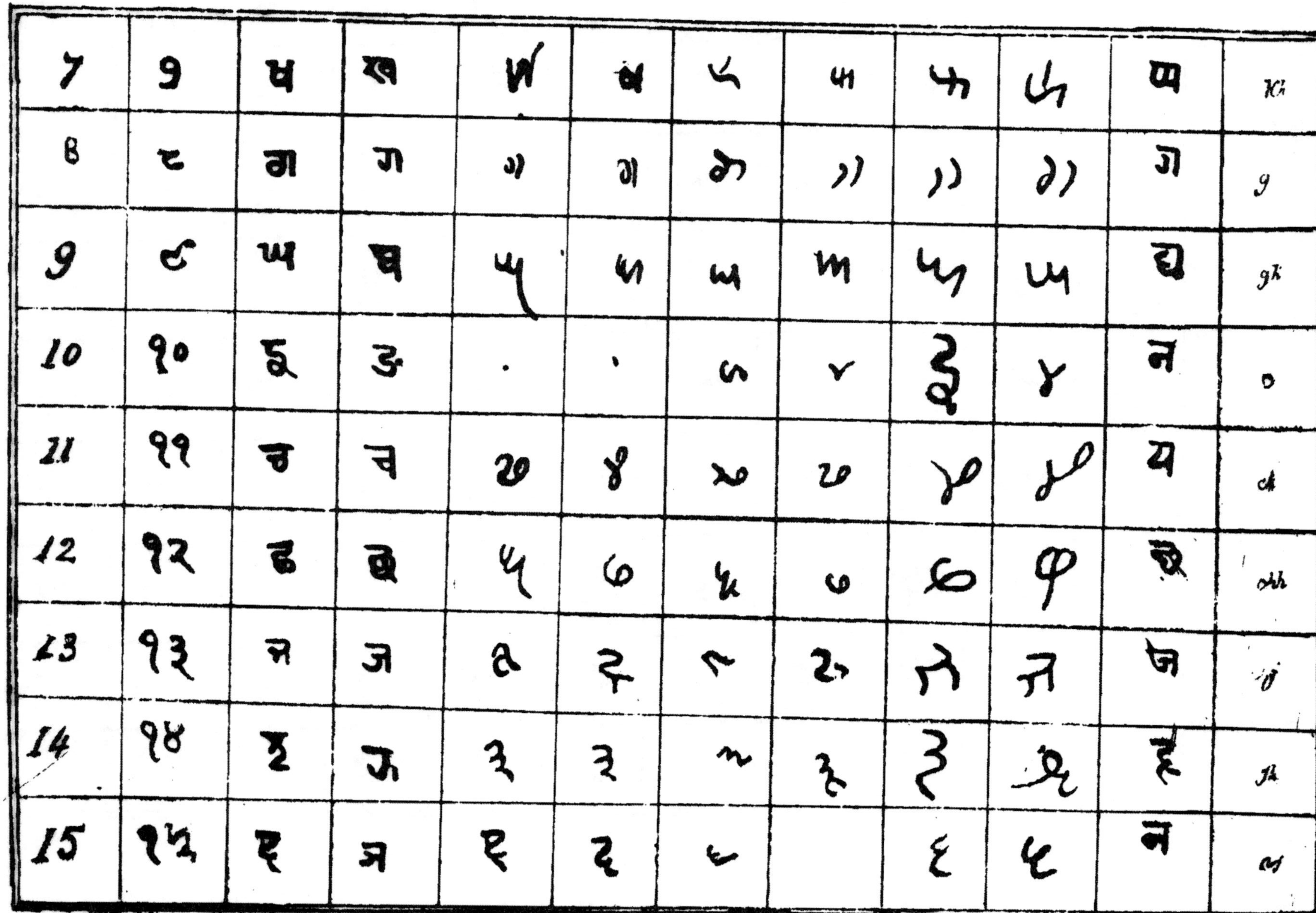

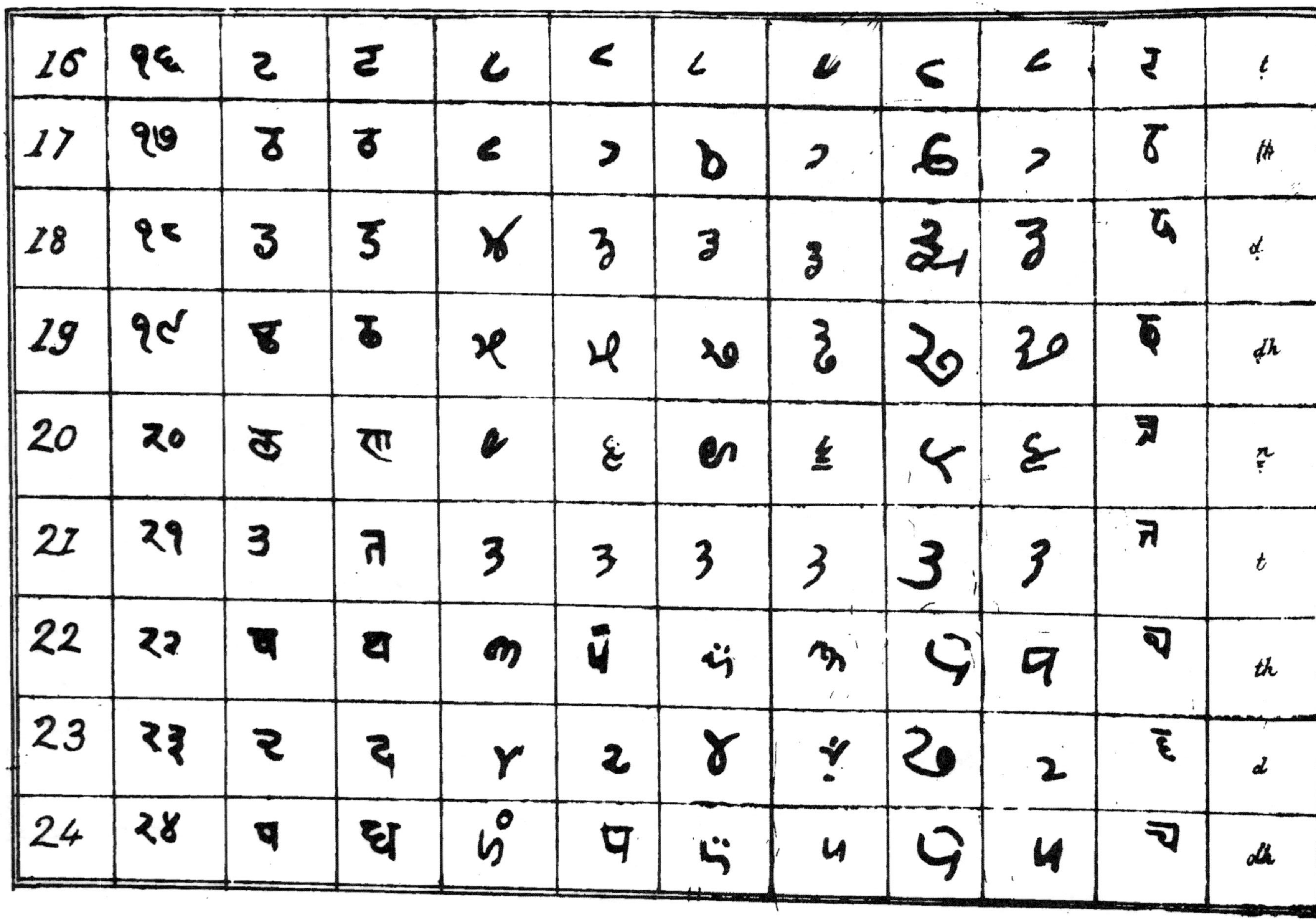
16 १६ t
17 १७ th
18 १८ d
19 १९ dh
20 २० n
21 २१ t
22 २२ th
23 २३ d
24 २४ dh

25	२५	ਨ	न	[illegible]	[illegible]	[illegible]	[illegible]	[illegible]	[illegible]	न	n
26	२६	ਪ	प	[illegible]	[illegible]	[illegible]	[illegible]	[illegible]	[illegible]	प	p
27	२७	ਫ	फ	[illegible]	[illegible]	[illegible]	[illegible]	[illegible]	[illegible]	फ	ph
28	२८	ਬ	ब	[illegible]	[illegible]	[illegible]	[illegible]	[illegible]	[illegible]	ब	b
29	२९	ਭ	भ	[illegible]	[illegible]	[illegible]	[illegible]	[illegible]	[illegible]	भ	bh
30	३०	ਮ	म	[illegible]	[illegible]	[illegible]	[illegible]	[illegible]	[illegible]	म	m
31	३१	ਯ	य	[illegible]	[illegible]	[illegible]	[illegible]	[illegible]	[illegible]	य़	y
32	३२	ਰ	र	[illegible]	[illegible]	[illegible]	[illegible]	[illegible]	[illegible]	र	r
33	३३	ਲ	ल	[illegible]	[illegible]	[illegible]	[illegible]	[illegible]	[illegible]	ल	l
34	३४	ਵ	व	[illegible]	[illegible]	[illegible]	[illegible]	[illegible]	[illegible]	व़	w
35	३५	ੜ	ड़	[illegible]	[illegible]	[illegible]	[illegible]	[illegible]	[illegible]		ṛ

Set No. 4

I Table of Interest

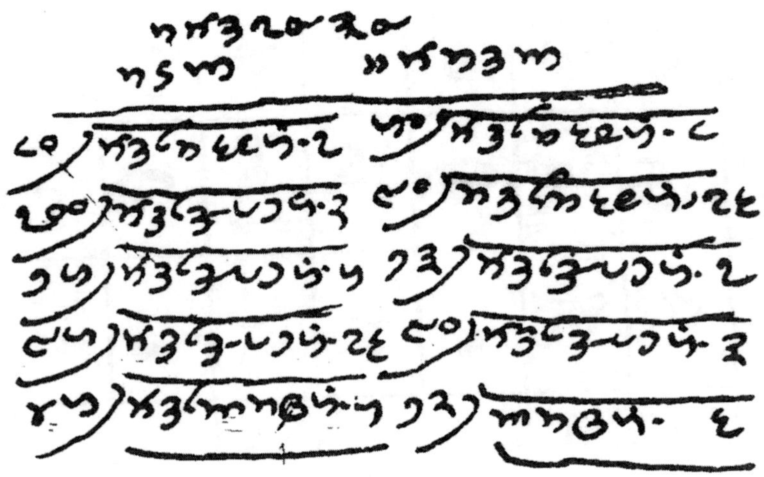

II Pahara or Multiplication Table of Rawalpindi

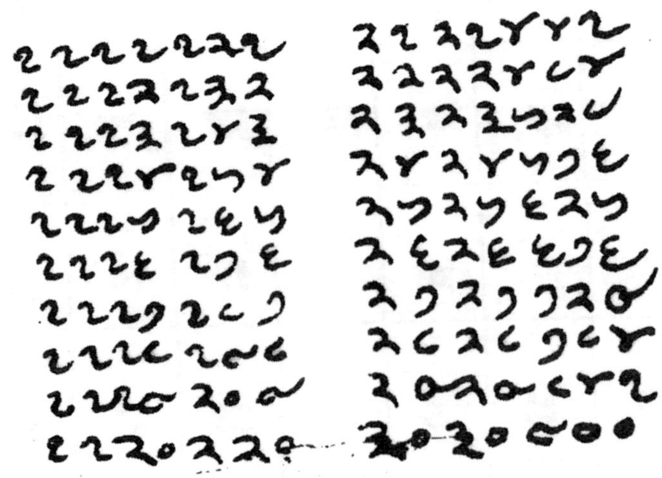

III Letter in the Rawalpindi Mahajani (?) character called the Local Panjabi characters

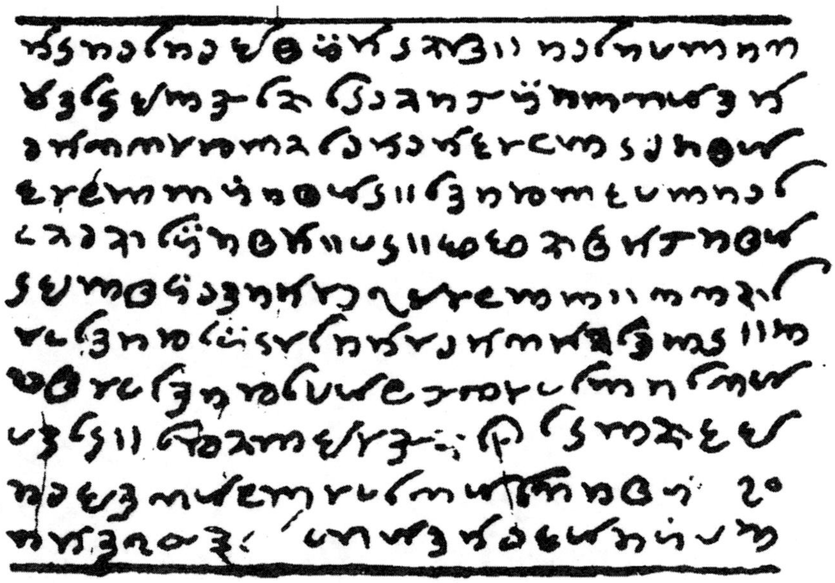

IV Table of Land Measurement

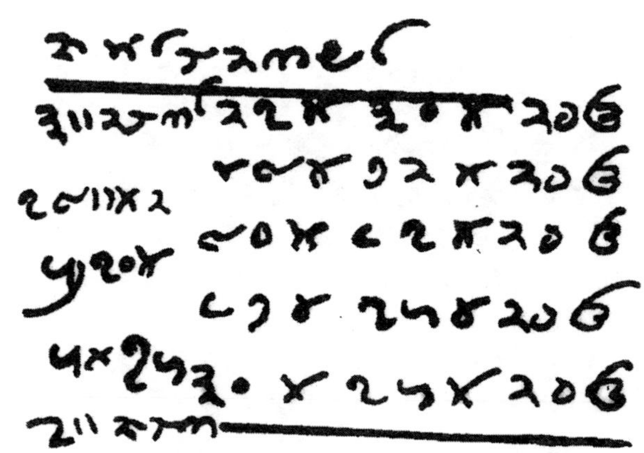

عبدالرحمٰن

V A letter in the Ráwalpindi Bániyá character

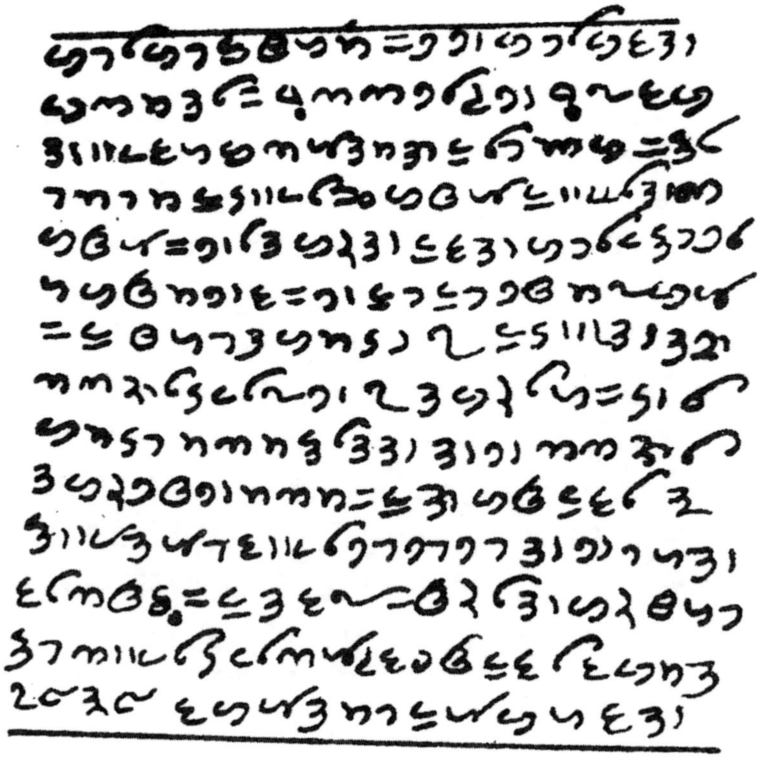

VI Specimen of a Hundi

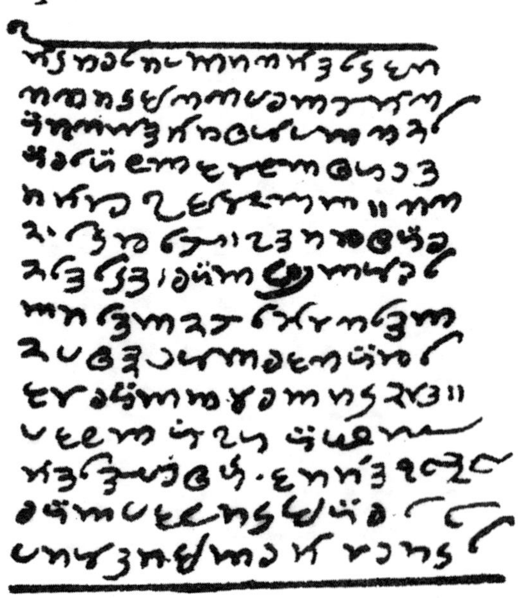

عبدالرحمٰن

VII Multiplication by 1, 1¼, 1½, 2½, 3½, 4½

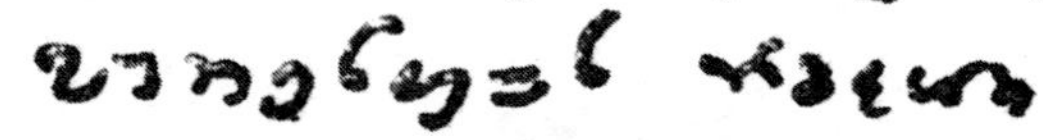

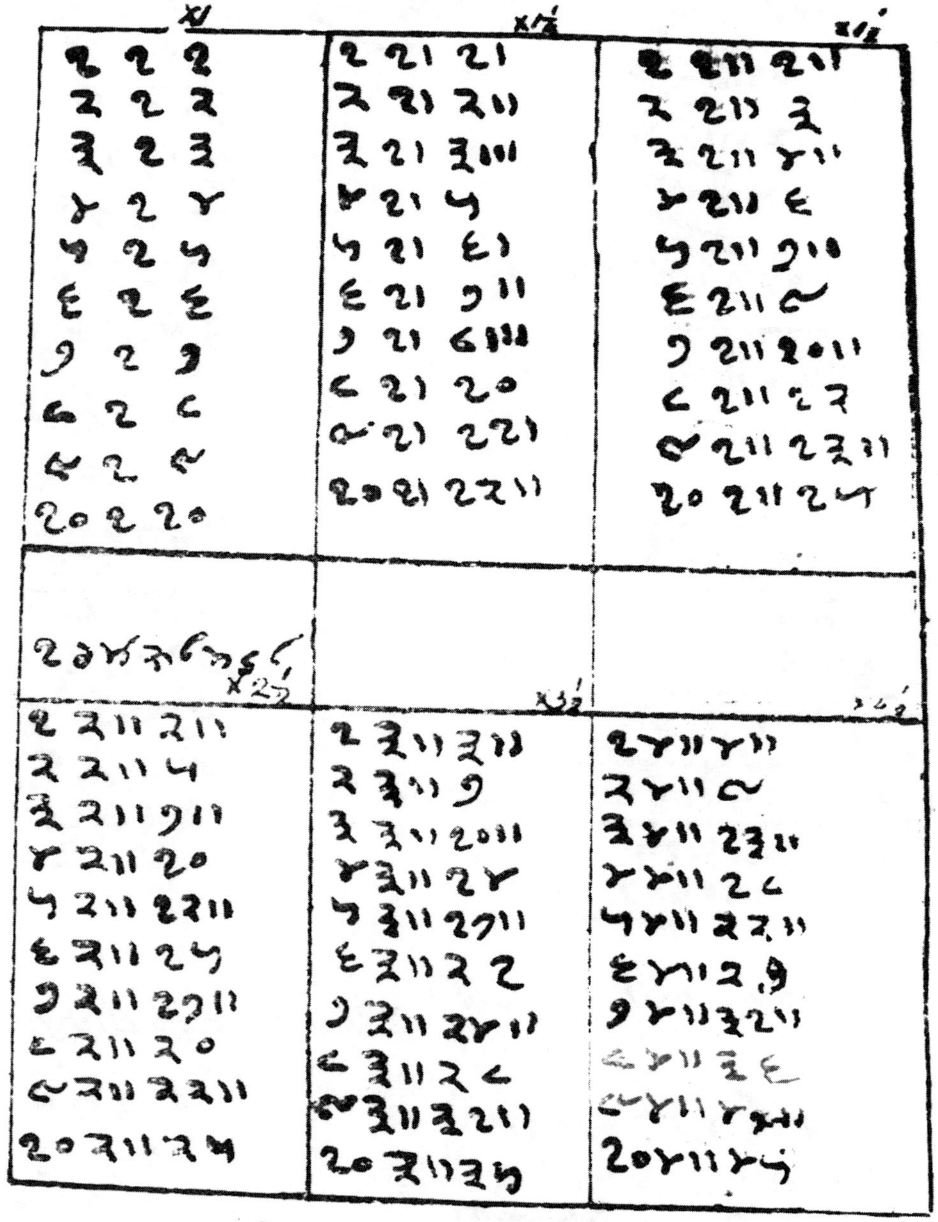

VIII . Rate Table

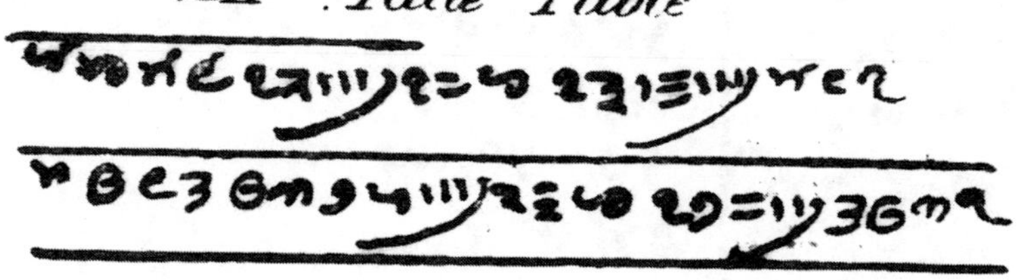

XII Addition

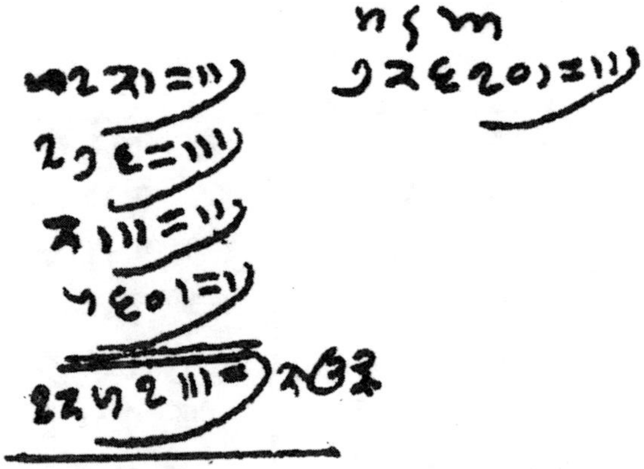

XV Banya letters

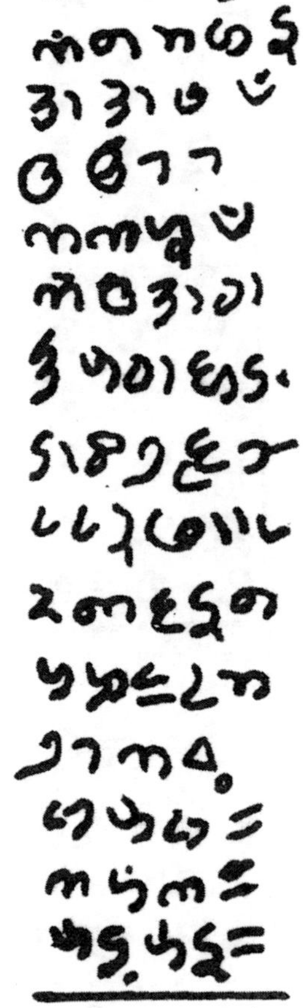

XIII Multiplication

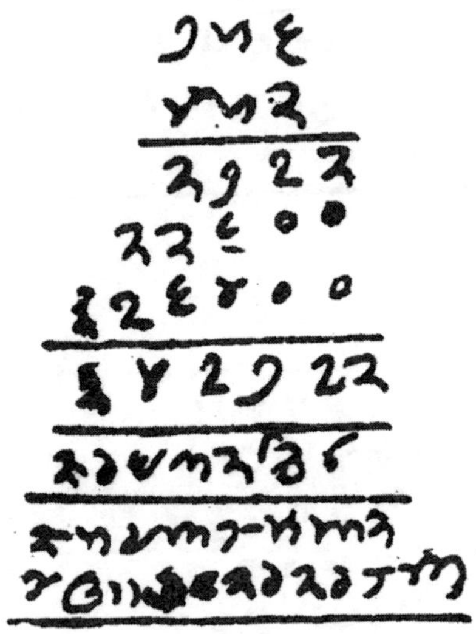

XIV Letters in local Panjabi

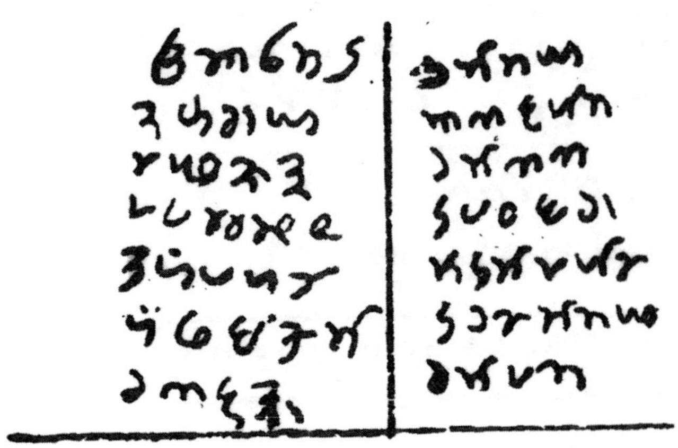

XVI Names in Banya letters

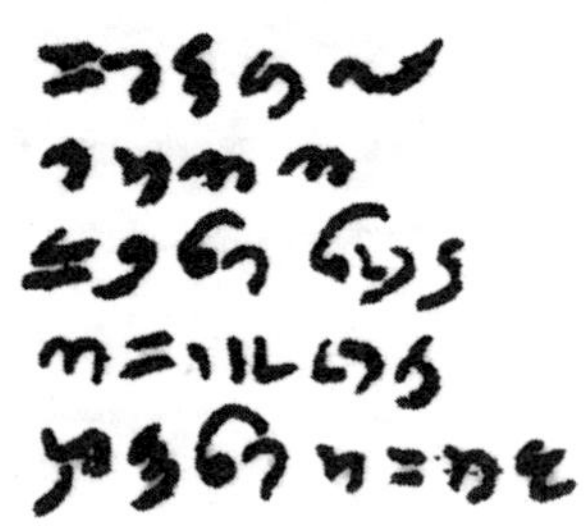

IX Fractional Multiplication Table

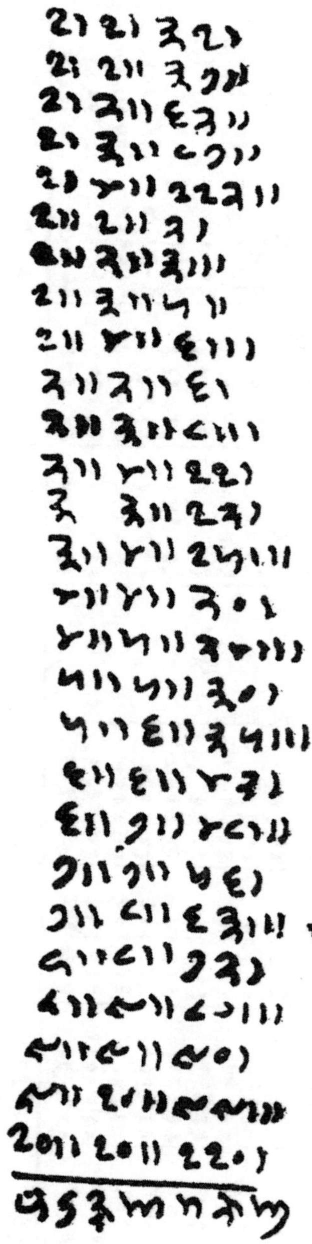

X Subtraction

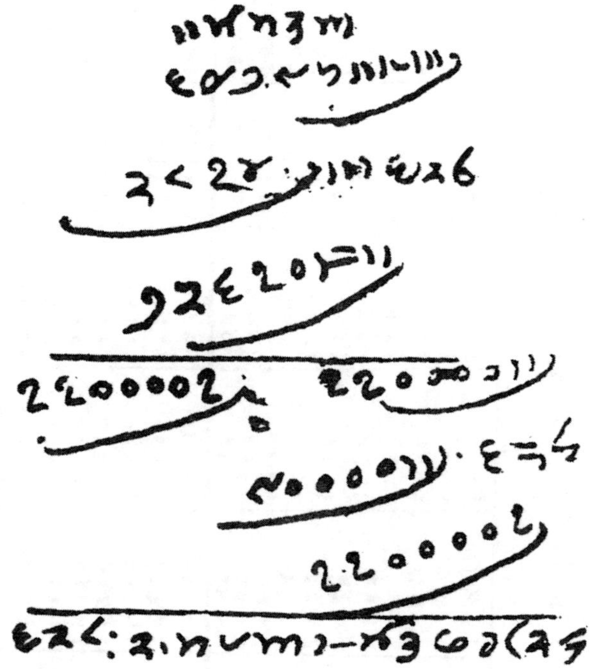

XI Division

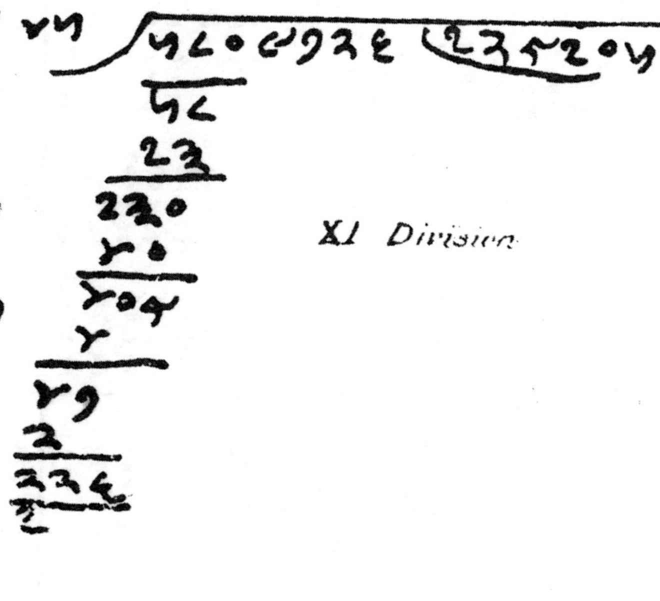

V *Multiplication Table Mithu Tiwana District Shahpur from 1 to 40*

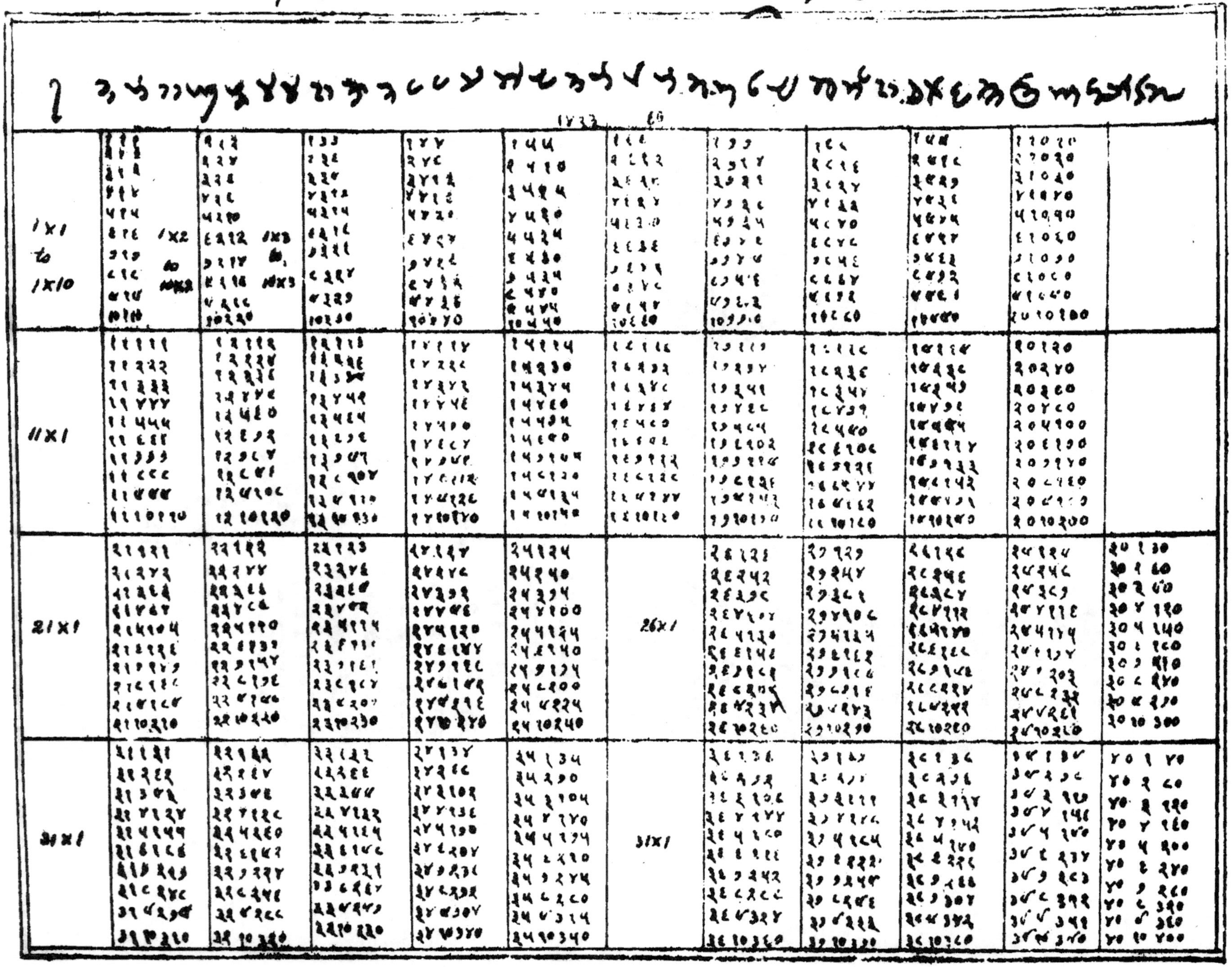

Fractional Multiplication Table

१	१।	१।	११	१।	१३॥।	२१	१।	२६।	३१	१।	३८॥।	४१	१।	५१।
२	१।	२॥	१२	१।	१५	२२	१।	२७॥	३२	१।	४०	४२	१।	५२॥
३	१।	३॥।	१३	१।	१६।	२३	१।	२८॥।	३३	१।	४१।	४३	१।	५३॥।
४	१।	५	१४	१।	१७॥	२४	१।	३०	३४	१।	४२॥	४४	१।	५५
५	१।	६।	१५	१।	१८॥।	२५	१।	३१।	३५	१।	४३॥।	४५	१।	५६।
६	१।	७॥	१६	१।	२०	२६	१।	३२॥	३६	१।	४५	४६	१।	५७॥
७	१।	८॥।	१७	१।	२१।	२७	१।	३३॥।	३७	१।	४६।	४७	१।	५८॥।
८	१।	१०	१८	१।	२२॥	२८	१।	३५	३८	१।	४७॥	४८	१।	६०
९	१।	११।	१९	१।	२३॥।	२९	१।	३६।	३९	१।	४८॥।	४९	१।	६१।
१०	१।	१२॥	२०	१।	२५	३०	१।	३७॥	४०	१।	५०	५०	१।	६२॥

५१	१।	६३॥।	६१	१।	७६।	७१	१।	८८॥।	८१	१।	१०१।	९१	१।	११३॥।
५२	१।	६५	६२	१।	७७॥	७२	१।	९०	८२	१।	१०२॥	९२	१।	११५
५३	१।	६६।	६३	१।	७८॥।	७३	१।	९१।	८३	१।	१०३॥।	९३	१।	११६।
५४	१।	६७॥	६४	१।	८०	७४	१।	९२॥	८४	१।	१०५	९४	१।	११७॥
५५	१।	६८॥।	६५	१।	८१।	७५	१।	९३॥।	८५	१।	१०६।	९५	१।	११८॥।
५६	१।	७०	६६	१।	८२॥	७६	१।	९५	८६	१।	१०७॥	९६	१।	१२०
५७	१।	७१।	६७	१।	८३॥।	७७	१।	९६।	८७	१।	१०८॥।	९७	१।	१२१।
५८	१।	७२॥	६८	१।	८५	७८	१।	९७॥	८८	१।	११०	९८	१।	१२२॥
५९	१।	७३॥।	६९	१।	८६।	७९	१।	९८॥।	८९	१।	१११।	९९	१।	१२३॥।
६०	१।	७५	७०	१।	८७॥	८०	१।	१००	९०	१।	११२॥	१००	१।	१२५

१	१॥	१॥	११	१॥	१६॥	२१	१॥	३१॥	३१	१॥	४६॥	४१	१॥	६१॥
२	१॥	३	१२	१॥	१८	२२	१॥	३३	३२	१॥	४८	४२	१॥	६३
३	१॥	४॥	१३	१॥	१९॥	२३	१॥	३४॥	३३	१॥	४९॥	४३	१॥	६४॥
४	१॥	६	१४	१॥	२१	२४	१॥	३६	३४	१॥	५१	४४	१॥	६६
५	१॥	७॥	१५	१॥	२२॥	२५	१॥	३७॥	३५	१॥	५२॥	४५	१॥	६७॥
६	१॥	९	१६	१॥	२४	२६	१॥	३९	३६	१॥	५४	४६	१॥	६९
७	१॥	१०॥	१७	१॥	२५॥	२७	१॥	४०॥	३७	१॥	५५॥	४७	१॥	७०॥
८	१॥	१२	१८	१॥	२७	२८	१॥	४२	३८	१॥	५७	४८	१॥	७२
९	१॥	१३॥	१९	१॥	२८॥	२९	१॥	४३॥	३९	१॥	५८॥	४९	१॥	७३॥
१०	१॥	१५	२०	१॥	३०	३०	१॥	४५	४०	१॥	६०	५०	१॥	७५

५१	१॥	७६॥	६१	१॥	९१॥	७१	१॥	१०६॥	८१	१॥	१२१॥	९१	१॥	१३६॥
५२	१॥	७८	६२	१॥	९३	७२	१॥	१०८	८२	१॥	१२३	९२	१॥	१३८
५३	१॥	७९॥	६३	१॥	९४॥	७३	१॥	१०९॥	८३	१॥	१२४॥	९३	१॥	१३९॥
५४	१॥	८१	६४	१॥	९६	७४	१॥	१११	८४	१॥	१२६	९४	१॥	१४१
५५	१॥	८२॥	६५	१॥	९७॥	७५	१॥	११२॥	८५	१॥	१२७॥	९५	१॥	१४२॥
५६	१॥	८४	६६	१॥	९९	७६	१॥	११४	८६	१॥	१२९	९६	१॥	१४४
५७	१॥	८५॥	६७	१॥	१००॥	७७	१॥	११५॥	८७	१॥	१३०॥	९७	१॥	१४५॥
५८	१॥	८७	६८	१॥	१०२	७८	१॥	११७	८८	१॥	१३२	९८	१॥	१४७
५९	१॥	८८॥	६९	१॥	१०३॥	७९	१॥	११८॥	८९	१॥	१३३॥	९९	१॥	१४८॥
६०	१॥	९०	७०	१॥	१०५	८०	१॥	१२०	९०	१॥	१३५	१००	१॥	१५०

१	२॥	२॥	११	२॥	२७॥	२१	२॥	५२॥	३१	२॥	७७॥	४१	२॥	१०२॥
२	२॥	५	१२	२॥	३०	२२	२॥	५५	३२	२॥	८०	४२	२॥	१०५
३	२॥	७॥	१३	२॥	३२॥	२३	२॥	५७॥	३३	२॥	८२॥	४३	२॥	१०७॥
४	२॥	१०	१४	२॥	३५	२४	२॥	६०	३४	२॥	८५	४४	२॥	११०
५	२॥	१२॥	१५	२॥	३७॥	२५	२॥	६२॥	३५	२॥	८७॥	४५	२॥	११२॥
६	२॥	१५	१६	२॥	४०	२६	२॥	६५	३६	२॥	९०	४६	२॥	११५
७	२॥	१७॥	१७	२॥	४२॥	२७	२॥	६७॥	३७	२॥	९२॥	४७	२॥	११७॥
८	२॥	२०	१८	२॥	४५	२८	२॥	७०	३८	२॥	९५	४८	२॥	१२०
९	२॥	२२॥	१९	२॥	४७॥	२९	२॥	७२॥	३९	२॥	९७॥	४९	२॥	१२२॥
१०	२॥	२५	२०	२॥	५०	३०	२॥	७५	४०	२॥	१००	५०	२॥	१२५

५१	२॥	१२७॥	६१	२॥	१५२॥	७१	२॥	१७७॥	८१	२॥	२०२॥	९१	२॥	२२७॥
५२	२॥	१३०	६२	२॥	१५५	७२	२॥	१८०	८२	२॥	२०५	९२	२॥	२३०
५३	२॥	१३२॥	६३	२॥	१५७॥	७३	२॥	१८२॥	८३	२॥	२०७॥	९३	२॥	२३२॥
५४	२॥	१३५	६४	२॥	१६०	७४	२॥	१८५	८४	२॥	२१०	९४	२॥	२३५
५५	२॥	१३७॥	६५	२॥	१६२॥	७५	२॥	१८७॥	८५	२॥	२१२॥	९५	२॥	२३७॥
५६	२॥	१४०	६६	२॥	१६५	७६	२॥	१९०	८६	२॥	२१५	९६	२॥	२४०
५७	२॥	१४२॥	६७	२॥	१६७॥	७७	२॥	१९२॥	८७	२॥	२१७॥	९७	२॥	२४२॥
५८	२॥	१४५	६८	२॥	१७०	७८	२॥	१९५	८८	२॥	२२०	९८	२॥	२४५
५९	२॥	१४७॥	६९	२॥	१७२॥	७९	२॥	१९७॥	८९	२॥	२२२॥	९९	२॥	२४७॥
६०	२॥	१५०	७०	२॥	१७५	८०	२॥	२००	९०	२॥	२२५	१००	२॥	२५०

Arowrah Lande
Used in Sind

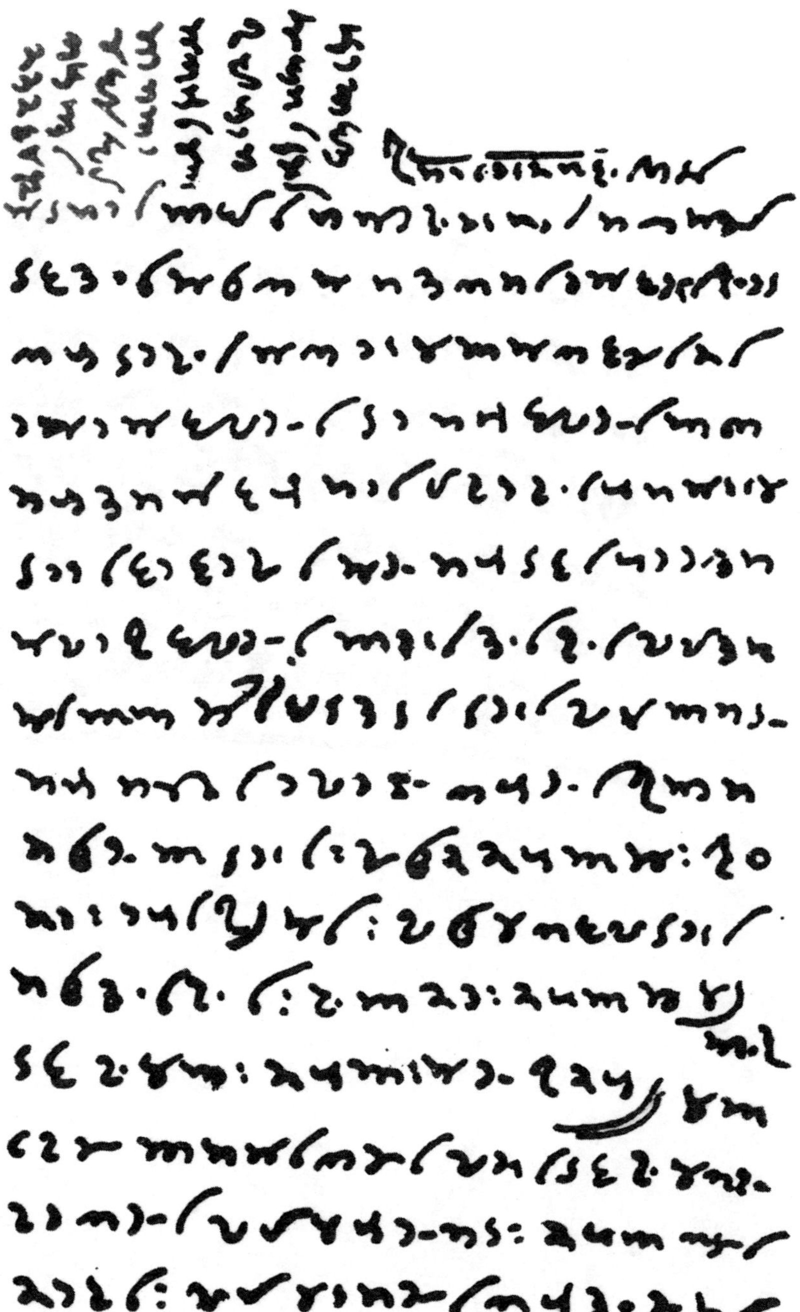

(2)

Baniah Lande

Used in the Districts of Sirsa, Hissar &c.

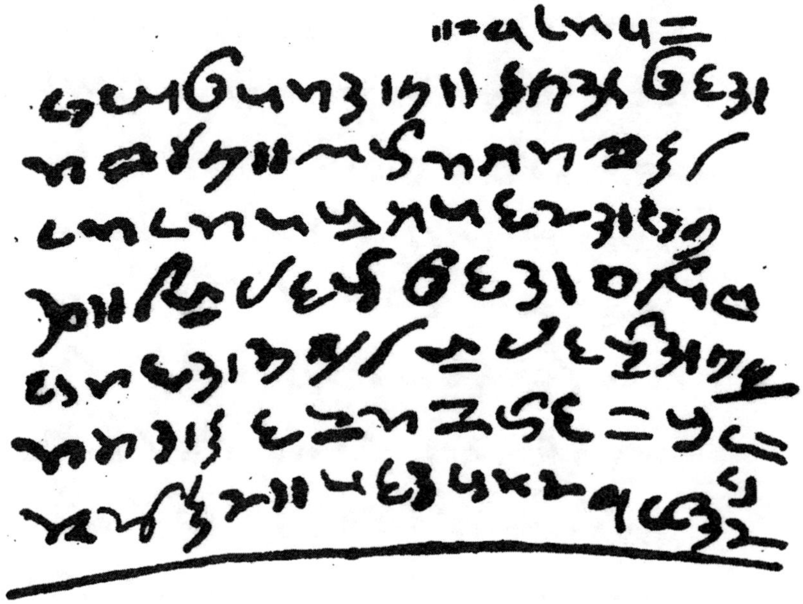

Bahawalpuri

Used in Bahawalpur

(This seems to be Sarrafi)

(4)

Bisati Lande
Used by Mahomedan marchants in the
North Western Provinces.

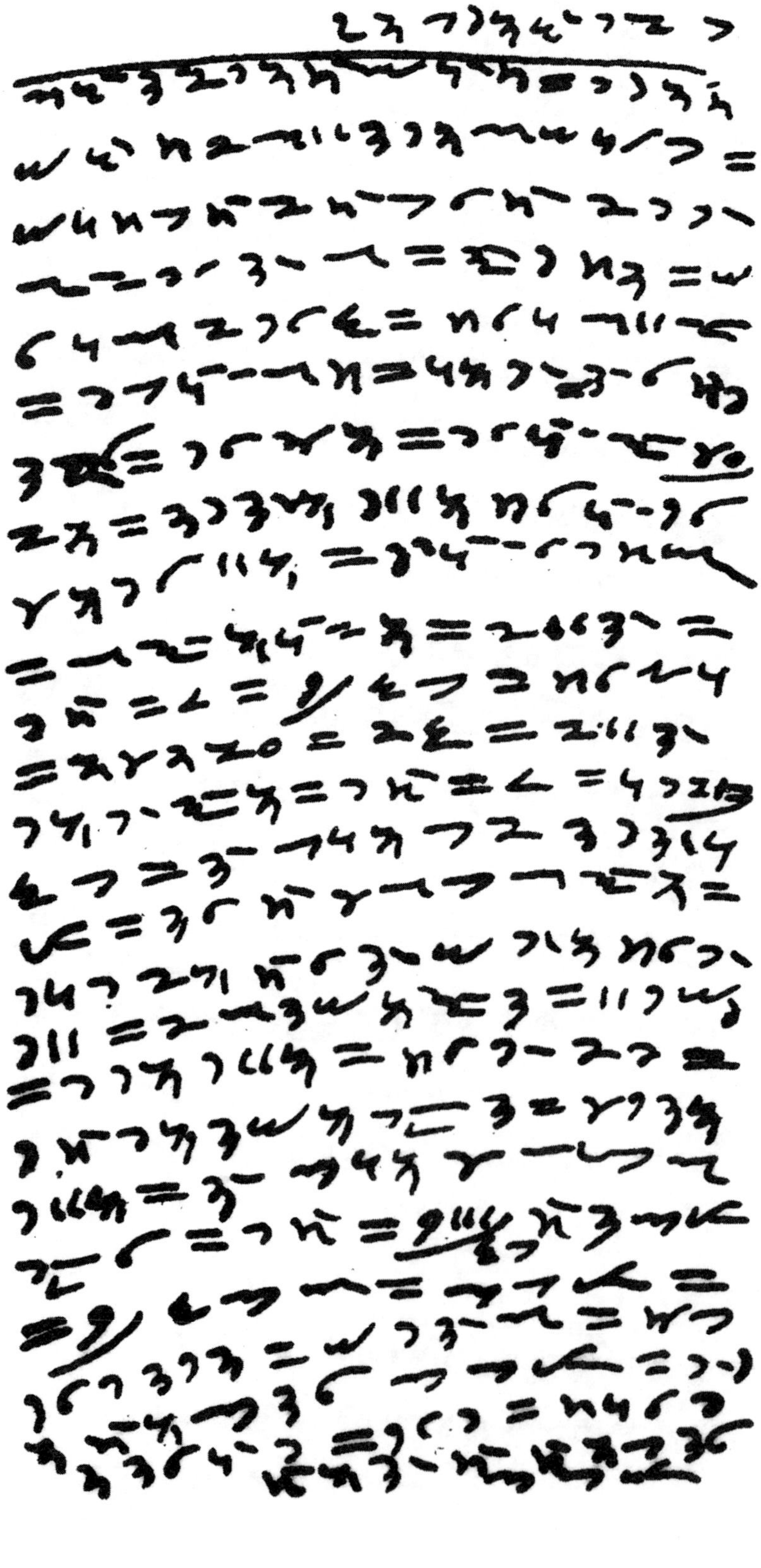

Kaithi

Used by partly educated Hindoos in Oudh the N. W. P. and upper Bengal.

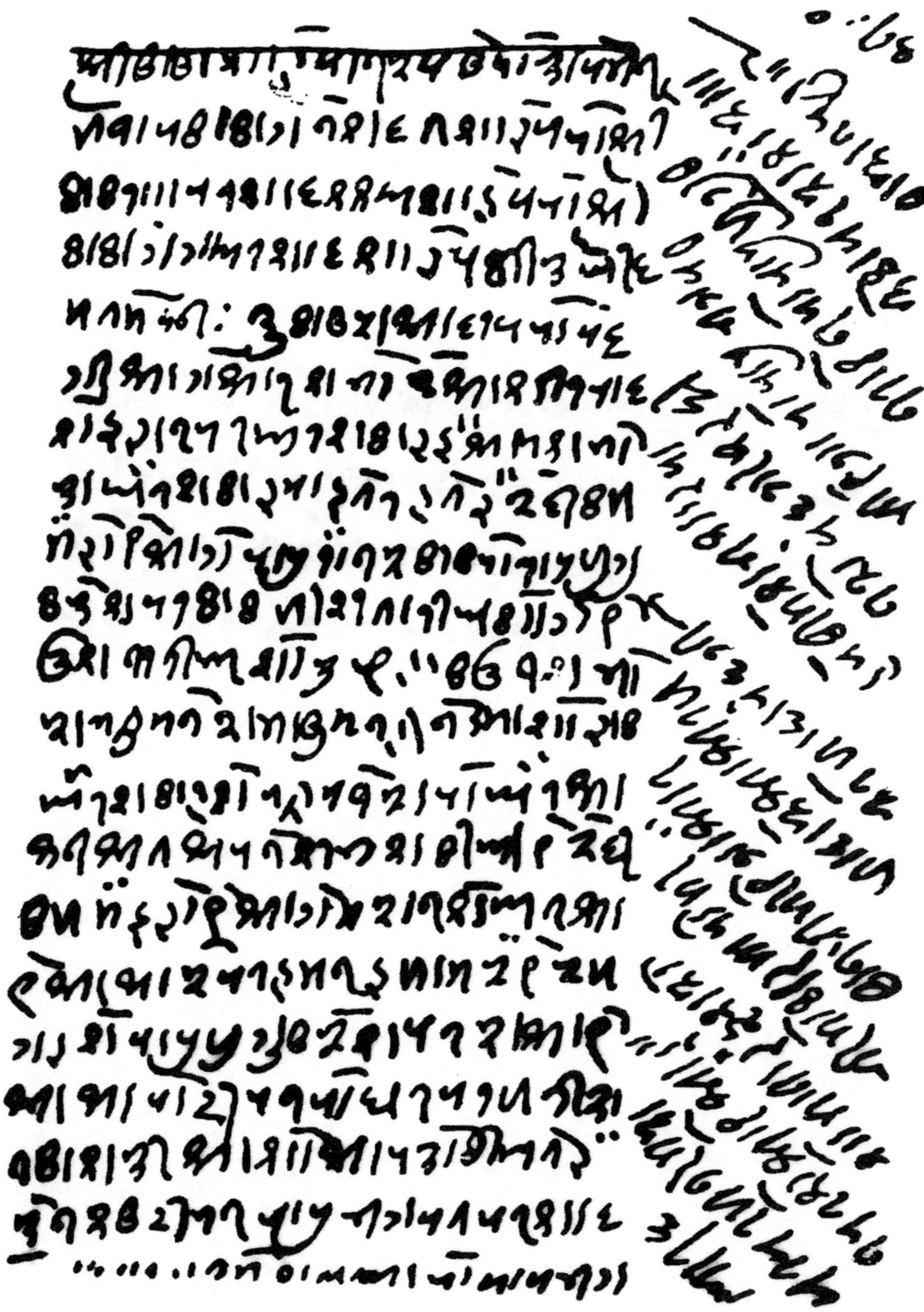

(6)

Karadi Lande
Used by Banyahs in Sind

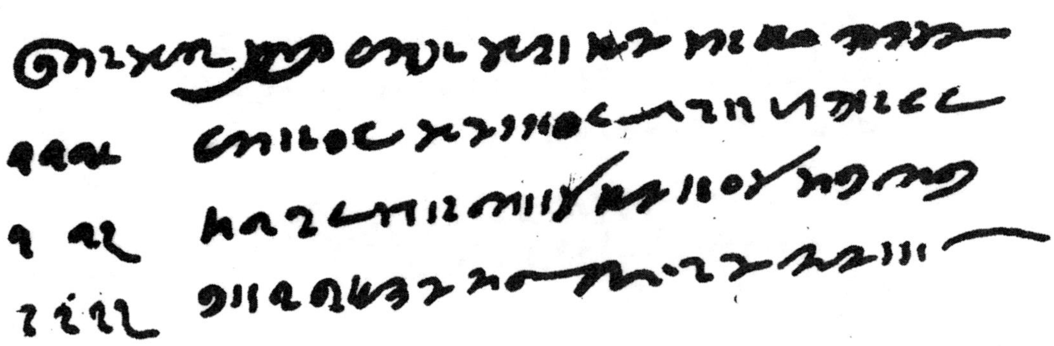

Khaja Lande

Used by Eunuchs in the service of Native States.

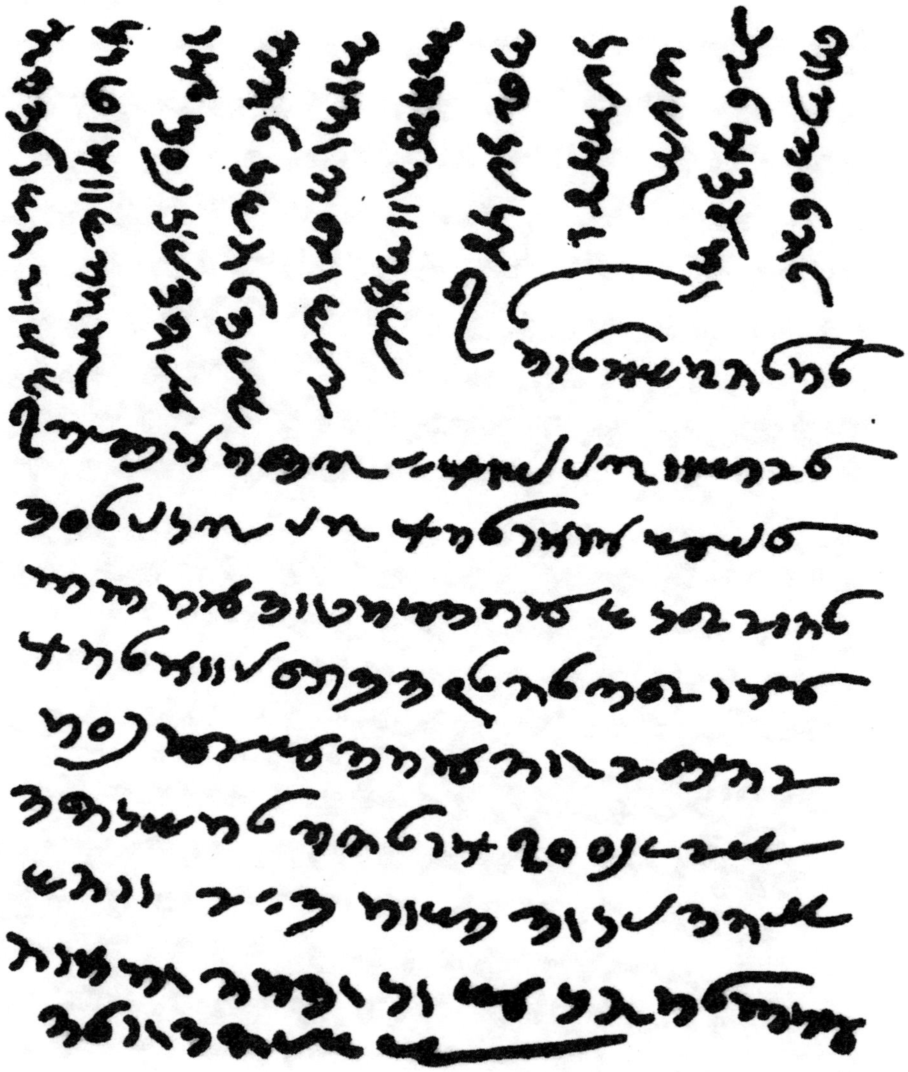

(8)

Lamawasi Lunde

Used in Pindi, Bhulian, Chunian, &c

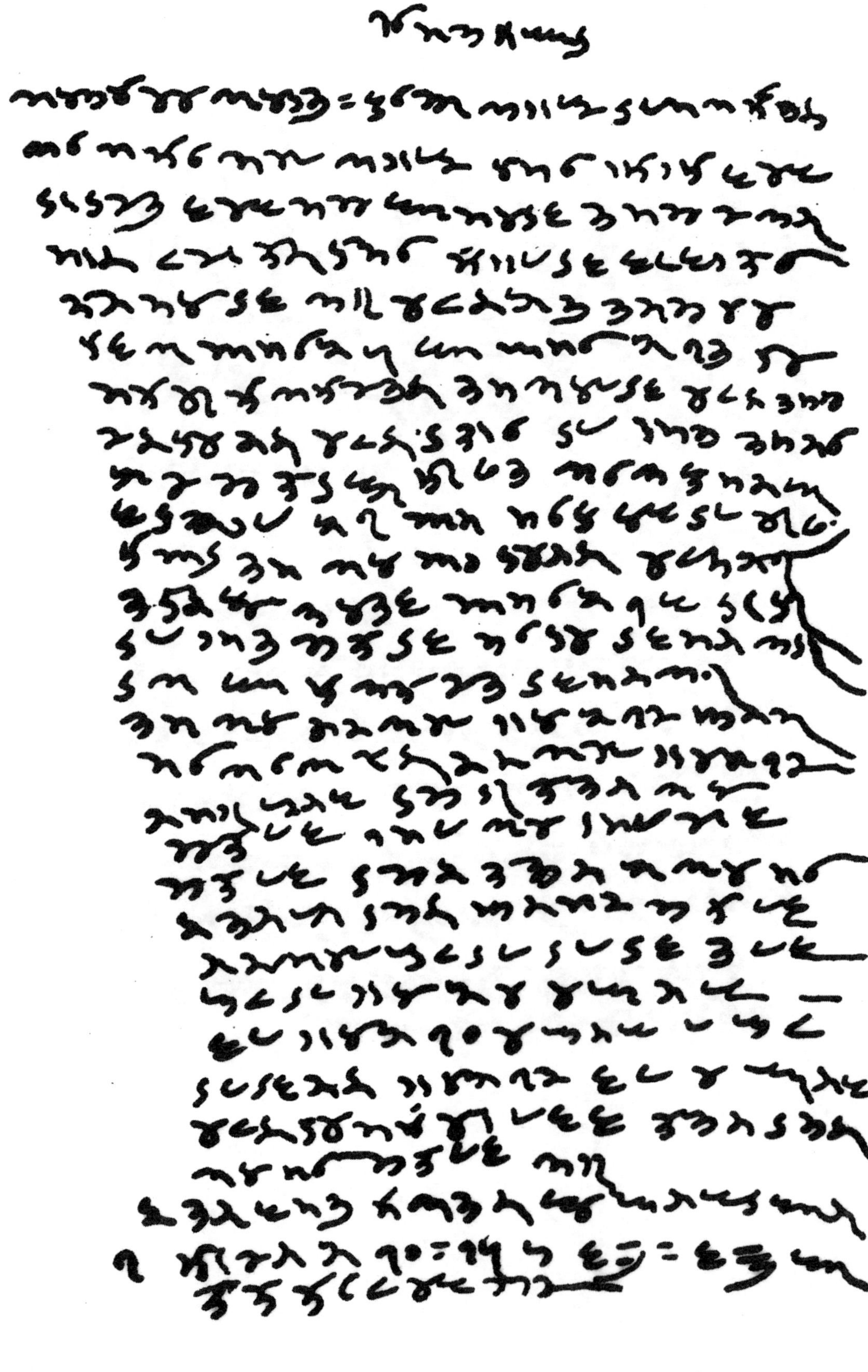

Lundas

Used in Sealkote Wazirabad &c.

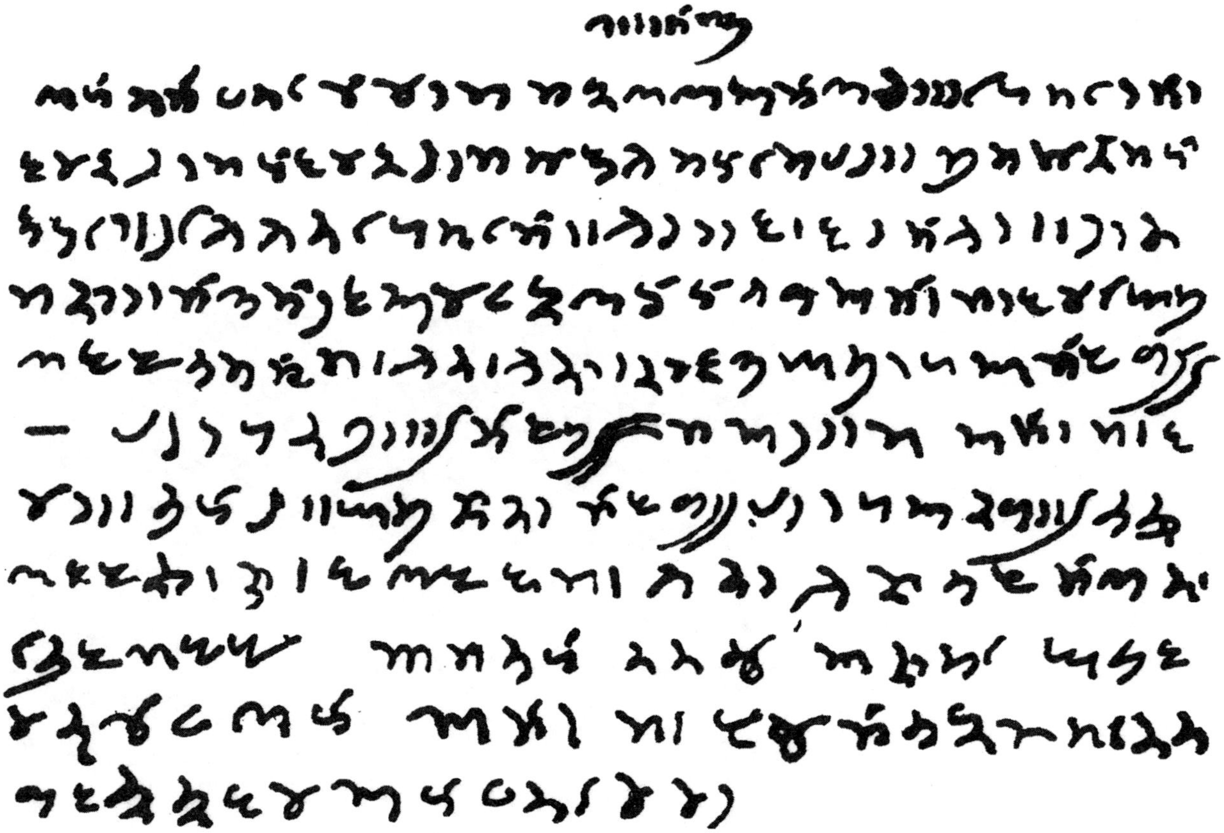

Marwari

Used in Rájputáná by Marwaries and by the trading class generally

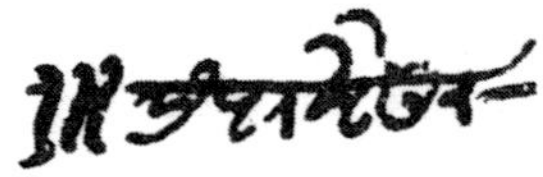

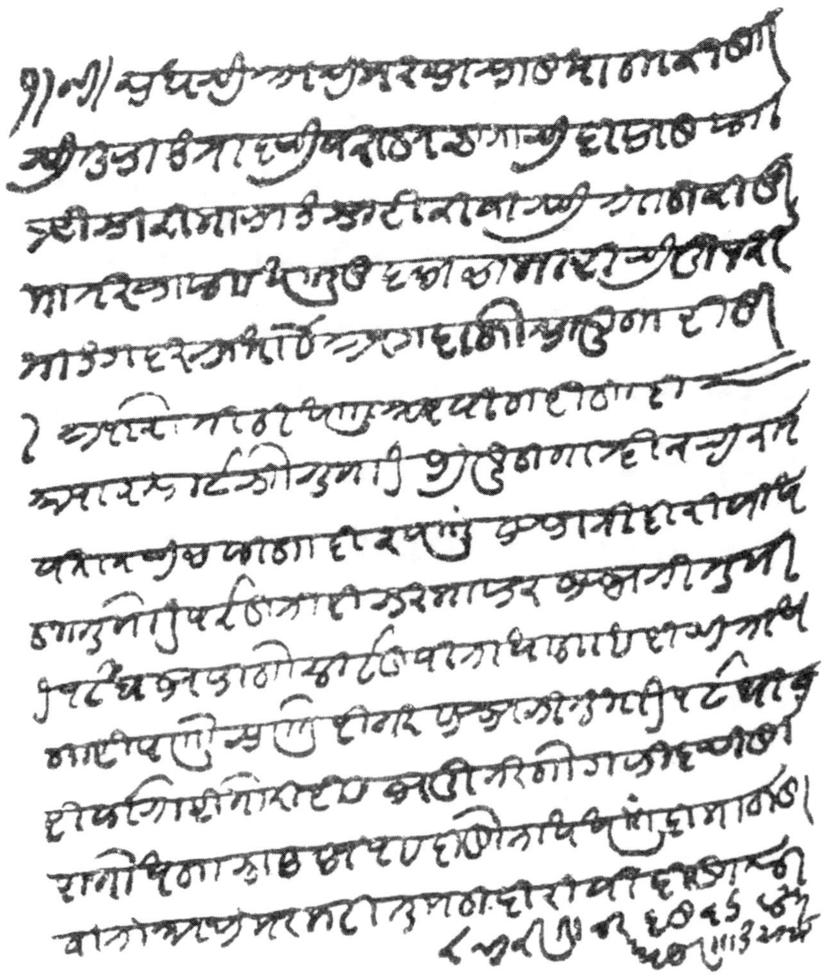

Márwári mixed with saráfi

Used in Ajmere Jeypore.

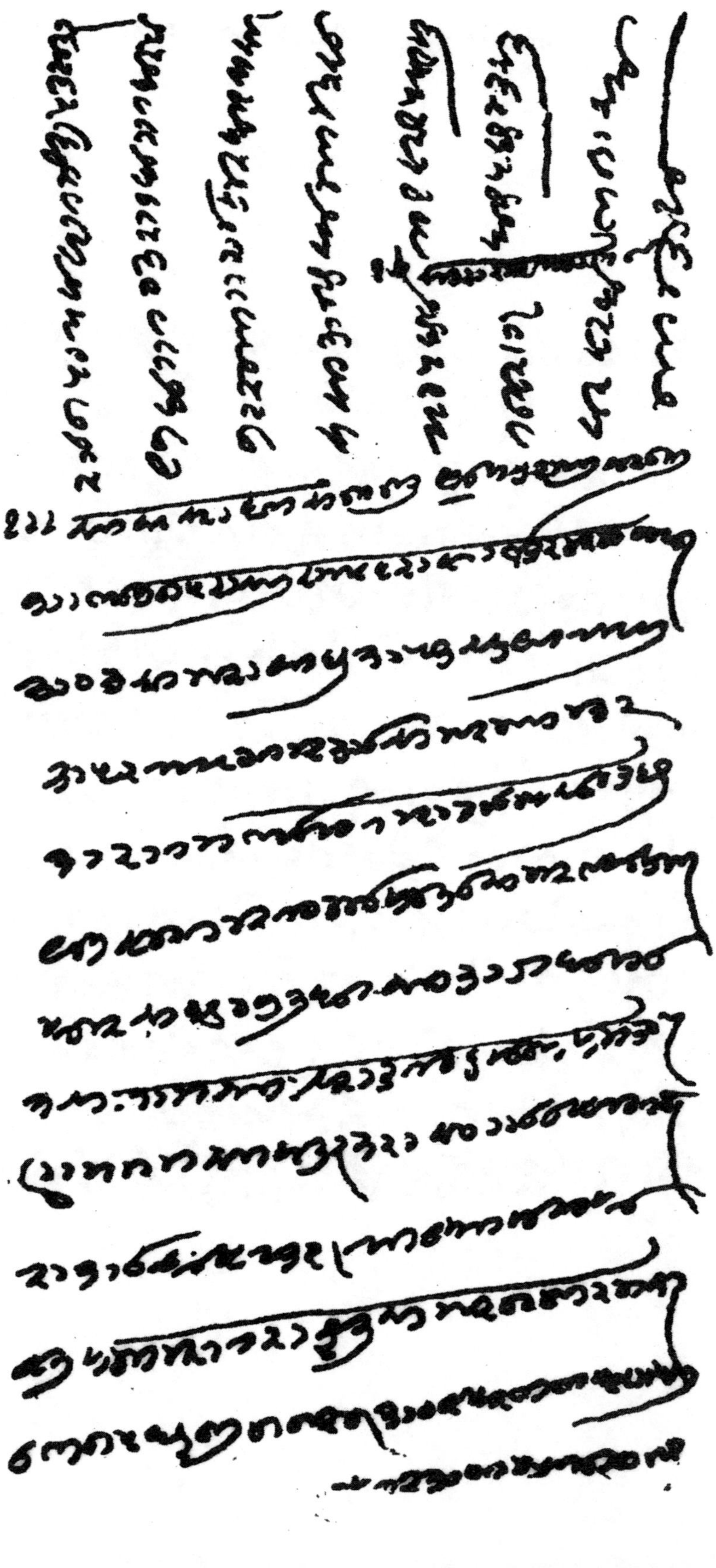

Blai

Mudia lande

Used in Oudh and Towns in the North Western Provinces below Allahabad and u. Garhwal

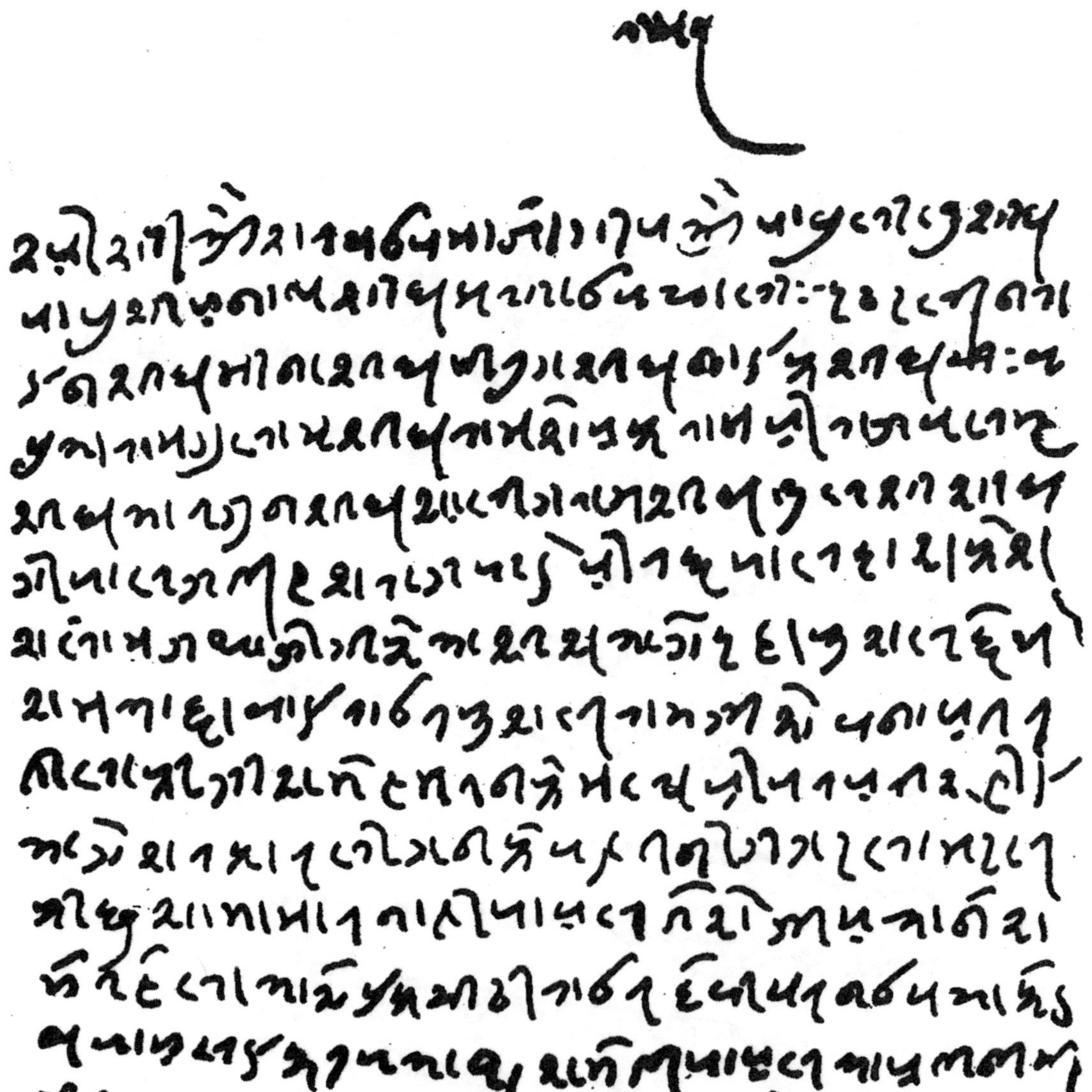

Multani Lande

Used in Multán and adjoining Towns

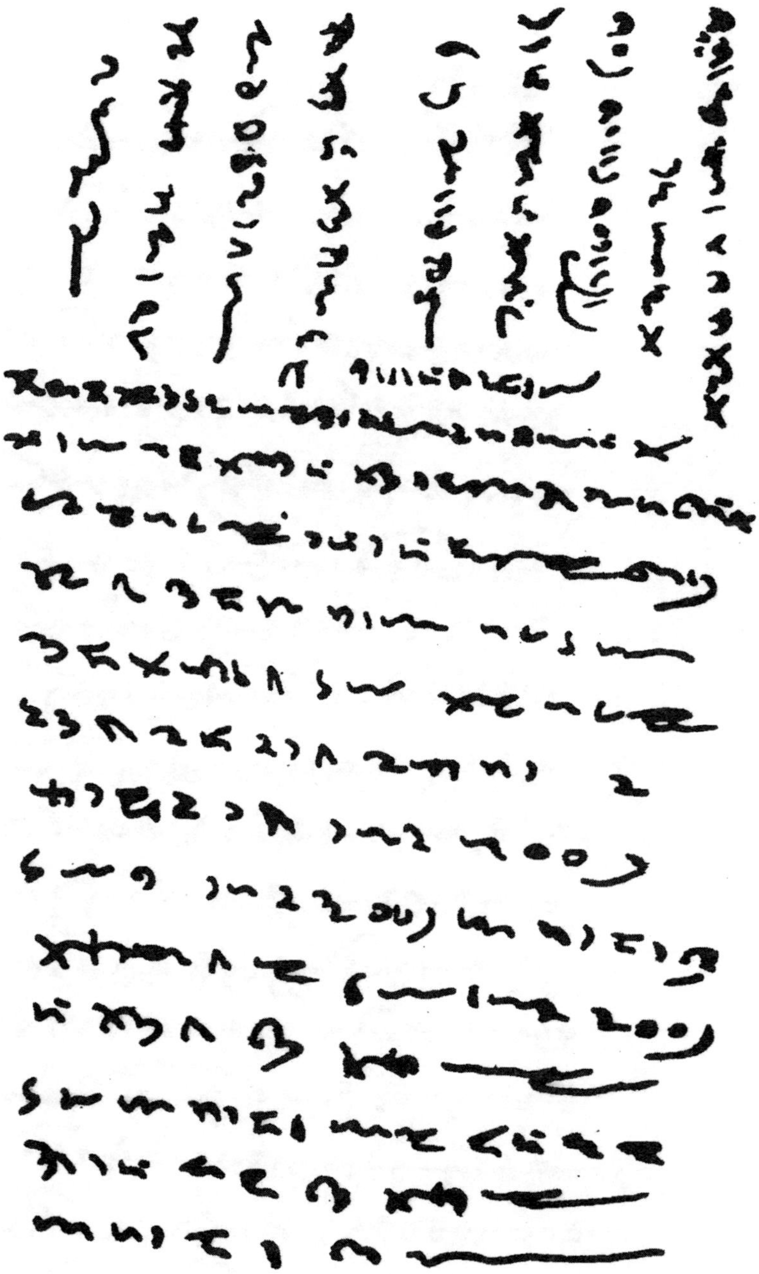

Muria

Used by Merchants in Behar and Benares &c.

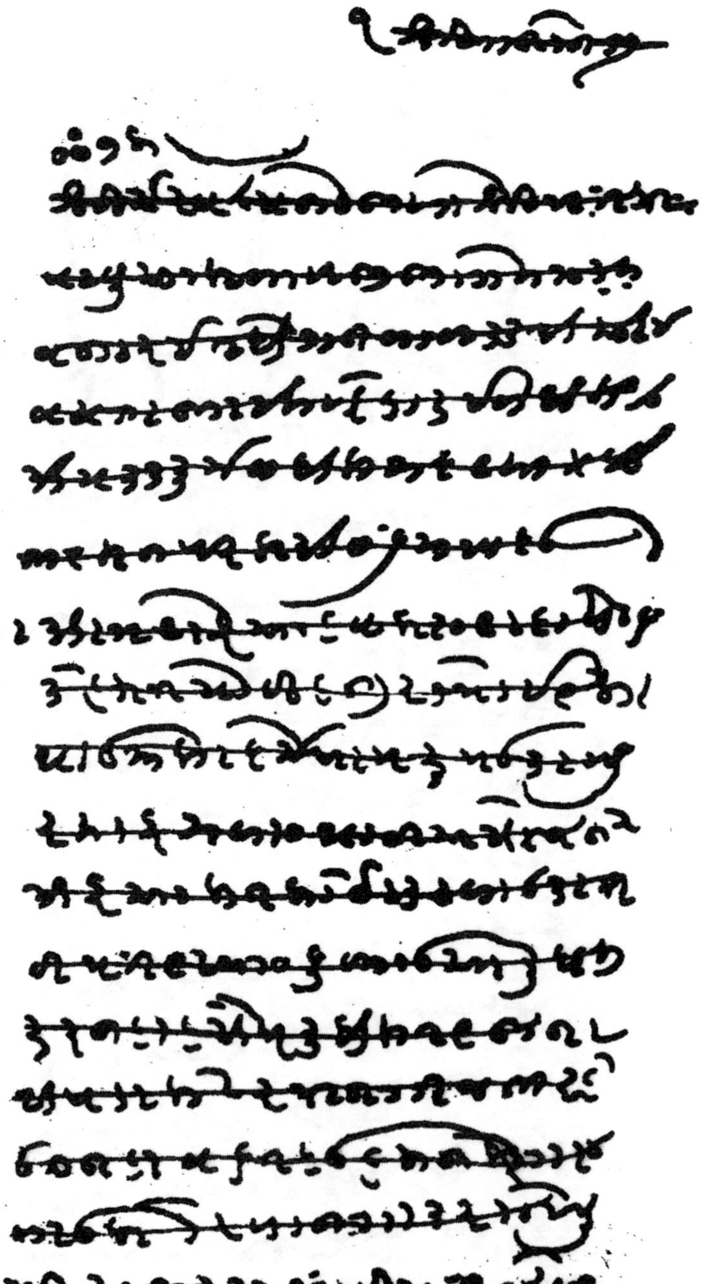

Parachi

Used in Bhera Khoshab &c.

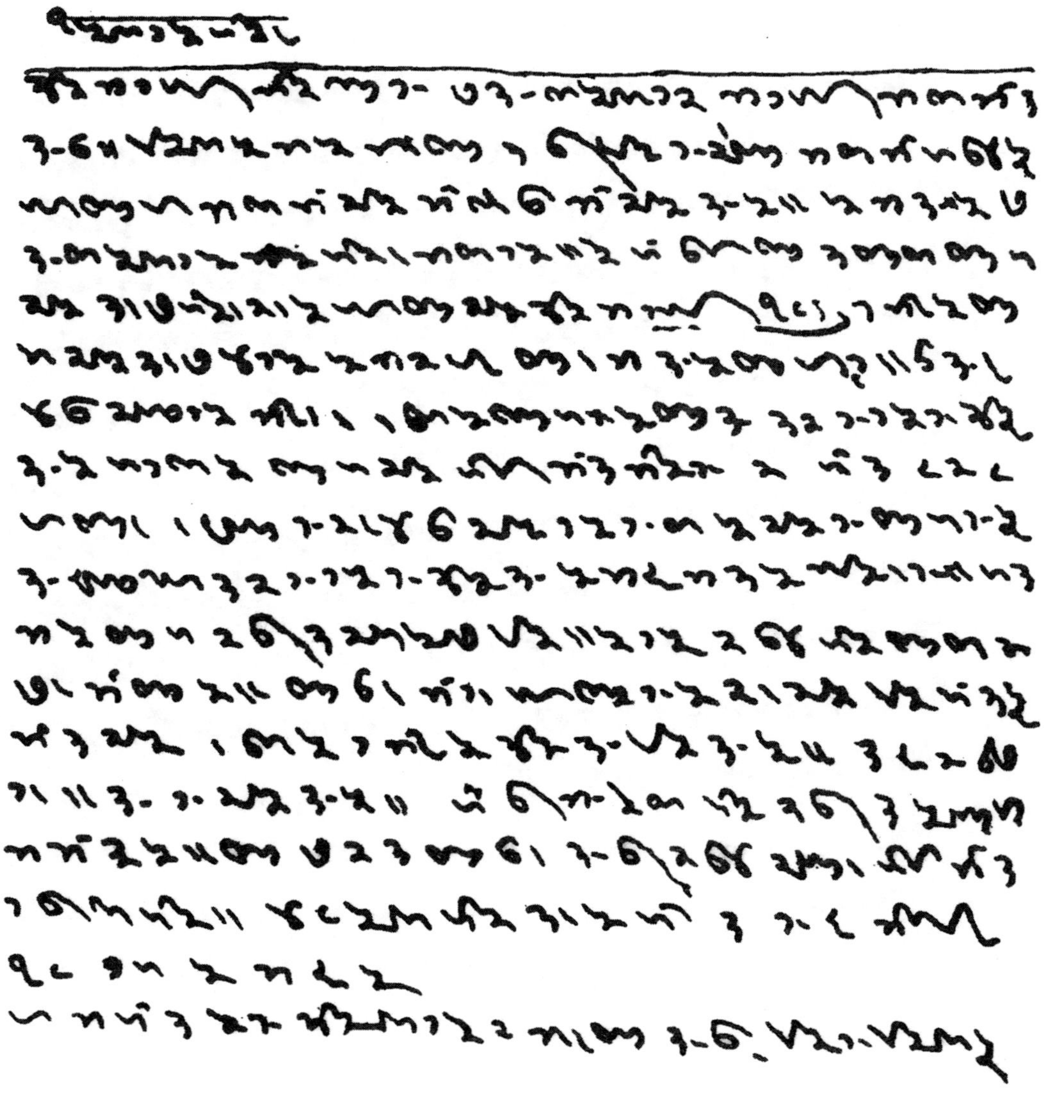

Roṛi Laṇḍe

Used by Bankers in the Panjab and Sindh

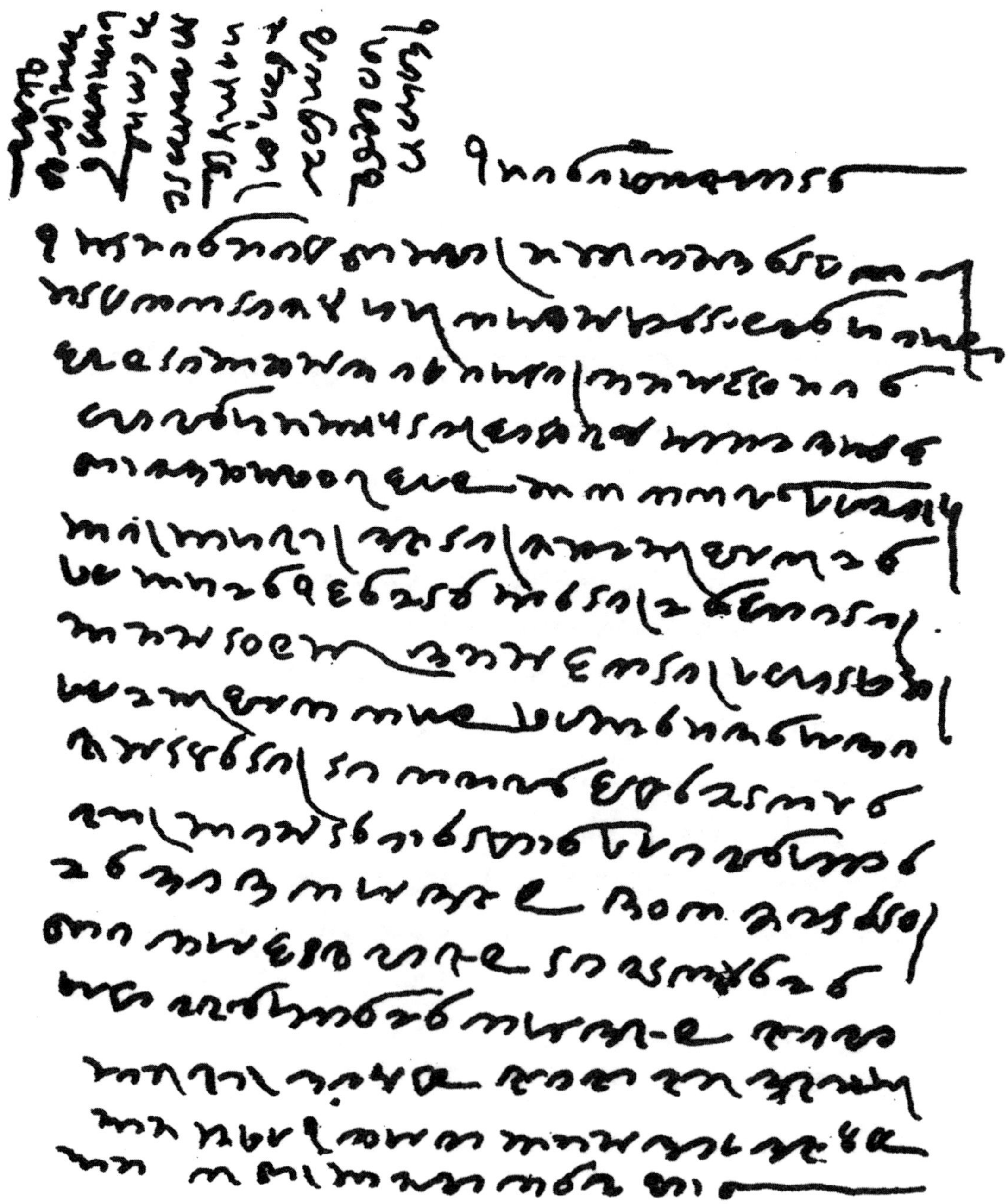

SARAFI

Used by the Bankers of the North Western Provinces and Oudh

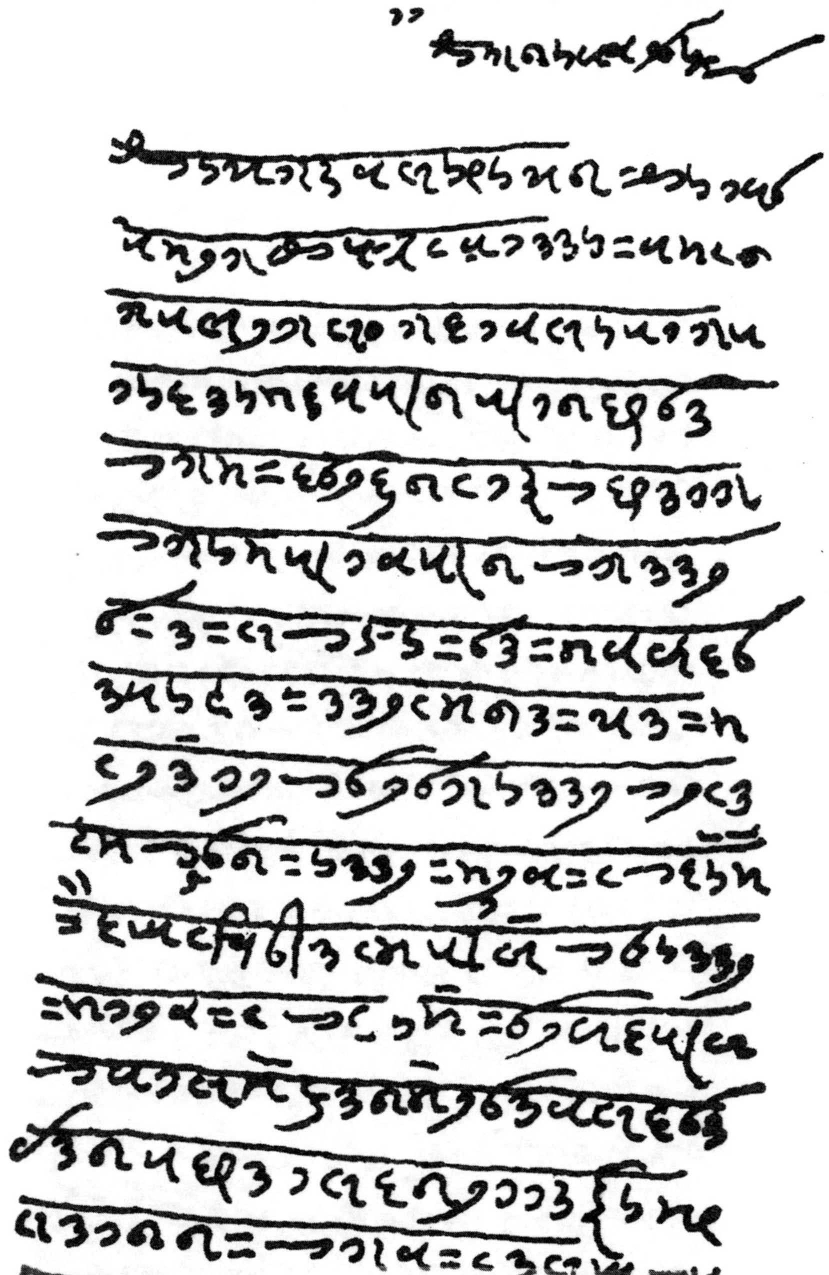

Sarika
Used in the Dehrajat of the Punjab

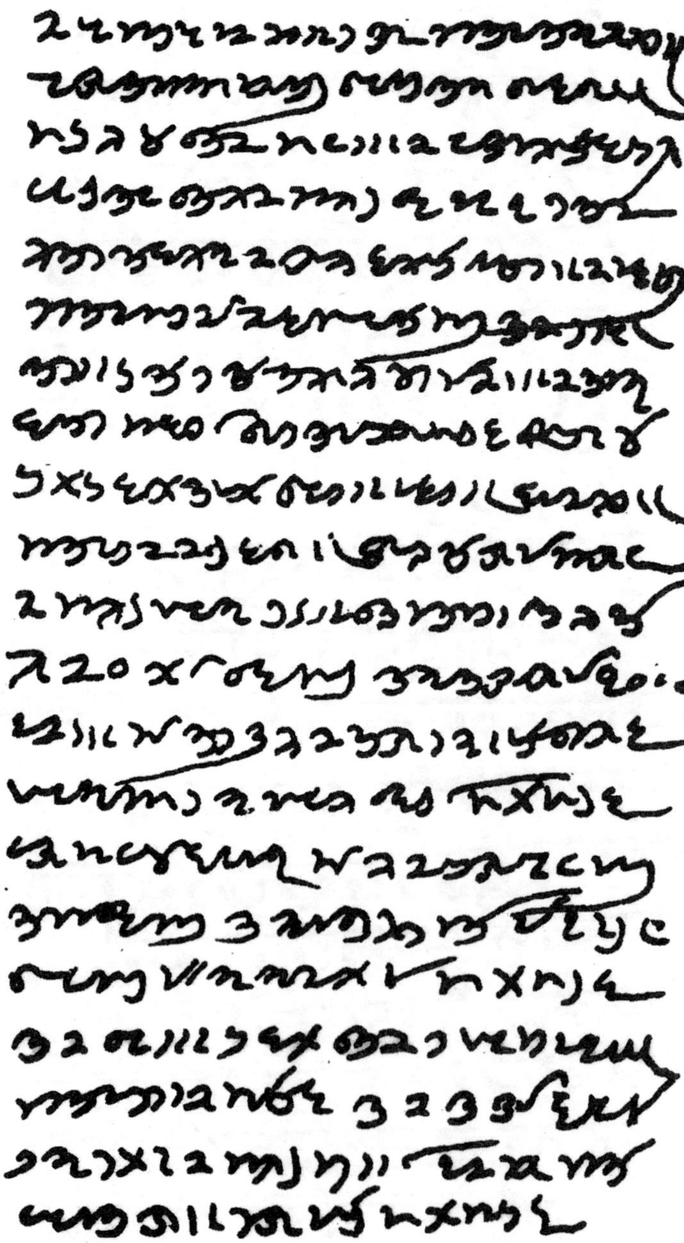

Shikarpuri

Used in Upper Sind

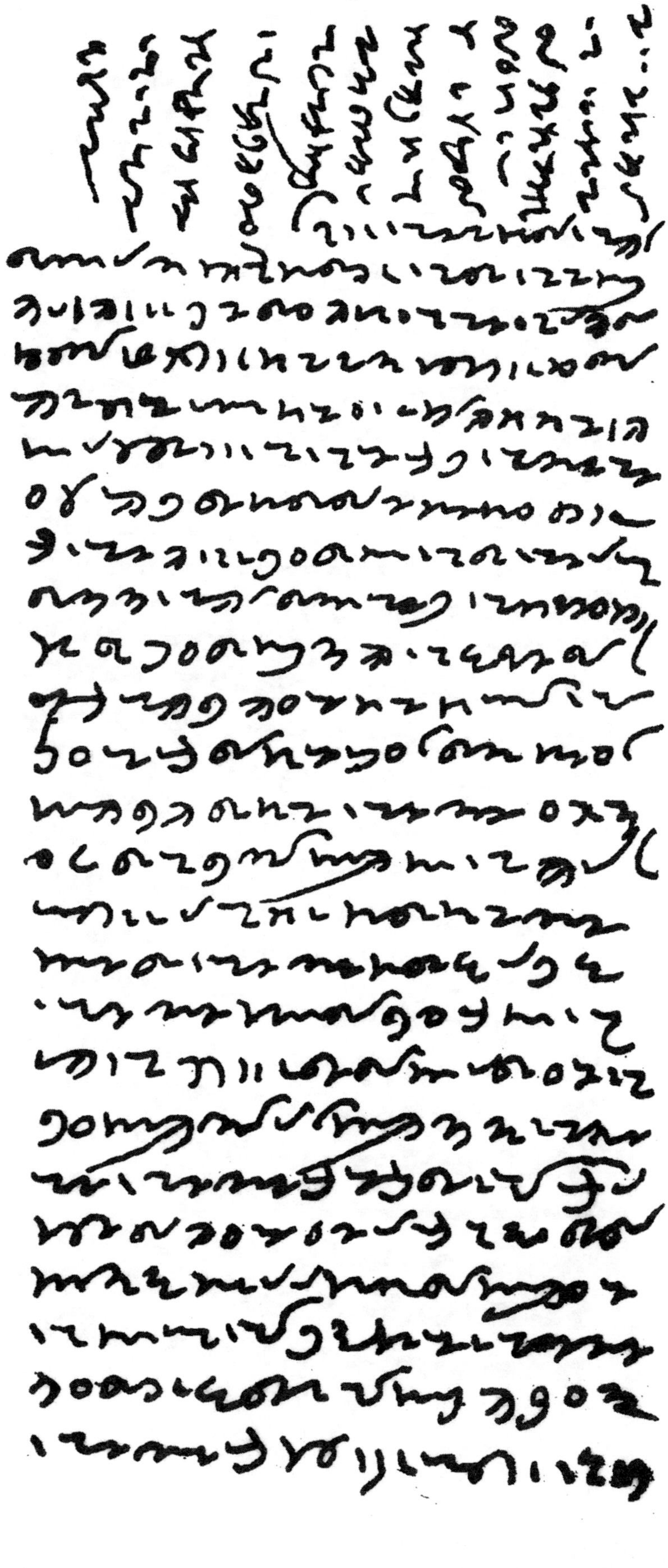

Sindi

Used in Sind

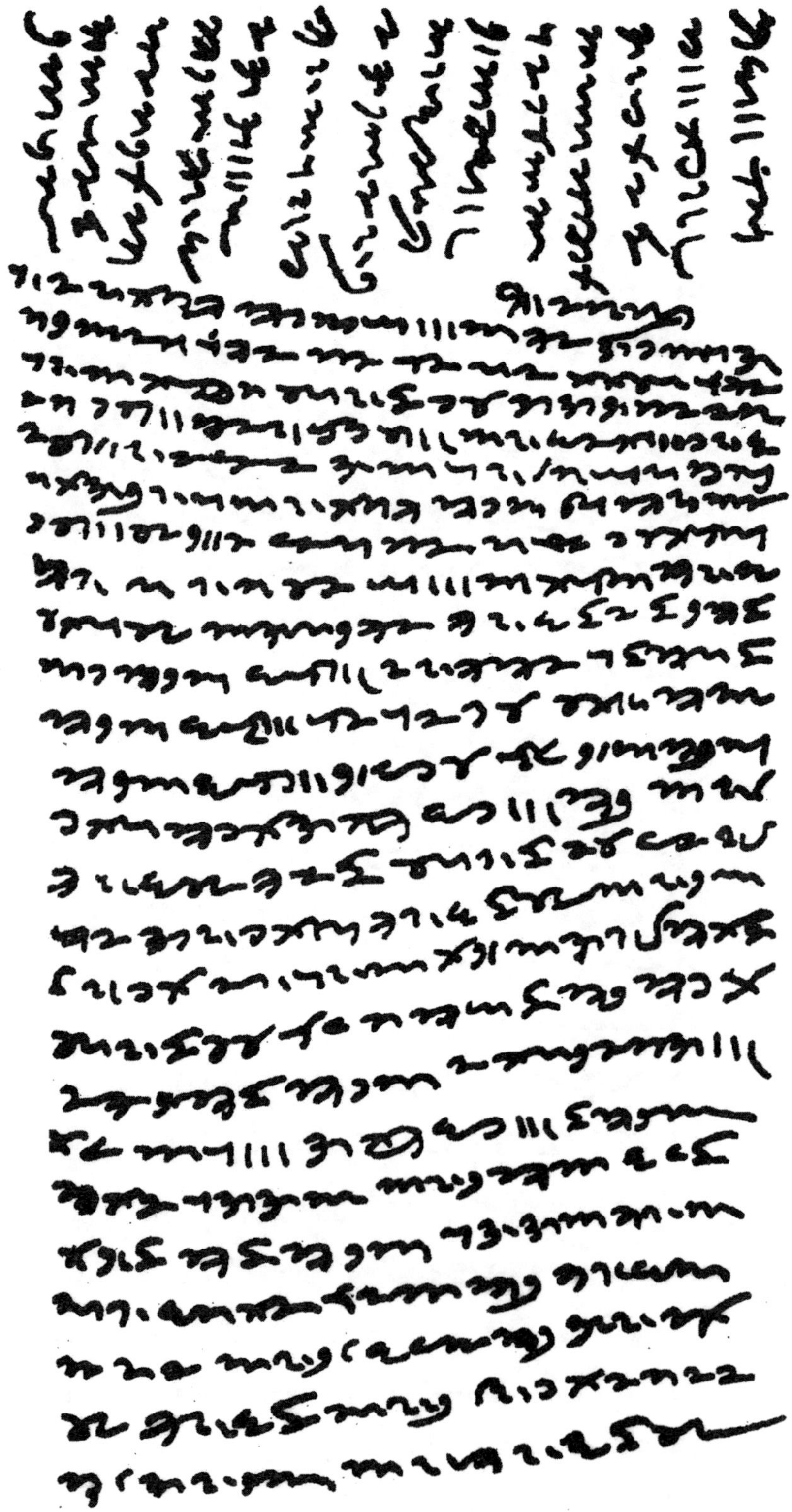

Thal

Used in the Dehrajat. of the Panjab

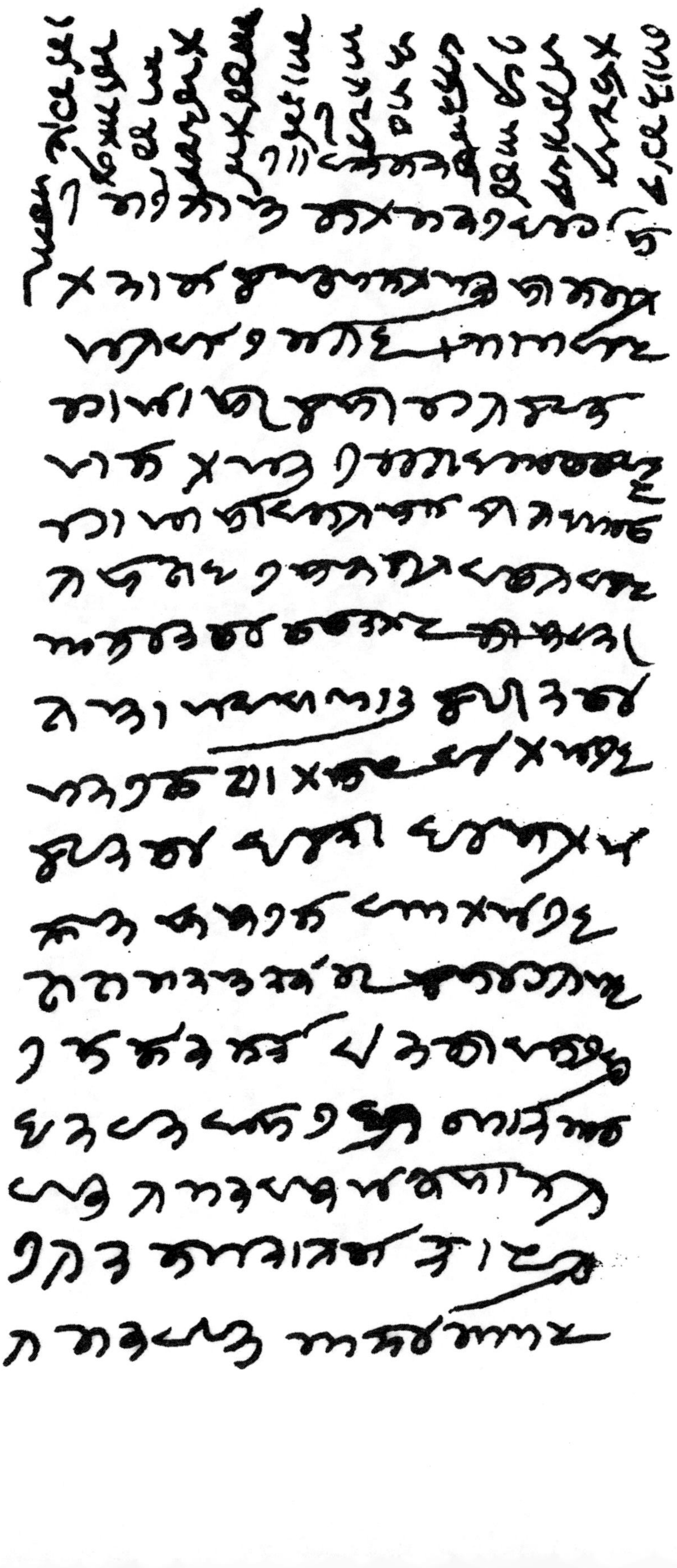

عبدالرحمن

Thakari or Thankri

Kangrā (and with some modifications in Kulu, Mandi, Suket)

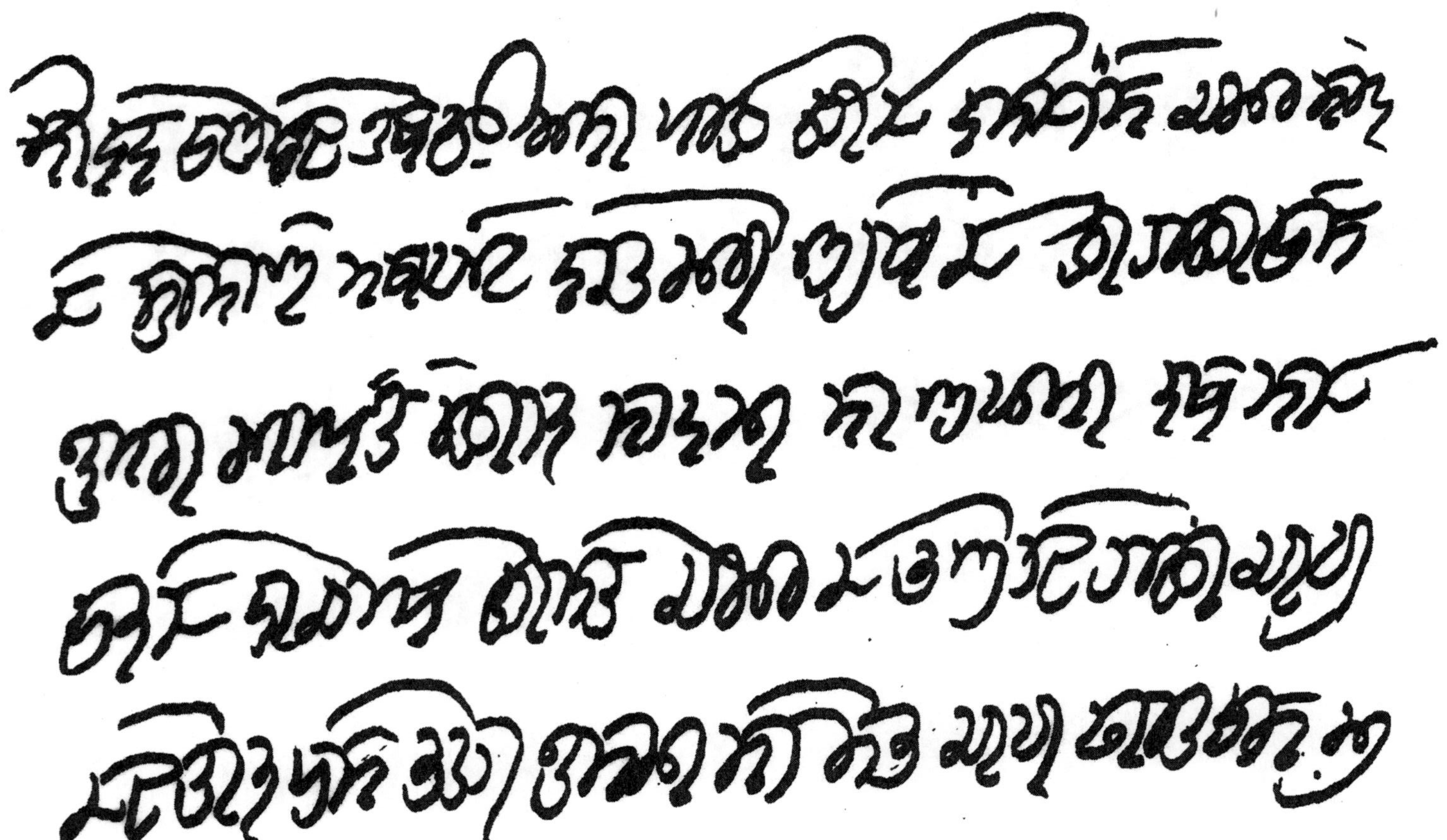

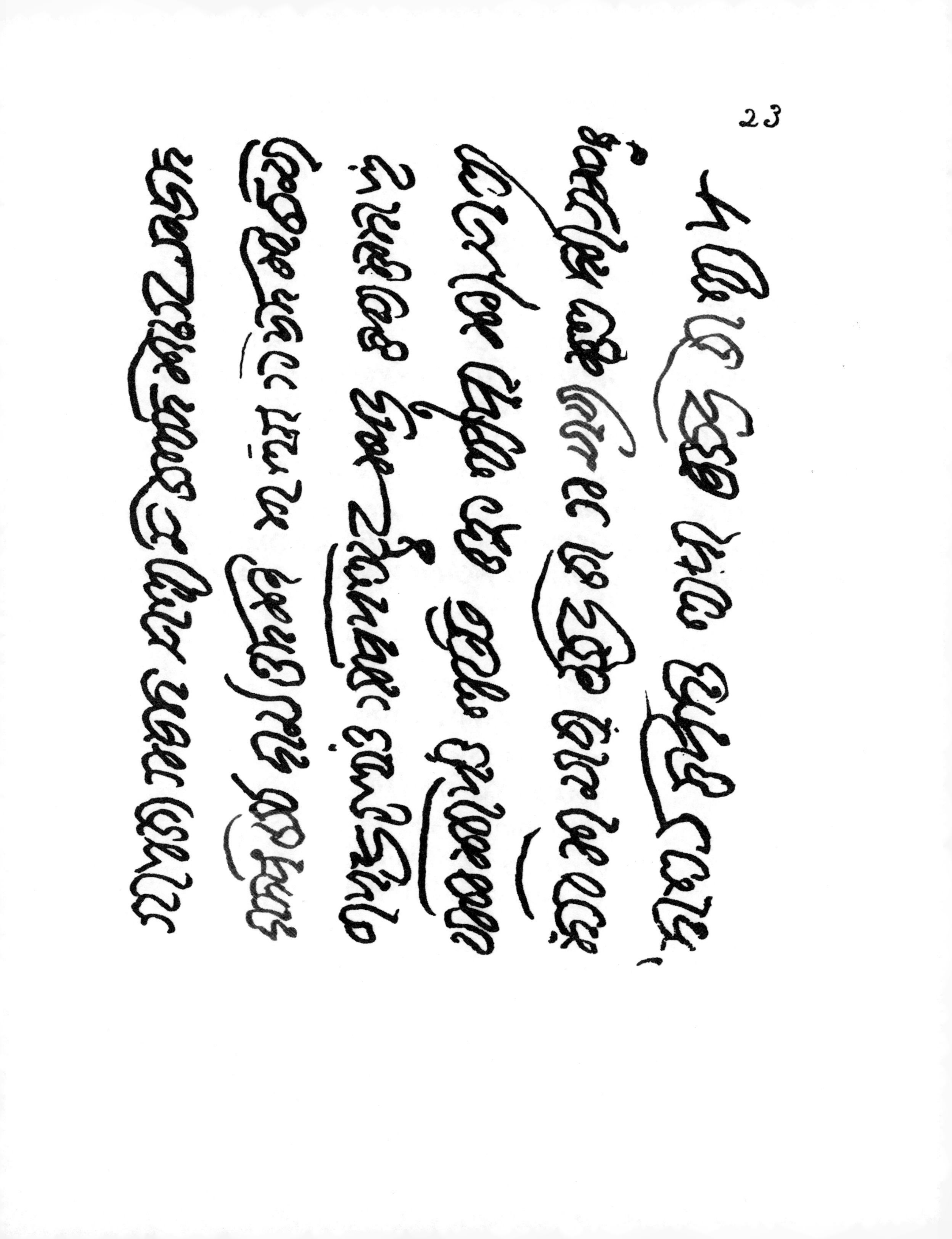

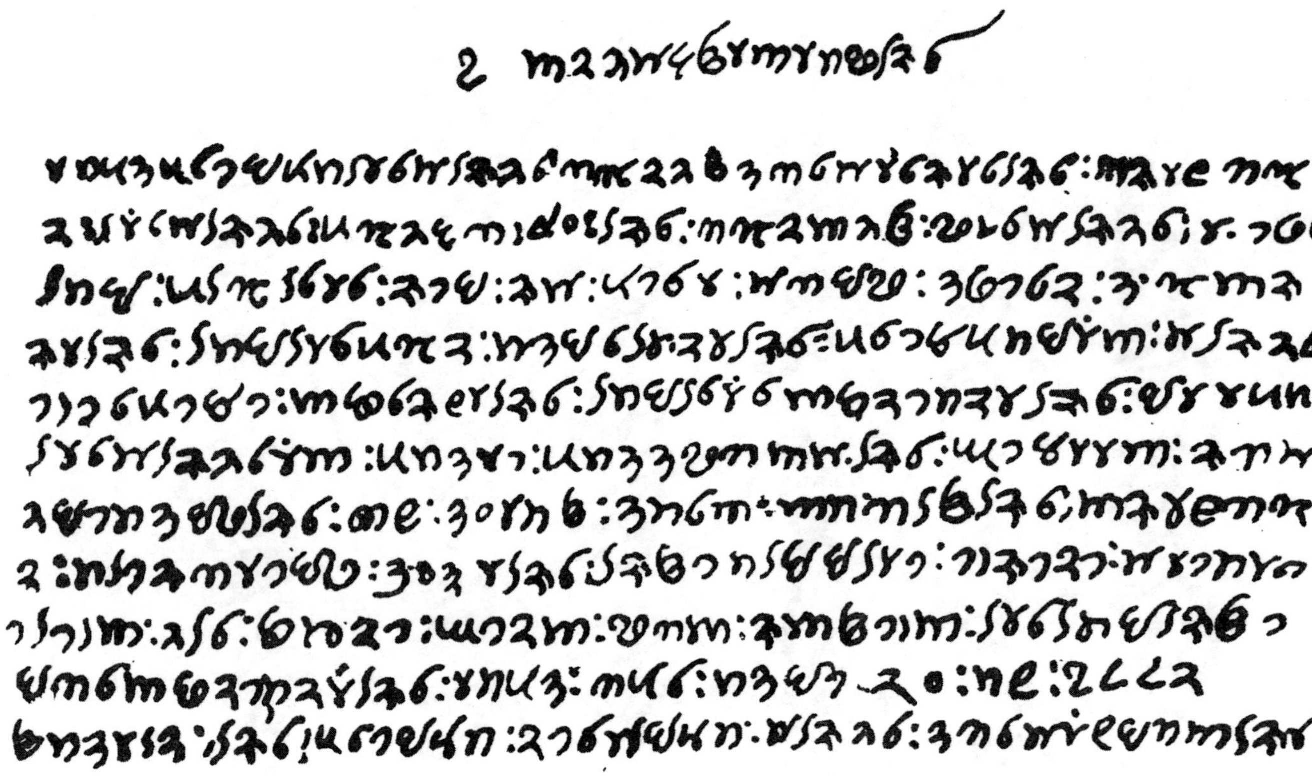

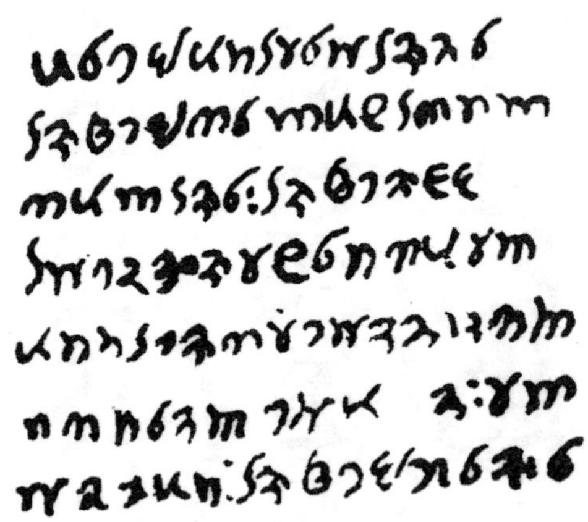

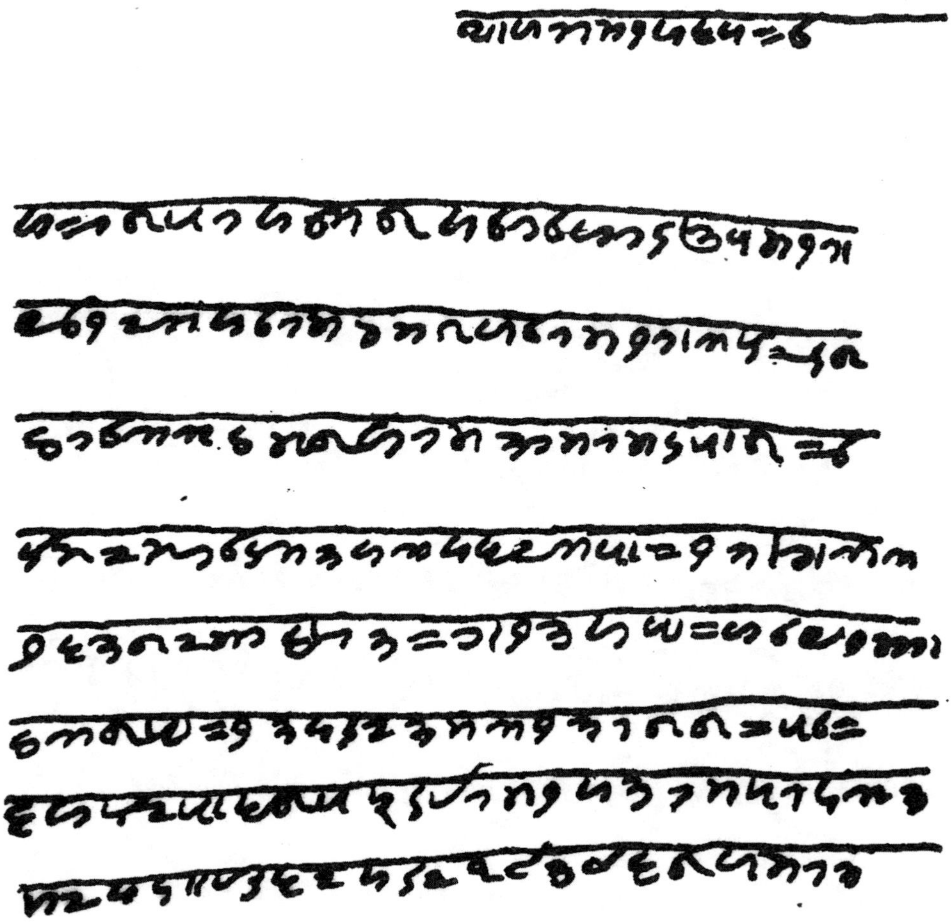

26

Kyunthali Thakari with the signature of the Raja of Kyunthal (Simla)

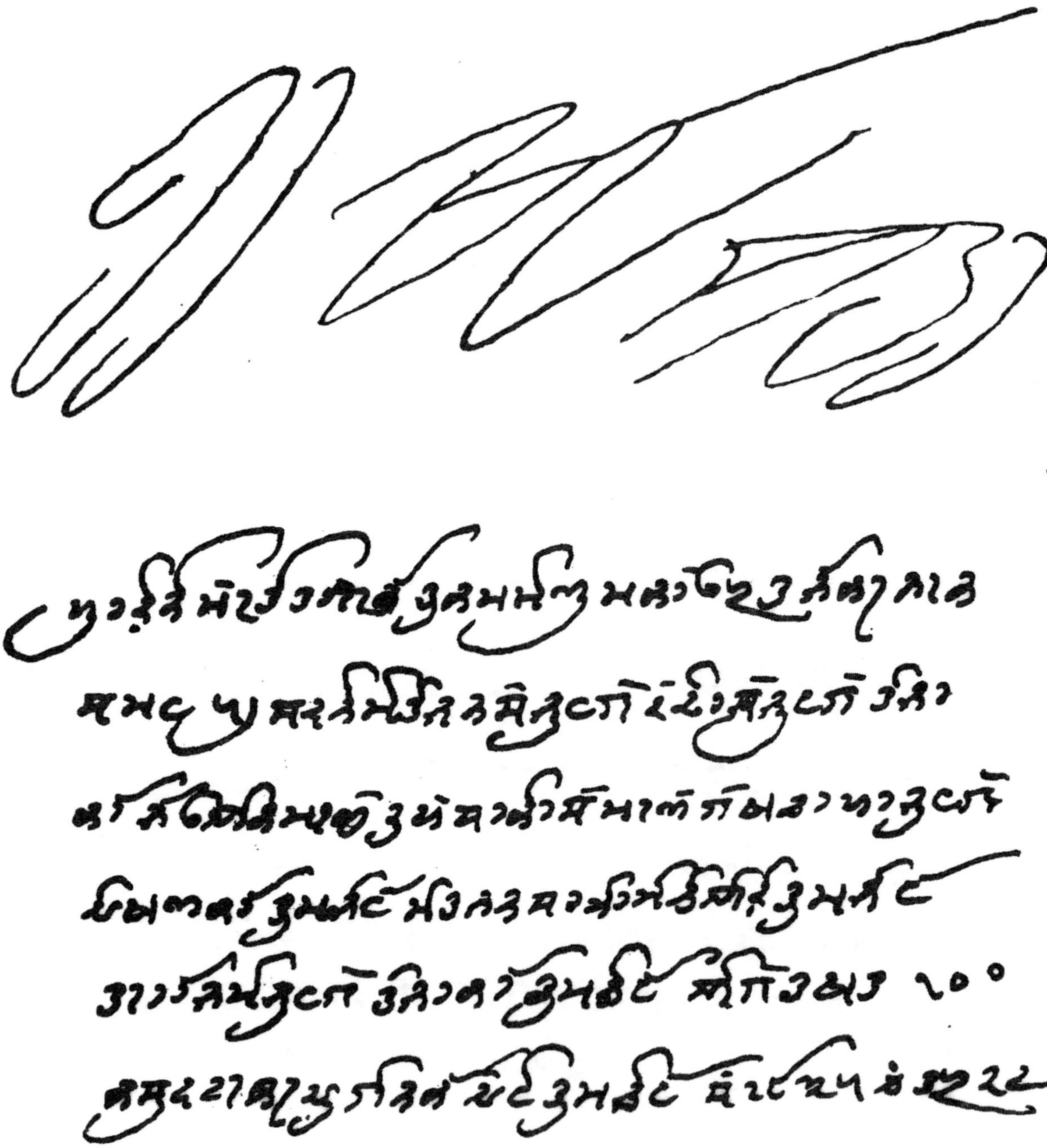

Lande of Jallandhar

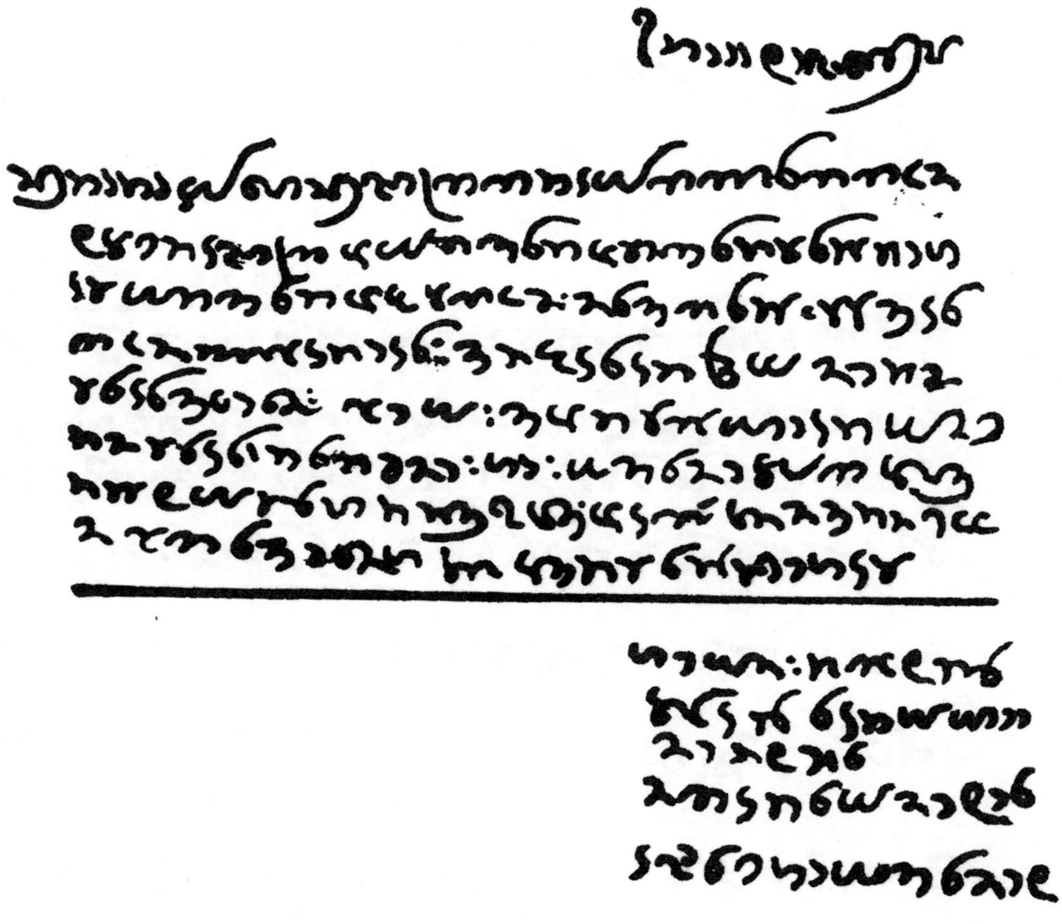

Letter in Landé of Jállandhar

حروف لنڈہ مستعملہ جالندہر

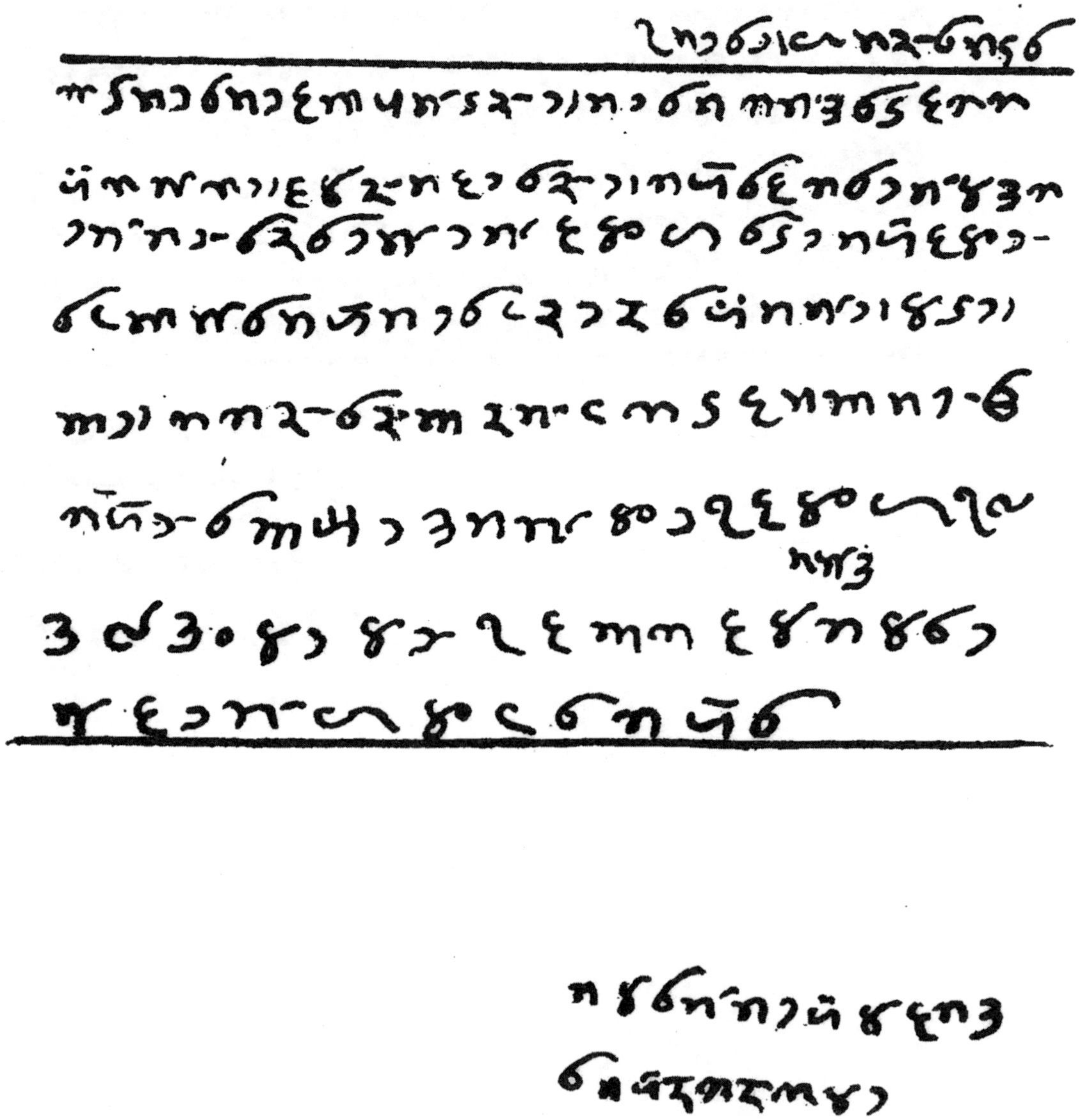

Jallandhar

نمونہ جات حروف لنڈہ و صرافی و مہاجنی

Lande Alphabet

حروف ابجد لنڈہ

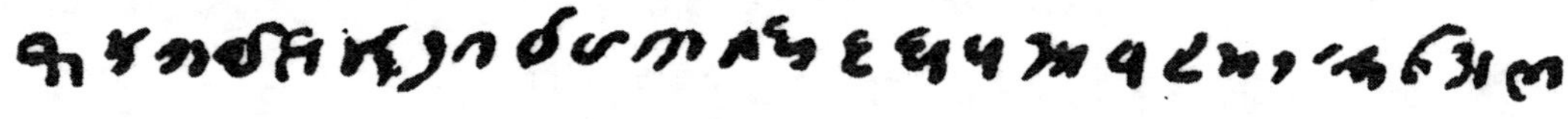

Lande II

قسم دیگر حروف ابجد لنڈہ

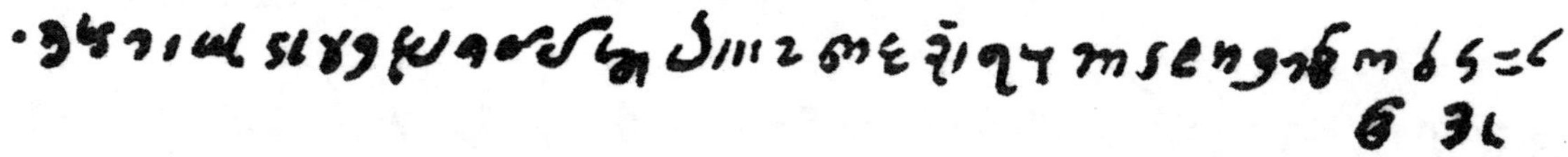

Sarrafi alphabet

حروف ابجد صرافی

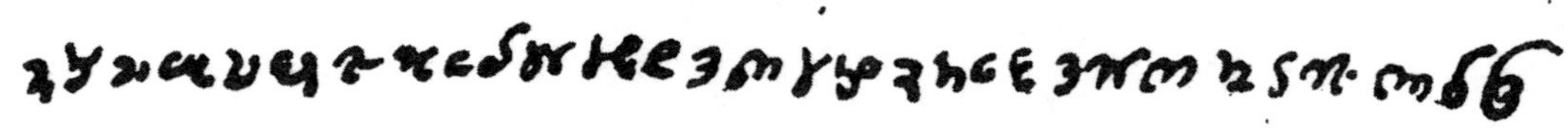

Mahajni alphabet

حروف ابجد مہاجنی

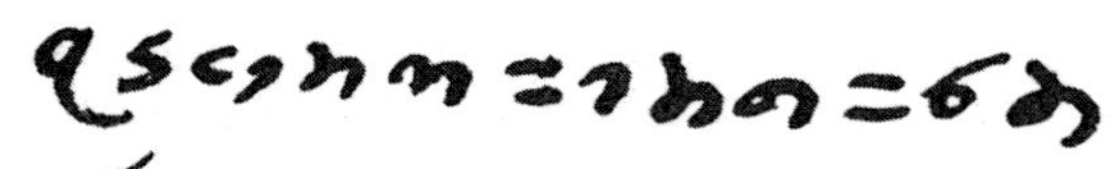

حروف مہاجنی کم استعمال شدہ یعنے جسکو استعمال بکثرت نہین *Mahajni (little used)*

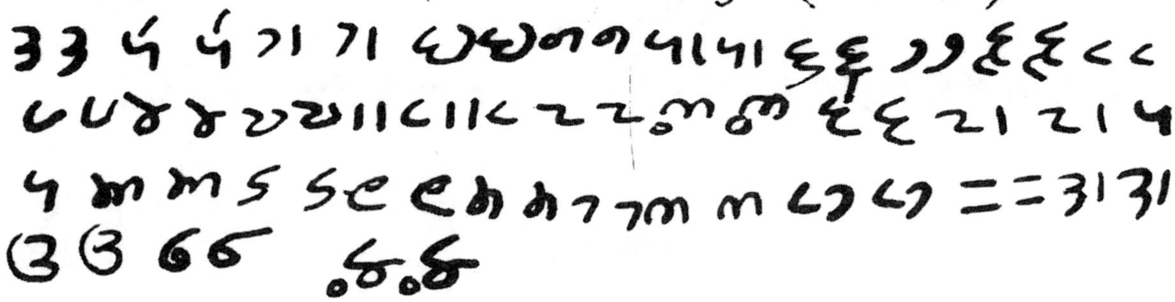

حروف صرافی مستعمل *Sarrafi (generally used)*

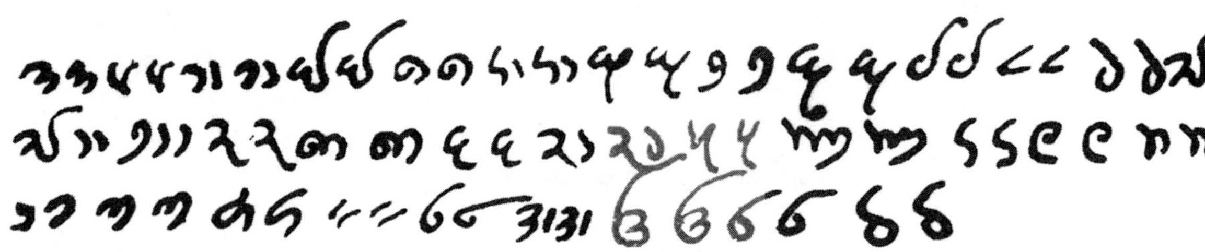

Lande of Dera Ghazi Khan

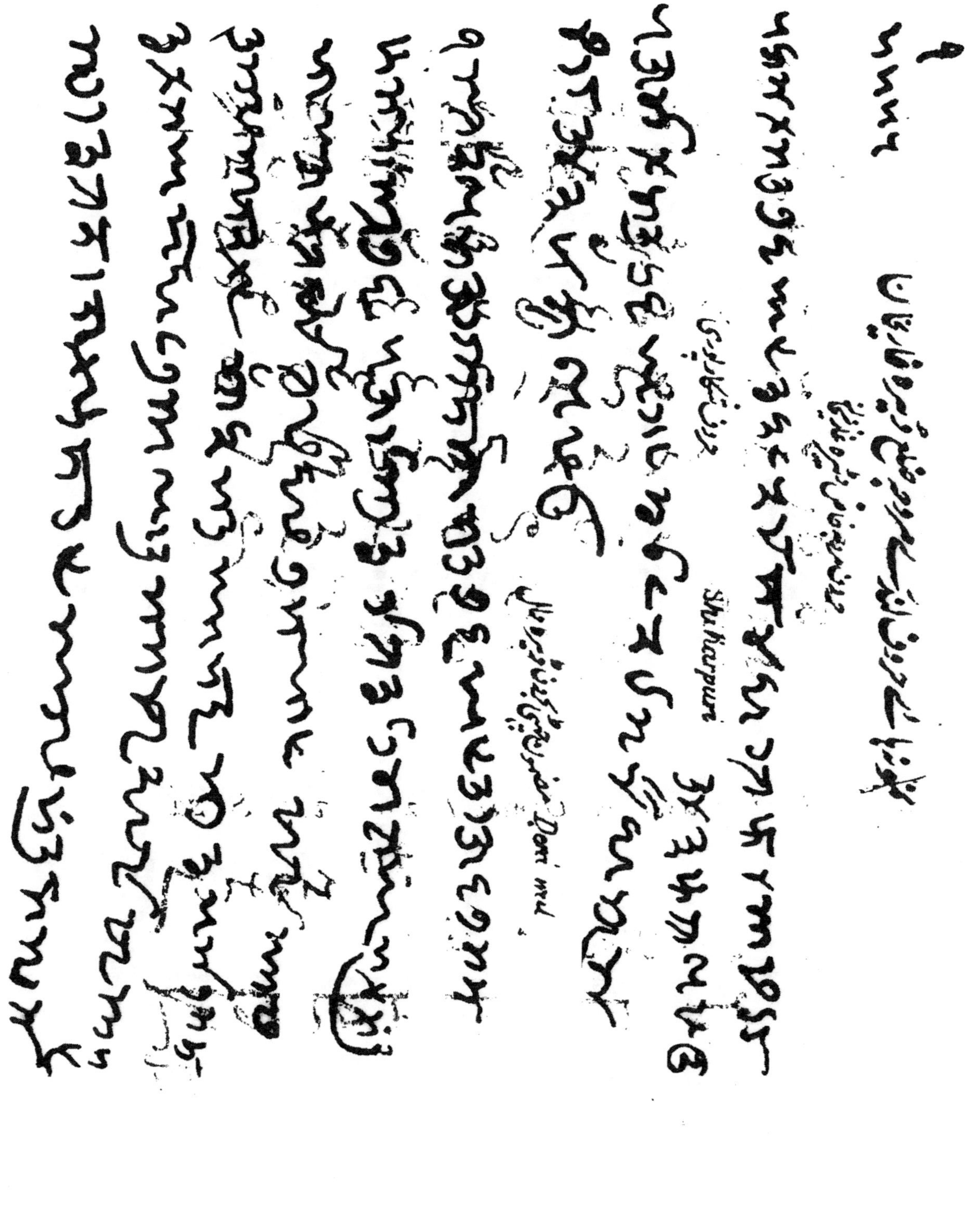

Lande used by Native Mahajans of Sirsá

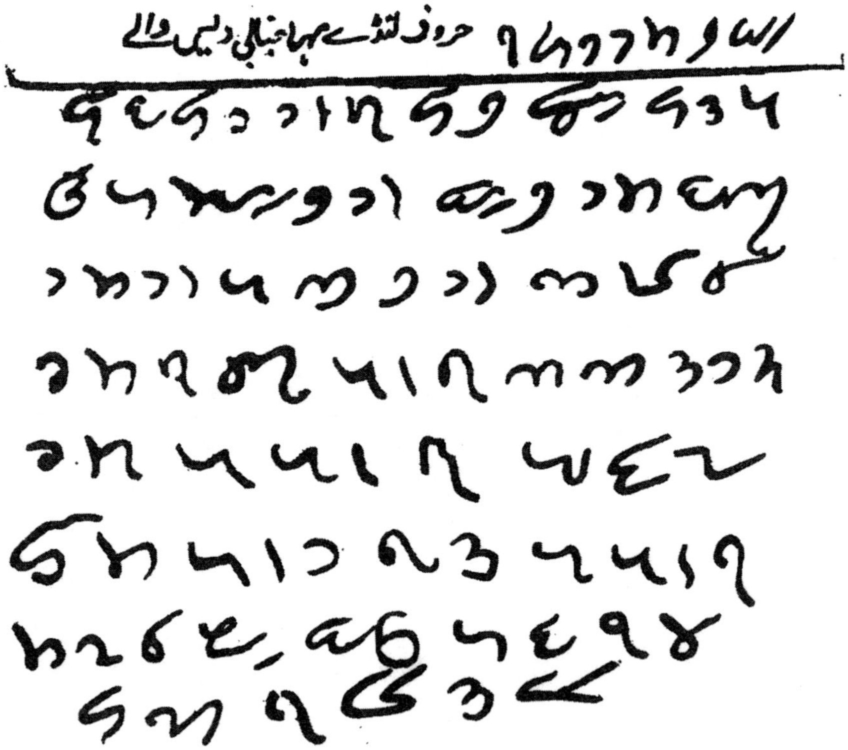

Letters used by Oswál Mahájans of Sirsá

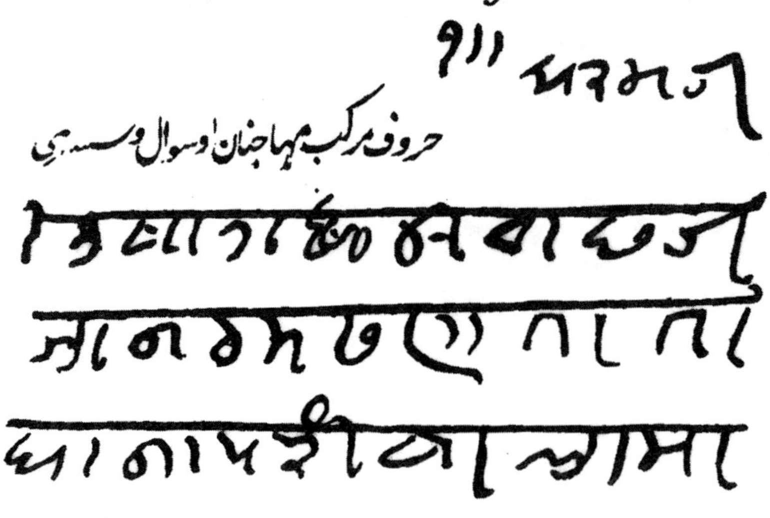

Names and meanings of the letters of the Lande alphabet

Lande	Nagri	Name of letter	Word illustrating name of letter	Meaning
	क	Kakká	Kubrá	Hump-backed.
	ख	Khakkha	Khatri	A Khatri.
	ग	Gaggá	Gualiya	Cowherd.
	घ	Ghaggá	Ghi-ka-ghurá	Pitcher full of Ghi.
	ङ	Nanná	Nái Ki Arsi	Barber's looking glass.
	च	Chachchá	Chuchalyá	Beaked.
	छ	Chhachchhá	Chhábaryá	Confectioner's tray.
	ज	Jajja	Janbú	Jummú
	झ	Jhajjá	Jhár Ki beri	Shrub
	ट	Tattá	* Adhi púri	Half a loaf of bread
	ठ	Thatthá	* Sawái púri	One and a quarter of bread
	ड	Daddá	Doli gánth	Double knot
	ढ	Dhaddá	Dhongar Bojhrá	
	ण	Ane	Tin lakir ko kahye	Says 3 lines.
	त	Tattá	Tuní	
	थ	Thatthá	Thálí	Plate.
	द	Daddá	Dál	Half a grain.
	ध	Dhad-dá	Dhuri-Kaman	Double bow.
	प	Pappá	Pawaryá	
	फ	Phupphá	Phuti Khari	
	ब	Babbá	Bindá	
	भ	Bhabbá	Bhár Ká Konchá	
	म	Mammá	Muchh-marorá	To twist moustaches.
	र	Rárá	Rám Katárá	Dagger.
	ल	Lal-lá	Lakhri	
	व	Vava.	Bindi wáná	Dotted
	स	Sassá.	* Teran	A spool
	ह	Háhá.	Hiran	
	ड़	Bhabbá.	Bindi Rará	
	ई	I i	* Ulti sáth ki ái	
	उ	U.	* Múnhmore ú	The mouth-rounding "U"?
	आ	Á	* Derh lakir ki á	

The above letters are first taught, but in the villages many Pádhás teach only these letters, but not the words added to them.

* The name refers to the form of the letter

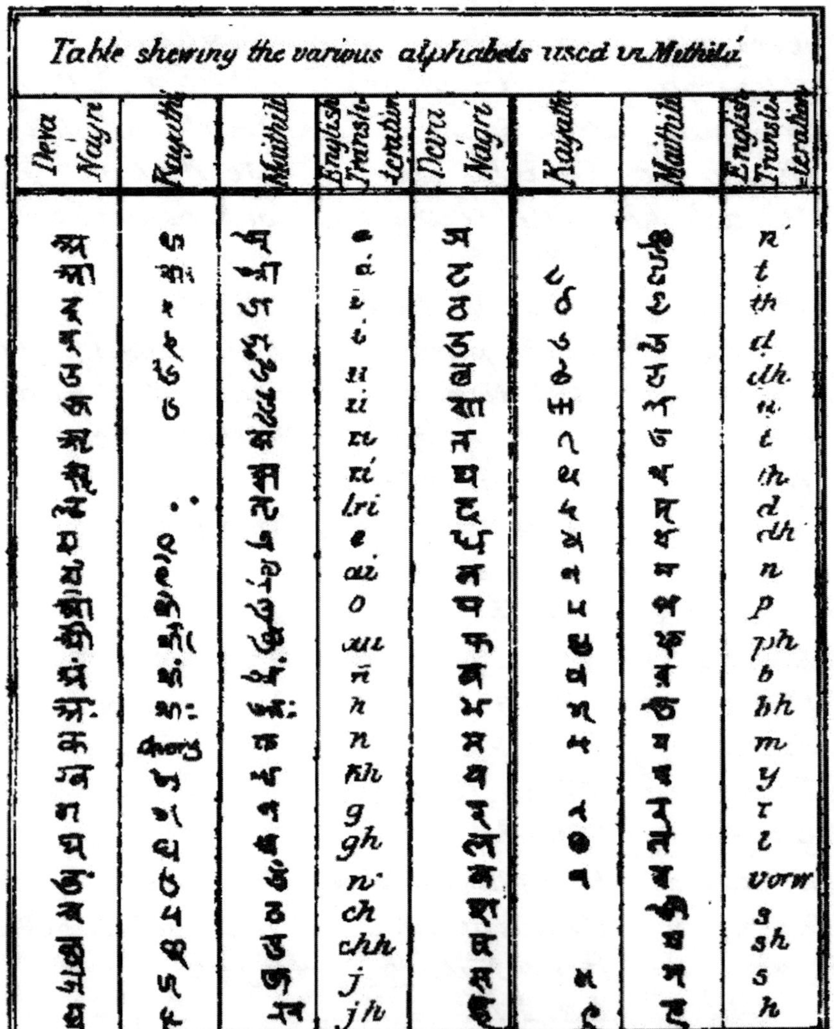

The semi-vowel व is not used by Kayasths in writing Maithili the vowel इ being substituted for it.

APPENDIX VII.

A COLLECTION OF SPECIMENS OF COMMERCIAL AND OTHER ALPHABETS AND HANDWRITINGS AS ALSO OF MULTIPLICATION TABLES CURRENT IN VARIOUS PARTS OF THE PANJAB, SIND AND THE NORTH WEST PROVINCES.

PART B.

Set No I

Comparison of different Kinds of Lande with Gurmukhi and Nagri

Numerals نمبر	Gurmukhi گورمکھی	Nagri ناگری	Sarafi Lande لنڈہ صرافی	Lande I. لنڈہ قسم اول	Lande II لنڈہ قسم دویم	Lande III لنڈہ قسم سیوم	Lande IV لنڈہ قسم چہارم	Lande V لنڈہ قسم پنجم	Dogre Kardari ڈوگرے قسم کارداری	Dogre Mahajani ڈوگری مہاجنی	
੧	ੳ	उ	[illegible]	[illegible]	[illegible]	[illegible]	[illegible]	[illegible]	[illegible]		
੨	ਅ	अ	[illegible]	[illegible]	[illegible]	[illegible]	[illegible]	[illegible]	[illegible]		
੩	ੲ	इ	[illegible]	[illegible]	[illegible]	[illegible]	[illegible]	[illegible]	[illegible]		
੪	ਸ	स	[illegible]	[illegible]	[illegible]	[illegible]	[illegible]	[illegible]	[illegible]		
੫	ਹ	ह	[illegible]	[illegible]	[illegible]	[illegible]	[illegible]	[illegible]	[illegible]		
੬	ਕ	क	[illegible]	[illegible]	[illegible]	[illegible]	[illegible]	[illegible]	[illegible]		

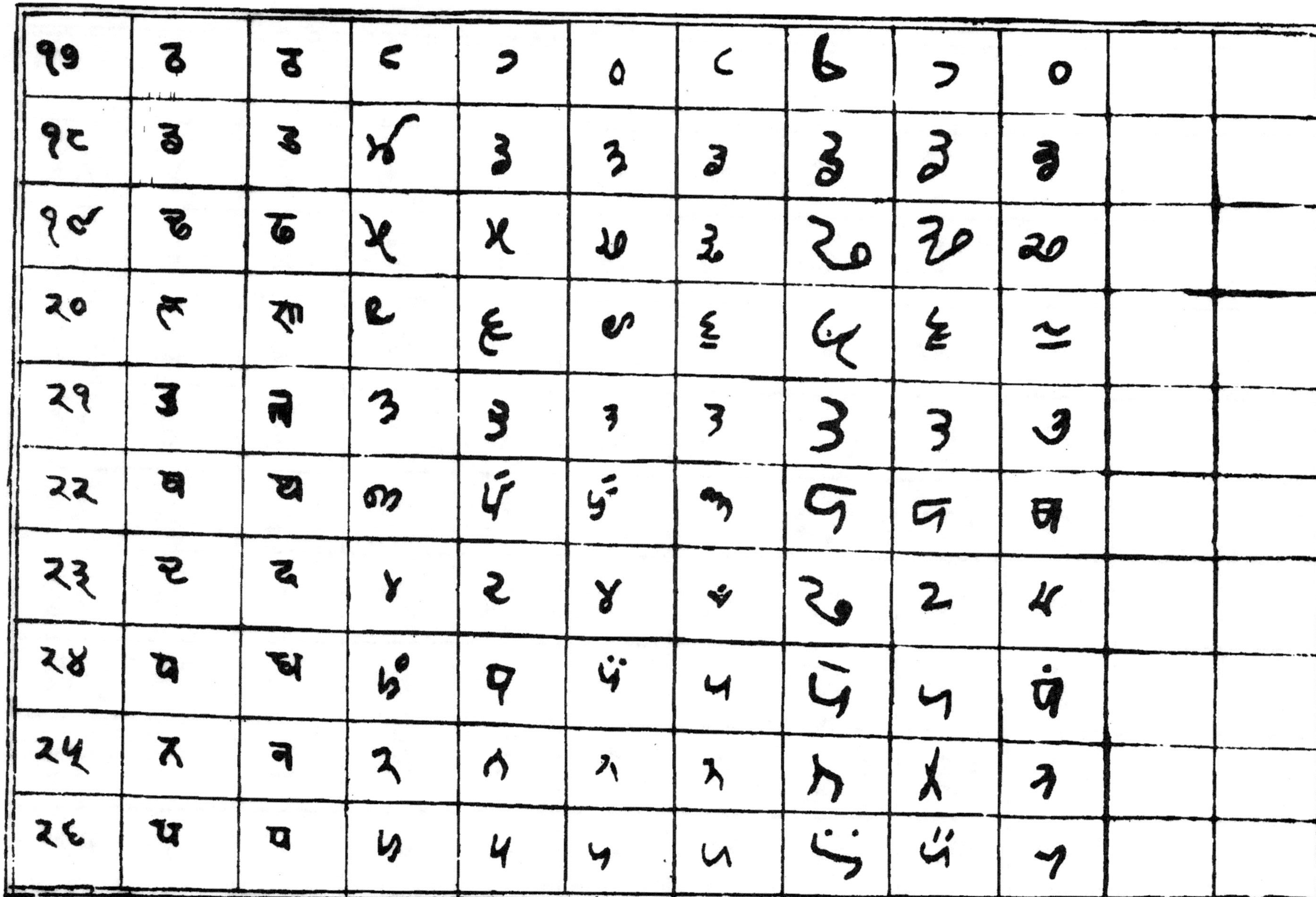
१७ ठ ठ
१८ ड ड
१९ ढ ढ
२० ण ण
२१ त त
२२ थ थ
२३ द द
२४ ध ध
२५ न न
२६ प प

२७	ठ	फ	[illegible]	[illegible]	[illegible]	[illegible]	[illegible]	[illegible]
२८	ब	ब	[illegible]	[illegible]	[illegible]	[illegible]	[illegible]	[illegible]
२९	भ	भ	[illegible]	[illegible]	[illegible]	[illegible]	[illegible]	[illegible]
३०	म	म	[illegible]	[illegible]	[illegible]	[illegible]	[illegible]	[illegible]
३१	य	य	[illegible]	[illegible]	[illegible]	[illegible]	[illegible]	[illegible]
३२	र	र	[illegible]	[illegible]	[illegible]	[illegible]	[illegible]	[illegible]
३३	ळ	ल	[illegible]	[illegible]	[illegible]	[illegible]	[illegible]	[illegible]
३४	व	व	[illegible]	[illegible]	[illegible]	[illegible]	[illegible]	[illegible]
३५	ड	ड	[illegible]	[illegible]	[illegible]	[illegible]	[illegible]	[illegible]

Sct № 2

I. Gurmukhi

ਕਬਿੱਤ

ਤਰੁਨਤਨੂਜਾਤੀਰ ਸੁਖਦ ਸਮੀਰ ਧੀਰ ਖਗਨ ਕੀ ਭੀਰ ਜੀਸੇ
ਹੇਰ ਹਰਖਤ ਹੈਂ। ਬੰਜੁਲ ਨਿਕੁੰਜਨ ਮੈਂ ਗੁੰਜਨ ਦ੍ਵਰੇਫ਼ਕੀ ਅਨੰਦ
ਸੋਂ ਪੁੰਜਨ ਪਰਾਗ ਪਰਖਤ ਹੈਂ। ਬਾਂਕੀ ਬਲਗੀਨੇ ਦੇਖਿ ਤਾਨ ਸੇ
ਬਿਲੋਕਯਤ ਪਰਮ ਪੁਨੀਤ ਮਨੀਮਨ ਕਖਤ ਹੈਂ। ਮੋਰ ਮਨ
ਭਾਈ ਸ੍ਰੀ ਅਭੀਰ ਸੁਖਦਾਈ ਤਾਂ ਸ੍ਯਾਮ ਘਨ ਚਪਲਾ ਮੈਂ
ਰਸ ਬਰਖਤ ਹੈਂ॥

੧ ਅਲਬਰ
ਹੀਰਾ ਨੰਦ ਬੇਟਾ ਗੁਲਜਾਰੀ
ਕਾ ਅਨੰਦਪੁਰ ਕਾ

ੳ ਅ ੲ ਸ ਹ ਕ ਖ ਗ ਘ ਙ ਚ ਛ ਜ ਝ ਞ ਟ ਠ
ਡ ਢ ਣ ਤ ਥ ਦ ਧ ਨ ਪ ਫ ਬ ਭ ਮ ਯ ਰ ਲ ਵ ੜ॥

II Nagri

अआइई उऊऋॠ ऌॡएऐ
ओऔअंअः
कखगघङ चछजझञ टठडढण
तथदधन पफबभम यरलव
शषसह क्षत्रज्ञ

ओम

कवित्त।

प्रथम पठन कीन स्वाध्याय नित्य काम
बहु रस आयुर्वेद नीके कै निकास्यो है।
काव्य कामिनी नवीन नायका प्रवीन चारु
अलंकार भाव वास रस नाय धार्यो है।
अंक कीन संकरीन चीन विपरीत विध
गुरस्वती सार स्वती विविध विचार्यो है।
हीरानंद नाम धाम सखा आनंद मांहि
बालक पढावन मैं आनंद विचार्यो है॥

दोहा।

वैद्यक विद्या काव्य मन अंक अनंत प्रकार
पाठन वाणी गुरस्वती सभ को करों उचार॥

Set No 3

I. Sealkot

Mahajani Lande

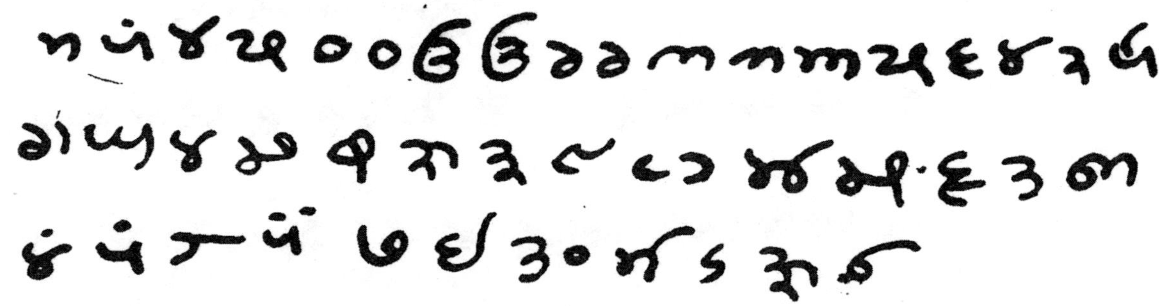

II Mahájani Dogre

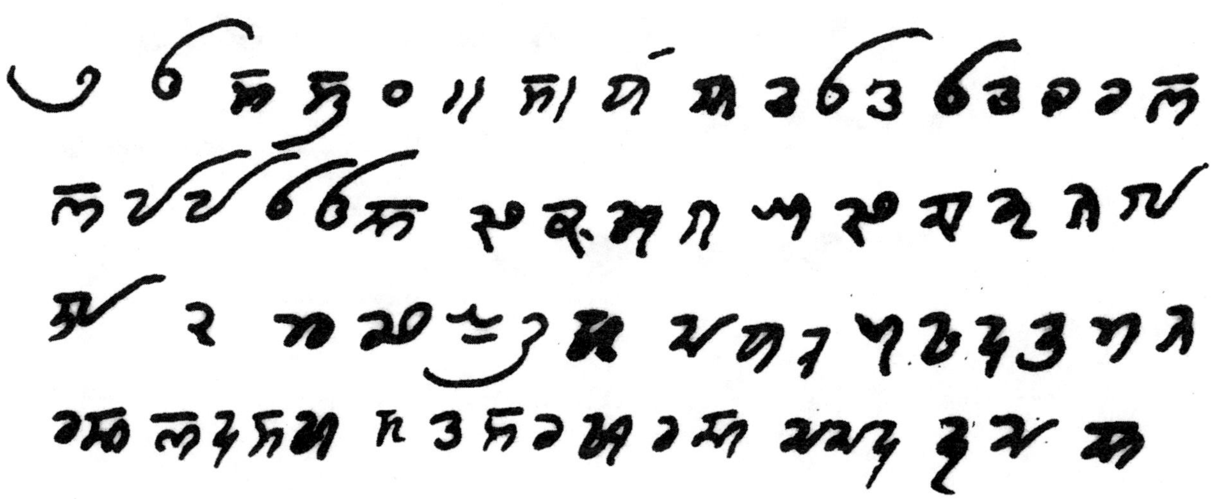

III. Lande characters of Amritsar

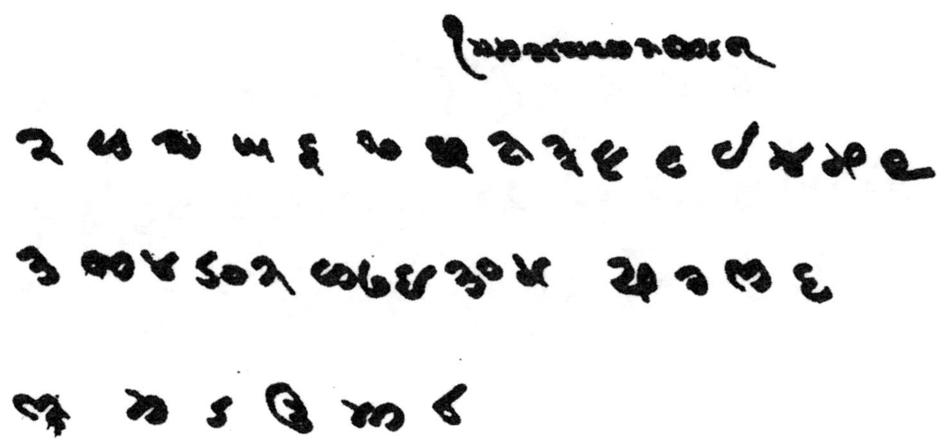

IV Bania characters of Amritsar

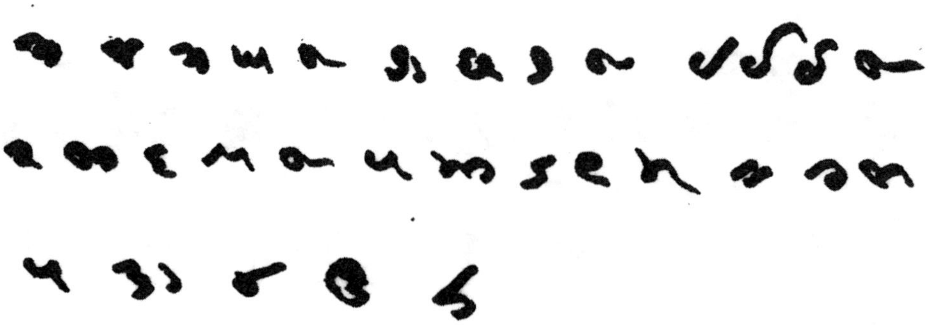

V Characters of the Bicaneris in Amritsar

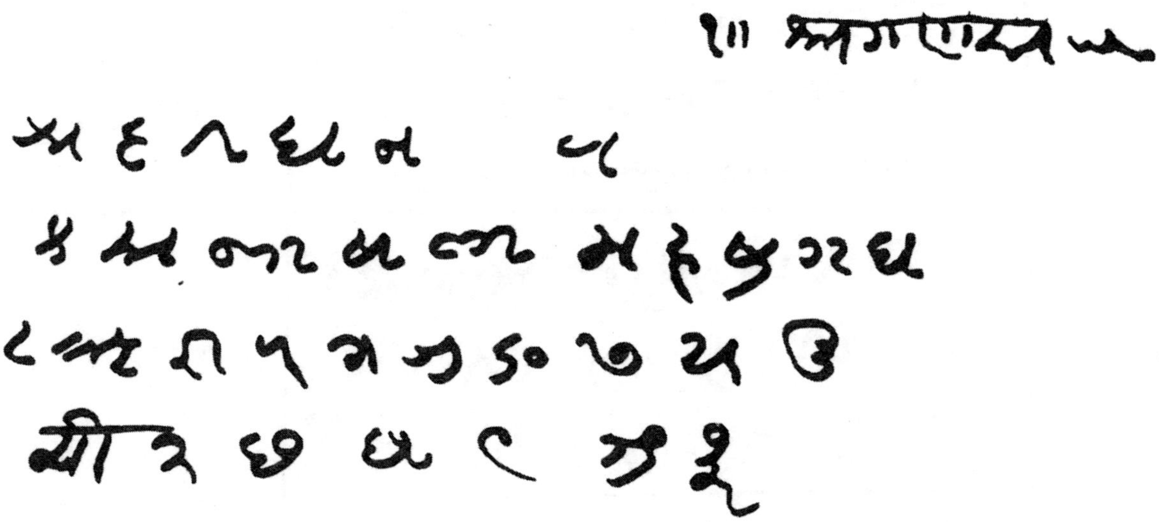

VI. Specimen of Landás

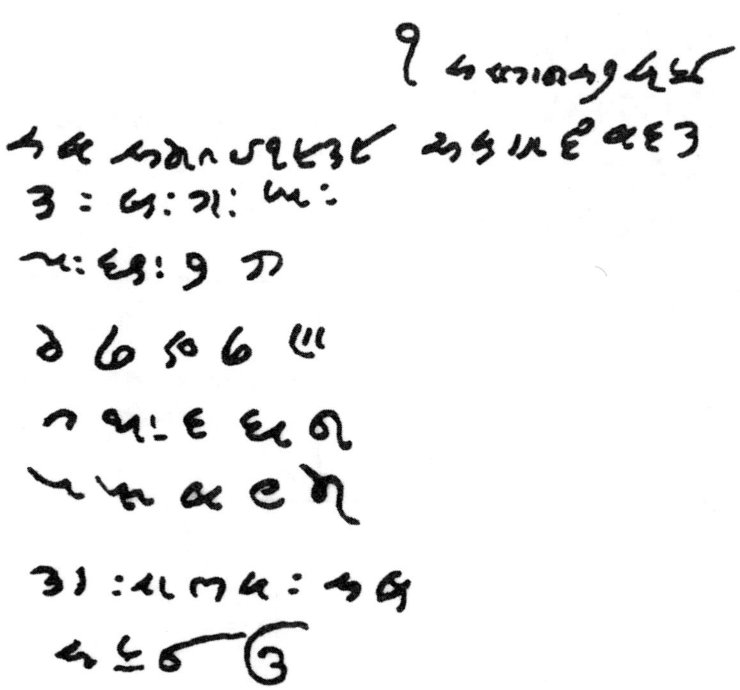

VII. Differs from Karnál

Mahajan

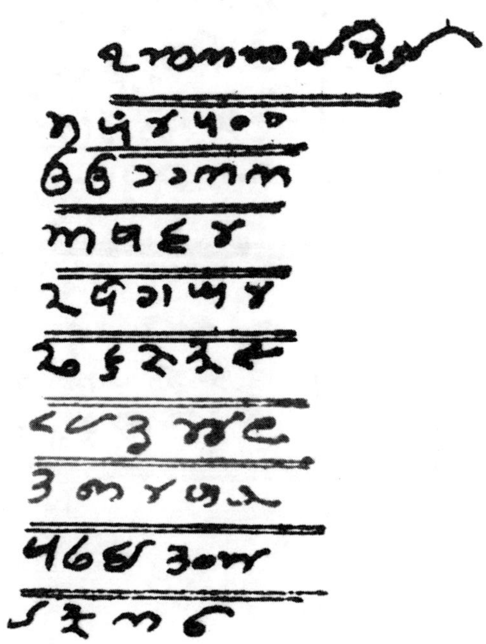

Taran táran District Amritsar

VIII Specimen of Lande

	Specimen	Script
	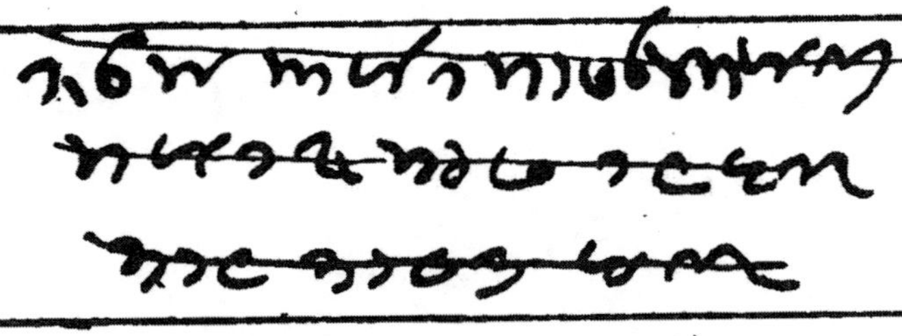	Sarrafi
	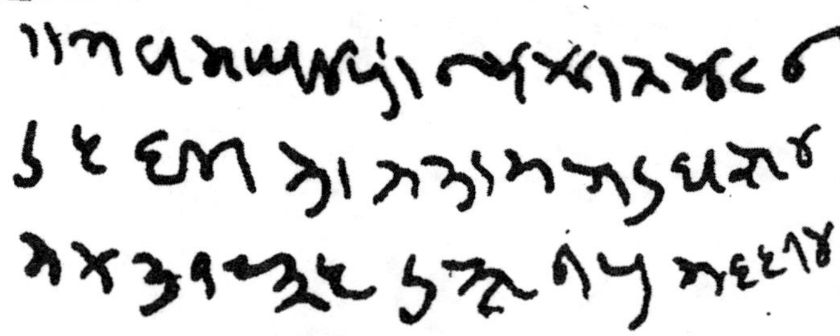	Lande
	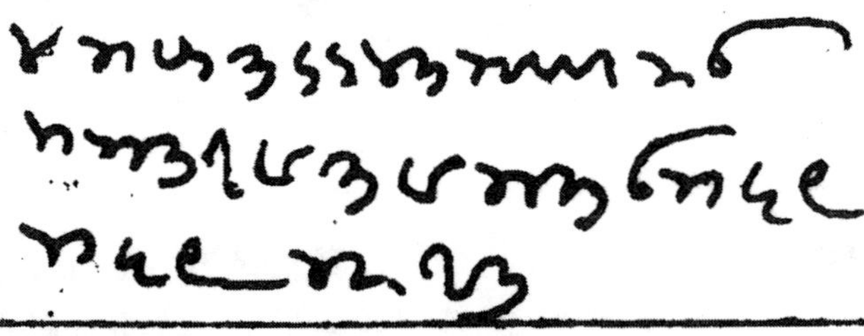	2nd Specimen of Lande
	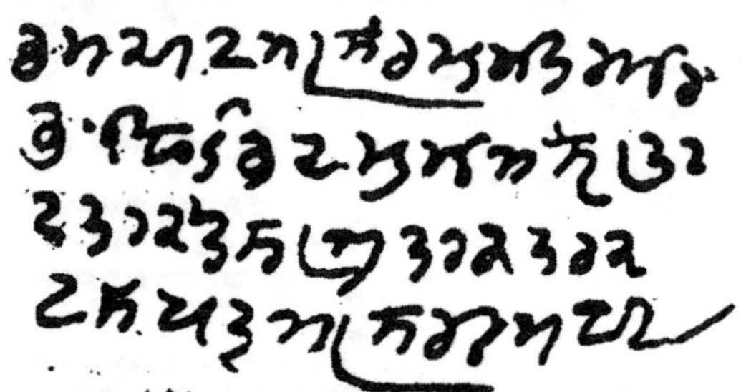	Lande Tionkari
	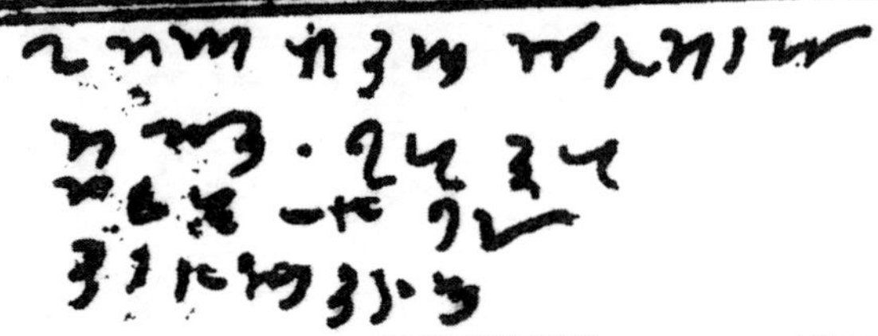	Lande of another kind

Set No 4

Mahajani used in Rohtak

1. Rohtak – Sarrafi

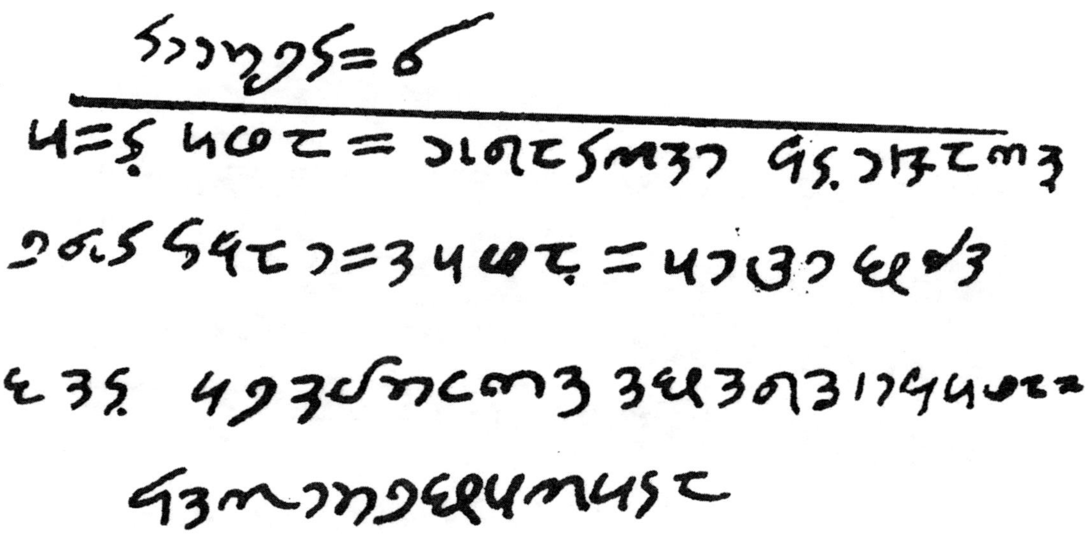

Set No. 5

Mahajani and Sarrafi used in the Dehli Karnal and Gurgaon Districts

I. Dehli Mahajani

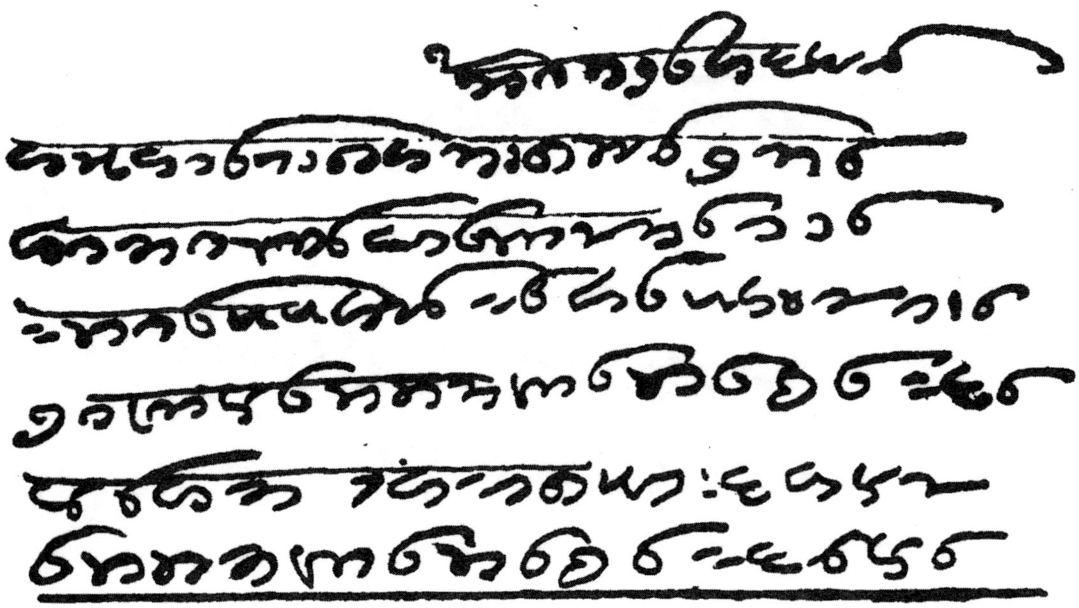

II. Dehli Sarrafi

III Gurgaon

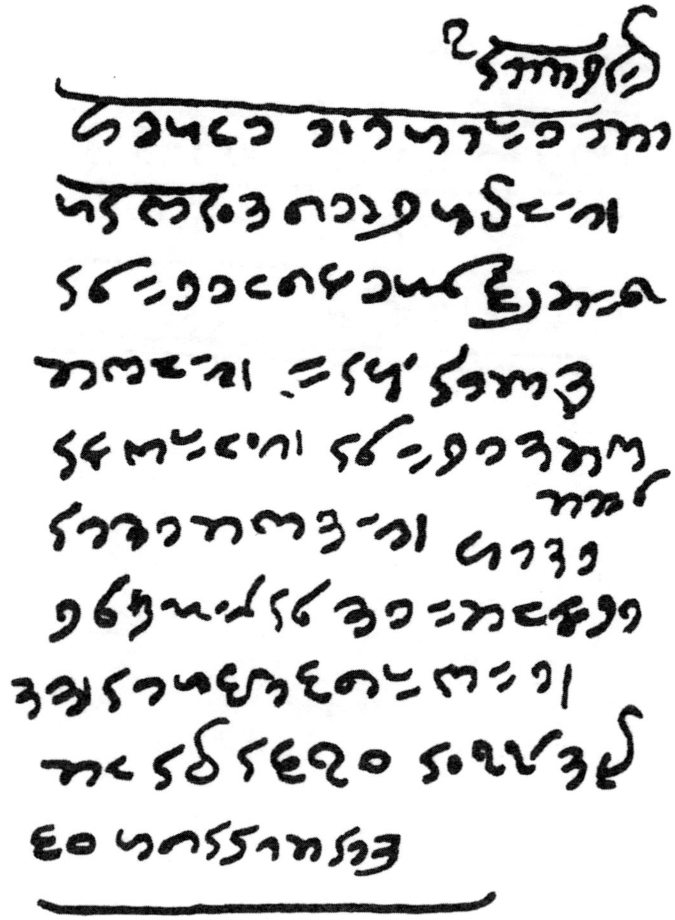

IV Gurgaon

Current Mahajani letter writing

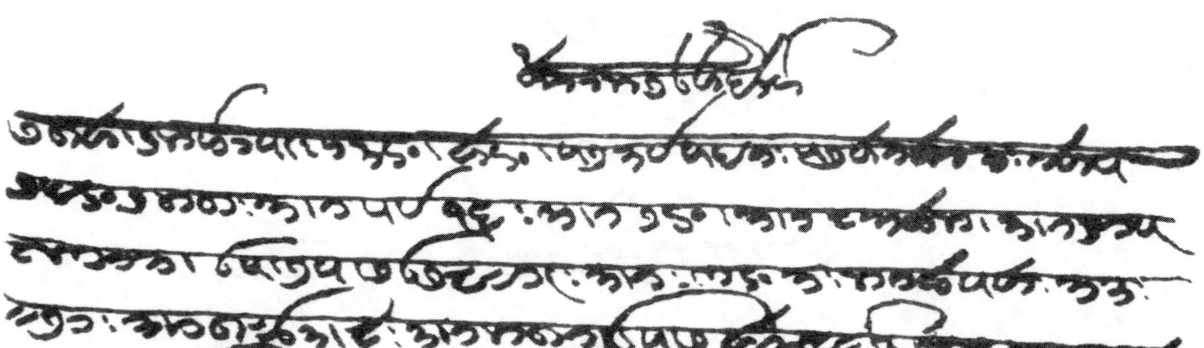

V. Gurgaon Mahajani

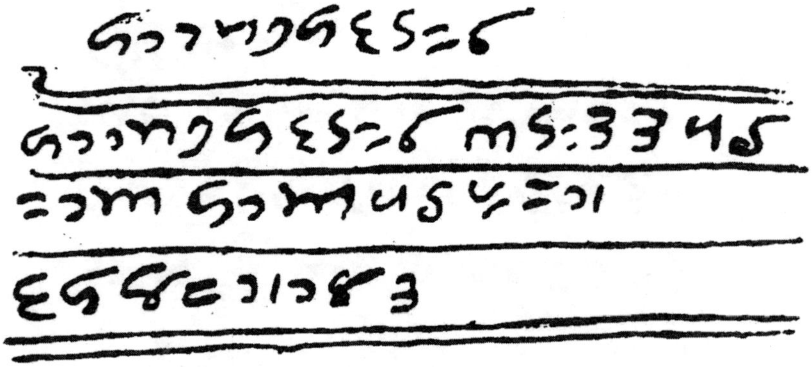

VI. Karnál

VII. Kurnal Mahajani

Set No 6

Landas used in the Multan Jhang Montyoumary Musaffargarh Districts

1. Massan ṭhāṇā

Jhang District

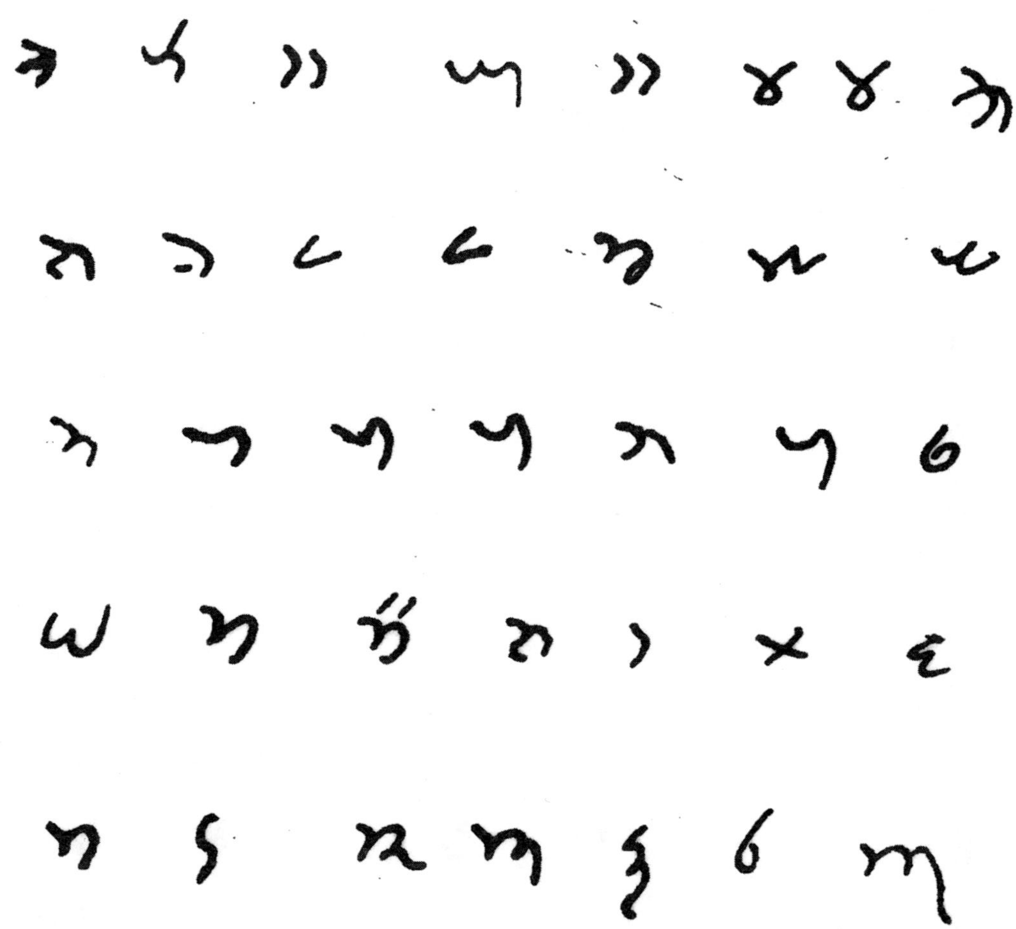

II Jhang District

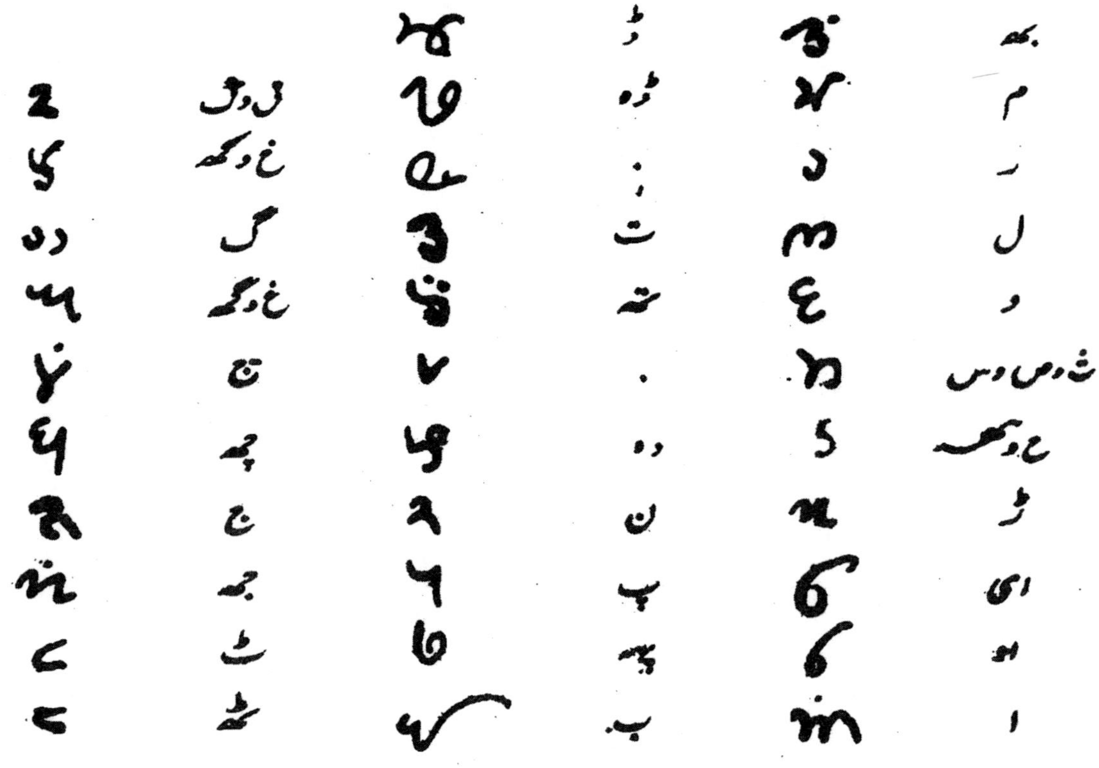

III Lande Uch Dist. Jhang

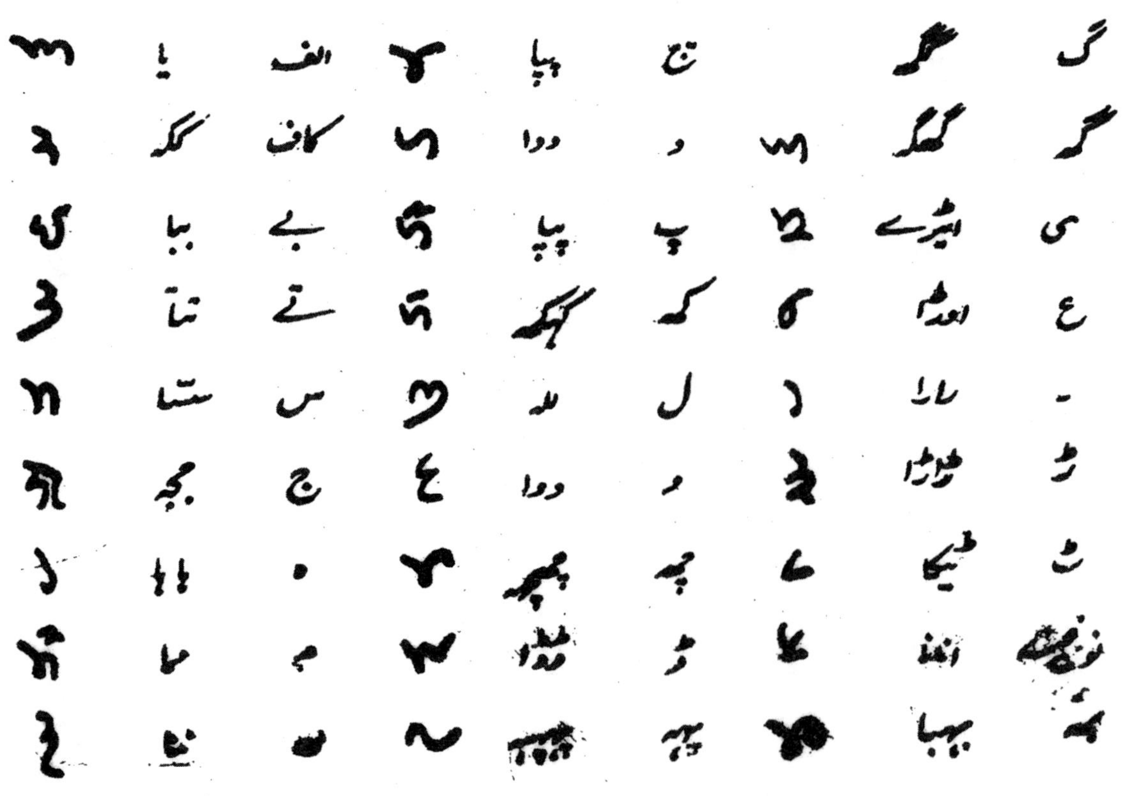

W Montgomery

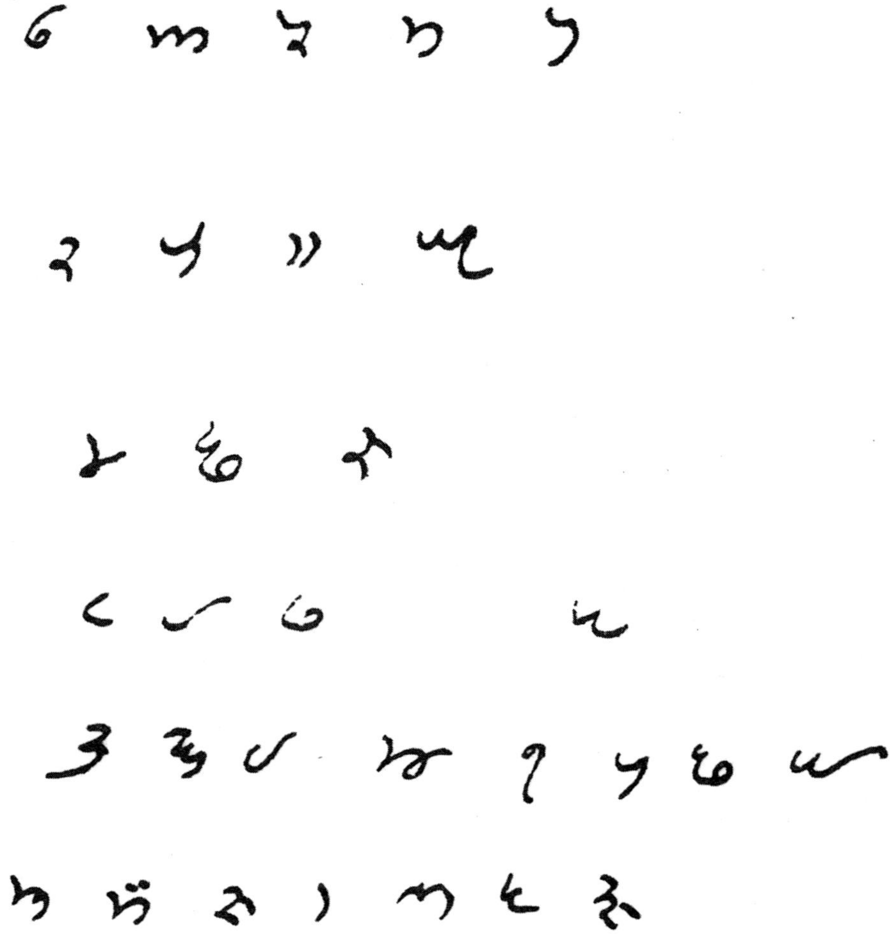

V Moltan Lunde

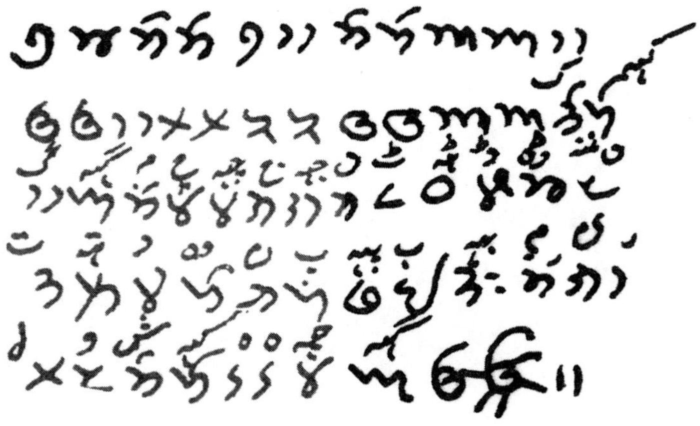

Lunde used in Multān

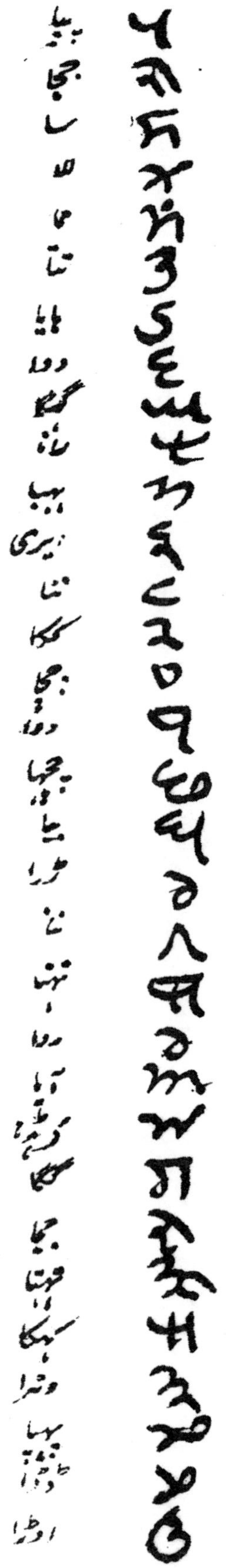

نورالدینه

VII Lande

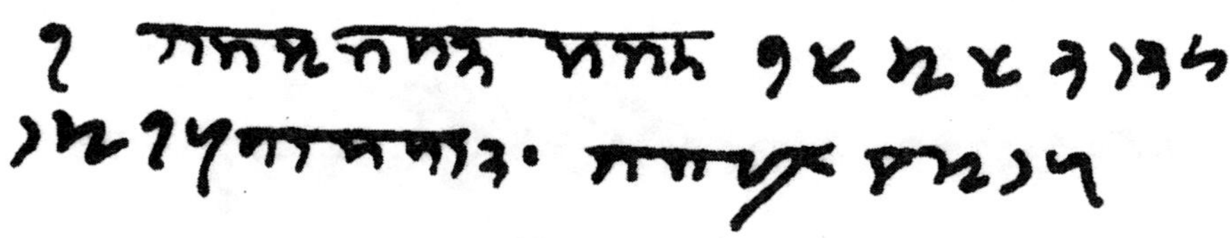

VIII Sarrafi

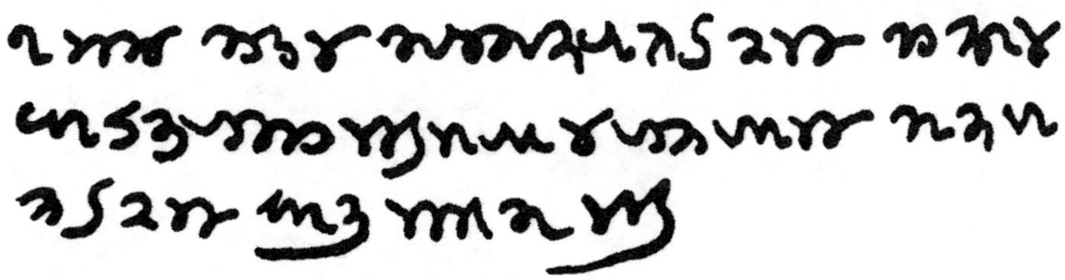

Set No. 7

Landas used in the Shimla (Tankari) & Ludhiyana Districts

Tankri character used in Simla

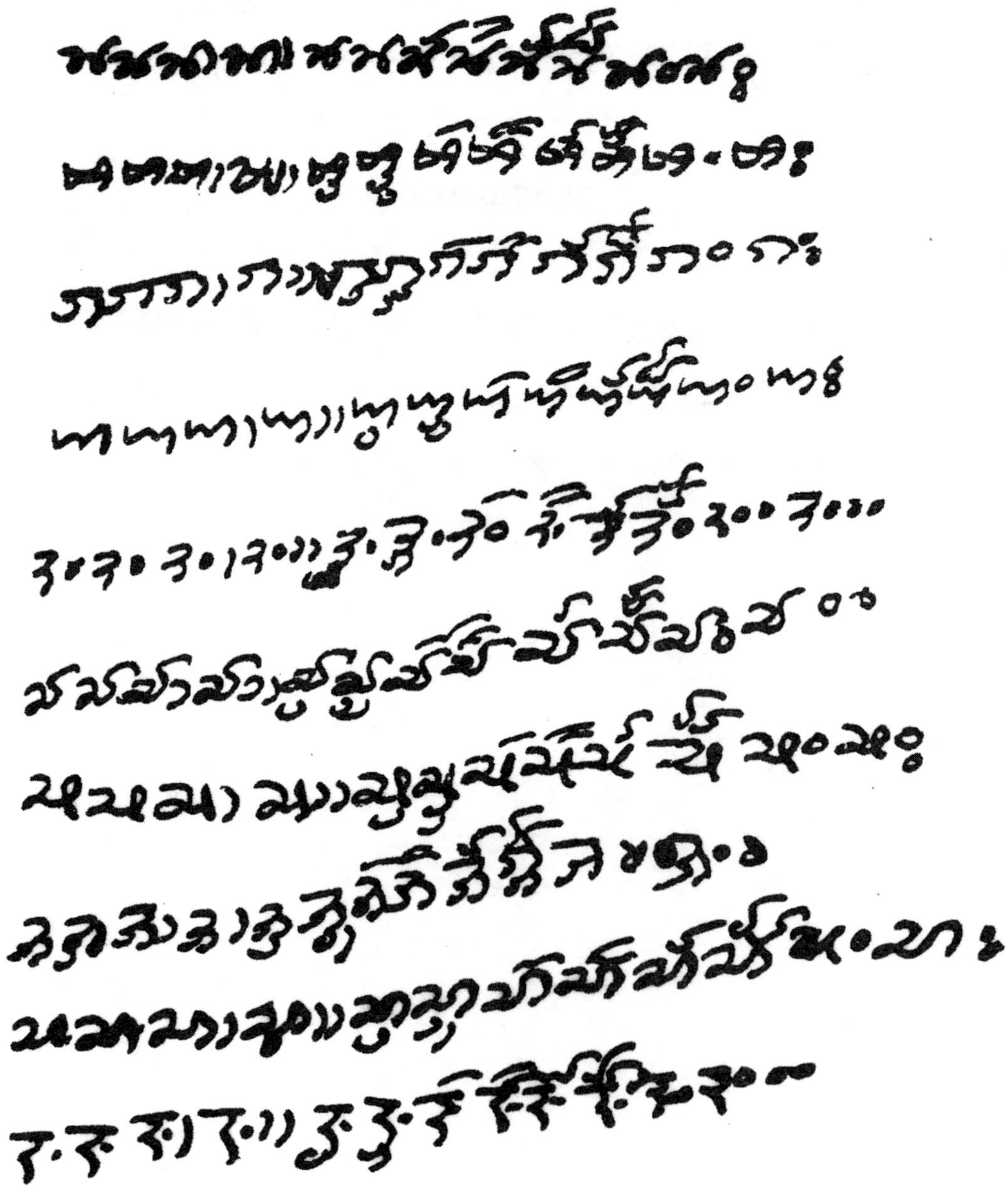

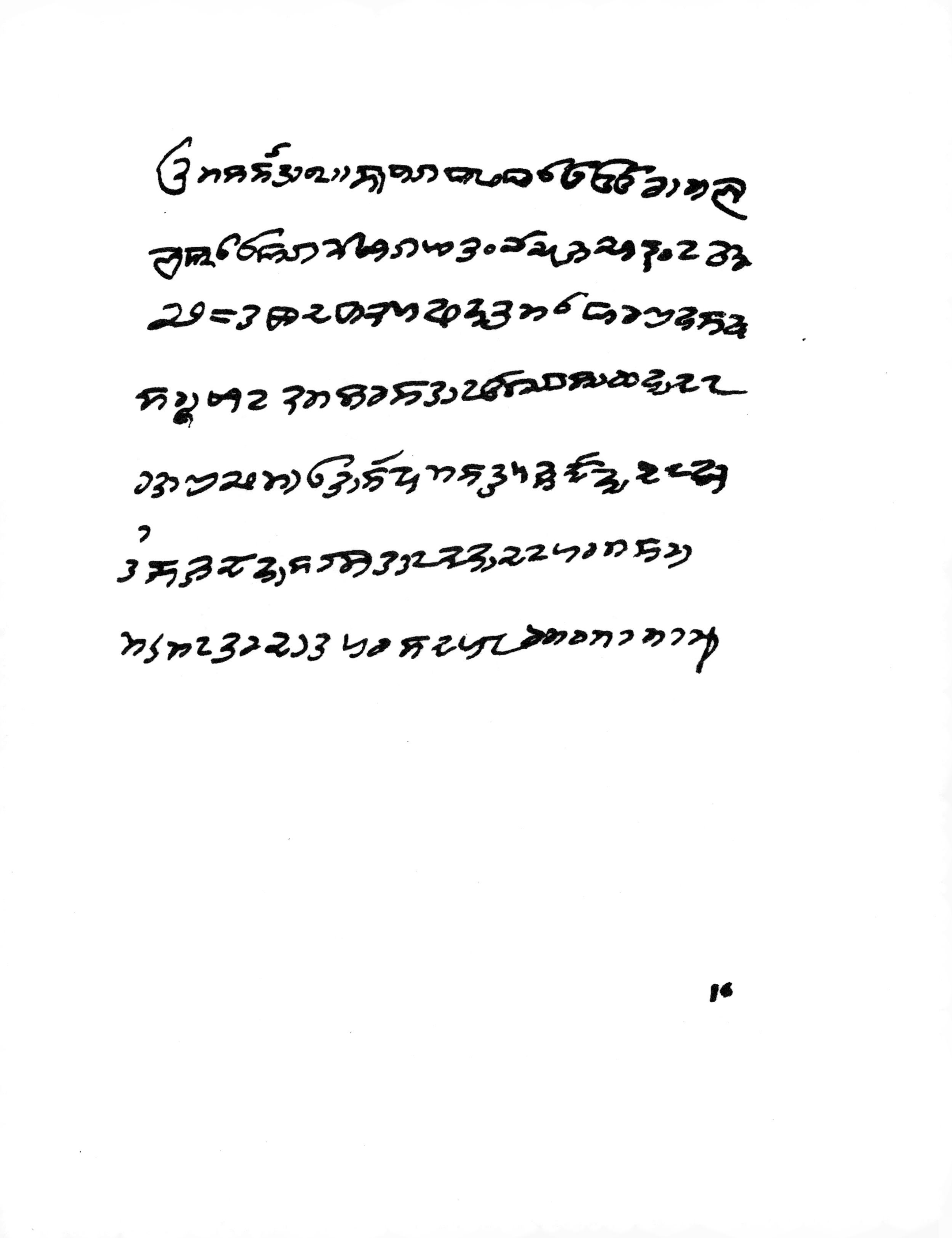

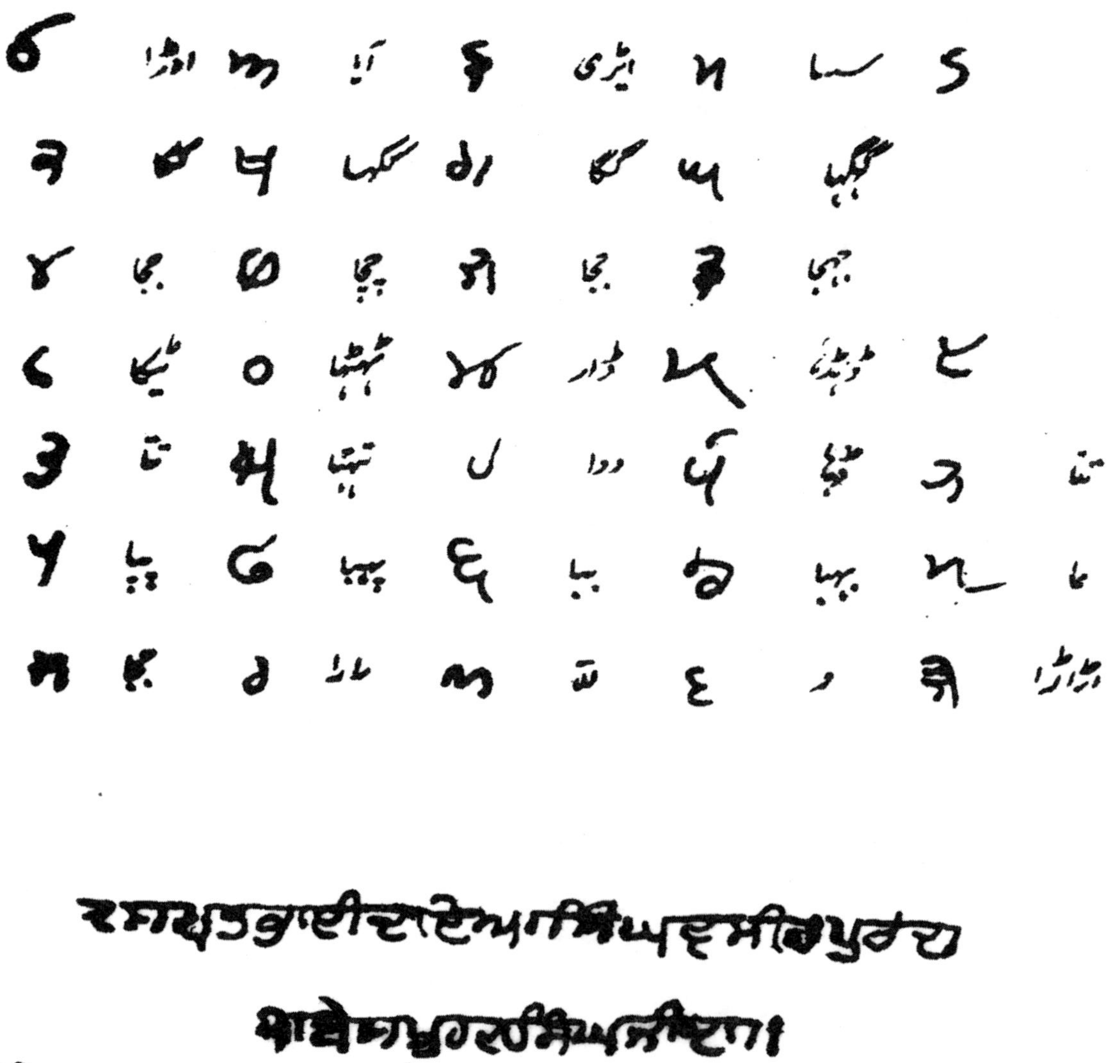

Set No 8

Mercantile characters

Used in the Lahore Gujranwala and Ferozpur Districts

I Gujranwala

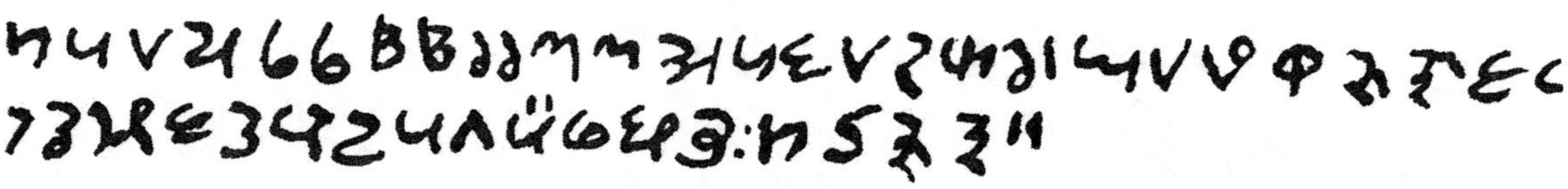

II Gujranwala

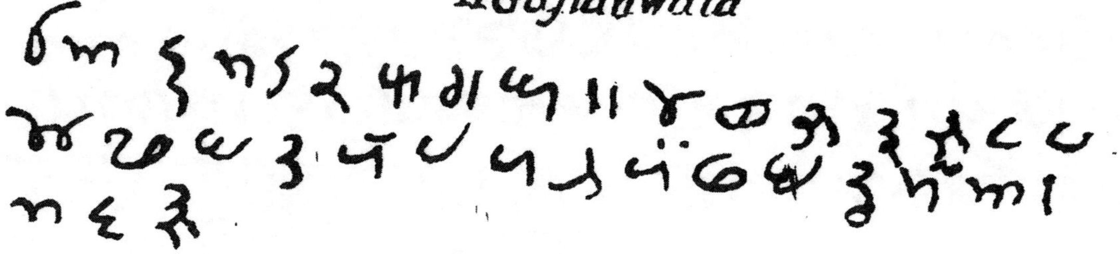

III Lande

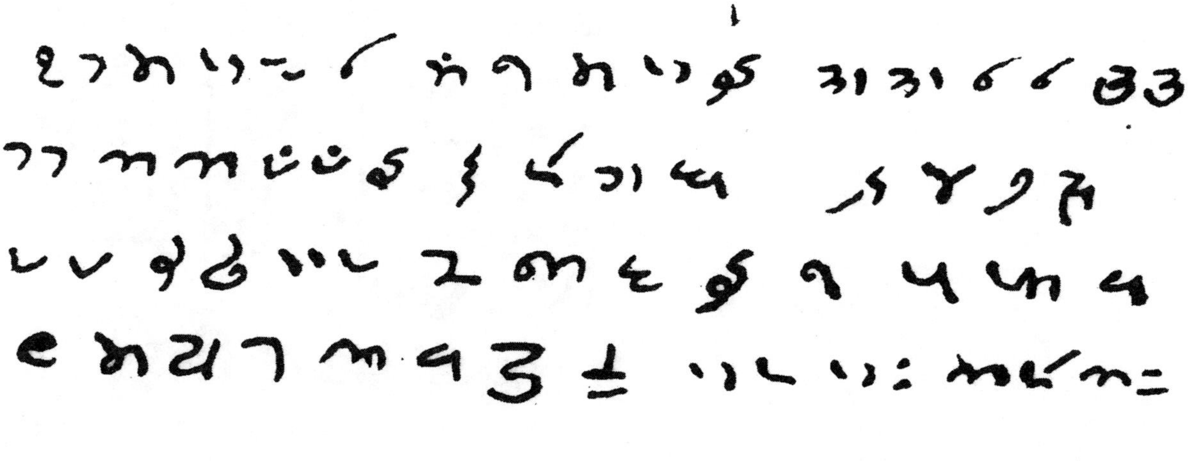

IV. Lahore

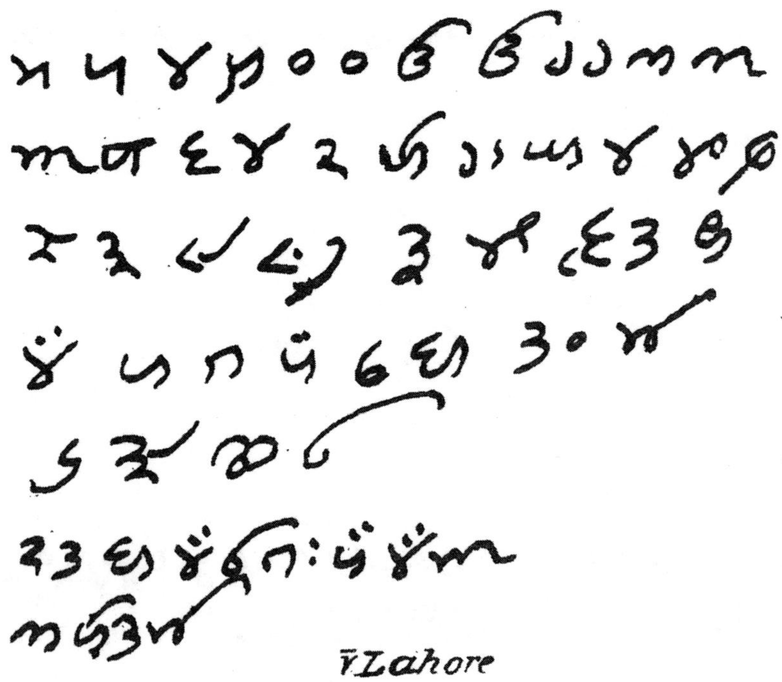

V. Lahore

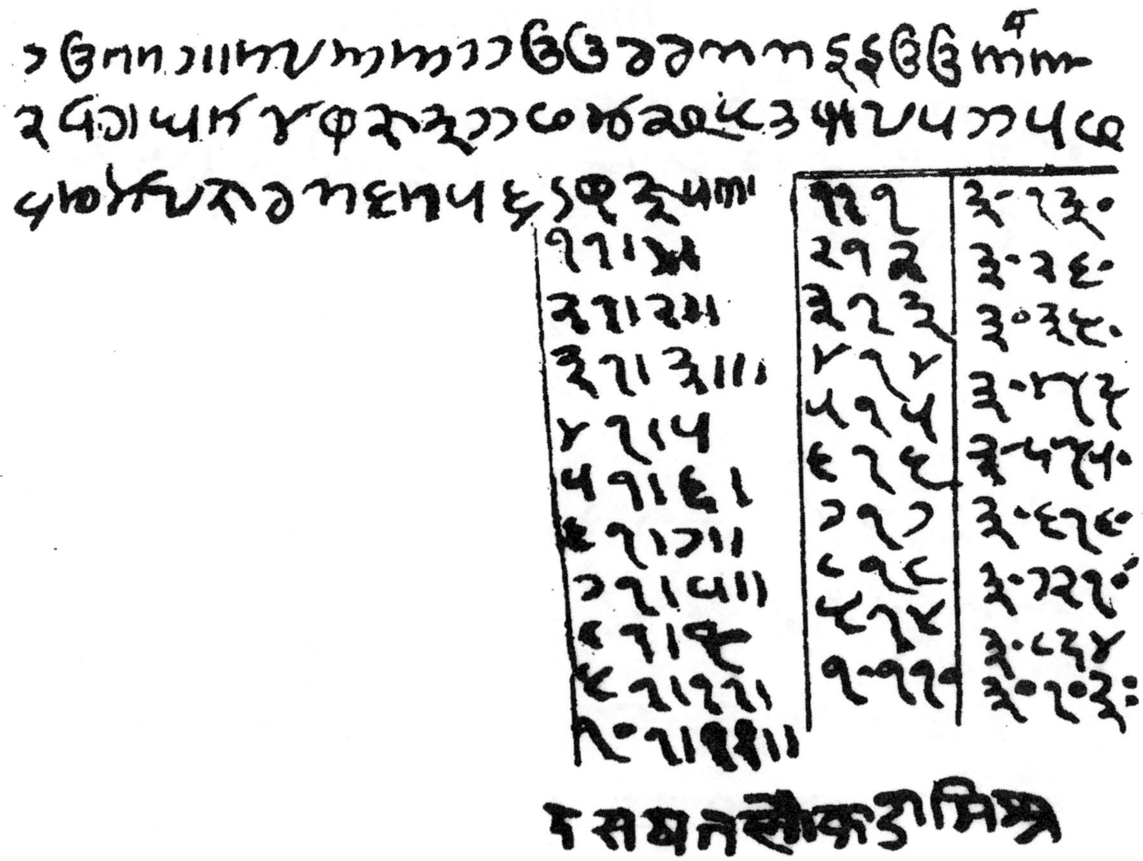

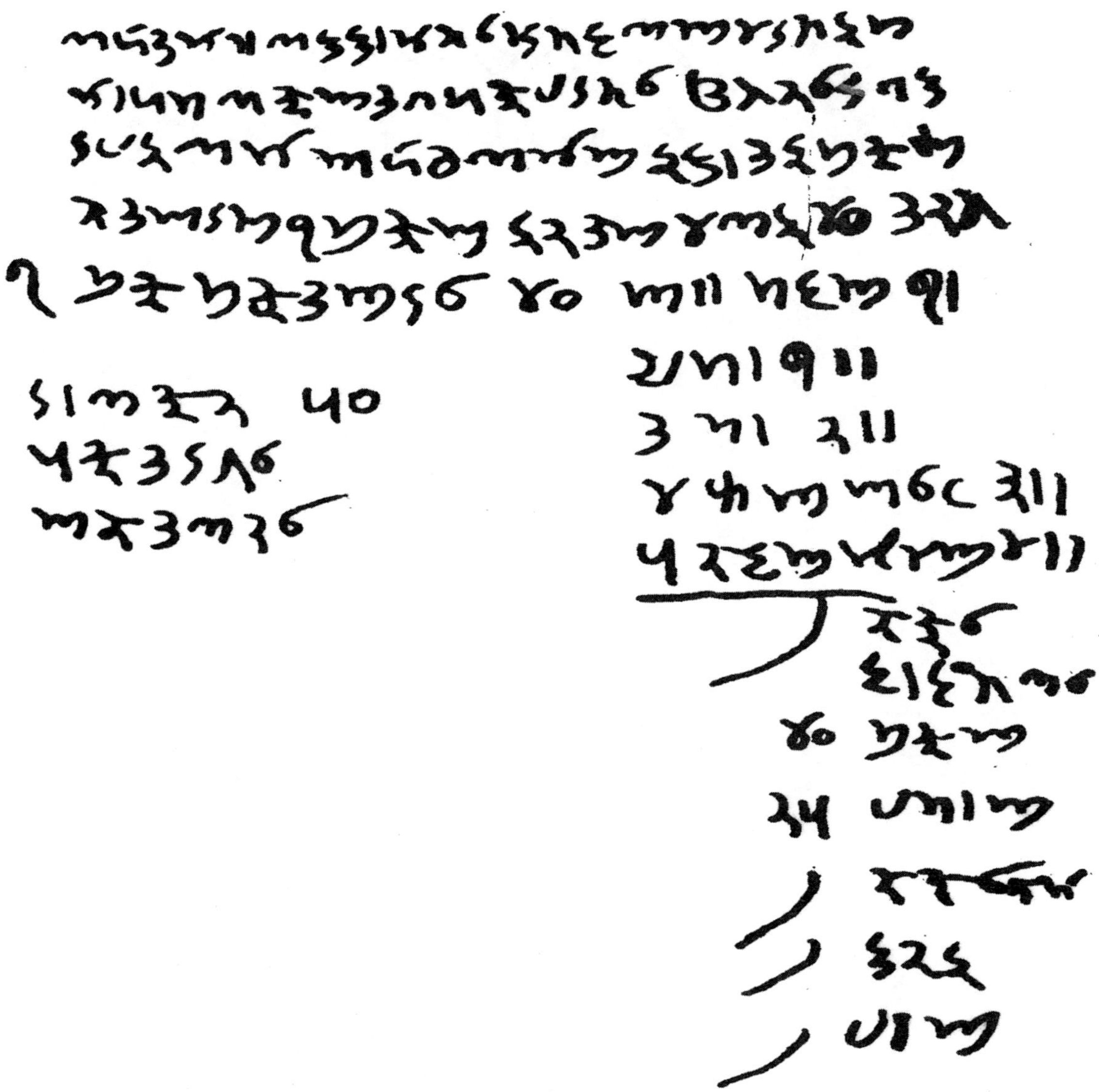

S-

VII Lahore

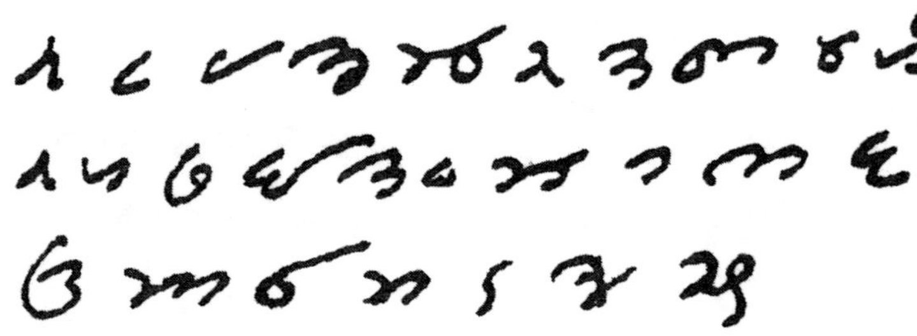

VIII Lahore

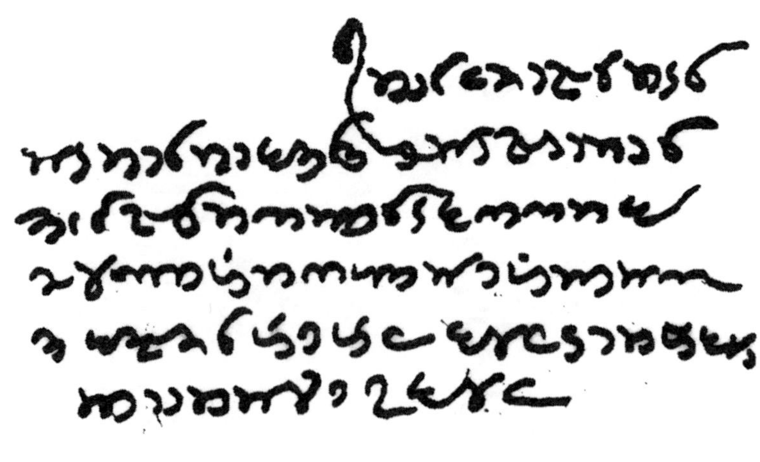

Set No. 1

Lande, Thakuri and Sarafi characters used in the Hushyarpur and Kangra Districts

I. Takri letters used in Kangra hills

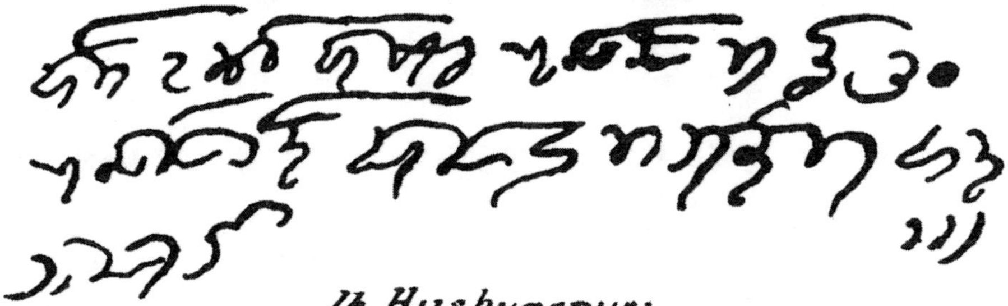

II. Hushyarpuri

Lande Sarafi Takari

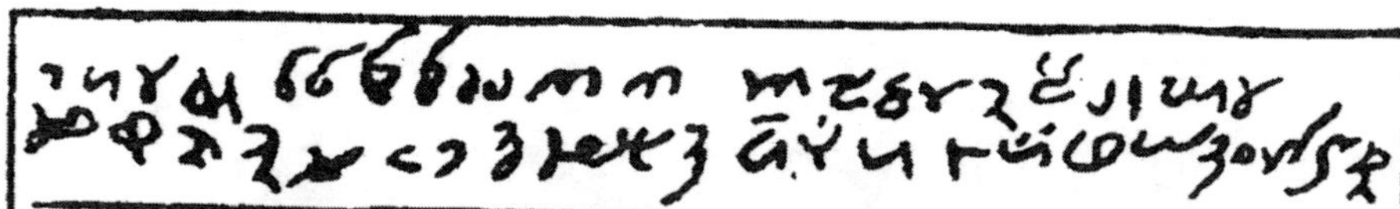	Lande
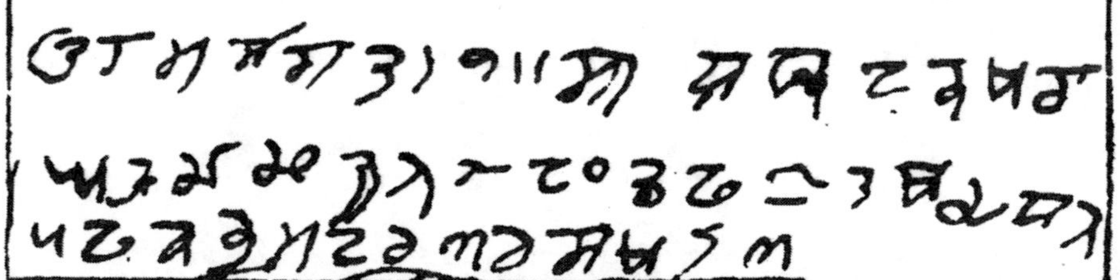	Takari Pahari
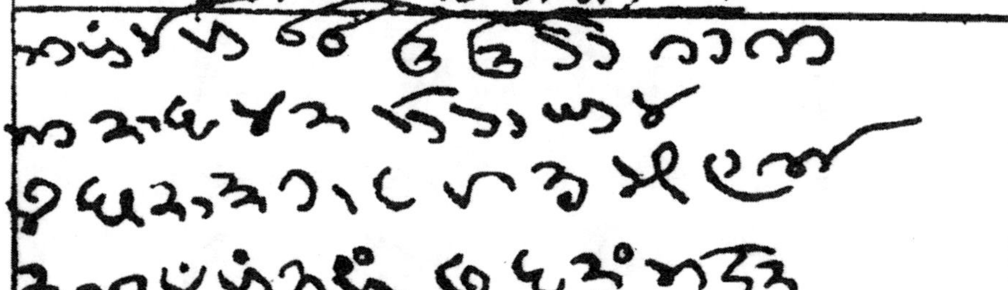	Sarafi
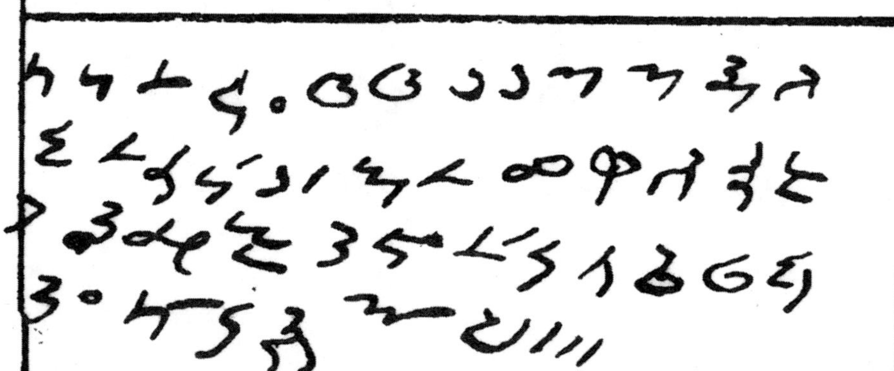	Lande

III Lande III used in Jejon District
Hushyárpur

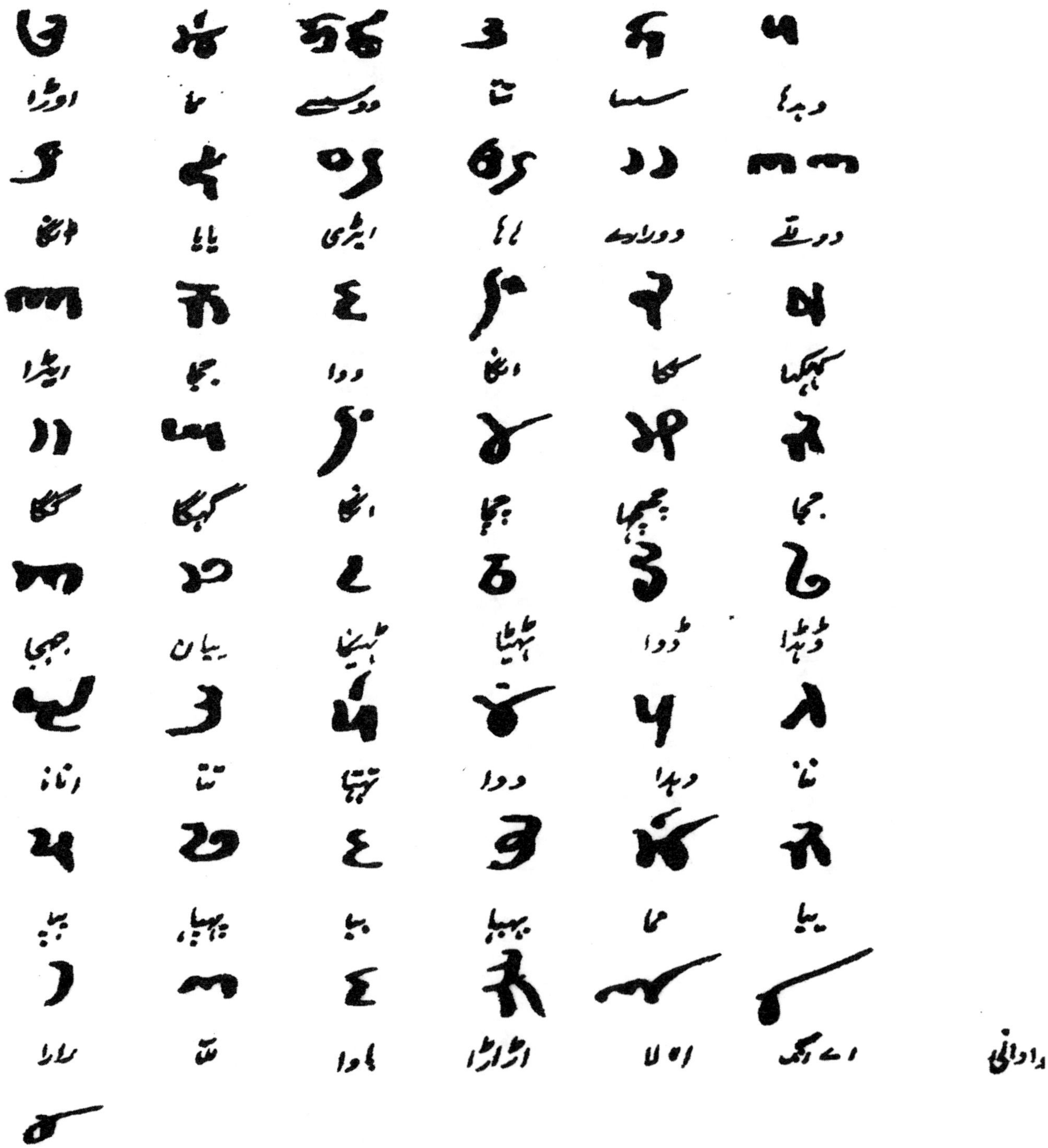

Mlande III used in Jejun District Hushyarpur

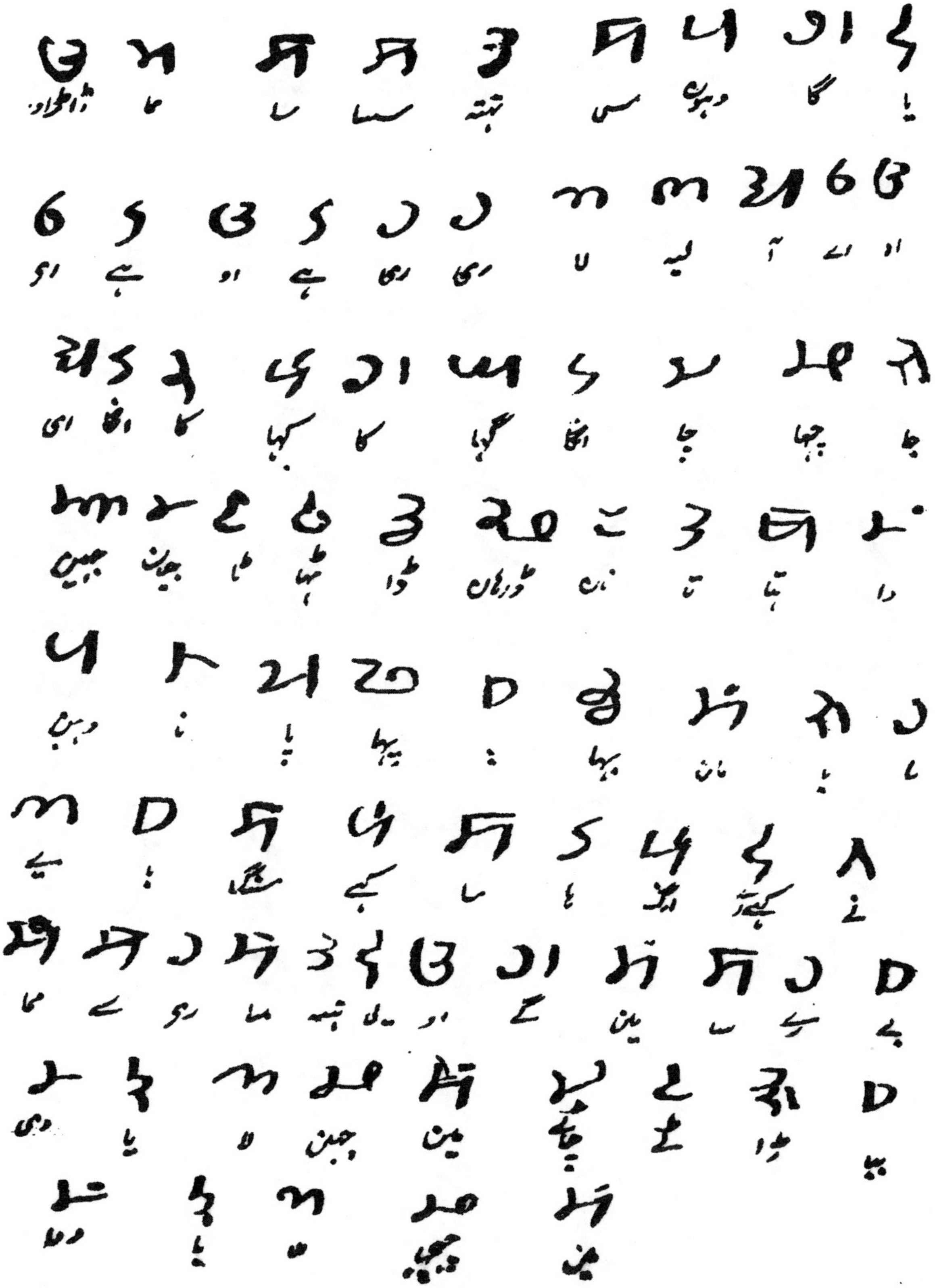

V. Lande I used in Jejun District Hushyarpur

V. Jejun village Mahilpur Ṭhánà Hushyárpur District

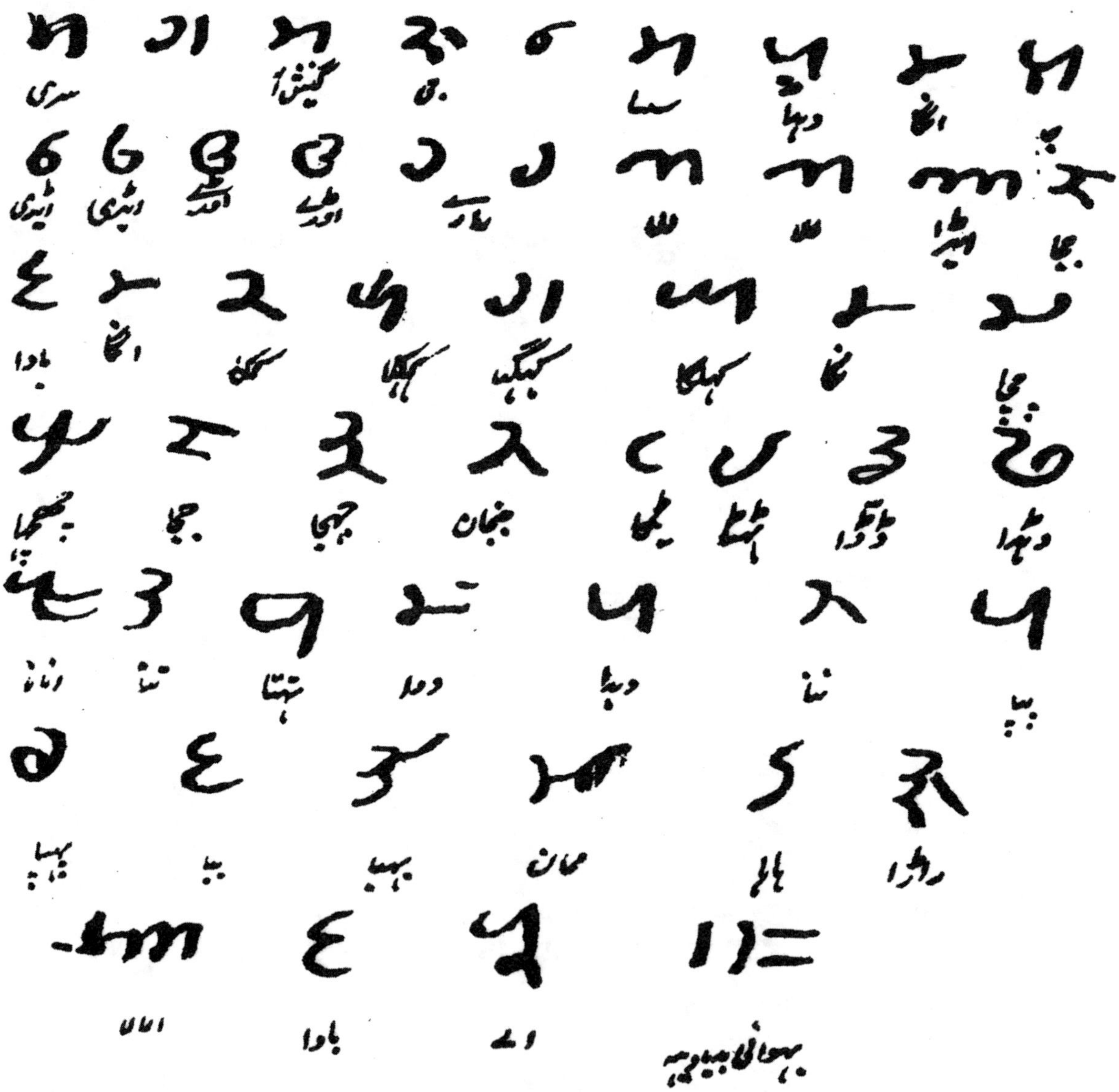

Set No 10

Multiplication Table and different Kinds of Landás used in the Gujrat, Shahpur, and Rawalpindi Districts

1. Ráwalpindi

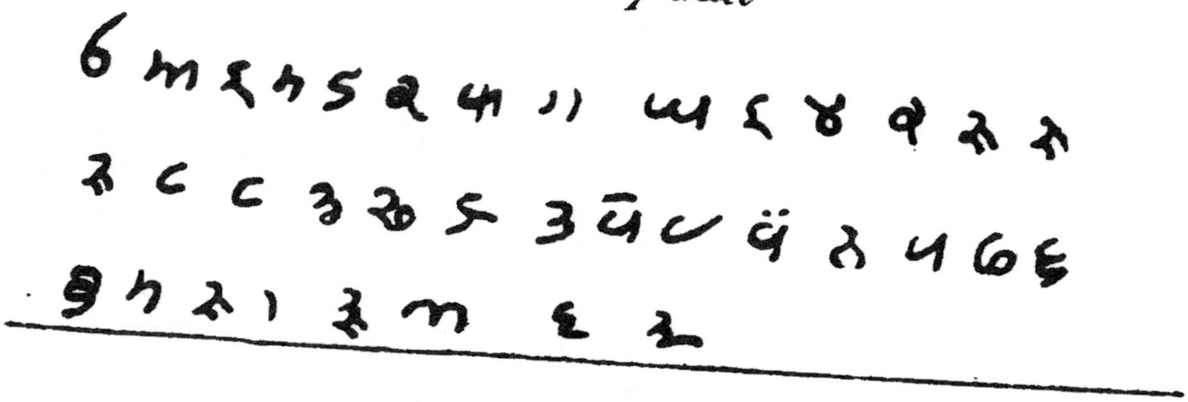

2 Rawalpindi

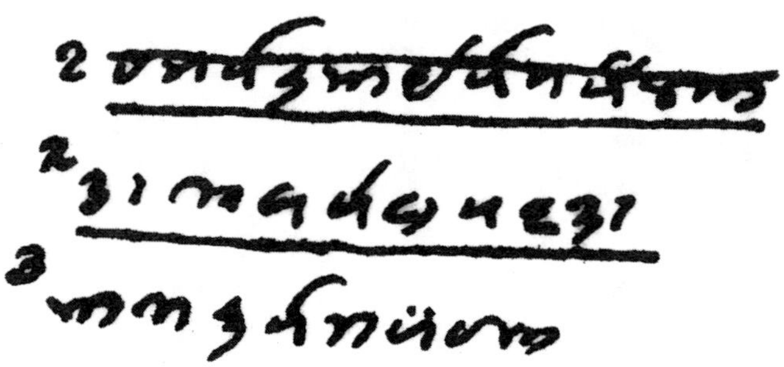

III Lande of Bhera Shahpur (seems somewhat different)

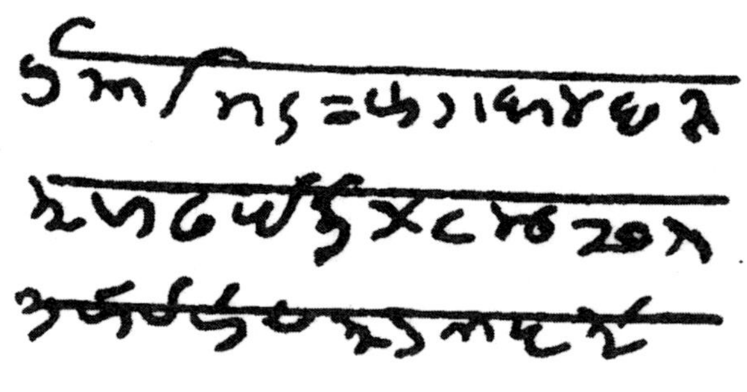

IV. Lande of Gujrat

بندی کا اوڑا آیا

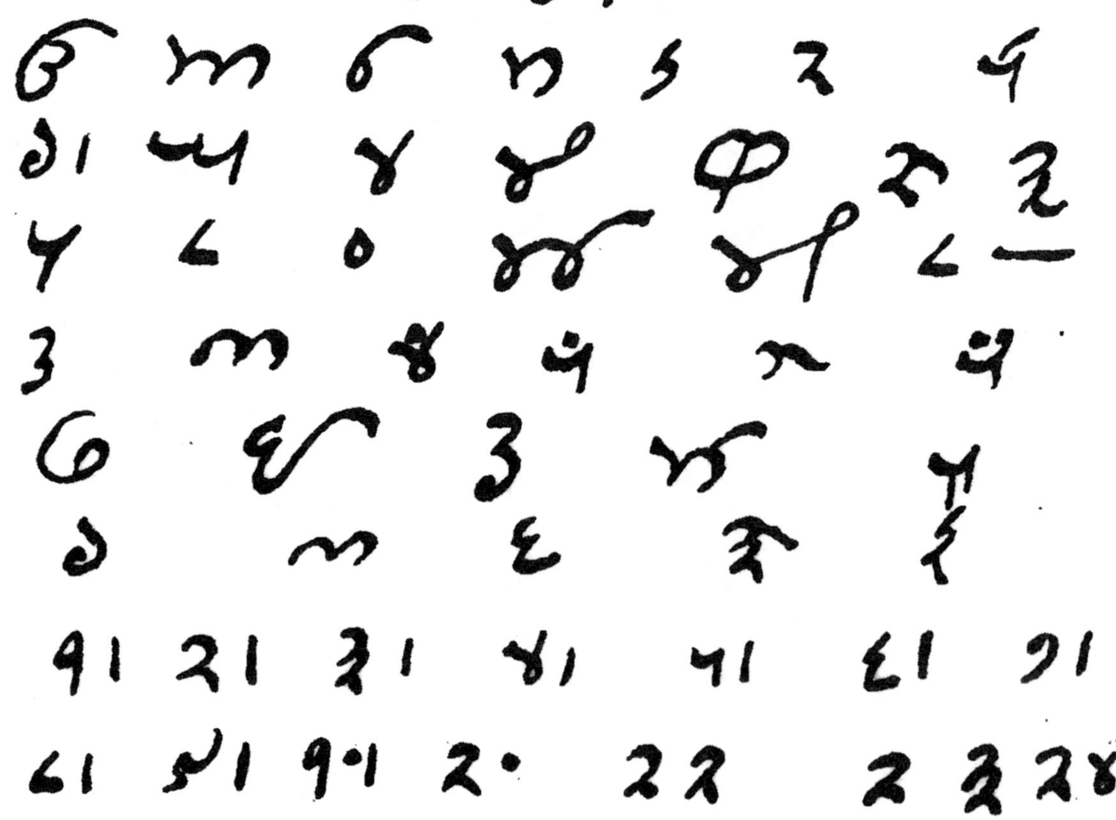

V. Multiplication Table ہندی پہاڑا

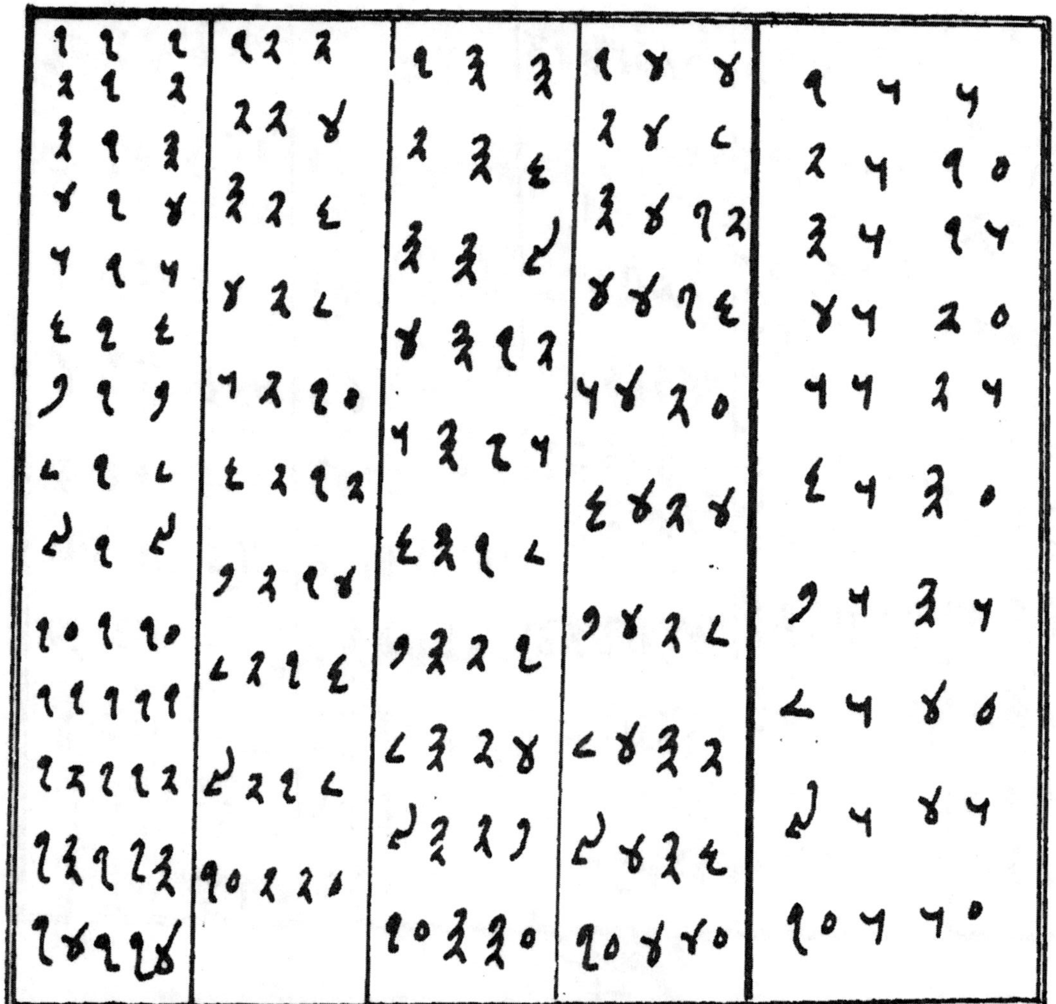

پہاڑا ڈیوڑھا

१ १॥ १॥	११ १॥ १६॥	२१ १॥ ३१॥	३१ १॥ ४६॥	४१ १॥ ६१॥
२ १॥ ३	१२ १॥ १८	२२ १॥ ३३	३२ १॥ ४८	४२ १॥ ६३
३ १॥ ४॥	१३ १॥ १९॥	२३ १॥ ३४॥	३३ १॥ ४९॥	४३ १॥ ६४॥
४ १॥ ६	१४ १॥ २१	२४ १॥ ३६	३४ १॥ ५१	४४ १॥ ६६
५ १॥ ७॥	१५ १॥ २२॥	२५ १॥ ३७॥	३५ १॥ ५२॥	४५ १॥ ६७॥
६ १॥ ९	१६ १॥ २४	२६ १॥ ३९	३६ १॥ ५४	४६ १॥ ६९
७ १॥ १०॥	१७ १॥ २५॥	२७ १॥ ४०॥	३७ १॥ ५५॥	४७ १॥ ७०॥
८ १॥ १२	१८ १॥ २७	२८ १॥ ४२	३८ १॥ ५७	४८ १॥ ७२
९ १॥ १३॥	१९ १॥ २८॥	२९ १॥ ४३॥	३९ १॥ ५८॥	४९ १॥ ७३॥
१० १॥ १५	२० १॥ ३०	३० १॥ ४५	४० १॥ ६०	५० १॥ ७५

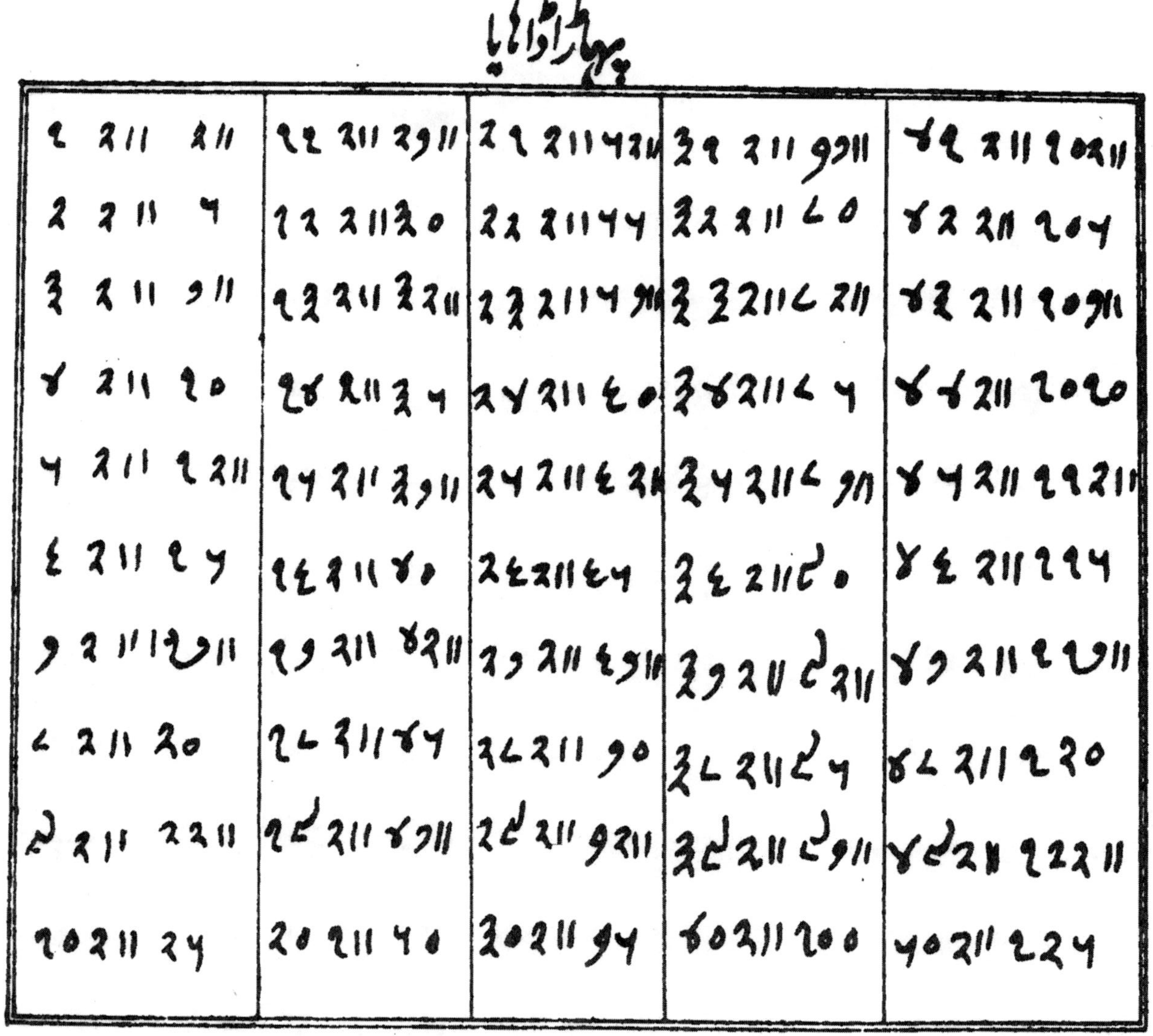

(*Gujrati Mahajani*)

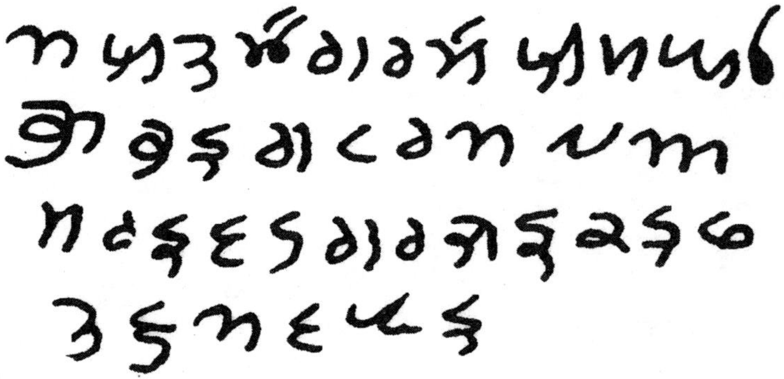

Dinga Zila Gujrat

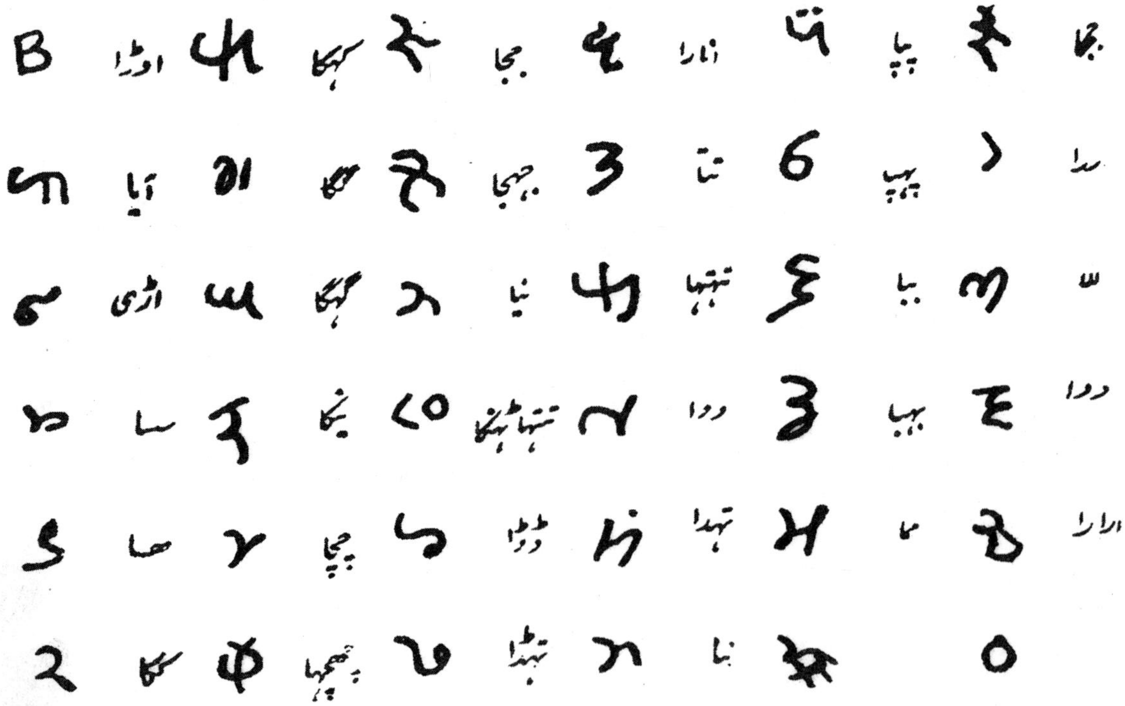